International Handbook of Emotions in Education

For more than a decade, there has been growing interest and research on the pivotal role of emotions in educational settings. This ground-breaking handbook is the first to highlight this emerging field of research and to describe in detail the ways in which emotions affect learning and instruction in the classroom as well as students' and teachers' development and well-being. Informed by research from a number of related fields, the handbook includes four sections. Section I focuses on fundamental principles of emotion, including the interplay among emotion, cognition, and motivation, the regulation of emotion, and emotional intelligence. Section II examines emotions and emotion regulation in classroom settings, addressing specific emotions (enjoyment, interest, curiosity, pride, anxiety, confusion, shame, and boredom) as well as social-emotional learning programs. Section III highlights research on emotions in academic content domains (mathematics, science, and reading/writing), contextual factors (classroom, family, and culture), and teacher emotions. The final section examines the various methodological approaches to studying emotions in educational settings. With work from leading international experts across disciplines, this book synthesizes the latest research on emotions in education.

Dr. Reinhard Pekrun holds the Research Chair for Personality and Educational Psychology at the University of Munich, Germany.

Dr. Lisa Linnenbrink-Garcia is an Associate Professor of Educational Psychology in the Department of Counseling, Educational Psychology, and Special Education at Michigan State University.

Educational Psychology Handbook Series
Series Editor: Patricia A. Alexander

International Handbook of Research on Conceptual Change, Second Edition
Edited by Stella Vosniadou

The International Guide to Student Achievement
Edited by John Hattie, Eric M. Anderman

The International Handbook of Collaborative Learning
Edited by Cindy E. Hmelo-Silver, Clark A. Chinn, Carol Chan, and Angela M. O'Donnell

Handbook of Self-Regulation of Learning and Performance
Edited by Barry J. Zimmerman, Dale H. Schunk

Handbook of Research on Learning and Instruction
Edited by Patricia A. Alexander, Richard E. Mayer

Handbook of Motivation at School
Edited by Kathryn Wentzel, Allan Wigfield

International Handbook of Research on Conceptual Change
Edited by Stella Vosniadou

Handbook of Moral and Character Education
Edited by Larry P. Nucci, Darcia Narvaez

Handbook of Positive Psychology in Schools, Second Edition
Edited by Michael Furlong, Rich Gilman, and E. Scott Huebner

International Handbook of Emotions in Education
Edited by Reinhard Pekrun, Lisa Linnenbrink-Garcia

Handbook of Moral and Character Education
Edited by Larry Nucci, Tobias Krettenauer, and Darcia Narvaez

International Handbook of Emotions in Education

Edited by
Reinhard Pekrun and Lisa Linnenbrink-Garcia

Routledge
Taylor & Francis Group

NEW YORK AND LONDON

First published 2014
by Routledge
711 Third Avenue, New York, NY 10017

and by Routledge
2 Park Square, Milton Park, Abingdon, Oxon OX14 4RN

Routledge is an imprint of the Taylor & Francis Group, an informa business

© 2014 Taylor & Francis

Library of Congress Cataloging-in-Publication Data

Handbook of emotions and education / [edited] by Reinhard Pekrun and
   Lisa Linnenbrink-Garcia.
      pages cm. — (Educational psychology handbook series)
   Includes bibliographical references and index.
   1. Educational psychology—Handbooks, manuals, etc.   2. Affective education—Handbooks, manuals, etc.   3. Emotions—Handbooks, manuals, etc.   I. Pekrun, Reinhard, 1952– editor of compilation.   II. Linnenbrink-Garcia, Lisa, editor of compilation.
   LB1072.H33 2013
   370.15—dc23
   2013032944

ISBN: 978-0-415-89501-9 (hbk)
ISBN: 978-0-415-89502-6 (pbk)
ISBN: 978-0-203-14821-1 (ebk)

Typeset in Minion
by Apex CoVantage, LLC

Printed and bound in the United States of America by
Edwards Brothers Malloy

CONTENTS

Preface   ix

Chapter 1   Introduction to Emotions in Education   1
REINHARD PEKRUN AND LISA LINNENBRINK-GARCIA

Part I   **FUNDAMENTAL PRINCIPLES**   **11**

Chapter 2   Concepts and Structures of Emotions   13
VERA SHUMAN AND KLAUS R. SCHERER

Chapter 3   Affect and Cognitive Processes in Educational Contexts   36
KLAUS FIEDLER AND SUSANNE BEIER

Chapter 4   The Experience of Emotions During Goal Pursuit   56
CHARLES S. CARVER AND MICHAEL F. SCHEIER

Chapter 5   Implicit Motives, Affect, and the Development of Competencies:
A Virtuous-Circle Model of Motive-Driven Learning   73
OLIVER C. SCHULTHEISS AND MARTIN G. KÖLLNER

Chapter 6   An Attributional Approach to Emotional Life in the Classroom   96
SANDRA GRAHAM AND APRIL Z. TAYLOR

Chapter 7   Control-Value Theory of Achievement Emotions   120
REINHARD PEKRUN AND RAYMOND P. PERRY

Chapter 8   Achievement Goals and Emotions   142
             LISA LINNENBRINK-GARCIA AND MICHAEL M. BARGER

Chapter 9   Emotional Intelligence in Education: From Pop
             to Emerging Science   162
             VELEKA ALLEN, CAROLYN MACCANN, GERALD MATTHEWS,
             AND RICHARD D. ROBERTS

Chapter 10   Emotion Regulation in Education: Conceptual Foundations,
             Current Applications, and Future Directions   183
             SCOTT E. JACOBS AND JAMES J. GROSS

Part II   EMOTIONS AND EMOTION REGULATION
             IN CLASSROOM SETTINGS   203

Chapter 11   Interest and Enjoyment   205
             MARY AINLEY AND SUZANNE HIDI

Chapter 12   Curiosity   228
             AMANDA MARKEY AND GEORGE LOEWENSTEIN

Chapter 13   Shame and Pride and Their Effects on Student Achievement   246
             GERALDINE V. OADES-SESE, TARA ANN MATTHEWS, AND MICHAEL LEWIS

Chapter 14   Anxiety in Education   265
             MOSHE ZEIDNER

Chapter 15   Confusion   289
             SIDNEY K. D'MELLO AND ARTHUR C. GRAESSER

Chapter 16   Academic Boredom   311
             THOMAS GOETZ AND NATHAN C. HALL

Chapter 17   The Role of Emotion in Engagement, Coping, and
             the Development of Motivational Resilience   331
             ELLEN SKINNER, JENNIFER PITZER, AND HEATHER BRULE

Chapter 18   Regulating Emotions Related to Testing   348
             PAUL A. SCHUTZ, HEATHER A. DAVIS, JESSICA T. DECUIR-GUNBY,
             AND DAVID TILLMAN

Chapter 19 Transforming Students' Lives With Social
and Emotional Learning   368
MARC A. BRACKETT AND SUSAN E. RIVERS

Part III   CONTENT DOMAIN, CONTEXT, AND CULTURE   389

Chapter 20 Perspectives on Emotion in Mathematical Engagement,
Learning, and Problem Solving   391
GERALD A. GOLDIN

Chapter 21 Emotions in Science Education   415
GALE M. SINATRA, SUZANNE H. BROUGHTON, AND DOUG LOMBARDI

Chapter 22 Emotion During Reading and Writing   437
CATHERINE M. BOHN-GETTLER AND DAVID N. RAPP

Chapter 23 Situating Emotions in Classroom Practices   458
DEBRA K. MEYER

Chapter 24 Emotions in Advanced Learning Technologies   473
ARTHUR C. GRAESSER, SIDNEY K. D'MELLO, AND AMBER C. STRAIN

Chapter 25 Teacher Emotions   494
ANNE C. FRENZEL

Chapter 26 Caregiving Influences on Emotion Regulation: Educational
Implications of a Biobehavioral Perspective   520
SUSAN D. CALKINS AND JESSICA M. DOLLAR

Chapter 27 The Influence of Culture on Emotions: Implications
for Education   539
JESSICA T. DECUIR-GUNBY AND MECA R. WILLIAMS-JOHNSON

Part IV   MEASUREMENT OF EMOTIONS IN ACADEMIC SETTINGS   559

Chapter 28 Self-Report Measures of Academic Emotions   561
REINHARD PEKRUN AND MARKUS BÜHNER

Chapter 29 Observational Approaches to the Measurement of Emotions   580
RAINER REISENZEIN, MARTIN JUNGE, MARKUS STUDTMANN, AND OSWALD HUBER

Chapter 30   Neuroscientific Contributions to Understanding and
              Measuring Emotions in Educational Contexts   607
              MARY HELEN IMMORDINO-YANG AND JOANNA A. CHRISTODOULOU

Chapter 31   Autonomic Nervous System Measurement of Emotion
              in Education and Achievement Settings   625
              SYLVIA D. KREIBIG AND GUIDO H. E. GENDOLLA

Chapter 32   Measuring Situated Emotion   643
              JULIANNE C. TURNER AND MEG TRUCANO

Chapter 33   Conclusions and Future Directions   659

Contributors List   677

Index   683

PREFACE

Emotions have emerged as one of the most salient topics in current educational research. This was not always the case. Traditionally, with few exceptions, educational researchers focused on the cognitive outcomes of schooling and neglected emotions. For many years, educational research ignored the dramatic progress in understanding emotions made by neighboring fields, such as psychology, sociology, economics, the neurosciences, and the humanities. Since the 1990s, however, educational science is experiencing an affective turn. Researchers have begun to recognize that emotions are ubiquitous in the classroom—students and teachers frequently experience both positive and negative emotions, and these emotions are often manifold, intense, and momentous. Accordingly, emotions are no longer regarded as epiphenomena that may occur in academic settings but lack any educational relevance. Rather, in the emerging field of educational emotion research, emotions are viewed as critically important for students' learning, developmental trajectories, and psychological health, as well as teachers' classroom instruction and professional careers, thus affecting the productivity of educational institutions around the world.

This handbook documents the progress in the field. In four sections, the volume highlights both existing, groundbreaking research on emotions in education as well as key basic research on emotions that informs this work. The first section focuses on fundamental principles, including the structure of emotion; the interplay among emotion, cognition, and motivation; and emotional intelligence and the regulation of emotion. A second group of chapters focuses on emotions, emotion regulation, and social-emotional learning programs in classroom settings. Chapters address emotions that are particularly relevant to these settings, including enjoyment and interest, curiosity, pride, shame, anxiety, confusion, and boredom. The third section highlights contextual factors relevant to studying emotions in education, focusing on educational content domains (mathematics, science, and reading/writing), learning environments, teacher emotions, family influences, and cultural perspectives. Chapters in the final section illustrate different methods to studying emotions in educational settings, including self-report, behavioral observation, neuroscientific and physiological analysis, and situated approaches.

Emotions in education are investigated from various disciplinary perspectives, including education, educational psychology, affective neuroscience, computer engineering, as well as mathematics and science education. It is an important mission of this handbook to bring together these divergent disciplinary perspectives in order to provide a more comprehensive view on emotions in educational settings. Researchers studying emotions in education have also employed various methodologies, such as laboratory-based behavioral experiments, neuroscience investigations, qualitative interviews, and quantitative field studies involving cross-sectional survey methods or longitudinal designs. By representing these various substantive and methodological approaches within one volume, our hope is that this handbook will be considered a key resource for guiding future research that is systematic, theoretically grounded, and empirically sound.

The handbook is targeted toward those in academia and research institutes, including advanced undergraduates, graduate students, postdoctoral fellows, lecturers, research scientists, and professors. It should also be of interest to educational practitioners, administrators, and policy-makers who want to obtain comprehensive information about the current state of the field. The level of assumed prior knowledge for comprehending the text varies across chapters, but most of the chapters contain easily readable sections that highlight the broad applicability of principles of emotion for educational practice. Furthermore, the volume can be used both as a personal resource for researchers and practitioners and as a textbook for advanced undergraduate and graduate seminars.

Finally, we extend our thanks and appreciation to our families for their encouragement over the extended period of time during which this handbook was conceptualized and produced. We are also grateful to each of the leading scholars in the field, whose names appear as authors in this volume, for their tireless work and invaluable insights into the function of emotions in education. Lastly, we thank the editor of the Educational Psychology Handbook series, Patricia Alexander, as well as Rebecca Novack, Lane Akers, and Trevor Gori from the publisher's side for their continued support of this project.

Reinhard Pekrun
Lisa Linnenbrink-Garcia

1

INTRODUCTION TO EMOTIONS IN EDUCATION

Reinhard Pekrun and Lisa Linnenbrink-Garcia,
University of Munich and Michigan State University

The classroom is an emotional place. The countless hours students spend attending class, completing projects, taking exams, and building social relationships translate into progress towards crucial life goals—holding a degree in education has never been of more personal, social, or financial significance than it is today. Accordingly, it is no wonder that educational settings abound with emotions. In these settings, emotions such as enjoyment of learning, curiosity, interest, hope, pride, anger, anxiety, shame, confusion, frustration, or boredom are frequent, pervasive, manifold, and often intense.

Emotions are both *experienced* in the educational setting as well as *instrumental* for academic achievement and personal growth. For instance, experiencing enjoyment while working on a challenging project can help a student envision goals, promote creative and flexible problem solving, and support self-regulation (Clore & Huntsinger, 2009; Fredrickson, 2001; Pekrun, Goetz, Titz, & Perry, 2002). On the other hand, experiencing excessive anxiety about exams can impede a student's academic performance, compel him to drop out of school, and negatively influence his psychological and physical health (Zeidner, 1998). The far-reaching consequences of emotional experiences are also likely reflected in the tragic numbers of attempted and committed suicides on academic campuses each year (Westefeld et al., 2005).

The importance of emotions in education equally extends to teachers, principals, and administrators. For example, teachers are not only responsible for imparting knowledge but also for inspiring passion for the discipline and excitement about learning. Of these outcomes, passion and excitement are the most elusive because teachers receive little or no training in the principles of affect and learning. If they succeed at inspiring excitement about the course content, the motivational benefits should extend far beyond the course itself. If they fail, however, the ensuing negative emotions, such as anxiety or boredom, can quickly undermine motivation and the will to remain in the class.

Despite the clear relevance of emotions for education, emotions have been neglected by educational research until the 1990s (Pekrun & Frese, 1992; Schutz & Lanehart, 2002).

The few exceptions include research on test anxiety (Zeidner, 1998) and on attributional antecedents of achievement emotions (Weiner, 1985). Since the 1970s, there has been a dramatic increase in attention to emotion in many scientific disciplines, including economics, the neurosciences, anthropology, and the humanities. By contrast, likely due to the strong focus of educational research on the cognitive outcomes of schooling, research on emotions in education was slow to emerge.

Over the past 15 years, however, the number of studies focusing on students' and teachers' emotions has steadily increased. There have been several calls for more research in this field; for example, in the concluding chapter of their *Handbook of Self-Regulation*, educational researchers Moshe Zeidner, Monique Boekaerts, and Paul Pintrich (2000, p. 754) asked the question: "How should we deal with emotions or affect?," and Martin Maehr (2001, p. 184) stated that we need to "rediscover the role of emotions." In response to these calls, researchers have begun to explore emotions related to learning and teaching. Starting with scarcely attended conference sessions on emotions at the annual meetings of the American Educational Research Association and the biannual conferences of the European Association for Research on Learning and Instruction in the mid to late 1990s to recent conferences with multiple, large sessions, it is clear that interest in research on emotions in education has grown substantially.

This handbook aims to document the progress made in this field. During the past 10 years, several edited volumes and special issues were published that covered select aspects of students' and teachers' emotions (Efklides & Volet, 2005; Linnenbrink, 2006; Linnenbrink-Garcia & Pekrun, 2011; Schutz & Lanehart, 2002; Schutz & Pekrun, 2007; Schutz & Zembylas, 2009). The present handbook provides a comprehensive attempt to review the progress that has been made. In the following sections, we first provide an overview of concepts of emotions that are used by educational researchers and addressed in the chapters of this handbook, and then we explain the structure of the sections of the handbook.

CONCEPTS OF EMOTIONS IN EDUCATION

Emotion, Mood, and Affect

As detailed by Vera Shuman and Klaus Scherer (2014), emotions can be defined as multifaceted phenomena involving sets of coordinated psychological processes, including affective, cognitive, physiological, motivational, and expressive components (Kleinginna & Kleinginna, 1981). For example, a students' anxiety before an exam can be comprised of nervous, uneasy feelings (affective), worries about failing the exam (cognitive), increased heart rate or sweating (physiological), impulses to escape the situation (motivation), and an anxious facial expression (expressive). As compared to intense emotions, *moods* are of lower intensity and lack a specific referent. Some authors define emotion and mood as categorically distinct (Rosenberg, 1998). Alternatively, since moods show a similar profile of components and similar qualitative differences as emotions (as in cheerful, angry, or anxious mood), they can also be regarded as low-intensity emotions (Pekrun, 2006).

In the educational research literature, different emotions and moods are often compiled in more general constructs of *affect*. Two variants of this term are used in the literature. In the broader educational literature, affect is often used to denote a broad variety of noncognitive constructs including emotion but also including self-concept, beliefs, motivation, and so on (e.g., McLeod & Adams, 1989; see Goldin, 2014; Shuman & Scherer, 2014). In contrast, in emotion research, affect refers to emotions and moods more specifically. In this research, the term is often used to refer to omnibus variables of positive versus negative emotions or moods, with *positive affect* referring to a compilation of various positive states (e.g., enjoyment, pride, satisfaction) and *negative affect* consisting of various negative states (e.g., anger, anxiety, frustration). For example, in research on students' achievement goals and emotions, most studies have compared the links between achievement goals and positive versus negative affect without further distinguishing between different emotions or moods (Huang, 2011).

Valence and Activation

Two important dimensions describing emotions, moods, and affect are *valence* and *activation* (see Shuman & Scherer, 2014). In terms of valence, positive (i.e., pleasant) states, such as enjoyment and happiness, can be differentiated from negative (i.e., unpleasant) states, such as anger, anxiety, or boredom. In terms of activation, physiologically activating states can be distinguished from deactivating states, such as activating excitement versus deactivating relaxation. These two dimensions are orthogonal, making it possible to organize affective states in a two-dimensional space. In circumplex models of affect, affective states are grouped according to the relative degree of positive versus negative valence and activation versus deactivation (e.g., Feldman Barrett & Russell, 1998). By classifying affective states as positive or negative, and as activating or deactivating, the circumplex can be transformed into a 2 × 2 taxonomy including four broad categories of emotions and moods (*positive activating*: e.g., enjoyment, hope, pride, excitement; *positive deactivating*: relief, relaxation, calmness; *negative activating*: anger, anxiety, shame, frustration; *negative deactivating*: hopelessness, sadness, boredom, exhaustion; Linnenbrink, 2007; Pekrun, 2006).

OBJECT FOCUS OF EMOTIONS

In addition to valence and activation, emotions can be grouped according to their object focus (Pekrun, 2006). For explaining the educational functions of emotions, this dimension is no less important than valence and activation. For example, regarding the functions of emotions for students' and teachers' engagement, object focus is critical because it determines if emotions pertain to the academic task at hand or not.

Traditionally, research on emotions in education focused on the achievement emotions experienced by students when they succeed or fail, or expect to succeed or fail, on academic tasks. Prime examples are students' hope, pride, anxiety, and shame related to academic accomplishments or failures. Similarly, early studies on teachers' emotions focused on the anxiety occurring when a teacher is afraid of failing in teaching classes (Coates & Thoresen, 1976; see Frenzel, 2014). However, emotions relevant to education extend far beyond the realm of achievement emotions. Emotions related to the contents of learning and teaching, to the process of cognitively generating knowledge, and to social interactions in the classroom are no less important, suggesting that there are at least four distinct groups of emotions that should be considered: achievement emotions, topic emotions, epistemic emotions, and social emotions. In addition, moods and incidental emotions that are brought into the classroom from outside can play a major role as well.

Achievement Emotions

We define achievement emotions as emotions that relate to activities or outcomes that are judged according to competence-related standards of quality. In education, achievement emotions can relate to academic activities, like studying, taking exams, or teaching, and to the success and failure outcomes of these activities. Accordingly, two groups of achievement emotions are activity-related emotions, such as enjoyment or boredom during learning and teaching, and outcome-related emotions, such as hope and pride related to success, or anxiety, hopelessness, and shame related to failure. Combining the valence, activation, and object focus (activity versus outcome) dimensions renders a 3 × 2 taxonomy of achievement emotions (see Pekrun, 2006, Pekrun & Perry, 2014). Traditionally, research on achievement emotions has focused on outcome emotions such as anxiety, pride, and shame (Weiner, 1985; Zeidner, 1998), but recently researchers have begun to attend to activity emotions, such as enjoyment or boredom as well (see Ainley & Hidi, 2014; Goetz & Hall, 2014).

Epistemic Emotions

Emotions can be caused by cognitive qualities of task information and of the processing of such information. A prototypical case is cognitive incongruity triggering surprise and curiosity. As suggested by Pekrun and Stephens (2011), these emotions can be called epistemic emotions since they pertain to the epistemic, knowledge-generating aspects of cognitive activities. During learning and teaching, many emotions can be experienced either as achievement emotions or as epistemic emotions, depending on the focus of attention. For example, the frustration experienced by a student not finding the solution to a mathematical problem can be regarded as an epistemic emotion if it is focused on the cognitive incongruity implied by a nonsolved problem, and as an achievement emotion if the focus is on personal failure and inability to solve the problem. A typical sequence of epistemic emotions induced by a cognitive problem may involve (1) surprise, (2) curiosity and situational interest if the surprise is not dissolved, (3) anxiety in case of severe incongruity and information that deeply disturbs existing cognitive schemas, (4) enjoyment and delight experienced when recombining information such that the problem gets solved, or (5) frustration when this seems not to be possible (D'Mello & Graesser, 2012, 2014).

Topic Emotions

During studying or attending class, emotions can be triggered by the contents covered by learning material. Examples are the empathetic emotions pertaining to a protagonist's fate when reading a novel, the emotions triggered by political events dealt with in political lessons, or the emotions related to topics in science class, such as the frustration experienced by American children when they were informed by their teachers that Pluto was reclassified as a dwarf planet (Sinatra, Broughton, & Lombardi, 2014). Similarly, teachers' emotions when preparing lessons and teaching classes can be aroused by the contents of materials. In contrast to achievement and epistemic emotions, topic emotions do not directly pertain to learning and teaching. However, they can strongly influence students' and teachers' engagement by affecting their interest and motivation in an academic domain (Ainley, 2007).

Social Emotions

Academic learning and teaching are situated in social contexts. Even when learning alone, students do not act in a social vacuum; rather, the goals, contents, and outcomes of learning are socially constructed. By implication, academic settings induce a multitude of social emotions related to other persons. These emotions include both social achievement emotions, such as admiration, envy, contempt, or empathy related to the success and failure of others, as well as nonachievement emotions, such as love or hate in the relationships with classmates or teachers (Weiner, 2007). Social emotions can strongly influence students' engagement, especially so when learning is situated in teacher–student or student–student interactions (Linnenbrink-Garcia, Rogat, & Koskey, 2011). Similarly, social emotions can profoundly affect teachers' classroom instruction and interaction with colleagues, parents, and supervisors.

Incidental Emotions and Moods

Students and teachers may experience emotions in the classroom that relate to events outside school, such as stress and problems in the family. These emotions do not relate to academic activities but have, nonetheless, the potential to influence students' and teachers' engagement, such as the worries about a parent's divorce that a student brings into the classroom. The same holds true for moods. While moods, by their very nature, may not be directly tied to a specific academic activity, they nonetheless can shape the way in which students and teachers engage academically. For instance, a student in a negative mood may have difficulty focusing on the task at hand, thus limiting engagement.

OVERVIEW OF CHAPTERS

This handbook aims to highlight both existing research on emotions in education as well as key basic research on emotions that informs this work. The first section focuses on fundamental concepts and theories of emotion. The second section addresses emotions, emotion regulation, and social-emotional learning programs in classroom settings. The chapters within this second section focus on specific emotions (enjoyment, interest, curiosity, pride, anxiety, confusion, shame, and boredom) that are particularly relevant to academic contexts. The third section highlights contextual factors relevant to studying emotions in education, focusing specifically on educational content domains (mathematics, science, and reading/writing), classroom context and learning environments, family influences, and cultural perspectives. This section also includes a chapter on teacher emotions, to highlight the importance of considering both teacher and student emotions. The fourth section includes chapters illustrating the various methodological approaches to studying emotions in educational settings, including self-report, observation, neuroscientific and physiological approaches, and situational perspectives. Finally, the concluding chapter provides a summary of the present state of research and addresses directions for future research.

Part I: Fundamental Principles

In this section, basic concepts and theories of emotion are discussed that lay the groundwork for research in this field. In Chapter 2 ("Concepts and Structures of Emotions"), Vera Shuman and Klaus Scherer explain the concept of emotion, discuss how emotions can be differentiated from other affective states, and address the ongoing controversy about how best to classify emotions in terms of dimensions of affect versus categories of discrete emotions. Chapter 3 ("Affect and Cognitive Processes in Educational Contexts") addresses the functions of emotions for cognitive processes that can explain their impact on academic performance. Susanne Beier and Klaus Fiedler review various theories of these functions, including Fiedler's approach addressing cognitive accommodation and assimilation, as well as related empirical findings. In Chapter 4 ("The Experience of Emotions During Goal Pursuit"), Charles S. Carver and Michael F. Scheier discuss antecedents of emotions in terms of the progress made when pursuing goals as well as implications for the dimensionality of emotions and the expenditure of effort. Chapter 5 ("Implicit Motives, Affect, and the Development of Competencies: A Virtuous-Circle Model of Motive-Driven Learning") addresses implicit motives as antecedents of emotion. Oliver C. Schultheiss and Martin G. Köllner discuss how motives such as the achievement motive amplify emotions and shape emotional learning. In Chapter 6 ("An Attributional Approach to Emotional Life in the Classroom"), Sandra Graham and April Z. Taylor consider B. Weiner's attributional theory, related evidence on the antecedents and development of students' emotions, and implications for issues of racial and ethnic minority students.

In Chapter 7 ("Control-Value Theory of Achievement Emotions"), Reinhard Pekrun and Raymond P. Perry discuss the control-value theory of achievement emotions describing how appraisals of control over achievement and the value of achievement instigate emotions in achievement settings and how these emotions influence learning and performance. In Chapter 8 ("Achievement Goals and Emotions"), Lisa Linnenbrink-Garcia and Michael M. Barger provide an overview of current theoretical approaches to understanding the relation between achievement goals and emotions and review current research on the topic. In Chapter 9 ("Emotional Intelligence in Education: From Pop to Emerging Science"), Veleka Allen, Carolyn MacCann, Gerald Matthews, and Richard Roberts discuss trait and ability constructs of emotional intelligence, methods to measure these constructs, and implications for emotional intelligence in educational settings. Finally, Chapter 10 ("Emotion Regulation in Education: Conceptual Foundations, Current Applications, and Future Directions") considers the regulation of emotions. Using Gross's model of emotion regulation, Scott E. Jacobs and James J. Gross outline how emotions can be regulated by selecting and modifying situations, changing one's appraisals, and modulating emotional responses, and how emotion regulation impacts resistance to temptation and one's anxiety in achievement situations.

Part II: Emotions and Emotion Regulation in Classroom Settings

The second section focuses on different emotions occurring in the classroom, ways to regulate these emotions, and social-emotional learning programs aimed at changing these emotions. Mary Ainley and Suzanne Hidi highlight students' interest and enjoyment, arguing that these two positive affects are conceptually and empirically distinct

(Chapter 11, "Interest and Enjoyment"). Amanda Markey and George Loewenstein use Loewenstein's information gap theory to discuss curiosity, an epistemic emotion that is critically important for students' conceptual change (Chapter 12, "Curiosity"). Self-conscious emotions are discussed by Geraldine V. Oades-Sese, Tara Ann Matthews, and Michael Lewis, who outline how pride and shame can be conceptualized and how they are shaped by classroom practices (Chapter 13, "Shame and Pride and Their Effects on Student Achievement"). Moshe Zeidner provides a review of research on test anxiety, addressing conceptual foundations, assessments, antecedents, performance consequences, and therapy for this well-researched emotion (Chapter 14, "Anxiety in Education"). Sidney K. D'Mello and Arthur C. Graesser target students' confusion, an under-researched epistemic emotion that is aroused by cognitive disequilibrium and can have beneficial effects on learning (Chapter 15, "Confusion"). Finally, Thomas Goetz and Nathan C. Hall review theories, assessment, functions, and development of students' boredom, an emotion that is frequently experienced by students and can undermine their learning and performance (Chapter 16, "Academic Boredom").

The remaining three chapters of this section address regulation and intervention related to emotions in the classroom. In Chapter 17 ("The Role of Emotion in Engagement, Coping, and the Development of Motivational Resilience"), Ellen Skinner, Jennifer Pitzer, and Heather Brule present a model of coping and motivational resiliency in the classroom, focusing on the role of students' emotions in the coping process. In Chapter 18 ("Regulating Emotions Related to Testing"), Paul A. Schutz, Heather A. Davis, Jessica T. DeCuir-Gunby, and David Tillman discuss how students regulate their emotions when taking tests and exams, focusing on various appraisal-oriented, emotion-focused, and task-focused ways to deal with these emotions. Finally, Marc A. Brackett and Susan E. Rivers provide an overview of social-emotional learning programs that aim to foster students' affective development, and they use the RULER program to illustrate the design of these programs, their implementation, and their impact on students' emotions (Chapter 19, "Transforming Students' Lives With Social and Emotional Learning").

Part III: Content Domains, Context, and Culture

The chapters in this section discuss emotions as situated in specific academic domains, social environments, and cultural contexts. In Chapter 20 ("Perspectives on Emotion in Mathematical Engagement, Learning, and Problem Solving"), Gerald A. Goldin reviews concepts of affect used in mathematics education and reviews studies on emotions in mathematics. Chapter 21 ("Emotions in Science Education") addresses students' emotions in science. Gale M. Sinatra, Suzanne H. Broughton, and Doug Lombardi discuss the role of emotions for science learning, with a specific focus on conceptual change in science. In Chapter 22 ("Emotion During Reading and Writing"), Catherine M. Bohn-Gettler and David N. Rapp address emotions related to reading and writing and review evidence on how emotions develop and influence the acquisition of skills in this domain.

The next three chapters address student emotions in specific learning environments as well as teacher emotions. Debra K. Meyer discusses emotions in classroom interaction and outlines how teacher–student interaction as well as peer interaction shape students' emotions (Chapter 23, "Situating Emotions in Classroom Practices"). Arthur C. Graesser, Sidney K. D'Mello, and Amber C. Strain address emotions in technology-based learning environments, which are of increasing importance in 21st-century education, outlining how these emotions can be assessed, how they unfold during learning, and how they can be influenced through pedagogical agents (Chapter 24, "Emotions in Advanced Learning Technologies"). Anne C. Frenzel addresses the emotions experienced by teachers (Chapter 25, "Teacher Emotions"). She discusses concepts of teacher emotions and how they relate to similar constructs, such as teacher burnout, and reviews research on the occurrence and functions of these emotions using Frenzel's model of teacher emotions as a conceptual framework.

Moving beyond academic settings, Susan D. Calkins and Jessica M. Dollar use a biobehavioral perspective to address the influence of caregivers and the family on the socialization of children's emotion and emotion regulation, with a focus on how early socialization processes support emotional functioning during schooling (Chapter 26, "Caregiving Influences on Emotion Regulation: Educational Implications of a Biobehavioral Perspective"). Finally, Jessica T. DeCuir-Gunby and Meca R. Williams-Johnson provide a broader perspective by discussing how sociocultural contexts shape the emotions occurring in education (Chapter 27, "The Influence of Culture on Emotions: Implications for Education"). Using the concepts of race, ethnicity, independent versus interdependent construals of the self, and individualism versus collectivism, the authors discuss how culture influences students' emotions, and the expression of emotions, in the classroom.

Part IV: Measurement of Emotions in Academic Settings

The fourth section includes chapters illustrating the various methodological approaches to studying emotions in academic settings. Reinhard Pekrun and Markus Bühner review self-report methodology to assess emotions, highlighting advantages as well as problems of self-report, and emphasizing the need to develop multidimensional instruments to capture the complexity of students' and teachers' emotions (Chapter 28, "Self-Report Measures of Academic Emotions"). Rainer Reisenzein, Martin Junge, Markus Studtmann, and Oswald Huber discuss observational methods to capture emotions (Chapter 29, "Observational Approaches to the Measurement of Emotions"). The authors outline how emotion can be inferred from observation, the pros and cons of objective, theory-based, and intuitive systems of observation, and the implementation of these systems in educational emotion research. Mary Helen Immordino-Yang and Joanna A. Christodoulou address neuroscientific methodology in the study of emotions (Chapter 30, "Neuroscientific Contributions to Understanding and Measuring Emotions in Educational Contexts"). The chapter focuses on neuroimaging techniques, such as fMRI, MEG, EEG, NIRS, PET, and TMS, and discusses their potential benefits as well as limitations for use in educational research on emotions. In Chapter 31 ("Autonomic Nervous System Measurement of Emotion in Education and Achievement Settings"), Sylvia D. Kreibig and Guido H. E. Gendolla consider principles of assessing arousal of the autonomic nervous system, the interaction of such arousal with emotion, and implications to measure emotions in educational settings. Finally, Julianne C. Turner and Meg Trucano discuss situated approaches to the study of emotions in education, addressing situated methods such as experience sampling, online questionnaires, situational interviews, and video recording, as well as ways to integrate situated data from multiple sources (Chapter 32, "Measuring Situated Emotion").

Conclusions

In the concluding chapter, we emphasize that substantial progress has been made in educational research on emotions during the past 15 years. We also outline, however, that this nascent field of research still is in a state fragmentation that needs to be overcome to make progress and to derive evidence-based recommendations for educational practice. We address the need to create more comprehensive theoretical frameworks integrating the multitude of prevailing small-scale models; to use multiple-methodology approaches to adequately assess students' and teachers' emotions; to consider the complexity of these emotions in terms of facets of emotions, academic domains, multilevel structures of education systems, and the specificity of sociocultural and historical contexts; and to advance educational intervention research through the development of approaches for preventing maladaptive and fostering adaptive emotions in school settings.

REFERENCES

Ainley, M. (2007). Being and feeling interested: Transient state, mood, and disposition. In P. A. Schutz & R. Pekrun (Eds.), *Emotion in education* (pp. 147–163). San Diego, CA: Academic Press.

Ainley, M., & Hidi, S. (2014). Interest and enjoyment. In R. Pekrun & L. Linnenbrink-Garcia (Eds.), *International handbook of emotions in education* (pp. 205–227). New York, NY: Taylor & Francis.

Clore, G. L., & Huntsinger, J. R. (2009). How the object of affect guides its impact. *Emotion Review, 1,* 39–54.

Coates, T. J., & Thoresen, C. E. (1976). Teacher anxiety: A review with recommendations. *Review of Educational Research, 46,* 159–184.

D'Mello, S., & Graesser, A. (2012). Dynamics of affective states during complex learning. *Learning and Instruction, 22,* 145–157.

D'Mello, S. K., & Graesser, A. C. (2014). Confusion. In R. Pekrun & L. Linnenbrink-Garcia (Eds.), *International handbook of emotions in education* (pp. 289–310). New York, NY: Taylor & Francis.

Efklides, A., & Volet, S. (Eds.). (2005). Feelings and emotions in the learning process [Special issue]. *Learning and Instruction, 15* (5).

Feldman Barrett, L., & Russell, J. A. (1998). Independence and bipolarity in the structure of current affect. *Journal of Personality and Social Psychology, 74,* 967–984.

Fredrickson, B. L. (2001). The role of positive emotions in positive psychology: The broaden-and-build theory of positive emotions. *American Psychologist, 56,* 218–226.

Frenzel, A. C. (2014). Teacher emotions. In R. Pekrun & L. Linnenbrink-Garcia (Eds.), *International handbook of emotions in education* (pp. 494–519). New York, NY: Taylor & Francis.

Goetz, T., & Hall, N. C. (2014). Academic boredom. In R. Pekrun & L. Linnenbrink-Garcia (Eds.), *International handbook of emotions in education* (pp. 311–330). New York, NY: Taylor & Francis.

Goldin, G. A. (2014). Perspectives on emotion in mathematical engagement, learning, and problem solving. In R. Pekrun & L. Linnenbrink-Garcia (Eds.), *International handbook of emotions in education* (pp. 391–414). New York, NY: Taylor & Francis.

Huang, C. (2011). Achievement goals and achievement emotions: A meta-analysis. *Educational Psychology Review, 23,* 359–388.

Kleinginna, P. R., & Kleinginna, A. M. (1981). A categorized list of emotion definitions, with suggestions for a consensual definition. *Motivation and Emotion, 5,* 345–379.

Linnenbrink, E. A. (Ed.). (2006) Emotion research in education: Theoretical and methodological perspectives on the integration of affect, motivation, and cognition [Special issue]. *Educational Psychology Review, 18*(4).

Linnenbrink, E. A. (2007). The role of affect in student learning: A multi-dimensional approach to considering the interaction of affect, motivation, and engagement. In P. Schutz & R. Pekrun (Eds.), *Emotion in education* (pp. 107–124). San Diego, CA: Academic Press.

Linnenbrink-Garcia, L., & Pekrun, R. (2011). Students' emotions and academic engagement [Special issue]. *Contemporary Educational Psychology, 36*(1).

Linnenbrink-Garcia, L., Rogat, T. K., & Koskey, K.L.K. (2011). Affect and engagement during small group interaction. *Contemporary Educational Psychology, 36,* 13–24.

Maehr, M. L. (2001). Goal theory is not dead—not yet anyway: A reflection on the special issue. *Educational Psychology Review, 13,* 177–185.

McLeod, D. B., & Adams, V. M. (Eds.). (1989). *Affect and mathematical problem solving: A new perspective.* New York, NY: Springer.

Pekrun, R. (2006). The control-value theory of achievement emotions: Assumptions, corollaries, and implications for educational research and practice. *Educational Psychology Review, 18,* 315–341.

Pekrun, R., & Frese, M. (1992). Emotions in work and achievement. In C. L. Cooper & I. T. Robertson (Eds.), *International review of industrial and organizational psychology* (Vol. 7, pp. 153–200). Chichester, United Kingdom: Wiley.

Pekrun, R., Goetz, T., Titz, W., & Perry, R. P. (2002). Academic emotions in students' self-regulated learning and achievement: A program of quantitative and qualitative research. *Educational Psychologist, 37,* 91–106.

Pekrun, R., & Perry, R. P. (2014). Control-value theory of achievement emotions. In R. Pekrun & L. Linnenbrink-Garcia (Eds.), *International handbook of emotions in education* (pp. 120–141). New York, NY: Taylor & Francis.

Pekrun, R., & Stephens, E. J. (2011). Academic emotions. In K. R. Harris, S. Graham, T. Urdan, S. Graham, J. M. Royer, & M. Zeidner (Eds.), *APA educational psychology handbook* (Vol. 2, pp. 3–31). Washington, DC: American Psychological Association.

Rosenberg, E. L. (1998). Levels of analysis and the organization of affect. *Review of General Psychology, 2,* 247–270.

Schutz, P. A., & Lanehart, S. L. (Eds.). (2002). Emotions in education [Special issue]. *Educational Psychologist, 37*(2).

Schutz, P. A., & Pekrun, R. (Eds.). (2007). *Emotion in education.* San Diego, CA: Academic Press.

Schutz, P. A., & Zembylas, M. (Eds.). (2009). *Advances in teacher emotion research: The impact on teachers' lives.* New York, NY: Springer.

Shuman, V., & Scherer, K. (2014). Concepts and structures of emotions. In R. Pekrun & L. Linnenbrink-Garcia (Eds.), *International handbook of emotions in education* (pp. 13–35). New York, NY: Taylor & Francis.

Sinatra, G. M., Broughton, S. H., & Lombardi, D. (2014). Emotions in science education. In R. Pekrun & L. Linnenbrink-Garcia (Eds.), *International handbook of emotions in education* (pp. 415–436). New York, NY: Taylor & Francis.

Weiner, B. (1985). *An attributional theory of achievement motivation and emotion. Psychological Review, 52,* 548–573.

Weiner, B. (2007). Examining emotional diversity on the classroom: An attribution theorist considers the moral emotions. In P. A. Schutz & R. Pekrun (Eds.), *Emotion in education* (pp. 73–88). San Diego, CA: Academic Press.

Westefeld, J. S., Homaifar, B., Spotts, J., Furr, S., Range, L., & Werth, J. L. (2005). Perceptions concerning college student suicide: Data from four universities. *Suicide and Life Threatening Behavior, 35,* 640–645.

Zeidner, M. (1998). *Test anxiety: The state of the art.* New York, NY: Plenum.

Zeidner, M., Boekaerts, M., & Pintrich, P. R. (2000): Self-regulation: Directions and challenges for future research. In M. Boekaets, P. R. Pintrich, & M. Zeidner (Eds.), *Handbook of self-regulation* (pp. 750–768). San Diego, CA: Academic Press.

Part I
Fundamental Principles

2

CONCEPTS AND STRUCTURES OF EMOTIONS

Vera Shuman and Klaus R. Scherer,
University of Lausanne and University of Geneva

What role do the emotions of students and teachers play in learning and teaching? Should the experience and expression of emotions be encouraged or discouraged? How can emotions be regulated in educational settings? Due to varying explanations of the cause, regulation, and measurement of emotions, different theories of emotions answer these questions in different ways. In order to better understand the role of emotions in an educational setting and in order to avoid misunderstandings from the very beginning, it is therefore important to be aware of the breadth of theoretical perspectives. In this chapter, we will (1) briefly discuss the desirability of emotions for learning; (2) present commonalities in how researchers from different theoretical backgrounds think about emotions—namely, that emotions are multicomponential episodes, which can be differentiated from other affective phenomena, such as moods; (3) discuss current controversies about the definition of emotion; (4) illustrate the implications of the different theoretical perspectives for the regulation of emotions, the structural relationships among emotions, the measurement of emotions, and the bodies of knowledge that have been generated; (5) and, finally, conclude with current and future directions in the research on emotions. This brief review chapter is selective by necessity, and we do not present in detail many important aspects about the concepts and structures of emotions. (For more information, see also Davidson, Scherer, & Goldsmith, 2003; Frijda, 1986; Lewis, Haviland-Jones, & Barrett, 2008; Moors, 2009; Niedenthal, Krauth-Gruber, & Ric, 2006; Oatley, Keltner, & Jenkins, 2006; and Sander & Scherer, 2009.)

EMOTIONS AND LEARNING: FRIENDS OR ENEMIES?

In early papers, the "passions," as they were called, were primarily seen as disruptive for behavior and intelligent thinking (Mandler, 2001). After all, how is a student to sit still at her desk and study when shaking with anxiety about an upcoming test? How can one hold a sensible lecture in front of a rowdy crowd? One implication of the view that emotions are disruptive is that humans should generally aim at suppressing emotions.

Current approaches to emotions advocate a more nuanced view. First, an *evolutionary perspective* on emotions suggests that emotions may actually be quite desirable. According to this view, emotions evolved because they have been adaptive (e.g., Izard, 2007; Plutchik, 2001; Tooby & Cosmides, 1990). For example, running away from an anxiety provoking situation, such as when facing an aggressive person, can be lifesaving. Also, feelings of curiosity trigger the active seeking of information and, in turn, lead to the broadening of one's knowledge required to ensure survival. Negative emotions are thought to trigger specific action tendencies—for example, attacking with anger, discarding with disgust, and running or freezing with fear (e.g., Plutchik, 2001). On the other hand, positive emotions, such as curiosity, love, and compassion, are thought to trigger rather broad thought–action repertoires to seek information, bond with others, and build resources (Fredrickson, 1998). In today's schools, when the school bully triggers fear and the teacher's curriculum arouses curiosity, the action tendencies to avoid the threatening student and to explore the course material may still be quite useful. However, due to new situations that did not exist 4,000 years ago, such as exams, the evolved action tendencies triggered by emotions may sometimes be counterproductive; for example, the tendency to avoid the situation associated with fear is not helpful when it comes to passing a test. Therefore, according to the evolutionary viewpoint, emotions can be good or bad for learning depending on how similar the requirements posed to us in modern situations are to the demands for survival in the past.

Second, a *cultural perspective* on emotions suggests that an individual's emotions are the result of sociocultural contexts that differ across social groups (families, peer groups, generations, nations, etc.). As a consequence, social groups may have different views on which emotions should normally be experienced and expressed in a particular situation. For example, whereas members of so-called individualistic cultures (e.g., North America) may view it as appropriate to experience and express pride after a personal achievement because it demonstrates the individual's success and may encourage others to follow suite, members of so-called collectivistic cultures (e.g., Japan) may not view it as appropriate to express pride in this situation because the singling out of the individual is seen as disruptive to group harmony (Markus & Kitayama, 1991). From a cultural perspective, which emotions are good or bad for learning depends on the fit with the current social conception of appropriate feelings. The educational setting and cultural practices outside the classroom mutually influence each other to establish, reinforce, or change cultural emotion norms (see Calkins & Dollar, 2014; DeCuir-Gunby & Williams-Johnson, 2014). Furthermore, the educational setting is a context in which teachers and students coregulate emotions to create context-specific emotion norms (see Meyer, 2014).

To conclude, researchers no longer view emotions as generally disruptive. Instead, they examine the specific causes of emotions (evolutionary and social contexts) and their consequences for cognition and behavior in different situations, focusing, for example, on identifying human universals and/or group differences.

EMOTIONS AS COMPONENTIAL EPISODES

To better understand the role of emotions in an educational setting, a closer look at the concept of emotion is useful.

Emotions Are Episodes

Emotion researchers generally view emotions as episodes that are evoked by a variety of stimuli (e.g., Ekman, 1992; Russell, 2003; Scherer, 2009). These can be actually occurring stimuli, such as feedback on an exam, as well as remembered or imagined stimuli, such as memories or fantasies of having failed an exam. Also, neurophysiological changes can cause changes in emotions. For example, some students take drugs to increase their positive affect or to reduce their negative affect.

Although individuals do not need to be consciously aware of the stimulus that caused their emotion, it is considered a defining characteristic of emotions that they are about something. This is also called the "event focus" of emotions (Scherer, 2005, p. 700). For example, a teacher may feel enthusiastic about a particular subject or about the activity of teaching (see Frenzel, 2014). Also, a student may be anxious about a test (see Zeidner, 2014). As the relation of the individual to the object of the emotion changes, so do the individual's emotions. Sources of change are the object (e.g., the teacher makes the test easier), the individual (e.g., the student studies for the test), the relation between the individual and the object (e.g., the student drops the class), or habituation (e.g., the student gets used to having tests and does not get upset by tests anymore).

As a result, emotions are commonly short-lived. For example, everyday fear episodes often last less than 15 minutes, and anger and joy episodes often last 15 to 60 minutes (Scherer, Wallbott, Summerfield, 1986; Verduyn, Delvaux, Van Coillie, Tuerlinckx, & Van Mechelen, 2009). Verduyn et al. (2009) find that the medium lifetime (the time when half of the episodes studied have ended) for anger and gratitude is shorter than the medium lifetime for joy and sadness. The study shows that the duration of everyday emotional episodes is longer the more intense the emotions are at the beginning of an episode, and is furthermore influenced by personality and situational variables. For example, ruminating about an emotion-eliciting event can lead to much longer lasting emotions.

Emotions Consist of Components

In addition to viewing emotions as episodes, researchers generally agree that these episodes consist of multiple components: a subjective feeling component, a motor component, a physiological component, an action tendency component, and an appraisal component (e.g., Plutchik, 2001; Russell, 2003; Scherer, 1984). Note that the words *affect* and *emotion* are sometimes used synonymously with the feeling component; more commonly though, affect is seen as a larger category that includes, among others, emotions and moods, and emotion is viewed as multicomponential and includes, among others, a feeling component. While there is a long tradition of regarding the subjective feeling, motor, and physiological components as central to emotions (see Scherer, 2001a), the action tendency component was advocated in the 1980s, in particular by Frijda (1986), and has since been included as an emotion component by most scientists. With the cognitive revolution in the social and behavioral sciences, the cognitive appraisal component has been increasingly recognized as an additional component of emotional experiences. However, some consider appraisals as antecedents and not components of emotions (for a detailed review of other disagreements among researchers concerning emotion components, see Moors, 2009).

The relevance of these components becomes obvious in self-reports and observations of emotions in others. Emotions are considered subjective experiences—that is, they are

Table 2.1 Examples of Emotion Components

Component	Primary Function	Examples
Subjective feeling	Monitoring	Sadness, happiness, gratitude, anger, feeling good
Action tendency	Motivation	Urge to weep, to jump up and down, to approach
Appraisal	Meaning-making	I just lost something, I just received a gift, I passed a difficult test, something good happened to me
Motor activity	Communication	Crying, smiling, raising one's chin, making oneself small, moving one's arms up and down quickly
Physiological	Support	Changes in pulse, blood flow, brain activity

primarily known only to the person experiencing them. Therefore, individuals' descriptions of emotional episodes greatly influence how scientists think about emotions. The multicomponential nature of emotions becomes evident in such self-reports. For example, "I am afraid," "I feel jittery," "I don't want to be here," or "I just don't have enough time to prepare for the final" refer to the different components of an emotion. The first expression (I am afraid) describes a subjective feeling of fear. The second example (I feel jittery) refers to the physiological component of emotion. The third example (I don't want to be here) indicates an avoidance action tendency, which may or may not be carried out. The fourth example describes several appraisals of the situation, including goal frustration (I am not prepared) and lack of power (I do not have enough time). Observable motor activities are also associated with emotions. For example, facial expressions, such as smiling or frowning, body postures, such as opening the arms or raising the fists, and changes in the voice, such as raised pitch, can be observed in emotional situations. See Table 2.1 for more examples of emotion components.

The individual is not always consciously aware of the activity in these components. For example, appraisals can be processed consciously or unconsciously by a conceptual, a schematic, and a sensory-motor system (e.g., Leventhal & Scherer, 1987; see Scherer, 2009, for a suggestion as to how to distinguish between schematic template matching and schematic associations). Similarly, the person can be more or less aware of her body posture or ongoing physiological changes.

The emotion components are associated with different functions. The subjective feeling component has been associated with a monitoring function. For example, feeling fear allows the individual to take regulatory efforts to reduce fear, and feeling less fear gives the individual feedback that the regulation was successful, such as when a student who feels scared before a test realizes that her fear decreases the more she prepares for the test. The monitoring function is not only important to regulate the individual's emotions but also to coordinate emotions in social interactions (for a review on the social functions of emotions, see Keltner & Haidt, 1999).

The appraisal component is associated with a meaning-making function. Cognitively processing an emotional event allows individuals to detect whether an event is relevant or not, to understand the causes and consequences of the event, to predict emotional reactions, to regulate the occurrence of emotions, and to communicate emotional knowledge to others. It is therefore highly important at the individual and the interindividual level. For example, a student may advise another student that studying before the test is very likely to reduce his fear.

The function of the action tendency component is to prioritize actions that are needed in a given situation. As a result, emotions bestow "control precedence" on some actions over others. This is seen as a defining feature of emotions (Frijda, 2007). For example, feeling curious is associated with approach rather than avoidant behavior. At the same time, as *action tendencies* are not actions (i.e., overt behavior), one has some flexibility to decide whether or not to carry out the action. This decoupling of stimulus and response distinguishes emotions from reflexes and allows for greater behavioral flexibility. For example, in a classroom, students sometimes need to wait before they can ask their questions. The action tendency associated with curiosity motivates students to ask questions, but it does not dictate that they immediately do so. Similarly, when feeling fear before a test for which one is not prepared, a student needs to suppress the urge to avoid the test and overcome the fear instead by, for example, studying for the test to increase her coping potential.

The motor component serves a communicative function, such as when we express our feelings of happiness by smiling at another person. This function is therefore particularly important at the interindividual level. Additionally, as suggested already by Darwin (1872/1998), the motor component has a function at the individual level because it can support adaptive action tendencies. For example, Susskind and Anderson (2008) demonstrate that expressions of disgust and anger lead to sensory closure. This may support the action tendencies to dispel the source of the disgust (e.g., unpleasant odor) and protect against the source of the anger. Conversely, fear and surprise motor activity in the face may increase sensory exposure and thereby support the gathering of information to reduce uncertainty.

The physiological component supports the activity of the other components. For example, appraising an event as relevant to the self is associated with increased amygdala activity (Sander, Grandjean, & Scherer, 2005). Also, an increase of blood flow to the hands and arms prepares the body for behavior when angry (Levenson, Ekman, & Friesen, 1990).

Emotional components can be measured at different *levels of analysis.* For example, subjective feelings can be assessed as more narrow categories, such as "gratefulness," or broad dimensions, such as "a positive feeling." Similarly, action tendencies can be assessed as concrete behaviors, such as "asking the teacher a question," or more broadly, such as "approaching the teacher." Also, appraisals can be more specific, such as "this might come up in the exam" or less specific, such as "this is relevant to me." The motor component may be assessed at a range of levels from muscle strand activity to expression in the entire body. Similarly, physiological changes can be measured at many different levels from single neuron activity to large-scale autonomic and motor systems involving the entire body.

Furthermore, the emotion components can be assessed using different *measurement paradigms.* Currently, research examining the brain activity associated with emotions is flourishing. However, one of the most important tools to measure emotions will probably remain self-report because of the inherent subjectivity of feelings, the easy applicability of self-report instruments for measuring emotions, and the richness of data that can be gathered using this method. Although most self-report instruments focus on the subjective feeling component of emotions, individuals can report information relevant to all components of an emotion associated with subjective feeling labels (Fontaine, Scherer, & Soriano, 2013; Scherer & Wallbott, 1994) and associated with facial expressions (e.g.,

Clark-Polner, Shuman, Meuleman, Sander, & Scherer, under review). For more details on measurements of emotion components, see Part IV of this book.

Differentiation of Emotions From Other Affective Phenomena

Knowing that emotions are componential episodes is useful to distinguish emotions from other affective phenomena, such as moods, attitudes, preferences, and affect dispositions (Scherer, 2005). First, moods tend to differ from emotions with regard to the associated components and the duration, although in some cases, it is difficult to make a sharp distinction. Whereas emotions are about something, moods generally do not have an object—in a bad mood, one just feels bad, often for no apparent reason, although moods do, of course, have a cause. For example, hormones may influence one's mood in adolescence (Buchanan, Eccles, & Becker, 1992). In contrast to moods, emotions have an object that is appraised. Also, moods last longer than emotions.

Second, attitudes, such as prejudice against students from certain sociocultural groups, also differ from emotions in duration and components. Similar to moods, attitudes are longer-lived than emotions. With regard to the associated components, attitudes may appear rather similar to emotions because both involve cognitive, affective, and motivational facets (Breckler, 1984). However, there are some important differences. First, the cognitive facet of attitudes is beliefs about the attitude object. Beliefs do not need to be triggered by an actually occurring, a remembered, or an imagined attitude object. For example, a student might believe that a particular cultural group is lazy without having met anybody from that group in an achievement context. Second, the structure of the affective component of attitudes consists mainly of general valence (positive–negative), and the structure of the behavioral component of attitudes consists mainly of approach–avoidance. The structures of the affective and the behavioral components of emotions are more complex. Third, the attitude behavior relation seems less direct than the emotion behavior relation. In a specific situation, attitudes may not predict concrete behavior well without taking other variables into account (see, e.g., Ajzen & Fishbein, 1977). For example, a student's belief that another cultural group is lazy might reduce the likelihood that the student will approach members of that group for collaborative projects, but it might not be a good predictor for the likelihood that she will ask a specific member of that group to collaborate with her on a particular project. In this situation, feelings of trust and liking show a stronger relation to behavior.

Third, preferences differ from emotions in similar ways as attitudes. That is, the associated affective states and behavioral tendencies are broader than those of emotions (valence, approach-avoidance), and they last longer than emotions. For example, students might have a general preference for learning Spanish over French, but they might feel rather excited about the French class offered by a particular teacher.

Finally, affect dispositions (also called trait emotions) are stable interindividual differences, such as an angry, anxious, depressed, or curious personality trait (Spielberger & Reheiser, 2009). Trait emotionality can be a precursor of enduring emotional disturbances such as depression. The disposition is, as the name indicates, not an affective experience itself but a tendency to experience a mood or emotion. The trait is reflected in the frequency that a particular emotion has been experienced in the past and the probability that it will be experienced in the future (Spielberger & Reheiser, 2009). For example, students with dispositions to experience and express anger may show more frequent aggressive behavior in a class setting than students without these dispositions (Spielberger & Reheiser, 2009); students with trait test anxiety may show an increased likelihood to experience anxiety in school settings (see Schutz, Davis, DeCuir-Gunby, & Tillmanand, 2014; Zeidner, 2014). A mechanism underlying the effects of trait emotionality consists of appraisal biases—for example, having a tendency of viewing out-group members as dangerous, or one's coping potential with tests as low. Such biases may be due to cognitive predispositions, cultural factors, or one's learning history (see Scherer & Brosch, 2009). Also, implicit motives may be a source of appraisal biases (see Schultheiss & Köllner, 2014).

CONTROVERSIAL THEORETICAL PERSPECTIVES

The previous section outlined what emotions are not. However, deciding what emotions are is still a controversial issue. Construing emotions as involving various interacting components makes it hard to define the boundaries of an emotion. After all, we often appraise our environment without feeling particularly emotional (e.g., the computer is goal conducive to writing a paper, but I am not happy right now), we show motor expressions without being in any particular emotion (e.g., when squinting at the sun), and we have action tendencies without feeling emotional (e.g., following habits or routines). It is necessary to further define how the different emotion components act together to bring about an emotion. This question is still hotly debated in the affective sciences.

Researchers generally agree that emotions are episodes with multiple components that are shaped by evolutionary and social contexts and can be expressed in a variety of ways (e.g., Ekman, 1992; Ellsworth & Scherer, 2003; Izard, 2007; Russell, 2003; Scherer, Schorr, & Johnstone, 2001). However, it is rather controversial how the different components hang together to form an emotion. To what extent is the component activity hard-wired? Which component drives changes in other components? How are emotions different from nonemotional states? Early emotion researchers suggested that emotions are the perception of bodily symptoms (James, 1884) or context-dependent attributions of unspecified arousal (Schachter & Singer, 1962). The major current emotion theories—basic emotion theories, appraisal theories, social constructionist theories, and nonlinear dynamic systems theories—still provide different answers to fundamental questions about emotions (see Figure 2.1).

Basic Emotions Theories

Basic emotions theories, also called discrete emotions theories (e.g., Ekman, 1992; Izard, 1994, 2007; Panksepp, 2007; Plutchik, 2001; Tomkins, 1962), were inspired by Darwin's (1872/1998) work on emotion expressions and propose the existence of a small number of basic emotions (affect programs). The notion of a program suggests that the different components of the emotion are strongly linked; some theorists indeed propose that affect programs have specific neural circuits (Panksepp, 2007). The components are triggered as one "package," resulting in an emotional sequence with a baseline, a stimulus, an emotion, and a return to the baseline ("equilibrium," Plutchik, 2001, p. 348). Basic emotions lead to prototypical changes in emotion components in specific types of situations. For example, in a threat situation, the subjective feeling of fear is associated with the appraisal of danger and an action tendency to escape the situation, but in a competitive

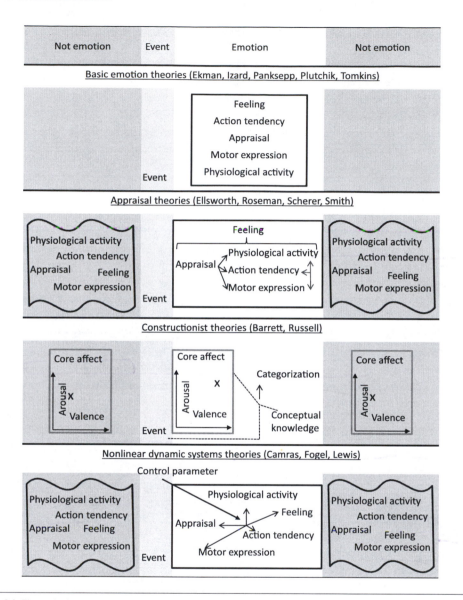

Figure 2.1 Theoretical perspectives on the relation among emotion components. Note that in Russell's (2003) theory, *emotion* would be replaced by *emotional meta-experience*.

situation, the subjective feeling of anger is associated with the appraisal of enemy and an action tendency of attack (Plutchik, 2001).

Basic emotions are seen as meeting fundamental needs of survival that reoccur throughout human evolution. Thus, basic emotions are thought to have evolved, to be universally shared by humans, and to occur in similar forms across related species. This view is bolstered by empirical similarities of emotion expression and perception when comparing cultures, when examining adult and child behavior, and when studying various species that are unlikely to have occurred by chance (e.g., Ekman, 1992).

There are only a few basic emotions (3 to 11; Plutchik, 2001). Other emotions are seen as variations within a basic emotion family (e.g., Ekman, 1992), mixtures of the more basic emotions (e.g., Plutchik, 2001), or other types of emotions (Izard, 2007). For example, Izard (2007) distinguishes basic emotions from emotion schemas. In his theory, basic emotions are associated with rudimentary appraisals and have their strongest influence in infancy and in critical situations. Emotion schemas, in contrast, are common in everyday adult life and involve more elaborate appraisals and variation as the result of social learning. Researchers who do not propose emotion schemas leave room for cultural influences by suggesting that cultures have specific display rules and that individuals' construals of a situation (which may be culturally influenced) determine which basic emotions are subsequently felt (Ekman, 1992). In other words, although basic emotion theories emphasize the evolutionary roots of emotions, they are compatible with cultural learning perspectives on emotion.

Appraisal Theories

Appraisal theories (e.g., Arnold, 1960; Ellsworth & Smith, 1988; Lazarus, 1968; Ortony, Clore, & Collins, 1990; Roseman, Antoniou, & Jose, 1996; Scherer, 1984, 2001b, 2009; see Scherer, Schorr, & Johnstone, 2001 for a comprehensive overview and Moors, Ellsworth, Scherer, & Frijda, 2013 for recent extensions) propose that emotions are driven by appraisals. Changes in other emotional components are caused by changes in appraisals. For example, when a student appraises the homework as too demanding and the time to do it as too short, the pulse starts to rise, she sweats, and feelings of panic arise. The causal path can be conceived as going from each appraisal to each component (e.g., Scherer, 2005) or from a pattern of appraisals to each component (e.g., Lazarus, 1991). Subjective feelings play a special role in appraisal theory because they are thought of as an integrative representation of changes in the other emotion components.

Treating appraisal both as a causal factor and a component of emotion is possible because appraisal theorists see emotion as a process with constantly interacting components. Appraisal, the cognitive component, plays a special role in that it starts the emotion. Due to the interaction between components, reactions in other components triggered by appraisal results will in turn be appraised in terms of their appropriateness (e.g., given sociocultural expectations) and may thus change the emotion process. In such a system of recursive causation between multiple components, simple models of unidirectional cause–effect sequences no longer apply.

The relation among appraisals has been further specified. Appraising an event as relevant to the individual's goals and needs is seen as central to arouse emotions; other appraisals then differentiate among emotions. For example, when an event is appraised as obstructive to reaching a highly relevant goal and one's potential to cope with that obstruction is appraised as low, an individual feels dejected and has the urge to hide and cry. This may happen, for instance, when a bad test score will result in failing a class and no more tests are scheduled that could improve the grade. Although appraisals have been conceptualized as discrete (e.g., a situation is either consistent or inconsistent with an individual's goals; Roseman et al., 1996), other theories and empirical evidence suggest that they are continuous (e.g., degrees of goal conduciveness; Scherer, 1984, 2001b; Tong & Tay, 2011). Furthermore, Scherer (2005, 2009) proposes that appraisals are processed in parallel but produce efferent effects on other components only after sufficient closure with respect to the evaluation is available to justify the involvement of many other components. This typically occurs in a specific sequence, as some appraisal checks can only lead to a result if preceding checks have produced the required background information. For example, individuals first have to appraise to what extent an event is obstructive to their goals before they can come to closure on whether or not they have the resources to cope with it: a student cannot know whether she has the capacity to finish her homework on time before knowing how much homework she will get.

Component activities, including appraisals, are continuously ongoing. Emotions occur when something happens that the organism considers of great relevance—that is, by being directly linked to its needs, goals, values, and general well-being, and that therefore requires the deployment of attention and further information processing (Frijda & Scherer, 2009). Furthermore, Scherer (2000, 2009) suggests that emotions differ from nonemotional states in that the components, which normally operate relatively independently, are synchronized for the duration of the emotion episode in order to prepare the appropriate action tendency.

Modal patterns of synchronized emotion components triggered by typical configurations of appraisal results that consistently occur with greater frequency in human social life are labeled with commonly known emotion terms, such as happiness or anger (providing evidence for the lexical sedimentation of common experiences in a culture; Scherer, 2013), but other combinations of appraisals and therefore of emotions are possible. There may be differences in emotions across cultures with regard to which stimuli cause emotions and which labels are used to describe them. However, researchers suggest that the appraisal–emotion link is evolved and consistent across cultures. Evidence for appraisal theory comes from research showing systematic links between appraisals and emotions (e.g., Ellsworth & Scherer, 2003; Fontaine et al., 2013; Scherer et al., 2001, Scherer & Wallbott, 1994) and appraisals and action tendencies (e.g., Frijda, Kuipers, & ter Schure, 1989).

Psychological Constructionist Theories

Central to psychological constructionist theories of emotions is the concept of core affect (Barrett, 2006a, 2006b; Russell, 2003). Core affect is an evolved neurophysiological state that is always present and consciously accessible as a subjective feeling of valence and arousal (Barrett, 2006b; Russell, 2003).

According to Russell (2003, personal communication March 19, 2013), an emotional episode consists of various components, typically including, among other components, appraisals, instrumental actions, motor expressions, and an emotional meta-experience. Core affect, being always present, is also a component of emotional episodes. In this theory, emotional episode is a rather heterogeneous class: not all components need to be present, and affective phenomena other than prototypical emotions are considered the rule rather than the exception. An emotional meta-experience is the categorization of one's perceived state based on the status of the other components of the emotional episode. The categories typically (not necessarily) map onto lexicalized emotion concepts (e.g., anger).

Barrett (2006a, 2006b) does not explicitly use the technical term emotional meta-experience. She suggests that emotions result when individuals associate a subjective feeling of core affect with an event and conceptual knowledge about emotions. The conceptual knowledge includes knowledge about emotion terms and emotion scripts that describe or prescribe which emotions are, or ought to be, felt in which situations. In her model, the conceptual knowledge contributes to the overall experience of the emotion (conceptual act).

Theories of the psychological construction of emotions generally emphasize cultural influences on emotions because knowledge about emotion terms and scripts is seen as culturally determined. As such, emotions are not considered natural entities or special in any way. Constructionist theories propose no natural relations between situation types and emotions (as in basic emotion theories) or between appraisals and emotions (as in appraisal theories). As a result, there is no reliable criterion to distinguish emotions from other categories constructed based on perceived core affect (e.g., feeling sick). Evidence in support of this view can be seen in empirically demonstrated differences across situations, individuals, and cultures in the expression, perception, and understanding of emotions, and in numerous studies that point to valence and arousal as the central underlying dimensions of emotional experiences (e.g., see reviews in Barrett, 2006c; Russell, 2003).

Nonlinear Dynamic Systems Theories

Nonlinear dynamic systems theories (Camras, 2011; Fogel et al., 1992; Lewis, 2005) emphasize nonlinear relations between emotion components. Emotions are seen as attractor states. Attractor states result from self-organization by nested positive and negative feedback loops; they are local energy minima and are therefore locally stable. Any emotion component may draw the other emotion components into an attractor state. For example, smiling may cause feelings, appraisals, and physiological changes to take on the attractor state of "happiness." An emotion is seen as a particular kind of state in a succession of attractor states that is "motivationally charged" (Fogel et al., 1992, p. 133).

Attractor states, once reached, may require a large change to move the system out of an attractor state and disturb it until a new attractor state is reached (so-called phase shift). For example, once students have reached an attractor state of disinterest, it may take a huge effort to move them away from that state to one of curiosity. Conversely, once students' curiosity is aroused, it may take quite a bit of slack in the teaching to move the class to utter boredom; the relation between stimulus and emotion is not linear (the quality of the teaching does not translate one-to-one to students' interest) but depends on the previous state of the system (boredom or curiosity). In other words, a nonlinear dynamic systems view emphasizes the importance of knowing the preceding state for predicting future states.

Another feature of this view is that control parameters determine the relation between input and output, such as whether they are linearly related or not. For example, when gazing upward, one already has a tendency to open one's mouth, and thus there may be a rather linear relation between the degree to which an event is surprising and one's surprise facial expression. However, when looking down, two attractor states may exist (closed mouth, open mouth) that show phase shifts that are not linearly related with the degree of a surprising event (compare Camras, 2011). Nonlinear dynamic systems are increasingly used to describe emotions (e.g., Lewis, 2005). However, hypothesis driven empirical studies following this perspective are still relatively scarce (e.g., Camras, 2011; Sacharin, Sander, & Scherer, 2012).

Summary

To summarize, basic emotion theory suggests that all emotion components are triggered jointly as packages; appraisal theory proposes that appraisals drive changes in other components that, when synchronized, build emotions; social constructionist theories suggest that the categorization of changes in core affect and other emotion component activity leads to emotions (emotional meta-experiences); and a nonlinear dynamic systems approach suggests that any one component can pull the other components into attractor states, which may correspond to emotions. Note that although this review suggests rather distinct differences between these perspectives, they can to some extent be reconciled. For example, the nonlinear systems approach has been partially incorporated by proponents of other theoretical traditions, such as basic emotions theory (Izard, 2007) and appraisal theory (Sander et al., 2005; Scherer, 2000).

IMPLICATIONS OF DIFFERENT THEORETICAL PERSPECTIVES

The different theoretical approaches have implications for the regulation of emotion, the relation between emotions, and the preferred measurement of emotions. Furthermore, researchers from the different theoretical traditions have brought forth specific bodies of knowledge because the theories focus research attention on particular aspects of emotional life.

Implications for the Regulation of Emotions

Emotion regulation research (see Jacobs & Gross, 2014) is not wed to one of the traditional emotion theories, and the primary focus of emotion theories is not on emotion regulation. However, in applied settings, such as educational settings, the question of emotion regulation is a central concern (see, e.g., Schutz et al., 2014). It is therefore useful to briefly sketch the implications of the different emotion theories for emotion regulation. The different theoretical perspectives suggest that attempts to regulate emotions target different components of the emotion (Gross & Barrett, 2011; see also Jacobs & Gross, 2014).

According to a basic emotions view, affect programs occur automatically. Emotion regulation can therefore take place primarily by changing which stimuli an individual is exposed to in the first place or by controlling the automatic action tendencies and suppressing motor expressions and respective physiological changes. Emotion generation and regulation can be quite clearly distinguished from a basic emotions perspective. Note that when Izard's (2007) emotion schemas are considered, regulation may also look similar to the processes suggested by appraisal theories.

Appraisal theories suggest that appraisals drive the emotion process. Consequentially, changing the way individuals appraise events seems key to changing an emotional experience. Once an event is appraised and the emotion emerges, emotion regulation can take place by reappraising the event. For example, a student who receives a bad grade might initially appraise that he did poorly on the test, and subsequently, in order to improve his feelings, reappraise the situation to think that the teacher wrote an unfair test. Subjectively, the difference between emotion generation and regulation can be quite clear—for example, when individuals conscientiously try to change their perspectives on a situation to influence their emotions. However, in the constant stream of appraisals and emotions, it can be difficult to objectively and systematically distinguish these processes. Furthermore, social contexts may influence how events are appraised, further blurring the line between emotion generation and regulation. Temporary social environments (e.g., being in school) and stable social environments (e.g., culture) may increase the likelihood to appraise situations in a particular way and thereby regulate the occurrence of particular emotions. For example, in a family setting, the situation where Anna asks John questions that Anna knows the answers to but John does not may lead John to blame Anna for asking difficult questions and subsequently arouse John's anger. In a school setting, however, John might rather blame himself for not knowing the answers and feel embarrassed.

Psychological constructionist theories regard valence and arousal as core affective building blocks that lead via categorization to emotions (emotional meta-experiences). Therefore, the regulation of core affect and of the constructed emotion concept might take place relatively independently. First, regulation can focus on core affect by changing the situation that caused the core affect. Second, regulation can target the categorization of the emotion, with regard to either the knowledge used to construct the emotion (e.g., knowledge of emotion words) or the process of the construction (e.g., interrupting it through cognitive load). Psychological constructionist theories are similar to appraisal theory in that both approaches are concerned with meaning making, but in appraisal theory, meaning making is mostly concerned with the evaluation of external events in the light of internal goals, values, and capacities, whereas in psychological constructionist theories, the meaning making is about internal body sensations. Similar to appraisal theory, the boundary between emotion emergence and regulation is not clear as emotions are continuously constructed.

A nonlinear dynamic systems approach proposes that any of the components can draw the remaining components into an emotional attractor state. Therefore, regulation can target any of the emotion components. Indeed, facial expressions and body postures influence individuals' self-reported affective state (e.g., Laird, 1974; Levenson et al., 1990).

Implications for the Emotion Space and the Measurement of Emotions

Knowing the different theoretical perspectives is important because they suggest different structures and measurements of emotions. We illustrate this with a few selected examples (see also Immordino-Yang & Christodoulou, 2014; Kreibig & Gendolla, 2014; Pekrun & Bühner, 2014; Reisenzein et al., 2014; Turner & Trucano, 2014).

First, a well-known structural model to describe the relation between emotions from a basic emotions perspective is Plutchik's circumplex model, which was developed in 1958 (Plutchik, 2001; Figure 2.2). In this model, eight basic emotions are arranged as four pairs of opposites (e.g., joy—sadness). Discrete emotion terms describe intensity differences within the basic emotions (e.g., serenity, joy, ecstasy) as well as mixtures between the basic emotions (e.g., joy and trust build love). Thus, the relation between emotions is organized by a systematic arrangement of discrete emotions. In basic emotions research, emotions are generally assessed as discrete categories (e.g., happiness, anger) with different response formats (e.g., multiple choice).

Second, in appraisal theory, emotions are structured in a space described by the underlying appraisals. For example, in Scherer's component process model (Scherer, 1984, 2005), four appraisal objectives are proposed: relevance, implication assessment, coping

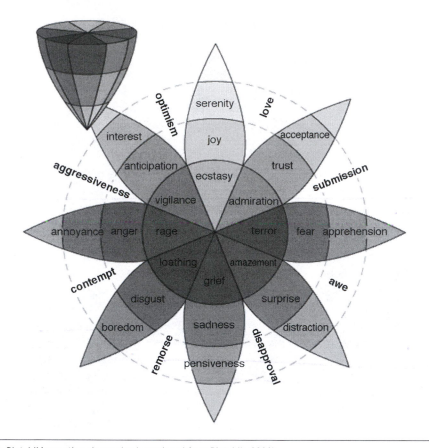

Figure 2.2 Plutchik's emotion circumplex (reproduced from Plutchik, 2001).

potential, and normative significance. Each of the objectives contains between two and six stimulus evaluation checks, resulting in a total of 14 possible dimensions. Specifically, relevance appraisals contain a novelty check, an intrinsic pleasantness check, and a goal/need relevance check; implications are assessed regarding the causal agent and the agent's motive, regarding the situational outcome probability, discrepancy from expectations, and goal conduciveness, and regarding the situational urgency; coping potential contains checks of the general controllability of the situation, the personal power of the individual, and the individual's potential to adjust to the situation; the normative significance is assessed with regard to internal and external standards. While this allows a high degree of specificity for differentiating emotions from each other, visualizing the appraisal space is difficult because of the number of dimensions considered important. As a result, though appraisals might be assessed for a limited number of emotions, emotions are not typically assessed as appraisals. Instead, appraisal researchers typically work with discrete emotion terms to study the appraisal–emotion relation.

Ortony et al. (1990), who are appraisal theorists in a broader sense, suggest a more specific structure of emotions. Based on a decision tree of several appraisals concerning the consequences of events, the actions of agents, and aspects of the objects, they differentiate various emotion types, such as prospect-based emotions (e.g., hope), attribution emotions (e.g., pride), and attraction emotions (e.g., love). The decision tree lends itself to computational approaches to emotions, such as computational analyses, simulations, and artificial intelligence.

Third, in psychological constructionist theories, emotions are primarily structured along the valence and arousal dimensions. Describing the structure of emotions on dimensions has a long tradition in psychological research. Early dimensional models of feelings included valence, arousal, and tension (tense-relaxed; Wundt, 1897) or valence, arousal, and attention-rejection (Schlosberg, 1954). Researchers and lay people alike distinguish between positive emotions, such as happiness, satisfaction, and pride, and negative emotions, such as anger, fear, and sadness. Note that upon closer inspection, this assignment is ambiguous because some emotions may be regarded as positive from one perspective (e.g., how they feel) but as negative from another (how virtuous they are; e.g., Solomon & Stone, 2002). Furthermore, some emotions, such as surprise, are neither positive nor negative. Nonetheless, the dimensional approach to emotions has been highly influential. A well-known measurement tool from this tradition is the Self-Assessment Manikin, which features valence, arousal, and dominance dimensions (Bradley & Lang, 1994).

With only one valence dimension, however, it is not possible to capture mixed positive–negative emotions. Some researchers therefore suggest that the structure of emotions can be better described by a rotation of the valence and arousal dimensions by 45 degrees, resulting in one dimension of Positive Activation and one dimension of Negative Activation (see Watson, Clark, & Tellegen, 1988). A commonly used measurement tool from this approach is the Positive and Negative Affect Schedule (PANAS; Watson et al., 1988). Others suggest that underlying the commonly used single valence dimension, which has a positive and a negative pole (*bipolar* valence), are two orthogonal valence dimensions—positive valence; and negative valence—each with a low and a high pole (*bivariate* valence; Cacioppo, Gardner, & Berntson, 1999). The Evaluative Space Grid (Larsen, Norris, McGraw, Hawkley, & Cacioppo, 2008) is a measurement tool that assesses bivariate valence in a single step.

Despite the apparent distinction between discrete and dimensional approaches, they can be seen as complementary (Izard, 2007; Scherer, 2005). For example, it is possible to project discrete emotions onto a dimensional model, such as Russell's (1980) circumplex model with a valence and arousal dimension (Figure 2.3). Indeed, it is quite common to assess discrete emotions that are then aggregated according to superordinate dimensions, factors, or clusters.

Taking a complementary approach much further, in an extensive study examining how emotion components assessed with 142 features are associated with 24 emotion terms in 34 samples and 25 languages, Fontaine et al. (2013) identify an underlying four-dimensional space with the dimensions valence, power/control, activation/arousal, and novelty (note that in this study, power/control emerges as a dimension with more predictive power than arousal). They then proceed to analyze their data from different perspectives—namely, regarding the emotion components, the 24 categorical emotion terms and the 4 higher order dimensions. They find, first, that the emotion domain can be represented from each of the different perspectives. Second, analyses from the different perspectives lead to unique insights. For example, the structure of the feeling component with a valence, power/control, and arousal dimension most closely resembles the structure across all emotion components, whereas the structure of the physiological component least resembles that structure.

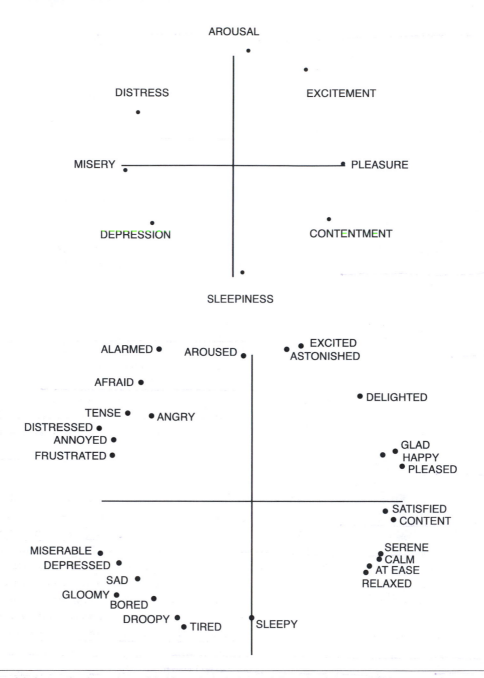

Figure 2.3 On top, the circumplex model with a valence and arousal dimension; below, multidimensional scaling results based on similarity judgments of emotion words, such as angry, happy, and sad, and the dimensions of the circumplex model (reproduced from Russell, 1980; reprinted with permission).

Data from this study has been used to further develop a self-report measure of emotions, the Geneva Emotion Wheel (GEW; Scherer, Shuman, Fontaine, & Soriano, 2013). The GEW (Figure 2.4) consists of discrete emotion terms corresponding to emotion families that are systematically aligned in a circle. Underlying the alignment of the

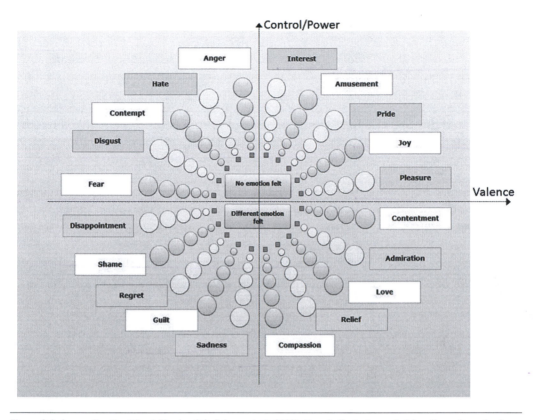

Figure 2.4 Geneva Emotion Wheel (Version 3.0; Scherer et al., 2013). Lines indicate the underlying dimensions of valence (negative–positive) and control/power (low–high).

emotion terms are the two dimensions of valence (negative to positive) and control/power (low to high), separating the emotions in four quadrants: negative-low control/power, negative-high control/power, positive-low control/power, and positive-high control/power. The response options are spikes in the wheel that correspond to different levels of intensity for each emotion family. These range from low intensity (towards the center of wheel) to high intensity (toward the circumference of the wheel). The response option "no emotion" and "other emotion" is also offered in the very center of the wheel. The GEW directly reflects the complementary approach to a discrete and dimensional assessment by visually combining discrete emotion terms in a dimensional structure.

Implications for the Knowledge Gained From Different Theoretical Traditions

The theoretical perspectives on emotions described above have stimulated rather different kinds of research programs and paradigms, which have generated unique bodies of knowledge. We include this brief, nonexhaustive illustration to demonstrate that the choice of theoretical paradigm influences the research findings and that knowing about different paradigms is therefore important to guide research on emotions in education.

With their emphasis on clearly distinguishable affect programs that have evolutionary roots, basic emotions theories lend themselves to researching questions such as:

Which and how many emotions are basic? How can the specificity of affect programs be described? How does the affect program increase evolutionary fitness? A concern with *the function of an emotion* is central. To identify evolutionary continua across ontogenetic and phylogenetic development, researchers from this tradition investigate which emotions are shared by human adults across different cultures, human children, and other species. Two examples of the research tools and knowledge gained from this research tradition are a detailed description of facial expressions, the highly influential Facial Action Coding System (Ekman, Friesen, & Hager, 2002), and the identification of happiness, anger, sadness, fear, disgust, and surprise as being similarly expressed and perceived across cultures (e.g., Ekman, 1992; Elfenbein & Ambady, 2002).

Furthermore, Fredrickson's (1998) highly influential broaden-and-build theory builds on the notion of the evolutionary route of emotions and emotion specific action tendencies. Fredrickson describes how the action tendencies associated with negative emotions typically studied by emotion theorists appear narrower (e.g., fight the enemy) and suggests that the action tendencies associated with positive emotions may be broader (explore the environment). Similarly, while negative emotions might solve a specific problem (e.g., get away from a fear-provoking stimulus), positive emotions might increase an organism's thought-action-repertoire, which may be of value for survival at a later time (e.g., bonding with others in love creates social resources). Her work has been highly influential in the growing field of positive psychology, which examines the processes and factors involved in human flourishing.

Appraisal theories enable us to study which appraisals most parsimoniously describe similarities and differences between emotions, identify the sequence of appraisals, assess physiological correlates of appraisals, and examine the links between appraisals and action tendencies. A concern with the *process that leads to an emotion* is central. The most important appraisals researchers have converged on include novelty (Is the event new/familiar?), valence (Is the event good/bad?), certainty (Is the outcome of the event certain/predictable?), goal significance (Is the event important to my goals/needs?), agency (Who is responsible for the event?), coping potential (Can I cope with the event?), and compatibility with norms (Is the event in accordance with mine/others' norms? Ellsworth & Scherer, 2003). Also, many cross-cultural differences in emotion experience can be explained by understanding the underlying appraisals (e.g., Scherer, 1997). Furthermore, researchers established that small changes in appraisals cause stronger changes in emotions at moderate levels (Tong & Tay, 2011).

Psychological constructionist theories lend themselves to examining how well affective stimuli and experiences can be structured along the underlying dimensions of valence and arousal, the variability and malleability of the emotion components associated with emotion categories due to the context specific construction of emotion categories, and the development of emotional understanding in children. A concern with *what influences the construal of an emotion category* is central. In the controversy about which theoretical approach is better, psychological constructionist researchers, similar to basic emotion theorists, focus much research attention on the expression and perception of emotion, but they also examine the influence of language on the understanding of emotions. Their research demonstrates, for example, that the valence dimension explains the most variance in the classifications of affective words, facial and vocal expressions, and affective states aroused by various stimuli across language and age groups (e.g., see review in Barrett, 2006c). Another example is research showing that the perception of emotion expressions is strongly influenced by the context, such as previously seen emotion expressions (e.g., Russell & Fehr, 1987). Furthermore, important issues for the study of emotions, such as the influence of the response format on the data, have been identified (e.g., Russell, 1994).

Nonlinear dynamic systems theory affords research describing organized patterns of emotional components in different contexts. A particular focus is on the temporal dynamics of emotions and on identifying control parameters. A concern with *the dynamics underlying emotional and nonemotional states* is central. However, only little empirical research exists from a nonlinear dynamic systems view. This research focuses on the development of emotions in infants; it shows, for example, how emotional components are increasingly differentiated and integrated to attractor states (Camras, 2011). Other studies examine the specific nature of the attractor states for anger (Hoeksma, Oosterlaan, Schipper, & Koot, 2007). Finally, research on phase shifts in emotion perception shows that the phase shifts depend on the emotion expression origin (Sacharin et al., 2012).

FUTURE DIRECTIONS

We now provide an outlook on selected future directions in research on the concepts and structures of emotion and their implications for research on emotions in education. First, an ongoing debate among affective scientists concerns the question of the extent to which emotions are universal or culture specific. This question has been widely debated since the beginning of systematic emotion research. For example, Paul Ekman (1998) reports heated discussions with Margaret Mead in the 1970s about whether emotions are universal or culture specific. The research paradigm of choice then was to study emotions via emotion expressions and perceptions. In a modern take on the same fundamental question, Lisa Feldman Barrett and Jaak Panksepp argue back and forth about whether emotions have emotion specific brain correlates (Panksepp, 2007 and responses). The debate is likely to continue in the near future. Our suggestion for researchers of emotions in education is to be aware of their own preconceptions and to clearly emphasize both human universals and cultural differences when interpreting their data.

A second major issue that is likely to affect future emotion research is the question of whether and how discrete and continuous structures of emotions should be combined. A central disagreement is whether dimensions such as valence and arousal are the more basic building blocks of emotional life (Barrett, 2006c) or whether these dimensions are higher order dimensions of emotions (e.g., Fontaine et al., 2013). Also, there is still no consensus on whether valence should be conceived of as bivariate or bipolar. Researchers are increasingly examining in more detail how lower and higher order dimensions of emotions might relate to one another both theoretically (e.g., Shuman, Sander, & Scherer, 2013) and empirically (e.g., Kuppens, Champagne, & Tuerlinckx, 2012). Our suggestion for researchers of emotions in education is to contribute to this discussion based on the insights from their research rather than to pick a particular camp.

Third, researchers are increasingly investigating aesthetic emotions (art related, such as emotions during listening to music) and epistemic emotions (knowledge related, such as wonder at intellectual prowess). Both aesthetic and epistemic emotions (e.g., wonder, admiration, rapture, interest) differ from the commonly studied utilitarian emotions because no particular action tendencies or adaptive functions seem to be associated with them

(Scherer, 2005). The study of these emotions may require the development of new research paradigms (e.g., Zentner, Grandjean, & Scherer, 2008) and contributes to the ongoing debate about the nature of emotions. Although it is not immediately apparent, research on epistemic emotions and their effect on motivation to learn may produce insights of great interest for educational settings. Furthermore, research on the mechanism underlying aesthetic emotions, such as entrainment by music through rhythm and coordination, may be directly applicable to classroom settings where students act together in time.

Finally, emotion researchers have traditionally examined the individual's face, voice, or self-report. Increasingly, they are using two additional approaches to understanding emotions: neural correlates of emotions and emotions in social contexts. The growing interest of basic emotions researchers in studying emotion in a social setting could create a more favorable climate for the integration of basic emotions research with more applied research from education settings. We hope that the current contribution in this handbook can facilitate and encourage such integration.

REFERENCES

Ajzen, I., & Fishbein, M. (1977). Attitude-behavior relations: A theoretical analysis and review of empirical research. *Psychological Bulletin, 84,* 888–918.

Arnold, M. (1960). *Emotion and personality.* New York, NY: Columbia University Press.

Barrett, L. F. (2006a). Are emotions natural kinds? *Psychological Science, 1,* 28–58.

Barrett, L. F. (2006b). Solving the emotion paradox: Categorization and the experience of emotion. *Personality and Social Psychology Review, 10,* 20–46.

Barrett, L. (2006c). Valence is a basic building block of emotional life. *Journal of Research in Personality, 40,* 35–55.

Bradley, M., & Lang, P. J. (1994). Measuring emotion: The self-assessment manikin and the semantic differential. *Journal of Behavior Therapy and Experimental Psychiatry, 25,* 49–59.

Breckler, S. J. (1984). Empirical validation of affect, behavior, and cognition as distinct components of attitude. *Journal of Personality and Social Psychology, 47,* 1191–1205.

Buchanan, C. M., Eccles, J. S., & Becker, J. B. (1992). Are adolescents the victims of raging hormones? Evidence for activational effects of hormones on moods and behavior at adolescence. *Psychological Bulletin, 111,* 62–107.

Cacioppo, J. T., Gardner, W. L., & Berntson, G. G. (1999). The affect system has parallel and integrative processing components: Form follows function. *Journal of Personality and Social Psychology, 76,* 839–855.

Calkins, S. D., & Dollar, J. M. (2014). Caregiving influences on emotion regulation: Educational implications of a biobehavioral perspective. In R. Pekrun & L. Linnenbrink-Garcia (Eds.), *International handbook of emotions in education* (pp. 520–538). New York, NY: Taylor & Francis.

Camras, L. A. (2011). Differentiation, dynamical integration and functional emotional development. *Emotion Review, 3,* 138–146.

Clark-Polner, E., Shuman, V., Meuleman, B., Sander, D., & Scherer, K. R. (under review). *Emotion perception from a componential perspective.* Manuscript submitted for publication.

Darwin, C. (1998). *The expression of emotions in man and animals.* P. Ekman (Ed.). London, UK: HarperCollins. (Original work published 1872)

Davidson, R., Scherer, K. R, &. Goldsmith, H. (Eds.). (2003). *Handbook of affective sciences.* New York, NY: Oxford University Press.

DeCuir-Gunby, J. T., & Williams-Johnson, M. R. (2014). The influence of culture on emotions: Implications for education. In R. Pekrun & L. Linnenbrink-Garcia (Eds.), *International handbook of emotions in education* (pp. 539–557). New York, NY: Taylor & Francis.

Ekman, P. (1992). An argument for basic emotions. *Cognition and Emotion, 6,* 169–200.

Ekman, P. (1998). Universality of emotional expression? A personal history of the dispute. In C. Darwin (Ed.), *The expression of the emotions in man and animals* (3rd ed., pp. 363–393). New York, NY: Oxford University Press.

Ekman, P., Friesen, W. V., & Hager, J. C. (2002). *Facial action coding system.* Salt Lake City, UT: A Human Face.

Elfenbein, H. A., & Ambady, N. (2002). On the universality and cultural specificity of emotion recognition: A meta-analysis. *Psychological Bulletin, 128,* 203–235.

Ellsworth, P. C., & Scherer, K. R. (2003). Appraisal processes in emotion. In R. J. Davidson, H. H. Goldsmith, & K. R. Scherer (Eds.), *Handbook of affective sciences* (pp. 572–595). New York, NY: Oxford University Press.

Ellsworth, P. C., & Smith, C. A. (1988). From appraisal to emotion: Differences among unpleasant feelings. *Motivation and Emotion, 12,* 271–302.

Fogel, A., Nwokah, E., Dedo, J. Y., Messinger, D., Dickson, K. L., Matusov, E., & Holt, S. A. (1992). Social process theory of emotion: A dynamic systems approach. *Social Development, 1,* 122–142.

Fontaine, J.R.J., Scherer, K. R., & Soriano, C. (2013), *Components of emotional meaning: A sourcebook.* Oxford: Oxford University Press.

Fredrickson, B. L. (1998). What good are positive emotions?? *Review of General Psychology, 2,* 300–319.

Frenzel, A. C. (2014). Teacher emotions. In R. Pekrun & L. Linnenbrink-Garcia (Eds.), *International handbook of emotions in education* (pp. 494–519). New York, NY: Taylor & Francis.

Frijda, N. H. (1986). *The emotions.* Cambridge: Cambridge University Press.

Frijda, N. H. (2007). *The laws of emotion.* Mahwah, NJ: Lawrence Erlbaum.

Frijda, N. H., Kuipers, P., & ter Schure, E. (1989). Relations among emotion, appraisal, and emotional action readiness. *Journal of Personality and Social Psychology, 57,* 212–228.

Frijda, N., & Scherer, K. R. (2009). Emotion definitions (psychological perspectives). In D. Sander & K. R. Scherer (Eds.). *Oxford companion to emotion and the affective sciences* (pp. 142–144). Oxford: Oxford University Press.

Gross, J. J., & Barrett, L. F. (2011). One or two depends on your point of view. *Emotion Review, 3,* 8–16.

Hoeksma, J. B., Oosterlaan, J., Schipper, E., & Koot, H. (2007). Finding the attractor of anger: Bridging the gap between dynamic concepts and empirical data. *Emotion, 7,* 638–648.

Izard, C. E. (1994). Innate and universal facial expressions: Evidence from developmental and cross-cultural research. *Psychological Bulletin, 115,* 288–299.

Izard, C. E. (2007). Basic emotions, natural kinds, emotion schemas, and a new paradigm. *Perspectives on Psychological Science, 2,* 260–280.

Jacobs, S. E., & Gross, J. J. (2014). Emotion regulation in education: Conceptual foundations, current applications, and future directions. In R. Pekrun & L. Linnenbrink-Garcia (Eds.), *International handbook of emotions in education* (pp. 183–201). New York, NY: Taylor & Francis.

James, W. (1884). What is an emotion? *Mind, 9,* 188–205.

Keltner, D., & Haidt, J. (1999). Social functions of emotions at four levels of analysis. *Cognition and Emotion, 13,* 505–521.

Kuppens, P., Champagne, D., & Tuerlinckx, F. (2012). The dynamic interplay between appraisal and core affect in daily life. *Frontiers in Psychology, Emotion Science, 3,* 1–8.

Laird, J. D. (1974). Self-attribution of emotion: The effects of expressive behavior on the quality of emotional experience. *Journal of Personality and Social Psychology, 29,* 475–486.

Larsen, J., Norris, C., McGraw, A. P., Hawkley, L., & Cacioppo, J. (2008). The evaluative space grid: A single-item measure of positivity and negativity. *Cognition & Emotion, 23,* 453–480.

Lazarus, R. S. (1968). Emotions and adaptation: Conceptual and empirical relations. *Nebraska Symposium on Motivation* (Vol. 16, pp. 175–270). Lincoln, NE: University of Nebraska Press.

Lazarus, R. S. (1991). Progress on a cognitive-motivational-relational theory of emotion. *The American Psychologist, 46,* 819–34.

Levenson, R. W., Ekman, P., & Friesen, W. V. (1990). Voluntary facial action generates emotion-specific autonomic nervous system activity. *Psychophysiology, 27,* 363–384.

Leventhal, H., & Scherer, K. R. (1987). The relationship of emotion to cognition: A functional approach to a semantic controversy. *Cognition and Emotion, 1,* 3–28.

Lewis, M. D. (2005). Bridging emotion theory and neurobiology through dynamic systems modeling. *Behavioral and Brain Sciences, 28,* 169–194. Retrieved from www.ncbi.nlm.nih.gov/pubmed/16201458

Lewis, M., Haviland-Jones, J. M., & Barrett, L. F. (2008). *Handbook of emotions* (3rd ed.). New York, NY: Guilford.

Mandler, G. (2001). Emotion: History of the concept. In N. J. Smelser & P. B. Baltes (Eds.), *International encyclopedia of the social and behavioral sciences* (pp. 4437–4440). Amsterdam, Netherlands: Elsevier.

Markus, H. R., & Kitayama, S. (1991). Culture and the self: Implications for cognition, emotion, and motivation. *Psychological Review, 98,* 224–253.

Meyer, D. K. (2014). Situating emotions in classroom practices. In R. Pekrun & L. Linnenbrink-Garcia (Eds.), *International handbook of emotions in education* (pp. 458–472). New York, NY: Taylor & Francis.

Moors, A. (2009). Theories of emotion causation: A review. *Cognition and Emotion, 23*(4), 625–662. doi: 10.1080/02699930802645739

Moors, A., Ellsworth, P., Scherer, K. R., & Frijda, N. H. (2013). Appraisal theories of emotion: State of the art and future development. *Emotion Review, 5*(2), 119–124.

Niedenthal, P. M., Krauth-Gruber, S., & Ric, F. (2006). *The psychology of emotion: Interpersonal, experiential, and cognitive approaches.* Principles of Social Psychology series. New York, NY: Psychology Press.

Oatley, K., Keltner, K., & Jenkins, J. M. (2006). *Understanding emotions* (2nd ed.). Malden, MA: Blackwell.

Ortony, A., Clore, G. L., & Collins, A. (1990). *The cognitive structure of emotions.* Cambridge: Cambridge University Press.

Panksepp, J. (2007). Neurologizing the psychology of affects: How appraisal-based constructivism and basic emotion theory can coexist. *Perspectives on Psychological Science, 2*, 281–296.

Plutchik, R. (2001). The nature of emotions: Human emotions have deep evolutionary roots, a fact that may explain their complexity and provide tools for clinical practice. *American Scientist, 89*, 344–350.

Roseman, I. J., Antoniou, A. A., & Jose, P. E. (1996). Appraisal determinants of emotions: Constructing a more accurate and comprehensive theory. *Cognition and Emotion, 10*, 241–278.

Russell, J. A. (1980). A circumplex model of affect. *Journal of Personality and Social Psychology, 39*, 1161–1178.

Russell, J. A. (1994). Is there universal recognition of emotion from facial expression? A review of the cross-cultural studies. *Psychological Bulletin, 115*, 102–41. Retrieved from www.ncbi.nlm.nih.gov/pubmed/8202574

Russell, J. A. (2003). Core affect and the psychological construction of emotion. *Psychological Review, 110*, 145–172.

Russell, J. A., & Fehr, B. (1987). Relativity in the perception of emotion in facial expressions. *Journal of Experimental Psychology: General, 116*, 223–237.

Sacharin, V., Sander, D., & Scherer, K. R. (2012). The perception of changing emotion expressions. *Cognition and Emotion, 26*, 1273–1300.

Sander, D., Grandjean, D., & Scherer, K. R. (2005). A systems approach to appraisal mechanisms in emotion. *Neural Networks, 18*, 317–352.

Sander, D., & Scherer, K. R. (Eds.). (2009). *The Oxford companion to emotion and the affective sciences.* Oxford: Oxford University Press.

Schachter, S., & Singer, J. E. (1962). Cognitive, social, and physiological determinants of emotional state. *Psychological Review, 69*, 379–399.

Scherer, K. R. (1984). On the nature and function of emotion: A component process approach. In K. R. Scherer & P. Ekman (Eds.), *Approaches to emotion* (pp. 293–317). Hillsdale, NJ: Lawrence Erlbaum.

Scherer, K. R. (1997). Profiles of emotion-antecedent appraisal: Testing theoretical predictions across culture. *Cognition and Emotion, 11*, 113–150.

Scherer, K. R. (2000). Emotions as episodes of subsystem synchronization driven by nonlinear appraisal processes. In M. D. Lewis & I. Granic (Eds.), *Emotion, development, and self-organization. Dynamic systems approaches to emotion development* (pp. 70–99). Cambridge: Cambridge University Press.

Scherer, K. R. (2001a). Emotion, the psychological structure of. In N. J. Smelser & P. B. Baltes (Eds.), *International encyclopedia of the social and behavioral sciences* (pp. 4472–4477). Amsterdam, Netherlands: Elsevier.

Scherer, K. R. (2001b). Appraisal considered as a process of multi-level sequential checking. In K. R. Scherer, A. Schorr, & T. Johnstone (Eds.). *Appraisal processes in emotion: Theory, methods, research* (pp. 92–120). New York, NY: Oxford University Press.

Scherer, K. R. (2005). What are emotions? And how can they be measured? *Social Science Information, 44*, 695–729.

Scherer, K. R. (2009). The dynamic architecture of emotion: Evidence for the component process model. *Emotion, 23*, 1307–1351.

Scherer, K. R. (2013). Measuring the meaning of emotion words: A domain-specific componential approach. In J.R.J. Fontaine, K. R. Scherer, & C. Soriano (Eds.), *Components of emotional meaning: A sourcebook* (pp. 7–30). Oxford, United Kingdom: Oxford University Press.

Scherer, K. R., & Brosch, T. (2009). Culture-specific appraisal biases contribute to emotion dispositions. *European Journal of Personality, 23*, 265–288.

Scherer, K. R., Schorr, A., & Johnstone, T. (Eds.). (2001). *Appraisal processes in emotion: Theory, methods, research.* New York, NY: Oxford University Press.

Scherer, K. R., Shuman, V., Fontaine, J.R.J., & Soriano, C. (2013). The GRID meets the wheel: Assessing emotional feeling via self-report. In J.R.J. Fontaine, K. R. Scherer, & C. Soriano (Eds.), *Components of emotional meaning: A sourcebook* (pp. 281–298). Oxford, United Kingdom: Oxford University Press.

Scherer, K. R., & Wallbott, H. G. (1994). Evidence for universality and cultural variation of differential emotion response patterning. *Journal of Personality and Social Psychology, 66,* 310–328.

Scherer, K. R., Wallbott, H. G., & Summerfield, A. B. (1986). *Experiencing emotion: A crosscultural study.* Cambridge, United Kingdom: Cambridge University Press.

Schlosberg, H. (1954). Three dimensions of emotion. *Psychological Review, 61,* 81–88.

Schultheiss, O. C., & Köllner, M. G. (2014). Implicit motives, affect, and the development of competencies: A virtuous-circle model of motive-driven learning. In R. Pekrun & L. Linnenbrink-Garcia (Eds.), *International handbook of emotions in education* (pp. 73–95). New York, NY: Taylor & Francis.

Schutz, P. A., Davis, H. A., DeCuir-Gunby, J. T., & Tillman, D. (2014). Regulating emotions related to testing. In R. Pekrun & L. Linnenbrink-Garcia (Eds.), *International handbook of emotions in education* (pp. 348–367). New York, NY: Taylor & Francis.

Shuman, V., Sander, D., & Scherer, K. R. (2013). Levels of valence. *Frontiers in Psychology, 46* (Article 261), 1–17. doi: 10.3389/fpsyg.2013.00261

Solomon, R. C., & Stone, L. D. (2002). On "positive" and "negative" emotions. *Journal for the Theory of Social Behaviour, 32,* 417–435.

Spielberger, C. D., & Reheiser, E. C. (2009). Assessment of emotions: Anxiety, anger, depression, and curiosity. *Applied Psychology: Health and Well-Being, 1,* 271–302.

Susskind, J. M., & Anderson, A. K. (2008). Facial expression form and function. *Applied Animal Behaviour Science, 1,* 1–2.

Tomkins, S. S. (1962). *Affect, imagery, consciousness: Vol. I. The positive affects.* New York, NY: Springer.

Tong, E.M.W., & Tay, K.L.H. (2011). S-shaped appraisal-emotion relationships: The role of neuroticism. *Social Psychological and Personality Science, 2,* 487–493.

Tooby, J., & Cosmides, L. (1990). The past explains the present: Emotional adaptations and the structure of ancestral environments. *Ethology and Sociobiology, 11,* 375–424.

Verduyn, P., Delvaux, E., Van Coillie, H., Tuerlinckx, F., & Van Mechelen, I. (2009). Predicting the duration of emotional experience: Two experience sampling studies. *Emotion, 9,* 83–91.

Watson, D., Clark, L. A., & Tellegen, A. (1988). Development and validation of brief measures of positive and negative affect: The PANAS scales. *Journal of Personality and Social Psychology, 54,* 1063–1070.

Wundt, W. (1897). *Outlines of psychology.* New York, NY: Wilhelm Engelmann.

Zeidner, M. (2014). Anxiety in education. In R. Pekrun & L. Linnenbrink-Garcia (Eds.), *International handbook of emotions in education* (pp. 265–288). New York, NY: Taylor & Francis.

Zentner, M., Grandjean, D., & Scherer, K. R. (2008). Emotions evoked by the sound of music: Characterization, classification, and measurement. *Emotion, 8,* 494–521.

3

AFFECT AND COGNITIVE PROCESSES IN EDUCATIONAL CONTEXTS

Klaus Fiedler and Susanne Beier, University of Heidelberg

Educational settings are replete with affective experiences, anxiety and fun, frustration and fulfillment, disappointment and pride. The relationship between affect and cognition is bidirectional. On the one hand, emotions are results of appraisal of academic success and failure, of pleasant or unpleasant personal and social experiences in educational encounters. On the other hand, learners' emotions energize but also restrict their achievement and achievement motivation. In the first two decades of most people's lives, educational settings are one of the most important sources of affective experience. Similarly, teachers' affective states are influenced by their success and failure in teaching, and these states in turn moderate their evaluations and attributions and impact their teaching behavior.

Although affect and cognition can influence each other in either direction, the vast majority of pertinent studies are concerned with influences of emotional states on cognitive and motivational functions. Evidence for the reverse influence of cognitive operations on emotional outcomes is largely confined to correlational evidence on appraisal influences, which is the topic of Chapters 6 and 7 (Graham & Taylor, 2014; Pekrun & Perry, 2014). Nevertheless, a growing interest in the investigation of affect regulation, conceived as a dialectical interplay of mental and emotional processes and behavioral outcomes, highlights the need to study all functions subserved by emotions in educational settings, be it as independent, dependent, or mediating variables.

TERMINOLOGY AND CONCEPTUAL EXPLICATIONS

Just as the affect–cognition interface can be approached from different perspectives, the educational domain can be defined in more or less restrictive ways. More specifically, the term education may refer to the cognitive process of learning and knowledge acquisition

Acknowledgement: The research and scientific work underlying this chapter was supported by a Koselleck Grant of the Deutsche Forschungsgemeinschaft awarded to the first author (Fi 294/23–1).

at school and in academic settings. Much more generally, though, education can also be conceptualized in a broad sense, referring to all kinds of social-learning and socialization mechanisms that together shape the socialization process, including the acquisition of moral, social, and cultural norms, attitudes, and habits. Research on affect and cognition has led to rich evidence and valuable insights at both levels of education, referred to as *academic learning* and *socialization*, respectively.

Types of Affective States

With regard to the terminology used to denote affective states, there is now wide agreement to distinguish between specific *emotions* and more diffuse *mood states*. Emotions are bound to specific eliciting stimuli and characterized by situation-specific appraisal functions. For instance, embarrassment is an emotion elicited by failure experience or revelation of intimate secrets but does not fit a frustrating or provocative situation. As a consequence, emotions are bound to a specific stimulus context and therefore unlikely to carry over to many other stimulus contexts. Moods, in contrast, are unspecific, typically quite enduring affective states, with often indeterminate origins. When people are in an elated or melancholic mood state, the origin or eliciting experience is often unknown, and maybe attributed to a wrong cause. Because of this unbounded, stimulus-independent nature, mood states are more likely to generalize over time and situations and are more difficult to evade or control than distinct emotions. While research on mood has been largely confined to one-dimensional comparisons of positive and negative states, more dimensions are needed to represent the qualitatively different contrasts that have been the focus of emotion research.

A prominent topic in recent research on metacognition (Schwarz & Clore, 2007) and embodiment (Niedenthal, 2007) are *feelings*. These affective states can be characterized as nonpropositional cues or signals that impact regulation functions. For instance, fluency is a cognitive feeling that signals flow and absence of obstacles or difficulties, whereas disfluency signals problems or sources of resistance that need to be tackled (Oppenheimer, 2008). The empirical study of feelings highlights the fact that subtle affective cues, or primes, may serve similarly important functions for the regulation of behavior as intensive moods or acute emotional reactions, particularly in the domain of learning and education (Koriat & Bjork, 2005). Finally, the term *affect* is used as a superordinate concept that covers all experientially nonneutral, hedonic or value-laden states or stimuli.

Chapter Preview

Providing a comprehensive review of the huge literature on affect and cognition would exceed the scope of this chapter. Its aim is rather to present a sensible but necessarily selective overview of findings that should meet two criteria. The reported evidence should be both practically useful and theoretically meaningful. In the absence of a sound theoretical framework to explain the reported evidence, it would be impossible to evaluate the validity, the limits, and the practical value of any empirical findings.

Therefore, the purpose of the next section is to outline a basic theoretical framework within which the interplay of emotional and cognitive processes can be understood. While this theoretical outline will draw on illustrative examples of educational behavior, another section will then be devoted to a broader review of convergent evidence. This major section will be subdivided into several subsections dealing with more specific research topics. Starting with an overview of the impact of positive versus negative mood on learning and memory, we will then examine the trade-off between reproductive (conservative) and productive (creative) cognitive functions, and we will also briefly point out distinct appraisal functions and the cognitive consequences of more specific emotions, beyond the mere distinction of positive and negative mood. (For a more comprehensive treatment of appraisal functions and appraisal theories, the reader is referred to Chapters 6 and 7; Graham & Taylor, 2014; Pekrun & Perry, 2014.) A final section will deal with research on affective behavior regulation, highlighting the basic insight that no particular emotional state is generally optimal for learning, education, and subjective well-being but that adaptive behavior calls for varying cognitive strategies and contrasting emotions rather than optimization of constant strategies and hedonic states.

OUTLINE OF A THEORETICAL FRAMEWORK

Two Basic Adaptive Functions: Accommodation and Assimilation

Central for understanding the interaction between affect and cognition is the analysis of adaptive behavior in terms of two distinct adaptive functions, accommodation and assimilation, with the terms borrowed from Piaget's (1954) theory of cognitive development. Accommodation refers to adaptive adjustments of the individual's internal representations to the external constraints imposed by the stimulus environment. Assimilation refers to the complementary process of adjusting (i.e., assimilating) the external world to the individual's internal structures. Accommodation can be characterized as a stimulus-driven bottom-up process that aims at reacting as sensitively as possible to new environmental data—that is, to the signals, threats, challenges, and opportunities of ongoing adaptation tasks. In contrast, assimilation is a knowledge-driven top-down process whereby the individual relies on his or her own theories in going beyond the given stimulus data to predict, explain, and control the external world. In other words, accommodation is essentially reproductive and conservative whereas assimilation is productive and generative.

Both functions are not mutually exclusive processing modes but complementary aspects that are jointly involved in all adaptive behavior. Every social or intellectual task calls for some degree of adherence to the constraints of the situation and the stimulus input (accommodation) but also some creative transformation of the given input into some new output, or solution, based on the individual's internalized knowledge, motives, and behavioral repertoire (assimilation). To solve a mathematical task means to keep the task instructions and the input text and data in memory, as a precondition for any reasonable response that might transform the input task into some creative output solution. Even a seemingly reproductive task as reading involves both stimulus-driven decoding of written text and knowledge-driven inference making and hypothesis testing.

However, while both adaptive functions are universal and mutually complement and constrain each other, the relative contribution of accommodation and assimilation can vary considerably across tasks. When conservative or reproductive tasks call for careful bottom-up assessment of all stimulus details, sticking to externally given facts and refraining from uncertain inferences, the emphasis is on accommodation. In contrast, success on creative or productive tasks depends on innovative interpretations, constructive top-down inferences, and creative enrichment of the information given, thus relying heavily on assimilation.

Crucial to understanding the role of affect in learning and education is the assumption that negative affective cues and moods support accommodation, whereas positive affect supports assimilation functions. This general rule received support from countless empirical studies. Negative affective states have been regularly shown to facilitate careful stimulus processing (Forgas, 1998), selective attention to task-relevant stimuli (Rowe, Hirsh, Anderson, & Smith, 2007), avoidance of careless mistakes (Sinclair & Mark, 1995), concrete and detailed representations (Beukeboom & Semin, 2006), discrimination of strong and weak arguments (Bless, Bohner, Schwarz, & Strack, 1990), and adherence to social and moral norms (Forgas, 1999). In contrast, positive affective states facilitate constructive inferences (Storbeck & Clore, 2005), priming effects and heuristic judgments (Storbeck & Clore, 2008), creative problem solving (Isen, Daubman, & Nowicki, 1987), stereotyping (Bodenhausen, 1994), flexible representations (Huntsinger, Clore, & Bar-Anan, 2010), and spontaneous and norm-independent behavior (Forgas, 1999).

While mood states may also affect the amount of available cognitive resources (Pekrun, 2006), this influence can operate in both directions: both the consumption of positive mood states (Mackie & Worth, 1989) and the administration of negative moods (Ellis & Ashbrook, 1988).

Affective States as Causes and Catalysts of Learning

As a consequence, there is no one-sided answer to the frequently asked question of whether learning is generally more effective in positive or negative emotional states. The answer depends, rather, on the type of learning task. As a general rule, task-specific performance can be expected to profit from negative states on accommodative (conservative stimulus-driven bottom-up) tasks and from positive states on assimilative (creative knowledge-driven top-down) tasks. Moreover, successful learning and development in the long run is a function of optimal variation between both stages of the creative cycle (Fiedler, 1988, 2001a; Kelly, 1955). On the one hand, "loosening" stages serve the assimilative function of broadening one's behavioral repertoire through exploration and creation of new ideas, analogous to the role of (random) variation in evolution. On the other hand, "tightening" stages serve the accommodative function of selecting and maintaining the most effective and least error-prone exemplars.

Affective States Resulting From Learning Experience

Affective states not only function as independent variables that motivate and facilitate learning processes, but they also appear as dependent variables that reflect (the appraisal of) success versus failure, or pleasant versus unpleasant outcomes of learning tasks. Indeed, (alleged) performance feedback is an effective means for the experimental induction of positive or negative mood states (Alter & Forgas, 2007). Similarly, disapproval and social exclusion (ostracism; Williams & Nida, 2011) have been shown to be a potent source of negative mood, whereas approval and social support induce happiness and life satisfaction (Kasprzak, 2010).

One intriguing implication of the adaptive-behavior framework is that the bidirectional causal relationship between affective influences on learning and learning on affect typically results in regulatory cycles. The assimilation effects of positive moods (e.g., enterprising exploration, impoliteness, constructive inferences) often raise the likelihood of errors, unwanted consequences, and negative social reactions that will down-regulate mood to more negative states. Conversely, the accommodative strategies, characteristic of negative states (e.g., careful stimulus monitoring, norm-adherence, refraining from idiosyncrasies), contribute to mood repair and upward regulation. Thus, ironically, the explorative and creative style fostered by positive mood entails the potential for mood impairment, and the cautious and compliant style in negative mood entails the potential for mood repair (Fiedler, 1988). To be sure, this is not to say that all feedback loops will reverse the current mood.

EMPIRICAL EVIDENCE RELATING MOOD TO COGNITION, BEHAVIOR, AND MOTIVATION: IMPACT OF POSITIVE AND NEGATIVE MOOD ON LEARNING

Fundamental research on learning and memory in laboratory settings reveals that, compared to positive mood, negative mood leads to increased accuracy (Forgas, Goldenberg, & Unkelbach, 2009), careful responding (Sinclair, 1988), and decreased heuristic mistakes (Bodenhausen, 1994; Koch & Forgas, 2012; Park & Banaji, 2000). These advantages are evident on accommodative tasks demanding discipline and careful stimulus processing. Conversely, the relative advantages of positive mood are visible on assimilative tasks that call for creative solutions (Isen et al., 1987), knowledge-based organization (Bless, Hamilton, & Mackie, 1992), self-generated inferences (Fiedler, Nickel, Asbeck, & Pagel, 2003), and selective forgetting as a precondition of the controlled acquisition of new knowledge (Bäuml & Kuhbandner, 2007).

The same basic pattern is obtained in actual academic-learning settings or in experimental tasks that resemble educational learning situations. Consistent with the notion that negative and positive affective cues function like stop and go signals (Clore, Schwarz, & Conway, 1994), several studies found that people in a positive mood make more errors than people in a negative mood on misleading tasks with high rates of premature responding. Using standard reasoning tasks, such as the Tower of London and the Wason selection task, Oaksford, Morris, Grainger, and Williams (1996) showed that mood states generally interfered with working memory capacity. However, the resulting performance suppression was stronger for positive than negative mood, as manifested in a more pronounced confirmation bias to respond positively to wrong solutions that ought to be rejected.

Conceptually, very similar results have been obtained in the false-memory paradigm (Forgas, Laham, & Vargas, 2005; Storbeck & Clore, 2005). Using a task created by Roediger and McDermott (1995), participants were presented with word lists in which various words (e.g., bed, pillow, rest, awake, dream) were related to a critical one (sleep) that was, however, not included. In a subsequent memory test, these critical lures are typically remembered equally well or even better than the actually presented stimuli. Storbeck and Clore (2005) found more false-memory effects in positive mood and, hence, higher accuracy under negative mood. However, inaccuracy on such a task only reflects the deeper assimilative processing of the stimulus lists by people in positive mood, whose false memories may also be interpreted as strong memories for self-generated information.

Consistent with this interpretation, the so-called generation effect—that is, the enhanced memory for self-generated as compared to externally provided information, was repeatedly shown to be stronger under positive than negative mood (Bless & Fiedler, 2006; Fiedler, 2001a). In a series of experiments by Fiedler et al. (2003), happy and sad participants who had been exposed to funny or sad film clips, respectively, received extended lists of positive and negative words. These either appeared in a complete format and only had to be read or in a degraded format with several missing letters, so that the word meaning had to be generated actively. As usual in this paradigm, which highlights the crucial role of active encoding for academic learning (Bjork, 1994; Metcalfe, 2009), subsequent free recall was higher for generated than for merely read words. However, crucially, the generation advantage was systematically stronger in positive than in negative mood, apparently because memory profits greatly from assimilative elaboration during learning.

In a related vein, positive mood was shown to facilitate the formation of knowledge-based memory for scripted behavior presented in narratives (Bless, Clore, Schwarz, Golisano, Rabe, & Wolk, 1996), for tightly organized, categorized lists (Fiedler, Pampe, & Scherf, 1986), and for spontaneous category learning (Nadler, Rabi, & Minda, 2010). The latter authors reasoned that the increased flexibility of people in a positive mood is associated with the prefrontal cortex and the anterior cingulate cortex. As both brain locations play crucial roles in rule selection, the authors instructed participants in positive, neutral, or negative mood states to learn either rule-based or nonrule-based category sets. Consistent with their hypothesis and with the notion that positive mood facilitates creative top-down hypothesis testing, Nadler et al. (2010) found that participants in a positive mood performed better than subjects in a neutral or negative mood in classifying stimuli from rule-described categories, but not from arbitrary, rule-independent categories.

MEMORY ORGANIZATION AS A KEY TO EFFECTIVE LEARNING

Thus, whether negative or positive mood produces better learning depends on the extent to which either given associations or new organization is the key to good learning and performance (cf. Mandler, 2011). Careful responding and avoidance of flawed responses at surface level, or detailed high-fidelity reports may certainly profit from cautious strategies that prevail under negative mood. However, whenever the criterion for successful learning depends on active organization and integration of complex stimulus material, as is typical for higher-order academic learning, a pronounced positive-mood advantage can be expected.

In a seminal study by Mandler and Pearlstone (1966), participants in a free group, who consistently used their own self-determined categories to sort 52 stimulus instances of various kinds, showed clearly superior recall compared to participants in a constrained group on whom the categories of the free group were imposed. Self-determined category coding led to fewer errors, less time required per trial, and more efficient learning than other-determined learning and retrieval processes (see also Bäuml & Kuhbandner, 2003; Rundus, 1973). Pertinent to this theoretical background, it has been shown that positive mood facilitates organization and clustering in memory (Bless et al., 1992; Fiedler & Stroehm, 1986; Lee & Sternthal, 1999). Moreover, embedding isolated pictures in self-generated picture stories has been shown to greatly increase the resulting recall performance (Fiedler, 1990).

Enduring memory not only depends on the assimilation of new information to existing schemas and knowledge structures but also on the strategic forgetting of old and obsolete stimuli that may interfere with new incoming information. An intriguing finding in this context is that retrieval-induced forgetting of lists of isolated items only works in positive but not in negative mood (Bäuml & Kuhbandner, 2007). Thus, the active suppression (inhibitory control) of unattended learning items, which serves to protect attended items from interference, is facilitated through assimilation in positive mood. This finding can be explained by the assumption that positive moods encourage relational processing that should increase interference from competing memory contents. Negative mood, in contrast, encourages item-specific processing, which in turn reduces interference and retrieval-induced forgetting of competing materials.

Perhaps, this convergent evidence for top-down organization and relational processing as the crucial principle of memory (Mandler, 2011) should not be overstated, and the importance of careful item-specific bottom-up processing should not be underestimated. Nevertheless, outside the realm of episodic memory for arbitrary lists, in meaningful problem environments, the available evidence emphasizes the crucial role of organization and generative coding. For example, many ordinary mathematics tasks cannot be solved by merely memorizing associations. Relying on analogies and inferences derived from organized knowledge is inevitable to come to a solution. With this insight in mind, it is not surprising that math performance was also found to profit from positive mood (Bryan & Bryan, 1991).

MOOD-CONGRUENCY EFFECTS

One particularly prominent consequence of an assimilative processing style is mood congruency (Bower, 1981; Clore, Schwarz, & Conway, 1994; Forgas, 1995)—that is, the processing advantage of mood-congruent information. In positive mood, pleasant information is more readily attended to, perceived, encoded, learned, retrieved, and inferred, and positive mood gives rise to more positive judgments and optimistic decisions. In contrast, negative mood produces a relative processing advantage for negative stimulus information. Although mood congruency is often treated as a separate phenomenon, it is but a special case of assimilation. Congruency effects are therefore asymmetrically stronger for positive than negative mood. Mood-congruent memory or judgment means that the affective value of target stimuli is assimilated to the individual's internal affective state.

To illustrate, in the aforementioned research by Fiedler et al. (2003) on mood and the generation effects, self-generated words were not only recalled better, particularly when people were in good mood, rather, this generation advantage came along with a marked bias to recall more mood-congruent words. This congruency advantage was almost totally confined to the recall of self-generated words by participants in the positive-mood condition. As summarized in Forgas's (1995) affect-infusion model, most evidence for mood-congruency effects is peculiar to assimilative tasks that leave many degrees of freedom for constructive processing (Forgas, 1992, 1995).

In educational settings, congruency effects are manifested in two consequential phenomena, self-efficacy judgments and achievement evaluations. Both phenomena are crucial for students' achievement motivation and self-attributions, which in turn affect their future achievement. First, several studies have shown that positive mood enhances self-efficacy, conceived as the optimistic and confident appraisal that one can master the task at hand if one mobilizes one's own talents and motivation (Kavanagh & Bower, 1985; Thelwell, Lane, & Weston, 2007). As a consequence, aspiration setting and self-confidence profit from this sort of mood-congruent self assessment.

Second, the enhanced confidence and optimistic attitude of learners in positive as opposed to negative affective states reflects their differential attribution styles. During elated states following the receipt of performance feedback, participants in a study conducted by Brown (1984) tended to attribute experienced success (induced by bogus feedback) to more stable causes than during negative states previously induced by failure feedback. In general, judgments of elated participants were biased in a self-enhancing direction following success, whereas manipulated performance outcomes had no effect on the causal attributions of participants who were temporarily induced to feel depressed.

THE MOOD-CREATIVITY RELATION

Creativity affords another influential consequence of an assimilative processing style. Creativity can be characterized as a top-down process whereby the given input stimulus is transformed and enriched with activated internal knowledge structures (Fiedler, 2001b) and (analogical or heuristic) inference tools. Pertinent research shows that happy mood leads to more unusual associations (Isen, Johnson, Mertz, & Robinson, 1985), facilitates problem solving, including combining material in a new and unusual way (Ashby, Isen, & Turken, 1999; Isen et al., 1987), and more flexible categorizations (Isen & Daubmann, 1984). All these effects reflect mood influences on creativity, operationalized as the ability of a person to generate new, potentially useful and original ideas, insights, and inventions (Amabile, 1983). Meta-analytic evidence suggests that creativity is most enhanced by activating positive mood, fostering an approach motivation, as is the case in the example of happiness (Baas, De Dreu, & Nijstad, 2008).

However, positive mood does not always lead to a better performance on creative generation tasks. Feeling-as information approaches (e.g., Schwarz, 1990) assume that negative mood signals a problematic situation, and—in line with an accommodation strategy—advises individuals to invest more cognitive effort but also prevents them from taking risks or using novel alternatives. Positive mood, in contrast, suggests that a situation is safe and thus—in line with an assimilative strategy—encourages individuals to seek stimulation and incentives. Based on these theoretical assumptions, Friedman, Förster, and Denzler (2007) analyzed the performance in a creative generation task that was either framed as silly and fun or as serious and important, thus making the task motivationally compatible with positive or negative mood, respectively. They found an increased effort for tasks fitting the subjects' affective state. Thus, subjects in negative mood showed an enhanced effort for tasks framed as important but in positive mood for tasks framed as fun. All these studies suggest that every student can be regarded as potentially creative (Isen et al., 1987) and, depending on auspicious situational conditions and appropriate task framing, students may enhance their performance on creative problems considerably.

PERSISTENCE, EFFORT EXPENDITURE, GOALS PURSUIT

Related to the aforementioned study by Friedman et al. (2007), Martin, Ward, Achee, and Wyer (1993) demonstrated that the influence of affect on peoples' persistence in regard to working on a task depended on the framing of the task. More precisely, when people were instructed to continue working on a task until they no longer enjoyed it, they showed higher persistence in a good in comparison to a bad mood. When they were instructed to continue working until they felt like having gained enough information, however, the opposite mood effect emerged. Good mood led them to stop earlier than bad mood. In both cases, these findings are in line with the notion that mood is used as information about whether or not to continue working on a task, although with different implications derived from positive and negative affective cues, depending on the framing of the question asked.

Conversely, how much effort is spent on a task can also influence the rate and strength of resulting mood effects. According to the affect infusion model (Forgas, 1995), mood effects on judgments vary depending on the dominant processing strategy in a given task situation. This model distinguishes between four processing strategies that are characterized by (a) variation in high versus low motivation and effort expended in a task and (b) variation in whether a task calls for closed or open-ended and constructive information search. The resulting four strategies are (1) direct access (low effort, closed information search), (2) motivated processing (high effort, closed information search), (3) heuristic processing (low effort, open-ended information search), and (4) constructive processing (high effort, open-ended information search). What strategy is chosen depends on the familiarity of the task, features of the person making a judgment, and situational features. There is ample empirical support for stronger affective influences when the task calls for open-ended information search, regardless of effort expenditure. That is, mood influences are strongest for heuristic and constructive processing strategies as compared to motivated processing and direct access (Fiedler, 2001b; Forgas, 1995).

Persistence and effort expenditure, two crucial preconditions of academic performance, are related to the students' goals. Performance increases for harder rather than easier goals and for challenging goals with a clearly specified set-up, in comparison to unspecific goals (Locke, Shaw, Saari, & Latham, 1981). Classroom related affective states are linked to the students' goal structure and their adoption of specific achievement goal orientations. The adoption of a mastery goal—that is, a goal to learn and understand (Dweck & Legget, 1988)—is associated with an increase in positive emotions like enjoyment of learning as well as a decrease in negative emotions like boredom (Pekrun, Elliot, & Maier, 2006). Adopting a performance approach goal—that is, the goal to be better than others (Elliot, 1999)—was found to be associated with the positive emotion pride. In contrast, the adoption of a performance avoidance goal—that is, a goal not to appear incompetent, stupid, or uninformed in comparison to others—was consistently related to the negative emotion test anxiety (Middleton & Midgley, 1997; Skaalvik, 1997) and was found to be associated with specific negative emotions like anxiety and hopelessness (Pekrun et al., 2006). However, the relation between goals and affect might not be a unidirectional but a reciprocal one as proposed in Linnenbrink and Pintrich's (2002) bidirectional model. Thus, affective states might also influence which goals a student adopts. In line with this assumption is the finding that students who experience positive affect are subsequently more likely to perceive their classroom as being focused on the goal to learn and understand (Kaplan & Midgley, 1999).

One specific cognitive activity that can interfere with academic achievement is engaging in unrealistically positive fantasies. Fantasies are freely occurring visualized images and thoughts concerning one's own future life and achievement, largely detached from actual past experiences (Klinger, 1990; Oettingen & Mayer, 2002). Oettingen and Mayer

(2002) argue that these positive fantasies allow people to experience a pleasant future at the moment while masking the necessary effort one has to invest to actually realize the idealized future. Such fantasies are correlated with lower effort expenditure and academic achievement (Kappes, Oettingen, & Mayer, 2012; Oettingen & Mayer, 2002). However, Langens and Schmalt (2002) argue that especially for people who have a high fear of failure, engaging in positive fantasies might not lead to positive affect due to an anticipatory experience of a pleasant future. These authors assume that people high in fear of failure experience negative emotions like depression when they engage in positive fantasies. Due to low success expectancies, positive fantasies might make the potential absence of the anticipated outcome in the future particularly clear. In line with these assumptions, the authors demonstrated higher feelings of depression after engaging in positive fantasies about attaining agentic personal goals and, possibly motivated by an effort to repair this negative mood repair, disengagement from this goal.

Distinct Appraisal Functions and Consequences of Specific Emotions

In educational settings, students experience a variety of emotions. Anxiety is one of the most commonly experienced emotions by students. However, positive emotions are experienced about as often as negative ones (Pekrun, Goetz, Titz, & Perry, 2002). Going beyond the broad distinction of positive and negative mood, it is worth considering various specific emotions, such as boredom, anxiety, and enjoyment of learning, and their association with specific situational appraisals as well as their effects on cognitive processing and academic outcomes. We choose these emotions because they represent distinct emotions representing positive (enjoyment) and negative (boredom, anxiety) as well as activating (enjoyment, anxiety) and deactivating (boredom) emotions important in the educational context (Goetz, Frenzel, Pekrun, & Hall, 2006). Appraisal theories generally assume a connection between the appraisal of an environment and the elicited emotion. As a result, the experienced emotion is shaped by the cognitive interpretation of the situation (Smith & Ellsworth, 1885).

Emotion Appraisal in Educational Settings

Smith and Ellsworth (1987), for example, illustrated that different emotions elicited before and after taking a college midterm exam were associated with distinct appraisals of that situation. For example, the experience of anger before or after the exam was predicted by an appraisal of the situation as unfair, the experience of fear by an appraisal of unpleasantness, and the experience of happiness, on the contrary, by an appraisal of the situation as pleasant. Hope and challenge experiences before or after the exam were predicted by an appraisal of anticipated effort in regard to the test situation, and the experience of apathy by an appraisal of agency other than oneself.

In educational contexts, an appraisal of the learning and achievement related activities are of primary relevance to determine what specific subsequent achievement emotion—that is, an emotion that is linked to achievement activities or outcomes (Pekrun, 2006)—is experienced. More precisely, Pekrun (2006) assumes in his control-value theory of achievement emotions that the perceived control of learning and the subsequent outcomes as well as the subjective value of the achievement activities and outcomes are of particular importance in this context. For example, enjoyment of learning is characterized by a subjective feeling of control over and positively valuing learning activities and outcomes, anxiety in regard to a test is characterized by rather low subjective control paired with a high subjective value of the test's outcome, and boredom is characterized by a either high or low subjective control paired with a lack of subjective value (Pekrun, Goetz, Daniels, Stupnisky, & Perry, 2010). Since the specific emotions experienced in achievement contexts are critically influenced by the specific appraisal pattern in these situations, it follows that the students' emotional experiences are domain specific (Pekrun, 2006). Goetz et al. (2006) tested this assumption for the emotional experience in regard to the domains mathematics, Latin, German, and English of students in the seventh to tenth grade. For the examined emotions academic enjoyment, anxiety, and boredom, the results indicated that a domain specific organization of emotions with academic enjoyment showed the highest domain specific organization. The relations between different emotions in the same domain were related stronger than experiences of a specific emotion across domains. These authors concluded that students might therefore especially benefit from domain specific counseling and interventions in regard to their emotional experiences in school.

Boredom

Boredom is a specific emotion that is abundantly experienced by students in educational settings but not yet thoroughly researched in this context. It is characterized by lack of stimulation in combination with low arousal (Harris, 2000; Pekrun et al., 2010). In line with the control-value theory of achievement emotions (Pekrun, 2006), Pekrun et al. (2010) demonstrated that the feeling of boredom was most of the time associated with a perception of a lack of control over and lack of value of achievement activities. Especially important in educational settings, these authors also showed that boredom predicted lower academic performance. Cognitive consequences of experiencing boredom are attention impairments. Students have problems concentrating when they are bored and are more prone to being distracted by task irrelevant things. As a negative emotion, boredom is negatively associated with assimilative task handling strategies like elaboration. However, boredom most likely does not induce the use of accommodative, repetitive learning strategies, but these rehearsive strategies might induce boredom. In accordance with the previously discussed adaptive function of emotions, boredom leads to lower intrinsic motivation, effort, and, in the end, a tendency to escape the boring situation. Trying to provide individual students more with tasks that match their abilities or guide them to self-regulate their study activities to make them feel more self-controlled might help to reduce their boredom and as a consequence to avoid the negative motivational and performance-related consequences associated with boredom (Pekrun et al, 2010).

Test Anxiety

Students' anxiety—in particular, test anxiety—is one of the most well researched achievement emotions, and it has been addressed in more than 1,000 studies (Pekrun et al., 2010). In line with the control-value theory, classroom variables that are associated with an appraisal of control- and value-related aspects of achievement outcomes and activities (for example, punishment after failure, high achievement expectations, and a competitive classroom) are correlated with students test anxiety (Pekrun et al., 2002). The construct of test anxiety has been differentiated in past research, and the components worrying about failure and negative consequences, automatic emotional reactions to test situation, interfering and distracting cognitions, and low confidence are distinguished. These components are differently associated with different coping styles. For female students, for example, worrying is associated with preparing more and low avoidance coping, and for both male and female students, the relationship is revered for the interference component (Stöber, 2004). A cognitive consequence of test anxiety is a reduction of the working memory capacity, which, as a result, impairs the performance on academic tasks. In general, test anxiety is associated with lower academic performance. In regard to motivational variables, test anxiety is negatively correlated with intrinsic and overall extrinsic motivation. However, test anxiety is positively associated with making an effort to avoid failure (extrinsic avoidance motivation; Pekrun et al., 2002). Meta-analytical evidence suggests that higher scores in test anxiety are associated with an adoption of performance goals—in particular, performance avoidance goals (Huang, 2011).

Enjoyment of Learning

Enjoyment of learning is the pleasure students experience while performing learning activities (Ainley & Ainley, 2011). Students experience enjoyment in specific learning situations and habitually associate a certain level of this emotion with learning activities in general. While on average, the learning enjoyment is on a positive level, students experience a decrease in this emotion with increasing school years (Hagenauer & Hascher, 2011). In line with the control-value theory (Pekrun, 2006), students' value of science predicted their enjoyment of learning in this school domain. Also, the students' enjoyment was closely related to their interest in learning more about science topics (Ainley & Ainley, 2011). In regard to students' motivation, the experience of enjoyment of learning is positively associated with their intrinsic and extrinsic motivation as well as their self-reports on academic effort. Not only is this positive emotion associated with beneficial motivational variables, but the experience of enjoyment of learning also predicts higher academic achievement (Pekrun et al., 2002). As a positive emotion, enjoyment is related to assimilative learning strategies, like elaboration, critical thinking, and metacognitive strategies (Pekrun et al., 2002). Similar to these findings, Goetz, Hall, Frenzel, & Pekrun (2006) showed that students' use of learning strategies, like self-regulated learning, learning from mistakes, and trying to tackle academic tasks in a creative and flexible way were positively correlated with their enjoyment of learning.

Regulation of Affective Behavior

Granting that mood states and specific emotions both reflect and influence social and academic learning, the bidirectional relation between emotion and cognition constitutes a regulatory cycle, within which longitudinal developments can be understood. As already mentioned, the adaptive interplay of accommodative and assimilative strategies that characterizes different affective states is intrinsically self-regulated. Careful and thorough accommodation strategies (e.g., caution, minimization of mistakes) preclude the perpetuation of negative states and support the reestablishment of positive states. Conversely, carefree and jaunty assimilation strategies (e.g., overconfidence, impoliteness) entail the potential to prevent positive states from perpetuation and to return to more negative styles. Apparently, such a regulatory cycle has several desirable and adaptive consequences that should ideally support an individual's motivation, learning potential, and well-being. The resulting variation in affect, cognition, and behavior should be a remedy of habituation and saturation and provide individuals with valuable contrast experiences, affect-related wisdom, and emotional intelligence (Salovey & Grewal, 2005). Frequent shifts in adaptive strategies dealing with ever-changing environmental settings, learning tasks, and social situations might serve to foster the individual's development and maturation.

Abnormal and pathological developments, such as depression or antisocial delinquency, seem to reflect anomalies in such a cyclic regulation process. Typical for a depressive loop, for instance, seems to be the inability to repair one's depressed mood and to reestablish positive affective states, self-worth, and the optimism that characterizes assimilative tendencies.

MOOD REPAIR: SELF-REGULATION OF AFFECT

The experience of a specific affective state itself may trigger the motivation to regulate one's own affective state. The mood repair hypothesis claims that people seek to maintain positive mood because of its hedonic value and to avoid negative moods experienced as aversive or unpleasant (Isen, 1984; Taylor, 1991). Thus, it is assumed that people deliberately try to improve their mood and that the experience of an unpleasant versus pleasant mood is the crucial cue that drives mood repair. However, as Erber and Erber (2001) have summarized, the empirical evidence suggests that effective mood repair depends both on motivation and appropriate skills. Both of these conditions are shaped by situational constraints. For example, a student's experience of happiness, who wants to console a friend because of a bad grade, is constrained by this situation motivating the student to regulate his/her feelings of happiness. Erber and Erber (2001) assume in their social-constraints model that goal attainment affords the most important principle for peoples' self-controlled mood regulation. The experience of a certain mood, even if it is a negative one, is not the main motivating reason for whether or not people engage in mood repair, according to the findings summarized by these authors. Without situational constraints making regulation of the own mood necessary, people do not show mood regulation and maintain their current positive or negative mood. However, if being in a happy mood, for example, distracts students from focusing on a learning task because of intruding thoughts regarding pleasant weekend plans, then they may want to regulate their happy mood state and try to achieve a more neutral mood state that is more appropriate to their learning and achievement goals.

PRIMING, SIGNALING, AND MINIMAL AFFECTIVE CUES

Regulation is not contingent on intensive or hedonically important affective states. Subtle and even subliminal affective cues can signal environmental changes, threats, or chances calling for adaptive reactions and appropriate strategies. Numerous studies have demonstrated that emotional treatments need not be incisive or intensive to exert systematic effects. Finding a dime in a Xerox machine (Isen & Levin, 1972), facial muscle activity that simulates a smile (Stepper & Strack, 1993), or the subtle feeling of fluency associated with a mental task (Schwarz, 1990) are examples of subtle affective cues that suffice to induce mood-congruency effects or mood-specific cognitive strategies. In contrast, experiencing a feeling of difficulty or simulating a frowning face is sufficient to trigger reactions associated with aversive situations.

Affective Priming

One pertinent paradigm here is affective priming (Fazio, 2001). The time required to categorize a target stimulus as either positive or negative is reduced when the valence of the preceding prime matches the valence of a subsequent target to be evaluated. This congruity effect in affective priming is remarkably similar to the congruency effects obtained in free recall and social judgments. Like the latter class of findings, congruity in affective priming is asymmetrically stronger for positive rather than negative primes, and affective primes need not be intensive or salient. If anything, affective priming (like semantic priming) was generally found to decrease or even disappear when too strong and blatant primes are attended to and consciously experienced as distinct entities, clearly separate from the target (Fiedler, Bluemke, & Unkelbach, 2011). This phenomenon is analogous to the disappearance of mood congruency when mood can be attributed to external origins (Schwarz & Clore, 1983).

One way to understand the analogy between mood congruency and priming congruity is to assume that affective primes constitute minimal mood treatments that have been associated with stronger mood treatments in the individual's learning history, much like conditional stimuli have been associated with unconditional stimuli. This assumption offers a simple account of the powerful impact of subtle affective cues on the regulation of behavior.

Fluency

In the realm of learning and education, for instance, an influential regulatory cue is fluency. The feeling of fluency, as, for example, induced by easy-to-solve puzzles, high color contrast of written text, or simple mental rotations, is not only experienced as hedonically pleasant but also induces a feeling of confidence, truth, and an illusion of learning (Koriat & Bjork, 2005; Unkelbach, 2006; Winkielman, Schwarz, Fazendeiro, & Reber, 2003).

In contrast, the feeling of disfluency or unease, as induced by hard to solve puzzles, insufficient color contrast, or difficult mental rotations, is typically experienced as unpleasant and serves to reduce self-confidence and subjective truth. An apparent adaptive function of the fluency cue is to discriminate easy and unproblematic situations from difficult and problematic ones. Whereas high fluency encourages organisms to continue performing ongoing actions, low fluency signals the need to overcome some obstacle and to change one's current strategy.

Disfluency and Cognitive Reflection

An intriguing ironic consequence of this regulatory mechanism is that experienced fluency can undermine effort expenditure and persistence motivation whenever the fluency cue creates an unrealistic illusion of learning and understanding (Koriat & Bjork, 2005). In contrast, the hedonically unpleasant feeling of disfluency may trigger extra efforts and deliberate attempts to try out new strategies and problem solutions. Such benevolent consequences of disfluency have been observed recently in several experimental studies. Alter, Oppenheimer, Epley, and Eyre (2007) manipulated fluency by presenting Frederick's (2005) cognitive reflection test (CRT) printed either in easy-to-read black Myriad Web 12-point font or in a difficult-to-read 10% gray italicized Myriad Web 10-point font.

Participants in the former (fluent) condition frequently chose the intuitively most plausible but wrong response options. Participants in the latter (disfluent) condition in contrast engaged in second thoughts and were thus more likely to find out the correct solutions.

In another experiment, fluency was manipulated by proprioceptive feedback from facial muscles in that participants were instructed either to puff their cheeks (fluent condition) or to furrow their brows (disfluent condition). The resulting feeling of disfluency helped participants to overcome the so-called base-rate neglect (i.e., the failure to take the base rates into account when judging the profession of a target person described in a vignette). According to Alter et al. (2007), feelings of task difficulty or disfluency reduce the danger of premature, heuristic judgments, unreflected reliance on misleading peripheral cues, and instead facilitate deeper and more analytic reasoning.

Distrust

In a related vein, Schul, Mayo, and Burnstein (2008) manipulated distrust in several ways, such as by presenting faces that had been pretested to convey different degrees of suspiciousness. Similar to disfluency, distrust led participants to avoid routine strategies and to try out new and unusual strategies. For instance, people exposed to distrust-inducing faces solved trickier matchstick problems than people exposed to trustworthy, safety-inducing faces. Thus, distrust was shown to benefit performance on tasks that call for nonroutine, innovative strategies.

Achievement Priming

In addition to these indirect influences of affective primes on learning and achievement goals, other studies have revealed direct influences of achievement-related cues. For example, in a series of studies by Hart and Albarracín (2009), achievement-denoting word primes were successfully used to increase self-reported task performance and task resumption following an interruption. However, achievement priming was only effective in participants with chronic high achievement motivation. The same primes inhibited a goal to achieve and instead activated fun goals in people with low achievement motivation.

CONCLUDING REMARKS

To summarize, with regard to both domains of education, formal learning and socialization, our theory-driven review of the cognition–emotion link leads to the same general conclusions.

Recapitulation of Basic Insights

First, it is useful to distinguish between the two complementary adaptive functions of accommodation and assimilation. Negative affective states increase the individual's accommodative attempts to deal with environmental constraints, fostering careful stimulus-driven processing in the learning domain and norm-conforming strategies in the social domain. These strategies, in turn, entail the potential for mood repair and variation in affect and associated strategies. Positive affective states will then give the individual the backing-up for assimilative strategies, characterized by knowledge-driven creative and exploratory behavior in the learning domain and independence of external norms in the social domain. Again, the consequences of these innovative and uncertain strategies entail the potential for mood impairment. Over time, as a consequence of this dialectic interplay of both adaptive functions, the individual has to deal with contrasting affective experiences and to acquire a rich repertoire of strategies, which in turn facilitates successful education and development in the long run. Malfunctioning regulation (inability to down-regulate assimilative strategies; failure of mood repair) can be the source of pathological developments.

Second, in regard to another consequence of this cyclic regulation process, the available evidence shows that any simplified, one-sided answer to the question of whether achievement and motivation profit from positive or negative mood is inappropriate. As a general rule, all things such as motivation or working memory capacity being equal, negative mood enhances performance on accommodative tasks that call for detailed stimulus assessment in accordance with externally provided rules. Positive mood, in contrast, benefits performance on assimilative tasks that depend on exploration and the creative ability to go beyond the given stimulus input. Although learning tasks and developmental tasks of both kinds are important for the individual's growth and maturation, it seems justified to conclude that higher-order intellectual functions of memory organization as well as self-determined behavior and emancipation are basically assimilative functions.

Third, it is important to note that affective states need not be enduring, intensive, or biologically significant to exert a systematic influence on achievement, motivation, and behavior regulation. Subtle affective cues have often been shown to be sufficient for inducing assimilation and accommodation effects, including mood congruency biases, as evident from numerous experiments using affective priming and symbolic stimuli associated with appetitive and aversive settings. Of particular relevance to education here is the role of fluency for learning and motivation. The feeling of flow or subjective ease, which signals proper functioning and lack of obstacles, has been shown to create an illusion of learning that can undermine motivation and effort expenditure. In contrast, the feeling of difficulty and impairment is actually a concomitant of good learning and effective learning transfer (Bjork, 1994).

Schools play a major role for the development of the ability to regulate emotions and to take them into account for information processing (McLaughlin, 2008). As already pointed out in the introduction, in the first two decades of most people's lives, there are not many similarly important sources of affective experience comparable to educational settings. While interacting with students and teachers, who might in some cases even serve as most important role models next to role models from families, children learn how to relate emotionally to others and to themselves (McLaughlin, 2008). Within such a socially challenging and emotionally rich school environment, calling for contrasting experiences with both adaptive functions of assimilation and accommodation, the psychological conditions should be met for effective learning, regulation, and personal growth.

REFERENCES

Ainley, M., & Ainley J. (2011). Student engagement with science in early adolescence: The contribution of enjoyment to students' continuing interest in learning about science. *Contemporary Educational Psychology, 36,* 4–12.

Alter, A. L., & Forgas, J. P. (2007). On being happy but fearing failure: The effects of mood on self-handicapping strategies. *Journal of Experimental Social Psychology, 43,* 947–954.

Alter, A. L., Oppenheimer, D. M., Epley, N., & Eyre, R. N. (2007). Overcoming intuition: Metacognitive difficulty activates analytic reasoning. *Journal of Experimental Psychology: General, 136,* 569–576.

Amabile, T. M. (1983). The social psychology of creativity: A componential conceptualization. *Journal of Personality and Social Psychology, 45,* 357–376.

Ashby, F., Isen, A. M., & Turken, A. U. (1999). A neuropsychological theory of positive affect and its influence on cognition. *Psychological Review, 106,* 529–550.

Baas, M., De Dreu, C.K.W., & Nijstad, B. A. (2008). A meta-analysis of 25 years of mood-creativity research: Hedonic tone, activation or regulatory focus? *Psychological Bulletin, 134,* 779–806.

Bäuml, K.-H., & Kuhbandner, C. (2003). Retrieval-induced forgetting and part-list cueing in associatively structured lists. *Memory & Cognition, 31,* 1188–1197.

Bäuml, K.-H, & Kuhbandner, C. (2007). Remembering can cause forgetting—but not in negative moods. *Psychological Science, 18,* 111–115.

Beukeboom, C. J., & Semin, G. R. (2006). How mood turns on language. *Journal of Experimental Social Psychology, 42,* 553–566.

Bjork, R. A. (1994). Memory and metamemory considerations in the training of human beings. In J. Metcalfe & A. P. Shimamura (Eds.), *Metacognition: Knowing about knowing* (pp. 185–205). Cambridge, MA: The MIT Press.

Bless, H., Bohner, G., Schwarz, N., & Strack, F. (1990). Mood and persuasion: A cognitive response analysis. *Personality and Social Psychology Bulletin, 16,* 331–345.

Bless, H., Clore, G. L., Schwarz, N., Golisano, V., Rabe, C., & Wolk, M. (1996). Mood and the use of scripts: Does a happy mood really lead to mindlessness? *Journal of Personality and Social Psychology, 71,* 665–679.

Bless, H., & Fiedler, K. (2006). Mood and the regulation of information processing and behavior. In J. P. Forgas (Ed.), *Affect in social thinking and behavior* (pp. 65–84). New York, NY: Psychology Press.

Bless, H., Hamilton, D. L., & Mackie, D. M. (1992). Mood effects on the organization of person information. *European Journal of Social Psychology, 22,* 497–509.

Bodenhausen, G. (1994). Emotions, arousal, and stereotypic judgments: A heuristic model of affect and stereotyping. In D. Mackie & D. Hamilton (Eds.), *Affect, cognition, and stereotyping: Interactive processes in group perception* (pp. 13–37). San Diego, CA: Academic Press.

Bower, G. H. (1981). Mood and memory. *American Psychologist, 36,* 129–148.

Brown, J. (1984). Effects of induced mood on causal attributions for success and failure. *Motivation and Emotion, 8,* 343–353.

Bryan, T., & Bryan, J. (1991). Positive mood and math performance. *Journal of Learning Disabilities, 24,* 490–494.

Clore, G. L., Schwarz, N., & Conway, M. (1994). Affective causes and consequences of social information processing. In R. S. Wyer & T. K. Srull (Eds.), *Handbook of social cognition, Vol. 1: Basic processes; Vol. 2: Applications* (2nd ed; pp. 323–417). Hillsdale, NJ: Lawrence Erlbaum.

Dweck, C., & Leggett, E. (1988). A social cognitive approach to motivation and personality. *Psychological Review, 95,* 256–273.

Elliot, A. J. (1999). Approach and avoidance motivation and achievement goals. *Educational Psychologist, 34,* 149–169.

Ellis, H. C., & Ashbrook, P. W. (1988). Resource allocation model of the effects of depressed mood states on memory. In K. Fiedler & J. P. Forgas (Eds.), *Affect, cognition, and social behavior* (pp. 25–43). Toronto, Canada: Hogrefe.

Erber, M. W., & Erber, R. (2001). The role of motivated social cognition in the regulation of affective states. In J. P. Forgas (Ed.), *Affect and social cognition* (pp. 275–290). Mahwah, NJ: Lawrence Erlbaum.

Fazio, R. H. (2001). On the automatic activation of associated evaluations: An overview. *Cognition and Emotion, 15,* 115–141.

Fiedler, K. (1988). Emotional mood, cognitive style, and behavior regulation. In K. Fiedler & J. P. Forgas (Eds.), *Affect, cognition, and social behavior* (pp. 100–119). Toronto, Canada: Hogrefe.

Fiedler, K. (1990). Mood-dependent selectivity in social cognition. In W. Stroebe & M. Hewstone (Eds.), *European review of social psychology.* New York, NY: Wiley.

Fiedler, K. (2001a). Affective states trigger processes of assimilation and accommodation. In L. L. Martin and G. L. Clore (Eds.), *Theories of mood and cognition: A user's guidebook* (pp. 85–98). Mahwah, NJ: Lawrence Erlbaum.

Fiedler, K. (2001b). Affective influences on social information processing. In J. P. Forgas (Ed.), *Affect and social cognition* (pp. 163–185). Mahwah, NJ: Lawrence Erlbaum.

Fiedler, K., Bluemke, M., & Unkelbach, C. (2011). On the adaptive flexibility of evaluative priming. *Memory and Cognition, 39,* 557–572.

Fiedler, K., Nickel, S., Asbeck, J., & Pagel, U. (2003). Mood and the generation effect. *Cognition and Emotion, 17,* 585–608.

Fiedler, K., Pampe, H., & Scherf, U. (1986). Mood and memory for tightly organized social information. *European Journal of Social Psychology, 16,* 149–164.

Fiedler, K., & Stroehm, W. (1986). What kind of mood influences what kind of memory: The role of arousal and information structure. *Memory and Cognition, 14*(2), 181–188.

Forgas, J. P. (1992). On mood and peculiar people: Affect and person typicality in impression formation. *Journal of Personality and Social Psychology, 62,* 863–875.

Forgas, J. P. (1995). Mood and judgment: The affect infusion model (AIM). *Psychological Bulletin, 117,* 39–66.

Forgas, J. P. (1998). On being happy and mistaken: Mood effects on the fundamental attribution error. *Journal of Personality and Social Psychology, 75,* 318–331.

Forgas, J. P. (1999). On feeling good and being rude: Affective influences on language use and request formulations. *Journal of Personality and Social Psychology, 76,* 928–939.

Forgas, J. P., Goldenberg, L., & Unkelbach, C. (2009). Can bad weather improve your memory? An unobtrusive field study of natural mood effects on real-life memory. *Journal of Experimental Social Psychology, 45,* 254–257.

Forgas, J. P., Laham, S. M., & Vargas, P. T. (2005). Mood effects on eyewitness memory: Affective influences on susceptibility to misinformation. *Journal of Experimental Social Psychology, 41,* 574–588.

Frederick, S. (2005) Cognitive reflection and decision making. *Journal of Economic Perspectives, 19,* 25–42.

Friedman, R. S., Förster, J., & Denzler, M. (2007). Interactive effects of mood and task framing on creative generation. *Creativity Research Journal, 19,* 141–162.

Goetz, T., Frenzel, A. C., Pekrun, R., & Hall, N. C. (2006). The domain specificity of academic emotional experiences. *The Journal of Experimental Education, 75,* 5–29.

Goetz, T., Hall, N. C., Frenzel, A. C., & Pekrun, R. (2006). A hierarchical conceptualization of enjoyment in students. *Learning and Instruction, 16,* 323–338.

Graham, S., & Taylor, A. Z. (2014). An attributional approach to emotional life in the classroom. In R. Pekrun & L. Linnenbrink-Garcia (Eds.), *International handbook of emotions in education* (pp. 96–119). New York, NY: Taylor & Francis.

Hagenauer, G., & Hascher, T. (2011). Schulische Lernfreude in der Sekundarstufe 1 und deren Beziehung zu Kontroll- und Valenzkognitionen. *Zeitschrift für Pädagogische Psychologie, 25,* 63–80.

Harris, M. B. (2000). Correlates and characteristics of boredom proneness and boredom. *Journal of Applied Social Psychology, 30,* 576–598.

Hart, W., & Albarracín, D. (2009). The effects of chronic achievement motivation and achievement primes on the activation of achievement and fun goals. *Journal of Personality and Social Psychology, 97,* 1129–1141.

Huang, C. (2011). Achievement goals and achievement emotions: A meta-analysis. *Educational Psychology Review, 23,* 359–388.

Huntsinger, J. R., Clore, G. L., & Bar-Anan, Y. (2010). Mood and global–local focus: Priming a local focus reverses the link between mood and global–local processing. *Emotion, 10,* 722–726.

Isen, A. M. (1984). Toward understanding the role of affect in cognition. In R. S. Wyer, Jr. & T. Srull (Eds.), *Handbook of social cognition* (pp. 179–236). Hillsdale, NJ: Lawrence Erlbaum.

Isen, A.M., & Daubman, K. A. (1984). The influence of affect on categorization. *Journal of Personality and Social Psychology, 47,* 1206–1217.

Isen, A. M., Daubman, K. A., & Nowicki, G. P. (1987). Positive affect facilitates creative problem solving. *Journal of Personality and Social Psychology, 52,* 1122–1131.

Isen, A. M., Johnson, M.M.S., Mertz, E., & Robinson, G. F. (1985). The influence of positive affect on the unusualness of word associations. *Journal of Personality and Social Psychology, 48,* 1413–1426.

Isen, A. M., & Levin, P. F. (1972). Effect of feeling good on helping: Cookies and kindness. *Journal of Personality and Social Psychology, 21*(3), 384–388.

Kaplan, A., & Midgley, C. (1999). The relationship between perceptions of the classroom goal structure and early adolescents' affect in school: The mediating role of coping strategies. *Learning and Individual Differences, 11,* 187–212.

Kappes, H. B., Oettingen, G., & Mayer, D. (2012). Positive fantasies predict low academic achievement in disadvantaged students. *European Journal of Social Psychology, 42,* 53–64.

Kasprzak, E. (2010). Perceived social support and life-satisfaction. *Polish Psychological Bulletin, 41,* 144–154.

Kavanagh, D. J., & Bower, G. H. (1985). Mood and self-efficacy: Impact of joy and sadness on perceived capabilities. *Cognitive Therapy and Research, 9,* 507–525.

Kelly, G. A. (1955). *The psychology of personal constructs. Vol. 1. A theory of personality. Vol. 2. Clinical diagnosis and psychotherapy.* Oxford, England: W. W. Norton.

Klinger, E. (1990). *Daydreaming: Using waking fantasy and imagery for self-knowledge and creativity.* Los Angeles, CA: Jeremy P. Tarcher.

Koch, A. S., & Forgas, J. P. (2012). Feeling good and feeling truth: The interactive effects of mood and processing fluency on truth judgments. *Journal of Experimental Social Psychology, 48,* 481–485.

Koriat, A., & Bjork, R. A. (2005). Illusions of competence in monitoring one's knowledge during study. *Journal of Experimental Psychology: Learning, Memory, and Cognition, 31,* 187–194.

Langens, T. A. & Schmalt, H.-D. (2002). Emotional consequences of positive daydreaming: The moderating role of fear of failure. *Personality and Social Psychology Bulletin, 28,* 1725–1735.

Lee, A. Y., & Sternthal, B. (1999). The effects of positive mood on memory. *Journal of Consumer Research, 26,* 115–127.

Linnenbrink, E. A., & Pintrich, P. R. (2002). Achievement goal theory and affect: An asymmetrical bidirectional model. *Educational Psychologist, 37,* 69–78.

Locke, E. A., Shaw, K. N., Saari, L. M., & Latham, G. P. (1981). Goal setting and task performance: 1969–1980. *Psychological Bulletin, 1,* 125–152.

Mackie, D. M., & Worth, L. T. (1989). Processing deficits and the mediation of positive affect in persuasion. *Journal of Personality and Social Psychology, 57,* 27–40.

Mandler, G. (2011). From association to organization. *Current Directions in Psychological Science, 20,* 232–235. doi:10.1177/0963721411414656

Mandler, G., & Pearlstone, Z. (1966). Free and constrained concept learning and subsequent recall. *Journal of Verbal Learning and Verbal Behavior, 5,* 126–131.

Martin, L. L., Ward, D. W., Achee, J. W., & Wyer, Jr. R. S. (1993). Mood as input: People have to interpret the motivational implications of their moods. *Journal of Personality and Social Psychology, 64,* 317–326.

McLaughlin, C. (2008). Emotional well-being and its relationship to schools and classrooms: A critical reflection. *British Journal of Guidance & Counselling, 36,* 353–366.

Metcalfe, J. (2009). Metacognitive judgments and control of study. *Current Directions in Psychological Science, 18,* 159–163.

Middleton, M., & Midgley, C. (1997). Avoiding the demonstration of lack of ability: An underexplored aspect of goal theory. *Journal of Educational Psychology, 89,* 710–718.

Nadler, R. T., Rabi, R., & Minda, J. P. (2010). Better mood and better performance: Learning rule described categories is enhanced by positive mood. *Psychological Science, 21,* 1770–1776.

Niedenthal, P. M. (2007). Embodying emotion. *Science, 316,* 1002–1005.

Oaksford, M., Morris, F., Grainger, B., & Williams, J.M.G. (1996). Mood, reasoning, and central executive processes. *Journal of Experimental Psychology: Learning, Memory, and Cognition, 22,* 477–493.

Oettingen, G., & Mayer, D. (2002). The motivating function of thinking about the future: Expectations versus fantasies. *Journal of Personality and Social Psychology, 83,* 1198–1212.

Oppenheimer, D. M. (2008). The secret life of fluency. *Trends in Cognitive Sciences, 12,* 237–241.

Park, J., & Banaji, M. R. (2000). Mood and heuristics: The influence of happy and sad states on sensitivity and bias in stereotyping. *Journal of Personality and Social Psychology, 78,* 1005–1023.

Pekrun, R. (2006). The control-value theory of achievement emotions: Assumptions, corollaries, and implications for educational research and practice. *Educational Psychology Review, 18,* 315–341.

Pekrun, R., Elliot, A. J., & Maier, M. A. (2006). Achievement goals and discrete achievement emotions: A theoretical model and prospective test. *Journal of Educational Psychology, 98,* 583–597.

Pekrun, R., Goetz, T., Daniels, L. M., Stupnisky, R. H., & Perry, R. P. (2010). Boredom in achievement settings: Exploring control-value antecedents and performance outcomes of a neglected emotion. *Journal of Educational Psychology, 102,* 531–549.

Pekrun, R., Goetz, T., Titz, W., & Perry, R. P. (2002). Academic emotions in students' self-regulated learning and achievement: A program of qualitative and quantitative research. *Educational Psychologist, 37,* 91–105.

Pekrun, R., & Perry, R. P. (2014). Control-value theory of achievement emotions. In R. Pekrun & L. Linnenbrink-Garcia (Eds.), *International handbook of emotions in education* (pp. 120–141). New York, NY: Taylor & Francis.

Piaget, J. (1954). *The construction of reality in the child.* New York, NY: Free Press.

Roediger, H., & McDermott, K. (1995). Creating false memories: Remembering words not presented in lists. *Journal of Experimental Psychology: Learning, Memory, and Cognition, 21,* 803–814.

Rowe, G. G., Hirsh, J. B., Anderson, A. K., & Smith, E. (2007). Positive affect increases the breadth of attentional selection. *PNAS Proceedings of the National Academy of Sciences of the United States of America, 104,* 383–388.

Rundus, D. (1973). Negative effects of using list items as recall cues. *Journal of Verbal Learning and Verbal Behavior, 12,* 43–50.

Salovey, P., & Grewal, D. (2005). The science of emotional intelligence. *Current Directions in Psychological Science, 14,* 281–285.

Schul, Y., Mayo, R., & Burnstein, E. (2008). The value of distrust. *Journal of Experimental Social Psychology, 44*(5), 1293–1302.

Schwarz, N. (1990). Feelings as information: Informational and motivational functions of affective states. In E. T. Higgins & R. M. Sorrentino (Eds.), *Handbook of motivation and cognition: Foundations of social behaviour* (Vol. 2, pp. 527–561). New York, NY: Guilford Press.

Schwarz, N., & Clore, G. L. (1983). Mood, misattribution, and judgments of well-being: Informative and directive functions of affective states. *Journal of Personality and Social Psychology, 45,* 513–523.

Schwarz, N., & Clore, G. L. (2007). Feelings and phenomenal experiences. In A. W. Kruglanski & E. Higgins (Eds.), *Social psychology: Handbook of basic principles (2nd ed.)* (pp. 385–407). New York, NY: Guilford Press.

Sinclair, R. C. (1988). Mood, categorization breadth, and performance appraisal: The effects of order of information acquisition and affective state on halo, accuracy, information retrieval, and evaluations. *Organizational Behavior and Human Decision Processes, 42,* 22–46.

Sinclair, R. C., & Mark, M. M. (1995). The effects of mood state on judgmental accuracy: Processing strategy as a mechanism. *Cognition and Emotion, 9,* 417–438.

Skaalvik, E. (1997). Self-enhancing and self-defeating ego orientation: Relations with task avoidance orientation, achievement, self-perceptions, and anxiety. *Journal of Educational Psychology, 89,* 71–81.

Smith, C. A., & Ellsworth, P. C. (1985). Patterns of cognitive appraisal in emotions. *Journal of Personality and Social Psychology, 48,* 813–838.

Smith, C. A., & Ellsworth, P. C. (1987). Patterns of appraisal and emotion related to taking an exam. *Journal of Personality and Social Psychology, 52,* 475–488.

Stepper, S., & Strack, F. (1993). Proprioceptive determinants of emotional and nonemotional feelings. *Journal of Personality and Social Psychology, 64,* 211–220.

Stöber, J. (2004). Dimensions of test anxiety: Relations to ways of coping with pre-exam anxiety and uncertainty. *Anxiety, Stress and Coping, 17,* 213–226.

Storbeck, J., & Clore, G. L. (2005). With sadness comes accuracy; with happiness, false memory: Mood and the false memory effect. *Psychological Science, 16,* 785–791.

Storbeck, J., & Clore, G. L. (2008). The affective regulation of cognitive priming. *Emotion, 8,* 208–215.

Taylor, S. E. (1991). The asymmetrical effects of positive and negative events: The mobilization-minimization hypothesis. *Psychological Bulletin, 110,* 67–85.

Thelwell, R. C., Lane, A. M., & Weston, N. V. (2007). Mood states, self-set goals, self-efficacy and performance in academic examinations. *Personality and Individual Differences, 42*(3), 573–583.

Unkelbach, C. (2006). The learned interpretation of cognitive fluency. *Psychological Science, 17,* 339–345.

Williams, K. D., & Nida, S. A. (2011). Ostracism: Consequences and coping. *Current Directions In Psychological Science, 20,* 71–75.

Winkielman, P., Schwarz, N., Fazendeiro, T., & Reber, R. (2003). The hedonic marking of processing fluency: Implications for evaluative judgment. In J. Musch & K. C. Klauer (Eds.), *The psychology of evaluation: Affective processes in cognition and emotion* (pp. 189–217). Mahwah, NJ: Lawrence Erlbaum.

4

THE EXPERIENCE OF EMOTIONS
DURING GOAL PURSUIT

Charles S. Carver and Michael F. Scheier,
University of Miami and Carnegie Mellon University

This chapter describes a viewpoint on the origins of emotions in the context of goal-directed behavior. This viewpoint treats emotions as part of a systematic network of influences on behavior, embedding the goal concept in a model of self-regulating systems. The systems regulate actions with respect to diverse kinds of goals (e.g., values, plans, strategies, intentions—even whims), so that life's many incentives are successfully approached and threats avoided.

The viewpoint we take construes behavior as the output function of feedback control processes. We propose that two layers of control manage two aspects of behavior, placing behavior in time as well as space. We believe that one of these layers is involved in the existence of affect, the core of emotion. We suggest that this arrangement is useful both for the successful attainment of a single goal and also for managing multiple tasks competing for attention. That is, the system described here can help transform simultaneous desire for many different goals into a stream of actions that shifts repeatedly from one goal to another over time.

BEHAVIOR AS GOAL DIRECTED AND
FEEDBACK CONTROLLED

We begin by describing a feedback-based view of action control. This description begins with the goal concept, a concept that is prominent in today's psychology (Austin & Vancouver, 1996; Elliot, 2008; Johnson, Chang, & Lord, 2006). The goal concept is broad

Acknowledgment: Preparation of this chapter was facilitated by support from the National Cancer Institute (CA64710), the National Science Foundation (BCS0544617), and the National Center for Complementary and Alternative Medicine (AT007262).

enough to cover both long-term aspirations (e.g., creating and maintaining good performance in a course one is taking) and the endpoints of very short-term acts (e.g., reaching to pick up a book). Goals generally can be reached in diverse ways, and a given action often can be done in the service of diverse goals. This results in potentially vast complexity in the organization of action.

Feedback Loops

The point here is actually less about the goals per se, however, than about the process of attaining them. Movement toward a goal can be seen as reflecting the operation of a discrepancy reducing feedback loop (MacKay, 1966; Miller, Galanter, & Pribram, 1960; Powers, 1973; Wiener, 1948). Such a loop is an organization among several component processes. It entails sensing some existing condition and comparing it to a desired or intended condition. If there is a discrepancy between the two, the discrepancy is countered by acting in some way to change the sensed condition. The overall effect is to bring the sensed condition into conformity with the intended one (Powers, 1973). If the intended condition is thought of as a goal, the effect is to bring behavior into conformity to the goal—thus, goal attainment.

There also exist discrepancy enlarging loops, which increase deviations rather than decrease them. The comparison point in this case is a threat, an antigoal to escape. Effects of discrepancy enlargement in living systems are typically constrained by discrepancy reducing processes. Thus, people often can avoid something aversive (e.g., failure) by the very act of approaching something else (success).

Some people mistakenly believe that feedback loops act only to create and maintain steady states and are therefore irrelevant to behavior. Some reference values (and goals) are static, but others are dynamic (e.g., taking a vacation trip across Europe, completing secondary school). In the latter cases, the goal is the process of traversing the changing trajectory of the activity, not just arrival at the endpoint. The principle of feedback control (matching behavior to goals or intentions) applies easily to moving targets (Beer, 1995).

What we bring to the conversation about goals, then (though we are far from the first to do so; see MacKay, 1966; Miller et al.,1960; Powers, 1973) is the idea that goal-directed action reflects feedback control. Why emphasize feedback control? The feedback concept has been useful in many fields, to the point that it is sometimes suggested that feedback processes are fundamental building blocks of all complex systems. We believe there is merit in recognizing similarities between processes that underlie behavior and those underlying other complex systems (cf. von Bertalanffy, 1968). Nature seems to be a miser. It seems likely that an organizational property that emerges in one complex system will emerge over and over in other complex systems. In part for these reasons, we have continued to use the principle of feedback control as a conceptual heuristic over the years.

Levels of Abstraction

But let us return now to goals. Goals exist at many levels of abstraction. You can have the goal of being at the top of your class; you can also have the goal of doing well in math—a more restricted goal that contributes to the broader goals of being at the top of your class. A behavior that contributes to doing well in math is mastering the ideas in the math textbook. This in turn entails more-concrete goals: arranging the lighting for studying, holding the book straight, concentrating on the terms. All of these are goals, values to be approached, but at varying levels of abstraction.

It is often said that people's goals form a hierarchy (Powers, 1973; Vallacher & Wegner, 1987) in which abstract goals are achieved by attaining the concrete goals that help define them. Lower-level goals are attained by briefer sequences of action (formed from subcomponents of motor control; e.g., Rosenbaum, Meulenbroek, Vaughan, & Jansen, 2001). Some sequences of action have a self-contained quality in that they run off fairly autonomously once triggered.

The hierarchy can also be viewed from the other direction. Sequences can be organized into programs of action (Powers, 1973). Programs are more planful than sequences and require choices at various points. Programs, in turn, are often enacted in the service of principles—more abstract values that provide a basis for making decisions within programs and which suggest that certain programs be undertaken or refrained from. Even greater complexity is possible. Patterns of values can coalesce to form a very abstract sense of desired (and undesired) self.

All these classes of goals, from very concrete to very abstract, can in principle serve as reference points for action. When self-regulation is undertaken regarding a goal at one level, it presumably invokes control at all levels of abstraction below that one. Control is not necessarily being exerted at higher levels than that one, however. Indeed, it is even possible for a person to knowingly take an action that turns out to conflict with a higher level goal. This creates problems when the person later attends to that higher goal.

FEEDBACK PROCESSES AND AFFECT

Production of action is the jumping off point for the main concern of this chapter, which is affect, the evaluative core of emotion (although distinctions can be made between affect and emotion, we will use these terms more or less interchangeably here). Two fundamental questions about affect are what it consists of and where it comes from. It is often said that affect pertains to one's desires and whether they are being met (e.g., Clore, 1994; Frijda, 1986, 1988; Ortony, Clore, & Collins, 1988). But what exactly is the mechanism by which it arises?

This question can be addressed in terms of neurobiology, cognition, and in other ways. We have proposed an answer that focuses on some of the functional properties that affect seems to display in the person who experiences it (Carver & Scheier, 1990, 1998, 1999a, 1999b). We used feedback control again as an organizing principle but applied it somewhat differently. Our idea was that the feelings forming the core of emotions emerge from a feedback process that runs automatically, simultaneously with the behavior-producing process, and in parallel to it. The easiest way to convey the sense of this second process is to say that it continuously checks on how well the first process (the behavioral loop) is doing at reducing its discrepancies (we focus first on approach loops). Thus, the input for the second loop is some representation of the *rate of discrepancy reduction in the action system over time.*

A physical analogy can be useful here. An action implies a change between states. A change between physical states is distance. Thus, behavior is analogous to traversing distance. If the action loop controls distance, and if the affect loop assesses the action loop's progress, then the affect loop is assessing the psychological analogue of velocity, the first derivative of distance over time. To the extent that this analogy is meaningful, the perceptual input to the affect loop should be the first derivative over time of the input used by the action loop.

Input in itself does not create affect (a given velocity has different implications in different circumstances). As in any feedback system, the input is compared to a reference value (Frijda, 1986, 1988). In this case, that reference value is an acceptable (or desired or intended) rate of behavioral discrepancy reduction. As in any feedback loop, the comparison checks for deviation from the standard. If there is one, the output function changes.

Our argument was that the comparison in this loop yields an error signal (a representation of the discrepancy) that is manifested subjectively as affect—positive or negative valence. If the sensed rate of progress is below the criterion, affect is negative. If the rate is high enough to exceed the criterion, affect is positive. If the rate is not distinguishable from the criterion, affect is neutral. In essence, the argument is that feelings with a positive valence tell you that you are doing better at something than you need to or expected to, and feelings with a negative valence tell you that you are doing worse than you need to or expected to (for detail see Carver & Scheier, 1998; Chapters 8 and 9).

This implies that for any given goal-directed action—taken by itself—at any moment in time, the potential for affective pertaining to that action should form a bipolar dimension. For any given action, affect can be positive, neutral, or negative, depending on how well or poorly the action is going. If you are studying math and you have an insight that jumps your overall understanding forward, you experience a flash of elation. If you realize it is taking you far longer than you had expected to get through today's assignment, you feel a sense of frustration and negativity.

What determines the criterion for this loop? When the activity is unfamiliar, the criterion is rather arbitrary and tentative. If the activity is familiar, the criterion is likely to reflect the person's accumulated experience in that activity, in the form of an expected rate (the more experience you have, the more you know what is reasonable to expect). Sometimes the criterion is instead a "desired" or "needed" rate of progress.

The criterion can also change. How fast it changes depends on additional factors. The less experience the person has in a domain, the more fluid the criterion is likely to be; in a familiar domain, change is slower. Still, it is likely that repeated overshoot of the criterion automatically yields an upward drift of the criterion (e.g., Eidelman & Biernat, 2007); repeated undershoots yield a downward drift. Thus, the system recalibrates over repeated experience in such a way that the criterion stays within the range of those experiences (Carver & Scheier, 2000). A somewhat ironic effect of such recalibration would be to keep the balance of a person's affective experience (positive to negative) in a given domain relatively similar across time, even when the rate criterion changes considerably.

Evidence

Evidence of the role of the velocity function in affective reactions to situations comes from several sources (see also Carver & Scheier, 1998). An early source was Hsee and Abelson (1991), who came to the velocity hypothesis independently. Participants read descriptions of paired hypothetical scenarios and indicated which they would find more satisfying. For example, would you be more satisfied if your class standing had gone from the 30th percentile to the 70th over the past six weeks, or if it had done so over the past three weeks? Given positive final outcomes, participants preferred improving to a high outcome over having a constant high outcome; they preferred a fast velocity over a slow one; they even preferred fast small changes to slower larger changes. When the change was negative (e.g., salaries got worse), they preferred a constant low salary to a salary that started high and fell to the same low level; they preferred slow falls to fast falls; and they preferred large slow falls to small fast falls. Thus, higher velocities toward desired outcomes were reflected in greater satisfaction (more positive affect), and higher velocities away from desired outcomes were reflected in less satisfaction (less positive affect).

Another early study that appears to bear on this view of affect was reported by Brunstein (1993). It examined subjective well-being among college students over an academic term as a function of several perceptions, including perception of progress toward goals. Of greatest interest at present, perceived progress at each measurement point was strongly and positively correlated with concurrent subjective well-being.

More recently, Chang, Johnson, and Lord (2010) reported another pair of studies on this topic. The first was a field study of employees' job satisfaction. Participants rated various aspects of their current jobs with respect to existing and desired job characteristics. They also rated their perceptions of how quickly each job characteristic was changing to more closely approximate the ideal, and they rated the desired velocity of change for each job characteristic. Results indicated that velocity considerations play an important role in participants' job satisfaction. In a second study using a laboratory, Chang et al. (2010) found that satisfaction with task performance was similarly affected by perceptions of velocity toward their performance goal. Thus, once again, velocity toward desired goals was related to more positive affect, expressed as satisfaction.

Two Kinds of Behavioral Loops, Two Dimensions of Affect

Thus far we have focused exclusively on discrepancy-reducing loops. Affect can also arise with regard to discrepancy-enlarging loops. The view just outlined rests on the idea that positive feeling results when an action system is making rapid progress in doing what it is organized to do. There is no obvious reason why the principle should not also apply to systems that enlarge discrepancies. If that kind of system is making rapid progress doing what it is organized to do, there should be positive affect. If it is doing poorly, there should be negative affect.

The idea that the potential exists for affects of both valences would seem to apply to both approach (discrepancy-reducing) and avoidance (discrepancy-enlarging) systems. That is, both approach and avoidance have the potential to induce positive feelings (by doing well) and the potential to induce negative feelings (by doing poorly). But doing well at approaching an incentive is not quite the same experience as doing well at moving away from a threat. Thus, the two positives may not be quite the same, nor may the two negatives.

Based on this line of thought and drawing on insights from Higgins (e.g., 1987, 1996) and his collaborators, we argue for two sets of affects, one relating to approach, the other to avoidance (Carver & Scheier, 1998). The former reflect doing well versus poorly at gaining an incentive; the latter reflect doing well versus poorly at avoiding a threat. Thus, approach can lead to such positive affects as eagerness, excitement, and elation, and to such negative affects as frustration, anger, and sadness (Carver, 2004; Carver &

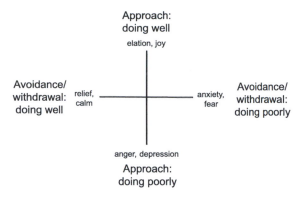

Figure 4.1 Carver and Scheier's (1998) view of two orthogonal dimensions of self-regulatory function and examples of the affects that can emerge from them (Carver & Harmon-Jones, 2009a).

Harmon-Jones, 2009a). Avoidance can lead to such positive affects as relief and contentment (Carver, 2009) and such negative affects as fear, guilt, and anxiety. The two sets of affects are assumed to have independent origins (Figure 4.1). Since approach and avoidance functions can occur simultaneously, however, the affects that people subjectively experience do not always reflect solely one or the other.

The view shown in Figure 4.1 is similar to the view proposed for different reasons by Rolls (1999, 2005). His theory starts with reinforcement contingencies, identifying emotions in terms of the occurrence of reinforcers and punishers and the omission or termination of reinforcers and punishers. Consistent with our view, Rolls (1999, 2005) differentiated between the occurrence of a punisher (which yields fear) and the omission of a reinforcer (which yields frustration and anger). Similarly, he distinguished between the occurrence of a reinforcer (which yields elation) and the omission of a punisher (which yields relief).

Merging Affect and Action

The view described in the previous section implies a natural connection between affect and action. If the input function of the affect loop is a sensed rate of progress in action, the output function must involve a change in progress of that action. Thus, the affect loop has a direct influence on what occurs in the action loop. Some changes in velocity are straightforward. If you are lagging behind, you try harder (Brehm & Self, 1989; Wright, 1996). Sometimes the changes are less straightforward. The rates of many behaviors are defined not by pace or intensity of physical action but by choices among actions or entire programs of action. For example, increasing the rate of progress on a school project may mean choosing to spend a weekend working on it rather than hanging out at the mall. Increasing one's rate of kindness may mean choosing to act in a way that reflects kindness when given the opportunity. Thus, adjustment in rate must often be translated into other terms, such as concentration or allocation of time and effort.

The idea of two feedback systems functioning in concert with one another is common in control engineering (e.g., Clark, 1996). Having two feedback systems functioning together—one controlling position, one controlling velocity—permits the overall device to respond in a way that is both quick and stable, without overshoots and oscillations (Carver & Scheier, 1998, pp. 144–145). The combination of quickness and stability is valuable in human experience as well. A person who is highly reactive emotionally is prone to overreact to events and to oscillate behaviorally. A person who is emotionally unreactive is slow to respond even to urgent events. A person whose reactions are between these extremes acts quickly but without overreaction and consequent oscillation. Responding quickly yet accurately confers a clear advantage. We believe this combination requires having both behavior-managing and affect-managing control systems. Affect allows people's responses to be quicker (because this control system is time-sensitive) and, provided that the affective system is not overresponsive, the responses are also stable.

Our focus here is on how affects influence behavior, emphasizing the extent to which affect and behavior are interwoven. Note, however, that the behavioral responses that the affects promote also lead to reduction of the affects. Thus, in a very basic sense, the affect system itself is self-regulating (cf. Campos, Frankel, & Camras, 2004). Certainly people also make voluntary efforts to regulate their emotions (Gross, 2007; Jacobs & Gross, 2014), but the affect system does a good deal of that self-regulation through its own normal functioning. Indeed, if the affect system is optimally responsive, affect will generally not be intense because the relevant deviations are countered before they become intense (cf. Baumeister, Vohs, DeWall, & Zhang, 2007).

AFFECT ISSUES

This view of affect is unusual in several ways. At least two points appear to have interesting and potentially important implications.

Dimensionality Behind Affect

One difference concerns relationships among affects. A number of theories (though not all) conceptualize affects as aligned along dimensions. Our view fits that picture, in a sense. That is, we argue that affect regarding any action—approach or avoidance—has the potential to be either positive or negative, to the extent that progress is going better than intended or worse than intended. Thus, we assume a bipolar dimension of potential affective valence for each of these two core motivational tendencies (Figure 4.1).

Most dimensional models of affect that relate to motivations take a different form, however. One set of widely known dimensional models assumes that each core motivational system is responsible for affect of one valence only. This view yields two *unipolar* dimensions, each linked to one motivational system (e.g., Cacioppo & Berntson, 1994; Cacioppo, Gardner, & Berntson, 1999; Gray, 1990, 1994; Lang, 1995; Lang, Bradley, & Cuthbert, 1990; Watson, Wiese, Vaidya, & Tellegen, 1999). In this view, greater engagement of the approach system is linked to greater positive affect, and greater engagement of the avoidance system is linked to greater negative affect.

Evidence distinguishing these views from each other is not fully consistent. Here are some relevant findings regarding doing well in avoidance of threat. Higgins, Shah, and Friedman (1997, Study 4) found that having an avoidance orientation to a task (try to avoid failing) plus a good outcome led to elevations in reports of calmness. Calmness was not affected, however, with an approach orientation (try to succeed). Thus, calmness was linked to doing well at avoidance but not to doing well at approach. In other studies, people responded to hypothetical scenarios in which a threat was introduced then removed (Carver, 2009). Reports of relief related principally to individual differences in threat sensitivity.

More frequently studied are links from certain negative affects to doing poorly at approach. For example, in the study by Higgins et al. (1997) just described, people with an approach orientation who failed reported elevated sadness. This did not occur with an avoidance orientation. This suggests a link between sadness and doing poorly at approach. The broader literature of self-discrepancy theory makes a similar point. Studies in that literature have found that sadness relates uniquely (controlling for anxiety) to discrepancies between actual selves and ideal selves (see Higgins, 1987, 1996, for reviews). Ideals are qualities the person intrinsically desires: aspirations, hopes, positive images for the self. Pursuing an ideal is an approach process (Higgins, 1996). Thus, this literature also suggests that sadness stems from a failure of approach.

Considerable evidence also links the approach system to anger (for review, see Carver & Harmon-Jones, 2009a). As one example, Harmon-Jones and Sigelman (2001) induced anger in some persons but not others then examined cortical activity. They found elevated left anterior activity, which previous research (e.g., Davidson, 1992) had linked to activation of the approach system. In other studies (Carver, 2004), people reported the feelings they experienced in response to hypothetical failures (Study 2) and after the destruction of the World Trade Center (Study 3). Reports of anger related to sensitivity of the approach system, whereas reports of fear and anxiety related to sensitivity of the avoidance system.

On the other hand, there is also an accumulation of evidence that contradicts our position, locating all negative affects on one dimension and all positive affects on another dimension. This evidence, briefly summarized by Watson (2009), consists primarily of studies in which people reported their moods at a particular time or across a particular span of time. As Carver and Harmon-Jones (2009b) pointed out, however, an affective response to a particular event (which is what we are discussing in this chapter) differs in important ways from a mood. Moods aggregate over multiple events. It seems likely that in the creation or maintenance of moods, influences come into play that differ from those underlying focused affective responses to specific events.

The issue of how affects relate to one another is an important one because it has implications for potential conceptual mechanisms underlying affect. Theories that posit two unipolar dimensions appear to equate greater activation of a motivational system to more affect of a corresponding valence. If the approach system actually relates instead to feelings of both valences, this mechanism is not tenable. A conceptual mechanism is needed that addresses both positive and negative feelings within the approach function (and, separately, the avoidance function). The mechanism described here is one that does so.

One final word about dimensionality. Our view is dimensional in that it is predicated on a dimension of how well things are going (from very well to very poorly). However, the affects that fall on that dimension do not themselves form a dimension, apart from having two valences and a neutral point (Figure 4.1). For example, depression (which arises when things are going extremely poorly) is not simply a more intense state of frustration (which arises when things are going poorly, but less poorly or for a more limited time). The identifiable emotions themselves appear to be nonlinear consequences of linear variation in system functioning. Anger and sadness are both potential consequences of approach going poorly. Which one emerges appears to depend in part on whether the goal seems lost or not (see also Rolls, 1999, 2005).

Coasting

A second potentially important issue also differentiates our view from most others on the meaning and consequences of affect (Carver, 2003). Recall the idea that affect reflects the error signal in a feedback loop. Given the nature of feedback processes, affect thus would be a signal to adjust progress. That would be true whether rate is above the criterion or below it. This is intuitive for negative feelings: Frustration leads to increase in effort. But what about positive feelings?

Here the theory becomes counterintuitive. Positive feelings, which arise when things are going better than they need to, still reflect a discrepancy, and the function of a negative feedback loop is to minimize sensed discrepancies. If this is a negative feedback loop, this system "wants" to see neither negative nor positive affect. Either one would represent an error and lead to changes in output that eventually would reduce it (see also Izard, 1977).

This view argues that exceeding the criterion rate of progress (thus creating positive feelings) automatically results in a tendency to reduce effort in this domain. The person coasts a little. This does not mean stopping altogether, but easing back, such that subsequent progress returns to the criterion. The impact on emotion would be that the positive feeling is not sustained for very long. It begins to fade.

We should be clear that expending effort to catch up when behind, and coasting when ahead, are both presumed to be specific to the goal to which the affect is linked. Usually (though not always) this is the goal from which the affect arises in the first place. We should also be clear about time frames. This view pertains to the ongoing episode. This is not an argument that positive affect makes people less likely to do the behavior again later on. That obviously is incorrect. Emotions have important effects on learning, but those effects of emotion are outside the scope of this chapter (see Baumeister et al., 2007).

A system of the sort we are postulating would operate in the same way as a car's cruise control. If progress is too slow, negative affect arises. The person responds by increasing effort, trying to speed up. If progress is better than needed, positive affect arises, leading to coasting. A car's cruise control displays similar properties. A hill slows you down; the cruise control feeds the engine more fuel, speeding back up. If you come across the crest of a hill and roll downward too fast, the system restricts fuel and the speed gradually falls back down.

The analogy is intriguing partly because both sides are asymmetrical in the consequences of deviation from the criterion. In both cases, to deal with the problem of going too slow requires expending further resources. To deal with the problem of going too fast entails only cutting back. A cruise control does not apply the brakes; it only reduces fuel. Friction is what eventually returns the car's speed to the set point. In the same fashion, people generally do not respond to positive affect by trying to dampen the feeling. They only ease back a little on resources that are devoted to the domain in which the affect arose.

The effect of a cruise control on an excessively high rate of speed thus depends partly on external circumstances. If the downward slope is steep, the car may exceed the set point all the way to the valley below. The same applies to positive feelings. The feelings may stay for a long time if momentum is high as the person coasts down the subjective hill. Eventually, though, the reduced resources would cause the positive affect to fade. In the long run, then, the system would act to prevent great amounts of pleasure as well as great amounts of pain (Carver, 2003; Carver & Scheier, 1998).

Does positive affect (or greater than expected progress) lead to coasting? To test this idea, a study must assess coasting toward the same goal as underlies the affect (or the high progress). A few studies satisfy these criteria. Louro, Pieters, and Zeelenberg (2007) examined the role of positive feelings from surging ahead in the context of multiple-goal pursuit. In three studies, they found that when people were relatively close to a goal, positive feelings prompted decrease in effort toward that goal and a shift of effort to an alternate goal. They also found a boundary on this effect; it occurred only when people were relatively close to their goal.

Another recent study used an intensive experience sampling procedure across a two-week period (Fulford, Johnson, Llabre, & Carver, 2010). Participants made a set of judgments three times a day about each of three goals that they were pursuing over that period. The ratings they made included perceptions of progress for each time block, which could be compared to expected progress for that block. The data showed that greater than expected progress toward a goal was followed by reduction in effort toward that goal during the next time period.

Coasting and Multiple Concerns

The idea that positive affect promotes coasting, which eventually results in reduction of the positive affect, might seem unlikely. Why should a process be built into people that limits positive feelings—indeed, that reduces them? After all, people do seek pleasure and avoid pain.

There are at least two potential bases for this tendency. First, it is not adaptive for organisms to spend energy needlessly (Brehm & Self, 1989; Gendolla & Richter, 2010). Coasting prevents that. Second, people have multiple simultaneous concerns (Atkinson & Birch, 1970; Carver, 2003; Carver & Scheier, 1998; Frijda, 1994). Given multiple concerns, people do not optimize performance on any one of them but rather "satisfice" (Simon, 1953)—do a good-enough job on each to deal with it satisfactorily. This lets the person handle many concerns adequately rather than just one (see also Fitzsimons, Friesen, Orehek, & Kruglanski, 2009; Kumashiro, Rusbult, & Finkel, 2008).

Coasting with respect to a given goal would virtually define satisficing regarding that goal. That is, reducing effort would prevent attainment of the best possible outcome for it. A tendency to coast would also promote satisficing regarding a broader array of goals. That is, if progress in one domain exceeds current needs, a tendency to coast in that particular domain (satisficing) would make it easier to devote energy to another domain. This would help ensure satisfactory goal attainment in the other domain and, ultimately, across multiple domains.

As an example, most students have both academic pursuits and social pursuits. There is a tendency for most students to do less than their very best at reaching their academic goals so that they can also devote time to their other interests. The result, for most people, is satisfactory levels of attainment in all of the relevant goal domains.

In contrast to this picture, continued pursuit of one goal without let-up can have adverse effects. Continuing at a rapid pace in one area may sustain positive affect pertaining to that area, but by diverting resources from other goals, it also increases the potential for problems elsewhere. This would be even truer of an effort to intensify the positive affect, which would further divert resources from other goals. Indeed, a single-minded pursuit of yet-more-positive feelings in one domain can even be lethal if it causes the person to disregard threats looming elsewhere.

A pattern in which positive feelings lead to easing back and an openness to shifting the focus of one's energies would minimize such problems. It is important to realize that this view does not require that positive feelings lead to a shift in goals. It simply holds that openness to a shift is a consequence—and a potential benefit—of the coasting tendency. This line of thought would, however, account for why people do eventually turn away from pleasurable activities.

PRIORITY MANAGEMENT

This line of argument begins to implicate positive emotion in a broad organizational function within the organism. This function is priority management across time: the shifting from one goal to another as focal in behavior (Dreisbach & Goschke, 2004; Shallice, 1978; Shin & Rosenbaum, 2002). This basic and very important function is often overlooked, but it deserves closer examination. Humans usually pursue many goals simultaneously, but only one can have top priority at a given moment. People attain their many goals by shifting among them. Thus, there are changes over time in which one goal has the top priority. An important question is how those changes are managed.

What we regard as an extremely insightful view of priority management was proposed many years ago by Simon (1967). He noted that, although goals with less than top prior-ity are largely out of awareness, ongoing events still can be relevant to them. Sometimes events that occur during pursuit of the top-priority goal create problems for a lower-priority goal. Indeed, the mere passing of time can create a problem for the lower-priority goal because passing of time may make its attainment less likely. If the lower-priority goal is also important, an emerging problem for its attainment must be taken into account. If there arises a serious threat to that goal, a mechanism is needed to change priorities, so that the second goal replaces the first one as focal.

Feelings and Reprioritization

Simon (1967) proposed that emotions are calls for reprioritization. He suggested that emotion arising with respect to a goal that is outside awareness eventually induces people to interrupt what they are doing and upgrade the priority of the neglected goal. The stronger the emotion, the stronger is the claim for upgrade. Simon did not address nega-tive affect that arises with respect to a currently focal goal, but the same principle seems to apply. In that case, negative affect seems to be a call for an even greater investment of resources and effort in that focal goal than is now being made.

Simon's analysis applies easily to negative feelings, cases in which a nonfocal goal demands a higher priority and intrudes on awareness. However, another way in which priority ordering can shift is that the currently focal goal can relinquish its place. Simon acknowledged this possibility obliquely, noting that goal attainment terminates pursuit of that goal. However, he did not address the possibility that an as-yet-unattained goal might also yield its place in line.

Carver (2003) expanded on that possibility, suggesting that positive feelings represent a cue to reduce the priority of the goal to which the feeling pertains. This view appears consistent with the sense of Simon's analysis but suggests that the prioritizing function of affect pertains to affects of both valences. Positive affect regarding an act of avoidance (relief or tranquility) indicates that a threat has dissipated, that it no longer requires as much attention as it did, and can now assume a lower priority. Positive affect regarding approach (happiness, joy) indicates that an incentive is being attained ahead of schedule. Even if it is not yet attained, the affect indicates that you could temporarily withdraw effort from this goal because you are doing so well.

What follows from a reduction in priority of a currently focal goal? This situation is less directive than the one that exists when a nonfocal goal demands higher priority. What happens in this case depends partly on what else is in line and whether the context has changed in important ways while you were absorbed with the focal goal. Opportunities to attain incentives sometimes appear unexpectedly, and people put aside their plans to take advantage of such unanticipated opportunities (Hayes-Roth & Hayes-Roth, 1979; Payton, 1990). It seems reasonable that positive affect should facilitate a tendency to shift goals now, if something else needs fixing or doing (regarding a next-in-line goal or a newly emergent goal) or if an unanticipated opportunity for gain has appeared.

On the other hand, sometimes neither of these conditions exists. In such a case, no shift in goal would occur. That is, even with the downgrade in priority, the focal goal still has a higher priority than the alternatives. Thus, positive feeling does not require that there be a change in direction. It simply sets the stage for such a change to be more likely.

Apart from evidence of coasting per se (discussed earlier), there is also other evidence that positive affect tends to promote shifting of focus to other areas that need attention (for broader discussion, see Carver, 2003). As an example, Trope and Neter (1994) induced a positive mood in some people but not others, gave all a social sensitivity test, then told them that they had performed well on two parts of the test but poorly on a third. Participants then indicated their interest in reading more about their performances on the various parts of the test. Those in a positive mood showed more interest in the part they had failed than did controls, suggesting that they were inclined to shift their focus to an area that needed their attention. This effect was conceptually replicated by Trope and Pomerantz (1998) and Reed and Aspinwall (1998).

Phenomena such as these have contributed to the emergence of the view that positive feelings represent psychological resources (see also Aspinwall, 1998; Fredrickson, 1998; Isen, 2000; Tesser, Crepaz, Collins, Cornell, & Beach, 2000). The idea that positive affect serves as a resource for exploration resembles the idea that positive feelings open people up to noticing and turning to emergent opportunities, to being distracted into enticing alternatives—to opportunistic behavior.

Indeed, there is some evidence that fits this idea more directly (Kahn & Isen, 1993). Kahn and Isen (1993) let people try out choices within a food category. Those who had been put into a state of positive affect beforehand switched among choices more than did controls. Isen (2000, p. 423) interpreted this as showing that positive affect promotes "enjoyment of variety and a wide range of possibilities," which sounds much like opportunistic foraging. Similarly, Dreisbach and Goschke (2004) found that positive affect decreased persistence on a task strategy and increased distractibility. Both of these findings are consistent with the reasoning presented in this section.

Priority Management and Depressed Affect

One more important aspect of priority management must be addressed. It concerns the idea that goals sometimes are not attainable and must be abandoned. Sufficient doubt about goal attainment creates an impetus to reduce effort to reach the goal and even to give up the goal itself (Carver & Scheier, 1998, 1999a, 1999b). This sense of doubt is accompanied by sadness or depressed affect. The abandonment of a goal reflects a decrease in its priority. How does this sort of reprioritization fit into the picture just outlined?

At first glance, this seems to contradict Simon's (1967) position that negative affect is a call for higher priority. After all, sadness is a negative affect. However, there seems to be an important difference between two classes of approach-related negative affects, which forces an elaboration of Simon's thinking. As noted earlier, our view on affect rests on a dimension that ranges from doing well to doing poorly, though the affects per se do not form a true continuum (sadness is not more intense anger). We argue that inadequate movement forward (or no movement, or reversal) gives rise first to frustration and anger. These feelings (or the mechanism underlying them) engage effort more completely, so as to overcome obstacles and enhance progress. This case clearly fits the priority management model of Simon (1967).

Sometimes, however, continued effort does not produce adequate movement. Indeed, if the situation involves loss, movement is impossible because the goal is gone. When failure is (or seems) assured, the feelings are sadness, depression, despondency, grief, and hopelessness. Behaviorally, this is paralleled by disengagement from effort toward the goal (Klinger, 1975; Lewis, Sullivan, Ramsay, & Allessandri, 1992; Mikulincer, 1988; Wortman & Brehm, 1975). Reduction of effort but retained commitment to the goal yields only greater distress. In adaptive functioning, the eventual result is disengagement from the goal altogether. This reflects a serious reduction in the goal's priority.

We reemphasize that these two kinds of negative feelings both have adaptive properties for the contexts in which they arise. In the first situation—when the person falls behind, but the goal is not seen as lost—feelings of frustration and anger induce an increase in effort, a struggle to gain the goal despite setbacks. This struggle is adaptive (and the affect thus is adaptive) to the extent that the struggle fosters goal attainment, which it often (though not always) does.

In the second situation—when effort appears futile—feelings of sadness and depression accompany reduction of effort. Sadness and despondency imply that things cannot be set right, that effort is pointless. Reducing effort in this situation is also adaptive (Carver & Scheier, 2003; Wrosch, Scheier, Carver, & Schulz, 2003; Wrosch, Scheier, Miller, Schulz, & Carver, 2003). It conserves energy rather than waste it in pursuit of the unattainable (Nesse, 2000). If reducing effort also helps diminish commitment to the goal (Klinger, 1975), it eventually readies the person to take up other goals in place of this one.

IMPLICATIONS FOR EDUCATIONAL SETTINGS

This chapter described a set of theoretical principles that were intended to apply to behavior in general. However, they are perhaps applied more easily to the achievement domain than to any other realm of behavior. As described earlier in the chapter, it is relatively intuitive to see how greater than expected progress toward an educational goal can lead to positive feelings and how falling behind can lead to negative feelings. It is also relatively intuitive to see how the distress that follows from falling behind can itself bifurcate into promoting renewed efforts to catch up versus abandoning the effort. Somewhat more complex is the idea that some efforts at educational achievement are motivated by the desire to attain goals and positive incentives, whereas others are motivated by the desire to avoid threats, but even this idea has been shown to be important in achievement settings (see Elliot, 2008).

This set of ideas also provides a framework for seeing how people can have mixed feelings in the course of educational efforts, when (for example) efforts toward one goal get in the way of exerting adequate efforts toward another goal. The multiple goals in question may both pertain to educational achievement, but as noted earlier in the chapter, people in educational settings typically have additional goals as well, which come into competition with their academic goals. Education attainment, whether considered narrowly or broadly, is a multigoal enterprise. Problems of scheduling and how to handle pursuit of the diverse activities that together form the matrix of any educational enterprise are among the most critical determinants of success in educational settings. And we are confident that these problems and issues are readily conceptualized in the terms used in this chapter.

REFERENCES

Aspinwall, L. G. (1998). Rethinking the role of positive affect in self-regulation. *Motivation and Emotion, 22,* 1–32.

Atkinson, J. W., & Birch, D. (1970). *The dynamics of action.* New York, NY: Wiley.

Austin, J. T., & Vancouver, J. B. (1996). Goal constructs in psychology: Structure, process, and content. *Psychological Bulletin, 120,* 338–375.

Baumeister, R. F., Vohs, K. D., DeWall, C. N., & Zhang, L. (2007). How emotion shapes behavior: Feedback, anticipation, and reflection, rather than direct causation. *Personality and Social Psychology Review, 11,* 167–203.

Beer, R. D. (1995). A dynamical systems perspective on agent–environment interaction. *Artificial Intelligence, 72,* 173–215.

Brehm, J. W., & Self, E. A. (1989). The intensity of motivation. *Annual Review of Psychology, 40,* 109–131.

Brunstein, J. C. (1993). Personal goals and subjective well-being: A longitudinal study. *Journal of Personality and Social Psychology, 65,* 1061–1070.

Cacioppo, J. T., & Berntson, G. G. (1994). Relationship between attitudes and evaluative space: A critical review, with emphasis on the separability of positive and negative substrates. *Psychological Bulletin, 115,* 401–423.

Cacioppo, J. T., Gardner, W. L., & Berntson, G. G. (1999). The affect system has parallel and integrative processing components: Form follows function. *Journal of Personality and Social Psychology, 76,* 839–855.

Campos, J. J., Frankel, C. B., & Camras, L. (2004). On the nature of emotion regulation. *Child Development, 75,* 377–394.

Carver, C. S. (2003). Pleasure as a sign you can attend to something else: Placing positive feelings within a general model of affect. *Cognition and Emotion, 17,* 241–261.

Carver, C. S. (2004). Negative affects deriving from the behavioral approach system. *Emotion, 4,* 3–22.

Carver, C. S. (2009). Threat sensitivity, incentive sensitivity, and the experience of relief. *Journal of Personality, 77,* 125–138.

Carver, C. S., & Harmon-Jones, E. (2009a). Anger is an approach-related affect: Evidence and implications. *Psychological Bulletin, 135,* 183–204.

Carver, C. S., & Harmon-Jones, E. (2009b). Anger and approach: Reply to Watson (2009) and Tomarken and Zald (2009). *Psychological Bulletin, 135,* 215–217.

Carver, C. S., & Scheier, M. F. (1990). Origins and functions of positive and negative affect: A control-process view. *Psychological Review, 97,* 19–35.

Carver, C. S., & Scheier, M. F. (1998). *On the self-regulation of behavior.* New York, NY: Cambridge University Press.

Carver, C. S., & Scheier, M. F. (1999a). Several more themes, a lot more issues: Commentary on the commentaries. In R. S. Wyer, Jr. (Ed.), *Advances in social cognition* (Vol. 12, pp. 261–302). Mahwah, NJ: Erlbaum.

Carver, C. S., & Scheier, M. F. (1999b). Themes and issues in the self-regulation of behavior. In R. S. Wyer, Jr. (Ed.), *Advances in social cognition* (Vol. 12, pp. 1–105). Mahwah, NJ: Erlbaum.

Carver, C. S., & Scheier, M. F. (2000). Scaling back goals and recalibration of the affect system are processes in normal adaptive self-regulation: Understanding "response shift" phenomena. *Social Science & Medicine, 50,* 1715–1722.

Carver, C. S., & Scheier, M. F. (2003). Three human strengths. In L. G. Aspinwall & U. M. Staudinger (Eds.), *A psychology of human strengths: Fundamental questions and future directions for a positive psychology* (pp. 87–102). Washington, DC: American Psychological Association.

Chang, C-H., Johnson, R. E., & Lord, R. G. (2010). Moving beyond discrepancies: The importance of velocity as a predictor of satisfaction and motivation. *Human Performance, 23,* 58–80.

Clark, R. N. (1996). *Control system dynamics.* New York, NY: Cambridge University Press.

Clore, G. C. (1994). Why emotions are felt. In P. Ekman & R. J. Davidson (Eds.), *The nature of emotion: Fundamental questions* (pp. 103–111). New York, NY: Oxford University Press.

Davidson, R. J. (1992). Anterior cerebral asymmetry and the nature of emotion. *Brain and Cognition, 20,* 125–151.

Dreisbach, G., & Goschke, T. (2004). How positive affect modulates cognitive control: Reduced perseveration at the cost of increased distractibility. *Journal of Experimental Psychology: Learning, Memory, and Cognition, 30,* 343–353.

Eidelman, S., & Biernat, M. (2007). Getting more from success: Standard raising as esteem maintenance. *Journal of Personality and Social Psychology, 92,* 759–774.

Elliot, A. J. (Ed.). (2008). *Handbook of approach and avoidance motivation.* Mahwah, NJ: Erlbaum.

Fitzsimons, G. M., Friesen, J., Orehek, E., & Kruglanski, A. W. (2009). Progress-induced goal shifting as a self-regulatory strategy. In J. P. Forgas, R. F. Baumeister, & D. M. Tice (Eds.), *Psychology of self-regulation: Cognitive, affective, and motivational processes* (pp. 183–197). New York, NY: Psychology Press.

Fredrickson, B. L. (1998). What good are positive emotions? *Review of General Psychology, 2,* 300–319.

Frijda, N. H. (1986). *The emotions.* Cambridge, United Kingdom: Cambridge University Press.

Frijda, N. H. (1988). The laws of emotion. *American Psychologist, 43,* 349–358.

Frijda, N. H. (1994). Emotions are functional, most of the time. In P. Ekman & R. J. Davidson (Eds.), *The nature of emotion: Fundamental questions* (pp. 112–126). New York, NY: Oxford University Press.

Fulford, D., Johnson, S. L., Llabre, M. M., & Carver, C. S. (2010). Pushing and coasting in dynamic goal pursuit: Coasting is attenuated in bipolar disorder. *Psychological Science, 21,* 1021–1027.

Gendolla, G.H.E., & Richter, M. (2010). Effort mobilization when the self is involved: Some lessons from the cardiovascular system. *Review of General Psychology, 14,* 212–226.

Gray, J. A. (1990). Brain systems that mediate both emotion and cognition. *Cognition and Emotion, 4,* 269–288.

Gray, J. A. (1994). Three fundamental emotion systems. In P. Ekman & R. J. Davidson (Eds.), *The nature of emotion: Fundamental questions* (pp. 243–247). New York, NY: Oxford University Press.

Gross, J. J. (Ed.). (2007). *Handbook of emotion regulation.* New York, NY: Guilford.

Harmon-Jones, E., & Sigelman, J. D. (2001). State anger and prefrontal brain activity: Evidence that insult-related relative left-prefrontal activation is associated with experienced anger and aggression. *Journal of Personality and Social Psychology, 80,* 797–803.

Hayes-Roth, B., & Hayes-Roth, F. (1979). A cognitive model of planning. *Cognitive Science, 3,* 275–310.

Higgins, E. T. (1987). Self-discrepancy: A theory relating self and affect. *Psychological Review, 94,* 319–340.

Higgins, E. T. (1996). Ideals, oughts, and regulatory focus: Affect and motivation from distinct pains and pleasures. In P. M. Gollwitzer & J. A. Bargh (Eds.), *The psychology of action: Linking cognition and motivation to behavior* (pp. 91–114). New York, NY: Guilford Press.

Higgins, E. T., Shah, J., & Friedman, R. (1997). Emotional responses to goal attainment: Strength of regulatory focus as moderator. *Journal of Personality and Social Psychology, 72,* 515–525.

Hsee, C. K., & Abelson, R. P. (1991). Velocity relation: Satisfaction as a function of the first derivative of outcome over time. *Journal of Personality and Social Psychology, 60,* 341–347.

Isen, A. M. (2000). Positive affect and decision making. In M. Lewis & J. M. Haviland-Jones (Eds.), *Handbook of emotions* (2nd ed., pp. 417–435). New York, NY: Guilford Press.

Izard, C. E. (1977). *Human emotions.* New York, NY: Plenum Press.

Jacobs, S. E., & Gross, J. J. (2014). Emotion regulation in education: Conceptual foundations, current applications, and future directions. In R. Pekrun & L. Linnenbrink-Garcia (Eds.), *International handbook of emotions in education* (pp. 183–201). New York, NY: Taylor & Francis.

Johnson, R. E., Chang, C. -H., & Lord, R. G. (2006). Moving from cognitive to behavior: What the research says. *Psychological Bulletin, 132*, 381–415.

Kahn, B. E., & Isen, A. M. (1993). The influence of positive affect on variety-seeking among safe, enjoyable products. *Journal of Consumer Research, 20*, 257–270.

Klinger, E. (1975). Consequences of commitment to and disengagement from incentives. *Psychological Review, 82*, 1–25.

Kumashiro, M., Rusbult, C. E., & Finkel, E. J. (2008). Navigating personal and relational concerns: The quest for equilibrium. *Journal of Personality and Social Psychology, 95*, 94–110.

Lang, P. J. (1995). The emotion probe: Studies of motivation and attention. *American Psychologist, 50*, 372–385.

Lang, P. J., Bradley, M. M., & Cuthbert, B. N. (1990). Emotion, attention, and the startle reflex. *Psychological Review, 97*, 377–395.

Lewis, M., Sullivan, M. W., Ramsay, D. S., & Allessandri, S. M. (1992). Individual differences in anger and sad expressions during extinction: Antecedents and consequences. *Infant Behavior and Development, 15*, 443–452.

Louro, M. J., Pieters, R., & Zeelenberg, M. (2007). Dynamics of multiple-goal pursuit. *Journal of Personality and Social Psychology, 93*, 174–193.

MacKay, D. M. (1966). Cerebral organization and the conscious control of action. In J. C. Eccles (Ed.), *Brain and conscious experience* (pp. 422–445). Berlin, Germany: Springer-Verlag.

Mikulincer, M. (1988). Reactance and helplessness following exposure to learned helplessness following exposure to unsolvable problems: The effects of attributional style. *Journal of Personality and Social Psychology, 54*, 679–686.

Miller, G. A., Galanter, E., & Pribram, K. H. (1960). *Plans and the structure of behavior*. New York, NY: Holt, Rinehart & Winston.

Nesse, R. M. (2000). Is depression an adaptation? *Archives of General Psychiatry, 57*, 14–20.

Ortony, A., Clore, G. L., & Collins, A. (1988). *The cognitive structure of emotions*. New York, NY: Cambridge University Press.

Payton, D. W. (1990). Internalized plans: A representation for action resources. In P. Maes (Ed.), *Designing autonomous agents: Theory and practice from biology to engineering and back* (pp. 89–103). Cambridge, MA: MIT Press.

Powers, W. T. (1973). *Behavior: The control of perception*. Chicago, IL: Aldine.

Reed, M. B., & Aspinwall, L. G. (1998). Self-affirmation reduces biased processing of health-risk information. *Motivation and Emotion, 22*, 99–132.

Rolls, E. T. (1999). *The brain and emotion*. Oxford, United Kingdom: Oxford University Press.

Rolls, E. T. (2005). *Emotion explained*. Oxford, United Kingdom: Oxford University Press.

Rosenbaum, D. A., Meulenbroek, R.G.J., Vaughan, J., & Jansen, C. (2001). Posture-based motion planning: Applications to grasping. *Psychological Review, 108*, 709–734.

Shallice, T. (1978). The dominant action system: An information-processing approach to consciousness. In K. S. Pope & J. L. Singer (Eds.), *The stream of consciousness: Scientific investigations into the flow of human experience* (pp. 117–157). New York, NY: Wiley.

Shin, J. C., & Rosenbaum, D. A. (2002). Reaching while calculating: Scheduling of cognitive and perceptual-motor processes. *Journal of Experimental Psychology: General, 131*, 206–219.

Simon, H. A. (1953). *Models of man*. New York, NY: Wiley.

Simon, H. A. (1967). Motivational and emotional controls of cognition. *Psychology Review, 74*, 29–39.

Tesser, A., Crepaz, N., Collins, J. C., Cornell, D., & Beach, S.R.H. (2000). Confluence of self-esteem regulation mechanisms: On integrating the self-zoo. *Personality and Social Psychology Bulletin, 26*, 1476–1489.

Trope, Y., & Neter, E. (1994). Reconciling competing motives in self-evaluation: The role of self-control in feedback seeking. *Journal of Personality and Social Psychology, 66*, 646–657.

Trope, Y., & Pomerantz, E. M. (1998). Resolving conflicts among self-evaluative motives: Positive experiences as a resource for overcoming defensiveness. *Motivation and Emotion, 22*, 53–72.

Vallacher, R. R., & Wegner, D. M. (1987). What do people think they're doing? Action identification and human behavior. *Psychological Review, 94*, 3–15.

von Bertalanffy, L. (1968). *General systems theory.* New York, NY: Braziller.

Watson, D. (2009). Locating anger in the hierarchical structure of affect: Comment on Carver and Harmon-Jones (2009). *Psychological Bulletin, 135,* 205–208.

Watson, D., Wiese, D., Vaidya, J., & Tellegen, A. (1999). The two general activation systems of affect: Structural findings, evolutionary considerations, and psychobiological evidence. *Journal of Personality and Social Psychology, 76,* 820–838.

Wiener, N. (1948). *Cybernetics: Control and communication in the animal and the machine.* Cambridge, MA: MIT Press.

Wortman, C. B., & Brehm, J. W. (1975). Responses to uncontrollable outcomes: An integration of reactance theory and the learned helplessness model. In L. Berkowitz (Ed.), *Advances in experimental social psychology* (Vol. 8, pp. 277–336). New York, NY: Academic Press.

Wright, R. A. (1996). Brehm's theory of motivation as a model of effort and cardiovascular response. In P. M. Gollwitzer & J. A. Bargh (Eds.), *The psychology of action: Linking cognition and motivation to behavior* (pp. 424–453). New York, NY: Guilford.

Wrosch, C., Scheier, M. F., Carver, C. S., & Schulz, R. (2003). The importance of goal disengagement in adaptive self-regulation: When giving up is beneficial. *Self and Identity, 2,* 1–20.

Wrosch, C., Scheier, M. F., Miller, G. E., Schulz, R., & Carver, C. S. (2003). Adaptive self-regulation of unattainable goals: Goal disengagement, goal re-engagement, and subjective well-being. *Personality and Social Psychology Bulletin, 29,* 1494–1508.

5

IMPLICIT MOTIVES, AFFECT, AND THE DEVELOPMENT OF COMPETENCIES

A Virtuous-Circle Model of Motive-Driven Learning

Oliver C. Schultheiss and Martin G. Köllner,
Friedrich-Alexander University

This chapter provides a conceptual framework for understanding how implicit motives—that is, nonconsciously operating motivational dispositions for the attainment of certain classes of incentives and the avoidance of certain classes of disincentives (Schultheiss, 2008)—influence successful goal pursuit and positive life outcomes through their effects on learning and memory. After a brief introduction to theory and measurement of implicit motives, we will review evidence that documents motives' critical involvement in affective responses to incentives and disincentives. We will argue that motive-dependent affect drives learning of stimuli, behaviors, and contexts associated with the affective experience and thus the development of integrated competencies across nondeclarative and declarative domains of knowledge. In doing so, we will also provide a brief review of the neurobiological substrates of the types of learning and memory influenced by motives and how these substrates interact with each other. Building on the literature on implicit motives and learning and memory, we will propose a virtuous-circle model of motive-driven learning according to which satisfaction of an implicit motive through incentive contact facilitates the acquisition of integrated competencies, which in turn promote successful pursuit of personal goals. Successful goal striving then translates into frequent opportunities for implicit motive satisfaction and closes the circle. We will review evidence in support of this model and, in closing, discuss its implications for educational settings.

IMPLICIT MOTIVES: A BRIEF INTRODUCTION

Research on implicit motives in the past 60 years has focused on three motive dispositions: the needs for achievement, power, and affiliation, often abbreviated as n Achievement, n Power, n Affiliation (Schultheiss, 2008). Although the existence of other implicit motives, like the needs for sex, food, or novelty, has also been postulated (see McClelland, 1987), much less is known about these dispositions within the research tradition we review here. We suggest that the processes, models, and conclusions presented in this chapter may also extend to these motives, but we will not discuss them further.

n Achievement

The achievement motive comprises a capacity for deriving satisfaction from autonomous mastery of moderately challenging tasks but also for dissatisfaction from failing to master such tasks (McClelland, 1987; see also Schultheiss, 2008) and the need to do well compared to a standard of excellence (Schultheiss & Pang, 2007). A strong achievement motive is the result of parents setting age-appropriate, yet challenging demands for their child and rewarding the child warmly for independent mastery of challenging goals but punishing her or him for failing to do so (for an overview, see Schultheiss & Brunstein, 2005). Over the years, effortful mastery of challenges becomes associated with the anticipation of positive feelings after success, while not succeeding on one's own becomes associated with aversive punishment. According to Schultheiss and Brunstein (2005), this is the dual root of n Achievement: it can be driven either by the prospect of satisfaction gained from mastery, by the relief from punishment associated with it, or both (see Gray & McNaughton, 2000, for a discussion of the functional equivalence of approach and active avoidance in reward). Individuals high in n Achievement prefer tasks of medium difficulty (Atkinson, 1957), but not easy or extremely difficult tasks, and seek feedback on their current performance vis-a-vis their past performance to gauge how much they are improving on a task (Brunstein & Schmitt, 2004). In doing so, they generally prefer an individual reference norm, comparing their current performance to their own past performance, as opposed to a social reference norm, which would require them to compare their performance to that of others (Brunstein & Maier, 2005).

n Power

The power motive represents a capacity for deriving pleasure from impact on others, be it physical, mental, or emotional, and an aversion to the impact of other people on oneself (Schultheiss, 2008). It has its roots in parents' permissiveness for sexual and socially aggressive behavior in early childhood—behaviors that presumably represent prototypical rewards for n Power (McClelland & Pilon, 1983). In adulthood, the need for attaining impact can manifest itself in a wide variety of phenomena, ranging from blunt aggression or dominance behavior to socially acceptable behaviors, like persuasive communication, impressing others, or eliciting strong emotions in others, such as when comedians make audiences scream with laughter or coaches inspire their protégées to superior performances (Schultheiss, 2008). Socially tamed power motivation is therefore associated with good management and leadership skills (McClelland & Boyatzis, 1982; Winter, 1991), whereas untamed power is associated with impulsive, egoistical, or profligate behavior (Winter, 1988).

n Affiliation

The affiliation motive is characterized by a concern for and a capacity for deriving satisfaction from establishing, maintaining, and restoring positive relationships with others (Atkinson, Heyns, & Veroff, 1958). Consistent with the observation that individuals high in this need tend to be clingy and show signs of rejection sensitivity (see Boyatzis, 1973; Winter, 1996), it appears to have its roots in childhood experiences of parents' lacking sensitivity for the child's needs (McClelland & Pilon, 1983) and thus perhaps to be associated with insecure attachment (see Schultheiss, 2008). However, few firm conclusions about its developmental precursors can be drawn so far. Individuals high in n Affiliation spend more time in contact with others, or wishing they had contact with others, and tend to alter their behavior in such a way that it makes them more similar to liked others. However, if others are perceived as too dissimilar or rejecting, affiliation-motivated individuals can also distance themselves and reject others (for a summary, see Winter, 1996).

Assessment

Because implicit motives are assumed to operate at the nonconscious level, they are most frequently assessed with a descendant of Morgan and Murray's (1935) Thematic Apperception Test, the Picture Story Exercise (PSE; McClelland, Koestner, & Weinberger, 1989). In the PSE, testees are shown pictures of persons in social situations, like a captain speaking to a passenger or persons seated on a park bench, and are instructed to write an imaginative story about each picture (Schultheiss, 2008; Schultheiss & Pang, 2007). Stories are later scored with content-coding systems (e.g., Smith, 1992; Winter, 1994), and the scores are interpreted as indicators of the strength of people's implicit motives (Schultheiss, 2008). Derivation and validation of these systems was accomplished empirically in experiments in which a given motivational need had been aroused in one group, but not in a control group, and themes that differed between these groups were identified and included in the coding systems (Winter, 1998). According to the validity concept proposed by Borsboom, Mellenbergh, and van Heerden (2004), a test is a valid measure if (a) the attribute it is supposed to assess actually exists and if (b) experimental manipulations of the attribute causally lead to variations in the measurement (see also McClelland, 1958, for a much earlier, almost identical argument). According to this criterion of validity, PSE content coding measures represent valid assessments of motives.

Reliability and Validity

The PSE demonstrates high interrater and a remarkable amount of retest-reliability (Schultheiss, Liening, & Schad, 2008; Schultheiss & Pang, 2007), and its predictive and criterion validity are well documented (see McClelland, 1987; Schultheiss, 2008; and Winter, 1996). At the biological level, implicit motives have been shown to be linked to hormone changes (Schultheiss, 2013), immune system functioning (McClelland, 1989), and activation of brain areas involved in motivation (Schultheiss, Wirth, Waugh, Stanton, Meier, & Reuter-Lorenz, 2008). At the individual level, implicit motive measures predict motivational phenomena in the laboratory, such as attentional orienting to incentive cues (Schultheiss & Hale, 2007; Wang, Liu, & Zheng, 2011), learning (see the section

"Implicit Motives and Learning" further on), task performance (Brunstein & Maier, 2005; Schultheiss & Brunstein, 1999, Study 2), and social behavior (e.g., McAdams & Powers, 1981; Schultheiss & Brunstein, 2002). They also predict life outcomes, such as career success (Jenkins, 1987, 1994; McClelland & Franz, 1992), sexual behavior (Hofer, Busch, Bond, Campos, Li, & Law, 2010; Zurbriggen, 2011), parental status (Peterson & Stewart, 1993), and mental and physical health (McAdams & Bryant, 1987; McClelland, 1979). At the societal level, implicit motive measures have been found to be valid predictors or correlates of economic growth (Engeser, Rheinberg, & Möller, 2009; McClelland, 1961), the behavior of political leaders (Winter, 2003), and the development and outcomes of international crises (Winter, 1993, 2010a).

Implicit Motives Are Fundamentally Distinct From Explicit Motives

While work on the validity of the PSE/content-coding approach to motive assessment has amassed an impressive array of findings, many researchers have attempted to replace this comparatively labor-intensive measurement approach with other methods, frequently based on self-report, claiming that these assess the same motive dispositions as the PSE. In most instances, however, this claim has either never been tested thoroughly or was not supported by the data (see Schultheiss, under revision). This practice has led to a Babylonian confusion of terms and concepts in the field of motivation research and particularly in its application in educational contexts. For instance, the term n Achievement, which was originally associated with the PSE measure of the implicit achievement motive (McClelland, Atkinson, Clark, & Lowell, 1953), is frequently used by researchers who use questionnaire measures of the self-attributed achievement motive (see, for instance, Steinmayr & Spinath, 2008). And the term achievement motive as viewed from the perspective of the PSE and its specific validity describes and explains phenomena that can be quite different from those that concern researchers using questionnaire measures. We mention this because psychologists and educational researchers should be aware of the fact that quite different phenomena are frequently presented under the guise of the same labels. McClelland et al. (1989) succinctly described the problem: "psychologists should not call by the same name two measures that do not correlate with one another" (p. 691). As we will show next, there is no justification for equating implicit motive measures with explicit motive measures, given the substantial differences between the measures of motive dispositions and their validities.

PSE motive measures typically show no or only slight correlations with questionnaire motive measures of the same domain (e.g., Pang & Schultheiss, 2005; Schultheiss & Brunstein, 2001). This result has been confirmed by two recent meta-analyses, one on n Achievement (Spangler, 1992) and one including all three motives (Köllner & Schultheiss, in preparation). These findings confirm the original premise of research using the PSE approach—namely, that motives may not be accessible to introspection and suggest that there are two kinds of motives, implicit ones that can be measured with the PSE and explicit or self-attributed ones that can be measured with various kinds of self-reports (McClelland et al., 1989).

These two types of motives respond to different kinds of incentives or cues (Schultheiss, 2008; Stanton, Hall, & Schultheiss, 2010). While implicit motives are particularly likely to respond to nonverbal cues, such as facial expressions of emotions, explicit motives are more likely to respond to verbal cues, like instructions, demands, and suggestions (McClelland et al.,

1989). As Spangler's (1992) meta-analysis shows, the implicit achievement motive is a particularly good predictor of behavior when combined with the right (i.e., nonverbal) incentive cues. However, in the presence of the wrong incentives (i.e., verbal–social), validity coefficients of n Achievement become zero or even negative. This may explain why students high in this motive generally do not perform better, and sometimes even worse, than low-motive students (e.g., McKeachie, Isaacson, Milholland, & Lin, 1968): they are not motivated by structured classroom situations in which teachers verbally communicate incentives to do well (see also the section "Application to Educational Settings" further on).

Implicit and explicit motives also influence different types of behavior (Schultheiss, 2008). Research documents a double dissociation in their predictive validity, with implicit motives influencing nondeclarative measures, such as task performance, attentional orienting, and physiological changes, but not declarative measures, such as choices, attitudes, and judgments, and with the reverse being true for explicit motives. An early study by deCharms, Morrison, Reitman, and McClelland (1955) exemplifies this dissociation. High n Achievement predicted recall and scrambled-word task performance, whereas a questionnaire measure of achievement motivation predicted the extent to which participants adjusted their judgments of artworks in the direction of a purported expert and negative attitudes towards an unsuccessful individual (see also Spangler, 1992, for a meta-analytical corroboration of these observations).

Summary

Implicit motives, such as the needs for achievement, power, and affiliation, can be assessed through content-coding of imaginative stories, but not via self-report, respond preferentially to nonverbal incentives, and predict nondeclarative outcome measures. They thus represent constructs that are distinct from the explicit beliefs that people hold about their motivational needs, which do not substantially correlate with implicit motive measures, respond preferentially to verbal incentives, and predict declarative criteria.

MOTIVES AND EMOTIONS: IMPLICIT MOTIVES AS AFFECT AMPLIFIERS

To truly understand how implicit motives operate and why they predict a vast array of physiological and behavioral phenomena, it is critical to examine the role of affect in implicit motivational processes. According to current theories of motivation based on biopsychology, affect is the defining feature of motivation, signaling the utility and survival value of certain types of stimuli and events for an organism (Berridge, 2004; Buck, 1999; Cabanac, 1992; Panksepp, 1998; Toates, 1986). It endows the stimuli an individual encounters with rewarding or punishing qualities and thus turns them into attractive or aversive stimuli. (Note that behavior can also be regulated without or against hedonically charged endpoints, but this does not represent motivation proper, but self-regulation; see, for instance, Muraven & Baumeister, 2000.)

The central role of affect has been acknowledged in implicit motive research from the very beginning. McClelland et al. (1953) made the expectation of a pleasant experience a core ingredient of their definition of n Achievement. Atkinson (1957) probably put it most succinctly, stating that "a motive is conceived as a disposition to strive for a certain kind of satisfaction, as a capacity for satisfaction in the attainment of a certain class of incentives" (p. 360). The definitions for the three major motives we gave in the preceding section represent specific instantiations of this fundamental principle. Thus, for instance, a person high in n Achievement is someone who is able to experience the mastery of a challenging task as particularly satisfying, whereas a person low in n Achievement is not—the difference in the affective response constitutes the difference in motive levels.

Given the centrality of the role of affect in motivation and individual differences in the capacity for affective responses in the concept of implicit motives, what evidence is there that implicit motives are associated with affective responses to incentives? Two lines of research document the affect-amplifying nature of implicit motives most clearly: studies on emotional well-being and research on facial expressions of affect.

Emotional Well-Being

Research on the role of implicit motives in emotional well-being, as assessed by self-report scales of hedonic feelings in everyday life (such as the hedonic tone scale by Matthews, Jones & Chamberlain, 1990, featuring items such as *happy, satisfied, contented*), consistently shows that higher levels of implicit motives predict higher well-being to the extent that people make good progress towards personal goals that match their motives and provide them with opportunities to harvest motive-specific incentives (e.g., think of an affiliation-motivated student succeeding with the goal of keeping in touch with his old friends at home; Brunstein, Lautenschlager, Nawroth, Pöhlmann, & Schultheiss, 1995; Brunstein, Schultheiss, & Grässmann, 1998; Schultheiss, Jones, Davis, & Kley, 2008; see Brunstein, 2010, for a review). In contrast, the successful pursuit of goals that are not supported by, or congruent with, a person's implicit motives appears to be hedonically irrelevant or even associated with negative mood (e.g., think of a person low in n Affiliation keeping in contact with friends at home or a high-affiliation student who pursues the power goal of becoming more independent of friends and family at home). Because of the striking differences in how the effect of progress on personal goals affects emotional well-being in individuals with different implicit motive levels, Schultheiss et al. (2008) have suggested that the pursuit of goals that are supported by a person's implicit motives represents a hot (i.e., affectively engaging) mode of goal striving, whereas the pursuit of goals that are not supported by a person's implicit motives represents a cold (i.e., affectively neutral) mode.

Analogous results for implicit motives influencing well-being come from studies examining motive–goal congruence and indicators of distress. Studies by Schultheiss et al. (2008) and Pueschel, Schulte, and Michalak (2011) show that people who succeed at goals that match their motives have fewer depressive symptoms than people who fail at such goals. In contrast, success or failure at motive-incongruent goals had no or even paradoxical effects (see Pueschel et al., 2011) on depressive symptoms.

Finally, cross-cultural research by Hofer and colleagues consistently shows that implicit motives are associated with higher life satisfaction, provided that individuals consciously endorse values and motivational orientations that match their implicit motives (e.g., Hofer & Chasiotis, 2003; Hofer, Chasiotis, & Campos, 2006). Why does holding a belief about oneself that matches one's motives promote well-being? Hofer, Busch, Bond, Li, and Law (2010) provide an answer: the endorsement of motive-congruent values (e.g., "Leading others is important to me") facilitates the derivation and pursuit of similarly motive-congruent goals (e.g., "I want to teach a section in this course"), which in turn provide opportunities for satisfying one's implicit motives.

Facial Affect

Whereas research focusing on emotional well-being relies heavily on subjective self-reports of affective states and thus depends critically on an accurate translation of a nondeclarative affective process into a declarative representation (see Schultheiss & Strasser, 2012), affect can also be assessed objectively by examining, via electromyography (EMG), facial muscle activity that is associated with positive and negative affective responses to stimuli and events (see Larsen, Norris, & Cacioppo, 2003). Here, too, reliable and consistent evidence for a critical role of implicit motives in affective responses to incentives can be found. Using EMG recordings of the corrugator muscle, which indexes negative affect by activation and positive affect by deactivation (see Larsen et al., 2003), Fodor and colleagues observed across several studies that individuals high in n Power respond with greater corrugator activation to power disincentives (e.g., watching a dominant job candidate) and less activation to power incentives (e.g., watching a submissive job candidate), whereas individuals low in n Power do not show these differences (e.g., Fodor & Wick, 2009; Fodor, Wick, & Hartsen, 2006). Similarly, Kordik, Eska, and Schultheiss (2012) found that individuals high in n Affiliation respond with corrugator activation to encountering an unsmiling experimenter and with corrugators deactivation to a smiling experimenter; individuals low in n Affiliation did not show this difference. A study by Kordik (2012) reveals that individuals high in n Achievement respond to failure feedback with stronger initial activation and subsequent dampening of corrugator activity than individuals low in n Achievement, a finding that is in line with conceptions of n Achievement as a capacity to master challenges (see Kuhl, 2001; McClelland et al., 1953).

Implications

Thus, although empirical work documenting the long-postulated affect-amplifying property of implicit motives has only been executed in the past 20 years, it consistently shows that Atkinson (1957) was right when he hypothesized that implicit motives represent capacities to derive satisfaction from incentives. Differences in how people experience incentives and disincentives at an affective level are prone to result in differences in how they deal behaviorally with such stimuli. McClelland (1987), in line with other theorists of motivation (e.g., Pfaff, 1999; Toates, 1986), specified two functions of affectively charged incentives for behavior: First, behavior is *oriented* preferentially towards such incentives and the cues that predict them, and, second, it is *energized* so that an incentive can be quickly reached and consummated (or a disincentive avoided). He also postulated a third function, which is of particular interest for the present discussion—namely, that the attainment of hedonically charged incentives *selects* behavior that was instrumental in attaining them and the stimuli that predicted them. In other words, motives influence learning, and this is the function that we will examine next in more detail.

IMPLICIT MOTIVES AND LEARNING

A central position that we take in this chapter is that because implicit motives determine how much pleasure can be gained from contact with incentives (i.e., reward) or displeasure from contact with disincentives (i.e., punishment), motives also influence how well

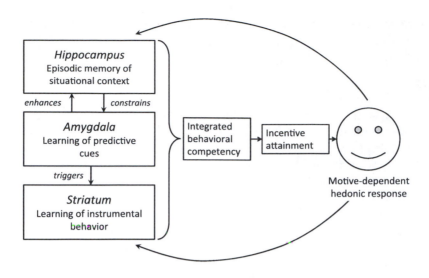

Figure 5.1 Overview of the role of implicit motives in learning processes and competency development. In individuals high in an implicit motive, incentive contact is associated with an affective response that leads to better memory for the episodic context in which incentive contact happened (a learning function mediated by the hippocampus), conditioning of specific cues that predict the rewarding experience (mediated by the amygdala), and reinforcement of motor behavior that led to incentive contact (mediated by the striatum). Jointly, these learning processes foster the development of an integrated behavioral competency consisting of memory for the context, trigger stimuli, and appropriate behaviors for the attainment of an incentive.

people learn stimuli, behaviors, and contexts associated with reward and punishment and thus how they develop integrated behavioral competencies for the further pursuit of incentives. To allow the reader to better digest the significance and meaning of research findings related to implicit motives and learning, however, we will first provide a brief foray into the functional neurobiology of learning and memory (see Figure 5.1 for an overview).

The Neurobiology of Learning and Memory

Although virtually the entire brain can be altered through experience and is thus capable of learning, research has identified three specific brain areas most closely related to learning and memory in the context of motivation: the amygdala for Pavlovian learning of the emotional meaning of stimuli, the striatum for instrumental learning based on reward and punishment, and the hippocampus for declarative learning of facts and events (for overviews, see Eichenbaum & Cohen, 2001; Squire, 2004).

Amygdala

The amygdala forges connections between stimuli endowed with unconditional affective properties—that is, natural born rewards and punishers, such as food or injury, and the stimuli that reliably predict them (i.e., conditioned stimuli). Due to LeDoux's (1996) seminal studies on fear conditioning, the amygdala has become primarily known for its ability to trigger stress responses when cued with conditioned stimuli predicting punishment. But it also mediates learning about stimuli that reliably predict reward (Baxter & Murray, 2002). The amygdala drives *emotional reactions* to stimuli via outputs to other brain areas, most notably the hypothalamus and the brainstem. But it can also trigger *motivated actions* by its output to the striatum (LeDoux, 2002).

Striatum

The striatum is sensitive to probabilistic contingencies between stimuli or events and their relation to the individual's own motor behavior (Delgado, 2007). It is critical for the nonconscious, procedural acquisition and execution of behavior sequences exploiting such predictable patterns, a process that has been termed implicit learning. Striatum-based implicit learning is boosted and turned into instrumental learning by salient affective consequences of behavior, such as pleasure associated with reward and pain associated with punishment. However, once a behavior has been learned well with the aid of reward and punishment, it turns into a habit that persists long after the affective consequences that have facilitated its acquisition have ceased to occur. Lieberman (2000) proposed that striatal learning of contingencies between social cues and appropriate behavioral responses is at the core of social intuition—that is, the fast, nonconscious learning and utilization of socially relevant information for socially adaptive behavior. Lieberman supported his hypothesis by evidence showing that individuals with damage to the striatum are not only impaired in their ability for implicit learning, but they are also likely to show socially inappropriate behavior.

Hippocampus

The hippocampus integrates perceptual information about the individual's current situational context and the complex relationships between the stimuli constituting it and thus provides the cognitive basis for conscious awareness of the situation in its entirety. In fact, conscious awareness of the association between stimuli critically depends on the hippocampus, as does memory for facts and events. Loss of the hippocampus leads to loss of the ability to learn new facts (i.e., anterograde amnesia) and consciously commit new information to memory. Although not dependent on emotion for fulfilling its learning functions, the hippocampus interacts with emotional learning in the amygdala in two important ways. First, it constrains the acquisition of Pavlovian-conditioned cues by contributing information about the situational context in which a learned cue is valid and in which it is not. Second, emotional responses triggered by amygdala responses to unconditioned or learned cues enhance memory encoding in the hippocampus, giving rise to stable and accessible emotional memories.

Interactions

Affective responses as elicited by reward and punishment play a critical role for learning in the striatum (particularly the anterior part, which includes the nucleus accumbens) and in the amygdala (LeDoux, 1996, 2002). In fact, Pavlovian learning in the amygdala crucially depends on the presence of stimuli that have immediate significance for survival and are therefore endowed with unconditional affective meaning (e.g., pain, food, sex) and would not occur in the absence of affectively charged stimuli. Although the striatum is able to learn stimulus-response contingencies in the absence of overt reward and punishment, as the phenomenon of implicit learning strongly suggests, learning is greatly enhanced by reinforcers. In contrast, the hippocampus represents a learning system that can operate efficiently without affective arousal, too, as, for instance, the ability to learn words in a new language illustrates.

How Implicit Motives Affect Learning and Memory

Because implicit motives determine which stimuli and events are affectively hot and which are not, they should be closely associated with Pavlovian conditioning of stimulus–stimulus associations that are forged in the amygdala and instrumental learning of complex stimulus-response associations mediated by the striatum (see Schultheiss, 2007; Schultheiss & Schiepe-Tiska, 2013). Take, for instance, a person with a strong need for power. Because this person is highly sensitive to dominance signaled by others (which may threaten his or her own claim to dominance), he or she should have a strong negative response to angry facial expressions, a social dominance signal (see Hess, Blairy, & Kleck, 2000), and therefore more readily learn stimuli that predict the occurrence of an angry face (amygdala-mediated Pavlovian conditioning) and learn to inhibit the execution of behavior that elicits anger in others (striatum-mediated instrumental avoidance learning). A person with a low need for power will not show these learning outcomes because angry faces do not have the same, strong affective meaning for that person. This is, in fact, what can be observed. Stanton, Wirth, and Schultheiss (2006) conducted a study in which participants learned to associate the spatial occurrence of angry faces on the computer screen with a predictive cue stimulus (a geometrical shape). As their performance on a dot-probe task of attention towards cues that during training preceded anger versus cues that during training preceded neutral expressions revealed, individuals high in n Power had become sensitive to anger-predicting cues, whereas individuals low in n Power had not. Although Stanton et al. (2006) did not measure amygdala activity during learning in this study, other studies with humans show that the amygdala is critically involved in similar learning experiments (e.g., Armony & Dolan, 2002). And Hall, Stanton, and Schultheiss (2010) report findings from a brain-imaging study that show that higher levels of n Power are associated with greater amygdala response to angry faces, an observation that is consistent with the interpretation of Stanton et al.'s (2006) findings being dependent on the amygdala.

In another study, Schultheiss, Pang, Torges, Wirth, and Treynor (2005) made the presentation of angry faces contingent on the execution of a visuomotor sequence in an implicit-learning paradigm. Individuals high in n Power showed impaired learning when the sequence was followed by an angry face but not when it was followed by a surprised face, which, as the authors argued, signals low dominance and thus does not represent a threat to power-motivated individuals. Individuals low in n Power did not show these differences in learning and were not expected to because angry and surprised faces should not have strong affective value for them. Schultheiss, Pang, et al. (2005) did not directly assess striatal involvement in learning in their study. But it is very well established that both implicit learning and reinforcement of instrumental behavior depend on an intact striatum (Delgado, 2007; Lieberman, 2000). Moreover, Schultheiss et al. (2008) later showed that n Power is positively associated with striatal activation in response to anger faces, a finding that might suggest that affectively charged motive-specific incentives not only reinforce but also trigger instrumental behavior aimed at dealing with the incentive.

In another line of research, Schultheiss and colleagues have obtained replicable evidence across three independent studies for enhanced implicit learning of visuomotor sequences during one-on-one competition among power-motivated winners and impaired implicit learning among power-motivated losers (Schiepe-Tiska, 2013; Schultheiss & Rohde, 2002; Schultheiss, Wirth, Torges, Pang, Villacorta, & Welsh, 2005). Together with the study by Schultheiss, Pang, et al. (2005) on reinforcing effects of facial expressions of emotion on motive-dependent implicit learning, these studies provide robust support for an involvement of striatal learning processes in the way that implicit motives shape behavior. Although presently evidence for such learning is strongest for the need for power, the study by Schultheiss, Pang et al. (2005) also suggests a role of n Affiliation in implicit learning. The role of n Achievement in implicit learning remains to be explored. Based on previous research by Brunstein and colleagues (e.g., Brunstein & Hoyer, 2002; Brunstein & Maier, 2005), we would expect n Achievement to predict implicit learning gains particularly well under conditions in which feedback is provided with reference to one's previous performance and that indicates that one's performance is deteriorating.

Finally, implicit motives also influence explicit memory and thus hippocampus-dependent learning. As McAdams (e.g., McAdams, 1982; McAdams, Hoffmann, Mansfield, & Day, 1996) and later Woike (see Woike, 2008, for a summary) have consistently shown, people are better at remembering affectively charged episodes and events in lab and life that correspond to their implicit motives than at remembering unrelated content. Thus, for instance, McClelland (1995) reported that achievement-motivated individuals are particularly likely to recall achievement-related content, but not other types of content, from a story they had read.

McAdams (1982) as well as Woike (1994) reported that power-motivated individuals are particularly likely to recall autobiographical peak experiences related to power, but not other types of episodes from their lives. Note, however, that the critical feature of the memory processes examined in these studies is their *affective* character. Findings by Woike, McLeod, and Goggin (2003) highlight this fact. These researchers asked participants to either report on emotionally charged experiences from their daily lives or to report experiences that were in some way self-descriptive for them. Memory for emotionally charged events was predicted well by participants' implicit motives (achievement and affiliation) but not by their self-ascribed, explicit motives, whereas memory for self-descriptive events was predicted well by their explicit motives but not as well by their implicit motives. Woike, Bender, and Besner (2009) could show that implicit motive effects on emotional memories depend on motivational-affective arousal during encoding: Higher n Achievement predicted better recall of achievement-related words participants had learned after vivid recollection of an achievement-related success (arousal condition) but not after recollection of a neutral life event (control condition). These findings suggest that explicit learning and memory are enhanced by implicit motives only when (a) the person has a strong motive and (b) the situation contains incentives for and thus arouses the motive. Although this was never directly tested, it appears very plausible that motive-dependent enhancement of memory for affective content is mediated by effects of the amygdala (affective arousal) on hippocampal learning (episodic encoding).

Implications

What can we conclude from this review of the role of implicit motives in learning and memory and the neurobiological substrates of learning? One conclusion is that implicit motives shape behavior through affect-based, nondeclarative learning of stimuli and particularly of instrumental responses, which, as Lieberman (2000) has argued, may be the basis of social intuition and thus of competent interpersonal behavior. Through emotional arousal associated with incentive stimuli, implicit motives also influence declarative learning about the situational context in which motivationally significant events (i.e., reward and punishment) occur.

However, a conclusion that should not be drawn from this discussion is that just because Pavlovian conditioning, instrumental conditioning, and declarative learning can be dissociated procedurally and neurobiologically, the effects of implicit motives on learning and memory are necessarily dissociated, too. Rather, we envision the effect of implicit motives on learning in naturally occurring situations as one in which all three types of learning go hand in hand, integrated by the affect-amplifying effect of a motive on all three, and thus enable the individual to respond emotionally and in a context-sensitive manner to learned stimuli, to intuitively recruit and execute instrumental behaviors, and to consciously recall and strategically seek out situational contexts in which motivational gratification has been obtained in the past (or avoid situations in which it has been forsaken). In interaction with situational incentives and demands, motives thus organize complex learning experiences that are only partly accessible to conscious awareness and that can generate complex know-how that operates at an intuitive level. It is this type of affect-based integration of learning across subsystems that we see as the basis of behavioral competence development and the kind of social intuitive know-how to which Lieberman (2000) referred. Viewed from this perspective, implicit motives may thus be the catalysts and accelerators for the development, over time and through repeated person-situation-transactions, of specific, integrated competencies (see Boyatzis & Kelner, 2010, for related arguments).

THE VIRTUOUS-CIRCLE MODEL OF MOTIVE-DRIVEN LEARNING AND GOAL ATTAINMENT

Pursuing the notion of implicit motives as catalysts of learning further, we propose a virtuous-circle model of motive-driven learning and successful goal pursuit (see Figure 5.2). The model starts with implicit motives' capacity to endow successful attainment of incentives with pleasure, thus turning the experience into one of reward. The pleasurable reward in turn provides a feedback signal to the parallel learning systems reviewed above, resulting in an integrated learning experience that leads to the Pavlovian acquisition of reward-predictive cues that automatically grab attention and induce emotional arousal, to the acquisition and energization of behavior that has been instrumental for obtaining the reward, and to affectively charged memories for the situational context in which the reward experience occurred. Such integrated learning experiences in turn make it easier for individuals to recognize situational opportunities for advancing the goals they have set for themselves and to use intuitive behavioral strategies to realize them. Evidence in support of the link between learning and enactment of motive-congruent goals comes from studies that show that although implicit motives do not per se predict people's goal

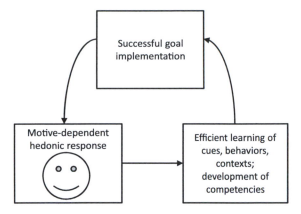

Figure 5.2 Virtuous-circle model of motive driven learning and successful goal pursuit. Motive-dependent hedonic responses to incentives (lower left box) lead to enhanced learning and the development of competencies (lower right box), which in turn promotes intuitive goal pursuit strategies (upper box). Successful goal pursuit entails the attainment of motive-specific incentives, which closes the circle.

choices, they do promote efficient progress towards personal goals (see Brunstein et al., 1998; Schultheiss, Jones, et al., 2008), particularly when people do not try too hard to reach their goals but leave goal enactment to their intuition (Schultheiss, Jones, et al., 2008). Progress towards motive-congruent goals in turn entails successful attainment of motive-specific incentives. Each time this happens, the circle closes through the elicitation of a pleasure response, and if it happens often, because a person is making rapid progress towards a goal, frequent pleasure responses can add up to lasting emotional well-being and rapid growth of competencies.[1]

Punishment

The virtuous-circle model of motive-driven learning also applies to the case of punishment or aversive outcomes because individuals with a strong implicit motive are not only sensitive to incentives but also to disincentives. Encounters with punishers lead to enhanced Pavlovian learning of predictive cues, too, and the emotional arousal associated with such cues then becomes a stress response that prepares the individual for dealing with the threat of punishment in the future. Such encounters also shape instrumental learning: they can lead to passive avoidance, the suppression of behavior that has led to an encounter with the punisher, but also to active avoidance—that is, learning of behavior that helps to escape the impending punishment. Finally, an encounter with a disincentive also enhances memory for the situational context of the motive-specific stressor, marking similar situations in a person's memory as those that need to be avoided or in which one has to tread carefully and avoid certain behaviors that may lead to punishment. Intuitive knowledge of what not to do or how to avoid or escape aversive situations is also critical for the successful enactment of personal goals and thus fosters well-being by avoiding deeply frustrating and stressful outcomes.

Thus, just as the reward version of the virtuous-circle model posits that implicit motives predict the acquisition of behavioral strategies that enable successful goal pursuit, the punishment version of the virtuous-circle model predicts that implicit motives drive the development of adaptive behavior by helping a person to learn what not to do and when not to do it. Both types of learning work in parallel to efficiently adapt a person's behavior to the opportunities, affordances, and threats associated with various situational contexts and to foster efficient intuitive goal pursuit.

No Virtuous Circle Without a Motive

Due to a motive's strong hedonic response to motive-specific incentives, the virtuous circle is easy to start and maintain in the presence of a strong implicit motive (e.g., achievement, affiliation, or power) and leads to rapid further growth of skills and knowledge through the principles of cue generalization and discrimination, shaping, Pavlovian-instrumental transfer, second-order conditioning, and so forth. In the absence of a strong motive, however, the circle is difficult to start or maintain because attaining a motive-specific incentive does not lead to pleasure (i.e., there is no reward), and encountering a motive-specific disincentive does not lead to displeasure (i.e., there is no punishment). As a consequence, learning of predictive cues through Pavlovian conditioning is less likely because there is no distinct, affectively charged unconditioned stimulus to begin with. For the same reason, the acquisition of instrumental behaviors is also hampered because these behaviors do not lead to an affectively rewarding experience. And the lack of emotional arousal associated with the episode also makes memories of the situation less likely to develop, or, if they do, more likely to be of a rather bland sort. In other words, a weak motive makes it difficult to learn and remember what stimuli, behaviors, and contexts would be conducive to a certain successful or unsuccessful outcome of a person-situation transaction because the outcome itself has little or no affective charge. As a consequence, people with a weak motive in a given motivational domain can rely less on their intuition and need to explicitly develop and implement plans for action when pursuing goals in that domain (see Cantor & Blanton, 1996). This mode of goal pursuit requires effort, and success is not associated with the pleasure of a motive-driven hedonic response. Thus, the circle cannot be closed, little emotional well-being can be reaped, and the development of competencies is not supported in the domain of a weak motive. Of course, within the same person, lacking development of competencies in one domain due to a weak motive does not preclude substantial competency development in other domains with strong motives.

Broaden-and-Build Effects of Motive Satisfaction

While our presentation of the virtuous-circle model of motive-driven learning relies heavily on findings and insights derived from biopsychology and neuroscience, we would like to point out that the beneficial effects of motive-driven hedonic experiences on adaptive behavior may also stem from effects of positive emotions that are not specifically related to learning and memory. For instance, in her broaden-and-build model of positive emotions, Fredrickson (1998) has argued that specific positive emotions, such as joy, contentment, interest, and love, which also occur in the context of implicit motive satisfaction, broaden the scope of attention and enhance cognitive processes, such as finding creative solutions to problems, help to build physical resources through enhanced health, and create enduring social alliances and resources. Evidence for the validity of the broaden-and-build model of positive emotions in the context of implicit motives comes from studies that show that positive feedback makes individuals high in n Power and n Achievement more creative than individuals low in these motives (Fodor & Carver, 2000; Fodor & Greenier, 1995). Evidence also comes from studies that show that satisfaction of implicit motives in everyday life is associated with enhanced immune system functions and health (summarized in McClelland, 1989). Thus, although there is considerably less research on the role of motive-dependent hedonic responses in broaden-and-build-type adaptations than there is on learning and memory, broaden-and-build effects of positive affect are also likely to contribute to the virtuous circle we have described.

Using the Model to Connect the Dots

The notion that implicit motives drive the acquisition of adaptive behavior and promote goal pursuit—a proposition that, as we have laid out, draws on many studies that link motives to learning—may help explain why individuals with strong motives tend to be successful in life. For instance, a large literature shows that individuals high in n Achievement excel as entrepreneurs in small-business contexts (see, for instance, Collins, Hanges, & Locke, 2004; McClelland, 1961). Other studies show that individuals high in n Power are successful as managers in business and political contexts (see McClelland & Burnham, 1976; Winter, 2010b). Furthermore, individuals characterized by high n Affiliation tend to be healthier than others (Jemmott, 1987; McClelland, 1989). However, these studies typically only measure motive dispositions and distal life outcomes, such as business growth, career success, or health status, but not the mediating processes that produce these outcomes, or, more specifically, the behavioral adaptations that people have developed and the goals that they pursue en route to these outcomes.

A few studies do provide glimpses of the specific competencies that may link implicit motives to life success. For instance, the work on n Power and implicit learning in the context of dominance contests we have reviewed previously suggests that power-motivated individuals quickly and intuitively learn to do whatever lets them dominate others and avoid whatever leads to a defeat (e.g., Schultheiss, Wirth, et al., 2005). Such a direct glimpse of the learning process helps explain how power-motivated individuals acquire strategies through which they can persuade and convince others without alienating them by coming across as particularly dominant or hostile: During discussions, they speak fluently, gesture a lot, and raise their eyebrows to underscore the importance of the arguments they are making (Schultheiss & Brunstein, 2002). It is reasonable to assume that power-motivated individuals have learned at some point to use these behaviors in the context of exchanging opinions because they had the desired effect of having an impact on others, which in turn was rewarding for the power-motivated individuals—an example of the virtuous circle in action. Persuasion skills like the ones identified by Schultheiss and Brunstein (2002) are a component of managerial influence competencies that Boyatzis and Kelner (2010) attribute to n Power and that may explain why power-motivated individuals are particularly likely to rise to the highest levels of management (Jacobs & McClelland, 1994; McClelland & Boyatzis, 1982).

Another set of studies that sheds light on what may actually happen along the way from an implicit motive disposition to beneficial life outcomes was published by McAdams and colleagues (McAdams & Constantian, 1983; McAdams, Jackson, & Kirshnit, 1984; McAdams & Powers, 1981). These researchers found that individuals high in n Intimacy, a love-oriented facet of the need to affiliate, were more likely to connect to others through smiling, the expression of positive affect, and relaxed chatting. These behavioral strategies may be critical for establishing and maintaining satisfying relationships with close others (Hagemeyer & Neyer, 2012) and more generally help build social resources and support, which are known to have beneficial effects on physical health (Uchino, 2004) and may explain the superior health of individuals high in the needs for affiliation and intimacy (McClelland, 1989). Thus, learning to connect to others through affiliative behavior is not only hedonically rewarding for affiliation-motivated individuals in the short term but may also engender long-term health benefits.

Summary

To conclude, the virtuous-circle model we have proposed here may help to bridge the gap between microlevel learning and memory processes associated with implicit motives and macrolevel outcomes, such as career success, relationship satisfaction, and health, by proposing that the competencies that motive-driven learning processes help to develop are instrumental for people to successfully realize their goals. Motive-supported goal implementation thus represents a critical midlevel process that connects motive-driven learning to motive-associated life outcomes.

APPLICATION TO EDUCATIONAL SETTINGS

What are some of the implications of the virtuous-circle model for educational psychology and educational research? The obvious first answer to this question is that learning and competence development will proceed rapidly and with strong affective support if it occurs in the context of a strong implicit motive. Learning environments that manage to engage students' implicit motives instill a sense of flow in the learner (e.g., Engeser & Rheinberg, 2008) and thus promote further motivation and learning in the classroom (see Shernoff, 2012). Such learning environments can also lead to superior academic outcomes.

McKeachie's (1961) Classic Study

A large-scale study by McKeachie (1961; see also McKeachie et al., 1968) shows that affiliation-motivated students achieve particularly good grades in classrooms in which the teacher fosters group work and other types of collaborative learning—that is, when affiliation incentives are provided. Power-motivated individuals benefit from teachers who provide power incentives by allowing them to have an impact on others through classroom discussion and opportunities to persuade others. Finally, achievement-motivated individuals do particularly well in classrooms in which the teacher does not attempt to set achievement incentives. This somewhat paradoxical outcome was corroborated meta-analytically: the presence of social-extrinsic cues for achievement can drive achievement-motivated individuals away from the superior performance they would show if no external incentives were given (Spangler, 1992).

We explain the effects of implicit motives, in conjunction with suitable incentives in the classroom, on academic outcomes that McKeachie (1961) observed as follows: The presence of motive-specific incentives in the classroom allowed individuals with the fitting implicit motives to frequently experience strong affective responses to learning situations. Affective arousal leads to better encoding of, and memory for, facts and events (i.e., a hippocampus-based learning function; see Cahill & McGaugh, 1998; Packard & Cahill, 2001; for a discussion of the complexities in the relationship between affect and learning, see Shuman & Scherer, 2014). Better memory is a critical determinant of exam performance and thus helps to achieve better grades. But this is not the only type of learning facilitated by instruction techniques that provide motivational incentives. At a nondeclarative level, students may also benefit by learning how to use social cues from others that trigger emotional processes and by learning intuitive behavioral skills (e.g., patterns of verbal and nonverbal communication) that help them succeed in the social context of the classroom. Thus, motive-driven learning in such a classroom is likely to go beyond mere academic achievement and to also entail the development of interpersonal skills. We believe that this is an important point if teachers aim not only to educate the minds but also the hearts of their students.

From this perspective, then, instructional methods that alternate between different incentives for different motives, and thus for students with different patterns of implicit motives, can help to boost learning in a maximum number of students. To illustrate this based on McKeachie's (1961) work, teachers who alternate providing students with opportunities to collaborate with others, to influence others, and to follow their own inclinations will enable more students to experience affectively charged, motivating learning situations and thereby also engender better learning than teachers who use only one of these methods or none of them.

Teachers' Effects on Students' Motives

Applied educational research reviewed by Rheinberg and Engeser (2010) suggests that by setting suitable incentives, teachers may even change their students' implicit motives. Teachers who instruct students based on an individual reference norm orientation by providing performance feedback that compares the student's current performance with her or his previous performance, by adjusting instruction to the student's current performance level, and by attributing setbacks to inappropriate instruction (rather than to factors in the student) foster higher n Achievement in their students. In contrast, teachers who use a social reference norm by comparing a student's performance to that of others, by using a one-size-fits-all instructional style, and by attributing failures and successes to stable, internal factors in the student effectively prevent students from developing high n Achievement.

Implications for Students' Learning Strategies

Students can also actively boost their learning by setting goals and creating learning activities for themselves that engage their implicit motives. For instance, a person high in n Affiliation may benefit from meeting with other students to exercise their vocabulary in a second language, a student high in n Power may benefit by trying to explain and teach a difficult topic to another student, and a student high in n Achievement may get a boost from trying to find new, more creative or more efficient ways to learn about a topic. Such active, intelligent management of one's own learning requires, of course, a willingness to experiment by the student and a certain freedom and encouragement to experiment provided by the instructor. Students not only need to learn, they also need to learn *how* to learn, and the individual-difference perspective we take here from the vantage point of implicit motives suggests that one size won't fit all. Every learner needs to explore and find out which learning strategies, environments, and activities are most likely to be motivationally engaging and thus learning-promoting for her or him. Unfortunately, this is not usually a learning experience traditional schools encourage students to have. As a consequence, many students continue to learn in the only way they have learned to learn—that is, alone and hunched over books—and thus in a way that requires a lot of tiring effort and promises comparatively little gain in terms of affectively charged learning experiences.

From a pedagogical point of view, then, it becomes a critical goal for students not only to learn content matter but also to learn to recognize, acknowledge, and use their affective responses to both the content matter of learning and the circumstances of learning because these responses signal the arousal of implicit motivational needs that can facilitate learning. Heeding such affective signals can help them optimize their learning so that it becomes engaging, lasting, and rapid. Ignoring such affective signals can hamper learning not only by failing to develop better, affectively engaging learning strategies but also by requiring additional self-regulatory effort and thereby inducing fatigue (see Muraven & Baumeister, 2000). The result is slow learning progress and, perhaps worse, a tendency to avoid the subject matter in the future. Thus, the value of understanding and using one's immediate affective responses to learning situations and contents itself needs to be conveyed to students. Affect is not the enemy of cognition, as some philosophers have claimed; it is in fact its close ally because it singles out experiences that are worth remembering, both at the level of declarative memory and at the level of unconscious, procedural learning.

NOTE

1. This account of motive-driven acquisition of integrated competencies may apply more to informal, nondeclarative learning of social skills than to the formal, declarative learning of rules and facts that dominates school contexts. Although work by Woike et al. (2009), McClelland (1995), and others seems to suggest that motives can also facilitate the declarative acquisition of factual knowledge, motive effects on formal leaning typically emerge only after appropriate situational arousal of the motive. The mere presence of motive-related verbal material in instructional texts may therefore not be sufficient to engage learners' implicit motives. As research by McKeachie (1961, reviewed further on) suggests, teachers need to provide suitable situational incentives that arouse students' motives and thus provide the necessary affective support for learning and mastering declarative material.

REFERENCES

Armony, J. L., & Dolan, R. J. (2002). Modulation of spatial attention by fear-conditioned stimuli: An event-related fMRI study. *Neuropsychologia, 40,* 817–826.

Atkinson, J. W. (1957). Motivational determinants of risk-taking behavior. *Psychological Review, 64,* 359–372.

Atkinson, J. W., Heyns, R. W., & Veroff, J. (1958). The effect of experimental arousal of the affiliation motive on thematic apperception. In J. W. Atkinson (Ed.), *Motives in fantasy, action, and society: A method of assessment and study* (pp. 95–104). Princeton, NJ: Van Nostrand.

Baxter, M. G., & Murray, E. A. (2002). The amygdala and reward. *Nature Reviews: Neuroscience, 3,* 563–573.

Berridge, K. C. (2004). Motivation concepts in behavioral neuroscience. *Physiology and Behavior, 81,* 179–209.

Borsboom, D., Mellenbergh, G. J., & van Heerden, J. (2004). The concept of validity. *Psychological Review, 111,* 1061–1071.

Boyatzis, R. E. (1973). Affiliation motivation. In D.C. McClelland & R. S. Steele (Eds.), *Human motivation – a book of readings* (pp. 252–276). Morristown, NJ: General Learning Corporation.

Boyatzis, R. E., & Kelner, S. P. (2010). Competencies as a behavioral manifestation of implicit motives. In O. C. Schultheiss & J. C. Brunstein (Eds.), *Implicit motives* (pp. 488–509). New York, NY: Oxford University Press.

Brunstein, J. C. (2010). Implicit motives and explicit goals: The role of motivational congruence in emotional well-being. In O. C. Schultheiss & J. C. Brunstein (Eds.), *Implicit motives* (pp. 347–374). New York, NY: Oxford University Press.

Brunstein, J. C., & Hoyer, S. (2002). Implizites und explizites Leistungsstreben: Befunde zur Unabhängigkeit zweier Motivationssysteme [Implicit versus explicit achievement strivings: Empirical evidence of the independence of two motivational systems]. *Zeitschrift fur Pädagogische Psychologie, 16,* 51–62.

Brunstein, J. C., Lautenschlager, U., Nawroth, B., Pöhlmann, K., & Schultheiss, O. (1995). Persönliche Anliegen, soziale Motive und emotionales Wohlbefinden [Personal goals, social motives, and emotional well-being]. *Zeitschrift für Differentielle und Diagnostische Psychologie, 16,* 1–10.

Brunstein, J. C., & Maier, G. W. (2005). Implicit and self-attributed motives to achieve: Two separate but interacting needs. *Journal of Personality and Social Psychology, 89,* 205–222.

Brunstein, J. C., & Schmitt, C. H. (2004). Assessing individual differences in achievement motivation with the Implicit Association Test. *Journal of Research in Personality, 38,* 536–555.

Brunstein, J. C., Schultheiss, O. C., & Grässmann, R. (1998). Personal goals and emotional well-being: The moderating role of motive dispositions. *Journal of Personality and Social Psychology, 75,* 494–508.

Buck, R. (1999). The biological affects: A typology. *Psychological Review, 106,* 301–336.

Cabanac, M. (1992). Pleasure: The common currency. *Journal of Theoretical Biology, 155,* 173–200.

Cahill, L., & McGaugh, J. L. (1998). Mechanisms of emotional arousal and lasting declarative memory. *Trends in Neurosciences, 21,* 294–299.

Cantor, N., & Blanton, H. (1996). Effortful pursuit of personal goals in daily life. In J. A. Bargh & P.M. Gollwitzer (Eds.), *The psychology of action: Linking cognition and motivation to behavior* (pp. 338–359). New York, NY: Guilford.

Collins, C. J., Hanges, P. J., & Locke, E. A. (2004). The relationship of achievement motivation to entrepreneurial behavior: A meta-analysis. *Human Performance, 17,* 95–117.

deCharms, R., Morrison, H. W., Reitman, W., & McClelland, D.C. (1955). Behavioral correlates of directly and indirectly measured achievement motivation. In D. C. McClelland (Ed.), *Studies in motivation* (pp. 414–423). New York, NY: Appleton-Century-Crofts.

Delgado, M. R. (2007). Reward-related responses in the human striatum. *Annals of the New York Academy of Sciences, 1104,* 70–88.

Eichenbaum, H., & Cohen, N. J. (2001). *From conditioning to conscious recollection: Memory systems of the brain.* New York, NY: Oxford University Press.

Engeser, S., & Rheinberg, F. (2008). Flow, moderators of challenge-skill-balance and performance. *Motivation and Emotion, 32,* 158–172.

Engeser, S., Rheinberg, F., & Möller, M. (2009). Achievement motive imagery in German schoolbooks: A pilot study testing McClelland's hypothesis. *Journal of Research in Personality, 43,* 110–113.

Fodor, E. M., & Carver, R. A. (2000). Achievement and power motives, performance feedback, and creativity. *Journal of Research in Personality, 34,* 380–396.

Fodor, E. M., & Greenier, K. D. (1995). The power motive, self-affect, and creativity. *Journal of Research in Personality, 29,* 242–252.

Fodor, E. M., & Wick, D. P. (2009). Need for power and affective response to negative audience reaction to an extemporaneous speech. *Journal of Research in Personality, 43,* 721–726.

Fodor, E. M., Wick, D. P., & Hartsen, K. M. (2006). The power motive and affective response to assertiveness. *Journal of Research in Personality, 40,* 598–610.

Fredrickson, B. L. (1998). What good are positive emotions? *Review of General Psychology, 2,* 300–319.

Gray, J. A., & McNaughton, N. (2000). *The neuropsychology of anxiety* (2 ed.). Oxford, United Kingdom: Oxford University Press.

Hagemeyer, B., & Neyer, F. J. (2012). Assessing implicit motivational orientations in couple relationships: The Partner-Related Agency and Communion Test (PACT). *Psychological Assessment, 24,* 114–128.

Hall, J. L., Stanton, S. J., & Schultheiss, O. C. (2010). Biopsychological and neural processes of implicit motivation. In O. C. Schultheiss & J. C. Brunstein (Eds.), *Implicit motives* (pp. 279–307). New York, NY: Oxford University Press.

Hess, U., Blairy, S., & Kleck, R. E. (2000). The influence of facial emotion displays, gender, and ethnicity on judgments of dominance and affiliation. *Journal of Nonverbal Behavior, 24,* 265–283.

Hofer, J., Busch, H., Bond, M. H., Campos, D., Li, M., & Law, R. (2010). The implicit power motive and sociosexuality in men and women: Pancultural effects of responsibility. *Journal of Personality and Social Psychology, 99,* 380–394.

Hofer, J., Busch, H., Bond, M. H., Li, M., & Law, R. (2010). Effects of motive-goal congruence on well-being in the power domain: Considering goals and values in a German and two Chinese samples. *Journal of Research in Personality, 44,* 610–620.

Hofer, J., & Chasiotis, A. (2003). Congruence of life goals and implicit motives as predictors of life satisfaction: Cross-cultural implications of a study of Zambian male adolescents. *Motivation and Emotion, 27,* 251–272.

Hofer, J., Chasiotis, A., & Campos, D. (2006). Congruence between social values and implicit motives: effects on life satisfaction across three cultures. *European Journal of Personality, 20,* 305–324.

Jacobs, R. L., & McClelland, D. C. (1994). Moving up the corporate ladder: A longitudinal study of the leadership motive pattern and managerial success in women and men. *Consulting Psychology Journal Practice and Research, 46,* 32–41.

Jemmott, J. B. (1987). Social motives and susceptibility to disease: Stalking individual differences in health risks. *Journal of Personality, 55,* 267–298.

Jenkins, S. R. (1987). Need for achievement and women's careers over 14 years: Evidence for occupational structure effects. *Journal of Personality and Social Psychology, 53,* 922–932.

Jenkins, S. R. (1994). Need for power and women's careers over 14 years: Structural power, job satisfaction, and motive change. *Journal of Personality and Social Psychology, 66,* 155–165.

Köllner, M., & Schultheiss, O. C. (in preparation). *A meta-analysis of the correlation between implicit and explicit measures of motivational needs for achievement, affiliation, and power.* Manuscript in preparation.

Kordik, A. (2012). *Implicit motives and affect: Facial EMG as an indicator of dispositional differences* (PhD diss.). Friedrich-Alexander University, Erlangen, Germany. Retrieved from http://opus4.kobv.de/opus4-fau/files/1810/Dissertation_Kordik.pdf

Kordik, A., Eska, K., & Schultheiss, O. C. (2012). Implicit need for affiliation is associated with increased corrugator activity in a non-positive, but not in a positive social interaction. *Journal of Research in Personality, 46,* 604–608.

Kuhl, J. (2001). *Motivation und Persönlichkeit: Interaktionen psychischer Systeme [Motivation and personality: Interactions of mental systems].* Göttingen, Germany: Hogrefe.

Larsen, J. T., Norris, C. J., & Cacioppo, J. T. (2003). Effects of positive and negative affect on electromyographic activity over zygomaticus major and corrugator supercilii. *Psychophysiology, 40,* 776–785.

LeDoux, J. E. (1996). *The emotional brain.* New York, NY: Simon & Schuster.

LeDoux, J. E. (2002). *The synaptic self.* New York, NY: Viking.

Lieberman, M. D. (2000). Intuition: A social cognitive neuroscience approach. *Psychological Bulletin, 126,* 109–137.

Matthews, G., Jones, D. M., & Chamberlain, A. G. (1990). Refining the measurement of mood: The UWIST mood adjective checklist. *British Journal of Psychology, 81,* 17–42.

McAdams, D. P. (1982). Experiences of intimacy and power: Relationships between social motives and autobiographical memory. *Journal of Personality and Social Psychology, 42,* 292–302.

McAdams, D. P., & Bryant, F. B. (1987). Intimacy motivation and subjective mental health in a nationwide sample. *Journal of Personality, 55,* 395–413.

McAdams, D. P., & Constantian, C. A. (1983). Intimacy and affiliation motives in daily living: An experience sampling analysis. *Journal of Personality and Social Psychology, 45,* 851–861.

McAdams, D. P., Hoffmann, B. J., Mansfield, E. D., & Day, R. (1996). Themes of agency and communion in significant autobiographical scenes. *Journal of Personality, 64,* 339–377.

McAdams, D. P., Jackson, J., & Kirshnit, C. (1984). Looking, laughing, and smiling in dyads as a function of intimacy motivation and reciprocity. *Journal of Personality, 52,* 261–273.

McAdams, D. P., & Powers, J. (1981). Themes of intimacy in behavior and thought. *Journal of Personality and Social Psychology, 40,* 573–587.

McClelland, D. C. (1958). Methods of measuring human motivation. In J. W. Atkinson (Ed.), *Motives in fantasy, action, and society: A method of assessment and study* (pp. 7–42). Princeton, NJ: Van Nostrand.

McClelland, D. C. (1961). *The achieving society.* New York, NY: Free Press.

McClelland, D. C. (1979). Inhibited power motivation and high blood pressure in men. *Journal of Abnormal Psychology, 88,* 182–190.

McClelland, D. C. (1987). *Human motivation.* New York NY: Cambridge University Press.

McClelland, D. C. (1989). Motivational factors in health and disease. *American Psychologist, 44,* 675–683.

McClelland, D. C. (1995). Achievement motivation in relation to achievement-related recall, performance, and urine flow, a marker associated with release of vasopressin. *Motivation and Emotion, 19,* 59–76.

McClelland, D. C., Atkinson, J. W., Clark, R. A., & Lowell, E. L. (1953). *The achievement motive.* New York, NY: Appleton-Century-Crofts.

McClelland, D. C., & Boyatzis, R. E. (1982). Leadership motive pattern and long-term success in management. *Journal of Applied Psychology, 67,* 737–743.

McClelland, D. C., & Burnham, D. H. (1976). Power is the great motivator. *Harvard Business Review, 54,* 100–110.

McClelland, D. C., & Franz, C. E. (1992). Motivational and other sources of work accomplishments in mid-life: A longitudinal study. *Journal of Personality, 60,* 679–707.

McClelland, D. C., Koestner, R., & Weinberger, J. (1989). How do self-attributed and implicit motives differ? *Psychological Review, 96,* 690–702.

McClelland, D. C., & Pilon, D. A. (1983). Sources of adult motives in patterns of parent behavior in early childhood. *Journal of Personality and Social Psychology, 44,* 564–574.

McKeachie, W. J. (1961). Motivation, teaching methods, and college learning. In M. R. Jones (Ed.), *Nebraska symposium on motivation* (Vol. 9, pp. 111–142). Lincoln, NE: University of Nebraska Press.

McKeachie, W. J., Isaacson, R. L., Milholland, J. E., & Lin, Y. G. (1968). Student achievement motives, achievement cues, and academic achievement. *Journal of Consulting and Clinical Psychology, 32*(1), 26–29.

Morgan, C. D., & Murray, H. A. (1935). A method for investigating fantasies: The thematic apperception test. *Archives of Neurology and Psychiatry, 34,* 289–306.

Muraven, M., & Baumeister, R. F. (2000). Self-regulation and depletion of limited resources: Does self-control resemble a muscle? *Psychological Bulletin, 126*(2), 247–259.

Packard, M. G., & Cahill, L. (2001). Affective modulation of multiple memory systems. *Current Opinion in Neurobiology, 11,* 752–756.

Pang, J. S., & Schultheiss, O. C. (2005). Assessing implicit motives in U.S. College students: Effects of picture type and position, gender and ethnicity, and cross-cultural comparisons. *Journal of Personality Assessment, 85,* 280–294.

Panksepp, J. (1998). *Affective neuroscience: The foundations of human and animal emotions.* New York, NY: Oxford University Press.

Peterson, B. E., & Stewart, A. J. (1993). Generativity and social motives in young adults. *Journal of Personality and Social Psychology, 65,* 186–198.

Pfaff, D. W. (1999). *Drive: Neurobiological and molecular mechanisms of sexual motivation.* Cambridge, MA: MIT Press.

Pueschel, O., Schulte, D., & Michalak, J. (2011). Be careful what you strive for: The significance of motive–goal congruence for depressivity. *Clinical Psychology and Psychotherapy, 18,* 23–33.

Rheinberg, F., & Engeser, S. (2010). Motive training and motivational competence. In O. C. Schultheiss & J. C. Brunstein (Eds.), *Implicit motives* (pp. 510–548). New York, NY: Oxford University Press.

Schiepe-Tiska, A. (2013). *In the power of flow: The impact of implicit and explicit motives on flow experience with a special focus on the power domain* (PhD diss.). Technical University, Munich, Germany. Retrieved from http://d-nb.info/1035502828/34

Schultheiss, O. C. (2007). A memory-systems approach to the classification of personality tests: Comment on Meyer and Kurtz (2006). *Journal of Personality Assessment, 89,* 197–201.

Schultheiss, O. C. (2008). Implicit motives. In O. P. John, R. W. Robins, & L. A. Pervin (Eds.), *Handbook of personality: Theory and research* (3 ed., pp. 603–633). New York, NY: Guilford.

Schultheiss, O. C. (2013). The hormonal correlates of implicit motives. *Social and Personality Psychology Compass, 7,* 52–65.

Schultheiss, O. C. (under revision). *Recommendations for the development and validation of implicit motive measures.* Manuscript submitted for publication.

Schultheiss, O. C., & Brunstein, J. C. (1999). Goal imagery: Bridging the gap between implicit motives and explicit goals. *Journal of Personality, 67*, 1–38.

Schultheiss, O. C., & Brunstein, J. C. (2001). Assessing implicit motives with a research version of the TAT: Picture profiles, gender differences, and relations to other personality measures. *Journal of Personality Assessment, 77*, 71–86.

Schultheiss, O. C., & Brunstein, J. C. (2002). Inhibited power motivation and persuasive communication: A lens model analysis. *Journal of Personality, 70*, 553–582.

Schultheiss, O. C., & Brunstein, J. C. (2005). An implicit motive perspective on competence. In A. J. Elliot & C. Dweck (Eds.), *Handbook of competence and motivation* (pp. 31–51). New York, NY: Guilford.

Schultheiss, O. C., & Hale, J. A. (2007). Implicit motives modulate attentional orienting to perceived facial expressions of emotion. *Motivation and Emotion, 31*, 13–24.

Schultheiss, O. C., Jones, N. M., Davis, A. Q., & Kley, C. (2008). The role of implicit motivation in hot and cold goal pursuit: Effects on goal progress, goal rumination, and depressive symptoms. *Journal of Research in Personality, 42*, 971–987.

Schultheiss, O. C., Liening, S., & Schad, D. (2008). The reliability of a picture story exercise measure of implicit motives: Estimates of internal consistency, retest reliability, and ipsative stability. *Journal of Research in Personality, 42*, 1560–1571.

Schultheiss, O. C., & Pang, J. S. (2007). Measuring implicit motives. In R. W. Robins, R. C. Fraley, & R. Krueger (Eds.), *Handbook of research methods in personality psychology* (pp. 322–344). New York, NY: Guilford.

Schultheiss, O. C., Pang, J. S., Torges, C. M., Wirth, M. M., & Treynor, W. (2005). Perceived facial expressions of emotion as motivational incentives: Evidence from a differential implicit learning paradigm. *Emotion, 5*, 41–54.

Schultheiss, O. C., & Rohde, W. (2002). Implicit power motivation predicts men's testosterone changes and implicit learning in a contest situation. *Hormones and Behavior, 41*, 195–202.

Schultheiss, O. C., & Schiepe-Tiska, A. (2013). The role of the dorsoanterior striatum in implicit motivation: The case of the need for power. *Frontiers in Human Neuroscience, 7*(141).

Schultheiss, O. C., & Strasser, A. (2012). Referential processing and competence as determinants of congruence between implicit and explicit motives. In S. Vazire & T. D. Wilson (Eds.), *Handbook of self-knowledge* (pp. 39–62). New York, NY: Guilford.

Schultheiss, O. C., Wirth, M. M., Torges, C. M., Pang, J. S., Villacorta, M. A., & Welsh, K. M. (2005). Effects of implicit power motivation on men's and women's implicit learning and testosterone changes after social victory or defeat. *Journal of Personality and Social Psychology, 88*, 174–188.

Schultheiss, O. C., Wirth, M. M., Waugh, C. E., Stanton, S. J., Meier, E., & Reuter-Lorenz, P. (2008). Exploring the motivational brain: Effects of implicit power motivation on brain activation in response to facial expressions of emotion. *Social Cognitive and Affective Neuroscience, 3*, 333–343.

Shernoff, D. J. (2012). Engagement and positive youth development: Creating optimal learning environments. In K. R. Harris, S. Graham, T. Urdan, S. Graham, J. M. Royer, & M. Zeidner (Eds.), *APA educational psychology handbook, Vol 2: Individual differences and cultural and contextual factors* (pp. 195–220). Washington, DC: American Psychological Association.

Shuman, V., & Scherer, K. R. (2014). Concepts and structures of emotions. In R. Pekrun & L. Linnenbrink-Garcia (Eds.), *International handbook of emotions in education* (pp. 13–35). New York, NY: Taylor & Francis.

Smith, C. P. (Ed.). (1992). *Motivation and personality: Handbook of thematic content analysis*. New York, NY: Cambridge University Press.

Spangler, W. D. (1992). Validity of questionnaire and TAT measures of need for achievement: Two meta-analyses. *Psychological Bulletin, 112*, 140–154.

Squire, L. R. (2004). Memory systems of the brain: A brief history and current perspective. *Neurobiology of Learning and Memory, 82*, 171–177.

Stanton, S. J., Hall, J. L., & Schultheiss, O. C. (2010). Properties of motive-specific incentives. In O. C. Schultheiss & J. C. Brunstein (Eds.), *Implicit motives* (pp. 245–278). New York, NY: Oxford University Press.

Stanton, S. J., Wirth, M. M., & Schultheiss, O. C. (2006). *Effects of perceivers' implicit power motivation on attentional orienting to Pavlovian-conditioned cues of anger and joy.* Paper presented at the Society for Personality and Social Psychology, Palm Springs, CA.

Steinmayr, R., & Spinath, B. (2008). The importance of motivation as a predictor of school achievement. *Learning and Individual Differences, 19*, 80–90.

Toates, F. (1986). *Motivational systems*. Cambridge, United Kingdom: Cambridge University Press.

Uchino, B. (2004). *Social support and physical health: Understanding the health consequences of relationships*. New Haven, CT: Yale University Press.

Wang, J., Liu, L., & Zheng, Y. (2011). Effects of implicit power motive on the processing of anger faces: An event-related potential study. *Journal of Research in Personality, 45*, 441–447.

Winter, D. G. (1988). The power motive in women—and men. *Journal of Personality and Social Psychology, 54*, 510–519.

Winter, D. G. (1991). A motivational model of leadership: Predicting long-term management success from TAT measures of power motivation and responsibility. *Leadership Quarterly, 2*, 67–80.

Winter, D. G. (1993). Power, affiliation, and war: Three tests of a motivational model. *Journal of Personality and Social Psychology, 65*, 532–545.

Winter, D. G. (1994). *Manual for scoring motive imagery in running text* (4th ed.). Unpublished manuscript, Department of Psychology, University of Michigan, Ann Arbor, MI.

Winter, D. G. (1996). *Personality: Analysis and interpretation of lives*. New York, NY: McGraw-Hill.

Winter, D. G. (1998). The contributions of David McClelland to personality assessment. *Journal of Personality Assessment, 71*, 129–145.

Winter, D. G. (2003). Measuring the motives of political actors at a distance. In J. M. Post (Ed.), *The psychological assessment of political leaders. With profiles of Saddam Hussein and Bill Clinton* (pp. 153–177). Ann Arbor, MI: University of Michigan Press.

Winter, D. G. (2010a). Political and historical consequences of implicit motives. In O. C. Schultheiss & J. C. Brunstein (Eds.), *Implicit motives* (pp. 407–432). New York, NY: Oxford University Press.

Winter, D. G. (2010b). Why achievement motivation predicts success in business but failure in politics: The importance of personal control. *Journal of Personality, 78*, 1637–1668.

Woike, B. A. (1994). Vivid recollection as a technique to arouse implicit motive-related affect. *Motivation and Emotion, 18*, 335–349.

Woike, B. A. (2008). A functional framework for the influence of implicit and explicit motives on autobiographical memory. *Personality and Social Psychology Review, 12*, 99–117.

Woike, B. A., Bender, M., & Besner, N. (2009). Implicit motivational states influence memory: Evidence for motive by state-dependent learning in personality. *Journal of Research in Personality, 43*, 39–48.

Woike, B. A., McLeod, S., & Goggin, M. (2003). Implicit and explicit motives influence accessibility to different autobiographical knowledge. *Personality and Social Psychology Bulletin, 29*, 1046–1055.

Zurbriggen, E. L. (2011). Implicit motives and sexual conservatism as predictors of sexual behaviors. *Journal of Social Psychology, 151*, 535–555.

6

AN ATTRIBUTIONAL APPROACH TO EMOTIONAL LIFE IN THE CLASSROOM

Sandra Graham and April Z. Taylor, University of California, Los Angeles and California State University, Northridge

Imagine this scenario. Mom picks her seventh-grade daughter Sarah up from middle school. Seeking an opportunity to spend quality time during the drive home, Mom initiates the following conversation:

Mom: What did you do in school today, Sarah?
Sarah (irritated): Mom, it's always about what I *did* in school today, like what grades I got on my quizzes or assignments. How come you don't ever ask me how I *felt*?
Mom: I'm sorry, dear. Let's start over. How did you feel in school today?
Sarah: Humiliated. All day. Do you want to know *why*?

This scenario captures three important themes of this chapter. The first theme is that children's emotional lives are just as important as their academic lives at school, and we cannot fully understand the determinants of achievement without knowing about the ways in which emotions shape experiences. Second, children's emotional lives are complex, playing pivotal roles in the way individuals define the self, maintain self-worth, manage relationships with others, and organize appropriate action. And third, many of the emotions experienced in classroom contexts follow causal appraisals about *why* outcomes occurred.

In this chapter, we elaborate on these themes as we outline an attributional approach to emotional life in the classroom. The chapter begins with a brief overview of causal attributions and their underlying properties, guided by attribution theory as formulated by Bernard Weiner (see reviews in Weiner, 1986, 1995, 2006). In the second section, we review research on the emotions most closely associated with attributions and their properties. As with most *Handbook* chapters, we aim for breadth rather than depth, and we acknowledge that we cannot do justice to a number of attribution-related emotions that have rich empirical literatures in their own right. Because emotions begin to have an impact early in life, in the third section, we examine developmental research on attribution-related emotions. In the fourth section, we turn to the larger racial/ethnic context of American schools as we ask whether an attributional approach to emotions can shed light on some of the unique challenges faced by racial and ethnic minority youth. We conclude the chapter by acknowledging some of the unanswered questions elicited by an attributional perspective.

ATTRIBUTION THEORY

Figure 6.1a and 6.1b show the main principles of an attributional theory of motivation and emotion. Think of the linkages as a temporal sequence that begins with an outcome interpreted as a success or failure. The first reaction is likely to be feelings akin to happiness following success and sadness following failure. Attribution theorists label happiness and sadness as outcome-dependent/attribution independent emotions. They are immediate and can be quite intense depending on the importance of the outcome, but they are not evoked by causal thoughts.

Causal Attributions

Following these outcome-based emotions, individuals may then undertake a causal search to determine why success or failure occurred. Attributions are answers to *why* questions, such as "Why I did I fail the exam?" when the motivational domain is achievement or "Why wasn't I invited to the party?" when the motivational domain is affiliation. Attributions are ubiquitous in everyday life, and people ask why questions about other people as well as themselves. As we were writing this chapter, for example, the American public was still riveted by the lethal school shooting in Newtown, Connecticut that left 20 young children and 6 adults dead. Most of the discourse associated with this horrific crime implicitly or explicitly asked *why*. Was the perpetrator mentally ill? Was he a victim of bullying? Were guns too readily available? As all of our examples illustrate, individuals especially make attributions about themselves and about other people following negative

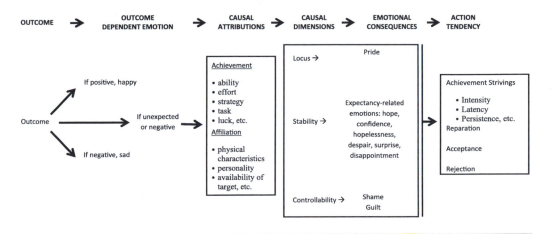

Figure 6.1a Partial representation of an intrapersonal attribution theory of motivation and emotion: Self-directed emotions.

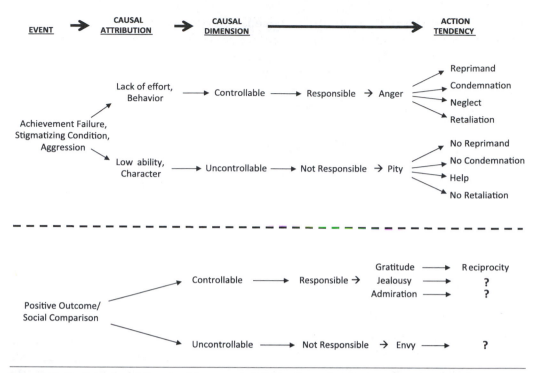

Figure 6.1b Partial representation of an interpersonal attribution theory of motivation and emotion: Other-directed emotions.

or unexpected outcomes (Gendolla & Koller, 2001). In general, negative events carry more weight than positive events (Taylor, 1991), and when they are unexpected, causal search can help us impose order on an unpredictable environment. It should therefore come as no surprise that more of the emotions amenable to an attributional analysis are negative rather than positive.

Causal search can lead to an infinite number of causes. In the achievement domain, which has served as a model for the study of causality in other contexts, Figure 6.1a shows that success and failure often are attributed to an ability factor that includes both aptitude and acquired skills, an effort factor that can be either temporary or sustained, the difficulty of the task, luck, mood, and help or hindrance from others. Among these causal ascriptions, in Western culture at least, ability and effort are the most dominant perceived causes of success and failure. When explaining one's own achievement outcomes or those of other people, individuals attach the most importance to their perceived competence and how hard they try. As we will demonstrate, understanding the conceptual distinctions between ability and effort, or *can* and *want*, as attributions about oneself or other people provides insight into a number of important emotions experienced in school contexts.

Causal Dimensions

Because attributional content will vary between motivational domains as well as between individuals within a domain, attribution theorists have focused on the underlying properties of causes in addition to specific causes per se. Three such properties, labeled causal dimensions, have been identified. These are *locus,* or whether a cause is internal or external to the individual; *stability,* which designates a cause as constant or varying over time; and *controllability,* or whether a cause is subject to volitional influence. A possible fourth dimension identified by learned helplessness theorists has been labeled *globality,* or the extent to which a cause generalizes across many or few situations (Abramson, Seligman, & Teasdale, 1978). For attribution theorists, however, globality (cross-situational consistency) is subsumed under the stability dimension (cross-time consistency).

All causes theoretically are classified into one of the eight cells of a locus X stability X controllability dimensional matrix. For example, ability is typically perceived as internal, stable, and uncontrollable. When we attribute our failure to low ability, we tend to see this as a characteristic of ourselves, enduring over time, and beyond personal control. Effort, on the other hand, is also internal but unstable and controllable. Failure attributed to insufficient effort indicates a personal characteristic that is modifiable by one's own volitional behavior. Whereas an older motivation literature from social learning theory merged the locus and controllability dimensions to describe individuals who are internal and external on locus of control (see Rotter, 1966), the conceptual distinctions between these two dimensions are very important in attribution theory. Both ability and effort are internal causes, but they differ on controllability. Thus, a cause may be internal to the person but quite uncontrollable.

Causal attributions about others are subject to the same dimensional analysis. For example, others' efforts tend to be judged as controllable by them, and their low abilities as uncontrollable. However, we prefer the label *responsibility* when referring to perceived controllability in others; this better captures the naïve understanding of the construct when applied to other-perception rather than self-perception. Individuals typically view their own outcomes as personally controllable or not, whereas they tend to hold others responsible or not for what they do.

Each causal dimension is uniquely linked to a set of emotional and behavioral consequences, some of which are also depicted in Figures 6.1a and 6.1b. We divide these linkages into attributions about oneself and self-directed emotions (e.g., pride and shame) and attributions about other people and emotions directed toward others (e.g., pity and anger). One strength of an attributional approach to emotions is that we study the psychology of emotions (how I feel about myself) and the social psychology of emotions (how I feel about other people) with the same unifying constructs. Note also that many of these emotions have behavioral consequences, or action tendencies. From an attributional perspective, causal thoughts determine feelings, and feelings, in turn, guide behavior. The study of thinking-feeling-action sequences is at the heart of attribution theory.

ATTRIBUTIONS AND SELF-DIRECTED EMOTIONS

Causal Locus and Esteem-Related Emotions

The locus dimension is related to self-esteem and esteem-related emotions. We have greater self-esteem and feel more pride when we can attribute our successes to internal causes, including ability and effort, than to external causes, such as good luck or unusual help from others. Similarly, we can maintain self-esteem when failures are attributed to external rather than internal causes. One of the most well-documented phenomena in all of attribution research is the hedonic bias, or the tendency to take credit for success and to blame failure on external causes (Miller & Ross, 1975). When students display a hedonic bias, they are making use of the locus–esteem relation.

Some researchers using attributional concepts are distinguishing between two distinct types of pride (Tracy & Robins, 2007). *Authentic* pride follows attributions for success to effort ("I won because I practiced") whereas *hubristic* pride follows self-ascriptions to ability ("I won because I'm really smart") (see Oades-Sese, Matthews, & Lewis, 2014). This latter form of pride bears close resemblance to narcissism and may not even be a positive emotion. Attribution theorists, however, have not made these finer distinctions between different types of pride because both would be elicited by internal attributions.

Pride is often associated with meeting or exceeding some standard of excellence through one's own actions and being recognized for those accomplishments (e.g., Mascolo & Fischer, 1995). Feelings of pride may therefore be intensified when there is an audience. For teachers, the child's need for recognition creates a delicate balance between publically praising and rewarding students for their achievements in order to promote feelings of pride and the possibility that such feedback might backfire and actually undermine esteem-related affect. A number of attribution studies with children and young adults have documented that praise for success at relatively easy tasks can lead to an inference of low ability and decrements in esteem-related affect (see review in Graham, 1990). Because ability and effort are perceived as compensatory causes of achievement in Western culture (high effort often implies low ability), and because high effort tends to be rewarded, it is possible that students can interpret too much praise—especially if others do not receive the same feedback—as evidence that they lack ability. Other motivation theorists working in the theories of intelligence tradition (e.g., Kamins & Dweck, 1999) and the intrinsic motivation tradition (e.g., Haimovitz & Corpus, 2011) have also documented that praise directed toward ability or effort can affect children's esteem-related affect and achievement strivings in unexpected ways. In their view, the direct focus on effort rather than ability (or *process praise* versus *person praise*) enhances self-worth and performance. The central message of our analysis is that pride can only be experienced when a success is attributed to internal causes. The main internal causes of achievement are ability and effort, but the relative strength of these two attributions in any given context as communicated by teacher praise will shape the experience of pride.

Causal Stability and Expectancy-Related Emotions

The stability dimension is related to expectancy for future success or failure; this linkage is a strong one in attribution theory (Weiner, 1986). Unstable causes for failure, such as a temporary illness or bad luck, allow us to maintain the belief that the failure need not occur again, whereas stable causes for failure, whether internal (e.g., low intelligence) or external (e.g., poverty) lead to the expectation that failure will be chronic. Attribution researchers believe that differences between ability and effort on the stability dimension, rather than the controllability dimension, account for expectancy increments and decrements (see Graham & Brown, 1988). As shown in Figure 6.1a, hopefulness and confidence are the emotions related to high expectations for future success in contrast to hopelessness and despair, which are emotions related to low expectations for success and high expectations for failure. Expectancies affect subsequent performance mainly because they influence how hard people are willing to try and how long they are willing to persist. Expectancy-related emotions mediate these expectancy-to-performance linkages.

Although it is not difficult to imagine the student with such low expectations for future success that she or he disengages from school, research on the linkage between hopeless-related emotions and achievement strivings is lacking (see Pekrun, Goetz, Frenzel, Barchfeld, & Perry, 2011 for an exception). The closest theoretical literature comes from clinical psychology and the hopelessness model of depression (Abramson, Metalsky, & Alloy, 1989). According to this formulation, hopelessness occurs when people attribute important negative outcomes to stable and global causes. The emotions associated with hopelessness depression include sadness, apathy, and low self-worth, and the behaviors that follow are passivity and withdrawal. Attributions for negative outcomes to unstable and specific causes lead to a more temporary state that Abramson et al. (1989) refer to as pessimism. Thus, if someone complains that "I feel hopeless" versus "I feel pessimistic," the inference would be that the cause of the negative outcomes that produced these feelings states differ on stability (and globality). Like attribution theory, it is the stability dimension and its relation to expectancy rather than the locus dimension that leads to hopelessness. While achievement failure is a type of negative outcome that can result in hopelessness depression, tests of the model in academic contexts are more conceptual than empirical at this point in time (see review in Au, Watkins, Hattie, & Alexander, 2009).

Unexpected outcomes also have emotional consequences. Success when failure was expected could generate surprise followed by relief, just as failure when success was expected will likely give rise to disappointment. For example, Marshall and Brown (2006) examined emotional reactions of high- and low-expectancy students to manipulated success or failure on a novel laboratory task. High-expectancy students reported more surprise and disappointment following failure than did low-expectancy students. Low-expectancy students were only surprised when they succeeded. However, they did not report increased confidence or esteem-related affect, suggesting that they realized that the causes of their success were unstable.

Causal Controllability: Shame Versus Guilt

The controllability dimension allows attribution theorists to make a distinction between shame and guilt. Like pride, shame and guilt are self-conscious emotions: They require self-awareness, self-representation ("it's *me*"), and self-evaluation as to whether the person lived up to a given standard, value, or goal (Tracy & Robins, 2006). In attribution terms, all three emotions therefore are linked to causal locus. As negative emotions, however, shame and guilt differ on the important dimension of controllability, which makes the distinction between ability and effort again important. Shame follows an attribution for failure to an internal and uncontrollable cause, such as low ability, while guilt follows an attribution for failure to an internal and controllable cause, such as lack of effort. Some emotion theorists also distinguish shame and guilt according to the degree to which the causes of failure implicate the self versus a specific behavior: We experience shame when the focus is on who we are and guilt when the focus is on what we did (Tangney, Stuewig, & Mashek, 2007). The experience of shame, then, is thought to be more painful than the experience of guilt. Shame and guilt are less theoretically linked to causal stability and expectancy, although repeated experiences of shame are likely to give way to hopelessness.

The distinct attributional antecedents of shame and guilt indicate that these emotions have very different motivational consequences. Shame, often accompanied by embarrassment or humiliation if the failure is public, is linked to withdrawal, disengagement, and the desire to be invisible. As one respondent disclosed when interviewed about what it is like to feel shame: "Shame is, like, give me a hole to crawl into. Let me just cover myself up and nobody can see me . . . shame is just total—you want to disappear" (Lindsay-Hartz, de Rivera, & Mascolo, 1995, p. 280). There are many studies in the achievement literature documenting that shame is the dominant emotional reaction to failure attributed to internal uncontrollable causes (e.g., Hareli & Weiner, 2002; Weiner, 1986). There are few studies, however, that examine a complete thinking-feeling-action sequence documenting that feelings of shame are directly predictive of a decline in achievement strivings. To the contrary, some models of achievement emotions propose that shame can actually increase achievement strivings by motivating students to avoid future failure (e.g., Pekrun, 2006; Turner & Schallert, 2001). However, it unclear in these models whether the causal antecedents of the emotion labeled as shame are actually internal and uncontrollable.

Linked to controllable causes, guilt is a moral emotion evoking notions of "ought" and "should," as when students lament that they should have tried harder or they ought to study more. For example, in our own research in which we asked children to recall a time that they experienced guilt, one 11-year-old disclosed: "I felt guilty when I didn't turn in my homework because I was too lazy to do it" (Graham, Doubleday, & Guarino, 1984). In attribution studies that manipulate the causes of failure and ask respondents how they would feel, guilt is the dominant reported emotion when the perceived cause is lack of effort or other factors perceived as personally controllable (see Peterson & Schreiber, 2012 for a recent review and empirical examples).

Guilt also has clear motivational consequences or action tendencies. As an emotion following moral "failure," there is a desire to make amends or set the record straight by taking personal responsibility for one's actions. Thus, guilt, unlike shame, is hypothesized to be a motivator of achievement strivings, propelled by the desire for corrective action. In the social domain, guilt can also be the motivator to repair damaged relationships. The skilled social perceiver, motivated by guilt, may offer an apology accepting responsibility for a transgression in order to gain forgiveness (Weiner, 2006). Later in this chapter, we discuss research on impression management strategies that help individuals manage the thoughts and feelings that others have about them.

PERCEIVED RESPONSIBILITY AND OTHER-DIRECTED EMOTIONS

The emotions reviewed above, although intrapersonal, also have interpersonal components in that they are partly shaped by the inferred reactions of others. For example, children may feel especially proud of their successes when their parents see how hard they have tried or especially humiliated when classmates see them fail despite high effort (implying low ability). In this section, we turn to a set of attribution-related emotions that are specifically interpersonal because they are directed toward other people in response to the perceived causes of their outcomes.

Pity and Anger

As Figure 6.1b shows, pity and anger following negative outcomes are linked to perceived controllability in other people. Here the perceiver asks: Is the person responsible? Was it his or her fault? Are there responses in the person's repertoire that could have altered the outcome? Judgments about responsibility then lead to other-directed emotions, such as pity and anger. Perceivers feel pity or sympathy toward a person whose failure is caused by uncontrollable causes like low ability (think of the teacher's reaction to the mentally handicapped child who struggles academically). In contrast, anger is aroused when another's failure is attributed to controllable causes (consider the teacher's feelings toward the gifted student who never completes assignments). These linkages are not confined to the achievement domain: In fact, they are among the most robust attribution principles documented across multiple domains (Weiner, 1995, 2006). For example, we pity the disabled but feel anger toward the able-bodied who are unwilling to work because they are perceived as responsible for their plight; social stigmas perceived as uncontrollable, such as blindness, Altzheimer's disease, or cancer, elicit pity, whereas controllable stigmas, such as drug addiction and child abuse, rarely elicit sympathy and almost always evoke anger. Anger is therefore a moral emotion, like guilt, that is directed toward someone who is seen to violate the "ought" and "should" of life and is capable of changing his or her behavior. Some stigmatizing conditions elicit disparate emotional reactions from pity to anger because their perceived causes can vary. Perceivers are generally more sympathetic to obese individuals when the cause of their weight status is a medical disorder (e.g., thyroid problems) than when attributed to willful overeating (Brownell & Puhl, 2003), just as persons with mental illness are perceived more sympathetically when the cause is a genetic abnormality rather than moral weakness (Corrigan, Markowitz, Watson, Rowan, & Kubiak, 2003).

Once pity and anger are aroused by perceived controllability in others, Figure 6.1b shows a vast set of interpersonal behaviors that follow, including reward versus punishment, help versus neglect, and prosocial versus antisocial behavior. Anger is more likely to result in punishment, neglect, and aggression or retaliation. Pity, on the other hand, is more likely to be followed by help or other prosocial gestures. Pity and anger are therefore the bridge between causal thinking and behavior. A recent meta-analysis of more than 60 studies and over 12,000 participants tested the predicted uncontrollability → pity → helping and controllability → anger → aggression sequences (Rudolph, Roesch, Greutemeyer, & Weiner, 2004). Both sequences were supported, with somewhat stronger evidence of the mediational role of sympathy than anger.

All of these phenomena are relevant to events that take place in classrooms and schools. The perceivers might be teachers making controllability attributions and responsibility inferences about their students' academic performance or peers making similar causal judgments about the social behavior of classmates who have stigmatizing conditions. We illustrate these attribution principles in three distinct domains.

Indirect Low-Ability Cues

When a teacher attributes student failure to lack of effort, the student is perceived as responsible, anger is elicited, and punishment or reprimand is meted out. In contrast, when failure is attributed to low aptitude, the student is perceived as not responsible, pity is aroused, and help may be offered. Now suppose a teacher does respond with pity as opposed to anger toward a failing student or with an unsolicited offer of help rather than neglect. It might be the case that the student will then use these affective and behavioral displays to infer why they failed. In a study that manipulated failure on a novel puzzle-solving task, sixth-grade failing students who received pity from an experimenter posing as a teacher were more likely to attribute their failure on the task to low ability, whereas students who received feedback that communicated anger were more likely to report lack of effort as the cause of failure (Graham, 1984). Using a methodology of observed rather than experienced failure to study unsolicited help, Graham and Barker (1990) had 6 to 12 year olds watch a videotape of two students working on a challenging achievement task, where one of the students was offered unsolicited help from the teacher. All participants perceived the helped student to be lower in ability than the student who was not helped. Thus, unsolicited help, like pity, can function as a low-ability cue. Earlier we suggested that praise for success at an easy task might also have this ability-implicating function. Note that the teacher who communicates pity (by helping or praising too much) can promote low ability attributions and feelings of shame in the student, just as the teacher who communicates anger (by withholding help and easy praise) can elicit low effort attributions and feelings of guilt in the student. Attribution principles about self-directed and other-directed emotions are closely interrelated.

Peer-Directed Aggression

Causal controllability and responsibility inferences have been prominent in the peer aggression literature. One very robust finding in the literature is that aggressive children display a *hostile attributional bias* to over-attribute negative intent to others, particularly in situations of ambiguously caused provocation (Dodge, Coie, & Lyman, 2006). To illustrate, imagine a situation where a student experiences a negative outcome, such as being pushed by a peer while waiting in line, and it is unclear whether the peer's behavior was intended or not. When asked whether the peer's action was hostile or benign, aggressive youth are more likely than their nonaggressive counterparts to infer that the push occurred "on purpose." Attributions to hostile intent (the person is responsible) then lead to anger and the desire to retaliate (e.g., Graham, Hudley, & Williams, 1992). If such attributions instigate a set of reactions that lead to aggression, then it should be possible to train aggressive-prone students to see ambiguous peer provocation as unintended. This should mitigate anger as well as the tendency to react with hostility. Hudley and Graham (1993) developed a six-week school-based attribution intervention for fourth to sixth grade boys labeled as aggressive. The intervention was designed to both strengthen aggressive boys' ability to accurately detect responsibility in others and increase the accessibility of attributions to nonresponsibility in ambiguously caused social predicaments. Later refinements incorporated a greater repertoire of social skills and more diverse populations. Across this series of studies, the intervention led to reductions in attributional bias and improved teacher ratings of social behavior, both concurrently and longitudinally (see review in Hudley, 2008).

Impression Management Strategies

Attribution principles about pity and anger also get expressed in the domain of impression management (Weiner, 1995, 2006). Impression management involves the individual shaping his or her responses in order to be viewed positively by others. A good example of impression management skills occurs in the domain of account giving. Accounts are explanations or reasons for social transgressions, and they include apology (confession), excuses, justifications, and denials (Scott & Lyman, 1968). Everyday expressions like "Excuse me, but . . ." or "What I meant was . . ." are examples of accounts that have the potential to remediate social predicaments. Effective account giving following a transgression protects relationships and helps individuals present themselves in a more favorable light. By shifting causal responsibility away from the self if there is a legitimate excuse, accounts have the potential to reduce anger and hostility from others. When guilt for a transgression is evident, transgressors who acknowledge responsibility and apologize for their misdeeds are more likely to evoke forgiveness (rather than anger) from the offended person than are individuals who deny wrongdoing.

Strategic account giving is clearly an important social skill, but there is not much evidence on how children in school settings effectively use accounts to manage others' impressions of them (see Darby & Schlenker, 1982, for an early example). More recent research suggests that aggressive boys have poor understanding of accounts. Graham, Weiner, and Benesh-Weiner (1995) reported that aggressive boys were less likely than nonaggressive boys to accept (honor) an apology from a remorseful peer or to recognize that perceivers are less angry when excuses for transgressions are uncontrollable. This limited understanding of accounts is not surprising given the hostile attributional bias that also is characteristic of aggressive youth. We are currently implementing a new attributional intervention with aggressive boys that includes training in the adaptiveness of accepting responsibility for one's misdeeds (apology) and honoring the accounts of others by showing greater forgiveness (Graham, Taylor, & Hudley, 2013).

Gratitude and Other Controllability-Related Emotions

From an attributional perspective, we feel grateful to others when they help us by their own volition—their actions are controllable by them. Having been ordered by the teacher to help a classmate finish a difficult assignment or required by the coach to select a classmate for the team will not elicit gratitude from that classmate. The motives of the benefactor are also relevant: The student who volunteers to help the classmate who is struggling just to win brownie points from the teacher is more likely to elicit indebtedness than gratitude (Watkins, Scheer, Ovnicek, & Kolts, 2006). The action tendency associated with feeling grateful is the desire to reciprocate the benefactor's good deed. In one experimental demonstration, participants were more likely to give a larger reward to an unseen fictitious "partner" in a resource distribution task if they were told that the partner had voluntarily given them a large reward compared to when they received the same reward by chance (Tsang, 2006). Although gratitude is associated with these prosocial tendencies, the experience of being helped even when the benefactor has good intentions does not always result in a positive emotion. Following success on a novel achievement task in which an unseen experimenter provided hints to the participant, Chow and Lowery (2010) reported that participants only felt grateful to their unseen benefactor if they had some personal responsibility for success on the novel task (e.g., the possibility to experience pride). Such findings underscore the complexity of emotional life when viewed from an attributional perspective and again illustrate the close intersection between other-directed and self-directed emotions. Even emotions that theoretically are other-directed and depend on perceived responsibility of others can have implications for self-directed emotions, especially in evaluative contexts where self-representations are salient.

Envy, admiration, and jealousy are three emotions relatively new to an attributional analysis (Hareli & Weiner, 2002; Weiner, 2007). Each is precipitated by an upward social comparison in which another person has something that the actor does not have and, by implication, wants. Hareli and Weiner (2002) propose that envy occurs when the actor covets qualities that are uncontrollable by the target, such as high aptitude. This causal argument is supported by research with gifted students who report that peers envy their intellectual talents (Masse & Gagne, 2002). Admiration, in contrast, is hypothesized to occur when actors compare themselves to others who have desired qualities that are controllable, such as high effort. Some emotion researchers have proposed that mild envy can coexist with admiration of the same person, suggesting that the attributional interpretation may be in need of refinement (see Miceli & Castelfranchi, 2007).

Finally, jealousy most often involves a triad: The jealous person feels that his or her favored position with a third party has been lost or jeopardized due to the behavior of the person who is the target of jealousy (Parrott & Smith, 1993). For example, Sarah may be jealous of Erica because *she* is now the teacher's classroom aide, a position Sarah had previously. Jealousy thus involves competition over a cherished good. Jealousy is more intense when the rival (Erica) is perceived to have engaged in some behavior to intentionally gain access to that cherished good (Miceli & Castelfranchi, 2007). From an attributional perspective, we feel jealous of our rivals whose behaviors to supplant us are controllable by them. The link to controllable versus uncontrollable causes is one of the theoretical distinctions between envy and jealousy.

There are rich individual literatures about the emotions of admiration, envy, and jealousy that are far beyond the scope of this chapter. We believe that these are emotions often experienced in the classroom, although the needed empirical studies of thinking-feeling-action sequences in actual achievement settings have not been carried out. Especially lacking are studies of the action tendencies associated with these emotions (hence the question marks in Figure 6.1b). It is evident that envy and jealousy in particular are most likely elicited in classrooms where competition and social comparison are heightened. The context will also shape the behavioral tendencies that follow each emotion—whether to denigrate the targets of envy and jealousy or strive for self-improvement.

Summary

A taxonomy of attribution-mediated emotions and their action tendencies was presented in this section. For self-directed emotions, causal thoughts about locus (pride), stability (e.g., hopelessness, surprise), and controllability (shame and guilt) in part determine particular feeling states. Other-directed emotions of pity, anger, and gratitude and a set of social comparison emotions (envy, jealousy, admiration) are elicited by attributions about the perceived controllability of others' behavior. Most of these emotions are also linked to particular action tendencies. The most robust findings involve perceived uncontrollability-pity-desire to help (going toward) versus perceived controllability-anger-desire to punish (going against). Emotions therefore have motivational significance: they summarize the past and provide direction for the future.

DEVELOPMENT OF ATTRIBUTION-RELATED EMOTIONS

Our naïve understanding of classroom emotional life tells us that even young children display at least some of the emotions that are linked to causal thoughts. At what point in development, we might ask, do children come to experience and understand the meaning of attribution-mediated emotions? Within the general field of emotion development, there are substantial literatures on the development of the self-conscious emotions of pride, shame, and guilt, tied largely to children's emerging self-representational abilities, awareness of an external standard against which their behavior can be evaluated, and display of facial expressions and postural gestures associated with particular emotions (Lagattuta & Thompson, 2007; Lewis, 2007; Stipek, 1995). Such research documents the relatively early experience of at least rudimentary forms of pride, shame, and guilt between two and three years of age.

The attributional perspective on emotional development is much more tied to children's emergent causal thinking and their growing awareness of the complexity of emotional life. Our basic position is that causal thoughts precede or change the experience of particular emotions. Therefore, developmental changes in the experience or understanding of these emotions are due to age-related changes in the understanding of attribution-emotion linkages (see Weiner & Graham, 1984). We have studied these linkages in children ranging in age between 4 and 12 years. We do this in two ways. In some studies, we ask participants to describe a time when they felt a particular emotion, state the cause, and then rate that cause on the relevant causal dimensions. In other studies, children are presented with vignettes about a story character experiencing an emotion-eliciting outcome (e.g., success on a test), and the cause of the outcome is manipulated. Respondents then report the likelihood that the target emotion would be experienced and particular actions would be undertaken.

Pride, Guilt, and Gratitude

The attribution-emotion linkages involving pride, guilt, and gratitude develop with age. In one pertinent study (Graham, 1988), 5- to 11-year-old children, tested individually, were presented with three scenarios involving exam success (pride story), a bicycle collision (guilt story), and making a baseball team (gratitude story). Two different story conditions varied the locus of the cause of exam success in the pride story and the controllability of the cause in the guilt and gratitude stories. For example, the pride story described a boy (girl) named Chris who got an "A" on the test either because he studied all the words (internal) or because the teacher gave a very easy test (external). The guilt story described a boy or girl (all stories matched the gender of the respondent) who crashed into another child on his bicycle and caused damage to the other child's bike either because he was doing tricks in a crowded section (controllable) or made a quick stop to avoid hitting a small child (uncontrollable). And the gratitude study involved getting selected to be on the baseball team by the team captain either because the captain wanted to (controllable) or because he had no choice (uncontrollable). For each story condition, respondents rated how much of the target emotion the story child would experience.

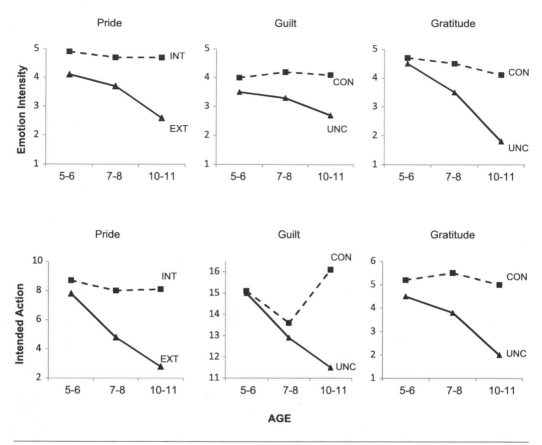

Figure 6.2 The development of attribution-emotion-action tendencies involving pride, guilt, and gratitude (data from Graham, 1988).

The top panels of Figure 6.2 display the emotion data for the three scenarios. Even though all children indicated some awareness that emotions varied in the two causal conditions, as children grew older, pride was less elicited by externality, and guilt and gratitude were less evoked given an uncontrollable cause. For the youngest children, the three emotions function more like outcome-dependent than attribution-dependent emotions (see Kornilaki & Chlouverakis, 2004, for a similar developmental pattern in feelings of pride).

To examine action tendencies (the motivational role of emotion), respondents also rated the likelihood that the story child would engage in a particular action theoretically linked to the emotion: self-reward in the pride story, repairing the person's bike in the guilt scenario, and reciprocation (giving a gift to the team captain) in the gratitude story. The bottom panel of Figure 6.2 displays the action tendency in each causal condition for the three scenarios. These age-related trends were very consistent with those documented for the emotions. The youngest participants were equally likely to reward themselves, make amends, or reciprocate in the two causal conditions. Correlational analyses revealed that the relations between causal thinking, feeling, and acting increased with age for all of the emotions. As children get older, more of the relation between what they think and how they intend to behave can be accounted for by how they feel.

Pity and Anger

We have conducted several developmental studies on the linkages involving pity, anger, and perceived controllability in others. Across every study, children as young as age five clearly understand that anger follows attributions to controllability. The pity-uncontrollability linkages have proven to show more interesting developmental change. For example, when the context is achievement, six year olds did not seem to make the connection between a teacher "feeling sorry for" a student (pity) and an attribution to low ability (Weiner, Graham, Stern, & Lawson, 1982). We reasoned that children of this age do not yet understand the causal properties of low ability—that it is a stable and uncontrollable cause (see Nichols, 1978). On the other hand, using a stimulated recall method, when we asked children to describe a time when they felt sorry for someone, 6 year olds were just as likely as 11 year olds to describe incidents for which the person was not responsible and to accurately rate the cause on controllability, operationalized as "made it happen-could not stop it from happening" (Graham et al., 1984). Therefore, it is not so much the uncontrollability-pity linkage that is changing with age, but the particular context in which it is expressed. When the context for experiencing the emotion is familiar and the eliciting thoughts are judged as uncontrollable, six year olds have the same understanding of pity as do older children and adults.

How young can we go? Graham and Hoehn (1995) tested pity-anger-(un)controllability linkages with four, five, and six year olds in the context of judgments about social stigmas. These young children were presented with simple scenarios describing two children, one of whom was socially isolated/shy (e.g., "This is Fred. He is usually alone. He doesn't play with the other kids very much.") or aggressive (e.g., "This is Max. He starts fights over nothing and gets in trouble a lot."). For each vignette, children made judgments about perceived responsibility ("does he act this way on purpose"), emotional reactions toward the person ("feel sorry for" and "mad"), and behavioral intentions ("would you be his friend?") on five-point scales. Extensive pilot testing was carried out to make the stimuli appropriate for the youngest participants (Graham & Hoehn, 1995, Study 2).

The data for each age group on the four attribution-related variables are shown in Figure 6.3. By age five, but not age four, children are quite skilled at making these judgments in ways consistent with attribution theory. The aggressive child is perceived as more responsible for his behavior, elicits more anger and less pity, and tends to be rejected. The shy child is perceived as not responsible for his shyness, elicits less anger and more pity, and the intention to form a friendship. These patterns are very similar to what we see in adult studies on social stigma (Weiner, 1995, 2006). At a surprisingly early age, if the context is familiar, children do understand the meaning of responsibility and its everyday operational definition (e.g., "on purpose," "meant to," "should have"), and they are capable of using this understanding to organize their thinking about the behavior of others and make decisions about how to interact with those peers.

Summary

In this section, we described the growing understanding of many of the emotions that are elicited by causal thinking. Children understand the causal meaning of anger and pity by about age five. Understanding the self-directed emotions of pride and guilt and the other-directed emotion of gratitude emerges more gradually over middle childhood; during

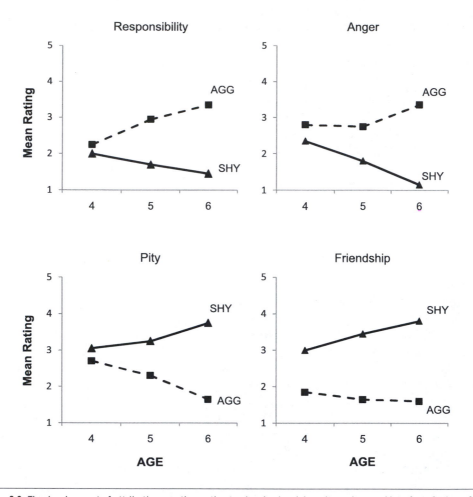

Figure 6.3 The development of attribution-emotion-action tendencies involving pity and anger (data from Graham & Hoehn, 1995).

early childhood, these emotions appear to be understood more as outcome-dependent, attribution-independent feeling states. It is not that young children are incapable of feeling proud, guilty, or grateful. Rather, the attributional interpretation is that these emotions are less cognitively complex at younger ages. Like outcome-dependent emotions, they may therefore be intense but more fleeting. There is no developmental attribution research that we know of on the social comparison emotions of envy, admiration, and jealousy. Given all the situations that can elicit these emotions in everyday life, we see this as an important direction for future research on emotional development from an attributional perspective.

THE CHALLENGES OF RACIAL/ETHNIC MINORITY YOUTH

The forces of immigration are redefining the racial/ethnic landscape of countries throughout the world. In the United States, for example, Latinos are the largest racial/ethnic group, and Asians are the fastest growing group. If these trends continue—

and there is every reason to think that they will, given immigration that is primarily non-White—within a generation, White students will no longer be the numerical majority in American schools, and public schools will be the first institution in this country without a majority of any one racial/ethnic group (Orfield & Lee, 2007). This growing diversity raises concerns about the ability of the public school system to meet the needs of ethnically diverse students. The achievement gap between different racial/ethnic groups is as entrenched as ever. African American and Latino students, particularly Black males, continue to lag behind Whites in the same grade on just about every indicator of educational attainment (NCES, 2012). Explanations for the achievement gap are complex, involving historical, cultural, structural, and individual factors. We make no attempt to take them on in this chapter. Instead, we want to call attention to a few attribution principles raised in this chapter that are relevant to understanding racial achievement disparities.

Attributions to Discrimination by Stigmatized Groups

The causal locus-to-self-esteem linkage has relevance to attributions to discrimination among socially stigmatized groups. By social stigma, we mean individuals who possess a social identity that is devalued in the eyes of others (Goffman, 1963). Among the prominent social stigmas are being a racial/ethnic minority, a sexual minority, obese, or mentally ill (Crocker, Major, & Steele, 1998). One of the most paradoxical findings in the social stigma literature is that stigmatized groups, such as African Americans, are able to maintain high self-esteem despite their low status in the larger society. In comparative racial research on motivation, for example, it is well-documented that African American youth report levels of self-esteem that are equal to or higher than that of their White counterparts, even when their achievement outcomes are much lower (see Graham, 1994; Twenge & Crocker, 2002).

What accounts for such high self-esteem even when there are pervasive achievement disparities? In an influential theoretical review, Crocker and Major (1989) drew on attribution research (and the locus-esteem linkage) to argue that attributing negative outcomes, including school failure, to external causes, such as the prejudice of others, is an important self-protective mechanism that members of stigmatized groups use to maintain their self-esteem. A number of laboratory-experimental studies that followed the Crocker and Major review supported that attributional analysis (see review in Major & Sawyer, 2009). On the other hand, there is a growing literature also documenting that perceived discrimination can take its toll on the mental and academic health of members of stigmatized groups (e.g., Benner & Graham, in press), suggesting that other causal appraisals might also be elicited. Cumulative experiences with discrimination, even when prejudiced others are blamed and one's self-esteem is intact, can lead to hopelessness and diminished motivation if the unfair treatment is expected to be chronic. Hence, the stability dimension may be at least as important as the locus dimension in explaining reactions to discrimination. We believe that attributions for failure to stable causes are probably more powerful predictors of academic disengagement for stigmatized youth than are attributions to locus and ensuing esteem-related affect (see van Laar, 2000). Thus, intervention approaches aimed directly at raising the self-esteem of stigmatized youth without impacting expectancy and expectancy-related emotions are probably misguided.

Indirect Low-Ability Cues

We reviewed research indicating that teachers can indirectly communicate low-ability cues via such behaviors and emotional reactions as praise for success at an easy task, unsolicited help, and displays of pity or sympathy following student failure. A number of principles from attribution theory about the causal determinants of pity and anger helped explained these findings. These ability cues communicated by teachers are believed to be unintended, in as much as the behaviors are often undertaken to protect the self-esteem of failure-prone ethnic minority students (see Graham, 1990). For example, in the teacher expectancy literature, Brophy and Good (1974) observed many years ago that a set of well-documented teacher behaviors toward low-expectancy minority students, such as teaching less difficult material, setting lower mastery levels, and praise for marginal or even incorrect answers, may be motivated, in part, by "excessive sympathy for the student" (p. 311). More contemporary analyses document that African American students receiving feedback on their intellectual abilities might be particularly susceptible to evaluations from authority figures that implicate their ability. In experimental research, for example, Black students reported lower academic self-esteem when they received unsolicited help on an intelligence test from a White confederate than did their African American counterparts who received no such help (Schneider, Major, Luhtanen, & Crocker, 1996). Consistent with our attributional analysis, the authors proposed that help that is not requested can confirm a "suspicion of inferiority" among African Americans who regularly confront the negative stereotypes about their group's intellectual abilities. In a related program of research (Cohen, Steele, & Ross, 1999, Study 1) the motivation of African American students to revise a challenging writing assignment was weaker in a feedback condition of unbuffered praise for performance compared to feedback that communicated criticism and high expectations for improved performance.

We are not arguing that teachers should never help their students or that they should always be angry rather than sympathetic or critical as opposed to complimentary. The appropriateness of any combination of behaviors or the achievement of what Cohen et al. (1999) label as "wise" feedback and the avoidance of what Rattan, Good, and Dweck (2012) label as "comforting" feedback will depend on many factors, including the characteristics of both students and teachers and the importance of the domain. Rather, we simply want to point out that attribution principles can aid our understanding of how some well-intentioned teacher behaviors can negatively impact achievement strivings of African American students and members of other stigmatized groups.

On Intervention Research

A number of recent interventions emerging from social psychology research have increased excitement about the potential of brief, even single-session treatments to increase achievement of African American youth. These interventions utilize constructs such as stereotype threat, theories of intelligence, and self-affirmation to deliver short but powerful treatments that not only boost immediate achievement but also reduce the racial achievement gap (see review in Yeager & Walton, 2011). We are firm believers in theory-guided interventions, and we applaud the social psychologists engaged in new intervention approaches that can better uncover the mechanisms underlying motivational change. However, we are less convinced that changing one set of beliefs—

be it worries about confirming racial stereotypes, entity theories of intelligence, or the importance of affirming personal values—will have lasting effects on motivation and achievement. The attribution principles reviewed in this chapter tell us that effective interventions will need to target changes in the stability and controllability of causal beliefs and their linked emotions. It is surprising to us how little of the achievement change literature—including attribution change programs—addresses emotions despite their known motivational properties. Because school failure and childhood aggression often go hand-in-hand, and both are more prevalent in African American boys (Dodge et al., 2006), we think that interventions need to include methods that can increase the motivation to achieve and decrease the motivation to aggress against others with a unifying conceptual framework. In other words, effective interventions need to target multiple causal beliefs and emotions about oneself and other people while addressing the close intersection between students' academic lives and their social lives (see Graham et al., 2013 for an example). We doubt that this can be achieved with very brief interventions no matter how powerfully they are delivered.

Causal Controllability and Racial Stereotypes

Stereotypes are culturally shared beliefs, both positive and negative, about the characteristics and behaviors of particular groups. Even though beliefs about African Americans have become more positive over the last 50 years, studies of cultural stereotypes continue to show that respondents associate being Black (and male) with hostility, aggressiveness, violence, and danger (e.g., Correll, Park, Judd, & Wittenbrink, 2002). The recent acquittal in Florida of George Zimmerman for the murder of Trayvon Martin, an unarmed Black youth, is a stark reminder of that fact. From an attributional perspective, stereotypes convey information about responsibility for a stigmatizing condition and therefore impact the way stigmatized individuals and the groups to which they belong are treated by others (Reyna, 2000). Moreover, racial stereotypes often are activated and used outside of conscious awareness (e.g., Bargh & Chartrand, 1999). By automatically categorizing people according to cultural stereotypes, perceivers can quickly make responsibility inferences, express their anger, and mete out punishment without using up their limited social information processing capacities.

In our own attribution research, one of us has been particularly interested in the consequences of negative racial stereotypes about African American adolescent males (Graham & Lowery, 2004). Using a priming methodology with police officers and probation officers in the juvenile justice system, Graham and Lowery (2004) examined the unconscious activation of racial stereotypes about adolescent males and their attributional consequences. Participants in whom racial stereotypes were unconsciously primed judged a hypothetical adolescent offender as more dangerous, responsible, and blameworthy for his alleged offense and more deserving of harsh punishment than participants in an unprimed control condition.

We believe that such findings also have implications for decision makers in our schools who make judgments about the social (mis)behavior of African American youth. Reviews of Zero Tolerance and related "get tough" policies in schools have produced racial disparities in the use of disciplinary practices, such that Black youth are more likely to be suspended or expelled from school than White youth who engage in similar transgressions (APA, 2008). Particularly among perceivers at the front end of a system, like teachers dealing with classroom disorder, decisions often must be made quickly, under conditions of cognitive and emotional overload, and where much ambiguity exists. These are the very conditions that are known to activate unconscious beliefs (Fiske, 1998). The consequences of unconscious racial stereotypes can be lethal. Attributional analyses provide an important framework for examining the stereotypes of even well-intentioned teachers and administrators.

CONCLUSIONS AND A FEW NOT FULLY ANSWERED QUESTIONS

In this final section, we turn to a few unanswered questions in conducting emotion research from an attributional perspective. We have no definitive answer to these questions, and our responses surely reflect our biases. Mainly, we want to acknowledge that we are aware of the questions and our hope that they will stimulate additional research.

Are We Really Studying Emotions?

Many of the studies reported in this chapter used a vignette methodology. Participants read about a hypothetical person who succeeds or fails, the cause of the failure is manipulated, and respondents then rate the likelihood that the person would feel a set of distinct emotions. In a more open-ended but less used method, participants recall a time when they experienced a particular emotion and then describe why they felt that way. All of these methods rely on verbal report of participants about how they once felt or what they or someone else would think, feel, or do if particular conditions were present. The methods do not allow us to examine emotions during their state of activation (see Robinson & Clore, 2002).

As attribution theorists, we draw on the experimental laboratory methods of social psychology; judgment studies that manipulate variables are a core part of those methods. We believe that what individuals (including children) say they would think, feel, or do in a particular situation maps closely onto how they actually think, feel, and behave in real-world contexts. Judgment studies about emotion are also valuable and needed when researchers are developing theory and testing hypotheses about that theory. We doubt that an attributional perspective on emotions that fits within a general theory of motivation would have been possible if researchers had started in the classroom with methods that try to capture feeling states "in the moment." On the other hand, we also resonate to some nonexperimental methods, such as daily diary or event sampling procedures that can be especially powerful for capturing emotional experiences as they unfold in everyday life (Reis & Gosling, 2010). We see this as a method that is very amenable to the study of attribution-mediated emotions in the classroom.

Do Causal Thoughts Always Precede Emotions?

This is the sequence question. The core tenet of the argument presented in this chapter is that causal thoughts determine how someone feels, and feelings, in turn, guide their behavior. But we also know from the more general emotion literature that feeling states influence numerous cognitive processes including selective attention, evaluative judgments, perceptions of risk, and *causal thinking* (see Keltner & Lerner, 2010). In one study, for example, people feeling sad were more likely to attribute ambiguous events to situational causes, whereas those feeling angry attributed the same outcome to the actions of other people (Keltner, Ellsworth, & Edwards, 1993). Emotions, then, can be a filter through which the perceiver may make rapid judgments in situations where there is much ambiguity.

It certainly is plausible that emotions can be antecedents to the causal sequences examined in this chapter. For example, do emotions such as sympathy and anger influence subsequent perceptions of responsibility in others? Does basking in pride bias the degree to which a person makes accurate assessments of their future expectancy of success? Does sadness affect the subjective meaning of attributions to discrimination over time ("maybe it really is something about *me*") such that there is a shift from external to internal causality and decreases in esteem-related affect? The answer to all of these questions is probably *yes*. A logical next step will be to test for bidirectional, cyclical, or cumulative relations over time. Such sequence questions can best be addressed with longitudinal research that tracks within-person change over time in causal beliefs and emotions about self and others. We do not know of any systematic programs of longitudinal research that have examined attribution-emotion sequences over time.

Traits Versus States?

In the literature on causal thinking, researchers have studied attributional traits in the form of attributional style and the tendency to endorse an entity (stable) versus incremental (unstable) theory about intelligence (see Graham & Williams, 2009). Similarly, in the emotion literature, dispositional tendencies to feel a particular way have been studied, and there are well-validated self-report measures of these tendencies (see review in Robins, Noftle, & Tracy, 2007). For example, individuals can be distinguished according to their degree of guilt-proneness and shame-proneness, with the latter trait associated with more negative outcomes (Stuewig & Tangney, 2007).

Attribution theorists are much more focused on the situational determinants of emotion than dispositional tendencies, and we suspect that these tendencies rarely overpower the situation. Once a causal attribution is endorsed, its theoretically linked emotion and action tendency are hypothesized to follow. Emotion traits may partly function as antecedents of attributions, or they may moderate one or more of the linkages in our temporal sequence. Thus, they can shed light on the conditions under which the consequences of causal thinking are strong versus weak. In studying emotions in the classroom with all of its complexity and fluidity, attribution theorists believe that it is more useful to first be guided by general principles of emotion that are robust and only then turn to how those principles vary between individuals or contexts.

What About Culture?

Earlier in the chapter, we made reference to the changing demographics of American society. If almost half of the school-aged population is indeed comprised of racial/ethnic minorities, this raises issues about the cultural universality versus specificity of the attribution-emotion relations examined here. Cross-cultural differences in the expression and meaning of the self-conscious emotions such as pride, shame, and guilt are well documented (e.g., Wong & Tsai, 2007). The comparisons are primarily between collectivist Asian cultures like China and Japan and individualistic cultures as typified by the

United States. For example, pride is less likely to be experienced for personal successes in collectivist societies and more likely to be felt in reaction to the successes of one's close ingroup members. Shame and guilt are less distinguished by attributional determinants in collectivist societies. Shame, in fact, may be a more commonly experienced and less negative emotion in collectivistic cultures because of the belief that self-criticism (self-effacement) is important to healthy development.

Whether these and other cultural determinants of emotion call into question the cross-cultural generality of attribution-emotion linkages is not yet known. If group rather than individual successes determine pride in collectivist cultures or shame functions more like guilt in terms of antecedents and motivational consequences, these are not challenges to basic attribution principles. Rather, the cross-cultural work to date should alert us to conceptualize culture as another important moderator of thinking-feeling-action sequences. Today's multicultural and multiethnic classrooms are ideal settings for conducting such moderation analyses. For the practitioner, such analyses can shed light on the types of self-construals and emotion-eliciting feedback that may be most motivating for particular cultural groups. For attribution theorists, the absence of cultural differences can lead to theory generality, while the presence of differences can lead to theory refinement.

As all of the chapters in this *Handbook* illustrate, the study of students' emotional lives in the classroom is rich and complex. The attributional approach begins with students' and teachers' beliefs about why outcomes occur as a framework for organizing some of that richness and complexity. We acknowledge in this concluding section that there are many unanswered questions in our approach, including the use of self-report of emotions (a methodological issue), whether causal thoughts precede or follow emotional experience (a conceptual issue), and the role of emotional traits, culture, and other individual differences (an empirical question). The *Handbook* chapters also reveal that there are other ways to conceptualize the emotions that fit within an attributional perspective, and some theoretical frameworks might offer different predictions about the function of those same emotions in achievement contexts. We view that as a good sign that the study of everyday experiences of emotions in classrooms and schools is a field with much theoretical vitality.

REFERENCES

Abramson, L. Y., Metalsky, G. I., & Alloy, L. B. (1989). Hopelessness depression: A theory-based subtype of depression. *Psychological Review, 96,* 358–372.

Abramson, L. Y., Seligman, M.E.P., & Teasdale, J. D. (1978). Learned helplessness in humans: Critique and reformulation. *Journal of Abnormal Psychology, 87,* 49–74.

American Psychological Association Zero Tolerance Task Force (APA). (2008). Are zero tolerance policies effective in the schools? Evidentiary review and recommendations. *American Psychologist, 63,* 852–862.

Au, R., Watkins, D., Hattie, J., & Alexander, P. (2009). Reformulating the depression model of learned hopelessness for academic outcomes. *Educational Research Review, 4,* 103–117.

Bargh, J., & Chartrand, T. (1999). The unbearable automaticity of being. *American Psychologist, 54,* 462–479.

Benner, A., & Graham, S. (in press). The antecedents and consequences of racial/ethnic discrimination during adolescence: Does the source of discrimination matter? *Developmental Psychology.*

Brophy, J., & Good, T. (1974). *Teacher-student relationships: Causes and consequences.* New York, NY: Holt, Rinehart, & Winston.

Brownell, K. D., & Puhl, R. M. (2003). Psychosocial origins of obesity stigma: Toward changing a powerful and pervasive bias. *Obesity Reviews, 4,* 213–227.

Chow, R. M., & Lowery, B. S. (2010). Thanks, but no thanks: The role of personal responsibility in the experience of gratitude. *Journal of Experimental Social Psychology, 46,* 487–493.

Cohen, J., Steele, C., & Ross, L. (1999). The mentor's dilemma: Providing critical feedback across the racial divide. *Personality and Social Psychology Bulletin, 25,* 1302–1318.

Correll, J., Park B., Judd, C. M., & Wittenbrink, B. (2002). The police officer's dilemma: Using ethnicity to disambiguate potentially threatening individuals. *Journal of Personality and Social Psychology, 83,* 1314–1329.

Corrigan, P., Markowitz, F. E., Watson, A., Rowan, D., & Kubiak, M. A. (2003). An attribution model of public discrimination towards persons with mental illness. *Journal of Health and Social Behavior, 44,* 162–179.

Crocker, J., & Major, B. (1989). Social stigma and self-esteem: The self-protective properties of stigma. *Psychological Review, 96,* 608–630.

Crocker, J., Major, B., & Steele, C. (1998). Social stigma. In D. Gilbert, S. Fiske, & G. Lindzey (Eds.), *The handbook of social psychology* (Vol. 2, pp, 504–553). Boston, MA: McGraw-Hill.

Darby, B. W., & Schlenker, B. R. (1982). Children's reactions to apologies. *Journal of Personality and Social Psychology, 43,* 742–753.

Dodge, K.A., Coie, J. D., & Lyman, D. (2006). Aggression and antisocial behavior in youth. In N. Eisenberg (Ed.), *Handbook of child psychology. Volume 3: Social, emotional, and personality development* (pp. 719–788). New York, NY: John Wiley.

Fiske, S. T. (1998). Stereotyping, prejudice, and discrimination. In D. T. Gilbert, S. T. Fiske, & G. Lindzey (Eds.) *Handbook of social psychology* (4th ed., pp. 357–411). New York, NY: McGraw-Hill.

Gendolla, G., & Koller, M. (2001). Surprise and causal search: How are they affected by outcome valence and importance? *Motivation and Emotion, 25,* 237–250.

Goffman, E. (1963). *Stigma: Notes on the management of a spoiled identity.* New York, NY: Simon & Schuster.

Graham, S. (1984). Communicating sympathy and anger to black and white children: The cognitive (attributional) antecedents of affective cues. *Journal of Personality and Social Psychology, 47,* 40–54.

Graham, S. (1988). Children's developing understanding of the motivational role of affect: An attributional analysis. *Cognitive Development, 3,* 71–88.

Graham, S. (1990). On communicating low ability in the classroom. In S. Graham & V. Folkes (Eds.), *Attribution theory: Applications to achievement, mental health, and interpersonal conflict* (pp. 17–36). Hillsdale, NJ: Lawrence Erlbaum.

Graham, S. (1994). Motivation in African Americans. *Review of Educational Research, 64,* 55–117.Graham, S., & Barker, G. (1990). The downside of help: An attributional-developmental analysis of help-giving as a low ability cue. *Journal of Educational Psychology, 82,* 7–14.

Graham, S., & Brown, J. (1988). Attributional mediators of expectancy, evaluation, and affect: A response time analysis. *Journal of Personality and Social Psychology, 55,* 873–881.

Graham, S., Doubleday, C., & Guarino, P. (1984). The development of relations between perceived controllability and the emotions of pity, anger, and guilt. *Child Development, 55,* 561–565.

Graham, S., & Hoehn, S. (1995). Children's understanding of aggression and shyness/withdrawal as social stigmas: An attributional analysis. *Child Development, 66,* 1143–1162.

Graham, S., Hudley, C., & Willams, E. (1992). Attributional and emotional determinants of aggression among African-American and Latino early adolescents. *Developmental Psychology, 28,* 731–740.

Graham, S., & Lowery, B. (2004). Priming unconscious racial stereotypes about adolescent offenders. *Law and Human Behavior, 28,* 483–504.

Graham, S., Taylor, A. Z., & Hudley, C. (2013). *A motivational intervention for aggressive African American boys.* Manuscript submitted for publication.

Graham, S., Weiner, B., & Benesh-Weiner, M. (1995). An attributional analysis of the development of excuse giving in aggressive and nonaggressive African-American boys. *Developmental Psychology, 31,* 274–284.

Graham, S., & Williams, C. (2009). An attributional approach to motivation in school. In K. Wentzel & A. Wigfield (Eds.), *Handbook of motivation at school* (pp. 11–33). Hillsdale, NJ: Lawrence Erlbaum.

Haimovitz, K., & Corpus, J. (2011). Effects of person versus process praise on student motivation: Stability and change in emerging adulthood. *Educational Psychology, 31,* 596–609.

Hareli, S., & Weiner, B. (2002). Social emotions and personality inferences: A scaffold for a new direction in the study of achievement motivation. *Educational Psychologist, 37,* 183–193.

Hudley, C. (2008). *You did that on purpose: Understanding and changing children's aggression.* New Haven, CT: Yale University Press.

Hudley, C., & Graham, S. (1993). An attributional intervention with African American boys labeled as aggressive. *Child Development, 64,* 124–138.

Kamins, M. L., & Dweck, C. S. (1999). Praise versus process praise and criticism: Implications for contingent self-worth and coping. *Developmental Psychology, 35,* 835–847.

Keltner, D., Ellsworth, P. C., & Edwards, K. (1993). Beyond simple pessimism: Effects of sadness and anger on social perception. *Journal of Personality and Social Psychology, 64,* 740–752.

Keltner, D., & Lerner, J. S. (2010). Emotion. In S. T. Fiske, D. T. Gilbert, & G. Lindzey (Eds.), *Handbook of social psychology* (5th ed., Vol. 1, pp. 317–352). Hoboken, NJ: John Wiley.

Kornilaki, E. N., & Chlouverakis, G. (2004). The situational antecedents of pride and happiness: Developmental and domain differences. *British Journal of Developmental Psychology, 22,* 605–619.

Lagattuta, K., & Thompson, R. A. (2007). The development of self-conscious emotions: Cognitive processes and social influences. In J. L. Tracy, R. W. Robins, & J. P. Tangney (Eds.), *The self-conscious emotions: Theory and research* (pp. 91–113). New York, NY: Guilford Press.

Lewis, M. (2007). Self-conscious emotional development. In J. L. Tracy, R. W. Robins, & J. P. Tangney (Eds.), *The self-conscious emotions: Theory and research* (pp. 134–149). New York, NY: Guilford Press.

Lindsay-Hartz, J., de Rivera, J., & Mascolo, M. F. (1995). Differentiating guilt and shame and their effects on motivation. In J. P. Tangney & K. W. Fischer (Eds.), *Self-conscious emotions: The psychology of guilt, shame, embarrassment, and pride* (pp. 274–321). New York, NY: Guilford Press.

Marshall, M. A., & Brown, J. D. (2006). Emotional reactions to achievement outcomes: Is it really better to expect the worse? *Cognition and Emotion, 20,* 43–63.

Major, B., & Sawyer, P. J. (2009). Attributions to discrimination: Antecedents and consequences. In T. D. Nelson (Ed.), *Handbook of prejudice, stereotyping, and discrimination* (pp. 89–110). New York, NY: Psychology Press.

Mascolo, M. F., & Fischer, K. W. (1995). Developmental transformations in appraisals for pride, shame, and guilt. In J. P. Tangney & K. W. Fischer (Eds.), *Self-conscious emotions: The psychology of guilt, shame, embarrassment, and pride* (pp. 64–113). New York, NY: Guilford Press.

Masse, L., & Gagne, F. (2002). Gifts and talents as sources of envy in high school settings. *Gifted Child Quarterly, 46,* 15–28.

Miceli, M., & Castelfranchi, C. (2007). The envious mind. *Cognition and Emotion, 21,* 449–479.

Miller, D., & Ross, L. (1975). Self-serving biases in the attribution of causality: Fact or fiction? *Psychological Bulletin, 82,* 213–225.

National Center for Educational Statistics (NCES). (2012). Condition of Education 2012. Retrieved from http://nces.ed.gov/pubs2012/2012045_3.pdf

Nichols, J. G. (1978). The development of the concepts of effort and ability, perception of academic attainment, and the understanding that difficult tasks require more ability. *Child Development, 49,* 800–814.

Oades-Sese, G. V., Matthews, T. A., & Lewis, M. (2014). Shame and pride and their effects on student achievement. In R. Pekrun & L. Linnenbrink-Garcia (Eds.), *International handbook of emotions in education* (pp. 246–264). New York, NY: Taylor & Francis.

Orfield, G., & Lee, C. (2007). *Historic reversals, accelerating resegregation, and the need for new integration strategies.* Los Angeles, CA: The Civil Rights Project.

Parrott, W. G., & Smith, R. H. (1993). Distinguishing the experience of envy and jealousy. *Journal of Personality and Social Psychology, 64,* 906–920.

Pekrun, R. (2006). The control-value theory of achievement emotions: Assumptions, corollaries, and implications for educational theory and practice. *Educational Psychology Review, 18,* 315–341.

Pekrun, R., Goetz, T., Frenzel, A. C., Barchfeld, P., & Perry, R. P. (2011). Measuring emotions in students' learning and performance: The Achievement Emotions Questionnaire (AEQ). *Contemporary Educational Psychology, 36,* 36–48.

Peterson, S. E., & Schreiber, J. B. (2012). Personal and interpersonal motivation for group projects: Replications of an attributional analysis. *Educational Psychology Review, 24,* 287–311.

Rattan, A., Good, V., & Dweck, C. S. (2012). "It's OK—Not everyone can be good at math": Instructors with an entity theory comfort (and demotivate) students. *Journal of Experimental Social Psychology, 48,* 732–737.

Reis, H. T., & Gosling, S. D. (2010). Social psychological methods outside the laboratory. In S. T. Fiske, D. T. Gilbert, & G. Lindzey (Eds.), *Handbook of social psychology* (5th ed., Vol. 1, pp. 82–114). Hoboken, NJ: John Wiley.

Reyna, C. (2000). Lazy, dumb, or industrious: When stereotypes convey attribution information in the classroom. *Educational Psychology Review, 12,* 85–110.

Robins, R. W., Noftle, E. E., & Tracy, J. L. (2007). Assessing self-conscious emotions: A review of self-report and nonverbal measures. In J. L. Tracy, R. W. Robins, & J. P. Tangney (Eds.), *The self-conscious emotions: Theory and research* (pp. 443–468). New York, NY: Guilford Press.

Robinson, R. D., & Clore. G. L. (2002). Belief and feeling: Evidence for an accessibility model of emotional self-report. *Psychological Bulletin, 128,* 934–960.

Rotter, J. (1966). Generalized expectancies for internal versus external control of reinforcement. *Psychological Monographs, 80* (1, Whole No. 609).

Rudolph, U., Roesch, S. C., Greitemeyer, T., & Weiner, B. (2004). A meta-analytic review of help giving and aggression from an attributional perspective. *Cognition and Emotion, 18,* 815–848.

Schneider, M., Major, B., Luhtanen, R., & Crocker, J. (1996). Social stigma and the potential cost of assumptive help. *Personality and Social Psychology Bulletin, 22,* 201–209.

Scott, M., & Lyman, S. (1968). Accounts. *American Sociological Review, 23,* 46–62.

Stipek, D. (1995). The development of pride and shame in toddlers. In J. P. Tangney & K. W. Fischer (Eds.), *Self-conscious emotions: The psychology of guilt, shame, embarrassment, and pride* (pp. 237–254). New York, NY: Guilford Press.

Stuewig, J., & Tangney, J. P. (2007). Shame amd guilt in antisocial and risky behaviors. In J. L. Tracy, R. W. Robins, & J. P. Tangney (Eds.), *The self-conscious emotions: Theory and research* (pp. 371–388). New York, NY: Guilford Press.

Tangney, J. P., Stuewig, J., & Mashek, D. J. (2007). Moral emotions and moral behavior. *Annual Review of Psychology, 58,* 345–372.

Taylor, S. E. (1991). Asymmetrical effects of positive and negative events: The mobilization-minimization hypothesis. *Psychological Bulletin, 110,* 67–85.

Tracy, J. L., & Robins, R. W. (2006). Appraisal antecedents of shame and guilt: Support for a theoretical model. *Personality and Social Psychology Bulletin, 32,* 1339–1351.

Tracy, J. L., & Robins, R. W. (2007). The nature of pride. In J. L. Tracy, R. W. Robins, & J. P. Tangney (Eds.), *The self-conscious emotions: Theory and research* (pp. 263–282). New York, NY: Guilford Press.

Tsang, J. (2006). Gratitude and prosocial behavior: An experimental test of gratitude. *Cognition and Emotion, 20,* 138–148.

Turner, J. E., & Schallert, D. L. (2001). Expectancy-value relationships of shame reactions and shame resiliency. *Journal of Educational Psychology, 93,* 320–329.

Twenge, J. M., & Crocker, J. (2002). Race and self-esteem: Meta-analyses comparing Whites, Blacks, Hispanics, Asians, and American Indians and comments on Gray-Little and Hafdahl (2000). *Psychological Bulletin, 128,* 371–408.

van Laar, C. (2000). The paradox of low academic achievement but high self-esteem in African American students: An attributional account. *Educational Psychology Review, 12,* 33–61.

Watkins, P. C., Scheer, J., Ovnicek, M., & Kolts, R. (2006). The debt of gratitude: Dissociating gratitude and indebtedness. *Cognition and Emotion, 20,* 217–241.

Weiner, B. (1986). *An attributional theory of motivation and emotion.* New York, NY: Springer.

Weiner, B. (1995). *Judgments of responsibility: A foundation for a theory of social conduct.* New York, NY: Guilford Press.

Weiner, B. (2006). *Social motivation, justice, and the moral emotions.* Mahwah, NJ: Lawrence Erlbaum.

Weiner, B. (2007). Examining emotional diversity in the classroom: An attribution theorist considers the moral emotions. In P. A. Schutz & R. Pekrun (Eds.), *Emotion in education* (pp. 75–88). San Diego, CA: Academic Press.

Weiner, B., & Graham, S. (1984). An attributional approach to emotional development. In C. Izard, J. Kagan, & R. Zajonc (Eds.), *Emotions, cognition, and behavior* (pp. 167–191). New York, NY: Cambridge University Press.

Weiner, B., Graham, S., Stern, P., & Lawson, M. (1982). Using affective cues to infer causal thoughts. *Developmental Psychology, 18,* 278–286.

Wong, Y., & Tsai, J. (2007). Cultural models of shame and guilt. In J. L. Tracy, R. W. Robins, & J. P. Tangney (Eds.), *The self-conscious emotions: Theory and research* (pp. 209–223). New York, NY: Guilford Press.

Yeager, D. S., & Walton, G. M. (2011). Social-psychological interventions in education: They're not magic. *Review of Educational Research, 81,* 267–301.

7

CONTROL-VALUE THEORY OF ACHIEVEMENT EMOTIONS

Reinhard Pekrun and Raymond P. Perry,
University of Munich and University of Manitoba

Success and failure in achievement settings are of critical importance throughout students' educational careers. Across various academic domains, individual achievement shapes opportunities and developmental trajectories. The overarching impact of educational achievement in a modern, meritocratic society implies that achievement fulfils a basic requisite for the arousal of intense emotion—success and failure in education are highly important to the individual student, to the extent that they influence completion versus drop-out, employment versus unemployment, affluence versus poverty, and health versus disease. Consequently, situations that contribute to educational accomplishment arouse a multitude of different emotions, including enjoyment, hope, pride, anger, anxiety, shame, boredom, and hopelessness. Similarly, success in performing teaching duties is critically important for teachers throughout their occupational careers, thus inducing a broad range of achievement emotions related to teaching and to interacting with colleagues, supervisors, and parents.

These emotions are not just mere epiphenomena of success and failure. Rather, they can strongly impact students' and teachers' performance as well as psychological and physical well-being. Consider, for example, the last time you took an important exam. You may have hoped for success, feared failure, or felt desperate because you were unprepared, but it is unlikely that you felt emotionally indifferent. Furthermore, your emotional arousal likely affected your motivation, concentration, and strategies used for studying—even if you were unaware of these developments. Similarly, think of the last time you worked on some project. Depending on the goals and tasks involved, you may have enjoyed working on it or felt bored, experienced a sense of flow or frustration about never-ending obstacles, felt proud of the outcome or ashamed of lack of accomplishment. Again, these emotions likely had profound effects on your involvement in the project, motivation to persist, and strategies for approaching the tasks involved.

Research on achievement emotions has begun to flourish over the past 15 years but is in a fragmented state to date. Different traditions of research pertain to achievement

120

anxiety that was studied since the inception of test anxiety research in the 1930s (Brown, 1938), to the attributional antecedents of achievement emotions (Weiner, 1985), and to achievement emotions experienced in specific settings, such as education, work, and sports (Boehm & Lyubomirsky, 2008; Schutz & Pekrun, 2007). Conceptual frameworks having the power to integrate the multitude of emerging findings are largely lacking, however. The control-value theory of achievement emotions (Pekrun, 2006) seeks to provide such a framework.

In this chapter, we provide an overview of the control-value theory. We first introduce the concept of achievement emotion used in the theory. Next, we provide a short summary outlining the structure of the theory. We then describe the theory's propositions to explain the origins of achievement emotions in terms of self-related appraisals. In subsequent sections, we discuss various implications and extensions of the theory pertaining to the situational specificity of these emotions, their individual antecedents, and their functions for task performance and achievement. In conclusion, we highlight the relative universality of achievement emotions across academic domains, genders, and cultures, and the need for research on emotion regulation and treatment interventions targeting achievement emotions in educational settings.

CONCEPT OF ACHIEVEMENT EMOTION

We define *achievement emotions* as affective arousal that is tied directly to achievement activities (e.g., studying) or achievement outcomes (success and failure; see Table 7.1). Most emotions pertaining to studying and to writing tests are seen as achievement emotions, since they relate to activities and outcomes that are typically judged according to competence-based standards of quality.

However, not all of the emotions triggered in academic settings are achievement emotions. For example, topic emotions, epistemic emotions, and social emotions are frequently experienced in these same settings, as outlined in the introductory chapter of this handbook (Pekrun & Linnenbrink-Garcia, 2014). Achievement emotions can overlap with other categories of emotion, as in social achievement emotions such as admiration, envy, or contempt related to the success and failure of others (Weiner, 2007).

Table 7.1 A Three-Dimensional Taxonomy of Achievement Emotions

	Positive[a]		Negative[b]	
Object Focus	Activating	Deactivating	Activating	Deactivating
Activity	Enjoyment	Relaxation	Anger	Boredom
				Frustration
Outcome/Prospective	Hope	Relief[c]	Anxiety	Hopelessness
				Joy[c]
Outcome/Retrospective	Joy	Contentment	Shame	Sadness
	Pride	Relief	Anger	Disappointment
				Gratitude

[a]Positive = pleasant emotion. [b]Negative = unpleasant emotion. [c]Anticipatory joy/relief.

Past research focused on emotions induced by achievement outcomes, such as hope and pride related to success, or anxiety and shame related to failure (Weiner, 1985; Zeidner, 2007). Certainly outcome emotions are of critical importance for achievement strivings. However, we argue that emotions directly pertaining to the activities performed in academic settings can also be considered as achievement emotions and are of equal relevance for students' and teachers' achievement strivings. The excitement arising from the commencement of a new class, boredom experienced when attending monotonous lectures, or anger felt when task demands seem unreasonable are examples of activity-related emotions.

In the three-dimensional taxonomy of achievement emotions that is part of the control-value theory (Pekrun, 2006; Pekrun, Goetz, Titz, & Perry, 2002), the differentiation of activity versus outcome emotions pertains to the object focus of these emotions. In addition, as emotions more generally, achievement emotions can be grouped according to their *valence* and to the degree of *activation* implied (Table 7.1). In terms of valence, positive (i.e., pleasant) emotions can be distinguished from negative (i.e., unpleasant) emotions, such as enjoyment versus anxiety. In terms of activation, physiologically activating emotions can be distinguished from deactivating emotions, such as excitement versus relaxation. By using the dimensions valence and activation, the taxonomy is consistent with circumplex models that arrange affective states in a two-dimensional (valence x activation) space (Feldman Barrett & Russell, 1998).

Exploratory research has documented that the emotions organized in this taxonomy are common in academic settings. For example, in a series of interview and questionnaire studies with high school and university students, anxiety was the emotion reported most often, constituting 15–27% of all emotional episodes experienced in various academic situations (such as attending class, studying, and taking tests and exams; Pekrun, 1992a; Spangler, Pekrun, Kramer, & Hofmann, 2002). This prevalence of anxiety corroborates the importance of achievement anxiety research. However, the vast majority of emotions reported in these studies pertained to emotion categories other than anxiety, with episodes of enjoyment, satisfaction, hope, pride, relief, anger, boredom, and shame reported frequently as well.

STRUCTURE OF THE CONTROL-VALUE THEORY

The control-value theory addresses origins, situational specificity, functions, regulation, and relative universality of achievement emotions as defined above (Figure 7.1). The basic propositions of the theory pertain to the appraisal antecedents of these emotions. It is assumed that appraisals of ongoing achievement activities, and of their past and future outcomes, are of primary importance in this respect. Succinctly stated, it is proposed that individuals experience specific achievement emotions when they feel in control of, or out of control of, achievement activities and outcomes that are subjectively important to them. This proposition implies that *control appraisals* and *value appraisals* are the proximal determinants of these emotions. Noncognitive factors underlying emotions are acknowledged by the theory, but appraisals are deemed to be critically important for achievement emotion arousal.

To the extent that control and value appraisals are organized in situation-specific ways, achievement emotions should also follow principles of situational specificity. Accordingly, the theory implies that students' and teachers' achievement emotions should be

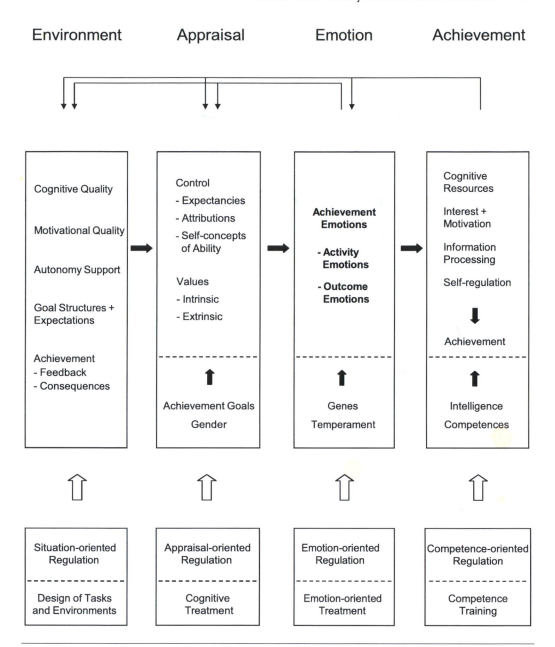

Figure 7.1 Basic propositions of the control-value theory of achievement emotions (adapted from Pekrun, 2006).

organized in domain- and subject-specific ways. Furthermore, to the extent that control and value appraisals function as proximal antecedents, any more distal antecedents should influence achievement emotions by affecting these appraisals to begin with. This is expected to be true both for more distal individual antecedents, such as achievement goals, beliefs, or gender, and for situational antecedents, such as tasks and features of the achievement setting (Figure 7.1).

In addition to the origins of achievement emotions, the theory targets their functions for achievement activities and performance, stipulating that these emotions affect learning and performance through various cognitive and motivational mechanisms. Consequently, it is expected that achievement emotions impact educational successes and failures and the developmental trajectories shaped by success and failure.

Furthermore, using principles of reciprocal causation, the theory acknowledges that achievement activities and their outcomes reciprocally influence achievement emotions and their antecedents, implying that achievement emotions, their origins, and their outcomes are linked by reciprocal causation (Figure 7.1). The cyclic nature of these processes implies that achievement emotions can be regulated by targeting any of the elements of the resulting feedback loops. Specifically, adapting current conceptions of emotion regulation to explain the regulation of achievement emotions, the theory distinguishes emotion-oriented, appraisal-oriented, situation-oriented, and competence-oriented regulation.

Finally, the theory also addresses the relative generality of achievement emotions across individuals, genders, domains of achievement, and sociohistorical contexts. It is argued that contents, frequency, and intensities of achievement can vary widely but that the functional mechanisms linking achievement emotions to their origins and outcomes are universal.

BASIC PROPOSITIONS: THE ROLE OF CONTROL AND VALUE APPRAISALS

Emotions can be caused and modulated by numerous individual factors, including situational perceptions, cognitive appraisals, neurohormonal processes, physiological feedback from autonomic nervous system activity, and sensory feedback from facial, gestural, and postural expression (Davidson, Scherer, & Goldsmith, 2003; Mauss, Bunge, & Gross, 2007). Among these factors, appraisals of personal competences, task demands, the probability of success and failure, and the value of these outcomes likely play a major role in the arousal of achievement emotions. In contrast to emotions induced in phylogenetically older and more constrained situations (e.g., enjoyment of physiological need fulfillment; anxiety of falling when perceiving heights; Campos, Bertenthal, & Kermoian, 1992), achievement emotions pertain to culturally defined demands in settings that are a recent product of civilization. In these settings, the individual has to learn how to adapt to situational demands while preserving individual autonomy—inevitably a process guided by appraisals.

Types of Control and Value Appraisals

Various types and dimensions of appraisals have been proposed to explain the arousal of emotions, including goal relevance, goal congruence, controllability, agency, probability, legitimacy, and so forth (Scherer, Schorr, & Johnstone, 2001). For achievement emotions specifically, the control-value theory proposes that perceived control and perceived values are most important. These two constructs integrate a number of the different appraisal dimensions considered in traditional appraisal theories. *Perceived control* refers to appraisals of control over actions and outcomes (controllability), whereby such control can be exerted by oneself or external factors (agency). Perceived control also determines the subjective likelihood to obtain outcomes (probability). *Perceived value* involves both perceived degree of importance for oneself (goal relevance) and perceived direction (positive versus negative; i.e., goal congruence in terms of events either supporting goal attainment or impeding goal attainment). As such, the concept of value used in the control-value theory is similar to the value concepts used in expectancy-value theories of motivation and decision making, which also integrate importance and direction (Heckhausen, 1991).

Appraisals of control can take prospective or retrospective forms. Prospective control appraisals consist of causal expectancies, including *action-control expectancies* whether one is able to successfully initiate and perform an action ("self-efficacy expectations"; Bandura, 1997), and *action-outcome expectancies* whether the action will produce desired outcomes (for details, see Pekrun, 1988, 2006). For example, a student's expectations about her capacity to adequately prepare for an exam is considered an action-control expectancy, and her expectation that this persistence will eventually help her to succeed on the exam is considered an action-outcome expectancy. Together, the two expectancies shape the subjective likelihood that the desired outcome will be attained.

Whereas prospective control appraisals imply cognitively linking a given cause to future effects, retrospective control appraisals as implied by *causal attributions* involve linking given effects to possible causes. In line with Weiner's (1985, 2007) attributional theory of achievement emotion, the control-value theory considers the perceived internal versus external location of causes for success and failure (such as one's effort versus help by others) as critically important for shaping the arousal of achievement emotions.

In addition to expectancies, competence appraisals are considered by the theory, with a specific focus on *self-concepts of ability*. These self-concepts imply judgments of one's abilities in a given domain (Marsh, 1993; e.g., "I'm good at math"). Ability judgments do not directly represent control as exerted by some agent over an effect (i.e., they do not represent cause–effect relationships). However, any expectancies to successfully pursue achievement activities, attain success, and avoid failure are shaped by these self-appraisals of ability, implying that they lay the foundations for perceived control in the achievement domain.

With regard to value appraisals, the control-value theory distinguishes between values of achievement activities and values of the outcomes of these activities. Both activities and outcomes can be valued in and of themselves (*intrinsic values*), such as valuing math because dealing with this subject is interesting, or valuing success at sports because success is intrinsically reinforcing (for intrinsic values of success, failure, and behavioral outcomes more generally, see Bandura, 1977; Heckhausen, 1991; also see Eccles's, 1983, concept of attainment value addressing the value of achievement for satisfying identity-related needs). Alternatively, activities and outcomes can be valued because of their instrumental functions for obtaining desired consequences (*extrinsic values*), such as a teacher valuing effort in preparing lessons because preparation encourages engagement on the students' part, or valuing success because success improves one's status among colleagues. Both intrinsic and extrinsic values can be either positive or negative (e.g., if learning is perceived as interesting and pleasant, it has positive intrinsic value; by contrast, to the extent that it is perceived as aversive, it has negative intrinsic value). One of the implications of these conceptual distinctions is that the value of success and failure is decomposed in its intrinsic and extrinsic elements in the control-value theory.

Appraisals as Proximal Antecedents of Achievement Emotions

Different kinds of control and value appraisals are assumed to instigate different achievement emotions, including prospective outcome emotions, retrospective outcome emotions, and activity emotions (Table 7.1). Prospective, anticipatory joy and hopelessness are expected to be triggered when there is high perceived control (joy) or a complete lack of perceived control (hopelessness). For example, a student who believes he has the necessary resources to master an exam may feel excited about the prospect of receiving a good grade. Conversely, a student who believes she is incapable of mastering the exam material may experience hopelessness. Prospective hope and anxiety are instigated when there is uncertainty about control, the attentional focus being on anticipated success in the case of hope, and on anticipated failure in the case of anxiety. For example, a student who is unsure about being able to master an important exam may hope for success, fear failure, or both.

Retrospective joy and sadness are considered control-independent emotions that immediately follow perceived success and failure, further cognitive elaboration being unnecessary (in line with B. Weiner's, 1985, assumptions; see Graham & Taylor, 2014). In contrast, disappointment and relief are assumed to depend on the perceived match between expectations and the actual outcome; disappointment being aroused when anticipated success does not occur and relief when anticipated failure does not occur. Finally, pride, shame, gratitude, and anger are seen to be induced by causal attributions of success and failure to oneself or others, respectively. For example, a student who wins an important competition will feel pride provided that he attributes the victory to his own ability or effort. Conversely, losing the competition can induce shame if attributed to lack of ability or effort.

The perceived controllability of *success and failure* is posited to trigger these outcome-related achievement emotions, rather than the controllability of the *causes* of success and failure as posited by Weiner (1985). Achievement outcomes may be controllable by use of causal factors that themselves are uncontrollable, such as ability. From this perspective, emotions like pride and shame are seen as being induced by success or failure caused by oneself, irrespective of the controllability of the underlying ability and effort. This perspective is similar to Weiner's view on pride but differs from his view on shame as being produced by failure attributions to uncontrollable causes only (such as lack of ability), but not by failure attributions to controllable causes (such as lack of effort; see Pekrun, Frenzel, Goetz, & Perry, 2007).

Furthermore, the control-value theory proposes that these outcome-related emotions also depend on the subjective importance of achievement outcomes, implying that they are a joint function of perceived control and value. For instance, a teacher should feel worried if she judges herself incapable of managing classes (low controllability) that are critically important for her career (high value). In contrast, if she feels that she is able to manage these classes (high controllability), or is indifferent about them (low value), her anxiety should be low.

Regarding activity emotions (Table 7.1), enjoyment of achievement activities (e.g., enjoyment of learning) is proposed to depend on a combination of positive competence appraisals as triggered by high self-concept of ability and positive appraisals of the intrinsic value of the action (e.g., studying) and its reference object (e.g., learning material). For example, a student is expected to enjoy learning if she feels competent to meet the

demands of the learning task and values the learning material. If she feels incompetent, or is disinterested in the material, studying is not enjoyable. Anger and frustration are aroused when the intrinsic value of the activity is negative (e.g., when working on a difficult project is perceived as taking too much effort that is experienced as aversive, thus taking on negative intrinsic value). Finally, boredom is experienced when the activity lacks any positive or negative intrinsic incentive value.

Importantly, the control-value theory does not imply that achievement emotions are always mediated by conscious appraisals. Rather, it is expected that recurring appraisal-based induction of emotions can become automatic and nonreflective over time. When achievement activities are repeated over and over again, appraisals and the induction of emotions can become routinized to the extent that there is no longer any conscious mediation of emotions—or no longer any cognitive mediation at all (Pekrun, 1988; Reisenzein, 2001). In the procedural emotion schemata established by routinization, situation perception and emotion are directly linked such that perceptions can automatically induce the emotion (e.g., the mere smell of a chemistry lab inducing joy). However, when the situation changes or attempts are made to change the emotion (as in psychotherapy), appraisals come into play again.

Empirical Evidence

Empirical evidence supports the importance of control and value appraisals for the arousal of achievement emotions. Specifically, numerous studies have corroborated that test anxiety is negatively related to variables involving perceived control, such as academic self-concepts, self-efficacy, and internal versus external locus of control (Davis, DiStefano, & Schutz, 2008; Hembree, 1988; Zeidner, 1998). A few longitudinal studies suggest that perceived lack of control causally influences test anxiety rather than simply being an epiphenomenon of students' anxiety or achievement (e.g., Krampen, 1988). Furthermore, research has confirmed that the perceived importance of academic achievement relates positively to test anxiety (e.g., Pekrun, 1992b).

For achievement emotions other than test anxiety, Folkman and Lazarus (1985) have shown that students' exam-related "challenge emotions" and "benefit emotions" (p. 154; e.g., hopeful, happy) related positively to perceived control over the exam, whereas "threat emotions" and "harm emotions" (p. 154; e.g., fearful, sad) related negatively to perceived control. Similarly, Smith and Ellsworth (1987) have shown that students' exam-related agency appraisals (self vs. other control) correlated positively with their happiness and hope and negatively with their anger, fear, guilt, and apathy.

Studies directly testing the control-value theory have confirmed that perceived control over achievement relates positively to students' enjoyment, hope, and pride, and negatively to their anger, anxiety, shame, hopelessness, and boredom, in university students (Ahmed, Minnaert, & van der Weerf, 2010; Hall, Perry, Ruthig, Hladkyj, & Chipperfield, 2006; Pekrun, Goetz, Frenzel, Barchfeld, & Perry, 2011; Pekrun, Goetz, Perry, Kramer, & Hochstadt, 2004; Perry, Hladkyi, Pekrun, & Pelletier, 2001; Turner & Schallert, 2001) as well as in middle and high school students (Dettmers et al., 2011; Frenzel, Pekrun, & Goetz, 2007; Goetz, Frenzel, Hall, & Pekrun, 2008; Goetz, Pekrun, Hall, & Haag, 2006). Similar links have been observed for students' emotions in online learning environments (Artino & Jones, 2012; Daniels & Stupnisky, 2012). Furthermore, some of these studies have corroborated that the perceived value of achievement is positively related to both positive and negative achievement emotions except boredom (Artino & Jones, 2012; Frenzel et al., 2007; Goetz et al., 2006; Pekrun et al., 2011), indicating that the importance of success and failure amplifies these emotions. For boredom, negative links with perceived value have been found, confirming that boredom is reduced when students value achievement (Vogel-Walcutt, Fiorella, Carper, & Schatz, 2012; Pekrun, Goetz, Daniels, Stupnisky, & Perry, 2010).

Goetz, Frenzel, Stoeger, and Hall (2010) evaluated the proposition implied by the control-value theory that control and value appraisals interact in triggering emotions. Using an experience sampling approach, they examined the links between university students' momentary control-value appraisals and three positive emotions (enjoyment, pride, and contentment) in everyday achievement and nonachievement settings. The results showed that the multiplicative interaction of control and value had positive effects on these emotions. In sum, the extant research confirms that perceived control and value appraisals are closely linked to students' achievement emotions, with control generally showing positive relations with positive emotions and negative relations with negative emotions, and value showing positive relations with both types of emotions.

SITUATIONAL SPECIFICITY OF ACHIEVEMENT EMOTIONS

Traditionally, achievement emotions such as test anxiety have been regarded as trait-like characteristics of the individual that are generalized across different achievement settings (Zeidner, 1998). However, the control and value appraisals that underlie these emotions can be situation-specific, pertaining to specific academic domains (e.g., mathematics), or to subdomains and tasks within these domains (e.g., geometry vs. algebra). To the extent that these appraisals are situation-specific, it follows from the control-value theory that achievement emotions should also be organized in domain-specific and task-specific ways.

Domain specificity has been shown for a number of variables related to control and value, such as competence appraisals, achievement goals, and interests (Bong, 2001). An especially robust body of evidence pertains to the domain specificity of students' academic self-concepts. Numerous studies have documented that students' self-concepts in math and languages show zero correlations, as predicted by H. Marsh's (1986) Internal/External Frame of Reference model (I/E model). As achievement emotions are thought to depend on control-related appraisals, such as self-concepts of ability, these emotions should also be organized in domain-specific ways. In a series of studies, Goetz and colleagues tested this hypothesis (e.g., Goetz, Frenzel, Pekrun, Hall, & Lüdtke, 2007). The findings show that the achievement emotions experienced by students, such as enjoyment, pride, anger, anxiety, and boredom, correlate positively across similar subjects like math and science, but show zero to small correlations across math and science subjects, on the one hand, and languages, on the other. In addition, the study by Goetz, Frenzel, Hall, and Pekrun (2008) suggests that the domain specificity of emotions in math versus languages is in fact due to the specificity of math and verbal self-concepts that function as antecedents of these emotions.

These studies provide robust evidence supporting the domain specificity of achievement emotions in education, thus corroborating one of the corollaries of the control-value theory. By implication, educational research and practice would be well advised to attend to principles of situational specificity. For example, teachers should know that it

[disciplines are independent]

is not possible to infer from a student's enjoyment or anxiety in math to what extent the student enjoys, or has trepidations about, other subjects such as language classes.

DISTAL INDIVIDUAL ANTECEDENTS

To the extent that cognitive appraisals are proximal determinants of achievement emotions, more distal individual antecedents, such as trait emotions, beliefs, goals, cognitive abilities, or gender should affect these emotions by first influencing appraisals (Figure 7.1; Pekrun, 2006). For example, the control-value theory implies that achievement goals and gender should influence emotions by affecting control and value appraisals in the first place.

In the achievement goal literature, *achievement goals* are conceptualized according to the standards used to define achievement, including intraindividual standards and absolute criteria (jointly called *mastery*) as well as normative standards comparing performance across individuals (called *performance*). This leads to a differentiation of mastery goals versus performance goals. In addition, both types of achievement goals can either focus on approaching success or on avoiding failure, thus rendering four types of goals within a 2 × 2 taxonomy as proposed by Elliot and McGregor (2001; mastery-approach, mastery-avoidance, performance-approach, performance-avoidance; for a recent extension, see Elliot, Murayama, & Pekrun, 2011).

In a model derived from the control-value theory, Pekrun, Elliot, and Maier (2006, 2009) argued that mastery-approach goals focus attention on the ongoing mastery of the activity and the positive value of the activity. By implication, these goals should foster positive activity emotions, such as enjoyment of learning, and reduce negative activity emotions, such as boredom (for mastery-avoidance goals, see Elliot & Pekrun, 2007). In contrast, performance-approach goals were posited to focus attention on the perceived controllability and positive value of success outcomes, implying they should facilitate positive outcome emotions such as hope and pride. Performance-avoidance goals focus attention on the perceived uncontrollability and negative value of failure outcomes, suggesting that they should evoke negative outcome emotions such as anxiety, shame, and hopelessness (for evidence supporting these propositions, see Pekrun et al., 2006, 2009).

Similarly, other individual variables are also thought to influence achievement emotions by shaping control and value appraisals. For example, *gender* is expected to influence the socialization of appraisals based on gender-linked stereotypes of competencies, thus making it possible to explain gender differences in achievement emotions by related differences in appraisals. One important case in point is differences between male and female students in the emotions they experience in various academic domains. For mathematics, Frenzel, Pekrun, and Goetz (2007) have shown that females reported more maladaptive emotions, such as anxiety, shame, and hopelessness, and less enjoyment (also see Goetz, Bieg, Lüdtke, Pekrun, & Hall, 2013). These differences proved to be mediated by differences in control and value appraisals, with female students reporting lower self-concepts of mathematics ability and less intrinsic value of the domain of mathematics.

THE INFLUENCE OF TASKS AND LEARNING ENVIRONMENTS

Similar to the role of distal individual antecedents, the impact of task demands and environments on achievement emotions is also thought to be mediated by individual control and value appraisals. Variables in the learning environment that affect these appraisals should influence the resulting emotions as well. The following groups of factors may be relevant for a broad variety of achievement emotions (Figure 7.1).

Cognitive Quality

The cognitive quality of tasks as defined by their structure, clarity, and potential for cognitive stimulation likely has a positive influence on perceived competence and the perceived value of tasks (e.g., Cordova & Lepper, 1996), thus positively influencing achievement emotions. In addition, the relative difficulty of tasks can influence perceived control, and the match between task demands and competences can influence subjective task value, thus also affecting emotions. If demands are too high or too low, the intrinsic value of tasks may be reduced to the extent that boredom is experienced (Csikszentmihalyi, 1975; Pekrun et al., 2010).

Motivational Quality

Teachers, parents, and peers deliver both direct and indirect messages conveying achievement values. Two indirect ways of inducing emotionally relevant values may be most important. First, if tasks and environments are shaped such that they meet individual needs, positive activity-related emotions should be fostered. For example, classroom environments that support cooperation should help students fulfill their needs for social relatedness, thus making classroom instruction more enjoyable. Second, teachers' own enthusiasm in dealing with instruction can facilitate the adoption of achievement values and related emotions (Frenzel, Goetz, Lüdtke, Pekrun, & Sutton, 2009). Observational learning and emotional contagion may be prime mechanisms mediating these effects (Hatfield, Cacioppo, & Rapson, 1994).

Autonomy Support

Tasks and environments supporting autonomy can increase perceived control and, by meeting needs for autonomy, the intrinsic value of related achievement activities (Tsai, Kunter, Lüdtke, Trautwein, & Ryan, 2008). However, these beneficial effects likely depend on the match between individual competences and needs for autonomy, on the one hand, and task demands, on the other. In case of a mismatch in terms of high demands on self-regulation and low competences to meet these demands, loss of control and negative emotions could result. For example, if a student who has difficulties in adequately planning and monitoring his learning activities is left alone to deal with difficult material, he may experience a loss of control, along with anxiety and hopelessness, in not reaching his learning goals.

Goal Structures and Social Expectations

Different standards for defining achievement can imply individualistic (mastery), competitive (normative performance), or cooperative goal structures (Johnson & Johnson, 1974). The goal structures provided in achievement settings conceivably influence emotions in two ways. First, to the extent that these structures are adopted, they influence individual achievement goals (Murayama & Elliot, 2009) and any emotions mediated by these goals (Kaplan & Maehr, 1999; Roeser, Midgley, & Urdan, 1996). Second, goal structures determine relative opportunities for experiencing success and perceiving control, thus influencing control-dependent emotions. Specifically, competitive goal structures imply, by definition, that some individuals have to experience failure, thus inducing negative outcome emotions such as anxiety and hopelessness in these individuals. Similarly, the demands implied by an important other's unrealistic expectancies for achievement can lead to negative emotions resulting from reduced subjective control.

Feedback and Consequences of Achievement

Cumulative success can strengthen perceived control, and cumulative failure can undermine control. In environments involving frequent assessments, performance feedback is likely critical to the arousal of achievement emotions. In addition, the perceived consequences of success and failure are important, since these consequences affect the extrinsic, instrumental value of achievement outcomes. Positive outcome emotions (e.g., hope for success) can be increased if success produces beneficial long-term outcomes (e.g., future career opportunities), provided sufficient contingency between one's own efforts, success, and these outcomes. Negative consequences of failure (e.g., unemployment), on the other hand, may increase achievement-related anxiety and hopelessness (Pekrun, 1992b).

FUNCTIONS FOR ACHIEVEMENT BEHAVIOR AND PERFORMANCE

In the cognitive-motivational model of emotion effects that is part of the control-value theory, it is argued that achievement emotions impact learning and achievement through cognitive and motivational mechanisms. The model is based on previous research showing that positive versus negative affective states influence cognitive processes underlying learning, including attention, memory storage and retrieval, decision making, and cognitive problem solving (Clore & Huntsinger, 2007; Loewenstein & Lerner, 2003; Parrott & Spackman, 2000). The model expands upon this research in two ways. First, it is argued that it is insufficient to just differentiate between positive versus negative states. Rather, it is important to consider the functional differences between various emotions within these categories. Second, to more fully capture the effects of emotions on achievement, it is necessary to also consider their impact on achievement-related motivation and behavior, in addition to their effects on cognitive processes.

With regard to the functions of emotions, the model proposes that it is necessary to consider both the valence and the arousal dimensions describing emotion. Using these dimensions, four broad categories of achievement emotions can be distinguished: *positive activating* (e.g., enjoyment, hope, and pride); *positive deactivating* (e.g., relief, relaxation); *negative activating* (e.g., anger, anxiety, and shame); and *negative deactivating* (e.g., hopelessness, boredom; Table 7.1). Furthermore, there may also be functional differences within these four categories, such as the differences between anger and anxiety. Both of these emotions are negative and activating, but anger is approach-related (Carver & Harmon-Jones, 2009), whereas anxiety relates to avoidance (Zeidner, 1998).

Functional Mechanisms of Emotion

The impact of emotions on achievement is thought to be mediated by a number of cognitive and motivational mechanisms. All of these mechanisms derive from the basic functions of emotions for adaptive behavior. To adapt to environmental demands and personal goals, emotions help to draw attention to the object of emotion, instigate motivation to deal with the object in appropriate ways, and trigger cognitive modes of processing information that support adaptive behavior. For example, anxiety can help to prioritize information about threat when attending to stimuli (Kuhbandner, Spitzer, & Pekrun, 2011), can motivate to avoid threat or escape from it, and can facilitate an analytical way of processing information that supports avoidance and escape. In terms of functions for learning and achievement, four mechanisms are supposed to be especially important.

Working Memory Resources

Focusing attention on the object of emotion implies that emotions draw on working memory resources. If the object of the emotion is the achievement activity itself, this attentional mechanism may help task performance. Specifically, enjoyment of achievement activities is thought to help in focusing attention on task performance and to support experiences of flow. However, if the object of emotion is external to the activity itself, using cognitive resources to attend to the emotion object implies that fewer resources are available to perform the task, and that performance is reduced for cognitively complex and difficult tasks that draw on working memory resources. This is supposed to be the case for incidental emotions not related to the achievement activity but brought to the situation from outside, and to achievement emotions that disrupt attentional focus, such as boredom, anxiety, or hopelessness. In many situations, the attentional effects of these emotions are adaptive. However, in achievement situations, they may be detrimental. Obviously, one of the basic functional mechanisms of emotion that generally serves adaption can have negative side effects in achievement settings.

Motivation to Achieve

Emotions are thought to influence students' and teachers' achievement motivation. Positive activating emotions, such as enjoyment of learning, hope for success, and pride in one's accomplishments, are thought to support motivation by serving as reinforcers for pursuing the activity per se (enjoyment) or because of its outcomes (pride), and by helping to activate optimistic control appraisals (hope). An opposite pattern is expected for negative deactivating emotions, such as hopelessness and boredom. These emotions can undermine any motivation to achieve due to the facilitation of low-control appraisals (hopelessness) or perceived lack of any incentives to perform the activity (boredom).

By contrast, the motivational effects of positive deactivating and negative activating emotions are proposed to be more complex. Positive deactivating emotions, such as relief, can undermine any immediate motivation to continue working on tasks but can serve as reinforcers for long-term commitment to achievement goals, thus promoting reengagement with the activity. Similarly, the effects of negative activating emotions can be variable. For example, anxiety and shame are expected to undermine interest and intrinsic motivation but can induce strong extrinsic motivation to invest effort in order to avoid failure (e.g., Turner & Schallert, 2001).

Information Processing

Emotions facilitate different modes of processing information. Specifically, positive affective states have been shown to promote top-down, relational, heuristic, and flexible processing, whereas negative affective states facilitate bottom-up, item-specific, analytical, and more rigid ways to process information. These different modes of processing are thought to have various consequences on cognitive performance. The effects on memory processes and strategies of learning and teaching are especially important.

By promoting relational versus item-specific processing, emotions impact storage and retrieval of memory material. For example, negative emotions can prevent retrieval-induced forgetting for items that are weakly related, likely because negative affect can reduce retrieval competition (Bäuml & Kuhbandner, 2007). Positive emotions can prevent retrieval-induced forgetting for material showing strong relations, such as coherent texts, and may even promote retrieval-induced facilitation for such materials (Kuhbandner & Pekrun, 2013).

Regarding strategy use, positive activating emotions are expected to promote use of flexible, deep strategies, whereas negative activating emotions facilitate rigid ways to solve problems. For example, enjoyment of learning relates positively to use of cognitive strategies involving deep learning, such as elaboration and organization of learning material (Pekrun et al., 2002), whereas anxiety and shame can facilitate rigid rehearsal of materials. By contrast, deactivating emotions can undermine any strategic efforts and just promote superficial processing of information. This may be especially true for negative deactivating emotions such as boredom (Pekrun et al., 2010).

Self-Regulation of Learning and Teaching

Self-regulation presupposes flexibility in adapting one's actions to task demands. Accordingly, because positive activating emotions are thought to promote flexible thought and action, they are also expected to promote students' self-regulation of learning. By contrast, negative activating emotions are expected to foster external regulation of learning, such as a test anxious student's reliance on external guidance by the teacher. Similarly, positive and negative activating emotions are expected to promote teachers' self-regulation versus external regulation, respectively.

Achievement Effects of Emotion

Given the multifaceted impact of emotions on the various functional mechanisms described above, their effects on overall learning, teaching, and achievement are inevitably complex. These effects depend on the interplay between task demands, characteristics of the individual (such as working memory capacity or knowledge about strategy use), and the different cognitive and motivational mechanisms triggered by emotion. The next sections describe effects thought to be typical for emotions of the four categories described earlier.

Achievement Effects of Positive Emotions

Traditionally, it was assumed that positive emotions, notwithstanding their potential to foster creativity, are maladaptive as a result of inducing unrealistic appraisals, fostering superficial information processing, and reducing motivation to pursue challenging goals.

From this perspective, "our primary goal is to feel good, and feeling good makes us lazy thinkers who are oblivious to potentially useful negative information and unresponsive to meaningful variations in information and situation" (Aspinwall, 1998, p. 7). From the perspective of the control-value theory, however, such a simplistic view needs to be modified by differentiating between activating and deactivating positive emotions as well as different emotions within these categories.

Specifically, the theory implies that enjoyment of achievement activities should preserve cognitive resources and focus attention on the activity, promote the development of interest and intrinsic motivation, facilitate the use of flexible strategies of learning and teaching, and perhaps promote beneficial memory processes such as retrieval-induced facilitation. In turn, these developments should exert positive effects on overall achievement under many task conditions. Similarly, positive outcome-related emotions, such as hope and pride, should typically exert positive effects by promoting motivation and creative problem solving, although there also may be negative side effects when excessive pride or hope draws too much attention on the self or desired outcomes. For example, a student may be preoccupied with basking in the glory of having won an important award to the extent that she neglects further pursuing her academic activities. By contrast, deactivating positive emotions, such as relief, can reduce task attention, can have ambiguous motivational effects as noted earlier, and can lead to superficial information processing, thus likely making effects on overall performance more variable.

Achievement Effects of Negative Emotions

Negative activating emotions, such as anxiety, shame, and anger, are expected to produce task-irrelevant thinking (e.g., worries about failure in test anxiety), thereby reducing cognitive resources available for task purposes, and to undermine interest and intrinsic motivation. However, as noted, anxiety and shame can induce motivation to avoid failure and can facilitate the use of analytical strategies to solve problems. Similarly, anger instigated by obstacles can motivate to overcome difficulties. For example, self-related anger about one's lack of accomplishments can induce motivation to persist and achieve. As a consequence, the overall effects of these emotions on achievement can be quite variable, even if the modal impact on indicators of performance, such as students' academic achievement scores, is negative (Hembree, 1988; Zeidner, 1998).

By contrast, the effects of deactivating negative emotions, such as hopelessness and boredom, are posited to be uniformly negative. These emotions distract attention, undermine task-related motivation, reduce any effortful use of strategies, and promote shallow information processing, thus negatively affecting achievement (e.g., Pekrun et al., 2010). However, one caveat pertains to more indirect effects that may be mediated by attempts to cope with these detrimental emotions. For example, coping with boredom may imply searching for more challenging cognitive activities, thus potentially leading to choices of achievement settings and tasks that better fit individual needs and that make the individual more productive (Nett, Goetz, & Hall, 2011).

In sum, these propositions imply that emotions exert profound effects on students' and teachers' achievement activities, task performance, and resulting achievement. To capture the complexity of these effects, it is imperative to attend to both the valence and arousal dimensions of emotions, as well as to functional differences between single emotions. Overall, with few exceptions, any emotion can prove to be either adaptive or maladaptive in terms of achievement outcomes—the control-value theory implies that it would be inadequate to simply equate positive (i.e., pleasant) emotions with positive achievement effects and negative (unpleasant) emotions with negative effects.

RECIPROCAL CAUSATION, EMOTION REGULATION, AND INTERVENTION

Reciprocal Causation

In the control-value theory, achievement emotions, their antecedents, and their outcomes are thought to be linked by reciprocal causation (Figure 7.1). As noted, task and achievement settings are assumed to shape the control and value appraisals that instigate achievement emotions, and these emotions in turn impact achievement activities and their outcomes. However, emotions reciprocally influence individual appraisals as well as one's environment. For example, positive emotions, such as hope, can facilitate the adoption of optimistic control appraisals, whereas negative emotions, such as hopelessness, can undermine these appraisals. With regard to environments, the emotions of different individuals, such as teachers' and students' emotions in the classroom, can also reciprocally influence each other (e.g., Frenzel et al., 2009). These linkages imply feedback loops between emotions, on the one hand, and antecedent appraisals and environmental factors, on the other.

Similarly, achievement activities and outcomes are thought to reciprocally influence emotions and their antecedents (Pekrun, Hall, Goetz, & Perry, in press). For example, success and failure outcomes influence control-related appraisals, such as self-concepts of ability, causal attributions of achievement, and expectancies of success and failure, with success strengthening confident appraisals and failure undermining them. Furthermore, success and failure also shape the reactions of others, such as teachers and parents, and influence the design and selection of tasks provided by them, thereby affecting subsequent emotions triggered by these tasks and reactions.

Emotion Regulation and Intervention

Given that achievement emotions impact outcomes such as task performance, achievement, and well-being, it is important for the individual to up-regulate adaptive emotions fostering these outcomes and to down-regulate maladaptive emotions. The reciprocal nature of the linkages between achievement emotions, their antecedents, and their outcomes implies that this can be done by targeting any of the elements of these cyclic feedback processes. Similarly, intervention by others, such as psychological therapists, can target these various elements as well.

Emotion Regulation

First, emotions can be regulated by changing component processes of the emotion itself (*emotion-oriented* regulation). Examples are relaxation techniques, drug use, and suppression to influence the affective and physiological processes that are part of emotions such as anxiety, or employing interest-enhancing strategies to reduce boredom (Sansone, Weir, Harpster, & Morgan, 1992). Second, it is possible to regulate emotions by changing antecedent appraisals (*appraisal-oriented* regulation), as in reinterpreting one's performance as successful. Third, emotion regulation can involve selecting and designing tasks and environments in order to foster adaptive emotions (*situation-oriented* regulation). For example, the choice between alternative schools can serve to improve a student's enjoyment of learning and pride in accomplishments. Finally, achievement emotions can be regulated by improving one's competencies (*competence-oriented* regulation), thus making it possible to experience the enjoyment that comes with competent pursuit of achievement activities and the success resulting from these activities. From the perspective of the model of reciprocal causation portrayed in Figure 7.1, appraisal- and situation-oriented regulation target the antecedents of emotion, whereas competence-oriented regulation targets achievement outcomes that affect these antecedents due to reciprocal effects.

Intervention

Strategies underpinning educational and clinical interventions can be grouped in similar ways. For example, teachers and therapists can influence students' achievement emotions by directly addressing these emotions; by changing underlying appraisals, as in cognitive treatments such as cognitive behavioral therapy; by appropriately selecting and designing tasks and academic settings; and by helping the student to improve competencies.

An example for an intervention that specifically aims to change control-related appraisals is *attributional retraining* (e.g., Perry, Hall, & Ruthig, 2005; Perry, Hechter, Menec, & Weinberg, 1993). Attributional retraining reframes maladaptive causal thinking by encouraging students and teachers to use controllable causes to explain failures (adaptive attributional reasoning) and by discouraging their use of uncontrollable causes (maladaptive reasoning). For example, Perry, Stupnisky, Hall, Chipperfield, and Weiner (2010) showed that attributional retraining led students to favor a controllable cause (use of bad strategy) to explain their failures and to downplay an uncontrollable cause (poor teaching).

As a consequence, attributional retraining fosters adaptive achievement emotions and resulting achievement outcomes. For example, such intervention can have positive effects on achievement emotions like pride, hope, anger, anxiety, and shame (Hall et al., 2007; Ruthig, Perry, Hall, & Hladkyj, 2004). Furthermore, in the Perry et al. (2010) study, attributional retraining produced noteworthy effects for diverse performance indicators over two semesters, including classroom tests ($d = .92$), grades ($d = .43$), and GPAs ($d = .51$). Consistent with the propositions of the control-value theory on the emotion-achievement link, Perry et al. (2012) showed that emotions mediated the effects of attributional retraining on performance indicators.

The present four-fold model of emotion regulation and intervention is generally consistent with traditional models of coping with stress and negative emotions. Models of coping highlight distinctions between emotion- and avoidance-oriented coping, on the one hand, and problem-oriented coping, on the other. Emotion- and appraisal-oriented regulation are conceptually equivalent with the former category of coping, situation- and competence-oriented regulation with the latter category.

Furthermore, this four-fold conception is also consistent with current models of emotion regulation. For example, emotion-, appraisal-, and situation-oriented regulation are equivalent to the respective categories in the model advanced by J. Gross (e.g., Gross & Thompson, 2007; Jacobs & Gross, 2014), with emotion-oriented regulation also comprising attentional deployment, which is considered a separate category in Gross's model. However, there is one important difference. The current model expands previous views of emotion regulation by also considering competence-oriented regulation that targets the skills and abilities making it possible to act successfully, beyond just changing appraisals of actions and outcomes. Competence-oriented regulation is of obvious importance in the achievement domain but likely is critically important in other settings as well.

RELATIVE UNIVERSALITY OF ACHIEVEMENT EMOTIONS

All things being equal, it makes sense to prefer parsimonious explanations over more complex ones. The generality of functional mechanisms of emotion is a case in point—unless there are good reasons to assume that different mechanisms work in different individuals, it is straightforward to expect that many of these mechanisms are universal within our species, or even across species. For achievement emotions specifically, the control-value theory proposes that the principles linking these emotions with their antecedents and outcomes are universal across individuals, genders, academic domains, and cultures. For example, the proposed connections between specific control and value appraisals, on the one hand, and different emotions, on the other, are thought to be universal (Pekrun, 2009).

However, universality of functional mechanisms notwithstanding, the base rates, contents, and process parameters (such as intensity) of achievement emotions are expected to differ widely, due to differences in individual dispositions, developmental trajectories, achievement settings, and cultures. For example, whereas the same proximal antecedents are assumed for female and male students' emotions experienced in academic domains such as mathematics, the frequency and intensity of these emotions may well differ between genders, as noted earlier.

In our own research, we have investigated principles of relative universality for the achievement emotions experienced by students across academic domains, genders, and cultures. For domains, achievement emotions show considerable variation across domains within students, but the linkages of different emotions (such as enjoyment, anxiety, and boredom) with antecedent appraisals and achievement outcomes show cross-domain universality (e.g., Goetz et al., 2007). Similarly, whereas male and female students' achievement emotions differed, their linkages with control and value appraisals, classroom climate, and academic achievement proved to be similar across genders (Frenzel, Pekrun, et al., 2007). As for culture, the study by Frenzel, Thrash, Pekrun, and Goetz (2007) showed substantial differences between the average math emotions experienced by Chinese and German students, with Chinese students reporting more enjoyment, pride, anxiety, and shame but less anger in mathematics. These differences notwithstanding, the relationships of these emotions with parental expectations, control and value appraisals, and students' achievement were virtually identical across cultures. Overall, these findings are consistent with the generality of functional principles as proposed by the control-value theory.

CONCLUDING COMMENT

Achievement emotions are among the most frequently experienced and functionally most important kinds of emotions in education. However, except for studies examining test anxiety, which has been a popular construct in personality research since the 1950s (Zeidner, 1998), research on students' and teachers' achievement emotions is clearly in a nascent stage. Educational and psychological researchers are just beginning to acknowledge the importance of achievement emotions, and the fragmented research efforts in this field need more integration. The control-value theory described in this chapter is an attempt to provide better integration of theoretical propositions. Our hope is that the theory can be used as a platform to advance research on achievement emotions across research traditions and disciplines.

As noted, major parts of the theory have empirically been corroborated during recent years, including the theory's propositions on the role of control and value appraisals, the domain specificity of achievement emotions, their links with individual and environmental antecedents, their functions for achievement behavior and performance, and their relative universality. However, emotion regulation and intervention targeting achievement emotions are just beginning to be explored (Nett, Goetz, & Hall, 2011; Perry et al., 2010). Specifically, there are few attempts to design academic environments that foster positive and reduce negative emotions (Glaeser-Zikuda, Fuss, Laukenmann, Metz, & Randler, 2005). More research on how to deal with achievement emotions is clearly needed—little is known to date about regulation, treatment, and design of academic settings targeting these emotions. However, there is one major exception: Test anxiety intervention proved to be highly successful. This seems true both for individual treatment and for the design of tasks and exams aiming to reduce students' anxiety (Zeidner, 1998). The success story of test anxiety intervention suggests that future research can be successful in developing ways to shape academic settings so that adaptive achievement emotions are promoted and maladaptive emotions prevented.

REFERENCES

Ahmed, W., Minnaert, A., & van der Weerf, G. (2010). The role of competence and value beliefs in students' daily emotional experiences. *Learning and Individual Differences, 20,* 507–511.

Artino, A. R., & Jones, K. D. (2012). Exploring the complex relations between achievement emotions and self-regulated learning behaviors in online learning. *Internet and Higher Education, 15,* 170–175.

Aspinwall, L. (1998). Rethinking the role of positive affect in self-regulation. *Motivation and Emotion, 22,* 1–32.

Bandura, A. (1977). Self-efficacy: Toward a unifying theory of behavorial change. *Psychological Review, 84,* 191–215.

Bandura, A. (1997). *Self-efficacy: The exercise of control.* New York, NY: Freeman.

Bäuml, K.-H., & Kuhbandner, C. (2007). Remembering can cause forgetting—but not in negative moods. *Psychological Science, 18,* 111–115.

Boehm, J. K., & Lyubomirsky, S. (2008). Does happiness promote career success? *Journal of Career Assessment, 16,* 101–116.

Bong, M. (2001). Between- and within-domain relations of academic motivation among middle and high school students: Self-efficacy, task value and achievement goals. *Journal of Educational Psychology, 93,* 23–34.

Brown, C. H. (1938). Emotional reactions before examinations: II. Results of a questionnaire. *Journal of Psychology, 5,* 11–26.

Campos, J. J., Bertenthal, B. I., & Kermoian, R. (1992). Early experience and emotional development: The emergence of wariness of heights. *Psychological Science, 3,* 61–64.

Carver, C. S., & Harmon-Jones, E. (2009). Anger is an approach-related affect: Evidence and implications. *Psychological Bulletin, 135,* 183–204.

Clore, G. L., & Huntsinger, J. R. (2007). How emotions inform judgment and regulate thought. *Trends in Cognitive Sciences, 11,* 393–399.

Cordova, D. I., & Lepper, M. R. (1996). Intrinsic motivation and the process of learning: Beneficial effects of contextualization, personalization, and choice. *Journal of Educational Psychology, 88,* 715–730.

Csikszentmihalyi, M. (1975). *Beyond boredom and anxiety.* San Francisco, CA: Jossey-Bass.

Daniels, L. M., & Stupnisky, R. H. (2012). Not that different in theory: Discussing the control-value theory of emotions in online learning environments. *Internet and Higher Education, 15,* 222–226.

Davidson, R. J., Scherer, K. R., & Goldsmith, H. H. (Eds.). (2003). *Handbook of affective sciences.* Oxford, United Kingdom: Oxford University Press.

Davis, H. A., DiStefano, C., & Schutz, P. A. (2008). Identifying patterns of appraising tests in first-year college students: Implications for anxiety and emotion regulation during test taking. *Journal of Educational Psychology, 100,* 942–960.

Dettmers, S., Trautwein, U., Lüdtke, O., Goetz, T., Frenzel, A. C., & Pekrun, R. (2011). Students' emotions during homework in mathematics: Testing a theoretical model of antecedents and achievement outcomes. *Contemporary Educational Psychology, 36,* 25–35.

Eccles, J. S. (1983). Expectancies, values and academic behaviors. In J. T. Spence (Ed.), *Achievement and achievement motives* (pp. 75–146). San Francisco, CA: Freeman.

Elliot, A. J., & McGregor, H. A. (2001). A 2 x 2 achievement goal framework. *Journal of Personality and Social Psychology, 80,* 501–519.

Elliot, A. J., Murayama, K., & Pekrun, R. (2011). A 3 x 2 achievement goal model. *Journal of Educational Psychology, 103,* 632–648.

Elliot, A. J., & Pekrun, R. (2007). Emotion in the hierarchical model of approach-avoidance of achievement motivation. In P. A. Schutz & R. Pekrun (Eds.), *Emotions in education* (pp. 57–73). San Diego, CA: Academic Press.

Feldman Barrett, L., & Russell, J. A. (1998). Independence and bipolarity in the structure of current affect. *Journal of Personality and Social Psychology, 74,* 967–984.

Folkman, S., & Lazarus, R. S. (1985). If it changes it must be a process: Study of emotion and coping during three stages of a college examination. *Journal of Personality and Social Psychology, 48,* 150–170.

Frenzel, A. C., Goetz, T., Lüdtke, O., Pekrun, R., & Sutton, R. (2009). Emotional transmission in the classroom: Exploring the relationship between teacher and student enjoyment. *Journal of Educational Psychology, 101,* 705–716.

Frenzel, A. C., Pekrun, R., & Goetz, T. (2007). Girls and mathematics—a "hopeless" issue? A control-value approach to gender differences in emotions towards mathematics. *European Journal of Psychology of Education, 22,* 497–514.

Frenzel, A. C., Thrash, T. M., Pekrun, R., & Goetz, T. (2007). Achievement emotions in Germany and China: A cross-cultural validation of the Academic Emotions Questionnaire-Mathematics (AEQ-M). *Journal of Cross-Cultural Psychology, 38,* 302–309.

Glaeser-Zikuda, M., Fuss, S., Laukenmann, M., Metz, K., & Randler, C. (2005). Promoting students' emotions and achievement: Instructional design and evaluation of the ECOLE-approach. *Learning and Instruction, 15,* 481–495.

Goetz, T., Bieg, M., Lüdtke, O., Pekrun, R., & Hall, N. C. (2013). Do girls really experience more anxiety in mathematics? *Psychological Science, 24,* 2079–2087.

Goetz, T., Frenzel, A. C., Hall, N. C., & Pekrun, R. (2008). Antecedents of academic emotions: Testing the internal/external frame of reference model for academic enjoyment. *Contemporary Educational Psychology, 33,* 9–33.

Goetz, T., Frenzel, A. C., Pekrun, R., Hall, N. C., & Lüdtke, O. (2007). Between- and within-domain relations of students' academic emotions. *Journal of Educational Psychology, 99,* 715–733.

Goetz, T., Frenzel, A. C., Stoeger, H., & Hall, N. C. (2010). Antecedents of everyday positive emotions: An experience sampling analysis. *Motivation and Emotion, 34,* 49–62.

Goetz, T., Pekrun, R., Hall, N., & Haag, L. (2006). Academic emotions from a socio-cognitive perspective: Antecedents and domain specificity of students' affect in the context of Latin instruction. *British Journal of Educational Psychology, 76,* 289–308.

Graham, S., & Taylor, A. Z. (2014). An attributional approach to emotional life in the classroom. In R. Pekrun & L. Linnenbrink-Garcia (Eds.), *International handbook of emotions in education* (pp. 96–119). New York, NY: Taylor & Francis.

Gross, J. J., & Thompson, R. A. (2007). Emotion regulation: Conceptual foundations. In J. J. Gross (Ed.), *Handbook of emotion regulation* (pp. 3–24). New York, NY: Guilford Press.

Hall, N. C., Perry, R. P., Goetz, T., Ruthig, J. C., Stupnisky, R. H., & Newall, N. E. (2007). Attributional retraining and elaborative learning: Improving academic development through writing-based interventions. *Learning and Individual Differences, 17,* 280–290.

Hall, N. C., Perry, R. P., Ruthig, J. C., Hladkyj, S., & Chipperfield, J. G. (2006). Primary and secondary control in achievement settings: A longitudinal field study of academic motivation, emotions, and performance. *Journal of Applied Social Psychology, 36,* 1430–1470.

Hatfield, E., Cacioppo, J. T., & Rapson, R. L. (1994). *Emotional contagion.* New York, NY: Cambridge University Press.

Heckhausen, H. (1991). *Motivation and action.* New York, NY: Springer.

Hembree, R. (1988). Correlates, causes, effects, and treatment of test anxiety. *Review of Educational Research, 58,* 47–77.

Jacobs, S. E., & Gross, J. J. (2014). Emotion regulation in education: Conceptual foundations, current applications, and future directions. In R. Pekrun & L. Linnenbrink-Garcia (Eds.), *International handbook of emotions in education* (pp. 183–201). New York, NY: Taylor & Francis.

Johnson, D. W., & Johnson, R. T. (1974). Instructional goal structure: Cooperative, competitive or individualistic. *Review of Educational Research, 4,* 213–240.

Kaplan, A., & Maehr, M. L. (1999). Achievement goals and student well-being. *Contemporary Educational Psychology, 24,* 330–358.

Krampen, G. (1988). Competence and control orientations as predictors of test anxiety in students: Longitudinal results. *Anxiety Research, 1,* 185–197.

Kuhbandner, C., & Pekrun, R. (2013). Affective state influences retrieval-induced forgetting for integrated knowledge. *PloS ONE, 8*(2), e56617.

Kuhbandner, C., Spitzer, B., & Pekrun, R. (2011). Read-out of emotional information from sensory memory: The longevity of threatening stimuli. *Psychological Science, 22,* 695–700.

Loewenstein, G., & Lerner, J. S. (2003). The role of affect in decision making. In R. J. Davidson, K. R. Scherer, & H. Hill Goldsmith (Eds.), *Handbook of affective sciences* (pp. 619–642). Oxford, United Kingdom: Oxford University Press.

Marsh, H. W. (1986). Verbal and math self-concept: An internal/external frame of reference model. *American Educational Research Journal, 23,* 129–149.

Marsh, H. W. (1993). Academic self-concept: Theory, measurement and research. In J. Suls (Ed.), *Psychological perspectives on the self* (Vol. 4, pp. 59–98). Hillsdale, NJ: Erlbaum.

Mauss, I. B., Bunge, S. A., & Gross, J. J. (2007). Automatic emotion regulation. *Social and Personality Psychology Compass, 1,* 146–167.

Murayama, K., & Elliot, A. J. (2009). The joint influence of personal achievement goals and classroom goal structures on achievement-relevant outcomes. *Journal of Educational Psychology, 101,* 432–447.

Nett, U. E., Goetz, T., & Hall, N. C. (2011). Coping with boredom in school: An experience sampling perspective. *Contemporary Educational Psychology, 36,* 49–59.

Parrott, W. G., & Spackman, M. P. (2000). Emotion and memory. In M. Lewis & J. M. Haviland-Jones (Eds.), *Handbook of emotions* (2nd edition, pp. 476–490). New York, NY: Guilford Press.

Pekrun, R. (1988). *Emotion, Motivation und Persönlichkeit* [Emotion, motivation and personality]. Munich, Germany: Psychologie Verlags Union.

Pekrun, R. (1992a). Kognition und Emotion in studienbezogenen Lern- und Leistungssituationen: Explorative Analysen [Cognition and emotion in academic learning and achievement: An exploratory analysis]. *Unterrichtswissenschaft, 20,* 308–324.

Pekrun, R. (1992b). Expectancy-value theory of anxiety: Overview and implications. In D. G. Forgays, T. Sosnowski, & K. Wrzesniewski (Eds.), *Anxiety: Recent developments in self-appraisal, psychophysiological and health research* (pp. 23–41). Washington, DC: Hemisphere.

Pekrun, R. (2006). The control-value theory of achievement emotions: Assumptions, corollaries, and implications for educational research and practice. *Educational Psychology Review, 18,* 315–341.

Pekrun, R. (2009). Global and local perspectives on human affect: Implications of the control-value theory of achievement emotions. In M. Wosnitza, S. A. Karabenick, A. Efklides, & P. Nenniger (Eds.), *Contemporary motivation research: From global to local perspectives* (pp. 97–115). Cambridge, MA: Hogrefe.

Pekrun, R., Elliot, A. J., & Maier, M. A. (2006). Achievement goals and discrete achievement emotions: A theoretical model and prospective test. *Journal of Educational Psychology, 98,* 583–597.

Pekrun, R., Elliot, A. J., & Maier, M. A. (2009). Achievement goals and achievement emotions: Testing a model of their joint relations with academic performance. *Journal of Educational Psychology, 101,* 115–135.

Pekrun, R., Frenzel, A., Goetz, T., & Perry, R. P. (2007). The control-value theory of achievement emotions: An integrative approach to emotions in education. In P. A. Schutz & R. Pekrun (Eds.), *Emotion in education* (pp. 13–36). San Diego, CA: Academic Press.

Pekrun, R., Goetz, T., Daniels, L. M., Stupnisky, R. H., & Perry, R. P. (2010). Boredom in achievement settings: Control-value antecedents and performance outcomes of a neglected emotion. *Journal of Educational Psychology, 102,* 531–549.

Pekrun, R., Goetz, T., Frenzel, A. C., Barchfeld, P., & Perry, R. P. (2011). Measuring emotions in students' learning and performance: The Achievement Emotions Questionnaire (AEQ). *Contemporary Educational Psychology, 36,* 36–48.

Pekrun, R., Goetz, T., Perry, R. P., Kramer, K., & Hochstadt, M. (2004). Beyond test anxiety: Development and validation of the Test Emotions Questionnaire (TEQ). *Anxiety, Stress and Coping, 17,* 287–316.

Pekrun, R., Goetz, T., Titz, W., & Perry, R. P. (2002). Academic emotions in students' self-regulated learning and achievement: A program of quantitative and qualitative research. *Educational Psychologist, 37,* 91–106.

Pekrun, R., Hall, N. C., Goetz, T., & Perry, R. P. (in press). Boredom and academic achievement: Testing a model of reciprocal causation. *Journal of Educational Psychology.*

Pekrun, R., & Linnenbrink-Garcia, L. (2014). Introduction to emotions in education. In R. Pekrun & L. Linnenbrink-Garcia (Eds.), *International handbook of emotions in education* (pp. 1–10). New York, NY: Taylor & Francis.

Perry, R. P., Chipperfield, J. G., Pekrun, R., Chuchmach, L., Stewart, T. L., & Murayama, K. (2012, January). *Attributional retraining in achievement settings: Longitudinal effects of a motivation treatment on cognition, emotion, and performance.* Paper presented at the Hawaiian International Conference on Education, Honolulu, HI.

Perry, R. P., Hall, N. C., & Ruthig, J. C. (2005). Perceived (academic) control and scholastic attainment in higher education. In J. Smart (Ed.), *Higher education: Handbook of theory and research* (Vol. 20, pp. 363–436). New York, NY: Springer.

Perry, R. P., Hechter, F. J., Menec, V. H., & Weinberg, L. (1993). Enhancing achievement motivation and performance in college students: An attributional retraining perspective. *Research in Higher Education, 34,* 687–723.

Perry, R. P., Hladkyi, S., Pekrun, R., & Pelletier, S. (2001). Academic control and action control in college students: A longitudinal study of self-regulation. *Journal of Educational Psychology, 93,* 776–789.

Perry, R. P., Stupnisky, R. H, Hall, N. C., Chipperfield, J. G., & Weiner, B. (2010). Bad starts and better finishes: Attributional retraining and initial performance in competitive achievement settings. *Journal of Social and Clinical Psychology, 29,* 668–700.

Reisenzein, R. (2001). Appraisal processes conceptualized from a schema-theoretic perspective. In In K. R. Scherer, A. Schorr, & T. Johnstone, T. (Eds.), *Appraisal processes in emotion* (pp. 187–201). Oxford, United Kingdom: Oxford University Press.

Roeser, R. W., Midgley, C., & Urdan, T. C. (1996). Perceptions of the school psychological environment and early adolescents' psychological and behavioral functioning in school: The mediating role of goals and belonging. *Journal of Educational Psychology, 88,* 408–422.

Ruthig, J. C., Perry, R. P., Hall, N. C., & Hladkyj, S. (2004). Optimism and attributional retraining: Longitudinal effects on academic achievement, test anxiety, and voluntary course withdrawal in college students. *Journal of Applied Social Psychology, 34,* 709–730.

Sansone, C., Weir, C., Harpster, L., & Morgan, C. (1992). Once a boring task always a boring task? Interest as a self-regulatory mechanism. *Journal of Personality and Social Psychology, 63,* 379–390.

Scherer, K. R., Schorr, A., & Johnstone, T. (Eds.). (2001). *Appraisal processes in emotion.* Oxford, United Kingdom: Oxford University Press.

Schutz, P. A., & Pekrun, R. (Eds.). (2007). *Emotion in education.* San Diego, CA: Academic Press.

Smith, C. A., & Ellsworth, P. C. (1987). Patterns of appraisal and emotion related to taking an exam. *Journal of Personality and Social Psychology, 52,* 477–488.

Spangler, G., Pekrun, R., Kramer, K., & Hofmann, H. (2002). Students' emotions, physiological reactions, and coping in academic exams. *Anxiety, Stress and Coping, 15,* 413–432.

Tsai, Y.-M., Kunter, M., Lüdtke, O., Trautwein, U., & Ryan, R. M. (2008). What makes lessons interesting? The role of situational and individual factors in three school subjects. *Journal of Educational Psychology, 100,* 460–472.

Turner, J. E., & Schallert, D. L. (2001). Expectancy-value relationships of shame reactions and shame resiliency. *Journal of Educational Psychology, 93,* 320–329.

Vogel-Walcutt, J. J., Fiorella, L., Carper, T., & Schatz, S. (2012). The definition, assessment, and mitigation of state boredom within educational settings: A comprehensive review. *Educational Psychology Review, 24,* 89–111.

Weiner, B. (1985). An attributional theory of achievement motivation and emotion. *Psychological Review, 92,* 548–573.

Weiner, B. (2007). Examining emotional diversity on the classroom: An attribution theorist considers the moral emotions. In P. A. Schutz & R. Pekrun (Eds.), *Emotion in education* (pp. 73–88). San Diego, CA: Academic Press.

Zeidner, M. (1998). *Test anxiety: The state of the art.* New York, NY: Plenum.

Zeidner, M. (2007). Test anxiety in educational contexts: What I have learned so far. In P. A. Schutz & R. Pekrun (Eds.), *Emotion in education* (pp. 165–184). San Diego, CA: Academic Press.

8

ACHIEVEMENT GOALS AND EMOTIONS

Lisa Linnenbrink-Garcia and Michael M. Barger,
Michigan State University and Duke University

Given the importance of motivation to schooling processes (Wigfield, Eccles, Schiefele, Roeser, & Davis-Kean, 2006), the goal of this chapter is to highlight how emotions relate to motivation in academic settings. We focus here on the relations between achievement goals and emotions and refer readers to other chapters within this volume for the consideration of emotions in relation to other motivational theories and constructs, such as interest and intrinsic motivation (Ainley & Hidi, 2014), attributions (Graham & Taylor, 2014), and implicit motives (Schultheiss & Köllner, 2014).

The interplay between achievement goals and emotions has been acknowledged since the inception of achievement goal theory (Dweck & Leggett, 1988). Indeed, many of the proposed relations build upon the foundational research on attributions and emotions conducted by Weiner (1985). Until recently, however, the links between emotions and achievement goals were largely ignored. In this chapter, we provide an overview of current theoretical models and empirical research relating achievement goals and emotions. Towards this end, we begin by presenting a general theoretical background, starting with a brief overview of achievement goal theory, briefly describing our terminology related to the study of emotions, and then presenting current theoretical models on achievement goals and emotions. We then provide an updated review of the extant literature, focusing on empirical research conducted from 2002 to present (see Linnenbrink & Pintrich, 2002 for a review of the literature prior to 2002). We conclude the chapter with suggestions for future research and theory.

THEORETICAL BACKGROUND

According to achievement goal theory, achievement goals provide a framework for interpreting and reacting to events (Dweck & Leggett, 1988). There are thought to be two primary goal orientations: mastery, where the focus is developing one's competence, and performance, where the focus is demonstrating one's competence often in comparison to others. These two primary dimensions can be further differentiated into approach and avoidance dimensions (Elliot, 1999; Pintrich, 2000). In this way, a student might be focused on trying to demonstrate competence (performance-approach) or avoiding the appearance of incompetence (performance-avoidance). The same approach-avoidance distinction can also be applied to mastery goals such that students can focus on developing competence (mastery-approach) or avoiding declining competence or not fulfilling one's potential (mastery-avoidance). Importantly, students can endorse multiple goal orientations at the same time (Barron & Harackiewicz, 2000; Pintrich, 2000), suggesting that there may be various profiles or combinations of simultaneously endorsed goal orientations.

With respect to affect and emotions, we draw largely from social psychological models. We use the term affect to refer to affective states, which shift and change as a function of the context, and include both general mood states and more discrete emotions (Rosenberg, 1998). We utilize the circumplex model of affect (Feldman Barrett & Russell, 1998), which differentiates affective states along two primary dimensions: valence (positive to negative) and activation (high to low). Accordingly, positive affect is differentiated into activated (excitement) and deactivated (relaxation) forms. A similar distinction between activated (anxious) and deactivated (tired) negative affect is also made. When relevant, we also focus on more specific emotions within these four quadrants to examine whether the patterns are similar among different types of emotions within that quadrant (e.g., angry and anxious).

MODELS OF ACHIEVEMENT GOALS AND EMOTIONS

With respect to the potential relations between achievement goals and emotions, researchers have put forth two largely complementary, yet distinct, models. One model, the asymmetrical bidirectional model, proposed by Linnenbrink and Pintrich (2002), draws upon Carver and Scheier's (1990) control-process model of self-regulation as well as research on achievement goal orientations more generally. The second model, proposed by Pekrun and his colleagues (2006, 2009), extends Pekrun's (2006, Pekrun & Perry, 2014) control-value theory of emotions to articulate how achievement goals predict discrete achievement emotions.

Asymmetrical Bidirectional Model

Linnenbrink and Pintrich's (2002) model of achievement goals and affect proposes that affect and achievement goals are reciprocally related (see Figure 8.1). On the left side of the figure, positive and negative affect shape students' perceptions of the classroom goal structure and subsequent goal endorsement. These effects, however, are only expected to occur for mastery goal structures and not performance goal structures, with positive moods supporting and negative moods undermining perceived mastery goal structures and subsequent mastery goal endorsement. Performance goal structures and personal performance goal endorsement are more readily influenced by other features of the context (competition) and individual differences (entity beliefs, fear of failure, need for achievement), and thus moods should not strongly influence them. Finally, based on the larger self-regulatory literature, positive moods are thought to predict approach goal endorsement while negative moods predict avoidance goal endorsement.

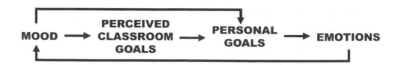

Figure 8.1 Linnenbrink and Pintrich's (2002) asymmetrical bidirectional model of achievement goals and affect.

On the right side of the figure, both mastery and performance goals predict emotions. The right side of the asymmetrical bidirectional model draws heavily on Carver and Scheier's (1990, 2014; Carver, Lawrence, & Scheier, 1996) control-process model of self-regulation. Thus, we first briefly describe the hypothesized role of emotions during self-regulation and then apply this model to a more specific type of goal pursuit, that of achievement goals.

The control-process model suggests that an individual's affective reaction during goal pursuit varies based on two factors (Carver et al., 1996; Carver & Scheier, 1990, 2014). The first is the type of goal, whether the person is trying to progress towards a goal (approach) or away from a goal (avoidance). The second is the perceived rate of progress. Approach goals are generally associated with elation (when one is approaching the goal at a standard or close to standard rate) and sadness (when one is not approaching the goal at a standard or close to standard rate). In contrast, avoidance goals are associated with relief when one is making sufficient progress and anxiety when one is not. Within this model, one's affect serves as a self-regulatory barometer, providing feedback to the self about perceived goal progress and thus helping to devote resources where appropriate (e.g., easing off on goals where sufficient progress is being made and towards goals with insufficient progress). Applied to achievement goals, the endorsement of mastery-approach or performance-approach goals would be associated with elation when successfully approaching one's goal and sadness with insufficient progress. Mastery-avoidance and performance-avoidance goals would be associated with relief with successful goal pursuit and anxiety when goal pursuit is not progressing at a sufficient rate.

Simply applying the approach/avoidance dichotomy to explain the emotions associated with achievement goals does not, however, account for the content of those goals. That is, one might expect different patterns of emotions depending on whether one pursues a goal with a mastery or performance focus. Thus, the asymmetrical bidirectional model further proposes that the expected pattern of emotions varies based not only the direction of the goal (approach/avoid) but also the content of the goal (mastery/performance).

Specifically, a student may be more successful in approaching a mastery goal (relative to a performance goal) in that the standard of progress is set relative to the self (improvement or learning), making it more likely that one would experience positive activated emotions, such as elation or joy, and less likely that one would experience negative deactivated emotions, such as sadness. Even with insufficient progress, a student with a mastery-approach goal may not experience much negative affect, as the lack of progress should signal that one is not trying hard enough and should not reflect negatively on one's view of oneself. That is, the attribution for lack of progress would likely be towards lack of effort rather than lack of ability and would thus help to protect a negative evaluation of the self and reduce the likelihood of negative emotions such as guilt, shame, or anxiety. Indeed, individuals with mastery goals often view difficult situations as challenging and may take pleasure in their attempts to master a difficult task, even when success is not readily apparent.

In contrast, students who endorse performance-approach goal orientations use normative standards for evaluating goal progress (Elliot, 2005; Elliot, Murayama, & Pekrun, 2011). When success is judged normatively, one may be less likely to make sufficient progress towards one's goal, as only a limited number of people can outperform their peers. Thus, performance-approach goals are hypothesized to positively predict sadness or depression (deactivated negative affect). However, when a student is making sufficient progress towards demonstrating competence (performance-approach), the student should experience activated positive emotions, such as elation and pride. Additionally, the emphasis on demonstrating one's competence is likely to produce anxiety, given that one is putting one's sense of self on the line. In this way, performance-approach goals are expected to give rise to negative activating (anxiety, frustration), negative deactivating (sadness), and positive activating (elation, pride) emotions, depending on the perceived progress towards the goal and threat to the self.

Performance-avoidance goal orientations should primarily give rise to negative activating emotions (anxiety), although students with these goal orientations may also experience positive deactivating emotions such as relief when sufficient progress is made. Similar to performance-approach goals, students with performance-avoidance goals may experience lack of progress more frequently, as success may only occur through outperforming others. Mastery-avoidance goals are also expected to relate to emotions such as anxiety and relief. However, as the standard of progress is internal or criterion-based, students endorsing mastery-avoidance goals may be more successful in making progress towards these goals and thus may tend to experience a sense of calm more than anxiety.

Control-Value Model

An alternative, but related, perspective is that proposed by Pekrun, Elliot, and Maier (2006, 2009). This perspective is based on Pekrun's (2006, Pekrun & Perry, 2014) control-value theory of achievement emotions, which argues that perceptions of control and subjective value for both achievement activities and outcomes shape achievement emotions. Based on this view, emotions emerge surrounding achievement-related activities (e.g., enjoyment) as well as retrospective (e.g., shame) and prospective (e.g., hope) achievement outcomes. The actual emotion that occurs depends on one's feelings of control and value. Experiencing both control (competence) and positive subjective value (perceived importance of the task) increase enjoyment and decrease boredom and anger during achievement activities. For emotions surrounding achievement outcomes, control (success) and positive subjective value can also give rise to prospective (hope) and retrospective (pride) emotions. In contrast, lack of control (failure) and negative subjective value are associated with prospective (hopelessness, anxiety) and retrospective (shame) outcome emotions.

Goal orientations relate to emotions by directing individuals' attention and thus their appraisals and self-related cognitions. In their model, Pekrun et al. (2006, 2009) employ the trichotomous model of achievement goals (mastery-approach, performance-approach, performance-avoidance; see Elliot & Pekrun, 2007 for an extension of the model to mastery-avoidance goals). Specifically, mastery-approach goals help to focus the individual on the positive value of the task and are associated with heightened feelings of control and competency. Thus, based on the control-value model, mastery goals are expected to positively predict positive activity emotions, such as enjoyment, and negatively predict negative activity emotions, such as anger and boredom. In contrast, performance goals, with the focus on demonstrating competence, tend to focus the individual on the outcome rather than the activity, but feelings of control and competence vary for approach versus avoidance goals. With performance-approach goals, the student feels in control and is focused on the positive value of attaining success. Thus, performance-approach goal orientations should be linked to positive prospective and retrospective outcome emotions such as hope and pride. On the other hand, individuals who endorse performance-avoidance goals may not feel in control, may doubt their competence, and may focus on the negative value of failure. Given these negative perceptions of control and value, individuals who endorse performance-avoidance goals are therefore expected to experience both prospective (anxiety and hopelessness) and retrospective (shame) negative outcome emotions.

Summary

While the underlying mechanisms to explain how achievement goals and emotions differ across these two models, the models make fairly similar predictions. Mastery goals are hypothesized to give rise to positive activated emotions (enjoyment) and either be unrelated to or reduce negative activated (anger, anxiety) and deactivated (bored, tired) emotions. Performance-avoidance goals heighten negative activated emotions, especially anxiety. According to Pekrun et al. (2006), performance-avoidance goals should also be associated with negative deactivated outcome emotions, such as hopelessness and shame. Performance-approach goals lead to feelings of hope, pride, and enjoyment but may also elicit activated (anxiety) and deactivated (sadness) negative emotions, at least based on Linnenbrink and Pintrich's (2002) model. While Pekrun et al. (2006) do not make hypotheses regarding mastery-avoidance goals, Linnenbrink and Pintrich (2002) hypothesize that these goals will be related to both deactivated positive emotions (calm) and activated negative emotions (anxiety). Finally, Linnenbrink and Pintrich's (2002) model also considers how emotions relate to perceived goal structures and subsequent personal goal endorsement. While Pekrun et al. (2006, 2009) do not focus on this in their work related to achievement goals, the control-value model includes feedback loops suggesting that emotions can also shape appraisal processes. With this broader theoretical framing in mind, we now turn to the extant literature to consider the empirical evidence for these theoretical models.

REVIEW OF EMPIRICAL EVIDENCE

In 2002, Linnenbrink and Pintrich reviewed the extant literature linking achievement goals and affect and utilized this review to develop their proposed model. Their review found that mastery-approach goals were consistently associated with positive affect and were either unrelated or negatively related to negative affect, including anxiety. The findings for performance-approach goals were more mixed. Performance-approach goals were positively, negatively, or unrelated to positive affect and either negatively or unrelated to negative affect. In contrast, performance-avoidance goals were consistently related to increased negative affect, especially test anxiety. In 2002, mastery-avoidance goals were positively related to anxiety as well, although there was not much empirical research to review at the time. Linnenbrink and Pintrich (2002) also reported on a few longitudinal studies that provided evidence that general measures of positive and negative affect were associated with students' perceptions of the classroom as mastery-oriented but were unrelated to the perceived environment as performance-oriented. Notably, the majority of research conducted prior to 2002 focused on positive and negative affect more generally rather than specific emotions and focused on goals as predictors of affect.

Since Linnenbrink and Pintrich's (2002) review, research on achievement goals and emotion has increased. However, these studies mostly focus on the effect of personal goals on emotions; few researchers investigate the influence of mood on perceptions of classroom goal structures or personal goals. Thus, our review of recent research on goals and emotions will focus on published research aimed at understanding how goals lead to emotions. A notable difference between the literature reviewed prior to 2002 and the current review is that many more studies now investigate specific emotions, or at least differentiate emotions based on both valence and activation. Thus, our more recent review allows a more careful evaluation of both Linnenbrink and Pintrich's (2002) and Pekrun and his colleagues' (2006, 2009) models.

Before turning to our review, it is important to note that a recent meta-analysis of studies through 2009 examined the relation between goals and affect (Huang, 2011). Findings generally supported both the asymmetrical-bidirectional model and the control-value model. Mastery-approach goals related strongly to positive emotions and negatively (though less strongly) to negative emotions. Mastery-avoidance goals related strongly to negative emotions. Performance-approach goals were more moderately related to positive and negative emotions. Performance-avoidance goals were strongly related to negative emotions and negatively (though less strongly) to positive emotions. Our current review expands on these findings in several ways. First, our review explicitly compares current findings to two theoretical models. Second, we make the distinction between activated and deactivated emotions, a theoretically important distinction. Third, given the potential for students to pursue multiple goals simultaneously, we also include studies that utilize person-centered techniques.

We divide our review based on whether the researchers employed a variable-centered or person-centered analytical approach. These two complimentary approaches provide somewhat different information about the relations between achievement goals and emotions. The variable-centered view is more aligned with both the asymmetrical bidirectional model and the control-value model—both of which focus on how each achievement goal relates independently to emotions. With this approach, researchers typically conduct multiple regression analyses or path analyses to examine the unique, independent relations of each achievement goal and emotions. However, there is also a growing body of research that considers how patterns or profiles of achievement goal endorsements (e.g., simultaneously endorsing both mastery-approach and performance-approach goals) relate to emotions, drawing from a multiple goal perspective (see Barron & Harackiewicz, 2000). Person-centered analyses typically employ cluster analysis or latent profile analysis to identify profiles of goals and then relate these clusters to emotions.

Variable-Centered View of Goals to Emotions

By far, the majority of research examining achievement goals and emotions can be characterized as variable-centered. In order to organize our review, we differentiate among four types of achievement goals (mastery-approach, mastery-avoidance, performance-approach,

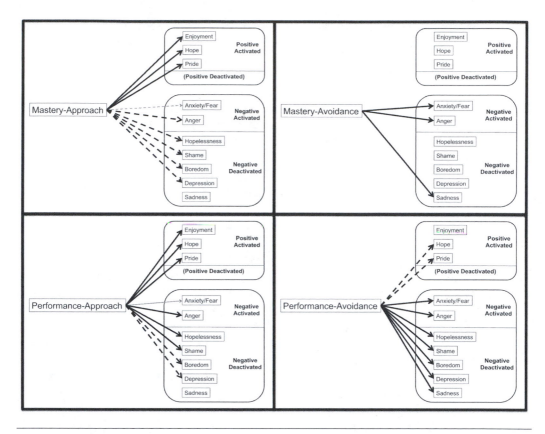

Figure 8.2 Summary of findings for the variable-centered relation between goals and emotions. Solid lines indicate a positive relation, while dashed lines indicate a negative relation. Gray lines indicate inconsistent findings.

performance-avoidance) and consider how these goals relate to emotions organized into the four quadrants of the circumplex model of affect (see Figure 8.2).[1]

Mastery-Approach Goals

In line with both theoretical models linking achievement goals and emotions, there is strong empirical support suggesting that mastery-approach goals relate positively to positive activated emotions, such as enjoyment (Daniels et al., 2008, 2009; King, McInerney, & Watkins, 2012; Pekrun et al., 2006, 2009; Shih, 2008), hope (King et al., 2012; Pekrun et al., 2006, 2009; Sapio, 2010), and pride (King et al., 2012; Pekrun et al., 2006, 2009). They are also related to positive affect when measured more broadly (Kalil & Ziol-Guest, 2008; Linnenbrink, 2005; Sideridis, 2007; Tulis & Ainley, 2011). Mastery-approach goals are negatively related to negative emotions, including both negative activated emotions, such as anxiety and anger (Bandalos, Finney, & Geske, 2003; Daniels et al., 2008, 2009; King et al., 2012; Pekrun et al., 2006, 2009; Shih, 2005, 2008) and negative deactivated emotions, like boredom, depression, shame, and hopelessness (Daniels et al., 2008, 2009; King et al., 2012; Pekrun et al., 2006, 2009; Shih, 2008; Tupper, 2008; Zychinski & Polo, 2012). Notably, the most common link of mastery-approach goals to emotions involved enjoyment and boredom. This pattern of findings suggests that the nature of mastery-approach goals intertwine with interest development and intrinsic motivation (Harackiewicz, Durik, Barron, Linnenbrink-Garcia, & Tauer, 2008). Thus, it is not surprising that mastery-approach goals are associated most frequently with heightened enjoyment and decreased boredom.

Given the larger number of studies that examined anxiety, we provide more detail regarding these findings. Several studies found a negative relation between mastery-approach and anxiety (Bandalos et al., 2003; Daniels et al., 2008, 2009; Shih, 2005, 2008). However, there was no significant relation in an equivalent number of studies (Bong, 2009; Linnenbrink, 2005; Pekrun et al., 2009; Putwain & Symes, 2012; Sideridis, 2007). Somewhat surprisingly, there was a positive relation between mastery-approach goals and anxiety in two studies (Gaudreau, 2012; Koul, Roy, Kaewkuekool, & Ploisawaschai, 2009). However, both studies were somewhat unique. One study investigated second language learning in Thailand (Koul et al., 2009). The other only found that mastery-approach goals related to anxiety among students who endorsed mastery goals for external reasons (such as wanting to study as much as possible not out of personal interest but because someone else tells them it is important; Gaudreau, 2012). In both of these studies, performance-approach and -avoidance goals were stronger predictors of anxiety than mastery goals.

In summary, just as with many academic outcomes, mastery-approach goals seem to be associated with adaptive patterns of emotions. They are consistently associated with heightened activated positive emotions. Moreover, there seems to be some benefit to endorsing mastery-approach goals in terms of decreased levels of negative activated and deactivated emotions, especially boredom. These findings are aligned with both the asymmetrical bidirectional model and the control-value model. Students with mastery-approach goals feel positive activated emotions as they successfully meet their goals of improvement or because mastery goals relate to perceptions of competency and control. When students believe their goals are being met and feel competent and in control, this precludes negative activated and deactivated emotions as well. Together, these results suggest that mastery-approach goals relate broadly to the types of emotional experiences that should help to sustain students' engagement and learning in school.

Mastery-Avoidance Goals

A relatively new arrival to the study of achievement goals, mastery-avoidance goals have only been studied in conjunction with emotions in a few studies. These studies found no statistically significant relation between mastery-avoidance goals and any kind of positive affect (Shih, 2008; Sideridis, 2008). However, mastery-avoidance goals were associated with several negative emotions, such as anxiety (Bong, 2009; Putwain & Symes, 2012; Sideridis, 2008), anger (Shih, 2008), and sadness (Sideridis, 2008). These results coincide very little with mastery-approach goals, suggesting that the approach/avoid dimension is key to differentiating the way in which these two types of mastery goals predict emotions.

The empirical findings generally support the asymmetrical bidirectional model, as mastery-avoidance goals were hypothesized to predict negative activated emotions like anxiety. However, mastery-avoidance goals were not expected to be associated with anger or sadness, and the hypothesized link to relief has not been investigated. Pekrun's control-value model did not include mastery-avoidance goals. Given the relative sparse empirical findings available for mastery-avoidance, there is a clear need for additional research to replicate these findings, consider the implications of the findings for both theoretical models, and determine if there are any similar patterns of emotions for the two types of mastery goals.

Performance-Approach Goals

Performance-approach goals and emotions are a more complicated story. Performance-approach goals in some studies relate to the positive emotions of enjoyment (Daniels et al., 2008; King et al., 2012), hope (King et al., 2012; Pekrun et al., 2009), and pride (King et al., 2012; Pekrun et al., 2006, Study 2; 2009). This generally supports the asymmetrical bidirectional model that predicts approach goals elicit positive activated emotions, assuming students make sufficient progress towards their goals. It also supports the control value model in which the focus on the outcome produces feelings of enjoyment and prospective and retrospective emotions like hope and pride.

Negative emotions, on the other hand, relate less consistently to performance-approach goals. Several studies have suggested that performance-approach goals are in fact related to anxiety, particularly test anxiety (Bandalos et al., 2003; Bong, 2009; Daniels et al., 2008, 2009; Gaudreau, 2012; King et al., 2012; Koul et al., 2009; Linnenbrink, 2005). However, a small number found just the opposite (Duchesne & Rattelle, 2010; Shih, 2005), and even more have found no relation at all (Pekrun et al., 2006, 2009; Putwain & Symes, 2012; Shih, 2008; Sideridis, 2007). Researchers have put so much effort into studying anxiety that it has been measured in a number of different ways, which might complicate the findings. Furthermore, the relation between performance-approach goals and anxiety may be suppressed, given the high correlation between performance-approach and -avoidance goals and the high correlation between performance-avoidance goals and anxiety (Linnenbrink-Garcia et al., 2012). When both performance-approach and performance-avoidance goals are entered into a regression, one predictor can control for irrelevant variance in the other, changing the size or direction of the relation with the criterion variable. In other words, the strong relation between performance-avoidance goals and anxiety, combined with the strong relation between performance-approach and -avoidance goals, may make it appear that performance-approach goals do not relate strongly to anxiety. Alternatively, one could argue that it is critical to control for performance-avoidance goals when assessing the effects of performance-approach goals to anxiety. The difficulty in interpreting these findings helps to highlight why a person-centered approach (see the section further on) may be particularly useful for teasing apart these findings. There is also some evidence for the relation between performance-approach goals and another positive activated emotion: anger (Shih, 2008), though this too has not been replicated in other studies (King et al., 2012; Pekrun et al., 2006, 2009).

As for negative deactivated emotions, performance-approach goals relate positively to hopelessness (King et al., 2012) and shame (King et al., 2012; Pekrun et al., 2006) but negatively to depression (Kalil & Ziol-Guest, 2008). Hopelessness and shame are more complex emotions than other negative deactivated emotions. Feelings of hopelessness and shame implicate the self. Performance-approach goals, once called *ego-involvement* (Nicholls, 1984), focus on demonstrating competence about oneself. Therefore, it makes sense that students who tend to be in this frame of mind might also experience negative, self-implicating emotions.

Overall, the findings align with both the asymmetrical bidirectional model and the control-value model. Both models predict that performance-approach goals relate to positive activated emotions, although this predicted relation is expected to be stronger in the control-value model. Current research also partially supports the asymmetrical bidirectional model's additional predictions about negative affect. Performance-approach goals often relate positively to negative activated emotions like anger and anxiety, and some forms of negative deactivated emotions (shame), but, in contrast to the asymmetrical bidirectional model, they negatively relate to other negative deactivated emotions (sadness). Notably, the control-value model does not predict a relation between performance-approach goals and negative affect. These complex findings remind us that the emotions students experience when endorsing performance-approach goals probably also depend on other factors, specifically whether or not they are making sufficient progress towards their goal or whether the emotion implicates the self. Variations may also be accounted for individual differences in the regulation of negative emotions (Tyson, Linnenbrink-Garcia, & Hill, 2009).

Performance-Avoidance Goals

Performance-avoidance goals predict less beneficial emotional outcomes. They relate negatively to positive activated emotions like hope and pride (Pekrun, 2009); however, they are consistently unrelated to enjoyment, another positive activated emotion (Pekrun et al., 2006, 2009; Puente-Díaz, 2012 (sport); Shih, 2008). Performance-avoidance goals also relate positively to negative deactivated emotions, such as hopelessness (Pekrun et al., 2006), boredom (Pekrun et al., 2006, Study 2; Shih, 2008), sadness (Sideridis, 2008), shame (Pekrun et al., 2009), and depression (Sideridis, 2007; Tupper, 2008; Zychinski & Polo, 2012). As for negative activated emotions, performance-avoidance goals are positively related to anger (Pekrun et al., 2009), and many studies have shown a positive association with anxiety (Bong 2009; Duchesne & Ratelle, 2010; Pekrun et al., 2006, 2009; Putwain & Symes, 2012; Shih, 2005, 2008; Sideridis, 2007, 2008).

When interpreting the findings for negative activated emotions, especially anxiety, it is important to keep in mind that earlier versions of performance-avoidance scales included phrases like "I worry . . ." and "I'm afraid that . . ." (e.g., Elliot & Church, 1997). Thus, the strong relation to anxiety may be due, at least in part, to measurement. However, more recent studies that have used performance-avoidance scales revised to eliminate affective elements still found a significant positive relation between performance-avoidance goals and anxiety (Pekrun et al., 2006, 2009), albeit not as strong a relation (β's ranged from 0.14 to 0.43) as earlier studies that included affective components (e.g., $\beta = 0.54$; Shih, 2005).

The consistent findings linking performance-avoidance goals to negative activated emotions supports both the asymmetrical bidirectional model and the control-value model. It also confirms the extension from control-value theory that performance-avoidance goals relate to negative deactivated outcome emotions. While neither model expressed clear expectations for performance-avoidance goals and positively valenced emotions, research suggests that performance-avoidance goals are associated with fewer feelings of hope and pride.

Summary

There are many studies that have not found significant relations between certain pairings of goals and affect. We have tried to simplify the picture by only presenting significant relations between goals and emotions that have been examined in multiple studies and are not contradicted by findings that suggest the variables relate in an opposing direction (see Figure 8.2). From this synthesis of current research, it is clear that achievement goals relate to emotions in fairly predictable patterns. Mastery-approach goals relate to more positive affect and less negative affect. Avoidance goals, both mastery and performance, either do not relate to positive emotions or negatively relate to them and relate strongly with negative emotions. Performance-approach goals have a more complicated relation with emotions, though it is possible to differentiate these connections by dividing emotions into positive, negative with a focus on the self (shame, anger), and negative without a focus on the self (sadness, boredom). Pursuing performance-approach goals implicates the self, therefore putting the self at risk for failure, eliciting negative self-related emotions. However, having this goal might also prevent negative emotions that do not implicate the self, such as depression and boredom. The asymmetrical bidirectional model also suggests that because not everyone can successfully meet performance-approach goals, the relation between performance goals and emotion likely depends on whether a student feels he or she is making sufficient progress towards his or her goals, although this has not been explicitly tested in the studies reviewed here. Indeed, despite the growing body of literature linking achievement goals to emotions, the presumed mediating processes (rate of progress, control-value appraisals) have not been examined for either of the two theoretical models.

Person-Centered View of Goals to Emotions

By focusing on variables like goals and emotions, prior research demonstrates the systematic relation between the two constructs. But what does this mean for an individual student, particularly if that student endorses multiple goals or, even, no goals at all? Students' goal orientations become increasingly complex as researchers conceptualize an increasing number of goal constructs. Instead of examining mean levels of goal endorsement and complex interactions among four or more goal orientations, person-centered analyses focus on different goal profiles with the individual at the center of analysis. In other words, what common types of goal endorsement exist, and how do these different goal profiles relate to students' emotional experiences in the classroom? Person-centered analyses (e.g., cluster analysis, latent profile analysis) are currently gaining traction in achievement goal theory as a meaningful way to interpret the intricate relations among goals at the level of the individual (Daniels et al., 2008; Liu, Wang, Tan, Ee, & Koh, 2009; Luo, Paris, Hogan, & Luo, 2011). These analyses group students into goal profiles based on the similarity in students' goal endorsement. Person-centered work is also uniquely suited to answer questions about multiple-goal pursuit. For example, researchers could compare a profile that shows high mastery-approach and performance-approach goals to a profile with high mastery goals and low performance goals. Doing so may be particularly useful for understanding the more complex pattern of findings observed for performance-approach goals.

Across studies, several reliable goal profiles have been identified such as high all goals, mastery-oriented (high on mastery goals but low or average on performance),

performance-oriented (high on performance-approach but low or average on mastery), and approach oriented (high on approach goals but low or average on avoidance goals) (Wormington & Linnenbrink-Garcia, 2013). However, the groups that arise in each data set vary somewhat and depend on which goals are included as clustering variables. Thus, we organize our discussion of person-centered analyses based on the types of goals included within the profile, starting with studies including mastery-approach and performance-approach goals only and then turning to those utilizing the trichotomous or 2 × 2 (four goals) models.

Mastery and Performance Profiles

When only mastery-approach and performance-approach goals are used to create the clusters, a clear pattern arises. Students in profiles where mastery goals are strongly endorsed either alone (mastery-oriented) or alongside performance-approach goals (multiple goals) experience greater enjoyment and less boredom (Daniels et al., 2008). With respect to anxiety, students in high performance goal profiles (both multiple goals and high performance with low mastery goals) tend to experience greater anxiety than students in high mastery, low performance profiles (Daniels et al., 2008; Ironsmith, Marva, Harju, & Eppler, 2003). These findings support the assumptions of both theoretical models that mastery goals relate to positive activated affect and the assertion by Linnenbrink and Pintrich (2002) that performance-approach goals relate to anxiety. However, these relations become more complex as more goals enter into the goal profile.

Trichotomous Goals Profiles

When mastery, performance-approach, and performance-avoidance goals were used to form the profiles, a difference emerged between two sets of multiple goal profiles. Students in profiles with high performance-approach and performance-avoidance goals and moderately high mastery goals experienced greater anxiety, negative affect, and depression than students in most other groups (Luo et al., 2011; Poulin, Duchesne, & Ratelle, 2010). However, a similar group of students with high performance-approach and performance-avoidance goals and high mastery goals experienced greater positive affect, less anxiety, and less depression than members of many other groups (Sideridis, 2007). This may indicate the importance of simultaneously endorsing mastery goals alongside performance goals. Without a strong buffering effect of relatively high mastery goals, students with high performance goals appear to be at risk for experiencing greater negative affect in school.

Differentiating between approach and avoidance goals in the trichotomous goals cluster analyses also provides interesting information. Students in profiles with high performance-avoidance goals tend to experience greater anxiety (Luo et al., 2011; Poulin et al., 2010) and generally lower positive affect and higher negative affect (Conley, 2012). This is even true for students in profiles with high performance-avoidance goals relative to amotivated students (low on all goals), who interestingly experience less anxiety than many other groups (Poulin et al., 2010), perhaps because they do not care about educational outcomes. With person-centered analysis, including other variables in the motivational profile may also inform the findings. For example, Conley (2012) included perceived cost in her analyses and discovered that students with moderate scores on all goals only experienced increased negative affect when they also perceived a high cost to learning math.

2 × 2 Goals Profiles

Only a few studies have examined goal profiles with the 2 × 2 goal structure in relation to emotional outcomes (Jang & Liu, 2012; Tuominen-Soini, Salmela-Aro, & Niemivirta, 2008). The clearest finding for these analyses is that students in a profile high on mastery-approach goals but low on all other goals experienced fewer depressive symptoms (Tuominen-Soini et al., 2008) as well as greater enjoyment, lower anxiety, and less boredom (Jang & Liu, 2012) than students in other goal profiles. In addition, students in the amotivated profile (low on all goals) experienced less enjoyment than all groups, while students in the high on all goals profiles actually experienced similar degrees of enjoyment compared to students in the mastery-approach only profile (Jang & Liu, 2012).

Summary

While the identified profiles can vary across studies, person-centered analysis provides useful information about the relation between achievement goals and emotions beyond the traditional variable-centered approach. A person-centered approach has become increasingly common in the achievement goal literature. It helps researchers test the value of multiple goals and the relative importance of approach and avoidance orientations for students' emotions. Person-centered analyses also represent a technique that allows researchers to examine the influence of other variables, like work-avoidance goals or cost in determining how goals relate to emotions within individuals (Conley, 2012; Tuominen-Soini et al., 2008).

To some extent, person-centered analyses produce similar results to variable-centered analyses. Both forms of analysis support the control-value model and the asymmetrical bidirectional model. Specifically, both methods find that mastery-approach goals and profiles with high levels of mastery-approach goals relate to more positive emotions and less negative emotions. Approach goals are generally associated with more adaptive patterns of emotions than avoidance goals across both analytical approaches. And, both approaches suggest that performance-avoidance goals are strongly related to negative emotions, especially anxiety. With both person-centered and variable-centered analyses, performance-approach goals relate to emotions in a complicated manner.

However, person-centered analyses provide insight into the function of performance-approach goals that variable-centered analyses cannot. Specifically, goal theorists have long acknowledged that students may simultaneously endorse more than one goal at a time (Barron & Harackiewicz, 2000). Person-centered analyses may better reflect how students endorse multiple goals simultaneously, as they allow both more nuanced patterns and help to identify the profiles of goal endorsement that are typically experienced in the classroom (Wormington & Linnenbrink-Garcia, 2013). One reason the relation between performance-approach goals and emotions may be more complex is because the relation of performance-approach goals to emotions varies as a function of the other goals that are endorsed. Profile studies suggest that performance goals relate to more positive activated and less negative activated and negative deactivated emotions when accompanied by strong mastery goals. Even with slightly lower levels of mastery goals, high performance-approach goals in a profile relate to less positive emotional outcomes (Luo et al., 2011; Poulin et al., 2010). Another interesting finding is the amotivated profile. Variable-centered analysis only looks at students' levels of different goals; however, person-centered analyses have uncovered students that are low on all goals. While students in amotivated profiles generally experience less positive activated emotions and more negative deactivated emotions (as would be predicted in variable-centered studies), they also experience less anxiety. Although positive deactivated emotions have not been linked to achievement goals by current research, it seems reasonable that these amotivated students might experience more emotions like relief and calm at the opposite region of the circumplex.

Finally, person-centered analyses allow researchers to examine the more complex amalgam of motivation students actually experience. Researchers have included other motivational constructs, such as perceived cost and avoidance goals, to better understand the relation between goals and emotions (Conley, 2012; Tuominen-Soini et al., 2008). Interestingly, both theoretical models discussed in this paper arise from variable-centered research. Future researchers may find that they need to expand on these models to include findings from person-centered research. Considering the complex motivational milieu students experience from day to day, profile analyses may be especially well-suited to understanding how achievement goals relate to emotions in the classroom.

CHALLENGES AND FUTURE DIRECTIONS

In our review, we have noted a number of consistent findings regarding the relation between achievement goals and emotions. Our review also helps to highlight several important future directions as well as challenges that must be addressed if we are to continue to make progress in the study of emotions and achievement goals. Accordingly, we outline several challenges and suggest areas for future research to address these challenges and to fill voids in the extant literature.

One particular challenge concerns how and when to assess emotions and goals. For instance, when in the goal pursuit process should emotions and moods be measured? To date, the majority of the studies we reviewed assessed achievement goals and emotions simultaneously and retrospectively. Yet, most studies make the claim that goals are predicting emotions, even without direct evidence regarding directionality. Moreover, there are very few studies that even considered whether emotions, moods, or general affective states predicted perceived goal structures or personal goal endorsement, as hypothesized by Linnenbrink and Pintrich (2002; see Daniels et al., 2009 and Tupper, 2008 for exceptions). Thus, given the current approach to research, we know very little about the directionality in the relation between achievement goals and emotions. One potential solution to this problem is to measure affective states, goals, and emotions over multiple time points. Doing so would enable researchers to better test reciprocal relations over time and thus make clearer claims regarding directionality and reciprocity.

In addition to needing longitudinal data with multiple time points, the field would benefit from moving beyond retrospective reports of goals and emotions. Given that both achievement goals and emotions may shift as a function of the context, one may want to consider varying units of time and level to more fully capture the dynamic, situated relations between achievement goals and emotions during goal pursuit. Measuring achievement goals and emotions in shorter time intervals or using experimental methodologies may help researchers to better understand the complex way in which performance-approach goals predict emotions. For example, in line with earlier research by Elliott and Dweck (1988), Linnenbrink-Garcia and Tyson (2007) observed that the relation of performance-approach goals to emotions varied as a function of perceived challenge or difficulty encountered when solving complex reasoning problems. More-over, the way in which achievement goals relate to emotions may also vary based on the context. For example, Ben-Eliyahu and Linnenbrink-Garcia (2011) observed different patterns of emotions associated with performance-approach goals depending on whether students reported on achievement goals and emotions in a favorite or least favorite class.

Taking a situated and dynamic perspective to studying achievement goals and emotions can be particularly challenging but can be facilitated by utilizing multiple levels of analysis and multiple methodologies (see Meyer & Turner, 2006; Turner & Trucano, 2014). Employing physiological indicators of emotion may also help to measure emotion as it occurs and prevent overreliance on survey measures. For instance, one recent study found that mastery-approach goals related to a decline in heart rate during an oral presentation (Sideridis, 2008). This aligns with findings that mastery-approach goals decrease self-reported anxiety. Additionally, the use of technology to collect real-time data may facilitate a more situated analysis, as it allows for moment-to-moment assessments (see D'Mello & Graesser, 2014; Graesser, D'Mello, & Strain, 2014).

The methodological approaches described above for studying achievement goals and emotions can also be employed to test the underlying psychological mechanisms that link achievement goals to emotions. The two theoretical models presented here, proposed by Linnenbrink and Pintrich (2000) and Pekrun et al. (2006, 2009), propose somewhat different mechanisms to explain the relation between achievement goals and emotions. Linnenbrink and Pintrich (2000) rely heavily on models of self-regulation and suggest that perceived rate of progress towards (or away from) one's goal is key, yet prior research has not specifically tested this hypothesis (see Linnenbrink-Garcia & Tyson, 2007 for the closest approximation). Similarly, Pekrun and his colleagues (2006, 2009) propose that control and value appraisals are the mechanisms through which achievement goals shape emotions; yet to date, these mediating processes have not been empirically tested. Future research should utilize study designs that not only allow for the testing of reciprocal relations between goals and emotions but also allow one to test the hypothesized underlying psychological mediators of these relations.

Another consideration with respect to assessment and analysis is the importance of accounting for multiple goal pursuit and addressing shared variance among goals when conducting variable-centered analyses. Given the high correlation between performance-approach and performance-avoidance goals, findings from multiple regression analyses may vary as a function of which goals are in the model (Linnenbrink-Garcia et al., 2012). For example, Pekrun et al. (2009) reported that the bivariate correlation between performance-approach goals and hope was nonsignificant but that the beta coefficient was statistically significant and positive, suggesting that this positive relation between performance-approach goals and hope may only occur when the shared variance between performance-approach and -avoidance goal orientations is removed. The potential problem with shared variance as well as the difficulty of accounting for multiple goal pursuit when conducting variable-centered analyses suggests that a person-centered perspective may be especially useful for unpacking the complex ways in which achievement goals and emotions relate. As mentioned previously, a person-centered perspective enables the researcher to examine how multiple patterns (or profiles) of goals relate to emotions. This may be particularly useful in better understanding some of the complex or contradictory findings observed, especially for performance-approach goals. Indeed, our review of the literature employing a person-centered approach suggests that performance-approach goals are more strongly associated with positive emotions (and less with negative emotions) when mastery-approach goals are also strongly endorsed.

Researchers must also consider what emotions to assess. Notably, researchers have largely ignored one type of affect: positive deactivated emotions, such as feeling calm or relieved. While students certainly experience positive deactivated emotions in the classroom (Pekrun, Goetz, Titz, & Perry, 2002), researchers have not yet examined these emotions in empirical studies relating achievement goals to emotions. Yet, their inclusion is important for fully assessing theoretical models. The asymmetrical bidirectional model suggests that positive deactivated emotions arise when sufficient progress is made towards mastery-avoidance and performance-avoidance goals. Moreover, given the evidence from person-centered studies, certain profiles of goals may be more likely to experience relief in the classroom, such as amotivated students.

Finally, researchers must also carefully consider what type or form of affect should be studied. Pekrun et al. (2006, 2009) make very specific hypotheses about particular achievement emotions that are expected to emerge as a function of achievement goals. Linnenbrink and Pintrich (2002), on the other hand, refer more broadly to positive and negative affect, although they do reference some specific emotions, such as anxiety. Moreover, Linnenbrink (2007) argued for the need to differentiate activated and deactivated forms of positive and negative affect but did not make differential hypotheses for discrete emotions or distinguish between activity emotions and outcome emotions. Several issues are important here. First, do we expect achievement goals to predict discrete emotions (e.g., anxiety, pride, shame, etc.) or a more general affective state (e.g., activated negative affect, deactivated positive affect, etc.)? The empirical evidence provides support for both views. Specifically, there is some evidence that particular forms of emotions may be relevant. For example, performance-approach goals are positively related to two forms of deactivated negative emotions (hopelessness and shame) but negatively related to depression (also a deactivated negative emotion). On the other hand, the overall pattern of findings for mastery-approach, mastery-avoidance, and performance-avoidance goals suggests that the valence (positive/negative) dimension may be all that is needed to explain the empirical findings.

So, is it enough to simply measure positive or negative affect? Does one even need to assess activation? Or to assess discrete emotion types? There is certainly utility in assessing the more discrete forms of emotion as this provides a more nuanced perspective, but this can also be quite cumbersome to assess as it requires multiple items to assess each form of emotion (see Pekrun, Goetz, Frenzel, Barchfeld, & Perry, 2011). Moreover, many of the alternatives to self-report, such as neurobiological and physiological indicators, may be more limited in terms of assessing particular emotions or even valence (see Immordino-Yang & Christodoulou, 2014; Kreibig & Gendolla, 2014). Thus, we suggest that the need to differentiate among different forms of affect may depend upon one's research question. A more nuanced assessment of emotions may be particularly useful for understanding the complex patterns observed between performance-approach goals and emotions but may not be necessary for understanding the relations for the other goals. Further, while valence seems more critical than activation, researchers interested in linking achievement goals and emotions to academic engagement are advised to differentiate based on both valence and activation, as this distinction does seem important when considering how emotions relate to academic engagement (Pekrun & Linnenbrink-Garcia, 2012). Finally, assessing discrete emotions may help to further advance theory, as it may provide further insight about the underlying mechanisms or reasons relating achievement goals and emotions.

CONCLUSION

As we have highlighted in this chapter, research on achievement goals and emotions is growing. By and large, the empirical findings are fairly consistent and align well with both Linnenbrink and Pintrich's (2002) asymmetrical bidirectional model and Pekrun's (2006) control-value model. Unsurprisingly, the research on performance-approach goals is the least clear, a problem not unique to emotions. Although the current theories account for much of the empirical evidence and a great deal of progress has been made, there is still more work to be done. Specifically, future research will need to move beyond variable-centered self-report studies examining achievement goals and emotions in a single time point to include longitudinal studies employing multiple methodologies to assess emotions and alternative analytic techniques such as person-centered analyses. Doing so may provide a more nuanced understanding of how achievement goals and emotions relate and may help to further refine and advance both theoretical models.

NOTE

1. While many of the studies conducted over the past decade have utilized different frameworks of goals, such as a simple performance-mastery distinction or a trichotomous model of achievement goals, we have classified the extant literature based on the 2 × 2 model for ease of interpretation across studies.

REFERENCES

Ainley, M., & Hidi, S. (2014). Interest and enjoyment. In R. Pekrun & L. Linnenbrink-Garcia (Eds.), *International handbook of emotions in education* (pp. 205–227). New York, NY: Routledge.

Bandalos, D. L., Finney, S. J., & Geske, J. A. (2003). A model of statistics performance based on achievement goal theory. *Journal of Educational Psychology, 95*, 604–616.

Barron, K. E., & Harackiewicz, J. M. (2000). Achievement goals and optimal motivation: A multiple goals approach. In C. Sansone & J. M. Harackiewicz (Eds.), *Intrinsic and extrinsic motivation: The search for optimal motivation and performance* (pp. 229–254). San Diego, CA: Academic Press.

Ben-Eliyahu, A., & Linnenbrink-Garcia, L. (2011, April). *Achievement goal orientations, emotions, and engagement: A focus on the varying role of emotions in favorite and least-favorite classes.* Poster presented at the Annual Meeting of the American Education Research Association, New Orleans, LA.

Bong, M. (2009). Age-related differences in achievement goal differentiation. *Journal of Educational Psychology, 101*, 879–896.

Carver, C. S., Lawrence, J. W., & Scheier, M. F. (1996). A control-process perspective on the origins of affect. In L. L. Martin & A. Tesser (Eds.), *Striving and feeling: Interactions among goals, affect, and self-regulation* (pp. 11–52). Hillsdale, NJ: Lawrence Erlbaum.

Carver, C. S., & Scheier, M. F. (1990). Origins and functions of positive and negative affect: A control-process view. *Psychological Review, 97*, 19–35.

Carver, C. S., & Scheier, M. F. (2014). The experience of emotions during goal pursuit. In R. Pekrun & L. Linnenbrink-Garcia (Eds.), *International handbook of emotions in education* (pp. 56–72). New York, NY: Routledge.

Conley, A. M. (2012). Patterns of motivation beliefs: Combining achievement goal and expectancy-value perspectives. *Journal of Educational Psychology, 104*, 32–47.

Daniels, L. M., Haynes, T. L., Stupnisky, R. H., Perry, R. P., Newall, N. E., & Pekrun, R. (2008). Individual differences in achievement goals: A longitudinal study of cognitive, emotional, and achievement outcomes. *Contemporary Educational Psychology, 33*, 584–608.

Daniels, L. M., Stupnisky, R. H., Pekrun, R., Haynes, T. L., Perry, R. P., & Newall, N. E. (2009). A longitudinal analysis of achievement goals: From affective antecedents to emotional effects and achievement outcomes. *Journal of Educational Psychology, 101,* 948–963.

D'Mello, S. K, & Graesser, A. C. (2014). Confusion. In R. Pekrun & L. Linnenbrink-Garcia (Eds.) *International handbook of emotions in education* (pp. 289–310). New York, NY: Routledge.

Duchesne, S., & Ratelle, C. (2010). Parental behaviors and adolescents' achievement goals at the beginning of middle school: Emotional problems as potential mediators. *Journal of Educational Psychology, 102,* 497–507.

Dweck, C. S., & Leggett, E. L. (1988). A social-cognitive approach to motivation and personality. *Psychological Review, 95,* 256–273.

Elliot, A. J. (1999). Approach and avoidance motivation and achievement goals. *Educational Psychologist, 34,* 169–189.

Elliot, A. J. (2005). A conceptual history of the achievement goal construct. In A. J. Elliot & C. S. Dweck (Eds.), *Handbook of competence and motivation* (pp. 52–72). New York, NY: Guilford Publications.

Elliot, A. J., & Church, M. A. (1997). A hierarchical model of approach and avoidance achievement motivation. *Journal of Personality and Social Psychology, 72,* 218–232.

Elliot, A. J., Murayama, K., & Pekrun, R. (2011). A 3 x 2 achievement goal model. *Journal of Educational Psychology, 103,* 632–648.

Elliot, A. J., & Pekrun, R. (2007). Emotion in the hierarchical model of approach-avoidance achievement motivation. In P. A. Schutz & R. Pekrun (Eds.), *Emotion in education* (pp. 57–73). San Diego, CA: Academic Press.

Elliott, E. S., & Dweck, C. S. (1988). Goals: An approach to motivation and achievement. *Journal of Personality and Social Psychology, 54,* 5–12.

Feldman Barrett, L., & Russell, J. A. (1998). Independence and bipolarity in the structure of current affect. *Journal of Personality and Social Psychology, 74,* 967–984.

Gaudreau, P. (2012). Goal self-concordance moderates the relationship between achievement goals and indicators of academic adjustment. *Learning and Individual Differences, 22,* 827–832.

Graesser, A. C., D'Mello, S. K., & Strain, A. C. (2014). Emotions in advanced learning technologies. In R. Pekrun & L. Linnenbrink-Garcia (Eds.), *International handbook of emotions in education* (pp. 473–493). New York, NY: Routledge.

Graham, S., & Taylor, A. Z. (2014). An attributional approach to emotional life in the classroom. In R. Pekrun & L. Linnenbrink-Garcia (Eds.), *International handbook of emotions in education* (pp. 96–119). New York, NY: Routledge.

Harackiewicz, J. M., Durik, A. M., Barron, K. E., Linnenbrink-Garcia, L., & Tauer, J. M. (2008). The role of achievement goals in the development of interest: Reciprocal relations between achievement goals, interest, and performance. *Journal of Educational Psychology, 100,* 105–122.

Huang, C. (2011). Achievement goals and achievement emotions: A meta-analysis. *Educational Psychology Review, 23,* 359–388.

Immordino-Yang, M. H., & Christodoulou, J. A. (2014). Neuroscientific contributions to understanding and measuring emotions in educational contexts. In R. Pekrun & L. Linnenbrink-Garcia (Eds.) *International handbook of emotions in education* (pp. 607–624). New York, NY: Routledge.

Ironsmith, M., Marva, J., Harju, B., & Eppler, M. (2003). Motivation and performance in college students enrolled in self-paced versus lecture-format remedial mathematics courses. *Journal of Instructional Psychology, 30,* 276–284.

Jang, L. Y., & Liu, W. C. (2012). 2 x 2 Achievement goals and achievement emotions: A cluster analysis of students' motivation. *European Journal of Psychology of Education, 27,* 59–76.

Kalil, A., & Ziol-Guest, K. M. (2008). Teacher support, school goal structures, and teenage mothers' school engagement. *Youth & Society, 39,* 524–548.

King, R. B., McInerney, D. M., & Watkins, D. A. (2012). How you think about your intelligence determines how you feel in school: The role of theories of intelligence on academic emotions. *Learning and Individual Differences, 22,* 814–819.

Koul, R., Roy, L., Kaewkuekool, S., & Ploisawaschai, S. (2009). Multiple goal orientations and foreign language anxiety. *System, 37,* 676–688.

Kreibig, S. D., & Gendolla, G. H. E. (2014). Autonomic nervous system measurement of emotion in education and achievement settings. In R. Pekrun & L. Linnenbrink-Garcia (Eds.) *International handbook of emotions in education* (pp. 625–642). New York, NY: Routledge.

Linnenbrink, E. A. (2005). The dilemma of performance-approach goals: The use of multiple goal contexts to promote students' motivation and learning. *Journal of Educational Psychology, 97,* 197–213.

Linnenbrink, E. A. (2007). The role of affect in student learning: A multi-dimensional approach to considering the interaction of affect, motivation, and engagement. In P. A. Schutz & R. Pekrun (Eds.), *Emotion in education.* (pp. 107–124). San Diego, CA: Elsevier Academic Press.

Linnenbrink, E. A., & Pintrich, P. R. (2002). Achievement goal theory and affect: An asymmetrical bidirectional model. *Educational Psychologist, 37,* 69–78.

Linnenbrink-Garcia, L., Middleton, M. J., Ciani, K. D., Easter, M. A., O'Keefe, P. A., & Zusho, A. (2012). The strength of the relation between performance-approach and performance-avoidance goal orientations: Theoretical, methodological, and instructional implications. *Educational Psychologist, 47,* 281–301.

Linnenbrink-Garcia, L., & Tyson, D. F. (2007, April). *Reactions to challenge: The interplay between achievement goal orientations and affect.* Paper presented at the annual meeting of the American Educational Research Association, Chicago, IL.

Liu, W. C., Wang, C., Tan, O. S., Ee, J., & Koh, C. (2009). Understanding students' motivation in project work: A 2 × 2 achievement goal approach. *British Journal of Educational Psychology, 79,* 87–106.

Luo, W., Paris, S. G., Hogan, D., & Luo, Z. (2011). Do performance goals promote learning? A pattern analysis of Singapore students' achievement goals. *Contemporary Educational Psychology, 36,* 165–176.

Meyer, D. K., & Turner, J. C. (2006). Re-conceptualizing emotion and motivation to learn in classroom contexts. *Educational Psychology Review, 18,* 377–390.

Nicholls, J. G. (1984). Achievement motivation: Conceptions of ability, subjective experience, task choice, and performance. *Psychological Review, 91,* 328–346.

Pekrun, R. (2006). The control-value theory of achievement emotions: Assumptions, corollaries, and implications for educational research and practice. *Educational Psychology Review, 18,* 315–341.

Pekrun, R., Elliot, A. J., & Maier, M. A. (2006). Achievement goals and discrete achievement emotions: A theoretical model and prospective test. *Journal of Educational Psychology, 98,* 583–597.

Pekrun, R., Elliot, A. J., & Maier, M. A. (2009). Achievement goals and achievement emotions: Testing a model of their joint relations with academic performance. *Journal of Educational Psychology, 101,* 115–135.

Pekrun, R., Goetz, T., Frenzel, A. C., Barchfeld, P., & Perry, R. P. (2011). Measuring emotions in students' learning and performance: The Achievement Emotions Questionnaire (AEQ). *Contemporary Educational Psychology, 36,* 36–48.

Pekrun, R., Goetz, T., Titz, W., & Perry, R. P. (2002). Academic emotions in students' self-regulated learning and achievement: A program of qualitative and quantitative research. *Educational Psychologist, 37,* 91–106.

Pekrun, R., & Linnenbrink-Garcia, L. (2012). Academic emotions and student engagement. In S. L. Christenson, A. L. Reschly, & C. Wylie (Eds.), *Handbook of research on student engagement* (pp. 259–282). New York, NY: Springer.

Pekrun, R., & Perry, R. (2014). Control-value theory of achievement emotions. In R. Pekrun & L. Linnenbrink-Garcia (Eds.), *International handbook of emotions in education* (pp. 120–141). New York, NY: Routledge.

Pintrich, P. R. (2000). Multiple goals, multiple pathways: The role of goal orientation in learning and achievement. *Journal of Educational Psychology, 92,* 544–555.

Poulin, R., Duchesne, S., & Ratelle, C. (2010). Profils de buts d'apprentissage et caractéristiques personnelles des élèves au début du secondaire. *Canadian Journal Of Behavioural Science/Revue Canadienne Des Sciences Du Comportement, 42,* 44–54.

Puente-Díaz, R. (2011). The effect of achievement goals on enjoyment, effort, satisfaction and performance. *International Journal of Psychology, 47,* 102–110.

Putwain, D. W., & Symes, W. (2012). Achievement goals as mediators of the relationship between competence beliefs and test anxiety. *British Journal of Educational Psychology, 82,* 207–224.

Rosenberg, E. L. (1998). Levels of analysis and the organization of affect. *Review of General Psychology, 2,* 247–270.

Sapio, M. (2010). *Mastery goal orientation, hope, and effort among students with learning disabilities* (unpublished doctoral dissertation). Fordham University, New York, NY.

Schultheiss, O. C., & Köllner, M. G. (2014). Implicit motives, affect, and the development of competencies: A virtuous-circle model of motive-driven learning. In R. Pekrun & L. Linnenbrink-Garcia (Eds.), *International handbook of emotions in education* (pp. 73–95). New York, NY: Routledge.

Shih, S.-S. (2005). Role of achievement goals in children's learning in Taiwan. *The Journal of Educational Research, 98,* 310–319.

Shih, S.-S. (2008). The relation of self-determination and achievement goals to Taiwanese eighth graders' behavioral and emotional engagement in schoolwork. *The Elementary School Journal, 108,* 313–334.

Sideridis, G. D. (2007). Why are students with LD depressed? A goal orientation model of depression vulnerability. *Journal of Learning Disabilities, 40,* 526–539.

Sideridis, G. D. (2008). The regulation of affect, anxiety, and stressful arousal from adopting mastery-avoidance goal orientations. *Stress and Health, 24,* 55–69.

Tulis, M., & Ainley, M. (2011). Interest, enjoyment and pride after failure experiences? Predictors of students' state-emotions after success and failure during learning in mathematics. *Educational Psychology, 31,* 779–807.

Tuominen-Soini, H., Salmela-Aro, K., & Niemivirta, M. (2008). Achievement goal orientations and subjective well-being: A person-centred analysis. *Learning and Instruction, 18,* 251–266.

Tupper, K. (2008). *Depressive symptoms, anxiety, and perceived competence as predictors of goal orientation* (unpublished doctoral dissertation). University of Victoria, Victoria, Canada.

Turner, J. C., & Trucano, M. (2014). Measuring situated emotion. In R. Pekrun & L. Linnenbrink-Garcia (Eds.), *International handbook of emotions in education* (pp. 643–658). New York, NY: Routledge.

Tyson, D. F., Linnenbrink-Garcia, L., & Hill, N. E. (2009). Regulating debilitating emotions in the context of performance: Achievement goal orientations, achievement-elicited emotions, and socialization contexts. *Human Development, 52,* 329–356.

Weiner, B. (1985). An attributional theory of achievement motivation and emotion. *Psychological Review, 92,* 548–573.

Wigfield, A., Eccles, J. S., Schiefele, U., Roeser, R. W., & Davis-Kean, P. (2006). Development of achievement motivation. In N. Eisenberg, W. Damon, & R. M. Lerner (Eds.), *Handbook of child psychology: Vol. 3, Social, emotional, and personality development* (6th ed., pp. 933–1002). Hoboken, NJ: John Wiley & Sons.

Wormington, S. V., & Linnenbrink-Garcia, L. (2013, April). *A new look at multiple goal pursuit: The promise of a person-centered approach.* Poster presented at the Annual Meeting of the American Education Research Association, San Francisco, CA.

Zychinski, K. E., & Polo, A. J. (2012). Academic achievement and depressive symptoms in low-income Latino youth. *Journal of Child and Family Studies, 21,* 565–577.

9

EMOTIONAL INTELLIGENCE IN EDUCATION

From Pop to Emerging Science

Veleka Allen, Carolyn MacCann, Gerald Matthews, and Richard D. Roberts, Law School Admission Council, The University of Sydney, University of Central Florida, and Educational Testing Service

Noncognitive factors such as working well with others, perseverance, and conscientiousness are critical to academic success. They enable individuals to be diligent on homework assignments, to collaborate with classmates, to study independently, and to exhibit other behaviors that appear imperative for academic achievement (Lipnevich, Roberts, & MacCann, 2013). Many educational stakeholders view noncognitive factors, such as leadership, motivation, and determination, as important determinants of success in the academic setting (e.g., Hoover, 2013). Empirical research supports this view. For example, a recent meta-analysis showed that noncognitive factors, such as conscientiousness, can predict academic achievement almost as strongly as can cognitive ability (Poropat, 2009).

Emotional intelligence (EI) is another noncognitive factor that appears to play a key role in students' experience of primary, secondary, and tertiary/higher education. While there are many different models and definitions, EI can be broadly defined as a set of abilities or tendencies to perceive, understand, and manage emotions in an accurate and productive way. EI may be involved in a range of issues relevant to educational success and therefore holds great promise for educational applications (Zeidner & Matthews, 2012). EI predicts K–12 student achievement, university GPA, and student attrition from university (e.g., MacCann, Fogarty, Zeidner, & Roberts, 2011; MacCann & Roberts, 2008; Márquez, Martín, & Brackett, 2006; Parker et al., 2004; Parker, Hogan, Eastabrook,

Author Note: All statements expressed in this article are the authors' and do not reflect the official opinions or policies of any of the authors' host affiliations.

Oke, & Wood, 2006). High EI is also associated with social competence, self-esteem, and coping with stress (Ciarrochi, Chan, & Caputi, 2000; MacCann et al., 2011; Márquez et al., 2006). Furthermore, students' EI predicts whether they are likely to be bullied or to bully others (Lomas, Stough, Hansen, & Downey, 2012). Stakeholders in primary and secondary education, including school administrators, teachers, and parents, thus see promise in applying EI to systemic issues, such as ameliorating low self-esteem, reducing bullying rates, and preventing youth suicide. Higher education stakeholders, including admission officers, are considering using EI to aid with program completion and professional success.

In the current chapter, we first explore the societal and historical precursors of EI before going on to explore fundamental historical models and principles that have shaped this field. Next, we discuss a number of different measurement approaches associated with each of these respective models. We then go on to discuss how these models and measures play out in a variety of educational applications, including programs singling out social and emotional learning, policies related to, in particular, the standards movement, and various current (and projected) assessment practices.

EMOTIONAL INTELLIGENCE: A BRIEF HISTORICAL OVERVIEW

Emotional Intelligence, Pop Science, and Positive Psychology

With the 1995 mainstream release of psychologist Daniel Goleman's book, *Emotional Intelligence: Why It Can Matter More than IQ*, the concept of EI developed an immense popularity and momentum long before the scientific community had the chance to adequately study the construct or develop rigorous measurement techniques. Goleman's proposal that EI is more important than cognitive ability in many areas of life received an enormous amount of media attention and public interest, including a *Time* magazine cover story and a segment on Oprah Winfrey's television show. Applications within organizational psychology became particularly popular, with many organizations starting to assess EI as an additional criterion for employment selection. In the absence of a strong research background, many organizations were using assessment procedures that had not yet been adequately tested for their psychometric properties or predictive utility (Matthews, Zeidner, & Roberts, 2002).

The urgency to embrace this new and potentially important construct led to a proliferation of definitions, applications, and theoretical models developed in parallel by different research teams that were not informed by each others' work (Mayer, Caruso, & Salovey, 2000). As a result, there were several competing theoretical models of EI, which researchers later classified into two distinct types: (a) ability models, which defined EI as a person's ability to identify and process emotions, similar to a person's ability to grasp musical or mathematical concepts; and (b) mixed models, which defined EI as a mix of qualities that might include character traits, motivations, abilities, and coping styles (Mayer et al., 2000). Another classification of the different EI traditions focused on the different methods of measurement, with EI instruments divided into: (a) *ability scales,* which use maximum performance ability scales; and (b) *trait EI* assessments that use rating scales (Petrides & Furnham, 2001). All ability scales are based on theoretical models of ability EI, but self-report scales can be based on either an ability conceptualization of EI or mixed models of EI. Currently, there is general consensus that EI is best described in terms of the four-branch hierarchical ability model (Mayer, Salovey, Caruso, & Sita-renios, 2001). In this model, EI is described as the ability to perceive or recognize emo-tions, to use emotions to facilitate thought, to understand emotional information, and to manage emotions in oneself and others (Mayer, Roberts, & Barsade, 2008).

EI has become particularly popular in the field of positive psychology, which focuses on human performance, happiness, and well-being. The ultimate goal of positive psy-chology is to help people live up to their potential in their personal and work lives (Selig-man, 1998). In education, positive psychology often translates into social and emotional learning (SEL; see Brackett & Rivers, 2014). SEL programs focus on building students' emotional skills, such as emotion regulation and resilience, with the ultimate aim to increase student well-being. EI has clear theoretical links to the continued experience of positive emotions as well as the management of interpersonal relationships and can therefore be considered a key concept within positive psychology (Salovey, Mayer, & Caruso, 2002). EI is also related to several cornerstone concepts within positive psy-chology, including subjective well-being, happiness, life satisfaction, coping, and close relationships (e.g., Bar-On, 2010; Brackett, Mayer, & Warner, 2004; Furnham & Petrides, 2003; MacCann et al., 2011). Given this, EI rightfully constitutes a major focus within the field of positive psychology.

The Emergence of a Science of Emotional Intelligence

Research on emotions and social intelligence includes several historical precursors to EI that date back nearly 150 years. It is possible to trace the emotion perception and expression aspects of EI back to Charles Darwin's (1872) book *The Expression of Emotions in Man and Animals*. In this work, Darwin proposed that expressions of emotions such as joy, happiness, fear, grief, and anger were universal across not only human cultures but also in the animal kingdom (Darwin, 1872). Another precursor to EI was the concept of social intelligence. In 1920, E. L. Thorndike introduced the term *social intelligence*, which he defined as the "ability to manage and understand men and women, boys and girls, to act wisely in human relations" (p. 228). Thorndike proposed that social intelligence was part of a tripartite model that included abstract and mechanical intelligence, with these abilities considered to be of equal importance. David Wechsler (1940) suggested that some of the Wechsler scale subtests, such as Picture Arrangement, assessed aspects of social intelligence. Social and emotional components of intelligence also featured in Howard Gardner's (1983) theory of mul-tiple intelligences, in the form of *interpersonal intelligence* (the capacity to understand the motivations of others) and *intrapersonal intelligence* (the capacity to understand one's own feelings and motivations).

The term *emotional intelligence* appeared in the peer-review literature as early as 1966 (see Leuner, 1966). However, the topic did not receive an explicit definition or mea-surement paradigm until 1990 when Salovey and Mayer (1990) published their seminal article. EI remained a fairly obscure topic for the next five years. Public interest and awareness in EI rapidly increased from nearly zero to saturation levels with the pub-lication of Daniel Goleman's book in 1995. The late 1990s thus saw both popular and academic interest in EI skyrocket. This rapid increase in EI research lead to confusion in the research literature as different teams defined and measured EI in different ways and came to different conclusions about what the concept meant. Classification of models and measures at the turn of the century lead to a bifurcation in the research literature, as it became obvious that trait and ability EI conceptualizations were quite different from each other (Mayer et al., 2000). Later meta-analysis showed that trait EI relates substantially to known personality traits, such as Neuroticism and Extraversion, but is unrelated to intelligence, whereas ability EI is unrelated to most personality traits (though showing a small relationship to Agreeableness) but relates to cognitive ability, particularly crystallized knowledge (Newman, Joseph, & MacCann, 2010; Roberts, Schulze, & MacCann, 2008). The most recent research treats trait and ability EI as separate constructs, with research on ability EI now incorporating the emerging research on emotion recognition and emotion appraisal from emotions researchers (e.g., Banziger, Grandjean, & Scherer, 2009; MacCann & Roberts, 2008; Roberts et al., 2006).

EMOTIONAL INTELLIGENCE: FUNDAMENTAL THEORETICAL PRINCIPLES

Mixed (and Trait) Models of Emotional Intelligence

One of the pivotal—and still unresolved—theoretical controversies surrounding EI is how broadly or narrowly the construct should be defined. Goleman's (1995) popular but influential account was notably inclusive of a wide range of personal qualities, including those such as empathy and hope, which were not abilities as conventionally understood. A later and more systematic treatment (Goleman, 1998a, 1998b) listed emotional competencies as falling within domains of Self-Awareness, Self-Regulation, Social Skill, Social Awareness, and Motivation. Only a few of the specific facets of EI in Goleman's model might be described as true abilities, such as accurate self-assessment (Self-Awareness). The majority seem like personality traits, such as self-confidence (Self-Awareness) and innovativeness (Self-Regulation), or belong with other types of psychological construct including learned social skills, such as teamwork, or motivations, such as achievement drive. Thus, the conceptualization of EI lacks psychological coherence.

Although Goleman's (1998a, 1998b) model might seem like a liquorice assortment of desirable but unrelated personal qualities, it can be defended as an instance of a "mixed model" of EI. In introducing the term *mixed model*, Bar-On (2000) argued that EI constitutes not only abilities but personality traits that allow the person to deploy their emotional competencies effectively in real life. According to Bar-On (2010, p. 57) "emotional-social intelligence is an array of interrelated emotional and social competencies and skills that determine how effectively individuals understand and express themselves, understand others and relate with them, and cope with daily demands, challenges and pressures." Bar-On (2000, 2013) went on to describe 15 specific skills that underlie five broad components, somewhat resembling Goleman's (1998a, 1998b) domains and labeled as Intrapersonal, Interpersonal, Stress Management, Adaptability, and General Mood. This model inspired a widely used questionnaire, the EQ-i, which we describe below. The conceptual issue that mixed models raise is whether there is really any clear distinction between EI, in this sense, and standard personality, motivational, and emotional constructs (Matthews et al., 2002; Zeidner, Roberts, & Matthews, 2009).

One resolution to the issue of how EI relates to personality traits is simply to define EI as an aspect of personality. Petrides and Furnham (2001, 2003) coined the term "trait EI" to describe their own theoretical model as well as a general measurement approach to EI that involved the use of rating scales. They proposed 16 underlying facets of EI: adaptability, assertiveness, emotion expression, emotion management, emotion perception, emotion regulation, empathy, happiness, low impulsiveness, optimism, relationship skills, self-esteem, self-motivation, social competence, and stress management. This model involves individuals' self-perceptions of their emotional abilities as well as character traits related to emotions and therefore places the construct of EI within the personality domain.

Mixed/Trait Emotional Intelligence: Not Much More Than Personality?

Mixed and trait models introduce conceptual uncertainty over whether EI is really an ability as normally understood. This uncertainty is exacerbated by the preference of their proponents (e.g., Bar-On, 2000; Petrides & Furnham, 2001) to measure EI using self-ratings, a technique normally considered highly suspect in ability assessment (Matthews et al., 2002). When EI is assessed using self-ratings, resulting scores are strongly correlated with existing broad personality traits (Brackett, Rivers, Shiffman, Lerner, & Salovey, 2006; Dawda & Hart, 2000; Freudenthaler & Neubauer, 2005). One key aspect of test validity is that correlations of test scores with conceptually different constructs should be low enough to indicate that different tests are measuring different things. In the case of EI and personality, very high correlations would indicate that EI is substantially the same thing as personality. Some degree of association between EI and emotion-related personality traits might be expected on a theoretical basis, given that EI should promote well-being.

However, the magnitude of relationships between trait EI and personality indicate that trait EI is redundant with personality. For example, the magnitude of correlations between trait EI and personality is extremely high (e.g., for the TEIque, $r = .68$ and $-.70$ with Extraversion and Neuroticism respectively, or .84 to .87 after correcting for attenuation; Petrides & Furnham, 2003). Small to moderate correlations might indicate a relationship, but correlations this large are more likely to indicate different measurements of essentially the same construct. In addition, there is theoretical overlap in the specification of trait EI models and the specification of personality facets from well-known models of personality. For example, the trait EI facets of Adaptability, Assertiveness, Empathy, Happiness, Impulse Control, and Optimism specified by Petrides and Furnham's (2001, 2003) model are also facets of personality in major personality models. Lastly, there is considerable overlap at the item level between trait EI and personality items. For example, the items "I get depressed" and "I am a fairly cheerful person" are drawn from the EQ-i, and the items "I am seldom sad or depressed" and "I am a cheerful, high-spirited person" are drawn from the public-domain measure of the Revised Neuroticism-Extraversion-Openness Personality Inventory (NEO-PI-R; Goldberg et al., 2006). Indeed, one of the reasons that trait EI measures predict levels of mental health and psychological well-being is because of item overlap, leading to exaggerated claims for the criterion validity of trait EI (Zeidner, Matthews, & Roberts, 2012).

Taken together, these forms of evidence suggest that trait EI models are contained within existing personality models and may not offer substantially different information than what can already be obtained from personality assessments. There are also fundamental concerns about whether people are even capable of reporting accurately on their own abilities (Zeidner et al., 2009). What trait EI may offer is a specific and detailed focus on the emotion-specific and emotion-relevant aspects of personality. Given the renewed interest in the specific facet level of personality, and the evidence that facets may be as or more predictive than broad domains of personality, trait EI might usefully add to the prediction of important emotion-related outcomes (O'Connor & Paunonen, 2007; Paunonen & Ashton, 2001; Weiss & Costa, 2005). However, it may be more productive, both empirically and conceptually, to differentiate the various subfactors of EI rather than some notional general EI (Zeidner et al., 2009).

Emotional Intelligence as an Ability Construct

Four-Branch Hierarchical Model

Mayer and Salovey (1997) proposed that EI comprises four sets of related emotional competencies that increase in order of complexity from the first to the fourth set. First, the branch *emotion perception* comprises the perception of emotions in facial expressions, body language, artwork, and other sources. Second, the branch *emotion facilitation* involves the use of emotions, mood, and other emotional information to aid performance. Third, *understanding emotions* involves understanding how emotions blend together, how they may change over time and situations, and having a wide vocabulary of emotion terms. Fourth, *managing emotions* is the apex of EI and involves the ability to regulate one's own emotions as well as the emotions of others. Together, the perception and facilitation branches are proposed to form the *experiential EI* area, relating to the direct experience of emotional stimuli unmediated by higher thought process. In contrast, the understanding and management branches are proposed to form the *strategic EI* area, which involves higher level strategic processing of the basic emotional information. The model is hierarchical in the sense that that higher level branches managing emotions rely on the lower level skills, such as perceiving and using emotions (e.g., Mayer et al., 2001, 2008).

A Suggested Revision: The Three-Branch Ability Model of EI

Although the original theory specifies four distinct branches, the second branch (facilitating emotions) may not be either conceptually or empirically distinguishable from the other three branches. Recent research has suggested that a three-branch model might be more appropriate (Joseph & Newman, 2010; MacCann, Joseph, Newman, & Roberts, in press). Indeed, a recent meta-analytic analysis of the four-branch hierarchical model structure found that the Facilitation factor was too highly correlated with other factors to suggest that it represented a separate construct (Fan, Jackson, Yang, Tang, & Zhang, 2010). Conceptually, the ability to use emotions for nonemotional tasks involves either: (a) generating the appropriate emotion for the task at hand or (b) strategically choosing a task to make use of a naturally occurring emotion (Mayer, Salovey, & Caruso, 2012). The ability to generate emotions is encompassed within the construct of emotion management: In some theories, regulating emotions includes the induction of a desired emotion at an appropriate time (Gross, 1998). The strategic choice of task to make use of an emotion involves understanding the links between situation and emotion, which is part of understanding emotions.

Summary and Conclusion

Theory and model development in EI has gone through several distinct stages. At the first stage, multiple differing theoretical models were developed in parallel, sharing many key components but all purporting to measure the same construct (EI). At the second stage, delineation between ability models and mixed models was clear, with the conclusion that mixed models are best placed as a specified area within the existing field of personality. We are now entering the third stage of theory development in EI, where modification to the four-branch hierarchical model of EI is being considered on the basis of structural research of existing data, as well as new research that is emerging from the new measurement paradigms described further on.

EMOTIONAL INTELLIGENCE: MEASUREMENT APPROACHES

In this section, we examine the psychometric properties of a wide variety of instruments currently used to assess EI. We begin with an evaluation of self-report approaches, which, in terms of number, dominate the field. Next, we discuss approaches anchored largely in multiple-choice approaches. In both of these sections and elsewhere in these passages, where appropriate, we discuss the importance of alternatives approaches, such as forced-choice, constructed response, and others-ratings.

Self-Report Rating Approaches

Bar-On EQ-i (and EQ-i-YV)

Bar-On's (e.g., 2000) EQ-i consists of 133 items and 15 scales (grouped into five areas) corresponding to 15 skills that are specified in the Bar-On model. There is also a youth version of the assessment (EQ-i-YV), which assesses the emotional functioning of children and adolescents between the ages of 7 and 18. The EQ-i-YV consists of 60 items and 5 scales (Intrapersonal, Interpersonal, Stress Management, Adaptability, and General Mood). Raw scores for both EQ-i-YV and EQ-i assessments are standardized and reported based on the mean of 100 and standard deviation of 15.

Across the 15 subscales of the EQ-i, reported internal consistencies ranged from .69 to .86, indicating reasonable reliability at the facet level (e.g., Bar-On, 2000). The EQ-i is also reasonably stable across time, with test-retest reliability estimates of .85 across a one-month period and .75 across a four-month period. For the youth version, internal consistency ranges from .65 to .90 and test-retest reliability from .77 to .89 over a three-week period (Bar-On & Parker, 2000). These levels of reliability are acceptable for most purposes, with the caveat that consequential decisions about individuals (e.g., acceptance into specialized or remedial programs or streams) should not be made on the basis of EQ-i scores alone.

Evidence for validity is somewhat weaker. On the positive side, correlations with other variables show that the EQ-i relates to lower levels of depression and alexithymia (Dawda & Hart, 2000) and that scores were related to achievement at high school and university as well as student retention in university (e.g., Parker et al., 2004, 2006). On the negative side, structural evidence does not support the theoretical model of five components with 15 underlying facets, but rather 10 facets (Bar-On, 2000). In addition, scores on the EQ-i show substantial overlap with personality traits: a multiple correlation of .79 with the Big Five, and correlations as large as –.72 with Neuroticism have been reported (Dawda & Hart, 2000; Grubb & McDaniel, 2007). Moreover, test takers are able to fake high scores on the EQ-i when instructed to do so, with a very large average score increase of 0.83 SDs, or 12.45 points (Grubb & McDaniel, 2007). An overall evaluation of the EQ-i's validity is poor. EQ-i scores provide little additional information that is not already obtainable from existing personality scales. In addition, it also suffers the same problems of fakability that plague personality assessments (Viswesvaran & Ones, 1999).

Petrides and Furnham's TEIQue

Petrides and Furnham (2001, 2003) developed the Trait Emotional Intelligence Questionnaire (TEIQue) assessment based on their trait emotional intelligence model. There are 153 items and 15 scales with four domains: Well-being, Self-Control, Emotionality, and Sociability. The 15 scales include adaptability, assertiveness, emotion appraisal (self and others), emotion expression, emotion management (others), emotion regulation, impulsiveness, relationship skills, self-esteem, self-motivation, social competence, stress management, trait empathy, trait happiness, and trait optimism. Similar to the EQ-i, the TEIQue shows good internal consistency, mostly around .85 and is reasonably stable over time, with test-retest reliability estimates ranging between .50 to .82 for global and four domain scores across a 12-month period (Pérez, Petrides, & Furnham, 2005). There is validity evidence for the four-factor structure of the TEIQue (Pérez et al., 2005). There is also strong overlap with known personality traits, which is expected as the TEIQue assessment was designed to conceptualize emotional intelligence as a personality trait (Petrides & Furnham, 2000, 2001, 2003). The TEIQue is predictive of mental health (e.g., depression), coping, stress, student behavior, and job performance. Much of the predictive validity of the TEIque derives from its overlap with standard personality traits (Zeidner et al., 2009, 2012), but, in some studies, TEIque scores provide incremental validity for affective moods beyond the Big-Five personality traits (see e.g., Pérez et al., 2005). The TEIQue also has been translated into other languages, with its four-factor structure and predictive validity evidence largely being retained (Freudenthaler, Neubauer, Gabler, Scherl, & Rindermann, 2008; Mikolajczak, Luminet, Leroy, & Roy, 2007).

Still Further Self-Report Assessments

Beyond these self-report assessments are a sheer plethora that has been developed by different research teams, with little attempt to test whether these are redundant with any of those reviewed previously. Exactly why this is the case is not clear, but elsewhere has led us to call for a moratorium on the development of self-report assessments (e.g., Zeidner et al., 2009). Nevertheless, any review of this approach would be remiss not to acknowledge two others that have been widely used in educational research settings: The Schutte Self-Report Scale (SSRS; Schutte et al., 1998) and the Wong and Law (2002) Emotional Intelligence Scale (WLEIS).

The SSRS is an example of a trait EI assessment that is based on an ability model. Content coverage for 33 items was based on the (then current) three-component definition of EI as: (a) the ability to appraise and express emotion, (b) using emotions to solve problems, and (c) regulating emotions. Internal consistency estimates range from .70 to .85 (Pérez et al., 2005). Sharing considerable content overlap, the WLEIS is a short self-report measure of EI, consisting of 16 items that cover the following four domains: Self-Emotion Appraisal, Emotion Appraisal of Others, Use of Emotion, and Regulation of Emotion. Internal consistency ranges from .70 to .85, and moderate correlations with the Big-Five personality traits have been reported (Pérez et al., 2005; Wong & Law, 2002). WLEIS also predicts life satisfaction, job performance, and job satisfaction (see Pérez et al., 2005; Wong & Law, 2002).

Forced-Choice as a Potential Solution for Faking

An issue compromising self-ratings is the possibility that test takers will "fake good" when the tests are used for high-stakes applications. As mentioned previously, research on instructed faking from a job selection perspective demonstrates that participants can increase their scores on self-rated EI instruments by over .80 SDs—the equivalent size of more than 12 IQ points (Grubb & McDaniel, 2007; Tett, Freund, Christiansen, Fox, & Coaster, 2012). This is clearly an issue for the use of trait EI assessments for high-stakes applications, such as college admissions, selection into advanced streams or programs, or admissions to highly selective private schools.

In the standard self-report rating scale, participants will rate the extent of their agreement with a statement (e.g., "I am a good judge of character"). In a forced-choice assessment, test takers are instructed to choose between equally desirable statements (e.g., Which is more like you: "I am a good judge of character" or "I can control my impulses"?). A test taker cannot then grade themselves highly on all positive statements but must choose between them. Research on personality scales indicates that forced-choice testing paradigms may reduce faking (e.g., Christiansen, Burns, & Montgomery, 2005).

A common criticism of forced-choice formats is that they produce ipsative scores. While ipsative scores can accurately provide a profile of relative strengths within an individual, they cannot be compared across different people. For example, a student with higher scores on empathy than impulse control and cheerfulness would know that empathy is their strong point. However, if scores are ipsative, it would not be possible to judge whether one student's empathy score was higher than another's. Normative scores are required to make judgments between people. Recent research has potentially resolved this issue by using item response theory models to estimate normative scores from forced-choice data (e.g., Chernyshenko, Stark, Prewett, Gray, Stilson, & Tuttle, 2009). This approach, which requires sophisticated modeling to calculate scores, would seem especially appropriate in high-stakes testing applications (e.g., selection into state-wide or nation-wide gifted programs or into university). Emotional intelligence researchers (including ourselves) might be well advised to consider this approach in the future.

Assessing Ability EI: Multiple Choice Approaches

Omnibus Assessments of Emotional Intelligence

Omnibus assessments of emotional intelligence combine several abilities to measure emotional intelligence as a whole. The Multifactor Emotional Intelligence Scale (MEIS; Mayer, Caruso, & Salovey, 1999) and the Mayer Salovey Caruso Emotional Intelligence Test (MSCEIT; Mayer, Salovey, & Caruso, 2002) appear as two examples of omnibus assessments. Mayer, Caruso, and Salovey (1999) created MEIS based on their four-branch model of emotional intelligence. Later, they updated and shortened the MEIS to create the MSCEIT.

The MSCEIT consists of 122 items, and respondents are given 15 scores. These scores include an overall MSCEIT emotional intelligence, two area scores (Experiential and Strategic emotional intelligence), four branch scores (Perceiving, Facilitating, Understanding, and Managing), and eight individual tasks scores (Faces, Pictures, Sensations, Facilitation, Blends, Changes, Emotional Management, and Emotional Relations). The MSCEIT uses a variety of item types, including asking respondents to identify emotions experienced when presented with pictures of landscapes and faces, asking respondents how emotions are related to other emotions and particular situations through the use of multiple choice questions, and asking respondents to rate the effectiveness of various actions based on the presentation of scenarios, similar to a situational judgment test. There are two ways of scoring the MSCEIT. First, items are scored according to the expert opinion of 21 members of the International Society for Research on Emotions (expert scoring). For example, if 86% of the experts thought the correct answer was "c" and 14% thought the correct answer was "d," a test taker would be awarded .86 for selecting option "c" but .14 if they selected option "d." Second, items are scored according to the general consensus of a group of 2,112 nonexperts, 58.6% of whom were female (general scoring). Reliability of the four MSCEIT branch scores ranges from .76 to .90 for expert scores and from .79 to .91 for general scoring (Mayer, Salovey, Caruso, & Sitarenios, 2001).

There is also a youth version of the MSCEIT, appropriate for testing youths aged between 10 and 17 years. The youth version consists of 97 items divided into four tasks, one for each branch (Rivers et al., 2012). Cronbach's alpha reliability estimates of the branch's reliability range from .70 to .79 (Rivers et al., 2012).

Unlike the self-report EI assessments, the MSCEIT shows evidence of discriminant validity with respect to personality. Meta-analyses show that correlations between the MSCEIT branches and Big-Five personality domains are all less than .30, and are highest for the association between Agreeableness and Emotion Management (Joseph & Newman, 2010; Roberts et al., 2008). In addition, recent research demonstrates that the three primary MSCEIT branches (perception, understanding, and management) collectively represent an ability that maps on to the known structure of human mental abilities (MacCann et al., in press). This represents convergent validity evidence for the MSCEIT, based on the premise that EI represents a type of intelligence related to processing emotional information. Importantly, EI was a distinct type of intelligence rather than a component of existing intelligence constructs. MSCEIT scores also predict emotion-related outcomes, such as life satisfaction, relationship quality, empathy, and effective dispositional coping styles (Ciarrochi et al., 2000; MacCann et al., 2011). As such, the validity evidence for the MSCEIT as a measure of EI is reasonable, particularly for the three branches of perception, understanding, and management.

Emotional Perception Assessments

Emotional perception is fundamental to EI, as it is the basic competency that must first be obtained in order to build more complex skills, such as emotional understanding and management (Mayer et al., 2008). The Diagnostic Analysis of Nonverbal Accuracy Scales (DANVA and DANVA-2; Nowicki & Duke, 1994) and the Japanese and Caucasian Brief Affect Recognition Test (JACBART; Matsumoto et al., 2000) are two commonly used emotional perception assessments. Both assessments present pictures of faces, postures, and gestures and audio recordings of vocal tones. Respondents are given a multiple choice list of emotions and are asked to identify the emotion presented in the picture and audio recording.

Emotional Understanding Assessments

The Situational Test of Emotional Understanding (STEU) is a situational judgment test developed by MacCann and Roberts (2008). Situational judgment tests (SJTs) present hypothetical scenarios, and respondents evaluate several possible responses to these scenarios. SJTs may use either knowledge instructional formats (e.g., "What is the best response?") or behavioral tendency instructional formats (e.g., "What would you do in this situation?"). The STEU uses a knowledge instructional format, as demonstrated in the following example item: *An irritating neighbor of Eve's moves to another state. Eve is most likely to feel? (a) Regret, (b) Hope, (c) Relief, (d) Sadness, (e) Joy.*

The theoretical basis for the STEU was Roseman's (2001) appraisal theory. Under this theory, particular emotions are generated according to a particular set of appraisals of the situation. This theory was used to develop the STEU items and to determine the correct answer to each item. For example, according to Roseman (2001), relief occurs when a motive-inconsistent event (i.e., something unwanted) ceases to occur. This combination of appraisals was used to develop and score the example item shown above. Cronbach's alpha reliability for the STEU is .71 (MacCann & Roberts, 2008). STEU scores show evidence of convergent validity, relating to other tests of EI ($r = .70$ with an emotion management test, and $r = .40$ with an emotion perception test). STEU scores predict lower levels of anxiety, depression, and stress ($r = -.25, -.15,$ and $-.17$, respectively) and also predict college GPA ($r = .37$; MacCann & Roberts, 2008).

Emotional Management Assessments

The Situational Test of Emotional Management (STEM) is a situational judgment test developed by MacCann and Roberts (2008). The STEM was developed in three stages. First, 50 semistructured interviews were conducted to collect emotional situations to be used as items. Second, response options were generated from free responses to the potential items by a second sample. This sample responded with both the best thing to do and what they would do in each situation. Third, items were scored according to the judgment of 12 experts (either emotions researchers or practitioners working in mental/ emotional health fields, such as psychiatry or clinical psychology). The STEM consists of 44 scenarios assessing respondents' ability to manage fear, anger, and sadness. The STEM may be administered either as a multiple-choice test (where test takers select the best answer to each situation) or using ratings (where test takers rate the effectiveness of each response). Cronbach's alpha reliability is .68 for the multiple-choice version and .92 for the ratings-based version (MacCann & Roberts, 2008). STEM scores correlate with emotional understanding ($r = .70$) and lower levels of externally oriented thinking ($r = -.43$).

An 11-item youth version of the STEM has been developed for children aged 12–16 (MacCann, Matthews, Wang, & Roberts, 2010). An example item from the Situational Test of Emotion Management—Youth (STEM-Y) is as follows: *You and James sometimes help each other with homework. After you help James on a difficult project, the teacher is very critical of this work. James blames you for his bad grade. You respond that James should be grateful, because you were doing him a favor. What would you do in this situation? (a) Tell him from now on he has to do his own homework, (b) Apologize to him, (c) Tell him "I am happy to help, but you are responsible for what you turn in," (d) Don't talk to him.* Note that the youth version uses behavioral tendency instructional format (i.e., "what would you do" rather than "what is the best answer"). STEM-Y reliability is .71, and STEM-Y scores are associated with more positive feelings about school, greater life satisfaction, and higher GPA.

The Future of Multiple-Choice Assessments? Multimedia Situational Judgment Tests

Multimedia or video-based situational judgment tests use video as a medium to present the situations and response options. Respondents are typically asked to endorse the best response or to rate the appropriateness of each response. Multimedia SJTs have high fidelity in that the situation and response format are consistent with the reality of how the situation would occur (Lievens, Peeters, & Schollaert, 2008). Respondents have viewed multimedia SJTs as more face valid, more enjoyable, and more modern than their written counterparts (e.g., Richman-Hirsch, Olson-Buchanan, & Drasgow, 2000). Multimedia SJT may be a good medium of testing emotional intelligence as it may allow test takers to use multiple sources of information in their answers. For example, test takers would be able to endorse a response option after seeing the emotions displayed through the actors' face, posture, mannerisms, and tone. In actuality, people gather emotional information from various sources within a situation, and using multimedia SJT may be able to tap into this reality. An additional advantage of multimedia SJTs may be that they have a lower reliance on reading ability. In text-based tests, such as the MSCEIT, test takers need to comprehend the written text in order to answer the question correctly. It is possible that a test taker with high EI but low reading ability would get a low EI score on a text-based test. This issue may be particularly important when testing children and adolescents (whose reading skills are still developing), particularly those with interrupted education or suspected reading disorders.

Assessing Ability EI: Constructed Response Approaches

Levels of Emotional Awareness Scale

Currently, only a few emotional intelligence instruments use a constructed response format, where test takers write or speak their answers to each item. Lane, Quinlan, Schwartz, and Walker (1990) created the Levels of Emotional Awareness Scale (LEAS) to measure emotional awareness among adults. The scale presents 20 scenarios and test takers involving two people. Items are phrased in second person, and test takers write how they and the other person in the scenario would feel. Scoring is based on the sophistication of the emotional awareness, with each item scored from zero (no mention of emotion) through to five (sophisticated differentiation between one's own and the other's emotions). LEAS scores are positively correlated with openness to experience and emotional functioning (e.g., recognizing emotional stimuli) but not with measures of specific emotions, suggesting that LEAS taps into the structure of emotional awareness as opposed to emotional content (Lane et al., 1990, 1996). A 12-item version of the LEAS was developed for children and administered to 10–11 year olds (Levels of Emotional Awareness for Children, LEAS-C; Bajgar, Ciarrochi, Lane, & Deane, 2005). Reliability of the LEAS-C was .93 for interrater reliability and .71 for internal consistency. Scores were related to emotion comprehension and to verbal ability, suggesting that the LEAS-C assesses emotional awareness but also may require test takers to have a reasonable level of verbal ability to successfully answer the items.

The LIWC Approach

Pennebaker, Booth, and Francis (2013) have designed a text analysis software approach known as the Linguistic Inquiry and Word Count). This software analyzes text, including emails and essays, and calculates the degree to which certain word types are utilized, including positive and negative emotions. A software program such as this can be used to analyze emotional intelligence constructed response items. It would allow for the scoring of responses varying in lengths from one sentence to an essay and would allow for large volume testing.

Other-Report Approaches

Other-Ratings

There are many instruments that assess a person's ability level through the ratings of other people (e.g., teachers, parents, and friends). Even though other-ratings approach to assessments can be subject to rating bias, other-ratings show stronger prediction of educational outcomes than self-ratings (e.g., Connelly & Ones, 2010; Wagerman & Funder, 2006). Instruments such as the Bar-On EQ-i are routinely administered as 360-degree feedback in organizational settings (i.e., ratings are obtained from colleagues, direct reports, and supervisors). The research on other-ratings of personality in educational settings indicates that an other-report approach to EI could also be useful in education.

Other-Report SJTs

The other-report approach can be applied to situational judgment tests. In this form, an evaluator (e.g., parent or teacher) would be given a situation and asked to indicate what would be the response of the person being evaluated. MacCann et al. (2010) demonstrated that SJTs can be delivered in other-report format. They administered self-report and parent-report versions of the STEM-Y to assess emotional management skills in middle school students. Similar to previous research, self-report and parent-report were weakly related, but both were predictive of academic performance, life satisfaction, and positive and negative emotional reactions to the school environment. Other-raters SJTs for measuring emotional intelligence can be beneficial as it offers the fidelity of situations and allows younger children (or those of limited verbal abilities) to be assessed in this domain.

EMOTIONAL INTELLIGENCE: FROM THEORY TO MEASUREMENT TO PRACTICE

Emotional Intelligence Predicts Educational Outcomes

A growing number of studies have examined whether both rating scales of EI and ability EI are associated with academic achievement. For self-reported EI, scores on the EQ-i, TEIque, and Adolescent Swinburne University Emotional Intelligence Test were significantly associated with high school GPA (Downey, Mountstephen, Lloyd, Hansen, & Stough, 2008; Parker et al., 2004; Petrides, Frederickson, & Furnham, 2004). The effect on college GPA is more mixed. An association between EQ-i scores and college GPA was obtained by Parker et al. (2005) but not by Brackett and Mayer (2003) nor Newsome, Day, and Catano (2000). Scores on the WLEIS and SSRI were unrelated to college GPA, but scores on the TEIque were significantly related (e.g., Brackett & Mayer, 2003; MacCann & Burrows, 2013; Petrides et al., 2004). Given the known relationships between personality and academic achievement (e.g., Poropat, 2009) and between self-reported EI and personality, it is likely that much of this prediction is due to the overlap between self-report EI and personality. Moreover, the direction of causality is not entirely clear. Correlations between trait EI and GPA may simply reflect effects of academic achievement on students' affective well-being rather than indicating that EI has an influence on achievement. That is, students may feel proud or happy that they are succeeding at school rather than succeeding at school due to superior emotional skills. Alternatively, emotionally intelligent students may gain higher grades due to their greater ability to cope with the stresses of the school environment (Downey, Johnston, Hansen, Birney, & Stough, 2010; MacCann et al., 2011). That is, coping styles, such as problem-focused coping, mediate the relationship between EI and academic achievement. Of course, causal relationships between EI and achievement may be bidirectional.

For ability-based EI, evidence of a relationship with academic outcomes is somewhat stronger, with most research finding a significant association between EI and GPA (e.g., Amelang & Steinmayr, 2006; Barchard, 2003; Brackett & Mayer, 2003; Brackett et al., 2004; MacCann & Roberts, 2008; MacCann et al., 2011; Márquez et al., 2006). Some branches of EI are more predictive of GPA than others. Emotional understanding shows the strongest relationship to academic achievement; emotion management is also substantially related to achievement, whereas perceiving and facilitating emotions show little relationship (Barchard, 2003; MacCann & Roberts, 2008; O'Conner & Little, 2003; Rode et al., 2008). However, the evidence for incremental validity of EI beyond intelligence and personality is equivocal. Some research demonstrates that ability EI does not predict GPA once the influence of intelligence and personality is accounted for (Amelang & Steinmayr, 2006; Barchard, 2003; Brackett & Mayer, 2003; O'Conner & Little, 2003; Rode et al., 2008). Other research suggests that EI does predict student achievement above and beyond personality and intelligence (e.g., Di Fabio & Palazzeschi, 2009; MacCann & Roberts, 2008; Márquez et al., 2006).

Emotional Intelligence Assessments and Social and Emotional Learning Programs

Social and emotional learning (SEL) programs have been developed for kindergarten through grade 12. SEL programs aim to train children in the skills needed to recognize and manage their emotions, exercise empathy towards others, and constructively work out differences with others. The objective is to increase the emotional intelligence of students as a part of the academic curriculum. The belief is that by increasing students' emotional intelligence, school climates would be more positive, resulting in an environment where students can thrive, academically and personally.

SEL programs are covered extensively in the chapter by Brackett and Rivers (2014), so we will not review them here. However, it would seem appropriate to acknowledge in this exposition that the ultimate value of these programs rests on the development of sound theoretical models, valid measurement approaches, and careful experimental designs. Without these three pillars, it is unlikely that these programs will be widely adopted by educational practitioners or educational policy-makers at scale.

Building Formative Emotional Intelligence Assessments

There is potential for EI tests to be used as formative assessments. Bell and Cowie (2001) defined formative assessment as a process used by both teachers and students to evaluate and address gaps in student learning. In the realm of EI, teachers could use the feedback gathered from EI assessments to understand the emotional needs and skill set of the students and to work with them to develop such skills. Assessments such as an SJT with items describing situations commonly encountered in the classroom could be a viable formative emotional intelligence assessment. Based on the students' emotional intelligence ability level, teachers could then attempt to fill in the gaps through direct and indirect instruction.

High-Stakes Applications of Emotional Intelligence: Ready Yet for Prime Time?

There is a strong interest for the use of EI in the higher educational admission process. Medicine is among several disciplines that have made efforts to include within its admission process instruments that validly measure emotional intelligence among medical school applicants. Medical schools would like to produce doctors who are sensitive and understanding of their patients' emotions as well as knowledgeable about medicine. Several studies have found that higher EI was positively associated with better doctor–patient relationships, stronger teamwork, communication, and leadership skills, better performance on medical examinations, and better stress management (e.g., Arora et al., 2010; Austin, Evans, Magnus, & O'Hanlon, 2007; Weng, Chen, Chen, Lu, & Hung, 2008). Researchers have explored the use of mini-interviews to measure noncognitive traits, including those associated with emotional intelligence among medical school applicants and have found them to be predictive of medical licensure performance (e.g., Lemay, Lockyer, Collin, & Brownell, 2007). Specifically, Lemay et al. (2007) developed a multiple mini-interview (MMI) assessment to assess 10 noncognitive traits among medical school applicants, including empathy. There were 10 mini-interviews or stations, each testing a noncognitive trait. Factor analysis revealed that each station loaded onto a single factor. Significant difference in MMI scores was found among applicants who were accepted to medical school versus applicants who were waitlisted. Perhaps, this may be a viable avenue for large-scale testing of emotional intelligence, as to date, objective assessments are unavailable.

While research efforts are made to develop assessments for high-stakes testing, some graduate programs have implemented the development of emotional intelligence competency into their curriculum (Boyatzis & Saatcioglu, 2008; Joyner & Mann, 2011). One MBA program, in particular, was successful in improving emotional intelligence as measured by the EQ-i assessment comparing scores at the beginning of the MBA and at its completion (Joyner & Mann, 2011). The pilot program consisted of seminars where topics, including personal development and self-awareness, were discussed. The authors asserted that increased emotional intelligence allows students to improve self-management skills and thus function more effectively in the business environment where integrative thinking is vital. Additionally, over a 20-year period, Boyatzis and Saatcioglu (2008) investigated if emotional, social, and cognitive intelligence competencies could be developed through MBA programs. Incoming graduate students learn about their strengths and weaknesses as a manager and leader and write a growth plan. Students try to implement their growth plan throughout the remainder of their graduate program and beyond. Self-Assessment (SAQ) and External Assessment questionnaires (EAQ) were administered during this class and at the completion of the graduate program. The SAQ asks respondents to report the frequency of various behaviors, while the EAQ asks an informant (e.g., boss, family, or friend) about the frequency of witnessing these behaviors. Significant improvements were seen in the areas of emotional self-control and empathy as rated by the students and others.

Emotional Intelligence, the Standards Movement, and Twenty-First-Century Skills

Many countries have now begun to develop a set of educational standards that outline the skills and knowledge students should attain throughout their K–12 education. The premise of the standards is that every high school graduate should possess the skills required to succeed in the workforce and to undertake college-level course work. What those skills should be is open to some debate. Currently, standardized assessments of traditional subjects, such as science, mathematics, reading and writing, are used annually to test students in selected grades. Given the demonstrated importance of social and emotional skills for workplace and college success (Mayer et al., 2008), tests of EI might be an appropriate addition to the standards framework. Standards need to be holistic, addressing not only the academic component but the emotional and social components as well. A high school graduate needs to be an individual who can read and write well, who is knowledgeable about mathematical and science concepts, and who can work well with others, communicate constructively, and is adaptable.

The changing nature of work in the twenty-first century also implies that educators require an expanded view of the skills requisite for students' readiness to participate effectively in the workplace. Factors related to cultural change, technological innovation, and the global economy have come together to make jobs both more challenging and more precarious (Schabracq & Cooper, 2000). High emotional intelligence may support the new graduate in working with diverse and changing teams, in changing career trajectory as the economy shifts, and in coping with unpredictable change. In the United States, the National Research Council (NRC, 2008) has taken the lead in attempting to define twenty-first-century skills and to articulate the implications for education, such as the extent to which resources should be diverted from the traditional curriculum to less familiar skills, including adaptability, complex communication/social skills, self-management/self-development, nonroutine problem-solving skills, and systems thinking. The first three of these skills, as defined by the NRC, appear to overlap with high emotional intelligence, although assessment challenges remain (NRC, 2011).

At a practical level, in the United States, the Partnership for 21st Century Skills is a national organization that brings together the US Department of Education together with the business community, education leaders, and policymakers to position twenty-first-century readiness at the center of US K–12 education. It advocates that every student should be educated in the following: (a) core subjects, which include English, reading, or language arts, mathematics, science, foreign languages, civics, government, economics, arts, history, and geography, (b) twenty-first-century content, which includes global awareness, financial, economic, business, and entrepreneurial literacy, civic literacy, health and wellness awareness, and environmental literacy, (c) learning and thinking skills, which consist of critical thinking and problem solving, communication, information and media literacy, contextual learning, collaboration, and creativity and innovation, (d) information and communications technology (ICT), (e) life skills, which include leadership, ethics, accountability, adaptability, personal productivity, personal responsibility, people skills, self-direction, and social responsibility (Partnership for 21st Century Skills, 2013). The organization advocates for the adoption of this framework in every school. The Life Skills component encompasses many aspects of emotional intelligence and can be viewed as addressing the emotional and social skills needed for success. From this standpoint, emotional intelligence is already gaining visibility in local, state, and federal policies that support Partnership for 21st Century Skill's approach to education.

CONCLUDING COMMENTS

Emotional intelligence is associated with academic achievement and life success. Students benefit when they are able to understand and regulate emotions and channel that ability to communicate and solve problems constructively. Several broad trends are now apparent. First, the most useful aspects of EI for educational applications seem to be those concerned with understanding and managing emotions rather than the simpler skills involved in accurately perceiving emotions. Second, self-report rating scales of EI may be problematic for applied use, both due to scores' overlap with personality and due to the propensity for test takers to fake high scores in high-stakes situations (e.g., admissions to medical school). There are several promising methods for ameliorating the latter issue. However, ability scales would seem the preferable alternative at the time of writing. Third, there are still some challenges as to the best way to measure EI in children and adolescents, but there are now many possible options, including several assessments designed specifically for youths. Multimedia assessments may be particularly important in this regard, providing both a multimodal platform to assess emotional competencies and limiting the dependence of EI scores on reading ability. In summary, there are many useful applications for EI in K–12 education, including both summative and formative assessment, inclusion into social and emotional learning programs, and potentially an addition to the standards-based movement in many educational systems across the globe.

REFERENCES

Amelang, M., & Steinmayr, R. (2006). Is there a validity increment for tests of emotional intelligence in explaining the variance of performance criteria? *Intelligence, 34*, 459–468.

Arora, S., Ashrafian, H., Davis, R., Athanasiou, T., Darzi, A., & Sevdalis, N. (2010). Emotional intelligence in medicine: A systematic review through the context of the ACGME competencies. *Medical Education, 8*, 749–764.

Austin, E. J., Evans, P., Magnus, B., & O'Hanlon, K. (2007). A preliminary study of empathy, emotional intelligence and examination performance in MBChB students. *Medical Education, 41*, 684–689.

Bajgar, J., Ciarrochi, J., Lane, R., & Deane, F. P. (2005). Development of the Levels of Emotional Awareness Scale for Children (LEAS-C). *British Journal of Developmental Psychology, 23*, 569–586.

Banziger, T., Grandjean, D., & Scherer, K. R. (2009). Emotion recognition from expressions in face, voice, and body: The Multimodal Emotion Recognition Test (MERT). *Emotion, 9*, 691–704.

Barchard, K. A. (2003). Does emotional intelligence assist in the prediction of academic success? *Educational and Psychological Measurement, 63,* 840–858.

Bar-On, R. (2000). Emotional and Social Intelligence: Insights from the Emotional Quotient Inventory. In R. Bar-On and J.D.A. Parker, (Eds.), *The handbook of emotional intelligence* (363–388). San Francisco, CA: Jossey-Bass.

Bar-On, R. (2010). Emotional Intelligence: An integral part of positive psychology. *South African Journal of Psychology, 40,* 54–62.

Bar-On, R. (2013). The 5 meta-factors and 15 sub-factors of the Bar-On model. Retrieved from www.reuvenbaron.org/bar-on-model/essay.php?i = 3.

Bar-On, R., & Parker, J.D.A. (2000). *The Bar-On Emotional Quotient Inventory: Youth Version (EQ-i:YV) technical manual.* Toronto, Canada: Multi-Health Systems.

Bell, B., & Cowie, B. (2001). *Formative assessment and science education.* Dordretch, Netherlands: Kluwer Academic Press.

Boyatzis, R. E., & Saatcioglu, A. (2008). A 20-year view of trying to develop emotional, social, and cognitive intelligence competencies in graduate management education. *Journal of Management Development, 27,* 92–108.

Brackett, M. A., & Mayer, J. D. (2003). Convergent, discriminant, and incremental validity of competing measures of emotional intelligence. *Personality and Social Psychology Bulletin, 49,* 1147–1158.

Brackett, M. A., Mayer, J. D., & Warner, R. M. (2004). Emotional intelligence and its relation to everyday behaviour. *Personality and Individual Differences, 36,* 1387–1402.

Brackett, M. A., & Rivers, S. E. (2014). Transforming students' lives with social and emotional learning. In R. Pekrun & L. Linnenbrink-Garcia (Eds.), *International handbook of emotions in education* (pp. 368–388). New York, NY: Taylor & Francis.

Brackett, M. A., Rivers, S. E., Shiffman, S., Lerner, N., & Salovey, P. (2006). Relating emotional abilities to social functioning: A comparison of self-report and performance measures of emotional intelligence. *Journal of Personality and Social Psychology, 91,* 780–795.

Chernyshenko, O. S., Stark, S., Prewett, M. S., Gray, A. A., Stilson, F. R., & Tuttle, M. D. (2009). Normative scoring of multidimensional pairwise preference personality scales using IRT: Empirical comparisons with other formats. *Human Performance, 22,* 105–127.

Christiansen, N. D., Burns, G. N., & Montgomery, G. E. (2005). Reconsidering forced-choice item formats for applicant personality assessment. *Human Performance, 18,* 267–307.

Ciarrochi, J. V., Chan, A.Y.C., & Caputi, P. (2000). A critical evaluation of the emotional intelligence construct. *Personality and Individual Differences, 28,* 539–561.

Connelly, B. S., & Ones, D. S. (2010). An other perspective on personality: Meta-analytic integration of observers' accuracy and predictive validity. *Psychological Bulletin, 136,* 1092–1122.

Darwin, C. (1872). *The expression of the emotions in man and animals.* London, United Kingdom: John Murray. Retrieved from http://darwin-online.org.uk/EditorialIntroductions/Freeman_TheExpressionoftheEmotions.html

Dawda, D., & Hart, S. D. (2000). Assessing emotional intelligence: Reliability and validity of the Bar-On Emotional Quotient Inventory (EQ-i) in university students. *Personality and Individual Differences, 28,* 797–812.

Di Fabio, A., & Palazzeschi, L. (2009). An in-depth look at scholastic success: Fluid intelligence, personality traits, or emotional intelligence? *Personality and Individual Differences, 46,* 581–585.

Downey, L. A., Johnston, P. J., Hansen, K., Birney, J., & Stough, C. (2010). Investigating the mediating effects of emotional intelligence and coping on problem behaviours in adolescents. *Australian Journal of Psychology, 62,* 20–29.

Downey, L. A., Mountstephen, J., Lloyd, J., Hansen, K., & Stough, C. (2008). Emotional intelligence and scholastic achievement in Australian adolescents. *Australian Journal of Psychology, 60,* 10–17.

Fan, H. Y., Jackson, T., Yang, X. G., Tang, W. Q., & Zhang, J. F. (2010). The factor structure of the Mayer-Salovey-Caruso Emotional Intelligence Test V 2.0 (MSCEIT): A meta-analytic structural equation modeling approach. *Personality and Individual Differences, 48,* 781–785.

Freudenthaler, H. H., & Neubauer, A. C. (2005). Emotional intelligence: The convergent and discriminant validities of intra- and interpersonal emotional abilities. *Personality and Individual Differences, 39,* 569–579.

Freudenthaler, H. H., Neubauer, A. C., Gabler, P., Scherl, W. G., & Rindermann, H. (2008). Testing and validating the trait emotional intelligence questionnaire (TEIQue) in a German-speaking sample. *Personality and Individual Differences, 45,* 673–678.

Furnham, A., & Petrides, K. V. (2003). Trait emotional intelligence and happiness. *Social Behavior and Personality: An international journal, 31,* 815–823.

Gardner, H. (1983). *Frames of mind: The theory of multiple intelligences*. New York, NY: Basic Books.

Goldberg, L. R., Johnson, J. A., Eber, H. W., Hogan, R., Ashton, M. C., Cloninger, C. R., et al. (2006). The international personality item pool and the future of public-domain personality measures. *Journal of Research in Personality, 40,* 84–96.

Goleman, D. (1995). *Emotional intelligence: Why it can matter more than IQ*. New York, NY: Bantam Books.

Goleman, D. (1998a). *Working with emotional intelligence*. New York, NY: Bantam Books.

Goleman, D. (1998b, November–December). What makes a leader? *Harvard Business Review,* 93–102.

Gross, J. J. (1998). The emerging field of emotion regulation: An integrative review. *Review of General Psychology, 2,* 271–299.

Grubb, W. L., & McDaniel, M. A. (2007). The fakability of Bar-On's Emotional Quotient Inventory Short Form: Catch me if you can. *Human Performance, 20,* 43–59.

Hoover, E. (2013, January 14). Colleges seek "noncognitive" measures of applicants: Admissions offices want to know about traits, like leadership, initiative, and grit, that the SAT doesn't test. *The Chronicle of Higher Education.* Retrieved from http://chronicle.com/article/Colleges-Seek-Noncognitive/136621

Joseph, D. L., & Newman, D. A. (2010). Emotional intelligence: An integrative meta-analysis and cascading model. *Journal of Applied Psychology, 95,* 54–78.

Joyner, F. F., & Mann, D.T.Y. (2011). Developing emotional intelligence in MBA students: A case study of one program's success. *Journal of Business Education, 10,* 59–72.

Lane, R. D., Quinlan, D. M., Schwartz, G. E., & Walker, P. A. (1990). The Levels of Emotional Awareness Scale: A cognitive-developmental measure of emotion. *Journal of Personality Assessment, 55,* 124–134.

Lane, R. D., Sechrest, L., Reidel, R., Weldon, V., Kasniak, A. W., & Schwartz, D. E. (1996). Impaired verbal and nonverbal emotion recognition in alexithymia. *Psychosomatic Medicine, 58,* 203–210.

Lemay, J. F., Lockyer, J. M., Collin, V. T., & Brownell, K. W. (2007). Assessment of non-cognitive traits through the admissions multiple mini-interview. *Medical Education, 41,* 573–579.

Leuner, B. (1966). Emotionale Intelligenz und Emanzipation [Emotional intelligence and emancipation]. *Praxis der Kinderpsychologie und Kinderpsychiatry, 15,* 196–203.

Lievens, F., Peeters, H., & Schollaert, E. (2008). Situational judgment tests: A review of recent research. *Personnel Review, 37,* 426–441.

Linguistic Inquiry and Word Count. (2013). Retrieved from www.liwc.net/

Lipnevich, A. A., Roberts, R. D., & MacCann, C. (2013). Assessing noncognitive constructs in education: A review of traditional and innovative approaches. In D. Saklofske (Ed.), *Oxford handbook of psychological assessment of children and adolescents* (pp. 750–772). New York, NY: Oxford University Press.

Lomas, J., Stough, C., Hansen, K., & Downey, L. A. (2012). Emotional intelligence, victimisation and bullying in adolescents. *Journal of Adolescence, 35,* 207–211.

MacCann, C., & Burrows, C. B. (2013). Does self-report emotional intelligence incrementally predict student affective outcomes and GPA beyond five-factor personality? *Psychology of Education Review.*

MacCann, C., Fogarty, G. J., Zeidner, M., & Roberts, R.D. (2011). Coping mediates the relationship between emotional intelligence (EI) and academic achievement. *Contemporary Educational Psychology, 36,* 60–70.

MacCann, C., Joseph, D. L., Newman, D. A., & Roberts, R. D. (in press). Emotional intelligence is a second-stratum factor of intelligence: Evidence from hierarchical and bifactor models. *Emotion.*

MacCann, C., Matthews, G., Wang, L., & Roberts, R. D. (2010). Emotional intelligence and the eye of the beholder: Comparing self- and parent-rated situational judgments in adolescents. *Journal of Research in Personality, 44,* 673–676.

MacCann, C. & Roberts, R. D. (2008). New paradigms for assessing emotional intelligence: Theory and data. *Emotions 8,* 540–551.

Márquez, P. G., Martín, R., & Brackett, M. A. (2006). Relating emotional intelligence to social competence and academic achievement in high school students. *Psicothema, 18* (Suplemento), 118–123.

Matsumoto, D., LeRoux, J. A.,Wilson-Cohn, C., Raroque, J., Kooken, K., et al. (2000). A new test to measure emotion recognition ability: Matsumoto and Ekman's Japanese and Caucasian Brief Affect Recognition Test (JACBART). *Journal of Nonverbal Behaviour, 24,* 179–209.

Matthews, G., Zeidner, M., & Roberts, R. (2002). *Emotional intelligence: Science and myth*. Cambridge, MA: MIT Press.

Mayer, J. D., Caruso, D. R., & Salovey, P. (1999). Emotional intelligence meets traditional standards for an intelligence. *Intelligence, 27,* 267–298.

Mayer, J. D., Caruso, D. R., & Salovey, P. (2000). Selecting a measure of emotional intelligence: The case for ability scales. In R. Bar-On & J.D.A. Parker (Eds.), *Handbook of emotional intelligence* (pp. 320–342). San Francisco, CA: Jossey-Bass.

Mayer, J. D., Roberts, R. D., & Barsade, S. G. (2008). Human abilities: Emotional intelligence. *Annual Review of Psychology, 59,* 507–536.

Mayer, J. D., & Salovey, P. (1993). The intelligence of emotional intelligence. *Intelligence, 17,* 433–442.

Mayer, J. D., & Salovey, P. (1997). What is emotional intelligence? In P. Salovey & D. Sluyter (Eds.), *Emotional development and emotional intelligence: Educational implications.* New York, NY: Basic Books.

Mayer, J. D., Salovey, P., & Caruso, D. R. (2002). *Mayer-Salovey-Caruso Emotional Intelligence Test MSCEIT user's manual.* North Tonawanda, NY: Multi-Health Systems.

Mayer, J. D., Salovey, P., & Caruso, D. R. (2012). The validity of the MSCEIT: Additional analyses and evidence. *Emotion Review, 4,* 403–408.

Mayer, J. D., Salovey, P., Caruso, D. R., & Sitarenios, G. (2001). Emotional intelligence as a standard intelligence. *Emotion, 1,* 232–242.

Mikolajczak, M., Luminet, O., Leroy, C., & Roy, E. (2007). Psychometric properties of the Trait Emotional Intelligence Questionnaire: Factor structure, reliability, construct, and incremental validity in a French-speaking population. *Journal of Personality Assessment, 88,* 338–353.

National Research Council. (2008). *Research on future skill demands: A workshop summary. Margaret Hilton, Rapporteur.* Washington, DC: The National Academies Press.

National Research Council. (2011). *Assessing 21st Century skills: Summary of a workshop. Judith Anderson Koenig, Rapporteur.* Washington, DC: The National Academies Press.

Newman, D. A., Joseph, D. L., & MacCann, C. (2010). Emotional intelligence and job performance: The importance of emotion regulation and emotional labor context. *Industrial and Organizational Psychology-Perspectives on Science and Practice, 3,* 159–164.

Newsome, S., Day, A. L., & Catano, V. M. (2000). Assessing the predictive validity of emotional intelligence. *Personality and Individual Differences, 29,* 1005–1016.

Nowicki, S. J, & Duke, M. P. (1994). Individual differences in the nonverbal communication of affect: the Diagnostic Analysis of Nonverbal Accuracy Scale. *Journal of Nonverbal Behaviour, 19,* 9–35.

O'Connor, M. C., & Paunonen, S. V. (2007). Big five personality predictors of post-secondary academic performance. *Personality and Individual Differences, 43,* 971–990.

Parker, J. D., Creque, R. E., Barnhart, D. L., Harris, J. I., Majeski, S. A., Wood, L. M., . . . Hogan, M. J. (2004). Academic achievement in high school: Does emotional intelligence matter? *Personality and Individual Differences, 37,* 1321–1330.

Parker, J. D., Duffy, J. M., Wood, L. M., Bond, B. J., & Hogan, M. J. (2005). Academic achievement and emotional intelligence: Predicting the successful transition from high school to university. *Journal of the First-Year Experience & Students in Transition, 17,* 67–78.

Parker, J.D.A., Hogan, M. J., Eastabrook, J. M., Oke, A., & Wood, L. M. (2006). Emotional intelligence and student retention: Predicting the successful transition from high school to university. *Personality and Individual Differences, 41,* 1329–1336.

Partnership for 21st century skills (2013). *Framework for 21st century Learning.* Retrieved from p21.org

Paunonen, S. V., & Ashton, M. C. (2001). Big five factors and facets and the prediction of behavior. *Journal of Personality and Social Psychology, 81,* 524–539.

Pérez, J. C., Petrides, K. V., & Furnham, A. (2005). Measuring trait emotional intelligence. In R. Schulze & R. D. Roberts (Eds.), *Emotional intelligence: An international handbook,* 181–201. Cambridge, MA: Hogrefe & Huber.

Pennebaker, J. W., Booth, R. J., & Francis, M. E. (2013). The linguistic inquiry and word count. Retrieved from www.liwc.net/

Petrides, K.V., Frederickson, N., & Furnham, A. (2004). The role of trait emotional intelligence in academic performance and deviant behaviour at school. *Personality and Individual Differences, 36,* 277–293.

Petrides, K. V., & Furnham, A. (2000). On the dimensional structure of emotional intelligence. *Personality and Individual Differences, 29,* 313–320.

Petrides, K. V., & Furnham, A. (2001). Trait emotional intelligence: Psychometric investigation with reference to established trait taxonomies. *European Journal of Personality, 15,* 425–448.

Petrides, K. V., & Furnham, A. (2003). Trait emotional intelligence: Behavioural validation in two studies of emotion recognition and reactivity to mood induction. *European Journal of Personality, 17,* 39–57.

Poropat, A. E. (2009). A meta-analysis of the five-factor model of personality and academic performance. *Psychological Bulletin, 135,* 322–338.

Richman-Hirsch, W. L., Olson-Buchanan, J. B., & Drasgow, F. (2000). Examining the impact of administration medium on examinee perceptions and attitudes. *Journal of Applied Psychology, 85,* 880–887.

Rivers, S. E., Brackett, M. A., Reyes, M. R., Mayer, J. D., Caruso, D. R., & Salovey, P. (2012). Measuring emotional intelligence in early adolescence with the MSCEIT-YV: Psychometric properties and relationship with academic performance and psychosocial functioning. *Journal of Psychoeducational Assessment, 30,* 344–366.

Roberts, R. D., Schulze, R., & MacCann, C. (2008). The measurement of emotional intelligence: A decade of progress? In G. Boyle, G. Matthews, & D. Saklofske (Eds.), *The Sage handbook of personality theory and assessment* (pp. 461–482). New York, NY: Sage.

Roberts, R. D., Schulze, R., O'Brien, K., MacCann, C., Reid, J., & Maul, A. (2006). Exploring the validity of the Mayer-Salovey-Caruso emotional intelligence test (MSCEIT) with established emotions measures. *Emotion, 6,* 663–669.

Rode, J. C., Mooney, C. H., Arthaud-Day, M. L., Near, J. P., Rubind, R. S., Baldwin, T. T., et al. (2008). An examination of the structural, discriminant, nomological, and incremental predictive validity of the MSCEIT V2.0. *Intelligence, 36,* 350–366.

Roseman, I. J. (2001). A model of appraisal in the emotion system: Integrating theory, research, and applications. In K. R. Scherer & A. Schorr (Ed.), *Appraisal processes in emotion: Theory, methods, research* (pp. 68–91). New York, NY: Oxford University Press.

Salovey, P., & Mayer, J. D. (1990). Emotional intelligence. *Imagination, Cognition and Personality, 9,* 185–211.

Salovey, P., Mayer, J. D., & Caruso, D. (2002). The positive psychology of emotional intelligence. In C. R. Synder & S. J. Lopez (Eds), *Handbook of positive psychology* (pp. 159–171). New York, NY: Oxford University Press.

Schabracq, M. J., & Cooper, C. L. (2000). The changing nature of work and stress. *Journal of Managerial Psychology, 15,* 227–241.

Schutte, N. S., Malouff, J. M., Hall, L. E., Haggerty, D. J., Cooper, J. T., Golden, C. J., & Dornheim, L. (1998). Development and validation of a measure of emotional intelligence. *Personality and Individual Differences, 25,* 167–177.

Seligman, M.E.P. (1998). *Learned optimism* (2nd ed.). New York, NY: Pocket Books.

Tett, R. P., Freund, K. A., Christiansen, N. D., Fox, K. E., & Coaster, J. (2012). Faking on self-report emotional intelligence and personality tests: Effects of faking opportunity, cognitive ability, and job type. *Personality and Individual Differences, 52,* 195–201.

Thorndike, E. L. (1920). Intelligence and its uses. *Harper's Magazine, 140,* 227–335.

Viswesvaran, C., & Ones, D. S. (1999). Meta-analyses of fakability estimates: Implications for personality measurement. *Educational and Psychological Measurement, 59,* 197–210.

Wagerman, S. A., & Funder, D. C. (2006). Acquaintance reports of personality and academic achievement: A case for conscientiousness. *Journal of Research in Personality, 41,* 221–229.

Wechsler, D. (1940). Non-intellective factors in general intelligence. *Psychological Bulletin, 37,* 444–445.

Weiss, A., & Costa, P. T. (2005). Domain and facet personality predictors of all-cause mortality among medicare patients aged 65 to 100. *Psychosomatic Medicine, 67,* 724–733.

Weng, H. C., Chen, H. C., Chen, H. J., Lu, K., & Hung, S. Y. (2008). Doctors' emotional intelligence and the patient-doctor relationship. *Medical Education, 42,* 703–711.

Wong, C. S., & Law, K. S. (2002). The effects of leader and follower emotional intelligence on performance and attitude: An exploratory study. *The Leadership Quarterly, 13,* 243–274.

Zeidner, M., & Matthews, G. (2012). Personality. In K. R. Harris, S. Graham, T. Urdan, S. Graham, J. M. Royer, & M. Zeidner (Eds.), *APA educational psychology handbook. Vol. 2: Individual differences and cultural and contextual factors.* Washington, DC: APA.

Zeidner, M., Matthews, G., & Roberts, R. D. (2012). The emotional intelligence, health, and well-being nexus: What have we learned and what have we missed? *Applied Psychology: Health and Well-Being, 4,* 1–30.

Zeidner, M., Roberts, R. D., & Matthews, G. (2009). *What we know about emotional intelligence: How it affects learning, work, relationships and our mental health.* Cambridge, MA: MIT Press.

10

EMOTION REGULATION IN EDUCATION
Conceptual Foundations, Current Applications, and Future Directions

Scott E. Jacobs and James J. Gross, Stanford University

Imagine a classroom in which your teacher slouches in late and begins scribbling an outline for a lecture on the chalkboard. Eventually he turns and starts an algebra lecture by reading directly from a textbook for the next 20 minutes. Your mind wanders, and you hear your classmates playing videogames on their cell phones and talking. You are brought back to attention when your teacher slams the book shut and calls you to the blackboard to complete one of the example problems.

Now imagine a very different classroom. Your teacher arrives with a step of confidence and a smile, and he dazzles you with thought-provoking concepts. Your teacher describes the science lesson as a path to understanding the universe and literature as a secret window into the minds of the authors. Andrew Motion, former poet laureate of the United Kingdom, describes such an experience:

> My background was very unbookish, and there was absolutely no expectation from my family of my ever reading very much or even writing anything. I wanted to bird-watch and be left alone. Then I was taught English by Peter Way (Mr. Way to me), and it was as though he walked into my head and turned all the lights on.
>
> (Jackson, 2010)

Boredom and interest are not the only emotions competing in the classroom. Whether one is anxiously anticipating a difficult test, angry at a fellow student, concerned about

Acknowledgments: The research reported here was supported by the Institute of Education Sciences, U.S. Department of Education, through Grant R305A120671 to Board of Trustees of the Leland Stanford Junior University. The opinions expressed are those of the authors and do not represent views of the Institute or the U.S. Department of Education.

fitting in socially, or sad at falling behind one's peers, emotions powerfully shape students' educational experiences. In this chapter, we make the case that developments in the study of emotion and emotion regulation may shed important new light onto the educational process. We begin with an introduction to emotion, emotion regulation, and the process model of emotion regulation. We then consider many of the ways in which emotion regulation might be relevant to education, with a focus on (1) developmental considerations, (2) the management of temptation, and (3) test anxiety. Finally, we comment on a number of exciting future directions that illustrate how education researchers can benefit from an emotion regulation framework.

CONCEPTUAL FOUNDATIONS

Before we can consider emotion regulation, we must address the question of what, exactly, is being regulated? Because so many responses, experiences, and behaviors can contribute to what we call an emotion, scientists often rely on a prototype approach to provide a common ground for the study of emotion.

Defining Emotion

William James sparked debate by asking "What is an emotion?" and researchers and philosophers ever since have wrestled with this question (James, 1884). Emotions can be simple or complex and range from low to high in intensity. Emotional responses can help or hinder, feel good or bad, and be easy or difficult to change. In spite of the many unique responses that can be labeled emotion, emotion theorists, while varied in their approaches, frequently agree on a number of core features (Gross & Thompson, 2007). When taken together, these features comprise the modal model of emotion (Figure 10.1).

The first core feature is that emotions are generated from person-situation transactions in which an individual understands a situation to impinge on a relevant goal (Scherer, Schorr, & Johnstone, 2001). These goals can be conscious (e.g., when a person wants to impress his peers) or unconscious (e.g., wanting to avoid the humiliation of failing a test) and can range from the simple (e.g., the bully nearby is dangerous) to the more complex (e.g., a poor test score will mean that I'm not as smart as my peers) (Gross, 2008). In spite of the objective features of a goal-relevant situation, it is a person's subjective interpretation of that situation that leads to a particular emotional response (Gross & Thompson, 2007).

A second core feature of an emotion is that it coordinates responses to the situation that generated it. Emotions are described as complex full-body responses that coordinate

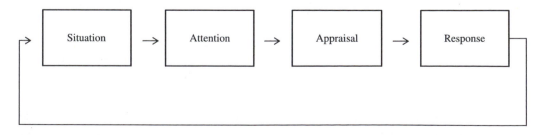

Figure 10.1 The modal model of emotion.

changes across physiology, subjective experience, and behavior (Mauss, Levenson, McCarter, Wilhelm, & Gross, 2005). Examples of these full-body changes include the physiological activation that accompanies anger (Mauss, Cook, Cheng, & Gross, 2007), the blushing that comes with embarrassment (Keltner & Anderson, 2000), and the smiling that comes with amusement (Giuliani, McRae, & Gross, 2008). These coordinated responses brought on by emotion can change the situation in adaptive ways (e.g., anger that motivates striking an aggressor). These instances in which emotion changes the situation that caused it are captured by the modal model through the arrow from the emotion response to the situation (Figure 10.1).

Third, the activation of response systems by emotion is characterized by a degree of malleability (Gross, 1998b; Gross & Thompson, 2007). While emotions can alter our own behaviors, including what we attend to (Öhman, Flykt, & Esteves, 2001), perceive (Phelps, Ling, & Carrasco, 2006), think about (Naqvi, Shiv, & Bechara, 2006), and remember (Philippot & Schaefer, 2001), these behaviors driven by emotion are not entirely fixed and can, in fact, be controlled. As a result, it is the malleable aspect of an emotional response that allows for the existence of emotion regulation.

Defining Emotion Regulation

In spite of the frequently useful aspects of our emotions, they can at times be unhelpful, such as when one's anxiety interferes with test performance or when one's anger in the classroom results in an after-school detention or a visit to the principal's office. It is in these cases that a student may be better off regulating his or her emotions, as emotional responses can be disruptive, attentionally demanding, or interfere with one's goals (see Pekrun & Linnenbrick-Garcia, 2012; Schutz & Davis, 2000).

The history of emotion regulation research has its origins in the study of psychological defenses (Freud, 1926/1959), stress and coping (Lazarus, 1966), with recent work growing out of the developmental (Thompson, 1991) and adult literature (Gross & Levenson, 1993; Gross & Thompson, 2007). *Emotion regulation* refers to "the processes by which individuals influence which emotions they have, when they have them, and how they experience and express these emotions" (Gross, 1998b, p. 275). This excludes processes by which emotions themselves coordinate various biological systems (regulation by emotions) and instead covers the set of processes by which emotions themselves can be regulated (regulation of emotions) (Gross, 2008). For present purposes, it is important to note that some instances of emotion regulation are intrinsic in the sense that they involve a person (e.g., a teacher) trying to influence his or her own emotions (e.g., trying to suppress feelings of annoyance at a disruptive and needy child). Other instances are extrinsic in the sense that they involve a person (e.g., a teacher) trying to influence another person's emotions (e.g., trying to help calm an anxious child).

Of course, there are many ways a specific emotional response can be regulated. Using the modal model as a starting point, the process model of emotion regulation holds that there are five points in the emotion generative process that may be targeted when an individual seeks to regulate an emotion (Gross & Thompson, 2007). Organizing emotion regulation strategies by the temporal point that they target yields five families of emotion regulation processes (see Figure 10.2). These families are: situation selection, situation modification, attentional deployment, cognitive change, and response modulation (Gross, 1998b).

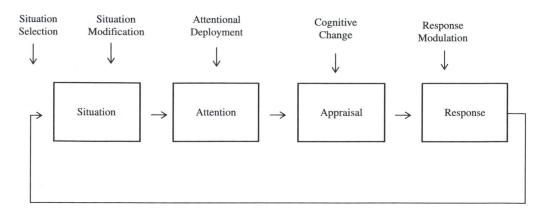

Figure 10.2 The process model of emotion regulation.

The earliest point one can begin to shift an emotional trajectory is before the emotion even takes place, and *situation selection* refers to "taking actions that make it more (or less) likely that one will end up in a situation one expects will give rise to desirable (or undesirable) emotions" (Gross & Thompson, 2007, p. 14). Intrinsic situation selection can come in the form of a student who avoids embarrassment by staying out of the bully-infested parts of the playground. Extrinsic situation selection can take the form of a teacher who isolates a disruptive student to maintain the class enjoyment of the other students.

When one is already in an emotional situation, aspects of that situation can be modified to change the emotional outcome. These strategies fall under the family of emotion regulation processes known as *situation modification*. The boundary between situation selection and situation modification is somewhat blurry, but situation modification is defined as "active efforts to directly modify the situation so as to alter its emotional impact" (Gross, 1998b, p. 283). A teacher who puts the more disruptive students in the back of the class to decrease the irritation they cause can be considered an act of situation modification. Intrinsic situation modification can come in the form of the student who asks a parent to turn off a noisy TV while he is studying. An act of extrinsic situation modification occurs when a parent, who, seeing their child trying to study in the midst of a distracting television, takes efforts to remove those distracters from the environment to decrease the child's frustration. There are many ways to modify a situation, and even emotional expressions themselves can modify situations, as when a student who frowns prompts a teacher's criticism to soften.

The third family of emotion regulatory processes is known as *attentional deployment*. Attentional deployment refers to "how individuals direct their attention within a given situation in order to influence their emotions" (Gross & Thompson, 2007, p. 18). One common strategy that falls under this category is distraction, which involves changing the focus of one's attention. Intrinsic examples of this include the student who ignores an annoying child who sits next to him. Attentional deployment is not limited to the external environment, as one can also change their internal focus by bringing to mind situations that are inconsistent with the emotions generated by an ongoing situation (e.g., the student who thinks about recess instead of paying attention to today's lessons).

Extrinsic examples of attentional deployment include the parent who soothes their child by directing his or her attention away from thoughts of poor grades, or the teacher who directs the class's attention toward the more positive aspects of learning new material.

Moving forward, strategies that target one's cognitive interpretation of a situation fall into the category of *cognitive change*. Cognitive change refers to "changing how one appraises the situation one is in so as to alter its emotional significance, either by changing how one thinks about the situation or about one's capacity to manage the demands it poses" (Gross & Thompson, 2007, p. 20). Intrinsic cognitive reappraisal (a type of cognitive change) includes the student who finds evaluative tests to be stressful and chooses to reinterpret this situation as an opportunity to show himself how much he has learned. Extrinsic cognitive reappraisal includes the teacher who soothes her students by informing them that today's pop quiz is just a way for her to get feedback on her teaching performance, and not a real test.

Finally, the components of emotional responses themselves can be subject to regulatory efforts, and this family of regulatory processes is called *response modulation*. Response modulation refers to "influencing physiological, experiential, or behavioral responding as directly as possible" (Gross & Thompson, 2007, p. 22). That is, each response channel can be a unique target of regulation. For example, students who engage in deep breathing while feeling anxious during a class speech have engaged response-focused modulation. However, physiology alone is not the only component that can be targeted by response-focused regulation; other examples include concealing facial expressions of emotion, as in the case of a student who attempts to conceal from his peers the happiness he feels from getting good grades. This strategy, known as expressive suppression, is one of the most frequently studied forms of response modulation, which is often invoked when one conceals behavioral displays of emotion (Gross & Thompson, 2007).

Key Findings From the Emotion Regulation Literature

One key insight from the emotion regulation literature is that not all regulation processes are created equal. Some strategies (e.g., cognitive reappraisal) are more effective than others at reducing the overall experience of emotion, while other strategies (e.g., expressive suppression) target specific components of the emotional response but have less influence on the subjective experience of emotion. As a general finding, regulatory processes that target earlier stages of the emotion generative cycle are more effective at decreasing the emotional response than later processes that target components of the emotional response itself (Gross, 1998a, 1998b, 2002; Gross & John, 2003; Gross & Thompson, 2007).

The two most widely studied emotion regulation strategies, cognitive reappraisal and expressive suppression, demonstrate the divergent effects of different regulation strategies. To illustrate the relative costs and benefits of emotion regulation strategies, we will summarize core findings in the affective, cognitive, and social consequences as revealed by studies that directly compared the strategy of cognitive reappraisal to the strategy of expressive suppression.

On the affective front, cognitive reappraisal has been shown to be more effective at decreasing the experience of emotion in comparison to expressive suppression, a strategy that targets only the expression of emotion (Gross, 1998a, 2002). Affective consequences of expressive suppression include elevations in physiological activity and decreases in the experience of positive but not negative emotion (Gross, 1998a, 2002). Cognitive reappraisal can be used to reinterpret the physiological responses triggered by stress, such that individuals who view their physiological activation as beneficial will yield a more adaptive cardiovascular response profile (Jamieson, Nock, & Mendes, 2012).

On the cognitive front, cognitive reappraisal is better for memory than expressive suppression. Early studies that investigated this found that expressive suppression decreased memory for emotional stimuli, whereas reappraisal maintained memory (Richards & Gross, 1999, 2000), indicating that cognitive reappraisal enhances the encoding of the emotional situation (Hayes et al., 2010). With respect to academic outcomes, expressive suppression is more cognitively costly relative to cognitive reappraisal, the latter of which can improve performance outcomes on stressful cognitive tasks if one reinterprets the meaning of the situation or views one's anxiety responses as adaptive (Jamieson, Mendes, Blackstock, & Schmader, 2010; Schmader, Johns, & Forbes, 2008).

On the social front, expressive suppression impairs social functioning relative to cognitive reappraisal (Gross, 2002). In particular, individuals who typically use suppression are less likely to share their experience of both negative and positive emotions, whereas individuals who frequently use reappraisal were more likely to share their emotions (Gross & John, 2003). Moreover, Butler et al. (2003) showed that expressive suppression causes social interactions to be more negative, interfering with one's ability to engage in rapport. These social consequences of expressive suppression may play out over time, as students who engage in expressive suppression when transitioning to college report less social support and less satisfaction with social interactions (Srivastava, Tamir, McGonigal, John, & Gross, 2009). This is important because the dissociation between experiencing positive emotions and expressing them is associated with lower levels of well-being and social connectedness (Mauss et al., 2011).

These differences between reappraisal and suppression may exert their effects in educational contexts across affective, cognitive, and social domains. The affective consequences of reappraisal versus suppression can determine whether a student finds school situations enjoyable and interesting or decreases their experience of positive emotions by concealing them. Cognitive consequences may come in the form of learning and performance effects accruing over time: The student who uses cognitive strategies to decrease negative thoughts and feelings during classroom instruction may have enhanced memory for the material relative to the student who suppresses emotional expressions. Conversely, students who tend to use suppression may find the cognitive costs disruptive to learning and performance outcomes. Socially, one's emotion regulation choices can influence whether one is perceived as a happy student who others want to be friends with and has consequences for one's social connectedness. Students who use suppression may go through education hiding feelings that would be helpful to share with others, both positive and negative. Students and teachers who employ cognitive reappraisal may form stronger connections and have more support through larger peer groups, whereas those who use suppression may be perceived of as less socially apt than others and have less social support.

CURRENT APPLICATIONS

The term education has a distinctly cognitive ring, but emotional processes may aid or interfere at many points throughout the educational process. This means that the opportunity for emotion regulation can be found in educational settings almost anytime you find an emotion. Whether it is the excitement or terror of making new friends, anxiety at achieving good grades, or frustration at trying to learn complex information, emotion regulation can be called on to either help or harm educational outcomes. It can be found by requesting a new seat in the classroom to move away from threatening bullies, distracting oneself from negative thoughts and feelings during a test, or concealing one's excitement at making the highest grade to prevent jealousy on behalf of friends or academic enemies.

We contend that nearly all of these situations can be understood more fully by adopting an emotion regulation framework. In particular, we argue that using an explicit model of emotion regulation, such as the process model, may make it possible to more systematically examine the role of emotion and emotion regulation in education. Historically, educational research related to emotion has primarily focused on the academic testing situation, and these typically invoke affective processes as a source of faulty test performance (i.e., choking under pressure, stereotype threat, or test anxiety). Recently, however, there is an increase in the consideration of emotion across a variety of educational domains (Davis, DiStefano, & Schutz, 2008; Schutz & Pekrun, 2007; Tyson, Linnenbrink-Garcia, & Hill, 2009). However, the temporal unfolding of emotion and explicit investigations of antecedent versus response forms of emotion regulation is less frequently a target of educational research. In the following, we selectively review literature on development, temptation management, and the testing situation to illustrate the potential value of an explicit emotion regulation perspective.

Developmental Considerations

Given the many triggers of emotional responses and all the points at which dysregulation can occur, it is amazing that teachers can ever get a roomful of children or adolescents to settle down and pay attention. Educators have a vested interest in understanding the development of emotion regulation, as students with poor emotion regulation will go on to have more difficulty adjusting to school settings (Eisenberg, Spinrad, & Smith, 2004); and proper emotion regulation contributes to successful academic outcomes over time (Graziano, Reavis, Keane, & Calkins, 2007).

Research has begun to show that emotion regulation is a core ingredient for the development of successful social behaviors in preschoolers (Blair, Denham, Kochanoff, & Whipple, 2004), such that understanding how to regulate emotions can be thought of as a crucial developmental milestone (Thompson, 1991). To this end, educators must be sensitive to the types of emotion regulation strategies that can capably be understood and employed by younger children given the constraints of their cognitive abilities, so that appropriate intervention programs can be developed (e.g., see Izard et al., 2008).

Developmentally, as children learn the causes and consequences of their emotions, they then can begin to initiate efforts to shape their emotional experience and expression (Thompson, 1991). That is, for a child to develop an understanding of emotion regulation, he must first understand what causes emotion. Studies have shown that around age 3 children can correctly identify the emotion that will follow from a given situation and can identify specific situation-emotion pairings (Harris, Olthof, Terwogt, & Hardman, 1987; Thompson, 1991). As a child gains a heightened understanding of how situations can generate thoughts that cause emotional responses, he or she can begin to regulate the emotion by changing situations, attention, or thoughts themselves (Thompson, 1991).

Early on in development, this situation-causes-emotion understanding guides the types of strategies one employs, such as targeting efforts to change or modify the situation. Evidence suggests that younger children see situations as the triggers of emotion, and they prefer strategies targeting situation selection and modification (McCoy & Masters, 1985), which emerges between the ages of 3 and 5 (Cole, Dennis, Smith-Simon, & Cohen, 2009). To move beyond situation selection and modification strategies requires an understanding that thoughts, and not situations alone, can cause changes in one's feelings, an understanding that does not seem to be fully in place until age 8 (Flavell, Flavell, & Green, 2001). In spite of mixed evidence at which age this understanding begins to first appear, a more recent study has shown that children as young as 5 and 6 can generate cognitive strategies (e.g., changing goals or thoughts) as a strategy to change one's feelings (Davis, Levine, Lench, & Quas, 2010). And older children (8 to 12 years old) are more likely to describe strategies that regulate attention or seek to alter one's appraisal directly (McCoy & Masters, 1985; Pons, Harris, & de Rosnay, 2004). Many of these developmental studies employed self-report scenarios in which a child is presented a story or scenario and asked to either generate or identify ways to change the emotional response of the character in the story. To illustrate the real-world importance of these findings, children who generated and recognized more emotion regulation strategies persisted in a frustrating task, such as continuing to try to open a locked box given by the experimenter (Cole et al., 2009).

The understanding of the triggers of emotion plays an important role in the development and use of emotion regulation strategies, but another important determinant of emotion regulation is an understanding of the consequences of a given emotional response. If a child sees an anger outburst as disrupting his social goals, he will forge efforts to decrease the experience or expression of that anger. For example, children who understand the negative consequences of an emotional display are more likely to control the expression of a particular emotion, such as anger (Fuchs & Thelen, 1988), and this ability to inhibit facial expressions of emotion have been documented in children as young as ages 3 and 4 (Cole, 1986).

Overall, the work on the development of emotion regulation provides initial evidence that cognitive reappraisal ability increases with age, but it is unclear whether this increase tracks cognitive development or other processes, such as determinants of strategy selection over time (McRae et al., 2012). From these studies in the developmental literature, the evidence indicates that younger children are quite capable of understanding and regulating emotional responses, and they prefer the strategies of situation selection and modification. Preferences for and engagement with more sophisticated strategies, such as cognitive reappraisal or attentional deployment, appear to develop later over time.

For educators, the developmental trajectories of emotion regulation is important because education interventions designed to train emotion regulation skills must be grounded in current theory, and an understanding of the origins and consequences of emotion regulation skills is a prerequisite for evidence-based interventions. Understanding the developmental trajectory of emotional intelligence, such as what drives the selection of one emotion regulation strategy over another, is a crucial area of research for understanding the role of emotion in education (Sheppes, Scheibe, Suri, & Gross, 2011; Zeidner, Matthews, Roberts, & MacCann, 2003). Future directions on the developmental aspect of emotion regulation must address how the development of cognitive skills supports emotion regulation ability and strategy selection and how improving emotion awareness influences emotion regulation strategies over time. While adaptive emotion regulation is associated with a variety of benefits in adulthood, it is not fully known how children, adolescents, and young adults flexibly employ emotion regulation, or the cognitive prerequisites needed. Given the benefits of flexible emotion regulation, this is a ripe area for investigation because in spite of the emerging evidence that focuses on the use of emotion regulation at early stages of development, only limited work has connected these developmental considerations to educational outcomes. Moreover, the majority of our research on emotion regulation processes comes from investigations of young children (preschool age) or adults (college-age and above). How one transitions through these crucial years in terms of emotion regulation development is a question researchers must address.

Management of Temptations

Feeling better about an emotional situation is not the only benefit of emotion regulation—harnessing the power of emotions in pursuit of one's goals is another useful application. In these contexts, it may be adaptive to engage with a negative task now to obtain a benefit later or to decrease positive feelings associated with a temporary reward to obtain a larger reward later. Here, we are talking about the management of temptation. At nearly every stage of education, temptation occurs. How are students supposed to maintain their focus on learning, given the many varieties of temptations? These questions can be addressed by empirical work investigating how one manages their responses to activities that are more pleasurable in the moment but come with negative consequences later.

Walter Mischel, in his famous "marshmallow studies," found that children often employed explicit strategies to achieve success in delaying gratification (Mischel, Shoda, & Rodriguez, 1989). The ability to delay gratification was also shown to predict important life outcomes, such that children who succeeded in delaying gratification (i.e., putting off a smaller, sooner reward to receive a larger, later reward) subsequently showed higher SAT scores (Mischel et al., 1989; Mischel, Shoda, & Peake, 1988). The ability to delay gratification is also an important skill, implicated in the management of motivation (Wolters, 2003). Evidence has accumulated showing that those who successfully delay gratification often employ various strategies to resist the temptation of waiting for a larger, delayed reward, indirectly implicating a role for emotion regulation processes. Often, these strategies focus on attentional control and the use of self-distraction (Mischel & Ebbesen, 1970; Mischel, Ebbesen, & Zeiss, 1972).

Related to these findings are studies that focus exclusively on *academic delay of gratification*, which occurs when a student resists an immediate temptation in order to pursue a task that advances one's academic goals (Bembenutty & Karabenick, 1998). These studies find that this crucial ability is associated with positive academic outcomes (Bembenutty & Karabenick, 1998). Can a process understanding of emotion regulation achieve greater understanding of academic delay of gratification? Only a limited number of studies have addressed the role of emotion regulation in the management of temptations that disrupt academic outcomes.

Employing an emotion regulation framework, Magen and Gross (2007) asked whether the strategy of cognitive reappraisal could be used to decrease the reward value associated with a temptation. Study 3 of Magen and Gross (2007) constructed a scenario in which a participant would receive a delayed monetary reward for high performance on a math test, which must be completed in the presence of an amusing video that is playing in the same room. The video was directly to the right of the participant, such that he or she had to turn away from the math test to watch it, allowing the researchers to quantify the amount of time spent looking away from the test toward the temptation. Half of the participants were instructed to reappraise the situation as a test of their willpower. Participants who received this instruction succeeded in decreasing the reward associated with the temptation as evidenced by having spent less time looking at the video and more time working on the test. These studies suggest that rather than constantly fighting temptation with effortful behavior modification strategies (Muraven & Baumeister, 2000), one can begin to target the reward associated with temptation with earlier attentional or cognitive reappraisal interventions.

Congruent with findings from Magen and Gross (2007), a more recent study by Leroy, Grégoire, Magen, Gross, and Mikolajczak (2012) shows that students can use reappraisal to increase study related behaviors. In Study 1, participants were asked to memorize study materials in the presence of a distracter (i.e., a poster on the wall). Participants in the reappraisal group were asked to reconstruct the situation as an opportunity to improve their memory. These participants showed improved enthusiasm for the task and obtained higher scores on the memory test. Following up on this study, Leroy et al. (2012) sought to tease apart which aspect of reappraisal was more important: (1) increasing the reward associated with the study task or (2) decreasing the pleasure associated with temptation. Regardless of the target of cognitive reappraisal, both groups obtained comparable improvements in task performance relative to a control group (Leroy et al., 2012). Under this framework, academic delay of gratification can be conceptualized as a process that unfolds over time and is driven by both the pursuit of positive and avoidance of negative emotions. With this in mind, emotion regulation strategies that either decrease the positive emotions associated with the temptation (reappraising television-watching as a negative event) or increase the reward associated with the negative (reinterpreting studying as a positive event) can improve academic achievement and mood outcomes.

Academically, delay of gratification has been shown to be important for learning and grades and has even been shown to be more important than IQ in predicting grades in adolescents (Duckworth & Seligman, 2005). Moreover, this self-discipline has been offered as an explanation for why girls have better grades than boys (Duckworth & Seligman, 2006).

Future work in this area may address how we can train appropriate emotion regulation strategies to be employed in the face of temptations. Other issues for future research include comparing and contrasting the relative effectiveness of each family of regulation strategies as interventions to improve academic delay of gratification. How can we get students to exercise their self-control and find distractions (e.g., use of smartphones) less tempting in the classroom? Educators must consider emotion regulation processes as they contribute to the value associated with temptations.

Test Anxiety

A third context of particular relevance to educators is the testing context. Anxiety about an upcoming test can be precisely what motivates some students to study harder and focus attention, while for other students, this response can cause them to withdraw from study-related behaviors and lead to excess worrying (Schutz & Davis, 2000; Zeidner,

1998, 2014). Given that anxious testing situations can both facilitate performance for those low in test anxiety and harm performance for those high in test anxiety, interventions must be careful to strike a delicate balance (Lang & Lang, 2010; Wine, 1971).

Early work in this area focused on the types of coping strategies reported by students facing stressful tests (Folkman & Lazarus, 1985). These coping strategies are frequently classified into global categories such as *problem-focused coping* and *emotion-focused coping*. Problem-focused coping refers to efforts to change or improve the situation that is causing the negative emotion, whereas emotion-focused coping refers to efforts to change one's emotional response elicited by the situation (Folkman & Lazarus, 1985). Evidence finds that while coping responses are generally associated with better affective outcomes, they are inconsistently related to performance outcomes (see Zeidner, 1998). Zeidner (1998) notes that these categories blur the lines, as actions typically described as problem-focused coping can change emotional outcomes, whereas actions performed in service of emotion-focused coping can change the nature of the problem.

More recent work has begun to address emotion regulation processes as they influence the testing scenario, including the development of emotion regulation questionnaires about test-taking (Schutz, Davis, DeCuir-Gunby, & Tillman, 2014; Schutz, DiStefano, Benson, & Davis, 2004). However, rarely is this work placed in context of a process model of emotion regulation. That is, the temporal unfolding of the anxiety response and the distinct stages at which it can be regulated are understudied. Which strategies do students use to regulate their emotions, which are most effective, and at what time point do they use them? These are questions driven exclusively by an emotion regulation perspective.

To illustrate the value of an emotion regulation framework, we will apply the process model of emotion regulation to organize the many studies that have investigated test anxiety. We acknowledge that anxiety can disrupt learning that comes prior to the test, and anxiety responses after test feedback can influence subsequent rounds of testing. For simplicity, we will apply the process model of emotion regulation to the actual test performance phase, where a student is engaging with an actual test. This framework will allow us to consider both how anxiety unfolds over time and how it can be regulated at each stage of the emotion generative process.

For the anxious student, *situation selection*—in the form of simply leaving the examination room—may be the fastest way to decrease anxiety. However, this comes with drastic consequences for performance, and students are aware of this insight: anxious test-takers report frequent thoughts of leaving the testing situation (Galassi, Frierson, & Sharer, 1981). Situation selection can also be achieved by students who rush though exam materials to escape the situation more quickly, but still at expense to successful test performance. Extrinsic situation selection can come in the form of teachers who structure test situations to be less stressful, by removing pressure-inducing time limits for students who are susceptible to anxiety about testing.

Students in the testing situation, instead of opting to leave the testing situation, may opt for *situation modification,* which involves modifying aspects of the situation to reduce anxiety. Here, a student could alter the order in which they complete the test items, such as completing easier questions first and only moving on to more threatening items later. Evidence suggests that this strategy may result in a less stressful testing experience (Covington & Omelich, 1987).

Other situation modification strategies include the extent to which students mark up the exam itself (i.e., making notes on the test). One study that led participants to write comments on the test directly led to improvements for anxious students (McKeachie, Pollie, & Speisman, 1955). While there are extrinsic situation modifications that educators can employ to decrease the stress of a testing situation (i.e., such as selecting multiple choice exams over essay exams; see Zeidner, 1998), limited work has addressed the types of intrinsic situation modifications that students employ to regulate achievement emotions.

Attentional deployment is also highly relevant to the test-taking context. An influential model of the anxiety-performance relationship argues that performance deficits accrue because of the attentional demands posed by anxiety (Wine, 1971). For example, anxiety is known to increase attention to threat cues, draining working memory of resources needed for test performance (Beilock, Jellison, Rydell, McConnell, & Carr, 2006; MacLeod & Mathews, 1988; Schmeichel, 2007). As a result, attentional deployment is a rich stage at which interventions may be directed, and some of the most successful interventions rely on altering one's attentional focus (Mueller, 1978).

Redirecting attention away from threatening aspects of a testing scenario may free up these cognitive resources. For example, in a sample of Asian women, one study manipulated whether they attended to female or Asian aspects of their identity: For those students who attended to Asian aspects of identity, performance was improved because the stereotype threat associated with being a female and taking a math test was attentionally reduced (Shih, Pittinsky, & Ambady, 1999).

Anxious students may also find relief through *cognitive change*, which involves changing the way they think about the testing situation, either by cognitively rendering the environment less threatening or by reevaluating one's capabilities to manage a threatening situation. The most extensive work addressing cognitive change has been investigations of different forms of cognitive therapy (Zeidner, 1998), with existing research generally showing it to be an effective treatment for test anxiety outcomes. Nevertheless, laboratory investigations of specific cognitive change processes engaged under actual testing procedures are lacking. As one example of the kind of laboratory research that is attempting to understand these processes, Johns, Inzlicht, and Schmader (2008) found that students who were directed to think about a testing scenario objectively and as personally irrelevant achieved less negative outcomes and improved test performance.

Not only can cognitive change be used to reinterpret aspects of the situation, but also it can be used to change the way one thinks about the emotional response itself. For example, individuals with test anxiety often view this response as negative (Hollandsworth, Glazeski, Kirkland, Jones, & Van Norman, 1979). Some studies have targeted this dimension of test anxiety, leading test-takers to view their responses as beneficial to performance or to attribute their responses to irrelevant sources. These interventions typically yield improvements in test outcomes when one's negative interpretations of anxiety responses are changed (Ben-Zeev, Fein, & Inzlicht, 2005; Jamieson et al., 2010; Johns et al., 2008; Weiner & Samuel, 1975). Taken together, emotion regulatory processes that target the meaning of the situation or one's response can improve outcomes.

Finally, with respect to the fifth family of emotion regulation processes, *response modulation*, what happens when test-takers suppress their emotional responses? Emerging evidence suggests that faulty emotion regulation efforts targeting the expression of emotion may contribute to the cognitive interference thought to be caused by anxiety responses themselves. Johns et al. (2008) conducted a series of studies to investigate the role of emotion regulation in targets of stereotype threat. Using a modified dot probe task, they were able to show that targets of stereotype threat spontaneously attempted to conceal information about their emotional state and that this response-focused regulation contributed to poorer performance outcomes. Giving evidence for a causal relationship, Johns et al. (2008) showed that when test-takers are directed to hide information about their emotions, they also obtain worse outcomes than those who do not.

It is clear that, in the case of the anxiety-performance relationship, a process model of emotion regulation can advance test anxiety research by distinguishing between the processes involved with the generation of anxiety and the processes involved with its regulation. Without this explicit emotion regulation framework, there would be no way to theoretically separate the negative effects of anxiety from the negative effects of faulty emotion regulation strategies. Future directions in this area must address which emotion regulation strategies are employed by the low and high test anxious, compare and contrast the effectiveness of each family of emotion regulation strategies, and understand how these test-taking anxieties unfold over the learning-testing cycle.

FUTURE DIRECTIONS

Traditional conceptions of education have focused on cognitive processes, but there is growing interest in the role of emotional processes in education (e.g., Linnenbrink-Garcia & Pekrun, 2011; Schutz & Pekrun, 2007). Given the increasing interest in emotion in educational contexts, it is crucial that we understand how emotions themselves are shaped or regulated by parents, teachers, and students.

So far in this chapter, we have argued that many issues in education can benefit from an up-to-date understanding of emotion regulation theory, and we have focused on three emerging domains for considering emotion regulation in an educational context. However, many new questions are suggested by our emotion regulation perspective, and in this section, we broaden our view and consider a number of directions for future research. First, we will consider the role of emotion regulation goals. Second, we will discuss interventions that appear to target emotional processes. Finally, we will address individual differences in emotion regulation.

Emotion Regulation Goals

Students are surrounded by opportunities to feel positive or negative, but it is less clear how students regulate their emotions in educational settings. Adding to this complexity, not all negative emotional responses are bad, and even bad emotions can have positive outcomes if they serve our goals. Some individuals may benefit from negative mood states, and even prefer to feel them in anticipation of a difficult cognitive task, such as a test (Tamir, 2005). What types of emotions do students believe influence test performance, and can we help them achieve their emotion regulatory goals? What motivates students to regulate their emotions? In addition, work must address how these regulatory goals change as a function of educational context. Certainly, students may have a goal to behave one way at home that changes once he or she arrives at school. These are the types of questions an education researcher armed with an up-to-date understanding of emotion regulation science would ask.

In addition to students, teachers also have their own emotion regulation goals, such as the desire to convey excitement and enthusiasm to students to help motivate them to learn the material, and at other times, the desire to conceal emotional responses that may hinder student achievement (Sutton, Mudrey-Camino, & Knight, 2009). A recent study found that a female teacher's math anxiety can come to influence female students' math performance (Beilock, Gunderson, Ramirez, & Levine, 2010). What emotion regulation processes might these educators engage to improve outcomes? Does cognitive reappraisal on behalf of a teacher reduce students' perceptions of anxiety? These are just a few of the types of questions researchers can ask when considering the importance of emotion regulation goals.

Emotion Regulation Interventions

Another important future direction is to develop and understand targeted interventions. The iterative nature of emotion regulation processes may advance our understanding of why some interventions seemingly have lasting effects (Blackwell, Trzesniewski, & Dweck, 2007; Cohen, Garcia, Apfel, & Master, 2006; Cohen, Garcia, Purdie-Vaughns, Apfel, & Brzustoski, 2009). For example, the process model of emotion regulation implies that the successful management of test anxiety at one time point can lead to recursive effects over time, putting vulnerable students in an upward trajectory. For example, consider the student who manages test anxiety by avoiding any reminders of the testing situation, by choosing to not attend review sessions or study. When a second round of the learning-testing cycle comes around, this student will be less prepared and still experience anxiety at the time of testing. Now consider a similar student who is the target of an intervention that teaches students to attack anxious thoughts of testing by employing cognitive change. This student goes on to attend review sessions and chooses to study. While he may feel a marginal amount of test anxiety the next time he encounters a test, he will not have predetermined failure with faulty emotion regulation choices. It is scenarios like this that demonstrate how an intervention at an initial time point can have recursive effects over time, putting targets of test anxiety into an upward trajectory.

Successful interventions appear to direct their efforts toward motivation and emotion regulation processes, and these interventions have been shown to improve either student mood, academic performance, or both. For example, Blackwell et al. (2007) found that students trained to adopt a malleable theory of intelligence showed improvements in academic outcomes over time. Walton and Cohen (2011) found that a short intervention focusing on making students feel more socially connected decreased feelings of threat and improved learning outcomes over time. Moreover, Ramirez and Beilock (2011) found that a short expressive writing intervention, in which students were directed to write about their worries about an upcoming test, improved test outcomes for anxious students. The processes by which these interventions have their effects are not yet well understood, but all appear to impinge upon particular emotion regulation processes, and it is our view that an explicit emotion regulation framework may be useful in conceptualizing and fashioning successful educational interventions. For example, by changing the meaning or interpretation of one's situation, each of these interventions may be targeting reappraisal processes that lead to the improved outcomes.

Individual Differences

Who benefits from a particular intervention? The process by which interventions interact with characteristics of the student must be more fully explored. As an example, a number of measures exist to predict test anxiety, but it is less clear which emotion regulation intervention is most beneficial: For example, is situation modification superior to attentional deployment, or does cognitive change trump all? Moreover, there are no measures that will predict which type of emotion regulation intervention will be appropriate for a given individual. Broadly speaking, this framework suggests that antecedent-focused emotion regulation will likely fare better than response-focused emotion regulation, but nevertheless, it is an open question whether strategies that target attentional processes, appraisal processes, or behavioral responses work best for the most highly test anxious. Researchers must be careful to consider that other forms of emotion regulation (e.g., expressive suppression) may even contribute to the deficits experienced by the test anxious or targets of stereotype threat. Because individuals differ in their use of emotion regulation strategies, an intervention that has its effects by decreasing the cognitive costs associated with suppression may not work for someone who rarely uses that strategy to begin with. Extending this logic, other interventions may suffer similar fates: Expressive writing interventions may be ineffective for the low test anxious, and training a malleable view of intelligence or teaching students to make different attributions in the face of failure will do nothing for those students who already hold those beliefs or make similar attributions for failure. In light of these issues, educators must keep in mind that students differ in their emotion regulatory needs, and interventions must consider individual differences to avoid harming students who already excel.

CONCLUSIONS

Think of what teachers, students, and parents with a keen understanding of emotion regulation can do to transform the educational process. Teachers can change their own behavior and classroom environments to extrinsically increase interest on the part of the students, turning a once boring environment into their very own educational theater with spellbinding lectures and student-centered learning activities. Students, on the other hand, can intrinsically guide their own attention to topics that excite them and change the way they think about classes to enhance the value in what they once found uninteresting. Parents can modify the home learning situation into a calm and soothing place for their children, and children can reinterpret temptations as unrewarding and a distraction from their educational goals. The classroom is a place full of emotion, and the educational context can be positively transformed when students, teachers, and parents effectively harness the power of emotion to enhance educational outcomes. There are many targets of regulation, and this is only the beginning for what benefits an emotion regulation perspective can provide for educators, parents, students, and educational researchers.

New questions emerge when education researchers consider the role of emotion regulation: Which emotions are optimal for the learning environment, and what strategies should students (and teachers) be using to create an affective climate beneficial to educational outcomes? How does emotion and its regulation contribute to the effects of various emotional responses on test performance, and what can be done about it? What processes contribute to changes in student well-being that last over time? These questions may not have clear answers yet, but giving equal treatment to emotion generation and emotion regulation processes is an important step in advancing the state of the art in education research.

REFERENCES

Beilock, S. L., Gunderson, E. A., Ramirez, G., & Levine, S. C. (2010). Female teachers' math anxiety affects girls' math achievement. *Proceedings of the National Academy of Sciences of the United States of America, 107*, 1860–1863. doi: 10.1073/pnas.0910967107

Beilock, S. L., Jellison, W. A., Rydell, R. J., McConnell, A. R., & Carr, T. H. (2006). On the causal mechanisms of stereotype threat: Can skills that don't rely heavily on working memory still be threatened? *Personality & Social Psychology Bulletin, 32*, 1059–1071. doi: 10.1177/0146167206288489

Bembenutty, H., & Karabenick, S. A. (1998). Academic delay of gratification. *Learning and Individual Differences, 10*, 329–346. doi: 10.1016/S1041–6080(99)80126–5

Ben-Zeev, T., Fein, S., & Inzlicht, M. (2005). Arousal and stereotype threat. *Journal of Experimental Social Psychology, 41*, 174–181. doi: 10.1016/j.jesp.2003.11.007

Blackwell, L. S., Trzesniewski, K. H., & Dweck, C. S. (2007). Implicit theories of intelligence predict achievement across an adolescent transition: A longitudinal study and an intervention. *Child Development, 78*, 246–263. doi: 10.1111/j.1467–8624.2007.00995.x

Blair, K. A., Denham, S. A., Kochanoff, A., & Whipple, B. (2004). Playing it cool: Temperament, emotion regulation, and social behavior in preschoolers. *Journal of School Psychology, 42*, 419–443. doi: 10.1016/j.jsp.2004.10.002

Butler, E. A., Egloff, B., Wilhelm, F. H., Smith, N. C., Erickson, E. A., & Gross, J. J. (2003). The social consequences of expressive suppression. *Emotion, 3*, 48–67. doi: 10.1037/1528–3542.3.1.48

Cohen, G. L., Garcia, J., Apfel, N., & Master, A. (2006). Reducing the racial achievement gap: A social-psychological intervention. *Science, 313*, 1307–1310. doi: 10.1126/science.1128317

Cohen, G. L., Garcia, J., Purdie-Vaughns, V., Apfel, N., & Brzustoski, P. (2009). Recursive processes in self-affirmation: Intervening to close the minority achievement gap. *Science, 324*, 400–403. doi: 10.1126/science.1170769

Cole, P. M. (1986). Children's spontaneous control of facial expression. *Child Development, 57*, 1309–1321. doi: 10.2307/1130411

Cole, P. M., Dennis, T. A., Smith-Simon, K. E., & Cohen, L. H. (2009). Preschoolers' emotion regulation strategy understanding: Relations with emotion socialization and child self-regulation. *Social Development, 18*, 324–352. doi: 10.1111/j.1467–9507.2008.00503.x

Covington, M. V., & Omelich, C. L. (1987). Item difficulty and test performance among high-anxious and low anxious students. In R. Schwarzer, H. M. Van Der Ploeg, & C. D. Spielberger (Eds.), *Advances in test anxiety research* (pp. 127–135). Hillsdale, NJ: Erlbaum.

Davis, E. L., Levine, L. J., Lench, H. C., & Quas, J. A. (2010). Metacognitive emotion regulation: Children's awareness that changing thoughts and goals can alleviate negative emotions. *Emotion, 10*, 498–510. doi: 10.1037/a0018428

Davis, H. A., DiStefano, C., & Schutz, P. A. (2008). Identifying patterns of appraising tests in first-year college students: Implications for anxiety and emotion regulation during test taking. *Journal of Educational Psychology, 100*, 942–960. doi: 10.1037/a0013096

Duckworth, A. L., & Seligman, M.E.P. (2005). Self-discipline outdoes IQ in predicting academic performance of adolescents. *Psychological Science, 16*, 939–944. doi: 10.1111/j.1467–9280.2005.01641.x

Duckworth, A. L., & Seligman, M.E.P. (2006). Self-discipline gives girls the edge: Gender in self-discipline, grades, and achievement test scores. *Journal of Educational Psychology, 98*, 198–208. doi: 10.1037/0022–0663.98.1.198

Eisenberg, N., Spinrad, T. L., & Smith, C. L. (2004). Emotion-related regulation: Its conceptualization, relations to social functioning, and socialization. In P. Philippot & R. S. Feldman (Eds.), *The regulation of emotion* (pp. 277–306). Mahwah, NJ: Erlbaum.

Flavell, J. H., Flavell, E. R., & Green, F. L. (2001). Development of children's understanding of connections between thinking and feeling. *Psychological Science, 12*, 430–432. doi: 10.1111/1467–9280.00379

Folkman, S., & Lazarus, R. S. (1985). If it changes it must be a process: Study of emotion and coping during three stages of a college examination. *Journal of Personality and Social Psychology, 48*, 150–170. doi: 10.1037/0022–3514.48.1.150

Freud, S. (1959). *Inhibitions, symptoms, anxiety* (A. Strachey, Trans., and J. Strachey, Ed.). New York, NY: Norton. (Original work published 1926).

Fuchs, D., & Thelen, M. H. (1988). Children's expected interpersonal consequences of communicating their affective state and reported likelihood of expression. *Child Development, 59*, 1314–1322. doi: 10.2307/1130494

Galassi, J. P., Frierson, H. T., & Sharer, R. (1981). Behavior of high, moderate, and low test anxious students during an actual test situation. *Journal of Consulting and Clinical Psychology, 49*, 51–62. doi: 10.1037/0022–006X.49.1.51

Giuliani, N. R., McRae, K., & Gross, J. J. (2008). The up- and down-regulation of amusement: experiential, behavioral, and autonomic consequences. *Emotion, 8*, 714–719. doi: 10.1037/a0013236

Graziano, P. A., Reavis, R. D., Keane, S. P., & Calkins, S. D. (2007). The role of emotion regulation and children's early academic success. *Journal of School Psychology, 45*, 3–19. doi: 10.1016/j.jsp.2006.09.002

Gross, J. J. (1998a). Antecedent- and response-focused emotion regulation: Divergent consequences for experience, expression, and physiology. *Journal of Personality and Social Psychology, 74*, 224–237. doi: 10.1037/0022–3514.74.1.224

Gross, J. J. (1998b). The emerging field of emotion regulation: An integrative review. *Review of General Psychology, 2*, 271–299. doi: 10.1037/1089–2680.2.3.271

Gross, J. J. (2002). Emotion regulation: Affective, cognitive, and social consequences. *Psychophysiology, 39*, 281–291. doi: 10.1017.S0048577201393198

Gross, J. J. (2008). Emotion regulation. In M. Lewis, J. M. Haviland-Jones, & L. F. Barrett (Eds.), *Handbook of emotions* (3rd ed., pp. 497–512). New York, NY: Guilford Press.

Gross, J. J., & John, O. P. (2003). Individual differences in two emotion regulation processes: Implications for affect, relationships, and well-being. *Journal of Personality and Social Psychology, 85*, 348–362. doi: 10.1037/0022–3514.85.2.348

Gross, J. J., & Levenson, R. W. (1993). Emotional suppression: Physiology, self-report, and expressive behavior. *Journal of Personality and Social Psychology, 64*, 970–986. doi: 10.1037/0022–3514.64.6.970

Gross, J. J., & Thompson, R. A. (2007). Emotion regulation: Conceptual foundations. In J. J. Gross (Ed.), *Handbook of emotion regulation* (pp. 3–24). New York, NY: Guilford Press.

Harris, P. L., Olthof, T., Terwogt, M. M., & Hardman, C. E. (1987). Children's knowledge of the situations that provoke emotion. *International Journal of Behavioral Development, 10*, 319–343. doi: 10.1177/016502548701000304

Hayes, J. P., Morey, R. A., Petty, C. M., Seth, S., Smoski, M. J., McCarthy, G., & LaBar, K. S. (2010). Staying cool when things get hot: Emotion regulation modulates neural mechanisms of memory encoding. *Frontiers in Human Neuroscience, 4*, 230. doi: 10.3389/fnhum.2010.00230

Hollandsworth, J. G., Glazeski, R. C., Kirkland, K., Jones, G. E., & Van Norman, L. R. (1979). An analysis of the nature and effects of test anxiety: Cognitive, behavioral, and physiological components. *Cognitive Therapy and Research, 3*, 165–180. doi: 10.1007/BF01172603

Izard, C. E., King, K. A., Trentacosta, C. J., Morgan, J. K., Laurenceau, J. P., Krauthamer-Ewing, E. S., & Finlon, K. J. (2008). Accelerating the development of emotion competence in Head Start children: Effects on adaptive and maladaptive behavior. *Development and Psychopathology, 20*, 369–397. doi:10.1017/S0954579408000175

Jackson, N. (2010). *The teacher who inspired me. Guardian.* Retrieved from www.guardian.co.uk/education/2010/jan/19/teacher-inspired-me

James, W. (1884). What is an Emotion? *Mind, 9*, 188–205.

Jamieson, J. P., Mendes, W. B., Blackstock, E., & Schmader, T. (2010). Turning the knots in your stomach into bows: Reappraising arousal improves performance on the GRE. *Journal of Experimental Social Psychology, 46*, 208–212. doi: 10.1016/j.jesp.2009.08.015

Jamieson, J. P., Nock, M. K., & Mendes, W. B. (2012). Mind over matter: Reappraising arousal improves cardiovascular and cognitive responses to stress. *Journal of Experimental Psychology: General, 141*, 417–422. doi: 10.1037/a0025719

Johns, M., Inzlicht, M., & Schmader, T. (2008). Stereotype threat and executive resource depletion: Examining the influence of emotion regulation. *Journal of Experimental Psychology: General, 137*, 691–705. doi: 10.1037/a0013834

Keltner, D., & Anderson, C. (2000). Saving face for Darwin: The functions and uses of embarrassment. *Current Directions in Psychological Science, 9*, 187–192. doi: 10.1111/1467–8721.00091

Lang, J.W.B., & Lang, J. (2010). Priming competence diminishes the link between cognitive test anxiety and test performance. *Psychological Science, 21*, 811–819. doi: 10.1177/0956797610369492

Lazarus, R. S. (1966). *Psychological stress and the coping process.* New York, NY: McGraw Hill.

Leroy, V., Grégoire, J., Magen, E., Gross, J. J., & Mikolajczak, M. (2012). Resisting the sirens of temptation while studying: Using reappraisal to increase focus, enthusiasm, and performance. *Learning and Individual Differences, 22*, 263–268. doi: 10.1016/j.lindif.2011.10.003

Linnenbrink-Garcia, L., & Pekrun, R. (2011). Students' emotions and academic engagement: Introduction to the special issue. *Contemporary Educational Psychology, 36*, 1–3. doi: 10.1016/j.cedpsych.2010.11.004

MacLeod, C., & Mathews, A. (1988). Anxiety and the allocation of attention to threat. *The Quarterly Journal of Experimental Psychology Section A: Human Experimental Psychology, 40*, 653–670. doi: 10.1080/14640748808402292

Magen, E., & Gross, J. J. (2007). Harnessing the need for immediate gratification: Cognitive reconstrual modulates the reward value of temptations. *Emotion, 7*, 415–428. doi: 10.1037/1528–3542.7.2.415

Mauss, I. B., Cook, C. L., Cheng, J.Y.J., & Gross, J. J. (2007). Individual differences in cognitive reappraisal: Experiential and physiological responses to an anger provocation. *International Journal of Psychophysiology, 66*, 116–124. doi: 10.1016/j.ijpsycho.2007.03.017

Mauss, I. B., Levenson, R. W., McCarter, L., Wilhelm, F. H., & Gross, J. J. (2005). The tie that binds? Coherence among emotion experience, behavior, and physiology. *Emotion, 5*, 175–190. doi: 10.1037/1528–3542.5.2.175

Mauss, I. B., Shallcross, A. J., Troy, A. S., John, O. P., Ferrer, E., Wilhelm, F. H., & Gross, J. J. (2011). Don't hide your happiness! Positive emotion dissociation, social connectedness, and psychological functioning. *Journal of Personality and Social Psychology, 100*, 738–748. doi: 10.1037/a0022410

McCoy, C. L., & Masters, J. C. (1985). The development of children's strategies for the social control of emotion. *Child Development, 56*, 1214–1222. doi: 10.2307/1130236

McKeachie, W. J., Pollie, D., & Speisman, J. (1955). Relieving anxiety in classroom examinations. *The Journal of Abnormal and Social Psychology, 50*, 93–98. doi: 10.1037/h0046560

McRae, K., Gross, J. J., Weber, J., Robertson, E. R., Sokol-Hessner, P., Ray, R. D., . . . Ochsner, K. N. (2012). The development of emotion regulation: An fMRI study of cognitive reappraisal in children, adolescents and young adults. *Social Cognitive and Affective Neuroscience, 7*, 11–22. doi: 10.1093/scan/nsr093

Mischel, W., & Ebbesen, E. B. (1970). Attention in delay of gratification. *Journal of Personality and Social Psychology, 16*, 329–337. doi: 10.1037/h0029815

Mischel, W., Ebbesen, E. B., & Zeiss, A. R. (1972). Cognitive and attentional mechanisms in delay of gratification. *Journal of Personality and Social Psychology, 21*, 204–218. doi: 10.1037/h0032198

Mischel, W., Shoda, Y., & Peake, P. K. (1988). The nature of adolescent competencies predicted by preschool delay of gratification. *Journal of Personality and Social Psychology, 54*, 687–696. doi: 10.1037/0022–3514.54.4.687

Mischel, W., Shoda, Y., & Rodriguez, M. L. (1989). Delay of gratification in children. *Science, 244*, 933–938. doi: 10.1126/science.2658056

Mueller, J. H. (1978). The effects of individual differences in test anxiety and type of orienting task on levels of organization in free recall. *Journal of Research in Personality, 12*, 100–116. doi: 10.1016/0092–6566(78)90087–9

Muraven, M., & Baumeister, R. F. (2000). Self-regulation and depletion of limited resources: Does self-control resemble a muscle? *Psychological Bulletin, 126*, 247–259. doi: 10.1037/0033–2909.126.2.247

Naqvi, N., Shiv, B., & Bechara, A. (2006). The role of emotion in decision making: A cognitive neuroscience perspective. *Current Directions in Psychological Science, 15*, 260–264. doi: 10.1111/j.1467–8721.2006.00448.x

Öhman, A., Flykt, A., & Esteves, F. (2001). Emotion drives attention: Detecting the snake in the grass. *Journal of Experimental Psychology: General, 130*, 466–478. doi: 10.1037/0096–3445.130.3.466

Pekrun, R., & Linnenbrink-Garcia, L. (2012). Academic emotions and student engagement. In S. L. Christenson, A. L. Reschly, & C. Wylie (Eds.), *Handbook of research on student engagement* (pp. 259–292). New York, NY: Springer.

Phelps, E. A., Ling, S., & Carrasco, M. (2006). Emotion facilitates perception and potentiates the perceptual benefits of attention. *Psychological Science, 17*, 292–299. doi: 10.1111/j.1467–9280.2006.01701.x

Philippot, P., & Schaefer, A. (2001). Emotion and memory. In T. J. Mayne & G. A. Bonanno (Eds.), *Emotions: Currrent issues and future directions* (pp. 82–122). New York, NY: Guilford Press.

Pons, F., Harris, P. L., & de Rosnay, M. (2004). Emotion comprehension between 3 and 11 years: Developmental periods and hierarchical organization. *European Journal of Developmental Psychology, 1*, 127–152. doi: 10.1080/17405620344000022

Ramirez, G., & Beilock, S. L. (2011). Writing about testing worries boosts exam performance in the classroom. *Science, 331*, 211–213. doi: 10.1126/science.1199427

Richards, J. M., & Gross, J. J. (1999). Composure at any cost? The cognitive consequences of emotion suppression. *Personality and Social Psychology Bulletin, 25*, 1033–1044. doi: 10.1177/01461672992511010

Richards, J. M., & Gross, J. J. (2000). Emotion regulation and memory: The cognitive costs of keeping one's cool. *Journal of Personality and Social Psychology, 79*, 410–424. doi:10.1037/0022–3514.79.3.410

Scherer, K. R., Schorr, A., & Johnstone, T. (2001). *Appraisal processes in emotion: Theory, methods, research.* New York, NY: Oxford University Press.

Schmader, T., Johns, M., & Forbes, C. (2008). An integrated process model of stereotype threat effects on performance. *Psychological Review, 115*, 336–356. doi: 10.1037/0033–295X.115.2.336

Schmeichel, B. J. (2007). Attention control, memory updating, and emotion regulation temporarily reduce the capacity for executive control. *Journal of Experimental Psychology: General, 136*, 241–255. doi: 10.1037/0096–3445.136.2.241

Schutz, P. A., & Davis, H. A. (2000). Emotions and self-regulation during test taking. *Educational Psychologist, 35*, 243–256. doi: 10.1207/S15326985EP3504_03

Schutz, P. A., Davis, H. A., DeCuir-Gunby, J. T., & Tillman, D. (2014). Regulating emotions relating to testing. In R. Pekrun & L. Linnenbrink-Garcia (Eds.), *International handbook of emotions in education* (pp. 348–367). New York, NY: Taylor & Francis.

Schutz, P. A., Distefano, C., Benson, J., & Davis, H. A. (2004). The emotional regulation during test-taking scale. *Anxiety, Stress & Coping: An International Journal, 17*, 253–269. doi: 10.1080/10615800410001710861

Schutz, P. A., & Pekrun, R. (Eds.). (2007). *Emotion in education.* San Diego, CA: Academic Press.

Sheppes, G., Scheibe, S., Suri, G., & Gross, J.J. (2011). Emotion-regulation choice. *Psychological science, 22*, 1391–1396. doi:10.1177/0956797611418350

Shih, M., Pittinsky, T. L., & Ambady, N. (1999). Stereotype susceptibility: Identity salience and shifts in quantitative performance. *Psychological Science, 10*, 80–83. doi: 10.1111/1467–9280.00111

Srivastava, S., Tamir, M., McGonigal, K. M., John, O. P., & Gross, J. J. (2009). The social costs of emotional suppression: A prospective study of the transition to college. *Journal of Personality and Social Psychology, 96*, 883–897. doi: 10.1037/a0014755

Sutton, R. E., Mudrey-Camino, R., & Knight, C. C. (2009). Teachers' emotion regulation and classroom management. *Theory Into Practice, 48*, 130–137. doi: 10.1080/00405840902776418

Tamir, M. (2005). Don't worry, be happy? Neuroticism, trait-consistent affect regulation, and performance. *Journal of Personality and Social Psychology, 89*, 449–461. doi: 10.1037/0022–3514.89.3.449

Thompson, R. A. (1991). Emotional regulation and emotional development. *Educational Psychology Review, 3*, 269–307. doi: 10.1007/BF01319934

Tyson, D. F., Linnenbrink-Garcia, L., & Hill, N. E. (2009). Regulating debilitating emotions in the context of performance: Achievement goal orientations, achievement-elicited emotions, and socialization contexts. *Human Development, 52*, 329–356. doi: 10.1159/000242348

Walton, G. M., & Cohen, G. L. (2011). A brief social-belonging intervention improves academic and health outcomes of minority students. *Science, 331*, 1447–1451. doi: 10.1126/science.1198364

Weiner, M. J., & Samuel, W. (1975). The effect of attributing internal arousal to an external source upon test anxiety and performance. *The Journal of Social Psychology, 96*, 255–265. doi: 10.1080/00224545.1975.9923291

Wine, J. (1971). Test anxiety and direction of attention. *Psychological Bulletin, 76*, 92–104. doi: 10.1037/h0031332

Wolters, C. A. (2003). Regulation of motivation: Evaluating an underemphasized aspect of self-regulated learning. *Educational Psychologist, 38*, 189–205. doi: 10.1207/S15326985EP3804_1

Zeidner, M. (1998). *Test anxiety: The state of the art.* New York, NY: Plenum Press.

Zeidner, M. (2014). Anxiety in education. In R. Pekrun & L. Linnenbrink-Garcia (Eds.), *International handbook of emotions in education* (pp. 265–288). New York, NY: Taylor & Francis.

Zeidner, M., Matthews, G., Roberts, R. D., & MacCann, C. (2003). Development of emotional intelligence: Towards a multi-level investment model. *Human Development, 46*, 69–96. doi: 10.1159/000068580

Part II

Emotions and Emotion Regulation
in Classroom Settings

11

INTEREST AND ENJOYMENT

Mary Ainley and Suzanne Hidi,
University of Melbourne and University of Toronto

> Education systems aim to enable students not just to acquire knowledge but also to become capable, confident and enthusiastic learners. . . . Beyond school, children and adults who have developed the ability and motivation to learn on their own initiative are well-placed to become lifelong learners.
>
> (Artelt, Baumert, McElvany, & Peschar, 2003)

Implicit in Artelt et al.'s (2003) statement is the belief that sound education is based on positive learning experiences. Hence, the character of the experiences and the conditions that generate and support learning experiences are important issues for 21st-century educators. At the same time, it is important to acknowledge that students' motivation and engagement with core learning domains continues to be of concern to educators throughout the world (Kuenzi, Matthews, & Mangan, 2006). Whether an educator's focus is on positive educational development or on students' disengagement with education, knowledge of how interest and enjoyment might contribute to desired educational outcomes is part of the 21st-century educational agenda.

The underlying issue for this chapter is to give shape to concepts of interest and enjoyment as they contribute to students' learning and achievement. First, we consider whether both interest and enjoyment can be considered to be emotions and whether they overlap or are different concepts. As part of this analysis, we examine the feeling states and facial expressions associated with interest and enjoyment. In the following section, contemporary neuroscientific evidence distinguishing wanting and liking within brain reward mechanisms is presented, and implications for the distinction between interest and enjoyment are explored. Next, we consider how the relation between interest and enjoyment may differ according to whether the perspective is an in-the-moment experience or a more general predisposition and draw on the Four-Phase model of interest development to highlight the different relations between interest and enjoyment at different phases of interest development. This leads into a consideration of how interest and enjoyment are viewed from the perspective of the control-value theory of achievement emotions, followed by a brief discussion of how interest and enjoyment currently are measured. The final section considers recent findings on interest and enjoyment as factors contributing to learning and achievement. We conclude that feelings of interest and enjoyment often and ideally co-occur but may also occur independently. Experiencing interest motivates exploration and information seeking especially when faced with novel or puzzling situations; feelings of enjoyment signal pleasure and satisfaction with what is achieved.

SO WHAT IS INTEREST, AND WHAT IS ENJOYMENT?

Clear descriptions of the affective states or feelings associated with basic emotions are found in Izard's early writings (e.g., Izard, 1977). He describes feeling interested as the experience of being engrossed with, or absorbed in, an activity. Interest "is the feeling of being engaged, caught-up, fascinated, curious. There is a feeling of wanting to investigate, become involved" (Izard, 1977, p. 216). On the other hand, to feel enjoyment is to feel satisfied with, or pleased about, one's participation in an activity:

> Joy is not the same as having fun. Joy may be involved in having fun and games, but the experience of fun probably includes interest-excitement as a principal ingredient . . . Joy is characterized by a sense of confidence and significance . . . feeling that you are capable of coping with the problems and pleasures of living.
>
> (Izard, 1977, p. 240)

According to Izard, interest and enjoyment are separate feelings, but it is likely that the experience of having fun is generated when interest and enjoyment occur together.

In his classic work on emotion, Tomkins (1962) proposed that interest and enjoyment are positive affects within the category of "primary affects." He used the terminology of interest-excitement and enjoyment-joy where the first of the pair of terms indicated the relatively lower, and the second term the relatively higher intensity form. Interest-excitement can be identified through a facial expression of "eyebrows down, track, look, listen," while enjoyment-joy is identified by an expression of "smile, lips widened up and out" (Tomkins, 1962, p. 337). With these differences in expression, there are differences in function. While interest motivates exploration of what is novel and intriguing, enjoyment is the sense of satisfaction and reward generated from the activity and/or the outcome of the activity. Tomkins (1962) also proposed that the relation between these two variables may be reciprocal: "In short, one can enjoy excitement, and become excited by enjoyment" (p. 368).

Enjoyment and joy are included in all listings of emotions, whether referred to as "basic emotions," "primary affects," or simply emotions. As Tomkins (1962) acknowledged, there has been considerable debate over the existence of "primary affects," and some researchers questioned interest being considered a primary affect. A number of writers who have made major contributions to the study of emotion do not include interest as a basic emotion. For example, Darwin (1872) did not refer to interest in his classic study of emotions. Nor was it included by Ekman (Ekman & Freisan, 1971) in the set of six basic emotions used in his cross-cultural research on the universality of basic emotions.

In the context of documenting excitement as one of the "enjoyable emotions," Ekman referred to Tomkin's characterization of excitement as the more intense form of interest, arguing that "interest is largely cerebral, a thinking state rather than an emotion" (Ekman, 2003, p. 193). Recently, in response to a paper raising questions concerning the status of feelings of confusion, concentration, and worry within the structure of emotion (Rozin & Cohen, 2003), Ellsworth (2003), a former student of Ekman, argued that interest was not included in the set of basic emotions defined by Ekman (see Ekman, 1994; Ekman, Friesen, & Ellsworth, 1972) because at the time there was a stark divide between emotion and cognition—interest seemed "too cognitive." With the wisdom of hindsight, Ellsworth concluded that "concentration, confusion, absorbed meditation, and perplexed reflection are feelings that are inseparable from thought, feelings that most clearly exemplify the inseparability of cognition and emotion. They are all manifestations of interest" (2003, p. 84). At the core of this proposition is a commitment to understanding the evolutionary significance of interest by virtue of its role in learning, creativity, and activities that require sustained effort, and critically, that it has both affective and cognitive components.

This latest stance by Ellsworth (2003) is consistent with Izard's writings on emotion that extend from the early 1970s. In his recent writings, Izard (2007, 2009) reasserts the importance of interest as an emotion in human behavior. Expressions of interest appear in the early months of life and:

[interest] is most likely to be present in the healthy individual in ordinary conditions. That a simple change in the perceptual field can contribute to the activation or maintenance of interest helps account for its tendency to be omnipresent. Its ubiquity is further enhanced by its effectiveness in engaging and sustaining the individual in person–environment interactions that facilitate exploration, learning, and constructive endeavors and in detecting events and situations (sources of information) that lead to new emotions.

(Izard, 2007, p. 272)

Izard (2007, 2009), reflecting on his early work (e.g., 1977; Izard & Malatesta, 1987), summarized the potential reciprocal and complimentary functions of interest and enjoyment in his description of combinations of interest, joy, and contentment underpinning constructive and creative activities. In his view, interest and joy are part of the conditions associated with exercise of and expansion of ideas and knowledge at all developmental levels.

A similar perspective on a complementary relation between interest and enjoyment occurs in research on general well-being and positive development. For example, Fredrickson's (2001) broaden-and-build theory of positive emotions draws attention to distinct roles of interest and joy as positive emotions contributing to expanding experience and acquisition of adaptive knowledge: "Joy, for instance, broadens by creating the urge to play, push the limits, and be creative. . . . Interest, a phenomenologically distinct positive emotion, broadens by creating the urge to explore, take in new information and experiences, and expand the self in the process" (p. 220). While there are many settings where interest and enjoyment occur independently, the significance of these models for understanding achievement is that interest and enjoyment may also be complementary and reciprocal components of the experience when an individual is pursuing an idea, exploring and seeking new information, or creating a novel solution to a problem.

With recent research focused on the role of positive emotions in behavior, there is an increasing trend to look beyond global positive emotion, and consistent with Fredrickson's (2001) theory, to distinguish the role of specific positive emotions. This is happening with both situational and generalized measures. For example, Egloff, Schmukle, Burns, Kohlmann, and Hock (2003) identified three positive affect dimensions—joy, interest, and activation—when factoring responses to the Positive and Negative Affect Schedule (PANAS; Watson, Clark, & Tellegen, 1988). Responses recorded during an exam, in a classroom, and when affect was induced through success and failure experience treatments, indicated different trajectories for positive affect dimensions of joy, interest, and activation across the target situations. This supported the researchers' contention that measures of global positive affect can usefully be supplemented by investigating the separate trajectories of specific positive affect dimensions. Around the same time, Consedine, Magai, and King (2004) distinguished general tendencies to experience interest and to experience joy in their investigation of how they were differentially associated with lifestyle patterns in the elderly. After allowing for the positive association between interest and joy, key findings were that higher interest scores were associated with higher educational attainment in the elderly, while more frequent joy experiences were associated with fewer health symptoms.

At the same time as researchers are distinguishing separate dimensions within positive affect, attention is also being directed to reexamining differences between the facial expressions associated with specific positive emotions. While facial features that express enjoyment have been widely researched, the facial expression that is characteristic of interest has not been explored as extensively. In addition to Tomkin's description of the facial expressions associated with interest and enjoyment mentioned above, both Ekman (e.g., 1994, 2003) and Izard (e.g., 1977, 2007) proposed prototypes of discrete facial expressions associated with each basic emotion. They codified these in their facial coding systems, Facial Action Coding Scheme, FACS (Ekman, Friesen, & Hager, 2002), and the Maximally Discriminative Affect Coding System, MAX (Izard, 1983/1995). However, identification of feeling states associated with facial expression is complicated by variations in displays across individuals, social groups, and cultures that emerge as a function of the need for effective communication in social contexts.

Investigations of the facial expression correlates for specific positive emotions are ongoing and more attention is being given to specific positive emotions. Of significance for our examination of the relation between interest and enjoyment is research exploring features of facial expressions that are distinctive to interest. For example, Reeve (1993) videotaped undergraduate students' responses to both interesting and uninteresting film clips and coded their facial expressions using Ekman's FACS (Ekman et al., 2002). Reeve reported finding significant differences in patterns of upper facial behavior—for example, a greater incidence of eyelid widening during interesting films than uninteresting films. Importantly, he found that identification of interest expressions required observations over several seconds: "Our findings suggest that one must monitor facial behavior for several seconds before many of the interest-associated facial movements begin to provide the data necessary to discriminate interested from disinterested faces" (Reeve, 1993, p. 373). A further study (Reeve & Nix, 1997) used these findings to explore the potential of using upper face activity as a behavioral measure of interest. The incidence of upper face indicators of interest were recorded when students were solving spatial relations manipulation puzzles and were examined in relation to self-report and persistence indicators of interest. Reeve and Nix reported that these interest indicators related positively to the amount of eye contact with the puzzle and related negatively to the amount of time eyes were closed. As they pointed out, "the two facial displays did not correlate with each other, which suggests that a coherent cluster of interest-associated facial displays might not exist" (Reeve & Nix, 1997, p. 247). One implication of this finding currently being investigated is that facial expressions associated with feelings of interest and enjoyment may not be static displays but may be "the cumulative result of a series of individual facial actions" (Mortillaro, Mehu, & Scherer, 2011, p. 269).

According to Scherer (2009), facial expressions associated with specific feelings consist of a dynamic process whereby facial expression is constantly open to minute changes in the combinations of features that are activated as a result of constant reappraisals of the ongoing stimulus event. This is in contrast to the "discrete language labels referring to steady states" (Scherer, 2000, p. 75) used to classify emotional expressions. Hence, specific positive emotions may not be distinguished through a discrete static display but by a sequence of facial action units. For example, Mortillaro et al. (2011) investigated facial patterning produced by professional actors when instructed to express four positive affective states: pride, joy, interest, and sensory pleasure. Specific definitions were provided for each affect. Interest was described to the actors as "being attracted, being fascinated, or having one's attention captured," while joy was specified as having a "feeling of great happiness caused by an unexpected event" (Mortillaro et al., 2011, p. 263). The duration of defined action units within the expressions produced by the actors were coded using Ekman's FACS (Ekman et al., 2002). While judges were able to reliably classify the set of expressions, findings for comparisons between the interest and joy expressions point to both specificity and to overlap in facial patterning: "systematic differences in the expression of positive discrete emotions, but no-emotion specific prototype emerged from the analysis" (p. 268). For example, one action unit referred to as "cheek raiser," typically associated with "the family of enjoyable emotion," was present in both sets of expressions. This action unit was expressed more frequently and for a longer duration for joy than for interest. Similarly, there was a longer duration of the action unit representing a tightening of the eyelid in interest expressions than in joy expressions. On this basis, it appears that the temporal sequence of facial actions is critical for distinguishing facial expression that accompanies feeling states of interest and enjoyment. Further research into facial patterning associated with positive emotions will help clarify both the distinctiveness and complementarity of interest and enjoyment. We now turn to the recent neuroscientific evidence on the relation between interest and enjoyment.

INTEREST, ENJOYMENT, AND REWARD: THE NEUROSCIENTIFIC EVIDENCE

Contemporary neuroscientific evidence has been used by Hidi (2006) to argue that interest is a unique motivational variable. She cites Panksepp's (1998) propositions concerning the SEEKING system as the major biological basis for the state or subjective experience of interest.

The mammalian brain contains a foraging/ exploration/ investigation/ curiosity/ interest/ expectancy SEEKING system that leads organisms to eagerly pursue the fruits of their environment from nuts to knowledge, so to speak. . . . Although this brain state, like all other basic emotional states, is initially without intrinsic cognitive content, it gradually helps cement the perception of casual connections in the world and thereby creates ideas.

(Panksepp, 1998, p. 145)

alignment for more critical inquiry

The distinctive feeling tone for the emotional derivatives of the SEEKING system involves feeling energized and invigorated anticipation, suggesting that when exposed to novel, uncertain, or ambiguous events there is a "prewired" tendency to experience interest as an emotion and feelings of interest are a key motivator of action. Furthermore, it has been suggested that brain activation is different when a learner feels an interest in what they are doing compared with activities where they feel no interest (Hidi, 2006; Panksepp, 1998; Renninger & Hidi, 2011).

While much of the research on interest has been conducted at the level of behavioral observation and self-report, the evidence emerging from neuroscientific research that involves tracking and recording brain activity using scanning techniques and neural imaging, such as functional magnetic resonance imaging (fMRI) (Damasio, 2003), provides further support for the above assumptions. One particular direction in this research has relevance for our understanding of the relation between interest and enjoyment—namely, research into the characteristics of the basic reward mechanisms. More specifically, Hidi (2011, 2012) suggested that interest is related to the reward system and may function as a reward.

The existence of an endogenous reward system in mammals has been demonstrated by a multitude of fMRI studies that examined the neural correlates of reward anticipation and delivery. An important study emerging from this literature is that of Kang et al. (2009). As is also the case in a number of other studies in this area, their work refers to curiosity rather than early phases of situational interest. However, their findings bear equally on early phases of interest and curiosity, as both are characterized by an internally driven search for novelty (Quintanilha, 2010). When humans and other mammals seek information about an object that has aroused their curiosity, it has been assumed that the anticipated information is rewarding (Kang et al., 2009; Loewenstein, 1994). Based on this assumption, Kang et al. (2009) examined the underlying neural mechanisms of curiosity states—that is, states comparable to states of situational interest (Renninger & Hidi, 2011). The researchers collected fMRI measures while individuals were reading trivia questions that varied in the levels of curiosity elicited. Their data showed level of curiosity was correlated with activation of the caudate in the striatum, a component of the reward circuitry that previously has been associated with anticipated rewards. In addition, both imaging and behavioral data suggested that curiosity enhanced memory for novel information, pointing to cognitive benefits of activation of the reward circuitry. The researchers concluded that curiosity involves anticipation of rewarding information and may enhance learning of new information. In addition, Kang et al. (2009) made the following important suggestion:

Having established that curiosity is a form of reward anticipation, we can also tie this research to the work of Adcock, Thangavel, Whitfield-Gabrieli, Knutson, and Gabrieli (2006) who showed anticipated monetary rewards modulate activations in the mesolimbic and parahippocampal regions and promote memory formation prior to learning. Our results complement theirs by showing that endogenous internal motivation manifested in curiosity recruits neural circuits similar to those that are recruited by exogenous incentives, and has a similar effect on learning.

(Kang et al., 2009, p. 971)

As Hidi (submitted) has demonstrated, recently neuroscientists have focused on identifying brain mechanisms that link novelty and reward processing. For example, Wittmann, Bunzeck, Dolan, and Düzel (2007) reported that anticipation of novelty recruits the reward system and the hippocampus while promoting recognition memory. They noted that early findings showed that the dopaminergic midbrain, which comprises the substantianigra and ventral tegmental area (SN/VTA), plays a central role in the anticipation of rewards and that this area is also activated by anticipation of novel stimuli leading to enhanced encoding of events. The researchers concluded that dopaminergic processing of novelty might be important in driving exploration of new environments. Subsequently, Krebs, Schott, Schutze, and Düzel (2009) hypothesized that novel stimuli provide salient learning signals that motivate exploration in search for potential rewards. More specifically, in two fMRI experiments, they investigated whether novel stimuli enhanced reward anticipation signals in brain areas that are part of dopaminergic circuitry and whether this in turn would reduce responses to reward outcomes. Participants viewed images of complex natural outdoor and indoor scenes associated with monetary reward or neutral outcomes. Half of the images in each condition were novel and half were familiar. The predicted pattern was observed when both the task involved novel images and reward-predictive properties of the images were explicit. In a follow-up study, Krebs, Heipertz, Schuetze, and Düzel (2011) also found that novelty increased the mesolimbic functional connectivity of the SN/VTA during reward anticipation. These studies provide evidence supporting the argument that the experiences of interest, curiosity, exploration, and information seeking generated in novel situations also activate the reward circuitry and that activation of the reward circuitry has cognitive benefits. In addition, linking the reward mechanism with interest may explain Izard's argument that interest is omnipresent in a wide range of human behavior.

To highlight the psychological components of rewards and their underlying neural mechanisms, Berridge and colleagues (Berridge, 2012; Berridge & Kringelbach, 2011; Berridge, Robinson, & Aldridge, 2009) demonstrated that rewards have three dissociable psychological components: liking (hedonic impact), wanting (incentive salience), and learning (predictive associations and cognitions) and noted that each component has conscious and nonconscious subcomponents. It should be noted that incentive salience is not considered to be the same as perceptual salience that has been the focus of some other investigations reported above. Incentive salience refers to a strong motivational "wanting" (Berridge, personal communication). Based on a series of intricate brain studies, the researchers suggested that a single hedonic circuit may combine together neuroanatomical and neurochemical mechanisms to produce liking reactions and pleasure. In addition, wanting, also referred to as incentive salience that has been demonstrated to be distinct from liking, is a type of motivation that promotes approach toward rewards as well as their consumption and has been shown to be mediated by a specific neural system.

Berridge (2012) noted that although "wanting" typically coheres with "liking" for the same reward, the two can also be disassociated. He and his colleague (Berridge & Kringelbach, 2011) emphasized that hedonic systems are well developed in the brain, spanning subcortical and cortical levels, and the capacity for pleasure has fundamental, evolutionary importance. In addition, Berridge et al. (2009) also argued that the brain substrates for wanting are more widely distributed and more easily activated than substrates for liking and that a stimulus cue's predictive value that leads to learning is different from its ability to elicit incentive salience. Importantly, the researchers concluded that the three components of rewards have distinct psychological identities and distinguishable neural substrates.

These findings are suggestive for analysis of the relation between interest and enjoyment in educational contexts. In response to some situations, interest and enjoyment can occur as separate feelings. In response to other situations, through experience, interest and enjoyment become linked and occur together. In addition, the finding that repeated actions to ensure specific stimulation continues are not always pleasurable, that wanting without liking can occur, explains one of the paradoxes of interest research. Originally, it was assumed that all types of interest had a positive emotional component and asking people whether or not they liked an activity was a valid way to measure interest. However, in the early stages of interest development, negative emotions may be activated. For example, in an early paper, Iran-Nejad (1987) noted that a snake could be interesting without being liked. Hidi and Harackiewicz (2000) noted that although interest-based actions are often associated with positive emotional experiences, situational interest does not necessarily generate positive emotion. Students in medical school who find dissecting cadavers to be interesting may simultaneously experience negative affect. At later phases of interest development, the enjoyment associated with achievement of a solution to a problem may only be experienced after persisting through earlier frustrating moments when the solution seemed elusive (Renninger, 2000). Hidi and Harackiewicz (2000) concluded that only as the interest persists across time can we confidently assume that positive emotions, such as enjoyment and liking, are part of the interest experience.

Further neuroscientific exploration of the reward system will add to understanding of the relation between interest and enjoyment contributing to knowledge of how positive affect is involved both at the level of in-the-moment experiences, and when they function in combination across developing phases of interest.

IMMEDIATE EXPERIENCE AND DYNAMIC ORGANIZED UNITS IN ACHIEVEMENT CONTEXTS

To this point, we have considered the character of interest and enjoyment at the level of experiential states. However, more commonly in the context of learning and achievement both interest and enjoyment can also be conceptualized as generalized ways of responding.

Research on interest and its role in achievement mostly is located in the motivation literature (e.g., Sansone & Thoman, 2005), and to examine the relation between experiences of interest and enjoyment within the broader literature on interest, we consider how they are represented in the Four-Phase model of interest development (Hidi & Renninger, 2006). This model is informative because it encompasses interest as both immediate experience and as predisposition. Across the four phases of development, from triggered and maintained situational interest to emerging and well-developed individual interest, most often the affective component of interest is referred to simply as positive affect. The primary focus in the description of this model concerns how affect, knowledge, and value vary across the four phases and how the relation between the three components changes across the phases of interest development. Apart from its general description as positive affect, there is only passing reference to the specific character of affect at each of the four phases. For example, in relation to triggered situational interest, the feelings are described as having "a highly energized positive affective character" (Hidi & Renninger, 2006, p. 112). A slightly more general characterization used in reference to both triggered and maintained situational interest is "focused attention and positive feelings" (p. 114). As has already been pointed out, situational interest can be triggered in situations that also arouse negative affect (Bergin, 1999; Hidi & Harackiewicz, 2000; Iran-Nejad, 1987).

The character of affective processes across the phases of development of interest is more explicitly discussed in an associated paper where Hidi (2006) argues that interest is a unique motivational variable through its linking of affective and cognitive components. ✱

> It seems to me that if we only consider the moment in which the psychological state of interest is triggered, interest may be appropriately considered as an emotion. However, as interest develops and is maintained, both affect and cognition contribute to the experience.
>
> (Hidi, 2006, pp. 70–71)

The in-the-moment experience is one of feeling alert, concentrating, and being absorbed with the triggering object. But this is transient. If interest persists over time, more information is acquired through exploration of the object of interest, and interest becomes elaborated into a structure that is likely to include other feelings as well as extended cognitions and value components. Thus, what is triggered in the initial situation develops through maintained situational interest into a more enduring predisposition. Other interest researchers (Krapp, 2003; Schiefele, 1991) have defined individual interest in terms of feeling-related and value-related components. When examples are given of the feeling-related components they are specified as feelings of enjoyment and excitement, and sometimes as enjoyment and involvement (Krapp, 2003; Schiefele, 1991).

On the other hand, in the literature on emotions in achievement settings, most commonly enjoyment has been conceptualized as a general tendency to feel enjoyment in a specific subject domain (see Pekrun, Goetz, Titz, & Perry, 2002). Goetz, Cronjaeger, Frenzel, Lüdke, and Hall (2010) included enjoyment as one the achievement emotions in their profiling of patterns of emotions students reported across subject domains. Goetz, Hall, Frenzel, and Pekrun (2006) have also argued that enjoyment as an achievement emotion can be located within a hierarchical structure of enjoyment. At the base of the hierarchy are general experiences of enjoyment that are activity-specific. At the next level are enjoyment experiences that are situation-specific and include learning, instruction, exams, and extracurricular activities. At the third level are enjoyment experiences that are context-specific differentiating between school, family, peers, and alone. The apex of the hierarchy represents the most general level—enjoyment of life. This approach distinguishes enjoyment as it is generally experienced in terms of its breadth of focus, from the micro level of a particular educational activity to the all-encompassing category of life. In contrast, the major models of interest focus on defining the changing structure of an interest across the course of its development, including its knowledge and value components (Renninger, 2000). However, whether conceptualized as traits or as predispositions, both interest and enjoyment draw meaning from the affective states that students recognize and describe. Hence, further exploration of processes that are involved in the onset and development of states of interest and enjoyment can inform understanding of their roles in learning and achievement.

In recent writings, Izard (2007, 2009) has used the term emotion schema to designate the complex unit formed out of the dynamic combinations of affect and cognition acquired through experience. The dynamic organizations of affect, knowledge, and value that develop from triggered situational interest described in the Four-Phase model of interest development (Hidi & Renninger, 2006) can also be viewed in this way (Ainley, 2006). In addition, Krapp (2005) cites a tradition of using the concept of a "cognitive-affective synthesis" (see Dewey, 1913; Rathunde & Csikszentmihalyi, 1993) to support his proposal that combinations of cognitive-rational evaluations and emotional feedback contribute to the emergence of strong individual interests.

In infancy and early childhood, interest and enjoyment typically can be identified by facial expressions associated with particular activities and social situations (Izard, 1977; Izard & Malatesta, 1987). However, with children's developing experience, co-occurrence of each emotion with specific events can generate distinct organizations consisting of combinations of affects and combinations of affects and cognition. For example, the boy who has developed an interest in dinosaurs displays feelings of excitement, delight, and concentration when taken to a new museum dinosaur exhibit. In addition, the existing knowledge base of his interest guides his exploration of the exhibit to find species he has not previously encountered.

What we have described is consistent with Izard's (2007) propositions highlighting the difference between basic emotions and emotion schema. Basic emotions refers to "those emotions that have been characterized as having evolutionarily old neurobiological substrates, as well as an evolved feeling component and capacity for expressive and other behavioral actions of evolutionary origin" (Izard, 2007, p. 261). On the other hand, Izard's (2007) term emotion schema refers to "processes involved in the dynamic interplay of emotion, appraisals, and higher order cognition" (p. 261).

Accordingly, the relation between interest and enjoyment at different points in development, for different activities and domains, and for different individuals will vary reflecting whether it draws on the in-the-moment experiences or developed organizations, which have their own distinct structure. At the level of momentary experience with relatively novel stimuli, Silvia's (2005, 2008; Turner & Silvia, 2006) findings from experiments with undergraduates providing ratings of paintings, demonstrated that paintings rated as interesting were not necessarily rated as pleasant. The researchers concluded that the immediate experience of feeling interest in a painting was a response to two appraisals. The first was an appraisal of novelty or complexity and the second was an appraisal that the content could be comprehended. This same conclusion, that interest does not require pleasantness, was also demonstrated in an earlier experiment in which Reeve (1989) had undergraduate students respond to anagrams that were characterized as being "more irregular" and "less irregular." Using anagrams in these experiments assumes that the stimuli were unfamiliar to the participants. Feelings of interest in response to the anagrams were related to differences in collative variability (more versus less irregular), while feelings of enjoyment were related to whether students found the anagrams easy or difficult.

When referring to in-the-moment experience, interest initiates and directs attention and exploration (see, e.g., Sansone & Thoman, 2005). Enjoyment comes with successful performance of the activity and sustains persistence. In a wide variety of behaviors, including learning and achievement, these may or may not be complementary and reciprocal processes. On the other hand, when the situation is one that draws on dynamic organizations or predispositions, and on general or habitualized emotions, there is substantial evidence for a strong positive association between reports of interest and enjoyment. For example, Pinquart and Sorensen (2009) reported positive associations between interest and enjoyment when undergraduate participants respond to remembered experiences. Such recollections are likely to be influenced by participants' in-the-moment experience as well as the dynamic organization developed from their similar experiences in the past. Hence, observing that experiences of interest and enjoyment can be triggered by the same stimuli, and that experiences of interest and enjoyment can be triggered separately by different types of stimuli, may both have pertinence for different parts of the interest development trajectory.

What does this say about the development of interest for educational achievement? When the affective state of interest is triggered by a novel event, exploratory behavior occurs. When exploration exposes new information about the triggering object, this may generate pleasant feelings of satisfaction and a sense of achievement. These feelings become linked in the dynamic unit associated with the triggering object. Future appraisals of objects from the same domain will then trigger both interest and enjoyment; interest as the alertness and concentration for further exploration, and enjoyment as the anticipation of similar knowledge acquisition and successful performance. Therefore, when points on the trajectory from triggered situational interest to well-developed individual interest are considered, it is likely that the positive affect component will combine alert concentration, absorption, and feelings of pleasure and satisfaction.

Examples of this development can be found when children's involvements with specific learning domains are monitored. Nolen's (2007) research into children's early writing development captures this interdependence of enjoyment and interest in the pursuit of learning and achievement. In first grade, Aidan expressed enjoyment with his success and his teachers providing topics to write about ("Why [writing's] fun is because—hmm. I just like it and I think I'm good or something. I just like it," p. 234). In third grade, Aidan spoke about writing as an activity that involved enjoyment, seeking out and exploring new information, and writing about his new knowledge ("I like to put ideas down on paper and I like to make up stories and stuff. [At home] I made a nonfiction book and I got books from the library and wrote about tigers and elephants. I like to write nonfiction books," p. 234).

While interest and enjoyment serve different adaptive functions, when they are bound together in the one unit, such as an individual interest, their combined functioning makes for powerful achievement. For example, in our own work, we found that students with stronger individual interest in the task topic were more likely to respond with higher initial interest, reported positive on-task feelings, persisted longer, and achieved higher scores for task performance (e.g., Ainley, Hidi, & Berndorff, 2002; Ainley, Hillman, & Hidi, 2002). In another study (Tulis & Ainley, 2011), success and failure experiences were defined by students' performance on sets of individualized mathematics problems; successful sets were those where the students scored more than 60% correct answers and failure sets, less than 60% correct answers. Across the sample of fifth-grade students, higher ratings of positive feelings of interest, enjoyment, and pride were recorded following success experiences than following failure experiences. However, these responses also drew on past experiences of being successful in solving problems in mathematics classes and having experiences that support the development of individual interest in mathematics. One group of students showed strong positive feelings in response to both success and failure experiences. Other measures confirmed that these students valued expanding their skills and knowledge in mathematics. In particular, these students reported positive attitudes to learning from their mistakes. Similar patterns of response to success and failure were found in a second study and were associated with higher mastery goal scores.

In sum, feelings of interest and enjoyment need to be considered together to appreciate their contribution to engagement with educational activities and achievements. When the situation is relatively novel, appraisals of properties of the situation differentially trigger feelings of interest, feelings of enjoyment, and sometimes negative feelings of frustration or anxiety. However, with repeated engagements, positive feelings of interest and enjoyment become interconnected with the cognitions and values generated from experience in the domain. The outcomes of these processes are the dynamic organizations typical of the different phases of development from situational interest to well-developed individual interest, and under such conditions feelings of interest and enjoyment are generally complementary.

INTEREST AND ENJOYMENT AS ACHIEVEMENT EMOTIONS

Although interest was one of the emotions reported in the exploratory research with university students for the development of the AEQ (Academic Emotions Questionnaire, Pekrun et al., 2002), "emotions reported frequently included enjoyment, interest, hope, pride, anger, anxiety, frustration and boredom in academic settings" (Pekrun & Linnenbrink-Garcia, 2012, pp. 259–260), enjoyment, but not interest, is included as an emotion in the control-value theory of achievement emotions (Pekrun, Frenzel, Goetz, & Perry, 2007; Pekrun et al., 2002; Pekrun & Perry, 2014). Pekrun et al. (2007) define achievement emotions as those emotions tied directly to academic activities or academic outcomes that are judged by competence standards. Control and value appraisals are the "proximal determinants" of achievement emotions. Pekrun's three-way taxonomy (see, e.g., 2007, Table 1, p. 16) distinguishes emotions in terms of their focus, activity or outcome; their valence, positive or negative; and their activation features, activating or deactivating. According to this taxonomy, enjoyment and joy are activity focused, are positive, and are activating. A further dimension distinguishes prospective from retrospective emotions. When emotions are focused on an activity or outcome that is yet to occur, emotions are anticipatory—for example, anticipatory joy when students feel in control and expect success. When emotions occur as the result of reflection on performance, joy may also be experienced as a retrospective achievement emotion: pleasure following a successful outcome. In what follows, we examine a number of features of the control-value theory to understand how interest and enjoyment are related from the perspective of this theory and point to how this differs from the interest researchers' perspectives we have presented.

First, examination of the criterial attributes of enjoyment indicates considerable overlap with attributes that other models of emotion use to identify the affective state of interest (e.g., Izard, 1977, 2007; Tomkins, 1962). Pekrun, Elliot, and Maier (2006) define emotions as "multi-component, coordinated processes of psychological subsystems including affective, cognitive, motivational, expressive, and peripheral physiological processes" (p. 316). For task-related enjoyment, these component processes are specified as "to feel excited when taking the task, appraise the task as challenging, experience physiological arousal, and be motivated to work on the task" (Pekrun et al., 2002, p. 155). There are strong similarities here with the emotion "interest-excitement" in the writings of Tomkins (1962) and Izard (1977): to feel caught up, fascinated, curious about the task, appraise the task as new or puzzling, experience physiological arousal, and be motivated to explore and investigate the task. Importantly, one of the key similarities concerns feelings of excitement. The control-value theory, like Ekman (e.g., 1994, 2003), includes feelings of excitement as part of the experience of enjoyment and anticipatory joy rather than identifying interest as a distinct affective experience.

Second, the control-value theory of achievement emotions positions interest as a motivation dimension mediating the influence of achievement emotions on achievement outcomes: "positive activating emotions such as enjoyment of learning are assumed to increase interest and strengthen motivation" (Pekrun et al., 2007, p. 26). According to control-value theory, processes such as motivation, cognitive resources, learning strategies and self-regulation are influenced by achievement emotions, and the effects of achievement emotions on achievement are mediated by these processes (Pekrun et al., 2007, Figure 1, p. 17). From this theoretical perspective, interest is viewed as a motivational variable that follows the activation of achievement emotions, such as anticipatory joy, and because this theory excludes interest from the set of achievement emotions, does not consider that interest may initiate achievement activity.

Third, feedback loops (reciprocal causation) allow for the influence that mediating processes (including interest) may have on emotions. Just as goals can give rise to appraisals of controllability and value, personal interest in the activity domain can give rise to appraisals of controllability and value—promoting positive activity emotions, such as enjoyment of learning. From this perspective, interest consists of a developed orientation toward particular domains with regulatory motivational function, akin to individual interest as presented in the Four-Phase model of interest development (Hidi & Renninger, 2006).

Pekrun (2005) acknowledged that there are still some ambiguities and unresolved aspects to the relation between interest and enjoyment in his commentary included in a special issue of *Learning and Instruction* dealing with emotions in education. He suggests that one of the issues to be addressed in the future should be clarification of the boundaries of "concepts such as 'emotions', 'interest', 'well-being' and 'feelings' . . . For example, should interest be regarded as an emotion . . . or as being comprised of component structures including both emotional and non-emotional components?" (2005, p. 504). One step towards achieving such clarification would be to distinguish between phases in the trajectory of interest development, more specifically between the transient state and the developed predisposition, allowing that relations between component processes might vary (Hidi & Renninger, 2006).

MEASURING INTEREST AND ENJOYMENT

We now consider measurement issues to identify what assumptions are being made about the relation between interest and enjoyment. In a recent review, Wigfield and Cambria (2010) detail the content and structure of self-report scales designed to measure values, goal orientation, and interest as they represent motivation of achievement. Following their findings of substantial overlaps between measures and underlying lack of clarity in the main constructs, they recommended that researchers give more attention to identifying the distinctive character of each of these motivational constructs. Our analysis of the relation between interest and enjoyment in learning and achievement contexts suggests that they are often complimentary and reciprocal, and it is likely that the relative importance of feelings of interest and enjoyment in this relation may vary according to specific areas of achievement, such as reading or mathematics, and to students' developmental level. In addition, as Renninger and Hidi (2011) have pointed out in relation to the development of measures distinguishing the four phases of interest development, part of the difficulty of producing sound measures involves the changing relation between and balance of the affective, cognitive, and value components. It is our contention that distinguishing between experiences of interest and enjoyment will add to understanding of the dynamics of students' positive affect in achievement settings and thereby provide stronger guidance for educational practice.

We have argued that interest and enjoyment each can occur both as basic feeling states and as components of more complex organizations of experience that initiate and guide action. Overlap between these constructs, confirmed by widely reported positive correlations, is to be expected due to shared components. Feelings of both interest and enjoyment may simultaneously be components within the set of processes that constitute motivational constructs, such as task orientation, mastery goals, and intrinsic value as described in expectancy-value theory (Eccles et al., 1993; Wigfield & Eccles, 1992). For example, all of the constructs dealing with intrinsic motivation involve positive feeling states of interest and enjoyment. Hence, the relevance of items using terms such as "interest," "like," "enjoy," or "enjoyment" in the scale items (see Wigfield & Cambria, 2010, p. 14). Differences between the constructs adhere in relative balance of interest and enjoyment and in the constellation of additional components that define them. Hence, for the construct of intrinsic value, sometimes referred to in expectancy-value theory as interest value (Eccles et al., 1993), focus is on valuing the activity. Intrinsic value because the activity is valued for the attention and concentration (feelings of interest) that are afforded by the activity. Simultaneously, investment in the activity feels pleasing and enjoyable. On the other hand, a well-developed individual interest combines positive feelings of concentration, excitement, and enjoyment with substantial knowledge and value for the interest domain or activity (Hidi & Renninger, 2006).

When scales have been designed to measure different phases of interest, the inclusion of an enjoyment component in the items recognizes the potentially complementary and reciprocal relation between feelings of interest and enjoyment in the structure and content of both situational interest and individual interest. For example, Mitchell's (1993) measures of interest in mathematics included separate situational interest factors of catch (trigger) and hold (maintain), as well as personal (individual) interest. Situational interest included both positive and negative items. The positive items specified experiences of "fun," "look forward to," and "like," while the negative items specified "class is dull," "nothing interesting," and "other classes more interesting." Only one of Mitchell's five catch and hold factors, the hold factor of meaningfulness, does not explicitly include terms such as "fun," "enjoy," or "enjoyable." In addition, the personal or individual interest items specify generally feeling relaxed, enjoyment, and excitement in relation to mathematics.

More recently, Linnenbrink-Garcia et al. (2010) developed measures of different phases of situational interest (SI): triggered-SI, maintained-SI-feeling, and maintained-SI-value. Although intended to be applied across academic domains, the items used in refining the scales refer specifically to mathematics. Of significance for this discussion is the content of the triggered-SI and maintained-SI-feeling items. Triggered-SI items refer to the affective experiences that initiate interest, specifying experiences in class that are "exciting," "entertaining," and "that grab my attention." Maintained-SI-feeling items refer to experiences that build connections with the domain content and refer to "what we are learning in math this year." Specific feeling terms are "fascinating," "excited," "like," and "interesting." As was the case with Mitchell's (1993) measure, the individual interest items refer to feeling relaxed, enjoyment, and excitement. Hence, the affective experiences are forms of excitement and enjoyment. However, because these are self-report scales where the score is generated by summing across items, the balance of excitement and enjoyment across the scales is informative. Three of the triggered-SI items refer to excitement or attention, or both, and one to enjoyment (entertaining). The maintained-SI-feeling items include "fascinating," "interesting," "I am excited," and "I like." Interpreted from the standpoint of in-the-moment feelings, this measure gives more weight to feelings of interest-excitement than to enjoyment-joy.

Further insight into the relation between interest and enjoyment can be seen in Nolen's (2007) detailed analyses of how motivation contributes to development of early reading and writing skills. Framed within an analysis of the interdependence of development and the instructional context of their classrooms, Nolen coded salient motivation categories as they emerged when children were interviewed about their reading and writing experiences, and interest and enjoyment are two of the main codes.

The major code of interest for reading included the minor codes of situational, genre, topic, and activity. The major code of enjoyment included minor codes of reading is fun, reading time as a social good, and fun to use imagination. The main experience terms that appear in sample quotations coded as interest were "It's fun to . . . " "It's fun," "I like reading," and "I love reading." In addition, some of the statements under this code included reference to being involved or absorbed with the content of the stories: "It's fun to like go inside the story, and it's like you get involved."[1] The sample quotations for enjoyment had similar themes: "I like reading. It's fun." Key terms used by the children to describe their experience were "I like (writing) when I can write a story or something that is exciting," "I love to write about animals," and "I just like it, and it's very interesting" (p. 269).

The language these young students used when describing reading and writing as fun is reminiscent of our earlier reference to Izard's (1977) distinction between joy and fun, attributing the experience of fun to a combination of interest-excitement and enjoyment-joy. Fun is the feeling of enjoyment when caught up in, or involved in, an activity. Following this line of reasoning, the overlap between the enjoyment and interest codes in Nolen's (2007) analysis reflects a complementary and reciprocal relation between feelings of interest and enjoyment; concentration, attention, and pleasure all focused within the one activity—here, the activity of writing.

Specific features of the affective and cognitive experiences of students at different developmental levels in different achievement domains have also been reported. Qualitative analysis of interview responses has been used to identify shifts in what students of different ages mean when they respond to the items on a measure of interest in mathematics (Frenzel, Pekrun, Dicke, & Goetz, 2012). Students were interviewed to identify the personal concepts that informed their item responses. Answers from the fifth-grade students included significantly more references to a range of positive affective experiences than did ninth graders. On the other hand, ninth graders made significantly more references to aspects of competence in mathematics. However, this grade difference was in the context of references to positive affect being the most frequent category in the answers for both grade levels. The specific marker words for the affective category were "enjoy," "fun," "like," and "love," which as we have seen above have been used to measure both interest and enjoyment. In the domain of physical education, Chen and colleagues (Chen, Darst, & Pangrazi, 1999; Sun, Chen, Ennis, Martin, & Shen, 2008) identified a number of critical task dimensions that trigger situational interest: novelty, attention demand, optimal challenge, exploration opportunity, and instant enjoyment. For third- to fifth-grade students, all dimensions appeared equally likely to trigger situational interest. However, when participants were middle school students (Sun et al., 2008), it was found that instant enjoyment, a factor measured by items referring to activities that are "enjoyable," "exciting," "inspires me to participate," and "appealing" was the strongest of the factors triggering situational interest. In many achievement contexts, what is being measured by these scales are the developed units that combine both interest and enjoyment components.

Recently (Ely, Ainley, & Pearce, 2013) a new interactive measure has been used to explore the combinations of feelings and experiences across different phases of interest development. From a large pool of interest items, participants explore and select a small number (minimum three and maximum eight) that they are interested in or that have triggered their interest during the exploratory process. Selected interest items are then described using textboxes and ratings on cognitive and affective scales to generate a profile of the experience associated with each chosen interest, whether just triggered or of longer standing. Excited, happy, and proud were, in order, the affective dimensions receiving high ratings for these interest choices. Of significance for the current discussion is the close association between excited and happy in the profiles of feelings irrespective of whether the interests were newly triggered or relatively longer term.

This brief look at a range of measures points to the close association between feelings of interest (excitement) and enjoyment in the measurement of interest whether at the level of triggered situational interest or the more general organization of affect, cognition, and value that constitutes a well-developed interest.

INTEREST AND ENJOYMENT AS FACTORS CONTRIBUTING TO LEARNING AND ACHIEVEMENT

Through this examination of the relation between interest and enjoyment, we have identified parts of the network of positive emotion and motivation processes contributing to strong learning outcomes. While feelings of interest motivate exploration of what is novel and intriguing, feelings of enjoyment are the sense of satisfaction that accompanies achievement. Whether in the words researchers use when constructing items to measure interest and enjoyment or the words students use to describe their positive learning experiences, there is frequent use of the word fun. While at one level this appears to blur the lines between these concepts, at another level it has been suggested that when interest and enjoyment occur together the experience is fun (Izard, 1977). Interest engages the student with the new and puzzling task and contributes to the sustained effort required for achieving satisfying outcomes. At times this may involve persisting through negative feelings of frustration engendered by a very challenging task (Renninger, 2000). When students have experienced the co-occurrence of absorbed focus of interest and enjoyment in achievement, new learning situations trigger anticipatory interest and enjoyment processes, then students expect to find the new topic interesting and expect to enjoy participating in the learning activity:

> Our class is fun. Our teacher has fun activities to learn the stuff that we need to know.
>
> (Mitchell, 1993, p. 436)

> I like reading. It's fun.
>
> (Nolen, 2007, p. 267)

As we have indicated throughout this chapter, there is a strong literature that dates back to the early 1990s on the positive association between interest, both situational and individual, and learning outcomes (Hidi, 1990). Recently, this has been updated in two comprehensive reviews (see Hidi & Renninger, 2006; Renninger & Hidi, 2011). In a similar vein, there has been a growing literature on achievement emotions, and the role of enjoyment in learning has been well-documented in reviews of the research growing out of the control-value theory of achievement emotions (see Pekrun, Goetz, Frenzel, Barchfeld, & Perry, 2011; Pekrun et al., 2002; Pekrun & Linnenbrink-Garcia, 2012). Here, we will present some selected examples from this research literature to highlight developing research directions examining how interest and how enjoyment are related to learning behavior and to achievement outcomes. It should be noted that rarely are both interest and enjoyment the focus in any one research project, but as we have pointed out in our consideration of measurement issues, the items used in this research often reflect feelings of interest and enjoyment that are complementary.

One of the most important conditions for learning to occur is that students engage with activities that allow them to acquire the information and skills required for performance on whatever the task may be. This directs attention to the part played by both interest and enjoyment in students becoming involved in learning activities, and to research monitoring on-task experiences of interest and enjoyment. Earlier we referred to our own studies tracking how interest as experienced during the course of a reading activity is associated with learning behavior such as task persistence (see Ainley, Hidi, & Berndorff, 2002; Ainley, Hillman, & Hidi, 2002). Other researchers have adopted similar strategies and plotted the trajectory of situational interest across learning activities as diverse as ninth-grade inquiry-based lessons (Palmer, 2009) and college-age students undertaking full-day problem-based learning workshops (Rotgans & Schmidt, 2011).

Using a single item measure of situational interest that consisted of a five-point rating scale with the end points anchored as "very boring" to "very interested," Palmer (2009) found that ninth-grade students' interest was highest for the demonstration and experiment segments of lessons. During demonstration segments, students were giving attention to direct instruction concerning the topic of the lesson, while in experiment segments students were hands-on participants in experiments.

With polytechnic students, Rotgans and Schmidt (2011) identified a trajectory whereby situational interest was heightened immediately after the problem was presented and from there steadily decreased across the course of the day's program of activities until the end of the day when there was a significant increase. In this research, the measure of situational interest was based on Hidi and Renninger's (2006) definition, and items included "I think today's topic is interesting" as well as "I will enjoy working on today's topic." Rotgans and Schmidt also modeled the impact of successive recordings of situational interest for achievement on the learning workshop problem task. They found that the effect of situational interest on achievement was indirect and operated through the positive relation between interest and achievement-related classroom behaviors as recorded by classroom tutors.

Other researchers have monitored composite variables that include interest components as they occur in particular lessons. For example, Buff, Reusser, Rakoczy, and Pauli (2011) monitored eighth and ninth graders' positive affective experiences in mathematics lessons. The positive affective experiences variable consisted of excitement, stimulation, appeal, and interest items. Buff et al. (2011) found that positive affective experiences were predictive of on-task cognitive activity in the classroom but did not have a direct effect on achievement. Effects on achievement were mediated by levels of task-related cognitive activity. As these research findings demonstrate, tracking students' on-task experience and aligning it with learning behavior provides a window into the processes whereby affective experiences influence learning behavior and achievement. A common pattern of results has been that interest is related to learning strategies and cognitive activity, while learning strategies and cognitive activity predict achievement.

One of the most detailed examples of on-task monitoring of affective experience recently has been reported by D'Mello and Graesser (2012) working with undergraduate psychology students using Autotutor, an interactive and fully automated tutor. Students were required to undertake a computer literacy task while their facial movements and body posture as well as all of the screen activity for the entire session were recorded. This extensive monitoring of micro processes provided very fine-grained data from which the researchers were able to plot the real-time dynamics of students' affective states. The researchers' objective was to observe the transitions between affective states across the course of the computer literacy tutorial, and they defined a number of affects to be observed: boredom, confusion, engagement/flow, frustration, delight, and neutral. Engagement/flow was defined as "a state of interest that results from involvement in an activity" and delight defined as "a high degree of satisfaction" (D'Mello & Graesser, 2012, p. 150). The complex and very challenging task presented by Autotutor is comparable to the situations described earlier (Reeve, 1993; Turner & Silvia, 2006) that differentiated interest and enjoyment. In keeping with their assessment of the challenging character of the task, D'Mello and Graesser (2012) found a very low incidence of expressions of delight. On the other hand, transitions between states of engagement/flow (interest) and confusion, boredom and frustration were observed frequently. Further research of this kind will identify the dynamic patterns relating affective experience, learning strategies, and achievement with tasks that present students with different levels of challenge.

We will conclude with one further example to illustrate how interest and enjoyment come together in 15 year olds' responses to science problems. Across a variety of countries, Ainley and Ainley (2011) demonstrated how wanting to find out more about specific science topics is contingent on the mix of enjoyment and focused attention characteristic of interest. Using Programme for International Student Assessment (PISA) 2006 data, the relations between interest and enjoyment were modeled both as general predispositions toward science and as situational interest in the specific science problems used to assess science achievement. Both the general and the situational measures used only the term "interest" in the item stem: general—"How much interest do you have in learning about the following topics?" followed by a list of topic areas and situational—"How much interest do you have in the following information?" followed by a set of aspects of further issues on the specific topic. The six enjoyment of science items specified general experiences of have "fun," "like," "am happy," "enjoy," and "am interested" (OECD, 2009). Notwithstanding the overlap of interest and enjoyment in the item content of the enjoyment of science scale, the results demonstrated the close association between interest and enjoyment in students' perspectives on their engagement with science studies. The strongest predictive path suggested that enjoyment predicted to general interest in learning science, which in turn mediated the prediction from enjoyment to situational interest in the specific science topics. In addition, science knowledge and personal value of science made significant contributions to the prediction of situational interest. These findings confirm theories such as Fredrickson's (2001) broaden-and-build theory of positive emotions. Interest and enjoyment are often complementary and reciprocal components of the experience when an individual is pursuing an idea, exploring and seeking new information, or creating a novel solution to a problem.

CONCLUSION

Our examination of the literature on interest and enjoyment suggests that the nature and the strength of the relation between these two constructs may vary with different learning domains, with students' developmental level, and with students' past experience in the domain. The latest neuroscientific research is providing evidence of separate systems that underpin wanting and liking, and together with research into brain systems that process novelty, this growing body of knowledge about brain functions supporting learning and achievement will undoubtedly expand our rudimentary understanding of the relation between interest and enjoyment. Current evidence suggests that feelings of interest and enjoyment may be triggered separately at different points as students undertake new and complex learning tasks. Feelings of interest motivate exploration and information seeking, while feelings of enjoyment signal pleasure and satisfaction with what is achieved. However, the development of the relatively enduring individual interest that supports achievement is contingent on students experiencing both interest and enjoyment in their learning. Whether at the level of immediate experience or as predisposition, interest and enjoyment are a hallmark of capable, confident and enthusiastic learners.

NOTE

1. Notice that "like," as used a number of times by this student, is filling the pause while the student thinks of what she wants to say, or while she finds the right word.

REFERENCES

Adcock, R. A., Thangavel, A., Whitfield-Gabrieli, S., Knutson, B., & Gabrieli, J.D.E. (2006). Reward-motivated learning: Mesolimbic activation precedes memory formation. *Neuron, 50*, 507–517.

Ainley, M. (2006). Connecting with learning: Motivation, affect and cognition in interest processes. *Educational Psychology Review, 18*, 391–405.

Ainley, M., & Ainley, J. (2011). Student engagement with science in early adolescence: The contribution of enjoyment to students' continuing interest in learning about science. *Contemporary Educational Psychology, 36*, 4–12.

Ainley, M., Hidi, S., & Berndorff, D. (2002). Interest, learning and the psychological processes that mediate their relationship. *Journal of Educational Psychology, 94*, 545–561.

Ainley, M., Hillman, K., & Hidi, S. (2002). Gender and interest processes in response to literary texts: Situational and individual interest. *Learning and Instruction, 12*, 411–428.

Artelt, C., Baumert, J., McElvany, N. J., & Peschar, J. (2003). *Learners for life: Student approaches to learning: Results from PISA 2000*. Paris, France: OECD.

Bergin, D. A. (1999). Influences on classroom interest. *Educational Psychologist, 34*, 87–98.

Berridge, K. C. (2012). From prediction error to incentive salience: Mesolimbic computation of reward motivation. *European Journal of Neuroscience, 35*, 1124–1143.

Berridge, K. C., & Kringelbach, M. L. (2011). Building a neuroscience of pleasure and well-being. *Psychology of Well-Being: Theory, Research and Practice 1*, 1–26.

Berridge, K. C., Robinson, T. E., & Aldridge, J. W. (2009). Dissecting components of reward: 'Liking', 'wanting', and learning. *Current Opinion in Pharmacology, 9*, 65–73.

Buff, A., Reusser, K., Rakoczy, K., & Pauli, C. (2011). Activating positive affective experiences in the classroom: "Nice to have" or something more? *Learning and Instruction, 21*, 452–466.

Chen, A., Darst, P. W., & Pangrazi, R. P. (1999). What constitutes situational interest? Validating a construct in physical education. *Measurement in Physical Education and Exercise Science, 3*, 157–180.

Consedine, N. S., Magai, C., & King, A. R. (2004). Deconstructing positive affect in later life: A differential functionalist analysis of joy and interest. *International Journal of Aging and Human Development, 58*, 49–68.

Damasio, A. R. (2003). The person within. *Nature, 423*, 227.

Darwin, C. (1872). *The expression of the emotions in man and animals*. Cambridge, United Kingdom: Cambridge University Press.

Dewey, J. (1913). *Interest and effort in education*. Boston, MA: Houghton Mifflen.

D'Mello, S., & Graesser, A. (2012). Dynamics of affective states during complex learning. *Learning and Instruction, 22*, 145–157.

Eccles, J. S., Midgley, C., Wigfield, A., Buchanan, C. M., Reuman, D., & Flanagan, C. (1993). Development during adolescence: The impact of stage–environment fit on young adolescents' experiences in schools and in families. *American Psychologist, 48*, 90–101.

Egloff, B., Schmukle, S. C., Burns, L. R., Kohlmann, C.-W., & Hock, M. (2003). Facets of dynamic positive affect: Differentiating joy, interest, and activation in the positive and negative affect schedule (PANAS). *Journal of Personality and Social Psychology, 85*, 528–540.

Ekman, P. (1994). All emotions are basic. In P. Ekman & R. J. Davidson (Eds.), *The nature of emotion: Fundamental questions.* (pp. 15–19). New York, NY: Oxford University Press.

Ekman, P. (2003). *Emotions revealed*. New York, NY: Henry Holt and Company.

Ekman, P., & Freisan, W. V. (1971). Constants across cultures in the face and emotion. *Journal of Personality and Social Psychology, 17*, 124–129.

Ekman, P., Friesen, W. V., & Ellsworth, P. C. (1972). *Emotions in the human face: Guidelines for research and a review of the findings*. New York, NY: Pergamon Press.

Ekman, P., Friesen, W. V., & Hager, J. C. (2002). *Facial Action Coding System*. London, United Kingdom: Weidenfeld & Nicholson.

Ellsworth, P. (2003). Confusion, concentration, and other emotions of interest: Commentary on Rozin and Cohen (2003). *Emotion, 3*, 81–85.

Ely, R., Ainley, M., & Pearce, J. (2013). More than enjoyment: Identifying the positive affect component of interest that supports student engagement and achievement. *Middle Grades Research Journal, 8*, 13–32.

Fredrickson, B. L. (2001). The role of positive emotions in positive psychology: The broaden-and-build theory of positive emotions. *American Psychologist, 56*, 218–226.

Frenzel, A., Pekrun, R., Dicke, A., & Goetz, T. (2012). Beyond quantitative decline: Conceptual shifts in adolescents' development of interest in mathematics. *Developmental Psychology, 48*, 1069–1082.

Goetz, T., Cronjaeger, H., Frenzel, A., Lüdtke, O., & Hall, N. (2010). Academic self-concept and emotion relations: Domain specificity and age effects. *Contemporary Educational Psychology, 35*, 44–58.

Goetz, T., Hall, N., Frenzel, A., & Pekrun, R. (2006). A hierarchical conceptualization of enjoyment in students. *Learning and Instruction, 16*, 323–338.

Hidi, S. (1990). Interest and its contribution as a mental resource for learning. *Review of Educational Research, 60*, 549–571.

Hidi, S. (2006). Interest: A unique motivational variable. *Educational Research Review, 1*, 69–82.

Hidi, S. (2011, May). *Interest development: Psychological and neuroscientific considerations.* Paper presented at the Keynote address 2011 bMRI Symposium on Motivation Korea University, Seoul, Korea.

Hidi, S. (2012, June). *Interest and rewards.* Paper presented at the session Developing Interest: Research Results and Questions (K.A. Renninger, Chair). Meetings of the Jean Piaget Society, Toronto, Canada.

Hidi, S. (submitted). Revisiting the role of rewards in motivation and learning: Implications of neuroscientific research. Manuscript submitted for publication.

Hidi, S., & Harackiewicz, J. M. (2000). Motivating the academically unmotivated: A critical issue for the 21st. century. *Review of Educational Research, 70*, 151–179.

Hidi, S., & Renninger, K. A. (2006). The four-phase model of interest development. *Educational Psychologist, 41*, 111–127.

Iran-Nejad, A. (1987). Cognitive and affective causes of interest and liking. *Journal of Educational Psychology, 79*, 120–130.

Izard, C. E. (1977). *Human emotions.* New York, NY: Plenum Press.

Izard, C. E. (1983/1995). *The maximally discriminative facial movement coding system (MAX-revised edition).* Newark, DE: Instructional Resources Center.

Izard, C. E. (2007). Basic emotions, natural kinds, emotion schemas, and a new paradigm. *Perspectives on Psychological Science, 2*, 260–280.

Izard, C. E. (2009). Emotion theory and research: Highlights, unanswered questions, and emerging issues. *Annual Review of Psychology, 60*, 1–25.

Izard, C. E., & Malatesta, C. E. (1987). Perspectives on emotional development I: Differential emotions theory of early emotional development. In M. Lewis & J. M. Haviland-Jones (Eds.), *Handbook of infant development* (2nd ed., pp. 494–510). New York, NY: John Wiley & Sons.

Kang, M. J., Hsu, M., Krajbich, I. M., Loewenstein, G., McClure, S. M., Wang, J. T., & Camerer, C. F. (2009). The wick in the candle of learning: Epistemic curiosity activates reward circuitry and enhances memory. *Psychological Science, 20*, 963–973.

Krapp, A. (2003). Interest and human development: An educational-psychological perspective. *Development and Motivation, BJEP Monograph Series, Series II, 2*, 57–84.

Krapp, A. (2005). Basic needs and the development of interest and intrinsic motivational orientations. *Learning and Instruction, 15*, 381–395.

Krebs, R. M., Heipertz, D., Schuetze, H., & Düzel, E. (2011). Novelty increases the mesolimbic functioning connectivity of the substantia nigra/ventral tegmental area (SN/VTA) during reward anticipation. *Neuroimage, 58*, 647–655.

Krebs, R. M., Schott, B. H., Schütz, H., & Düzeld, E. (2009). The novelty exploration bonus and its attentional modulation. *Neuropsychologia, 47*, 2272–2281.

Kuenzi, J., Matthews, C., & Mangan, B. (2006). *Science, technology, engineering, and mathematics (STEM) education issues and legislative options.* Washington, DC: Congressional Research service, the Library of Congress.

Linnenbrink-Garcia, L., Durik, A. M., Conley, A. M., Barron, K. E., Tauer, J. M., Karabenick, S. A., & Harackiewicz, J. M. (2010). Measuring situational interest in academic domains. *Educational and Psychological Measurement, 70*, 647–671.

Loewenstein, G. (1994). The psychology of curiosity: A review and reinterpretation. *Psychological Bulletin, 116*, 75–98.

Mitchell, M. (1993). Situational interest: Its multifaceted structure in the secondary school mathematics classroom. *Journal of Educational Psychology, 85*, 424–436.

Mortillaro, M., Mehu, M., & Scherer, K. R. (2011). Subtly different positive emotions can be distinguished by their facial expressions. *Social Psychological and Personality Science, 2*, 262–271.

Nolen, S. B. (2007). Young children's motivation to read and write: Development in social contexts. *Cognition and Instruction 25*, 219–270.

OECD. (2009). *PISA 2006 Technical report*. Paris, France: OECD.

Palmer, D. H. (2009). Student interest generated during an inquiry skills lesson. *Journal of Research in Science Teaching, 46*, 147–165.

Panksepp, J. (1998). *Affective neuroscience: The foundations of human and animal emotion*. New York, NY: Oxford University Press.

Pekrun, R. (2005). Progress and open problems in educational emotion research. *Learning and Instruction, 15*, 497–506.

Pekrun, R., Elliot, A. J., & Maier, M. A. (2006). Achievement goals and discrete achievement emotions: A theoretical model and prospective test. *Journal of Educational Psychology, 98*, 583–597.

Pekrun, R., Frenzel, A., Goetz, T., & Perry, R. P. (2007). The control-value theory of achievement emotions: An integrative approach to emotions in education. In P. Schutz & R. Pekrun (Eds.), *Emotion in education* (pp. 13–36). Amsterdam, Netherlands: Elsevier.

Pekrun, R., Goetz, T., Frenzel, A., Barchfeld, P., & Perry, R. P. (2011). Measuring emotions in students' learning and performance: The Achievement Emotions Questionnaire (AEQ). *Contemporary Educational Psychology, 36*, 36–48.

Pekrun, R., Goetz, T., Titz, W., & Perry, R. P. (2002). Academic emotions in students' self-regulated learning and achievement: A program of qualitative and quantitative research. *Educational Psychologist, 37*, 91–105.

Pekrun, R., & Linnenbrink-Garcia, L. (2012). Academic emotions and student engagement. In S. L. Christenson, A. L. Reschly, & C. Wylie (Eds.), *Handbook of research on student engagement* (pp. 259–282). New York, NY: Springer.

Pekrun, R., & Perry, R. P. (2014). Control-value theory of achievement emotions. In R. Pekrun & L. Linnenbrink-Garcia (Eds.), *International handbook of emotions in education* (pp. 120–141). New York, NY: Taylor & Francis.

Pinquart, M., & Sorensen, S. (2009). Influences of socioeconomic status, social network, and competence on subjective well-being in later life: A meta-analysis. *Psychology and Aging, 15*, 187–224.

Quintanilha, A. (2010, September). *Promoting curiosity and understanding risk*. Paper presented at the International Conference on Motivation, Porto, Portugal.

Rathunde, K., & Csikszentmihalyi, M. (1993). Undivided interest and the growth of talent: A longitudinal study of adolescents. *Journal of Youth and Adolescence, 22*, 385–405.

Reeve, J. (1989). The interest-enjoyment distinction in intrinsic motivation. *Motivation and Emotion, 13*, 83–103.

Reeve, J. (1993). The face of interest. *Motivation and Emotion, 17*, 353–375.

Reeve, J., & Nix, G. (1997). Expressing intrinsic motivation through acts of exploration and facial displays of interest. *Motivation and Emotion, 21*, 237–250.

Renninger, K. A. (2000). Individual interest and its implications for understanding intrinsic motivation. In C. Sansone & J. M. Harackiewicz (Eds.), *Intrinsic and extrinsic motivation: The search for optimal motivation and performance* (pp. 373–404). San Diego, CA: Academic Press.

Renninger, K. A., & Hidi, S. (2011). Revisiting the conceptualization, measurement, and generation of interest. *Educational Psychologist, 46*, 168–184.

Rotgans, J. I., & Schmidt, H. G. (2011). Situational interest and academic achievement in the active-learning classroom. *Learning and Instruction 21*, 58–67.

Rozin, R., & Cohen, A. B. (2003). High frequency of facial expressions corresponding to confusion, concentration, and worry in an analysis of naturally occurring facial expressions of Americans. *Emotion, 3*, 68–75.

Sansone, C., & Thoman, D. B. (2005). Interest as the missing motivator in self-regulation. *European Psychologist, 10*, 175–186.

Scherer, K. R. (2000). Emotions as episodes of subsystem sychronization driven by nonlinear appraisal processes. In M. D. Lewis & I. Granic (Eds.), *Emotion, development, and self-organization: Dynamic approaches to emotional development* (pp. 70–99). Cambridge, United Kingdom: Cambridge University Press.

Scherer, K. R. (2009). The dynamic architecture of emotion: Evidence for the component process model. *Cognition and Emotion, 23*, 1307–1351.

Schiefele, U. (1991). Interest, learning and motivation. *Educational Psychologist, 26*, 299–323.

Silvia, P. J. (2005). What is interesting? Exploring the appraisal structure of interest. *Emotion, 5*, 89–102.

Silvia, P. J. (2008). Interest—The curious emotion. *Current Directions in Psychological Science, 17*, 57–60.

Sun, H., Chen, A., Ennis, C. D., Martin, R., & Shen, B. (2008). An examination of the multidemensionality of situational interest in elementary school physical education. *Research Quarterly for Exercise and Sport, 79*, 62–70.

Tomkins, S. S. (1962). *Affect, imagery and consciousness* (Vol. 1: The positive affects). New York, NY: Springer.

Tulis, M., & Ainley, M. (2011). Interest, enjoyment and pride after failure experiences? Influences on students' state-emotions after success and failure during learning in mathematics. *Educational Psychology, 31*, 779–807.

Turner, S.A.J., & Silvia, P. J. (2006). Must interesting things be pleasant? A test of competing appraisal structures. *Emotion, 6*, 670–674.

Watson, D., Clark, L. A., & Tellegen, A. (1988). Development and validation of brief measures of positive and negative affect: The PANAS scales. *Journal of Personality and Social Psychology, 54*, 1063–1070.

Wigfield, A., & Cambria, J. (2010). Students' achievement values, goal orientations, and interest: Definitions, development, and relations to achievement outcomes. *Developmental Review, 30*, 1–35.

Wigfield, A., & Eccles, J. S. (1992). The development of achievement task values: A theoretical analysis. *Developmental Review, 12*, 265–310.

Wittmann, B.C., Bunzeck, N., Dolan, R. J., & Düzel, E. (2007). Anticipation of novelty recruits reward system and hippocampus while promoting recollection. *Neuroimage, 38*, 194–202.

12

CURIOSITY

Amanda Markey and George Loewenstein,
Carnegie Mellon University

It is a miracle that curiosity survives formal education.

—*Albert Einstein*

Curiosity, which has been defined as a desire for information in the absence of extrinsic reward, has long been recognized as a crucial motivation driving educational attainment. Cicero (1914, p. 48), for example, referred to curiosity as an "innate love of learning and of knowledge . . . without the lure of any profit." Aristotle (1947, p. 243) wrote that, "All men by nature desire to know," and in a different treatise noted that men study science "not for any utilitarian end" (Posnock, 1991, p. 40). Yet, many of the most fundamental questions regarding this key motivation remain largely or totally unanswered. Why are people so often strongly attracted to information that, by the definition of curiosity, bears no extrinsic benefit? What are curiosity's situational determinants? Are there ways to encourage and cultivate curiosity in the classroom? These questions have been the focus of limited empirical research over the past half century, much of which we review.

We organize our review of the literature into four sections. In the first section, we discuss the definition of curiosity, outlining what is, and what is not, included in the construct. The second section describes the information-gap theory proposed by the second author (Golman & Loewenstein, 2012; Loewenstein, 1994). This theory posits that curiosity develops when people become aware of a gap between what they know and what they don't know. We discuss the theoretical predictions generated by the information gap theory, and we discuss an expansion of the theory that outlines three categories of determinants of curiosity: importance, salience, and surprise. We then review empirical research on situational determinants of curiosity, focusing specifically on studies conducted in educational settings. We begin by discussing environments that can lead to the *suppression* of curiosity but then discuss, more constructively, how instructors can actively foster curiosity through capitalizing on curiosity's three factors. The final section concludes the chapter with a discussion of potentially fruitful directions for future research.

CURIOSITY'S DEFINITION AND DIMENSIONALITY

What do we mean by "curiosity?" "Absent a clear definition of curiosity," Jirout and Klahr (2012, p. 126) note, in a paper on children's scientific curiosity, "our understanding of developmental mechanisms that underlie it cannot be advanced, and the effectiveness of instructional processes aimed at stimulating and increasing it . . . cannot be assessed." The fact that the field has, in fact, not coalesced around a single clear definition of the construct can be seen in the diversity of methods used to measure curiosity—for example, by the number of questions a person asks, the amount of interaction with novel objects in a waiting room, a preference for complex visual stimuli as determined by eye gaze, a desire to see images repeatedly, and explicit ratings of the desire to obtain information. Yet, there has been some convergence over time in researchers' interpretation of the construct. Such convergence has often resulted from researchers' recognition that the construct was being used in different ways, and consequent narrowing of the definition by discarding specific interpretations as not being commensurate with curiosity.

One important refinement to the construct was proposed by D. E. Berlyne (1950, 1954a, 1954b), who was the first researcher to devote sustained attention to the topic. As his research on, and thinking about, curiosity progressed from the 1950s through the 1970s, Berlyne began to distinguish between two quite different phenomena: (1) "specific exploration," when "an animal is disturbed by a lack of information" (1966, p. 26) and (2) "diversive exploration," when "an animal seeks out stimulation, regardless of source or content, that offers something like an optimum amount of novelty, surprisingness, complexity, change or variety" (p. 26). Ultimately, Berlyne came to view only the first of these—specific exploration—as commensurate with curiosity. Drawing an explicit comparison to specific exploration, Berlyne (1966, p. 27) wrote that diversive exploration "is not preceded by receipt of partial information about the stimulus patterns . . . and thus seems to be *motivated by factors quite different from curiosity* [emphasis added]" (see, also, Berlyne, 1978, p. 144). As will be evident, Berlyne's implicit suggestion that specific exploration is preceded by a receipt of partial information hints at what is the key ingredient of the information gap account of curiosity that forms the basis of the current paper.

Berlyne's definition of curiosity is as useful for what it excludes as for what it includes. Specifically, it excludes varieties of information search in which an animal (including a human) is engaged in an unfocused attempt to acquire information. Dashiell (1925), for example, observed that, even when hungry, rats would pay little to no attention to food and instead explore a new environment, a phenomenon that he attributed to an "instinct of curiosity" triggered by "novelty in the environment" (p. 208). Nissen (1930) likewise observed that rats would go so far as to cross an electrified grid to explore a maze, and Pavlov (1927) observed that dogs reflexively respond to changes in the world around them by orienting their eyes, head, and trunk toward the source of stimulation. Beyond the fact that one cannot know whether these animals' desire for information really was intrinsic, it is perfectly possible that they were seeking information so as to better be able to navigate their environment, rule out potential threats, or search for sources of food—Berlyne's distinction between diversive and specific exploration, and his association of curiosity with only the latter, suggests that such exploratory, or orienting, phenomena should not be treated as manifestations of curiosity. That is not to say that information seeking by nonhuman animals should never be interpreted as specific exploration and curiosity per se; anyone who has observed the propensity of cats to explore anything they have restricted access to—that is, from which they have experienced "receipt of partial information"—will be unlikely to blithely dismiss the idea that nonhuman animals engage in specific exploration.

Berlyne and other behaviorists maintained a focus on state curiosity, which refers to the temporary experience of curiosity in a given situation. This is contrasted with trait curiosity, which corresponds to an individual's personality disposition toward experiencing curiosity. Many trait curiosity scales have been developed in the past 50 years (e.g., Perceptual Curiosity Scale [Collins, Litman, & Spielberger, 2004]; Curiosity and Exploration Inventory [Kashdan, Rose, & Fincham, 2004]; Epistemic Curiosity Scale [Litman & Spielberger, 2003]; Melbourne Curiosity Inventory [Naylor, 1981]; Curiosity/Interest in the World Scale [Peterson & Seligman, 2004]). As one can infer from the scale titles, these trait curiosity scales measure a diversity of constructs, and this diversity is also manifest in the questions composing the scales, which range from, "I really enjoy learning about other countries and cultures" to "When I am participating in an activity, I tend to get so involved that I lose track of time" to "When I see a new fabric, I like to touch and feel it."

While trait curiosity scales are useful for examining the correlates—for example, life-outcomes and other measured traits—of the diversity of constructs they measure, they are limited in their ability to inform educational practices. Individuals with high trait curiosity probably do make superior students and scientists, on average, but this ability to measure differences would, at best, aid in sorting or tracking students on the basis of their curiosity. These scales have limited capability to inform practices to encourage and capitalize on curiosity. In contrast, an improved understanding of state curiosity has the potential to suggest practical methods to stimulate curiosity, and, furthermore, if trait differences reflect the cumulative effect of situational factors, then these interventions, if effective in stimulating state curiosity, might ultimately serve to enhance trait curiosity. Therefore, in this chapter, we focus on the state curiosity, its situational determinants, and its application to educational settings and specific instructional techniques.

Drawing both on the historic interpretation of curiosity and Berlyne's refinement in what follows, we adopt the definition of curiosity as a desire for specific information in the absence of extrinsic reward.[1] Few researchers would exclude such a desire for specific information as a variant of curiosity, but some would deem the definition to be excessively narrow. We agree with Berlyne, however, that a more parsimonious definition of the curiosity that excludes, for example, unfocused exploration or a preference for novelty provides a superior foundation for development of an empirically grounded understanding of the phenomenon. We also believe it provides for a more effective application to instruction in education.

AN INFORMATION-GAP ACCOUNT OF CURIOSITY

In the mid-twentieth century, two different, although not inherently contradictory, theoretical accounts of curiosity were proposed. One, of which Berlyne was the most prominent advocate, viewed curiosity as a drive motivating information acquisition, much as hunger motivates seeking of food and thirst motivates seeking of drink. Like hunger, thirst, and other drives, Berlyne noted, curiosity produces a negative feeling when not satisfied but is pleasurable when satisfied by the acquisition of desired information. An important difference between curiosity and many other drives, such as hunger and thirst, however, is that curiosity does not tend to intensify over time when it is not satisfied. In this respect, curiosity is more like the sex drive, which (although it does tend to intensify if not satisfied for some interval) is largely stimulus bound.

Skirting these features of curiosity that the drive theory was intended to highlight, "incongruity" theories focused on the question of what stimuli arouse curiosity. Just as sexual desire is activated by any kind of sensory contact with any sexually charged object (typically a person), the incongruity theories posited that curiosity was triggered by incongruity in the environment, and specifically by a violation of expectations (e.g., Hebb, 1949; Hunt, 1963).

The information gap account of curiosity proposed by Loewenstein (1994) was an attempt to integrate insights from drive theory, incongruity theory and decision theory. Curiosity, according to this account, arises when people become aware of the gap between what they know and what they don't know. Such a gap could be triggered by violated expectations, as posited by incongruity theories, but it could also be triggered by many other varieties of stimuli, such as hearing snippets of a conversation at an adjoining table in a restaurant, or, somewhat trivially, being asked a question to which one does not know the answer. Like drive theories, the information gap account assumes that unsatisfied curiosity is aversive and that satisfying curiosity is pleasurable.

To make sense of these, and a variety of other features of curiosity, the information gap account draws on the concept of an informational reference point—a salient state of knowledge. Curiosity, according to this account, arises when an individual's attention is drawn to a potential state of knowledge different from, and specifically greater than, their current state. The information gap is then the difference between the individual's current state of knowledge and this salient alternative state of knowledge. Curiosity, which according to this account results from the desire to close an information gap, can be distinguished from interest. In Chapter 11, interest has been defined as "the feeling of being engaged, caught-up, fascinated, curious . . . a feeling of wanting to investigate, become involved" (Izard, 1977, p. 216). As is quite explicit, this definition encompasses curiosity within the larger construct of interest. In contrast, we view curiosity and interest as distinct phenomena. We define interest as a psychological state that involves a desire to become engaged in an activity or know more, in general, about a subject. If an individual is interested in pottery, for example, that person may want to sit down and throw pots, or that person may want to know more about the technique, the materials, and the history. Curiosity, in contrast, according to our definition, only arises when a specific knowledge gap occurs, such as, "What is the difference between high and low fire pottery?" Thus, curiosity and interest differ by their objects of desire (specific knowledge vs. general knowledge/activity engagement). Furthermore, while interest is often subdivided based on its causal source—situational interest is generated by particular conditions in the environment, and individual interest is generated by relatively enduring predispositions—curiosity is agnostic about its origin. A final distinction is phenomenology, which refers to what each state feels like. Interest is often, though not always, associated with positive affect (Hidi, 2000, p. 312). In contrast, while the satisfaction of curiosity provides pleasure, curiosity itself is an aversive state associated with deprivation (e.g., Day, 1982; Litman & Jimerson, 2004; Loewenstein, 1994; Todt & Schreiber, 1998).[2]

What, then, determines the intensity of curiosity? In a recent elaboration of the theory (as well as an attempt to integrate curiosity with a wide range of other informational phenomena), Golman and Loewenstein (2012) specify that curiosity depends on three factors: (1) importance, (2) salience, and (3) surprise.

Importance indicates how much the information matters to the individual—that is, how differently the individual will feel if the information gap is filled in different ways. Because most people care more about themselves than about other people, missing information about anything relating to the self—for example,, whether one is a good person, good looking, intelligent or even an above-average driver—will tend to be important, and hence to evoke curiosity. In general, people will tend to be especially curious about things that matter to them. An investor will be curious about the state of the market, parents about the welfare of their children, and a botanist about the name or characteristics of a plant. In the common situation in which individuals face myriad information gaps, the importance of a missing piece of information, and hence the individuals' curiosity to obtain it, will naturally be increasing in the number of gaps the information can address.

One implication of the latter prediction is that insight problems should generally evoke greater curiosity than incremental problems because, with insight problems, there is a possibility that a single piece of information can throw light on the entire problem. With incremental problems, in contrast, any single piece of information is unlikely to yield a sudden solution. To test this prediction, participants in a study conducted early in the days of the personal computer were asked to click on 5 of 45 squares on a screen, ostensibly to familiarize themselves with the operation of the mouse (Loewenstein, Adler, Behrens, & Gillis, 1992). For half of the participants, the 45 squares, when exposed, formed an image of a single animal, but several squares had to be exposed before the identity of the animal could be determined. For the other participants, each square, when clicked on, revealed a different animal. Curiosity was measured by how many excess squares participants voluntarily turned over, beyond the required 5. As predicted, based on the information-gap perspective, participants voluntarily turned over more squares in the single animal condition than in the multiple animal condition.

Salience refers to the degree to which the individual's environment highlights a particular information gap. The conversation happening at the next table is likely to evoke curiosity because the proximity of the table, the unusual appearance of the diners, and the tantalizing snippets of conversation overheard, all make that conversation especially salient. The conversations happening at more distant tables, or even at the most interesting tables around the world, in contrast, fail to evoke much curiosity at all. Salience will tend to be high when a question is asked explicitly, and it will be even higher if there is another identifiable and proximate individual who knows the answer. By the same token, curiosity will decline almost instantly if attention is drawn away from an information gap.

Finally, surprise captures the central insight of incongruity theories—that the receipt of information can trigger (or in some cases squelch) curiosity. A person who views another person as intelligent, for example, might be surprised when the latter person gives an obviously wrong answer to a simple question, which would open an information gap in the form of a desire for an explanation for the discrepancy. Consistent with such a role for surprise, Berlyne (1954b, 1957) found that questions subjects indicated to be "surprising" coincided closely with those they reported to be evoking of curiosity.

An important implication of this framework for education is that curiosity will tend to be positively related to one's knowledge in a particular domain; thus, the accumulation of knowledge tends to beget a desire for further knowledge. First, when one has more knowledge of a topic one tends to have more information gaps, so that new knowledge is more likely to address a larger number of gaps. This is exemplified by the classic mystery novel; revealing the killer's identity promises to immediately unlock the key to all of the seemingly inconsistent and inexplicable clues, allowing the reader to make sense of multiple puzzles at once. Second, the more one knows, the more salient a gap is likely to become. When a botanist walks along a trail in a densely packed forest, an undiscovered plant would capture her attention and likely elicit questions of its species, its unique markings, its growth conditions, and so forth. A casual hiker, on the other hand, will likely not even notice the unusual plant, and even if informed of its presence, will be unlikely to request further details. Third, the more one knows, the more likely one is to be surprised when one acquires new knowledge. If you see a speaker you don't know at a conference who is obviously suffering from stage-fright, you are unlikely to be surprised; it is a common occurrence. If you do know the speaker, however, and know that she is a superb teacher, is comfortable in social situations, or generally has a blasé attitude, the stage-fright is much more surprising, and, as a result, curiosity evoking.

To test the relationship between knowledge and curiosity, Loewenstein et al. (1992) randomly assigned experimental participants to view photographs of parts of an individual person (hands, feet, and torso). Participants viewed between one to three photographs, and afterwards, they were given a choice to see a photograph of the whole person or receive a bonus payment of $0.50. Participants who had uncovered more body parts were more likely to view the picture and forsake the money, even though they had objectively less to learn from doing so.

A final important, if somewhat obvious, implication of the information gap account is that curiosity should be directly related to the perceived ability of a piece of information to close the gap. Large information gaps will generally not tend to evoke much curiosity because the individual will perceive closing the gap as an unattainable goal. Smaller gaps will more likely be perceived as closeable and subsequently arouse more curiosity, a phenomenon that resembles the notion of an approach gradient, whereby motivation tends to increase as an organism nears a goal (e.g., Hull, 1932; for a reference point-as-goals account, see Heath, Larrick, & Wu, 1999).

Loewenstein et al. (1992) found evidence for the prediction that curiosity will tend to increase as one perceives oneself as close to filling an information gap. Participants in an experiment were given words and definitions and asked to match them. For words they were unable to identify, they rated their "feeling of knowing" and whether the answer was on the tip of their tongue. Self-reported curiosity was highly correlated to these measures. Litman, Hutchins, and Russon (2005) also found a positive correlation between self-reported curiosity to answer a question and the degree to which the answer was perceived to be at the tip-of-the-tongue. Other research that we discuss below shows that children's curiosity is enhanced in environments that boost their self-confidence, self-esteem, and agency. These findings could be explained by the idea that all of these states are likely to increase the child's confidence that they will be capable of answering questions—of closing information gaps—hence, leading to intensified motivation to make the attempt (e.g., Kashdan, 2009).

In sum, Loewenstein's original information gap theory describes curiosity as the desire to reach an informational reference point, which is established when it becomes apparent that what one wants to know exceeds what one currently knows. This theoretical reference point account, with the additional insight that curiosity's intensity is a product of importance, salience, and surprise, generates specific predictions about what will, and what will not, evoke curiosity as well as who will, and who will not, be prone to curiosity. In the remaining sections of this chapter, we use the information gap theory to discuss how to foster curiosity and exploit its motivational power in educational settings.

CURIOSITY IN EDUCATION

When presented with a prepopulated list of character traits, over 75% of teachers chose curiosity as one of the top five characteristics they strive to encourage in their students (Hackmann & Engel, 2002, as cited in Engel, 2011).[3] Additionally, various science curricula explicitly aim to encourage curiosity (e.g., The University of Chicago Laboratory School Science Curriculum, n.d.; National Science Teachers Position Statement, Association Curriculum Recommendation, 2003), and the National Education Goals Panel proposes that "openness and curiosity about new tasks and challenges" affect children's learning and is an indicator of school readiness (Kagan, Moore, & Bredekamp, 1995, p. 23). There is evidence that this encouragement of curiosity is warranted, given its facilitation of memory, attention, and information-seeking behavior. In one fMRI study, researchers demonstrated that level of curiosity is correlated with activation in regions that have been associated with anticipated rewards and memory, and when answers were provided to curiosity-inducing questions, there was a stronger neural activation overall (Kang et al., 2009). Furthermore, they found that curiosity was correlated with pupil dilation, a common measure of attention. Numerous behavioral studies have shown that answers to questions that elicit curiosity are much more likely to be remembered minutes, days, and weeks later (Berlyne, 1954b,1966; Kang et al., 2009) and that individuals who experience curiosity are more likely to exert effort to learn an answer (Litman et al., 2005; Loewenstein et al., 1992). In sum, there is widespread agreement that curiosity is a valuable form of motivation promoting learning in and outside of the classroom and that curiosity should be actively fostered in and outside the classroom.

The question of how curiosity can be fostered, however, may inadvertently distract us from an important insight. Beyond the techniques they can use to stimulate curiosity (a point we turn to momentarily), an even more fundamental goal for educators should be to not get in the way of a powerful and innate drive that is evident both in children and in other animals. As Parvanno (1990; quoted in Jirout & Klahr, 2012, p. 126) observed, "Children are born scientists. From the first ball they send flying to the ant they watch carry a crumb, children use science's tools—enthusiasm, hypotheses, tests, conclusions—to uncover the world's mysteries." But many commentators on education, including Einstein in his opening quote, have suggested that education somehow gets in the way. Parvanno continues, "somehow students seem to lose what once came naturally." Consistent with such a perspective, although admittedly open to alternative interpretations, many scholars have either commented upon (Hall & Smith, 1903) or even documented empirically (Engel, 2009; Labella, 2009; Tizard & Hughes, 1984) the tendency for children who ask questions at home to dramatically reduce such question asking when they enter the classroom.

John Locke (1909–1914, pp. 209–211), who early on proposed techniques that parents could use to stimulate their children's curiosity, advised parents "not to check or discountenance any enquiries he shall make, nor suffer them to be laugh'd at; but to answer all his questions, and explain the matter he desires to know, so as to make them as much intelligible to him." These same two prescriptions that Locke applied within the family apply equally well to educational settings. Considerable research supports Locke's proposals that, to avoid suppressing curiosity, authority figures should create a safe and welcoming environment in which children feel comfortable taking risks, and they should answer questions clearly and accurately.

Moore and Bulbulian (1976) randomly assigned a confederate to encourage and approve of, or aloofly criticize, preschoolers' organization of a miniature farm set. The researchers found children in the aloof-critical condition took significantly longer before beginning exploration, engaged in less exploratory behavior overall, and were less likely to volunteer guesses in a game. Similarly, Henderson (1984) found that children explored significantly less when adults showed indifference as opposed to watching children explore, and actively encouraging exploration with smiles, eye contact, and positive verbal responses. Hackmann and Engel (2002, cited in Engel, 2011) found patterns of systematic variation in students' curiosity levels, as measured by their willingness to explore a "curiosity box" with many drawers containing different items. Approving teacher behavior, such as encouragement to examine the box and positive feedback in response to exploration, facilitated exploration, while a lack of approval discouraged it.

Information seeking by even characteristically curious students can be squelched in the right (or wrong) environment. Peters (1978) examined the behavior of college students measured to be low or high in trait curiosity, in classrooms with intimidating or nonintimidating professors. In low-threat classrooms, students with high trait curiosity asked more questions, but in high-threat classrooms, this difference disappeared because both groups asked few questions.

It would be an overstatement, however, to state that adults can only get in the way of children's natural curiosity. Indeed, other researchers have found that the absence of adults can suppress children's exploration. In one study, Hutt (1966) found that children were more apprehensive of novelty when an adult was absent from the room, and subsequent research has observed similar patterns specifically for children and parents. For example, Henderson, Charlesworth, and Gamradt (1982) observed children in a natural science museum, either in peer groups or with a parent, and found that children in the company of their parents explored exhibits more thoroughly and asked more questions than children who were with peers but with parents absent.

The information gap theory suggests that this relationship between welcoming and supportive environments and children's curiosity is due, in part, to the impact of self-efficacy and confidence. A supportive environment likely promotes students' feelings of self-efficacy and confidence, which increases students' perceived ability to close gaps and increases their level of curiosity. Additionally, a safe environment allows children to focus their attention on knowledge gaps as opposed to threatening stimuli, such as bullying peers or critical teachers. It is important to note that there is no research, which we know of, that directly measures self-efficacy and confidence, though numerous studies are consistent with the perspective proposed above. Rodrigue, Olson, and Markley (1987), for example, found that inducing negative affect stifles the desire for knowledge. Participants in the experiment were randomly assigned to a control condition or a negative mood condition in which they read statements aloud (e.g., "Every now and then I feel so tired and gloomy that I'd rather just sit than do anything") that became increasingly negative (see Velten, 1968). After this induction, participants read scientific studies and then rated the value of experiments and their desire to know more. Individuals in whom a negative mood had been induced rated the experiments as less valuable and showed a diminished desire to learn more, as compared with the control condition, and a third condition with a positive mood induction. These studies suggest that environments that breed negativity, low self-efficacy, and confidence, whether via peer bullying, threatening teachers, or negligent parents, can suppress curiosity. As Todd Kashdan observes, "At any age, we are more curious when we possess secure, safe havens," and when these safe havens are comprised, so is curiosity (2009, n.p.).

In addition to the creation of a safe haven, to avoid suppressing curiosity, educators should also directly answer questions or encourage students to answer questions themselves. Curiosity is reinforced when individuals receive concrete answers because stronger associations are formed between the positive feeling of closing the information gap (the "aha moment") and the feeling of curiosity itself. Additionally, satisfying curiosity should be reinforcing because it increases confidence in one's ability to close gaps and builds competence in the subject domain, both of which, the information gap theory predicts, should increase curiosity. Consistent with this prediction, research has found that unsatisfying answers stifle curiosity. Children who receive "I don't know" responses are less likely to ask subsequent questions than those who receive concrete answers (Endsley & Clarey, 1975). In an observational study, children who were offered less information by their parents, when playing in a room filled with different types of toys, explored less than students provided with more information. Even a promise of "not now, but later" can diminish curiosity, according to a study by Henderson and Moore (1980). The researchers simulated the response pattern of a busy, yet attentive, parent in their "unresponsive condition," in which an adult invited a child to play in a play area while she worked off to one side. When the child asked a question or tried to get the adult's attention, she indicated in a friendly way that she was too busy, but that the child should have fun playing and they would talk later. Children asked fewer questions in this condition than when the adult responded with factual, yet brief, answers, as well as a condition in which the adult didn't even answer the question, but instead asked the child back, "What do *you* think?" and then listened intently to the child's answer.

When given insufficient or vague answers, students' attention often wanders, and their desire for knowledge dissipates. Curiosity is a natural drive, but one that is easily suppressed. A lack of encouragement, an absence of adult figures, and insufficient answers can all extinguish curiosity's flame. The most basic goal of educators, insofar as curiosity is concerned, should be to not get in its way.

IMPORTANCE, SALIENCE, AND SURPRISE

Beyond the, perhaps obvious, goal of not suppressing curiosity by eliminating threats in an environment and avoiding unsatisfying answers, how can curiosity be actively cultivated by educators? The information gap perspective points to several approaches that facilitate learning through capitalizing on the three factors of curiosity discussed earlier: importance, salience, and surprise.

Importance specifies how much a piece of information matters to an individual; the more important the information, the more curiosity aroused. Research demonstrates that interest, a key input to importance, is associated with higher comprehension and retention, and recent trends in education on tailoring instruction and culturally responsive teaching also reflect how importance can stimulate curiosity and learning. Interest is defined as "a motivational variable [that] refers to the psychological state of engaging or the predisposition to reengage with particular classes of objects, events, or ideas over time" (Hidi & Renninger, 2006, p. 112). A topic of interest is, by definition, a topic of importance, and, across studies, interest has been shown to facilitate curiosity and subsequent memory for assimilated information.

Asher, Hymel, and Wigfield (1978) evaluated fifth graders' interests by having them rank photographs of different topics (e.g., jet planes, butterflies, cats). One week later, children read either high- or low-interest passages, based on their previously indicated interests, and, while reading the passage, filled out a single-word blank that measured their comprehension. The high-interest groups demonstrated significantly higher comprehension than the low-interest group. In another study, Bernstein (1955) assigned ninth graders to read one of two passages, previously rated as high- or low-interest by a group of independent peers, and then to take a comprehension test with both objective and free response components. High-interest passages were associated with significantly better comprehension as well as greater reading speed. In another study, Hidi and Baird (1988) created a text to accentuate characteristics believed to be determinants of interest: activity level (i.e., material that describes more intense actions and feelings), character identification, and novelty. Students reading the version intended to enhance interest recalled more information and experienced less forgetting one week later than a control group of typical, unmodified texts. This pattern of interest facilitating learning holds for a variety of ages, from young children to college students, and across a variety of domains (for a review, see Hidi, 1990).

Teachers commonly tailor content in curricula to appeal to individual students' interests, background, and culture, in an effort to increase curiosity by increasing the relevance of content to students' lives. Inner-city teachers, for example, often seek to include course materials, such as readings, that convey the perspectives of individuals with similar ethnic backgrounds as their students' (e.g., Gay, 2010; Wlodkowski & Ginsberg, 1995) or history texts that give voice to marginalized characters (for a review of the impact of culturally responsive practices on student outcomes, see Irvine & Hawley, 2011).

Salience, the degree to which the individual's environment highlights a particular information gap, is commonly utilized in educational environments. Diverse research suggests that instructional techniques that increase the salience of gaps result in better student outcomes. For example, in one focusing treatment in the previously discussed study in which children explored more when exposed to an attentive adult who smiled and made eye contact (Henderson, 1984), adults actively pointed out novel features and asked leading questions, thereby highlighting the salience of information gaps. Children in this condition explored as much as the active interest condition, and children in both groups explored significantly more than those in the control group. Similarly, Bonawitz and colleagues (2011) found that children whose attention was drawn to incomplete information were more likely to explore novel features of a toy. In two conditions, children were either explicitly shown uses of a toy by an adult or saw an adult accidentally discover a use, and then were given the opportunity to play with the toy. In the latter condition, children were more likely to explore other features of the toy and discover other uses. When information is portrayed, implicitly or explicitly, as being complete, then the formation of a reference point, along with curiosity, is stifled, but when an information gap is highlighted, curiosity is aroused and exploration increases.

Instructional techniques that capitalize on salience are diverse and include questioning and highlighting controversy. As Berlyne (1960, p. 289) observed, "the skillful lecturer excites curiosity in his audience by putting questions to them . . . which it has never occurred to them to ask themselves." Questions serve a multitude of purposes in the classroom, not only sparking curiosity but also serving as a check for students' understanding so that teachers can diagnose whether students comprehend the material presented. By bringing information gaps to the attention of students, question asking has been shown to increase retention of material (e.g., King, 1994; Redfield & Rousseau, 1981; Rosenshine, Meister, & Chapman, 1996; Wong, 1985).

While question asking generally promotes curiosity and retention, not all questions are created equal; the questioner, timing, and type of question all matter. In one study, Ross and Killey (1977) showed children slides and allowed them to ask questions about them. Children had the highest retention for answers to their own questions, as contrasted with questions asked by peers. Although it is possible that this result simply reflects the fact that children tend to ask questions about topics they are interested in, other research has found that encouraging students to generate their own questions, specifically through the cognitive strategy of "self-questioning," is an effective strategy for enhancing curiosity and improving comprehension and retention (King, 1989; Rosenshine et al., 1996; Wong, 1985). In another study examining the impact of timing and content of questions, Rickards (1976) found that conceptual questions asked before readers engage with a text are more effective in promoting recall than conceptual or verbatim questions administered after such engagement. Questioning is effective in promoting the salience of information gaps, which in turn seems to promote deep engagement with material and, ultimately, understanding and retention.

Another educational technique that capitalizes on salience is to highlight controversy. In one study, Lowry and Johnson (1981) assigned elementary school students to small groups to learn about a topic in social studies. In one condition, children were encouraged to focus on controversy and uncertainty, whereas in another, children were encouraged to work together to learn the facts. Children in the controversy condition learned more and were more likely to forgo recess to watch a film on the topic after the unit was over. By highlighting controversy, an obvious information gap is highlighted: which view is right and which view is wrong.

While many existing educational techniques, including question asking, naturally play on salience, a more explicit understanding of how and why salience affects learning, via its impact on curiosity, could be a useful insight to impart to teachers. Imagine, for example, a teacher who was introducing a unit on the topic of simple machines. She could present students with the machine and ask them to try to figure out what it does before demonstrating its operation, or she could demonstrate its operation and ask them to try to figure out how it works before providing the answer. Teachers attuned to the importance of salience as a stimulus of curiosity might themselves benefit from asking themselves, and trying to answer, the question: How can I make manageable information gaps salient to my students?

A final educational technique that capitalizes on salience and has been shown to increase learning is the Know-Want-to-know-Learned chart (KWL; see Deck, 2012, and Ogle, 1986, for a case study of its effectiveness). A KWL chart is a graphic organizer that exemplifies building curiosity through increasing salience. The chart is a table with three columns titled something like: What I Know, What I Want To Know, and What I Learned.

Before students begin a unit, book, or daily lesson, they fill out the chart, beginning with what they know and what they want to know. Then, either throughout the content or at the very end, students revisit the chart and write what they have learned, often in ways that directly relate to what they wanted to know. For example, suppose a seventh-grade social studies class is learning about the Kobe Earthquake in Japan in 1995 as part of a larger unit on when and how governments are useful in society. First, the teacher would have students brainstorm what they know about earthquakes and government involvement. Students might write in the first column, "Earthquakes occur when tectonic plates collide" or "Governments sometimes evacuate cities because of natural disasters." Following this activation of prior knowledge, the class would then brainstorm things they want to learn about the 1995 Kobe Earthquake, such as "How many people were injured or killed?" or "How long did it take the Japanese government and aid organizations to respond?" Finally, throughout the lesson or after, students would fill out knowledge they gained in the third column: "Japan has strict building codes and regularly holds earthquake drills" or "The Kobe Earthquake had a magnitude of 7.2." Through this process of activating prior knowledge, generating information gaps and then explicitly writing out information that fills the gaps, students are more likely to retain the material in this format. Making information gaps salient, whether through teacher questioning, highlighting controversy, or using graphic organizers, effectively engages student attention, builds curiosity, and ultimately facilitates learning.

Surprise, which occurs when expectations are violated, can open information gaps, thereby stimulating curiosity and information seeking. A number of studies support the idea that surprise stimulates curiosity (Berlyne, 1957; Charlesworth, 1964; Minton, 1963), and facilitates memory and learning (e.g., Pearce & Hall, 1980; Rescorla and Wagner, 1972; Schultz & Dickinson, 2000). In one rather complicated study on surprise, curiosity, and recall, Berlyne (1954b) had participants read multiple-choice questions on various animals, rate whether each question surprised them, and mark questions that they would most likely have answered. In a second phase of the experiment, subjects received statements, a subset of which answered the original questions. Subjects then rated whether the statements were surprising and whether they believed that the statement answered a previous question. In the third phase of the experiment, the questions were presented in open-ended format, and subjects attempted to provide answers. Berlyne (1957) found that questions originally marked as surprising were more likely to elicit curiosity, which was directly measured by asking participants to mark 12 questions "whose answers they most wanted to know" (p. 258). He also found some evidence that statements marked as surprising were more likely to be recalled in phase three. Beyond theory and basic research in the lab, utilizing surprise to facilitate learning is a common prescription in teaching guides.

In the book *How Learning Works*, Susan Ambrose and her colleagues (2010) argue that explicitly pointing out and correcting inaccurate prior knowledge is beneficial and results in students updating their understanding. Beyond the usual benefits of feedback, such feedback is likely to initiate surprise when students find they were wrong about topics they believed they knew; as a result, curiosity is likely to be aroused. Another instructional technique that plays on surprise is to have students make predictions. The Center for Research on Learning and Teaching (Brown, Hershock, Finelli, & O'Neal, 2009), for example, suggests that, to increase retention, teachers should "ask students to make predictions by applying course concepts to unfamiliar situations." When predictions turn out wrong, the resulting surprise can, again, stimulate curiosity and motivate learning. For example, a physics teacher, who has been teaching for 28 years, asks his students, every year, on the first day, "Which will hit the ground first—this paper or this textbook, and why?" After students share their forecasts that the textbook will hit first because it weighs more, he crumples up the paper, drops both, and, to the amazement of the students, they hit the ground at exactly the same time. Thus begins the conversation of kinematics. Unfortunately, unlike the instructional techniques described above that capitalize on salience and importance, in the case of surprise, there are no empirical studies (which we know of) that measure the effectiveness of surprise-inducing techniques in classroom or other educational settings.

In conclusion, the three factors of curiosity—importance, salience, and surprise—can each be fostered in educational settings in order to maximize curiosity and to maximize learning. By modifying content to make it interesting and relevant to students, by explicitly or implicitly pointing out information gaps, and by violating students' expectations through correcting prior knowledge and utilizing prediction, teachers, parents, and other educators can harness the power of curiosity and maximize learning.

CONCLUSION

As our review of the literature has hopefully highlighted, research in curiosity, including that which focuses specifically on education, is still at an early stage. On the one hand, given how long philosophers, social scientists, and educators have been discussing curiosity, this is both surprising and disappointing. On the other hand, researchers, including education researchers, should be encouraged that curiosity remains wide open in offering opportunities for those ready to use rigorous methods to attack the wide range of unaddressed, or inadequately addressed, important questions. Some of these opportunities include:

- *Uncovering the relationship between state and trait curiosity.* At the beginning of the chapter, we suggested that if trait differences reflect the cumulative effect of situational factors, then interventions that stimulate state curiosity might ultimately serve to enhance trait curiosity. There is no research, which we know of, that examines state curiosity over time or its relationship to trait curiosity, despite the obvious and important educational implications.
- *Determining what instructional methods are most effective in promoting curiosity.* We discussed instructional methods that capitalize on importance, salience, and surprise. However, studies that examine the effectiveness of these instructional techniques rarely measure the impact on curiosity directly. In addition, it is difficult to determine which techniques are most effective. Is it more effective to begin a novel with a KWL chart, or is it better to provide students with surprising facts and generate interest? Teachers have a limited amount of time, and while different techniques will work better for different teachers, it is also useful to have larger scale empirical comparisons between different instructional methods and curricula.
- *Exploring alternate methods to increase curiosity.* One blog classifies rearranging toys in a child's room as one of their "top five" strategies to increase curiosity. Another recommends imaginative play. A third stresses the importance of lengthening a child's attention span. There is a lot of advice out there, and most likely, a

lot of it is good. However, the advice to experimental support ratio is low. There are relatively few studies that manipulate children's (or adult's) environments and then measure the impact on curiosity. We've cited the majority of state curiosity studies conducted, and none of them address the propositions above.

- *Measuring self-efficacy, confidence, and other potential mediators of curiosity.* As discussed, there is reason to believe confidence and self-efficacy increase curiosity, yet there is limited research directly supporting this claim due to a lack of measurement and manipulation. It is critical to understand what interventions increase curiosity, but it is also valuable to understand why, and how, these interventions work.
- *Exploring the neurophysiological correlates of curiosity.* Does curiosity have a distinct neurophysiological signature? How does the neurophysiology of curiosity relate to interest, flow, and drive states, such as hunger and sex? In what conditions, if any, is curiosity painful? Few researchers have explored the neurophysiological correlates of curiosity (for an exception, see Kang et al., 2009), yet such studies have the potential to shed light on these, and many other, intriguing questions.
- *Examining the potential harms of curiosity.* While curiosity is commonly viewed as a desirable trait (for many good reasons, as we discussed), this was not always the case. Berlyne (1978, p. 99) observed that, traditionally, "curiosity meant lack of self-restraint, encroachment on other people's privacy, prying into matters that did not concern one," and Pandora, Eve, and the cat provide a few cautionary tales. Curiosity is sometimes cited as the culprit motivating teenage drug use (Lee, Neighbors, & Woods, 2007), yet this line of research remains largely uncharted. In addition, morbid curiosity, the desire to view disgusting and unnatural phenomena, has received relatively little attention despite its long-standing prevalence.[4] While curiosity can be a powerful motivating force in education due to its facilitation of memory, attention, and learning, it is valuable to understand when, and why, this force drives undesirable behavior.

Despite the still raw state of research on curiosity in education, educators should nevertheless be able to derive a few relatively confident conclusions from the research just reviewed. These include:

- *Curiosity increases in supportive environments.* Students ask more questions and are more likely to explore novel environments in the presence of their parents and other supportive adults. Students also ask more questions when educators show encouragement through smiling, eye contact, and positive verbal responses, and more generally, when educators are perceived as nonthreatening.
- *Curiosity is naturally reinforcing when questions are answered effectively.* Students tend to ask fewer questions when adults fail to provide answers, or answer them only after a delay. By the same token, students tend to ask more questions when adults answer their questions directly or pose the question back and listen intently to the student's answer.
- *Curiosity increases on topics of importance.* Students demonstrate higher comprehension and retention when reading high-interest passages and experience better academic outcomes when teachers tailor curriculum to reflect students' experiences and identities.

- *Curiosity increases when gaps are made salient.* Students exhibit greater curiosity when adults ask leading questions, or otherwise draw students' attention to open problems, unanswered questions, or controversies. Instructor questioning is especially effective when questions are asked before students interact with content. Self-questioning, a meta-cognitive strategy whereby students pose questions to themselves while reading, also promotes better comprehension and retention. Utilizing KWL charts, which activate and record prior knowledge before generating questions and answers, is an effective instructional technique that promotes curiosity and retention.
- *Curiosity increases when students are surprised.* Teachers should challenge students with questions and facts that are at variance with their existing knowledge and beliefs. Questions and facts that students find surprising elicit curiosity and, when answered, are associated with higher levels of retention.

In sum, while the literature on curiosity remains at a relatively primitive state, several consistent themes, as well as recommendations for educators who are interested in fostering curiosity, do emerge from existing research. In this review, we have sought to identify some of these themes and providing a conceptual framework for thinking about curiosity as an information gap. In addition, we propose the three core determinants of curiosity, which we term importance, salience, and surprise. As our review of the literature has made salient, however, there remain large gaps in our understanding of how curiosity can be instilled, and exploited, in the classroom. Hopefully, making these gaps salient will encourage curious researchers to pursue this vitally important topic.

NOTES

1. The editors of this volume asked us how curiosity relates to broader concepts, such as motivation, emotion, affect, and epistemic feeling. Such questions are always difficult to answer and involve a certain element of subjective judgment, but our answer is as follows.

   Curiosity's relationship to motivation is straightforward. It follows from our definition that curiosity is a motivational state and is included in the broader catalog of intrinsic motivation. We would also define curiosity as an emotion. The evolutionary account of emotion, which we advocate (Loewenstein, 2007), defines emotions as "superordinate programs" that orchestrate a concerted psycho-physiological response to recurrent situations of adaptive significance in our evolutionary past, such as fighting, falling in love, escaping predators, and experiencing a loss in status (Cosmides & Toobey, 2000). Curiosity can readily be viewed as a kind of program that evolved to orchestrate information-seeking in specific situations. Izard (1991, p. 14) characterizes an emotion as "a feeling that motivates, organizes, and guides perception, thought, and action." Certainly, curiosity would also fit this popular description. The terms "affect" and "affective processes" are sometimes used as superordinate labels that encompass emotion. In this case, it is obvious that affect would encompass curiosity. Additionally, the satisfaction of curiosity is typically associated with positive affect. The term "epistemic feelings," like emotions, has different definitions, though fortunately, not as many. Some scholars define it as a feeling about knowledge, hypotheses, and beliefs and associate it with certainty and doubt (e.g., de Sousa, 2008). Other scholars define it as a feeling that depends on unknown knowledge and associate it with fear and hope (e.g., Gordon, 1990). Using either definition, curiosity can be classified as an epistemic feeling because it is a feeling about the value of knowledge, and it is a feeling that depends on the existence of unknown knowledge. Although we were not asked if curiosity is a "drive," we address this question in the next section.

2. This is not to say that curiosity cannot take on a bittersweet flavor. Just as the anticipation of a lover's arrival at an airport can be simultaneously pleasurable and aversive, so can the anticipation of desired information. However, curiosity, like anticipation, is never purely pleasurable.

3. Less encouragingly, when teachers were asked to generate a list of characteristics they sought to encourage, rather than choosing characteristics from a given list, not one teacher's list included curiosity.

4. Over 2,000 years ago, St. Augustine observed that the object of curiosity can be distasteful and disgusting, such as when men seek out "the sight of a lacerated corpse." He didn't coin the term morbid curiosity, but he certainly knew about it.

REFERENCES

Ambrose, S. A., Bridges, M. W., DiPietro, M., Lovett, M. C., & Norman, M. K. (2010). *How learning works: Seven research-based principles for smart teaching.* San Francisco, CA: Jossey-Bass.

Aristotle. (1947). *Metaphysics.* In R. McKeon (Ed.), *Introduction to Aristotle* (pp. 238–296). New York, NY: Modern Library.

Asher, S. R., Hymel, S., & Wigfield, A. (1978). Influence of topic interest on children's reading comprehension. *Journal of Literacy Research, 10,* 35–47.

Berlyne, D. E. (1950). Novelty and curiosity as determinants of exploratory behavior. *British Journal of Psychology, 41,* 68–80.

Berlyne, D. E. (1954a). A theory of human curiosity. *British Journal of Psychology, 45,* 180–191.

Berlyne, D. E. (1954b). An experimental study of human curiosity. *British Journal of Psychology, 45,* 256–265.

Berlyne, D. E. (1957). Conflict and information-theory variables as determinants of human perceptual curiosity. *Journal of experimental psychology, 53,* 399.

Berlyne, D. E. (1960). *Conflict, arousal, and curiosity.* New York, NY: McGraw-Hill.

Berlyne, D. E. (1966). Curiosity and exploration. *Science, 153,* 25–33.

Berlyne, D. E. (1978). Curiosity and learning. *Motivation and Emotion, 2,* 97–175.

Bernstein, M. R. (1955). Relationship between interest and reading comprehension. *The Journal of Educational Research, 49,* 283–288.

Bonawitz, E. B., Shafto, P., Gweon, H., Goodman, N., Spelke, E., & Schulz, L. E. (2011). The double-edged sword of pedagogy: Teaching limits children's spontaneous exploration and discovery. *Cognition, 120,* 322–330.

Brown, M. K., Hershock, C., Finelli, C. J., & O'Neal, C. (2009). Teaching for retention in science, engineering, and math disciplines: A guide for faculty. Occasional Paper No. 25. Ann Arbor, MI: Center for Research on Learning and Teaching, University of Michigan.

Charlesworth, W. R. (1964). Instigation and maintenance of curiosity behavior as a function of surprise versus novel and familiar stimuli. *Child Development, 35,* 1169–1186.

Cicero. (1914). *De finibus bonorum et malorum* (Trans. H. Rackham). Cambridge, MA: Harvard University Press.

Collins, R. P., Litman, J. A., & Spielberger, C. D. (2004). The measurement of perceptual curiosity. *Personality and Individual Differences, 36,* 1127–1141.

Cosmides, L., & Tooby, J. (2000). Evolutionary psychology and the emotions. In M. Lewis & M. Haviland-Jones (Eds.), *Handbook of emotions* (pp. 91–115). New York, NY: The Guilford Press.

Dashiell, J. F. (1925). A quantitative demonstration of animal drive. *Comparative Psychology, 5,* 205–208.

Day, H. I. (1982). Curiosity and the interested explorer. *Performance and Instruction, 21,* 19–22.

Deck, A. L. (2012). *The ffects of KWL on ELL middle school students' listening comprehension of science content.* (Unpublished doctoral dissertation). The Ohio State University, Columbus, OH.

de Sousa, R. (2008). Epistemic feelings. In G. Brun, U. Doğuoğlu, & D. Kuenzle (Eds.), *Epistemology and emotions* (pp. 185–204). Burlington, VT: Ashgate Publishing Company.

Endsley, R. C., & Clarey, S. A. (1975). Answering young children's questions as a determinant of their subsequent question-asking behavior. *Developmental Psychology, 11,* 863.

Engel, S. (2009). Is curiosity vanishing? *Journal of the American Academy of Child & Adolescent Psychiatry, 48,* 777–779.

Engel, S. (2011). Children's need to know: Curiosity in schools. *Harvard Educational Review, 81,* 625–645.

Gay, G. (2010). *Culturally responsive teaching: Theory, research, and practice.* New York, NY: Teachers College Press.

Golman, R., & Loewenstein, G. F. (2012). Curiosity, Information Gaps, and the Utility of Knowledge. (Unpublished manuscript.) Department of Social and Decision Sciences, Carnegie Mellon University, Pittsburgh, PA.

Gordon, R. M. (1990). *The structure of emotions: Investigations in cognitive philosophy.* Cambridge, England: Cambridge University Press.

Hackmann, H., & Engel, S. (2002). Curiosity in context: The classroom environment examined. (Unpublished honors thesis). Williams College, Williamstown, MA. In Engel, S. (2011). Children's need to know: Curiosity in schools. *Harvard Educational Review, 81,* 625–645.

Hall, S. G., & Smith, T. (1903). Curiosity and interest. *The Pedagogical Seminary, 10,* 315–358.

Heath, C., Larrick, R. P., & Wu, G. (1999). Goals as reference points. *Cognitive Psychology, 38,* 79–109.

Hebb, D. O. (1949). *The organization of behavior.* New York, NY: Wiley.

Henderson, B. B. (1984). Social support and exploration. *Child Development, 55,* 1246–1251.

Henderson, B. B., Charlesworth, W. R., & Gamradt, J. (1982). Children's exploratory behavior in a novel field setting. *Ethology and Sociobiology, 3,* 93–99.

Henderson, B., & Moore, S. G. (1980). Children's responses to objects differing in novelty in relation to level of curiosity and adult behavior. *Child development, 51,* 457–465.

Hidi, S. (1990). Interest and its contribution as a mental resource for learning. *Review of Educational research, 60,* 549–571.

Hidi, S. (2000). An interest researcher's perspective: The effects of extrinsic and intrinsic factors on motivation. In C. Sansone & J. M. Harackiewicz (Eds.), *Intrinsic and extrinsic motivation: The search for optimal motivation and performance* (pp. 309–339). San Diego, CA: Academic Press.

Hidi, S., & Baird, W. (1988). Strategies for increasing text-based interest and students' recall of expository texts. *Reading Research Quarterly, 23,* 465–483.

Hidi, S., & Renninger, K. A. (2006). The four-phase model of interest development. *Educational Psychologist, 41,* 111–127.

Hull, C. L. (1932). The goal-gradient hypothesis and maze learning. *Psychological Review, 39,* 25–43.

Hunt, J. M. (1963). Motivation inherent in information processing and action. In O. J. Harvey (Ed.), *Motivation and social interaction* (pp. 35–94). New York, NY: Ronald Press.

Hutt, C. (1966). Exploration and play in children. *Symposia of the Zoological Society of London, 18,* 61–81.

Irvine, J. J., & Hawley, W. D. (2011) Culturally responsive pedagogy: An overview of research on student outcomes. *Culturally responsive teaching awards celebration.* Retrieved from www.edweek.org/media/crt_research.pdf

Izard, C. E. (1977). *Human emotions.* New York, NY: Plenum Press.

Izard, C. E. (1991). *The psychology of emotions.* New York, NY: Plenum Press.

Jirout, J., & Klahr, D. (2012). Children's scientific curiosity: In search of an operational definition of an elusive concept. *Developmental Review, 32,* 125–160.

Kagan, S. L., Moore, E., & Bredekamp, S. (Eds.) (1995). Reconsidering children's early development and learning: Toward common views and vocabulary. *Goal 1 Technical Planning Group Report 95–03.* Washington, DC: National Education Goals Panel. Retrieved from http://govinfo.library.unt.edu/negp/reports/child-ea.htm

Kang, M. J., Hsu, M., Krajbich, I. M., Loewenstein, G., McClure, S. M., Wang, J.T.Y., & Camerer, C. F. (2009). The wick in the candle of learning: Epistemic curiosity activates reward circuitry and enhances memory. *Psychological Science, 20,* 963–973.

Kashdan, T. (2009, August 4). Six ways for parents to cultivate strong, curious, creative children. *Huffington Post.* Retrieved from www.huffingtonpost.com/todd-kashdan/six-ways-for-parents-to-c_b_249031.html

Kashdan, T. B., Rose, P., & Fincham, F. D. (2004). Curiosity and exploration: Facilitating positive subjective experiences and personal growth opportunities. *Journal of Personality Assessment, 82,* 291–305.

King, A. (1989). Effects of self-questioning training on college students' comprehension of lectures. *Contemporary Educational Psychology, 14,* 366–381.

King, A. (1994). Guiding knowledge construction in the classroom: Effects of teaching children how to question and how to explain. *American educational research journal, 31,* 338–368.

Labella, M. (2009). *Encouraging exploration: The effects of teacher behavior on student expressions of curiosity* (unpublished honors thesis). Williams College, Williamstown, MA.

Lee, C. M., Neighbors, C., & Woods, B. A. (2007). Marijuana motives: Young adults' reasons for using marijuana. *Addictive Behaviors, 32,* 1384–1394.

Litman, J. A., Hutchins, T. L., & Russon, R. K. (2005). Epistemic curiosity, feeling-of-knowing, and exploratory behaviour. *Cognition and Emotion, 19,* 559–582.

Litman, J. A., & Jimerson, T. L. (2004). The measurement of curiosity as a feeling of deprivation. *Journal of Personality Assessment, 82,* 147–157.

Litman, J. A., & Spielberger, C. D. (2003). Measuring epistemic curiosity and its diversive and specific components. *Journal of Personality Assessment, 80,* 75–86.

Locke, John. *Some thoughts concerning education.* (1909–1914). Vol. 37, Part 1. The Harvard Classics. New York, NY: P.F. Collier & Son. Retrieved from www.bartleby.com/37/1

Loewenstein, G. (1994). The psychology of curiosity: A review and reinterpretation. *Psychological Bulletin, 116,* 75–98.

Loewenstein, G. (2007). Defining affect (commentary on Klaus Scherer's "What is an emotion?"). *Social Science Information, 46,* 405–410.

Loewenstein, G., Adler, D., Behrens, D., & Gillis, J. (1992). *Why Pandora opened the box: Curiosity as a desire for missing information.* Working paper, Carnegie Mellon University, Pittsburgh, PA.

Lowry, N., & Johnson, D. W. (1981). Effects of controversy on epistemic curiosity, achievement, and attitudes. *The Journal of Social Psychology, 115,* 31–43.

Minton, H. L. (1963). A replication of perceptual curiosity as a function of stimulus complexity. *Journal of Experimental Psychology, 66,* 522–524.

Moore, S. G., & Bulbulian, K. N. (1976). The effects of contrasting styles of adult- child interaction children's curiosity. *Developmental Psychology, 12,* 171–172.

National Science Teachers Association. (2003). *NSTA position statement: Science education for middle level students.* Retrieved from www.nsta.org/about/positions/middlelevel.aspx?lid=ms

Naylor, F. D. (1981). A state-trait curiosity inventory. *Australian Psychologist, 16,* 172–183.

Nissen, H. W. (1930). A study of exploratory behavior in the white rat by means of the obstruction method. *Journal of Genetic Psychology, 37,* 361–376.

Ogle, D. M. (1986). KWL: A teaching model that develops active reading of expository text. *The Reading Teacher, 39,* 564–570.

Pavlov, I. P. (1927). *Conditioned reflexes.* Oxford, England: Clarendon Press.

Pearce, J. M., & Hall, G. (1980). A model for Pavlovian learning: Variations in the effectiveness of conditioned but not of unconditioned stimuli. *Psychological Review, 106,* 532–552.

Peters, R. A. (1978). Effects of anxiety, curiosity, and perceived instructor threat on student verbal behaviors in the college classroom. *Journal of Educational Psychology, 70,* 388–395.

Peterson, C., & Seligman, M. E. (2004). *Character strengths and virtues: A handbook and classification.* New York, NY: Oxford University Press.

Posnock, R. (1991). *The trial of curiosity: Henry James William James, and the challenge of modernity.* New York, NY: Oxford University Press.

Redfield, D. L., & Rousseau, E. W. (1981). A meta-analysis of experimental research on teacher questioning behavior. *Review of educational research, 51,* 237–245.

Rescorla, R. A., & Wagner, A. R. (1972). A theory of Pavlovian conditioning: Variations in the effectiveness of reinforcement and nonreinforcement. In A. H. Black & W. F. Prokasy (Eds.), *Classical conditioning II* (pp. 64–99). New York, NY: Appleton-Century-Crofts.

Rickards, J. P. (1976). Interaction of position and conceptual level of adjunct questions on immediate and delayed retention of text. *Journal of Educational Psychology, 68,* 210.

Rodrigue, J. R., Olson, K. R., & Markley, R. P. (1987). Induced mood and curiosity. *Cognitive therapy and research, 11,* 101–106.

Rosenshine, B., Meister, C., & Chapman, S. (1996). Teaching students to generate questions: A review of the intervention studies. *Review of educational research, 66,* 181–221.

Ross, H. S., & Killey, J. C. (1977). The effect of questioning on retention. *Child Development, 48,* 312–314.

Schultz, W., & Dickinson, A. (2000). Neuronal coding of prediction errors. *Annual Review of Neuroscience, 23,* 473–500.

Tizard, B., & Hughes, M. (1984). *Young children learning.* London, England: Fontana.

Todt, E., & Schreiber, S. (1998). *Development of interests.* In L. Hoffmann, A. Krapp, K. A. Remminger, & J. Baumert (Eds.), *Interest and learning: Proceedings of the Seeon Conference on Interest and Gender* (pp. 25–40). Kiel, Germany: IPN.

University of Chicago Laboratory Schools. (n.d.). *Educational Program: Curriculum: Science.* Retrieved from www.ucls.uchicago.edu/schools/lower-curriculum/index.aspx

Velten, E. (1968). A laboratory task for the induction of mood states. *Behaviour Research and Therapy, 6,* 473–482.

Wlodkowski, R. J., & Ginsberg, M. B. (1995). *Diversity and motivation: Culturally responsive teaching.* San Francisco, CA: Jossey-Bass.

Wong, B. Y. (1985). Self-questioning instructional research: A review. *Review of Educational Research, 55,* 227–268.

13

SHAME AND PRIDE AND THEIR EFFECTS ON STUDENT ACHIEVEMENT

*Geraldine V. Oades-Sese, Tara Anne Matthews,
and Michael Lewis, Rutgers University*

If we think back to our early education experience and about the teachers who made an impact on our lives, we remember some of them and not others. Why some and not others? We asked some people to recall their experiences; here are three examples of what we heard:

Part of the reason I went into this profession was due to my own school experience. I had a wonderful experience with an elderly woman who was a volunteer. She helped me with reading. She was so encouraging and patient and above all said I was "smart." In junior high I had a number of encouraging teachers. Mr. S., a social studies teacher and Mr. C., a science teacher. They were such great teachers who were very supportive and above all listened to my concerns. I will always remember them.

(Sarah, 38-year-old psychologist)

Sister L was for sure old school and I remembered that she sent me to the board and embarrassed me when I didn't know an answer to a math question. Instead of explaining it, she scolded me. It made me develop a dislike for math. On the other hand, Mr. Z made class fun and I enjoyed his class. He made it easy to understand and he influenced me to become a teacher.

(Janet, 45-year-old teacher)

In a positive way, it was Ms. G. in the first grade who, back in 1947 before people knew much about learning disorders, diagnosed me with a reading problem and left-eye dominance. She worked with my parents and helped me learn to read and write (and allowed me to be left handed). I was, by then, a step behind everyone else but if she hadn't stepped in I might never have learned to read or write.

(Tom, 65-year-old lawyer)

We heard many answers about early school experiences and found many commonalities across people's early education experiences. Teachers who made a positive impact on students' lives were described as being warm, nurturing, caring, and encouraging, and it was these teachers that impacted their learning experiences. Many years later, people report that they can vividly remember their teacher's face and smile. A common thread among them was how these teachers built self-confidence and competence and instilled a sense of pride. Even though the person may not have liked or performed well in a particular subject, these teachers inspired them to become interested in a subject, do well, and in some cases, pursue a career in that domain years later.

In contrast, teachers who had a negative impact on students' lives were described as mean, harsh, and strict. These teachers tend to embarrass or yell at students in front of others, which made them want to roll up in a ball and hide, or even die. These negative experiences generated shame, which had a long-lasting effect on how individuals' viewed themselves as well as how they evaluated their ability. These few stories about peoples' experiences capture the essence of shame and pride and their resulting effects on students. We will refer to these stories throughout the text as we examine the role of shame and pride in educational settings and academic achievement.

THE ROLE OF EMOTIONS IN LEARNING

In schools, learning occurs within the social-emotional context of teacher–student relationships (Lewis, 1977). Within the interactions between a teacher and students, emotions are involved in the exchange of information and knowledge and have a significant impact on students' academic learning and performance. In order to examine the effects of emotions on learning, we need to understand what we mean by the term emotion, which can be best understood by separating the term into its constituent parts: emotional elicitors, emotional action patterns including expressions, and emotional experience (Lewis, 2014; Lewis & Michaelson, 1983). Each of these features of emotions is important to understand in their relation to achievement. Emotions are fundamentally important in cognitive processes that contribute to how we learn, such as perception, attention, memory, decision making, and problem-solving skills (Clore & Huntsinger, 2007; Pekrun, 2011). Emotions even affect our motivation level, psychological health, and neuroimmunological functioning and determine whether learning can actually occur (Lewis, Haviland-Jones, & Barrett, 2008). For example, emotions are associated with the levels of dopamine in the brain, which affects one's capacity to store and retrieve information from long-term memory (Ashby, Isen, & Turken, 1999), which is essential for academic subjects.

We benefit from positive emotions embedded within teacher–student relationships and the learning environment in a number of ways. Positive emotions, such as enjoyment of learning and pride, have been linked to intrinsic motivation and interest in students across all ages, including college (Pekrun, 2011). These emotions foster positive self-appraisals, which can increase a student's motivation to learn and perform better as well as facilitate retrieval and learning of information (Parrott & Spackman, 2000). Thus, in part, the consequences of positive emotions are flexibility in thinking, creativity, and holistic ways of problem solving, which all foster an optimal learning experience (Fredrickson, 2001).

Negative emotions, such as anxiety, shame, and boredom, on the other hand, can hamper students' motivation to learn and affect their performance (Pekrun, 2011). They can also promote negative self-appraisals of one's ability, skills, and performance, impede the learning of materials, likeability of the subject matter, and taint the student's overall learning experience.

While children's school experiences are important in affecting their emotions as well as performance, experiences in the home with parents, either prior to school or during school, are also important. Parents, after all, are not only the initial determiners of children's achievement behavior (Eccles, 1997), but they are also important in terms of children's emotional life, which affect their academic performance. Parental behaviors, such as verbal comments about behavior early in life, are likely to have a long-term impact on how children orient to learning tasks and respond to success or failure (Alessandri & Lewis, 1996; Lewis, 1992). Moreover, parents foster the development of a positive sense of self when they have positive and reaffirming interactions with their children (Kaufman, 1992). Thus, early parent–child relationships, prior to school as well as school experiences themselves, play an important role; both need to be considered when we study the role of emotions and self-attributions as they affect achievement in school.

Given the importance of the effects of emotion on learning and achievement, it would seem reasonable that emotions would be considered most important in the theories of learning, teacher training, and the educational curriculum. Historically, the consideration of emotions and its association with academic learning was not considered (see Lewis, 1977, for an exception). More recently, the idea that promoting a positive learning climate, close positive teacher–student relationships, and the incorporation of social-emotional learning into the curriculum are essential to a child's social-emotional and academic development (see Brackett & Rivers, 2014; Zins, Weissberg, Wang, & Walberg, 2004). In this chapter, we focus on the emotion of shame as well as pride and the self-attributions that are likely to generate them. Before we do so, it is important to look at both the primary emotions and these self-conscious emotions, since it is our belief that the self-conscious emotions, such as shame and pride, are equally, if not more so, related to achievement than are the primary emotions of fear or anger.

THE DEVELOPMENT OF EMOTIONAL LIFE

Lewis has articulated a theory of emotional development where during the first half year of life the primary emotions can be readily seen. With the onset of consciousness at about 18 to 24 months, a new class of emotions emerges that follows Darwin; these are called the self-conscious emotions, which include shame and pride (Lewis, 1997, 2008). Primary emotions can be divided into approach and withdrawal action patterns; approach patterns designed for infant engagement with its social and object world, while withdrawal patterns designed to allow infants to withdraw from it. The primary emotions can be observed within the first 6 to 8 months of life using the facial coding schemas of Izard and Ekman (Ekman, Friesen, & Ellsworth, 1972; Izard, 1995). These emotions exist prior to the emergence of consciousness, since the level of cognitive processing that is required for them is limited (Lewis & Sullivan, 2005). Fear, for example, while requiring memory about past experiences of the fearful stimuli, such as a doctor's office, does not require elaborate cognition, such as consciousness or self-attributions.

At around 15 to 24 months, using the emergence of self-referential behavior as a measure of consciousness, children show the ability to recognize themselves in mirrors, use personal pronouns such as me and mine, and engage in pretend play (Lewis & Ramsay, 2004). These measures indicate that they have developed a mental representation of the idea of "me." However, in addition to the emergence of consciousness, the self-conscious emotions require self-attributions and can be readily seen by 36 months.

Self-Attribution

Attribution about the self refers to what a child takes to be the cause of his or her behavior (see Weiner, Russell, & Lerman, 1978, 1979). These attributions include factors that are stable and uncontrollable, such as natural ability, intelligence, or height (if you are a basketball player) as well as attributions of unstable and controllable factors, such as effort exerted, strategy used, or amount of practice. These attributions are in contrast to those attributions thought to be externally caused such as luck, teacher preference, and task difficulty, which can also be stable/unstable and controllable/uncontrollable. Weiner (2010) has suggested that these self-attributions affect a person's self-conscious emotions.

These self-attributions seem to emerge around three years of age (Lewis, 1995; Lewis, Alessandri, & Sullivan, 1992; Lewis & Sullivan, 2005; Stipek, Recchia, & McClintic, 1992). For Lewis, these attributions include (1) the evaluation of their behavior, thoughts, or feelings as success or failure vis-à-vis some standard, rule, or goal, (2) perceived responsibility for their success or failure, and (3) the belief about whether their performance was related to global or specific traits. These beliefs are shaped by children's cognitive ability and to the standards, rules, and goals that they have acquired from their family, friends, and culture. By three years of age, children have the cognitive capacity for these self-attributions and show self-conscious emotions such as shame and pride during achievement-like tasks (Lewis, Alessandri, & Sullivan, 1992).

The different self-conscious emotions are elicited by these aspects of self-attributions. For example, Lewis's model suggests that the self-conscious emotion of shame, embarrassment, and guilt are associated with attributions of failure, while pride is associated with attributions of success. While the attributions of success and failure vis-à-vis standards, rules, and goals (SRG) are needed for all the self-conscious emotions, the specific attribution of a global or specific focus of attention differentiate shame from guilt as well as between authentic and hubristic pride.

Global and Specific Attributions

Global and specific attributions specify the focus of the child in regard to evaluations about the self (Lewis, 1995). Having a global attribution refers to a child's propensity to focus on the total self, reflected in such comments as "Because I failed, I am a loser." Because shame is the consequence of such a global attribution, the child wants to hide, disappear, or avoid the task that caused this attribution. In contrast, a specific attribution allows the child to examine and judge specific behaviors that may have led to the failure. Notice that specific attributions around failure allow the child to produce specific behaviors (i.e., effort, practice). Children differ to the degree that they make specific or global self-attributions. Specific-focused children tend to make evaluative statements such as "What I did was wrong and I must avoid doing it again" (Weiner, 1974).

Specific or global evaluations have also been referred to as task versus performance self-attributions (Lewis, 2014). Dweck was more interested in self-attributions' effect on achievement rather than on emotions. Dweck and colleagues have discussed two self-attributions, the "helpless" and "mastery-oriented" patterns (Diener & Dweck, 1978, 1980; Kamins & Dweck, 1999). Dweck suggests that children who display a helpless response view their failure as a result of poor ability. These children, who blame failure on their global self, have low expectations and subsequently show impaired strategies and performance (Elliot & Dweck, 2005). Children who show the helpless pattern also under-report their past performances and expect poor performance in the future (Elliot & Dweck, 2005; Smiley & Dweck, 1994). Mastery-oriented children, in contrast, focus on specific behaviors, such as effort, process, or strategy, needed for the task. They accurately recall past experiences, maintain high expectations for future performance, maintain positive self-assessments of their ability, and continue to exhibit constructive behaviors even when a setback occurs (Diener & Dweck, 1978, 1980; Dweck & Reppucci, 1973; Elliot & Dweck, 2005; Kamins & Dweck, 1999; Smiley & Dweck, 1994). Dweck's two reactions to failure are similar to Lewis's and Weiner's global and performance attributions.

To capture the tendency of children to show these two patterns of helpless and mastery-orientation, Dweck developed a measure of children's self-beliefs about whether they perceive outcomes as resulting from perception of the self as helpless or task-related factors (Dweck, Chiu, & Hong, 1995; Elliot & Dweck, 2005; Smiley & Dweck, 1994). Unlike children who focus on specific tasks, children who focus on their performance contemplate on "how I did" and blame themselves for doing badly. These responses reflect children's belief that ability is a stable, unchanging trait. For these children, a failed task leads them to experience more negative affect and be less confident that they can succeed at challenging tasks in the future. They view failure as the result of an incompetent, stable self. Children who believe that ability is a fixed, stable quality are more likely to adopt a performance-avoidance or extrinsic motivational style, characterized by a concern about how others evaluate them and a strong desire to perform successfully and avoid failure; that is, they have a performance self focus. Children who adopt a performance-avoidance orientation have the proclivity to avoid situations or tasks that may lead to failure in order to preserve the perception of the self.

Dweck's view of children's self-attributions about competence bears some similarities to Lewis's theory about attributions and emotional development and in particular his ideas about the emotions of shame, guilt, and pride (Lewis, 1992). As described in the next section, these self-conscious emotions are the result of the self-attributions children make about their achievement. Lewis's cognitive-emotional view emphasizes that what children think about their performance determines their response rather than the actual success or failure on the task (Lewis 1992; Lewis & Sullivan, 2005). In Lewis's theory, the performance (global) orientation is likely to lead to shame in failure situations, while task (specific) orientation is more likely to lead to guilt.

SHAME AND OTHER SELF-CONSCIOUS EMOTIONS

What Is Shame?

Following Darwin, Lewis has proposed that self-conscious emotions emerge after self-reference or consciousness (Lewis & Brooks, 1974). Moreover, the self-conscious emotions, at least shame, pride, guilt, and evaluative embarrassment require the acquisition of self-evaluation on the part of the child. These self-attributions lead to different self-conscious emotions (Lewis, 1992). This is unlike the early self-conscious emotions of empathy, envy, and exposure embarrassment, which require consciousness but little self-attribution (Lewis, 1995, 2000, 2003).

Shame is a consequence of how children think about themselves. Phenomenologically, shame causes a child to hide, disappear, or even die. The physical manifestation of shame can be seen in a lowered or dropped head, a collapse of the shoulders, and an avoidance of eye contact. Shame is caused by children's belief that their behavior, feelings, or actions do not meet their own standards, rules, and goals as well as those of their parents, peers, and teachers. It is also caused when children hold themselves responsible for their failure and when they make a global attribution. These cognitive attributional processes lead to shame. Because of the fleeting nature of the emotional experience, it is often difficult to observe (Monroe, 2009). Moreover, because of its powerful negative feeling, it is often converted into another emotion, which Helen B. Lewis (1971) called unfelt shame. More recently, Lewis and colleagues showed that for adolescents, shame can be converted into blame of others through altering the attribution of responsibility. Young juvenile delinquents often blamed others for their failure and instead of having felt shame they converted their feelings into aggression (Gold, Sullivan, & Lewis, 2011).

Shame is often observed in the parent–child interaction (Alessandri & Lewis, 1996; Lewis, 1992). Some children suffer from prolonged shame, both as a result of parental verbal and physical abuse (Alessandri & Lewis, 1996; Gold et al., 2011) but also because of temperament differences (Kochanska, 1991). While all children and adults experience shame to some degree, it is the prolonged shame that leads to individual differences in children's emotional problems and school and performance difficulties. For example, prolonged shame leads to hormone dysfunction, such as excessive cortisol response (Lewis & Ramsey, 1995) as well as mental health problems. Tomkins (1963) suggested that shame is stored as scenes that can be re-experienced by the child and adult.

Shame around failure is readily seen in early childhood, both at home with parents and siblings, among peers, and also in school. It is prolonged shame, however, that is most pathological and that has the most serious consequences (Lewis, 1997, 2000). In our example of teachers' remarks and their effects on students' subsequent development, think of Janet's story. Janet's capacity to learn math concepts was inhibited by her negative experiences in school, which resulted in a dislike of math for the rest of her life. From Lewis's theory, we can say that shame is elicited depending on whether students are more likely performance-oriented rather than task-oriented; that is, focused on the global self rather than focused on a specific behavior. Performance-oriented students are likely to show shame if they failed in a school task; likewise, they may overestimate their successes as in hubristic pride. Task-oriented students, who fail a school task, will focus on improving a grade by practicing more or asking for help. This is what we see in Tom's example. The literature on self- attributions supports our belief. For example, Thompson, Altmann, and Davidson (2004) found that high-shame prone students tend to put less effort in practicing to improve performance and are likely to make unproductive self-attributions following a failure.

How Does Shame Differ From Guilt and Embarrassment?

The emotions of guilt and shame have often been confused. However, the work of H. B. Lewis (1971), Lewis (1992), and Tangney and Dearing (2002) provide a clear way to distinguish between them. While shame is caused by focusing on the global self, guilt, on the other hand, focuses on the failed event or on the specific task rather than the global self. Because the self-attribution is focused on the task, guilt leads to repair and therefore to action, which in turn leads to making more effort to amend the failure (Lewis, 1992; Russell & McCauly, 1986; Tangney & Dearing, 2002; Weiner, Russell, & Lerman, 1978). For example, we see four- and five-year-old children when they do not finish a task on time request more time to be able to finish it. This is an example of a guilt response, whereas shame-prone children are likely to exhibit bodily collapse and make no attempt for repair. The elicitation of guilt is produced when students evaluate their behavior as failure but focus on the self's action that led to the failure. Because guilt focuses on the specific task and because the self is not damaged, students have the capacity to rid themselves of this emotional state by means of corrective action. Unlike shame, an emotion in which the self is associated with both subject and object, in guilt, the self is differentiated from the object. As such, the emotion is less paralyzing and more capable of dissipation. Expression of guilt is similar to expression of shame in that children expressing guilt will avert their eye gaze and show tense facial expressions, but their bodily behavior is different. In shame, the body collapses, while in guilt, it does not. Guilt feelings allow for repair, and thus action of repair is what ultimately distinguishes guilt from shame (Lewis, 1995). Because guilt can be easily repaired, it is a less insidious negative emotion than shame in educational settings (McGregor & Elliot, 2005).

Lewis (1992) has suggested that there are two types of embarrassment, which he has called exposure and evaluative embarrassment. Exposure embarrassment, similar to shyness, occurs only when one recognizes that they are the focus of attention (Darwin, 1872) once self referential behavior emerges (Lewis, Sullivan, Stanger, & Weiss, 1989). For example, a child may experience exposure embarrassment when she is praised, pointed to, or asked to perform such as dancing or singing. Exposure embarrassment does not require self-attributions and is seen before self- attributions and the internalization of standards, rules, and goals occur. Exposure embarrassment, unlike evaluative embarrassment, does not lead to an increase in stress as measured by cortisol response (Lewis, Stranger, Sullivan, & Barone, 1991).

Evaluative embarrassment, unlike exposure embarrassment, does not emerge until children have developed internalized standards, rules, and goals and the capacity to make self-attributions. Thus, while exposure embarrassment can be seen in toddlers between 15 to 24 months of life, evaluative embarrassment is not seen until 30 months or more. Evaluative embarrassment results from the negative evaluation of one's performance. The evaluative form of embarrassment is similar to shame, although not as intense and as such does not lead to a marked decrease in action or the desire to hide, disappear, or die (Lewis, 2014).

THE ROLE OF SHAME IN ACHIEVEMENT

Self-attributions about achievement produce self-conscious emotions. Bernard Weiner (1977) suggests that:

> Pride and shame, as well as interpersonal evaluation, are absolutely maximized when achievement outcomes are ascribed internally and are minimized when success and failures are attributed to external causes. . . . In sum, locus of causality influences the emotional consequences of achievement outcomes.
>
> (p. 183)

Furthermore, he believed that one's perception of effort was important in guiding emotional reaction; greater shame was experienced when students with high ability, for example, attributed failure to the lack of effort (Weiner & Kukla, 1970).

Covington and Omelich (1979, 1985) argue, however, that self-perception of ability determines self-worth and emotional reactions. They state that effort and certainty and uncertainty of ability are the eliciting factors of emotions after failure. For example, greater shame is experienced when a student puts in high effort but fails on a task. The association between high effort and failure implies low ability, which produces shame. This was especially true if the student is uncertain about his/her perceived low ability status, referred to as failure-avoidance. There were no differences in shame, however, between high ability students who were certain or uncertain about their ability status.

In young children, Lewis's cognitive-emotional and Dweck's motivational views emphasize that what children think about their performance determines their emotional responses as well as their achievement (Lewis 1992; Lewis & Sullivan, 2005). To look at self-attributions related to mastery or helplessness, Dweck examined children's responses to the question, "Do you want to do the task again?" She used this question to measure the child's performance or task orientation (Smiley & Dweck, 1994). To get at the same attribution question, Lewis asked children, "Was the task easy or hard?" How children respond in particular to failure of an easy task determines whether they have a global or specific orientation. For example, children show a specific or task-oriented response when they fail an easy task if they state that the task was "easy." It is specific because the task they failed was easy and so their answer reflects their focus on the task. However, if they answer that the task was hard, they are focusing on their performance, so this is a global orientation. In other words, these children state that the task was hard, despite being easy, as a response to preserve their perceptions about their own ability.

In a recent study using both Dweck's and Lewis's measures, Matthews, Sullivan, and Lewis (in press) examined in four year olds the relation between measures of self-attribution and emotional behavior in response to failure on easy tasks. While there has been some work on young children's self-attributions, most of it has been concerned with at what age children first make self- attributions (e.g., Dweck & Leggett, 1988; Elliot & Dweck, 1988; Stipek et al., 1992). What these studies have shown is that a three-year-old child's response to failure is related to shame with failure on an easy task eliciting more shame then failure on a difficult task (Lewis, Alessandri, & Sullivan, 1992; Lewis & Sullivan, 2005). In this study of four year olds, Matthews et al. (in press) looked at whether children made specific or global attributes around their failures on an easy task, as well as asking the question used by Dweck: whether they wanted to do the task again. The answers to these attribution questions were related to emotions they exhibited when they failed their other tasks. The two measures of specific or task versus global or performance attributions were found to be weakly related. Of importance to our interest in shame was the result that the specific versus global measures developed by Lewis were more correlated with shame than Dweck's measures. Children who showed the global attributions were the ones who showed more shame and support our belief that shame is likely to interfere with intrinsic motivation.

Gender Differences

Gender differences in attribution orientation have been reported. Dweck and Leggett (1988) found that girls attribute their failures to a lack of ability, a global factor, and are therefore more performance focused. In contrast, boys often view their failures as more specific, related to the situation at hand, and are therefore more task focused. Lewis et al. (1992) found that boys attribute success to their own efforts and are more likely to make an internal attribution ("I am fantastic"). Girls, however, are more likely to attribute their success to luck, the situation, or the task at hand, an external attribution ("I was lucky that the test was easy"). Females are more likely than males to make self-blame attributions of failure, and this global orientation in response to failure leads to more expression of shame in girls than boys (Lewis et al.,1992). Gender differences appear to be age related. Differences in shame expression were not seen in three year olds (Lewis et al., 1992) or in the study of four year olds (Matthews et al., in press). After the age of five, girls consistently demonstrate more shame than boys after failing a task, particularly when the task was difficult (Alessandri & Lewis, 1996; Lewis et al., 1992).

These gender differences appear to be enduring across childhood and extend into adulthood (Lewis, 1995). A recent meta-analysis of 697 effect sizes from 382 journal articles, dissertations, and unpublished data sets indicates that women have more guilt and shame when they do not live up to standards, rules, or goals, while there were negligible gender differences found for embarrassment, hubris, and pride (Else-Quest, Higgins, Allison, & Morton, 2012). While gender differences may be a function of age, they may also be explained by the academic environment. It may be related to how adults behave toward children as a function of gender, more specifically, teachers' reactions to children's performance and behaviors, despite evidence that boys' and girls' performance are equivalent (Deaux & Emswiller, 1974).

PRIDE, HUBRIS, AND ACHIEVEMENT

Two Facets of Pride: Authentic and Hubristic Pride

Pride and hubris are considered the emotional responses to success as well as to failure. When success is attributed to the global self, hubris or "pridefulness" occurs. This form of pride is referred to as hubristic pride (Tracy & Robbins, 2007). However, when success is due to children making a task or specific attribution about themselves, they show authentic pride (Tracy & Robbins, 2007). Lewis (1993) among others views authentic pride as adaptive, while hubristic pride maladaptive. Authentic pride in one's success promotes achievement because it is associated with task orientation, and it is this focus on the task that leads to achievement and motivation. Hubristic pride is related to narcissism and its disorders (Lewis, 1995). Although we view pride as a self-conscious emotion, others have argued that it may be considered a primary emotion (Tracy & Robbins, 2006; Tracy, Robins, & Lagattuta, 2005) because it may enhance a person's social status or group acceptance, thus averting social rejection (Leary, Tambor, Terdal, & Downs, 1995). Exactly how a child has knowledge of social status and its position in that status suggests that such an analysis does not rest on cognitive attributional processes.

The physical manifestation of pride is characterized by having an erect posture (i.e., shoulders back and head up), hands often thrown into the air, which is accompanied by a broad smile and comments about success. For example, either pointing at or displaying the results, applauding, and/or a positive statement, such as "aah!" or "I did it!" (Lewis, 1995). In order to experience authentic pride, a sense of personal responsibility is critical in self-evaluation, such as "I won because I practiced for hours" or "I used a good strategy for calculating numbers in my head." The student focuses on the specific behavior leading to the success. As a consequence, a student can identify the means by which they can recreate this rewarding state at a future date. Accordingly, authentic pride has been likened to the construct of achievement motivation (Heckhausen, 1984; Stipek et al., 1992). Also, authentic pride motivates altruism and achievement, while its loss may incite aggression, hostility, relational conflicts, and other antisocial behaviors because it threatens the self (Bushman & Baumeister, 1998).

Hubristic pride is the arrogant form of pride, which is experienced when one assumes an internal responsibility for a success and a global focus on the self. Hubristic pride is a distorted and less authentic view of self (I am the best, and that's why I'm always the winner). These individuals are described as "full of themselves" or conceited, and in extreme cases are associated with grandiosity or narcissism (Morrison, 1989). Although hubristic pride is highly rewarding to the person who is experiencing it, others who are watching view it as painfully unpleasant and off putting. Therefore, hubristic pride appears to be a socially undesirable self-conscious evaluative emotion (Lewis, 2014). Some have argued, however, that hubristic pride may be desirable or advantageous in situations where competitiveness and boastfulness communicate superiority in order to intimidate the competition (Tracy & Robins, 2007). Also, hubristic pride may be part of a dynamic regulatory process or defense mechanism through which narcissistic individuals use to suppress feelings of shame (Lewis, 1992).

There is support for authentic and hubristic pride. Tracy and Robbins (2007) found that authentic pride was associated with words such as accomplished, successful, achieving, fulfilled, self-worth, confident, and productive, while hubristic pride was associated with words such as snobbish, pompous, stuck-up, conceited, egotistical, arrogant, and smug. In terms of personality traits, they found that authentic pride was significantly correlated with extraversion, agreeableness, conscientiousness, and emotional stability, while negatively correlated with proneness to shame. Hubristic pride was associated with shame proneness, but negatively correlated with agreeableness and conscientiousness. It would seem that extraverted, agreeable, and conscientious people tend to experience authentic pride after a success and experience it in everyday life as it relates to effort (unstable, controllable). While self-aggrandizing, shame-prone, disagreeable, and non-conscientious individuals are likely to experience hubristic pride in everyday life as it relates to one's ability (stable, uncontrollable).

Pride and Achievement

Authentic pride is related to achievement constructs such as "efficacy," "mastery," and "personal satisfaction" (Lewis, 2014). Among students from grade K to college, authentic pride is positively correlated to interests, effort invested in studying, elaboration of learning material, self-regulation of learning, and academic performance (Pekrun, 2011). In terms of achievement motivation, authentic pride is linked to mastery goals, while hubristic pride is related to performance goals (Dweck, 1999). Mastery goals are important to student learning because they relate to the joys of learning, such as taking the time to understand and process class materials and emphasizing effort on improving one's skills to receive a good grade or achieve mastery (Pekrun, Elliot, & Maier, 2006). As a consequence, the learner experiences joy over the behavior, thought, or feeling well-done (Lewis, 2014).

Children with hubristic pride, however, may have difficulty with interpersonal relationships because they tend to interfere with the wishes, needs, and desires of others. This may lead to interpersonal conflicts and deficits in performance, which affect achievement outcomes. Parents and teachers who praise children too much may lead to global evaluations of success, which can easily turn to shame or the fear of being shamed if they fail (Baumeister, Campbell, Kreuger, & Vohs, 2003; Kamins & Dweck, 1999; Mueller & Dweck, 1998). Hubristic pride can be an addictive emotion that is unrelated to any specific action and thus requires one to redefine success or alter goals. This type of pride emphasizes performance goals, which are concerned about how others evaluate one's performance.

The presence of an audience to judge whether a performance is worthy of pride depends on age. Young children experience pride when others such as parents, teachers, coaches, and peers are present to make evaluative judgments. They feel proud of their accomplishments when they have shown improvements when doing something ("I am getting better at coloring") or if they have reached their goal ("I finally finished building my Lego truck all by myself"). As standards for evaluation are internalized, the presence and judgments of others become less important. Seidner, Stipek, and Feshback (1988) have shown that once children reach second grade, hubristic pride is experienced as a result of comparing their performances and behaviors to other children and that mastery, as a source of authentic pride, appears to decline from Kindergarten to grade six. This is likely due to the competitive nature of the classroom and teachers' comments such as, "Why can't you do as well as Vivian?" Therefore, are parents and teachers moving children way from experiencing authentic pride toward hubristic pride as they get older?

MOVING AWAY FROM SHAME AND PRIDE: HOW TO SUCCEED

Shame in the Classroom

Schools have used a number of pedagogical and behavioral management methods that trigger shame in students (Monroe, 2009; Nathanson, 2000). These methods historically include the dunce cap, ruler slaps, soaps for washing "dirty" mouths, and wooden paddle boards. One of the authors (GVO) recalls her mother's account of a classmate kneeling on a bed of uncooked rice in front of the class while holding two heavy textbooks in each hand with arms outstretched. These older methods have evolved into sending children to time-out corners, shaming them by writing students' names on the board, sending students to the principal's office, and preventing them from participating in school activities.

Students with learning problems or disabilities are subjected to even more shame in the classroom. They are removed from the classrooms for one-on-one instruction or asked to sit near the teacher's desk or in front or back of the classroom. Teachers' use of ability tracking also undermines student's self-concept and exposes their weaknesses to others (Monroe, 2009). No matter what labels are used to separate students according to ability (e.g., Bluebirds, Cardinals, Canaries, or Green Parrots), students can differentiate between the advanced-level group from the beginner's group in academic areas such as reading, math, and writing. Lower ability groupings are found to be typically lower in instructional quality, inhibit the development of critical thinking and problem-solving skills, and are likely to promote shame.

However, according to the Big-Fish-Little-Pond Effect (Marsh & Parker, 1984), how students view their performance in school depends on the ability of other students in the classroom. Goetz, Preckel, Zeidner, and Schleyer (2008) showed that gifted students placed in regular or mixed ability classrooms (big fish in a little pond) are likely to exhibit greater academic self-concept and reduced test anxiety unlike gifted students placed in similar ability classrooms (small fish in a big pond). Moreover, the effect of the peer reference group on academic self-concept hold for both low and high achieving groups and in both regular and gifted classrooms (Zeidner & Schleyer, 1999).

Students from economically disadvantaged and or culturally and/or linguistically diverse backgrounds and immigrant children new to the country are also exposed to many shaming situations in schools (see DeCuir-Gunby & Williams-Johnson, 2014). These students do not live up to the standards, rules, and goals of mainstream society, hence they look and dress differently, have limited English proficiency, and have accents (Shaunessy & McHatton, 2008). Some of these students are subjected to teacher apathy and low teacher expectations, creating a self-fulfilling prophecy (Ferguson, 2003). These students are often referred for disciplinary actions (Fenning & Rose, 2007) and overrepresented in referrals to special education placement, especially African Americans, Hispanics, Native Americans, and Native Alaskans (Artiles, Rueda, Salazar, & Higareda, 2005; U.S. Commission on Civil Rights, 2009). English language learners are consistently found to perform below their peers and are at risk of school failure and dropout (Duran, 2008). School problems are caused by factors beyond learning problems or disabilities (Lesaux, 2006) and may be related to the shame of being different and being considered inferior.

Although there is little research in this area of classroom observation, a powerful producer of shame may be the "language" teachers use in the classroom when interacting with their students (Jenson, Olympia, Farley, & Clark, 2004; Wilson, 2012). Insults, hurtful words and phrases, statements that compare students, and negative evaluative feedback all contribute to shame. Peers also are sources of shame; for example, students laughing at a peer who responds with an incorrect answer or giggling at a student who stumbles on words while reading a passage. Cliques, teasing, and bullying from peers may also contribute to shame, which lead to serious psychological, emotional, and educational consequences (Delara, 2012; Olthof, 2012; Yeager, Trzesniewski, Tirri, Nokelainen, & Dweck, 2011). In sum, shame threatens the social-emotional and academic resilience of students.

Reparation of Shame

Lewis (1995) discussed various ways of recovery from a shameful event. There are a number of methods a student can use to prevent, reduce, or eliminate shame. The simplest method of riding shame is to "own it" and allow shame to dissipate with time. For example, a student can accept that his paper was rejected and put it away in a drawer, but then later look at it again. To prevent shame, students also can use denial, "I didn't want it anyway," after losing a science competition. A student can use confession to reduce shame, such as by saying, "I have to confess that I've never read the book, so I wasn't able to do the assignment." Laughing at oneself or with others at a humiliating situation can also reduce or eliminate shame.

Recovery from prolonged shame, however, involves "rebuilding the self," which includes the process of understanding and gaining awareness of shame, connecting with supportive others, and refocusing from the global self to specific behaviors and tasks. The shaming event, such as a failed test or a negative comment from a teacher, represents for the student a loss of the "ideal self" or self-image. In the process of repairing the "injured" self, the student must recognize that the emotion felt after a failure event is indeed shame by recognizing bodily responses and identifying associated emotions that may mask shame, such as anger, sadness, or denial. For example, a student's body is slumped over with his head looking down, with a need to hide. The student may vacillate between negative self statements such as "I hate this course! The professor hates me," "I just don't have what it takes. So what's the point in continuing," and/or "I can't believe this is happening to me!" Once shame is identified, felt shame leads to an ultimate attempt to deal with the emotion. Some felt shame are appropriate and will help alter behavior in order for the student to move on or progress, while others are inappropriate as in making global attributions of "I am not a good student," which leaves the student paralyzed. In extreme cases, shame may be transformed into rage, grandiosity, and depression. When shame is transformed, it can never be dealt with because shame is unknown to the student, only the consequences of the shame. Nathanson (1992) states that shame can only be seen by the trail it leaves. Possible examples of this include the Columbine High School massacre in 1999 or the Virginia Tech shooting in 2007.

In the process of understanding shame, it is essential that the student "connect" with supportive others, such as teachers, peers, and parents, to prevent from feeling isolated. These supportive others help the student understand the shaming event. Others may support the student by validating the student's beliefs and feelings about the shaming event or by providing insights that challenge the student's belief, leading to a change of perspective. Through awareness, self- reflection, and consideration or integration of others' beliefs into one's own belief system, the student is able to understand what has happened and move toward acceptance of shame.

In the process of acceptance, the student acknowledges and understands the shaming event, therefore "owning it." In owning it, the student takes on the responsibility of doing something about it. For example, "Okay, I failed! Now what can I do to fix it?" In doing so, the focus from the self is shifted toward taking a specific action. This may involve remembering positive behaviors, skills, resources, and strategies that led to past successful outcomes. The student pulls from a variety of resources from utilizing learning and study strategies and/or reaching out to others for tutoring. By focusing on the task or behavior, the student becomes proactive in dealing with the shaming event and a little more skilled at facing similar events in the future. Through action, shame dissipates, and the student moves toward reparation of the injured self.

Paving the Way for Pride

Attributions about the self are learned through socialization and interactions with others. Parents and teachers' use of evaluative feedback has an effect on student motivation and achievement. Alessandri and Lewis (1993) found that Caucasian mothers make different attribution statements according to the gender of their three-year-old children. Mothers were found to make more global attribution statements than fathers, while fathers made more specific behavioral attribution statements. Boys, in general, received more specific attribution statements than girls from both parents. This may explain why males make more specific attribution statements and why females are more likely to blame themselves for failure. Similarly, these findings have also been observed in schools. For boys, teachers made specific and nonintellectual behavioral attributions, such as misbehavior, distraction, or lack of motivation, as causes of poor academic performance. Generally, girls, however, were provided with global attribution statements, such as "You're no good at math" or other statements that suggest a lack of understanding or poor cognitive ability (Dweck & Leggett, 1988).

In order to move away from shame toward pride, parents and teachers must focus on making specific behavioral statements rather than global statements in reaction to both children's successes and failures. Global statements such as "You're so smart!" or "You're the best!" are not conducive to increasing authentic pride but are likely to increase hubristic pride. Rather, using statements that comment on specific behaviors are more productive and useful while saving the self from the downward spiral of negative appraisals and academic disengagement. For example, a teacher can say, "All your hard work and preparations for the test really paid off. Wow, such good planning and perseverance!" Or "That's a very good strategy you used, but it didn't seem to work for this particular problem, can you think of something else you can do in this situation?" This is consistent with research that indicates acknowledgement for effort, strategy, and persistence may allow for a fuller recognition of achievement, which leads toward a mastery orientation (Kamins & Dweck, 1999). Furthermore, school environments that involve providing choice, decision making, peer interaction, peer cooperation, and groups based on interests and needs are likely to espouse a task orientation rather than a focus on ability (Maehr & Midgley, 1991).

Students who are less prone to shame or less likely to experience hubris are goal-directed in their approach to academic setbacks (Turner & Husman, 2008). Teachers and parents can provide learning strategies along with specific evaluative statements to help students focus on what they can do rather than on personal, global inadequacies. Teachers and parents can help students develop study and goal-striving motivation strategies that regulate stressful emotions and perceptions of failure. Study strategies include taking notes in your own words to monitor understanding of materials, making flashcards, and applying information to real-life situations. Students are able to connect current tasks with future goals by using goal-striving motivation strategies, which are task oriented—self thoughts that can bolster self-efficacy. These methods can also be coupled with methods that relieve anxiety, such as deep breathing and listening to calm music. Teachers can guide students' self thoughts to remind themselves of their past goal-oriented strengths. Examples of goal-striving motivation strategies include saying to oneself: "I did this task before and if I get stuck I can ask for help." By recalling past successes and reaching out to others for help or by modifying one's behavior to prevent future occurrences of similar situations, a student can defend against shame as a result of failure.

CLASSROOM APPLICATIONS

The instructional methods used by teachers may have an influence on students' self-attribution. A child-centered approach in early childhood school settings may be more likely to produce pride than a teacher-centered instructional approach. A classroom that is child-centered (constructivist model) emphasizes self-motivation and self-determination in learning by allowing a student to become an active, responsible participant to think, experience, explore, inquire, and search for answers. This approach focuses on a student's needs, abilities, and interests with the teacher as the facilitator of learning. Compared to students in didactic or teacher-centered classrooms, students in child-centered classrooms (high on social climate) rated their abilities higher, had higher expectations for success on academic tasks, selected more challenging math problems, were less dependent on adults for permission and approval, experienced more pride in their accomplishments, and were less anxious about school (Stipek, Feiler, Daniels, & Milburn, 1995). Students in child-centered classrooms were also more likely to choose a school readiness task over another kind of activity, suggesting that they found learning about numbers and letters more interesting than students in didactic programs. For high school students, placement in student-centered general biology classrooms resulted in higher grades and greater comprehension of materials (Lord, 1997), as well as higher level thinking skills and increased interest in the subject matter (Burrowes, 2003).

Self-Brown and Matthews (2003) found that teacher instructional methods and evaluation approaches also have an influence on the type of achievement goals that students set, which promote pride. Classrooms that used a contingency-contract approach in their study, where students determined their achievement goals and are evaluated individually, were significantly more mastery goal oriented by setting more learning goals than performance goals. This approach may reduce the threat of failure because students evaluate themselves as either having met or not met their own goals. If students meet their goals, this can result in pride and personal satisfaction. If they have not, students are able to reconsider, revise, or change their goals in order to achieve success.

In contrast, classrooms using a token economy-based approach in the study, where students were rewarded for meeting normative standards, set significantly more performance goals than learning goals—that is, they were performance oriented. Students in these classrooms were usually not motivated by the same tokens, preferred less challenging tasks, worked to please the teacher, and depended on others to evaluate their work. This type of approach is also troublesome for students who have learning difficulties because these students are likely to feel frustrated and helpless for not meeting standards placed on them, hence shame is inevitable. Therefore, classrooms that emphasize individual-set goals and effort in this study lead to better learning strategies, motivation, self-evaluation of ability and competence (Self-Brown & Mathews, 2003).

To conclude, shame producing failures are inevitable. However, the home and educational environments can be modified to prevent and reduce shame by providing specific behavioral attribution statements that help students move forward in place of global evaluative feedback that leaves students paralyzed or helpless. Specific attribution statements are strengthened by providing students with study, goal-striving motivation, and anxiety-reducing strategies. The classroom environment can also be modified so that students create their own goals, thereby increasing goal-directed behaviors, motivation, competence, and pride in one's accomplishments. Just like Sarah's, Janet's, and Tom's experiences in the beginning of this chapter, teachers who provide words of encouragement and help students believe in themselves have a profound effect on their destiny.

REFERENCES

Alessandri, S. M., & Lewis, M. (1993). Parental evaluation and its relation to shame and pride in young children. *Sex Roles, 29*, 335–343.

Alessandri, S. M., & Lewis, M. (1996). Differences in pride and shame in maltreated and nonmaltreated preschoolers. *Child Development, 67*, 1857–1869.

Artiles, A. J., Rueda, R., Salazar, J. J., & Higareda, I. (2005). Within-group diversity in minority disproportionate representation: English language learners in urban school districts. *Exceptional Children, 71*, 283–300.

Ashby, F. G., Isen, A. M., & Turken, A. U. (1999) A neuropsychological theory of positive affect and its influence on cognition. *Psychological Review, 106*, 529–550.

Baumeister, R. F., Campbell, J. D., Kreuger, J. I., & Vohs, K. D. (2003). Does high self-esteem cause better performance, interpersonal success, happiness, or healthier lifestyles? *Psychological Science in the Public Interest, 4*, 1–44.

Brackett, M. A., & Rivers, S. E. (2014). Transforming students' lives with social and emotional learning. In R. Pekrun & L. Linnenbrink-Garcia (Eds.), *International handbook of emotions in education* (pp. 368–388). New York, NY: Taylor & Francis.

Burrowes, P. A. (2003). A student-centered approach to teaching general biology that really works: Lord's constructive model put to a test. *The Americal Biology Teacher, 65*, 491–502.

Bushman, B. J., & Baumeister, R. F. (1998). Threatened egotism narcissism, self esteem, and direct and displaced aggression: Does self-love or self-hate lead to violence? *Journal of Personality and Social Psychology, 75*, 219–229.

Clore, G. L., & Huntsinger, J. R. (2007). How emotions inform judgment and regulate thought. *Trends in Cognitive Science, 11*, 393–399.

Covington, M. V., & Omelich, C. L. (1979). Effort: The double-edged sword in school achievement. *Journal of Educational Psychology, 71*, 169–182.

Covington, M. V., & Omelich, C. L. (1985). Ability and effort valuation among failure-avoiding and failure-accepting students. *Journal of Educational Psychology, 77*, 446–459.

Darwin, C. (1872). *The expression of the emotions in man and animals.* London, England: John Murray.

Deaux, K., & Emswiller, T. (1974) Explanations of successful performance on sex-linked tasks: What is skill for male is luck for the female. *Journal of Personality and Social Psychology, 29*, 80–85.

DeCuir-Gunby, J., & Williams-Johnson, M. (2014). The influence of culture on emotions: Implications for education. In R. Pekrun & L. Linnenbrink-Garcia (Eds.), *International handbook of emotions in education* (pp. 539–557). New York, NY: Taylor & Francis.

Delara, E. W. (2012). Why adolescents don't disclose incidents of bullying and harassment. *Journal of School Violence, 11*, 288–305.

Diener, C. I., & Dweck, C. S. (1978). An analysis of learned helplessness: Continuous changes in performance, strategy, and achievement cognitions following failure. *Journal of Personality and Social Psychology, 36*, 451–462.

Diener, C. I., & Dweck, C. S. (1980). An analysis of learned helplessness II: The processing of success. *Journal of Personality and Social Psychology, 39*, 940–952.

Duran, R. P. (2008). Assessing English-language learners' achievement. *Review of Research in Education, 32*, 292–327.

Dweck, C. S. (1999) *Self theories: Their Role in motivation, personality and development.* Philadelphia, PA: Taylor & Francis.

Dweck, C. S., Chiu, C., & Hong, Y. (1995). Implicit theories and their role in judgments and reactions: A world from two perspectives. *Psychological Inquiry, 6*, 267–285.

Dweck, C. S., & Leggett, E. L. (1988). A Social-cognitive approach to motivation and personality. *Psychological Review, 95*, 256–272.

Dweck, C. S., & Reppucci, N. (1973). Learned helplessness and reinforcement responsibility in children. *Journal of Personality and Social Psychology, 25*, 109–116.

Eccles, J. (1997). School and family effect on the ontogeny of children's interests, self perception, and activity choices. In J. Jacobs (Ed.), *Nebraska symposium on motivation* (vol. 40, pp. 145–208). Lincoln, NE: Lincoln University of Nebraska Press.

Ekman, P., Friesen, W. V., & Ellsworth, W. V. (1972). *Emotion in the human face: Guidelines for research and an integration of findings.* New York, NY: Pergamon.

Elliot, E. S. & Dweck, C. S. (1988). Goals: An approach to motivation and achievement. *Journal of Personal Social Psychology, 54,* 5–12.

Elliot, A., & Dweck, C. S. (2005). Competence and motivation. In A. Elliot & C. S. Dweck (Eds.), *Handbook of competence and motivation* (pp. 3–12). New York, NY: The Guilford Press.

Else-Quest, N. M., Higgins, A., Allison, C., & Morton, L. C. (2012). Gender differences in self-conscious emotional experience: A meta-analysis. *Psychological Bulletin, 138,* 947–981

Fenning, P., & Rose, J. (2007). Overrepresentation of African American students in exclusionary discipline: The role of school policy. *Urban Education, 42,* 536–559.

Ferguson, R. F. (2003). Teachers perceptions and expectations and the black-white test score gap. *Urban Education, 38,* 460–507.

Fredrickson, B. L. (2001). The role of positive emotions in positive psychology: The broaden-and-build theory of positive emotions. *American Psychologists, 56,* 218–226.

Goetz, T., Preckel, F., Zeidner, M., & Schleyer E. (2008). Big fish in big ponds: A multivariable analysis of test anxiety and achievement in special gifted classes. *Anxiety, Stress and Coping: An International Journal, 21,* 185–198.

Gold, J., Sullivan, M. W., & Lewis, M. (2011). The relation between abuse and violent delinquency: The conversion of shame to blame in juvenile offenders. *Child Abuse and Neglect, 33,* 459–467.

Heckhausen, H. (1984). Emergent achievement behavior: Some early developments. In J. Nicholls (Eds.). *The development of achievement motivation* (pp. 1–32). Greenwich, CT: JAI Press.

Izard, C. E. (1995). *Maximally discriminative movement system* (Rev.). Newark, DE: University of Delaware.

Jenson, W., Olympia, D., Farley, M., & Clark, E. (2004). Positive psychology and externalizing students in a sea of negativity. *Psychology in the Schools, 41,* 51–66.

Kamins, M. L., & Dweck, C. S. (1999). Person versus process praise and criticism: Implications for contingent self-worth and coping. *Developmental Psychology, 3,* 835–847.

Kaufman, G. (1992). *Shame: The power of caring.* 3rd ed. Rochester, NY: Schenkman Books.

Kochanska, G. (1991). Socialization and temperament in the development of guilt and conscience. *Child Development, 62,* 1379–1392.

Leary, M. R., Tambor, E. S., Terdal, S. K., & Downs, D. L. (1995). Self-esteem as an interpersonal monitor: The sociometer hypothesis. *Journal of Personality and Social Psychology, 68,* 518–530.

Lesaux, N. K. (2006). Building consensus: Future direction for research on English language learners at risk for learning disabilities. *Teachers College Record, 108,* 2406–2438.

Lewis, H. B. (1971). *Shame and guilt in neurosis.* New York, NY: International Universities Press.

Lewis, M. (1977). Early social-emotional development and its relevance for curriculum. *Merrill-Palmer Quarterly, 23,* 279–286.

Lewis, M. (1992). The self in self-conscious emotions. A commentary. In D. Stipek, S. Recchia, & S. McClintic (Eds.). Self-evaluation in young children. *Monographs of the Society for Research in Child Development, 57,* (1, Serial No. 226, pp. 85–95).

Lewis, M. (1993). The development of deception. In M. Lewis & C. Saarni (Eds.), *Lying and deception in everyday life* (pp. 90–105). New York, NY: Guilford Press.

Lewis, M. (1995). *Shame: The exposed self.* New York, NY: Free Press.

Lewis, M. (1997). *Altering fate: Why the past does not predict the future.* New York, NY: Guilford Press.

Lewis, M. (2000). Self-conscious emotions: Embarrassment, pride, shame, and guilt. In M. Lewis & J. Haviland-Jones (Eds.), *Handbook of emotions* (2nd ed., pp. 623–636). New York, NY: Guilford Press.

Lewis, M. (2003). The role of shame and the self. *Social Research, Winter, 70,* 1181–1204.

Lewis, M. (2008). The emergence of human emotions. In M. Lewis, J. Haviland-Jones, & L. Feldman Barrett (Eds.), *Handbook of emotions, 3rd Edition* (pp. 304–319). New York, NY: Guilford Press.

Lewis, M. (2014). *The rise of consciousnesses and the development of emotion life..* New York, NY: Guilford Press.

Lewis, M., Alessandri, S. M., & Sullivan, M. W. (1992). Differences in pride and shame as a function of children's gender and task difficulty. *Child Development, 63,* 630–638.

Lewis, M. & Brooks, J. (1974). Self, others and fear: Infants' reactions to people. In M. Lewis & L. Rosenblum (Eds.), *The origins of fear: The origins of behavior* (Vol. 2, pp. 195–227). New York, NY: Wiley.

Lewis, M., Haviland-Jones, J. M., & Barrett, L. (2008). *Handbook of emotions* (3rd edition). New York, NY: Guilford Press.

Lewis, M., & Michaelson, L. (1983). *Children's emotion and moods.* New York, NY: Plenum Press.

Lewis, M., & Ramsay, D. (1995). Developmental change in infants' response to stress. *Child Development, 66,* 657–670.

Lewis, M., & Ramsay, D. (2004). Development of self-recognition, personal pronoun use, and pretend play during the 2nd year. *Child Development, 75,* 1821–1831.

Lewis, M., Stranger, C., Sullivan, M. W., & Barone, P. (1991). Changes in embarrassment as a function of age, sex and situation. *British Journal of Developmental Psychology, 9,* 485–492.

Lewis, M., & Sullivan, M. W. (2005). The development of self-conscious emotions. In A. Elliot & C. S. Dweck (Eds.), *Handbook of competence and motivation* (pp.185–201). New York, NY: The Guilford Press.

Lewis, M., Sullivan, M.W., Stanger, C., & Weiss, M. (1989). Self-development and self-conscious emotions. *Child Development, 25,* 439–443.

Lord, T. R. (1997). A comparison between traditional and constructivist teaching in college biology. *Innovative Higher Education, 21,* 197–216.

Maehr, M. L., & Midgley, C. (1991). Enhancing student motivation: A schoolwide approach. *Educational Psychologist, 26,* 399–427.

Marsh, H. W., & Parker, J. W. (1984). Determinants of student self-concept: Is it better to be a relatively large fish in a small pond even if you don't learn to swim as well? *Journal of Personality and Social Psychology, 47,* 213–231.

Matthews, T. A, Sullivan, M. W., & Lewis, M. (2014). *Young children's self-evaluation and emotional behavior during achievement tasks.* Manuscript submitted for publication.

McGregor, H. A., & Elliot, A. J. (2005). The shame of failure: Examining the link between fear of failure and shame. *Personality and Social Psychology Bulletin, 31,* 218–231.

Monroe, A. (2009). Shame solutions: How shame impacts school-aged children and what teachers can do to help. *The Educational Forum, 73,* 58–66.

Morrison, A. P. (1989). *Shame: The underside of narcissism.* Hillsdale, NJ: Analytic Press.

Mueller, C. M., & Dweck, C. S. (1998). Praise for intelligence can undermine children's motivation and performance. *Journal of Personality and Social Psychology, 75,* 33–52.

Nathanson, D. L. (1992). *Shame and pride: Affect, sex, and the birth of the self.* New York, NY: Norton.

Nathanson, D. L. (2000, December). The name of the game is shame. Report to the Academic Advisory Council of the National Campaign Against Youth Violence. Washington, DC.

Olthof, T. T. (2012). Anticipated feelings of guilt and shame as predictors of early adolescents' antisocial and prosocial interpersonal behavior. *European Journal of Developmental Psychology, 9,* 371–388.

Parrott, W. G., & Spackman, M. P. (2000). Emotion and memory. In M. Lewis & J. M. Haviland-Jones (Eds.), *Handbook of emotions* (2nd ed., pp. 476–490). New York, NY: Guilford Press.

Pekrun, R. (2011). Emotions as drivers of learning and cognitive development. In R. A. Calvo & S. K. D'Mello (Eds.), *New perspectives on affect and learning technologies: Vol. 3.Explorations in the learning sciences, instructional systems, and performance technologies* (pp. 23–39). New York, NY:Springer.

Pekrun, R., Elliot, A. J., & Maier, M. A. (2006). Achievement goals and discrete achievement emotions: A theoretical model and prospective test. *Journal of Educational Psychology, 98,* 583–597.

Russell, D., & McCauly, E. (1986). Causal Attributions, causal dimensions, and affective reactions to success and failure. *Journal of Personality and Social Psychology, 50,* 1174–1185.

Seidner, L. B., Stipek, D. J., & Feshbach, N. D. (1988, April). A developmental analysis of elementary school-aged children's concepts of pride and embarrassment. *Child Development, 59,* 367–377.

Self-Brown, S. R., & Mathews, S., II. (2003, November/December). Effects of classroom structure on student achievement goal orientation. *The Journal of Educational Research, 97,* 106–111.

Shaunessy, E., & McHatton, P. A. (2008). Urban students? perceptions of teachers: Views of students in general, special, and honors education. *Urban Review, 41,* 486–503.

Smiley, P. A., and Dweck, C. S. (1994). Individual difference in achievement goals among young children. *Child Development, 65,* 1723–1743.

Stipek, D., Feiler, R., Daniels, D., & Milburn, S. (1995). Effects of different instructional approaches on young children's achievement. *Child Development, 66,* 209–223.

Stipek, D., Recchia, S., & McClintic, S. (1992). Self evaluation in young children. *Monographs of the Society for Research in Child Development, 57*(1, serial no. 226), 1–84.

Tangney, J., & Dearing, R. (2002) *Shame or guilt.* New York, NY: Guilford Press.

Thompson, T., Altmann, R., & Davidson, J. (2004). Shame-proneness and achievement behavior. *Personality and Individual Differences, 36,* 613–627.

Tomkins. S. S. (1963). *Affect, imagery, consciousness* (Vol. 2). New York, NY: Springer.

Tracy, J. L., & Robins, R. W. (2007). The psychological structure of pride: A tale of two facets. *Journal of Personality and Social Psychology, 92,* 506–525.

Tracy, J. L., Robins, R. W., & Lagattuta, K. H. (2005). Can children recognize the pride expression? *Emotion, 5,* 251–257.

Tracy, J. P., & Robins, R. W. (2003) Death of (narcissistic) salesman: An integrative model of fragile self esteem. *Psychological inquiry, 15,* 103–125.

Tracy, J. P., & Robins, R. W. (2006) Appraisal antecedents of shame and guilt: Support for a theoretical model. *Personality and Social Psychology Bulletin, 32,* 1339–1351.

Turner, J. E., & Husman, J. (2008). Emotional and cognitive self-regulation following academic shame. *Journal of Advanced Academics, 20,* 138–173.

U.S. Commission on Civil Rights. (2009). *Minorities in special education: A briefing before the United States Commission on Civil Rights.* Retrieved from www.usccr.gov/pubs/MinoritiesinSpecialEducation.pdf

Weiner, B. (1974). *Achievement motivation and attribution theory.* Morristown, NJ: General Learning Press.

Weiner, B. (1977). Attribution and affect: Comments on Sohn's Critique. *Journal of Educational Psychology, 69,* 506–511.

Weiner, B. (2010). The development of an attribution-based theory of motivation: A history of ideas. *Educational Psychologist, 45,* 28–36.

Weiner, B., & Kukla, A. (1970). An attributional analysis of achievement motivation. *Journal of Personality and Social Psychology, 15,* 1–20.

Weiner, B., Russel, D., & Lerman, D. (1978). Affective consequences of causal ascriptions. In J. Harvey, W. Ickles, & R. Kidd (Eds.), *New directions in attribution research* (Vol. 2., pp. 59–90). Hillsdale, NJ: Lawrence Erlbaum.

Weiner, B., Russel, D., & Lerman, D. (1979). The cognition-emotion process in achievement-related contexts. *Journal of personality and Social Psychology, 37,* 1211–1220.

Wilson, M. (2012). What do we say when a child says . . . "Look at my drawing!" *Educational Leadership, 69,* 52–56.

Yeager, D. S., Trzesniewski, K. H., Tirri, K., Nokelainen, P., & Dweck, C. S. (2011). Adolescents' implicit theories predict desire for vengeance after peer conflicts: Correlational and experimental evidence. *Developmental Psychology, 47,* 1090–1107.

Zeidner, M. & Schleyer, E. J. (1999). The big-fish-little-pond effect for academic self concept, test anxiety, and school grades in gifted children. *Contemporary Educational Psychology, 24,* 305–329.

Zins, J. E., Weissberg, R. P., Wang, M. C., & Walberg, H. J. (Eds.). (2004). *Building academic success through social and emotional learning: What does the research say?* New York, NY: Teachers College Press.

14

ANXIETY IN EDUCATION

Moshe Zeidner, University of Haifa

Anxiety has figured prominently in the literature as one of the most ubiquitous and researched emotions in the educational arena. In fact, school-aged individuals are frequently exposed to a myriad of stressful and anxiety-evoking stimuli (parental pressures for high achievement, classroom competition for high grades, experiences of frustration and failure, teacher disapproval, peer conflict, social isolation and rejection, bullying, verbal aggression, etc.) at practically every level of their educational experience (Schutz & Pekrun, 2007). The growth of high stakes testing coupled with an audit culture in many Western school systems, characterized by performance and accountability pressures, publicized test scores, and high target standards, has prompted a renewed focus on the consequences of school assessments, such as evaluative anxiety (Putwain, 2008). Likewise, college students are often bombarded with a myriad of stressors, including exposure to novel and challenging experiences in a low control academic environment, high competition, social pressure to excel, and the need to make critical career and social choices. Indeed, even a bright high school student may be unable to adjust to the increased demands for self-initiative and autonomy in the transition to the demanding academic environment of college (Perry, Hladkyj, Pekrun, & Pelletier, 2001).

Clearly, many students have the potential to do well in educational settings but perform poorly because of their debilitating levels of anxiety, thus limiting educational or vocational development. The loss to society of the full contribution of potentially capable students through anxiety-related distress and somatic ailments as well as underachievement and failure at school constitutes an important problem for educational practitioners.

CHAPTER GOALS AND STRUCTURE

This chapter discusses current thinking and research on anxiety in educational contexts. Although a wide array of particular forms of anxiety have been discussed in the literature (e.g., school phobias, math and computer anxiety, language anxiety, willingness to communicate anxiety, social anxiety, sports anxiety), due to space constraints, I focus my discussion on the broad manifestations of evaluative anxiety in educational settings. I also draw liberally upon the general anxiety literature in surveying the nature, antecedents, consequences, and treatment of anxiety in educational settings. Following a brief historical and conceptual overview, I survey a number of conceptual models and then present some of the distal and proximal determinants of anxiety. I then assess evaluative anxiety and the anxiety-performance interface. Following a discussion of individual differences in anxiety, a number of critical clinical parameters are then surveyed. I conclude by presenting some promising directions for future research.

HISTORICAL AND CONCEPTUAL BACKDROP FOR ANXIETY RESEARCH

Anxiety, as a basic human emotion, refers to a loosely coupled ensemble of cognitive, affective, somatic arousal, and behavioral components, evoked in response to mental representations of future threat or danger in the environment. The *Diagnostic and Statistical Manual of Mental Disorders*, Fifth Edition (DSM-5; American Psychiatric Association, 2013) views *anxiety* as an anticipation of future danger or misfortune, which is often associated with muscle tension and vigilance in preparation for future danger and cautious or avoidant behaviors. The term seems to have been derived from the Indo-Germanic root, angh, which also appears in the Greek, and means a feeling of tightness or constriction under duress. Related words, such as anguish and anger, come from the same root.

Prior to 1950 there was relatively little systematic empirical research on anxiety, particularly in educational settings. Among the factors contributing to the scant research on anxiety were: the complexity and multidimensionality of the phenomena, the ambiguity and vagueness in theoretical conceptions of anxiety, the lack of appropriate measuring instruments, and ethical problems associated with inducing anxiety in laboratory settings. However, since the 1950s, studies of human anxiety have appeared in the psychological, educational, and psychiatric literatures with increasing regularity. The anxiety construct was dramatically advanced by a number of important conceptual distinctions, discussed below, which helped refine thinking and research in the area.

One useful distinction, originally introduced by Raymond Cattell (1950) and popularized by Charles Spielberger (1972), differentiates between anxiety as a relatively stable personality *trait* and anxiety as a more transitory *state* reaction to specific ego-threatening situations. Thus, state anxiety is a palpable, temporary reaction to a stressful event characterized by subjective feelings of tension, apprehension, nervousness, and worry, and by activation or arousal of the nervous system. Although anxiety state reactions are transitory, they can recur when evoked by appropriate stimuli, and they may endure over time when the evoking situation persists. Trait-anxiety, by contrast, refers to relatively stable individual differences in anxiety-proneness—that is, to differences between people in the tendency to perceive stressful situations as dangerous and threatening and to respond to these situations with varying amounts of state anxiety. Trait anxiety may be regarded as a temporal cross-section in the stream-of-life of a person, with specific anxiety reactions construed as expressions of trait anxiety.

A particularly useful conceptual distinction was advanced by Liebert and Morris (1967), differentiating between *worry* and *emotionality* components of evaluative anxiety. This distinction proved to be instrumental in shifting anxiety theory and research, mainly in the area of test anxiety research, toward a more cognitive orientation. Specifically, the cognitive component of anxiety— that is, worry—was viewed primarily as a cognitive concern about the consequences of the stressful situation. It is the individual's perception of the degree of threat to his sense of adequacy and merit that affects the level of the cognitive component (Covington, 1992). By contrast, the affective component of anxiety— that is, emotionality—was construed as perceptions of autonomic reactions evoked by stress. These two components are revealed to be empirically distinct, though correlated, and worry relates more strongly to cognitive performance than does emotionality.

Lazarus's transactional theory of stress and coping (Lazarus, 1999; Lazarus & Folkman, 1984) provided a fundamental conceptual framework for the analysis of stress, both general and evaluative anxiety, and coping. According to this framework, stress and emotions are primarily about person–environment relationships. Thus, the quality and intensity of an emotion are products of actual or anticipated adaptational encounters with the environment, which are appraised by the individual as having either positive or negative significance for well-being. Underlying each emotion are core themes, which refer to personal meanings attributed to events (e.g., harm, loss, threat, benefit). Any evoked emotion reflects a high-level synthesis of several appraisals relating to the individual's adaptational status in the current environment. The core theme in anxiety is *danger* or *threat* to ego or self-esteem, especially when a person is facing an uncertain, existential threat. Emotions, such as anxiety, tell us something of a person's goal hierarchy and belief system and how events in the immediate environment are appraised by the anxious person. Thus, the very presence of anxiety in a stressful encounter is informative because it tells us that an existential threat has not been controlled very well, thus providing the researcher and clinician with critical diagnostic information.

Speilberger (Spielberger & Vagg, 1995) adapted Lazarus's transactional model specifically to the study of anxiety in general and evaluative anxiety in particular. Accordingly, whether or not people who differ in trait anxiety will show corresponding differences in state anxiety depends on the extent to which each of them appraises a specific situation as psychologically dangerous or threatening, and this is influenced by each individual's constitution and past experiences (Trait anxiety × Situation → Perceived Threat → State anxiety).

I now move on to discuss in greater detail a number of conceptual models that inform research on anxiety in general and evaluative anxiety in particular.

KEY CONCEPTUAL ISSUES AND THEORETICAL MODELS OF ANXIETY

A plethora of conceptual models of anxiety (psychodynamic, developmental, motivational, cognitive-attentional, self-merit, self-regulation, goal-orientation) have been proposed in the literature to account for the phenomenology of anxiety, its antecedents, and cognitive and behavioral consequences (see Zeidner & Matthews, 2011, for a recent review). I suffice by presenting two contemporary state-of-the-art models of anxiety.

Interactional Model of Anxiety

The interactional model of stress and anxiety (Endler & Parker, 1992) assumes that the dynamic interaction among personal traits (i.e., trait anxiety) and the characteristics of situations (i.e., social-evaluative, physical harm, ambiguous) determine situational anxiety in a particular context. This model identifies four different potentially stressful environmental contexts—that is, daily routine, social evaluation, ambiguity, and physical danger, as sources of stress. Comparably, this model identifies the same four isomorphic facets of trait anxiety. Furthermore, two facets of state anxiety—that is, worry and emotionality, are distinguished. The differential hypothesis of the interactional model (cf. Endler & Parker, 1992) postulates that state anxiety will be experienced in a given situation when there is a congruency or fit between the nature of a person's vulnerability (e.g., high social evaluation) and the nature of the situation (e.g., important final exam).

The differential hypothesis was supported by Zeidner (1998) in a study conducted among 198 Israeli college students preparing for midterm exams. It was predicted that significant differences in state anxiety would be found between high versus low social evaluative trait-anxious students in evaluative conditions, while at the same time, non-significant differences in state anxiety would be observed between high versus low social evaluative trait-anxious students under neutral conditions. Students were assessed for anxiety and coping during two phases: (a) a neutral phase, in which students were assessed during midsemester and (b) an evaluative phase, in which students were assessed during an evaluative period, prior to midterm exams. State anxiety and situational coping served as criterion measures. Overall, the evidence supports the differential hypothesis of the interactional model of anxiety. Thus, any account of determination of coping and anxiety in test situations needs to consider individual difference variables and situational variables (Zeidner, 1998).

Self-Regulation Model

Carver and Scheier (1991) proposed a control-system self-regulation model of anxiety in order to better understand the nature of anxiety, mainly in evaluative contexts, and its impact on human performance. This model is based on the assumption that intentional goal-directed behavior in humans displays the functional characteristics of a feedback control system (Carver & Scheier, 1988a, 1988b, 2014). Accordingly, people establish goals and standards for themselves, which they use as reference points in guiding and monitoring their behavior. Present behaviors are continuously sensed and brought to mind and then compared against situationally salient reference values and goals. Any observed discrepancies encountered between present behaviors or states and salient reference values or behavioral standards are handled by adjusting behavior in the direction of the latter.

The basic unit in this suggested cybernetic model is a feedback loop. A feedback loop refers to a sensed value—for example, consider the student realizing that today is Friday, March 23rd, and he has just begun his term paper; this state of affairs is then compared to a reference value or standard—for example, the lecturer's request to "Have the paper submitted by Monday, March 26th." Whenever people consistently move towards salient reference values they use to guide behaviors, they manifest the functions of a negative feedback loop, which is designed to bridge the gap between intended and actual qualities of behavior. The control system makes adjustments, if necessary, to reduce the discrepancy by shifting the sensed value in the direction of the standard ("Finish up the paper in four days"). However, a great many circumstances exist in which people encounter impediments and are therefore unable to make desired adjustments in their behavior in order to match behavior to goals. These impediments toward reaching the goal, such as skill deficits, serious doubts about self-adequacy or efficacy, and situational constraints, tend to be anxiety evoking (Carver & Scheier, 1990). Anxiety states are viewed as a common obstacle to goal attainment, thus generating further anxiety. A number of studies by Carver and his coworkers have provided empirical support for their model (Carver, Peterson, Follansbee, & Scheier, 1983; Carver & Scheier, 1984; Carver, Scheier, & Klahr, 1987).

It is underscored that whereas no single theoretical perspective on anxiety at present can readily account for the complex and multifaceted nature of anxiety, these models have shaped subsequent research; understanding these theoretical approaches is useful for advancing the field. Next, I delve into the nature of anxiety in the classroom.

EVALUATIVE ANXIETY IN EDUCATIONAL SETTINGS

A host of different types of anxiety may be relevant to specific educational settings (test anxiety, math and computer anxiety, social anxiety, communication and second language anxiety, dating anxiety, sports anxiety, etc.). These forms of anxiety are frequently encountered in education and share the prospect of personal evaluation in real or imagined social situations, particularly when a student perceives a low likelihood of obtaining satisfactory evaluations from others (Leitenberg, 1990; Zeidner & Matthews, 2005). Anxiety researchers accept that individuals differ in their susceptibility to anxiety in different contexts. Below, I briefly discuss test anxiety—the most salient form of anxiety researched in educational contexts.

Test Anxiety

When one considers the many uses of tests in our culture, their high stakes, and the numerous ways in which they can determine the lives of people who take them, it comes as no great surprise that tests and testing situations often evoke anxiety reactions in many students (Cassady, 2010). Recent examinations of the prevalence for test anxiety suggest estimates close to 25%–40% of the population. Higher prevalence rates have consistently been reported for females and ethnic minorities (Carter, Williams, & Silverman, 2008; Putwain, 2007). Early in life, many children in our culture become test-oriented and test anxious.

Test-anxious behavior is typically evoked when a person believes that their intellectual, motivational, and social capabilities are taxed or exceeded by demands stemming from the test or evaluative situation (Reeve, Bonaccio, & Charles, 2008). Test-anxious students interpret a wide range of situations as evaluative and react with cognitive concern and preoccupation with past failure and future negative consequences (Wine, 1980; Zeidner, 2010). These students have been reported to manifest a host of deficits in information processing during encoding, processing, and retrieval of information (Cassady, 2004). During assessment sessions, test-anxious students are reported to suffer from heightened emotional arousal, worry excessively about exam failure, suffer from cognitive interference and task-irrelevant thoughts, and are highly susceptible to distraction (Zeidner, 2010). These self-related cognitions and interfering thoughts preempt the examinee's attentional resources, which could have been used for task-relevant mental activities. Also, due to their negative self-schemata, high test-anxious students constantly perceive a threat to their ego; they are said to be biased in processing more self-detrimental than self-enhancing information in test situations (Wong, 2008).

In my own theorizing (e.g., Zeidner & Matthews, 2005), I have emphasized the distinction between test anxiety as an attribute of the person and as a dynamic process. From the first perspective, dispositional test anxiety may be construed as a *contextualized personality trait*. Accordingly, test anxiety refers to the individual's disposition to react with extensive worry, intrusive thoughts, mental disorganization, tension, and physiological arousal when exposed to evaluative contexts or situations (Spielberger, Anton, & Bedell, 1976). The more transient state expressions of anxiety may be assessed separately from the more stable trait. From the second, process-oriented perspective, test anxiety depends on the reciprocal interaction of a number of distinct elements at play in the ongoing stressful encounter between a person and an evaluative situation (Zeidner, 1998). These elements include: the evaluative context, individual differences in vulnerability (trait anxiety), threat perceptions, appraisals and reappraisals, state anxiety, coping patterns, and adaptive outcomes. Events that elicit test anxiety consist of a number of distinct temporal phases, including preparation, confrontation, anticipation, and resolution (Carver & Scheier, 1989; Zeidner, 1998). In addition, high test anxiety has been shown to accompany lower study skills and academic acumen (Reeve et al., 2008). Many test-anxious students are also reported to experience deficits in study skills and test taking, with poor preparation a major catalyst for anxiety in evaluative situations (Zeidner, 1998). Evaluative situations appear to be particularly detrimental to the performance of students low in perceived competence (Van Yperen, 2007).

Recent research suggests that test anxiety is associated with detrimental perceptions and behaviors in all phases of the learning-testing cycle (Cassady, 2004). During the test preparation stage, students experience an inability to employ effective study skills, to encode and store information and develop conceptual representation of core content during the test preparation phase, and monitor test preparation. In addition, they experience a tendency to adopt performance-avoidance goals, driven by a fragile or low self-efficacy. During the test performance phase, students experience worry, emotionality, and anxiety blockage, failures at retrieval, distractibility, poor cue-utilization, and decreased performance.

Discussions of test anxiety in the literature are commonly guilty of a "uniformity myth," conveying the impression that test anxiety is a rather homogeneous or unidimensional category. However, under the assumption that test anxiety is a multidimensional and multidetermined phenomenon, it stands to reason that a variety of different types of test-anxious examinees may be identified (Zeidner, 2007). This simple fact is often overlooked when writers present theory and research relating to the "test-anxious" student—typically treated as a uniform category. Some examinees may be anxious in test situations because they have high motivation to succeed on academic tasks given the likelihood of failure, some may have poor study or test-taking skills, some may be anxious because they have low intellectual ability, some tend to be perfectionist overachievers and will be dissatisfied with anything less than a perfect score, while others are anxious because they fail to meet social expectations or fear parental punishment.

DETERMINANTS OF ANXIETY

For the purposes of our discussion, it is useful to distinguish between *distal* and *proximal* antecedents of anxiety (Zeidner, 1998). *Distal* factors would include biological givens and environmental factors (e.g., specific patterns of the parent–child relationship, preschool and early school experiences, cumulative success and failure experiences, etc.), which contribute more indirectly to anxiety reactions as responses to stressful or threatening conditions. They are indirect in the sense that they are the factors that have their major initial impact as antecedents of anxiety in the early years of life, although their influence continues to be felt throughout life. By contrast, *proximal* antecedents are those factors that are specific to the stressful situation and directly responsible for anxiety reactions in specific settings. For example, certain contextual factors, such as school atmosphere, subject difficulty, time pressure to complete assignments, and the like, would appear to be proximal factors in the development of anxiety.

Distal Factors

In the paragraphs to follow, I discuss two key distal factors in the development of anxiety: (a) biology and (b) family environment and early socialization.

Biological Factors

Current research points to a meaningful genetic component underlying the development of trait anxiety, with heredity shown to contribute about half of the variance in explaining individual differences in the major personality factor of neuroticism, or its midlevel trait expression, trait anxiety (Eysenck, 1992). Comparably, two studies (Eley, Bolton, O'Connor, Perrin, Smith, & Plomin, 2003; van Beijsterveldt, Verhulst, Molenaar, & Boomsma, 2004), using large twin registry samples (n = 4,564 and 7,600), report heritability estimates around .50 for anxiety problems in children. Taken together, these studies suggest that about 50% of the observed variance in trait anxiety can be accounted for by genetic factors. Thus, it is a plausible hypothesis that individuals are born with a basic "wired in" propensity to react with increased arousal and elevated worry when confronted with stressful conditions. At the same time, heredity is much less than 100%, demonstrating the important role of the environment in anxiety development. Further, studies show that the nonshared environment (biological and social environmental influences that affect one sibling but not another) might account for a substantial proportion of additional variance of trait anxiety (van Beijsterveldt et al., 2004).

In addition, anxiety may be influenced by the *interaction* of genes and environment. Genes may influence how the brain develops in response to environmental threats during childhood. As noted by Caspi et al. (2003), genes do not directly cause anxiety or anxiety disorders but rather serve as a form of vulnerability to environmental stress of pathology. The diathesis x stress model posits an interaction between stressful conditions and personal vulnerability (diathesis) in precipitating maladaptive outcomes. In keeping with this model, trait anxiety may be expressed across different threatening situations as a function of traumatic or stressful life experiences in interaction with genetic vulnerability (Lau, Gregory, Goldwin, Pine, & Eley, 2007).

Furthermore, current research suggests that anxiety is not localized in any single specific brain structure or neural circuit. Instead, several cortico-limbic neural structures working in a parallel and holistic manner subserve the experience of normal anxiety and support the neural circuits underlying the pathophysiology of anxiety disorders. These include the amygdala (LeDoux, 1996; Panksepp, 1998), the septo-hippocampal circuit (Gray & McNaughton, 2003), the interior and medial hypothalamus (Panksepp, 1998), and cingulum (Eysenck, 1967).

Biologically based temperament may play an important role in the development of anxiety. Thus, early work on inhibition (Kagan, Reznick, & Snidman, 1988) linked the behavioral inhibition feature of temperament to excessive reactivity of the sympathetic nervous system in response to novel stimuli. A longitudinal study by Rende (1993) demonstrated that higher levels of negative emotionality in infancy and early childhood were significantly related to mother's reports of their children's anxiety and depression at age seven. Follow-ups of inhibited toddlers and young children into late childhood and adolescence suggest that early behavioral inhibition is more specifically related to social anxiety (Biederman et al., 2001). Regrettably, there is very little work focusing directly on the neurobiological substrata of test anxiety; future research is clearly warranted in this important area.

Family Environment and Primary Socialization

Researchers studying anxiety and test anxiety have emphasized the importance of family influences in interaction with temperament in understanding the developmental background of children's disposition to experience anxiety (Degnan, Almas, & Fox, 2010). It is now readily apparent that early childhood experiences play a major role in determining individual differences in trait anxiety. Potentially important environmental factors contributing to the development of anxiety include maternal uterine environment, family climate, childrearing patterns, modeling, specific conditioning episodes, and acute and chronic stressors (Krohne, 1992; Rapee, 1997). A review by Van den Bergh, Mulder, Mennes, and Glover (2005) of 14 prospective studies has shown a substantial link between antenatal maternal anxiety and cognitive, behavioral, and emotional problems in the child.

Measurements of attachment style provide a further basis for exploring the childhood antecedents of trait anxiety (van Ijzendoorn & Bakermans-Kranenburg, 2004). It is assumed that the child's attachment style carries forward as a kind of template for the intimate relationships of adulthood; insecure children may be vulnerable to insecurity and ambivalence in adult partnerships. Attachment style does indeed show some continuity from childhood to adulthood in longitudinal studies (Fraley, 2002). It is believed that early attachment experiences are internalized as cognitive schemas that help the adult make sense of close relationships. However, in place of Ainsworth's separate categories of attachment, contemporary research most often uses dimensional models. The leading model (Shaver & Mikulincer, 2009) discriminates level of anxiety and level of avoidance as independent dimensions. The securely attached child (or adult) is then someone who experiences little anxiety in intimate relationships and seeks closeness with the parent or partner. Indeed, research has confirmed that attachment relates to standard personality dimensions (Noftle & Shaver, 2006).

A recent meta-analysis (Mcleod, Wood, & Weisz, 2007) showed that parenting practices accounted for only 4% of the variance in child anxiety. The weighted mean effect size was .21 for association between parenting and childhood anxiety, reflecting a relation in which more negative parenting was associated with more child anxiety. Parental control was found to be slightly more strongly related to anxiety than parental rejection (effect sizes of .20 and .25, respectively). Higher levels of parental warmth and autonomy granting were associated with less child anxiety, and higher levels of parental withdrawal, aversiveness, and overinvolvement were associated with childhood anxiety. The data suggest that the presence of aversiveness and/or withdrawal may have a greater impact on anxiety than the absence of positive parenting (i.e., warmth). As a rule, high levels of family dysfunction are associated with childhood anxiety (Drake & Kearney, 2008).

With respect to test anxiety in specific, S. B. Sarason and coworkers (Sarason, Davidson, Lighthall, Waite, & Ruebush, 1960) saw the child as motivated to avoid potential parental rejection due to underperformance, within a psychodynamic theory. The child's overdependence on parents for approval and support leads to a strong fear of failure, together with unconscious hostility. Similar emotions may be transferred to teachers. Anxious children tend to avoid situations in which the likelihood of criticism is high, and they tend to leave such situations as soon as possible. Family climate and parental socialization practices have also been claimed to bear important influences on the development of children's emotional and social behaviors, including test anxiety (Krohne, 1992).

Proximal Factors

Although a good number of proximal factors (cultural norms, parental pressures, testing conditions, etc.) may impact on anxiety, in the paragraphs to follow, I discuss one major proximal factor in the development of anxiety in school settings—the school environment. The most obvious source of anxiety is failure on school tasks—or anticipated failure—in academic work. However, school poses additional threats and challenges. The student may also be anxious about social relationships with others, reflecting motivations to make friends, to be popular, and to avoid being bullied.

Expectancy formulations of anxiety (Pekrun, 1992) predict that the strength of students' anxious reactions to evaluative classroom contexts is a complex function of the perceptions and appraisals of both the objective features of the classroom environment as well as cognitive factors, such as outcome expectancies. Accordingly, the classroom climate may enhance students' anxiety by reducing success expectations for specific academic tasks, by rendering failure outcomes as extremely negative, or by decreasing perceived control over outcomes.

A highly competitive and evaluative classroom environment may foster an unhealthy orientation among students in which trying to outperform other students becomes more important than mastery of the school material (Church, Elliot, & Gable, 2001). Since anxious children are already apprehensive about failure, an emphasis on outperforming or not doing worse than others should make the consequences of failure even more devastating (Pekrun, Elliot, & Maier, 2009). Students who do not perform well in such competitive environments often come to see themselves as failures and ruminate about their performance deficits rather than focusing on the task at hand (Harter, Whitesell, & Kowalski, 1987). The presence of an evaluation-focused classroom atmosphere, coupled with harsh evaluations, often leads to performance avoidance goal orientations (Church, Elliot, & Gable, 2001).

A body of research evidence suggests that the teacher's predominant mode of evaluating children's performance in the classroom impacts upon children's motivation and self-perception. Thus, children evaluated in terms of individual reference norms (i.e., their own previous performance) showed less fear of failure, more realistic goal setting, and less low ability attribution compared to those evaluated in terms of classroom group reference norms (Boggiano & Ruble, 1986). Also, teachers, like parents, who set overly high standards, or criticize their students too harshly, are also more likely to foster anxiety in their students than other teachers (Wigfield & Eccles, 1990). Evaluation practices, such as emphasizing letter grades, can promote a focus on ability perceptions, competition, social comparisons, and negative self-evaluations, which may elicit anxiety in students (Wigfield & Eccles, 1990). Such concerns are especially salient in educational practice in the United States, which increasingly stresses the importance of standardized testing through initiatives such as No Child Left Behind.

Furthermore, some research (Mueller & Dweck, 1998) suggests that children who are praised for their intelligence rather than effort in the context of achievement strivings, perceived failure on a test as being due to their low ability. In fact, praise for achievement due to ability may leave children vulnerable to developing anxiety in educational settings if they subsequently fail in a school subject and may be more resilient to the effects of poor performance if the intelligence aspect of achievement is minimized. As children move up the educational system, they experience greater expectation and pressure from parents and school to perform well, expectations that may become internalized as evaluative anxiety dispositions.

Social comparison helps shape a student's self-perceptions of ability and achievement, which, in turn, may influence emotions such as anxiety (Regner, Escribe, & Dupeyrat, 2007; Suls, Martin, & Wheeler, 2002). Social comparison theory would suggest that children who believe they are competent relative to their peers should feel more positive about themselves and less anxious compared to those who believe they are less competent than their peers. Peers may influence anxiety by setting minimal expected norms of academic performance, by actually passing judgment on peers' performance, or by deriding and humiliating fellow students when these fail to meet set standards. Because a students' classroom typically serves as the most salient reference group for social comparison processes, it stands to reason that students who rank below the norm of the reference group should suffer from low self-concept and higher anxiety (Zeidner & Schleyer, 1999). By contrast, students achieving above the norms would be expected to see themselves as competent and therefore more likely to appraise academic demands as challenging rather than threatening.

The *accumulation* as well as *timing* of failure experiences are key concepts to consider in our efforts to understand failure-induced anxiety (Wigfield & Eccles, 1990). Although one may theoretically develop a generalized anxiety reaction to physically dangerous, evaluative, or social situations because of some shattering one-time experience, anxiety is generally shaped by repeated failure during critical developmental periods, eventually producing a generalizable apprehension of all achievement activities. Whereas a single failure experience represents a challenge to overcome, continual poor performance over time typically evokes self-directed negative affect, causing a person who repeatedly fails in academic settings to experience aversive emotional states, such as anxiety, shame, and humiliation (Covington & Omelich, 1979).

ANXIETY AND COGNITIVE PERFORMANCE

A virtual flood of studies have probed the pattern of relationships between anxiety and a wide array of cognitive performances. Increased anxiety has been shown to negatively impact performance within domains of functioning that include mathematical ability, academic tests, working memory tasks, reading comprehension, social interactions, sporting behaviors, and musical performance (Eysenck, Derakshan, Santos, &

Calvo, 2007). Furthermore, numerous lab-based studies indicate that various processing deficits are related to anxiety, including general impairments of attention and working memory, together with more subtle performance changes, such as failure to organize semantic information effectively (Zeidner, 1998).

A meta-analytic review by Hembree (1998), based on 562 North American studies, demonstrated that evaluative anxiety correlated negatively, though modestly, with a wide array of conventional measures of school achievement and ability at both high school and college levels. Data collected on students from upper elementary school level through high school showed that anxiety scores were significantly related to grades in various subjects, although the correlation was typically about −0.20. Cognitive measures (i.e., aptitude and achievement measures combined) correlated more strongly with the worry than emotionality component of test anxiety ($r = -0.31$ vs. -0.15). Furthermore, anxiety correlated inversely with performance on laboratory cognitive tasks, such as problem solving ($r = -0.20$) and memory ($r = -0.28$). Another meta-analysis (Ackerman & Heggestad, 1997) showed a mean r of -0.33 between test anxiety and general intelligence test performance. Test anxiety was also correlated in the -0.20–0.30 range with other broad intellectual abilities including fluid and crystallized intelligence, learning and memory, visual perception, and math ability. Also, a recent meta-analysis (Byron & Khazanchi, 2011) showed that trait anxiety was modestly associated with performance on creative tasks ($r = -0.17$), a finding consistent with the idea that anxiety and creativity present competing cognitive demands.

The information-processing components (see Table 14.1) found to be sensitive to anxiety in lab experiments relate to encoding, information storing and processing, and information retrieval and production. These anxiety-related deficits at various stages of processing suggest some general impairment in attention and/or working memory. I now detail a number of mediating and moderating effects in the anxiety-performance relationship.

Mediating and Moderating Effects

The whole process by which anxiety serves to debilitate cognitive performance is highly complex, with a variety of factors possibly mediating the effects of anxiety on performance (McFall, Jamieson, & Harkins, 2009). As suggested in Table 14.1, deficits related to anxiety have been identified at various stages of information processing (input, cognitive processing, output), suggesting some general impairment in attention and/or working memory. As reviewed by Zeidner and Matthews (2011), these various performance deficits are often attributed to high levels of worry and cognitive interference or to loss of functional working memory. Cognitive interference has also been implicated in detrimental effects of computer anxiety, math anxiety, social anxiety, and sports anxiety (Zeidner & Matthews, 2005).

Also, it is noted that correlations between anxiety and performance do not always reflect a causal effect of anxiety. In some test-anxious individuals, it is poor study skills and preparation that cause poor examination performance (Zeidner, 1998). Accordingly, anxiety is merely a by-product of poor preparation with no direct effect on performance (and hence there is no mediating process). Anxiety can also be caused by failure. This would amount to reciprocal causation of anxiety and performance (e.g., Pekrun, 1992).

Table 14.1 Information Processing Deficits in Anxious Students

Deficit Area	Brief Description
I. Information Encoding	
1. Encoding Difficulties	Anxious individuals report experiencing more encoding difficulties than their low anxious counterparts.
2. Interpretive Bias	Anxious individuals exhibit selective attentional bias favoring threat.
3. Restricted Range of Cue-Utilization	Anxious individuals attend to fewer environmental features and have a narrow range of cue-utilization.
4. Distractibility	Anxious students have difficulty in concentrating on cognitive tasks. They typically find themselves dividing their attention between the multiple requirements of the complex task and various task-irrelevant activities.
II. Information Storage and Processing	
5. Short-Term Storage	Anxious arousal causes a reduction in cognitive capacity devoted to the task, thus reducing resources for short-term memory tasks in anxious students. Working memory is particularly affected.
6. Long-Term Storage	Anxiety may impair retention of information in long-term memory, leading to greater retention loss over time.
7. Depth of Processing	Anxiety leads to a relative emphasis on processing superficial features of verbal stimuli at the expense of deeper semantic processing. Anxious students tend to focus on shallow or physical features rather than deep or semantic features of stimuli.
8. Elaboration and Rehearsal	Anxious students fail to adequately rehearse or elaborate upon information.
9. Conceptual Organization	Anxiety may shallow the encoding and organization of semantic material by reducing the quality of elaborations and associative paths. Anxious students cluster less on free recall tasks than those lower in anxiety for taxonomic categories, acoustic categories, and associative categories.
10. Strategic Processing	Automatic or highly learned operations are relatively unaffected by anxiety, whereas complex tasks requiring rehearsal or strategic operations will be hindered by arousal.
11. Language Processing	Anxious students often have vocabulary deficits and are deficient in their comprehension and reading efficiency. Anxiety is selectively detrimental to the efficiency of text-level processes, such as those involving integrating information across sentences.
12. Decision Making	High anxious students have difficulty in absorbing decision-relevant information, tend to have difficulty in scanning of alternatives, and adopt more cautious decisional criteria.
13. Metacognition	Anxious subjects are often deficient in metacognitive knowledge, including knowledge and executive processes used to control learning.
III. Information Retrieval and Production	
14. Interference and Anxiety Blockage	Anxious subjects suffer from cognitive interference and are self-preoccupied with task-irrelevant information.
15. Information Retrieval	Anxiety impairs retrieval of material and thus lowers performance during social-evaluative encounters.

Associations between anxiety and performance do indeed vary from study to study, and there seem to be a number of moderating variables that accentuate or reduce deficits in performance. First, the nature of the task may play an important moderating role, with subtle effects related to the qualitative nature of the task. Generally, anxiety is more detrimental to attentionally demanding and complicated tasks and may even facilitate performance on easy tasks (Zeidner, 1998). In addition, highly evaluative environments and speeded time conditions, compared to neutral and nonspeeded conditions, respectively, may accentuate the depressing effects of anxiety on performance (Zeidner, 1998). Furthermore, negative feedback appears to be especially detrimental to anxious subjects. Also, metacognitive processes of labeling and interpretation of arousal could moderate the effects of arousal and anxiety on cognitive processing and performance. Thus, a student who experiences arousal and nervous energy but is confident about her performance and interprets anxiety as sign that the task is a challenge should be less impaired on the task than the student plagued by self-doubt, who assumes that arousal signals a state of impending failure (Schmader, Forbes, Zhang, & Mendes, 2009).

I now briefly discuss a number of individual differences in anxiety in the classroom, including gender, socioeconomic and ethnic background, and culture.

INDIVIDUAL DIFFERENCES

Evaluative anxieties in educational settings are quite prevalent in contemporary society, generalizing across gender, age, and culture, although relatively minor group differences are sometimes reported.

Gender Differences

Overall, females typically show higher levels of anxiety on average than males (Seipp & Schwarzer, 1996). Women tend to report higher levels of test, math, and computer anxiety than men, but the gender difference often does not translate into objective performance differences (Cassady & Johnson, 2002; Zeidner, 1998).

Socioeconomic and Ethnic Differences

Minority group children show higher levels of anxiety than majority school students (see Zeidner, 1998). A massive body of literature suggests that the intellectual performance of minority groups is particularly sensitive to the situational context in which tests are usually administered (*Stereotype threat*), possibly due to a disruptive mental load. Evidence is accumulating that stereotypic reputations of intellectual inferiority (e.g., blacks or Hispanics in the United States), which usually target ethnic group members and people from lower social classes, can undermine performance on cognitive tasks due to anxiety beyond any actual differences in cognitive ability. In particular, when individuals who are targeted by allegations of inferiority are in an evaluative situation in which the stereotype-laden characteristic (i.e., intelligence or cognitive ability) will be explicitly assessed, their performance suffers. According to Steele (1997), such a performance deficit would result from the extra cognitive and emotional load generated by the anxiety of substantiating the allegation of inferiority conveyed by the stereotype. Thus, cultural group differences can reflect different situational burdens and not necessarily actual differences in cognition (Croizet, Després, Gauzins, Huguet, Leyens, & Méot, 2004).

Cultural Differences

Current research suggests that cultural background plays a pivotal factor in determining how people experience, display, and are affected by anxiety (Good & Kleinman, 1985). Although research evidence indicates that anxiety is universal, the experience and form of expression in anxiety may vary from one society and culture to another. For example, anxiety related to school may be a more significant problem for some Asian children due to feelings of shame and disgrace to oneself and one's family associated with school failure (Bodas & Ollendick, 2005). Thus, anxiety may be evoked by different factors, show different display rules and degrees of intensity, and have different consequences as a function of cultural group membership.

Furthermore, anxiety in educational settings may be closely linked to the competitive nature of individualistic cultures. In our achieving society, governed by competition and normative evaluation at school, sports, and at work, anxiety may be part and parcel of daily competitive life. However, perceived threat of evaluative encounters in the classroom may be lower in some societies where success is guaranteed to all citizens and the learning environment is based upon a collectivist social structure, as is the case in Kuwait (Cassady, Mohammed, & Mathieu, 2004).

Having discussed the nature of anxiety, its aversive effects on cognitive performance, and individual differences in anxiety, in the next section, I address a number of clinical parameters related to anxiety. I begin by differentiating between normal and clinical anxiety and move on to discuss key interventions for treating anxiety.

CLINICAL PARAMETERS

Normal Versus Abnormal Anxiety

Clearly, it is perfectly normal for students to experience some degree of anxiety when faced with stressful or threatening situations. In fact, normal anxiety has considerable utility and adaptive value in that the rapid and early detection of warning signs of danger in the immediate surroundings enables the individual to avoid, prepare for, and cope more effectively with future threatening encounters (Eysenck, 1982). It would be fair to say that anxiety, like most things in life, may be good in small to moderate amounts but becomes bad and maladaptive in extremely excessive amounts.

Overall, the major anxiety disorders are characterized by grossly exaggerated versions of normal anxiety and distress that we all have experienced. At the same time, researchers (see Zeidner & Matthews, 2011, for a review) have attempted to distinguish normal from abnormal anxiety using a multitude of differentiating criteria. These include: intensity of affective reaction, appropriateness of anxiety level to the threat, rationality of response, duration and recurrence of emotional state, degree of suffering from the anxiety, perceived controllability, severity of cognitions, coping styles, and effects of anxiety on coping and functioning. Thus, in the face of a threatening event, normal anxiety reactions are more or less proportional to the threat, entail reasonable worry about the consequences, moderate arousal, and a minimal disruption to daily life and coping abilities. In contradistinction, anxiety reactions that are excessive and disproportional to the threat involve extremely high levels of arousal, and seriously disrupt coping and social functioning are labeled as an anxiety disorder.

Excessive anxiety is a common problem facing school children that can harm them in many areas of their lives, including social functioning and school performance (Wood, 2006). Thus, when anxiety goes awry and becomes excessive, irrational, or leads to a dread of daily routine situations or events, it can cause untold psychic pain and discomfort and develop into a host of disabling and costly anxiety disorders (panic attacks, generalized anxiety disorders, obsessive behaviors, social phobia, PTSD, etc.).

Selected Interventions

A bewildering array of anxiety treatment programs have been developed and evaluated over the past three decades for normative, subclinical, and clinical forms of anxiety with student populations. Treatment fashions and orientations have swayed sharply from the psychodynamic to the behavioral, and more recently to the cognitive perspective— essentially mirroring the evolution of the behavior therapies.

As I previously pointed out (Zeidner, 1998; Zeidner & Matthews, 2011), there is no simple organizing principle with which to categorize the plethora of therapeutic techniques and approaches that have proliferated over the past few decades for treating evaluative/test anxiety. Current attempts have typically focused either on treatments directed toward the emotional, cognitive, or behavioral facets of anxiety. Thus, treatment programs typically include both *emotion-focused* treatments, designed largely to alleviate negative emotional affect experienced by anxious students, *cognitive-focused* treatments, designed to help the anxious student cope with worry and task-irrelevant thinking, and *skills training,* designed to improve various skills among students (social, athletic, motor, study, test-taking skills) and enhance their performance. Following Zeidner (1998) and Zeidner and Matthews (2011), I now briefly describe each of these salient forms of intervention for evaluative anxiety in the classroom.

Emotion-Focused Interventions

The emotionally oriented therapies aim primarily at reducing the arousal and heightened emotional reactions of anxious individuals when faced with stressful evaluative situations. Based on the assumption that anxiety comprises a physiological component, attempts to alleviate anxiety symptoms should prove successful, in part, if they focus on reducing levels of arousal or on altering ways in which people appraise their arousal in evaluative situations. The basic strategy in these treatments is directed to teach the client certain skills (mainly relaxational) so that when confronted by stress-inducing evaluative situations in the future, he or she will be able to handle them adequately. The therapies also provide opportunities for application of training either within the therapy setting or in real-life situations.

These emotion-focused procedures typically include a number of common components, such as theoretical explanations of anxiety as a conditioned response and the deconditioning rationale for treatment, instructions in specific methods for reducing anxiety, such as relaxation and guided imagery, guided practice in therapeutic methods, and practice (homework, in vivo practice). By and large, these emotion-focused treatments rely on key behavioral learning principles (counterconditioning, reciprocal inhibition, extinction, observational and coping skill learning, etc.) and also draw from an arsenal of behavioral techniques, such as deep muscle relaxation, guided imagery, and graduated hierarchies. For example, relaxation and guided imagery is not unique to a particular anxiety behavioral intervention method but is employed in several methods, including relaxation as self-control, systematic desensitization, and anxiety management training.

As reviewed by Zeidner and Matthews (2011), procedures designed to reduce emotionality, while clearly useful in modifying subjectively experienced anxiety, by themselves, appear to have little effect on cognitive performance. Overall, emotion-focused treatments appear to be relatively ineffective in reducing evaluative anxiety unless these treatments contain cognitive elements. It may therefore be necessary to combine such approaches with therapy modes focusing specifically on cognitive change in order to reliably elicit improvement in cognitive performance.

Cognitive-Focused Interventions

Recent years have witnessed a proliferation of cognitively oriented intervention programs that emphasize the mediating role of cognitive processes in sustaining or eliminating anxiety in evaluative situations. In part, the documented failure of emotionally oriented behavioral therapies to markedly improve the academic performance of students suffering from evaluative anxiety, coupled with the inconsistent relation reported between emotional arousal and school performance, has led to a greater emphasis on cognitive factors in evaluative anxiety intervention. Indeed, reviews of the literature conclude that cognitively based treatment strategies are more powerful than direct behavioral therapies in effecting test anxiety and performance changes.

Cognitive therapy is a generic term that refers to a wide array of therapeutic approaches directed towards modifying the worry and irrational thought patterns of test-anxious clients. Broadly speaking, cognitively oriented approaches to anxiety intervention are quite similar in assuming that cognitive processes are determining factors in test anxiety, although they differ in terms of actual intervention procedures. A fundamental assumption shared by contemporary cognitive models of anxiety is that cognitive processes mediate the person's emotional and behavioral responses to stressful evaluative situations. It follows that in order to modify the negative emotional reactions of anxious students to evaluative situations, therapy needs to be directed at reshaping the faulty premises, assumptions, and negative attitudes underlying maladaptive cognitions of anxious subjects. Given their multiple emphasis on modifying emotional processes, irrational thoughts and cognitions, and behavioral deficits, this results in a powerful approach that merges emotionally oriented, cognitively oriented, and behaviorally oriented techniques to alleviate student's anxiety and enhance their scholastic performance.

The benefits of cognitive therapies seem to hold up over time (Butler, Chaptman, Forman, & Beck, 2006), although few studies have investigated periods longer than 12 months.

Study Skills Training

This method focuses on improving students' study and test-taking skills. Study skills training differs from the other cognitive therapies in that it does not directly focus on modifying the cognitive component of anxiety but rather centers on improving students' study and test-taking skills. Presumably, improvement of these skills should have a direct impact upon performance through improved mastery of the test material and also indirectly impact performance through the reduction of worries surrounding inadequate exam preparation.

Recent reviews (Zeidner & Matthews, 2011) conclude that these programs have been successful in mainly enhancing the performance of high anxious students with poor study skills. It is now apparent that when anxious students suffer from serious study skill or test-taking deficits, alternative forms of treatment would not be expected to lead to performance gains, inasmuch as the behavioral deficit still exists. At the same time, skill training alone may lead a person to performance gains, but it may still leave the student distressed.

It is noted, however, that the distinction between the various treatment orientations is quite fuzzy, and these approaches are becoming increasingly difficult to distinguish (Meichenbaum, 1972). Although there may be highly specific interventions that have an affective (e.g., relaxation therapy), cognitive (e.g., Rational Emotive Therapy), or skills (test-taking counseling) focus, most methods are normally embedded in a multidimensional context. At present, a combination of procedures (whether combined in a truly integrative manner or in the stance of technical eclecticism, Alford & Norcross (1991) seems to best represent the nature of the evaluative anxiety intervention process; see Meichenbaum, 1972; cf. Deffenbacher, 1977). The effectiveness of cognitive and behavioral therapies increased when combined with skill-focused techniques.

Anxiety is more than a combination of physiological arousal, negative self-preoccupation, and a deficit in stress-related coping skills and poor study habits. It is the complex interaction among these diverse components that seems to define anxiety. Because the cognitive, affective, and behavioral components of anxiety interweave in contributing to the problem of evaluative anxiety and its treatment, it is predicted that an induced change in one system would generally be followed by a change in the other. Therapeutic approaches, which emphasize cognition, often extend to the emotional life, too, and vice versa. For example, it is likely that emotion-focused training (e.g., progressive relaxation) may make the client less anxious and result in a decrease in anxiety-focused, task-irrelevant ideation. By the same token, some forms of cognitive therapy may provide anxious subjects with an increased sense of perceived control, which might spill over into the emotional domain and result in lower emotional arousal in an evaluative situation.

CONCLUSIONS AND DIRECTIONS FOR FUTURE RESEARCH

In this concluding section, I point to potential directions for future research. Although contemporary anxiety research has made important strides in mapping out the anxiety terrain, there is still much uncharted territory that needs to be explored and more extensively mapped out by future research. I therefore highlight a number of these important areas, pointing out needed directions for future research.

Conceptualizations and Basic Issues

A variety of models and theoretical perspectives have been proposed over the past 50 years or so to account for anxiety in educational settings; no single unifying model is able to account for the multiple facets (antecedents, phenomenology, consequences) of this phenomenon and the many complex empirical findings. Given the multivariate nature of anxiety, its various channels of expression, and its myriad causes and consequences, it is reasonable to assume that not one but several conceptual models and mechanisms are needed to account for the anxiety phenomenon. At the same time, there is an urgent need for more comprehensive and integrative models of anxiety that cover a larger number of facets of the anxiety domain and synthesize many of the conceptual frameworks appearing in the literature.

Some of the best candidates for the key components that should probably be included in more comprehensive models, as they are essential for the anxiety process, would include trait anxiety, stressful situations, state anxiety, confidence-devaluing experiences in home or at school, poor social skills, arousal and emotionality, worry, cognitive interference, chronic self-doubts and feelings of incompetence, outcome expectancies, failure and success attributions, poor cue-utilization and retrieval, cognitive disengagement, withdrawal of attention, avoidance behaviors, and self-regulatory strategies. Furthermore, future research could benefit from developing a more comprehensive model of test anxiety, integrating cognate concepts, such as fear of failure, low self-concept and self-competence, and avoidance performance goal orientations.

Addressing Different Levels of Analyses

Future work needs to address different grain sizes and levels of discourse with respect to anxiety in students. Cognitive science recognizes that cognition requires different levels of explanation. Following the tri-level hypothesis (Pylyshyn, 1986), future research should focus on three complementary ways to understand the operation of anxiety. The lowest level is to study the biological hardware and develop biological theories that relate anxiety to specific brain systems. The next level is one of programming, with explanations referring to virtual computations, like the lines of code in a computer program. Most of the cognitive psychology of anxiety assumes that anxiety relates to steps in the mental programs for encoding and analyzing stimulus input—for example, the subroutines that evaluate how threatening a stimulus is. At present, most standard cognitive theories are expressed at the intermediate, programming level, based on information-processing models of attention, memory, and so on. At the top level is the knowledge level, which refers to the students' high level personal and learning goals and beliefs about how to attain those goals. For example, an anxious student might place a high priority on avoiding perceived threats, as well as beliefs that they are highly vulnerable. This level of analysis often features in clinical accounts of anxiety as well as in social-cognitive models. Further work also needs to differentiate levels related to current distinctions between explicit and implicit processes.

Developing Viable Taxonomies

Anxiety among school children is clearly not a unified phenomena, and a variety of different types of anxious students have been identified (Zeidner & Matthews, 2005). Development of a comprehensive taxonomy of anxious students would be useful for both theoretical, research, and intervention purposes. Furthermore, despite earnest efforts by practitioners to individualize treatments to the particular needs and problems of anxious students, we still do not have clear evidence to indicate which of the various intervention approaches is most effective for particular types of anxious students or for treating different manifestations of anxiety. This stems, in part, from the absence of an established typology of anxious students—which is sorely needed.

Research Methodology

There is a strong need for large-scale and systematic research relating to various facets of anxiety, based on multiple observations of various student target groups, at various time points, and in various educational and social contexts and cultural settings. Future research would benefit from application of sophisticated longitudinal and multivariate experimental designs in particular. In addition, research could make more frequent and profitable use of qualitative methodologies and emergent paradigm, such as in-depth interviews, to capture more rich detail of the anxious experience along with contextual and situation features.

Overall, the assessment of anxiety in educational settings has not kept pace with the theoretical advances in conceptualizing the construct. Thus, much of the construct domain (e.g., task-irrelevant thinking, off-task thoughts, and poor academic self-concept) is underrepresented in current measures of anxiety. However, work by Pekrun and coworkers (2004) on the *Test Emotions Questionnaire* and the *Achievement Emotions Questionnaire* have improved upon prior measures by taking motivational components of test anxiety (and other test emotions) into account.

Empirical Research in Natural Settings

Further research is needed on the specific kinds of school-related encounters that shape children's anxiety reactions and avoidance behaviors in school settings. Although the application of lab-based information-processing research has been informative, it has failed to capture the dynamic nature of processing, both with regard to internal interactions between different processing systems and to the interplay between processing and the external environment. Furthermore, research would benefit from more large-scale systematic and controlled studies that would pinpoint the effects of a wide array of classroom and school environmental variables (e.g., group climate and norms, evaluation and grading practices, tracking and streaming, transitional periods, teacher characteristics, teacher–student interactions, peer-pressures, and expectations, etc.) on the development of anxiety in general and different anxiety components (e.g., worry, emotionality, self-blame, nontask interference), in particular. Additional research is also needed on the relationship between a child's failure-induced anxiety experiences in the preschool and elementary school years and their anxiety and cognitive performance later on in life (e.g., high school, college, and on-the-job performance). Also, the interaction between teacher anxiety and student anxiety is worthy of systematic investigation (e.g., see Beilock, Gunderson, Ramirez, & Levince, 2010).

Anxiety-Performance Relationship

Research has been quite successful in identifying a range of processes that may contribute to performance deficits in anxiety. Cognitive neuroscientists are also making progress in delineating the brain systems sensitivity to anxiety, such as prefrontal areas that support executive processing. More research is needed detailing how anxiety influences the more complex processing competencies that are often important in real-life settings, including various facets of judgment and decision making, inductive and deductive processes, ideation, and creative behavior.

Perhaps the greatest challenge for research is to develop understanding of dynamic processes in anxiety, especially in real-life settings. Broadly, it seems that anxiety relates to multiple internal processes and to ways of coping with external threat that may exacerbate performance difficulties. However, it remains somewhat mysterious how the influence of anxiety on cognition plays out over extended time periods, such as taking a demanding semester-long course or completing a critical research project in college. Research is also needed in the area of remediation of the cognitive deficits associated with anxiety.

Research on Resilient Students

Although I have focused on high anxious students in this chapter, future research would benefit from examining the developmental and situational determinants of students who are on the low end of the anxiety continuum. Thus, more research is needed focusing on resilient and low anxious students, who tend to view school tasks more as challenges than threats and who show adaptive coping responses to social evaluation situations. Furthermore, little research has been devoted to uncovering students' coping resources and factors that may serve to buffer negative emotions prior to and during stressful evaluative encounters in student populations. Future research would also benefit from examining the additive and interactive effects of evaluative anxiety and other emotions (e.g., anger, sadness, guilt, pride, envy, joy) in impacting upon student's success and well-being (cf. Pekrun & Frese, 1992).

In Sum

This chapter aimed at providing a comprehensive overview of current and recurrent issues in anxiety theory, research, development, performance, individual differences, and interventions in educational settings. As amply demonstrated, evaluative anxieties are quite prevalent in contemporary society, with cognitive aspects of evaluative anxiety fundamental; in each case, the anxious person fears that they will not be able to meet accepted performance standards and will be found deficient or inadequate by others, thus resulting in negative social consequences or sanctions. Also, the trait–state distinction is fundamental to understanding evaluative anxiety. Over shorter time spans, the state response is a product of dispositional anxiety and situational cues that are congruent with the person's specific vulnerabilities. Over longer time spans, the dynamic unfolding of the anxiety process depends on both the individual's social learning history and basic temperament, influenced by biological factors. It seems that dispositional evaluative anxiety feeds back into the social learning process, with potentially malignant results if the child becomes avoidant of academic environments.

The nature of the anxiety-performance relationship is best viewed as reciprocal in nature. Thus, high levels of anxiety, accompanied by elevated levels of worry and cognitive interference, absorb part of the capacity needed for attention, working memory, problem solving, or other cognitive processes required for successful completion of a task. Evaluative anxiety also produces avoidant patterns of motivation, coping, and task strategies that interfere with learning and performance. The result is that competence and self-efficacy suffers, thus leading to further anxiety over time, and generating a vicious circle of increasing anxiety and degrading competence for students.

A vast number of intervention programs targeting anxiety in general and test anxiety in particular have proliferated over the years. Whereas specific interventions have an affective, cognitive, or skills focus, most methods are normally embedded in a multidimensional context, and procedures that specifically address the etiology underlying the students' anxiety (anxiety blockage, lack of preparation, low self-esteem, procrastinaton, etc.) seems to be the optimal intervention policy at present.

Finally, I delineated a number of promising areas for future research that may shed additional light on evaluative anxiety—a ubiquitous and critical phenomena that impacts student learning and well-being in educational settings across the globe.

REFERENCES

Ackerman, P. L., & Heggestad, E. D. (1997) Intelligence, personality and interests: Evidence for overlapping traits. *Psychological Bulletin, 121,* 219–245.

Alford, B. A., & Norcross, J. C. (1991). Cognitive therapy as integrative therapy. *Journal of Psychotherapy Integration, 1,* 175–189.

American Psychiatric Association. (2013). *Diagnostic and statistical manual of mental disorders* (5th ed.). Washington, DC: Author.

Beilock, S. L., Gunderson, E. A., Ramirez, G., & Levince, S. C. (2010). Female teachers' math anxiety affects girls' math achievement. *PNAS, 107,* 1860–1863.

Biederman, J., Hirshfeld-Becker, D. R., Rosenbaum, J. F., Hérot, C., Friedman, D., Snidman, N. . . . Faraone, S. V. (2001). Further evidence of association between behavioral inhibition and social anxiety in children. *The American Journal of Psychiatry, 158,* 1673–1679.

Bodas, J., & Ollendick, T. H. (2005). Test anxiety: A cross-cultural perspective. *Clinical Child and Family Psychology Review, 8,* 65–88.

Boggiano, A. K., & Ruble, D. N. (1986). Children's responses to evaluative feedback. In R. Schwarzer (Ed.), *Self related cognitions in anxiety and motivation* (pp. 195–227). Hillsdale, NJ: LEA.

Butler, A. C., Chapman, J. E., Forman, E. M., & Beck, A. T. (2006). The empirical status of cognitive-behavioral therapy: A review of meta-analyses. *Clinical Psychology Review, 26,* 17–31.

Byron, K., & Khazanchi, S. (2011). A meta-analytic investigation of the relationship of state and trait anxiety to performance on figural and verbal creative tasks. *Personality and Social Psychology Bulletin, 37,* 269–283.

Carter, R., Williams, S., & Silverman, W. K. (2008). Cognitive and emotional facets of test anxiety in African American school children. *Cognition and Emotion, 22,* 539–551.

Carver, C. S., Peterson, L. M., Follansbee, D. J., & Scheier, M. F. (1983). Effects of self-directed attention on performance and persistence among persons high and low in test anxiety. *Cognitive Therapy and Research, 7,* 333–353.

Carver, C. S., & Scheier, M. F. (1984). Self-focused attention in test anxiety: A general theory applied to a specific phenomenon. In H. M. Van der Ploeg, R. Schwarzer, & C. D. Spielberger (Eds.), *Advances in test anxiety research* (Vol. 3, pp. 3–20). Lisse, Netherlands: Swets & Zeitlinger.

Carver, C. S., & Scheier, M. F. (1988a). A control-process perspective on anxiety. *Anxiety Research, 1,* 17–22.

Carver, C. S., & Scheier, M. F. (1988b). A model of behavioral self-regulation: Translating intention into action. *Advances in Experimental Social Psychology, 21,* 303–346.

Carver, C. S., & Scheier, M. F. (1990). Principles of self-regulation: Action and emotion. In E. T. Higgins & R. M. Sorrentino (Eds). *Handbook of motivation and cognition: Foundations of social behavior, Vol. 2* (pp. 3–52). New York, NY: Guilford Press.

Carver, C. S., & Scheier, M. F (1991). A control-process perspective on anxiety. In R. Schwarzer & R. A. Wicklund (Eds). *Anxiety and self-focused attention* (pp. 3–8). Amsterdam, Netherlands: Harwood Academic Publishers.

Carver, C. S., & Scheier, M. F. (2014). The experience of emotions during goal pursuit. In R. Pekrun & L. Linnenbrink-Garcia (Eds.), *International handbook of emotions in education* (pp. 56–72). New York, NY: Taylor & Francis.

Carver, C. S., Scheier, M. F., & Klahr, D. (1987). Further explorations of a control-process model of test anxiety. In R. Schwarzer, H. M. Van der Ploeg, & C. D. Spielberger (Eds.), *Advances in test anxiety research* (Vol. 6, pp. 15–22). Lisse, Netherlands: Swets & Zeitlinger.

Caspi, A., Sugden, K., Moffitt, T. E., Taylor, A., Craig, I. W., Harrington, H. . . . Poulton, R. (2003). Influence of life stress on depression: Moderation by a polymorphism in the 5-HTT gene. *Science, 301,* 386–389.

Cassady, J. C. (2004). The influence of cognitive test anxiety across the learning-testing cycle. *Learning and Instruction, 14,* 569–592.

Cassady, J. C. (2010). Test anxiety: Contemporary theories and implications for learning. In J. C. Cassady (Ed.), *Anxiety in schools: The causes, consequences, and solutions for academic anxieties* (pp. 7–26). New York, NY: Peter Lang.

Cassady, J. C., & Johnson, R. E. (2002). Cognitive test anxiety and academic performance. *Contemporary Educational Psychology, 27,* 270–295.

Cassady, T. C., Mohammed, A., & Mathieu, L. (2004). Cross-cultural differences in test perceptions: Women in Kuwait and the United States. *Journal of Cross-Cultural Psychology, 35,* 713–718.

Cattell, R. B. (1950). *Personality: A systematic theoretical and factual study.* New York, NY: McGraw Hill.

Church, M. A., Elliot, A. J., & Gable, S. L. (2001). Perceptions of classroom environment, achievement goals, and achievement outcomes. *Journal of Educational Psychology, 93,* 43–54.

Covington, M. V. (1992). *Making the grade.* New York, NY: Cambridge University Press.

Covington, M. V., & Omelich, C. L. (1979). Effort: The double edged sword in school achievement. *Journal of Educational Psychology, 71,* 169–182.

Croizet, J.-C., Després, G., Gauzins, M.-E., Huguet, P., Leyens, J.-P., & Méot, A. (2004). Stereotype threat undermines intellectual performance by triggering a disruptive mental load. *Personality and Social Psychology Bulletin, 30,* 721–731.

Deffenbacher, J. L. (1977). Test anxiety: The problem and possible responses. *Canadian Counsellor, 11,* 59–64.

Degnan, K. A., Almas, A. N., & Fox, N. A. (2010). Temperament and the environment in the etiology of childhood anxiety. *Journal of Child Psychology and Psychiatry, 51,* 497–517.

Drake, K. L., & Kearny, C. A. (2008). Child anxiety sensitivity and family environment as mediators of the relationship between parent psychopathology, parent anxiety sensitivity, and child anxiety. *Journal of Psychopathology and Behavioral Assessment, 30,* 79–86.

Eley, T. C., Bolton, D., O'Connor, T. G., Perrin, S., Smith, P., & Plomin, R. (2003). A twin study of anxiety-related behaviours in pre-school children. *Journal of Child Psychology and Psychiatry, 44,* 945–960.

Endler, N. S., & Parker, J. (1992). Interactionism revisited: Reflections on the continuing crisis in the personality area. *European Journal of Personality, 6,* 177–198.

Eysenck, H. J. (1967). *The biological basis of personality.* Springfield, IL: C. C. Thomas.

Eysenck, H. J. (1982). *Personality, genetics, and behavior.* New York, NY: Praeger.

Eysenck, M. W. (1992). *Anxiety: The cognitive perspective.* Hove, United Kingdom: Lawrence Erlbaum.

Eysenck, M. W., Derakshan, N., Santos, R., & Calvo, M. G. (2007). Anxiety and cognitive performance: Attentional control theory. *Emotion, 7,* 336–353.

Fraley, R. C. (2002). Attachment stability from infancy to adulthood: Meta-analysis and dynamic modeling of developmental mechanisms. *Personality and Social Psychology Review, 6,* 123–151.

Good, B. J., & Kleinman, A. M. (1985). Culture and anxiety: Cross-cultural evidence for the patterning of anxiety disorders. In H. Tuma & J. Master (Eds.), *Anxiety and the anxiety disorders* (pp. 297–323). Hillsdale, NJ: Lawrence Erlbaum.

Gray, J. A., & McNaughton, N. (2003). *The neuropsychology of anxiety: An inquiry into the functions of the septohippocampal system.* New York, NY: Oxford University Press.

Harter, S., Whitesell, N., & Kowalski, P. (1987). The effects of educational transitions on childrens perceptions of competence and motivational orientation. Unpublished manuscript. University of Denver, Denver, Colorado.

Hembree, R. (1998). Correlates, causes, effects, and treatment of test anxiety. *Review of Educational Research, 58,* 7–77.

Kagan, J., Reznick, J. S., & Snidman, N. (1988). Biological bases of childhood shyness. *Science, 240,* 167–171.

Krohne, H. W. (1992). Developmental conditions of anxiety and coping: A two-process model of child-rearing effects. In K. A. Hagtvet & B. T. Johnsen (Eds.), *Advances in test anxiety research* (Vol. 7, pp. 143–155). Lisse, Netherlands: Swets and Zeitlinger.

Lau, J.Y.F., Gregory, A. M., Goldwin, M. A., Pine, D. S., & Eley, T. C. (2007). Assessing gene-environment interactions on anxiety symptom subtypes across childhood and adolescence. *Development and Psychopathology, 19,* 1129–1146.

Lazarus, R. S. (1999). *Stress and emotion: A new synthesis.* New York, NY: Springer.

Lazarus R. S., & Folkman, S. (1984). *Stress, appraisal, and coping.* New York, NY: Springer.

LeDoux, J. E. (1996). *The emotional brain: The mysterious underpinnings of emotional life.* New York, NY: Simon & Schuster.

Leitenberg, H. (Ed.). (1990). *Handbook of social and evaluation anxiety.* New York, NY: Plenum.

Liebert, R. M., & Morris, L. W. (1967). Cognitive and emotional components of test anxiety: A distinction and some initial data. *Psychological Reports, 20,* 975–978.

McFall, S. R., Jamieson, J. P., & Harkins, S. G. (2009). Testing the mere effort account of the evaluation-performance relationship. *Journal of Personality and Social Psychology, 96,* 135–154.

Mcleod, B. D., Wood, J. J., & Weisz, J. R. (2007). Examining the association between parenting and childhood anxiety: A meta-analysis. *Clinical Psychology Review, 27,* 155–172.

Meichenbaum, D. H. (1972). Cognitive modification of test anxious college students. *Journal of Consulting and Clinical Psychology, 39,* 370–380.

Mueller, C. M., & Dweck, C. S. (1998). Praise for intelligence can undermine children's motivation and performance. *Journal of Personality and Social Psychology, 75,* 33–52.

Noftle, E. E., & Shaver, P. R. (2006). Attachment dimensions and the big five personality traits: Associations and comparative ability to predict relationship quality. *Journal of Research in Personality, 40,* 179–208.

Panksepp, J. (1998). *Affective neuroscience: The foundations of human and animal emotions.* New York, NY: Oxford University Press.

Pekrun, R. (1992). The expectancy-value theory of anxiety: Overview and implications. In D. G. Forgays, T. Sosnowski, & K. Wrzesniewski (Eds.), *Anxiety: Recent developments in self-appraisal, psychophysiological and health research* (pp. 23–41). Washington, DC: Hemisphere.

Pekrun, R., Elliot, A. J., & Maier, M. A. (2009). Achievement goals and achievement emotions: Testing a model of their joint relations with academic performance. *Journal of Educational Psychology, 101,* 115–135.

Pekrun, R., & Frese, M. (1992). Emotions in work and achievement. *International Review of Industrial and Organizational Psychology, 7,* 153–200.

Pekrun, R., Goetz, T., Perry, R. P., Kramer, K., & Hochstadt, M. (2004). Beyond test anxiety: Development and validation of the Test Emotions Questionnaire (TEQ). *Anxiety, Stress and Coping, 17,* 287–316.

Perry, R. P., Hladkyj, S., Pekrun, R. H., & Pelletier, S. T. (2001). Academic control and action control in the achievement of college students: A longitudinal field study. *Journal of Educational Psychology, 93,* 776–789.

Putwain, D. W. (2007). Test anxiety in UK schoolchildren: Prevalence and demographic patterns. *British Journal of Educational Psychology, 77,* 579–593.

Putwain, D. W. (2008). Deconstructing test anxiety. *Emotional and Behavioral Difficulties, 13,* 145–155.

Pylyshyn, Z. W. (1986). *Computation and cognition: Toward a foundation for cognitive science.* Cambridge, MA: The MIT Press.

Rapee, R. M. (1997). Potential role of childrearing practices in the development of anxiety and depression. *Clinical Psychology Review, 17,* 47–67.

Reeve, C. L, Bonaccio, S., & Charles, J. E. (2008). A policy-capturing study of the contextual antecedents of test anxiety. *Personality and Individual Differences, 45,* 243–248.

Regner, I., Escribe, C., & Dupeyrat, C. (2007). Evidence of social comparison in mastery goals in natural academic settings. *Journal of Educational Psychology, 99,* 575–583.

Rende, R. D. (1993). Longitudinal relations between temperament traits and behavioral syndromes in middle childhood. *Journal of the American Academy of Child & Adolescent Psychiatry, 32,* 287–290.

Sarason, S. B., Davidson, K. S., Lighthall, F. F., Waite, R. R., & Ruebush, B. K. (1960). *Anxiety in elementary school children.* Oxford, England: John Wiley.

Schmader, T., Forbes, C. E., Zhang, S., & Mendes, W. B. (2009). A metacognitive perspective on the cognitive deficits experienced in intellectually threatening environments. *Personality and Social Psychology Bulletin, 35,* 584–596.

Schutz, P., & Pekrun, R. (Eds.). (2007). *Emotions in education.* Beverly Hills, CA: Sage.

Seipp, B., & Schwarzer, C. (1996). Cross-cultural anxiety research: A review. In C. Schwarzer & M. Zeidner (Eds.), *Stress, anxiety, and coping in academic settings* (pp. 13–68). Tubingen, Germany: Francke-Verlag.

Shaver, P. R., & Mikulincer, M. (2009). Attachment theory: I. Motivational, individual-differences and structural aspects. In P. J. Corr & G. Matthews (Eds.), *The Cambridge handbook of personality psychology* (pp. 228–246). New York, NY: Cambridge University Press.

Spielberger, C. D. (1972). *Anxiety: Current trends in theory and research.* New York, NY: Academic Press.

Spielberger, C. D., Anton, W. D., & Bedell, J. (1976). The nature and treatment of test anxiety. In M. Zuckerman & C. D. Spielberger (Eds.), *Emotions and anxiety: New concepts, methods, and applications* (pp. 317–344). New York, NY: LEA/Wiley.

Spielberger, C. D., & Vagg, P. R. (1995). Test anxiety: A transactional process model. In C. D. Spielberger & P. R. Vagg (Eds.), *Test anxiety: Theory, assessment, and treatment.* Series in clinical and community psychology (pp. 3–14). Philadelphia, PA: Taylor & Francis.

Steele, C. M. (1997). A threat in the air: How stereotypes shape intellectual identity and performance. *American Psychologist, 52,* 613–629.

Suls, J., Martin, R., & Wheeler, L. (2002). Social comparison: Why, with whom, and with what effect? *Current Directions in Psychological Science, 11,* 159–163.

van Beijsterveldt, C.E.M., Verhulst, F. C., Molenaar, P.C.M., & Boomsma, D. I. (2004). The genetic basis of problem behavior in 5-year-old dutch twin pairs. *Behavior Genetics, 34,* 229–242.

Van den Bergh, B.R.H., Mulder, E.J.H, Mennes, M, & Glover, V. (2005). Antenatal maternal anxiety and stress and the neurobehavioural development of the fetus and child: Links and possible mechanisms: A review. *Neuroscience and Biobehavioral Reviews, 29,* 237–258.

Van Ijzendoorn, M. H. V., & Bakermans-Kranenburg, M. J. (2004). Maternal sensitivity and infant temperament in the formation of attachment. In G. Bremner & A. Slater (Eds.), *Theories of infant development* (pp. 233–257). Malden, MA: Blackwell Publishing.

Van Yperen, N. W. (2007). Performing well in an evaluative situation: The roles of perceived competence and task-irrelevant interfering thoughts. *Anxiety, Stress, and Coping, 20,* 409–419.

Wigfield, A., & Eccles, J. S. (1990). Test anxiety in the school setting. In M. Lewis & S. M. Miller (Eds.), *Handbook of developmental psychopathology: Perspectives in developmental psychology* (pp. 237–250). New York, NY: Plenum Press.

Wine, J. D. (1980). Cognitive-attentional theory of test-anxiety. In I. G. Sarason (Ed.), *Test anxiety: Theory, research, and applications* (pp. 349–385). Hillsdale, NJ: Erlbaum.

Wong, S. S. (2008). The relations of cognitive triad, dysfunctional attitudes, automatic thoughts, and irrational beliefs with test anxiety. *Current Psychology, 27,* 177–191.

Wood, J. (2006). Effect of anxiety reduction on children's school performance and social adjustment. *Developmental Psychology, 42,* 345–349.

Zeidner, M. (1998). *Test anxiety: The state of the art.* New York, NY: Plenum Press

Zeidner, M. (2007). Test anxiety: Conceptions, findings, conclusions. In P. Schutz & R. Pekrun (Eds.), *Emotion in education* (pp. 165–184). Beverly Hills, CA: Sage.

Zeidner, M. (2010). Test anxiety. In I. B. Weiner & E. Craighead (Ed.), *Corsini's Encyclopaedia of Psychology* (4th ed., pp. 1766–1768). New York, NY: Wiley.

Zeidner, M. & Matthews, G. (2005). Evaluation anxiety: Current theory and research. In A. J. Elliot & C. S. Dweck (Eds.), *Handbook of competence and motivation* (pp. 141–163). New York, NY: Guilford Publications.

Zeidner, M. & Matthews, G. (2011). *Anxiety101.* New York, NY: Springer.

Zeidner, M. & Schleyer, E. (1999). The big-fish-little-pond effect for academic self-concept, test anxiety, and school grades in gifted children. *Contemporary Educational Psychology, 24,* 305–329.

15

CONFUSION

Sidney K. D'Mello and Arthur C. Graesser,
University of Notre Dame and University of Memphis

A man may be absorbed in the deepest thought, and his brow will remain smooth until he encounters some obstacle in his train of reasoning, or is interrupted by some disturbance, and then a frown passes like a shadow over his brow.

(Darwin, 1872, p. 220)

Almost a century and a half ago, Darwin published his seminal book *The Expression of Emotions in Man and Animals* that arguably launched the scientific study of emotion. In that book, he made a number of astute observations on frowns, the contexts that elicit them, their evolutionary value, their special status in the arsenal of human expressions, and their ubiquity as a form of emotional expression from infancy to mortality. Darwin observed that frowns often accompanied incongruence during deep thought and effortful deliberation, but not during simple reflection, orientation of attention, or meditation. He reasoned that frowns were an expressive correlate of the intention to focus attention on distant objects, which can be achieved by contracting the eye muscles so as to restrict incoming light to objects of immediate relevance. Though once associated with voluntary muscle control in the service of visual perception, Darwin hypothesized that through millions of years of evolution, the frown was involuntarily associated with information seeking, as is the case when one encounters a disruption in a train of thought.

Although not explicitly mentioned by Darwin, in some contexts, the furrowed brow is accompanied by feelings of *cognitive disequilibrium* (Piaget, 1952), or *cognitive*

Author Notes: The authors are grateful to members of the Emotive Computing Lab who have contributed to the research synthesized in this chapter (http://emotion.autotutor.org). This research was supported by the National Science Foundation (NSF) (ITR 0325428, HCC 0834847, DRL 1235958). Any opinions, findings and conclusions, or recommendations expressed in this paper are those of the authors and do not necessarily reflect the views of the NSF.

dissonance (Festinger, 1957), and the experience of *confusion*. Cognitive disequilibrium and confusion are triggered when individuals encounter incongruence in the form of impasses, anomalies, contradictions, disruptions of goals, extreme novelty that cannot be comprehended, and interruptions of organized sequences of actions. The importance of cognitive disequilibrium and cognitive dissonance in learning has a long history in psychology that spans the developmental, social, and cognitive sciences (Berlyne, 1960; Chinn & Brewer, 1993; Collins, 1974; Festinger, 1957; Graesser & Olde, 2003; Laird, Newell, & Rosenbloom, 1987; Mandler, 1976; Mugny & Doise, 1978; Piaget, 1952; Schank, 1999). The notion that cognitive disequilibrium extends beyond cognition and into emotions has also been acknowledged and investigated for decades. What is less clear, however, is the nature of the affective processes that are spawned by cognitive disequilibrium and how affect and cognition interact during learning. The focus on this chapter is on *confusion,* which is hypothesized to be the affective signature of cognitive disequilibrium and is expected to be highly relevant to both the processes and products of learning.

In our view, confusion is central to complex learning activities, such as comprehending difficult texts, generating cohesive arguments, solving challenging problems, and modeling complex systems. It is an inevitable consequence of effortful information processing, yet it has received considerably less attention in the mainstream scientific literature. Within the affective sciences, studies on confusion are essentially nonexistent when compared to emotions such as disgust and anger. Fortunately, there have been some recent efforts to investigate the phenomenon of confusion more carefully. This chapter synthesizes some of this literature with an emphasis on research on emotions and learning that we have conducted over the last decade. Our analysis of confusion is organized around seven fundamental questions: (a) What is confusion? (b) What are the appraisals that lead to confusion? (c) How is confusion expressed? (d) What are the temporal dynamics of confusion? (e) How is confusion regulated? (f) Why is confusion relevant to learning? and (g) When is confusion beneficial to learning? We conclude by discussing some of the implications of the findings, list open issues, and highlight opportunities in the scientific study of confusion.

WHAT IS CONFUSION?

The theoretical status of confusion in the affective sciences is quite mixed. Confusion has been considered to be a bona fide emotion (Rozin & Cohen, 2003a), a knowledge emotion (Silvia, 2010), an epistemic emotion (Pekrun & Stephens, 2011), an affective state but not an emotion (Hess, 2003; Keltner & Shiota, 2003), and a cognitive feeling state (Clore, 1992). It is beyond the scope of this chapter to go into these various conceptualizations of confusion, but the reader is referred to Rozin and Cohen (2003a, 2003b), Ellsworth (2003), Keltner and Shiota (2003), and Hess (2003) for an informative debate on the reasons for and against categorizing confusion as an emotion versus an affective or feeling state. In general, the confusion about the theoretical status of confusion as an emotion arises from (a) a lack of a clear definition of emotion, (b) multiple perspectives of emotion (Izard, 2010), and (c) a general paucity of basic research on confusion within the affective sciences (Rozin & Cohen, 2003b). This suggests that it might be useful to first ask a more basic question, "What is an emotion?" and then examine if, and to what extent, available data supports the classification of confusion as an emotion.

It is not surprising that the term emotion has stubbornly resisted any formal and widely accepted definition. To address this, Carroll Izard (2010), a noted emotion researcher, recently adopted a somewhat innovative approach to identify the defining characteristics of emotion. He asked 37 leading emotion researchers to provide written responses to six fundamental questions related to emotion. The question of interest to this chapter is "What is an emotion?" The results of a qualitative analysis of the written responses, published in a manuscript aptly titled "The Many Meanings/Aspects of Emotion: Definitions, Functions, Activation, and Regulation," yielded that emotions (a) involve neural circuits partially dedicated to "emotional processing" (8.92), (b) activate response systems in preparation for action (8.61), (c) have distinct feeling states (7.84), (d) play a role in expressive behavior and signaling systems (i.e., social functions) (6.56), (e) arise from results of appraisal processes (6.54), and (f) may involve cognitive interpretation of feelings (4.79). The numbers in parentheses beside each component reflect the extent to which a subset of the 37 respondents agreed on each of these six components in a subsequent survey on a scale ranging from 1 (not at all) to 10 (completely).

The six components identified by Izard (2010) reflect a number of different traditions, theories, and perspectives that have emerged over the last century (see Gross & Barrett, 2011, for a review). Hence, it is useful to consider whether confusion shares these six characteristics of an emotion. The case can easily be made for four of the components (items a, c, d, and e). First, it is clear that confusion arises from some form of neural interaction, as is the case when anomalies trigger EEG activities of the N400 (a negative event-related potential with a 400 ms post-stimulus onset) (Halgren et al., 2002; Kutas & Hillyard, 1980). Although the field of affective neuroscience is still in its infancy, it is unlikely that there is specific neural circuit or substrate dedicated solely to confusion. However, this should not weaken the status of confusion as an emotion because there is considerable debate as to whether specialized neural circuits exist for widely accepted emotions such as anger and disgust (Lindquist, Wager, Kober, Bliss-Moreau, & Barrett, 2011). Second, there is a distinct feeling state (subjective experience) that accompanies confusion (Rozin & Cohen, 2003a), although it is important to distinguish the form of short-term confusion that we are referring to here with long-term *mental confusion*. The latter is a pathological condition associated with mental disorientation and is symptomatic of dementia and other mental disorders (de Smet et al., 1982). Third, confusion has an expressive component consisting of the furrowed brow as initially noted by Darwin and subsequently confirmed in research studies (Craig, D'Mello, Witherspoon, & Graesser, 2008; Grafsgaard, Boyer, & Lester, 2011; McDaniel et al., 2007). Observers can also detect confusion from facial cues (Graesser et al., 2006). It is too early to say if there is a distinct facial expression for confusion, although failure to find one should not disqualify it as an emotion because despite decades of research, it is unclear if distinct facial expressions accompany emotions such as anger and disgust (Barrett, 2006; Russell, Bachorowski, & Fernandez-Dols, 2003). Fourth, as will be discussed in the next section, there is evidence to suggest that confusion arises from a cognitive appraisal of a mismatch between incoming information and existing knowledge (D'Mello, Lehman, Pekrun, & Graesser, 2014; Silvia, 2010).

It is unclear to what extent confusion involves bodily response systems via changes in physiology and priming of actions (item b). The lack of available data is not due to a failure to associate confusion with specific bodily changes, but rather stems from the lack of systematic research on how confusion is manifested in the body and how it recruits action systems (Rozin & Cohen, 2003a). As will be subsequently discussed in the section on expression, physiological-based machine learning models have recently achieved some success in distinguishing confusion from the neutral state and discriminating confusion from other emotions (AlZoubi, D'Mello, & Calvo, 2012). Though far from conclusive, this suggests that there is a link between confusion and the underlying physiology. Finally, it is unclear if confusion is a cognitive interpretation of a feeling (item f), an idea that originated with James (1884) and has been in and out of fashion for over a century. This was the sixth criteria listed by Izard (2010), and it obtained the lowest ratings (4.79 out of 10), so we will not let it influence confusion's fate as an emotion.

In summary, it is possible to make an initial case for confusion as an emotion because it arises out of neural interactions, involves bodily response systems, has a distinct feeling state, has an expressive component, and is an antecedent of cognitive appraisal. Confusion might also be considered to be an epistemic emotion or a knowledge emotion (Pekrun & Stephens, 2011; Silvia, 2010) since it arises out of information-oriented appraisals of external or internal knowledge (see next section). Some evidence indicates that confusion is likely perceived as a negative activating emotion (i.e., negative valence + moderate arousal) (Sazzad, AlZoubi, Calvo, & D'Mello, 2011) and can be positioned in the upper left quadrant of the Circumplex (see Russell, 1980 for details on the Circumplex model of affect). This categorization of confusion as an emotion should be taken to be tentative until there is more data to support or refute this position.

WHAT ARE THE APPRAISALS THAT LEAD TO CONFUSION?

The categorization of confusion as a knowledge emotion or an epistemic emotion implies that it has something to do with the state of an individual's knowledge. Indeed, confusion is hypothesized to occur when there is a mismatch of information, a violation of expectations, and other clashes of cognition during the processing of information. According to Mandler's interruption (discrepancy) theory (Mandler, 1990), individuals are constantly assimilating new information into existing knowledge schemas (e.g., an existing mental model). When new or discrepant information is detected (e.g., a conflict with prior knowledge or expectations), attention shifts to discrepant information, arousal increases in the autonomic nervous system, and the individual experiences a variety of possible emotions, depending on the context, the amount of change, and other relevant appraisals. Surprise is expected to occur when the degree of unexpectedness is high. Confusion is hypothesized to occur when there is a mismatch between incoming information and prior knowledge, or when new information cannot be integrated into existing mental models, thereby initiating cognitive disequilibrium. Confusion and surprise need not be mutually exclusive since surprise can precede confusion when an unexpected stimulus is appraised as being incomprehensible (Silvia, 2010).

Kagan (2009) provides a useful framework to discriminate among different states of uncertainty that are induced when low probability events are encountered. He identifies eight distinct states that emerge from appraising stimuli with respect to *familiarity* (familiar vs. unfamiliar), *expectation* (expected vs. unexpected), and *outcome* (desired vs. aversive). For example, a sudden clash of thunder while taking a stroll on a sunny day can be categorized as familiar (because one has heard thunder before), unexpected (because it is a sunny day), and aversive (because one has no umbrella). Uncertainty and confusion are expected to be maximized when the situation is unfamiliar, unexpected, and somewhat aversive, but this is entirely an empirical question.

Kagan also distinguishes *stimulus novelty,* which occurs when the unexpected events pertain to sensory information, from *conceptual novelty,* which is related to a mismatch of expectations in terms of an individual's knowledge structures and existing schemas. For example, hearing an unexpected high-pitched tone while learning Newtonian physics would be an example of stimulus novelty. On the other hand, watching a simulation of an elephant and a pebble being dropped from a skyscraper and noting that they both hit the ground at the same time would be conceptually novel if the individual has a fundamental misconception of Newton's second law of motion (i.e., the individual believes that heavier objects accelerate faster during free fall). The confusion that stems from conceptually novel events is of relevance to learning.

We have conducted a number of experiments to test the claim that confusion is elicited when there is conceptual novelty stemming from expectation violations and the presence of discrepancies in the information stream. In one set of experiments, confusion was induced while individuals performed a device comprehension task, such as trying to understand how toasters, doorbells, and other devices work from studying technical illustrated texts (D'Mello & Graesser, in review). The experimental trials consisted of presenting individuals with descriptions of device breakdowns (e.g., "When a person rang the bell there was a short *ding* and then no sound was heard") and asking them to diagnose the malfunction after they had studied a functioning device and had constructed a mental model of how it functions under normal operating conditions. The control trials simply involved comprehending the illustrated text without any breakdown descriptions. Confusion was measured via online self-reports after studying each device and was reported at significantly higher levels in the experimental trials than the control trials.

Contradictions are hypothesized to be another class of discrepant events that can induce confusion. We tested this hypothesis in three experiments that induced confusion by planting contradictory information during the learning of research methods. Specifically, learners discussed the scientific merits of sample research studies with two animated pedagogical agents: a tutor agent and a peer learner agent (D'Mello et al., 2014; Lehman et al., 2011). Contradictory trials involved the two animated agents expressing divergent opinions (one inaccurate and the other accurate or both inaccurate) and asking the (human) learners to decide which opinion had more scientific merit. Confusion was measured via a cued-recall procedure where participants made affect judgments by viewing videos of their faces and screens that were recorded during the learning task, with online self-reports, and by analyzing their response patterns (accuracy and consistency) immediately following contradictory trials. There was significantly higher confusion in the contradictory trials compared to the control trials that had no contradictions or inaccuracies.

Feedback plays an important role in learning because it is *directive* (i.e., tells learners what needs to be fixed), *facilitative* (i.e., helps learners conceptualize information), and has *motivational* functions (Shute, 2008). What are the consequences of false or inaccurate feedback? Will the novelty and violation of expectations caused by false feedback yield confusion? Indeed, a recent experiment indicated that learners self-reported more confusion and had longer response times when they received inaccurate feedback (i.e., correct responses received negative feedback from the computer tutor) (Lehman, D'Mello, & Graesser, 2012) compared to accurate feedback.

Earlier we categorized confusion as a knowledge emotion because it involves appraisals of information. It is useful to ascertain the extent to which the appraisal structure of confusion is aligned with other knowledge emotions, such as interest and surprise. Silvia (2010) posits that confusion and interest share an appraisal space consisting of novelty (familiar vs. unfamiliar) and comprehensibility (low vs. high). While both confusion and interest are expected to be triggered by highly novel events, Silvia hypothesized that confusion would be associated with appraisals of low comprehensibility, while interest would arise from high comprehensibility appraisals. In other words, a novel stimulus that could not be understood would be confusing, but a novel stimulus that could be understood would spark interest. This hypothesis was confirmed in an experiment involving comprehension of novel poems that were either comprehendible because background information required to understand the poem was provided (thereby triggering interest) or not comprehendible when participants had no background information (triggering confusion).

In summary, these experiments indicate that unexpected discrepant events induce confusion. This has been observed when the discrepancy is in the form of breakdowns, contradictions, false feedback, or the presentation of novel information that cannot be easily comprehended.

HOW IS CONFUSION EXPRESSED?

As Williams James (1884) put it so eloquently, "if we fancy some strong emotion, and then try to abstract from our consciousness of it all the feelings of its characteristic bodily symptoms, we find we have nothing left behind, no 'mind-stuff' out of which the emotion can be constituted, and that a cold and neutral state of intellectual perception is all that remains" (p. 193). Taking a cue from James that emotions and their expressions are inextricably coupled, we consider how confusion is expressed via the face, speech, posture, physiology, and language. Our emphasis is on studies that investigate naturalistic expressions of confusion instead of acted or posed expressions.

There are two primary methods of investigating the expressive components of emotion. The *theory-guided* approach focuses on a small set of expressions or actions (e.g., puckered lips, rises in pitch, forward leans) that have some theoretical-grounding as an expressive component of an emotion (see Russell et al., 2003, for a review). The advantage of this approach is that it affords the systematic testing of theory and yields highly interpretable expressive models of emotion. The disadvantage of this approach is that a large number of potential cues are ignored because they have no adequate grounding in theory. For example, it might be difficult to advance a theory as to why the kurtosis of the third formant of a speech signal is diagnostic of confusion. Should this feature simply be ignored in our quest for the vocal correlates of confusion?

The second is more of a *data-driven approach* that consists of computing large feature sets (potentially in the thousands) and applying automated data mining techniques (specifically machine learning) to narrow the feature space by identifying features that correlate with human-provided judgments of confusion, such as self-reports, online observations by researchers, or coding of video (see Calvo & D'Mello, 2010, for a review of these studies). The advantage is that this method has the potential to identify complex features that no theoretician would conjure a priori. The disadvantages are the potential lack of alignment with theory, the increased risk of Type I errors (although this risk can be eliminated with appropriate cross-validation methods), and problems interpreting some of the predictive models (as is the case when a neural network is used for prediction). The subsequent review includes both approaches. Aside from philosophical differences that are unlikely to ever be resolved, both systematic decoding studies (theory-guided approach) and data mining (data-driven approach) offer useful insights into how confusion is expressed.

Several of our findings pertaining to the expressive components of confusion were obtained in a study involving 28 learners who completed a 32-minute tutorial session with AutoTutor (D'Mello, Craig, Witherspoon, McDaniel, & Graesser, 2008; D'Mello & Graesser, 2009, 2010b), an intelligent tutoring system with conversational dialogue (Graesser, Chipman, Haynes, & Olney, 2005). This study is henceforth referred to as the *AutoTutor Multiple Judge Study*. Videos of the learners' faces, their computer screens, posture patterns, and logs of the interaction were recorded during the tutorial session. Approximately 100 judgments of each learner's emotions (boredom, flow/engagement, confusion, frustration, delight, surprise, and neutral) were provided by the learners themselves (self-report), untrained peers, and two trained judges via a cued-recall protocol (Graesser et al., 2006). The primary analysis consisted of extracting features from each of the informational streams and linking them to specific emotions using traditional statistical techniques as well as more advanced machine learning methods. The findings specific to different modalities are discussed below.

Facial Expressions

Darwin's (1872) observations about the emergence of frowns during disruptions of thought has been systematically confirmed in the few studies that have investigated the facial correlates of confusion. Using a theory-guided approach, Craig and colleagues (2008) performed an emote-aloud study where seven learners verbally expressed their emotions (as they occurred) during interactions with AutoTutor. Video recordings of learners' faces were manually coded for facial movements using the Facial Action Coding System (FACS; Ekman & Friesen, 1978). The Action Units (AUs) were correlated with online verbal reports of confusion. They found that a lowered brow (AU4), tightened lids (AU7), and combinations of these two facial movements (AU4 + AU7) were associated with confused expressions (see Figure 15.1). The lip corner puller (AU12) yielded a weaker but notable association with confusion. In a subsequent study (McDaniel et al., 2007),

Figure 15.1 Facial expressions of confusion.

FACS coding was performed on the videos collected in the *AutoTutor Multiple Judge Study*, and the observed AUs were correlated with affect judgments provided by two trained judges (as stated previously). Once again, the furrowed brow with tightened lids (AU4 + AU7) was predictive of confusion, although there was a notable lack of a link between AU12 and the expression of confusion. There is some additional converging evidence that is suggestive of the link between brow movements and confusion (Grafsgaard et al., 2011; Rozin & Cohen, 2003a), but more work is needed to identify additional facial indicators of confusion if they exist.

Speech Contours

Speech transmits affective information through the explicit linguistic message (what is said) and the implicit paralinguistic features of the expression (how it is said). Although it is clear that affective information is encoded and decoded through speech, there is also some ambiguity with respect to how different acoustic features communicate different emotions. One reliable finding is that pitch (*fo* or fundamental frequency) appears to be a reliable index into arousal (Johnstone & Scherer, 2000). Pitch has also been identified as a positive predictor of uncertainty (Forbes-Riley & Litman, 2011). This finding was obtained via a data-driven approach that involved regressing human-provided judgments of uncertainty on several acoustic and lexical features extracted from learner responses during one-on-one human-computer tutorial dialogues with the ITSpoke speech-enabled intelligent tutoring system. Future research is needed to replicate this finding and to identify additional vocal correlates of confusion.

Body Movements

Bodily movements are a much neglected but excellent channel to study the expression of emotion because the body is large and has multiple degrees of freedom. Bodily movements are presumably unconscious so they are less susceptible to social editing, at least when compared to the face and speech. We have analyzed how specific postures, as well as subtle changes in bodily fluctuations, are indicative of confusion and other emotions. For example, in the *AutoTutor Multiple Judge Study*, the pressure exerted on the back and seat of a pressure-sensitive chair was recorded during a tutorial session with AutoTutor (D'Mello & Graesser, 2009). When compared to the neutral state, confusion was accompanied by a decrease in the pressure exerted on the back of the chair without any accompanying increase on the seat. This is suggestive of an upright or alert posture (D'Mello & Graesser, 2010a).

In addition to specific postures, we have also investigated how subtle, presumably unconscious, bodily fluctuations covary with the experience of confusion and other emotions. We recently (D'Mello, Dale, & Graesser, 2012) tracked these movement dynamics using 1/f noise, pink noise, or fractal scaling during naturalistic experiences of affect in two studies involving deep learning and effortful problem solving. The results indicated that body movement fluctuations of individuals experiencing cognitive equilibrium was characteristic of correlated pink noise (i.e., an expected balance between determinism and randomness), but there was a whitening (i.e., more disorder or randomness) of the signal when individuals experienced states that are diagnostic of cognitive distress such as confusion.

Physiology

One of the key evolutionary functions of emotion is to prepare for rapid action in response to relevant environmental events. This call to action is accompanied by higher activation of the sympathetic nervous system. A large body of research has attempted to identify how different emotions are manifested in a number of physiological channels and devices such as electrocardiogram (ECG), electromyogram (EMG), galvanic skin response (GSR), respiration (RESP), skin temperature (ST), blood volume pressure (BVP), photoplethysmograph (PPG), impedance cardiogram (ICG), and electroencephalographs (EEG) (see Larsen, Berntson, Poehlmann, Ito, & Cacioppo, 2008, for a review). Although there has been some difficulty associated with identifying specific physiological responses for each emotion, physiological changes have been reliably linked to variations in arousal and sometimes valence (Barrett, 2006). The classification of confusion as a knowledge emotion raises the question of whether it has a specific physiological correlate, at least when compared to the more visceral emotions like disgust and fear.

This question was recently addressed by AlZoubi et al. (2012) who attempted to discriminate among several nonbasic emotions (e.g., confusion, curiosity) using ECG (electrical activity of the heart), EMG from the corrugator (brow) muscle, and GSR from finger tips. The physiological signals were collected while 27 learners completed a 45-minute tutorial session with AutoTutor. A total of 117 features were extracted from these three physiological channels and were used to predict self-reports of emotion obtained at 15-second intervals using a cued-recall procedure. They were able to obtain moderate accuracy in discriminating confusion from neutral and from other emotions. This suggests that confusion is to some extent manifested in physiology, although the exact nature of this manifestation is still unclear because the internals of machine learning models used in this research are not readily interpretable.

Language

Communication is one of the functions that is shared by language and emotions. It is perfectly clear that emotional content is routinely encoded in language as is the case when individuals write movie reviews, product reviews, blogs, and e-mail messages (see Pang & Lee, 2008, for an extensive review of sentiment analysis). But to what extent do individuals express emotions (particularly confusion) during learning? This question was investigated by analyzing 1,167 learner responses collected over the course of 28 tutorial interactions collected in the *AutoTutor Multiple Judge Study* (D'Mello & Graesser, 2012). We were only able to identify one occurrence of an explicit emotional expression ("I'm confused") in this corpus of learner utterances. Therefore, individuals experiencing confusion very rarely overtly label this emotion to a computer tutor. A similar finding was obtained in an analysis of transcripts from 50 tutorial sessions between learners and human tutors (D'Mello & Graesser, 2012). The lack of verbal emotion expressions in these learner utterances is somewhat surprising because an in-depth analysis of videos of both the human-computer and human-human sessions indicated that there were numerous emotional episodes (D'Mello & Graesser, 2012; Lehman, Matthews, D'Mello, & Person, 2008). This suggests that a more systematic textual analysis of tutorial dialogues might be necessary to uncover cues that might be diagnostic of learner emotions.

We explored this possibility by investigating the extent to which particular emotions are reflected in learner responses by considering a broad profile of language characteristics measured by the Linguistic Inquiry and Word Count (LIWC) (Pennebaker, Francis, & Booth, 2001) and Coh-Metrix (Graesser, McNamara, Louwerse, & Cai, 2004). LIWC is a validated computer tool that analyzes bodies of text using a large lexicon of words that have been rated on approximately 80 psychological and linguistic features. Coh-Metrix automatically analyzes text with respect to hundreds of measures of different types of cohesion (e.g., co-reference, referential, causal), genre, syntactic complexity, characteristics of words, and readability. Confusion was predicted by learner responses that were lacking in connectives (e.g., "hence," "because"), which is indicative of fragmented and less-cohesive responses. Confusion was also predicted by an increased use of inhibitory terms akin to "block," "constrain," and "stop" as measured by LIWC. This analysis revealed that although learners do not directly express their confusion, their responses inevitably convey their confusion by the words they use and by the connectives that hold their responses together.

Discourse Features and Contextual Cues

One advantage of investigating emotions with a dialogue-based intelligent tutoring system like AutoTutor is that the dialogue history provides a rich trace into the contextual underpinnings of learners' emotional experiences. To what extent is confusion manifested in these features of discourse and other conversational cues? To address this question, we analyzed the interaction logs collected in the *AutoTutor Multiple Judge Study*. Specifically, we examined the tutorial dialogue (i.e., the context) over 15-second intervals that culminated in episodes of confusion (D'Mello, Craig, Witherspoon, McDaniel, & Graesser, 2008). An event triggering confusion could either be tutor generated (e.g., the tutor provided a vague hint), learner generated (e.g., the learner has a misconception), or session related (e.g., early vs. late in the session). The results indicated that confusion occurred earlier in the session, within the first few attempts to answer a question, with slower and less verbose responses, with responses that had low conceptual quality, with frozen expressions (e.g., "I don't care" or "Please repeat" instead of domain-related contributions), when the tutor was less direct (i.e., more vague hints rather than explanations), and when the tutor provided negative feedback. These relationships between the various discourse features and confusion are generally in the expected directions.

WHAT ARE THE TEMPORAL DYNAMICS OF CONFUSION?

One aspect of confusion and of emotions in general that has not received sufficient attention is the chronometry or temporal dynamics of emotion. As an initial step to understanding temporal dynamics, we present a sketch of a model that predicts specific confusion trajectories on the basis of the severity of the discrepant event that triggers confusion and the results of confusion regulation processes. We also present some preliminary data that supports parts of the model.

The model assumes that individuals encounter discrepancies at multiple levels as they attempt to assimilate incoming information into existing mental models. There is some threshold T_a that needs to be exceeded before the individual is confused. Discrepancies that are not severe enough to exceed T_a are not detected by the individual, and there is no confusion. Sometimes the severity of the discrepancy greatly exceeds T_a, and the individual is bewildered or flustered. Let us denote this threshold as T_b.

A moderate level of confusion is experienced when the severity of the discrepancy meets or exceeds T_a but is less than T_b. The individual may not elect to attend to the confusion and shift attentional resources elsewhere. When this occurs, confusion is alleviated very quickly, and the length of confusion is less than duration D_a. If the length of the confusion episode exceeds D_a, then the individual has begun to attempt to identify the source of the discrepancy in order to resolve the confusion. When confusion resolution fails and the individual is confused for a long enough duration D_b, then there is the risk of frustration. With a longer duration D_c, there is a persistent frustration and the risk of disengagement and boredom (i.e., the learner gives up). There is potentially a *zone of optimal confusion*, which occurs when: $T_a >$ *discrepancy* $< T_b$ and $D_a >$ *duration* $< D_b$.

Some evidence in support of this model can be obtained from some recent research that identified *confusion-engagement, confusion-frustration,* and *frustration-boredom* oscillations during interactions with AutoTutor (D'Mello & Graesser, 2012). These oscillations are depicted in Figure 15.2. The confusion-engagement transition is presumably linked to experiencing discrepancies (engagement to confusion) and successfully resolving the confusion (confusion to engagement). The confusion-frustration transition likely occurs when a learner experiences failure when attempting to resolve an impasse (confusion to frustration) and experiences additional impasse(s) when frustrated (frustration to confusion). Transitions involving boredom and frustration are ostensibly related to a state of being stuck due to persistent failure to the point of disengaging (frustration to boredom) and annoyance from being forced to persist in the task despite having mentally disengaged (boredom to frustration).

In addition to these transitions across states, we have also made some progress towards fitting exponential decay curves to study the decay characteristics of confusion

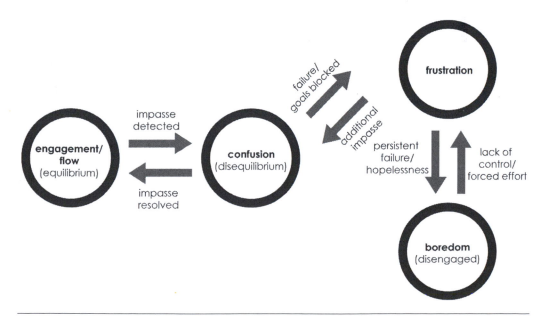

Figure 15.2 Affect transitions.

trajectories of individual learners (D'Mello & Graesser, 2011). What is missing, however, is the task of specifying and testing the various durations and thresholds of the model, which likely depend on some interaction between individual differences and the complexity of the materials and task. Systematically fitting these parameters in a manner that is sensitive to constraints of the individual, the environment, and their interaction is an important item for future work.

HOW IS CONFUSION REGULATED?

Individuals who are confused ideally pursue effective ways to regulate their confusion in order to restore equilibrium. Emotions theorists have identified a number of strategies that individuals enact to regulate their emotions. These include situation selection, situation modification, attentional deployment, cognitive change, and response modulation (Gross, 2008; see also Jacobs & Gross, 2014). The first two strategies, situation selection and situation modification, are regulatory strategies aimed at selecting and modifying contexts (situations) that minimize or maximize the likelihood of experiencing certain emotions. Attentional deployment involves either attending to (e.g., ruminating) or avoiding (e.g., distraction) an object or event that can trigger an emotion. Cognitive reappraisal (Dandoy & Goldstein, 1990) involves changing the perceived meaning of a situation in order to alter its emotional content. Finally, response modulation involves a sustained effort to either overemphasize or minimize (e.g., suppression) the expression of an emotion.

There undoubtedly are individual differences in how learners experience and regulate confusion. Some learners might attempt to avoid confusion (and other negative emotions) by seeking out tasks with minimal intellectual challenges (situation selection), immediately seeking help when challenged (situation modification), avoiding attending to events within a situation that might be challenging (distraction/attentional deployment), intentionally ignoring or misattributing the cause of discrepant events to avoid confusion (reappraisal), and even withholding bodily expressions by adopting a poker face when confused (response modification). In contrast to these cautious learners, academic risk takers (Clifford, 1988) might engage in tasks that are intellectually stimulating (situation selection and modification), persevere on difficult problems, and consider challenges and failure to be necessary conditions to develop proficiency (reappraisal).

At this point in science, it is unclear if and to what extent learners utilize these strategies to regulate confusion. It is likely that confusion is perceived to be an aversive state, so learners who experience cognitive disequilibrium must resolve their confusion in order to restore equilibrium. Hence, one way to regulate confusion is to engage in cognitive activities to resolve the confusion, but this is only an assumption at this time. Four possible (but nonexclusive) trajectories of confusion dynamics as a function of the outcome of effortful resolution processes are shown in Figure 15.3.

One possibility is that confusion quickly rises, but it rapidly dissipates soon after (*quick rise and rapid dissipation* trajectory, see Figure 15.3a). It is possible that a learner might never fully resolve his or her confusion, and it might even increase as time progresses, thereby producing the *slow rise but never peak* trajectory depicted in Figure 15.3b. Alternately, confusion might adopt a *rise, peak, hold, decay* model (see Figure 15.3c) (Davidson, 1998; Rosenberg, 1998). According to this model, confusion gradually rises

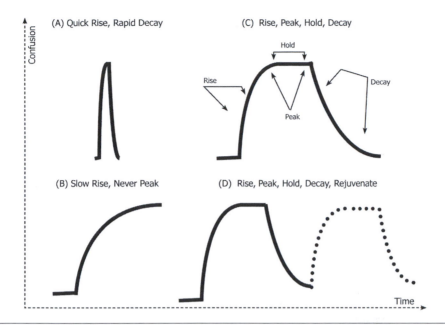

Figure 15.3 Confusion growth and decay dynamics.

until it peaks, presumably when an impasse is fully detected. Confusion is then held at its peak as the learner tries to resolve his or her confusion. Confusion begins to decay if and when the impasse is resolved or the source of a discrepancy is discovered. There is also the possibility that the learner might have not correctly resolved the impasse, and the rise, peak, hold, decay cycle is rejuvenated if a discrepancy is discovered (Figure 15.3d). Of critical importance is the observation that confusion is never fully resolved in the slow rise but never peak trajectory. This form of unresolved (hopeless) confusion is expected to accompany poor performance when compared to situations where confusion is immediately or eventually resolved.

The data from the device comprehension study (D'Mello & Graesser, in review) described earlier (see section on appraisals) was used to assess whether learners adhered to any or some of these trajectories and on the relationship between confusion resolution and learning. Specifically, learners participated in a cued-recall task in which they provided continuous confusion judgments by viewing videos of their faces that were recorded while they were attempting to diagnose the cause of device malfunctions. A second-by-second analysis of these confusion time series yielded two characteristic trajectories that successfully distinguished those learners who partially resolved their confusion (*rise, peak, hold, decay*) from those who remained confused (*slow rise but never peak*). As predicted, learners who partially resolved their confusion performed significantly better on a subsequent comprehension test than learners who remained confused. In addition to this study, Rodrigo and colleagues have reported some converging evidence to support this distinction between resolved and unresolved confusion and the differential impact of these processes on learning in more authentic contexts, such as learning computer programming in computer labs in schools (Lee, Rodrigo, Baker, Sugay, & Coronel, 2011; Rodrigo, Baker, & Nabos, 2010).

WHY IS CONFUSION RELEVANT TO LEARNING?

We have described a number of studies that have investigated different but related aspects of confusion. Although the context of these studies has been learning and problem-solving tasks, we now turn to the fundamental question of why confusion is relevant to learning. In our view, confusion plays a prominent role in learning activities that are pitched at deeper levels of comprehension and especially when the learner needs to bridge the gap between an existing (and usually faulty) mental model and an ideal conceptual model (Chi, 2008; Chinn & Brewer, 1993; Nersessian, 2008) (also see Sinatra, Broughton, & Lombardi, 2014). For example, a learner who has the faulty mental model that heavier objects accelerate faster than lighter objects during free-fall must confront this misconception in order to arrive at a mental model that is consistent with Newton's second law. The learner will be in a state of cognitive disequilibrium and experience confusion when they detect the misconception. The next section discusses some of the conditions where confusion might be beneficial to learning. Here, we focus on the incidence of confusion across multiple learning contexts.

In general, confusion is expected to be more the norm than the exception for complex learning tasks, such as learning the principles of ecological succession, comprehending a legal document, fixing a broken piece of equipment, and debugging errors in a computer program. Some compelling evidence to support this claim can be found in a recent meta-analysis that analyzed 24 studies that used a mixture of methodologies to systematically monitor the emotions (15 emotions plus neutral) of 1,740 middle school, high school, college, and adult learners in five countries over the course of more than 1,000 hours of continuous interactions with a range of learning technologies including intelligent tutoring systems, serious games, and simulation environments (D'Mello, 2013). The incidence of confusion was consistent with small or larger effects (i.e., Cohen's $d > 0.2$) compared to the other emotions in approximately half of the studies, which is reasonable given that the different learning environments varied with respect to the complexity of the learning task (e.g., writing an essay vs. learning about computer architecture). Confusion was found to be less frequent than engagement/flow, as frequent as boredom and happiness, somewhat more frequent than curiosity and frustration, and substantially more frequent than anxiety, contempt, delight, disgust, fear, sadness, and surprise. In addition to its prevalence during human-computer interactions, confusion has also been found to be quite frequent in human-human tutoring sessions. For example, Lehman and colleagues (2008) coded videos collected over the course of 50 hours of interactions between students and expert human tutors. They found that confusion was the most frequent emotion, comprising one third of all recorded emotion instances.

It should be noted that confusion is more than a mere incidental corollary of complex learning activities. Confusion is also related to learning outcomes. In a detailed analysis of human-human tutorial dialogues, VanLehn and colleagues (2003) reported that learning of conceptual physics concepts was rare if learners did not reach an impasse (which we assume to involve some level of confusion) irrespective of the explanations provided by the tutor. Craig, Graesser, Sullins, and Gholson (2004) conducted an online observational study in which the affective states (frustration, boredom, engagement/flow, confusion, eureka) of 34 learners were coded by observers every five minutes during interactions with AutoTutor. When learning gains were regressed on the incidence of the individual emotions, confusion was the only emotion that significantly predicted learning. This finding of a positive correlation between confusion and learning has subsequently been replicated in follow-up studies with AutoTutor that used different methods to monitor emotions (D'Mello & Graesser, 2011; Graesser, Chipman, King, McDaniel, & D'Mello, 2007). Some recent data has also causally linked confusion and learning gains, but this depends on how confusion is attended to and the extent to which it is effectively regulated. This data is discussed in the next section.

WHEN IS CONFUSION BENEFICIAL TO LEARNING?

Confusion is expected to be beneficial to learning because it signals that there is something wrong with the current state of the world. This jolts the cognitive system out of equilibrium, focuses attention on the anomaly or discrepancy, and motivates learners to effortfully deliberate, problem solve, and restructure their cognitive system in order to resolve the confusion and return to a state of equilibrium. These activities inspire greater depth of processing, more durable memory representations, more successful retrieval, and consequently enhanced learning. It is not the confusion itself, but the cognitive activities that accompany its experience, that presumably influence learning. In this respect, confusion may not have a direct causal effect on learning, but rather serves as some form of a moderator on learning outcomes.

We have recently conducted three experiments to test for a moderation effect of confusion on learning (D'Mello et al., 2014; Lehman et al., 2011). These experiments were briefly introduced in the section on appraisals but are discussed in more detail in this section. The learning context for these experiments was the teaching of conceptual skills pertaining to scientific reasoning, such as stating hypotheses, identifying dependent and independent variables, isolating potential confounds in designs, interpreting trends in data, determining if data support predictions, and understanding effect sizes (Halpern, 2003; Millis et al., 2011). We developed a multimedia learning environment that attempted to teach these fundamental scientific inquiry skills by presenting example cases of studies (including the research design, participants, methods, results, and conclusions) that were frequently flawed because they violated principles of good research. Learners were instructed to evaluate the merits of the studies and point out flaws in the design.

The critiques of sample research studies were accomplished by holding multiturn trialogues with two embodied conversational agents and the human learner. One agent called the *tutor agent,* or *Dr. Williams,* led the tutorial lessons and served as an expert on scientific inquiry. The second agent, *Chris,* was the *peer-agent,* who simulated a peer of the human learner (i.e., the participant in the experiment). The human learners interacted with both agents by holding conversations in natural language that were designed to mimic human-human tutorial interactions.

Confusion was experimentally manipulated over the course of these multiturn trialogues by a manipulation of contradictory information. This occurred by having the animated agents occasionally disagreeing on ideas by voicing inaccurate information (experimental trials) and asking the human learner to intervene and decide which opinion had the most scientific merit. The source, timing, and content of the contradictions varied across conditions and experiments, details of which are beyond the scope of this chapter. What is important is that confusion was induced by providing misleading and sometimes incorrect information. However, all misleading information was corrected over the course of the trialogues, and learners were fully debriefed at the end of the experiment.

The results were illuminating in a number of respects. One finding was that the contradictions were quite effective in inducing confusion. Interestingly, the learners were somewhat reticent to admit that they were confused, but their underlying confusion was revealed through more objective measures consisting of their responses to probe questions immediately following the contradictions. As predicted, confusion moderated the effect of the contradictions on learning gains. Learning gains for contradictory trials were statistically equivalent to no-contradiction control trials when learners were not confused by the contradictions. However, learners who were confused by the contradictions had substantially higher learning gains in the contradictory trials than in the control trials. This effect was observed for simple multiple choice tests of knowledge and on subsequent transfer tests, some of which consisted of identifying flaws in case studies that were radically different than the case studies discussed during the trialogues.

Some of these effects have also been observed in a recently completed study where confusion was induced via a false feedback manipulation in lieu of contradictions (Lehman et al., in 2012). Learners who initially provided correct answers but received negative feedback reported more confusion, had longer response times immediately following the false feedback (processing incongruities), and spent more time studying an explanatory text (greater depth of processing) than controls. Importantly, learners demonstrated enhanced learning gains compared to those who received accurate feedback (positive feedback for correct responses), but only when they reported being confused by the feedback.

In summary, although systematic research on the potential facilitative effects of confusion on learning is in its infancy, there appear to be some measurable benefits to productively confusing learners in order to promote deeper inquiry. These findings, which highlight the beneficial role of confusion to learning, are consistent with Piaget's (1952) notion of *accommodation* because learners must, to some extent, alter their mental models in order to resolve their confusion. These findings also contribute to an impressive body of evidence on the facilitative effects of negative mood states on the process of accommodation; this literature is surveyed in considerable detail by Fiedler and Beier (2014). Although it is tempting to merely attribute the facilitative effects of confusion to the fact that it is a negatively valenced emotion, it is important to note that all negative affective states are not created alike. Indeed, there is a world of difference between a background negative mood state that subtly biases cognition and an intense experience of a negative emotion that overtakes cognition (Rosenberg, 1998). Frustration, for example, is a negative activating emotion (similar to confusion), but it is unlikely to yield any of the learning benefits associated with confusion. For that matter, neither are disgust, fear, or contempt.

SUMMARY, IMPLICATIONS, FUTURE WORK, AND CONCLUSIONS

The last decade has ushered in considerable excitement for research on emotions in the affective, learning, and computer sciences. Some landmarks include the launch of the APA journal *Emotion* in 2001, the launch of *Emotion Review* in 2009, Schutz and Pekrun's (2007) edited volume *Emotions in Education,* and numerous special issues on affect and its relationship with learning (e.g., Linnenbrink-Garcia & Pekrun, 2011).

Computer scientists and engineers are also fascinated by emotion, a movement that can be traced to Picard's (1997) book *Affective Computing*. The 2010 launch of *Transactions in Affective Computing*, a scholarly journal published by the Institute for Electrical and Electronic Engineers (IEEE), offers further evidence that we now live in a world of *computational emotions* (systems that sense, induce, respond to, and synthesize emotions).

We are also living in an era of interdisciplinary research as emotion, education, and computing researchers forgo traditional disciplinary boundaries in a collaborative effort to do basic research on emotions during learning and to leverage these insights towards the development of technologies that help students learn by coordinating emotion and cognition. Some of this emerging interdisciplinary research has been compiled in Calvo and D'Mello's (2011) edited volume *New Perspectives on Affect and Learning Technologies*. As with any burgeoning research area, there are currently more open questions than answers, but this only fuels interest and enthusiasm for more research.

In keeping with this interdisciplinary spirit, much of the research described in this chapter has adopted an interdisciplinary approach that has encompassed multiple theoretical frameworks, methodologies, and instruments to shed light on one ubiquitous but inconspicuous emotion—confusion. We made an effort to argue in favor of categorizing confusion as an emotion, discussed the appraisals that lead to confusion, examined how confusion is expressed across multiple modalities that encompass the mind and body, explored the temporal dynamics of confusion, and described how confusion might be regulated. After examining these interrelated aspects of confusion, we discussed why confusion is very relevant to learning and explored circumstances in which confusion moderates learning outcomes.

Many of the studies on confusion featured in this chapter have been laboratory studies with limited ecological validity. These studies have been instrumental in confirming some expected patterns (e.g., the link between a furrowed brow and expressions of confusion) and revealing some nonobvious patterns (e.g., positive correlation between confusion and learning). However, it is unclear whether these patterns will be observed in more authentic learning contexts where a large number of extraneous variables come into play. Replicating and extending these initial laboratory findings in classrooms and other learning situations would represent an important step forward. It is also highly likely that previously unforeseen patterns will be discovered when confusion is investigated in more authentic learning contexts.

We conclude this chapter by briefly describing some of the important implications, challenges, and opportunities for a research program centered on confusion. Although such a discussion can warrant a chapter in itself, we focus on three major points. First, the empirical status of confusion as an emotion currently suffers from a lack of positive evidence rather than a surplus of negative evidence. Hence, there is a pressing need for basic research to validate or disprove our tentative categorization of confusion as an emotion. The phenomenon of confusion itself is completely oblivious to its categorization as an emotion, a cognition, or a blend of the two, so one might question the utility of advancing a research program to test the *confusion as an emotion* hypothesis. Although we are sympathetic to this view, and have previously argued against the false cognition versus emotion dichotomy (Graesser & D'Mello, 2011), the reality is that the scientific study of confusion is likely to flourish if there is sufficient empirical evidence to elevate it to the privileged status of a bona fide emotion, on par with the basic emotions of happiness, sadness, fear, disgust, anger, and surprise. It is somewhat paradoxical that one must first conduct a large body of research on confusion to show that it is an emotion before researchers are encouraged to scientifically investigate confusion as an emotion.

Second, within the educational realm, there appear to be some learning benefits associated with confusion. A somewhat controversial implication of our research is that pedagogical practices that attempt to productively confuse learners might be attractive alternatives to the typical information delivery systems that are comfortable for passive learning but rarely promote deep insight. One can imagine a world where interventions that expose misconceptions might be cherished instead of chastised, complexity might be a valuable substitute or complement for clarity, and less cohesive texts and lectures might replace the polished information deliveries of textbooks and formal lectures. Learning of difficult conceptual material is chaotic, gritty, and confusing, so there might be advantages to interventions with embedded challenges and other desirable difficulties (Bjork & Bjork, 2011), especially if the goal is to promote learning at deeper levels of comprehension. We have not formally studied this issue, but we suspect that most students and teachers perceive confusion to be reflective of failure and negativity, so there is an initial challenge of changing this simplistic and somewhat inaccurate mindset.

To be clear, we are not advocating learning environments that intentionally confuse low-achieving learners, learners with minimal motivation, and learners who risk dropping out when there is hopeless and unproductive confusion. It is worth noting, however, that stemming from Piaget's (1952) theory of cognitive development, there have been several attempts at promoting conceptual change by inducing cognitive conflict in classrooms (see Limón, 2001, for a review of these studies), so our suggestions are not entirely radical. Nevertheless, there obviously is no one-size-fits-all approach to learning, so these somewhat unconventional interventions should be differentially and dynamically sensitive to individual learners. Adapting pedagogical strategies to individual learners is difficult to achieve in formal learning contexts, but this is precisely the niche in which advanced learning technologies excel. Intelligent tutoring systems have made significant advances in creating fine-grained models of learner knowledge and have leveraged these models to select learning trajectories that are optimized to individual learners (Corbett & Anderson, 1994; Koedinger & Corbett, 2006). These systems can be augmented with the ability to induce confusion at the appropriate time and with the appropriate level of discrepancies, track the induced confusion using state-of-the art affect detection systems (Calvo & D'Mello, 2010; D'Mello & Graesser, 2010b), and implement scaffolds that help learners regulate their confusion so that they correct problematic misconceptions, resolve impasses, and revise faulty mental models. This is exactly the sort of scientific and technological infrastructure that is needed to design interventions that keep learners balanced between the extremes of boredom and bewilderment by selecting materials and challenges within their *zones of optimal confusion*.

REFERENCES

AlZoubi, O., D'Mello, S. K., & Calvo, R. A. (2012). Detecting naturalistic expressions of nonbasic affect using physiological signals. *IEEE Transactions on Affective Computing, 3*, 298–310.

Barrett, L. (2006). Are emotions natural kinds? *Perspectives on Psychological Science, 1*, 28–58.

Berlyne, D. (1960). *Conflict, arousal, and curiosity.* New York, NY: McGraw-Hill.

Bjork, E. L., & Bjork, R. A. (2011). Making things hard on yourself, but in a good way: Creating desirable difficulties to enhance learning. In M. A. Gernsbacher, R. W. Pew, L. M. Hough, & J. R. Pomerantz (Eds.), *Psychology and the real world: Essays illustrating fundamental contributions to society* (pp. 56–64). New York, NY: Worth Publishers.

Calvo, R. A., & D'Mello, S. K. (2010). Affect detection: An interdisciplinary review of models, methods, and their applications. *IEEE Transactions on Affective Computing, 1,* 18–37.

Calvo, R. A., & D'Mello, S. K. (2011). *New perspectives on affect and learning technologies.* New York, NY: Springer.

Chi, M. (2008). Three types of conceptual change: Belief revision, mental model transformation, and categorical shift. In S. Vosniadou (Ed.), *International handbook of research on conceptual change* (pp. 61–82). New York, NY: Routledge.

Chinn, C., & Brewer, W. (1993). The role of anomalous data in knowledge acquisition—A theoretical framework and implications for science instruction. *Review of Educational Research, 63,* 1–49.

Clifford, M. (1988). Failure tolerance and academic risk-taking in ten- to twelve-year-old students. *British Journal of Educational Psychology, 58,* 15–27.

Clore, G. L. (1992). Cognitive phenomenology: Feelings and the construction of judgment. In L. L. Martin & A. Tesser (Eds.), *The construction of social judgments* (pp. 133–163). Hillsdale, NJ: Erlbaum.

Collins, A. (1974). Reasoning from incomplete knowledge. *Bulletin of the Psychonomic Society, 4,* 254–254.

Corbett, A., & Anderson, J. (1994). Knowledge tracing—Modeling the acquisition of procedural knowledge. *User Modeling And User-Adapted Interaction, 4,* 253–278.

Craig, S., D'Mello, S., Witherspoon, A., & Graesser, A. (2008). Emote aloud during learning with AutoTutor: Applying the facial action coding system to cognitive-affective states during learning. *Cognition & Emotion, 22,* 777–788.

Craig, S., Graesser, A., Sullins, J., & Gholson, J. (2004). Affect and learning: An exploratory look into the role of affect in learning. *Journal of Educational Media, 29,* 241–250.

Dandoy, A. C., & Goldstein, A. G. (1990). The use of cognitive appraisal to reduce stress reactions—A replication. *Journal of Social Behavior and Personality, 5,* 275–285.

Darwin, C. (1872). *The expression of the emotions in man and animals.* London, England: John Murray.

Davidson, R. J. (1998). Affective style and affective disorders: Perspectives from affective neuroscience. *Cognition & Emotion, 12,* 307–330.

de Smet, Y., Ruberg, M., Serdaru, M., Dubois, B., Lhermitte, G., & Agid, Y. (1982). Confusion, dementia and anticholinergics in Parkinson's disease. *Journal of Neurology, Neurosurgery and Psychiatry, 45,* 1161–1164.

D'Mello, S. K. (2013). A selective meta-analysis on the relative incidence of discrete affective states during learning with technology, *Journal of Educational Psychology, 105,* 1082–1099.

D'Mello, S., Craig, S., Witherspoon, A., McDaniel, B., & Graesser, A. (2008). Automatic detection of learner's affect from conversational cues. *User Modeling and User-Adapted Interaction, 18,* 45–80.

D'Mello, S., Dale, R., & Graesser, A. (2012). Disequilibrium in the mind, disharmony in the body. *Cognition & Emotion, 26,* 362–374.

D'Mello, S., & Graesser, A. (2009). Automatic detection of learners' affect from gross body language. *Applied Artificial Intelligence, 23,* 123–150.

D'Mello, S., & Graesser, A. (2010a). Mining bodily patterns of affective experience during learning. In A. Merceron, P. Pavlik, & R. Baker (Eds.), *Proceedings of the third International Conference on Educational Data Mining* (pp. 31–40). International Educational Data Mining Society.

D'Mello, S., & Graesser, A. (2010b). Multimodal semi-automated affect detection from conversational cues, gross body language, and facial features. *User Modeling and User-adapted Interaction, 20,* 147–187.

D'Mello, S., & Graesser, A. (2011). The half-life of cognitive-affective states during complex learning. *Cognition & Emotion, 25,* 1299–1308.

D'Mello, S., & Graesser, A. (2012). Dynamics of affective states during complex learning. *Learning and Instruction, 22,* 145–157.

D'Mello, S. K. & Graesser, A. C. (2012). Language and discourse are powerful signals of student emotions during tutoring. *IEEE Transactions on Learning Technologies, 5,* 304–317.

D'Mello, S., & Graesser, A. (in review). Confusion and its dynamics during device comprehension with breakdown scenarios.

D'Mello, S. K., Lehman, B. Pekrun, R., & Graesser, A. C. (2014). Confusion can be beneficial for learning, *Learning & Instruction, 29,* 153–170.

Ekman, P., & Friesen, W. (1978). *The Facial Action Coding System: A technique for the measurement of facial movement*. Palo Alto, CA: Consulting Psychologists Press.

Ellsworth, P. C. (2003). Confusion, concentration, and other emotions of interest: Commentary on Rozin and Cohen (2003). *Emotion, 3,* 81–85.

Festinger, L. (1957). *A theory of cognitive dissonance*. Stanford, CA: Stanford University Press.

Fiedler, K., & Beier, S., (2014). Affect and cognitive processes in educational contexts. In R. Pekrun & L. Linnenbrink-Garcia (Eds.), *International handbook of emotions in education* (pp. 36–55). New York, NY: Taylor & Francis.

Forbes-Riley, K., & Litman, D. J. (2011). Benefits and challenges of real-time uncertainty detection and adaptation in a spoken dialogue computer tutor. *Speech Communication, 53,* 1115–1136.

Graesser, A., Chipman, P., Haynes, B., & Olney, A. (2005). AutoTutor: An intelligent tutoring system with mixed-initiative dialogue. *IEEE Transactions on Education, 48,* 612–618.

Graesser, A., Chipman, P., King, B., McDaniel, B., & D'Mello, S. (2007). Emotions and learning with AutoTutor. In R. Luckin, K. Koedinger & J. Greer (Eds.), *Proceedings of the 13th International Conference on Artificial Intelligence in Education* (pp. 569–571). Amsterdam, Netherlands: IOS Press.

Graesser, A., & D'Mello, S. (2011). Theoretical perspectives on affect and deep learning. In R. Calvo & S. D'Mello (Eds.), *New perspective on affect and learning technologies* (pp. 11–22). New York, NY: Springer.

Graesser, A., McDaniel, B., Chipman, P., Witherspoon, A., D'Mello, S., & Gholson, B. (2006). Detection of emotions during learning with AutoTutor. In R. Sun & N. Miyake (Eds.), *Proceedings of the 28th Annual Conference of the Cognitive Science Society* (pp. 285–290). Austin, TX: Cognitive Science Society.

Graesser, A., McNamara, D., Louwerse, M., & Cai, Z. (2004). Coh-Metrix: Analysis of text on cohesion and language. *Behavior Research Methods, Instruments, & Computers, 36,* 193–202.

Graesser, A., & Olde, B. (2003). How does one know whether a person understands a device? The quality of the questions the person asks when the device breaks down. *Journal of Educational Psychology, 95,* 524–536.

Grafsgaard, J., Boyer, K., & Lester, J. (2011). Predicting facial indicators of confusion with hidden markov models. In S. D'Mello, A. Graesser, B. Schuller, & J. Martin (Eds.), *Proceedings of the 4th International Conference on Affective Computing and Intelligent Interaction (ACII 2011)* (pp. 97–106). Berlin Heidelberg, Germany: Springer.

Gross, J. (2008). Emotion regulation. In M. Lewis, J. Haviland-Jones, & L. Barrett (Eds.), *Handbook of emotions* (3rd ed., pp. 497–512). New York, NY: Guilford.

Gross, J. J., & Barrett, L. F. (2011). Emotion generation and emotion regulation: One or two depends on your point of view. *Emotion Review, 3,* 8–16.

Halgren, E., Dhond, R. P., Christensen, N., Van Petten, C., Marinkovic, K., Lewine, J. D., & Dale, A. M. (2002). N400-like magnetoencephalography responses modulated by semantic context, word frequency, and lexical class in sentences. *NouroImage, 17,* 1101–1116.

Halpern, D. F. (2003). *Thought and knowledge: An introduction to critical thinking* (4th ed.). Mahwah, NJ: Erlbaum.

Hess, U. (2003). Now you see it, now you don't—the confusing case of confusion as an emotion: Commentary on Rozin and Cohen (2003). *Emotion, 3,* 76–80.

Izard, C. (2010). The many meanings/aspects of emotion: Definitions, functions, activation, and regulation. *Emotion Review, 2,* 363–370.

Jacobs, S. E., & Gross, J. J. (2014). Emotion regulation in education: Conceptual foundations, current applications, and future directions. In R. Pekrun & L. Linnenbrink-Garcia (Eds.), *International handbook of emotions in education* (pp. 183–201). New York, NY: Taylor & Francis.

James, W. (1884). What is an emotion? *Mind, 9,* 188–205.

Johnstone, T., & Scherer, K. (2000). Vocal communication of emotion. In M. Lewis & J. Haviland-Jones (Eds.), *Handbook of emotions* (2nd ed., pp. 220–235). New York, NY: Guilford Press.

Kagan, J. (2009). Categories of novelty and states of uncertainty. *Review of General Psychology, 13,* 290–301.

Keltner, D., & Shiota, M. (2003). New displays and new emotions: A commentary on Rozin and Cohen (2003). *Emotion, 3,* 86–91.

Koedinger, K., & Corbett, A. (2006). Cognitive tutors: Technology bringing learning sciences to the classroom. In R. K. Sawyer (Ed.), *The Cambridge handbook of the learning sciences* (pp. 61–78). New York, NY: Cambridge University Press.

Kutas, M., & Hillyard, S. A. (1980). Reading senseless sentences: Brain potentials reflect semantic incongruity. *Science, 207,* 203–205.

Laird, J. E., Newell, A., & Rosenbloom, P. S. (1987). Soar—an architecture for general intelligence. *Artificial Intelligence, 33*, 1–64.

Larsen, J., Berntson, G., Poehlmann, K., Ito, T., & Cacioppo, J. (2008). The psychophysiology of emotion. In M. Lewis, J. Haviland-Jones, & L. Barrett (Eds.), *Handbook of emotions* (3rd ed., pp. 180–195). New York, NY: Guilford.

Lee, D. M., Rodrigo, M. M., Baker, R. S., Sugay, J., & Coronel, A. (2011). Exploring the relationship between novice programmer confusion and achievement. In S. D'Mello, A. Graesser, B. Schuller, & J. Martin (Eds.), *Proceedings of the 4th bi-annual International Conference on Affective Computing and Intelligent Interaction* (pp. 175–184). Berlin, Germany: Springer.

Lehman, B., D'Mello, S., Chauncey, A., Gross, M., Dobbins, A., Wallace, P.... Graesser, A. C. (2011). Inducing and tracking confusion with contradictions during critical thinking and scientific reasoning. In S. Bull & G. Biswas (Eds.), *Proceedings of the 15th International Conference on Artificial Intelligence in Education* (pp. 171–178). New York, NY: Springer.

Lehman, B., D'Mello, S. K., & Graesser, A. C. (2012). Confusion and complex learning during interactions with computer learning environments, *The Internet and Higher Education, 15*, 184–194.

Lehman, B., Matthews, M., D'Mello, S., & Person, N. (2008). What are you feeling? Investigating student affective states during expert human tutoring sessions. In B. Woolf, E. Aimeur, R. Nkambou, & S. Lajoie (Eds.), *Proceedings of the 9th International Conference on Intelligent Tutoring Systems* (pp. 50–59). Berlin, Germany: Springer.

Limón, M. (2001). On the cognitive conflict as an instructional strategy for conceptual change: a critical appraisal. *Learning and Instruction, 11*, 357–380.

Lindquist, K. A., Wager, T., D., Kober, H., Bliss-Moreau, E., & Barrett, L. F. (2011). The brain basis of emotion: A meta-analytic review. *Behavioral and Brain Sciences, 173*, 1–86.

Linnenbrink-Garcia, L., & Pekrun, R. (2011). Students' emotions and academic engagement: Introduction to the special issue. *Contemporary Educational Psychology, 36*, 1–3.

Mandler, G. (1976). *Mind and emotion.* New York, NY: Wiley.

Mandler, G. (1990). Interruption (discrepancy) theory: Review and extensions. In S. Fisher & C. L. Cooper (Eds.), *On the move: The psychology of change and Transition* (pp. 13–32). Chichester, United Kingdom: Wiley.

McDaniel, B., D'Mello, S., King, B., Chipman, P., Tapp, K., & Graesser, A. (2007). Facial features for affective state detection in learning environments. In D. McNamara & G. Trafton (Eds.), *Proceedings of the 29th Annual Meeting of the Cognitive Science Society* (pp. 467–472). Austin, TX: Cognitive Science Society.

Millis, K., Forsyth, C., Butler, H., Wallace, P., Graesser, A., & Halpern, D. (2011). Operation ARIES! A serious game for teaching scientific inquiry. In M. Ma, A. Oikonomou, & J. Lakhmi (Eds.), *Serious games and edutainment applications* (pp. 169–196). London, United Kingdom: Springer.

Mugny, G., & Doise, W. (1978). Socio-cognitive conflict and structure of individual and collective performances. *European Journal of Social Psychology, 8*, 181–192.

Nersessian, N. (2008). Mental modeling in conceptual change. In S. Vosniadou (Ed.), *International handbook of research on conceptual change* (pp. 391–416). New York, NY: Routledge.

Pang, B., & Lee, L. (2008). Opinion mining and sentiment analysis. *Foundations and Trends in Information Retrieval, 2*, 1–135.

Pekrun, R., & Stephens, E. J. (2011). Academic emotions. In K. Harris, S. Graham, T. Urdan, S. Graham, J. Royer, & M. Zeidner (Eds.), *APA educational psychology handbook, Vol 2: Individual differences and cultural and contextual factors* (pp. 3–31). Washington, DC: American Psychological Association.

Pennebaker, J., Francis, M., & Booth, R. (2001). *Linguistic inquiry and word count (LIWC): A computerized text analysis program.* Mahwah, NJ: Erlbaum.

Piaget, J. (1952). *The origins of intelligence.* New York, NY: International University Press.

Picard, R. (1997). *Affective computing.* Cambridge, MA: MIT Press.

Rodrigo, M., Baker, R., & Nabos, J. (2010). *The relationships between sequences of affective states and learner achievement.* Paper presented at the Proceedings of the 18th International Conference on Computers in Education, Putrajaya, Malaysia.

Rosenberg, E. (1998). Levels of analysis and the organization of affect. *Review of General Psychology, 2*, 247–270.

Rozin, P., & Cohen, A. (2003a). High frequency of facial expressions corresponding to confusion, concentration, and worry in an analysis of naturally occurring facial expressions of Americans. *Emotion, 3*, 68–75.

Rozin, P., & Cohen, A. B. (2003b). Reply to commentaries: Confusion infusions, suggestives, correctives, and other medicines. *Emotion, 3*, 92–96.

Russell, J. (1980). A circumplex model of affect. *Journal of Personality and Social Psychology, 39*, 1161–1178.

Russell, J. A., Bachorowski, J. A., & Fernandez-Dols, J. M. (2003). Facial and vocal expressions of emotion. *Annual Review of Psychology, 54*, 329–349.

Sazzad, M. S., AlZoubi, O., Calvo, R. A., & D'Mello, S. K. (2011). Affect detection from multichannel physiology during learning. In S. Bull & G. Biswas (Eds.), *Proceedings of the 15th International Conference on Artificial Intelligence in Education* (pp. 131–138). New York, NY: Springer.

Schank, R. (1999). *Dynamic memory revisited.* Cambridge, England: Cambridge University Press.

Schutz, P., & Pekrun, R. (Eds.). (2007). *Emotion in education.* San Diego, CA: Academic Press.

Shute, V. (2008). Focus on formative feedback. *Review of Educational Research, 78*, 153–189.

Silvia, P. J. (2010). Confusion and interest: The role of knowledge emotions in aesthetic experience. *Psychology of Aesthetics Creativity and the Arts, 4*, 75–80.

Sinatra, G. M., Broughton, S. H., & Lombardi, D. (2014). Emotions in science education. In R. Pekrun & L. Linnenbrink-Garcia (Eds.), *International handbook of emotions in education* (pp. 415–436). New York, NY: Taylor & Francis.

VanLehn, K., Siler, S., Murray, C., Yamauchi, T., & Baggett, W. (2003). Why do only some events cause learning during human tutoring? *Cognition and Instruction, 21*, 209–249.

16

ACADEMIC BOREDOM

Thomas Goetz and Nathan C. Hall, University of Konstanz/Thurgau University of Teacher Education and McGill University

The present chapter addresses academic boredom—an emotion that is highly common in educational settings, consistently detrimental for learning and achievement in students, and receiving increasing attention in the research literature. Following a discussion of how boredom is defined and operationalized in an academic context, we outline empirical findings with respect to its frequency and intensity in student populations. Theoretical considerations and empirical findings are then addressed concerning the effects and antecedents of academic boredom as well as how students attempt to cope with it. From a research perspective, we then describe efforts to empirically assess academic boredom. Finally, this chapter concludes with recommendations for how academic boredom can be prevented in the classroom as well as suggestions for future research on boredom in students.

DEFINITION OF BOREDOM

What is boredom? Is it an emotion, a cognition, a motivational orientation, a type of fatigue, a unique experience, or simply the absence or opposite of interest? The answers to these questions are not clear and depend largely on the field of psychological research (e.g., motivation vs. emotion research). What is clear, however, is increasing research interest in this construct, particularly with respect to defining what boredom actually is and whether or not boredom can be defined as an emotion given that it is not a proto-typical or basic emotional experience, such as anxiety, anger, or happiness (e.g., Ekman, 1984; Rosch, 1978; Shaver, Schwartz, Kirson, & O'Connor, 1987). For example, boredom has often been classified as a feeling-oriented construct, such as affect or mood, and has been described in the literature as an unpleasant affective state corresponding with low physiological arousal and cognitive stimulation as well as slow and monotonous speech (Harris, 2000; Mikulas & Vodanovich, 1993). Moreover, this emotion has been associated with specific subjective experiences, such as time slowing down ("time stands still") as well as action tendencies that typically involve escaping the boredom-inducing situation through behavioral and/or cognitive disengagement (e.g., distraction, daydreaming; Goetz & Frenzel, 2006; Johnstone & Scherer, 2000).

To account for these varied descriptions and definitional approaches to boredom, the contemporary component process model of emotions suggests that emotional experiences are best understood in terms of their underlying constituent processes (Kleinginna & Kleinginna, 1981; Scherer, 2000). From the perspective of this model, boredom is regarded as a specific emotional experience comprised of five components: *affective* (an unpleasant, aversive sensation), *cognitive* (altered perceptions of time), *motivational* (desire to modify or withdraw from the activity), *physiological* (reduced arousal), and *expressive* (facial, vocal, and postural expressions; Pekrun, Goetz, Daniels, Stupnisky, & Perry, 2010).

It is important to note that according to the component perspective, boredom is not understood simply as the absence of positive emotions or interest (see Pekrun et al., 2010). First, there exist numerous affective states that are not experienced as enjoyable, but would not be described as boredom (e.g., anger, anxiety, shame, hopelessness). Second, whereas lack of interest can reasonably be assumed to be an important antecedent of boredom, it is clear that the two constructs are not identical in that lack of interest is affectively neutral, whereas boredom is prototypically negative in valence (e.g., the "torments of boredom"; Berlyne, 1960, p. 192). Third, when comparing lack of interest or enjoyment with boredom, they are also found to have discrepant motivational consequences due to differences in affective load (Goetz & Frenzel, 2006). Whereas lack of interest or enjoyment does not imply an intention to engage in an activity, or to withdraw from it, boredom is consistently associated with impulses to escape the situation. Thus, it is possible to differentiate these constructs in a manner similar to how a lack of approach tendencies can be distinguished from the presence of avoidance in achievement goal research (Pekrun et al., 2010).

If boredom is experienced in the academic domain, it can be classified as an *academic emotion*. More specifically, academic emotions are defined as emotions experienced by individuals in educational settings that directly correspond with learning behaviors, classroom activities, and achievement outcomes (Pekrun, Goetz, Titz, & Perry, 2002). Given the primarily process-oriented nature of boredom experiences, *academic boredom* is typically experienced during learning activities in academic settings—for example, while completing homework or during classroom-based learning exercises.

Referring back to the initial question of "What is academic boredom," it is important to understand not only what boredom is but also what it is not, and as such, how boredom relates to other emotions in academic contexts. To date, several empirical studies have examined the relations between academic boredom and other emotions (e.g., Goetz, Frenzel, Pekrun, Hall, & Lüdtke, 2007; Goetz, Lüdtke, Nett, Keller, & Lipnevich, 2013; Pekrun, Goetz, Frenzel, Barchfeld, & Perry, 2011). These studies show a rather consistent picture of results—namely, that academic boredom is negatively related to positive emotions (e.g., enjoyment, pride) and positively related to negative emotions (e.g., anxiety, anger). Given that these relations are generally moderate in magnitude, these findings suggest that boredom does indeed differ from other emotional experiences and does not simply represent a lack of positive emotions (e.g., enjoyment) or overlap with negative emotions (e.g., anxiety).

In addition to the need to operationally define what boredom is (and is not), there remains the need to also explore the conceptual dimensions underlying experiences of boredom. As opposed to operational definitions, this approach reflects a more specific way of classifying emotional experiences along multiple dimensions. This dimensional approach is highlighted in well-known circumplex models of affect (Russell, 1980; see also Watson & Tellegen, 1985) in which affective states are characterized by two orthogonal dimensions of valence (positive/pleasant vs. negative/unpleasant) and arousal.

In dimensional approaches, boredom has primarily been classified and assessed as an unpleasant emotional state having a relatively low negative *valence* (slightly unpleasant, on average; e.g., Fisher, 1993; Goetz, Frenzel, Pekrun, et al., 2007; Perkins & Hill, 1985). While the valence assumption has been consistently supported by limited research to date, findings concerning the *arousal* dimension as it relates to boredom are mixed. For example, several researchers have classified boredom as a low-arousal emotion (e.g., Hebb, 1955; Mikulas & Vodanovich, 1993), whereas others have described it as high in arousal (e.g., Berlyne, 1960; London, Schubert, & Washburn, 1972; Rupp & Vodanovich, 1997; Sommers & Vodanovich, 2000). Consequently, there exists ongoing debates in the research literature as to whether boredom is best understood as a low- or high-arousal emotion (Pekrun et al., 2010; for both low and high arousal, see Harris, 2000) and why extant findings concerning the arousal associated with boredom are so varied in nature.

One explanation for these conflicting results may be that arousal is itself not a well-defined construct and may actually be multidimensional in nature, resulting in it being assessed in different ways (see Schimmack & Grob, 2000; Schimmack & Reisenzein, 2002; Watson, Wiese, Vaidya, & Tellegen, 1999). Another possible explanation is that there exist different types of boredom, as implied in psychoanalytic literature from the 1930s in which the multifaceted nature of boredom was hypothesized ("*it is probable that the conditions and forms of behavior called 'boredom' are psychologically quite heterogeneous*"; Fenichel, 1951, p. 349; see also Fenichel, 1934). This sentiment was echoed over six decades later by Phillips (1993), who suggested that boredom does not appear to represent a single entity but instead to consist of multiple "boredoms" (p. 78).

In line with this assumption, a recent empirical study conducted by Goetz et al. (in press) in which boredom was evaluated using in vivo assessments in real-life achievement settings, suggests an alternate conceptualization of this emotion in which different types of boredom (boredom in achievement and nonachievement situations) are proposed. More specifically, this study suggests that individuals could experience up to five types of boredom in achievement settings, including (1) *indifferent boredom* (relaxed, withdrawn, indifferent) having slightly positive valence and very low arousal, (2) *calibrating boredom* (uncertain, receptive to change/distraction), (3) *searching boredom* (somewhat restless, active pursuit of change/distraction) with slightly negative valence and higher arousal than indifferent boredom, (4) *reactant boredom* (highly restless and motivated to leave the situation for specific alternatives) having high levels of negative valence and relatively high levels of arousal, and (5) *apathetic boredom* (highly aversive) characterized by a high level of negative valence and very low arousal.

In sum, above and beyond existing operational definitions of academic boredom based on component approaches, ongoing research based on dimensional approaches suggests that different types of boredom may be experienced by students in the classroom. It is important to note that although these types of boredom may differ based on valence and arousal, they all share essential elements of the common operational definition of this emotion. In other words, whereas significant variance within the experience of boredom may be observed with respect to multiple boredoms, these differences do not qualitatively contradict the underlying operational definitions of this emotion.

FREQUENCY AND INTENSITY OF ACADEMIC BOREDOM

International research consistently shows boredom to be one of the most commonly experienced emotions in educational settings (e.g., United States [Csikszentmihalyi & Larson, 1984; Farrell, Peguero, Lindsey, & White, 1988]; Europe [Gjesme, 1977; Robinson, 1975]; Africa [Vandewiele, 1980]; Asia [Won, 1989]). In a study with high school students (fifth and ninth graders), for example, Larson and Richards (1991) found boredom to be experienced during 32% of the time spent in class. The prevalence of this emotion is further highlighted by findings from Goetz, Frenzel, and Pekrun (2007), who found ninth graders, on average, to be bored during almost half of the time spent in class. Similarly, Nett, Goetz, and Hall (2011) found eleventh-grade students to report at least some degree of boredom 58% of the time in math class using real-life assessment methods (experience sampling). With respect to university students, Goetz and Nett (2012) utilized retrospective measures to ask students how strongly they experienced a given emotion in situations related to learning and achievement (Likert scale: 1 *not at all* to 5 *very strongly*) and found mean levels of 3.02 for boredom, 2.90 for anxiety, and 3.30 for enjoyment, suggesting that boredom may be experienced as least as often, and just as intensely, as anxiety.

In a larger study conducted with German secondary school students, eighth and eleventh graders were asked to indicate how strongly they experienced the emotions of boredom, anxiety, and enjoyment in the domains of mathematics, physics, German (native language), history, and music (trait assessment; Likert scale: 1 = *not at all* to 5 = *very strongly*). As outlined in Figure 16.1, mean levels for boredom were above the scale

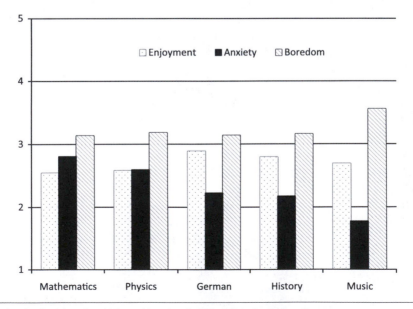

Figure 16.1 Levels of enjoyment, anxiety, and boredom in different academic domains.

midpoint as well as higher than the mean levels observed for anxiety and enjoyment in each of the subject domains. As such, these findings underscore not only the prevalence of boredom relative to other emotions in educational settings but also the salience of this emotional experience for students across academic domains.

EFFECTS OF BOREDOM ON LEARNING BEHAVIOR AND ACHIEVEMENT

Theoretical Considerations

Through what mechanisms is academic boredom assumed to impact learning behavior and achievement outcomes? According to Pekrun's (2006) control-value theory of achievement emotions, the effects of boredom (and other emotions) on performance are mediated by (1) students' motivation to engage in achievement striving, (2) the accessibility of cognitive resources, and (3) the nature and extent of the learning strategies employed, which includes the higher-order self-regulation of learning strategy use. Concerning *cognitive resources,* boredom is assumed to withdraw attention from boring activities and redirect it toward other, more rewarding and highly valued pursuits. Thus, boredom is hypothesized to reduce the cognitive resources that can be directed toward the boring task, thereby causing attention deficits. As for *motivation,* it is hypothesized that boredom corresponds with a desire to escape the boredom-inducing activity. Given the inverse relationship between avoidance and intrinsic motivation as well as effort, it can be expected that boredom should similarly impair engagement and persistence in the activity. With respect to *learning strategies* and *self-regulation,* boredom is assumed to lead to shallow information processing and lower use of effective learning-related cognitive and metacognitive strategies. Specifically, boredom is expected to reduce learners' use of deep and flexible learning strategies, such as cognitive elaboration. In fostering a passive approach to learning, boredom is further expected to inhibit learners' abilities to regulate their own achievement striving with respect to setting goals, selecting learning strategies, and monitoring their learning progress.

As a consequence of the negative effects of boredom on cognitive resources, motivation, learning strategies, and self-regulation, boredom is further expected to have uniformly negative effects on performance on both simple and complex tasks and therefore contribute to poorer achievement outcomes. However, Vodanovich (2003a; see also Seib & Vodanovich, 1998) argues that under specific situational conditions, boredom can in fact have positive effects on learning and achievement outcomes—for example, by enabling creative processes (holistic ways of thinking), providing opportunities for self-reflection (e.g., identifying alternate learning activities or domains in which greater success can be achieved), prompting learners to seek variety and change (e.g., enhancing innovation), and allowing for relaxation (e.g., renewal of cognitive resources and emotional well-being). The idea that boredom might have achievement benefits is also consistent with approaches highlighting the evolutionary benefit of being able to cognitively disengage from nonrewarding or nonthreatening situations to which one is repeatedly exposed (Bornstein, Kale, & Cornell, 1990). Despite the intuitive appeal of arguments in favor of the benefits of boredom, however, there at present exists little empirical support for this assertion in the existing research literature on learning and achievement (see Vodanovich, 2003a).

Empirical Findings

Concerning the observed effects of boredom on learning and achievement in published empirical research, findings from the few interview and survey studies conducted to date show clear negative relations between boredom and attention (e.g., Farmer & Sundberg, 1986; Hamilton, Haier, & Buchsbaum, 1984), effort in achievement settings (e.g., Jarvis & Seifert, 2002; Roseman, 1975; Watt & Vodanovich, 1999), and strategy use (e.g., Goetz, 2004; Pekrun et al., 2010, 2011).With respect to performance outcomes, experimental studies have consistently shown higher levels of boredom to predict lower task performance in addition to greater variability in performance over time (e.g., Cantor, 1968; Hamilton et al., 1984; Kass, Vodanovich, Stanny, & Taylor, 2001; Pan, Shell, & Schleifer, 1994; Sawin & Scerbo, 1995). Similarly, a study conducted by Wallace, Vodanovich, and Restino (2003) showed boredom proneness and self-reports of everyday cognitive failures, such as memory lapses and distractibility, to be positively related. However, there is at present a notable lack of research on the relation between boredom and performance as assessed using more complex tasks, as well as between boredom and cumulative academic achievement more generally.

Of the few studies exploring the relations between boredom and achievement in the academic domain, nearly all of them show greater boredom to correspond with lower achievement (e.g., Daniels et al., 2009; Goetz, 2004; Goetz, Cronjaeger, Frenzel, Lüdtke, & Hall, 2010; Goetz, Frenzel, Pekrun et al., 2007; Maroldo, 1986; Pekrun, Elliot, & Maier, 2009; Pekrun et al., 2010, 2011). One exception in this regard is a study by Larson and Richards (1991) in which a weak, positive relation was found between academic achievement (grade point average) and boredom as experienced by upper elementary students during school hours. Concerning the magnitude of the relationship between academic boredom and academic achievement, the correlations are generally around −.30 across subject domains and performance indicators (cf. Goetz & Hall, 2013).

ANTECEDENTS OF ACADEMIC BOREDOM

Theoretical Considerations

With respect to causes of academic boredom, three theoretical models are particularly relevant due to their explicit focus on the critical determinants of boredom experiences. Whereas Pekrun's (2006) control-value approach and Robinson's (1975) model focus explicitly on boredom in the context of learning and achievement, a third model by Hill and Perkins (1985) pertains to experiences of boredom more generally. In addition to these models, the results from scattered empirical findings on boredom suggest additional antecedent variables based on more general theories on the antecedents of emotional experiences (e.g., cognitive appraisals; Lazarus, 1991; Scherer, 1993).

Pekrun's (2006) Control-Value Theory

Pekrun's (2006) control-value theory posits that subjective control and value appraisals related to achievement activities and outcomes represent the two most important psychosocial antecedents of boredom experiences (and other academic emotions). The term *subjective control* refers to the perceived causal influence of an agent over actions and outcomes (Skinner, 1996), whereas the term *subjective value* refers to the perceived valences and personal relevance of actions and outcomes. The theory posits that boredom is elicited when achievement activities are perceived by the individual as lacking in importance or subjective value. As such, this model hypothesizes an inverse relationship between the intensity and frequency of feelings of boredom and the subjective value of these academic activities. In this regard, boredom clearly differs from other positive and negative emotions that, in contrast, are assumed to increase in intensity with increasing value.

With respect to subjective control, the theory also assumes a curvilinear relationship between subjective control and feelings of boredom, such that greater boredom is anticipated under conditions of very high or low control, and considered unlikely under conditions affording moderate control levels. Thus, it is expected that boredom may occur if one's perceived control is very high (task is not sufficiently challenging) or very low—namely, when task demands exceed one's capabilities (Acee et al., 2010; Goetz & Frenzel, 2010). This approach differs from Csikszentmihalyi's (1975) conception of "flow" experiences in which boredom is hypothesized to occur only when individual capabilities significantly exceed task demands (i.e., high perceived control). With respect to additional, more distal antecedents of boredom experiences, Pekrun's (2006) model further asserts that aspects of the social environment (e.g., classroom goal structures, parental support) can impact students' control and value beliefs (proximal antecedents) that, in turn, directly predict boredom experiences (e.g., parental support in a given domain should enhance the subjective value of that domain and consequently reduce boredom).

Robinson's (1975) Model of Academic Boredom

In this model, three critical classes of antecedent variables with respect to academic boredom are proposed. The first two antecedents include (1) the *monotony* of class activities, and, similar to Pekrun's theory, (2) students' perceived *uselessness* of class subjects. The third type of antecedent identified in Robinson's model involves (3) the *social environment*. As such, the model asserts that teachers (e.g., having low interest in student development and/or teaching, low interest in assigned teaching subjects), the school environment (e.g., available learning resources and amenities), peers (e.g., valuing of the subject domain), parents (e.g., demonstrated value of education; interest in child's academic progress), and the home environment (e.g., learning resources in the home) can significantly impact boredom experiences.

Hill and Perkin's (1985) General Boredom Model

The primary assumption in this theoretical model is that *monotonous situations* lead to experiences of boredom. However, it is further assumed that the magnitude of this effect is moderated by (1) characteristics of the *situation* (i.e., allows for additional/alternative stimulation), (2) characteristics of the *person* (i.e., neuroticism, extroversion—extroverts are more inclined to search for alternative stimulation in monotonous situations), and (3) characteristics of the *tasks* (i.e., potential for selecting an alternate activity).

Additional Antecedents of Boredom Experiences

In addition to the antecedent variables outlined above, various possible predictors of academic boredom have been proposed in the research literature. From a historical perspective (see Smith, 1981), *environmental characteristics* have received consistent

Table 16.1 Assumed Antecedents of Boredom

Environment	Person	Fit Environment/Person
• Monotony, Low Stimulation	• Lack of Control	• Suboptimal Stimulation
• Repetitive Tasks	• Low Value	• Suboptimal Difficulty (too high/ too low)
• Uselessness, Senselessness	• Boredom Susceptibility	• Poor Content/Interest Fit
• Isolation	• Boredom Proneness	
• Low available learning resources and amenities	• Achievement Goals (lack of mastery-approach goals)	
• Repeated Task Interruption	• Age (decreasing with age)	
• Teachers' Lack of Interest	• Gender (stronger in males)	
• Low Value in Peers Group and Family	• Intelligence (mixed results)	
• Lack of Alternative Opportunities	• Neuroticism	
	• Extraversion	

empirical attention since the 1930s, particularly in the domain of occupational psychology (see Fisher, 1993). Moreover, *dispositional characteristics* have been increasingly investigated since the 1950s, with the fit between environmental and personal characteristics having received greater attention in boredom research since the 1980s (e.g., O'Hanlon, 1981; cf. challenge/competency fit in flow research; Csikszentmihalyi, 1975). These antecedent variables, as well as those proposed in the aforementioned theories, are outlined in Table 16.1 and delineated according to environmental, personal, and environment-person "fit" determinants of boredom experiences.

Empirical Findings

There are numerous scattered empirical results concerning the effects of antecedent variables on academic boredom. As for control and value antecedents, high levels of perceived *control* (e.g., academic self-concept, self-efficacy) typically correspond with lower boredom levels. In achievement settings, the observed relations between control and boredom are also predominantly linear in nature (not curvilinear, as is often assumed), likely due to the intended difficulty of achievement activities limiting the extent to which overly high perceptions of control, and resulting feelings of boredom, are experienced (Dicintio & Gee, 1999; Goetz et al., 2010; Goetz, Nett et al., 2012; Goetz, Pekrun, Hall, & Haag, 2006; Pekrun et al., 2010, 2011). Perceptions of subjective *value* (intrinsic and extrinsic) with respect to learning- and achievement-related content, tasks, situations, and outcomes also show clear negative relations with boredom levels (Goetz, 2004; Goetz et al., 2006; Pekrun et al., 2010, 2011).

Concerning approach achievement *motives* and mastery achievement *goals*, these motivational variables have been found to negatively correspond with boredom levels (Duda, Fox, Biddle, & Armstrong, 1992; Gjesme, 1977; Jagacinski & Duda, 2001; Pekrun, Elliot, & Maier, 2006, 2009). Indicators of *teaching quality* (e.g., teacher enthusiasm, elaborative instruction, clarity and structure, understandability) have also been found to correspond with lower levels of student boredom (Frenzel, Pekrun, & Goetz, 2007; Goetz, 2004; Goetz, Lüdtke, Nett, Keller, & Lipnevich, 2013; Goetz et al., 2006). Finally, *task characteristics* that have been found to positively correspond with boredom levels include monotony and repetition as well as lack of complexity, variety, and intellectual stimulation (Coury & Drury, 1986; Fisher, 1993; Roseman, 1975; Scerbo, 1998).

COPING WITH ACADEMIC BOREDOM

Theoretical Considerations

Very little systematic research has examined the types and effects of strategies used by individuals to cope with experiences of boredom (Nett, Goetz, & Daniels, 2010; Strain & Graesser, 2012; Vodanovich, 2003b). In contrast, the research literature on coping with stress and general negative affect has produced various typologies and classification systems (e.g., Lazarus, & Folkman, 1984, 1987; Skinner, Edge, Altman, & Sherwood, 2003). Thus, to address this research gap with respect to how individuals cope with boredom, recent research has explored the extent to which existing models of coping can successfully be applied to feelings of boredom. In Nett et al. (2010, 2011), the utility of a classification system commonly used in stress research (Holahan, Moos, & Schaefer, 1996) to identify and categorize the strategies students use to cope with boredom was assessed. According to this classification system, four classes of coping strategies are proposed that can be differentiated according to two underlying dimensions. The first dimension involves the focus of the strategy being either to approach or avoid the aversive situation. Whereas approach strategies involve attempts to remediate the situation, avoidance strategies are used to withdraw from the situation. The second dimension distinguishes between strategies that are cognitive as opposed to behavioral in nature, resulting in a 2 × 2 factorial in which strategies for coping with boredom (and other negative emotions) can be classified (see Table 16.2).

Examples for each type of coping strategy, as applied by Nett et al. (2010) to boredom, are as follows: "When I am bored in mathematics class," "I make myself aware of the importance of the issue" (*cognitive approach*), "I ask my teacher for more interesting tasks" (*behavioral approach*), "I study for another subject" (*cognitive avoidance*), and "I talk to my classmates" (*behavioral avoidance*). It is important to note that although this model represents only one of several ways in which boredom-related coping strategies can be conceptually organized, there at present exist no theories on this topic beyond that suggested by Nett et al. (2010, 2011). More specifically, whereas self-report measures for assessing how individuals cope with boredom have occasionally been proposed (e.g., Hamilton et al., 1984), such measures have yet to be based on clear theoretical models

Table 16.2 Classification of Students' Strategies for Coping With Boredom

Type of Coping	Approach Coping	Avoidance Coping
Cognitive	Changing one's perception of the situation.	Focusing on thoughts not related to the situation.
Behavioral	Taking actions to change the situation.	Taking actions not related to the situation.

allowing for specific strategies to be effectively operationalized, evaluated, and compared (Vodanovich, 2003b).

Empirical Findings

There at present exist very few empirical findings on the types and effects of strategies used by students to cope with boredom. In a study by Vandewiele (1980) on boredom experienced outside the academic domain, students aged 13–14 years were asked how they avoid feelings of boredom. The frequencies of specific strategies were as follows: reading (20%), homework (9%), visiting friends (9%), music (8%), debates (8%), shows (7%), sports (6%), walks (4%), and games (4%). Similarly, a study by Harris (2000) on nonacademic boredom in university students (mean age: 28 years) revealed the following coping strategies: reading (39%), thinking/daydreaming (26%), socializing (21%), watching television (20%), physical activity (18%), learning/trying something new (16%), engaging in a specific activity (16%), sleeping (15%), refocusing attention (15%), planning/organizing (14%), cleaning (10%), doing something different (9%), listening to music (9%), studying (7%), smoking/drinking/drugs (5%), eating (3%), watching people (3%), singing (3%), exploring (2%), and other techniques (9%).

In an effort to evaluate boredom-related coping strategies in the academic domain, Goetz, Frenzel, and Pekrun asked ninth graders how they responded to boredom during class. The strategies reported for dealing with academic boredom were as follows: distraction (86%), acceptance (23%), increasing attention (15%), relaxation (8%), attempting to change the situation (2%), and behavioral avoidance (1%). Based on the conceptual model outlined in Table 16.2, the two most common types of strategies reported by German students for coping with boredom in the classroom can be classified as cognitive avoidance followed by cognitive approach strategies.

In the study by Nett et al. (2010; fifth to tenth graders, questionnaire format), the utility of self-report measures developed to assess each type of coping strategy outlined in Table 16.2 was evaluated. Results showed the classificatory structure of the *Coping with Boredom Scale* to be corroborated by confirmatory factor analysis. Latent profile analysis findings further differentiated between groups of students based on their use of boredom-related coping strategies, with the first group, referred to *Reappraisers,* preferring cognitive approach strategies over other strategies (e.g., bolstering their perceived value and importance of the material). The second group, labeled *Criticizers,* focused primarily on behavioral-approach strategies in opting to first try to change the learning situation (e.g., suggest potential modifications to learning tasks to their teacher).

The third group, the *Evaders,* had behavioral avoidance as their strategy of choice (occupying themselves with an unrelated activity). An analysis of differences between these three groups with respect to the frequency of boredom, academic performance, as well as other academic emotions, cognitions, and motivation variables suggested that Reappraisers experience less boredom and have a more positive academic profile (emotional, motivational, cognitive) relative to the other groups. In sum, these few empirical findings suggest that although cognitive avoidance may be a common way of coping with academic boredom, cognitive-approach strategies, in which boring situations are cognitively reframed as more interesting or valuable (cf. Fraughton, Sansone, Butner, & Zachary, 2011), are likely to be most effective in reducing boredom and improving academic development.

ASSESSMENT OF ACADEMIC BOREDOM

Academic boredom has primarily been assessed through standardized questionnaires (e.g., Daschmann, Goetz, & Stupnisky, 2011) and interviews (e.g., Farrell et al., 1988; Goetz, Frenzel, & Pekrun, 2007; Kanevsky & Keighley, 2003). With respect to questionnaires, academic boredom has typically been evaluated using single-item measures (e.g., Geiwitz, 1966; Gjesme, 1977; Perkins & Hill, 1985; Shaw, Caldwell, & Kleiber, 1996), with multi-item scales measuring various facets of academic boredom being increasingly used (for an overview, see Vodanovich, 2003b). Existing self-report measures commonly used to evaluate boredom, both within and outside academic settings, are outlined in Table 16.3.

As a sample measure of class-related academic boredom, items from a short boredom scale adapted from the Academic Emotions Questionnaire—Mathematics (AEQ-M; Pekrun et al., 2011) are as follows: *"I get bored in* [DOMAIN] *classes"*; *"I can't concentrate in* [DOMAIN] *class because I am so bored"*; *I am so bored in* [DOMAIN] *class that I can't stay awake"*; *"Just thinking of my* [DOMAIN] *class makes me feel bored."* Descriptive statistics for this scale as well as relations with other academic emotions (enjoyment, pride, anxiety, anger), academic self-concept, and academic achievement are outlined in Goetz et al. (2010) with respect to the domains of mathematics, physics, German, and English

Table 16.3 Self-Report Measures of Boredom

Scale	References
Boredom subscale; Achievement Emotions Questionnaire (AEQ; mathematics related version: AEQ-M)[a]	Pekrun, Goetz, Frenzel, Barchfeld, and Perry (2011)
Class-related Boredom (short version from the AEQ-M)[a]	Goetz, Cronjaeger, Frenzel, Lüdtke, and Hall (2010)
Homework Boredom Scale (based on the AEQ-M)[a]	Goetz, Nett, Martiny, Hall, Pekrun, Dettmers, and Trautwein (2012)
Academic Boredom Scale (ABS)	Acee et al. (2010)
Precursors to Boredom Scales (academic context)[a]	Daschmann, Goetz, and Stupnisky (2011)
Coping with Boredom Scale (academic context)[a]	Nett, Goetz, and Daniels (2010); Nett, Goetz, and Hall (2011)
Boredom Coping Scale (nonacademic context)	Hamilton, Haier, and Buchsbaum (1984)
Boredom Proneness Scale	Farmer and Sundberg (1986)
Boredom Susceptibility Scale (subscale of the Sensation Seeking Scale)	Zuckerman (1979)
Occupational Boredom Scales	Grubb (1975); Lee (1986)
Leisure Boredom Scale	Iso-Ahola and Weissinger (1990)
Free Time Boredom Scale	Ragheb and Merydith (2001)
Sexual Boredom Scale	Watt and Ewing (1996)

[a]Scales explicitly developed for the context of learning and achievement.

(eighth and eleventh graders). For example, the reliability of this boredom scale for the domain of mathematics in the eighth-grade sample ($N = 973$) was .86 with a mean level (referring to the sum of the scale divided by the number of items) of 2.49 ($SD = 1.12$; response format: 5-point Likert scale ranging from 1 = *strongly disagree* to 5 = *strongly agree*). The zero-order correlations of this scale with other measures were –.68 for enjoyment, –.43 for pride, .52 for anxiety, .74 for anger, –.42 for academic self-concept, and –.28 for academic achievement (all correlations $p < .001$).

Concerning the assessment of academic boredom, it is important to note that the cumulative empirical evidence suggests that achievement emotions (including academic boredom) are largely organized in domain-specific ways (e.g., Goetz, Frenzel, Pekrun et al., 2007). As such, a domain-specific assessment of academic boredom is highly recommended for future research as the most appropriate approach for evaluating boredom in students during academic activities (e.g., in mathematics vs. language classes). Moreover, future studies utilizing real-time (state) assessments of academic boredom (i.e., the experience sampling method; Goetz, Frenzel et al., 2013; Larson & Richards, 1991; Nett et al., 2011) are recommended as state assessments tend to be less biased by subjective beliefs as compared to trait assessments (see Robinson & Clore, 2002). Further, more objective measures of academic boredom might also be employed in the future, such as facial recognition technology.

HOW TO PREVENT/REDUCE ACADEMIC BOREDOM

Based on the theoretical approaches and empirical findings previously discussed, there exist numerous possibilities for reducing or preventing academic boredom in students.

Value Induction

Increasing students' perceived value of activities in academic settings, and their interest in the learning material, can be an especially effective means of minimizing boredom experience—for example, by highlighting the relevance of the learning material to students' daily lives (cf., Durik & Harackiewicz, 2007; Hidi & Renninger, 2006; Hulleman & Harackiewicz, 2009).

Appropriate Control Levels

It is important to adequately match task demands with individual competencies to maintain adaptive levels of subjective control in students (e.g., for boredom due to insufficient challenge in gifted students, see Preckel, Goetz, & Frenzel, 2010). However, as a perfect fit between the challenge level of a single classroom activity and the varied competency levels of students in that class is of course not attainable, some degree of mismatch in classroom settings is inevitable. As such, it becomes important in classroom settings to promote students' competencies by attending to individual student differences, modifying tasks, and encouraging self-regulated approaches to learning through which students can better identify their own learning needs and seek appropriate modifications to learning tasks (Rohrkemper & Corno, 1988; also see Nett et al., 2010; Sansone, Weir, Harpster, & Morgan, 1992).

Teacher Enthusiasm

Demonstrating enthusiasm while teaching has consistently been found to result in greater enjoyment in students—an emotion that is incompatible with academic boredom and promotes motivated achievement striving (see Frenzel, Goetz, Lüdtke, Pekrun, & Sutton, 2009).

Troubleshooting

One possible benefit of identifying boredom in students is the potential to also identify how class content and activities can be modified to minimize boredom and improve student engagement. It is therefore important for teachers to realize when students are bored in class and further, to consider the underlying reasons for their boredom. In this regard, the diagnostic competencies of teachers with respect to students' academic boredom are critical.

Teaching Coping Strategies

Helping students to identify and anticipate feelings of boredom, as well as informing them of (and modeling) appropriate coping strategies, should also help students better prepare for and reduce academic boredom. However, it can be difficult for teachers to talk to their students about how to deal with boredom in class as it may require teachers to acknowledge suboptimal learning activities or the limits of their efforts to promote student engagement at the classroom level. Nevertheless, by addressing the heterogeneous nature of students' interests, the inevitability of a mismatch with class content, and highlighting how some coping strategies can be used to effectively reduce boredom levels, students can be encouraged to assume greater responsibility and control over their feelings of boredom in academic settings.

AVENUES FOR FUTURE RESEARCH ON ACADEMIC BOREDOM

Following from existing lines of research on academic boredom are multiple potentially advantageous avenues for future research in this domain as outlined below.

Frequency and Intensity of Academic Boredom

It is recommended that future studies more clearly differentiate, both conceptually and in assessment methods, between the frequency versus intensity of boredom experiences. As afforded by experience sampling methods, it is suggested that both components be assessed in future research to better determine if the effects of boredom are due to how frequently it is experienced (e.g., moderate yet consistent levels of boredom), its intensity level (e.g., stronger boredom over shorter durations), or both (cf. Diener, Sandvik, & Pavot, 2009; Schimmack & Diener, 1997).

Consequences and Antecedents of Boredom

There is at present a lack of empirical research in which the causal nature of the relations between boredom and assumed antecedent/dependent variables is explicitly addressed (an exception is the research by Pekrun, Hall, Perry, & Goetz, in press). With respect to

Cantor, G. N. (1968). Effects of a "boredom" treatment on children's simple RT performance. *Psychonomic Science,* *10,* 299–300.

Coury, B. G., & Drury, C. G. (1986). The effects of pacing on complex decision-making inspection performance. *Ergonomics, 29,* 489–508.

Csikszentmihalyi, M. (1975). *Beyond boredom and anxiety.* San Francisco, CA: Jossey-Bass.

Csiksztenmihalyi, M., & Larson, R. (1984). *Being adolescent.* New York, NY: Basic Books.

Daniels, L. M., Stupnisky, R. H., Pekrun, R., Haynes, T. L., Perry, R. P., & Newall, N. E. (2009). A longitudinal analysis of achievement goals: From affective antecedents to emotional effects and achievement outcomes. *Journal of Educational Psychology, 101,* 948–963.

Daschmann, E. C., Goetz, T., & Stupnisky, R. H. (2011). Testing the predictors of boredom at school. Development and validation of the Precursors to Boredom Scales. *British Journal of Educational Psychology, 81,* 421–440.

Dicintio, M. J., & Gee, S. (1999). Control is the key: Unlocking the motivation of at-risks students. *Psychology in the Schools, 36,* 231–237.

Diener, E., Sandvik, E., & Pavot, W. (2009) Happiness is the frequency, not the intensity, of positive versus negative affect. In E. Diener (Ed.), *Assessing well-being: The collected works of Ed Diener* (pp. 213–231). New York, NY: Springer Science + Business Media.

Duda, J. L., Fox, K. R., Biddle, S. J., & Armstrong, N. (1992). Children's achievement goals and beliefs about success in sport. *British Journal of Educational Psychology, 62,* 313–323.

Durik, A. M., & Harackiewicz, J. M. (2007). Different strokes for different folks: How individual interest moderates the effects of situational factors on task interest. *Journal of Educational Psychology, 99,* 597–610.

Ekman, P. (1984). Expression and the nature of emotion. In K. S. Scherer & P. Ekman (Eds.), *Approaches to emotion* (pp. 319–343). Hillsdale, NJ: Erlbaum.

Farmer, R., & Sundberg, N. D. (1986). Boredom proneness: The development and correlates of a new scale. *Journal of Personality Assessment, 50,* 4–17.

Farrell, E., Peguero, G., Lindsey, R., & White, R. (1988). Giving voice to high school students: Pressure and boredom, ya know what I'm sayin'? *American Educational Research Journal, 25,* 489–502.

Fenichel, O. (1934). Zur Psychologie der Langeweile. *Imago, 20,* 20270–20281.

Fenichel, O. (1951). On the psychology of boredom. In D. Rapaport (Ed.), *Organization and pathology of thought: Selected sources* (pp. 349–361). New York, NY: Columbia University Press.

Fisher, C. D. (1993). Boredom at work: A neglected concept. *Human Relations, 46,* 395–417.

Fraughton, T., Sansone, C., Butner, J., & Zachary, J. (2011). Interest and performance when learning online: Providing utility value information can be important for both novice and experienced students. *International Journal of Cyber Behavior, Psychology and Learning, 1,* 1–15.

Frenzel, A. C., Goetz, T., Lüdtke, O., Pekrun, R., & Sutton, R. E. (2009). Emotional transmission in the classroom: Exploring the relationship between teacher and student enjoyment. *Journal of Educational Psychology, 101,* 705–716.

Frenzel, A. C., Pekrun, R., & Goetz, T. (2007). Perceived learning environment and students' emotional experiences: A multilevel analysis of mathematics classrooms. *Learning and Instruction, 17,* 478–493.

Geiwitz, P. J. (1966). Structure of boredom. *Journal of Personality and Social Psychology, 3,* 592–600.

Gjesme, T. (1977). General satisfaction and boredom at school as a function of the pupils' personality characteristics. *Scandinavian Journal of Educational-Research, 21,* 113–146.

Goetz, T. (2004). *Emotionales Erleben und selbstreguliertes Lernen bei Schuelern im Fach Mathematik* [Students' emotions and self-regulated learning in mathematics]. Munich, Germany: Utz.

Goetz, T., Bieg, M., Lüdtke, O., Pekrun, R., & Hall, N. C. (2013). Do girls really experience more anxiety in mathematics? *Psychological Science, 24,* 2079–2087.

Goetz, T., Cronjaeger, H., Frenzel, A. C., Lüdtke, O., & Hall, N. C. (2010). Academic self-concept and emotion relations: Domain specificity and age effects. *Contemporary Educational Psychology, 35,* 44–58.

Goetz, T., & Frenzel, A. C. (2006). Phänomenologie schulischer Langeweile [Phenomenology of boredom at school]. *Zeitschrift für Entwicklungspsychologie und Pädagogische Psychologie, 38,* 149–153.

Goetz, T., & Frenzel., A. C. (2010). Über- und Unterforderungslangeweile im Mathematikunterricht [Boredom due to excessive and insufficient academic demands in the context of mathematics instruction]. *Empirische Pädagogik, 24,* 113–134.

Goetz, T., Frenzel, A., C., Hall, N. C., Nett, U., Pekrun, R., & Lipnevich, A. (in press). Types of boredom: An experience sampling approach. *Motivation and Emotion.*

Goetz, T., Frenzel, A. C., & Pekrun, R. (2007). Regulation von Langeweile im Unterricht. Was Schuelerinnen und Schueler bei der 'Windstille der Seele' (nicht) tun [Regulation of boredom in class. What students (do not) do when experiencing the 'Windless Calm of the Soul']. *Unterrichtswissenschaft, 35,* 312–333.

Goetz, T., Frenzel, A. C., Pekrun, R., Hall, N. C., & Lüdtke, O. (2007). Between- and within-domain relations of students' academic emotions. *Journal of Educational Psychology, 99,* 715–733.

Goetz, T., & Hall, N. C. (2013). Emotion and achievement in the classroom. In J. Hattie and E. M. Anderman (Eds.), *International guide to student achievement* (pp. 192–195). New York, NY: Routledge.

Goetz, T., Lüdtke, O., Nett, U. E., Keller, M., & Lipnevich, A. A. (2013). Characteristics of teaching and students' emotions in the classroom: Investigating differences across domains. *Contemporary Educational Psychology, 38,* 383–394.

Goetz, T., & Nett, U. E. (2012). *Boredom in university students.* Unpublished codebook, University of Konstanz, Konstanz, Germany.

Goetz, T., Nett, U. E., Martiny, S. E., Hall, N. C., Pekrun, R., Dettmers, S., & Trautwein, U. (2012). Students' emotions during homework: Structures, self-concept antecedents, and achievement outcomes. *Learning and Individual Differences, 22,* 225–234.

Goetz, T., Pekrun, R., Hall, N. C., & Haag, L. (2006). Academic emotions from a social-cognitive perspective: Antecedents and domain specificity of students' affect in the context of Latin instruction. *British Journal of Educational Psychology, 76,* 289–308.

Hall, N. C., Perry, R. P., Goetz, T., Ruthig, J. C., Stupnisky, R. H., & Newall, N. E. (2007). Attributional retraining and elaborative learning: Improving academic development through writing-based interventions. *Learning and Individual Differences, 17,* 280–290.

Hamilton, J. A., Haier, R. J., & Buchsbaum, M. S. (1984). Intrinsic enjoyment and boredom coping scales: Validation with personality, evoked potential, and attention measures. *Personality and Individual Differences, 5,* 183–193.

Harley, J. M., Bouchet, F., & Azevedo, R. (2012, April). *Measuring learners' unfolding, discrete emotional responses to different pedagogical agent scaffolding strategies.* Paper presented at the annual meeting of the American Educational Research Association, Vancouver, BC, Canada.

Harris, M. B. (2000). Correlates and characteristics of boredom proneness and boredom. *Journal of Applied Social Psychology, 30,* 576–598.

Hebb, D. O. (1955). Drives and the C.N.S. (conceptual nervous system). *Psychological Review, 62,* 243–254.

Hidi, S., & Renninger, A. (2006). The four-phase model of interest development. *Educational Psychologist, 41,* 111–127.

Hill, A. B., & Perkins, R. E. (1985). Towards a model of boredom. *British Journal of Psychology, 76,* 235–240.

Holahan, C. J., Moos, R. H., & Schaefer, J. A. (1996). Coping, stress resistance, and growth: Conceptualizing adaptive functioning. In M. Zeidner & N. S. Endler (Eds.), *Handbook of coping. Theory, research, applications* (pp. 24–43). New York, NY: John Wiley & Sons.

Hulleman, C. S., & Harackiewicz, J. M. (2009). Promoting interest and performance in high school science classes. *Science, 326,* 1410–1412.

Jagacinski, C. M., & Duda, J. L. (2001). A comparative analysis of contemporary achievement goal orientation measures. *Educational and Psychological Measurement, 61,* 1013–1039.

Jarvis, S., & Seifert, T. (2002). Work avoidance as a manifestation of hostility, helplessness, and boredom. *Alberta Journal of Educational Research, 48,* 174–187.

Johnstone, T., & Scherer, K. R. (2000). Vocal communication of emotion. In M. Lewis & J. M. Haviland-Jones (Eds.), *Handbook of emotions* (2nd ed., pp. 220–235). New York, NY: Guilford Press.

Kahneman, D. (2011). *Thinking, fast and slow.* London, United Kingdom: Allen Lane.

Kanevsky, L., & Keighley, T. (2003). On gifted students in school. To produce or not to produce? Understanding boredom and the honor in underachievement. *Roeper Review, 26,* 20–28.

Kass, S. J., Vodanovich, S. J., Stanny, C. J., & Taylor, T. M. (2001). Watching the clock: Boredom and vigilance performance. *Perceptual and Motor Skills, 92,* 969–976.

Kleinginna, P. R., & Kleinginna, A. M. (1981). A categorized list of emotion definitions, with suggestions for a consensual definition. *Motivation and Emotion, 5,* 345–379.

Watt, J. D., & Vodanovich, S. J. (1999). Boredom proneness and psychosocial development. *Journal of Psychology: Interdisciplinary and Applied, 133,* 303–314.

Won, H. J. (1989). *The daily leisure of Korean school adolescents and its relationship to subjective well-being and leisure functioning.* (Unpublished PhD diss.). University of Oregon, Eugene, OR.

Wrosch, C., Scheier, M. F., Miller, G. E., Schulz, R., & Carver, C. S. (2003). Adaptive self-regulation of unattainable goals: Goal disengagement, goal reengagement, and subjective well-being. *Personality and Social Psychology Bulletin, 29,* 1494–1508.

17

THE ROLE OF EMOTION IN ENGAGEMENT, COPING, AND THE DEVELOPMENT OF MOTIVATIONAL RESILIENCE

Ellen Skinner, Jennifer Pitzer, and Heather Brule,
Portland State University

Learning in school is hard work. It requires effort, determination, and persistence in the face of challenges and setbacks. In order to learn, students must focus their attention, listen to their teachers, and expend mental energy participating constructively in academic tasks. In fact, this kind of wholehearted (and whole-headed) participation in academic work is considered by many educators and researchers to be a necessary condition for learning and a precondition for students' long-term success in school (Fredricks, Blumenfeld, & Paris, 2004). As a result, researchers in education and psychology have long focused on the question of how to promote and sustain students' engagement in academic work (Christenson, Reschly, & Wylie, 2012).

The goal of this chapter is to present one set of answers to this question, grounded in self-determination theory (SDT; Connell & Wellborn, 1991; Deci & Ryan, 1985) and our research on motivational resilience (Skinner & Pitzer, 2012). Our work fits squarely within the study of motivation more generally, which is fundamentally concerned with psychological processes that underlie the energy (i.e., vigor, intensity), direction (i.e., guidance, purpose), and durability (i.e., tenacity, commitment) of human activity. For us, *motivational resilience,* at its core, entails constructive energy focused on the hard work of learning: effort, enthusiasm, interest, and commitment, sustained on a daily basis and robust even in the face of obstacles and setbacks. As a result, the process of motivational resilience includes the quality and intensity of students' ongoing engagement as well as what happens to their engagement when they run into trouble: how they react and cope, and how they can maintain or recover their forward momentum so they can re-engage with challenging academic tasks. We are also concerned with processes of motivational *vulnerability,* including the ways that students become disaffected, how disaffection can trigger emotional reactivity and maladaptive coping when students encounter challenges or problems, and how these reactions can compromise students' capacity to recover from setbacks, and so lead them to give up in the face of demanding academic work.

In this chapter, we focus especially on the role of students' emotions in motivational resilience. Emotions provide both fuel and guidance for students' behaviors, and they are markers of the quality of students' participation and coping, informing researchers and teachers about whether students are building motivational resources or are at risk for burnout. We examine how supportive relationships with teachers, along with authentic academic work and constructive interpretations of failure, can protect and promote children's emotional investment in learning, eventually contributing to the development of durable academic assets during adolescence, such as a sense of ownership for one's own progress in school. We make suggestions for teacher practices that support positive emotional and motivational dynamics in the classroom, and counteract student disaffection, with special attention to the important role that teachers' own emotions and motivation play in the development of resilience.

SELF-DETERMINATION THEORY MODEL OF MOTIVATIONAL RESILIENCE

The model of motivational resilience used in this chapter is based in SDT and organized around the assumption that all people come with fundamental organismic psychological needs, focused on competence, relatedness, and autonomy, akin to the physiological needs for hunger, thirst, and safety (Connell & Wellborn, 1991; Deci & Ryan, 1985). According to this perspective, humans innately desire to seek out opportunities to fulfill these needs. They feel energized and joyful during interactions in which their needs are met and frustrated and dejected when they are thwarted. Based on their history of experiences in particular settings, people construct views of themselves and the world in relation to these needs. Over time, these expectations come to shape their participation in these settings.

Three Fundamental Psychological Needs as Sources of Energy and Emotion

As would be expected if they represent fundamental human commitments, the needs for competence, relatedness, and autonomy have long histories of study under a variety of labels. The programs of research organized around each need are described briefly in the next section, along with their applications to the study of motivation in schools.

Competence

In schools, the most obvious psychological need is for *competence,* which refers to the desire to experience oneself as effective in producing positive and preventing negative outcomes. Studied for many decades under labels such as self-efficacy, expectancies of success, perceived competence or ability, and sense of control (all of which can be considered facets of competence; Skinner, 1996), research has demonstrated that children who are convinced that they have what it takes to succeed in school show higher levels of effort, engagement, persistence, and cumulative academic performance (Elliot & Dweck, 2005). In the same vein, research on helplessness reveals that the experience of noncontingency and the lack of self-confidence can undermine students' investment and performance and can lead to passivity, sadness, and eventually, to giving up (Peterson, Maier, & Seligman, 1993).

To these large bodies of work, SDT adds the idea that concerns with control are ubiquitous and powerful because they represent the workings of underlying intrinsic needs for competence or effectance (White, 1959), which are present from birth (Watson, 1979) and are manifest as neurophysiological responses to opportunities for and losses of control (Maier & Watkins, 2005). According to this reasoning, perceptions of self-efficacy derive their potency in fueling emotion, engagement, and coping because they mark students' cumulative experience of the extent to which school is a place where their needs for competence can (or cannot) be met.

Relatedness

The need for relatedness has been studied most thoroughly by attachment researchers, who posit that infants are born with biobehavioral predispositions to seek proximity and derive comfort from their caregivers (Bowlby, 1969/1973). Apparent across the life span (Baumeister & Leary, 1995), the need for relatedness has only recently been studied as a force in schools, where students' sense of belonging—that is, of feeling welcome and treated like valued members of a learning community—has been shown to predict their engagement, self-esteem, achievement, and psychological and behavioral functioning (Osterman, 2000; Roeser, Midgley, & Urdan, 1996). According to SDT, a sense of relatedness is not simply a self-perception but instead comprises a compelling conviction about whether school (or specific teachers and peers) can serve as a secure base, a place where one feels at home, embodied by people who are dependable sources of support in times of trouble. If students feel like unwelcome outsiders, they will be alienated from school and may seek to fulfill their relatedness needs elsewhere.

Autonomy

Studied now for over 40 years, the need for autonomy reflects the human desire to be the author of one's own actions, to freely express one's genuine preferences, and to think and act from one's true self (Deci & Ryan, 1985). Of the three needs, this one seems to be the most controversial, sometimes accused of representing a Western predilection, but it also seems to be the one that students most consistently report as being thwarted by the demands and pressures of teachers and schools (Reeve, 2009). Reflection upon how this need might manifest during infancy, prior to any possible socialization, suggests that even newborns a few minutes old have access to their genuine preferences and are motivated to express them (loudly). The clearest evidence of the importance of autonomy in schools comes from observational and experimental research documenting that teacher autonomy support influences student engagement, enthusiasm, motivation, and deep learning (Su & Reeve, 2011).

Needs as a Source of Energy and Emotion

The notion that humans inherently seek out and enthusiastically engage in activities that fulfill these three needs and naturally feel dejected, helpless, and frustrated when these needs are thwarted, suggests that intrinsic motives are the origin of a deep source of energy, invigoration, and emotion. When students are given opportunities to fulfill their needs in school, they should be eager to participate and, when they do, should feel energizing emotions, such as joy, interest, curiosity, and excitement about the academic tasks they undertake. When their needs are unfulfilled, students should be passive and bored, and when needs are actively obstructed, students may experience vigorous negative emotions, such as anger and anxiety. According to SDT, students are not socialized to these reactions. Needs comprise intrinsic wellsprings of energy and emotion available to all students. They are always in play, for better or for worse, and can be supported intentionally by thoughtful teaching and sound educational practices.

The general model of motivation postulated by SDT is organized around these three needs (see Figure 17.1). Students' histories of experiences with school, including their interactions with parents, teachers, and peers who support or undermine their needs, cumulatively shape their academic identities, or their personal convictions about whether they truly belong in school (relatedness), have what it takes to succeed (competence), and genuinely endorse the goals and values of schooling (autonomy). These self-system processes, along with the nature of the academic work students are given (i.e., whether it is authentic, relevant, purposeful, and important) are the proximal predictors

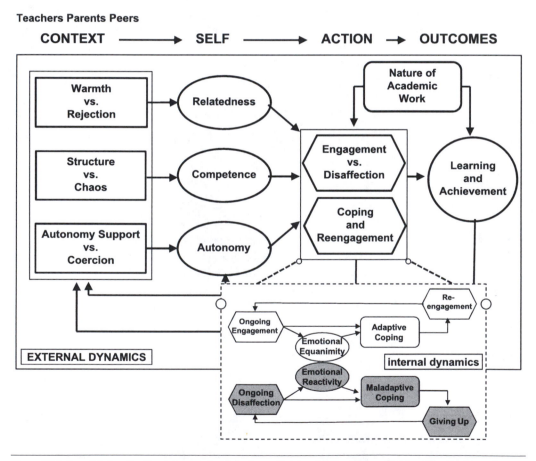

Figure 17.1 A model of motivational development based on self-determination theory, which specifies the internal dynamics among the processes of motivational resilience, including engagement, emotional reactivity, coping, re-engagement, as well as the external dynamics, or reciprocal connections among the social context (teachers, parents, and peers), students' self-system processes, authentic academic work, motivational resilience, learning, and achievement.

of students' motivational resilience (or vulnerability), including their engagement, coping, and re-engagement. These components of resilience, each of which contains emotions as essential constituents, are in turn necessary conditions for students' continued learning, development, and long-term success in school.

MOTIVATIONAL RESILIENCE: ENGAGEMENT, COPING, AND RE-ENGAGEMENT

In this model, the processes of motivational resilience include students' engagement, coping, and re-engagement with challenging tasks (see Figure 17.1). The key idea is that students' encounters with everyday obstacles and setbacks in school can exert a downward pressure on their motivation. When students are highly engaged, they are not only less affected by these stressful episodes, but they also have access to more constructive coping strategies (such as strategizing or help-seeking), leading to increased persistence and re-engagement with difficult academic material. In contrast, students who are disaffected may become even more discouraged in the face of problems, leaving them prone to utilize more maladaptive coping strategies (such as concealment or blaming others) that, in turn, make it more likely that they will give up.

Emotion as Central to Motivational Resilience

As depicted in Figure 17.2, emotions are embedded in all the components of motivational resilience. Engagement, coping, and re-engagement all represent "patterns of action" that combine behaviors (i.e., motor responses) with emotions, attention, and intentions into

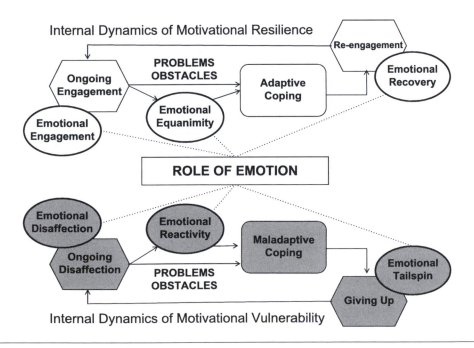

Figure 17.2 The role of emotion in the internal dynamics of motivational resilience and vulnerability.

goal-directed, emotion-laden functional packages (Brandtstädter, 2006). According to this perspective, goals and emotions energize and direct attention and behavior, and it is this amalgam—these actions—that reflect an individual's motivation. Examples of such actions are *approach* (which depicts positive, interested, focused movement toward interactions with a person, object, or event) or *flight* (which captures fearful, energized movement away from interactions). Action theorists argue that the natural unit of analysis for conceptualizing transactions between people and their social contexts are actions, and that it is individuals' actions (and not behaviors) to which social contexts respond (Brandtstädter, 2006). The next sections consider how emotions participate in each of the components of motivational resilience.

Engagement and Disaffection as Ongoing Motivated Actions

Engagement and disaffection, as we use the concepts, include emotion as part of their core definitions (Reeve, 2012; Skinner, Kindermann, & Furrer, 2009). The behavioral dimension of engagement involves effort, exertion, persistence, and determination; emotional or affective engagement encompasses enthusiasm, enjoyment, interest, fun, and satisfaction. Behavioral disaffection comprises physical withdrawal of effort, such as passivity or avoidance as well as their mental counterparts, such as inattention or daydreaming. Emotional disaffection includes withdrawal based on anxiety, boredom, frustration, or apathy.

These definitions differ from other conceptualizations in which emotional engagement is couched in terms of identification with school (Voelkl, 1997) or feelings of connectedness (Fredricks et al., 2004). The emotional features of engagement depicted in our conceptualization are labeled "activity-focused positive activating emotions" by emotion researchers (Pekrun & Linnenbrink-Garcia, 2012), and the emotional features of disaffection are labeled "activity-focused negative activating" and "de-activating" emotions. In our own studies, as suggested by emotion researchers, we have found that these emotions seem to fuel and direct engaged and disaffected behaviors (Skinner, Furrer, Marchand, & Kindermann, 2008).

Coping as Action Regulation under Stress

Like other developmentalists, we view coping as an adaptive self-regulatory process that involves the management of complex actions under stress (Compas, 2009; Skinner & Zimmer-Gembeck, 2007). In challenging situations, multiple facets of action, including behavior, attention, emotion, and physiological reactions, are typically activated so that children need to coordinate and sequence these (sometimes competing) action tendencies, or stress reactivity will overwhelm regulation (Compas, Connor, Salzman, Thomsen, & Wadsworth, 1999).

The role of emotion in motivational resilience is seen most clearly in the study of emotional reactivity in the face of stress in which children's coping and emotion regulation are shaped by the intensity of their initial negative emotional reactions to stressful events. Consistent with decades of work on emotion regulation (Jacobs & Gross, 2014), research on academic coping has found that when students show high levels of distress, it is more difficult for them to cope constructively with stressful academic events in school. For example, in one study of third to fifth graders, students' initial emotional reactions to academic stressors predicted changes in their subsequent coping across the school year, with students who reported high distress reactions in fall showing decreases in the use of constructive coping and an increasing reliance on maladaptive coping as the year progressed (Skinner, Pitzer, & Steele, 2013b).

Appraisals of Personal Resources and Liabilities

Important predictors of students' emotional reactivity and coping are their appraisals of the meaning of stressful encounters. The motivational model, not surprisingly, posits that students' appraisals (or self-systems) of relatedness, competence, and autonomy act as resources for emotional equanimity and constructive coping. That is, students who feel high levels of connection to others in the school setting (relatedness), academic self-efficacy (competence), and personal investment in learning (autonomy) are more likely to maintain their composure and cope adaptively with the problems they face (Skinner, Pitzer, & Steele, 2013a).

In contrast, students can appraise demanding academic events in ways that amplify their stressful qualities and threatening implications. These appraisals, which we refer to as *catastrophizing*, are also organized around the three basic needs—that is, catastrophizing of (1) relatedness, which magnifies the harmful interpersonal consequences of the event (e.g., "When something bad happens at school, I feel like nobody will like me"), (2) competence, which underscores the event's significance for ability (e.g., "I feel totally stupid"), and (3) autonomy, which accentuates self-blame and guilt (e.g., "I feel like it's all my fault"). Catastrophizing functions as a liability when students are dealing with problems in school because it intensifies emotional reactivity and triggers maladaptive ways of coping (Skinner et al., 2013a).

Emotional Recovery as Part of Re-engagement

Emotion is also an essential ingredient in the fourth component of motivational resilience in which students bounce back from academic difficulties and problems and re-engage with the challenging material. Also referred to as "buoyancy" (Martin & Marsh, 2008) or mastery (Dweck, 1999), the behavioral marker of re-engagement is the maintenance or intensification of one's efforts and determination. Adaptive coping strategies (such as problem solving, information seeking, and self-encouragement) seem to provide both guidance and a boost of energy towards those ends (Boekarts, 1993; Skinner et al., 2013b).

Figuring less prominently in discussions of these concepts, however, is the emotional recovery implied by re-engagement. When students run into difficulties, they can become frustrated, discouraged, or disinterested in continuing. At this juncture, they can cope in ways that leave them mired in negative emotions, eventually leading them to give up (Peterson et al., 1993). And, in fact, several ways of coping, such as rumination and projection, are considered maladaptive precisely because they amplify negative emotions, adding distress to an already stressful situation and potentially sending students into an emotional tailspin (Compas et al., 1999). Alternatively, to meaningfully re-engage, students can cope in ways that allow them to keep going despite worry or frustration (such as through help-seeking or self-encouragement), or that allow them to regain their enthusiasm for challenging tasks (such as through problem solving). Hence, constructive coping and emotional recovery may be keys to re-engagement.

Emotions as Organizers of Profiles of Motivational Resilience and Vulnerability

It is even possible that emotions are the leading edge in organizing and differentiating motivational profiles (or prototypes) of engagement, reactivity, coping, and re-engagement in the classroom (Connell & Wellborn, 1991). The fully engaged profile, which includes positive emotions (enthusiasm, interest), engaged behaviors (effort, attention), emotional equanimity, adaptive coping, and high re-engagement, characterizes the prototypically motivated student and both reflects and elicits corresponding motivational support from teachers (Furrer & Skinner, 2009; Skinner & Belmont, 1993). Anxiously engaged or enmeshed students might show a pattern that also includes high behavioral engagement but is colored by high levels of worry, emotional reactivity and confusion, concealment, or rumination in the face of problems and setbacks. Despite the presence of behavioral engagement, these students, based on their emotional reactivity and maladaptive coping, may be at risk for helplessness.

Emotions as Part of Profiles of Motivational Vulnerability

Emotions may also be critical in distinguishing diverse kinds of unmotivated students, furnishing clues about different routes to passivity or disruptive classroom behavior. The emotional culprit most commonly responsible for undermining students' engaged behaviors is boredom (Pekrun, Goetz, Daniels, Stupnisky, & Perry, 2010), which is likely accompanied by half-hearted attempts at coping or simply by escape, and a low threshold for giving up. More activating negative emotions, like anger and frustration, may organize a profile that also includes more active disaffected behavior in class, such as off-task and disruptive behaviors, along with maladaptive ways of coping that are also externalizing, like blaming others (i.e., projection) and giving up.

The most serious pattern of motivational vulnerability may be one referred to as *amotivation* (Vallerand et al., 1993), which has been tapped using self-report items like "I just don't care about school." Because it is characterized by the absence or loss of energetic resources dedicated to academic activities, amotivation likely includes not only passivity and lack of initiative but also a scarcity of coping of any sort and a high probability of giving up, perhaps even before running into resistance. It is important to note that the low levels of reactivity likely to accompany this profile cannot be considered good news, since they reflect the underlying emotional states of apathy or indifference.

The Development of Purpose as a Durable Motivational Resource

In the long term—that is, by the time they reach adolescence—students' enthusiastic engagement, adaptive coping, and constructive re-engagement may give rise to the development of an overarching sense of purpose or ownership for their own academic progress. Researchers have long discussed the benefits brought to learning when "wholeheartedness of purpose is present" (Kilpatrick, 1918, p. 334). The combination of personal fulfillment and satisfaction in serving others implied by purpose (Damon, Menon, & Bronk, 2003) seems to have the potential to inspire positive emotions and to galvanize action. In fact, as explained by McKnight and Kashdan (2009), purpose can be seen as "a central, self-organizing life aim that organizes and stimulates goals, manages behaviors, and provides a sense of meaning" (p. 242). If students believe that their schoolwork is important and meaningful, these commitments may serve as energetic anchors, especially if other aspects of their motivational systems are fragile. Because of the energy and organization that purposefulness provides to the whole motivational system, researchers recognize it as key to students' academic resilience (Morrison & Allen, 2007).

Even when academic subjects themselves do not arouse emotions connected with long-term purposes, a sense of academic ownership may arise out of the realization that school itself represents a meaningful goal. Especially as students enter secondary school, their academic achievement has real consequences, directly influencing their college and career opportunities (Anderman & Maehr, 1994). For at-risk students, in particular, school success is one of the few pathways to financial assistance with otherwise prohibitive college costs or as a means to improve their families' lives. When students are convinced that academic success is centrally important to their own futures, these commitments can serve as a powerful organizing force for helping students sustain their emotional and motivational investments in learning.

INTERNAL AND EXTERNAL DYNAMICS OF MOTIVATIONAL DEVELOPMENT

How do motivational resilience and vulnerability develop over time? The feedforward and feedback arrows among the components of motivational resilience depicted in Figure 17.2 suggest that these elements create a dynamic system of reciprocal relationships. If engagement is an energetic resource that supports students' constructive coping and re-engagement in the face of setbacks, this suggests an *internal dynamic,* which builds resilience. If, at the same time, student disaffection acts as a drain on energetic resources and leads students to cope maladaptively, withdraw, and give up after setbacks, this also suggests a dynamic that magnifies motivational vulnerabilities over time.

As shown in Figure 17.1, students' self-systems are closely coupled to these processes: Students who feel competent, connected, and autonomous also engage in academic work and react to challenges in ways that allow them to learn and succeed, thus cementing their positive views of themselves and school. In contrast, students who feel incompetent, unconnected, and coerced become disaffected and are more likely to react to problems and cope with demanding academic tasks in ways that amplify their distress and preempt learning, making failure more likely, and thus validating students' negative views of themselves and school. Hence, students' personal resources or liabilities tend to become part of self-perpetuating systems.

External Dynamics

However, these internal dynamics play out in the social contexts of classrooms and schools. As depicted in Figure 17.1, these *external dynamics,* involving students' interactions with teachers, parents, peers, and the academic work they are assigned, play key roles in supporting or undermining students' innate psychological needs for relatedness, competence, and autonomy in school, and so are decisive in magnifying or counteracting the internal dynamics of risk and resilience. Teachers are especially important interaction partners; the tasks they assign and the interpersonal climates they help to create on a daily basis are critical in supporting or undermining student motivation.

Although empirical evidence is sparse, so far it appears as if feedforward and feedback loops between the classroom (teacher, peers, academic work) and the student (academic identity, motivational resilience, learning) are also largely positive (Jang, Kim, & Reeve, 2012; Reeve, 2012; Skinner et al., 2008). That is, more engaged students also join peer groups who are more engaged and elicit more motivational support from teachers, whereas disaffected students tend to join peer groups of other students who are also more disaffected, and to receive less support and more controlling responses from teachers (Furrer & Skinner, 2009; Kindermann, 2007; Skinner & Belmont, 1993). Some researchers suggest that these recursive internal and external dynamics, as they are played out daily in classrooms, may combine to contribute to an overall developmental pattern of increasingly high interindividual stability with increasingly diverging pathways for students who start off "rich" (in any component) compared to those who start off "poor" (Marcoulides, Gottfried, Gottfried, & Oliver, 2008; Marks, 2000; Skinner et al., 2008).

It is important to note that because these components form a system of reciprocal feedback loops, the directionality of the system can be guided by any of its initial conditions. For example, vicious cycles can be initiated by student disaffection, but they can also be initiated by low teacher support, peer cultures of disaffection, student learning disabilities, or lack of preparation for academic work. Of course, the systems most likely to lead to problems are ones that contain multiple risk factors in students, teachers, parents, peer groups, and neighborhoods.

Educational Implications for Promoting Emotional Engagement and Motivational Resilience

What can teachers do to promote students' engagement, adaptive coping, and recovery from setbacks and failure? According to SDT, teachers can contribute to motivational development by meeting students' needs for relatedness, competence, and autonomy. As depicted in Figure 17.1, SDT focuses on whether teachers offer their students *warmth, structure,* and *autonomy support.* These qualities of classroom interactions are strong predictors of students' views of themselves, as well as their intrinsic motivation, emotional and behavioral engagement, self-regulated learning, and achievement (Elliot & Dweck, 2005; Jang, Reeve, & Deci, 2010; Niemiec & Ryan, 2009; Skinner et al., 2008; Su & Reeve, 2011).

Warmth or Pedagogical Caring

Teachers can promote students' feelings of relatedness by fostering caring and trusting relationships with their students (i.e., pedagogical caring; Wentzel, 1997), through means such as expressing affection, enjoyment, and concern, being available and dependable sources of emotional support, paying attention to, spending time with, and learning about individual students, and considering the whole student in curricular and disciplinary decisions. Relatedness is undermined by rejecting interactions in which teachers communicate to students that they are not welcome in class. Teachers can convey disinterest or neglect by overlooking students, not having time for them, disregarding their input, or not listening to their perspectives. More overt dislike can also be communicated by an irritated or disapproving tone of voice, or by criticism directed at a student's personality or abilities.

Structure

Teachers can promote students' perceived competence by providing appropriate levels of *structure*, including high and reasonable standards, clear expectations, and appropriate limits for students' behaviors and performance, and consistent follow-through on demands (Jang et al., 2010). Structure also includes helping students figure out how to reach high levels of performance and the provision of informational feedback, so that when students do not meet expectations, teachers explain how to improve. Perceived competence is undermined by *chaotic* interactions with teachers in which students view teachers as unpredictable, inconsistent, or arbitrary in their expectations or follow-through, especially in grading or discipline. Students can also experience teachers as chaotic if educators do not thoroughly explain to students how to succeed in learning tasks, explain in ways students cannot understand, or do not provide help when it is needed. Feedback about performance can also be experienced as chaotic if it is absent or focuses only on what is wrong rather than how to improve.

Autonomy Support

Teachers can bolster students' autonomy by offering students choices, listening to their opinions, and explaining the relevance of work to students' own goals (Reeve, 2009). Autonomy supportive teachers treat students with respect, seek out and value their views, encourage them to work on issues that are important to them, and provide explanations for why activities that are not intrinsically fun are nevertheless critical to learning. Classrooms attuned to students' needs can lead to *internalization* or ownership of what were once extrinsically motivated activities; students are no longer doing a task simply because the teacher assigned it but rather, because they can see how it is connected to their own personal goals or interests (Deci & Ryan, 1985). Student autonomy is undermined by *coercive* or controlling interactions in which students are pressured, bossed, or pushed around (Reeve, 2009). Coercive tactics rely on external sources of motivation, such as commands, deadlines, incentives, and threats of punishment and use pressuring language (e.g., "should," "have to"), including impatience and guilt-inducing criticism. Coercive reactions to students' negative affect (such as boredom or discouragement) include power assertions in which teachers deny their validity, and instead insist on compliance using authoritarian reasons ("because I said so").

Nature of Academic Work

While teachers can support or hinder students' motivation, engagement itself is a function of students' interactions with the actual academic tasks they encounter in the classroom. Hence, one of the most important avenues through which teachers can support motivational resilience is by providing students with authentic academic work—that is, with challenging, meaningful, hands-on, project-based, social, real-world activities that naturally capitalize on students' inherent motivation to learn (Newmann, King, & Carmichael, 2007; Swarat, Ortony, & Revelle, 2012). These activities seem to capture students' enthusiasm and energy through two related channels. First, certain task structures inherently seem like "fun." Active hands-on activities, where students work together to make something happen (such as writing and producing an opera, building a robot, or setting up a store) seem more likely to meet students' needs for relatedness and competence. Second, tasks that are connected to meaningful real-world concerns (such as reporting information to working scientists, creating a school garden so produce can be contributed to a food bank, or helping to create an exhibit in a local museum) tap into students' needs for purpose and service to the wider world. Thus, activities that are interesting, fun, relevant, clear, and interactive—tasks based in real actions and real settings, designed to involve students cognitively and emotionally—should provide a key pathway for promoting resilience.

Fostering Emotional and Motivational Resilience

When classrooms are focused on fun, meaningful, demanding learning tasks that not only invite interest and curiosity but are also worthy of hard work, many of teachers' motivational and management concerns disappear because students are naturally more engaged. And, because these activities are already aligned with students' own motivational proclivities, it is easier for teachers to provide pathways to success, relevance, choices, and warm interactions. Even normally disaffected students should find it easier to engage with intrinsically motivating academic tasks (Newmann et al., 2007).

The availability of a teacher who can act as a warm and caring guide attuned to students' interests and learning should allow students to deal constructively with demanding work and the failures and setbacks it necessarily entails. Teachers who can validate students' anxious, frustrated, or discouraged reactions to difficulties as well as provide emotional and instrumental support encourage students to persevere with emotional equanimity, using adaptive coping that accesses social and personal resources (through help and comfort seeking, or problem solving and self-encouragement). As a result, students can bounce back emotionally and recover their interest and enthusiasm for challenging academic tasks.

Over time, these interactions can foster student ownership for their own academic progress. Close caring relationships with teachers provide a secure base for students, fostering a sense of commitment to one's school or community and the trust needed for students to reveal their deeply held interests. Moreover, if commitment to a meaningful purpose is to thrive, students must gain the actual competencies they need to successfully pursue their interests, finding and using effective strategies and pathways for action via their teachers and their own personal efforts. Finally, these actions must tie back into students' genuine beliefs and feelings, informing students' identities as well as reflecting them. The emotions driving a sense of purpose—whether inspired by commitment to a particular cause or to school success in and of itself—should help organize a student's identity (Hill & Burrow, 2012), perhaps as reflected by self-perceptions such as "I am a person who helps others in my community," or "I will show others that people like me can succeed in life."

COUNTERACTING DISAFFECTION AND MOTIVATIONAL VULNERABILITIES

If teachers wish to promote motivational resilience, it is especially important for them to consider how they respond to students' negative emotions and behaviors in their classrooms. Teachers directly experience student disaffection every day, and they rate dealing with unmotivated and disruptive students as among the most stressful features of their jobs (Chang, 2009). Although research on teacher reactions to student motivation is sparse (Frenzel, Goetz, Ludtke, Pekrun, & Sutton, 2009; Reeve, 2012), the few studies examining student engagement as a predictor of changes in subsequent teacher support suggest that teachers typically respond to students in kind by becoming more involved, responsive, and autonomy supportive with engaged students, and responding to disaffected students by withdrawing their own involvement and becoming more coercive (Furrer & Skinner, 2009; Skinner & Belmont, 1993).

Teachers' Psychological Needs, Appraisals, and Engagement

In order to understand teachers' reactions to disaffected students, it is important to consider teachers' own emotions. According to SDT, teachers, just like students, have needs for relatedness, competence, and autonomy, and their interactions with students are an important venue in which those needs are satisfied or thwarted (Spilt, Koomen, & Thijs, 2011). It is easy to imagine how unmotivated students could undermine teachers' basic needs. Bored students can make teachers feel as if they themselves are boring or incompetent in creating engaging learning activities. Students' expressions of negative affect can make teachers feel as if students do not like them. And disruptive students, who argue or talk back, can be experienced as coercive, interrupting the flow of a class and forcing teachers into confrontations they prefer to avoid. In general, students, who are not cooperating with a teacher's plans for instruction (whatever their reasons), can easily derail a teacher's own enjoyment and engagement with teaching.

Teachers' Appraisals of Students' Disaffection

SDT maintains that it is not only actual objective events that shape teachers' experiences of whether their needs are being met by interactions with students. It is also, and perhaps as importantly, their interpretations of those experiences. These appraisals, and especially interpreting students' behaviors as personal affronts, are considered to be one important source of teachers' disaffected emotions (Chang, 2009). If, however, teachers can begin to view students' unmotivated or unruly behaviors not as insults or roadblocks but instead as useful information (about students' views of themselves, states of mind, and motivation) that is not only helpful, but essential to teachers in guiding their next interpersonal or curricular steps—then they can find students' emotions interesting and enlightening and come to appreciate their expression, whether positive or negative.

If teachers encourage students to communicate their true emotions and opinions, and also listen openly and respond warmly when they do, this should allow students and teachers to genuinely get to know and value each other as "whole persons." Such knowledge is the basis for close relationships and the provision of autonomy support. The more accurate the information that teachers receive, the more easily they can tailor the social-emotional climate, instruction, and management practices to meet students' needs (Jang et al., 2010). Even if a student really does not like a teacher and even if a student actually is trying to disrupt instruction, teachers can either take these actions personally (in the sense of a blow to the ego) or recognize them as the culmination of the students' experiences at school (and home). These interpretations can make a substantial difference to whether teachers react with negative emotions and disaffection of their own or with renewed warm, structured, and autonomy supportive engagement (Chang, 2009).

Teacher Coping, Re-engagement, and Emotional Recovery

Just as with students, the overall quality of a teacher's engagement with teaching can be seen as a protective factor that allows them, when they run into challenges and problems, to react with adaptive coping—such as problem solving, searching for more information, or seeking social support from friends or colleagues (Skinner & Beers, in press). Constructive coping (including self-encouragement and determination) allows teachers to persist in the face of difficult student behaviors and emotions and to re-engage even with challenging students. In contrast, teachers who are already somewhat disaffected should be more likely to fall into maladaptive ways of coping (such as escape, blaming others, rumination, or self-pity) when they run into trouble in the classroom. These reactions are likely to undermine teachers' energy and enthusiasm for teaching even more, putting them at risk for further disengagement, burn-out, and even desistence from the profession (Chang, 2009). Teachers need to develop the capacity to maintain their emotional composure and recover their emotional equanimity after stressful episodes if they are to remain resilient and authentically engaged in high-quality teaching over the course of their professional careers (Roeser, Skinner, Beers, & Jennings, 2012).

The Larger Context of the School and the Educational System

In order to fully understand teachers' emotional reactions to students in their classrooms, it is necessary to consider not only the individual players discussed so far (that is, the issues presented by students and teachers' interpretations of students' actions) but also the larger context of the school and profession in which these teacher–student interactions take place. For example, students' willingness to express their genuine emotions as well as teachers' capacities to accurately read students' emotional reactions both depend on how well teachers and students actually know and like each other; this in turn depends on how many students a teacher has been assigned to teach and how much class time can be allotted to cultivating relationships. If teachers are assigned multiple classes of 45–50 students (as is often the case in secondary schools), it is simply not possible to get to know each student individually. Likewise, if in order to meet accountability standards for external testing, instruction is packed full and subject-centered (instead of student-centered), time for building social-emotional connections is very hard to find.

Larger institutional and political forces help determine whether teachers can meet their needs for relatedness, competence, and autonomy in their chosen profession, and thus in very real ways shape the emotions they experience when teaching and interacting with students in the classroom (Niemiec & Ryan, 2009). External pressures from above (e.g., based on increases in workload, stressful external evaluations, or threats of job cuts) combine with the bottom-up pressures created by students who are unmotivated, unhappy, or unprepared to learn. These coercive forces operating on teachers can eventually lead them to become more controlling in their classrooms (Reeve, 2009). Such tactics not only backfire in terms of supporting student motivation, but they also undercut teachers' own enjoyment and engagement in teaching.

In this chapter, we have tried to highlight what is at stake for students and teachers in their daily work together in the classroom. If teachers can tune their interpersonal relationships and instructional activities to students' motivational needs, they can help students unlock energetic and emotional resources, including sustained positive engagement, productive coping, and the construction of an academic identity that allows students to take responsibility for their own academic success. The development of motivational resilience is not only a life-long gift from teachers to students, it also represents a gift teachers give themselves, since student engagement and excitement in learning are precious resources for teachers, and ones that can spark (or rekindle) their own joy in the challenging and ultimately rewarding profession of teaching.

REFERENCES

Anderman, E. M., & Maehr, M. L. (1994). Motivation and schooling in the middle grades. *Review of Educational Research, 64,* 287–309.

Baumeister, R. F., & Leary, M. R. (1995). The need to belong: Desire for interpersonal attachments as a fundamental human motivation. *Psychological Bulletin, 117,* 497–529.

Boekarts, M. (1993). Being concerned with well-being and with learning. *Educational Psychologist, 28,* 149–167.

Bowlby, J. (1969/1973). *Attachment and loss. Vols. 1 and 2.* New York, NY: Basic Books.

Brandtstädter, J. (2006). Action perspectives on human development. In W. Damon (Series Ed.) & R. M. Lerner (Vol. Ed.), *Handbook of child psychology: Vol. 1. Theoretical models of human development* (pp. 516–568). New York, NY: Wiley.

Chang, M.-L. (2009). An appraisal perspective of teacher burnout: Examining the emotional work of teachers. *Educational Psychology Review, 21,* 193–218.

Christenson, S. L., Reschly, A. L., & Wylie, C. (2012). *Handbook of research on student engagement.* New York, NY: Springer Science.

Compas, B. E. (2009). Coping, regulation, and development during childhood and adolescence. In E. A. Skinner & M. J. Zimmer-Gembeck (Eds.), *Coping and the development of regulation* (pp. 87–99). A volume for the series, R. W. Larson & L. A. Jensen (Eds.-in-Chief), *New Directions in Child and Adolescent Development.* San Francisco, CA: Jossey-Bass.

Compas, B. E., Connor, J. K., Saltzman, H., Thomsen, A. H., & Wadsworth, M. (1999). Getting specific about coping: Effortful and involuntary responses to stress in development. In M. Lewis & D. Ramsay (Eds.), *Soothing and stress* (pp. 229–256). Mahwah, NJ: Erlbaum.

Connell, J. P., & Wellborn, J. G. (1991). Competence, autonomy and relatedness: A motivational analysis of self-system processes. In M. Gunnar & L. A. Sroufe (Eds.), *Minnesota Symposium on Child Psychology: Vol. 23. Self processes in development* (pp. 43–77). Chicago, IL: University of Chicago Press.

Damon, W., Menon, J., & Bronk, K. C. (2003). The development of purpose during adolescence. *Applied Developmental Science, 7,* 119–128.

Deci, E. L., & Ryan, R. M. (1985). *Intrinsic motivation and self-determination in human behavior.* New York, NY: Plenum Press.

Dweck, C. S. (1999). *Self-theories: Their role in motivation, personality, and development.* Philadelphia, PA: Psychology Press.

Elliot, A. J., & Dweck, C. S. (Eds.). (2005). *Handbook of competence and motivation.* New York, NY: Guilford.

Fredricks, J. A., Blumenfeld, P. C., & Paris, A. H. (2004). School engagement: Potential of the concept, state of the evidence. *Review of Educational Research, 74,* 59–109.

Frenzel, A. C., Goetz, T., Lüdtke, O., Pekrun, R., & Sutton, R. E. (2009). Emotional transmission in the classroom: Exploring the relationship between teacher and student enjoyment. *Journal of Educational Psychology, 101,* 705–716.

Furrer, C. J., & Skinner, E. A. (2009, April). *Reciprocal effects of student engagement in the classroom on changes in teacher support over the school year.* Poster presented at the biennial meeting of the Society for Research in Child Development, Denver, CO.

Hill, P. L., & Burrow, A. L. (2012). Viewing purpose through an Eriksonian lens. *Identity, 12,* 74–91.

Jacobs, S. E., & Gross, J. J. (2014). Emotion regulation in education: Conceptual foundations, current applications and future directions. In R. Pekrun & L. Linnenbrink (Eds.), *Handbook of emotions and education.* Taylor & Francis.

Jang, H., Kim, E. J., & Reeve, J. (2012). Longitudinal test of self-determination theory's motivation mediation model in a naturally occurring classroom context. *Journal of Educational Psychology, 104,* 1175–1188.

Jang, H., Reeve, J., & Deci, E. L. (2010). Engaging students in learning activities: It is not autonomy support or structure but autonomy support and structure. *Journal of Educational Psychology, 102,* 588–600.

Kilpatrick, W. (1918). The project method: The use of the purposeful act in the educative process. *The Teachers College Record, 19,* 319–335.

Kindermann, T. A. (2007). Effects of naturally-existing peer groups on changes in academic engagement in a cohort of sixth graders. *Child Development, 78,* 1186–1203.

Maier, S. F., & Watkins, L. R. (2005). Stressor controllability and learned helplessness: The roles of the dorsal raphe nucleus, serotonin, and corticotropin-releasing factor. *Neuroscience and Behavioral Reviews, 29,* 829–841.

Marcoulides, G. A., Gottfried, A. E., Gottfried, A. W., & Oliver, P. H. (2008). A latent transition analysis of academic intrinsic motivation from childhood through adolescence. *Educational Research and Evaluation, 14,* 411–427.

Marks, H. M. (2000). Student engagement in instructional activity: Patterns in the elementary, middle, and high school years. *American Educational Research Journal, 37,* 153–184.

Martin, A. J., & Marsh, H. W. (2008). Academic buoyancy: Towards an understanding of students' everyday academic resilience. *Journal of School Psychology, 46,* 53–83.

McKnight, P. E., & Kashdan, T. B. (2009). Purpose in life as a system that creates and sustains health and well-being: An integrative, testable theory. *Review of General Psychology, 13,* 242–251.

Morrison, G. M., & Allen, M. (2007). Promoting student resilience in school contexts. *Theory into Practice, 46,* 162–169.

Newmann, F. M., King, M. B., & Carmichael, D. L. (2007). *Authentic instruction and assessment: Common standards for rigor and relevance in teaching academic subjects.* Des Moines, IA: Iowa Department of Education.

Niemiec, C. P., & Ryan, R. M. (2009). Autonomy, competence, and relatedness in the classroom: Applying self-determination theory to educational practice. *Theory and Research in Education, 7,* 133–144.

Osterman, K. F. (2000). Students' need for belonging in the school community. *Review of Educational Research, 70,* 323–367.

Peterson, C., Maier, S. F., & Seligman, M.E.P. (1993). *Learned helplessness: A theory for the age of personal control.* New York, NY: Oxford University Press.

Pekrun, R., Goetz, T., Daniels, L. M., Stupnisky, R. H., & Perry, R. P. (2010). Boredom in achievement settings: Exploring control–value antecedents and performance outcomes of a neglected emotion. *Journal of Educational Psychology, 102,* 531–549.

Pekrun, R., & Linnenbrink-Garcia, L. (2012). Academic emotions and student engagement. In S. L. Christenson, A. L. Reschly, & C. Wylie (Eds.), *Handbook of research on student engagement* (pp. 259–282). New York, NY: Springer.

Reeve, J. (2009). Why teachers adopt a controlling motivating style toward students and how they can become more autonomy supportive. *Educational Psychologist, 44,* 159–175.

Reeve, J. (2012). A self-determination theory perspective on student engagement. In S. L. Christenson, A.L. Reschly, & C. Wylie (Eds.), *Handbook of research on student engagement* (pp. 149–172). New York, NY: Springer.

Roeser, R. W., Midgley, C., & Urdan, T. C. (1996). Perceptions of the school psychological environment and early adolescents' psychological and behavioral functioning in school: The mediating role of goals and belonging. *Journal of Educational Psychology, 88,* 408–422.

Roeser, R. W., Skinner, E. A., Beers, J., & Jennings, P. A. (2012). Mindfulness training and teachers' professional development: An emerging area of research and practice. *Child Development Perspectives, 6,* 146–153.

Skinner, E. A. (1996). A guide to constructs of control. *Journal of Personality and Social Psychology, 71,* 549–570.

Skinner, E. A., & Beers, J. (in press). Mindfulness and teachers' coping in the classroom: A developmental model of teacher stress, coping, and everyday resilience. In K. Schonert-Reichl & R. W. Roeser (Eds.), *Handbook on mindfulness in education: Emerging theory, research, and programs.* New York, NY: Springer-Verlag.

Skinner, E. A., & Belmont, M. J. (1993). Motivation in the classroom: Reciprocal effects of teacher behavior and student engagement across the school year. *Journal of Educational Psychology, 85,* 571–581.

Skinner, E. A., Furrer, C., Marchand, G., & Kindermann, T. (2008). Engagement and disaffection in the classroom: Part of a larger motivational dynamic? *Journal of Educational Psychology, 100,* 765–781.

Skinner, E. A., Kindermann, T. A., & Furrer, C. (2009). A motivational perspective on engagement and disaffection: Conceptualization and assessment of children's behavioral and emotional participation in academic activities in the classroom. *Educational and Psychological Measurement, 69,* 493–525.

Skinner, E. A., & Pitzer, J. (2012). Developmental dynamics of engagement, coping, and everyday resilience. In S. L. Christenson, A.L. Reschly, & C. Wylie (Eds.), *Handbook of research on student engagement* (pp. 21–44). New York, NY: Springer Science.

Skinner, E. A., Pitzer, J. R., & Steele, J. S. (2013a). Coping as part of motivational resilience in school: A multi-dimensional measure of families, allocations, and profiles of academic coping. *Journal of Educational and Psychological Measurement, 73*, 803–835.

Skinner, E. A., Pitzer, J. R., & Steele, J. S. (2013b, April). *Academic coping in elementary school: The dynamics of motivational resilience.* Poster presented at the biennial meeting of the Society for Research in Child Development, Seattle, WA.

Skinner, E. A., & Zimmer-Gembeck, M. J. (2007). The development of coping. *Annual Review of Psychology, 58*, 119–144.

Spilt, J. L., Koomen, H.M.Y., & Thijs, J. T. (2011). Teacher well-being: The importance of teacher-student relationships. *Educational Psychology Review, 23*, 457–477.

Su, Y.-L., & Reeve, J. (2011). A meta-analysis of the effectiveness of intervention programs designed to support autonomy. *Educational Psychology Review, 23*, 159–188.

Swarat, A., Ortony, A., & Revelle W. (2012). Activity matters: Understanding student interest in science. *Journal of Research in Science Teaching, 49*, 515–537.

Vallerand, R. J., Pelletier, L. G., Blais, M. R., Brière, N. M., Senécal, C. B., & Vallières, E. F. (1993). On the assessment of intrinsic, extrinsic, and amotivation in education: Evidence on the concurrent and construct validity of the Academic Motivation Scale. *Educational and Psychological Measurement, 53*, 159–172.

Voelkl, K. (1997). Identification with school. *American Journal of Education, 105*, 294–318.

Watson, J. S. (1979). Perception of contingency as a determinant of social responsiveness. In E. Thoman (Ed.), *Origins of the infant's social responsiveness* (pp. 33–64). Hillsdale, NJ: Erlbaum.

Wentzel, K. R. (1997). Student motivation in middle school: The role of perceived pedagogical caring. *Journal of Educational Psychology, 89*, 411–419.

White, R. W. (1959). Motivation reconsidered: The concept of competence. *Psychological Review, 66*, 297–333.

18

REGULATING EMOTIONS RELATED TO TESTING

*Paul A. Schutz[a], Heather A. Davis[b], Jessica T. DeCuir-Gunby[b],
and David Tillman[c], University of Texas at San Antonio[a],
North Carolina State University[b], and Campbell University[c]*

Test taking and test performance are a central component of the primary, secondary, and collegiate academic cultures in the United States, Europe, and around the world. From the time children enter their local school district until the time they finish schooling, exams are part of the daily fabric of their school experience. Students around the world learn early in their academic careers that to win at school they must be successful in playing the testing game. Many students prevail in mastering the rules and a few even feel comfortable when taking tests:

> Compare it to rock climbing. If I feel like if I couldn't climb the rock or complete the triathlon then maybe I should have prepared better for it. The same is true of a test. . . . If it is challenging, if I feel like I am being challenged and I am doing well on it, then that makes me—I feel like I am confident.
>
> (Brad, low anxiety)[1]

However, for others, test taking is an excruciating experience:

> I try and study a lot for tests, but . . . I start second guessing myself and get confused. . . . I start to fidget. *(Her face goes flush. Her voice quivers.)* I mess with my hands a lot. . . . I can't sit still necessarily. . . . Little things start to bug me. Um, like my hair, like I have to get my hair up into a ponytail, or out of my face. *(She takes her long hair, wrings it in her hands, and twists it up into a ponytail.)* . . . I like to feel like I am just stripped down. You know, like my hair is out of my face, nothing is on my arms, or nothing is making me hot or contributing so that I can try to get a little more comfortable, a little less self-conscious. So I can just concentrate better.
>
> (Jennifer, high anxiety)

Researchers have labeled the anguish that students like Jennifer feel *test anxiety.* Researchers have also provided evidence for an inverse relationship between student success on tests and the anxiety they experience related to testing (Carver & Scheier, 1994; Chapell et al. 2005; Folkman & Lazarus, 1985; Stober & Pekrun, 2004; Zeidner, 1998, 2007, 2014). Understanding the phenomenon of test anxiety and the impact of unpleasant emotions on testing has become an interest for researchers concerned about the consequences of the increased emphasis being placed on high stakes testing. In fact, in addition to students, teachers and school districts are increasingly being held accountable for their scores on various tests (Nichols & Berliner, 2007), which means it is important that students' scores reflect their knowledge and skills in an area.

The increased focus on testing combined with the potential adverse effect of unpleasant emotions on test scores has resulted in our interest in students' emotional episodes related to testing and how students regulate during those emotional episodes. In order to address how students regulate emotions related to testing, we begin this chapter by discussing the emotional landscape of testing. Next, we discuss the work of researchers who have investigated the self-regulation of emotions related to testing, which will be followed by a discussion of research on social-contextual constraints and affordances related to emotion and emotion regulation. Finally, we will draw some conclusions and make some suggestions for future research.

EMOTIONAL LANDSCAPE OF TESTING

Dominance of Research on Test Anxiety

Traditionally, researchers interested in test emotions have focused on test anxiety. In fact, Stober and Pekrun (2004) noted that there were well over 1,000 such publications since 1952 and that number has only increased. In addition, research in this area has been conducted in countries all over the world (see O'Neil & Fukumura, 1992). Generally, test anxiety has been defined as anxiety subjectively relating to taking tests and exams, including anxiety related to the threat of failing an exam and the associated negative consequences (Zeidner, 1998, 2007, 2014).

Researchers in this area tend to make a distinction between *trait* and *state* anxiety. Trait test anxiety has been conceptualized as an individual disposition to react to tests and exams in habitual ways through the experience of anxiety (Spielberger & Vagg, 1995). Thus, to say someone is a test-anxious person implies that she or he has a tendency to see the testing in a manner that generally results in anxious feelings. On the other hand, state anxiety has been referred to the momentary context-specific emotions that emerge during a particular test.

However, in spite of researchers' focus on anxiety related to testing, the testing process has the potential for a variety of other emotional experiences both unpleasant (e.g., anger, anxiety) and pleasant (e.g., hope and pride) that can occur before, during, or after a test (DeCuir-Gunby, Aultman, & Schutz, 2009; Pekrun et al., 2004). In addition, emotional episodes are dynamic processes that can change from anxiety to anger to hope or to pride within a particular event, depending on a number of different factors, including appraisals, attributions, emotion regulation processes, or contextual constrains or affordances.

Affective Experiences

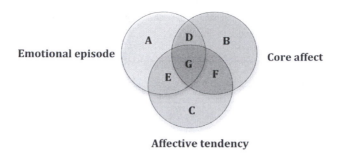

Figure 18.1 Relationship among emotional episodes, core affect, and affective tendency emotional episodes.

Affect as Dynamic Process

Prior to discussing our current conceptions of emotion regulation related to testing, we first describe how we conceptualize affective experiences. Currently, there are a number of concepts used to describe affective experiences in both the academic literature and in everyday speech. Thus, for clarity, we use the term *affective experiences* as an overarching construct to describe several transactional affective processes including *emotional episodes, core affect,* and *affective tendencies.* We use Figure 18.1 to represent how we see the transactions among affective experiences.

Emotional Episodes

Although there is a great deal of discussion about what constitutes an emotion, some common themes have emerged. For example, most scholars suggest that an emotion, at minimum, consists of physiological responses, cognitive appraisals, affective feelings, and behavioral tendencies (e.g., Frijda, 2000; Izard, 2007; Russell & Barrett, 1999; Scherer, 1993) (see "A" in Figure 18.1). Schutz and colleagues (2006) also emphasized social and historical aspects when they described an emotion as a "socially constructed, personally enacted ways of being that emerge from conscious and/or unconscious judgments regarding perceived successes at attaining goals or maintaining standards or beliefs during transactions as part of social-historical contexts" (p. 344).

When discussing emotions related to testing, it is clear that testing is increasingly becoming a way of life for students throughout the world. Thus, students tend to consider tests as central to their academic goals and self-worth (Bolger, 1990; Schutz, Benson, & DeCuir, 2008; Zeidner, 1998, 2007). With that in mind, and in order to capture the potential range of emotional episodes associated with the testing context, we will, like Pekrun and colleagues (2004), focus on four potential categories of emotional episodes: (A) pleasant-high activation (e.g., the *hope* of being successful while preparing for the test, the *enjoyment* of knowing the answers while taking the test, or, the *pride* in receiving a good grade after the test), (B) pleasant-low activation (e.g., *calmness* while preparing for a test, *relief* related to turning in the test, or, *pleasant* relaxation after the test is over), (C) unpleasant-high activation (e.g., *anger* at the instructor for the material to be studied, *anxiety* about not doing well during the exam, or *shame* related to being unsuccessful after the exam), and (D) unpleasant-low activation (e.g., *hopelessness* when not understanding the material, *sadness* about not being prepared during the test, or *despair* related to the score you received).

Core Affect

Developed from the work of Barrett (2006) and Russell (2003), we use the concept of *core affect* to describe how students generally feel at any particular point in time (see "B" in Figure 18.1). Core affect is generally described as a continuous and fluctuating state with two dimensions: *valence,* which ranges from pleasant to unpleasant, and *arousal,* which ranges from high to low activation (Barrett, 2006; Linnenbrink, 2007; Pekrun, et al., 2004; Russell, & Barrett, 1999; Schutz, Aultman, & Williams-Johnson, 2009). Core affect tends to function at an unconscious level (Barrett, 2006). So, although students may not be aware of their core affect at any particular point in time, Russell (2003) suggests that students can talk about their core affect, just as they can talk about their felt temperature (i.e., being hot or cold). So, if asked, students can describe how they feel at any particular point in time (e.g., happy, a little tired, or a bit tense), yet if not asked, they may not reflect on those current feelings.

With respect to emotion regulation surrounding testing, core affect represents the continuous range of ever-present feeling states that have the potential to become more prominent and intense based on the person's judgments (i.e., appraisal, attributions) related to a particular test. Thus, students' current core affect has the potential to influence not only if students have an emotion but also how that episode might be labeled (see "D" in Figure 18.1). For example, if a student's current core affect included being tense, an unexpected test question may result in increased feelings of anxiety. However, if the student's core affect was happy, like Brad from the beginning of the chapter, the same unexpected question may be met with feelings of challenge and excitement and a continuation of the test-taking process with little or no anxious thoughts.

Affective Tendencies

We use the term *affect tendencies* to refer to reasonably stable predispositions towards certain ways of emoting (Rosenberg, 1998; Schutz et al., 2009) (see "C" in Figure 18.1). In the testing context, affective tendencies such as trait emotions act as lenses through which students generally view testing. For example, Jennifer tends to be predisposed to view testing as fearful and unpleasant, which means she is more likely to experience core affects such as being tense during test preparation (see "F" in Figure 18.1) as well experiencing anxiety while testing (see "E" in Figure 18.1). As such, affective tendencies represent biases towards emotional episodes that resemble those propensities (Rosenberg, 1998; Schutz et al., 2009).

One dimension of an affective tendency is the potential for attentional bias (Eysenck, 1992). This particular bias involves seeing test situations as representing a threat for failure. As such, students tend to scan the test environment for evidence of threat (Edwards, Burt, & Lipp, 2010; Eysenck, 1992). Over time, students' with this affective tendency may perceive threat in even nonthreatening or ambiguous situations. For example, Schutz, Davis, and Schwanenflugel (2002) found that students who scored high on a measure of trait test anxiety tended to see task-focused test-taking strategies such as reading directions or checking ones answers as more closely related to the term test anxiety than moderate and low test-anxious participants. Thus, even potentially useful test-taking strategies were viewed as related to test anxiety, which may predispose students' towards having anxious emotional episodes.

It is also important to keep in mind that someone like Jennifer, whose affective tendencies may predispose her for test anxiety, is likely to have been preparing and ruminating about that test for several days before the test. Thus, she is more likely to enter the testing situation feeling tired from a lack of sleep and tension (core affect), which may contribute to her increased likelihood of experiencing an anxious emotional episode. The area in Figure 18.1 labeled "G" shows this transaction among *affective tendenc*ies, *core affect*, and *emotional episodes*. We acknowledge that other factors play a role in predicting affective valence and level of arousal of emotional episodes, with affective tendencies and core affect being only two of the potential influencing factors. As such, Figure 18.1 is presented as a conceptual model to guide readers in teasing out potential different distinctions that emotion researchers might use in studying emotion regulation related to testing.

REGULATING EMOTIONS RELATED TO TESTING

As a teacher, some of my personal observations of my students with test anxiety include watching students get flushed and profusely sweat, erasing so hard they created holes, and crying throughout tests. I have also witnessed, on three separate occasions, students between the ages of 8–10 urinating on themselves during end of grade testing. But, I will never forget one particular incident that took place during my first year teaching. One of my students had a meltdown. I believe she came upon a question that she was not completely confident with or was unsure of how to attack it. She gently laid her pencil down and placed her head in her hands. I initially felt this might be a good sign because I could see her doing the breathing exercises we had worked on to lower her heart rate and attempt to calm down. Then suddenly, she gripped her pencil like a knife and began tearing into the paper up and down and across, violently slashing and ripping through the pages, angrily grunting as though in a physical attack.
(Ms. Laudano, elementary teacher, North Carolina)

One of the challenges of studying emotion regulation related to testing is the dynamic nature of students' emotion experiences during the test-taking process. In the incident above, Ms. Laudano describes how one student's experience of anxiety quickly turned to anger when her regulation strategies "failed." We put the term failed in quotations to signify that the situation above can be viewed from different perspectives. Ahn (2010) reminds us that children can reclaim a great deal of social power when they perceive control over their emotion experiences. For example, the experience of anger can serve as a protective function within the context of testing, alerting children that an important boundary has been crossed. As such, we view emotional episodes as potentially playing critical roles in the broader process of self-direction or regulation related to testing. Self-regulation occurs as students make comparisons about how successful they see themselves in their attempts to reach their goals. Their judgments have been associated with the emergence of emotions and the emotion regulation that can influence the success of those self-directed attempts (Boekaerts, 2007; Schutz & Davis, 2000). Therefore, emotion regulation related to testing plays an important role in self-directions related to students' life-task goals of being successful in school and reaching their occupational goals. This suggests that if we were able to understand how students regulated their emotions, we may be able to better assist students during the testing process and assist them towards their other life goals.

We see emotion regulation as a set of the processes students use to monitor, evaluate, and modify their emotions (Gross & Thompson, 2007; Jacobs & Gross, 2014; Schutz & Davis, 2000; Thompson, 1994). Students' attempts to regulate their emotions during testing reflect their efforts to accomplish their academic goals by influencing the type, intensity, and timing of emotional episodes. Thus, useful emotion regulation involves flexible, situationally responsive, and performance-enhancing strategies that help move students towards their academic goals (Gross & Thompson, 2007; Schutz & Davis, 2000; Thompson, 1994).

Just as affective experiences have the potential to become affective tendencies, there is also the potential for emotion regulation approaches during testing processes to become habitualized. As such, like other regulatory processes, it is useful to think about emotion regulation efforts related to testing as being on a continuum from more explicated, conscious, effortful, and controlled emotion regulation to implicit, unconscious, effortless, and automatic regulation (Gross & Thompson, 2007; Gyurak, Gross, & Etkin, 2011; Koole & Rothermund, 2011).

When taking an exam, it would be useful for students to see the test as important but not overly important. It would also be useful for students to see themselves as being in control of the testing situation with confidence in their ability to handle any type of question that emerges. This mind set has the potential to facilitate a test focused, cognitive and physiological, state that involves a moderate level of activation with pleasant affect. In essence, the ideal test-taking state would resemble what Csikszentmihalyi (1990) talks about as a flow experience. This would involve an immersion in the test-taking process resulting from a balance among the skills needed (e.g., test taking strategies) and knowledge level (e.g., subject matter knowing) of the students, as well as the difficulty or challenge level of the test (Schutz & Davis, 2000). From this perspective, as students' perceptions of what is going on during a particular test move away from that ideal state, the potential need for explicit or implicit emotion regulation efforts tend to emerge.

Four Dimensions of Regulation of Emotions Related to Testing

Our conceptualization of emotional regulation related to testing emerged out of the stress and coping literature (e.g., Carver, Scheier, & Weintraub, 1989; Lazarus & Folkman, 1984). As such, several of the dimensions that we discuss are similar to labels used in the coping literature (e.g., Task-Oriented, Emotion-Oriented, and Avoidance-Oriented Coping). However, it is important to keep in mind that from that perspective, coping strategies (styles) tend to be conceptualized as a response to particular stressful or negative events. We take a broader, more goal-directed self-regulation perspective, where ultimately student goals are not to simply cope with a particular test but to also move students closer to their academic goals. On the surface, this may seem like a small difference in perspective; however, we think it has important implications for how we approach emotion regulation. For example, we see avoiding anxiety related to testing before it emerges as the goal and not just trying to cope with the emotions after they emerge. Therefore, from our perspective, we currently conceptualize the self-regulation of emotions related to testing with four dimensions: *cognitive appraising process, task focusing processes, emotion focusing processes,* and *regaining task-focusing processes.*

Cognitive Appraisals Related to Testing

Researchers who have investigated *cognitive appraisal processes* have suggested that the judgments students make about events in their environment and their potential to be able to manage event challenges are related to their emotional episodes (Davis, DiStefano & Schutz, 2008; Lazarus, 1991; Pekrun & Perry, 2014; Roseman & Smith, 2001; Smith, 1991). These continuous judgments tend to occur rapidly and often without conscious awareness but are viewed as essential for emotions to emerge (Panksepp, 2005; Schutz & Davis, 2000). In addition, these appraisals tend to be related to the students' goals that provide the direction to self- and potentially emotional-regulation.

Lazarus (1991, 1999) made an important distinction between primary (i.e., judging the significance of the event) and secondary appraisals (i.e., judging one's ability to handle the event). He associated primary appraisals with the likelihood and intensity of the emotion experience and secondary appraisals to specific emotion episode(s). For primary appraisals, we have investigated two important judgments: goal importance and goal congruence (Davis et al., 2008; DeCuir-Gunby et al., 2009; Schutz, DiStefano, Benson, & Davis, 2004). For students, goal importance appraisals are related to the question: "How important is this test to my goals and standards?" Whereas, goal congruence appraisals are related to the question: "Am I being successful on this test?" If students perceive a test as important and not going well, goal-incongruent emotions, such as anger or anxiety, are more likely to emerge. On the other hand, if the test is perceived as important and going well then goal-congruent emotions, such as happiness or pride, may be more likely to emerge (Schutz & Davis, 2000; Schutz & DeCuir, 2002; Smith, 1991; Smith, & Ellsworth, 1987). It is important to keep in mind that students use their own goals and standards when judging both the importance of the test and their test performance. Doing well for one student might involve getting a "C," whereas for other students with perfectionist tendencies, having to reason through a single item may produce feelings of threat and anxiety (Davis et al., 2008; Schutz & Davis, 2000).

We have also investigated two unique but interdependent secondary appraisals related to testing: agency and testing problem efficacy (Davis et al., 2008; DeCuir-Gunby et al., 2009; Schutz, DiStefano, Benson, & Davis, 2004). We define agency as the extent to which students judge themselves as being in control or responsible for their performance on tests. In attribution theory, this is the locus dimension (Weiner, 2007). We define testing problem efficacy as the judgments students make about their ability to handle the problems that can emerge during tests (i.e., difficult or unexpected questions, confusion, etc.). Although somewhat related, our research suggests that these are different constructs. For example, a student could see themselves as being in control of the outcome of a test, but the same student may not be confident in their ability to handle any problems during an exam (i.e., I am in control—but I am not good a test taking).

Researchers have found that unpleasant emotions, such as anxiety and anger, are more likely to emerge when students think that they have little or no agency and/or confidence in their ability to manage the problems or their emotions during tests (Davis et al., 2008;

Kondo, 1997; Schutz & Davis, 2000; Schutz et al., 2004). Pleasant emotions, such as hope and pride, are more likely to emerge when students perceive the test they are taking as more relevant to their lives, that their scores align with their goals, and that they have the resources and ability to manage the test and any problems that arise (DeCuir-Gunby et al., 2009).

Finally, cognitive appraisals, like other aspects of the emotion processes, have the potential to become habitualized, or as we discussed earlier, become part of affective tendencies. In essence, as appraisals become associated with particular tasks or events, the appraisal process has the potential to be automatic, which basically means that for any particular test, students not only evaluate the demands of that specific test but also past test-taking experiences. This also suggests that development of useful emotion regulation strategies for someone with those particular affective tendencies (e.g., lack of agency or test problem efficacy) may require a longer term decoupling from the way they approach testing events. For example, over time, consistent low testing problems efficacy appraisals may result in an affective tendency to experience anxiety in most or all testing contexts (i.e., trait test anxiety). In this case, a long-term, more permanent emotion regulation could occur if the student's level of efficacy for dealing with problems during test taking is improved. So, what may be at one point a tendency for low efficacy—with different strategies, some successes with those strategies, and potential attributional retraining, may help him or her to change towards higher appraisal of efficacy and potential for less test anxiety (Bandura, 1997; Schunk, 1996).

As such, one important aspect to longer term self-regulation towards academic goals may be the identification of the appraisals, beliefs, cognitions, and efforts aimed towards changing those habitual appraisals, beliefs, and cognitions about testing (Beck, 1993; Ellis, 1993; Schutz & Davis, 2000). There is the potential that by changing an appraisal of test problem efficacy from low to high, a person may eliminate and therefore regulate their test anxiety before it even begins. For example, Zeidner (1998, 2007) describes interventions that have been shown to have some success over time with the regulation of test anxiety when a cognitive component, such as the identification of anxiety-facilitating beliefs, was included in the treatment (Hembree, 1988). In other words, the introduction of more useful appraisals about testing may have the potential to help students avoid anxiety related to testing before it starts (see Jacobs & Gross, 2014).

Task-Focusing Processes

In an effort to monitor or regulate what is occurring during the test (including emotional experiences), students may attempt to gain and maintain their focus on the test by using task-focusing type strategies. In Gross's (1998) terminology, these would be classified as attentional deployment strategies, and in the coping literature, this would be referred to as task-focused coping. For example, during testing, students who try to manage their time by looking for key terms in questions and/or trying to eliminate multiple-choice alternatives are more likely to stay focused on the test. Thus, the focus of students' internal talk is on activities that get or keep their focus on the actual taking of the test. Ideally, these test-taking type strategies would be useful in getting and keeping students task-focused.

It is important to keep in mind that these task-focusing strategies are useful test-taking strategies, and as such, there are a number of students who may deploy these strategies as an effort to be successful on a given test without much thought to any potential emotion episodes that might be associated with the process of taking a test. For these students, task-focusing strategies may simply be habitual approaches to taking an exam with the added bonus of deploying their attention to the actual test and not to potential thoughts about taking the test. Thus, as indicated, the goal from our perspective is to use task-focused strategies as a way of preventing anxiety related to testing from emerging in the first place.

Emotion-Focusing Processes

Emotion-focusing processes involve students disengaging from the actual task and focusing on their feelings (pleasant or unpleasant), on thoughts about their performance on the test, and/or on the potential causes for that performance. In the coping litera-ture, scholars have referred to these as emotion-oriented coping. These processes tend to increase unpleasant emotions related to testing, and as such, from the perspective presented here, it would be useful for students to avoid indulging in those processes. Schutz and colleagues have provided evidence for two key emotion-focused processes that occur during testing: Wishful thinking and Self-blame (Davis et al., 2008; Schutz et al., 2004, 2008). Wishful thinking occurs when students indulge in thoughts like hop-ing their problems would go away or that the teacher would decide not to count particu-lar items or the whole test. Self-blame, on the other hand, involves students' indulgent self-criticisms about how successful they see themselves on the test or about how they should have prepared differently for the exam.

As indicated, emotion-focusing processes have the potential to up-regulate, or increase unpleasant emotions, such as anger and anxiety. Researchers found that both test anger and anxiety were positively related to self-blame and wishful thinking (Schutz et al., 2004, 2008). In fact, in a recent study by DeCuir-Gunby et al. (2009), a correlation between test anger and wishful thinking and self-blame was .50 and .47, respectfully, and the correlation between test anxiety and wishful thinking and self-blame was .57 and .56. In terms of emotion regulation, efforts to avoid these emotion-focusing processes by using task-focusing strategies would be important. However, when students participate in blaming themselves for engaging in wishful thinking, it may be necessary to use strate-gies that help them to regain their task focus.

Regaining Task-Focusing Processes

In attempting to develop construct validity for the emotional regulation related to teach-ing scale, Schutz and colleagues (Schutz et al. 2004, 2008) identified a fourth dimension of emotion regulation related to testing. Regaining task-focusing processes related to testing involve students' attempts at recovering their task focus during the act of taking the test when students recognize they are feeling tense or concerned about the outcome. We have identified two key regaining task-focusing processes, including tension reduc-tion and importance reappraisal (Davis et al., 2008; DeCuir-Gunby et al. 2009; Schutz et al., 2004). Tension reduction involves students' attempts to slow their breathing or to stop and stretch in an attempt to slow off-task self-talk. Tension reduction attempts have the potential to change the focus from the self, or emotions related to the self, hopefully back to the test-taking process itself.

Importance reappraisal involves students' attempts to reevaluate the importance of this particular test in the context of the class and other life-goals. Within the context of the testing situation, we see reappraisal as being different than the original appraisal we talked about earlier in that, if the original appraisal were creating the context for anxiety, the process of reappraisal may help in getting the student back to being task focused. As such, ideally reappraising the importance of the test may help stop or reduce off-task self-talk and move the student towards returning their focus back to the test. With that in mind, reminding oneself that a particular test is only one part of the course may help to change the self-talk from self-focusing to task-focusing (Lazarus & Folkman, 1984; Schutz et al., 2004). Research on regaining task-focused processes by Schutz and colleagues has demonstrated that, as theoretically suggested, regaining task-focused processes are positively correlated to task-focused processes but not emotion-focused processes (Davis et al., 2008; DeCuir-Gunby et al. 2009; Schutz et al., 2004). In addition, DeCuir-Gunby et al. (2009) found positive correlations between tension reduction and both test hope and test pride. As such, it is useful to think about regaining task-focused processes as a potential way for students who are experiencing unpleasant off-task test emotions, such as anger or anxiety, to regain focus and return to the more useful task-focused processes.

Regulation Across the Phases of Testing

In terms of tests and testing, we conceptualize the testing process as a prearranged evaluative activity that we, like others, discuss in three phases: (A) a forethought phase, which involves the activities and strategies used to prepare for the test; ideally, this would begin early in the semester or school year, (B) a performance phase, where the test is actually taken, and (C) a self-reflection phase, where students receive feedback on the results and develop an understanding of what those results mean to students (Cassady, 2004; Schutz & Davis, 2000; Pekrun et al, 2004; Zimmerman, 1998). As such, emotion and emotion regulation as discussed here have the potential to emerge in all three of those phases.

For example, Folkman and Lazarus (1985) assessed students' emotions and coping at three phases of the examination process: anticipation of the exam, the wait for grades to be posted, and the time after grades were posted. At each stage, students were asked to describe their state of mind and rate their experience of emotions associated with perceiving threat (i.e., unpleasant-high activation—worry, fear, and anxiety), challenge (i.e., pleasant-high activation—confidence, hope, and eagerness), harm (i.e., unpleasant-high activation—anger; unpleasant-low activation—sadness, disappointment, and guilt), and benefit (i.e., pleasant-high activation—exhilaration, pleasure, and happiness; pleasant-low activation—relief). They found that there were significant changes in the emotions students experienced, including seemingly contradictory emotions as well as changes in the coping strategies they deployed. These findings suggested that students' appraisal and attributional processes were ongoing throughout the entire examination process, resulting in fluctuations in the emotions they experienced.

Forethought Phase

The forethought phase is the preparatory part of the intended testing transaction. Researchers have indicated that the emotions that are most prevalent during this preparatory phase are anticipatory emotions that involve a perceived threat (e.g.,

and mastery-approach goals (wanting to improve compared to their own standards) (Putwain & Symes, 2011). Recently, Putwain and Best (2011) examined the impact of teachers' fear messages on primary school students' test performance. Results indicated students who felt more threatened by their teachers' use of fear messages did, in fact, report greater anxiety over the test and tended to perform worse. These findings affirm the manner in which teachers talk about testing has the potential to influence or regulate how testing is seen in particular classroom contexts.

Still, there may be other, less direct measures of the effects of teacher emotion on students' emotions and emotional regulation. Underlying cultural values and assumptions about the nature of emotions, what Hoffman (2009) and colleagues call "emotion culture," in classrooms and testing are also likely to be transmitted to students. Hoffman (2009) found parents are often encouraged to interpret, label, and model for children how not to feel unpleasant affect. She noted popular discourses (e.g., discussions in parent magazines) about emotion often caution parents about losing their own emotional control. Although we have not found any parallel studies regarding teachers, our experience as instructors and observers of classrooms finds similar ways in which teachers may be encouraged to suppress their own emotions regarding tests as well as to interpret and label emotions they observe in their students as a means to get children not to feel (see Frenzel, 2014).

In sum, the findings from these studies suggest that teachers have the potential to (co-)regulate various emotional classroom climates. This also implies that how teachers approach or talk about emotions and emotion regulation may have the potential to mediate some of the problems associated with test emotions, suggesting that if teachers are able to create an emotional climate where there are fewer unpleasant test emotions, they have in essence regulated those emotions before they occurred. Therefore, this may also be an important area for future investigation.

Impact of Culture

Another area to explore is the impact of culture on emotions and emotion regulation. Culture can be defined as the norms, beliefs, and customs that are shared by a group of people (Triandis & Suh, 2002). Culture groups often share similar race/ethnic backgrounds and/or regional affiliations. Because cultural groups have different backgrounds and approaches to understanding their experiences, researchers should examine how these cultural differences influence emotions and emotion regulation related to testing. For example, within the United States and other countries where there are majority and minority groups, we need to examine more diverse populations including groups from lower SES groups and various racial/ethnic groups (see DeCuir-Gunby & Williams-Johnson, 2014). This suggests it is necessary to use culturally inclusive methodological approaches to explore testing because it cannot be assumed that all cultures engage in testing in the same manner (Zeidner, 1998).

For example, Bodas and Ollendick (2005; see also Bodas, Ollendick, & Sovani, 2008) recently developed a comprehensive framework for conducting cross-cultural studies of test anxiety. They indicate that Western measures of test anxiety have been translated into over 14 different languages. Often researchers deploy simple translations of items, with some scholars recognizing limitations in the translations of certain items and creating alternative wordings. A few studies are emerging using approaches to examine the latent structure of the scales across multiple groups. Often cross-cultural studies are aimed at interpreting mean-differences in scores.

Bodas and Ollendick (2005) argued that to really understand why and how emotion episodes occur—and we would include the regulation of those emotions—during testing in different cultures, we must attempt to identify the underlying causes. In their recent mixed-methodology study of Indian students' understandings of test anxiety, students attributed the causes of anxiety to their fear of disapproval and shaming their family as well as their fear of the punishments and consequences of failing the exam (Bodas et al., 2008). In addition to coping (i.e., emotion regulation) with exam anxiety by studying, students frequently reported engaging in prayer. "While the qualitative data indicate that a high-stake school environment and stressful nature of the exams are present in the lives of these children, the quantitative data suggest that these factors do not appear to be associated specifically with [Western measures] of test-anxiety" (p. 399). Their interpretation of both the qualitative data and mean scores attempts to take into account specific components of Indian culture: potential desensitization to stress and enhanced coping with stress by parents and schools.

From our perspective, future research not only needs to account for the individual, interpersonal, and ecological contributors (see Bodas & Ollendick, 2005), but also employ methodological approaches that allow for culturally relevant interpretations of findings. Finally, we could find no cross-cultural studies of emotion and emotion regulation experiences of test taking other than anxiety. Thus, we call to researchers to broaden the scope of emotions studied across cultures.

Unique Emotional Experiences of Undeserved Populations—Stereotype Threat

Stereotype threat is a situational quandary in which an individual's identification with a group and identification with a particular domain of performance conflict in ways that add additional psychological burden (Schmader, Johns, & Forbes, 2008; Steele, 1997; Steele & Aronson, 1995; Tillman, 2012). Stereotype threat is a social psychological phenomenon wherein the performances of members of a stigmatized group are impaired simply by awareness of a pervasive, relevant negative stereotype. Under the conditions of threat, members of stigmatized groups who identify closely with the task experience evaluation apprehension that goes well beyond performance anxiety, as these individuals attempt to avoid reinforcing negative stereotypes with their performances. The members of stigmatized groups who are theoretically most susceptible to threat are those who also most identify with the task's domain.

Understanding emotion to be a mediator of threat, the extent to which a task is self-definitional could theoretically intensify both the need for increased vigilance for threatening social information and performance feedback as well as increased suppression of emotions. That is, when an individual is highly identified both with the domain and with their membership in a relevantly stigmatized group, stereotype threat triggers these emotional responses that impair both performance and learning (Mangels, Good, Whiteman, Maniscalco, & Dweck, 2012). As a result, researchers have suggested that interventions such as emotional expression can neutralize the effects of stereotype threat on academic tasks (Burns & Friedman, 2011). This area of research both provides evidence for the cultural nature of emotion and emotion regulation and suggests another area where more research is needed related to emotion regulation related to testing.

CONCLUSION

Over the last few decades, we have learned a lot about emotion and emotion regulation related to testing. And we are optimistic that research in this area has the potential to make important contribution to our understanding of student learning and motivation. There still are many unanswered questions and potential areas that need to be explored. Specifically, as assessment practices become more prolific in primary grades, more research is needed regarding younger students. More research is needed to examine developmental differences both across developmental periods and longitudinally, as students become more inculcated in the testing process. The majority of work on Emotion Regulation During Testing (ERDT) within the US context has been done using white, middle-class students. We need to increase the diversity of our research samples, increase the variety of tests studied, examine the relationship between ERDT and other test anxiety-related constructs, and attempt to capture other social-contextual variables at play. In order to grow the field, researchers need to expand their methodological approaches. Finally, it is important to further expand the nomological network of ERDT (Cronbach & Meehl, 1955). For example, it would be helpful to explore the relationship between ERDT and stereotype threat.

In addition, we would also suggest that as we continue to research in the area that we also broaden the focus from a "self," intraindividual perspective, to also include research related to teachers, their classroom emotional environments, and the even broader social-historical context. It is clear that emotions related to testing do not occur in a vacuum. At this point, there is much debate around the world regarding the importance and usefulness of high-stakes testing and their influence on the teaching and learning process. This suggests that researchers in this area should also consider these broader policy issues in their work. As such, research in this area continues to be a challenge.

In expanding the exploration in this area, it is critically important to consider our responsibilities to our student participants. Research conducted in this area largely has relied on the use of retrospective reports of students' emotion experiences and processes. We acknowledge the inherent limitations of using retrospective reports (see Pekrun & Bühner, 2014). However the dominance of this approach in the United States and other countries largely reflects regulations requiring that the risks of conducting the research (i.e., the potential to negatively affect the students' ability to perform on the test) cannot outweigh the benefits. This is the cost of doing ecologically valid emotion research in the United States and other countries. As such, it is important that researchers continue to develop creative was to approach emotion and emotion regulation related to testing.

NOTE

1.   Both quotes are from unpublished interview data regarding emotions related to testing. Both names are pseudonyms.

REFERENCES

Abella, R., & Heslin, R. (1989). Appraisal processes, coping, and the regulation of stress-related emotions in a college examination. *Basic and Applied Social Psychology, 10,* 311–327.

Ahn, J. (2010). "I'm not scared of anything": Emotion as social power in children's worlds. *Childhood, 17,* 94–112.

Bandura, A. (1997). *Self-efficacy: The exercise of control.* New York, NY: Freeman.

Barrett, L. F. (2006). Valence is a basic building block of emotional life. *Journal of Research in Personality, 40,* 35–55.

Beck, A. T. (1993). Cognitive therapy: Past, present and future. *Journal of Consulting and Clinical Psychology, 61,* 194–198.

Bodas, J., & Ollendick, T. H. (2005). Test anxiety: A cross-cultural perspective. *Clinical Child and Family Psychology Review, 8,* 65–88.

Bodas, J., Ollendick, T. H., & Sovani, A. V. (2008). Test anxiety in Indian children: A cross-cultural perspective. *Anxiety, Stress & Coping, 21,* 387–404.

Boekaerts, M. (2007). Understanding students' affective processes in the classroom. In P. A. Schutz & R. Pekrun, *Emotion in education* (pp. 223–241). San Diego, CA: Elsevier.

Bolger, N. (1990). Coping as a personality process: A prospective study. *Journal of Personality and Social Psychology, 59,* 525–537.

Burns, K. C., & Friedman, S. L. (2011). The benefits of emotional expression for math performance. *Cognition and Emotion, 26,* 245–251.

Carver, C. S., & Scheier, M. F. (1994). Situational coping and coping dispositions in a stressful transaction. *Journal of Personality and Social Psychology, 66,* 184–195.

Carver, C. S., & Scheier, M. F. (1998). *On the self-regulation of behavior.* New York, NY: Cambridge University Press.

Carver, C. S., Scheier, M. E, & Weintraub, J. K. (1989). Assessing coping strategies: A theoretically based approach. *Journal of Personality and Social Psychology, 56,* 267–283.

Cassady, C. C. (2004). The influence of cognitive test anxiety across the learning–testing cycle, *Learning and Instruction, 14,* 569–592.

Chapell, M., Blanding, B., Silverstein, M., Takahashi, M., Newman, B., Gubi, A., & McCann, N. (2005). Test anxiety and academic performance in undergraduate and graduate students. *Journal of Educational Psychology, 97,* 268–274.

Cronbach, L. J., & Meehl, P. E. (1955). Construct validity in psychological tests. *Psychological bulletin, 52,* 281.

Csikszentmihalyi, M. (1990). *Flow: The psychology of optimal experience.* New York, NY: Harper & Row.

Davis, H. A., DiStefano, C., &. Schutz, P. A. (2008). Patterns of appraisal and emotion regulation during test taking in first-year college students. *Journal of Educational Psychology, 100,* 942–960.

DeCuir-Gunby, J. T., Aultman, L. P., &. Schutz, P. A. (2009). Investigating transactions among approach/avoidance motives, emotions and emotional regulation during testing. *Journal of Experimental Education, 77,* 409–436.

DeCuir-Gunby, J. T., & Williams-Johnson, M. R. (2014). The influence of culture on emotions: Implications for education. In R. Pekrun & L. Linnenbrink-Garcia (Eds.), *International handbook of emotions in education* (pp. 539–557). New York, NY: Taylor & Francis.

Edwards, M. S., Burt, J. S., & Lipp, O. V., (2010). Selective attention for masked and unmasked emotionally toned stimuli: Effects of trait anxiety, state anxiety, and test order. *British Journal of Psychology, 101,* 325–343.

Ellis, A. (1993). Reflections on rational-emotive therapy. *Journal of Consulting and Clinical Psychology, 61,* 199–201.

Eysenck, M. W. (1992). *Anxiety: The cognitive perspective.* Hove, United Kingdom: Erlbaum.

Folkman, S., & Lazarus, R. S. (1985). If it changes it must be a process: Study of emotion and coping during three stages of a college examination. *Journal of Personality and Social Psychology, 48,* 150–170.

Frenzel, A. C. (2014). Teacher emotions. In R. Pekrun & L. Linnenbrink-Garcia (Eds.), *International handbook of emotions in education* (pp. 494–519). New York, NY: Taylor & Francis.

Frenzel, A. C., Goetz, T., Lüdtke, O., Pekrun, R., & Sutton, R. E. (2009). Emotional transmission in the classroom: Exploring the relationship between teacher and student enjoyment. *Journal of Educational Psychology, 101,* 705–716.

Frijda, N. H. (2000). The psychologists' point of view. In M. Lewis & J. M. Haviland-Jones (Eds.), *Handbook of emotions* (2nd ed., pp. 59–74). New York, NY: Guilford.

Galassi, J. P., Frierson, H. T., & Sharer, R. (1981). Behavior of high, moderate and low test anxious students during an actual test situation. *Journal of Consulting and Clinical Psychology, 49,* 51–62.

Gross, J. J. (1998). The emerging field of emotion regulation: An integrative review. *Review of General Psychology, 2,* 271–299.

Gross, J. J., & Thompson, R. A. (2007). Emotion regulation: Conceptual foundations. In J. J. Gross (Ed.), *Handbook of emotion regulation* (pp. 3–26). New York, NY: Guilford.

Gyurak, A., Gross, J. J., & Etkin, A. (2011). Explicit and implicit emotion regulation: A dual-process framework. *Cognition and Emotion, 25,* 400–412.

Hembree, R. (1988). Correlates, causes, effects and treatment of test anxiety. *Review of Educational Research, 58,* 47–77.

Hoffman, D. M. (2009). How (not) to feel: Culture and the politics of emotion in the American parenting advice literature. *Discourse: Studies In The Cultural Politics Of Education, 30,* 15–31.

Izard, C. E. (2007). Basic emotions, natural kinds, emotion schemas, and a new paradigm. *Perspectives on Psychological Science, 2,* 260–280.

Jacobs, S. E., & Gross, J. J. (2014). Emotion regulation in education: Conceptual foundations, current applications, and future directions. In R. Pekrun & L. Linnenbrink-Garcia (Eds.), *International handbook of emotions in education* (pp. 183–201). New York, NY: Taylor & Francis.

Klinger, E. (1984). A consciousness-sampling analysis of test anxiety and performance. *Journal of Personality and Social Psychology, 47,* 1376–1390.

Kondo, D. S. (1997). Strategies for coping with test anxiety. *Anxiety, Stress, and Coping, 10,* 203–215.

Koole, S. L., & Rothermund, K. (2011). "I feel better but I don't know why": The psychology of implicit emotion regulation. *Cognition and Emotion, 25,* 389–399.

Lang J.W.B., & Lang, J. (2010). Priming competence diminishes the link between cognitive test anxiety and test performance: Implications for the interpretation of test scores. *Psychological Science, 21,* 811–819.

Lazarus, R. S. (1991). *Emotion and adaptation.* New York, NY: Oxford University Press.

Lazarus, R. S. (1999). *Stress and emotions: A new synthesis.* New York, NY: Springer.

Lazarus, R. S., & Folkman, S. (1984). *Stress, appraisal, and coping.* New York, NY: Springer.

Linnenbrink, E. A. (2007). The role of affect in student learning: A multi-dimensional approach to considering the interaction of affect, motivation, and engagement. In P. A. Schutz & R. Pekrun (Eds.), *Emotions in education* (pp 107–124). San Diego, CA: Academic.

Mangels, J. A., Good, C., Whiteman, R. C., Maniscalco, B., & Dweck, C. S. (2012). Emotion blocks the path to learning under stereotype threat. *Social Cognitive & Affective Neuroscience, 7,* 230–241.

McCaslin, M. (2009). Co-regulation of student motivation and emergent identity. Educational *Psychologist, 44,* 137–146.

Nelson, D. W., & Knight, A. E. (2010). The power of positive recollections: Reducing test anxiety and enhancing college student efficacy and performance. *Journal of Applied Social Psychology, 40,* 732–745.

Nichols, S. L., & Berliner, D. C. (2007). *Collateral damage: How high-stakes testing corrupts America's Schools.* Cambridge, MA: Harvard Education Press.

O'Neil, H. F., & Fukumura, T. (1992). Relationship of worry and emotionality to test performance in a Juku environment. *Anxiety, stress, and coping, 5,* 241–251.

Panksepp, J. (2005). Affective consciousness: Core emotional feelings in animals and humans. *Consciousness and Cognition, 14,* 30–80.

Pekrun, R., & Bühner, M. (2014). Self-report measures of academic emotions. In R. Pekrun & L. Linnenbrink-Garcia (Eds.), *International handbook of emotions in education* (pp. 561–579). New York, NY: Taylor & Francis.

Pekrun, R., Frenzel, A. C., Goetz, T. & Perry, R. P. (2007). The control-value theory of achievement emotions: An integrative approach to emotions in education. In P. A. Schutz and R. Pekrun (Eds.), *Emotions in education* (pp. 13–36). San Diego, CA: Elsevier.

Pekrun, R., Goetz, T., Perry, R. P., Kramer, K., Hochstadt, M., & Molfenter, S. (2004). Beyond test anxiety: Development and validation of the Test Emotions Questionnaire (TEQ). *Anxiety, Stress and Coping, 17,* 287–316.

Pekrun, R., & Perry, R. P. (2014). Control-value theory of achievement emotions. In R. Pekrun & L. Linnenbrink-Garcia (Eds.), *International handbook of emotions in education* (pp. 120–141). New York, NY: Taylor & Francis.

Putwain, D., & Best, N. (2011). Fear appeals in the primary classroom: Effects on test anxiety and test grade. *Learning & Individual Differences, 21,* 580–584.

Putwain, D. W., & Symes, W. (2011). Classroom fear appeals and examination performance: facilitating or debilitating outcomes? *Learning and Individual Differences, 21,* 227–232.

Roseman, I., & Smith, C. A. (2001). Appraisal theory: Overview, assumptions, varieties, and controversies. In K. R. Scherer, A. Schorr, & T. Johnstone (Eds.), *Appraisal processes in emotion* (pp. 3–19). New York, NY: Oxford University Press.

Rosenberg, E. L., (1998). Levels of analysis and the organization of affect. *Review of General Psychology, 2,* 247–270.

Russell, J. A. (2003). Core affect and the psychological construction of emotion. *Psychological Review, 110,* 145–172.

Russell, J. A., & Barrett, L. F. (1999). Core affect, prototypical emotional episodes, and other things called emotion: Dissecting the elephant. *Journal of Personality and Social Psychology, 76,* 805–819.

Scherer, K. R. (1993). Studying the emotion antecedent appraisal process: An expert system approach. *Cognition and Emotion, 7,* 325–355.

Schmader, T., Johns, M., & Forbes, C. (2008). An integrated process model of stereotype threat effects on performance. *Psychological Review, 115,* 336–356.

Schunk, D. H. (1996). Goal and self-evaluative influences during children's cognitive skill learning. *American Educational Research Journal, 33,* 359–382.

Schutz, P. A., Aultman, L. P., & Williams-Johnson, M. R. (2009). Educational psychology perspectives on teachers' emotions. In P. A. Schutz & M. Zembylas (Eds.), *Advances in teacher emotion research: The impact on teachers' lives* (pp. 195–214). New York, NY: Springer.

Schutz, P. A., Benson, J., & DeCuir, J. T. (2008). Approach/Avoidance motives, test emotions, and emotional regulation during testing. *Anxiety, Stress and Coping: An International Journal, 21,* 263–281.

Schutz, P. A., & Davis, H. A. (2000). Emotions during self-regulation: The regulation of emotions during test taking. *Educational Psychologist, 35,* 243–256.

Schutz, P. A., Davis, H. A., & Schwanenflugel, P. J. (2002). Personal theories of emotion and emotional regulation during test taking. *Journal of Experimental Education, 70,* 316–342.

Schutz, P. A., & DeCuir, J. T. (2002). Inquiry on emotions in education. *Educational Psychologist, 37,* 125–134.

Schutz, P. A., DiStefano, C., Benson, J., & Davis, H. A. (2004). The emotional regulation during test taking scale. *Anxiety, Stress, and Coping, 17,* 253–259.

Schutz, P. A., Hong, J. Y., Cross, D. I., & Osbon, J. N. (2006). Reflections on investigating emotions among educational contexts. *Educational Psychology Review, 18,* 343–360.

Smith, C. A. (1991). The self, appraisal and coping. In C. R. Snyder &D. R. Forsyth (Eds.), *Handbook of social and clinical psychology: The health perspective* (pp. 116–137). Elmsford, NY: Pergamon.

Smith, C. A., & Ellsworth, P. C. (1987). Patterns of appraisal and emotions related to taking exams. *Journal of Personality and Social Psychology, 52,* 475–488.

Spielberger, C. D., & Vagg, P. R. (1995). Test anxiety: A transactional process. In C. D. Spielberger & P. R. Vagg (Eds.), *Test anxiety: Theory, assessment, and treatment* (pp. 3–14). Washington, DC: Taylor & Francis.

Steele, C. M. (1997). A threat in the air: How stereotypes shape intellectual identity and performance. *American Psychologist, 52,* 613–629.

Steele, C. M., & Aronson, J. (1995). Stereotype threat and the intellectual test performance of African-Americans. *Journal of Personality and Social Psychology, 69,* 797–811.

Stober, J., & Pekrun R. (2004). Editorial: Advances in test anxiety research. *Anxiety, Stress, and Coping, 17,* 205–211.

Stowell, J. R., Tumminaro, T., & Attarwala, M. (2008). Moderating effects of coping on the relationship between and test anxiety and negative mood. *Stress and Health, 24,* 313–321.

Thompson, R. A. (1994). Emotional regulation: A theme in search of definition. In N. A. Fox (Ed.), *The development of emotional regulation: Biological and behavioral considerations* (pp. 25–52). Chicago, IL: University of Chicago Press.

Tillman, D. (2012, February). Domain identification and math performance: Analysis of TIMSS 2007, by Gender. Paper presented at the annual meeting of the Southwest Educational Research Association, New Orleans, LA.

Triandis, H. C., & Suh, E. M. (2002). Cultural influences on personality. *Annual Review of Psychology, 53,* 133–160.

Turner, J. C., & Trucano, M. (2014). Measuring situated emotion. In R. Pekrun & L. Linnenbrink-Garcia (Eds.), *International handbook of emotions in education* (pp. 643–658). New York, NY: Taylor & Francis.

Weiner, B. (1994). Integrating social and personal theories of achievement striving. *Review of Educational Research, 64,* 557–573.

Weiner, B. (2007). Examining emotional diversity in the classroom: An attribution theorist considers the moral emotions. In P. A. Schutz and R. Pekrun (Eds.), *Emotions in education* (pp. 75–88). San Diego, CA: Elsevier.

Zeidner, M. (1998). *Test anxiety: The state of the art.* New York, NY: Plenum.

Zeidner, M. (2007). Test anxiety in educational contexts: Concepts, findings, and future directions. In P. A. Schutz & R. Pekrun (Eds.), *Emotion in education* (pp. 13–36). Amsterdam, Netherlands: Elsevier.

Zeidner, M. (2014). Anxiety in education. In R. Pekrun & L. Linnenbrink-Garcia (Eds.), *International handbook of emotions in education* (pp. 265–288). New York, NY: Taylor & Francis.

Zimmerman, B. J. (1998). Developing self-fulfilling cycles of academic regulation: Analysis of exemplary instructional models. In D. H. Schunk & B. J. Zimmerman (Eds.), *Self-regulation of learning and performance: Issues and educational applications* (pp. 3–21). Mahwah, NJ: Erlbaum.

19

TRANSFORMING STUDENTS' LIVES WITH SOCIAL AND EMOTIONAL LEARNING

Marc A. Brackett and Susan E. Rivers,
Yale University

How educators and students process and respond to emotions influences children's education in ways that affect their social, emotional, and cognitive development. A recent meta-analysis of research on programs focused on social and emotional learning (SEL) shows that a systematic process for promoting students' social and emotional development is the common element among schools that report an increase in academic success, improved quality of relationships between teachers and students, and a decrease in problem behavior (Durlak, Weissberg, Dymnicki, Taylor, & Schellinger, 2011). SEL can be especially powerful when grounded in theory and empirical evidence and when adult stakeholders in children's education are actively involved in cultivating and modeling their own social and emotional competencies (Brackett et al., 2009). As this chapter illustrates, SEL programming results in significant shifts in social, emotional, and academic competencies as well as improvements in the quality of learning environments.

There is growing recognition at the local, state, and federal levels in the United States and around the world that schools must meet the social and emotional developmental needs of students for effective teaching and learning to take place and for students to reach their full potential (http://casel.org/research/sel-in-your-state/). Efforts to promote SEL in schools align with the views of leading economists who have been calling for a greater focus on what have been traditionally referred to as soft skills. Nobel Laureate James Heckman has written that early investments in children's non-cognitive skills yield undeniable payoffs in societal and workforce productivity later in life (Heckman & Masterov, 2007). Heckman argues that investing in emotional skills is a cost-effective approach to increasing the quality and productivity of the workforce through fostering workers' motivation, perseverance, and self-control.

As increasing efforts move toward better preparing youth to enter and contribute to a competitive and global workforce, epidemiological evidence suggests that the basic needs of youth still are not being met. For example, the incidence of emotional disturbances among youth in the United States is widespread. Approximately one in five American adolescents experience problems with anxiety or depression (e.g., Benjamin, Costello, & Warren, 1990; Kessler & Walters, 1998), and prescribed antidepressants are being used at exceedingly high rates (Delate, Gelenberg, Simmons, & Motheral, 2004; Olfson & Marcus, 2009). Adolescents with a history of anxiety and depression are more likely to engage in risky and maladaptive behaviors, such as using illicit drugs, withdrawing from friends, disconnecting from school, and bullying classmates (Substance Abuse and Mental Health Services Administration [SAMHSA], 2005). Youth in the United States are more likely to experience intimidation or verbal abuse from peers at school compared to those in other developed countries (e.g., England, Italy, Japan; Miller, Malley, & Owen, 2009), and recent trends show that 28% of students aged 12–18 years report being victims of bullying (DeVoe & Murphy, 2011). These behaviors are problematic, threatening the physical and psychological health of youth, diminishing their ability to engage in learning and in society, and underscoring the need for SEL programming.

In this chapter, we describe the objectives and theoretical underpinnings of SEL, highlight research findings demonstrating the evidence supporting SEL programming, and advocate for comprehensive and systematic implementation of SEL programming in schools. We also provide overviews of several SEL programs with evidence of success, and present one program in particular, The RULER Approach to SEL (RULER), that incorporates both the science of emotions and ecological systems theory into its theory of change, content, and methods of implementation and sustainability.

WHAT IS SEL?

SEL refers to the process of integrating thinking, feeling, and behaving in order to become aware of the self and of others, make responsible decisions, and manage one's own behaviors and those of others (Elias et al., 1997). Intervention programs focused on SEL are designed to facilitate this process in systematic and comprehensive ways within schools and districts. The SEL movement stems, in part, from scientific research on emotional intelligence (EI; Salovey & Mayer, 1990), which was later popularized by Daniel Goleman (1995). EI refers to the mental abilities associated with processing and responding to emotions, including recognizing the expression of emotions in others, using emotions to enhance thinking, and regulating emotions to drive effective behaviors (Mayer & Salovey, 1997; Salovey & Mayer, 1990). These abilities are likely to be associated with social competence, adaptation, and academic success (see review by Mayer, Roberts, & Barsade, 2008; also, see Allen, MacCann, Matthews, and Roberts, 2014).

Schools increasingly are implementing school-wide SEL policies and curricula in order to foster caring relationships between teachers and students, cooperation and conflict reduction among students, a greater sense of school safety, and the development of social and emotional skills in students, teachers, and school leaders (Greenberg et al., 2003; Zins, Weissberg, Wang, & Walberg, 2004). However, some of these efforts have been limited in that they (1) focus too narrowly on specific social or emotional variables, such as preventing bullying, substance abuse, unhealthy sexual practices, delinquency, or violence; or promoting character development, career preparation, family life, community service, or physical or mental health or (2) are introduced in a piecemeal, unsystematic fashion. These, often disjointed, efforts do not fall under the umbrella of SEL programming (Devaney, O'Brien, Resnik, Keister, & Weissberg, 2006).

Self-awareness: Accurately assessing one's feelings, interests, values, and strengths; maintaining a well-grounded sense of self-confidence

Self-management: Regulating one's emotions to handle stress, control impulses, and persevere in overcoming obstacles; setting and monitoring progress toward personal and academic goals; expressing emotions appropriately

Social awareness: Taking the perspective of and empathizing with others; recognizing and appreciating individual and group similarities and differences; recognizing and using family, school, and community resources

Relationship skills: Establishing and maintaining healthy and rewarding cooperative relationships; resisting inappropriate social pressure; preventing, managing, and resolving interpersonal conflict; seeking help when needed

Responsible decision making: Making decisions based on consideration of ethical standards, safety concerns, appropriate social norms, respect for others, and probable consequences of various actions; applying decision-making skills to academic and social situations; contributing to the well-being of one's school and community

Figure 19.1 CASEL SEL competencies.

SEL programming offers a more unified and coordinated approach that targets a broader spectrum of positive youth outcomes that extend into lifelong success, including enhancing the social-emotional climates of classrooms, schools, and districts (Greenberg et al., 2003). Specifically, SEL programs are designed to create learning environments that meet the developmental needs of students, including feelings of belonging, safety, and community, and thus provide ideal conditions for success across the domains of their lives—academics, relationships, and ultimately in the workforce (Becker & Luthar, 2002; Catalano, Berglund, Ryan, Lonczek, & Hawkins, 2004).

The Collaborative for Academic, Social, and Emotional Learning (CASEL), a non-profit entity that advocates and provides leadership for high-quality SEL programming and learning standards, identifies five core competencies associated with SEL: self-awareness, self-management, social awareness, relationship skills, and responsible decision making (Zins, Weissberg, et al., 2004). Figure 19.1 illustrates and describes these competencies.

The design of SEL programs helps schools use curricular tools and strategies to develop in students the competencies delineated in Figure 19.1 (Zins, Bloodworth, Weissberg, & Walberg, 2004). Thus, SEL is one entryway for educators to influence student outcomes by teaching competencies that contribute to optimal outcomes. Although limited research shows that changing a student's IQ may be possible (Becker, Ludtke, Trautwein, Koller, & Baumert, 2012; Brinch & Galloway, 2012), copious research shows that students can learn how to use their emotions to make healthy decisions and to manage behavior effectively (Durlak et al., 2011; Durlak & Weissberg, 2011). For example, self-management, which includes controlling one's impulses, is a critical component of success in school and in life. Children who are better able to self-regulate have greater impulse control and pay more attention in school (Lane, Pierson, & Givner, 2003; McClelland et al., 2007). Self-regulation in childhood is related to better concentration during adolescence, which leads to higher academic grades as well as better performance on standardized tests (Eigsti et al., 2006; Mischel, Shoda, & Rodriguez, 1989). There also is some evidence that children who are poor at self-regulation are more likely to spend time in prison later in life compared to their peers who are better at self-regulation (Mischel & Ayduk, 2004).

A number of investigations, including large-scale experiments, support the notion that targeted SEL interventions can both improve the social-emotional attributes of classrooms and facilitate students' social-emotional and academic well-being (e.g., Brackett, Rivers, Reyes, & Salovey, 2012; Brown, Jones, LaRusso, & Aber, 2010; Raver et al., 2011). For example, a meta-analysis of 213 studies evaluating SEL programming efforts demonstrates its benefits to youth from elementary through high school and across urban, suburban, and rural schools in the United States (Durlak et al., 2011). Almost half (47%) of the reviewed interventions were tested by randomizing students or classrooms to either receiving the SEL program or to functioning as a control group. Primary outcomes were increases in students' social and emotional skills, improvements in students' prosocial attitudes and behavior, better mental health, and improved academic performance, including an 11-percentile-point gain in achievement assessed through report card grades and test scores.

THEORETICAL FOUNDATIONS OF SEL

The concept of SEL is grounded in the field of positive youth development, which upholds that the needs of youth must be addressed by creating environments or settings that promote outcomes like school achievement, mutually supportive relationships with adults and peers, problem solving, and civic engagement (Catalano et al., 2004; Greenberg et al., 2003). Efforts to promote positive youth development differ from those aimed at reducing risk factors in that they are focused on enhancing skills, building assets, and promoting resilience to achieve positive outcomes (Catalano, Hawkins, Berglund, Pollard, & Arthur, 2002). Positive youth development interventions like SEL programming typically utilize a skill-building, whole-child approach that is focused on cultivating assets, not on preventing problems. Schools are predominant settings that serve the educational and developmental needs of youth, and thus are compelling targets for universal efforts to promote positive youth development.

To accomplish this broader educational agenda, school-based programming needs to meet two standards: (1) enhance the social and emotional assets and learning of students across the curriculum and (2) improve the quality of the environments in which academic, social, and emotional learning occurs (Greenberg et al., 2003; Zigler & Bishop-Josef, 2006; Zins, Elias, Greenberg, & Weissberg, 2000). Thus, the success of any attempt to educate the whole child is dependent upon the extent to which learning occurs in caring, supportive, safe, and empowering settings. This premise has roots in ecological systems theory and self-determination theory. Ecological systems theory posits that the settings youth inhabit, like school, shape their development (Bronfenbrenner, 1979). Features of school settings that are related to positive youth development include opportunities for empowerment and skill building, the presence of supportive adults and peers, and being safe and orderly (Catalano et al., 2004). According to self-determination theory, youth are more likely to flourish when in settings that address their social and emotional needs, such as experiencing meaningful relationships, having confidence in their abilities, and feeling autonomous (Deci & Ryan, 1985). Students are more likely to thrive in classrooms that foster meaningful, caring, safe, and empowering interactions (e.g., Battistich, Solomon, Watson, & Schaps, 1997; McNeely, Nonnemaker, & Blum, 2002; Osterman, 2000).

It is the responsibility of schools to provide enriching environments for young people to assimilate into and contribute to society. Convincing empirical evidence indicates that schools can be highly effective in promoting positive youth development even in (and perhaps especially in) the presence of other contextual variables, such as low family socioeconomic status and segregated, economically depressed neighborhoods (McEvoy & Welker, 2000; Solomon, Battistich, Kim, & Watson, 1997). Learning climates can also thwart development if they are not well designed (Bronfenbrenner, 1979; Moos, 1979). A powerful example comes from the high-stakes testing environment prevalent in the No Child Left Behind (NCLB) era. This climate may very well have damaged the potential for protective emotional connections between youth and their schools and teachers (Mulvenon, Stegman, & Ritter, 2005). When youth do not feel connected to school, their grades slip, they become disruptive in class, and they are unlikely to aspire to higher educational goals. Struggling students are most vulnerable to the anxiety and frustrations accompanying standardized tests, and over time, they are more likely to give only token efforts in school (Paris, 1993). Such environments pose real threats to the availability of school resources like caring relationships and empowerment-building opportunities (Ravitch, 2010).

Teachers, as the primary actors in classroom settings, have a significant opportunity to affect the positive development of youth, not only through the content of their instruction but also through the quality of their social interactions and relationships with youth, including how they both manage behavior in the classroom and model social and emotional processes (e.g., Hamre & Pianta, 2001; Jennings & Greenberg, 2009). However, few professional development opportunities exist that help teachers improve their interactions with youth along these lines (Hargreaves, 1998). In the next section, we describe examples of SEL programming efforts as a promising approach for fostering positive youth development.

EXAMPLES OF SEL PROGRAMS

CASEL's best practices guidelines for SEL programming include the development of a specific set of skills related to social and emotional development using active learning techniques that are connected and coordinated (CASEL, 2003). CASEL further advocates that quality SEL programming needs to include a comprehensive and systematic approach, one that involves all the stakeholders involved in the students' education (Devaney, O'Brien, Resnik, Keister, & Weissberg, 2006). By definition, programs that can be classified as addressing SEL integrate emotions in some way, such as helping students identify, talk about, and regulate feelings. Here, we briefly review four SEL programs that provide emotion skill-building opportunities for students. One program will be explored in depth in the final section of the chapter to more fully illustrate how quality SEL programming is grounded in emotions theory, has an articulated theory of change that is supported by empirical evidence, has a detailed implementation plan that includes children and the adult stakeholders in their education, and has in place practices for sustainability. Information on other programs can be found in reviews by CASEL (2003).

Promoting Alternative Thinking Strategies (PATHS)

PATHS is an SEL program for preschool and elementary school designed to increase social and emotional competence; prevent violence, aggression, and other behavior problems; improve critical thinking skills; and enhance classroom climate (Greenberg, Kische, & Mihalic, 1998). PATHS derives from the affective-behavioral-cognitive dynamic (ABCD) model of development, which postulates that social competence is achieved when affect, behavior, and cognition work together (Greenberg, Kusche, & Riggs, 2004). This collaborative networking of emotional, behavioral, and cognitive systems occurs over the course of development as emotional responses begin to be verbalized and processed cognitively so that behavior can be controlled. Teachers trained on PATHS teach lessons on self-control, social problem solving, and emotional awareness and understanding. PATHS also includes lessons on labeling and expressing feelings using drawings of faces expressing different feelings and through conversations about feelings (Greenberg, Kusche, Cook, & Quamma, 1995). Teachers using PATHS typically teach three 20–30 minute lessons per week.

PATHS for the elementary level has been shown to improve children's feelings vocabulary and their understanding of their own feelings and those of others (Greenberg et al., 1995), increase children's inhibitory control and their verbal fluency, and reduce behavioral problems (Riggs, Greenberg, Kusche, & Pentz, 2006). Among high-risk children, PATHS has positive effects on academic, social, and emotional skills; peer interactions; and engagement in problem behaviors (Conduct Problems Prevention Research Group [CPPRG], 1999). Preschool PATHS has been shown to increase social competence and reduce social withdrawal (Domitrovich, Cortes, & Greenberg, 2007).

The Responsive Classroom (RC) Approach

The RC approach is a way of teaching that integrates the social, emotional, and academic needs of children. RC includes 10 classroom practices designed for both optimal learning and creating a classroom where children feel "safe, challenged, and joyful" (www.responsiveclassroom.org). Examples of classroom practices include (1) the morning meeting wherein children and teachers greet each other, share the day's news, and prepare for the day ahead and (2) use of teacher-led collaborative problem-solving strategies, such as role-playing and conferencing. Central to these classroom practices are a balanced emphasis on children's academic and social learning, as well as creating an environment that is academically challenging and builds social skills (Rimm-Kaufman, Fan, Chiu, & You, 2007). RC offers myriad resources and training supports to help with implementation and sustainability. Once classroom practices are in place, extensions to the larger school and family community are made.

Emerging evidence suggests that RC impacts the social and emotional climate of the classroom as well as student outcomes. Students in third- to fifth-grade classrooms that adopt RC report liking their school more and having more positive feelings toward learning, their teachers, and their classmates (Brock, Nishida, Chiong, Grimm, & Rimm-Kaufman, 2008). Results from quasiexperimental studies have shown an increase in reading and math scores as well as closer relationships with teachers, more prosocial skills, more assertive behavior, and less fear among children in RC classrooms compared to those in comparison classrooms after multiple years of exposure to the RC approach (Rimm-Kaufman et al., 2007; Rimm-Kaufman & Chiu, 2007). Teachers using the RC approach also report engaging in more collaboration with other teachers and having more positive perceptions of the school (Sawyer & Rimm-Kaufman, 2007).

The Reading, Writing, Respect, and Resolution (4Rs) Program

4Rs trains teachers to use a literacy-based curriculum that includes lessons on conflict resolution, cultural differences, and cooperation (Jones, Brown, & Aber, 2008). 4Rs is designed to combine specific instructional, skill-building techniques, and also model positive social norms. A randomized control trial of 18 schools with 82 third-grade classrooms showed evidence that 4Rs impacts the social and emotional climate of the classroom, which reflects the extent to which the interactions between teachers and students reflect warmth and support, a lack of anger and hostility, consistent response from teachers to the needs of students, and teacher integration of students' ideas and interests into learning activities (Brown et al., 2010). Encouraging effects have been found (Aber, Jones, Brown, Chaudry, & Samples, 1998). After the first year, trained, independent observers rated 4Rs classrooms higher in quality of student–teacher interactions and teacher's sensitivity to student needs (Brown et al., 2010). After two years in the program, children were rated as more socially competent, more attentive, and less aggressive than their peers in comparison classrooms (Jones, Brown, & Aber, 2011).

The RULER Approach to SEL

RULER is anchored in research that shows that acquiring and valuing the knowledge and skills of recognizing, understanding, labeling, expressing, and regulating emotion (i.e., the RULER skills) is critical to youth development, academic engagement and achievement, and life success (Rivers & Brackett, 2011). RULER's sustainability model includes systematic professional development for the adults involved in the education of children, including teachers, support staff, school and district leaders, and parents. RULER provides opportunities for adults and students to practice applying and modeling their RULER skills in ways that make emotions central to learning, teaching, and leading. Learning tools and lessons are integrated into the standard academic curriculum from preschool through high school. RULER is the focus of the case study included in the next section.

CASE STUDY: THE RULER APPROACH TO SEL

RULER is a multiyear, structured approach that combines a curriculum for students with comprehensive professional development for school leaders, teachers, and support staff, as well as training for families (Brackett et al., 2009; Brackett, Rivers, & Salovey, 2011; Maurer & Brackett, 2004). RULER focuses on developing each stakeholder's attitudes, knowledge, and expertise regarding five key emotional skills: recognizing emotions in the self and others, understanding the causes and consequences of emotions, labeling emotional experiences with an accurate and diverse vocabulary, and expressing and regulating emotions in ways that promote both intra- and interpersonal growth (Brackett et al., 2009; Brackett, Rivers, Maurer, Elbertson, & Kremenitzer, 2011; Mayer & Salovey, 1997). Research shows that RULER skills are important for effective teaching and learning, decision making, relationship quality, and both health and well-being for children and adults (e.g., Mayer et al., 2008).

RULER is an outgrowth of the ability model of emotional intelligence (EI; Mayer & Salovey, 1997; Salovey & Mayer, 1990) and is anchored in research on emotional development (e.g., Denham, 1998) and emotional competence (e.g., Saarni, 1999). EI theory proposes that the ability to reason about and leverage emotion enhances thinking, problem solving, relationships, and personal growth (Mayer & Salovey, 1997; Salovey & Mayer, 1990). Indeed, individuals with higher EI tend to perform better in school (Gil-Olarte Marquez, Palomera Martin, & Brackett, 2006; Rivers, Brackett, & Salovey, 2008), have better quality relationships (Brackett, Warner, & Bosco, 2005; Lopes et al., 2004), resolve conflict in more constructive ways (Brackett, Rivers, Shiffman, Lerner, & Salovey, 2006), solve social reasoning problems more effectively (Reis et al., 2007), and engage less frequently in unhealthy behaviors (Brackett, Mayer, & Warner, 2004; Trinidad & Johnson, 2002).

RULER focuses on the malleable aspects of emotional intelligence—the attitudes, knowledge, and skills that are acquired through experience and formal instruction. In other words, according to RULER, the development of emotional intelligence results from the acquisition and utilization of essential emotional skills, similar to how children learn to write and communicate effectively.

Developmental literature on emotion-related abilities has informed RULER in myriad ways. Based on the idea that emotion-related skills emerge in infancy, grow in preschool, continue to develop through the school-age years, and parallel the increase in cognitive capacities over the life course (Eccles, 1999), emotional intelligence provides a framework for tailoring lessons to age, in order to match the levels of cognitive, social, and emotional development necessary to learn important emotion-related skills. For instance, Saarni (1999) found that five year olds can only describe situations that lead to the expression of basic emotions, whereas seven year olds can describe situations that lead to the expression of more complicated emotions of pride, worry, and guilt. However, only by age 10 can children describe situations that elicit relief or disappointment. These increases in emotional understanding over time inform the scaffolded approach that RULER supports.

According to RULER, emotional intelligence develops through (1) an appreciation of the significance of emotions in learning, relationships, and personal growth; (2) the acquisition of knowledge and skills related to the full range of emotions; (3) being in environments that are safe and supportive for experiencing a wide range of emotions and practicing RULER skills; (4) frequent exposure to adults and peers expressing a range of emotions and modeling RULER skills; and (5) consistent opportunities to practice using RULER skills in social interactions with accompanied feedback on their application so that their use becomes refined and more automatic.

The RULER Skills

RULER represents five interrelated emotional skills. The acronym is not intended to reflect a hierarchy in which one skill precedes another in a progressive chain as the development of one RULER skill likely influences another. For example, as a young boy's emotion vocabulary (labeling emotion) becomes more sophisticated, he likely will become more skilled at reading a friend's facial expression (recognizing emotion) because language helps to shape the sensory processing involved in seeing another person's face (Feldman Barrett, Lindquist, & Gendron, 2007). Here, for simplicity, we describe briefly each skill separately.

Recognizing Emotion

Recognizing the occurrence of an emotion—by noticing a change in one's own thoughts or body, or in someone else's facial expression or voice—is the first clue that something important is happening in the environment. Students who accurately recognize emotional cues, both their own and those expressed by others, are able to modify their own behavior and respond in ways that are socially appropriate and helpful (Ekman, 2003). For example, the student skilled at recognizing emotions likely would behave differently toward a friend who is smiling than toward a classmate with pressed lips and furrowed brows. The smile reveals joy and invites the student to approach, whereas the latter cues represent anger and inform the student to stay away or approach with caution.

Understanding Emotion

Emotions are triggered by appraisals of events and lead to relatively distinct patterns of physiology, thoughts, and behaviors. Students with a deeper understanding of emotion know the causes and consequences of different emotions, as well as how discrete emotions like disappointment, excitement, and anger may influence their attention, thoughts, decisions, and behavior. This skill helps students to interpret situations more readily from others' perspectives and to develop empathy (Denham, 1998). For instance, a teenager who understands that his friend's unusual angry outburst is likely related to the divorce of his parents, might empathize with him, and encourage him to talk about his feelings.

Labeling Emotion

Labeling emotion refers to making connections between an emotional experience and emotion words. Students with a mature feelings vocabulary can differentiate among related emotions like peeved, annoyed, angry, and enraged. Labeling emotions accurately helps students communicate effectively, reducing misunderstanding in social interactions. Indeed, students who can label emotions properly have more positive social interactions and perform better in school, whereas students with deficits in labeling emotions are known to have behavioral and learning problems (Rivers, Brackett, Reyes, Mayer, Caruso, & Salovey, 2012).

Expressing Emotion

Expressing emotion refers to knowledge about how and when to express diverse emotions with different people and in multiple contexts. Children who are skilled in this area understand that unspoken rules for emotional expression, also called *display rules,* often direct how emotions are expressed and tend to modify their behavior accordingly. Display rules, often codified in childhood as manners, vary across contexts (home and school) and often are culturally specific. For example, it is generally less acceptable in Asian cultures than in Western cultures to express negative emotions like anger to others (Argyle, 1986). For many emotions, there also are gender-specific norms for expression (Shields, 2002); expressing anger is generally considered acceptable for boys, but not for girls, while expressing sadness is more acceptable for girls than for boys.

Regulating Emotion

Regulating emotion refers to the strategies used to manage the thoughts, feelings, and behaviors related to an emotional experience (Eisenberg, Fabes, Guthrie, & Reiser, 2000). Emotions can be prevented (test anxiety can be avoided), reduced (frustration toward someone can be lessened), initiated (inspiration can be generated to motivate a group), maintained (tranquility can be preserved to stay relaxed), or enhanced (joy can be increased to excitement when sharing important news) (Brackett et al., 2011). Students who know and use a wide range of emotion regulation strategies are able to meet different goals, such as concentrating on a difficult test, dealing with disappointing news, and managing challenging relationships. For a more detailed review of the emotion regulation literature, see Jacobs and Gross (2014).

RULER Theory of Change

RULER's theory of change for student development and outcomes is rooted in decades of research on emotional intelligence (Rivers & Brackett, 2011) and ecological systems theory (Bronfenbrenner, 1979). The theory specifies a set of pathways through which RULER influences emotional intelligence skill development and positive shifts in school and home communities, as illustrated in Figure 19.2. Accordingly, RULER

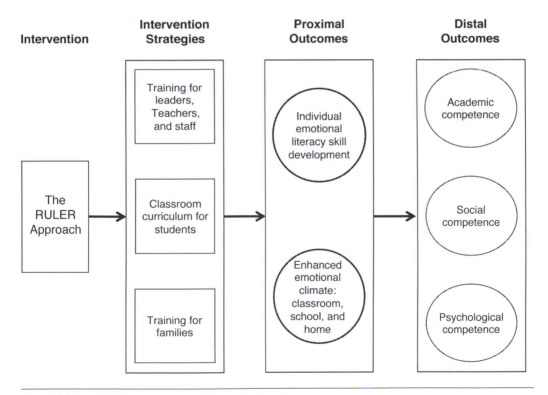

Figure 19.2 The RULER Approach theory of change for students.

both integrates the teaching of emotional intelligence into the academic curriculum and provides opportunities for students and all adult stakeholders—school leaders, teachers, staff, and family members—to learn and then apply these skills in their daily interactions. The integration into existing curriculum and training of both students and adults is the cornerstone of RULER. Moreover, the focus on both shifting the attitudes and developing the skills of the adults who create learning environments in addition to training them how to teach lessons to students makes RULER unique.

The intervention strategy for RULER is to integrate it into both the classroom and system (school or district) in ways that sustain it (CASEL, 2003; Catalano et al., 2004). First, adult stakeholders participate in professional development and program training so that emotional intelligence is being developed, modeled, and practiced regularly. This ensures RULER is embedded into all aspects of the school environment, including social interactions, self-reflective activities, and teaching. Only then do teachers begin using the student-level curriculum in the classroom and involve family members in their own training.

As Figure 19.2 illustrates, RULER has two proximal outcome targets: (1) enhanced emotional intelligence (RULER) skills among students and all adult stakeholders and (2) enhanced emotional climate (quality of social and emotional interactions) across settings, including the classroom, school, district, and home. These proximal outcomes mutually reinforce each other so that individual skill development enhances the emotional quality in each setting and vice versa.

RULER also has three primary distal outcomes for students: (1) academic performance, (2) relationship quality, and (3) health and well-being. The simultaneous development of students' emotional skills and enriched emotional climate are the bases for these distal outcomes (Brackett et al., 2012; Reyes, Brackett, Rivers, White, & Salovey, 2012). The theoretical rationale for this proposition is multifold. First, emotional skills among youth and adolescents are associated positively with each of the distal outcomes. Accumulating empirical evidence shows that children and youth with more developed RULER skills have greater social competence, psychological well-being, and academic performance (Denham, 1998; Fine, Izard, Mostow, Trentacosta, & Ackerman, 2003; Rivers et al., 2012; Saarni, 1999). Those with less developed emotional skills are more likely to experience depression and anxiety, engage in violent behaviors such as bullying, drug and alcohol use, destructive relationships, and poor academic performance (e.g., Eisenberg et al., 2000; Halberstadt, Denham, & Dunsmore, 2001; Saarni, 1999). Thus, becoming emotionally intelligent can be critical to developing into a healthy and productive adult. Second, as stated earlier in this chapter, a positive emotional climate in the classroom meets students' basic development needs for caring and supportive relationships, including the feeling that their opinions count and are respected (Deci & Ryan, 1985; Deci, Vallerand, Pellietier, & Ryan, 1991). There are also numerous plausible mediating variables between RULER's proximal and distal outcomes, among which may include student engagement, decision making, problem-solving ability, and enhanced mental health (Brackett, Reyes, Rivers, Elbertson, & Salovey, 2011; Reyes, Brackett, Rivers, White, et al., 2012).

Implementation of RULER

Initial implementation of RULER typically extends across a two-year period. By the third year, schools gradually become independent from the program developers, and sustainable, positive effects are expected. The comprehensive sustainability model is

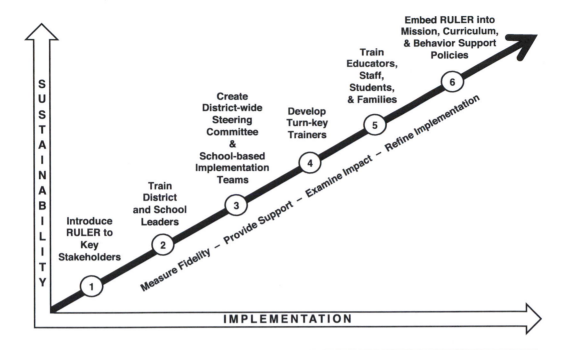

Figure 19.3 Year 1 implementation plan for RULER.

designed to build capacity within schools using a train-the-trainer approach to preserve the programs over time. Figure 19.3 depicts the action steps for the first year of implementation.

Briefly, the first action step involves securing the commitment from key stakeholders, including the superintendent, school board, building-level administrators, teachers, and support staff (e.g., school counselors and psychologists). These stakeholders, who are more likely to champion the program if they are included in the early planning phase, need to (1) understand the program's evidence base, (2) make explicit the links between the program's principles and the philosophy, policies, and current practices of the school, and (3) understand how the program can help the school enhance the social, emotional, and academic growth of students and staff.

The second action step involves training for both district- and building-level administrators who learn how emotions impact relationships and organizational climate, as well as how they can harness the wisdom of emotions to both become more effective leaders and create optimal learning environments. Administrators hone their RULER skills, learn how to use program tools, and work toward developing a long-term sustainability plan. This training also gives leaders the credibility to promote the program.

The creation of a district-wide steering committee and school-based implementation teams marks the third action step. The steering committee functions in an advisory and decision-making capacity to the implementation teams at each school and the district itself. Generally, schools appoint a coordinator to manage the rollout and key contact for the program developers, steering committee, and implementation teams.

School districts ultimately want to develop the internal capacity to sustain and enhance program implementation. Thus, the fourth action step involves the development of turn-key trainers, usually implementation team members, who learn about program concepts and tools in order to expedite and monitor the rollout at individual schools. Turnkey trainers should represent educators from different grade levels and areas of expertise (e.g., science, language arts, and pupil support personnel), and who are known for their social, emotional, and leadership skills and for being excellent presenters and group facilitators. Turnkey trainers attend a 30-hour institute led by RULER experts and then receive online support and coaching. Schools and districts with greater readiness for RULER often send a team of trainers to a RULER institute in advance of rolling out the program. These turnkey trainers can become the internal change agents that guide the school or district throughout the implementation process.

Action step five involves training and support first for teachers and support staff and then for students and families. Adult educators first develop their own RULER skills and learn how emotions influence learning, relationships, and health before they begin teaching students about emotional intelligence. Thus, in the initial rollout year, teachers first learn and use and then teach their students the Anchors of emotional intelligence, four tools that were designed to help both adults and children to develop their RULER skills, self-and social awareness, empathy, and perspective-taking ability, as well as to foster a healthy emotional climate. Once the Anchors are implemented with fidelity, teach-ers learn how to integrate the *Feeling Words Curriculum,* a language-based emotional intelligence program for students. The next section includes descriptions of these com-ponents. The success of RULER is dependent, in part, on adult family members being active participants. Like educators and students, RULER includes training for family members on how to develop and apply each of the RULER skills at home in order to foster healthy relationships, greater bonding among family members, academic perfor-mance, and well-being.

Mistakenly, some school leaders separate emotional intelligence programming from the essential components of instruction, jeopardizing its perceived importance and sustainability. For this reason, step six focuses on embedding RULER into the school's mission, overarching curriculum and instruction, and behavior support policies. For example, the Anchor Tools, described in the next section, become part of each school's approach to managing conflict.

Finally, because optimal professional development is ongoing, collaborative, and reflective (National Staff Development Council [NSDC], 2001), turnkey trainers and other educators' learning continues after initial training. Advanced training includes skill-building modules, individualized coaching sessions, support from RULER staff, and online resources, including model lessons conducted by both the program develop-ers and teachers in various grade levels as well as professional learning communities for teachers to share lesson plan ideas and examples of stellar student work.

Components of RULER

The Anchor Tools

The RULER Anchor Tools are designed to promote CASEL's competencies, RULER's proximal and distal outcomes, including the prevention of bullying, and also to align with Common Core State Standards. They provide a common language and set of strategies that

Table 19.1 RULER Anchor Tools for Developing Emotional Intelligence Skills and Fostering Supportive Learning Environments

Charter	A document with a mission statement at its core, developed collaboratively by all members of the learning community. Leaders and teachers create a faculty charter; teachers and students create individual classroom charters.
	Critical components: • Feelings each stakeholder wants to have in the community, such as feeling valued, empowered, and respected • Identification of behaviors that foster those feelings • Guidelines for handling uncomfortable feelings and conflict
Mood Meter	A self-awareness tool to develop RULER skills.
	Helps students and adult stakeholders to: • Identify their feelings accurately • Build self-and social awareness • Develop a sophisticated emotion vocabulary • Set daily goals for how they want to feel in school • Strategize effectively in order to achieve their goals
	Teachers use the tool to help: • Differentiate instruction • Enhance student memory and learning by considering the best mood states for different learning activities
Meta-Moment	A process to improve reflective practices and self-regulation.
	Helps students and adult stakeholders to: • Recognize "triggers" and respond to challenging emotional experiences with effective strategies • Cultivate one's "best self" to react more positively when triggered • Be more preventative than reactive when regulating emotions
Blueprint	A problem-solving tool for complex interpersonal situations.
	Helps students and adult stakeholders to: • Problem solve effectively about challenging situations • Build more empathy and understanding of others' perspectives • Reduce conflict and bullying

integrate into all aspects of learning at school and at home, including the standard curriculum and its physical spaces and learning environments. Table 19.1 briefly describes the four Anchor Tools. For example, morning meetings use tools such as the Charter and the Mood Meter to help teachers and students to identify the feelings they are bringing to the classroom, determine the best feelings and mood states for specific lessons and activities, and then to select effective strategies to modify or maintain these feelings and moods in order to achieve the learning goals for the day.

The Feeling Words Curriculum

The *Feeling Words Curriculum* includes units that each focus on exploring one feeling word in myriad ways (Brackett, Maurer, et al., 2011). The lessons that comprise each unit are calibrated for each grade level and are designed to integrate seamlessly into and across the core curriculum, including English language arts, social studies, humanities, math, and science. The feeling words in the program characterize the gamut of human emotions and were selected from a systematic review of research (e.g., Plutchik, 2003) on basic emotions (e.g., joy, fear), more complex, self-evaluative emotions (e.g., guilt, pride), and other, emotion-laden terms that describe motivational and relationship states (e.g., empowerment, alienation). Words are grouped into families that maintain continuity across grade levels and reflect the basic developmental needs of children (i.e., the need to feel connected to others, to feel competent in one's abilities, and to feel that one's behavior is self-directed; Deci & Ryan, 1985). Vocabulary plays a pivotal role in social and emotional development (e.g., Harre, 1986; Russell, 1990), and acquiring a sophisticated feelings vocabulary helps children to become consciously aware of their own and others' emotions, communicate effectively about emotions, and better regulate emotions and their behavior (e.g., Feldman Barrett, Lindquist, & Gendron, 2007; Hesse & Cicchetti, 1982; Lieberman et al., 2007).

The steps in the Feeling Words Curriculum encourage differentiation of instruction, address each student's unique thinking and learning style, and are aligned with Common Core State Standards. The activities represented by the steps are highly interactive and engage students in a creative, multifaceted approach that incorporates personalized and integrated learning, divergent thinking, both teacher-student and parent-child bonding, creative writing, and collaborative problem solving to develop strategies for regulating emotions. RULER is a spiraled curriculum; the complexity and number of steps in each program vary as a function of students' cognitive, emotional, and social development (Brackett, Kremenitzer, et al., 2011; Maurer & Brackett, 2004).

RULER Impact

Monitoring the progress and impact of an SEL program like RULER is an integral part of the implementation process. RULER has been adopted by hundreds of schools and is being evaluated rigorously. Thus far, research suggests that embedding RULER into a school or district fosters a range of behaviors and shifts in school climate that are essential to both positive development and academic achievement. Here, we review some of the research findings.

Results from numerous studies align with the program's theoretical model. In one study, students in middle school classrooms integrating RULER for one academic year had higher year-end grades and higher teacher ratings of social and emotional competence (e.g., leadership, social skills, and study skills) compared to students in the comparison group (Brackett et al., 2012). A randomized control trial in 62 schools tested the hypothesis that RULER improves the social and emotional climate of classrooms (Rivers, Brackett, Reyes, Elbertson, & Salovey, 2013). After one academic year, schools that had RULER as compared to those that used the standard curriculum were rated by independent observers as having higher degrees of warmth and connectedness between teachers and students, more autonomy and leadership, less bullying among students, and teachers who focused more on students' interests and motivations. Additional research examined the extent to which these first-year shifts in the emotional qualities of classrooms were followed by improvements in classroom organization and instruction at the end of the second year (Hagelskamp, Brackett, Rivers, & Salovey, 2013). The results supported RULER's theory of change. Compared to classrooms in the comparison schools, classrooms in RULER schools exhibited greater emotional support, better classroom organization, and more instructional support at the end of the second year of program delivery. Improvements in classroom organization and instructional support at the end of Year 2 were partially explained by RULER's impacts on classroom emotional support at the end of Year 1. Other research shows that, consistent with RULER's implementation plan, mere delivery of RULER lessons is not sufficient for cultivating benefits for students. In one study, students had more positive outcomes, including higher emotional intelligence and more developed social problem-solving skills when they were in classrooms with teachers who had attended more training, taught more lessons, and were rated by independent observers as high-quality program implementers, as compared to their counterparts (Reyes, Brackett, Rivers, Elbertson, & Salovey, 2012). Thus, SEL programs like RULER must be taught authentically, consistently, and with high quality in order to achieve intended outcomes. Though the proper implementation of RULER and other similar SEL programs comes with a price to schools as they must pay for instructional materials, trainings, and ongoing support, programs that target cognitive, behavioral, and academic changes are likely to generate large benefits that can be translated into savings to society in the short and long run in the form of enhanced educational attainment and achievement, reduced aggression, crime, and drug use, less welfare needs, reduced costs for social workers and counselors, and increases in earnings (Karoly, 2010; Schweinhart et al., 2005).

SUMMARY AND CONCLUSIONS

Over the last two decades, the field of SEL programming has come a long way. Numerous evidence-based programs have been developed, validated, refined, and disseminated across the United States and in other countries. Research that demonstrates the benefits of SEL training for both students and educators is also well documented (Durlak et al., 2011). Why, then, are SEL programs not a part of everyday practice in all schools? With ongoing changes in educational policy over the last decade, such as the No Child Left Behind act and initiatives like the Common Core State Standards in the United States, academic demands and pressure on teachers to raise test scores have become more stringent, and schools have less time to integrate, nevertheless consider SEL programming. Major progress in SEL likely will not happen until legislation such as the reauthorization of the Elementary and Secondary Education Act is passed, which holds schools accountable for the social and emotional development of students. Above all, educators, researchers, and parents must champion the SEL cause and the efforts toward enduring SEL programming in schools. As this chapter demonstrates, keeping SEL separate from academics is a disservice to educators, students, and families. The time has come to ensure that all children and adults develop skills to maximize their full potential—academically, socially, and emotionally.

REFERENCES

Aber, J. L., Jones, S. M., Brown, J. L., Chaudry, N., & Samples, F. (1998). Resolving conflict creatively: Evaluating the developmental effects of a school-based violence prevention program in neighborhood and classroom context. *Development and Psychopathology, 10*, 187–213.

Allen, V., MacCann, C., Matthews, G., & Roberts, R. D. (2014). Emotional intelligence in education: From pop to emerging science. In R. Pekrun & L. Linnenbrink-Garcia (Eds.), *International handbook of emotions in education* (pp. 162–182). New York, NY: Taylor & Francis.

Argyle, M. (1986). Rules for social relationships in four cultures. *Australian Journal of Psychology, 38*, 309–318.

Battistich, V., Solomon, D., Watson, M., & Schaps, E. (1997). Caring school communities. *Educational Psychologist, 32*, 137–151.

Becker, B. E., & Luthar, S. S. (2002). Social-emotional factors affecting achievement outcomes among disadvantaged students: Closing the achievement gap. *Educational Psychologist, 37*, 197–214.

Becker, M., Ludtke, O., Trautwein, U., Koller, O., & Baumert, J. (2012). The differential effects of school tracking on psychometric intelligence: Do academic-track schools make students smarter? *Journal of Educational Psychology, 104*, 682–699.

Benjamin, R. S., Costello, E. J., & Warren, M. (1990). Anxiety disorders in a pediatric sample. *Journal of Anxiety Disorders, 4*, 293–316.

Brackett, M. A., Kremenitzer, J. P., Maurer, M., Rivers, S. E., Elbertson, N. A., & Carpenter, M. D. (Eds.). (2011). *Creating emotional literate classrooms: An introduction to The RULER Approach to Social and Emotional Learning.* Port Chester, NY: National Professional Resources, Inc.

Brackett, M. A., Maurer, M., Rivers, S. E., Elbertson, N. A., Carpenter, M. D., Kremenitzer, J. P. . . . Bauer, J. (2011). The feeling words curriculum. In M. A. Brackett, J. P. Kremenitzer, M. Maurer, S. E. Rivers, N. A. Elbertson, & M. D. Carpenter (Eds.), *Creating emotionally literate classrooms: An introduction to the RULER Approach to Social and Emotional Learning* (pp. 23–48). Port Chester, NY: National Professional Resources, Inc.

Brackett, M. A., Mayer, J. D., & Warner, R. M. (2004). Emotional intelligence and its relation to everyday behaviour. *Personality and Individual Differences, 36*, 1387–1402.

Brackett, M. A., Patti, J., Stern, R., Rivers, S. E., Elbertson, N. A., Chisholm, C., & Salovey, P. (2009). A sustainable, skill-based approach to building emotionally literate schools. In D. Thompson, M. Hughes, & J. Terrell (Eds.), *The handbook of developing emotional and social intelligence: Best practices, case studies, & tools* (pp. 329–358). New York, NY: Pfeiffer.

Brackett, M. A., Reyes, M. R., Rivers, S. E., Elbertson, N. A., & Salovey, P. (2011). Classroom emotional climate, teacher affiliation, and student conduct. *Journal of Classroom Interaction, 46*, 27–36.

Brackett, M. A., Rivers, S. E., Maurer, M., Elbertson, N. A., & Kremenitzer, J. P. (2011). Creating emotionally literate learning environments. In M. A. Brackett, J. P. Kremenitzer, M. Maurer, S. E. Rivers, N. A. Elbertson, & M. D. Carpenter (Eds.), *Creating emotionally literate learning environments* (pp. 1–21). Port Chester, NY: National Professional Resources, Inc.

Brackett, M. A., Rivers, S. E., Reyes, M. R., & Salovey, P. (2012). Enhancing academic performance and social and emotional competence with the RULER Feeling Words Curriculum. *Learning and Individual Differences, 22*, 218–224.

Brackett, M. A., Rivers, S. E., & Salovey, P. (2011). Emotional intelligence: Implications for personal, social, academic, and workplace success. *Social and Personality Compass, 5*, 88–103.

Brackett, M. A., Rivers, S. E., Shiffman, S., Lerner, N., & Salovey, P. (2006). Relating emotional abilities to social functioning: A comparison of self-report and performance measures of emotional intelligence. *Journal of Personality and Social Psychology, 91*, 780–795.

Brackett, M. A., Warner, R. M., & Bosco, J. S. (2005). Emotional intelligence and relationship quality among couples. *Personal Relationships, 12*, 197–212.

Brinch, C., & Galloway, T. (2012). Schooling in adolescence raises IQ scores. *Proceedings of the National Academy of Sciences of the United States of America, 109*, 425–30.

Brock, L. L., Nishida, T. K., Chiong, C., Grimm, K. J., & Rimm-Kaufman, S. E. (2008). Children's perceptions of the classroom environment and social and academic performance: A longitudinal analysis of the contribution of the *Responsive Classroom* approach. *Journal of School Psychology, 46*, 129–149.

Bronfenbrenner, U. (1979). *The ecology of human development: Experiments by nature and design.* Cambridge, MA: Harvard University Press.

Brown, J. L., Jones, S. M., LaRusso, M. D., & Aber, J. L. (2010). Improving classroom quality: Teacher influences and experimental impacts of the 4Rs program. *Journal of Educational Psychology, 102*, 153–167.

Catalano, R. F., Berglund, L., Ryan, J.A.M., Lonczek, H. S., & Hawkins, J. D. (2004). Positive youth development in the United States: Research findings on evaluations of positive youth development programs. *The Annals of the American Academy of Political and Social Science, 591*, 98–124.

Catalano, R. F., Hawkins, J. D., Berglund, L., Pollard, J. A., & Arthur, M. W. (2002). Prevention science and positive youth development: Competitive or cooperative frameworks? *Journal of Adolescent Health, 31*, 230–239.

Collaborative for Academic Social and Emotional Learning [CASEL]. (2003). *Safe and sound: An educational leader's guide to evidence-based social and emotional learning (SEL) programs.* Chicago, IL: Author.

Conduct Problems Prevention Research Group (CPPRG). (1999). Initial impact of the Fast Track Prevention Trial for Conduct Problems: I. The high-risk sample. *Journal of Consulting and Clinical Psychology, 67,* 631–647.

Deci, E. L., & Ryan, R. M. (1985). *Intrinsic motivation and self-determination in human behavior.* New York, NY: Plenum.

Deci, E. L., Vallerand, R. J., Pellietier, L. G., & Ryan, R. M. (1991). Motivation and education: The self-determination perspective. *Educational Psychologist, 26,* 325–346.

Delate, T., Gelenberg, A. J., Simmons, V. A., & Motheral, B. R. (2004). Trends in the use of antidepressants in a national sample of commercially insured pediatric patients, 1998–2002. *Psychiatric Services, 55,* 387–391.

Denham, S. A. (1998). *Emotional development in young children.* New York, NY: Guilford Press.

Devaney, E., O'Brien, M. U., Resnik, H., Keister, S., & Weissberg, R. P. (2006). *Sustainable schoolwide social and emotional learning (SEL): Implementation guide and toolkit.* Chicago, IL: CASEL.

DeVoe, J., & Murphy, C. (2011). *Student reports of bullying and cyber-bullying: Results from the 2009 school crime supplement to the National Crime Victimization Survey.* Washington, DC: National Center for Education Statistics.

Domitrovich, C. E., Cortes, R. C., & Greenberg, M. T. (2007). Improving young children's social and emotional competence: A randomized trial of the preschool "PATHS" curriculum. *Journal of Primary Prevention, 28,* 67–91.

Durlak, J. A., and Weissberg, R. P. (2011). Promoting social and emotional development is an essential part of students' education. *Human Development, 54,* 1–3.

Durlak, J. A., Weissberg, R. P., Dymnicki, A. B., Taylor, R. D., & Schellinger, K. B. (2011). The impact of enhancing students' social and emotional learning: A meta-analysis of school-based universal interventions. *Child Development, 82,* 405–432.

Eccles, J. S. (1999). The development of children ages 6 to 14. *The Future of Children, 9,* 30–44.

Eigsti, I., Zayas, V., Mischel, W., Shoda, Y., Ayduk, O., Dadlani, M. B. . . . Casey, B. J. (2006). Predicting cognitive control from preschool to late adolescence and young adulthood. *Psychological Science, 17,* 478–484.

Eisenberg, N., Fabes, R. A., Guthrie, I. K., & Reiser, M. (2000). Dispositional emotionality and regulation: Their role in predicting quality of social functioning. *Journal of Personality and Social Psychology, 78,* 136–157.

Ekman, P. (2003). *Emotions revealed.* New York, NY: Henry Holt and Company.

Elias, M. J., Zins, J. E., Weissberg, R. P., Frey, K. S., Greenberg, M. T., Haynes, N. M. . . . Shriver, T. P. (1997). *Promoting social and emotional learning: Guidelines for educators.* Alexandria, VA: Association for Supervision and Curriculum Development.

Feldman Barrett, L., Lindquist, K. A., & Gendron, M. (2007). Language as context for the perception of emotion. *TRENDS in Cognitive Science, 11,* 327–332.

Fine, S. E., Izard, C. E., Mostow, A. J., Trentacosta, C. J., & Ackerman, B. P. (2003). First grade emotion knowledge as a predictor of fifth grade self-reported internalizing behaviors in children from economically disadvantaged families. *Development and Psychopathology, 15,* 331–342.

Gil-Olarte Marquez, P., Palomera Martin, R., & Brackett, M. A. (2006). Relating emotional intelligence to social competence and academic achievement in high school students. *Psichothema, 18,* 118–123.

Goleman, D. (1995). *Emotional intelligence.* New York, NY: Bantam Books.

Greenberg, M. T., Kische, C. A., & Mihalic, S. F. (1998). *Promoting alternative thinking strategies (PATHS).* Boulder, CO: Center for the Study and Prevention of Violence, University of Colorado.

Greenberg, M. T., Kusche, C. A., Cook, E. T., & Quamma, J. P. (1995). Promoting emotional competence in school-aged children: The effects of the PATHS curriculum. *Development and Psychopathology, 7,* 117–136.

Greenberg, M. T., Kusche, C. A., & Riggs, N. (2004). The PATHS curriculum: Theory and research on neurocognitive development and school success. In J. E. Zins, R. P. Weissberg, M. C. Wang, & H. J. Walberg (Eds.), *Building academic success on social and emotional learning: What does the research say?* (pp. 170–188). New York, NY: Teachers College Press.

Greenberg, M. T., Weissberg, R. P., O'Brien, M. U., Zins, J. E., Fredericks, L., Resnik, H., & Elias, M. J. (2003). Enhancing school-based prevention and youth development through coordinated social, emotional, and academic learning. *American Psychologist, 58,* 466–474.

Hagelskamp, C., Brackett, M. A., Rivers, S. E., & Salovey, P. (2013). Improving Classroom Quality with The RULER Approach to Social and Emotional Learning: Proximal and Distal Outcomes. *American Journal of Community Psychology, 51,* 530–543.

Halberstadt, A. G., Denham, S. A., & Dunsmore, J. C. (2001). Affective social competence. *Social Development, 10,* 79–119.

Hamre, B. K., & Pianta, R. C. (2001). Early teacher-child relationships and the trajectory of children's school outcomes through eighth grade. *Child Development, 72,* 625–638.

Hargreaves, A. (1998). The emotional practice of teaching. *Teaching and Teacher Education, 14,* 835–854.

Harre, R. (1986). *The social construction of emotions.* Oxford, England: Basil Blackwell.

Heckman, J. J., & Masterov, D. V. (2007). The productivity argument for investing in young children. *Applied Economic Perspectives and Policy, 29,* 446–493.

Hesse, P., & Cicchetti, D. (1982). Perspectives on an integrated theory of emotional development. *New Directions for Child Development, 1982,* 3–48.

Jacobs, S. E., & Gross, J. J. (2014). Emotion regulation in education: Conceptual foundations, current applications, and future directions. In R. Pekrun & L. Linnenbrink-Garcia (Eds.), *International handbook of emotions in education* (pp. 183–201). New York, NY: Taylor & Francis.

Jennings, P. A., & Greenberg, M. T. (2009). The prosocial classroom: Teacher social and emotional competence in relation to student and classroom outcomes. *Review of Educational Research, 79,* 491–525.

Jones, S. M., Brown, J. B., & Aber, J. L. (2008). Classroom settings as targets of intervention and research. In M. Shinn & H. Yoshikawa (Eds.), *Toward positive youth development: Transforming schools and community programs.* New York, NY: Oxford University Press.

Jones, S. M., Brown, J. L., & Aber, J. L. (2011). Two-year impacts of a universal school-based social-emotional and literacy intervention: An experiment in translational developmental research. *Child Development, 82,* 533–554.

Karoly, L. A. (2010). Toward standardization of benefit-cost analyses of early childhood interventions. RAND Working Paper No. WR-823. Available at http://dx.doi.org/10.2139/ssrn.1753326

Kessler, R. C., & Walters, E. E. (1998). Epidemiology of DSM-III-R major depression and minor depression among adolescents and young adults in the National Comorbidity Survey. *Depression and Anxiety, 7,* 3–14.

Lane, K. L., Pierson, M. R., & Givner, C. C. (2003). Teacher expectations of student behavior: Which skills do elementary and secondary teachers deem necessary for success in the classroom? *Education and Treatment of Children, 26,* 413–430.

Lieberman, M. D., Eisenberger, N. I., Crockett, M. J., Tom, S. M., Pfeifer, J. H., & Way, B. M. (2007). Putting feelings into words: Affect labeling disrupts amygdala activity in response to affective stimuli. *Psychological Science, 18,* 421–428.

Lopes, P. N., Brackett, M. A., Nezlek, J. B., Schutz, A., Sellin, I., & Salovey, P. (2004). Emotional intelligence and social interaction. *Personality and Social Psychology Bulletin, 30,* 1018–1034.

Maurer, M., & Brackett, M. A. (2004). *Emotional literacy in the middle school: A 6-step program to promote social, emotional, and academic learning.* Port Chester, NY: National Professional Resources.

Mayer, J. D., Roberts, R. D., & Barsade, S. G. (2008). Human abilities: Emotional intelligence. *Annual Review of Psychology, 59,* 507–536.

Mayer, J. D., & Salovey, P. (1997). What is emotional intelligence? In P. Salovey & D. J. Sluyter (Eds.), *Emotional development and emotional intelligence: Educational implications* (pp. 3–34). New York, NY: Basic Books.

McClelland, M. M., Cameron, C. E., Connor, C. M., Farris, C. L., Jewkes, A. M., & Morrison, F. J. (2007). Links between behavioral regulation and preschoolers' literacy, vocabulary, and math skills. *Developmental Psychology, 43,* 947–959.

McEvoy, A., & Welker, R. (2000). Antisocial behavior, academic failure, and school climate: A critical review. *Journal of Emotional and Behavioral Disorders, 8,* 130–140.

McNeely, C. A., Nonnemaker, J. M., & Blum, R. W. (2002). Promoting school connectedness: Evidence from the National Longitudinal Study of Adolescent Health. *Journal of School Health, 72,* 138–146.

Miller, D. C., Malley, L. B., & Owen, E. (2009). *Comparitive indicators of education in the United States and other G-8 Countries: 2009.* Washington, DC: U.S. Department of Education.

Mischel, W., & Ayduk, O. (2004). Willpower in a cognitive-affective processing system: The dynamic of delay of gratification. In R. F. Baumeister & K. D. Vohs (Eds.), *Handbook of self-regulation: Research theory and applications* (pp. 99–129). New York, NY: Guilford Press.

Mischel, W., Shoda, Y., & Rodriguez, M. L. (1989). Delay of gratification in children. *Science, 244,* 933–938.

Moos, R. H. (1979). *Evaluating educational environments.* San Francisco, CA: Jossey-Bass.

Mulvenon, S. W., Stegman, C. E., & Ritter, G. (2005). Test anxiety: A multifaceted study of the perceptions of teachers, principals, counselors, students and parents. *International Journal of Testing, 5,* 37–61.

National Staff Development Council (NSDC). (2001). *Standards for staff development, revised.* Oxford, OH: NSDC.

Olfson, M., & Marcus, S. C. (2009). National patterns in antidepressant medication treatment. *Archives of General Psychiatry, 66,* 848–856.

Osterman, K. E. (2000). Students' need for belonging in the school community. *Review of Educational Research, 70,* 323–367.

Paris, S. (1993). Four perspectives on educational assessment. *International Journal of Disability, Development and Education, 39,* 95–105.

Plutchik, R. (2003). *Emotions and life: Perspectives from psychology, biology, and evolution.* Washington, DC: American Psychological Association.

Raver, C. C., Jones, S. M., Li-Grining, C., Zhai, F., Bub, K., & Pressler, K. (2011). CSRP's impact on low-income preschoolers' preacademic skills: Self-regulation as a mediating mechanism. *Child Development, 82,* 362–378.

Ravitch, D. (2010). *The death and life of the great American school system: How testing and choice are undermining education.* New York, NY: Basic Books.

Reis, D. L., Brackett, M. A., Shamosh, N. A., Kiehl, K. A., Salovey, P., & Gray, J. R. (2007). Emotional intelligence predicts individual differences in social exchange reasoning. *NeuroImage, 35,* 1385–1391.

Reyes, M. R., Brackett, M. A., Rivers, S. E., Elbertson, N. A., & Salovey, P. (2012). The interaction effects of program training, dosage, and implementation quality on targeted student outcomes for The RULER Approach to Social and Emotional Learning. *School Psychology Review, 41,* 82–99.

Reyes, M. R., Brackett, M. A., Rivers, S. E., White, M., & Salovey, P. (2012). Classroom emotional climate, student engagement, and academic achievement. *Journal of Educational Psychology, 104,* 700–712.

Riggs, N. R., Greenberg, M. T., Kusche, C. A., & Pentz, M. A. (2006). The mediational role of neurocognition in the behavior outcomes of a social-emotional prevention program in elementary school students: Effects of the PATHS curriculum. *Prevention Science, 7,* 91–102.

Rimm-Kaufman, S. E., & Chiu, Y. I. (2007). Promoting social and academic competence in the classroom: An intervention study examining the contribution of the responsive classroom approach. *Psychology in the Schools, 44,* 397–413.

Rimm-Kaufman, S. E., Fan, X., Chiu, Y.-J., & You, W. (2007). The contribution of the Responsive Classroom Approach on children's academic achievement: Results from a three year longitudinal study. *Journal of School Psychology, 45,* 401–421.

Rivers, S. E., & Brackett, M. A. (2011). Achieving standards in the English language arts (and more) using The RULER Approach to social and emotional learning. *Reading & Writing Quarterly, 27,* 75–100.

Rivers, S. E., Brackett, M. A., Reyes, M. R., Elbertson, N. A., & Salovey, P. (2013). Improving the social and emotional climate of classrooms: A clustered randomized controlled trial testing The RULER Approach. *Prevention Science, 14,* 77–87.

Rivers, S.E., Brackett, M.A., Reyes, M.R., Mayer, J.D., Caruso, D.R., & Salovey, P. (2012). Measuring emotional intelligence in early adolescence with the MSCEIT-YV: Psychometric properties and relationship with academic performance and psychosocial functioning. *Journal of Psychoeducational Assessment, 30,* 344–366.

Russell, J. A. (1990). The preschoolers' understanding of the causes and consequences of emotion. *Child Development, 61,* 1872–1881.

Saarni, C. (1999). *The development of emotional competence.* New York, NY: Guilford Press.

Salovey, P., & Mayer, J. D. (1990). Emotional intelligence. *Imagination, Cognition and Personality, 9,* 185–211.

Sawyer, L.B.E., & Rimm-Kaufman, S. E. (2007). Teacher collaboration in the context of the responsive classroom approach. *Teachers and Teaching: Theory and Practice, 13,* 211–245.

Schweinhart, L. J., Montie, J., Xiang, Z., Barnett, W. S., Belfield, C. R., & Nores, M. (2005). *Lifetime effects: The High-Scope Perry Preschool study through age 40.* Monographs of the HighScope Educational Research Foundation, 14. Ypsilanti, MI: HighScope Press.

Shields, S. A. (2002). *Speaking from the heart: Gender and the social meaning of emotion.* New York, NY: Cambridge University Press.

Solomon, D., Battistich, V., Kim, D.-I., & Watson, M. (1997). Teacher practices associated with students' sense of the classroom as a community. *Social Psychology of Education, 1,* 235–267.

Substance Abuse and Mental Health Services Administration [SAMHSA]. (2005). *Overview of Findings from the 2004 National Survey on Drug Use and Health* (Office of Applied Studies, NSDUH Series H-27, DHHS Publication No. SMA 05-4061). Rockville, MD: SAMHSA.

Trinidad, D. R., & Johnson, C. A. (2002). The association between emotional intelligence and early adolescent tobacco and alcohol use. *Personality and Individual Differences, 32,* 95–105.

Weissberg, R. P., Caplan, M. Z., & Bennetto, L. (1988). *The Yale-New Haven Middle-School Social Program Solving (SPS) Program*. New Haven, CT: Yale University.

Zigler, E. F., & Bishop-Josef, S. J. (2006). The cognitive child vs. the whole child: Lessons from 40 years of Head Start. In D. G. Singer, R. M. Golinkoff, & K. Hirsh-Pasek (Eds.), *Play = learning: How play motivates and enhances children's cognitive and social-emotional growth* (pp. 15–35). New York, NY: Oxford University Press.

Zins, J. E., Bloodworth, M. R., Weissberg, R. P., & Walberg, H. J. (2004). The scientific base linking social and emotional learning to school success. In J. E. Zins, R. P. Weissberg, M. C. Wang, & H. J. Walberg (Eds.), *Building academic success on social and emotional learning: What does the research say?* (pp. 3–22). New York, NY: Teachers College Press.

Zins, J. E., Elias, M. J., Greenberg, M. T., & Weissberg, R. P. (2000). Promoting social and emotional competence in children. In K. M. Minke & G. C. Bear (Eds.), *Preventing school problems—promoting school success: Strategies and programs that work* (pp. 71–100). Bethesda, MD: National Association of School Psychologists.

Zins, J. E., Weissberg, R. P., Wang, M. C., & Walberg, H. J. (Eds.). (2004). *Building academic success on social and emotional learning: What does the research say?* New York, NY: Teachers College Press.

Part III

Content Domain, Context, and Culture

conceptual knowledge and the prevalence in the wider culture of certain beliefs about mathematics and mathematical ability.

The third section contrasts distinct interpretations of emotion in mathematics education: *traits* (characterizing different individuals' most typical emotional responses in mathematical situations), and *states* (emotions as they occur in-the-moment when doing mathematics). These enter into the *architecture* (the nature and functions of emotions in interaction with other affective, cognitive, or social constructs in mathematical environments). Such interpretations sometimes appear as competing or opposed research emphases, but here I regard them as fully compatible if appropriately distinguished.

The fourth section surveys some empirical findings pertaining to *math anxiety,* the most studied mathematical emotion. The larger scale, quantitative research on math anxiety and other emotions in mathematics has tended to focus on its trait-like interpretation. The results illustrate both the value and inherent limitations of studying trait emotions through questionnaire methods. The fifth section discusses research focusing on state-like interpretations, where the predominant mode has been to report qualitative descriptions and illustrative examples—suggesting important theoretical ideas but entailing a different set of inherent limitations.

The last section highlights theoretical ideas about affective architecture particularly important to mathematics education, which, in my view, should be central to future research.

THE COMPLEXITY OF MATHEMATICALLY SITUATED EMOTION

Mathematics classrooms present an extraordinary variety of contexts for students' emotional experiences. During individual work, small-group problem solving, or whole-class activity, a student may be presenting or listening, following directions, just thinking, or attending to something other than mathematics. Activity may be routine or cognitively challenging, with conceptions correct or incorrect, incomplete, confused, or nonstandard. Technology tools require additional, domain-specific skills. The experienced social environment exerts "press" through teacher and peer expectations and immediate events. Different students experience each social interaction differently, as personality traits vary. Events outside school, related or unrelated to mathematics, affect emotional responses. Students' emotions in similar contexts differ sharply. And the contexts for teachers' emotions are just as diverse—different comfort levels with the topics they teach, challenging classroom situations, demands associated with standardized tests, and so forth. In this manifold of mathematically related contexts, the emotions of different individuals also interact dynamically with each other: some labeled positive (e.g., curiosity, enthusiasm, fascination, love, pleasure, pride, satisfaction); some negative (e.g., anger, anxiety, boredom, fear, frustration, hatred, humiliation); and some variable or harder to classify (e.g., surprise).

Evidence for such emotion comes from questionnaires, from coding and analyzing expressions of emotion in videotaped activity, and other sources. Pekrun's Achievement Emotions Questionnaire–Mathematics (AEQ-M) (Frenzel, Pekrun, & Goetz, 2007; Pekrun, Goetz, Frenzel, Barchfeld, & Perry, 2011) includes items pertaining to enjoyment, pride, anxiety or fear, shame, anger, boredom, and hopelessness. The coding scheme of Else-Quest, Hyde, and Hejmadi (2008) identifies positive interest (described as involving interest, eagerness), tension (involving nervousness, anxiety, worry), frustration, sadness, anger, boredom, contempt, joy/pleasure, pride, and other emotions and related behaviors. Note that these extend beyond the "basic emotions" (Ekman, 1992; Ekman & Friesen, 2003) of anger, fear, joy, sadness, disgust, and surprise. Op't Eynde, De Corte, and Verschaffel (2006) consider facial actions, vocalizations, bodily actions, and most importantly, subjects' retrospective appraisals. They identify emotional sequences—for example, in one episode (Op't Eynde & Hannula, 2006), worry is followed by frustration, panic, and anger, but ultimately happiness.

We see also in these descriptions variation along other well-known dimensions—from mild (e.g., worry) to intense (e.g., panic) and from activating (e.g., eagerness) to deactivating (e.g., boredom). Some felt emotion can have depth and importance to the individual, while other emotions may be only fleetingly meaningful. And emotions can *recur*—Else-Quest et al. (2008) report children most often expressing tension and positive interest; sadness, boredom, anger, contempt, affection, joy, humor, and pride occurred on average less than once per session. Of course, such findings are highly dependent on the study's context (in this case, mother–child out-of-school mathematics sessions with American children, mean age 11.4 years, who had completed fifth grade).

Despite such complexities, certain *patterns* or regularities in emotions and their influence seem to stand out in mathematics education. Some not only jibe with plausible expectation but are substantiated by quantitative research—for example, the direct relation of math anxiety to students' perceptions of their math ability and their objective performance (e.g., Meece, Wigfield, & Eccles, 1990; see below). "Attitude toward mathematics," taken to have affective, behavioral, and motivational components, may include a propensity toward emotions such as enjoyment, liking, or the absence of boredom, as well as toward approach (vs. avoidance) behaviors. Favorable attitude (implicitly, positive emotion) is associated with school achievement (e.g., Mullis et al., 2008). Such identifiable, persistent, and widespread correlations of emotions with important goals of mathematics education constitute part of "what we know." But the details of the interactions among emotions, behaviors, and motivational orientations are crucial and should not be glossed over just by defining attitude as a composite.

Emotional sequence patterns are reported in qualitative studies in particular contexts. More complex patterns—for example, idealized *affective pathways* where sequences of emotional states interact with heuristics during mathematical problem solving (Goldin, 2000)—are proposed as plausible theoretical conjectures based on qualitative observations and teachers' and students' widely shared experiences. Some patterns—such as the association of mathematics with painful experience—also manifest themselves in the media and the wider culture.

There is much to learn about how in-the-moment emotions that students experience during mathematical activity contribute to longer term effects and about how teachers may skillfully influence them. For example, a student may become angry when another student says that her group's method of solving a problem is wrong (e.g., Schorr, Epstein, Warner, & Arias, 2010a, 2010b)—but public challenges to a student's ideas by the teacher or a peer can evoke on one occasion defensiveness, anger, or humiliation, and on another, excitement or determination. Such examples of situated emotion and accompanying behavior patterns are familiar to mathematics teachers, and their characterization is essential to understanding how emotions affect students' longer term mathematical development. But we must take into account how at different times a person experiences different emotional sequences, even in similar circumstances.

DOMAIN-SPECIFIC FEATURES

Let us next consider certain features with emotional implications that may be particular to mathematics as compared with other school subjects. I would highlight: (a) the central role of *impasse,* (b) the frequently occurring disconnection of procedural from conceptual knowledge, (c) embedded conceptual challenges, (d) the hierarchical nature of the curriculum, (e) the importance of correct answers and the frequent unreliability of attaining them, and (f) the prevalence in the wider culture of certain beliefs about mathematics and mathematical ability.

Problem solving is central to mathematical activity. But a problem is a situation in which the person has a goal but does not immediately know how to reach it (Schoenfeld, 1985), experiencing some kind of impasse or obstacle, some cognitive incongruity not easily resolved. Such impasse is likely to evoke *bewilderment,* or if it persists, *frustration* and an accompanying spectrum of emotions, from anxiety to increased interest and curiosity (Goldin, 2000; see also D'Mello & Graesser, 2014). Op 't Eynde, De Corte, and Verschaffel (2007) report students feeling annoyance, anger, anxiety, frustration, nervousness, happiness, and relief during problem solving, with frustration and nervousness occurring most frequently.

Mathematics involves procedures (rules for symbol-manipulation) as well as concepts (meanings, representations, and interpretations including why procedures work) (Lesh & Landau, 1983). Skemp (1976) calls these "instrumental" and "relational" understanding respectively. Tests often focus on fluency in arithmetic algorithms or algebraic manipulations, procedures that can often be acquired with minimal conceptual understanding (cf. Lesh & Lamon, 1992). But teaching well-established routines to ensure skills proficiency or to increase test performance (e.g., Firestone, Schorr, & Monfils, 2004; Handal, 2003; Ma, 1999; Smith, 1996) may leave some students *bored* and *disinterested* (Mora, 2011). Performance disconnected from concepts can lead to *discomfort, dislike,* and/or *anxiety* as the student follows rules without knowing why she is to do so (e.g., Nardi & Steward, 2003) or to *satisfaction* when and if she acquires a relational understanding (or succeeds using an algorithm with only instrumental understanding). Concept development in mathematics requires pressure-free exploration and discussion time, the unavailability of which in school can evoke *frustration,* while achieving conceptual understanding may lead to *elation.*

When new concepts (e.g., fractions, negative numbers, unknowns in algebra, formal geometry proofs, functions, limits, derivatives, and integrals) are first introduced, they typically require cognitive restructuring, the reinterpretation of existing representations or construction of new ones (e.g., Davis, 1984). This may lead to *confusion* and self-doubt or to *pride, satisfaction, appreciation,* and *self-confidence,* according to the degree of success and the social environment (e.g., Lewis, 2011, 2012; McCulloch, 2011; Schorr & Goldin, 2008).

The mathematics curriculum and its subfields (algebra, geometry, analysis, etc.) are typically organized hierarchically, so that failure to master prior concepts and prerequisite skills impedes subsequent learning. *Discouragement* may occur and a sense of falling behind when, for whatever reason, the learning sequence is interrupted.

Mathematics involves frequent evaluation of students' work as correct or incorrect, providing negative as well as positive feedback. Such evaluation may lead alternately to *elation* and *disappointment.* Forsyth (1986) describes a range of emotional reactions to examination scores, with failing students experiencing *unhappiness, tension,* and *guilt.* If the context is competitive or public, emotions easily extend to *pride* or *humiliation.* But mathematical correctness has an unreliable aspect even when the concepts and procedures are well understood—namely, the likelihood of oversight, clerical error, or miscommunication. Mathematical notation is highly nonredundant, so that a single misplaced character changes an expression's meaning. Many routine mathematical steps are expected to be taken mentally. Thus, the student has limited control of the outcome, leading possibly to *frustration* and a sense of *despair.*

Finally, certain prevailing, mathematics-specific beliefs can meet emotional needs, providing *comfort,* a sense of *security,* and some justification for experienced emotion and/or defenses from pain (Handal, 2003; Leder, Pehkonen, & Törner, 2002; Maasz & Schlöglmann, 2009). Mathematics is widely seen as requiring special ability, intelligence, or genius, often believed to be inherited or innate. Such beliefs, reflected in educational practice in many countries, may affect self-expectations and the expectations of others, influencing in turn success or failure emotions—for example, helping protect an unsuccessful student (as well as his teacher) from feeling *guilt, frustration,* or *despondency,* as lack of success is then neither one's fault (Goldin, Rösken, & Törner, 2009, p. 11). Alternatively, it may offer someone a sense of *pride* and family connection in being "mathematically gifted."

Mathematics is often believed to be purely rational, so that emotion is irrelevant—encouraging its suppression. Historically, mathematics has been male-dominated, with a continuing undercurrent of belief that women are less able than men to excel in it. Black and Hispanic students in the United States are greatly underrepresented in mathematical fields. These aspects may lead to phenomena such as stereotype threat (Aronson et al., 1999; Steele & Aronson, 1995), where consequent emotions inhibit performance.

TRAITS, STATES, AND ARCHITECTURE

Next, let us distinguish explicitly two different interpretations of what one means by emotions, and the different sorts of research questions and methods those interpretations suggest.

Trait-Like and State-Like Interpretations

The distinction between *state* (a person's in-the-moment psychological particulars, which can change rapidly) and *trait* (a longer term, relatively stable characteristic) is long-standing in the psychology of personality (Cattell & Scheier, 1961). Emotional states involve highly variable, situation- and event-dependent feelings (see Shuman & Scherer, 2014; Turner & Trucano, 2014). *Mood* states change less rapidly and may also be less specifically attached to an identifiable cause or referent (cf. Linnenbrink & Pintrich, 2004). Emotional traits refer to how someone typically feels and how his or her feelings characteristically differ from someone else's (e.g., Izard, 1991). The term *local affect* (Goldin, 2000; Gómez-Chacón, 2000) includes state emotions and mood states but also their moment-by-moment interactions with cognition, with the social environment, with the emotions of others, and with the individual's traits. *Global affect* includes trait emotions as well as stable structures that incorporate emotions—not only attitudes, beliefs, and values, but constructs such as mathematical self-identity.

The preponderance of large-scale questionnaire-based research in mathematics education has focused on trait emotions. Some instruments treat such emotions as components of attitudes or orientations (e.g., Fennema & Sherman, 1976); others, like the Math Anxiety Questionnaire (MAQ), address emotions directly (Wigfield & Meece, 1988). Trait-like emotions are not necessarily defined to be as enduring as the term trait might suggest. Thus, when Frenzel et al. (2007) use the AEQ-M to study German high school students' enjoyment, anxiety, anger, and boredom, the contextualized questions might be read to refer to emotions typically felt just that year or that term in connection with school mathematics, and not necessarily longer lasting. The MAQ item, "I dread having to do math," suggests a more permanent domain-specific trait emotion than the AEQ-M item, "I enjoy my math class." Trait emotions can also be assessed through interviews and field observations (cf. Tobias, 1993), although large-scale qualitative studies of trait emotions are more costly and therefore rare. Research goals include measuring correlations (positive or negative) between trait emotions and mathematical engagement, learning, and problem solving success, studying their association with age, gender, or other population characteristics, characterizing the underlying structure of the traits themselves, identifying their origins, and discovering how one may influence them through interventions.

Techniques for the study of state emotions in the mathematics education literature most often feature inference and analysis from close, in-the-moment observation (usually, but not always, qualitative analysis)—for example, videotaped classes or task-based and retrospective interviews, including stimulated recall interviews (e.g., Zan, Brown, Evans, & Hannula, 2006). The researcher seeks to infer, often with considerable uncertainty or unreliability, the shifting emotions such as curiosity, frustration, anger, anxiety, elation, or satisfaction actually felt in particular situations—their origins, functions, and consequences. Experience sampling methods (ESM) have been used less frequently (e.g., Schiefele & Csikszentmihalyi, 1995), but ESM is likely to become more influential as clickers and more sophisticated mobile devices come into use. Employing questionnaire methods to study state emotions in authentic mathematical contexts is more difficult; to ask state-anxiety questions such as "find the word or phrase that best describes how you feel right now, *at this very moment*" (Spielberger, Edwards, Montuori, & Lushene, 1973, emphasis in original) is impractical during engaged activity without disruption. Questionnaires given immediately after activity can provide insight into emotional states, but few such studies have thus far been done in mathematics education. Research goals include understanding and modeling how and why emotions in students or teachers arise, their relation to problem solving, learning, and teaching, and how they influence or are influenced by mathematical motivation, achievement, attitudes, beliefs, or other variables. Recurrent patterns in state emotions invite theoretical characterization, with potential for effective teacher interventions—strategies for turning in-the- moment emotions toward constructive learning goals, even without detailed knowledge of individual students' traits. Parallel comments can be made about mathematics teachers' emotions.

Sometimes these two strands seem to exemplify conflicting research paradigms (see discussion further on). But the research questions asked about emotion are quite parallel, albeit in different time frames and on different levels of situation-specificity. A contention in this chapter is that they can contribute in a mutually consilient way to a unifying theory of mathematical affect.

An interesting question is how to interpret the long-term *recollection* of earlier emotion in mathematics (e.g., Karsenty, 2004). The emotions recalled are, in principle, prior states; the feelings reported during recall are current state emotions. Yet, the possibly selective recall of emotion after a long interval and the incorporation of emotions accompanying such recall into what Karsenty terms "mathematical self-schema," suggests that they also have trait-like aspects.

Affective Architecture

Both state and trait emotions form a part of the architecture of affect. Architecture refers to the universal or near-universal functions of emotion, including structures within which emotions occur in human beings: how emotions are constituted, how they link with cognition, attitudes, beliefs, or values, social interactions, cultural norms and roles, and engagement (cf. Pekrun & Linnenbrink-Garcia, 2012), how they encode information, their communicative function and its relevance to cooperation or competition, and their domain-specificity versus generality (e.g., Goetz, Frenzel, Pekrun, Hall, & Lüdtke, 2007), reciprocal aspects of emotions, the role of meta-affect (see further on), and so forth. The focus here is neither on identifying traits nor describing states but on the nature and mechanisms of the interactions between emotions and mathematical learning, teaching, and problem solving.

Note that the words we use for emotions have different meanings when interpreted as states or traits, or when taken to be descriptive of architecture. "The student is *angry* because he missed solving an algebra problem," describes (partially) his state. "The student is *in an angry mood*," whether triggered by her mathematics test result or for an unidentifiable reason, suggests a state likely to persist. "He has a lot of *anger toward mathematics*," describes (partially) an emotional *trait*; he may not feel angry now, but he will probably continue to have a lot of anger toward mathematics. "He is an *angry person*," suggests a much less domain-specific emotional trait. But to say, "*Anger* [as a human emotion] combines strong disapproval and distress" (paraphrasing Ortony, Clore, & Collins, 1988, pp. 146–149) is to make a theoretical assertion about the nature of anger in general, and its possible place (as a compound, in this description) in the spectrum of human emotion. No person is mentioned, nor is mathematics mentioned, but ways of interpreting a person's anger in mathematical contexts are strongly implied.

Questions posed in mathematics education—for example, how curiosity, bewilderment, frustration, or relief interact with strategic decisions during problem solving (e.g., DeBellis & Goldin, 2006), addressed through qualitative analyses of individual episodes, how achievement emotions such as enjoyment anxiety, anger, or boredom relate to perceptions of mathematics classroom contexts (e.g., Frenzel et al., 2007; Pekrun, 2006), addressed through large-scale studies, or how anxiety, comfort, or satisfaction influence and help sustain a student's or teacher's beliefs about her mathematical ability (e.g., Leder et al., 2002; Philipp, 2007), addressed through surveys or interviews—rest on assumptions or theories about the architecture of affect. Their answers, of course, require empirical research on state and/or trait emotions.

Competing Emphases in Mathematics Education

One of the dichotomies in mathematics education research has been a tension between the focus on obtaining broad, generalizable findings about the occurrence of various emotions and their correlates, with an eye to developing structural models descriptive of populations (but possibly disregarding essential complexities), and the focus on under-standing and influencing the complex, dynamic emotional episodes that occur during learning and problem solving (but possibly disregarding the goal of scientific generaliz-ability). Prior to the late 1980s and early 1990s, most research on mathematical affect centered on the development and measurement of attitudes (e.g., Fennema & Sherman, 1976) and/or math anxiety (e.g., Richardson & Suinn, 1972) and their relation to learn-ing and performance—that is, trait-like emotion. This work goes on, and some findings are summarized below. However, a growing segment of the research community ques-tions the value of such research. For example, Zan et al. (2006, p. 114) remark that the theory underlying it is not only limited but drawn mainly from other disciplines:

> The driving force in much research seemed to be "the statistical methodology rather than the theory" (McLeod, 1987); researchers rarely gave explicit definitions of their construct, often leaving the definition to be inferred from the type of instrument used. This lack of conceptual clarity was related to the borrowing of instruments and constructs from psychology, without specific theoretical elaboration for mathematics education.

McLeod's evident intent, as well as that of Zan et al., is to criticize the questionnaire-based study of attitude and of trait emotions of the kind summarized below for math anxiety. Inspired partly by successes in the cognitive analysis of problem solving (e.g., Schoenfeld, 1985), McLeod had proposed to focus on the qualitative, fine-grained study of affect. His characterization took emotions, attitudes, and beliefs to be in order of increasing temporal stability and linkage with cognition, and decreasing intensity, thus positing a certain architecture of affect—emotions exclusively as states (with trait emo-tions incorporated into attitudes). This encouraged a then-new direction in mathemat-ics education—studying in-the-moment emotion in its own right, distinct from longer term constructs. During the subsequent decades, with few exceptions, there seems to have been quite little interaction between those continuing to study trait emotion, using questionnaires and to a much lesser extent qualitative interviews (e.g., Ho et al., 2000; Jain & Dowson, 2009), and those focusing on the fine-grained analysis of state emotion, using qualitative methods (e.g., Gómez-Chacón, 2000; Hannula, 2002, 2006).

To exemplify the study of a trait emotion, let us focus next on the most well-studied domain of emotion in mathematics education—that of students' math anxiety.

THE STUDY OF A TRAIT-LIKE EMOTION TOWARD MATHEMATICS: ANXIETY

Anxiety is a widespread, negative emotion promoting aversion to mathematics (e.g., Baloğlu & Koçak, 2006; Tobias, 1993) in which gender differences are also found (Devine, Fawcett, Szűcs, & Dowker, 2012). The apparent prevalence of anxiety in relation to mathematics (and/or manifestations such as unease, nervousness, and apprehension, or related emotions such as fear or unhappiness) favors its research study as a trait emotion.

Beasley, Long, and Natali (2001) enumerate various measures of mathematics anxi-ety. The Fennema-Sherman Mathematics Attitude Scale (Fennema & Sherman, 1976) incorporates nine different Likert-type attitude scales hypothesized as important either for all students or for females specifically; the "Mathematics Anxiety Scale" is one. The

Mathematics Anxiety Rating Scale (MARS) takes different forms (Plake & Parker, 1982; Richardson & Suinn, 1972; Suinn, 1988); the original consists of 98 items designed to assess anxiety in situations involving numbers and mathematical problems using a five-point Likert-type scale. The Mathematics Anxiety Scale for Children (MASC) is a shortened version, correlating highly with the MARS, designed for younger children with shorter attention spans (Chiu & Henry, 1990). The Math Anxiety Questionnaire (MAQ) items reported by Wigfield & Meece (1988) include 11 items addressing worry, uneasiness or nervousness, and fear, scored on a seven-point scale. They omit four items that prior factor analysis identified as assessing dislike of mathematics as distinct from anxiety.

A meta-analysis by Hembree (1990) of 151 studies of mathematics anxiety using validated instruments identifies correlating variables, reports population variables exhibiting different levels of mathematics anxiety, considers the relation between mathematics anxiety and performance, and examines the effects of treatments. Higher math anxiety correlates inversely with mathematical performance, variously measured, at all grade levels, with mean correlations of $r = -.36$ ($p < .01$) for males and $r = -.30$ ($p < .01$) for females in grades 5–12. It correlates inversely with the intentions by students in grades 7–12 to take more math ($r = -.35$, $p < .01$ for males, $r = -.25$, $p < .01$ for females). Much greater negative correlations are found between math anxiety and other attitude-related variables, such as enjoyment of math in grades 5–12 (mean $r = -.75$, $p < .01$), self-confidence in math in grades 6–11 ($r = -.82$, $p < .01$, a high negative value derived from 4 studies involving 514 subjects), self-concept in math ($r = -.71$, $p < .01$), and motivation in math ($r = -.64$, $p < .01$).

Correlations of math anxiety with other measures of anxiety are positive at the post-secondary level (where most such studies were conducted): with trait anxiety ($r = .38$, $p < .01$), state anxiety ($r = .42$, $p < .01$), and test anxiety ($r = .52$, $p < .01$). Math anxiety is higher for females than males at all grade levels according to Hembree's analysis, generally increasing from middle school into grades 9–10 and then leveling off. Some interventions (e.g., systematic desensitization, cognitive-behavioral) are highly successful in achieving math anxiety reduction, with significant positive effects on mathematics test performance.

Hembree (1990) believes there is evidence that math anxiety reduces performance, but "no compelling evidence that poor performance causes math anxiety" (p. 44). Comparing math anxiety with (general) test anxiety, he concludes, "only 37 percent of one construct's variance is predictable from the variance of the other. . . . Hence, it seems unlikely that mathematics anxiety is purely restricted to testing. Rather the construct appears to comprise a general fear of contact with mathematics, including classes, homework, and tests" (p. 45).

A subsequent meta-analysis by Ma (1999) addresses the relationship of mathematics anxiety and mathematical achievement in 26 studies of students in grades 5–12, both published and unpublished. Ma (1999) determines that "published studies tended to indicate a significantly weaker relationship than unpublished articles" (p. 531), while:

the common population correlation for the relationship between anxiety toward mathematics and achievement in mathematics was −.27. . . . Results show that [this relationship] is consistent across gender groups (male, female, and mixed), grade-level groups (Grades 4 through 6, Grades 7 through 9, and Grades 10 through 12), ethnic groups (mixed and unmixed), instruments used to measure anxiety (MARS and others), and years of publication. . . . Researchers using standardized achievement tests tended to report a significantly weaker relationship than those using researcher-made achievement tests and mathematics teachers' grades.

(Ma, 1999, p. 531)

Lee (2009) reports the correlations with mathematics scores and conducts factor analyses of the self-constructs of math self-concept, math self-efficacy, and math anxiety based on the 2003 Program for International Student Assessment (PISA) data. Participants included over 250,000 15 year olds from 41 participating countries. Within-country correlations of math anxiety with math scores range from $r = -.51$ (Denmark) to $r = -.12$ (Indonesia), mean correlation $r = -.39$; for comparison, the mean correlation for math self-efficacy is $r = .43$ and for math self-concept $r = .23$; all correlations are significant ($p < .01$). The between-country correlation for math anxiety with math score was large ($r = -.65, p < .001$), greater than that for math self-efficacy ($r = .42, p < .001$), while the between country correlation for math self-concept was negative ($r = -.45, p < .001$). In addition, factor-analytic results seem to well support the hypothesis that math self-concept, math self-efficacy, and math anxiety are separate, empirically distinguishable constructs across and within countries.

Math anxiety as measured may or may not consist of more than one factor. In a cross-national study of 671 sixth-grade students in China, Taiwan, and the United States, the distinction between affective and cognitive dimensions of math anxiety was supported in each of the three populations, with the affective factor negatively related to achievement (Ho et al., 2000). Here the analogy is with test anxiety (see Zeidner, 2014); the affective factor refers to "the emotional component of anxiety, feelings of nervousness, tension, dread, fear, and unpleasant physiological reactions" while the cognitive factor is defined as "the worry component of anxiety, which is often displayed through negative expectations, preoccupation with and self-deprecatory thoughts about an anxiety-causing situation" (Ho et al., 2000, p. 363). Other authors have suggested as many as six factors; for example, Bessant (1995) gives an 80-item version of the MARS to 173 college students and identifies dimensions labeled General Evaluation Anxiety, Everyday Numerical Anxiety, Passive Observation Anxiety, Performance Anxiety, Mathematics Test Anxiety, and Problem-Solving Anxiety. In contrast, Beasley et al. (2001) conclude from their study of 278 sixth-grade children using the MASC that math anxiety may be unidimensional. Devine et al. (2012) use the Abbreviated Math Anxiety Scale (AMAS) (Hopko, Mahadevan, Bare, & Hunt, 2003) to look for gender differences in the relation of math anxiety to mathematical performance in 433 British students in school years seven, eight, and one. Controlling for test anxiety, they find that math anxiety correlates negatively with performance only for girls.

Rayner, Pitsolantis, and Osana (2009) investigate math anxiety in preservice teachers. Administering the Revised Mathematics Anxiety Rating Scale (RMARS, Baloğlu, 2002) to 32 preservice teachers, as well as instruments designed to assess procedural and conceptual knowledge of fractions, they report that increasing math anxiety was associated with decreasing procedural as well as conceptual knowledge. This finding is against a background of earlier research:

where prospective and practicing teachers were requested to identify the source of their mathematics anxiety, none of the participants attributed his mathematics anxiety to difficulties in recalling mathematical procedures during anxiety-evoking situations . . . they reported that instruction that was procedurally focused while at the same time lacking in conceptual support was a salient factor that played a role in the development of their mathematics anxiety (Bowd & Brady, 2003; Brady & Bowd, 2005; Harper & Daane, 1998; Trujillo & Hadfield, 1999; Uusimaki & Nason, 2004; Widmer & Chavez, 1982).

(Rayner, Pitsolantis, & Osana, 2009, p. 63)

Moving beyond the study of correlates of mathematics anxiety, researchers have sought to establish structural or causal models (e.g., Akin & Kurbanoglu, 2011; Ma & Xu, 2004; Meece et al., 1990). Sherman and Wither (2003) report on a longitudinal study by Wither, testing whether math anxiety causes impairment of math achievement (as conjectured by Hembree), or absence of math achievement causes math anxiety, or a third condition is responsible for both. The study applies cross-lagged panel analysis to nine pairs of tests of math achievement and math anxiety, administered to a common group of students from three schools in suburban Adelaide, Australia over five years; 96 of the original 156 students completed all nine test sessions. The hypothesis that math anxiety causes a reduction in math achievement is rejected, while the evidence is insufficient to distinguish between the other two possibilities. Jain & Dowson (2009) consider self-regulation and self-efficacy variables in relation to math anxiety, testing a structural equation model based on questionnaire data from 232 eighth-grade students in India. They conclude:

(a) the survey scales represent substantially good measures of the factors they are intended to measure; (b) gender and age can be accurately modeled as influences on self-regulation, self-efficacy, and mathematics anxiety; and (c) mathematics anxiety can be accurately modeled as an outcome of multidimensional self-regulation mediated by self-efficacy.

(Jain & Dowson, 2009, p. 245)

The last conclusion differs from, but does not necessarily contradict, Lee's (2009) result that self-efficacy and math anxiety are consistently empirically distinguishable. A valuable recent bibliographic source on math anxiety is Devine et al. (2012).

Studies of positive trait emotions toward mathematics, such as enjoyment, are less extensive. The 2003 PISA data include a scale measuring interest and enjoyment; on average, this trait accounts for only 1.5% of the variance in students' mathematics performance (with greater enjoyment associated with better performance scores), although within certain countries the correlation is greater—as much as 15.5% of the variance in Korea and 16.1% in Norway. In Mexico, Indonesia, and Brazil, the reported relationship (albeit small) is in the opposite direction (OECD, 2004). Overall, only about a third of the study participants reported enjoyment of mathematics, while about half reported interest.

Limitations

The accessibility of generalizable results about trait emotions—even when correlations are relatively weak—creates a powerful pull toward theories in which trait emotions play the leading roles. The focus then becomes mainly or exclusively students' *characteristic* responses toward mathematics and how to develop them positively or change them when they are aversive. The example of math anxiety also suggests how a variable defined by a single trait-like emotion comes to subsume related emotional feelings in its definition—nervousness, frustration, worry, and fear tend to become part of the same construct as it is operationalized through different instruments. Certain features of emotional architecture are suppressed by the assumption (and correspondingly, the abundance of apparently supporting data) that emotions can be interpreted independently of many of the specifics of their context, that possibly distinct negative emotions serve equivalent functions, and that the role of a negative trait emotion such as anxiety is mainly to impede mathematical learning or performance (e.g., Maloney & Beilock, 2012). The difficulty in ascertaining whether math anxiety is comprised of one or several factors exemplifies a limitation in trying to understand the psychological makeup of a trait emotion (in individuals) through patterns of questionnaire responses across populations.

When self-reported emotions are surveyed, positive emotions typically correlate with each other, as do negative emotions (e.g., Laurent et al., 1999). It is then overly easy to reify the positive valence of emotion as the construct most worth studying or to use self-reported positive emotions as one's measure of affective engagement in mathematics and negative emotions as one's measure of disaffection (e.g., Skinner, Kindermann, & Furrer, 2009, adapted from Wellborn, 1991). But the amount of variance in important outcome variables for mathematics education that is attributable to trait emotions remains, at best, modest.

THE STUDY OF IN-THE-MOMENT EMOTION TOWARD MATHEMATICS

Following McLeod's call for fine-grained analyses of affect, there ensued much greater attention to the role of emotional complexity in mathematical problem solving, self-regulation, and motivation (e.g., DeBellis & Goldin, 2006; Goldin, 2000; Gómez-Chacón, 2000; Hannula, 2002; Malmivuori, 2006; Op't Eynde et al., 2006, 2007) and the interaction of emotions with beliefs (e.g., Leder et al., 2002; Maasz & Schlöglmann, 2009; Philipp, 2007). Because studies of this nature describe individual episodes of emotion, the findings usually take the form of detailed descriptions, together with suggested theoretical constructs or conjectures about affective architecture important to mathematics education. Most of this work deemphasizes quantitative methods and is based on videotaped observation and open-ended task-based and retrospective interviews. But in describing this trend, let me make my own opinion clear that both qualitative and quantitative methods are appropriate—and, ultimately, necessary—to the domain-specific study of both emotional traits and states. The method should depend on the questions asked, which in turn depend on the theory underlying the research.

Let us consider just a few examples (out of dozens of relevant investigations). Nardi and Steward (2003) describe a one-year study in England of three Year Nine middle-ability classes (in schools labeled N, C, and T). They conduct classroom observations and group student interviews, coding student statements and considering the frequencies with which certain statements occur. They focus on students whose mathematical engagement appears due mainly to obligation or pressure, with little joy, and seek the "sources of this disaffection" (p. 349). Student responses include many descriptions of recent or frequently felt emotions. An example illustrates absence of satisfaction in the disconnection of conceptual from procedural learning in mathematics:

Rosanna (N): . . . Yeah, I don't understand it all, like exactly how it would all like work together. I just . . . I'm just like told that that's how you do it but I don't understand how really you do it. I just do it like that.
Interviewer: Right, so it's not . . . so it's not satisfying for you? [Rosanna says yes] Because of that.
Rosanna (N): So you . . . you . . . you know how to do it because you've been told to do it like that but you don't really understand why it's done like that.

(Nardi & Steward, 2003, p. 357)

Other statements pertain either to trait emotions or to frequently or recently experienced states, for example: "*I hate maths because I'm not very good at it.* Rebecca (N)" (Nardi & Steward, 2003, p. 357), or "*I want to enjoy maths but I can't because it's so boring.* Noel (T)" (p. 351) (emphases in original). Supported by such examples, Nardi and Steward (2003) profile "quiet disaffection" in mathematics as a composite of "Tedium, Isolation, Rote learning (rule and cue following), Elitism and Depersonalisation" (p. 350), to form the acronym TIRED.

Lewis (2012) reports in detail on interview data with "Helen," a college student highly disaffected with mathematics. "Her relationship with maths ebbs and flows in tandem with her confidence . . . there is no sense of agency or internal regulation for her confidence or competence " (Lewis, 2012, p. 117). She describes her feelings as involving (variously) hatred, anger, frustration, humiliation, and boredom associated with low self-efficacy beliefs. Occasional positive emotions are associated with group activity and helping others with the mathematics. Lewis (2012) interprets the case as illustrating "the motivational and emotional complexity of students' relationship to mathematics" (p. 121); he describes aspects of this complexity using "reversal theory" (Apter, 2001), which involves shifts between oppositional pairs of motivational states.

Efforts to connect longer-term traits with emotional responses during problem solving are exemplified by Op't Eynde et al. (2007), who classify students into "types" according to the positivity/negativity of their belief profiles (based on the authors' Mathematics-Related Beliefs Questionnaire). They conclude that task-specific perceptions and emotions (including task attractiveness and anxiety) are closely related to students' beliefs: those with more negative belief profiles generally found tasks less attractive and experienced higher anxiety. They also emphasize the complexity and the context-dependence of affect. They embed self-regulation of emotion in a sociocultural model for mathematical problem solving, where what they term "meta-emotional competencies" are essentially *situated* in classroom contexts: "Students' competence to self-regulate [their] unpleasant emotions in effective ways might be an important determinant of successful mathematical problem solving" (Op't Eynde et al., 2007, p. 199). Malmivuori (2006) also highlights self-regulatory functions of mathematical affect in relation to the social environment.

DeBellis and Goldin (1993, 1997, 1999, 2006) focus on the interaction of emotion with cognition in videotaped mathematical task-based interviews with children in grades four to six, inferring emotion from children's statements, interjections, tone of voice, and also using Izard's (1983) Maximally Discriminative Facial Movement Coding Scheme (MAX). Affective pathways (sequences of emotions interacting with mathematical cognition) are reported; for example, a boy's surprise/enjoyment blend moving to a possible anger/enjoyment blend as he achieves a mathematical insight inconsistent with his prior expectation (1993, pp. 60–61). McCulloch (2011) studies six high school calculus students using graphing calculators. The calculators help maintain productive affective pathways (e.g., frustration shifting to curiosity/comfort and then to contentment) versus unproductive ones (e.g., comfort shifting to curiosity and nervousness, then to discouragement, then helplessness and annoyance, discomfort, and finally embarrassment) only when their use is *instrumentalized* in the sense of Artigue (2002)—that is, they are progressively transformed from artifacts to instruments through a process of "loading" with potentialities.

Walen and Williams (2002) describe in detail situated emotions of two adult women and one grade three child in the context of timed mathematics tests, drawing some implications regarding inequitable access to mathematics due to timed performance. Their subjects display neither math anxiety nor test anxiety as trait emotions, but the time limit situation evokes great fear. The value placed on speed in the social context of school leads the child to an experience of humiliation.

State emotion emerges as very important to other constructs in mathematics education. Heyd-Metzuyanim and Sfard (2012) study a small group in a grade seven class working on an unfamiliar problem involving fractions. They code the participants' utterances, mapping "the moment-by-moment alterations of the emotional hue . . . aiming at capturing a 'flow of emotional expressions' " (2012, p. 133). After the analysis, they conclude, "Above all, we were struck by the amount and emotional intensity of the subjectifying activity that took place in the classroom. As a result, our whole interpretation of what happened changed" (2012, p. 141). They interpret the episode as exemplifying "identity struggles."

Our group at Rutgers studies the mathematical engagement of middle school students during small-group, in-class activity, using pre- and post-interviews with teachers, videotaped class activity and small-group activity, retrospective stimulated-recall interviews with selected students, and the use of questionnaires asking about students' desires, thoughts, actions, and emotional feelings during the just-completed math class (Alston et al., 2007; Epstein et al., 2007; Goldin, Epstein, & Schorr, 2007; Goldin et al., 2011; Schorr et al., 2010a, 2010b). Initially, we sought to create a coherent narrative via analysis through four lenses: the flow of mathematical ideas, key affective events (where strong emotion or change in emotion is expressed or inferred), social interactions among the students, and significant teacher interventions; but despite the use of detailed codings, we came to see these perspectives alone as insufficient to understand what was governing students' engagement or disengagement. In one episode (Epstein et al., 2007), a short boy ["Will"] crumpled and threw away the paper on which he had written his solution to the mathematics problem under discussion, and he shared his ideas only reluctantly:

[Will:] . . . mine could have been wrong, and theirs could have just been right. So, if they had chosen my wrong one, and the right one they tossed it away, they might'd get mad at me. So I just left it like that . . .

[Describing] how he was feeling when he crumpled the paper, he said that his "level of happiness went down."

[Will]: I didn't like, saying anything. [Int]: Why not? [Will]: Because, it might just cause an argument in the first place. [Int]: And how do you feel when there's an argument? [Will]: I don't like arguing with people, because mostly, they become more like a fight.

(Epstein et al., 2007, p. 654)

Based on the qualitative analysis of numerous videotaped episodes, we identify several recurring patterns—"behavioral/affective/social constellations"—of in-the-moment desires, emotions, behaviors, and social interactions, which we term *engagement structures* (Goldin et al., 2011).

In analogy with cognitive structures, engagement structures are situated in the individual and become active in certain social/mathematical situations. Each is comprised of as many as 10 interwoven, mutually interacting strands that characterize it: (a) an immediate goal or motivating desire,(b) a pattern or patterns of behavior toward fulfilling the desire, including social interactions, (c) a sequence of emotional states (affective pathway), (d) expressions of affect by the person, (e) meanings that the emotional feelings encode, (f) meta-affect, (g) self-talk or inner speech, (h) interactions with systems of beliefs and values, (i) interactions with attitudes and other longer term traits, and (j) interactions with problem-solving strategies and heuristics.

Examples of engagement structures (and the corresponding motivating desires, which lend their names to the structures) include: (a) Get The Job Done: the desire is to complete an assigned mathematical task correctly, fulfilling an obligation; (b) Look How Smart I Am: the desire is to impress with one's mathematical ability; (c) Check This Out: the desire is to obtain a payoff, which may be an intrinsic or extrinsic reward (Wigfield & Eccles, 2000; Zimmerman & Schunk, 2008); (d) I'm Really Into This: the desire is to experience the mathematical activity, entering flow (Csikszentmihalyi, 1990); (e) Don't Disrespect Me: the desire is to save face, meeting a challenge or threat to one's status or sense of well-being, as may occur in a highly charged discussion or argument; (f) Stay Out Of Trouble: the desire is to avoid possible conflict, distress, or embarrassment; (g) It's Not Fair: the desire is to correct an inequity; (h) Let Me Teach You: the desire is to assist someone else to understand the mathematics or solve the problem; (i) Pseudo-Engagement: the desire is to look good by appearing engaged, but avoid real participation. Instances of structures' activation are inferred from coded videotapes, while confirmation of motivating desires, behavior, and accompanying emotions comes from retrospective interviews with students and from questionnaire responses.

Limitations

The predominantly qualitative work focusing on state emotions, exemplified in these studies, suggests the desirability of far more complex descriptions of affective architecture in the study of emotion in mathematics education. But that very complexity, a consistent theme, points also to a degree of unpredictability in students' emotions. Some features of the psychological and social contexts influencing the inferred mathematical emotions are likely to be unknown and possibly unknowable. Replication of classroom situations where emotions occur is difficult to achieve and rarely attempted. The question of how reliably one can infer emotions from observations, especially complicated, subtle, or partially suppressed emotions, remains open—even with apparently corroborative questionnaire data and/or retrospective interview data. Findings tend to be anecdotal, so that we do not know how generalizable they may be to other contexts or wider populations, and we cannot easily distinguish any that are spurious.

FUTURE DIRECTIONS: TOWARD THE UNIFICATION OF RESEARCH PERSPECTIVES

Quantitative studies can measure population characteristics and correlations, testing structural relations among trait emotions or between them and other easily quantifiable variables, and investigating whether a mathematical emotion is more often about mathematics or about something else (such as testing). But they leave out or average over the psychosocial contexts for emotions and disregard important possibilities of positive feelings about negative emotions (see further on). Fine-grained qualitative studies point to such complexities, but are small scale and labor intensive with high scale-up costs. Each such study illuminates at best a particular aspect of emotion in a specific mathematical context. And the methods of observation tend to influence researchers' theoretical perspectives profoundly. In my view, models based on still deeper ideas are needed: constructs sufficiently sophisticated to be able to address the domain-specific issues pertinent to mathematics, taking account of complex, situation-dependent interactions, yet at the same time providing a framework for generalizable descriptions of population characteristics, and offering systematic, research-based ways to improve the affective side of mathematics instruction through teachers' professional development.

In the balance of this chapter, I want to highlight four ideas that have been essential to the approach my collaborators and I have taken, which in my view deserve increased attention in mathematics education research: (a) the *representational* function of emotions, (b) emotions as functional components of *affective structures,* (c) the importance of *meta-affect,* and (d) the development of *mathematically powerful* affect. These pertain to both state and trait emotions.

Emotion as Representational

Emotional states continually encode and exchange information with cognitive systems of internal representation (Rogers, 1983; Zajonc, 1980). Emotions also serve *communicative* functions—sharing information and providing feedback among people in social situations. The *semantic content* of emotional feelings is implicit in constructs such as achievement emotions and essential to understanding the role state and trait emotions play in mathematical activity. For instance, during mathematical problem solving, *curiosity* may encode the possibility of new learning, evoking exploratory strategies for overcoming impasse. *Frustration* may serve to encode repeated failure of a strategy; as this emotion reaches a certain threshold strength, it can serve as a cue to the problem solver to try a different approach. The information encoded or exchanged through emotional expression may be about mathematical objects, the people engaged in mathematical discourse, the context of the activity, or where the problem solver stands in relation to expectations. Shared or interacting emotions carry information associated with mathematical cooperation, competition, or group processes during learning and problem solving.

State emotions typically encode complex information regarding the state of the learner or problem solver in relation to the problem environment—how likely one is to be able to learn something new or solve the problem in a reasonable length of time (*confidence, enthusiasm*), how others see the problem solver (*pride, exuberance, bashfulness, shame*), the possibility of failure, including public failure (*apprehension, anxiety*), absence of the possibility of new learning or stimulating experience (*boredom*), the effectiveness of a team effort (*security, satisfaction*), how one measures up to another's success (*jealousy*), and so forth. All of these interpretations are *context-dependent*—an emotion such as satisfaction in different contexts may signify problem solving success, fulfillment of the desire to be acknowledged by others, success in conveying a mathematical concept or problem solution to another student, a sense that hard work has paid off, the failure of someone else who was envied or resented, or having gotten away with pretending to be engaged while doing something else.

Similarly, trait emotions encode longer-term information that is drawn on in mathematical situations. Both state and trait emotions carry complex meanings only minimally captured by their valence. And an emotion's importance is not necessarily proportional to its intensity.

Emotions Within Affective Structures

A promising theoretical direction is the characterization of *affective structures* with which trait emotions are interwoven and with which state emotions interact in characteristic ways. These are components of architecture whose specifics differ from person to person but for which some features are more-or-less invariant. Domain-specific structures involving emotion include mathematical self-concept and identity, mathematical intimacy (a valued, personally vulnerable, emotional relation between an individual and mathematics), mathematical integrity (a psychological posture valuing understanding and honesty in one's relation to mathematics) and their interactions (DeBellis & Goldin, 1997, 1999, 2006), sociocultural norms (Grouws & Lembke, 1996), and systems of beliefs and values in relation to mathematics (Goldin, 2002; Philipp, 2007). Some structures may be fundamentally relational with other people—for example, Hackenberg (2010) provides detailed qualitative analyses of *mathematical caring relations* she establishes with two students. Such structures may be deemed "high level," describing global features of personality or relationship. The engagement structures discussed are termed "mid-level." Their role is analogous to that of cognitive structures, such as proportional reasoning, which influence sequences of problem-solving steps or interactions. Just as describing cognitive structures and schemas has helped us to interpret both students' immediate problem solving and longer term mathematical understanding, characterizing affective structures can help us to interpret both students' state and trait emotions. This research direction suggests ways to address calls for extending the theory of motivation (Middleton & Spanias, 1999) and provides an alternative to considering cognitive, affective, and behavioral engagement as three distinct types of mathematical engagement (cf. Fredricks, Blumenfeld, & Paris, 2004).

Meta-Affect

The concept of *meta-affect*, in analogy with that of metacognition (Flavell, 1976), refers to affect about affect, affect about cognition about affect, and the monitoring and control of affect (DeBellis & Goldin, 1997, 2006; Goldin, 2002; Gómez-Chacón, 2000). With respect to emotions in mathematics education, meta-affect thus includes (context-dependent) competencies pertaining to the control of the person's own emotional feelings, such as ways of coping with negative emotions—that is, what has been termed "meta-mood" and studied in the context of emotional intelligence (e.g., Fitness & Curtis, 2005). The "meta-emotional competencies" described by Op't Eynde et al. (2007) pertain to such self-regulation of emotion.

However, the idea of meta-affect involves far more than self-regulation—it incorporates the idea, familiar from everyday experience, that the experience of an emotion can be wholly transformed by the emotions one has about the emotion. For example, *fear* can be experienced with *elation,* as during a spectacular amusement park ride or a scary movie. *Pain* can be experienced with *joy,* as during strenuous physical activity. On the other hand, *pleasure* can be experienced *painfully, shamefully,* or *guiltily,* if it is undeserved, illicit, or lacks integrity. This kind of meta-affect is not typically voluntary, and as far as I know, has not been systematically investigated in the education literature.

During problem solving, the pivotal emotion of *frustration* may be experienced negatively (with the meta-affect of *apprehension*) when it encodes likely failure; we see this in qualitative studies of state anxiety. However, frustration can also be experienced positively (with the meta-affect of *anticipatory pleasure*) when it encodes the likelihood of the problem being intriguing—the solver, on becoming stuck, responding in effect, "This is a good one, don't tell me, I want to figure it out!" Likewise the *pleasure* of solving a problem correctly using a taught procedure can be experienced with discomfort, frustration, or even guilt when the solver does not understand an underlying concept. There can be many levels—conscious, preconscious, and unconscious—to such meta-affect. A student may describe *test anxiety* as about the immediate fear of failure under pressure. But behind it may lurk *pain,* the *shame* of acknowledging he did not earn the right to be *proud* in the face of expectations of a father whom he *loves.* The student is not consciously experiencing emotions of love or pride or shame in that moment, yet for this student in that context, the anxiety is about all of these other emotions—not simply about the test.

Meta-affect thus plays an essential role in the moment, so that emotions of either valence can be experienced positively or negatively. Both possibilities contribute to encoding strategic information. One may likewise conjecture that negative trait emotions toward mathematics can be experienced positively and contribute positively and vice versa. Such possibilities are typically averaged over, and thus unseen, in correlational studies.

Powerful Mathematical Affect

One explicit goal of research in mathematics education has been to characterize powerful problem-solving heuristics and strategies, insightful methods of visualization, and so forth. We need similarly far more detailed characterizations of *powerful affect* in mathematics—the emotional states and traits, the meta-affect, and the affective structures that enable one to ask questions, take the risk of being wrong, persevere in the face of impasse, create or engage with new representations, bring heuristic processes to bear, or plan anew. We need a new focus on how such powerful affect develops. And just as an explicit goal of research has been to characterize in detail mathematical misconceptions and how they may be corrected, we need a focus on how to intervene to correct disempowering affect—affect that interrupts concentration, enables avoidance, impedes understanding, or prevents its recognition when it occurs.

Feelings of negative valence—impatience, frustration, anxiety, or anger—occur during successful affective pathways, in expert problem solvers as well as students. It is a plausible conjecture that up to a point, negative emotions en route foster greater eventual pride, pleasure, and satisfaction in having attained a concept or solved a problem and that the experience of productive affective pathways in association with conceptually challenging mathematics contributes to the development of powerful global affective structures and trait emotions.

To sum up, there is much potential value in an integrated approach that draws on but distinguishes carefully the different characterizations of emotion and regards both state and trait emotion in the more sophisticated ways suggested here. The most immediate practical consequence, in my opinion, could be improved, research-based professional development of mathematics teachers that addresses the affective domain.

REFERENCES

Akin, A., & Kurbanoglu, I. N. (2011). The relationships between math anxiety, math attitudes, and self-efficacy: A structural equation model. *Studia Psychologia, 53,* 263–273.

Alston, A., Goldin, G. A., Jones, J., McCulloch, A., Rossman, C., & Schmeelk, S. (2007). The complexity of affect in an urban mathematics classroom. In T. Lamberg & L. R. Wiest (Eds.), *Exploring mathematics education in context: Proceedings of the 29th annual meeting of PME-NA, Lake Tahoe, NV* (pp. 326–333). Reno, NV: University of Nevada.

Apter, M. J. (Ed.). (2001) [cited in Lewis (2012)]. *Motivational styles in everyday life: A guide to reversal theory.* Washington, DC: American Psychological Association.

Aronson, J., Lustina, M. J., Good, C., Keough, K., Steele, C. M., & Brown, J. (1999). When white men can't do math: Necessary and sufficient factors in stereotype threat. *Journal of Experimental Social Psychology, 35,* 29–46.

Artigue, M. (2002) [cited in McCulloch (2011)]. Learning mathematics in a CAS environment: The genesis of a reflection about instrumentation and the dialectics between technical and conceptual work. *International Journal of Computers for Mathematical Learning, 7,* 245–274.

Baloğlu, M. (2002) [cited in Rayner et al. (2009)]. Construct and concurrent validity and internal consistency, split-half, and parallel-model reliability of the revised mathematics rating scale. *Dissertation Abstracts International, 63,* 6-B (UMI No. 3058162).

Baloğlu, M., & Koçak, R. (2006).A multivariate investigation of the differences in mathematics anxiety. *Personality and Individual Differences, 40,* 1325–1335.

Beasley, T. M., Long, J. D., & Natali, M. (2001). A confirmatory factor analysis of the mathematics anxiety scale for children. *Measurement and Evaluation in Counseling and Development, 34,* 14–26.

Bessant, K. C. (1995). Factors associated with types of mathematics anxiety in college students. *Journal for Research in Mathematics Education, 26,* 327–345.

Bowd, A.D., & Brady, P. H. (2003) [cited in Rayner et al. (2009)]. Gender differences in mathematics anxiety among preservice teachers and perceptions of their elementary and secondary school experience with mathematics. *Alberta Journal of Educational Research, 49,* 24–36.

Brady, P., & Bowd, A. (2005) [cited in Rayner et al. (2009)]. Mathematics anxiety, prior experience and confidence to teach mathematics among pre-service education students. *Teachers and Teaching: Theory and Practice, 11,* 37–46.

Cattell, R. B., & Scheier, I. H. (1961). *The meaning and measurement of neuroticism and anxiety.* New York, NY: Ronald Press.

Chiu, L. H., & Henry, L. L. (1990). Development and validation of the Mathematics Anxiety Scale for Children. *Measurement and Evaluation in Counseling and Development, 23,* 121–127.

Csikszentmihalyi, M. (1990). *Flow: The psychology of optimal experience.* New York, NY: Harper & Row.

Davis, R. B. (1984*). Learning mathematics: The cognitive science approach to mathematics education.* Norwood, NJ: Ablex.

DeBellis, V. A., & Goldin, G. A. (1993). Analysis of interactions between affect and cognition in elementary school children during problem solving. In J. R. Becker & B. J. Pence (Eds.), *Procs. of the 15th Annual Meeting of*

PME-NA, Vol. 2 (pp. 56–62). San Jose, CA: Center for Mathematics and Computer Science Education, San Jose State University.

DeBellis, V. A. & Goldin, G. A. (1997).The affective domain in mathematical problem solving. In E. Pehkonen (Ed.), *Procs. of the 21*st *Annual Meeting of PME, Vol. 2* (pp. 209–216). Lahti, Finland: Univ. of Helsinki.

DeBellis, V. A., & Goldin, G. A. (1999). Aspects of affect: Mathematical intimacy, mathematical integrity. In O. Zaslavsky (Ed.), *Procs. of the 23*rd *Annual Meeting of PME, Vol. 2* (pp. 249–256). Haifa, Israel: Technion Printing Center.

DeBellis, V. A., & Goldin, G. A. (2006). Affect and meta-affect in mathematical problem solving: A representational perspective. *Educational Studies in Mathematics, 63,* 131–147.

Devine, A., Fawcett, K., Szűcs, D., & Dowker, A. (2012). Gender differences in mathematics anxiety and the relation to mathematics performance while controlling for test anxiety. *Behavioral and Brain Functions, 8,* 33. Retrieved from www.behavioralandbrainfunctions.com/content/8/1/33

D'Mello, S. D., & Graesser, A. C. (2014). Confusion. In R. Pekrun & L. Linnenbrink-Garcia (Eds.), *International handbook of emotions in education* (pp. 289–310). New York, NY: Taylor & Francis.

Dweck, C. S. (2000). *Self-theories: Their role in motivation, personality, and development.* Philadelphia, PA: Taylor & Francis.

Ekman, P. (1992). An argument for basic emotions. *Cognition and Emotion, 6,* 169–20.

Ekman, P., & Friesen, W. V. (2003). *Unmasking the face: A guide to emotions from facial expressions.* Cambridge, MA: Malor Books.

Else-Quest, N. M., Hyde, J. S., & Hejmadi, A. (2008) Mother and child emotions during mathematics homework. *Mathematical Thinking and Learning, 10,* 5–35.

Epstein, Y. M., Schorr, R. Y., Goldin, G. A., Warner, L. B., Arias, C., Sanchez, L., Dunn, M., & Cain, T. R. (2007). Studying the affective/social dimension of an inner-city mathematics class. In T. Lamberg & L. R. Wiest (Eds.), *Exploring mathematics education in context: Proceedings of the 29th annual meeting of PME-NA, Lake Tahoe, NV* (pp. 649–656). Reno, NV: University of Nevada.

Fennema, E., & Sherman, J. A. (1976). Fennema-Sherman mathematics attitude scales: Instruments designed to measure attitudes toward the learning of mathematics by females and males. *Journal for Research in Mathematics Education, 7,* 324–326.

Firestone, W. A., Schorr, R. Y., & Monfils, L. F. (Eds.) (2004). *The ambiguity of teaching to the test.* Mahwah, NJ: Erlbaum.

Fitness, J., & Curtis, M. (2005). Emotional intelligence and the Trait Meta-Mood Scale: Relationships with empathy, attributional complexity, self-control, and responses to interpersonal conflict. *E-Journal of Applied Psychology: Social Section, 1,* 50–62.

Flavell, J. H. (1976). Metacognitive aspects of problem solving. In L. B. Resnick (Ed.), *The nature of intelligence* (pp. 231–236). Hillsdale, NJ: Erlbaum.

Forsyth, D. R. (1986). An attributional analysis of students' reactions to success and failure. In R. S. Feldman (Ed.), *The social psychology of education: Current research and theory* (pp. 17–38). Cambridge, United Kingdom: Cambridge University Press.

Fredricks, J. A., Blumenfeld, P. C., & Paris, A. H. (2004). School engagement: Potential of the concept, state of the evidence. *Review of Educational Research, 74,* 59–109.

Frenzel, A. C., Pekrun, R., & Goetz, T. (2007). Perceived learning environment and students' emotional experiences: A multilevel analysis of mathematics classrooms. *Learning and Instruction, 17,* 478–493.

Goetz, T., Frenzel, A. C., Pekrun, R., Hall, N. C., & Lüdtke, O. (2007). Between- and within-domain relations of students' academic emotions. *Journal of Educational Psychology, 99,* 715–733.

Goldin, G. A. (2000). Affective pathways and representation in mathematical problem solving. *Mathematical Thinking and Learning, 2,* 209–219.

Goldin, G. A. (2002). Affect, meta-affect, and mathematical belief structures. In G. Leder, E. Pehkonen, & G. Törner (Eds.), *Beliefs: A hidden variable in mathematics education?* (pp. 59–72). Dordrecht, Netherlands: Kluwer.

Goldin, G. A., Epstein, Y. M., Schorr, R. Y., & Warner, L. B. (2011). Beliefs and engagement structures: Behind the affective dimension of mathematical learning. *ZDM Mathematics Education, 43,* 547–556.

Goldin, G. A., Rösken, B., & Törner, G. (2009). Beliefs—no longer a hidden variable in mathematics teaching and learning processes. In J. Maasz & W. Schlöglmann (Eds.), *Beliefs and attitudes in mathematics education: New research results* (pp. 1–18). Rotterdam, Netherlands: Sense.

Gómez-Chacón, I. M. (2000). Affective influences in the knowledge of mathematics. *Educational Studies in Mathematics, 43,* 149–168.

Grouws, D. A., & Lembke, L. O. (1996). Influential factors in student motivation to learn mathematics: The teacher and classroom culture. In M. Carr (Ed.), *Motivation in mathematics* (pp. 39–62). Cresskill, NJ: Hampton Press.

Hackenberg, A. J. (2010). Mathematical caring relations in action. *Journal for Research in Mathematics Education, 41,* 236–273.

Handal, B. (2003). Teachers' mathematical beliefs: A review. *The Mathematics Educator, 13,* 47–57.

Hannula, M. S. (2002). Attitude towards mathematics: Emotions, expectations and values. *Educational Studies in Mathematics, 49,* 25–46.

Hannula, M. S. (2006). Motivation in mathematics: Goals reflected in emotions. *Educational Studies in Mathematics, 63,* 165–178.

Harper, N. W., & Daane, C. J. (1998) [cited in Rayner et al. (2009)]. Causes and reduction of math anxiety in pre-service elementary teachers. *Action in Teacher Education, 19,* 29–38.

Hembree, R. (1990). The nature, effects, and relief of mathematics anxiety. *Journal for Research in Mathematics Education, 21,* 33–46.

Heyd-Metzuyanim, E., & Sfard, A. (2012). Identity struggles in the mathematics classroom: On learning mathematics as an interplay of mathematizing and identifying. *International Journal of Educational Research, 51–52,* 128–145.

Ho, H.-Z., Senturk, D., Lam, A. G., Zimmer, J. M., Hong, S., & Okamoto, Y. (2000). The affective and cognitive dimensions of math anxiety: A cross-national study. *Journal for Research in Mathematics Education, 31,* 362–379.

Hopko, D. R., Mahadevan, R., Bare, R. L., & Hunt, M. K. (2003) [cited in Devine et al. (2012)]. The abbreviated math anxiety scale (AMAS): Construction, validity, and reliability. *Assessment, 10,* 178–182.

Izard, C. E. (1983 revised) [cited in DeBellis & Goldin (1993)]. *The maximally discriminative facial movement coding system.* Newark, DE: University of Delaware, Instructional Resources Center.

Izard, C. E. (1991*). The psychology of emotions.* New York, NY: Plenum.

Jain, S., & Dowson, M. (2009).Mathematics anxiety as a function of multidimensional self-regulation and self-efficacy. *Contemporary Educational Psychology, 34,* 240–249.

Karsenty, R. (2004). Mathematical self-schema: A framework for analyzing adults' retrospection on high school mathematics. *Journal of Mathematical Behavior, 23,* 325–349.

Kelly, A. E., & Lesh, R. A. (Eds.). (2000). *Handbook of research design in mathematics and science education.* Mahwah, NJ: Erlbaum.

Laurent, J., Catanzaro, S. J., Joiner, T. E., Jr., Rudolph, K. D., Potter, K. I., & Lambert, S. (1999). A measure of positive and negative affect for children: Scale development and preliminary validation. *Psychological Assessment, 11,* 326–338.

Leder, G. C., Pehkonen, E., & Törner, G. (Eds.). (2002). *Beliefs: A hidden variable in mathematics education?* Dordrecht, Netherlands: Kluwer.

Lee, J. (2009).Universals and specifics of math self-concept, math self-efficacy, and math anxiety across 41 PISA 2003 participating countries. *Learning and Individual Differences, 19,* 355–365.

Lesh, R. A., & Lamon, S. J. (Eds.) (1992). *Assessment of authentic performance in school mathematics.* Washington, DC: American Association for the Advancement of Science.

Lesh, R. A., & Landau, M. (Eds.) (1983). *Acquisition of mathematics concepts and processes.* New York, NY: Academic Press.

Lewis, G. (2011). Mixed methods in studying the voice of disaffection with school mathematics. *Proceedings of the British Society for Research into Learning Mathematics, 31,* 101–106.

Lewis, G. (2012). A portrait of disaffection with school mathematics: The case of Helen. In T. Y. Tso (Ed.), *Proceedings of the 36th conference of the International Group for the Psychology of Mathematics Education* (Vol. 3, pp. 115–122). Taipei, Taiwan: PME.

Linnenbrink, E. A., & Pintrich, P. R. (2004). Role of affect in cognitive processing in academic contexts. In D. Y. Dai & R. J. Sternberg (Eds.), *Motivation, emotion, and cognition: Integrative perspectives on intellectual functioning and development* (pp. 57–87). Mahwah, NJ: Erlbaum.

Ma, X. (1999). A meta-analysis of the relationship between anxiety toward mathematics and achievement in mathematics. *Journal for Research in Mathematics Education, 30,* 520–554.

Ma, X., & Xu, J. (2004). The causal ordering of mathematics anxiety and mathematics achievement: A longitudinal panel analysis. *Journal of Adolescence, 27,* 165–179.

Maasz, J., & Schlöglmann, W. (Eds.). (2009). *Beliefs and attitudes in mathematics education: New research results.* Rotterdam, Netherlands: Sense.

Malmivuori, M.-L. (2006). Affect and self-regulation. *Educational Studies in Mathematics, 63,* 149–164.

Maloney, E. A., & Beilock, S. L. (2012). Math anxiety: Who has it, why it develops, and how to guard against it. *Trends in Cognitive Sciences, 16,* 404–406.

McCulloch, A. W. (2011). Affect and graphing calculator use. *Journal of Mathematical Behavior, 30,* 166–179.

McLeod, D. B. (1987) [cited in Zan et al. (2006)]. A constructivist approach to research on attitude toward mathematics. In J. Bergeron, N. Herscovics, & C. Kieran (Eds.), *Proceedings of the 11th PME, Montreal,* Vol. 1, pp. 133–139. ERIC Clearinghouse (eric.ed.gov), *ED 383 532.*

McLeod, D. B. (1989). Beliefs, attitudes and emotions: New views of affect in mathematics education. In D. McLeod and V. Adams (Eds.), *Affect and mathematical problem solving: A new perspective* (pp. 245–258). New York, NY: Springer.

McLeod, D. B. (1992). Research on affect in mathematics education: A reconceptualization. In D. Grouws (Ed.), *Handbook of research on mathematics teaching and learning: A project of the National Council of Teachers of Mathematics* (pp. 575–596). New York, NY: Macmillan.

McLeod, D. B. (1994). Research on affect and mathematics learning. *Journal for Research in Mathematics Education, 25,* 637–647.

Meece, J. L., Wigfield, A., & Eccles, J. (1990). Predictors of math anxiety and its influence on young adolescents' course enrollment intentions and performance in mathematics. *Journal of Educational Psychology, 82,* 60–67.

Middleton, J. A., & Spanias, P. A. (1999). Motivation for achievement in mathematics: Findings, generalizations, and criticisms of the research. *Journal for Research in Mathematics Education, 30*(1), 65–88.

Mora, R. (2011). "School is so boring": High-stakes testing and boredom at an urban middle school. *Penn GSE Perspectives on Urban Education, 9*(1), www.urbanedjournal.org

Mullis, I.V.S., Martin, M. O., & Foy, P. (with Olson, J. F., Preuschoff, C., Erberber, E., Arora, A., & Galia, J.) (2008). *TIMMS (Trends in International Mathematics and Science Study) 2007 International Mathematics Report,* Chapter 4. Chestnut Hill, MA: TIMMS & PIRLS International Study Center, Boston College.

Nardi, E., & Steward, S. (2003). Is mathematics T.I.R.E.D.? A profile of quiet disaffection in the secondary mathematics classroom. *British Educational Research Journal, 29,* 345–367.

OECD [Organization for Economic Co-operation and Development] (2004). Student learning: Attitudes, Engagement, and Strategies. In *Learning for Tomorrow's World – First Results from PISA 2003* (pp. 109–158). Retrieved from www.oecd.org/edu/school/programmeforinternationalstudentassessmentpisa/learningfortomorrowsworldfirstresultsfrompisa2003.htm

Op't Eynde, P., De Corte, E., & Verschaffel, L. (2006). Accepting emotional complexity: A socioconstructivist perspective on the role of emotions in the mathematics classroom. *Educational Studies in Mathematics, 63,* 193–207.

Op't Eynde, P., De Corte, E., & Verschaffel, L. (2007). Students' emotions: A key component of self-regulated learning? In P. Schutz & R. Pekrun (Eds.), *Emotion in education* (pp. 185–204). Burlington, MA: Academic Press.

Op 't Eynde, P., & Hannula, M. S. (2006). The case study of Frank. *Educational Studies in Mathematics, 63,* 123–129.

Ortony, A., Clore, G. L., & Collins, A. (1988). *The cognitive structure of emotions.* Cambridge, United Kingdom: Cambridge University Press.

Pekrun, R. (2006). The control-value theory of achievement emotions: Assumptions, corollaries, and implications for educational research and practice. *Educational Psychology Review, 18,* 315–341.

Pekrun, R., Goetz, T., Frenzel, A. C., Barchfeld, P., & Perry, R. P. (2011). Measuring emotions in students' learning and performance: The Achievement Emotions Questionnaire (AEQ). *Contemporary Educational Psychology, 36,* 36–48.

Pekrun, R., & Linnenbrink-Garcia, L. (2012). Academic emotions and student engagement. In S. L. Christenson, A. L. Reschly, & C. Wylie (Eds.), *Handbook of research on student engagement* (pp. 259–282). New York, NY: Springer. doi: 1.1007/978–1–4614–2018–7_12

Philipp, R. A. (2007). Mathematics teachers' beliefs and affect. In F. K. Lester (Ed.), *Second handbook of research on mathematics teaching and learning* (pp. 257–318). Charlotte, NC: Information Age Publishing.

Plake, B. S., & Parker, C. S. (1982). The development and validation of a revised version of the Mathematics Anxiety Rating Scale. *Educational and Psychological Measurement, 42,* 551–557.

Rayner, V., Pitsolantis, N., & Osana, H. (2009). Mathematics anxiety in preservice teachers: Its relationship to their conceptual and procedural knowledge of fractions. *Mathematics Education Research Journal, 21,* 60–85.

Richardson, F. C., & Suinn, R. M. (1972). The Mathematics Anxiety Rating Scale: Psychometric data. *Journal of Counseling Psychology, 19,* 551–554.

Rogers, T. B. (1983). Emotion, imagery, and verbal codes: A closer look at an increasingly complex interaction. In J. Yuille (Ed.), *Imagery, memory. and cognition: Essays in honor of Alan Paivio* (pp. 285–305). Hillsdale, NJ: Erlbaum.

Schiefele, U., & Csikszentmihalyi, M. (1995). Motivation and ability as factors in mathematics experience and achievement. *Journal for Research in Mathematics Education, 26,* 163–181.

Schoenfeld, A. H. (1985). *Mathematical problem solving.* New York, NY: Academic Press.

Schorr, R. Y., Epstein, Y. M., Warner, L. B., & Arias, C. C. (2010a). Don't disrespect me: Affect in an urban math class. In R. Lesh, P. L. Galbraith, C. R. Haines, & A. Hurford (Eds.), *Modeling students' mathematical modeling competencies: ICTMA 13* (pp. 313–325). New York, NY: Springer.

Schorr, R. Y., Epstein, Y. M., Warner, L. B., & Arias, C. C. (2010b). Mathematical truth and social consequences: The intersection of affect and cognition in a middle school classroom. *Mediterranean Journal for Research in Mathematics Education, 9,* 107–134.

Schorr, R. Y., & Goldin, G. A. (2008). Students' expression of affect in an inner-city Simcalc classroom. *Educational Studies in Mathematics, 68,* 131–148.

Sherman, B. F., & Wither, D. P. (2003). Mathematics anxiety and mathematics achievement. *Mathematics Education Research Journal, 15,* 138–15.

Shuman, V., & Scherer, K. R. (2014). Concepts and structures of emotions. In R. Pekrun & L. Linnenbrink-Garcia (Eds.), *International handbook of emotions in education* (pp. 13–35). New York, NY: Taylor & Francis.

Skemp, R. R. (1976). Relational understanding and instrumental understanding. *Mathematics Teaching, 77,* 20–26.

Skinner, E., Kindermann, T., & Furrer, C. (2009). A motivational perspective on engagement and disaffection: Conceptualization and assessment of children's behavioral and emotional participation in academic activities in the classroom. *Educational and Psychological Measurement, 69,* 493–525.

Smith, J. P. III. (1996). Efficacy and teaching mathematics by telling: A challenge for reform. *Journal for Research in Mathematics Education, 27,* 387–402.

Spielberger, C. D., Edwards, C. D., Montuori, J., & Lushene, R. (1973). *State-trait anxiety inventory for children.* Palo Alto, CA: Mind Garden.

Sriraman, B., & English, L. (Eds.) (2010), *Theories of mathematics education: Seeking new frontiers.* New York, NY: Springer.

Steele, C. M., & Aronson, J. (1995). Stereotype threat and the intellectual test performance of African Americans. *Journal of Personality and Social Psychology, 69,* 797–811.

Steffe, L., Nesher, P., Cobb, P., Goldin, G. A., & Greer, B. (Eds.) (1996). *Theories of mathematical learning.* Hillsdale, NJ: Erlbaum.

Suinn, R. M. (1988) [cited in Beasley et al. (2001)]. *Mathematics Anxiety Rating Scale—E (MARS-E).* Fort Collins, CO: Rocky Mountain Behavioral Science Institute.

Tobias, S. (1993). *Overcoming math anxiety.* New York, NY: W. W. Norton & Company.

Trujillo, K. M., & Hadfield, O. D. (1999) [cited in Rayner et al. (2009)]. Tracing the roots of mathematics anxiety through in-depth interviews with preservice teachers. *College Student Journal, 33,* 219–232.

Uusimaki, L., & Nason, R. (2004) [cited in Rayner et al. (2009)]. Causes underlying pre-service teachers' negative beliefs and anxieties about mathematics. In M. J. Høines & A. B. Fuglestad (Eds.), *Proceedings of the 28th conference of the International Group for the Psychology of Mathematics Education* (Vol. 4, pp. 369–376). Bergen, Norway: Bergen University.

Walen, S. B., & Williams, S. R. (2002). A matter of time: Emotional responses to timed mathematics tests. *Educational Studies in Mathematics, 49,* 361–378.

Wellborn, J. G. (1991) [cited in Skinner et al. (2009)]. *Engaged and disaffected action: The conceptualization and measurement of motivation in the academic domain.* Unpublished doctoral dissertation, University of Rochester, NY.

Widmer, C. C., & Chavez, A. (1982) [cited in Rayner et al. (2009)]. Math anxiety and elementary school teachers. *Education, 102,* 272–276.

Wigfield, A., & Eccles, J. S. (2000). Expectancy-value theory of achievement motivation. *Contemporary Educational Psychology, 25,* 68–81.

Wigfield, A., & Meece, J. L. (1988). Math anxiety in elementary and secondary school students. *Journal of Educational Psychology, 80,* 210–216.

Zajonc, R. B. (1980). Feeling and thinking: Preferences need no inferences. *American Psychologist, 35,* 151–175.

Zan, R., Brown, L., Evans, J., & Hannula, M. S. (2006). Affect in mathematics education: An introduction. *Educational Studies in Mathematics, 63,* 113–121.

Zeidner, M. (2014). Anxiety in education. In R. Pekrun & L. Linnenbrink-Garcia (Eds.), *International handbook of emotions in education* (pp. 265–288). New York, NY: Taylor & Francis.

Zimmerman, B. J., & Schunk, D. H. (2008). Motivation: An essential dimension of self-regulated learning. In D. H. Schunk & B. J. Zimmerman (Eds.), *Motivation and self-regulated learning: Theory, research, and applications* (pp. 1–30). New York, NY: Routledge.

21

EMOTIONS IN SCIENCE EDUCATION

Gale M. Sinatra, Suzanne H. Broughton, and Doug Lombardi,
University of Southern California, Utah State University,
and Temple University

Science is often mischaracterized as a dispassionate discipline. So much so that scientists who exhibit passion about their work are portrayed in popular culture as evil, unethical, villainous, or worse, "mad." Science is often introduced to students as a rational, cold, methodical, and solitary process, where only observations and data have an impact on the findings and conclusions scientists draw. The image of the lone scientist toiling away in a laboratory with mysteriously bubbling beakers in the background may align with some students' attitudes and views about science.

However, the idea of science as a dispassionate and emotionless pursuit is belied by the fact that science is a human endeavor. Like all human endeavors, science is conducted and learned with the full range of emotions present in all human pursuits, including joy, wonder, amazement, surprise as well as anxiety, anger, fear, and hopelessness. These emotions are as present in the science classroom as they are in all learning environments. But are they important? Do they matter?

Research has shown that emotions are not only present in the classroom but that they have a significant impact on learning outcomes (Pekrun & Stephens, 2012). Moreover, emotions have been shown to be discipline specific (Goetz, Frenzel, Pekrun, & Hall, 2006), suggesting they must be explored and examined in each domain, including science.

At a moment in time when we are confronted with such complex and dynamic challenges as the threat of climate change, demands for sustainable energy, and global pandemics, measures of science achievement show U.S. students lagging behind their peers in European and Asian countries (National Center for Education Statistics, 2007). Moreover, the pipeline demands for new scientists to enter the workforce are not being met (National Center for Education Statistics, 2009). It is important to explore all avenues that influence learning and achievement in science, including those that may widen the pipeline by making science more attractive to more students, particularly women and

415

minorities who have been traditionally underrepresented in science careers. In order to broaden participation in science, we must capitalize on student emotions that are adaptive for science learning and those that promote sustained interest and pursuit of science careers. We must also understand what emotions serve as barriers to learning about science and may discourage engagement in the scientific enterprise and science careers. It is also important to consider which emotions are present in formal and informal science learning environments and what impact these constructs have on science learners and teachers.

To consider these issues, we first turn to how researchers have described emotions and attitudes when learning science. Because students often come to the science classroom with ideas that conflict with those they are learning, we then turn to how emotions impact conceptual change, a key construct in science learning. Next, we provide a brief review of relevant empirical studies on emotions in science learning, including research on anxiety, enjoyment, and interest. We also examine how emotions play out when learning about specific science topics. This is followed by an examination of methodological issues in research and then implications for instruction. We conclude with a discussion of next steps in this area of research.

CONCEPTUAL ISSUES: EMOTIONS AND ATTITUDES DURING SCIENCE LEARNING

Emotions and Science Learning

Emotions are powerful influences on cognitive processes and how individuals interpret events (Damasio, 1994; Lazarus, 1984). The definition of emotions is not consistent throughout the research literature (Linnenbrink, 2006); however, emotions are commonly viewed as affective responses occurring in relation to a specific referent that are quick, automatic, and often occurring unconsciously (Rosenberg, 1998). Pekrun (2006) proposes a more complex definition of emotions, describing them as "multi-component, coordinated processes of psychological subsystems including affective, cognitive, motivational, expressive, and peripheral physiological processes" (p. 316). We view emotions as mediating the science learning experience, through their impact on cognitive processing, motivation, engagement, and learning outcomes.

Emotions in the science classroom can be examined by considering the type of emotion (such as confusion) and how these emotions play out when learning in a particular class or domain of study (such as Earth science class or biology class). However, given the controversial nature of specific science topics within domains of scientific study (i.e., human evolution within biology or human-induced climate change within Earth science) it may be particularly important to consider emotions triggered by the study of specific topics, or *topic emotions*. Topic emotions are those that are experienced by students in relation to a specific topic within a domain of study (Broughton, Sinatra, & Nussbaum, 2013; Pekrun & Stephens, 2012). Topic emotions are a subtype of academic emotions (emotions experienced during learning and test taking) that are characterized by the object of focus that sparked the emotion.

Academic emotions are those emotions that pertain to classroom learning contexts, such as studying for an exam or receiving instruction from a teacher (i.e., whether they enjoy listening to the lecture) (Pekrun, Goetz, Titz, & Perry, 2002) and may be experienced in different types. For example, in science classrooms, a type of academic emotions, topic emotions, can include anger, frustration, and fear when learning about genetically modified foods (Broughton & Nadelson, 2012) or sadness and anger when learning about Pluto's reclassification to a dwarf planet (Broughton et al., 2013). Topic emotions might differ from other forms of academic emotions that students' experience within the same learning environment. Just as a student may have positive emotions about a class, but negative emotions around the assessments in that class, topic emotions may differ from the overarching emotions students typically experience when learning about a domain. In other words, a student could have positive academic emotions about biology class but negative topic emotions when the discussion turns towards evolution.

Topic emotions can be epistemic in nature. Epistemic emotions are those triggered by the characteristics of the to-be-learned information as well as the processing of that information (Pekrun & Linnenbrink-Garcia, 2012). Curiosity, interest, and frustration are examples of epistemic emotions that students may experience in science classrooms in relation to learning particular science topics. For example, students reported experiencing curiosity and interest in relatively high levels when thinking about genetically modified foods and climate change (Broughton, Pekrun, & Sinatra, 2012) and frustration in relation to the scientists' decision to reclassify Pluto to a dwarf planet (Broughton et al., 2013). Research on this more fine-grained aspect of emotions is relatively new, and further investigations are needed to explore how topic emotions may influence students' willingness to engage, interest in the topic, goals for learning more or resisting learning about the topic, and learning outcomes.

It is important to distinguish topic emotions so they may be measured apart from other types of academic emotions as they may provide a unique contribution to understanding the learning environment. For example, a high school student may enjoy Earth science class (class-related emotion), is interested and engaged in an inquiry activity using ice core data to examine paleoclimatic relationships between atmospheric carbon concentrations and temperatures (epistemic emotion), but when the discussion turns to the topic of human induced climate change, the student may become angry, frustrated, anxious, or fearful (topic emotions). Each of these emotion types (class-related, epistemic, and topic) may differentially contribute to cognitive processes during learning. Without directing our attention to topic emotions, we could very well overlook the negative emotions or misunderstand the origin of these emotions and their impact on learning.

Cognitive Engagement and Science Learning

Cognitive engagement serves as a mediator between emotions and academic achievement (Linnenbrink & Pintrich, 2004; Pekrun, 2006; Pekrun & Linnenbrink-Garcia, 2012). There are multiple perspectives on how to characterize cognitive engagement. Some have described cognitive engagement as willingness to engage in effortful tasks, purposiveness, strategy use, and self-regulation (Fredricks, 2011). Others have described it as "the quality of one's thinking in terms of cognitive strategies (e.g., elaboration, rehearsal), metacognitive strategy use, and self-regulated learning" (Linnenbrink, 2007, p. 113). Some researchers posit a continuum ranging from "low cognitive engagement to high metacognitive engagement" (Dole & Sinatra, 1998, p. 121). According to this view, high engagement is associated with deep, systematic, and intentional processing of information and increased opportunities for learning and conceptual change to occur (Sinatra & Pintrich, 2003; Sinatra & Taasoobshirazi, 2011). Low engagement may result in superficial processing, little or no reflection, and decreased opportunities for learning or conceptual change.

The relationship between emotions and cognitive engagement is described in the Control-Value Theory of Achievement Emotions (Pekrun, 2006; Pekrun et al., 2002). According to this theory, academic emotions can be described using two dimensions: valence (positive/negative) and activation (activating/deactivating). Activation refers to arousal, energy, and mobilization (Linnenbrink, 2007). Positive activating emotions include enjoyment and hope, whereas negative activating emotions include anger, anxiety, and shame. Boredom and hopelessness are considered to be negative deactivating emotions.

According to Pekrun (2006), positive activating emotions are associated with positive learning outcomes. Positive activating emotions (e.g., enjoyment) can promote elaboration, metacognitive strategy use, critical thinking, and likely facilitate positive overall achievement (Pekrun & Linnenbrink-Garcia, 2012). These higher level cognitive processes are likely to result in positive learning outcomes when studying science topics, especially topics that are viewed as controversial. Negative activating emotions (e.g., anxiety) can strengthen extrinsic motivation when overall learning expectancies are positive (Pekrun et al., 2002). Students who feel anxiety or shame may experience increased motivation to carefully process the information associated with a learning task in order to succeed. However, negative activating emotions can also foster off-task thinking and decreased motivation. Similarly, negative and positive deactivating emotions (e.g., boredom, relief) may diminish motivation and lead to superficial cognitive processing and lower achievement outcomes (Pekrun & Linnenbrink-Garcia, 2012).

Attitudes and Science Learning

Attitudes are distinct from emotions in that attitudes are described as general evaluations of entities (e.g., objects, people, ideas, processes) consisting of cognitive beliefs, affect, and behavior (Eagly & Chaiken, 1993; Hynd, 2003; Petty & Cacioppo, 1986). For example, a student may have both positive attitudes about learning (a process) and climate change (also a process). When learning about climate change, the student may experience positive emotions in relation to that topic as well as in relation to the learning activity. The behavior component of the positive attitude may, in turn, lead to deeper engagement while studying climate change.

It is important to differentiate between *attitudes towards science* and *scientific attitudes*. *Scientific attitudes* develop as a consequence of working in science and are rooted in beliefs about the nature of science, including the central tenant of empirical evidence as the bases of scientific knowledge (Tytler & Osborne, 2012). In contrast, *attitude toward science* is a complex construct that includes concepts such as enjoyment towards learning science, interest in science and science activities, and positive attitudes towards scientists. The classroom learning environment, the teacher's character, and whether the content is perceived as personally relevant to the student, affects students' attitudes toward school science (Osborne & Collins, 2001). Designing learning activities that foster positive attitudes towards science is important because students' attitudes toward science have been shown to correlate with enrollment in advanced science courses and science achievement (Lee & Burkam, 1996) and are likely to influence whether they will pursue careers in science-related fields (Baker & Leary, 1995; Jones, Howe, & Rua, 2000).

A challenge related to students' attitudes toward science and potential choice of science related careers is that students' positive attitudes can decline over time as they advance through elementary and secondary school as they often do for school subjects other than science (Murphy & Beggs, 2003; Sullins, Hernandez, Fuller, & Tashiro, 1995; Tytler & Osborne, 2012). This trend of decreased student interest in learning science is often associated with their perceptions of school science as being predominantly delivered through lectures and demonstrations, lacking authentic purpose or challenge, and repetition of content in elementary, middle and high school courses (Lyons, 2006; Osborne & Collins, 2001; Raved & Assaraf, 2011). Although much of the research suggests that K–12 students commonly hold unfavorable attitudes towards science, there exists a large population of students who hold favorable attitudes towards school science. Tytler and Osborne (2012) reported that students' attitudes toward their experiences in school science courses were predominantly favorable and that students often preferred biology courses to chemistry or physics courses.

Students' attitudes toward school science also show distinct gender differences with males typically holding more positive attitudes towards engaging in science learning activities than females (Brotman & Moore, 2008; Raved & Assaraf, 2011). However, much of that difference may actually be only in the physical sciences and engineering (Tytler & Osborne, 2012). Furthermore, the recent appreciable reduction in the gap between women and men in medical, biological, and social science careers suggests a relatively strong interest in the life sciences among females (Eccles, 2011a). Jones and colleagues (2000) found that sixth-grade boys had more experiences with physical science than sixth-grade girls, which in turn, likely increased the boys' interest and positive attitudes towards school science. Jones et al. (2000) suggested that providing girls with frequent and early experiences with physical science might increase their attitudes towards and enjoyment of school science as they progress through secondary school.

Similarly, Chen and Howard (2010) identified a gender gap between tenth-grade males' and females' attitudes toward science. Students in the Chen and Howard study participated in inquiry-based science activities in which they were asked to access and interpret satellite data collected during a volcanic eruption on a Caribbean island. The findings showed that after engaging in the learning activities, males held significantly more positive attitudes towards science than females and showed higher interest in pursuing science related careers than their female counterparts.

A wide body of literature has investigated the effects of attitudes and interest on learning in science (for a recent review of research about attitudes toward science see, Tytler & Osborne, 2012; also see Krapp & Prenzel, 2011, for a recent review of research on interest in science). Much of the work on attitudes—as exemplified by the research we have discussed above—has been of a descriptive nature (e.g., looking at trends in attitudes over time, examining differences in attitudes among subgroups students), with less research about the influence of attitudes on science learning, and also, how instruction can promote positive attitudes toward school science. Recent research on socioscientific issues has revealed that instruction can impact students' attitudes toward science (Lee & Erdogan, 2007; Yager, Lim, & Yager, 2006), but the research in promoting

positive attitudes is limited, perhaps due to the relatively long duration needed in changing attitudes toward science (e.g., Gibson & Chase, 2002). Another reason for the lack
of findings in science attitude instruction may be the conflation of attitudes and interest
that is common in the literature. As we have discussed earlier, we view attitudes and
interest as distinct constructs, with attitudes related to individuals' cognitive, affective,
and behavioral "evaluation viewpoints . . . toward a particular" entity (e.g., science) and
interest related to individuals' more "subjective value[s] attached to the knowledge about
this" entity (Krapp & Prenzel, 2011, p. 31). Whereas interest may be sparked in a particular topic of science and result in deeper learning (Maltese & Tai, 2010), promoting a positive attitude about science may require a sustained instructional setting that is relevant
to students' daily lives and experiences (Zacharia & Calabrese Barton, 2004). Moreover,
outside of attitudes and interest, there is a lack of research investigating the broad array
of emotions that may impact science learning.

ROLE OF EMOTIONS IN CONCEPTUAL CHANGE LEARNING

The role of emotions in science learning is most evident when students are confronted
with scientific ideas that conflict with their own. The restructuring of students' previously
formed misconceptions to align with the scientific point of view has been described as
conceptual change (Dole & Sinatra, 1998; Duit, 1999; Posner, Strike, Hewson, & Gertzog,
1982; Vosniadou, 1999). Conceptual change researchers propose that personal characteristics of the learner, including affective responses to a message, influence the change
process (Dole & Sinatra, 1998; Gregoire, 2003).

Researchers have traditionally described mechanisms for conceptual change through
Piaget's notions of assimilation and accommodation. For example, Linnenbrink and Pintrich (2004) explain that assimilation processes rely on prior knowledge structures to
understand new information. In contrast, accommodation is the process of restructuring
prior knowledge by focusing more attention on the new, incoming information. Conceptual change is similar to accommodation because each involves the restructuring of the
learner's prior knowledge to align with the accepted scientific viewpoint (Vosniadou &
Brewer, 1987).

Research on how emotions may play a factor in conceptual change is relatively new.
However, social psychologists have theorized models of how emotions may influence the
mechanisms of assimilation and accommodation. In the following section, we describe
Fiedler's dual-process model (2000) as it provides a framework for possible connections
between emotions and conceptual change learning.

Positive and Negative Emotions: Which Facilitate Change?

Fiedler's dual-process model (2000) draws upon processes of assimilation and accommodation for describing how emotions may influence learning. The central assumption
of the dual-process model is that negative moods are associated with accommodation,
which facilitates deeper processing of specific message details. Negative moods may signal to the learner that modifying current knowledge structures is not progressing correctly and that the individual may need to attend more closely to the information in
order to change existing schemes appropriately. According to Fiedler, negative moods
generally lead to careful, detail-oriented processing. In relation to conceptual change

processes, negative moods (i.e., frustration, confusion) may signal to the learner that his or her prior knowledge contrasts with the new information and thus lead to more careful weighing of the two conflicting explanations.

Alternatively, Fiedler (2000) suggests that positive moods are associated with assimilation and the reliance on general knowledge structures to process information. Positive moods signal that learning is proceeding well and that prior knowledge is appropriate for the task. In such instances, the learner will likely use prior knowledge, which can include misconceptions, to integrate new information with that prior knowledge. This can result in the formation of new iterations of the misconception rather than restructuring of knowledge necessary for conceptual change (see Vosniadou & Brewer, 1987). In sum, the dual-process models suggest that negative moods are beneficial for accommodation tasks, such as those involved with conceptual change learning. To date, this hypothesis has yet to find empirical support in the conceptual change literature. In fact, several studies have shown that negative emotions are associated with a lack of conceptual change, whereas positive emotions are either related to conceptual change or show no association (Broughton et al., 2013; Heddy & Sinatra, 2013; Linnenbrink & Pintrich, 2002; Lombardi & Sinatra, 2013). Several of these studies are reviewed in the "Topic Emotions and Conceptual Change" section further on.

Consistent with this dual-process perspective, the Cognitive-Affective Model of Conceptual Change (CAMCC; Gregoire, 2003) describes how mood may impact the change process. Gregoire explains that moods determine the type of processing an individual will direct towards a message, and that "positive moods are more likely to result in heuristic processing and negative moods in systematic processing" (2003, p. 166). Consistent with Fiedler's view, Gregoire suggests that positive or neutral moods will lead to superficial (or heuristic) cognitive processing of the message and that such processing is insufficient to bring about change, whereas negative moods promote the kind of deeper, systematic cognitive processing of the message required for conceptual change. Gregoire does caution, however, that negative emotions, such as anxiety and fear, if not tempered by positive beliefs about ability and efficacy for success, can lead to avoidance, minimal processing, and no change.

A different perspective comes from Bless (2000). According to this view, positive emotional responses such as enjoyment and curiosity may serve to promote deeper engagement if the individual notices a discrepancy between their prior knowledge and the scientific explanation. Bless (2000) suggests that learners in positive moods use less complex processing strategies until they notice the conflict between their current knowledge and the scientific viewpoint. Once that contrast is noticed, the learner is more likely to engage in deeper, critical processing. Alternatively, negative emotions, such as frustration or anger, may lead the individual to perceive the incoming scientific information as a threat, which may foster attitudes of resistance towards learning (Gregoire, 2003; Linnenbrink & Pintrich, 2002).

Linnenbrink and Pintrich (2002) also describe positive moods as being beneficial for conceptual change learning. They explain that students who are in a good mood may be willing to engage with anomalous information, be more open to new ideas, and not be threatened by information that conflicts with their prior knowledge. Alternatively, students who experience negative feelings, including anxiety or sadness, may be less likely to carefully consider the new information because it is perceived as a threat. Students in negative moods may also disregard the new information altogether because it contradicts with their prior knowledge. This perspective has so far been supported by the empirical studies to date relating emotions to the likelihood of conceptual change (Broughton et al., 2013; Heddy & Sinatra, 2013; Linnenbrink & Pintrich, 2002; Lombardi & Sinatra, 2013).

In contrast to these views, the Cognitive Reconstruction of Knowledge Model (CRKM) (Dole & Sinatra, 1998) proposes that change is determined by the strength (not the valence) of the learner's emotions. According to the CRKM, the learner is less likely to experience conceptual change when they have a strong commitment to their prior beliefs. Often, these commitments have a positive or negative emotional component. As an example, individuals may have a strong positive emotional commitment to a political candidate they favor, even if they are misinformed about one of the candidates' key political positions. If confronted with this misconception, the individual may reject the new information about the candidate's actual position because of their strong emotional commitment to the candidate. Or an individual may be angry about stem cell research and be committed to the prior misconception that all stem cells are embryonic. In this way, strong emotions (either positive or negative) may act to increase resistance to changing ideas about a nonembryonic stem cell's utility in medical treatment.

EMPIRICAL STUDIES OF EMOTIONS AND SCIENCE LEARNING

Empirical work in the full range of academic emotions and science learning is just emerging. However, there is relevant and informative research on anxiety and science learning, as well as enjoyment and interest experienced in the science classroom. We begin this section with a discussion of empirical work in the area of anxiety, enjoyment, and interest in science and then move to a review of empirical work in the emerging area of topic emotions, or emotions elicited by specific science topics (stem cell research, biological evolution, climate change).

Anxiety About Science

Science anxiety was first described by Mallow (1978) as a fearful emotional state about science in general, which results in poor performance in science courses, antiscientific attitudes, scientific illiteracy, and avoidance of careers in science. Mallow and colleagues have conducted an appreciable amount of research since the late 1970s (see, e.g., Mallow & Greenburg, 1982; Mallow et al., 2010) revealing that science anxiety is disproportionality greater among women. Furthermore, undergraduate education majors (who are predominately female) expressed some of the highest levels of science anxiety compared to several other categories of nonscience majors (e.g., business, nursing, and humanities; see Udo, Ramsey, Reynolds-Alpert, & Mallow, 2004). This finding was of particular concern because many of these teachers who are science anxious would be responsible for their future students' science learning.

Individuals may also feel anxiety about particular domains of science. For example, Eddy (2000) coined the term "Chemophobia" to represent students' anxiety about chemistry classes, above and beyond their general anxiousness (trait anxiety) and anxiety towards mathematics (mathematics anxiety). Eddy found a weak correlation between trait and chemistry anxieties but a moderate correlation between mathematics and chemistry anxiety. In-depth interviews revealed that students were also anxious about demonstrating adequate chemistry laboratory skills, as well as anxious about potential harmful effects of laboratory chemicals.

Similar to chemistry, anxiety about physics may be strongly related to mathematics anxiety. Gungor, Eryılmaz, and Fakıoglu (2007) found that overall physics anxiety (consisting of two subdimensions: physics course anxiety and physics test anxiety) was a significant predictor of motivation and achievement in introductory undergraduate physics courses, where lower levels of anxiety were associated with greater motivation and achievement. In developing their instrumentation, Gungor et al. (2007) patterned items measuring physics test anxiety after mathematics test anxiety items (Kazelskis, 1998).

Engagement with physics and chemistry may be limited because of high anxiety that individuals have about these domains. In turn, the issue of anxiety may provide some explanation about the continuing underrepresentation of women and minorities in physics, chemistry, and other physical science domains (Eccles, 2011b; Mallow et al., 2010; Newcombe et al., 2009). The National Research Council (2011) has recently proposed three goals for science, technology, engineering, and mathematics (STEM) education, with the first goal focused on increasing the number of individuals—specifically women and minorities—who seek degrees and careers in STEM. To meet this goal, instruction may need to focus on reducing anxiety, especially in physical science disciplines (Mallow et al., 2010).

Enjoyment of and Interest in Science

At the opposite end of the valence spectrum, there is appreciable work on students' enjoyment of science and their interest in science as a topic, field of study, and even career objective. Enjoyment of science is defined as the extent to which an individual enjoys science classes in general (Wang & Berlin, 2010), whereas interest in science is generally characterized as the extent to which an individual is interested in the knowledge generated by scientists and the practices in which scientists engage (Maltese & Tai, 2010; Osborne, Simon, & Collins, 2003; Swarat, Ortony, & Revelle, 2012).

A recent study by Ainley and Ainley (2011) found that an individual's personal value for science has a strong relationship with enjoyment of science, where a higher value is associated with a greater degree of enjoyment. Furthermore, Ainley and Ainley suggest that science enjoyment acts as a mediator between personal value and interest in science. In other words, "when students believe that the topics they are dealing with in science have personal relevance and meaning for their lives [i.e., greater personal value] they are more likely to experience enjoyment and interest from engaging with science content" (Ainley & Ainley, 2011, p. 11).

Overall enjoyment of science may not result in studying science at higher levels (i.e., pursuing a science major in college or STEM-related career). Archer et al. (2010) discuss the divide between "doing science" (i.e., students engaging in hand-on science activities in a classroom setting) and "being a scientist" (i.e., students adopting a science identity). The elementary students involved in their analysis generally enjoyed science class—especially engaging in hands-on investigations—but did not see future careers in science as desirable. Clearly, a variety of factors beyond emotion affect students' career choices.

In adolescence, enjoyment experienced during a science class is more strongly related to practical aspects and relevance of a particular science topic (Bennett & Hogarth, 2009) rather than to overall enjoyment of science. Sadler (2009) specifically states that socio-scientific issues (e.g., global climate change) generate interest in the science classroom because these issues "have the potential to affect the lives of individuals with competing perspectives" and "can be informed by scientific data and theory, but they are also subject to economic, social, political and/or ethical considerations" (p. 11). Therefore, enjoyment of science may develop from specific topics that are particularly relevant to an individual.

Enjoyment of science class is related closely to interest in science (Osborne et al., 2003). However, some researchers consider interest and enjoyment to be distinct emotions, with interest not necessarily involving enjoyment, and vice versa (Krapp & Prenzel, 2011). Researchers in science learning have examined interest somewhat specifically as interest in the practices of scientists and the knowledge generated by scientists (for broader perspectives on interest and interest development, see Ainley & Hidi, 2014, and Renninger, 1992).

In a science classroom, interest is often associated with a particular science topic (see, e.g., Baram-Tsabari & Yarden, 2005; Dawson, 2000; Schreiner & Sjøberg, 2004; Swarat et al., 2012). Topics of interest are generally characterized as those that students perceive to be personally relevant or relevant to their society. Furthermore, many topics of interest are controversial (e.g., global climate change). Gender is also an appreciable factor in determining interest about a particular science topic (Tytler & Osborne, 2012) with girls generally interested in life science topics (e.g., why we dream when we are sleeping) and boys generally interested in physical science topics (e.g., weightlessness in space). It is important to note that the gender gap appears to be closing in the life sciences but remains a problem for an equitable pipeline of future scientists in the physical sciences (Mallow et al., 2010).

Confusion and Science Learning

One emotion that may be of particular importance when learning science is confusion. Confusion has been found to play an important role in learning, especially during complex learning activities that are a common part of science courses. For example, learning about seasonal change involves a conceptual understanding of Earth having an axis, the degree of the tilt of Earth's axis, Earth's orbital path around the Sun, and the effects of direct and indirect sunlight on Earth's surface.

D'Mello, Lehman, Pekrun, and Graesser (2014) have proposed a theoretical model that describes how confusion may serve as a catalyst for engagement and positive learning outcomes during complex learning situations. According to the theory, confusion is likely to arise when a learner recognizes an ongoing discrepancy between their prior knowledge and the new information that is not immediately resolved. Confusion may also result when the learner is unable to integrate the discrepant information with existing knowledge or when contradictions in the information stream disrupt information processing. These conditions that trigger cognitive disequilibrium may result from anomalous events (Chinn & Brewer, 1993), activation of misconceptions (Kendeou & van den Broek, 2005), or impasses (VanLehn, Siler, Murray, Yamauchi, & Baggett, 2003), among others. When the learner detects impasses and subsequent confusion, he or she will need to engage in effortful cognitive processes in order to resolve the confusion. Effortful processes in this instance would include the learner pausing, reflecting, and engaging in critical thinking to problem solve and revise their prior knowledge (D'Mello et al.,

2014). Thus, confusion may serve as a catalyst for conceptual change, a hypothesis that warrants investigation.

Topic Emotions and Conceptual Change

Recent research has begun to shed light on the role of topic emotions in science learning. It is important to remember that whereas topic emotions are a form of academic emotions, they can be opposite in valence from other academic emotions (i.e., a student can experience positive emotions about geoscience class but negative emotions about human-induced climate change). In our own research, we have found that both students and teachers who exhibit enjoyment of science may experience very different emotions when they encounter specific topics in science classrooms. As noted previously, this is not unlike a student who enjoys his mathematics class but experiences anxiety when it comes to exam day. When students view a topic as controversial or identity threatening, such as biological evolution or climate change, they can experience negative emotions. This can even be the case when the topic seems disconnected from personal experience or identity (such as Pluto's demotion to dwarf status).

Students' Topic Emotions

Broughton et al. (2013) conducted a study focusing on students' topic emotions about Pluto's reclassification from a major to a dwarf planet. Fifth- and sixth-grade students were asked to read a refutation text passage on the scientists' rationale for developing a new definition of "planet" and the subsequent reclassification of Pluto to a dwarf planet. Students were then randomly assigned to one of two conditions: reread the text or reread the text during small group discussions. The small group discussions were structured using Questioning the Author (Beck & McKeown, 2006) in which the researcher stopped at key points of the text and posed questions to the students intended to deepen their understanding of the central ideas presented in the text. Prior to instruction, elementary students expressed they were disappointed, sad, and irritated as well as experiencing other negative emotions about Pluto's demotion. After engaging in instruction designed to promote understanding about the scientific reasoning behind the reclassification, the intensity of students' negative emotions was reduced in both groups. These elementary students concurrently changed their conceptual understanding of planets toward a more scientific view. Broughton et al. (2013) speculated that this conceptual change may be due in part to "a more accepting attitude towards Pluto's dwarf planet status" (p. 18) initiated by a dampening of negative emotions as evidenced by self-reported attitudes toward the reclassification.

Linnenbrink and Pintrich (2002) similarly showed that reduction in negative emotions may support conceptual change. In their study, undergraduate students' changing conceptions of projectile motion were examined in relation to achievement goals and emotions. The findings suggested that students who held mastery goals experienced a reduction in negative emotions, which, in turn, seemed beneficial for conceptual change learning. Linnenbrink and Pintrich (2002) explain that as negative emotions such as anxiety decrease, learners are more likely to focus on the information to be learned.

Heddy and Sinatra (2013) also found that instruction may impact topic emotions. In a study exploring the impact of Teaching for Transformative Experience in Science (TTES)

pedagogical approach to teaching about biological evolution, they found that students' emotions about the topic shifted with instruction. Transformative experience describes situations where students actively engage with science concepts they are learning about in class in out-of-school contexts (Pugh, 2011). TTES involves three general methods: (a) framing content in terms of its experiential value, (b) modeling transformative experiences, and (c) scaffolding re-seeing concepts in a new way in everyday contexts (Pugh, Linnenbrink-Garcia, Koskey, Stewart, & Manzey, 2010).

Heddy and Sinatra (2013) found a significant interaction between instructional group and topic enjoyment. Those students who learned about evolution through the TTES method showed a significant increase in their self-reported enjoyment for learning about biological evolution, whereas, those that experienced a more traditional lecture, reading, and discussion-based pedagogical approach reported a significant decrease in their reported enjoyment for the topic from pre- to post-instruction.

Intensity of emotions may also be closely related to greater misunderstanding about a topic. Broughton et al. (2012) found that graduate students "were more curious, interested, and anxious about topics with greater numbers of misconceptions (climate change, genetically modified foods) than those with fewer total misconceptions (airport body scanners)" (p. 8). Interestingly, both positive emotions (interest) and negative emotions (anxiety) were associated with misconceptions. This suggests that cognitive conflict may be associated—at least in part—with a degree of conflicting emotions about the topic. In terms of science instruction, teachers may want to consider creating a classroom environment where controversial topics are used to promote students' engagement and learning while simultaneously using strategies that dampen negative emotions associated with the topic that may act as a barrier to learning. Teachers should also consider their own emotions when teaching about a particular topic and how that impacts their science instruction (Broughton & Nadelson, 2012; Lombardi & Sinatra, 2013).

It is important to note that interest may play a critical role when learning about non-controversial science topics even when other topic emotions, such as anger and enjoyment, play less of a role in learning about that topic. In a study exploring self-efficacy and conceptual change on the topic of seasonal change, a topic that is generally considered noncontroversial by the public, Cordova, Sinatra, Broughton, Taasoobshirazi, and Lombardi (2013) created profiles of individuals using cluster analysis. These profiles were based on their degree of self-efficacy, prior knowledge, confidence in their knowledge, and topic interest. Cordova et al. (2013) used these profiles to predict conceptual change. The profiles showed that those high in all of the constructs (self-efficacy, prior knowledge, confidence, and interest) actually experienced less conceptual change than those with an all low profile or those with a mixed profile (high in self-efficacy, interest, and confidence, but low in prior knowledge). The mixed profile was most optimal. They interpret these findings to suggest that the high profile may reflect overconfidence in one's prior knowledge and result in less openness to change. In terms of implications for topic emotions, they found that interest played a role in creating the profiles of learners on this noncontroversial topic, even as other topic emotions did not play a significant role.

Topic interest may also facilitate deeper cognitive engagement, which, in turn, increases the likelihood of conceptual change (Dole & Sinatra, 1998). For example, Broughton, Sinatra, and Reynolds (2010) had participants read either a refutation text or traditional expository text about the causes of seasonal change on Earth. The structure of a refutation text differs from traditional expository texts in that the refutation texts states a common misconception, directly refutes it, and then provides the scientific explanation in a plausible, intelligible manner (Hynd, 2003; Sinatra & Broughton, 2011). The refutation text format likely promotes coactivation of the reader's misconception along with the information in the text (Kendeou & van den Broek, 2007). In turn, the coactivation of the misconception and the scientific explanation may act as a trigger for cognitive conflict, which may lead to deeper processing of the information as the reader strives to resolve the conflict. Broughton and colleagues (2010) found that interest played a role in promoting deeper engagement and conceptual change among participants who read the refutation text. Participants identified the refutation sentence as being the most interesting sentence in the passage. Further, participants explained that the reason the sentence was so interesting to them is that it contradicted what they knew. In addition, participants who read the refutation text had fewer misconceptions and increased science understanding at posttest than participants who read the traditional expository text.

Teachers' Topic Emotions

Many teachers may have positive emotions about science in general (e.g., love) but intense and potentially adverse emotions (e.g., fear and anger) about particular topics they may be asked to teach, particularly if these topics are controversial in nature. Griffith and Brem (2004) examined stress and emotions that arise when teaching about biological evolution. Griffith and Brem sorted the 15 secondary science teachers who participated in this study into three categories: "scientist, selective, and conflicted" (2004, p. 795). Whereas most of the teachers expressed a general love for science, each category differentiated teachers based on levels of fear and anxiety felt when teaching about evolution. "Scientist" teachers demonstrated fear that groups opposed to evolution would prevent instruction of the theory in their classrooms. However, these teachers have relatively low levels of anxiety about teaching evolution because of high confidence in their own content knowledge and abilities to keep instruction focused away from students' personal beliefs and experiences. Both "selective" and "conflicted" teachers had fears of conflict arising when teaching about evolution and associated higher levels of anxiety. The anxiety level for "conflicted" teachers was greater because they feared the "grave consequences for them and their students" (Griffith & Brem, 2004, p. 801) as they fully explored the topic, whereas selective teachers lowered their anxiety by avoiding the more controversial aspects of evolution (e.g., human evolution).

A research study by Lombardi and Sinatra (2013) investigated teachers' topic emotions about human-induced climate change. In this study, three groups of teachers (preservice, in-service teachers not currently teaching about climate change, and in-service teachers who were responsible for teaching about climate change) each responded to surveys measuring teachers' emotions about and plausibility perceptions of climate change, background knowledge of weather and climate distinctions (a principle related to understanding climate change), and their inclinations toward knowledge and thinking (i.e., needs for cognition and closure). Two teachers were selected for interviews to probe their thoughts about these variables in greater depth than was provided by the surveys. The findings showed that all groups expressed some degree of negative emotions. The nature of those negative emotions differed based on their teaching status and their agreement or disagreement with the scientific views on anthropogenic climate change. In-service science teachers who were not currently teaching about climate change and preservice elementary teachers expressed significantly greater anger about human-induced climate change than in-service teachers who were currently teaching about climate change. This result may emerge from an increased potential for critical evaluation—and an associated dampening of negative emotions—as teachers who currently teach about climate change prepare lessons about the topic and potentially have greater opportunity for reflection about the evidence supporting human-induced climate change.

Lombardi and Sinatra (2013) also created two predictive models, with one model focusing on teachers' personal emotions about climate change and the other model focusing on emotions they have about teaching the topic. In both models, anger was found to be a significant predictor of plausibility perceptions about human-induced climate change, with greater intensity of anger associated with lower plausibility.

Lombardi and Sinatra (2013) also found that more hopelessness about climate change was associated with greater plausibility that humans are the primary cause of current climate change. We speculate that this emotion may be associated with increased awareness about the notion of the "tipping point." Individuals who express greater hopelessness and consider human-induced climate to be more plausible than other alternatives may also know of the possibility that "global warming will lead to some impacts that are abrupt or irreversible, such as massive polar ice melt" (i.e., beyond a "tipping point," Intergovernmental Panel on Climate Change, 2007, p. 13).

The studies conducted by Griffith and Brem (2004) and Lombardi and Sinatra (2013) show that many teachers, who may have a love for science, also can have strong and negative emotions about a particular topic. These strong emotions may—in turn—likely impact the depth and quality of instruction about these topics.

METHODOLOGICAL CHALLENGES IN EMOTIONS RESEARCH IN SCIENCE EDUCATION

Certainly, the best avenue for progress on understanding adaptive emotions for science learning is to conduct further research. Emotions research in science classrooms has all the challenges of emotions research in general, such as construct definition, issues of measurement, self-report accuracy, triangulation with physiological data, and so on (for an extended discussion of these challenges, see Pekrun & Linnenbrink-Garcia, 2014). However, conducting emotions research in science learning environments has some added challenges over and above those on more general academic emotions.

First, emotions can be elicited in science learning when students are presented with controversial topics about which they have strong feelings. This presents a challenge in and of itself as researchers may experience some push back from teachers and school administrators regarding the introduction of controversial topics into the science curriculum. Second, physiological measures are difficult to collect in classroom settings, leaving classroom-based emotions researchers more reliant on self-report than researchers working with adults or in laboratory settings. The reliance on self-report presents the challenge of triangulating emotions data with other measures, such as interviews, observations, or behavioral data.

Third, emotions are not necessarily recognized as a positive part of the science learning experience on the part of teachers or school administrators, who may view science as more rational than affective. In addition, exploring controversial science topics such as climate change, stem cell research, or biological evolution, which can evoke strong emotional responses on the part of students, can cause stress and anxiety on the part of the teachers (Griffith & Brem, 2004). Examining emotions in science, whether positive or negative, may require collaboration with teachers as research partners who appreciate the role of emotions in the science classroom.

EMOTIONS AS AN INSTRUCTIONAL ENHANCEMENT

Popular culture has led many of us to believe that science proceeds effectively with emotionless reasoning, such as the fictional Vulcans in *Star Trek* who abandoned emotions to obtain pure logic. However, in reality, scientists' emotions factor quite heavily into their reasoning (e.g., the happiness, fear, and anger expressed in James Watson's account of the discovery of DNA; Thagard, 2006). Emotions may be particularly important in controlling the process of cognitive evaluation by limiting the number of alternatives that an individual may consider when making a judgment (Hookway, 2002; Stanovich, 2010). Correspondingly, critical evaluation is one of "three spheres of activity" that characterize the practices conducted by scientists and engineers, and specifically as a practice, "all ideas are evaluated against alternative explanations and compared with evidence . . . [and] acceptance of an explanation is ultimately an assessment. . .about which explanation is the most satisfactory" (National Research Council, 2011, pp. 3–2). Emotions, therefore, may play a potentially critical role in promoting productive science. On one hand, emotions may lead to critical evaluation of evidence, but on the other hand, strong emotions may be too restrictive in limiting alternatives (i.e., only considering one alternative explanation) and decrease scientific productivity.

The U.S. National Research Council (2011) has recently developed a framework for K–12 science education recommending that students engage in authentic science and engineering practices (e.g., critical evaluation) during schooling. Consequently, science instruction should consider how emotions influence critical evaluation in the classroom, both from a positive and negative standpoint. Emotions about a particular topic could restrict students' evaluation of the connections between evidence and different alternatives, thus requiring a transformation in emotions in order to promote science learning. Reciprocally, use of critical evaluation in the classroom may alter students' topic emotions. Such was the case with the study conducted by Broughton et al. (2013) where elementary students who engaged in instruction promoting critical evaluation (i.e., engaging in collaborative argumentation and reading refutation texts) tempered negative emotions. The study also showed shifts in students' attitudes about Pluto's demotion toward a position more in accord with the reclassification, as well as knowledge reconstruction about the concept of planet. Whereas Broughton et al. (2013) could not definitively link change in topic emotions to conceptual change, their study suggests that students' negative emotions were acting as a barrier to deeper understanding, and also, this emotional barrier may have been appreciably weakened through instruction promoting critical evaluation.

Using collaborative argumentation (Nussbaum, 2011; Osborne, 2010) and refutation text (Sinatra & Broughton, 2011) in the science classroom may engender evaluation because these techniques represent the authentic scientific practice of weighing evidence to alternative theories. Other instructional strategies, such as critical questioning (Nussbaum & Edwards, 2011), model-evidence link diagrams (Chinn & Buckland, 2012), and alternative argument flaw identification (Glassner & Schwarz, 2005) may also be similarly effective. These instructional techniques also promote critical evaluation by engaging students in connecting evidence to alternative claims. Not only may students' negative emotions (e.g., anger about discussing only the scientific alternative) be ameliorated when engaging in critical evaluation, but positive emotions (e.g., surprise, curiosity, wonder, and joy) about a topic may be potentially strengthened because students may experience empowerment through systematic consideration of various alternatives (Zembylas, 2005). Alternatively, negative emotions may be tempered through critical evaluation by developing an appreciation of the scientific rational for claims (as was seen in the students learning about Pluto's reclassification (Broughton et al., 2013). Cognitive and emotional processes are linked in a way that may actively engage students through deeper elaboration, thereby promoting knowledge construction and reconstruction (Dole & Sinatra, 1998; Olitsky & Milne, 2012). Engagement may be increased further when the topic is controversial and compelling alternatives are juxtaposed.

Several research studies show that students have great interest in science topics that may have both personal and societal relevance (i.e., "socio-scientific issues;" Schreiner & Sjøberg, 2004, p. 52). In one study listing the top five items that adolescent boys and girls would like to learn about in science (Jenkins & Nelson, 2005), two of the boys' items—nuclear bombs and biological/chemical weapons—and two of the girls'—cancer and sexually transmitted diseases—were topics of high relevance, and also potentially controversial. Many of these controversial issues also provide opportunities to learn about fundamental scientific principles. For example, climate change relates to the water cycle and energy transfer within the Earth system; human evolution relates to heredity, specialized cell structure, and ecosystems and biodiversity; and the Big Bang relates to expansion and structure of the universe and the formation of the elements.

Because of the expanding body of evidence showing the relationship between increased interest and socioscientific issues, Sadler (2009) recommended that science teachers develop a community of practice around controversial and meaningful topics in their classrooms. Whereas, interest in a socioscientific issue is not necessarily equivalent to emotions that students may have about a particular topic, interest and other emotions about a topic are closely related (Silvia, 2008). Therefore, instructional strategies that promote topic interest—particularly when the topic is controversial—may provide a guide for emotionality in science learning.

Controversial topics provide an opportunity for science teachers to facilitate both an emotional transformation toward a more positive stance and knowledge reconstruction toward scientifically accepted understanding. Teachers who avoid controversy in the classroom because of potential adverse emotions may therefore be doing a disservice to students. Such was the case for biology teachers identified by Griffith and Brem (2004) as "selective." Teachers who were categorized as "selective" (i.e., selective because they limit the amount of biological evolution content they teach to limit controversial elements) may be depriving students of opportunities to deeply engage with the topic of evolution. Avoiding the more controversial aspects of biological evolution may also keep strong negative emotions in place, both from the teachers' and students' perspective. Therefore, with a lower possibility of change in understanding and emotions about the topic, classroom time may have been wasted and an opportunity for science learning lost.

Science teachers do not need to be psychologically trained to facilitate emotional change about controversial topics, rather science teachers need to provide opportunities for students to engage in epistemic cognitive processes that are practiced by scientists (e.g., critical evaluation through connection of evidences to alternative explanations and making judgments about the quality of the connections between evidences and explanations). They also should strive to avoid dogmatic presentation of scientifically accepted content (e.g., discussing science as factual information or participation in "cookbook" laboratories).

To successfully integrate controversial topics and scientific habits of thought, teachers should have strong content knowledge about issues that are relevant to their students. Osborne et al. (2003) report on several research studies that support strong positive relationship among science teachers' understanding about a particular topic, their interest and enthusiasm for that topic, and corresponding interest expressed by their students. In situations where teachers may have adverse emotions about a topic (Griffith & Brem, 2004; Lombardi & Sinatra, 2013), both in-service and preservice professional development should engage teachers in activities designed to increase content understanding through critical evaluation and reflection on how these activities will influence students' emotions. Such training should be in addition to professional development, which develops teachers who actively ensure a cooperative environment, which also has been found to increase students' enjoyment and other positive emotions about their science classes (den Brok, Fisher, & Scott, 2005; Xu, Coats, & Davidson, 2012).

ADVANCING UNDERSTANDING OF EMOTIONS AND SCIENCE LEARNING

Significant advances in our understanding of emotions during science learning have been made in the last 10 years. However, much work remains to be done before we can capitalize on adaptive emotions to promote science learning and students' identification with science as a potential career option.

Several areas of future research should prove fruitful to advance this objective. First, additional controversial topics should be explored. Evolution and climate change have been examined, but there are many other topics that warrant research attention (i.e., stem cell research, pandemics, nuclear energy). It is important to explore an array of topics to promote a richer understanding of the complex interplay of topic emotions, academic emotions, interest, motives for learning, and learning outcomes.

More research is needed on emotions in informal and free choice learning environments, such as museums, zoos, science centers, and planetariums. As controversial topics are given short shift in the science curriculum, informal and free choice learning environments have begun to pick up the slack (see, e.g., Diamond, Evans, & Speigel, 2012) and are now a significant source of learning about science for children and their parents. Anyone who has been to a museum recently and seen children interacting with exhibits knows that many emotions appear to be present in these settings. Yet, research has yet to extensively examine the role of emotions in these settings as it relates to motivation and science learning outcomes.

Given the methodological challenges of exploring topic and academic emotions, researchers should continue to work towards developing measures that are sensitive to capturing the range, type, and intensity of emotions experienced during science learning. In addition, better methods of triangulation of multiple forms of evidence are needed, given the challenges of using physiological measures in either formal or informal learning environments.

More research is needed on how emotions function in the science classroom. In our review, it was clear that there are competing hypotheses for the role of negative and positive emotions in facilitating engagement and conceptual change. More work is needed on the mechanism(s) mediating the effects of emotion on science learning. In particular, researchers should explore the impact of emotional valence (positive and negative) on science learning outcomes. Further, researchers need to clarify the conditions under which emotions play a facilitative or inhibitory effect on science learning. This would allow further investigations to focus on emotion interventions that reduce or prevent maladaptive emotional responses to science learning situations, topics, and activities.

Finally, much more research is needed on the range of emotions teachers experience regarding science topics and how their emotions relate to their attitudes towards and willingness to teach science topics, especially those that are controversial. How teachers feel about science likely impacts their students' emotions, attitudes, and motivations for engaging in science. Given the import of teachers influence on our future scientists, the influence of teacher emotions on science learning should be a focus of additional investigation.

REFERENCES

Ainley, M., & Ainley, J. (2011). Student engagement with science in early adolescence: The contribution of enjoyment to students' continuing interest in learning about science. *Contemporary Educational Psychology, 36*, 4–12.

Ainly, M., & Hidi, S., (2014). Interest and enjoyment. In R. Pekrun & L. Linnenbrink-Garcia (Eds.), *International handbook of emotions in education* (pp. 205–227). New York, NY: Taylor & Francis.

Archer, L., DeWitt, J., Osborne, J., Dillon, J., Willis, B., & Wong, B. (2010). "Doing" science versus "being" a scientist: Examining 10/11-year-old school children's constructions of science through the lens of identity. *Science Education, 94*, 617–639.

Baker, D., & Leary, R. (1995). Letting girls speak out about science. *Journal of Research in Science Teaching, 32*, 3–27.

Baram-Tsabari, A., & Yarden, A. (2005). Characterizing children's spontaneous interests in science and technology. *International Journal of Science Education, 7*, 803–826.

Beck, I. L., & McKeown, M. G. (2006). *Improving comprehension with questioning the author: A fresh and expanded view of a powerful approach.* New York, NY: Scholastic.

Bennett, J., & Hogarth, S. (2009). Would you want to talk to a scientist at a party? High school students' attitudes to school science and to science. *International Journal of Science Education, 31*, 1975–1998.

Bless, H. B. (2000). The interplay of affect and cognition: The mediating role of general knowledge structure. In J. P. Forgas (Ed.), *Feeling and thinking: The role of affect in social cognition* (pp. 201–222). Cambridge, United Kingdom: Cambridge University Press.

Brotman, J. S., & Moore, F. M. (2008). Girls and science: A review of four themes in the science education literature. *Journal of Research in Science Teaching, 45*, 971–1002.

Broughton, S. H., & Nadelson, L. S. (2012, April). *Food for thought: Pre-service teachers' knowledge, emotions, and attitudes toward genetically modified foods.* Paper presented at the American Educational Research Association, Vancouver, Canada.

Broughton, S. H., Sinatra, G. M., & Nussbaum, E. M. (2013). "Pluto has been a planet my whole life!" Emotions, attitudes, and conceptual change in elementary students' learning about Pluto's reclassification. *Research in Science Education, 43*, 529–550.

Broughton, S. H., Pekrun, R., & Sinatra, G. M. (2012, April). *Climate change, genetically modified foods, airport body scanners: Investigating students' emotions related to science topics.* Paper presented at the American Educational Research Association, Vancouver, Canada.

Broughton, S. H., Sinatra, G. M., & Reynolds, R. E. (2010). The nature of the refutation text effect: An investigation of attention allocation. *The Journal of Educational Research, 103*, 407–423.

Chen, C. H., & Howard, B. (2010). Effect of live simulation on middle school students' attitudes and learning toward science. *Educational Technology & Society, 13*, 133–139.

Chinn, C. A., & Brewer, W. F. (1993). The role of anomalous data in knowledge acquisition: A theoretical framework and implications for science instruction. *Review of Educational Research, 63,* 1–49.

Chinn, C. A., & Buckland, L. A. (2012). Model-based instruction: Fostering change in evolutionary conceptions and in epistemic practices. In K. Rosengren, E. M. Evans, S. K. Brem, & G. M. Sinatra (Eds.), *Model-based instruction: Fostering change in evolutionary conceptions and in epistemic practices.* New York, NY: Oxford University Press.

Cordova, J., Sinatra, G. M., Broughton, S. H., Taasoobshirazi, G., & Lombardi, D. (2013). Self-efficacy, prior knowledge, interest, and confidence in prior knowledge: Influences on conceptual change. Manuscript submitted for publication.

Damasio, A. (1994). *Descartes' error: Emotion, reason, and the human brain.* New York, NY: Penguin Books.

Dawson, C. (2000). Upper primary boys' and girls' interests in science: Have they changed since 1980? *International Journal of Science Education, 22,* 557–570.

den Brok, P., Fisher, D., & Scott, R. (2005). The importance of teacher interpersonal behavior for student attitudes in Brunei primary science classes. *International Journal of Science Education, 27,* 765–779.

Diamond, J., Evans, E. M., & Speigel, A. N. (2012). Walking whales and singing flies: An evolution exhibit and assessment of its impact. In K. S. Rosengren, S. K. Brem, E. M. Evans, & G. M. Sinatra (Eds.), *Evolution challenges: Integrating research and practice in teaching and learning about evolution* (pp. 586–614). New York, NY: Oxford University Press.

D'Mello, S., Lehman, B., Pekrun, R., & Graesser, A. (2014). Confusion can be beneficial for learning. *Learning and Instruction, 29,* 153–170.

Dole, J. A., & Sinatra, G. M. (1998). Reconceptualizing change in the cognitive construction of knowledge. *Educational Psychologist, 33,* 109–128.

Duit, R. (1999). Conceptual change approaches in science education. In W. Schnotz, S. Vosniadou, & M. Carretero (Eds.), *New perspectives on conceptual change* (pp. 263–282). Oxford, United Kingdom: Elsevier.

Eagly, A. H., & Chaiken, S. (1993). *The psychology of attitudes.* Ft. Worth, TX: Harcourt Brace.

Eccles, J. S. (2011a). Understanding educational and occupational choices. *Journal of Social Issues, 67,* 644–648.

Eccles, J. S. (2011b). Understanding women's achievement choices: Looking back and looking forward. *Psychology of Women Quarterly, 35,* 510–516.

Eddy, R. M. (2000). Chemophobia in the college classroom: Extent, sources, and student characteristics. *Journal of Chemical Education, 77,* 514–517.

Fiedler, K. (2000). Toward an integrative account of affect and cognition phenomena using the BIAS computer algorith. In J. P. Forgas (Ed.), *Feeling and thinking: The role of affect in social cognition* (pp. 223–252). Cambridge, United Kingdom: Cambridge University Press.

Fredricks, J. A. (2011). Engagement in school and out-of-school contexts: A multidimensional view of engagement. *Theory into Practice, 50,* 327–335.

Gibson, H. L., & Chase, C. (2002). Longitudinal impact of an inquiry-based science program on middle school students' attitudes toward science. *Science Education, 86,* 693–705.

Glassner, A., & Schwarz, B. B. (2005). The antilogos ability to evaluate information supporting arguments. *Learning and Instruction, 15,* 353–375.

Goetz, T., Frenzel, A. C., Pekrun, R., & Hall, N. C. (2006). The domain specificity of academic emotional experiences. *Journal of Experimental Education, 75,* 5–29.

Gregoire, M. (2003). Is it a challenge or a threat? A dual-process model of teachers' cognition and appraisal process during conceptual change. *Educational Psycholology Review, 15,* 117–155.

Griffith, J., & Brem, S. K. (2004). Teaching evolutionary biology: Pressures, stress, and coping. *Journal of Research on Science Teaching, 41,* 791–809.

Gungor, A., Eryılmaz, A., & Fakıoglu, T. (2007). The relationship of freshmen's physics achievement and their related affective characteristics. *Journal of Research in Science Teaching, 41,* 791–809.

Heddy, B.C., & Sinatra, G. M. (2013). Transforming misconceptions: Using transformative experience to promote positive affect and conceptual change in students learning about biological evolution. *Science Education, 97,* 723–744.

Hookway, C. (2002). Emotions and epistemic evaluations. In P. Carruthers, S. Stitch, & M. Siegal (Eds.), *The cognitive basis of science* (pp. 251–262). Cambridge, United Kingdom: Cambridge University Press.

Hynd, C. (2003). Conceptual change in response to persuasive messages. In G. M. Sinatra & P. R. Pintrich (Eds.), *Intentional conceptual change* (pp. 291–315). Mahwah, NJ: Lawrence Erlbaum Associates.

Intergovernmental Panel on Climate Change. (2007). *Climate change 2007: Synthesis report—summary for policy-makers*. Geneva, Switzerland: World Meteorological Organization.

Jenkins, E. W., & Nelson, N. W. (2005). Important but not for me: Students' attitudes towards secondary school science in England. *Research in Science and Technology Education, 23,* 41–57.

Jones, M. G., Howe, A., & Rua, M. J. (2000). Gender differences in students' experiences, interests, and attitudes toward science and scientists. *Science Education, 84,* 180–192.

Kazelskis, R. (1998). Some dimensions of mathematics anxiety: A factor analysis across instruments. *Educational and Psychological Measurement, 58,* 623–633.

Kendeou, P., & van den Broek, P. (2005). The effects of readers' misconceptions on comprehension of scientific text. *Journal of Educational Psychology, 97,* 235–245.

Kendeou, P., & van den Broek, P. (2007). The effects of prior knowledge and text structure on comprehension processes during reading of scientific texts. *Memory & Cognition, 35,* 1567–1577.

Krapp, A., & Prenzel, M. (2011). Research on interest in science: Theories, methods, and findings. *International Journal of Science Education, 33,* 27–50.

Lazarus, R. S. (1984). On the primacy of cognition. *American Psychologist, 39,* 124–129.

Lee, M. K., & Erdogan, I. (2007). The effect of science-technology-society teaching on students' attitudes toward science and certain aspects of creativity. *International Journal of Science Education, 11,* 1315–1327.

Lee, V. E., & Burkam, D. T. (1996). Gender differences in middle grade science achievement: Subject domain, ability level, and course emphasis. *Science Education, 86,* 613–650.

Linnenbrink, E. A. (2006). Emotion research in education: Theoretical and methodological perspectives on the integration of affect, motivation, and cognition. *Educational Psychology Review, 18,* 307–314.

Linnenbrink, E. A. (2007). The role of affect in student learning: A multi-dimensional approach to considering the interaction of affect, motivation, and engagement. In A. Schutz & R. Pekrun (Eds.), *Emotion in education* (pp. 107–124). Burlington, MA: Elsevier.

Linnenbrink, E. A., & Pintrich, P. R. (2002). The role of motivational beliefs in conceptual change. In M. Limon & L. Mason (Eds.), *Reconsidering conceptual change: Issues in theory and practice* (pp. 115–135). Dordrecht, Netherlands: Kluwer Academic.

Linnenbrink, E. A., & Pintrich, P. R. (2004). Role of affect in cognitive processing in academic contexts. In D. Y. Dai (Ed.), *Motivation, emotion, and cognition: integrative perspectives on intellectual development and functioning* (pp. 57–87). Mahwah, NJ: Lawrence Erlbaum Associates.

Lombardi, D., & Sinatra, G. M. (2013). Emotions when teaching about human-induced climate change. *International Journal of Science Education, 35,* 167–191.

Lyons, T. (2006). Different countries, same science classes: Students' experience of school science classes in their own words. *International Journal of Science Education, 28,* 591–613.

Mallow, J. V. (1978). A science anxiety program. *American Journal of Physics, 46,* 862.

Mallow, J. V., & Greenburg, S. L. (1982). Science anxiety: Causes and remedies. *Journal of College Science Teaching, 11,* 356–358.

Mallow, J. V., Kastrup, H., Bryant, F. B., Hislop, N., Shefner, R., & Udo, M. (2010). Science anxiety, science attitudes, and gender: Interviews from a binational study. *Journal of Science Education and Technology, 19,* 356–369.

Maltese, A. V., & Tai, R. H. (2010). Eyeballs in the fridge: Sources of early interest in science. *International Journal of Science Education, 32,* 669–685.

Murphy, C., & Beggs, J. (2003). Children's attitudes towards school science. *School Science Review, 84,* 109–116.

National Center for Education Statistics. (2007). *Trends in international mathematics and science study*. Retrieved from http://nces.ed.gov/timss/results07_science07.asp

National Center for Education Statistics. (2009). *Students who study Science, Technology, Engineering, and Mathematics (STEM) in postsecondary education*. Washington, DC: U.S. Department of Education, Institute for Education Sciences.

National Research Council. (2011). *A framework for K-12 science education: Practices, crosscutting concepts, and core ideas*. Washington, DC: National Academies Press.

Newcombe, N. S., Ambady, N., Eccles, J. S., Gomez, L., Klahr, D., Linn, M. . . . Mix, K. (2009). Psychology's role in mathematics and science education. *American Psychologist, 64,* 538–550.

Nussbaum, E. M. (2011). Argumentation, dialogue theory, and probability modeling: Alternative frameworks for argumentation research in education. *Educational Psychologist, 46,* 84–106.

Nussbaum, E. M., & Edwards, O. V. (2011). Critical questions and argument stratagem: A framework for enhancing and analyzing students' reasoning practices. *Journal of the Learning Sciences, 20,* 443–488.

Olitsky, S., & Milne, C. (2012). Understanding engagement in science education: The psychological and the social. In B. J. Fraser, K. Tobin, & C. J. McRobbie (Eds.), *Second international handbook of science education* (pp. 19–33). Dordrecht, Netherlands: Springer Publishing.

Osborne, J. (2010). Arguing to learn in science: The role of collaborative critical discourse. *Science, 328,* 463–466.

Osborne, J., & Collins, S. (2001). Pupils' views of the role and value of the science curriculum: A focus-group study. *International Journal of Science Education, 23,* 441–468.

Osborne, J., Simon, S., & Collins, S. (2003). Attitudes towards science: A review of the literature and its implications. *International Journal of Science Education, 25,* 1049–1079.

Pekrun, R. (2006). The control-value theory of achievement emotions: Assumptions, corollaries, and implications for educational research and practice. *Educational Psychology Review, 18,* 315–341.

Pekrun, R., Goetz, T., Titz, W., & Perry, R. P. (2002). Academic emotions in students' self-regulated learning and achievement: A program of qualitative and quantitative research. *Educational Psychologist, 37,* 91–106.

Pekrun, R., & Linnenbrink-Garcia, L. (2012). Academic emotions and student engagement. In S. L. Christensen, A. L. Reschley, & C. Wylie (Eds.), *Handbook of research on student engagement* (pp. 259–282). New York, NY: Springer.

Pekrun, R., & Linnenbrink-Garcia, L. (2014). Emotions in education: Conclusions and future directions. In R. Pekrun & L. Linnenbrink-Garcia (Eds.), *International handbook of emotions in education* (pp. 659–675). New York, NY: Taylor & Francis.

Pekrun, R., & Stephens, E. J. (2012). Academic emotions. In K. R. Harris, S. Graham, T. Urdan, S. Graham, J. M. Royer, & M. Zeidner (Eds.), *APA handbooks in psychology* (pp. 3–31). Washington, DC: American Psychological Association.

Petty, R. E., & Cacioppo, J. T. (1986). The elaboration likelihood model of persuasion. In L. Berkowitz (Ed.), *Advances in experimental social psychology* (Vol. 19, pp. 123–205). New York, NY: Academic Press.

Posner, G. J., Strike, K. A., Hewson, P. W., & Gertzog, W. A. (1982). Accommodation of a scientific conception: Towards a theory of conceptual change. *Science Education, 67,* 489–508.

Pugh, K. J. (2011). Transformative experience: An integrative construct in the spirit of Deweyan pragmatism. *Educational Psychologist, 46,* 107–121.

Pugh, K. J., Linnenbrink-Garcia, L., Koskey, K. L. K., Stewart, V. C., & Manzey, C. (2010). Motivation, learning, and transformative experience: A study of deep engagement in science. *Science Education, 94,* 1–28.

Raved, L., & Assaraf, O.B.Z. (2011). Attitudes towards science learning among 10th grade students: A qualitative look. *International Journal of Science Education, 33,* 1219–1243.

Renninger, R. A. (1992). Individual interest and development: Implications for theory and practice. In R. A. Renninger, S. Hidi, & A. Drapp (Eds.), *The role of interest in learning and development* (pp. 361–396). Hillsdale, NJ: Lawrence Erlbaum Associates.

Rosenberg, E. L. (1998). Levels of analysis and the organization of affect. *Review of General Psychology, 2,* 247–270.

Sadler, T. D. (2009). Situated learning in science education: Socio-scientific issues as contexts for practice. *Studies in Science Education, 45,* 1–42.

Schreiner, C., & Sjøberg, S. (2004). Sowing the seeds of ROSE: Background, rationale, questionnaire development and data Collection for ROSE (the relevance of science education): A comparative study of students' views of science and science education. Retrieved from http://roseproject.no/publications/english-pub.html

Silvia, P. J. (2008). Interest: The curious emotion. *Current Directions in Psychological Science, 17,* 57–60.

Sinatra, G. M., & Broughton, S. H. (2011). Bridging reading comprehension and conceptual change in science: The promise of refutation text. *Reading Research Quarterly, 46,* 374–393.

Sinatra, G. M., & Pintrich, P. R. (2003). *Intentional conceptual change.* Mahwah, NJ: Lawrence Erlbaum Associates.

Sinatra, G. M., & Taasoobshirazi, G. (2011). Intentional conceptual change: The self-regulation of science learning In D. Shunk (Ed.), *Handbook of self-regulation of learning and performance* (pp. 203–216). New York, NY: Routledge.

Stanovich, K. E. (2010). *Decision making and rationality in the modern world.* New York, NY: Oxford University Press.

Sullins, E., Hernandez, D., Fuller, C., & Tashiro, J. (1995). Predicting who will major in a science discipline: Expectancy-value theory as part of an ecological model for studying academic communities. *Journal of Research in Science Teaching, 32,* 99–119.

Swarat, S., Ortony, A., & Revelle, W. (2012). Activity matters: Understanding student interest in school science. *Journal of Research in Science Teaching, 49*, 515–537.

Thagard, P. (2006). The passionate scientist: Emotion in scientific cognition. In P. Thagard (Ed.), *Hot thought: Mechanisms and applications of emotional cognition* (pp. 171–188). Cambridge, MA: MIT Press.

Tytler, R., & Osborne, J. (2012). Student attitudes and aspirations towards science. In B. J. Fraser, K. Tobin, & C. J. McRobbie (Eds.), *Second international handbook of science education* (pp. 597–625). New York, NY: Springer International.

Udo, M., Ramsey, G. P., Reynolds-Alpert, S., & Mallow, J. V. (2004). Science anxiety and gender in students taking general education science courses. *Journal of Science Education and Technology, 13*, 435–466.

VanLehn, K., Siler, S., Murray, C., Yamauchi, T., & Baggett, W. (2003). Why do only some events cause learning during human tutoring? *Cognition and Instruction, 21*, 209–249.

Vosniadou, S. (1999). Conceptual change research: State of the art and future directions. In W. Schnotz, S. Vosniadou, & M. Carretero (Eds.), *New perspectives on conceptual change* (pp. 3–13). Amsterdam, Netherlands: Pergamon.

Vosniadou, S., & Brewer, W. F. (1987). Theories of knowledge restructuring in development. *Review of Educational Research, 57*, 51–67.

Wang, T., & Berlin, D. (2010). Construction and validation of an instrument to measure Taiwanese elementary students' attitudes toward their science class. *International Journal of Science Education, 32*, 2413–2428.

Xu, J., Coats, L. T., & Davidson, M. L. (2012). Promoting student interest in science: The perspectives of exemplary African American teachers. *American Educational Research Journal, 49*, 124–154.

Yager, S. O., Lim, G., & Yager, R. (2006). The advantages of an STS approach over a typical textbook dominated approach in middle school science. *School Science and Mathematics, 106*, 248–260.

Zacharia, Z., & Calabrese Barton, A. (2004). Urban middle-school students' attitudes toward a defined science. *Science Education, 88*, 197–122.

Zembylas, M. (2005). Three perspectives on linking the cognitive and the emotional in science learning: Conceptual change, Socio-constructivism and poststructuralism. *Studies in Science Education, 41*, 91–115.

22

EMOTION DURING READING AND WRITING

Catherine M. Bohn-Gettler and David N. Rapp,
Wichita State University and Northwestern University

Effective literacy skills are of critical importance for academic and professional success. In formal educational settings, many of the tasks in which students are engaged involve reading and comprehending written materials to build content knowledge. These tasks also involve organizing and communicating written thoughts (Hagaman & Reid, 2008). A large body of research on learning has focused on the cognitive processes that underlie reading and writing in an effort to better understand and potentially improve student development and achievement.

More recently, however, emphasis is being placed on how academic learning involves conative alongside cognitive factors, as learning experiences are often infused with emotions for students and teachers. Calls for research emphasize the need for understanding students as affective beings and how emotion can influence learning (Meyer & Turner, 2006). Documenting the interplay between emotion and literacy will help refine our understandings of the factors that guide learning, which will help fulfill the general goal of integrating emotion and cognition in theoretical and methodological accounts of thinking, learning, and behaving (Zajonc, 1980).

In this chapter, we will consider the existing literature on literacy and affect, identifying ways in which emotion influences the processes and products underlying reading and writing. We will begin by first describing accounts of the mechanisms hypothesized to underlie reading, writing, and then emotion. Next, we will integrate these literatures with an identification of how emotion can interact with reading and writing. Finally, we will discuss methodological considerations, future directions, and applications of this work for educational settings.

MODELS OF READING AND WRITING

Reading

Whether a student is reading a novel, learning scientific facts, or studying history, a variety of skills are required to successfully comprehend text. Students must decode words, possess adequate vocabulary knowledge, and engage in comprehension strategies to ensure they understand what they are reading. We now provide a brief description of these skills in turn.

First, knowledge of alphabetic principles is necessary for decoding a text and is related to achievement. Readers must identify letters and their sounds and match combinations of letters with those sounds (phonemes; Ehri, Nunes, Stahl, & Willows, 2001; National Reading Panel, 2000). Practice and experience with decoding enables readers to become more automatic or fluent with reading. A reader is considered to be fluent when he or she can read the words in a text quickly, accurately, and with the appropriate expression. Fluency enables a reader to focus on the content of the text rather than on decoding the words (Rasinski, 2004).

Being able to fluently decode words, however, is not enough to successfully comprehend text. Activating knowledge about what words refer to is a necessary component of meaning construction (National Reading Panel, 2000). To do this, students must have breadth of knowledge of a large body of different words. For example, to understand the sentence, "Suzie went to the grocery store," a reader must know the definition of each word. A reader must also possess a depth, or quality, of vocabulary knowledge. This includes understanding the meanings, forms (i.e., spelling, pronunciation), and uses (i.e., functions, constraints) of words. For example, the word "went" means "to go" but comes in various forms (i.e., went, goes). The word "grocery" involves the semantic knowledge that a grocery is a place to buy food with different types of groceries exhibiting different characteristics depending on context and setting (e.g., size, cost, brand). Both breadth and depth of vocabulary knowledge are important, with breadth traditionally related to decoding skills and depth related to comprehension (Ouellette, 2006).

Decoding, fluency, and vocabulary all serve the purpose of helping readers derive meaning from text, referred to as comprehension. Comprehension necessitates more than simply having and activating knowledge of words and word meanings, though: Readers can go beyond the meanings provided in a text to produce inferences, which involve using background knowledge to deduce information that was not explicitly stated in the text (Graesser, Singer, & Trabasso, 1994). Inferences are generated based on what the text describes, what a reader knows, and what logic is deemed appropriate. Thus, comprehension represents a group of interrelated skills, including decoding and inferencing, that interact with each other (Oakhill, Cain, & Bryant, 2003; van den Broek, Rapp, & Kendeou, 2005).

As a necessary part of comprehension, readers attempt to build a mental representation of text content by encoding what they are reading into memory (Gernsbacher, 1997). According to the *tripartite* theory (Kintsch & van Dijk, 1978), which is a popular account of reading and mental representation, there are multiple levels of representation at which a reader will encode the text into memory. To contextualize this theory, consider the example sentences: "Donna placed her shoes in a bag and folded her jacket into a suitcase. An hour later, she locked her door and drove to the airport."

According to the tripartite theory, the most superficial level is the surface structure, which involves the reader encoding every single word, in the exact order presented, into memory. The second level is the textbase in which the reader can encode the meanings and ideas conveyed in the text. The textbase representation creates a longer-lasting memory representation than the surface structure, but it is still focused specifically on information from the text. For our example, the reader would encode gist ideas such as Donna is packing a bag and going to the airport. The third and most complex type of representation is the situation model. At this level, the reader can elaborate upon the text, engage in problem solving, and generate inferences by going beyond what was described to include prior knowledge, expectations, expertise, and logical assumptions. At the situation model level, a reader might infer that Donna is going on either a vacation or a business trip. These two possible explanations exemplify that, at the situation model level, a number of different inferences could be generated depending on the surrounding text and reader expectations.

Creating a situation model is necessary for comprehension, precisely because it requires that readers make connections between information presented within the text and the background knowledge that readers possess. Well-organized representations that encode the causal relationships signified in texts and that contain accurate inferences are associated with successful comprehension (Kintsch & van Dijk, 1978). Situation model research, including projects distinguishing the three levels of representation described above, have helped clarify an important point: Higher order thinking processes, such as inference generation and reasoning, are critical for successful comprehension.

Related to this notion, a number of other higher order strategies can improve text comprehension, and these strategies are related to those that improve learning and memory processes in general. For example, learning is enhanced when strategies such as elaboration and organization are applied (Craik & Lockhart, 1972; Mandler, 1967; Neath & Surprenant, 2003; Woloshyn, Willoughby, Wood, & Pressley, 1990). Applied specifically to reading, organization processes, such as focusing attention on what is important and summarizing previously read material, can foster successful comprehension. Elaborative processes, such as activating relevant background knowledge, making predictions, engaging in reflective metacognition, and evaluating are also related to successful comprehension. These activities promote deeper understanding by encouraging the construction of associations and connections between text content and reader knowledge (National Reading Panel, 2000).

Beyond these cognitive processes, a variety of other factors can influence comprehension. These include properties of the text, reader characteristics, and the instructional context (van den Broek & Kremer, 1999). For example, properties of the text can affect comprehension, such as the text structure (Wolfe & Mienko, 2007) and text difficulty (McNamara, 2001). Consider that more coherent texts help readers construct more coherent mental representations (Beck, McKeown, Omanson, & Pople, 1984; Britton & Gulgoz, 1991; McNamara, 2001; McNamara & Kintsch, 1996). Several projects have specifically looked at how the design of a text, including the particular words used and the associations between words (Keenan, Baillet, & Brown, 1984; van den Broek, 1994), as well as the organization of topics and themes (Hyönä & Lorch, 2004; Lorch & Lorch, 1995), influence readers' processing and comprehension of content.

When considering individual differences in reader characteristics, comprehension requires sufficient mental resources for readers to manage multiple processes simultaneously, such as activating background knowledge, tracking information, and generating inferences. Thus, readers with greater working memory capacity more easily manage these processes than do readers with lower working memory capacity (Just & Carpenter, 1992). In addition, readers approach texts with varying degrees of knowledge, expectations, and reading goals, all of which can affect text processing (van den Broek, Bohn-Gettler, Kendeou, Carlson, & White, 2011; van den Broek, Lorch, Linderholm, & Gustafson, 2001). Furthermore, the motivational orientation of a reader can affect comprehension. When intrinsic motivation to read is high, accompanied by supportive beliefs about reading competency (i.e., self-efficacy), a reader is more likely to employ background knowledge to understand text and persist longer when reading challenging texts (Deci, 1992; Guthrie & Wigfield, 2000). Of course, affect plays an important role here, a core point to which we will return in later sections of this chapter.

Finally, the instructional context plays an important role in determining reading successes and failures. For example, prereading instructions provided by a teacher or as provided by a text can guide inference generation and orient readers towards where they might direct attention (Kaakinen & Hyönä, 2011; McCrudden & Schraw, 2007; van den Broek et al., 2001). Likewise, the motivational features of the environment and instructional context can affect comprehension (Meyer & Turner, 2006). For example, a teacher consistently exhibiting positive emotions, positively responding to and supporting students, and establishing reasonable and appropriately challenging tasks, can encourage student motivation to learn and help promote mastery goals (Meyer & Turner, 2002; Patrick, Turner, Meyer, & Midgley, 2003; Pintrich & Schunk, 2002). And again, to foreshadow later sections of the chapter, these features are also infused with affect.

This brief description highlights some of the representations, skills, and factors that underlie comprehension of written text. However, comprehension and production are separable activities, and thus it is also important to consider how students produce their own written products. Research demonstrates that although reading and writing skills are correlated, simply improving one set of skills does not necessarily improve the other (Fitzgerald & Shanahan, 2000).

Writing

Composing a text is a complex process that requires writers to engage in a variety of behaviors. They must utilize knowledge of language and linguistic structures, form coherent thoughts, and organize and communicate information. To complete these tasks, writers make decisions about how to organize the composition and which language tokens and types to utilize that best embody their goals (Hacker, Keener, & Kircher, 2009). The cognitive processes involved in writing can involve directed thinking (i.e., goal oriented, such as writing a structured paper), undirected thinking (i.e., without a definable goal, such as free-writing), and recurrent thinking (i.e., repetitious thoughts, such as iteratively writing the same thing; Kellogg, 1994).

Cognitive accounts of writing have identified several core steps in the process: prewriting (or planning), writing (translating, or production), and rewriting (revision and refinement). These stages do not represent discrete, temporally ordered categories, as writers constantly move between the stages, and stages can interrupt each other. Many cognitive activities can occur at each step of the writing process, although some can recur in multiple stages. During the planning stage, the writer reinstates relevant knowledge to be included in the composition and develops and organizes an internal representation of what the final draft will include. This involves generating ideas, reading to build long-term memory, activating relevant prior knowledge, organizing ideas to create a meaningful structure, making decisions, and setting goals (Bereiter & Scardamalia, 1987; Flower & Hayes, 1981; Kellogg, 1994).

In the production stage of writing, individuals translate the planned ideas and organization into written language. This requires knowledge of grammatical conventions, spelling, and vocabulary. For example, writers must construct grammatically correct sentences in which the words are spelled correctly. Writers must also select the appropriate vocabulary that best exemplifies their thoughts (Flower & Hayes, 1981; Hillocks, 1987).

The reviewing stage involves evaluating the written product and making revisions. Writers, especially expert writers, often review their goals in this stage and may amend or reconsider their goals. For revision to be successful, the evaluation of the written product must involve critical reading such that the writer is able to find and correct any issues in the text (Brunyé, Mahoney, Rapp, Ditman, & Taylor, 2012; Flower, Hayes, Carey, Schriver, & Stratman, 1986; Hayes, Flower, Schriver, Stratman, & Carey, 1987).

At any of these stages, a variety of factors can affect writing. It is worth noting that the types of factors that influence writing are analogous to those for reading: individual variables and features of the text and instructional context. As with reading, individual variables, such as the writer's limited cognitive resources, are employed as individuals retrieve information from long term memory and organize this information to form coherent prose. Thus, individual differences, such as working memory, topic knowledge, and writing skills, affect writing behaviors. Motivation and affect can also influence writing through the instantiation and maintenance of beliefs and self-appraisals. For example, students with low self-efficacy in writing who believe that writing and effort are unrelated often experience writing anxiety. As another example, individual experiences of positive affect can lead to improved planning and information gathering during the writing process (Lynton & Salovey, 1997; Pajares, 2003).

Regarding features of the text and the instructional context, individuals behave differently as a function of the type of text they are composing (i.e., research papers versus narratives for different audiences; Bereiter & Scardamalia, 1987; Hayes, 1996). Instructors can provide task assignments and establish social environments that can motivate particular sets of writing behaviors. Consider the following examples. When composing a scientific text, writers often utilize their own knowledge, research other related scientific studies, interpret data, engage in revision, and utilize technical writing skills. In contrast, when composing a diary entry, writers engage in introspection but less revision. Narratives can similarly reveal a diversity of approaches for different text types. Writing narratives for different audiences often involves learning about the audience and developing an engaging plot and story structure for that particular readership. Consider that when writing a story for a teacher, writers often choose a more formal tone and utilize traditional structures to a greater degree than when writing the same story for a friend (Bereiter & Scardamalia, 1987; Hayes, 1996). These examples all illustrate how writing requirements and expectations can influence writing products.

Overall, characteristics of the writer, properties of a composition, and features of an instructional context are crucial considerations in accounts of literacy, memory, and learning. We next turn to an influence that we necessarily referred to as part of the above discussions and that is the focus of the current volume—emotion.

MODELS OF THE IMPACT OF EMOTION
ON COGNITIVE PROCESSES

Numerous activities underlie and influence reading and writing. However, emotion is a potential variable that, to date, has received far less attention than it warrants with regard to literacy. Broadly speaking, a variety of theories describe how emotion might affect the mental strategies individuals employ during problem-solving. These theories thus have direct implications for reading and writing, which allows for connecting the previously described work with emotion.

At the outset, it is important to note that many studies differentiate between the constructs of affect, mood, and emotion. Affect is considered a broad category of experiences, which includes the phenomenological interpretation and display of emotions, moods, and feelings. Emotions are specific feelings that often have a clearly perceived cause (or object), whereas moods are unfocused and without a clearly perceived cause (Batson, Shaw, & Oleson, 1992). However, many studies examining affect and literacy do not carefully account for the differences between moods and emotions, and thus the terminology used varies across projects. An attempt to disentangle these definitions and concepts is beyond the scope of the current chapter (although see the first chapter of this book, written by Pekrun & Linnenbrink-Garcia, for further elaboration of this issue). Rather, this chapter considers broadly how projects that examine these constructs, necessarily focused on affect, have implications for literacy activities. In this section, we utilize theories of emotion in making specific connections to accounts of comprehension and production.

Semantic Network Theories

Semantic memory represents a person's prior knowledge. This knowledge appears to be organized akin to a network, with different pieces of information connected through semantic relations. When considered as a function of this theoretical view, emotions represent information within the network and are thus connected to relevant knowledge and experiences. When feeling a particular mood, the experiences and knowledge that are related to and connected to that mood become available through a spread of activation in semantic memory (Bower, 1981).

This spread of activation can lead to memory facilitation for mood-congruent information (Bower, Gilligan, & Monteiro, 1981). For example, when remembering word lists, happy-induced participants often exhibit better memory for words with happy meanings, such as "cheerful." Individuals are also more apt to interpret ambiguous words as having a mood-congruent meaning. For example, when hearing homophones (i.e., "mourning" vs. "morning"), sad-induced participants more often write down the sad meaning (to grieve), whereas happy-induced participants more often write the happy connotation (Ferraro, King, Ronning, Pekarski, & Risan, 2003; Halberstadt, Niedenthal, & Kushner, 1995). Individuals are also more likely to notice stimuli in the environment (Mayer, 1986) and make evaluations that are congruent with their current mood (Schwarz & Skurnik, 2003). Memory facilitation thus can arise as a function of congruence between an individual's mood and external and internal representations.

It is important to note that the mood-congruency effects just described are somewhat controversial in that the evidence for their occurrence has been less than consistent.

Nevertheless, some replicated findings have emerged that are worth noting. For example, congruency effects are more likely to occur for positive as compared to negative moods. Furthermore, the effects are likely to occur when an individual is attempting to recall self-generated information in which constructive processing is necessary. Thus, mood-congruency effects, when they are obtained, seem to be a function of the particular methodological task (Fiedler, Nickel, Asbeck, & Pagel, 2003). We will revisit this point in greater detail when we consider the Affective Infusion Model (Forgas, 1995). (For additional discussion, see Fiedler & Beier, 2014).

The spread of activation associated with semantic networks can also result in state-dependent learning, which occurs as a person exhibits enhanced memory when their mood at the time of learning (encoding) matches their mood at the time of remembering (retrieval). For example, individuals in a happy mood are more likely to remember happy personal experiences, and individuals in a sad mood are more likely to remember sad experiences (Bower, Monteiro, & Gilligan, 1978). When learning word lists, participants are more likely to remember words when they are experiencing the same mood they were in when they originally studied the items, as compared to when they experience different moods at study and test (de l'Etoile, 2002; Thaut & de l'Etoile, 1993). However, like mood-congruency, the effects of mood state-dependent learning have not always been consistently obtained. Nevertheless, when the effects have emerged, they appear stronger for positive than negative moods and appear stronger when the stimuli are personally relevant to the participants (Ucros, 1989). The effects also do not always emerge for cued-recall tasks, in contrast to more consistent findings with free-recall tasks (Kenealy, 1997), which again suggests that self-generated, constructive processing plays a crucial role with respect to mood findings (Fiedler & Beier, 2014; Forgas, 1995). The purpose of describing these findings is to demonstrate that at least some evidence indicates that mood can influence learning (albeit only under certain conditions) and that mood can be infused into mechanistic accounts (i.e., semantic network theories) that have classically informed our understandings of cognitive processes and are quite relevant for the processes of reading and writing.

Resource Allocation Models

Aside from potentially being directly represented in memory, emotional information has been characterized as distinct from other types of representations, largely because emotional information is more salient and memorable to individuals than nonemotional information. For example, participants are more likely to remember emotional as compared to nonemotional photos (Payne & Corrigan, 2007). In addition, viewing emotional pictures or imagining emotionally intense events drains mental resources because these experiences are given high priority for processing as compared to more mundane materials and events. As a result, nonemotional events and information are not as privileged in memory as emotional events and information (Meinhardt & Pekrun, 2003).

This is the core idea that underlies models of resource allocation that are associated with emotion: Emotional information drains mental resources. Theorists hypothesize that our everyday experience of emotions thus places a burden on our limited cognitive resources. Our individual emotional experiences, though, differ from simply processing externally derived emotional presentations because the experience of emotion often involves generating appraisals, bodily reactions, facial expressions, and action tendencies (Parkinson, 1994). Our individual experiences of emotions thus create burden as we generate thoughts focused on the emotion but irrelevant to the task at hand, which causes interference with task performance (Ellis & Ashbrook, 1988). These intrusive, irrelevant thoughts can emerge in both positive and negative affective states (Rowe, Hirsh, & Anderson, 2007).

When an individual's cognitive resources are allocated toward processing emotions, this usually still leaves enough mental resources to successfully engage in simple tasks. However, performance on more demanding tasks may suffer. This can make it challenging to engage in mental activities that facilitate learning, such as identifying which information is relevant versus irrelevant in a problem-solving task. For example, when compared to neutral moods, negative moods increase the likelihood that an individual will focus attention on task-irrelevant information (Ellis & Ashbrook, 1989). This can lead to decreased problem-solving performance and inefficiencies when using, learning, and transferring problem-solving strategies (Seibert & Ellis, 1991). However, more recent research suggests that positive versus negative moods lead to differential processing styles, which may be functional depending on the type of task (see Fieldler & Beier, 2014). We now turn to research addressing these processing styles.

Affect Infusion Model

Resource allocation theorists hypothesize that attention is differentially focused as a function of mood. Building upon this view, the affect infusion model hypothesizes that moods and emotions are linked with the strategies and processes that individuals rely on to complete tasks (Fiedler, 2000; Forgas, 1995). The affect infusion model proposes that negative moods encourage individuals to process information methodically and analytically. Individuals in a negative mood engage in local, selective, attentional activity. Thus, in various tasks, memory for relevant stimuli is not always impaired, but rather memory for other stimuli can be enhanced (Corson, 2002; von Hecker & Meiser, 2005). In some cases, however, this attention to detail can tax an individual's limited cognitive capacities because of the additional focus on local information (Gunther, Ferraro, & Kirchner, 1996; Schwarz & Skurnik, 2003). While such a focus would restrict attention to the broader features of a task or stimuli, local, analytic processing can nevertheless improve performance for certain types of tasks, particularly those that require attention to detail (Fiedler & Beier, 2014; Forgas, 1998).

Positive moods, in contrast, are associated with a processing style that encourages a wider activation of information within the semantic network. This encourages individuals to perceive connections between concepts. As such, positive moods tend to be associated with more global, creative thinking (Bless & Fiedler, 1995; Gasper & Clore, 2002; Isen, 2008). Such processing can be particularly helpful for tasks that require inference generation or flexible processing to solve problems (Fiedler & Beier, 2014; Isen, Daubman, & Nowicki, 1987; Storbeck & Clore, 2005). However, this processing can impede performance for tasks that require more detail-oriented processing. To summarize, research examining the processing styles associated with positive and negative affect have identified performance enhancements and decrements that emerge through interactions between mood and tasks, rather than solely as a function of mood.

EMOTION APPLIED TO READING AND WRITING

In the previous sections, we have identified several accounts of emotion and cognition. These accounts, crucially, have relevant implications for the processes that underlie reading and writing. Literacy tasks involve a variety of different activities, including encoding, organization, inference generation, and retrieval. Previous research has described how mood can affect these particular activities, but with a focus on tasks different from those associated with literacy, or for very simple literacy tasks, such as recalling word lists. However, a growing body of work has examined how mood-driven responses arise during reading and writing. In this section, we describe research that makes specific connections between literacy and emotion.

Inferences About Emotion

According to semantic network theorists, emotions can be represented as information and connections in memory. Likewise, character emotions are represented in memory for texts, particularly when those emotions prove informative for understanding narrative events. Readers identify and infer the causes of events when they encode situation models (Gernsbacher, 1997; Kintsch & van Dijk, 1978). These models also encode characters' emotions, which is perhaps unsurprising as they can motivate or cause events to happen, with readers paying attention to emotions as a means for understanding plot (Gernsbacher, Goldsmith, & Robertson, 1992).

Because emotions can motivate a character's actions, readers will often encode and infer a character's emotional state and changes in that state into their situation models. This is in an effort to explain the causes of events (de Vega, Leon, & Diaz, 1996; Gernsbacher et al., 1992). Readers often take the mental perspective of a protagonist (Horton & Rapp, 2003) and try to simulate what he or she is thinking (Goldman, 2001; Rapp & Gerrig, 2001). Through the act of taking the mental perspective of the protagonist, stories can therefore change the emotions a reader experiences while proceeding through a text (Gerrig, 1993; Green & Brock, 2000; Komeda, Kawasaki, Tsunemi, & Kusumi, 2009). Thus, readers encode emotional information in their memory representations, linking emotion to the causes and consequences of events.

Mood Congruency and Emotional Salience

As in nonliteracy tasks, attention and memory are enhanced for mood-congruent information in reading and writing. When reading, individuals more easily learn and remember mood-congruent information, identify with and have better memory for characters in a congruent mood, and have better memory for texts written in a mood-congruent tone (Bower, 1981; Bower et al., 1981). When writing, individuals in a positive mood are more likely to write about positively (compared to negatively) valenced information, whereas the reverse is the case for individuals in a negative mood (Lynton & Salovey, 1997). Finally, during the planning stage of writing, writers experiencing positive affect are more likely to generate plans and gather information that anticipates a positive outcome, whereas individuals experiencing negative affect gather information in anticipation of a negative outcome (Mayer, 1986).

There are situations in reading, however, in which mood congruency effects are overridden. Readers often exhibit a *negativity bias* in which negatively valenced information receives more careful processing than positively valenced information. Readers spend more time processing negative than positive endings of stories, regardless of their naturalistic or induced mood. Thus, although mood congruency effects translate to literacy tasks, these effects can sometimes be overcome by more general tendencies associated with privileged types of information (Egidi & Gerrig, 2009).

Processing During Literacy Tasks

The ways in which emotion can occupy readers' and writers' limited cognitive resources have implications for processing. Recall that negative moods lead to a local focus of attention and can promote task-irrelevant thoughts. In some situations, this can interfere with literacy tasks. Because participants in a sad mood experience task-irrelevant thoughts, they are less accurate when identifying contradictions in texts, show poorer memory for certain texts, and are less accurate in judging their own comprehension (Ellis, Ottaway, Varner, Becker, & Moore, 1997; Ellis, Varner, Becker, & Ottaway, 1995). Negative emotions, such as anxiety, can interfere with the writing process by stymieing creativity and making it difficult to generate ideas (Brand & Powell, 1986). Thus, in reading and writing, a local focus of attention combined with increased irrelevant thoughts can interfere with the task at hand.

The affect infusion model specifies that individuals in positive moods are more likely to be creative, make connections between elements of tasks, and more broadly focus attention (Fiedler, 2000; Forgas, 1995). Based on this, we might expect readers in a positive mood to make inferential connections between elements of tasks and texts but not necessarily to have better memory for the important parts of a text. Bohn-Gettler and Rapp (2011) examined how induced moods affect the strategies readers engage in when reading expository texts. Happy-induced readers were more likely than sad-induced readers to generate causal inferences by utilizing relevant information contained within the text. In addition, both happy- and sad-induced participants engaged in the same amount of rehearsal of the text, and memory for the main ideas of the texts was equivalent. This indicates that sad moods do not result in a processing decrement for task-relevant information but may impair inferential processing.

Also consistent with the affect infusion model, positive affect leads to increased creativity in writing (Larson, 1989–1990). For example, when writing a persuasive text, individuals in a positive mood produce more arguments and are more convincing than are individuals in a negative mood (Bohner & Schwarz, 1993). Writers in a positive mood are also more likely to write forward-moving stories that follow the traditional format of having a beginning, middle, and an end with closure in which conflicts are resolved. Writers in a negative mood are less likely to follow this organized format—for example, writing in a diary style with incomplete sentences (Lynton & Salovey, 1997).

Emerging theories thus provide clear predictions regarding the effects of emotion on reading and writing. To restate, the findings with respect to affective influences on literacy activities align with the notion that negative affect results in a local focus of attention and methodological thinking. In contrast, positive affect results in a wider activation of information and flexible, creative processing. This work demonstrates the utility of examining the role of emotion in reading and writing.

Consideration of Individual Differences

An important consideration is that characteristics of the individual may interact with emotions during literacy experiences. For example, the amount of reading and/or writing skill and proficiency a person possesses can play a role in the types of emotions they experience. Skilled writers display a higher degree of positive affect throughout the writing process, whereas unskilled writers experience intense negative emotions, such as boredom and sadness at the beginning of the writing process, often because they do not feel prepared to write. Near the end of the writing process, these negative feelings dissipate, and the positive emotions of both groups are more similar (Brand & House, 1987; Brand & Powell, 1986).

Working memory is another critical variable to consider. During literacy tasks, individuals must maintain important information in working memory, activate related concepts from their long-term memory, and engage in processing strategies such as inferencing, organizing information in memory, and so on. Considering that the experience of emotion places an additional load on individuals' already limited cognitive resources (Ellis et al., 1997; Seibert & Ellis, 1991), working memory should drive effects of emotion on reading and writing. In fact, when compared to individuals with lower working memory resources, individuals with higher working memory resources are better at regulating their emotions, making them less likely to allow mood to affect processing (Schmeichel, Volokhov, & Demaree, 2008). In line with this, work from our own labs has shown that readers with high working memory generate text-based inferences regardless of mood; in contrast, readers with low working memory generate text-based inferences when induced to feel a happy mood but not a sad mood (Bohn-Gettler & Rapp, 2011). Thus, working memory can influence the degree to which mood affects processing.

Although a variety of other individual difference variables likely influence the interplay of emotion and literacy, the findings regarding skill and working memory highlight the importance of considering individual differences. Some readers and writers may be better equipped to handle their emotional experiences when engaging in academic tasks, whereas others may need assistance overcoming the effects of emotion.

METHODOLOGICAL CONSIDERATIONS AND CHALLENGES

The previously described projects were intended as investigations into how mood might influence the cognitive activities associated with reading and writing. Much of that work relied on specific methodologies intended to induce and evaluate mood, collecting and assessing performance data as a function of those instantiated moods. Whenever researchers elect to study the influences of affect on reading and writing, there are several crucial issues that need to be considered. In this section, we outline some of these issues most relevant to both previous work and future work in this area.

An important consideration is that not all tasks are equally likely to be influenced by mood. Tasks vary on a continuum of the depth of processing required for successful completion. Simpler tasks do not require many mental resources, and thus performance on these tasks is not likely to be shaped by affect. However, tasks that require deeper, more substantive processing, especially tasks that require elaboration, are more likely to be influenced by mood (Forgas, 1995). This suggests one reason why literacy studies prove particularly useful for understanding the nature of cognition and emotion: literacy studies often require deeper thinking than do other types of perceptual tasks.

Another consideration is the need to utilize multiple methods to provide converging evidence for the effects of mood on reading and writing. In discourse research, theorists advocate for a three-pronged approach (Magliano & Graesser, 1991) in which evidence is sought from verbal protocols, theoretical work, and behavioral measures. It is also important to study different types of tasks to account for variance in mood (Mayer & Volanth, 1985). Doing so can help to provide multiple forms of evidence to ensure that research findings adequately describe how various tasks can potentially lead to differential effects as a function of mood.

In addition to the need for converging evidence and controlling for depth of processing, instantiating a successful mood induction can be challenging. Mood induction procedures are not equally effective for all individuals. As one example, the effectiveness of musical mood inductions varies as a function of an individual's music preferences (Carter, Wilson, Lawson, & Bulik, 1995). Once a mood is successfully induced, it is also unclear how long the induced mood will last. Many studies that utilize mood inductions ask participants to complete shorter tasks, which might speak to the amount of time for which the mood induction is expected to last. Manipulation checks for mood induction often occur immediately after the induction procedure but not following the intervening task (P. Gomez, Zimmerman, Guttormsen Schar, & Danuser, 2009), which also leaves open whether the induction adequately influences performance across the entire task. Research suggests that mood manipulations can be quite fragile and short-lived. For example, mood manipulations utilizing the Velten procedure show decreased effectiveness after 10 minutes (Frost & Green, 1982), and when an intervening task as short as four minutes is introduced, the Velten procedure shows no effects (Isen & Gorgoglione, 1983). Thus, intervening tasks can interfere with mood induction. Other studies have expressed more optimism, particularly with video induction procedures. For these inductions, induced change in valence (i.e., feeling pleasant versus unpleasant) persists despite intervening tasks of up to nine minutes, although arousal (i.e., activation or energy levels) decreases much more rapidly (P. Gomez et al., 2009; Murray, Sujan, Hirt, & Sujan, 1990). Thus, the intervening tasks following a mood induction procedure should be relatively short in order for the induced mood valence to be effective (Gorn, Pham, & Sin, 2001). Future work will benefit from carefully outlining the temporal continuity of mood inductions (Frost & Green, 1982; P. Gomez et al., 2009).

Even if a mood is successfully induced and lasts for an adequate time period, the topic of the learning material, the task, or incidental emotions that students bring into the classroom may guide an individual's mood above or instead of any intended induction. This can occur in several ways. First, emotions may emerge in relation to the content of the text or writing topic (Pekrun & Stephens, 2012). For example, reading a text that is sad versus funny can induce a reader to feel sad or happy, over and above any preceding induction procedure. When comprehending narratives, readers also feel empathy for protagonists and experience emotions as a function of a protagonist's emotional state: Anxiety, surprise, and fear can arise with respect to concern about a protagonist in a narrative (Ferstl, Rinck, & Cramon, 2005; Komeda & Kusumi, 2002). When comprehending expository materials, the topic of science or political texts can also encourage emotional responses as a function of students' experiences and beliefs (Broughton et al.,

2013). When applied to writing, writing about adventurous and confusing experiences increases positive mood, writing descriptive essays increases negative mood, and writing about personal experiences heightens emotional responses (Brand & House, 1987). Thus, the particular tasks that participants are asked to engage in might rarely prove neutral, potentially strengthening or subverting any intended mood manipulations that precede the task activity.

Learners also experience emotions through the process of reading and writing, which can complement or override any intended induction. Recall that conflict in a narrative can lead to surprise, anxiety, and fear. These feelings dissipate and are replaced by relief toward the end of the story when the narrative conflicts are resolved (Komeda & Kusumi, 2002). The writing process likewise elicits an array of emotions. At the beginning of the process, writers are more likely to experience passive negative emotions, such as boredom, shyness, loneliness, and depression. As writing progresses, these passive negative emotions decrease, and happiness, relief, and excitement increase. As described earlier, this temporal effect is stronger for less experienced writers (Brand & House, 1987; Brand & Powell, 1986).

Other aspects of the task itself can also affect the emotional experiences of learners. For example, offering participants a monetary compensation can encourage positive moods regardless of the intended mood induction (R. Gomez, Cooper, & Gomez, 2000). Or, if tasks take too long to complete, or participants do not understand a text, they may experience boredom or frustration (D'Mello & Graesser, 2012). Thus, features of the task might instantiate moods.

Finally, readers and writers bring a variety of different emotions into the classroom from their lives outside of the classroom. As a few examples, students may feel elation from winning a sports match, sadness about a death in the family, confusion and anxiety regarding family or friendship conflicts, or any of a host of other incidental emotions. Thus, examining the effects of mood on reading and writing can be a challenging task, requiring consideration of the broader emotional experiences of learners.

FUTURE DIRECTIONS

In the next section, we describe a few topics for which we believe research can substantially extend our understanding of the effects of emotion on literacy. This list is by no means exhaustive; we have opted to focus on particular issues given our own research interests, the potential of this work for having important theoretical implications for research on cognition, and the possibility of developing practical implications for educational settings.

The Role of Arousal

The valence of an emotion refers to whether the emotion is generally pleasant or unpleasant. However, arousal refers to activation level and can vary from feeling calm to excited. For example, some emotions are considered more activated (such as feeling anger or fear), whereas others are considered more deactivated (such as feeling tired or bored) (Matthews & Margetts, 1991; Pekrun, Frenzel, Goetz, & Perry, 2007). Arousal may be important to reading and writing. For example, frustration, fatigue, and sadness are all negatively valenced emotions but have different activation levels. Feeling frustrated may challenge reading comprehension or writing production to a greater degree than feeling tired or sad.

Consider research in which individuals approach a text with various goals for reading. In some of those experiments (e.g., van den Broek et al., 2001), participants reading for study sit at a desk in brightly lit rooms, surrounded by textbooks. This may instantiate higher levels of arousal, thus making participants more alert and attentive. In contrast, participants reading for entertainment are placed in more subdued settings, such as on a couch surrounded by magazines. This may encourage readers to feel calm and thus experience lower levels of arousal. Therefore, reading goal manipulations may also manipulate arousal.

Mood induction techniques may likewise inadvertently manipulate arousal levels. Bohn-Gettler and Rapp (2011) induced readers to feel a neutral mood by asking them to watch nature documentary films. Unexpectedly, these participants engaged in reading activities that were less likely to help with comprehension, such as incorporating irrelevant background knowledge. It is possible that the films fostered relaxation or boredom, thus lowering arousal (Revelle & Loftus, 1992).

These findings highlight that arousal may be an important variable to account for when examining the effects of mood on literacy. However, research has also found that arousal plays a greater role when completing simple tasks but not necessarily more creative and complex problem-solving tasks (Schimmack, 2005). Similarly, arousal might affect simple reading and writing tasks but play less of a role for complex reading and writing situations. Either way, the role of arousal represents an interesting avenue for future research when examining emotion and literacy.

Discrete Emotions

In addition to considering valence and arousal, it is important to consider the array of emotions that individuals can feel. Emotional experiences involve more than simply feeling good or bad but instead can involve discrete emotions, which are more specific. There are a variety of discrete emotions that are commonly associated with learning contexts, such as boredom, confusion, curiosity, hopelessness, shame, anxiety, anger, surprise, relief, hope, pride, and enjoyment of learning (D'Mello & Graesser, 2012; Pekrun, Goetz, Frenzel, Barchfield, & Perry, 2011). These emotions are related to achievement, self-regulation, motivation, and several other processes in a variety of ways.

As one example, students experience boredom when the learning material is not appealing. This hinders productivity, learning, and creativity (Belton & Priyadharshini, 2007). On the opposite end of the spectrum from boredom are interest and curiosity. These foster engagement and are thus critical positive emotions for learning because they are related to achievement and motivation (D'Mello & Graesser, 2012). Curiosity can be encouraged by offering choices, such as allowing learners to select what they want to read or write about (Lepper & Woolverton, 2002).

As another example, students experience confusion when they have difficulty comprehending material and are unsure of how to proceed. Although cognitive disequilibrium can result with a learner making efforts to resolve the discrepancy through problem solving (resulting in delight), unsuccessfully solving the problem can lead to confusion, disengagement, and frustration (D'Mello & Graesser, 2014). When this occurs repeatedly, it can lead to despair, anxiety, and decreased learning (Craig, Graesser, Sullins, & Gholson, 2004; Linnenbrink & Pintrich, 2002). It is important to support students in their learning such that their confusion leads to positive learning experiences. One way to accomplish this in the context of reading and writing may be to provide appropriately challenging assignments. This can encourage students to feel a greater sense of control over their abilities to comprehend and produce written text. Another way to accomplish this can involve providing reading and writing tasks that are of interest to students and that students find valuable. This combination may help students to feel motivated to overcome their confusion and is supported by research in motivation—in particular, the control-value theory of achievement emotions (Pekrun, 2006; Pekrun, Goetz, Wolfram, & Perry, 2002).

The control-value theory of achievement emotions describes how discrete achievement related emotions can be a result of the amount of perceived control a student has within a learning situation combined with whether or not the student considers the topic and their performance to be of value (Pekrun et al., 2002, 2011). Within this context, positively valenced activating emotions (such as enjoyment, hope, or pride) can be induced when a student feels control over an academic task and values the task. These emotions are usefully related to intrinsic and extrinsic motivation, the use of flexible learning strategies, and improved academic performance. Negatively valenced deactivating emotions (such as boredom or hopelessness) can be induced when either a student does not feel control or does not value the task. These emotions are negatively correlated with motivation and academic performance. Positively valenced deactivating emotions (such as relief) and negatively valenced activating emotions (such as anger, anxiety, or shame) show complex relationships to motivation and achievement. For example, anger should decrease achievement because of task-irrelevant thinking, but in some situations, anger can also motivate an individual to increase effort (Pekrun et al., 2002, 2011; Pekrun & Stephens, 2012). The organizing framework of accounting for the valence and activation of emotions, situated within the control-value theory of achievement emotions, demonstrates that a wide variety of emotions are experienced in learning and assessment settings and suggests how such emotions can play a role in motivation, achievement, learning strategies, and a variety of other factors.

Future research should continue to expand upon the role of discrete emotions during reading and writing. It will be important to examine how these emotions are associated with different levels of arousal, how they can be instantiated in diverse educational settings through different instructional tasks, and how they may vary as a function of individual differences.

Classroom Climate and Instructor Feedback

Another important avenue for future work will involve examination of how instructors and their feedback can establish particular classroom climates and emotions. Classroom climates that consistently support learning and positive achievement emotions demonstrate the best conditions for motivation and support reading and writing (Meyer & Turner, 2006). Aside from the general learning environment, instructors believe they teach more effectively when experiencing a positive mood, just as a teacher's enthusiasm is positively correlated with students' enjoyment of instruction (Frenzel, Goetz, Lüdtke, Pekrun, & Sutton, 2009).

The feedback that instructors provide students also elicits emotion. One way this has been studied is with regard to intelligent tutoring systems in which an animated tutor provides feedback to learners as they read (D'Mello & Graesser, 2012). Although positive classroom environments have been found to be supportive of student learning, students actually perform better when the face of the automated tutor is designed to look more negatively than positively valenced (Sullins, Craig, & Graesser, 2009). This may occur because positive and negative feedback can convey different types of information. When learners receive positive instructor feedback after providing an incorrect answer, it communicates that their learning is going well, giving students an "illusion of knowing" and thus decreasing their efforts toward learning (Sullins et al., 2009). This suggests that affect as engendered by classroom situations might exhibit complex interactions depending upon tasks, contexts, and motivation.

The fields of artificial and computer-based learning environments will be particularly relevant in future studies of the effects of emotion on literacy. Not only do they offer useful tools for testing hypotheses about feedback and emotions in educational settings, they also represent the ways in which many individuals will comprehend and produce texts ever more regularly.

APPLICATIONS TO ACADEMIC SETTINGS

The study of emotion in the context of reading and writing is not only important theoretically but also has many practical applications for academic settings. Understanding how emotion can affect cognition and learning, and specifically the activities that underlie reading and writing, can help elucidate why some students may struggle with literacy tasks. Given the strong base of literature on how emotion can lead to more versus less effective literacy activities, it will be important to more clearly tease apart how emotion can affect processing in a variety of contexts. This work is, without a doubt, highly applicable to instructional settings. Understanding how to promote classroom settings that support appropriate emotions and thus encourage learning and achievement will be useful in determining best practices for individualizing instruction. Our understandings of cognitive influences on reading and writing can be enriched by considering conative factors that both arise from and guide our literacy experiences.

REFERENCES

Batson, C. D., Shaw, L. L., & Oleson, K. C. (1992). Differentiating affect, mood, and emotion: Toward functionally-based conceptual distinctions. In M. S. Clarke (Ed.), *Emotion* (pp. 294–326). Newbury Park, CA: Sage.

Beck, I. L., McKeown, M. G., Omanson, R. C., & Pople, M. T. (1984). Improving the comprehensibility of stories: The effect of revisions that improve coherence. *Reading Research Quarterly, 19*, 263–277.

Belton, T., & Priyadharshini, E. (2007). Boredom and schooling: A cross-disciplinary exploration. *Cambridge Journal of Education, 37*, 579–595.

Bereiter, C., & Scardamalia, M. (1987). *The psychology of written composition.* Hillsdale, NJ: Erlbaum.

Bless, H., & Fiedler, K. (1995). Affective states and the influence of activated general knowledge. *Personality and Social Psychology Bulletin, 21*, 766–778.

Bohn-Gettler, C. M., & Rapp, D. N. (2011). Depending on my mood: Mood-driven influences on text comprehension. *Journal of Educational Psychology, 103*, 562–577.

Bohner, G., & Schwarz, N. (1993). Mood states influence the production of persuasive arguments. *Communication Research, 20*, 695–722.

Bower, G. H. (1981). Mood and memory. *American Psychologist, 36,* 129–148.

Bower, G. H., Gilligan, S. G., & Monteiro, K. P. (1981). Selectivity of learning caused by affective states. *Journal of Experimental Psychology: General, 110,* 451–473.

Bower, G. H., Monteiro, K. P., & Gilligan, S. G. (1978). Emotional mood as a context for learning and recall. *Journal of Verbal Learning and Verbal Behavior, 17,* 573–585.

Brand, A. G., & House, G. (1987). Relationships between types of assignments, writer variables, and emotions of college composition students. *Alberta Journal of Educational Research, 33,* 21–32.

Brand, A. G., & Powell, J. L. (1986). Emotions and the writing process: A description of apprentice writers. *Journal of Educational Research, 79,* 280–285.

Britton, B. K., & Gulgoz, S. (1991). Using Kintsch's computational model to improve instructional text: Effects of repairing inference calls on recall and cognitive structures. *Journal of Educational Psychology, 83,* 329–345.

Broughton, S. H., Sinatra, G. M., & Nussbaum, E. M. (2013). "Pluto has been a planet my whole life!" Emotions, attitudes, and conceptual change in elementary students learning about Pluto's reclassification. *Research in Science Education, 43,* 529–550.

Brunyé, T. T., Mahoney, C. R., Rapp, D. N., Ditman, T., & Taylor, H. A. (2012). Caffeine enhances real-world language processing: Evidence from a proofreading task. *Journal of Experimental Psychology: Applied, 18,* 95–108.

Carter, F. A., Wilson, J. S., Lawson, R. H., & Bulik, C. M. (1995). Mood induction procedure: Importance of individualising music. *Behaviour Change, 12,* 159–161.

Corson, Y. (2002). Effects of positive, negative, and neutral moods on associative and semantic priming. *Current Psychology of Cognition, 21,* 33–62.

Craig, S., Graesser, A. C., Sullins, J., & Gholson, B. (2004). Affect and learning: An exploratory look into the role of affect in learning with AutoTutor. *Journal of Educational Media, 29,* 241–250.

Craik, F. I. M., & Lockhart, R. S. (1972). Levels of processing: A framework for memory research. *Journal of Verbal Learning and Verbal Behavior, 11,* 671–684.

D'Mello, S. K., & Graesser, A. C. (2012). Emotions during learning with Autotutor. In P. Durlach & A. Lesgold (Eds.), *Adaptive technologies for training and education.* Cambridge, United Kingdom: Cambridge University Press.

D'Mello, S. K., & Graesser, A. C. (2014). Confusion. In R. Pekrun & L. Linnenbrink-Garcia (Eds.), *International handbook of emotions in education* (pp. 289–310). New York, NY: Taylor & Francis.

de l'Etoile, S. K. (2002). The effect of a musical mood induction procedure on mood state-dependent word retrieval. *Journal of Music Therapy, 39,* 145–160.

de Vega, M., Leon, I., & Diaz, J. M. (1996). The representation of changing emotions in reading comprehension. *Cognition and Emotion, 10,* 303–321.

Deci, E. L. (1992). The relation of interest to the motivation of behavior: A self-determination theory perspective. In E. L. Deci (Ed.), *The role of interest in learning and development* (pp. 43–70). Hillsdale, NJ: Erlbaum.

Egidi, G., & Gerrig, R. J. (2009). How valence affects language processing: Negativity bias and mood congruence in narrative comprehension. *Memory & Cognition, 37,* 547–555.

Ehri, L. C., Nunes, S. R., Stahl, S. A., & Willows, D. M. (2001). Systematic phonics instruction helps students learn to read: Evidence from the National Reading Panel's meta-analysis. *Review of Educational Research, 71,* 393–447.

Ellis, H. C., & Ashbrook, P. W. (1988). Resource allocation model of the effect of depressed mood states on memory. In K. Fiedler & J. P. Forgas (Eds.), *Affect, cognition, and social behavior* (pp. 25–43). Toronto, Canada: Hogrefe International.

Ellis, H. C., & Ashbrook, P. W. (1989). The "state" of mood and memory research: A selective review. *Journal of Social Behavior and Personality, 4,* 1–21.

Ellis, H. C., Ottaway, S. A., Varner, L. J., Becker, A. S., & Moore, B. A. (1997). Emotion, motivation, and text comprehension: The detection of contradictions in passages. *Journal of Experimental Psychology, 126,* 131–146.

Ellis, H. C., Varner, L. J., Becker, A. S., & Ottaway, S. A. (1995). Emotion and prior knowledge in memory and judged comprehension of ambiguous stories. *Cognition and Emotion, 9,* 363–382.

Ferraro, F. R., King, B., Ronning, B., Pekarski, K., & Risan, J. (2003). Effects of induced emotional state on lexical processing in younger and older adults. *The Journal of Psychology, 137,* 262–272.

Ferstl, E. C., Rinck, M., & Cramon, D. Y. (2005). Emotional and temporal aspects of situation model processing during text comprehension: an event-related fMRI study. *Journal of Cognitive Neuroscience, 17,* 724–739.

Fiedler, K. (2000). Toward an integrative account of affect and cognition phenomena using the BIAS computer algorithm. In J. P. Forgas (Ed.), *Feeling and thinking: The role of affect in social cognition* (pp. 223–252). New York, NY: Cambridge University Press.

Fiedler, K., & Beier, S. (2014). Affect and cognitive processes in educational contexts. In R. Pekrun & L. Linnenbrink-Garcia (Eds.), *International handbook of emotions in education* (pp. 36–55). New York, NY: Taylor & Francis.

Fiedler, K., Nickel, S., Asbeck, J., & Pagel, U. (2003). Mood and the generation effect. *Cognition & Emotion, 17,* 585–608.

Fitzgerald, J., & Shanahan, T. (2000). Reading and writing relations and their development. *Educational Psychologist, 35,* 39–50.

Flower, L., & Hayes, J. R. (1981). A cognitive process theory of writing. *College Composition and Communication, 32,* 365–387.

Flower, L., Hayes, J. R., Carey, L., Schriver, K. A., & Stratman, J. F. (1986). Detection, diagnosion, and the strategies of revision. *College Composition and Communication, 37,* 16–55.

Forgas, J. P. (1995). Mood and judgment: The affect infusion model (AIM). *Psychological Bulletin, 117,* 39–66.

Forgas, J. P. (1998). On being happy and mistaken: Mood effects on the fundamental attribution error. *Journal of Personality and Social Psychology, 75,* 318–331.

Frenzel, A. C., Goetz, T., Lüdtke, O., Pekrun, R., & Sutton, R. E. (2009). Emotional transmission in the classroom: Exploring the relationship between teacher and student enjoyment. *Journal of Educational Psychology, 101,* 705–716.

Frost, R. O., & Green, M. C. (1982). Duration and postexperimental removal of Velten mood-induction procedure effects. *Personality and Social Psychology Bulletin, 8,* 341–347.

Gasper, K., & Clore, G. L. (2002). Attending to the big picture: Mood and global versus local processing of visual information. *Psychological Science, 13,* 33–39.

Gernsbacher, M. A. (1997). Two decades of structure building. *Discourse Processes, 23,* 265–304.

Gernsbacher, M. A., Goldsmith, H. H., & Robertson, R. R. W. (1992). Do readers mentally represent character's emotional states? *Cognition and Emotion, 6,* 89–111.

Gerrig, R. J. (1993). *Experiencing narrative worlds: On the psychological activities of reading.* Boulder, CO: Westview Press.

Goldman, A. I. (2001). Desire, intention, and the simulation theory. In B. F. Malle, L. J. Moses, & D. A. Baldwin (Eds.), *Intentions and intentionality: Foundations of social cognition* (pp. 207–224). Cambridge, MA: MIT Press.

Gomez, P., Zimmerman, P. G., Guttormsen Schar, S., & Danuser, B. (2009). Valence lasts longer than arousal: Persistence of induced moods as assessed by psychophysicological measures. *Journal of Psychophysiology, 23,* 7–17.

Gomez, R., Cooper, A., & Gomez, A. (2000). Susceptibility to positive and negative mood states: Test of Eysenck's, Gray's and Newman's theories. *Personality and Individual Differences, 29,* 351–366.

Gorn, G., Pham, M. T., & Sin, L. Y. (2001). When arousal influences ad evaluation and valence does not (and vice versa). *Journal of Consumer Psychology, 11,* 43–55.

Graesser, A. C., Singer, M., & Trabasso, T. (1994). Constructing inferences during narrative text comprehension. *Psychological Review, 101,* 371–395.

Green, M. C., & Brock, T. C. (2000). The role of transportation in the persuasiveness of public narratives. *Journal of Personality and Social Psychology, 79,* 701–721.

Gunther, D. C., Ferraro, F. R., & Kirchner, T. (1996). Influence of emotional state on irrelevant thoughts. *Psychonomic Bulletin & Review, 3,* 491–494.

Guthrie, J. T., & Wigfield, A. (2000). Engagement and motivation in reading. In J. T. Guthrie & A. Wigfield (Eds.), *Handbook of reading research, Vol. III* (pp. 403–422). Mahwah, NJ: Erlbaum.

Hacker, D. J., Keener, M. C., & Kircher, J. C. (2009). Writing is applied metacognition. In D. J. Hacker, J. Dunlosky, & A. C. Graesser (Eds.), *Handbook of metacognition in education* (pp. 154–174). New York, NY: Routledge.

Hagaman, J. L., & Reid, R. (2008). The effects of paraphrasing strategy on the reading comprehension of middle school students at risk for failure in reading. *Remedial and Special Education, 29,* 222–234.

Halberstadt, J. B., Niedenthal, P. M., & Kushner, J. (1995). Resolution of lexical ambiguity by emotional state. *Psychological Science, 6,* 278–282.

Hayes, J. R. (1996). A new framework for understanding cognition and affect in writing. In M. C. Levy & S. Ransdell (Eds.), *The science of writing: Theories, methods, individual differences, and applications* (pp. 1–27). Hillsdale, NJ: Erlbaum.

Hayes, J. R., Flower, L., Schriver, K. A., Stratman, J. F., & Carey, L. (1987). Cognitive processes in revision *Advances in applied psycholinguistics: Reading, writing, and language learning* (Vol. 2, pp. 176–240). New York, NY: Cambridge University Press.

Hillocks, G. (1987). Synthesis of research on teaching writing. *Educational Leadership, 44,* 71–82.

Horton, W. S., & Rapp, D. N. (2003). Out of sight, out of mind: Occlusion and the accessibility of information in narrative comprehension. *Psychonomic Bulletin and Review, 10,* 104–110.

Hyönä, J., & Lorch, R. F. (2004). Effects of topic heading on text processing: Evidence from adult readers' eye fixation patterns. *Learning and Instruction, 14,* 131–152.

Isen, A. M. (2008). Some ways in which positive affect influences decision making and problem solving. In M. Lewis, J. M. Haviland-Jones, & L. F. Barrett (Eds.), *Handbook of emotions* (3rd ed., pp. 548–573). New York, NY: Guilford Press.

Isen, A. M., Daubman, K. A., & Nowicki, G. P. (1987). Positive affect facilitates creative problem solving. *Journal of Personality and Social Psychology, 52,* 1122–1131.

Isen, A. M., & Gorgoglione, J. M. (1983). Some specific effects of four affect-induction procedures. *Personality and Social Psychology Bulletin, 9,* 136–143.

Just, M. A., & Carpenter, P. A. (1992). A capacity theory of comprehension: Individual differences in working memory. *Psychological Review, 99,* 122–149.

Kaakinen, J. K., & Hyönä, J. (2011). Online processing of and memory for perspective relevant and irrelevant text information. In M. T. McCrudden, J. P. Magliano & G. Schraw (Eds.), *Text relevance and learning from text* (pp. 223–242). Charlotte, NC: Information Age Publishing.

Keenan, J. M., Baillet, S. D., & Brown, P. (1984). The effects of causal cohesion on comprehension and memory. *Journal of Verbal Learning and Verbal Behavior, 23,* 115–126.

Kellogg, R. T. (1994). *The psychology of writing.* New York, NY: Oxford University Press.

Kenealy, P. M. (1997). Mood-state-dependent retrieval: The effects of induced mood on memory reconsidered. *The Quarterly Journal of Experimental Psychology, 50,* 290–317.

Kintsch, W., & van Dijk, T. A. (1978). Toward a model of text comprehension and production. *Psychological Review, 85,* 363–394.

Komeda, H., Kawasaki, M., Tsunemi, K., & Kusumi, T. (2009). Differences between estimating protagonists' emotions and evaluating readers' emotions in narrative comprehension. *Cognition and Emotion, 23,* 135–151.

Komeda, H., & Kusumi, T. (2002). Reader's changing emotions related to the construction of a situational model. *Tohoku Psychologica Folia, 61,* 48–54.

Larson, R. W. (1989–1990). Emotions and the creative process: Anxiety, boredom, and enjoyment as predictors of creative writing. *Imagination, Cognition, and Personality, 9,* 275–292.

Lepper, M. R., & Woolverton, M. (2002). The wisdom of practice: Lessons learned from the study of highly effective tutors. In J. Aronson (Ed.), *Improving academic achievement: Impact of psychological factors on education* (pp. 135–158). San Diego, CA: Academic Press.

Linnenbrink, E. A., & Pintrich, P. R. (2002). Motivation as an enabler for academic success. *School Psychology Review, 31,* 313–327.

Lorch, R. F., & Lorch, E. P. (1995). Effects of organizational signals on text processing strategies. *Journal of Educational Psychology, 87,* 537–544.

Lynton, H., & Salovey, P. (1997). The effects of mood on expository writing. *Imagination, Cognition, and Personality, 17,* 95–110.

Magliano, J. P., & Graesser, A. C. (1991). A three-pronged approach for studying inference generation in literary text. *Poetics, 20,* 193–232.

Mandler, G. (1967). Organization and memory. In K. W. Spence & J. T. Spence (Eds.), *The psychology of learning and motivation* (Vol. 1, pp. 328–372). New York, NY: Academic Press.

Matthews, G., & Margetts, I. (1991). Self-report arousal and divided attention: A study of performance operating characteristics. *Human Performance, 4,* 107–125.

Mayer, J. D. (1986). How mood influences cognition. In N. E. Sharkey (Ed.), *Advances in cognitive science* (Vol. 1, pp. 290–314). Chichester, United Kingdom: Ellis Horwood Limited.

Mayer, J. D., & Volanth, A. J. (1985). Cognitive involvement in the mood response system. *Motivation and Emotion, 9,* 261–275.

McCrudden, M. T., & Schraw, G. (2007). Relevance and goal-focusing in text processing. *Educational Psychology Review, 19,* 113–139.

McNamara, D. S. (2001). Reading both high-coherence and low-coherence texts: Effects of text sequence and prior knowledge. *Canadian Journal of Experimental Psychology, 55,* 51–62.

McNamara, D. S., & Kintsch, W. (1996). Learning from texts: Effects of prior knowledge and text coherence. *Discourse Processes, 22,* 247–288.

Meinhardt, J., & Pekrun, R. (2003). Attentional resource allocation to emotional events: An ERP study. *Cognition and Emotion, 17,* 477–500.

Meyer, D. K., & Turner, J. C. (2002). Discovering emotion in classroom motivation research. *Educational Psychologist, 37,* 107–114.

Meyer, D. K., & Turner, J. C. (2006). Re-conceptualizing emotion and motivation to learn in classroom contexts. *Educational Psychology Review, 18,* 377–390.

Murray, N., Sujan, H., Hirt, E. R., & Sujan, M. (1990). The influence of mood on categorization: A cognitive flexibility interpretation. *Journal of Personality and Social Psychology, 59,* 411–425.

National Reading Panel. (2000). Teaching children to read: An evidence-based assessment of the scientific research literature on reading and its implications for reading instruction. National Reading Panel, Bethesda, MD.

Neath, I., & Surprenant, A. M. (2003). *Human memory* (2nd ed.). Belmont, CA: Wadsworth.

Oakhill, J. V., Cain, K., & Bryant, P. E. (2003). The dissociation of word reading and text comprehension: Evidence from component skills. *Language and Cognitive Processes, 18,* 443–468.

Ouellette, G. P. (2006). What's meaning got to do with it: The role of vocabulary in word reading and reading comprehension. *Journal of Educational Psychology, 98,* 554–566.

Pajares, F. (2003). Self-efficacy beliefs, motivation, and achievement in writing: A review of the literature. *Reading & Writing Quarterly, 19,* 139–158.

Parkinson, B. (1994). Emotion. In A. M. Coleman (Ed.), *Companion encyclopedia of psychology* (Vol. 1, pp. 485–505). London: Routledge.

Patrick, J., Turner, J. C., Meyer, D. K., & Midgley, C. (2003). How teachers establish psychological environments during the first days of school: Associations with avoidance in mathematics. *Teachers College Record, 105,* 1521–1558.

Payne, B. K., & Corrigan, E. (2007). Emotional constraints on intentional forgetting. *Journal of Experimental Social Psychology, 43,* 780–786.

Pekrun, R. (2006). The control-value theory of achievement emotions: Assumptions, corrollaries, and implications for educational research and practice. *Educational Psychology Review, 18,* 315–341.

Pekrun, R., Frenzel, A. C., Goetz, T., & Perry, R. P. (2007). The control-value theory of achievement emotions: An integrative approach to emotions in education. In P. A. Schutz & R. Pekrun (Eds.), *Emotion in education. Educational psychology series* (pp. 13–36). San Diego, CA: Elsevier.

Pekrun, R., Goetz, T., Frenzel, A. C., Barchfield, P., & Perry, R. P. (2011). Measuring emotions in students' learning and performance: The Achievement Emotions Questionnaire (AEQ). *Contemporary Educational Psychology, 36,* 36–48.

Pekrun, R., Goetz, T., Wolfram, T., & Perry, R. P. (2002). Academic emotions in students' self-regulated learning and achievement: A program of qualitative and quantitative research. *Educational Psychologist, 37,* 91–105.

Pekrun, R., & Linnenbrink-Garcia, L. (2014). Introduction to emotions in education. In R. Pekrun & L. Linnenbrink-Garcia (Eds.), *International handbook of emotions in education* (pp. 1–10). New York, NY: Taylor & Francis.

Pekrun, R., & Stephens, E. J. (2012). Academic emotions. In K. Harris, S. Graham, & T. Urdan (Eds.), *APA Educational Psychology Handbook: Vol. 2. Individual differences and cultural and contextual factors* (pp. 3–31). Washington, DC: American Psychological Association.

Pintrich, P. R., & Schunk, D. H. (2002). *Motivation in education: Theory, research, and applications.* Englewood Cliffs, NJ: Merrill.

Rapp, D. N., & Gerrig, R. J. (2001). Readers' trait-based models of characters in narrative comprehension. *Journal of Memory and Language, 45,* 737–750.

Rasinski, T. V. (2004). Creating fluent readers. *Educational Leadership, 61,* 46–51.

Revelle, W., & Loftus, D. A. (1992). The implications of arousal effects for the study of affect and memory. In S. A. Christianson (Ed.), *The handbook of emotion and memory: Research and theory* (pp. 113–149). Hillsdale, NJ: Erlbaum.

Rowe, G., Hirsh, J. B., & Anderson, A. K. (2007). Positive affect increases the breadth of attentional selection. *PNAS, 104,* 383–388.

Schimmack, U. (2005). Attentional interference effects of emotional pictures: Threat, negativity, or arousal? *Emotion, 5,* 55–66.

Schmeichel, B. J., Volokhov, R. N., & Demaree, H. A. (2008). Working memory capacity and the self-regulation of emotional expression and experience. *Journal of Personality and Social Psychology, 95,* 1526–1540.

Schwarz, N., & Skurnik, I. (2003). Feeling and thinking; Implications for problem solving. In J. Davidson & R. Sternberg (Eds.), *The nature of problem solving* (pp. 263–290). Cambridge, United Kingdom: Cambridge University Press.

Seibert, P. S., & Ellis, H. C. (1991). Irrelevant thoughts, emotional mood states, and cognitive task performance. *Memory & Cognition, 19,* 507–513.

Storbeck, J., & Clore, G. L. (2005). With sadness comes accuracy; with happiness, false memory: Mood and the false memory effect. *Psychological Science, 16,* 785–791.

Sullins, J., Craig, S., & Graesser, A. C. (2009). Tough love: The influence of an agent's negative affect on students' learning. In V. Dimitrova, R. Mizoguchi, B. Du Boulay, & A. C. Graesser (Eds.), *Artificial intelligence in education: Building learning systems that care* (pp. 677–679). Amsterdam, Netherlands: IOS Press.

Thaut, M. H., & de l'Etoile, S. K. (1993). The effects of music on mood state-dependent recall. *Journal of Music Therapy, 30,* 70–80.

Ucros, C. G. (1989). Mood state-dependent memory: A meta-analysis. *Cognition and Emotion, 3,* 139–167.

van den Broek, P. (1994). Comprehension and memory of narrative texts: Inferences and coherence. In M. A. Gernsbacher (Ed.), *Handbook of psycholinguistics* (pp. 539–588). San Diego, CA: Academic Press.

van den Broek, P., Bohn-Gettler, C. M., Kendeou, P., Carlson, S., & White, M. J. (2011). The role of standards of coherence in reading comprehension. In M. T. McCrudden, J. P. Magliano, & G. Schraw (Eds.), *Text relevance and learning from text* (pp. 123–139). Charlotte, NC: Information Age Publishing.

van den Broek, P., & Kremer, K. E. (1999). The mind in action: What it means to comprehend during reading. In B. Taylor, M. Graves, & P. van den Broek (Eds.), *Reading for meaning* (pp. 1–31). New York, NY: Teachers College Press.

van den Broek, P., Lorch, R. F., Linderholm, T., & Gustafson, M. (2001). The effects of readers' goals on inference generation and memory for texts. *Memory & Cognition, 29,* 1081–1087.

van den Broek, P., Rapp, D. N., & Kendeou, P. (2005). Integrating memory-based and constructionist processes in accounts of reading comprehension. *Discourse Processes, 39,* 299–316.

von Hecker, U., & Meiser, T. (2005). Defocused attention in depressed mood: Evidence from source monitoring. *Emotion, 5,* 456–463.

Wolfe, M.B.W., & Mienko, J. A. (2007). Learning and memory of factual content from narrative and expository text. *British Journal of Educational Psychology, 77,* 541–564.

Woloshyn, V. E., Willoughby, T., Wood, E., & Pressley, M. (1990). Elaborative interrogation facilitates adult learning of factual paragraphs. *Journal of Educational Psychology, 82,* 513–524.

Zajonc, R. B. (1980). Feelings and thinking: Preferences need no inferences. *American Psychologist, 35,* 151–175.

23

SITUATING EMOTIONS IN CLASSROOM PRACTICES

Debra K. Meyer, Elmhurst College

As ubiquitous as emotions are in daily classroom life, scholarship that prioritizes their development and roles in teaching and learning have been relatively sparse until the last decade (Hagenauer & Hascher, 2010; Schutz & Pekrun, 2007). At the same time, the belief that emotions have a central role in classroom learning seems to have always been acknowledged, especially the benefits of an enjoyable learning environment. For example, published in 1976, Santrock reported an experimental study with 108 first and second graders in which he manipulated the (a) physical setting via happy, sad, or neutral decorations, (b) "affective tone" by asking students to think happy, sad, or neutral thoughts, and (c) "social agent's affect" through the experimenter telling a happy, sad, or neutral story. Santrock (1976) concluded that the children's self control, measured by their persistence on a boring task, was influenced by the affective tone of their thoughts, physical space, and relationship with the social agent. He saw these findings as suggesting strong implications for classroom practice.

> There is no reason to believe that the child's self-control in a classroom setting with a teacher would be substantially different from the type of situation evaluated in the present study. Thus, students who think about happy things, have happy interchanges with teachers, and who work in a happy room could be expected to persevere longer as tasks become repetitive and boring to them than students who experience less positively valenced affective situations.
>
> (Santrock, 1976, p. 534)

Interrelationships among student emotions and classroom practices are examined in this chapter from the perspective that emotions are a part of dynamic systems of interactions within classrooms. Within these systems, emotions represent intricate mash-ups of appraisals, action tendencies, desires, feelings, and physiological responses (Ortony & Turner, 1990). Emotions give meaning to thoughts, actions, and relations by drawing upon what has been experienced, is being experienced, and is anticipated (Ford, 1992; Pekrun, Goetz, Titz, & Perry, 2002; Schutz & Zembylas, 2009). Moreover, when specific emotions reappear frequently, they become linked to learning experiences, classroom characteristics, and interpersonal interactions that span school years.

To situate emotion in classroom experiences, the research chosen for this chapter focused on emotion within traditional P–12 classroom settings (e.g., a head teacher instructing a group of children or adolescents). Because other chapters in this *Handbook* address the role of content area in classroom emotions, there was no attempt to speak to disciplinary influences, which have been widely documented in the literature (e.g., Goetz, Frenzel, & Pekrun, 2006; Goetz, Pekrun, Hall, & Haag, 2006). Moreover, the chapter reflects the imbalance in the prominent role of mathematics in classroom motivation research (Turner & Meyer, 2009). Classroom studies that utilized multimethod approaches and triangulated data were deemed especially relevant as were studies comparing across classroom settings, time, or representing a program of research. In sum, the goal was not to provide a historical or theoretical analysis of classroom emotion research but a contemporary synthesis of themes within the literature to highlight what is known about relationships between emotions and teacher practices in P–12 settings.

The chapter is organized around two related but distinct bodies of research on classroom emotions: "Emotions During Classroom Learning" and the "Learning About Emotions in School." Research chosen within the emotions during learning section illustrates the interplay between P–12 classroom practices and student emotions primarily using a motivation theory as a theoretical framework. The second area of research, learning about emotions in school, was drawn from the developmental literature on student well-being and school adjustment, which examines student understanding and regulation of emotions in school contexts (see Jacobs & Gross, 2014, for a review of emotion regulation). The developmental research suggests that classroom practices also promote an informal but powerful *emotion curricula* related to students' socioemotional development as they move through school and learn about the opportunities and consequences of expressing their emotions in classroom contexts (see Bracket & Rivers, 2014, for a review of socioemotional development). Although the developmental research is comprised mostly of studies involving young children, the findings offer complementary evidence to the emotions during learning classroom research by emphasizing how emotions covey critical information on which teachers base instructional decisions and students use to guide their interactions in school settings.

EMOTIONS DURING CLASSROOM LEARNING

The most accessible and largest research base for examining classroom emotions has grown out of studies primarily focused on student motivation for learning. Whereas several motivation theories explicitly explain the central role of emotions in learning, such as attribution theory (Weiner, 1986), control-value theory (Pekrun, 2000), flow theory (Csikszentmihalyi, 1975), and motivation systems theory (Ford, 1992), the empirical links between emotions and motivation have mostly been implicit (Brophy, 2008; Pintrich, 2003) and even serendipitous (Meyer & Turner, 2002). Today, as Hagenauer and Hascher (2010) noted, the integral roles of emotions in learning are widely acknowledged. Pleasant emotions are recognized as impacting cognition, motivation, and well-being in highly reciprocal ways. However, our knowledge remains fragmented about what teachers and students actually do to create supportive classroom contexts (Anderman, Andrzejewski, & Allen, 2011; Meyer & Turner, 2007).

What the current research offers are the conceptual beginnings of an ecological model for organizing the emerging literature connecting student emotions and instructional practices. Imagine a set of concentric circles; in the center circle, the context for understanding student emotions is the *instructional activity* (i.e., lesson). The next circle going outward represents patterns of experiences that have coalesced over time to establish *classroom climates* linking emotions and practices. A third, larger circle, represents *student–teacher relations* that help to sustain enjoyable learning environments as well as support lesson-level interactions. If the three concentric circles are given depth, then these levels of instructional support for student emotions can be conceptualized over time, like the "chronosystem" in Bronfenbrenner's model of development (Bronfenbrenner, 1979). This ecological organization of the research highlights short-term and longer term interactions between emotions and classroom practices at the lesson, classroom, and interpersonal levels.

Emotions During Instructional Activities

The complex interrelationship among learning, motivation, and emotion is a primary reason emotion is commonplace in classroom motivation research (Meyer & Turner, 2002). A benefit of these interconnections is that when classroom researchers describe instruction, they commonly capture emotions during lessons, and instructional patterns emerge. To illustrate how research informs lesson-level practices, two sets of findings are described: (a) teacher support for the level of challenge in a learning activity and (b) teacher expression of emotions during teaching.

Instructional Challenge and Emotions

Challenge is essential for learning, yet it is accompanied by a variety of emotions, such as pride and happiness with success or anxiety and frustration with failure. Researchers have suggested that unpleasant emotions experienced after failure may be some of the more memorable experiences for students (e.g., *negative affect after failure*, Turner, Thorpe, & Meyer 1998). Therefore, student emotions, especially during challenging learning, are associated with beliefs about competence and efficacy (e.g., Ahmed, van der Werf, Minnaert, & Kuyper, 2010; Schweinle, Turner, & Meyer, 2008; Usher, 2009). Over time, the emotions experienced during academic challenges may not only be connected to the current lesson but also experienced in anticipation of similar anxiety or enjoyment in future lessons (Ahmed et al., 2010), in a discipline (Usher, 2009), or with teachers (Meyer, Turner, & Spencer, 1997; Turner & Patrick, 2004).

Although differences in the challenge level of lessons have been found in lesson-to-lesson changes in emotions and associated perceptions of competence or efficacy, associated instructional practices have been less frequently examined. Turner, Schweinle, and colleagues' research program explicitly connected emotions, challenge, and instructional practice (Turner, Meyer, Cox, et al., 1998, Turner et al., 2002; Schweinle, Turner, & Meyer, 2006, 2008) by applying flow theory to explain relationships between student emotions and instructional practices with different levels of challenge during mathematics lessons. An assumption of flow theory is that optimal learning experiences are intrinsically motivated and associated with pleasant emotions, enhanced cognitive processing, and best possible match between students' current skills and the lesson's challenge

(Csikszentmihalyi & Csikszentmihalyi, 1988; Csikszentmihalyi & Nakamura, 1989; Csikszentmihalyi, Rathunde, & Whalen, 1993). In Turner, Meyer, Cox, et al. (1998), the experience of *flow* was examined in seven upper-elementary mathematics classrooms using the experience sampling method by asking students to report their skill levels, the level of challenge during the observed lessons, their emotions, intrinsic motivation, and cognitive focus at the end of the lesson. The primary goal was to study involvement, which was defined as a moderate to high match between skill and challenge.

Using discourse analysis of the observed lessons during which student experiences were reported in their mathematics journals, Turner, Meyer, Cox, et al. (1998) described "high involvement" and "low involvement" classroom practices. Three common instructional patterns were found, which all related emotions to involvement and described how teachers negotiated the level of challenge in the high involvement classrooms. First, teachers balanced the press for understanding during challenging learning with humor and encouragement, seeming to acknowledge student emotions such as anxiety or frustrations. Second, teachers emphasized the constructive nature of errors, reducing negative affect after failure (see Turner, Thorpe, & Meyer, 1998). Third, teachers shared their own interest in and enthusiasm for learning mathematics, which may have provided a model of how to approach challenge positively or served as a buffer to student anxiety or frustration due to the level of challenge.

Challenge with support for student skill levels, therefore, appears to be a critical practice for enhancing student emotion and motivation. For example, as Schweinle et al. (2006) used finer-grained instructional analysis, they found that student self-reported happiness during a lesson was the major indicator of challenge with support. If challenge was high but students reported insufficient teacher support, then happiness declined. However, student reports of happiness also were found to be higher in a low challenge classroom, where students reported that their skills exceeded the challenge. Subsequently, Schweinle et al. (2008) concluded that balancing challenge and skill was a critical instructional practice for student emotion, motivation, and learning. When students perceived skills too low to meet challenges, they reported decreased efficacy, less happiness, and more anxiety, but if their skills were sufficient (moderate or high) to meet challenges, there were no consequences for efficacy or emotion. The instructional dilemma, however, was that if teachers adjusted the challenge level below students' skills, students responded with higher efficacy and more happiness, but opportunities for learning had been compromised.

Teacher Emotions During Instruction

A second instructional practice that motivation researchers frequently observe in classroom lessons is how teachers display their own emotions. Teacher displays of emotion, as mentioned previously in Turner, Meyer, Cox, et al. (1998), appear to be positively associated with student emotion, learning, and motivation through teachers' enthusiasm for teaching, content-related humor, and teachers' intrinsic motivation for their own learning (Turner, Meyer, Midgley, & Patrick, 2003). In addition, motivation researchers have observed unpleasant teacher emotions as part of evaluation practices and differential treatment, such as teacher displays of anger, sarcasm, gruffness, dissatisfaction, or aloofness (Stipek et al., 1998). Two approaches to investigating teacher emotion as an instructional practice seem to have emerged: (a) examining teachers' general affective stance during instruction and, more recently, (b) examining specific teacher emotions.

Teacher Emotions as Affective Stance

Although a teacher's emotions during instruction may simultaneously reflect the general classroom climate as well as serve to influence student emotions and learning during a lesson, researchers have rarely connected both student and teacher emotions during instruction. An illustrative exception is Stipek et al. (1998). Stipek et al. videotaped 24 fourth-, fifth-, and sixth-grade mathematics teachers during a fractions unit and then coded lessons across nine dimensions of which two specifically rated teacher emotion during instruction: (a) valence of negative affect versus positive (e.g., sarcasm vs. sensitivity) and (b) level of teacher enthusiasm and interest. The researchers also collected student self-reports on seven subscales, three of which were positive emotions, negative emotions, and enjoyment. Then they chose target students to analyze student self-reports with classroom observations. Three classroom practices were associated with student achievement and motivation: (a) practices that promoted a learning orientation, (b) teacher displays of positive affect, and (c) the absence of differential treatment. Of these practices, Stipek et al. concluded that "affective climate" (i.e., ratings of teacher emotion displays) was the best predictor of student affect (interest, pride, enjoyment) and motivation to learn fractions: "A positive affective climate that promoted risk-taking was positively associated with students' mastery orientation, help-seeking, and positive emotions associated with learning fractions" (Stipek et al., 1998, p. 483).

Transmission of Emotion

The aggregation of emotions for students and for teachers appears to be a common methodological practice in the classroom motivation research. However, generalized coding categories do not help us understand which displays of teacher emotion might have been the most influential. Therefore, research that focuses on specific emotions in classrooms is equally important. An example of such research is Frenzel, Goetz, Lüdtke, Pekrun, and Sutton's (2009) study of what is believed to be the first investigation combining self-reported student enjoyment and teacher enthusiasm with teacher self-reported enjoyment. Frenzel et al. (2009) used a diverse sample of students, who self-reported their enjoyment of mathematics in grade seven and again in grade eight, as well as perceptions of their mathematics teachers' enthusiasm in grade eight. After controlling for student enjoyment in seventh-grade mathematics, there was a significant positive relationship between eighth-grade student and teacher reports of enjoyment. Frenzel et al. (2009) concluded that teacher enjoyment was transmitted through teacher enthusiasm, and positive displays of teacher emotion could make a difference in student enjoyment, regardless of enjoyment in the previous year. Although Frenzel et al. (2009) acknowledged the reciprocal effect of student enjoyment on teacher enjoyment and the generalized nature of the self-reports (i.e., perceptions of mathematics class not specific lessons), their work corroborates more aggregate findings that teacher enthusiasm is an important teaching strategy for encouraging student enjoyment.

Emotional Support and Classroom Climate

As lessons unfold over time, classroom practices that have provided consistent emotional support appear to become integral features of positive learning environments. The formation of a classroom climate that reflects the development of emotional support through instructional practices is illustrated in Turner and colleagues' research program. For example, Turner, Meyer, and Schweinle (2003) described teacher discourse patterns that supported positive emotions. Although labeled a motivational discourse category, these specific whole-class teacher practices included displays of emotion (e.g., teacher enthusiasm, use of humor) along with practices for reducing student anxiety and addressing their emotional needs. Later, Schweinle, Turner, and Meyer (2006) created the instructional discourse category of "affective support" and suggested that a combination of instructional practices were related to four distinct factors found in student perceptions of supportive classrooms: challenge/importance, efficacy, social affect, and personal affect. The five classroom practices reflecting emotional support were: (a) encouraging effort and persistence, (b) alleviating frustration, (c) promoting enjoyment of mathematics, (d) encouraging peer cooperation, and (e) acknowledging student displays of emotion. Schweinle et al. (2006) found that when students perceived challenging mathematics as important, teachers supported them "affectively," which correlated positively with students' social affect (i.e., reports of feeling cooperative, alert, involved, part of the group, open) and personal affect (i.e., reports of excitement, pride, happiness, cheerfulness).

One of the most important findings on teacher emotional support reported by Turner and colleagues was that its consistent presence was a necessary characteristic of instruction associated with positive student outcomes, such as positive coping and low negative affect after failure. For example, Turner, Meyer, Midgley, and Patrick (2003) investigated two grade six mathematics classrooms that were perceived by students to be high in both mastery and performance goals. In comparing teacher discourse during whole-class instruction, however, emotional support in one classroom was intertwined with cognitive support, and students reported less negative affect after failure and less use of self-handicapping. However, in the classroom where students perceived primarily cognitive support, they reported more negative affect after failure and more use of self-handicapping. Using whole-class discourse analysis, Turner et al. (2003) described how a classroom could be cognitively rich but emotionally impoverished, lacking pleasant affective support (e.g., encouragement, humor, laughter) and interspersed with unpleasant interactions (e.g., scolding, sarcasm, humiliation). For example, when students made progress, the teacher remained silent or gave limited positive comments, and when they encountered difficulties, her discourse was "peppered with negative statements in their efforts and competence" (Turner et al., 2003, p. 375). Turner et al. (2003) concluded that it was both the presence of negative statements and the low frequency of positive ones that distinguished this classroom. From the students' perspective, this emotionless classroom was viewed more similarly to an emotionally unpleasant climate and negatively influenced their motivation to learn, although they reported that the teacher cared about their learning. Therefore, as important as teacher practices are to a supportive classroom climate for student emotions, research suggests that teachers need to be consistently supportive and aware of nonsupportive practices, even if infrequent and coupled with supportive practices (e.g., see also Patrick et al.'s, 2003, "ambivalent classrooms"; Stipek et al., 1998; Turner et al., 2003).

Emotion and Student-Teacher Relations

Teacher practices during lessons in combination with emotionally supportive classroom climates contribute to and are embedded in student–teacher relations. In the motivation literature, student–teacher relations have been studied by examining associations among student emotions, engagement, and well-being with student–teacher relatedness and teacher caring (e.g., Patrick, Anderman, Ryan, Edelin, & Midgley, 2001; Skinner & Belmont, 1993; Wentzel, 1997). The research suggests that when students have unpleasant experiences, positive student–teacher relations provide continuity and support because students know their teachers will personally attend to their needs, and teachers know how to engage individual students. At the intersection of motivation, sociological, and developmental research, the research literature in the areas of relatedness and teacher caring is vast and growing. However, while the research documents how teachers engage with students (Skinner & Belmont, 1993) and how they demonstrate care through respecting individual differences and democratic interactions (Wentzel, 1997), researchers have infrequently connected relatedness to classroom practices. Therefore, three illustrative research studies are discussed to highlight what teachers do within lessons as part of creating classroom climate helps establish relatedness, which then serves as a: (a) buffer for unpleasant emotions, (b) a foundation for adjustment to school, and (c) support for emotions experienced in school transitions.

Relatedness as a Buffer for Unpleasant Emotions

Furrer and Skinner (2003) were among the first to emphasize in their research that a student's sense of relatedness is associated with the pleasant emotions (see also Skinner, Furrer, Marchand, & Kindermann, 2008). Drawing from their findings of positive correlations among relatedness, engagement/disaffection, and achievement, Furrer and Skinner (2003) suggested that relatedness induces student enthusiasm for participation with others who "they like and by whom they feel liked in return" (p. 158). A strong sense of relatedness was found to evoke "fun" and other pleasant emotions, therefore Furrer and Skinner conjectured that relatedness could serve as a buffer against unpleasant emotions, such as boredom, anxiety, or frustration. A primary way relatedness might buffer unpleasant emotions is through teacher practices that most efficiently and effectively establish relations with students and among students early in the school year through interactions that communicate warmth, sensitivity, and "emotional availability."

Moreover, a student's perception of relatedness to teachers and peers provides a positive trajectory for more pleasant emotions and engagement. For example, Furrer and Skinner (2003) reported that grade three to six students who began the school year with a high sense of relatedness were more engaged and displayed fewer unpleasant emotions, becoming the recipients of more teacher, parent, and peer support. Similarly, Skinner and colleagues also have found that pleasant emotions (happiness, interest, enthusiasm) drive students' behavioral engagement, and their perceptions of teacher support for competence and autonomy are associated with their sense of relatedness (Skinner & Belmont, 1993; Skinner et al., 2008). Ongoing support for engagement strengthens students' feelings of relatedness and their pleasant emotions such as enjoyment, thus perpetuating a positive cycle of relationships, engagement, and learning, which may improve engagement over time and provide a buffer against declines in school motivation in early adolescence (Skinner et al., 2008).

Relatedness and Adjustment to School

A second way student–teacher relations have been connected to emotion and classroom practice is during early adjustment to school. In their research at the primary level, Pianta and colleagues have repeatedly emphasized the importance of understanding how young student–teacher relations predict student achievement and social and emotional adjustment to school (Hamre & Pianta, 2001; Pianta 1999, 2006; Stuhlman & Pianta, 2001). Their research on how early student–teacher relations are formed clearly reveals the critical relationship between early primary teachers' practices and student emotions. For example, Hamre and Pianta (2006) also emphasized developmental differences in early student–teacher relations, noting that young children's school adjustment is better predicted by relational stressors than supports and that early relational difficulties are predictors of future problems in school (e.g., low achievement, frequent disciplinary actions). Therefore, a central component of Pianta and colleagues' *Classroom Assessment Scoring System* (CLASS) *Framework* is the domain of "emotional support," which has four dimensions: (a) positive climate (e.g., warmth, enjoyment, enthusiasm); (b) negative climate (i.e., frequency, quality, and intensity of negativity); (c) teacher sensitivity (i.e., responsiveness to academic and emotional needs); and (d) regard for student perspectives (e.g., involving student interests and points of view; encouraging student autonomy and supporting student initiations).

An example of how the CLASS framework has been developed and informs a better understanding of emotions and teacher practices in primary classrooms was Stuhlman and Pianta's (2001) investigation of kindergarten and first-grade classrooms. Through observation as well as self-report, they found teachers' negative interactions with students and their expressions of negativity about the children outside the classroom had created relationships of "mutual negativity." In other words, the children were observed behaving more negatively in the classroom and their teachers responded more frequently and more negatively to them. As Stuhlman and Pianta explained, "when teachers talk about children, it is their emotional responses to the children that are most closely related to behavior in the classroom" (p. 160). They also observed patterns of decreased teacher sensitivity in the classroom for children about whom teachers had expressed more negativity. Furthermore, these interaction patterns were most evident with more experienced teachers, suggesting that student noncompliance and unpleasant emotional expressions may become more salient for primary teachers over time and influence how they approach interactions with new students in their classrooms.

Relatedness and School Transitions

Researchers also need to examine how school transitions represent opportunities to establish new relations and the degree to which the success of transitions is influenced by past student–teacher relations. School as well as teacher transitions have important implications for student emotions and teacher practices, especially as students transition to different types of school or classroom environments. For example, Hagenauer and Hascher (2010) used student surveys and daily diaries to follow students' enjoyment over a transition period from March and June of their sixth-grade year to November and April during their seventh-grade year. Using a multimethod approach, the researchers assumed that surveys revealed more habitual factors, while daily diaries described learning situations. Their findings further explained the research literature documenting the declines in self-efficacy and enjoyment during middle school (e.g., Anderman & Maher, 1994) and the importance of teachers fulfilling the basic student needs of autonomy, competence, and social relatedness, as explained in self-determination theory (e.g., Deci & Ryan, 1985).

Hagenauer and Hascher (2010) concluded that changes in instructional practice from one classroom context to the next, even in the same discipline, were contributing to declines in enjoyment and efficacy because learning environments had become less supportive of autonomy, less caring, and lower in instructional quality (i.e., practices that supported competence). Students' diaries specifically documented that the absence of teacher relatedness (i.e., either the student did not feel accepted by the teacher or felt rejected the teacher) interfered with the students' enjoyment in learning. The researchers also reported that teacher care and instructional quality were the most common characteristics of classrooms in which students reported higher self-efficacy and enjoyment for learning.

LEARNING ABOUT EMOTIONS IN SCHOOL

Classroom practices, whether embedded in lessons, in classroom climate or student–teacher relations, are simultaneously supporting the development of emotional competence and instructing students about school norms regarding emotions. For example, the developmental literature describes how young students learn to adapt to classroom norms of emotional expression (Miller et al., 2006) as well as to their teachers' instructional styles (e.g., LaBillois & Lagacé-Séguin, 2009). Student well-being and development thrive in emotionally pleasant classroom environments in which teacher practices ensure that their needs are met in developmentally appropriate ways (see the Brackett & Rivers, 2014). Similarly, research targeting socioemotional learning informs classroom practices because of its focus on students' social and emotional well-being in the early years of schooling (Baker, Dilly, Aupperlee, & Patil, 2003). This research explains how the emotions experienced during learning activities become lessons about emotions in school by describing the development of emotional understanding and regulation in classrooms, which allows young students to cope emotionally, engage in learning, and relate to their teachers and peers.

Emotional Competence and Peer Interactions

Emotional competence is commonly defined by the combined abilities to understand emotions and to regulate one's own emotions (Lindsey & Colwell, 2003; Mahady Wilton, Craig, & Pepler, 2000; Miller et al., 2006). The development of emotional competence is therefore important for successful interactions in classroom activities, such as young children's play, and in the development of early friendships and student–teacher relations (see Jacobs & Gross, 2014). For example, Lindsey and Colwell (2003) found early differences in the development of emotional competence and the type of play. They studied preschoolers' (ages 43–80 months) interactions with nominated "friend" classmates during unstructured play. Teacher emotional competence ratings were collected using a combination of (a) a positive emotion scale (e.g., cooperation with or comforting of peers), (b) an aggression scale, and (c) a withdrawal scale, which included anxiousness. The emotional competence was compared to mothers' ratings of emotional regulation and interviews with the children to determine their understanding of emotions (i.e., identification of happy, sad, angry, afraid in photographed faces and of the same emotions after listening to a vignette). Then children were videotaped during play with a same-sex friend. Lindsey and Colwell (2003) found that preschoolers who participated in pretend play demonstrated more understanding of their emotions, higher levels of regulation, and were rated as more emotionally competent by their teachers. Their findings highlight how unintentional classroom practices may promote or hinder emotional development. The common practice of allowing children to choose gender-related play (e.g., physical play for boys; pretend play for girls) was associated with girls' demonstrating more highly developed emotional understanding and regulation. Therefore, how teachers structure learning activities, or leave them unstructured, could impact development of emotional knowledge and regulation.

Emotional Competence and Student–Teacher Interaction

As previously discussed in Pianta and colleagues' research, emotions are highly salient in the earliest classroom experiences and contribute to the quality of classroom interactions, which are foundational for student–teacher relations. A critical aspect of classroom interactions that represents an important early lesson because of teacher attention to it is emotional expression. For example, Miller et al. (2006) investigated emotional competence in three to five year olds to determine how negative emotion expression, emotion regulation, and emotion knowledge were related. Using observations of children interacting in learning centers, child interviews to assess understanding of emotion, and teacher ratings of emotion knowledge, Miller et al. (2006) found that negative emotion expression was a strong predictor of teacher ratings of low emotion regulation. In addition, the children's emotion knowledge (i.e., identifying emotion expressions and emotions in situations) also predicted teacher ratings of their emotion regulation.

More importantly, although Miller et al. (2006) observed that the preschoolers infrequently displayed negative emotions, they found that even rare displays were highly relevant for teachers. Their findings appear to corroborate those of Stuhlman and Pianta's (2001) student–teacher "mutual negativity." Thus, a child's expression of unpleasant emotions, such as anger, may establish an early trajectory in student–teacher relations because the teacher perceives the child's emotional regulation as less developed. As Miller et al. (2006) stated, "Children who spent more time in negative emotional states were rated by teachers as less socially skilled and more aggressive" (p. 1186), even though they may have demonstrated emotional understanding. This finding suggests that children's emotional expression rather than any knowledge about their socioemotional skills had more influence on teacher perceptions. Therefore, as Miller et al. (2006) concluded, for children who learn to avoid expressing unpleasant emotions, their "more advanced emotion knowledge skills in the initial years of formal schooling may be able to lay the groundwork for positive social interactions and relationships early" (p. 1187).

Coping With Unpleasant Emotions and Sustaining Enjoyment

Research on emotion regulation also emphasizes the importance of coping with unpleasant emotions in school learning with respect to peer relations and teaching practices. For example, students' emotional competencies are important for their socioemotional well-being and motivational self-regulation, and studies have documented how emotions are indicative of student coping in peer interactions, such as peer bullying (e.g., Hunter & Borg, 2006; Mahady Wilton et al., 2000). For example, Mahady Wilton et al. (2000) found that students in grades one through six coped with bullying in one of two ways: (a) they problem solved to resolve the situations, or (b) they used aggression, which escalated the bullying. Mahady Wilton et al. (2000) saw the two strategies as reflecting effective and maladaptive emotional regulation. Students' perceived control of the situation appears to be highly related to their emotional regulation and actions. And their accompanying emotions are important indicators of why and how they choose to respond to peers as well as teachers, such as in seeking help or not (Hunter & Borg, 2006) or choosing which emotions to express (Miller et al., 2006).

In addition to coping with negative school experiences, students' emotional regulation helps sustain enjoyable learning, even in classrooms in which teaching practices are not aligned with student needs. For example, LaBillois and Lagacé-Séguin (2009) reported that grade two and four students coping with emotion (i.e., emotional regulation) were able to buffer the negative effects of teaching styles by reducing their anxiety. Teachers completed a teaching style inventory that assessed five styles (expert, formal authority, personal model, facilitator, and delegator). Parents filled out a child behavior checklist, and students completed two scales on a temperament questionnaire assessing capacity for emotion regulation: activation control (i.e., performing an action one wants to avoid) and inhibitory control (i.e., planning and suppressing inappropriate responses). Three teaching styles were self-reported: the expert style (i.e., teacher as sole authority), formal authority (i.e., more rigid, less flexible), and facilitator (i.e., more flexible, student-centered). All three teaching styles and student reports of emotion regulation significantly predicted parent reports of student anxiety. Students with higher emotion regulation were reported to be less anxious, regardless of the teacher's style. Whereas "low regulators" were reported as more anxious with the formal authority and facilitator style teachers, LaBillois and Lagacé-Séguin concluded that "higher regulators" have the emotional knowledge and skills to cope in stressful instructional environments at a very young age and more readily adapt to teaching practices. They described their findings as supporting a "goodness of fit" model in that high regulators are able to adapt to different classroom practices whereas low regulators could not.

In summary, developmental studies of children's emotions provide a different and important lens for understanding how emotion competence and expression develops within a school context. This research also highlights how the interplay among teacher practices and student emotions is especially significant in preschool and primary classrooms. In fact, the findings suggest that teachers often expect emotional regulation and establish emotional norms when students are still developing their emotional competencies (e.g., Miller et al., 2006; Stuhlman & Pianta, 2001). For example, one of the most common classroom management practices in early education is also a powerful lesson in emotions. As Maxwell and Reichenbach (2005, pp. 291, 292) argued, the "shame corner" is actually a series of lessons in moral emotions because when a child is placed in "time out," the practice evokes an emotional education in being directed to reappraise one's actions (e.g., *Why did you do that?*), imagine the effects of those actions on others (e.g., *How do you think Juan feels?*), or imitate the designated emotion (e.g., *You should be ashamed!*). Therefore, in the very earliest of classroom experiences, every child's emotional education commences.

CONCLUSION

The current research on classroom emotions provides a broad base for improving class-room practices, but there is much work ahead. Three areas of future directions are proposed. First, classroom researchers need shared frameworks around which to set research goals that specifically focus on emotions. As Goetz, Pekrun, et al. (2006) summarized, there are (at least) four major reasons for studying emotions in classrooms: (a) emotions are related to student well-being, (b) emotions impact the quality of learning, (c) emotions impact the quality of student–teacher interactions, and (d) research on emotions helps to test and build theoretical frameworks for future research and practice. Although prioritizing any of these reasons as a research goal would be important, studies need to connect multiple levels of practice—lessons, classrooms, student–teacher relations, and across classrooms and schools—with emotion. Also central to building a more coherent literature is the goal of focusing on specific teacher and student emotions to investigate. Given the current literature, the emotions chosen for study should be the good ones—enjoyment, happiness, pride, and so on—to understand which ones through daily teacher practice most readily and effectively impact achievement and well-being.

Second, research must be designed to inform classroom practice and allow practice to inform it. As Shernoff, Csikszentmihalyi, Scheider, and Steele Shernoff (2003) reminded us, although high levels of student disengagement are often emphasized, there are many classrooms that promote "excitement, stimulation, and engagement in the learning process" (p. 159). The classroom motivation research provides several rich examples of teachers who were enthusiastic, emotionally supportive, relational, and highly effective. Their students were challenged with support and reported feeling competent, cared for, and happy. However, in almost all cases, finding these teachers appeared to be happenstance, and time spent in their classrooms was minimal, given what might be learned from them. In addition, we know little about how teachers develop emotionally supportive practices or how observed lesson-level practices advance in concert with broader classroom climate and student-teacher relations. Given the significance of strong student–teacher relations, it is surprising that students emotionally thrive in so many different classrooms with such a variety of teachers. How are positive relations established quickly for the relatively brief periods called school or class? How do students and teachers negotiate so many relationships? Therefore, understanding classroom emotions in relation to multiple classroom experiences over time is important for moving forward empirically and theoretically, but it will be essential for pedagogical advancements and student success.

Third, in combination with focusing on classroom practices, research on students' development of emotion understanding and competence needs to be expanded to include students at different levels of school and in different types of instructional environments (i.e., comparing organizational, social, and instructional structures and formats). The developmental trajectories of classroom emotions are clearly integral to children's and adolescents' motivational, social, moral, and cognitive development with the effects of stress and happiness having implications for their physical development (Baker et al., 2003) and future success in school (Hamre & Pianta, 2006). However, there appears to be an "Emotional Matthew Effect" (i.e., the emotionally competent become more competent) as early as the preschool years. Research needs to help educators better understand how daily practice supports developing emotional competence, especially which practices successfully alter negative trajectories at all levels of schooling.

Understanding emotions in classroom practices has never been more urgent. Educational reforms are growing exponentially in today's societies with high stakes accountability testing and teacher evaluation, value-added models, calls for scaling up, and economic incentives like the U.S. Department of Education's Race to the Top. In classrooms everywhere teachers and students feel the stress of insufficient resources (material, time, and human), and they are pressed to learn more . . . faster . . . earlier. But if classrooms are not happy places for learning and teaching, how can long-term success be imagined? The possibilities for researching classroom emotions and helping teachers examine their classroom practices are truly just beginning.

REFERENCES

Ahmed, W., van der Werf, G., Minnaert, A., & Kuyper, H. (2010). Students' daily emotions in the classroom: Intra-individual variability and appraisal correlates. *British Journal of Educational Psychology, 80,* 583–597.

Anderman, E. M., & Maehr, M. L. (1994). Motivation and schooling in the middle grades. *Review of Educational Research, 64,* 287–309.

Anderman, L., Andrzejewski, C. E., & Allen, J. (2011). How do teachers support students' motivation and learning in their classrooms? *Teachers College Record, 113,* 969–1003.

Baker, J. A., Dilly, L. J., Aupperlee, J. L., & Patil, S. A. (2003). The developmental context of school satisfaction: Schools as psychologically healthy environments. *School Psychology Quarterly, 18,* 206–221.

Brackett, M. A., & Rivers, S. E. (2014). Transforming students' lives with social and emotional learning. In R. Pekrun & L. Linnenbrink-Garcia (Eds.), *International handbook of emotions in education* (pp. 368–388). New York, NY: Taylor & Francis.

Bronfenbrenner, U. (1979). *The ecology of human development: Experiments by nature and design.* Cambridge, MA: Harvard University Press.

Brophy, J. (2008). Scaffolding appreciation for school learning: An update. In M. Maehr, S. Karabenick, & T. Urdan (Eds.), *Advances in motivation and achievement* (Vol. 15, pp. 1- 48). New York, NY: Elsevier.

Csikszentmihalyi, M. (1975). *Beyond freedom and anxiety.* San Francisco, CA: Jossey-Bass.

Csikszentmihalyi, M., & Csikszentmihalyi, I. S. (1988). *Optimal experience: Psychological studies of flow in consciousness.* Cambridge, United Kingdom: Cambridge University Press.

Csikszentmihalyi, M., & Nakamura, J. (1989). The dynamics of intrinsic motivation. In R. Ames & C. Ames (Eds.), *Handbook of motivation theory and research* (Vol. 3, pp. 45–71). New York, NY: Academic.

Csikszentmihalyi, M., Rathunde, K., & Whalen, S. (1993). *Talented teenagers: The roots of success and failure.* Cambridge, United Kingdom: Cambridge University Press.

Deci, E. L., & Ryan, R. M. (1985). *Intrinsic motivation and self-determination in human behavior.* New York, NY: Plenum.

Ford, M. E. (1992). *Motivating humans: Goals, emotions, and personal agency beliefs.* Newbury Park, CA: Sage.

Frenzel, A. C., Goetz, T., Lüdtke, O., Pekrun, R., & Sutton, R. (2009). Emotional transmission in the classroom: Exploring relationships between teacher and student enjoyment. *Journal of Educational Psychology, 101,* 705–716.

Furrer, C., & Skinner, E. (2003). Sense of relatedness as a factor in children's academic engagement and performance. *Journal of Educational Psychology, 95,* 148–162.

Goetz, T., Frenzel, A. C., & Pekrun, R. (2006). The domain specificity of academic emotional experiences. *The Journal of Experimental Education, 25,* 5–29.

Goetz, T., Pekrun, R., Hall, N., & Haag, L. (2006). Academic emotions from a social-cognitive perspective: Antecedents and domain specificity of students' affect in the context of Latin instruction. *British Journal of Educational Psychology, 76,* 289–308.

Hagenauer, G., & Hascher, T. (2010). Learning enjoyment in early adolescence. *Educational Research and Evaluation, 16*(6), 495–516.

Hamre, B., & Pianta, R. C. (2001). Early teacher-child relationships and the children's social and academic outcomes through eighth grade. *Child Development, 72,* 625–638.

Hamre, B. K., & Pianta, R. C. (2006). Student-teacher relationships as a source of support and risk in schools. In G. G. Bear & K. M. Minke (Eds.) *Children's needs III: Development, prevention, and intervention* (pp. 59–71). Bethesda, MA: National Association of School Psychologists.

Hunter, S. C., & Borg, M. G. (2006). The influence of emotional reaction on help seeking by victims of school bullying. *Educational Psychology, 26*, 813–826.

Jacobs, S. E., & Gross, J. J. (2014). Emotion regulation in education: Conceptual foundations, current applications, and future directions. In R. Pekrun & L. Linnenbrink-Garcia (Eds.), *International handbook of emotions in education* (pp. 183–201). New York, NY: Taylor & Francis.

LaBillois, J. M., & Lagacé-Séguin, D. G. (2009). Does good fit matter? Exploring teaching styles, emotion regulation, and child anxiety in the classroom. *Early Child Development and Care, 179*, 303–315.

Lindsey, E. W., & Colwell, M. J. (2003). Preschoolers' emotional competence: Links to pretend and physical play. *Child Study Journal, 33*, 39–52.

Mahady Wilton, M. M., Craig, W. M., & Pepler, D. J. (2000). Emotional regulation and display in classroom victims of bullying: Characteristic expressions of affect, coping styles and relevant contextual factors. *Social Development, 9*, 226–245.

Maxwell, B., & Reichenbach, R. (2005). Imitation, imagination and re-appraisal: Educating the moral emotions. *Journal of Moral Education, 34*, 291–307.

Meyer, D. K., & Turner, J. C. (2002). Discovering emotion in classroom motivation research. *Educational Psychologist, 37*, 107–114.

Meyer, D. K., & Turner, J. C. (2007). Scaffolding emotions in classrooms. In P. A. Schultz & R. Pekrun (Eds.), *Emotions in education* (pp. 243–258). Amsterdam: Academic Press/Elsevier.

Meyer, D. K., Turner, J. C., & Spencer, C. A. (1997). Challenge in a mathematics classroom: Student motivation and strategies in project-based learning. *The Elementary School Journal, 97*, 501–522.

Miller, A. L., Fine, S. E., Kiely Gouley, K., Seifer, R., Dickstein, S., & Shields, A. (2006). Showing and telling about emotions: Interrelations between facets of emotional competence and associations with classroom adjustment in Head Start preschoolers. *Cognition and Emotion, 20*, 1170–1192.

Ortony, A., & Turner, T. J. (1990). What's basic about basic emotions? *Psychological Review, 97*, 315–331.

Patrick, H., Anderman, L. H., Ryan, A.M., Edelin, K., & Midgley, C. (2001). Teachers' communication of goal orientations in four fifth-grade classrooms. *Elementary School Journal, 102*, 35–58.

Patrick, H., Turner, J. C., Meyer, D. K., & Midgley, C. (2003). How teachers establish psychological environments during the first days of school: Inviting engagement or avoidance? *Teachers College Record, 105*, 1521–1558.

Pekrun, R. (2000). A social cognitive, control-value theory of achievement emotions. In J. Heckhausen (Ed.), *Motivational psychology of human development* (pp. 143–163). Oxford, United Kingdom: Elsevier Science.

Pekrun, R., Goetz, T., Titz, W., & Perry, R. P. (2002). Academic emotions in students' self-regulated learning and achievement: A program of quantitative and qualitative research. *Educational Psychologist, 37*, 91–106.

Pianta, R. C. (1999). *Enhancing relationships between children and teachers.* Washington, DC: American Psychological Association.

Pianta, R. C. (2006). Classroom management and relationships between children and teachers: Implications for research and practice. In C. M. Evertson & C. S. Weinstein (Eds.), *Handbook of classroom management: Research, practice, and contemporary issues* (pp. 685–710). Mahwah, NJ: Lawrence Erlbaum Associates.

Pintrich, P. (2003). A motivational science perspective on the role of student motivation in learning and teaching contexts. *Journal of Educational Psychology, 95*, 667–686.

Santrock, J. W. (1976). Affect and facilitative self-control: Influence of ecological setting, cognition, and social agent. *Journal of Educational Psychology, 68*, 529–535.

Schutz, P. A., & Pekrun, R. (Eds.). (2007). *Emotions in education.* San Diego, CA: Academic Press.

Schutz, P. A., & Zembylas, M. (Eds.). (2009). *Advances in teacher emotion research: The impact on teachers' lives.* New York, NY: Springer Publications.

Schweinle, A., Turner, J. C., & Meyer, D. K. (2006). Striking the right balance: Students' motivational experiences and affect in upper elementary mathematics classes. *Journal of Educational Research, 99*, 271–293.

Schweinle, A., Turner, J. C., & Meyer, D. K. (2008). Understanding young adolescents' optimal experiences in academic settings. *Journal of Experimental Education, 77*, 125–146.

Shernoff, D. J., Csikszentmihalyi, M., Schneider, B., & Steele Shernoff, E. (2003). Student engagement in high school classrooms from the perspective of flow theory. *School Psychology Quarterly, 18*, 158–176.

Skinner, E. A., & Belmont, M. J. (1993). Motivation in the classroom: Reciprocal effects of teacher behavior and student engagement across the school year. *Journal of Educational Psychology, 85,* 571–581.

Skinner, E., Furrer, C., Marchand, G., & Kindermann, T. (2008). Engagement and disaffection in the classroom: Part of a larger motivational dynamic? *Journal of Educational Psychology, 100,* 765–781.

Stipek, D., Salmon, J. M., Givvin, K. B., Kazemi, E., Saxe, G., & MacGyvers, V. L. (1998). The value (and convergence) of practices suggested by motivation research and promoted by mathematics education reformers. *Journal for Research in Mathematics Education, 29,* 465–488.

Stuhlman, M. W., & Pianta, R. C. (2001). Teachers' narratives about their relationships with children: Associations with behavior in classrooms. *School Psychology Review, 31,* 148–163.

Turner, J. C., & Meyer, D. K. (1999). Integrating classroom context into motivation theory and research: Rationales, methods, and implications. In T. Urdan (Ed.), *Advances in motivation and achievement; Vol. 11. The role of context* (pp. 87–121). San Diego, CA: Elsevier Inc.

Turner, J. A., & Meyer, D. K. (2009). Understanding motivation in mathematics: What is happening in classrooms? In A. Wigfield & K. Wentzel (Eds.), *Handbook of motivation at school* (p. 527–552). New York, NY: Lawrence Erlbaum Publications.

Turner, J. C., Meyer, D. K., Cox, K. C., Logan, C., DiCintio, M., & Thomas, C. T. (1998). Creating contexts for involvement in mathematics. *Journal of Educational Psychology, 90,* 730–745.

Turner, J. C., Meyer, D. K., Midgley, C., & Patrick, H. (2003). Teacher discourse and students' affect and achievement-related behaviors in two high mastery/high performance classrooms. *Elementary School Journal, 103,* 357–382.

Turner, J. C., Meyer, D. K., & Schweinle, A. (2003). The importance of emotion in theories of motivation: Empirical, methodological, and theoretical considerations from a goal theory perspective. *International Journal of Educational Research, 39,* 375–393.

Turner, J. C., Midgley, C., Meyer, D. K., Gheen, M., Anderman, E. M., Kang, Y., & Patrick, H. (2002). The classroom environment and students' reports of avoidance strategies in mathematics: A multi-method study. *Journal of Educational Psychology, 94,* 88–106.

Turner, J. C., & Patrick, H. (2004). Motivational influences on student participation in classroom learning activities. *Teachers College Record, 106,* 1759–1785.

Turner, J. C., Thorpe, P. K., & Meyer, D. K. (1998). Relating students' reports of motivation and negative affect: A theoretical and empirical analysis. *Journal of Educational Psychology, 90,* 758–771.

Usher, E. L. (2009). Sources of middle school students' self-efficacy in mathematics: A qualitative investigation. *American Educational Research Journal, 46,* 275–314.

Weiner, B. (1986). *An attributional theory of motivation and emotion.* New York, NY: Springer.

Wentzel, K. R. (1997). Student motivation in middle school: The role of perceived pedagogical caring. *Journal of Educational Psychology, 89,* 411–419.

24

EMOTIONS IN ADVANCED LEARNING TECHNOLOGIES

Arthur C. Graesser, Sidney K. D'Mello, and Amber C. Strain,
University of Memphis, University of Notre Dame,
and University of Memphis

There is a vision that advanced learning technologies can optimize the delicate balance between emotions and the learning of academic material. Students are not prone to have much fun when they are expected to learn a dense array of new jargon, complex systems with many components, mental models with tradeoffs between variables, solutions to difficult problems, and other difficult academic content. The technology needs to be designed in some fashion that allows students to have emotionally satisfying experiences as they attempt to master material that is often viewed as tedious, pedantic, exceedingly challenging, or useless in their eyes. In an ideal world, the computer system would put the student in a zone of optimal concentration that targets relevant knowledge about the subject matter at a pace that delivers the right challenges to the particular student at the right time.

A serious game could be engineered that brilliantly manages the tradeoff between fun and work. However, one would need to be very clever in designing such a serious game because young learners are skeptical of games that have any semblance of academic content. The game designer would need to smuggle in the academic subject matter under the students' attitudinal radar.

The goal of this chapter is to describe some advanced learning technologies that consider student emotions in addition to the conventional focus on cognition. The design of *affect-sensitive learning technologies* is likely to be quite complex because the designers of these systems need to have some understanding of cognition, emotions, motivation, pedagogy, aesthetics, communication, social interaction, sociology, and technology.

Author Notes: The research on was supported by the National Science Foundation (0325428, 633918, 0834847, 0918409, 1108845, 1235958) and the Institute of Education Sciences (R305A080594, R305G020018). Any opinions, findings, and conclusions or recommendations expressed in this material are those of the authors and do not necessarily reflect the views of these funding sources.

Some design teams have reasonable intuitions on how to integrate these constraints into games, but most teams fail. The multibillion dollar game industry has not managed to market many games that incorporate important academic content. Our hope is that the social sciences can provide a better understanding of the mechanisms that underlie affect-sensitive learning technologies.

There is a broad landscape of technology features that hold some promise in coordinating emotions and cognition as students learn difficult academic content. Below is a glimpse of some technological approaches that might hook the student into deeper learning:

1. Create a state of flow (or intense engagement) to the point where fatigue and time disappear. This may be accomplished by a simulation or game that delivers information, tasks, and scenarios at the student's zone of optimal challenge: not too easy or too difficult but just right.
2. Provide an engaging story narrative to sustain interest and coherence. The narrative would be integrated with the academic subject matter and promote its value.
3. Reward the student with points/resources that are extrinsically reinforcing or with experiences that are intrinsically reinforcing if the student is not already intrinsically interested in the topic.
4. Give the active student control over the interaction in order to allow autonomy and self-regulation.
5. Give the insecure student materials he/she can successfully master in order to build confidence and self-efficacy.
6. Interact with the student in a turn-by-turn conversation or collaboration to promote interactivity and social presence.
7. Give the student timely feedback on his/her actions so it is clear where the student stands in mastering the complex material.
8. Give feedback and guidance on the student's emotions so he/she can monitor the coordination between emotions and learning. A discouraged student may need an explanation that difficult material is sometimes confusing, frustrating, or boring.

This chapter examines how learning technologies can be coordinated with emotion mechanisms to facilitate the learning of difficult academic content. We concentrate primarily on difficult academic content because that is what students struggle with, avoid, or escape. The designers of some learning environments have intentionally considered the students' emotions when creating the artifacts, such as affect-sensitive intelligent tutoring systems and serious games. This chapter focuses on those projects that collect empirical data on the learners' emotions, cognitive states, and learning rather than untested learning environments. Sometimes emotions help and sometimes they interfere with learning, so it is important to take stock of what we know about the emotions students experience and how these emotions are related to learning. The next section identifies moment-to-moment emotions that occur during complex learning, followed by a section on some theoretical frameworks to explain such emotions. The final section describes some advanced learning technologies that track, manipulate, and respond to student emotions with the goal of improving deep learning.

Our perspective on emotion is purposefully inclusive and broad in this chapter because there is not an abundance of research that has investigated moment-to-moment affective states during the learning of difficult material. We view emotion as an affective state or hybrid cognitive-affective state that deviates from a neutral affective state. A more nuanced classification of psychological states and dynamic processes will no doubt evolve as this research area matures. It is beyond the scope of this chapter to address enduring affective traits (e.g., curious, hostile), long-term moods (general anxiety), or motivational traits that span days, months, or years.

EMOTIONS THAT OCCUR DURING COMPLEX LEARNING

Contemporary psychological theories routinely assume that emotion and cognition are tightly integrated rather than loosely linked modules (Bower, 1992; Isen, 2008; Lazarus, 2000; Mandler, 1999; Ortony, Clore, & Collins, 1988; Pekrun, 2006; Scherer, Schorr, & Johnstone, 2001), but the focus has never been on moment-to-moment emotions during complex learning. This section documents what we know about the moment-to-moment emotions that students experience while interacting with advanced learning technologies that target complex material. The targeted learning environments require deep comprehension, reasoning, problem solving, and learning (hereafter called deep learning) in addition to the mastery and memory of simple facts, rules, and procedures (called shallow learning). Deep learning involves inferences, integration of information, conceptual elaboration of material through prior knowledge, reasoning strategies, problem solving heuristics, reflection, and other time-consuming, deliberate cognitive activities.

The active struggles of deep learning can be contrasted with the (typically) linear reading of textbooks in print or electronic media that are at low to intermediate levels of difficulty (Ainley, Hidi, & Berndorff, 2002; Reichle, Reineberg, & Schooler, 2010). For example, Ainley et al. (2002) collected reading times during the course of reading interesting versus uninteresting passages presented on the computer, followed by an assessment of comprehension. Their model predicted, and data confirmed, that topic interest and the associated curiosity from a title triggered positive affect, which in turn predicted persistent engagement during reading, whereas persistence predicted learning from text. It is likely that these trends will also apply to deep learning, but our assumption is that the cognitive disequilibrium of deep learning will give rise to a broader array of emotions.

Some moment-to-moment emotions during learning are intuitively obvious. For example, highly motivated students have the persistence to complete the expected tasks and experience positive emotions when the tasks are successfully accomplished. They experience curiosity when the topics interest them, eureka moments when there are deep insights and discoveries, delight when challenges are conquered, and flow when they are so engaged that time and fatigue disappear. However, sometimes there are counterintuitive trends. In route to these positive affective states, learners may experience a rough terrain of confusion, frustration, irritation, and other negative emotions as they confront various obstacles in comprehension, production, reasoning, and problem solving. The students with maladaptive motivation and little interest in the material experience much more negative emotions than positive emotions. They quickly become bored and disengage after encountering a small amount of obstacles and dense technical content. Those with adaptive motivation and interest may visit anger or even rage on the trajectory to deep mastery of the subject matter, such as those individuals who have written dissertations, books, or grant proposals.

How Are Moment-to-Moment Emotions Measured?

Researchers have used a variety of methods to measure the moment-to-moment emotions that students experience in technology-based learning environments (for reviews see Calvo & D'Mello, 2010; D'Mello, 2013; D'Mello, Craig, & Graesser, 2009; D'Mello & Graesser, 2010, 2012a, 2012b; D'Mello, Picard, & Graesser, 2007; Graesser & D'Mello, 2012; Du Boulay et al., 2010; Picard, 2010; Woolf et al., 2009). The primary methods are summarized in the following list:

1. *Trained observers during learning.* Trained observers periodically classify or rate the learner's emotions during the learning session (Baker, D'Mello, Rodrigo, & Graesser, 2010; Craig, Graesser, Sullins, & Gholson, 2004). The judges may have a checklist with discrete categories (e.g., boredom, confusion, frustration, etc.) or rating scales for dimensions of emotions or categories. The observers are trained on detecting emotions before they make their judgments on the emotions that students display during the process of interacting with the technology.

2. *Self-report ratings of affective states during learning.* The students are stopped periodically during the course of learning and give judgments on their current states of emotions. The judgments may be in the form of ratings on emotional dimensions, selections on an emotion checklist, or a mark on a two-dimensional affect grid that crosses valence (negative versus positive) and arousal, following the circumplex model (Barrett, 2006; Russell, 2003). Self-reports concurrent with learning are perhaps the most typical methodology in the literature on emotions in technology-advanced learning environments (Arroyo et al., 2009; McQuiggan & Lester, 2009; Sabourin, Rowe, Mott, & Lester, 2011; Woolf et al., 2009).

3. *Emote aloud protocols by learners during learning.* An *emote-aloud* procedure collects spoken verbal expressions of emotions while the students complete a task (Craig, D'Mello, Witherspoon, & Graesser, 2008). The emote-aloud procedure is analogous to the traditional think-aloud procedure (Ericsson & Simon, 1993) except that the students are instructed to articulate their emotions instead of the cognitive content that typically surfaces in think aloud protocols. Most students do not know what it means to express emotions, so they need some guidance on what the alternative emotions might be and how to label them (Craig et al., 2008). Therefore, emotions are listed and defined before they start the learning task.

4. *Retrospective identification of emotions by learners, peers, trained judges and teachers.* The observational and emote-aloud studies collect emotion judgments concurrently during learning, whereas the retrospective identification approach collects judgments after the learning session is completed. Various channels of communication and interaction are recorded, including facial expressions, conversation, computer displays, and interactions between the student and computer. A systematic polling procedure is implemented to sample emotion judgments by the original learner, peers of learners, trained judges, and teachers (D'Mello & Graesser, 2010; D'Mello, Lehman, & Person, 2011; Graesser & D'Mello, 2012).

5. *Noninvasive automated detection of emotions.* Noninvasive sensing methods do not attach sensing devices to the learner and do not disrupt the normal stream of learning by probing the students with questions about their emotions or learning. The computers detect emotions of the learner by analyzing different communication

channels and their interactions (Calvo & D'Mello, 2010; D'Mello & Graesser, 2010; Picard, 1997, 2010). The common communication channels include facial expression (D'Mello & Graesser, 2010; Grafsgaard, Boyer, Phillips, & Lester, 2011; Kapoor, Burleson, & Picard, 2007), speech parameters (Litman & Forbes-Riley, 2006), body posture (D'Mello, Dale, & Graesser, 2012; D'Mello & Graesser, 2009), and language and discourse interaction (D'Mello, Craig, Witherspoon, McDaniel, & Graesser, 2008; D'Mello & Graesser, 2012b). Accuracy of these automated detection methods is modest, ranging from slightly above random guessing to perfect detection.

6. *Biological detection of emotions by recording events in the brain and physiology.* These methods include the recording of heart rate, movements of the muscles, galvanic skin response, and brain activity (e.g., EEG, fMRI; Arroyo et al., 2009; Calvo & D'Mello, 2010; McQuiggan & Lester, 2009; Picard, 2010). Most of these methods are invasive in the sense that it is obvious to the students that they are being recorded by physical instruments that have contact with their bodies. However, recent biological detection methods have become progressively less invasive, such as wrist bands that record galvanic skin response (Poh, Swenson, & Picard, 2010) and the computation of heart rate from facial movements (Poh, McDuff, & Picard, 2010).

It is widely acknowledged that there is no gold standard for measuring what emotions the learners are actually experiencing during learning. None of these measures are perfect windows into emotional experience. The various measures correlate only modestly (kappas ranging from .2 to .5; see D'Mello & Graesser, 2010), with each measure having both virtues and liabilities. For example, the observational judgments (1) have the virtue of tapping into the emotions as they occur, but the liability of potential judge training biases and of inability to reexamine the events to refine the judgments. The self-report measures (2 and 3) have the advantage of reflecting the phenomenology of the individual learner but also come with the liabilities of disrupting or redirecting the learning process with probes, of sensitizing the learner to the experimenter's goals, and of learners having limited metaknowledge of emotions. The retrospective judgments (4) allow multiple judges to examine the events on multiple occasions, but again there are training biases, and some of the extended context of the learning experience may get missed. The automated judgments (5 and 6) have advantages of concurrent and systematic measurement, but the validity of the classification is often challenged, even when the reliability indices are comparable to humans. In light of these indeterminacies in measurement validity, researchers often collected multiple measures and adjust the confidence in their conclusions according to the consistency of the results.

What Emotions Occur During Deep Learning With Advanced Learning Technologies?

There is a growing literature of research that tracks moment-to-moment emotions that occur when students interact with advanced learning environments, such as intelligent tutoring systems and serious games with agents (Arroyo et al., 2009; Baker et al., 2010; Calvo & D'Mello, 2010; Conati & Maclaren, 2009; D'Mello & Graesser, 2010, 2012a, 2012c; Kapoor et al., 2007; Litman & Forbes-Riley, 2006; McQuiggan & Lester, 2009; McQuiggan, Robison, & Lester, 2010; Sabourin et al., 2011; Woolf et al., 2009). All of these studies have targeted difficult materials in STEM (science, technology, engineering, and mathematics) topics, such as physics, mathematics, biology, and computer science. The students have ranged from middle school to college students, primarily in sessions that last one to two hours. However, one limitation of these studies is that they have not spanned weeks or months, the normal time stretch for deep learning on STEM topics. They also have rarely been integrated with the course curriculum, so there is no academic incentive for performing well on the learning tasks.

Most of studies that we have conducted have tracked the emotions that college students experience when they interact with AutoTutor on the topic of computer literacy (D'Mello & Graesser, 2010, 2012a, 2012c; Graesser & D'Mello, 2012). AutoTutor is an intelligent tutoring system (ITS) that helps students learn topics in Newtonian physics, computer literacy, and critical thinking through a mixed-initiative conversational dialog between the student and the tutor (Graesser, Jeon, & Dufty, 2008; Graesser, Lu, et al., 2004; VanLehn et al., 2007). AutoTutor's dialogues are organized around difficult questions and problems (called main questions) that require reasoning and explanations in the answers. AutoTutor actively monitors the students' knowledge states and engages them in a multi-turn conversational dialogue as they attempt to answer these questions. It adaptively manages the tutorial dialogue by providing feedback (e.g., "good job," "not quite"), pumping the learner for more information (e.g., "What else"), giving hints (e.g., "What about X"), generating prompts to elicit specific words, correcting misconceptions, answering questions, and summarizing answers. The conversational moves of AutoTutor are guided by constructivist theories of pedagogy that scaffold students to actively generate answers rather than merely instructing students with well-organized information delivery.

A small set of *learning-centered* emotions were found to dominate learning experiences with AutoTutor on the STEM topics in learning sessions of one to two hours. The primary emotions were confusion, engagement/flow, boredom, and frustration, with delight and surprise occasionally occurring but considerably less frequently. These learner-centered emotions are very different than the six basic emotions investigated by Ekman (1992) that are readily manifested in facial expressions: sadness, happiness, anger, fear, disgust, and surprise. They are also different from the emotions that occur over longer stretches of time in academic, classroom, and social contexts, such as Pekrun's classification of academic emotions into epistemic, achievement, topic, and social emotions (which include anxiety, shame, pride, and other emotions tied to a student's self-concept)(Pekrun, 2006; Pekrun, Elliot, & Maier, 2006). One exciting direction for future research is to track the moment-to-moment emotions over longer intervals, which is entirely possible with current technologies that track emotions.

It is beyond the scope of this chapter to fully specify the conditions that trigger the different learner-centered emotions, but some major patterns are noteworthy (D'Mello & Graesser, 2010, 2012a; Graesser & D'Mello, 2012). One of the important positive emotions is what we will call engagement/flow, which is somewhere between the extremes of an enjoyable concentration on the material (engagement) and sustained focused attention to the point of flow— that is, immersion and altered perception as time and fatigue disappear (Csikszentmihalyi, 1990). We make no attempt to sharply distinguish between mere engagement and intense flow, but we do assume that these are both positive affective states. The positive emotion of engagement/flow tends to occur when the learner is quickly generating information and receives positive feedback. The negative emotion of boredom tends to occur later in the tutoring session as the student fatigues and also when AutoTutor is disseminating information (asserting, summarizing, lecturing) as the student becomes overwhelmed with content. Frustration tends to occur when students are producing information they believe is on the mark, but they receive negative feedback because AutoTutor does not give the student due credit. Confusion tends to occur relatively early in the tutoring session when the discourse cohesion is low, the learner does not produce much information, the student is slow to respond, the feedback is negative or contradictory, and the student is not understanding AutoTutor's hints. These are moments when the student is in thought and experiencing cognitive disequilibrium (see D'Mello & Graesser, 2014).

The research conducted by D'Mello and Graesser on AutoTutor revealed that three of these emotions have significant correlations with learning: confusion and engagement/flow have a positive correlation with learning, whereas boredom has a negative correlation (Craig et al., 2004; D'Mello & Graesser, 2012c; Graesser & D'Mello, 2012). Frustration and the other emotions have no significant correlations with learning. Whether the emotions have a causal impact on learning is of course a separate question that will be addressed later in this chapter.

Do these conclusions about moment-to-moment emotions generalize to other advanced learning environments? Baker et al. (2010) tracked the emotions in three different computerized learning environments in order to assess the generality of our claims about the prevalence of learning-centered emotions. The first environment was AutoTutor, as we have already reported. The second involved students interacting with an intelligent tutoring system for mathematics, the *Aplusix II Algebra Learning Assistant* (Nicaud & Saidi, 1990). The third was *The Incredible Machine: Even More Contraptions* (Ryan, 2001), a simulation environment in which students complete a series of logical puzzles. Together, these three environments included different populations (Philippines vs. United States, high school students versus college students), different methods (quantitative field observation vs. retrospective self-report), and different types of learning environments (dialogue tutor, an ITS with problem solving, and a problem-solving game). Baker et al. (2010) investigated the following affective states: confusion, frustration, boredom, engagement/flow, delight, surprise, and neutral. Learning gains or performance was also measured in some of these studies.

Baker et al. (2010) reported a number of conclusions about the relative prevalence of different emotions in the three environments. Boredom was frequent in all learning environments, was associated with poorer learning, and was associated with the dysfunctional behavior called *gaming the system*. Gaming the system consists of mechanically using system facilities to trick the system into providing answers rather than learning the domain knowledge. Frustration was considerably less frequent than boredom, engagement/flow, and confusion; it was not associated with poorer learning, nor was it an antecedent to gaming the system. Confusion was consistently observed in all learning environments, whereas there were informative differences in the occurrence of engagement/flow. Experiences of delight and surprise were rare. In essence, the distribution of emotions we found in AutoTutor was remarkably similar across the three learning environments, but there were some variations, as would be expected. Baker et al. (2010) also recommended that significant effort should be put into detecting and productively responding to boredom, frustration, and confusion. There should be a special emphasis on developing pedagogical interventions to disrupt the downward spiral of emotions that occur when a student becomes bored and remains bored for long periods of time to the point of frustration and eventual disengagement (D'Mello & Graesser, 2012a, 2012c).

In another study conducted by D'Mello, Lehman, and Person (2011), students were tracked on emotions as they prepared for a law school entrance examination. The computer tracked them in a session where they solved difficult analytical reasoning problems from the law school admissions test (LSAT). Their facial expressions were recorded in addition to the computer screen. Students later completed a retrospective emotion judgment procedure. Students judged their emotions from the following alternatives: confusion, frustration, boredom, flow, contempt, curiosity, eureka, anxiety, anger, disgust, fear, happiness, sadness, surprise, and neutral. The results revealed that boredom, confusion, frustration, curiosity, and happiness (e.g., delight) were the major emotions that students experienced during problem solving, whereas anxiety was another important emotion. The emotion of anxiety is expected to surface more frequently when students anticipate evaluation and high-stakes tests.

More recently, D'Mello (2013) performed a meta-analysis of 24 studies that used a mixture of methodologies to systematically monitor the emotions (15 emotions plus neutral). There were 1,740 middle school, high school, college, and adult learners in five countries over the course of more than 1,000 hours of continuous interactions, with a range of learning technologies, including intelligent tutoring systems, serious games, and simulation environment. Engagement/flow, confusion, boredom, and frustration were the most frequent emotions and collectively comprised an astonishing 69% of all emotion reports. Indeed, we are quite confident that these are the critical learning-centered emotions that students experience during somewhat short (30 minutes to 2 hours) but in-depth learning sessions with technology.

Duration and Sequences of Emotions

Moment-to-moment emotions either reflect, mediate, moderate, or cause learning, so it is important to understand the emotion dynamics that accompany complex learning. The affective experiences that accompany learning are transient and dynamically change during learning rather than being persistent and static (unless the student becomes bored and disengages, as documented by Baker et al., 2010). Researchers have rarely investigated emotion dynamics during learning at a fine-grain level. However, the occurrence, duration, and sequencing of these emotions has been investigated in the AutoTutor system (D'Mello & Graesser, 2011, 2012a) and occasionally some other technology-advanced learning environments (Baker et al., 2010; McQuiggan et al., 2010; Sabourin et al., 2011).

D'Mello and Graesser (2011) documented the duration of the learner-centered emotions while students interacted with AutoTutor on computer literacy. A precise temporal chronometry would specify a point in time that an emotion is started, a duration from the start-point to the peak of the emotion, a duration of emotional experience around the peak, and a decay of the emotion until base level is achieved. The analyses modeled the decay rates of the emotions with exponentially decreasing functions. The decay rates showed the following trend for the six learner-centered emotions (Delight = Surprise) < (Frustration) < (Confusion = Boredom = Engagement/Flow). We would expect delight and surprise to be short-lived in most contexts, but the other four emotions should very much depend on the particular characteristics of the learning environment. Ideally, we would want the system to lower the decay of engagement/flow and increase the decay of frustration and boredom. However, the status of confusion may be more complex. How long should a learner remain confused and thinking before the system generates an event to move the learner along?

Transitions from one emotion to another are undoubtedly influenced by the difficulty of the materials, the dialogue interaction between student and computer, the student's level of mastery, and a host of other factors. One way to test or discover the moment-to-moment transitions in emotions is to document the emotion transitions in a transition matrix and to identify the events in the learning environment that explain these transitions. These analyses have been conducted on the AutoTutor data sets (D'Mello & Graesser, 2012a) and the data collected in a serious game on biology called *Crystal Island* (McQuiggan et al., 2010; Sabourin et al., 2011).

The analysis of interest would compute the transition from one emotion to a different emotion but in a manner that adjusts for base rates and the repetition of the same emotion. The repetition of the same emotion is of course important and was captured in our previously reported analysis of emotion duration (D'Mello & Graesser, 2011). A statistical metric was devised to make the adjustments so that we could compute the likelihood of shifting from emotion category at time to another emotion category at time in a way that quantitatively adjusts for the base rate likelihood of the emotion category and also the removal of a repeated emotion state.

Figure 24.1 summarizes the discoveries about emotion transitions. The transitions were aligned with a model of emotions that emphasizes the phenomenon of *cognitive disequilibrium* in learning. The significant transitions are identified in this section, whereas the next section turns to theoretical explanations. Chapter 15 in this volume by D'Mello and Graesser (2014) discusses confusion and the cognitive disequilibrium theoretical framework in more detail. Learners start out experiencing either a neutral state or a state of engagement/flow, referred to as cognitive equilibrium. Eventually an obstacle

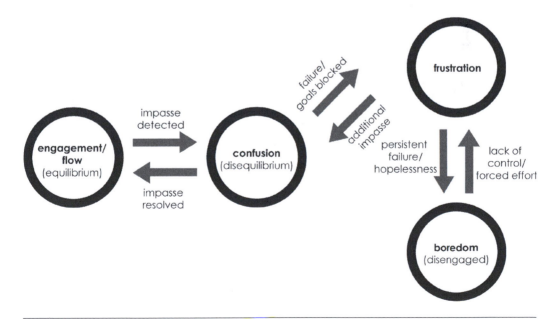

Figure 24.1 Cognitive disequilibrium framework.

or impasse is likely to occur, which triggers an emotion of confusion (and sometimes surprise, which is not depicted in Figure 24.1). The learner engages in effortful problem-solving activities in order to resolve the impasse and restore equilibrium. Confusion transitions into frustration when the impasse cannot be resolved, the student gets stuck, and important goals are blocked. Our analysis of emotion transitions confirmed these paths depicted in Figure 24.1. That is, sequences of emotions during learning with Auto-Tutor were analyzed and tested with alternative transition models. A theoretical explanation of these transitions is provided in the next section.

THEORETICAL FRAMEWORKS

This section builds on the cognitive disequilibrium framework and other theoretical frameworks that attempt to account for the emotions that occur during learning with advanced learning environments. It is beyond the scope of this chapter, and indeed the current state of available research, to present a comprehensive theory of emotions during deep learning. Instead, we present an initial sketch that does justice to what we currently know and that will hopefully stimulate future research.

The previous section offered a cognitive disequilibrium framework to account for the durations and transitions between emotions during deep learning (see Figure 24.1). These emotion sequences capture the microlevel analysis of emotions and cognition but fail to consider two theoretical components: moods (macrolevel emotions) and traits of learners. This section augments the cognitive disequilibrium framework by pulling in moods and learner traits.

A Cognitive Disequilibrium Theoretical Perspective

The cognitive disequilibrium framework summarized in Figure 24.1 explains the moment-to-moment emotions during complex learning (see D'Mello & Graesser, 2014). Cognitive disequilibrium is a state that occurs when people face obstacles to goals, interruptions, contradictions, incongruities, anomalies, uncertainty, and salient contrasts (D'Mello & Graesser, 2012a; Festinger, 1957; Graesser & D'Mello, 2011; Mandler, 1999; Piaget, 1952; Schwartz & Bransford, 1998). The handling of the cognitive disequilibrium depends on the learners' appraisal or reappraisal of their own abilities, their goals, the event that triggered the disequilibrium, and the context (Ortony et al., 1988; Scherer, et al., 2001; Strain & D'Mello, 2011). The learner is engaged and possibly in the zone of flow when the learning environment matches a student's zone of proximal development (Baumann, & Scheffer, 2010; Brown, Ellery, & Campione, 1998; Csikszentmihalyi, 1990). External events eventually create impasses, discrepancies, and the resulting cognitive disequilibrium, which in turn triggers confusion or surprise. When the cognitive disequilibrium and confusion persists, there is the risk of a downward spiral where the student becomes frustrated, eventually bored, and ultimately disengages from the task (Baker et al., 2010; D'Mello & Graesser, 2012a; Sabourin et al., 2011). When the challenges of cognitive disequilibrium are conquered, the student experiences the positive emotions of delight or engagement/flow (Csikszentmihalyi, 1990; D'Mello & Graesser, 2012a; Sabourin et al., 2011). There is an oscillation between cognitive disequilibrium and the resolution of the disequilibrium when the learner experiences flow (Baumann & Scheffer, 2010). The parameters of this oscillation vary among students and learning environments. For example, some students enjoy high levels of disequilibrium, confusion, and frustration over a lengthy time span when playing games. Other students are not comfortable with the disequilibrium even in game environments.

Augmenting the Cognitive Disequilibrium Framework With Traits and Moods

The learners' traits and moods would theoretically influence the occurrence, timing, and sequencing of the moment-to-moment emotions at the microlevel. Measures of enduring traits that are relevant to learning have tapped constructs of motivation, self-concept, and goal orientations (Daniels, et al., 2009; Frenzel, Pekrun, & Goetz, 2007; Linnenbrink, 2007; Pekrun, Elliot, & Maier, 2006; Schutz & Pekrun, 2007). The claims in this section are entirely theoretical, however, because investigation of microlevel emotions during learning is very much at its infancy. It is nevertheless important to briefly discuss how the cognitive disequilibrium framework would be expanded to incorporate traits and moods. The duration of the emotions and the likelihood of taking particular transitions depend on a host of factors, such as (1) the learner's interests, knowledge, self-concept, and traits, (2) the importance and difficulty of the subject matter in the learning environment, and (3) the mood that the learner starts out with prior to learning. Some examples are presented below.

1. Consider students who are mastery-oriented rather than performance-oriented (Deci & Ryan, 2002; Pekrun et al., 2006), have high intrinsic motivation in the task rather than extrinsic, are risk takers rather than cautious (Clifford, 1988; Meyer & Turner, 2006), and/or have a high degree of conscientiousness or persistence (Miserandino, 1996). These students would be able to handle more time in states of confusion and frustration when encountering impasses, setbacks, and negative feedback. In addition, they would be less prone to experiencing boredom and disengaging.

2. Consider students with a self-concept that they have low aptitude and interest in mathematics so they do not believe that effort will help them master the material (Dweck, 2002; Pekrun, Goetz, Daniels, Stupnisky, & Perry, 2010). These students will quickly become bored and disengage when assigned mathematics problems. They may not have enough skills and knowledge of math to experience much confusion other than an initial bewilderment and quick escape.

3. Consider a learning environment on a technical topic that is viewed by the students as being of little value and far above their heads. The students would attribute the challenge to a poor selection of materials and blame the instructional system and would quickly pursue the negative trajectory of frustration, boredom, and disengagement (Pekrun et al., 2010).

4. Consider the positive versus negative moods that mediate or moderate the experience of moment-to-moment emotions and deep learning. Theories of affect and cognitive processing highlight the important role of baseline mood valences (positive, negative, or neutral) on learning. For example, flexibility, creative thinking, and timely decision making in problem solving have been linked to experiences of positive affect (Clore & Huntsinger, 2007; Fredrickson & Branigan, 2005; Isen, 2008), whereas negative affect has been associated with a more methodical, focused, analytical approach to assessing the problem and finding the solution (Barth & Funke, 2010; Schwarz & Skurnik, 2003).

MANIPULATING AND RESPONDING TO EMOTIONS IN ADVANCED LEARNING TECHNOLOGIES

This section describes some advanced learning technologies that were designed to track, manipulate, or respond to learner emotions in an effort to promote deep learning. It is too early in this emerging research area to make firm conclusions on causal connections between emotions and learning, but the studies described here have measured both moment-to-moment emotions and deep learning with some directly testing causal relationships.

Emotion-Sensitive AutoTutor

An emotion-sensitive version of AutoTutor called *Affective AutoTutor* automatically detects student emotions based on multiple communication channels (D'Mello & Graesser, 2010; Graesser & D'Mello, 2012). It responds to the students' emotions by selecting appropriate discourse moves and displaying emotions through facial expressions and speech (D'Mello & Graesser, 2012c; D'Mello, Craig, Fike, & Graesser, 2009). The emotions of the students are automatically tracked by the features of their facial expressions, body posture, language, and discourse interaction. The primary student emotions that Affective AutoTutor tries to handle strategically are confusion, frustration, and boredom because these are the emotions that run the risk of leading to disengagement from the task. The tutor continues business as usual when the student is emotionally neutral or in the state of engagement/flow. The emotions of delight and surprise are fleeting, so there is no need to respond to these states in any special way.

The cognitive disequilibrium framework predicts that confusion is a critical juncture in the learning process that is sensitive to individual differences. Some students may give up when experiencing confusion because they have a self-concept that they are not good at the subject matter, or when they are trying to avoid negative feedback. For these kinds of students, encouragement, hints, and prompts may be the best strategy for helping them get over the hurdle. Other students treat confusion as a challenge to conquer and expend cognitive effort to restore equilibrium; these students can be left to their own devices. An adaptive tutor would treat these students differently. An Affective AutoTutor would ideally discriminate these two students by the automated detection of confusion together with the quantity and quality of the student contributions in the tutorial interaction. When frustration is detected, the tutor agent would express supportive empathetic comments to enhance motivation in addition to the usual hints or prompts to advance the student in constructing knowledge. It is important to minimize the likelihood of the student transitioning to boredom and disengagement in a downward trajectory; the Affective AutoTutor should respond to student boredom. When the student is bored, the tutor response would depend on the knowledge level of the student. Engaging material or challenging problems are appropriate for the more knowledgeable student, whereas easier problems are appropriate for the students with low subject matter knowledge so the student can build self-efficacy.

Affective AutoTutor has an emotion generator that enables the system to respond with suitable emotions. The agent speaks with intonation that is properly integrated with facial expressions that display emotions. The agent nods enthusiastically and expresses positive feedback language after the student has a correct contribution. The agent shakes its head in some versions or has a skeptical facial expression when the student contribution is low quality. There is an empathetic verbal message, kind facial expressions, and an encouraging demeanor when the student needs support. A small set of emotion displays like these examples went a long way in conveying the tutor's emotions.

A study was conducted to test the impact of different versions of Affective AutoTutor on learning gains (D'Mello, Craig, et al., 2009; D'Mello & Graesser, 2012c). The study compared the original AutoTutor without emotion tracking and emotional displays to an Affective AutoTutor version that is emotionally supportive. The *supportive* Affective AutoTutor had polite and encouraging positive feedback ("You're doing extremely well") or negative feedback after a low-quality student contribution ("Not quite, but this is difficult for most students"). When the student expressed low-quality contributions, the tutor attributed the problem to the difficulty of the materials to most students rather than blaming the student being tutored. There was also a *shake-up* version of Affective AutoTutor. This version tried to shake up the emotions of the student by being playfully cheeky and telling the student what emotion the student is having ("I see that you are frustrated"). The simple substitution of this feedback dramatically changed AutoTutor's personality.

The impact of the different AutoTutor versions on learning computer literacy depended on the phase of tutoring and the student's level of mastery. The supportive emotion-sensitive AutoTutor had either no impact (for low-knowledge students) or a negative impact (for high- knowledge students) on learning during early phases of the tutoring session (i.e., within the first 30 minutes of the session). During a later phase of tutoring (i.e., the next 30 minutes), the supportive AutoTutor improved learning but only for the low-knowledge students. Low-domain knowledge students also performed better on a transfer test when they interacted with the supportive AutoTutor. An analysis of learners' perceptions of both tutors indicated that their perceptions of how closely the computer tutors resembled human tutors increased over time, was related to the quality of tutor feedback, and was a powerful predictor of learning. Interestingly, the increase over time was greater for the Affective AutoTutor over the control condition.

These results suggest that supportive emotional displays by AutoTutor may not be beneficial during the early phases of an interaction when the student and agent are bonding but that a supportive tutor is appropriate at later phases for students who have low knowledge and encounter difficulties. In essence, there may be an optimal *time for emoting*—just like there is in interactions between humans. The shake-up AutoTutor had more complex patterns of results that were never fully tested because an initial study indicated learning gains were the same as the original AutoTutor. However, most adults have a positive initial impression of the shake-up AutoTutor. Perhaps the playful shake-up tutor is motivating when boredom starts emerging for the more confident, high-knowledge learners, but this needs to be tested with more research in diverse student populations and learning environments.

Stimulating Cognitive Disequilibrium in Operation ARIES

Earlier in the chapter, we reported that learning gains were positively correlated with confusion as long as the learner was not persistently confused (Craig et al., 2004; D'Mello & Graesser, 2012c). The question arises whether there is a causal relationship between confusion from cognitive disequilibrium and learning. Studies were conducted that manipulated cognitive equilibrium experimentally and measured the consequences on confusion and learning (D'Mello, Lehman, Pekrun, & Graesser, 2014; Lehman, D'Mello, & Graesser, 2012; Lehman et al., 2011). This research is reported in Chapter 15 by D'Mello and Graesser (2014) in this volume, so this work is succinctly covered in this section.

This research was conducted in the context of *trialogs* very similar to those developed in a serious game called *Operation ARIES* (Millis et al., 2011) and a commercialized version called *Operation ARA* (Halpern et al., 2012). ARIES teaches scientific critical thinking in college students through a series of game modules, including those with two or more animated pedagogical agents. In the trialogs, a three-way trialog conversation transpires among the human student, a tutor agent, and a student agent. The tutor agent is an expert on scientific inquiry, whereas the student agent is a peer of the human student. A series of cases are presented to the student that describe experiments with possible flaws with respect to scientific methodology. For example, one case study described an experiment that tested a new pill that purportedly helps people lose weight, but there was no control group. The goal of the student and agents in the trialog is to identify the flaws and express them in natural language.

As reported in the D'Mello and Graesser chapter, studies were conducted that attempted to plant cognitive disequilibrium by manipulating whether or not the tutor agent and the student agent contradicted each other during the trialog. That is, the tutor agent and student agent engaged in a short exchange about (1) whether there was a flaw in the study and (2) the nature of the flaw if there was a flaw. The tutor agent expressed a correct assertion, and the student agent agreed with the tutor in the *True-True* control condition. In the *True-False* condition, the tutor expressed a correct assertion, but the student agent disagreed with an incorrect assertion. The *False-True* condition was the flip side with the tutor expressing a false assertion, whereas the *False-False* condition had both the tutor and the student agreeing on incorrect information.

The central question is whether the contradictions would plant confusion and subsequent reasoning at deeper levels, which in turn would improve learning (contradiction → confusion → deep reasoning → deep learning). In one measure of confusion, the agents asked the student questions after particular points of agent contradiction in the conversation. For example, the agents turned to the human and asked "Do you agree with Chris (student agent) that the control group in this study was flawed?" A signal of confusion would be reflected in answers that were either incorrect or uncertain. This confusion would allegedly stimulate thinking, reasoning, and learning. The data indeed confirmed that the contradictions had an impact on the humans' answers to these forced-choice questions immediately following a contradiction. The correct responding showed the following order: True-True > True-False > False-True > False-False conditions. These findings indicated that learners typically agreed with the agents when the agents agreed (True-True, False-False) but were often confused when there was a contradiction between the two agents (True-False or False-True). Interestingly, there was also some evidence that disequilibrium and/or confusion caused more learning at deeper levels of mastery, as reflected in a delayed test on scientific reasoning. Specifically, experimental conditions with agent contradictions often produced higher performance on multiple choice questions that tapped deep levels of comprehension compared with performance in the true-true condition but only if learners were confused by the contradictions during training. Similarly, students who were confused by the contradictions during training were more likely to correctly identify flaws in new case studies at a test phase. These results are consistent with the hypothesis that there may be a causal relationship between cognitive disequilibrium and deep learning, with confusion playing a moderating role on the effect of the contradictions on learning.

Similar to our studies with trialogs, Forbes-Riley and Litman (2011) have used an intelligent tutoring system called *UNC-ITSPOKE* to examine whether automatic responses to learner uncertainty could improve learning outcomes. Uncertainty is an affective state that is similar to confusion and plays an important role on the process and products of learning. UNC-ITSPOKE was designed to teach students about various physics topics, with the capability to automatically detect and respond to learners' correctness/incorrectness, and certainty/uncertainty. Forbes-Riley and Litman (2011) compared learning outcomes between learners who received adaptive responses to uncertainty (adaptive), random responses to uncertainty (random), or no responses (control). The adaptive condition achieved slightly (but not significantly) higher learning outcomes than the random and control conditions. Interestingly, the results suggested that it is not the presence or absence of adaptive responses to uncertainty but how many adaptive responses were given. Learners who received a high frequency of adaptive responses to uncertainty achieved significantly higher learning outcomes than those who received a low frequency of adaptive responses. Forbes-Riley and Litman (2011) concluded that there is merit in offering adaptive feedback to uncertainty and that such feedback can improve learning outcomes.

A Serious Game With Narrative in Crystal Island

The links between emotions and learning are fundamental to the design of serious educational games that target complex academic topics (Conati, 2002; Forsyth et al., 2013; McNamara, Jackson, & Graesser, 2010). Educational games ideally are capable of turning work into play by minimizing boredom, optimizing engagement/flow, presenting challenges that reside within the optimal zone of confusion, preventing persistent frustration, and engineering delight and pleasant surprises (Lepper & Henderlong, 2000; Ritterfeld, Cody, & Vorderer, 2009). Although educational games increase learners' engagement, they may or may not provide instructional support that leads to improved learning (O'Neil & Perez, 2008; Tobias & Fletcher, 2011). Educators must balance a trade-off between game environments that are engaging but tangential to learning and environments that promote deep learning but fail to foster engagement. An analysis of moment-to-moment emotions is presumably needed to better understand the trade-offs.

Lester and his colleagues have recently conducted studies that track emotions while middle school children learn about biology in a serious game called *Crystal Island* (McQuiggan, Robison, & Lester, 2010; Sabourin et al., 2011). This is an immersive educational game that capitalizes on the principle of narrativity, which allegedly (1) motivates learners to initiate and persist in game play, (2) increases study time on academic content, and (3) increases learning. In Crystal Island, learners attempt to identify the source of an infectious disease that is spreading among the members of a research team on Crystal Island. Students make gradual steps toward diagnosing the cause of the disease through the generation of questions, generation of hypotheses, collection of data, and analysis of data. The affective states were tracked during the learning experience by having students self-report every seven minutes whether they are experiencing any of the following seven states: anxious, bored, confused, curious, excited, focused (engaged), and frustrated. The researchers also tracked off-task behavior during the game that is manifested by irrelevant actions. The transitions between emotions were found to interact with the off-task versus on-task behaviors along interesting trajectories. For example, students who remained on-task after reporting confusion tended to be focused (engaged) in the next stretch of time; students who were off-task after confusion tended to report boredom or frustration next. In contrast, frustration showed a very different profile. Frustrated students who went off-task ended up next being focused; frustrated students who went on-task ended up next being bored. Apparently, it was best for the frustrated students to take some time off from the primary task (see also Baker et al., 2010). It remains to be seen whether these results replicate, but they do illustrate the interesting and sometimes counterintuitive interactions between moment-to-moment emotions and learning activities. It is conceivable that a scientific understanding of these interactions will be necessary for any model that attempts to predict and explain successful serious games.

SUMMARY AND SPECULATIONS

This chapter has reviewed the available research investigating moment-to-moment emotions that occur in advanced learning technologies that target deep learning during relatively short, one to two hour time sessions. The primary learning-centered emotions are confusion, frustration, boredom, and engagement/flow, with occasional moments of curiosity, happiness, delight and surprise, and anxiety when students are preparing for tests. These emotions can be identified by the student, peers, teachers, and trained experts, but the different judges show modest agreement. There are automated methods of classifying emotions from the channels of tutorial dialogue history, language, speech, facial expressions, and body posture. The duration of emotions is longer for boredom, engagement/flow, and confusion than delight and surprise, with frustration in between. The occurrence and transitions between emotions are explained reasonably well by a cognitive disequilibrium theoretical framework. More specifically, the student experiences impasses that trigger cognitive disequilibrium and confusion. Confusion might be resolved and equilibrium restored; alternatively, unresolved confusion and persistent failure leads to frustration, boredom, and eventual disengagement. Engagement/flow occurs when the student is at the optimal level of challenge and manages to handle impasses that arise. There appears to be a causal relationship between cognitive disequilibrium and confusion, which in turn has a causal link to thoughtful reasoning and deeper learning. A number of learning environments have been developed that track, manipulate, and respond to students' emotions in order to promote deep learning. This chapter focused primarily on three of these learning environments: Affective AutoTutor, trialogs with agents similar to the serious game Operation ARIES, and the serious game Crystal Islands. Projects were conducted that systematically tracked learner emotions and tested whether learning is improved by manipulating emotions or by adaptively responding to the student emotions.

The research discussed in this chapter provides an initial sketch of moment-to-moment emotions during complex learning, but more research is needed on so many levels. The occurrence, duration, and sequencing of moment-to-moment emotions undoubtedly depend on characteristics of the student, the learning environment, and social context so future research needs to document such differences. A broader array of emotions is expected in the following example contexts:

1. Hours or days before a major test in courses that span a semester or year. In addition to anxiety, there should be irritation, anger, and other emotions associated with high stress.
2. Social interaction in a classroom or smaller groups. Pride, shame, embarrassment, and many other social emotions would be expected.
3. Writing a difficult paper under a deadline or high stakes. Rage is likely for those with writer's block, whereas a genuine flow experience occurs for the more gifted writers.

The traits of students are needed to predict what emotions occur in these situations, as has been documented over decades of research (Linnenbrink, 2007; Pekrun, 2006).

The cognitive disequilibrium framework is a good start in accounting for the emotions that occur in advanced learning environments that target deep learning. However, there needs to be a systematic investigation of how components in the framework are influenced by individual differences among students with respect to subject matter knowledge, general reasoning skills, academic risk taking, intrinsic motivation, persistence, emotional intelligence, self-concept, and the list goes on. These individual differences are undoubtedly mediating or moderating variables in the system, but this needs to be documented. For example, available evidence suggests that confusion is a pivotal emotion that sometimes leads to deeper learning, but there is uncertainty how particular types of students handle the confusion. Some students quickly escape confusion and conclude they are not very good at the subject matter; other students embrace confusion as a challenge to be conquered. There is the prospect of scaling the zone of optimal confusion for individual students. The learning technology would need to detect and be sensitive to these differences among students. Students who are prone to escape confusion will presumably need encouragement and good hints, whereas those who embrace confusion will benefit from a steeper gradient of challenge. Such interactions among emotions, student characteristics, and technological features await future research.

REFERENCES

Ainley, M., Hidi, S., & Berndorff, D. (2002). Interest, learning, and the psychological processes that mediate their relationship. *Journal of Educational Psychology, 94*, 545–561.

Arroyo, I., Woolf, B., Cooper, D., Burleson, W., Muldner, K., & Christopherson, R. (2009). Emotion sensors go to school. In V. Dimitrova, R. Mizoguchi, B. Du Boulay, & A. Graesser (Eds.), *Proceedings of 14th International Conference on Artificial Intelligence In Education* (pp. 17–24). Amsterdam, Netherlands: IOS Press.

Baker, R. S., D'Mello, S. K., Rodrigo, M. T., & Graesser, A. C. (2010). Better to be frustrated than bored: The incidence, persistence, and impact of learners' cognitive-affective states during interactions with three different computer-based learning environments. *International Journal of Human-Computer Studies, 68*, 223–241.

Barrett, L. (2006). Are emotions natural kinds? *Perspectives on Psychological Science, 1*, 28–58.

Barth, C. M., & Funke, J. (2010). Negative affective environments improve complex solving performance. *Cognition and Emotion, 24*, 1259–1268.

Baumann, N., & Scheffer, D. (2010). Seeing and mastering difficulty: The role of affective change in achievement flow. *Cognition and Emotion, 24*, 1304–1328.

Bower, G. (1992). How might emotions affect learning? In S. A. Christianson (Ed.), *Handbook of emotion and memory: Research and theory* (pp. 3–31). Hillsdale, NJ: Erlbaum.

Brown, A., Ellery, S., & Campione, J. (1998). Creating zones of proximal development electronically in thinking practices in mathematics and science learning. In J. Greeno & S. Goldman (Eds.), *Thinking practices in mathematics and science learning* (pp. 341–368). Mahwah, NJ: Lawrence Erlbaum.

Calvo, R. A., & D'Mello, S. K. (2010). Affect detection: An interdisciplinary review of models, methods, and their applications. *IEEE Transactions on Affective Computing, 1,* 18–37.

Clifford, M. (1988). Failure tolerance and academic risk-taking in ten- to twelve-year-old students. *British Journal of Educational Psychology, 58,* 15–27.

Clore, G. L., & Huntsinger, J. R. (2007). How emotions inform judgment and regulate thought. *Trends in Cognitive Sciences, 11,* 393–399.

Conati, C. (2002). Probabilistic assessment of user's emotions in educational games. *Journal of Applied Artificial Intelligence, 16,* 555–575.

Conati, C., & Maclaren, H. (2009). Empirically building and evaluating a probabilistic model of user affect. *User Modeling and User-Adapted Interaction, 19,* 267–303.

Craig, S. D., D'Mello, S., Witherspoon, A., & Graesser, A. (2008). Emote aloud during learning with AutoTutor: Applying the facial action coding system to cognitive-affective states during learning. *Cognition and Emotion, 22,* 777–788.

Craig, S. D., Graesser, A. C., Sullins, J., & Gholson, J. (2004). Affect and learning: An exploratory look into the role of affect in learning. *Journal of Educational Media, 29,* 241–250.

Csikszentmihalyi, M. (1990). *Flow: The psychology of optimal experience.* New York, NY: Harper-Row.

Daniels, L. M., Pekrun, R., Stupnisky, R. H., Haynes, T. L., Perry, R. P., & Newall, N. E. (2009). A longitudinal analysis of achievement goals: From affective antecedents to emotional effects and achievement outcomes. *Journal of Educational Psychology, 101,* 948–963.

Deci, E., & Ryan, R. (2002). The paradox of achievement: The harder you push, the worse it gets. In J. Aronson (Ed.), *Improving academic achievement: Impact of psychological factors on education* (pp. 61–87). Orlando, FL: Academic Press.

D'Mello, S. K. (2013). A selective meta-analysis on the relative incidence of discrete affective states during learning with technology, *Journal of Educational Psychology, 105,* 1082–1099.

D'Mello, S., Craig, S., Fike, K., & Graesser, A. (2009). Responding to learners' cognitive-affective states with supportive and shakeup dialogues. In J. Jacko (Ed.), *Human-computer interaction: Ambient, ubiquitous and intelligent interaction* (pp. 595–604). Berlin/Heidelberg, Germany: Springer.

D'Mello, S. K., Craig, S. D., & Graesser, A. C. (2009). Multi-method assessment of affective experience and expression during deep learning. *International Journal of Learning Technology, 4,* 165–187.

D'Mello, S. K., Craig, S. D., Witherspoon, A., McDaniel, B., & Graesser, A. C. (2008). Automatic detection of learner's affect from conversational cues. *User Modeling and User-Adapted Interaction, 18,* 45–80.

D'Mello, S. K., Dale, R. A., & Graesser, A. C. (2012). Disequilibrium in the mind, disharmony in the body. *Cognition & Emotion, 26,* 362–374.

D'Mello, S. K., & Graesser, A. C. (2009). Automatic detection of learners' emotions from gross body language. *Applied Artificial Intelligence, 23,* 123–150.

D'Mello, S., & Graesser, A. C. (2010). Multimodal semi-automated affect detection from conversational cues, gross body language, and facial features. *User Modeling and User-adapted Interaction, 20,* 147–187.

D'Mello, S., & Graesser, A. (2011). The half-life of cognitive-affective states during complex learning. *Cognition and Emotion, 25,* 1299–1308.

D'Mello, S. K. & Graesser, A. C. (2012a). Dynamics of affective states during complex learning, *Learning and Instruction, 22,* 145–157.

D'Mello, S., & Graesser, A. C. (2012b). Language and discourse are powerful signals of student emotions during tutoring. *IEEE Transactions on Learning Technologies, 5,* 304–317.

D'Mello, S. K. & Graesser, A. C. (2012c). AutoTutor and Affective AutoTutor: Learning by talking with cognitively and emotionally intelligent computers that talk back. *ACM Transactions on Interactive Intelligent Systems, 2,* 23:2–23:39.

D'Mello, S. D., & Graesser, A. C. (2014). Confusion. In R. Pekrun & L. Linnenbrink-Garcia (Eds.), *International handbook of emotions in education.* New York, NY: Taylor & Francis.

D'Mello, S., Lehman, S., Pekrun, R., & Graesser, A. (2014). Confusion can be beneficial for learning. *Learning and Instruction, 29,* 153–170.

D'Mello, S., Lehman, B., & Person, N. (2011). Monitoring affect states during effortful problem solving activities. *International Journal of Artificial Intelligence In Education, 20,* 361–389.

D'Mello, S., Picard, R., & Graesser, A. (2007). Towards an affect-sensitive AutoTutor. *Intelligent Systems, IEEE, 22,* 53–61.

D'Mello, S., Taylor, R., Davidson, K., & Graesser, A. (2008). Self versus teacher judgments of learner emotions during a tutoring session with AutoTutor. In B. Woolf, E. Aimeur, R. Nkambou, & S. Lajoie (Eds.), *Proceedings of the 9th international conference on Intelligent Tutoring Systems.* Berlin, Heidelberg, Germany: Springer.

du Boulay, B., Avramides, K., Luckin, R., Martínez-Mirón, E., Méndez, G. R., & Carr, A. (2010) Towards systems that care: A conceptual framework based on motivation, metacognition and affect. *International Journal of Artificial Intelligence in Education, 20,* 197–229.

Dweck, C. S. (2002). The development of ability conceptions. In A. Wigfield & J. S. Eccles (Eds.), *Development of achievement motivation: A volume in the educational psychology series,* (pp. 57–88). San Diego, CA: Academic Press.

Ekman, P. (1992). An argument for basic emotions. *Cognition and Emotion, 6,* 169–200.

Ericsson, K., & Simon, H. (1993). *Protocol analysis: Verbal reports as data.* Cambridge, MA: The MIT Press.

Festinger, L. (1957). *A theory of cognitive dissonance.* Stanford, CA: Stanford University Press.

Forbes-Riley, K., & Litman, D. J. (2011). Benefits and challenges of real-time uncertainty detection and adaptation in a spoken dialogue computer tutor. *Speech Communication, 53,* 1115–1136.

Forsyth, C. M., Graesser, A. C., Pavlik, P., Cai, Z., Butler, H., Halpern, D. F., & Millis, K. (2013). OperationARIES! Methods, mystery and mixed models: Discourse features predict affect in a serious game. *Journal of Educational Data Mining, 5,* 147–189.

Fredrickson, B., & Branigan, C. (2005). Positive emotions broaden the scope of attention and thought-action repertoires. *Cognition & Emotion, 19,* 313–332.

Frenzel, A. C., Pekrun, R., & Goetz, T. (2007). Perceived learning environment and students' emotional experiences: A multilevel analysis of mathematics classrooms. *Learning and Instruction, 17,* 478–493.

Graesser, A., & D'Mello, S. K. (2012). Emotions during the learning of difficult material. In B. Ross (Ed.), *Psychology of learning and motivation* (Vol. 57, pp. 183–226). Amsterdam, Netherlands: Elsevier.

Graesser, A. C., & D'Mello, S. K. (2011). Theoretical perspectives on affect and deep learning. In R. Calvo and S. D'Mello (Eds.). *New perspectives on affect and learning technologies.* New York, NY: Springer.

Graesser, A. C., Jeon, M., & Dufty, D. (2008). Agent technologies designed to facilitate interactive knowledge construction. *Discourse Processes, 45,* 298–322.

Graesser, A. C., Lu, S., Jackson, G. T., Mitchell, H., Ventura, M., Olney, A., & Louwerse, M. M. (2004). Auto-Tutor: A tutor with dialogue in natural language. *Behavior Research Methods, Instruments, and Computers, 36,* 180–193.

Grafsgaard, J., Boyer, K. E., Phillips, R., & Lester, J. (2011). Modeling confusion: Facial expression, task, and discourse in task-oriented tutorial dialogue. In G. Biswas, S. Bull, J. Kay, & A. Mitrovik (Eds.), *Proceedings of the 15th International Conference on Artificial Intelligence in Education* (pp. 98–105). Berlin, Germany: Springer-Verlag.

Halpern, D. F., Millis, K., Graesser, A. C., Butler, H., Forsyth, C., & Cai, Z. (2012). Operation ARA: A computerized learning game that teaches critical thinking and scientific reasoning. *Thinking Skills and Creativity, 7,* 93–100.

Isen, A. (2008). Some ways in which positive affect influences decision making and problem solving. In M. Lewis, J. Haviland-Jones, & L. Barrett (Eds.), *Handbook of emotions* (3rd ed., pp. 548–573). New York, NY: Guilford.

Kapoor, A., Burleson, W., & Picard, R. (2007) Automatic prediction of frustration. *International Journal of Human Computer Studies, 65,* 724–736.

Lazarus, R. (2000). The cognition-emotion debate: A bit of history. In M. Lewis & J. Haviland-Jones (Eds.), *Handbook of emotions* (2nd ed., pp. 1–20). New York, NY: Guilford Press.

Lehman, B., D'Mello, S. K., & Graesser, A. C. (2012). Confusion and complex learning during interactions with computer learning environments. *Internet and Higher Education, 15,* 184–194.

Lehman, B., D'Mello, S., Strain, A., Gross, M., Dobbins, A., Wallace, P., . . . Graesser, A.C. (2011). Inducing and tracking confusion with contradictions during critical thinking and scientific reasoning. In S. Bull, G. Biswas, J. Kay, & T. Mitrovic (Eds.), *Proceedings of the 15th International Conference on Artificial Intelligence in Education* (pp. 171–178). Berlin, Heidelberg, Germany: Springer.

Lepper, M. R., & Henderlong, J. (2000). Turning "play" into "work" and "work" into "play:" 25 years of research on intrinsic versus extrinsic motivation. In C. Sansone & J. M. Harackiewicz (Eds.), *Intrinsic and extrinsic motivation: The search for optimal motivation and performance* (pp. 257–307). San Diego, CA: Academic Press.

Linnenbrink, E. (2007). The role of affect in student learning: A muli-dimensional approach to considering the interaction of affect, motivation and engagement. In P. Schutz & R. Pekrun (Eds.), *Emotion in education* (pp. 107–124). San Diego, CA: Academic Press.

Litman, D. J., & Forbes-Riley, K. (2006). Recognizing student emotions and attitudes on the basis of utterances in spoken tutoring dialogues with both human and computer tutors. *Speech Communication, 48,* 559–590.

Mandler, G. (1999). Emotion. In B. M. Bly & D. E. Rumelhart (Eds.), *Cognitive science handbook of perception and cognition* (2nd ed., pp. 367–384). San Diego, CA: Academic Press.

McNamara, D. S., Jackson, G. T., & Graesser, A. C. (2010). Intelligent tutoring and games (ITaG). In Y. K. Baek (Ed.), *Gaming for classroom-based learning: Digital role-playing as a motivator of study* (pp. 44–65). Hershey, PA: IGI Global.

McQuiggan, S., & Lester, J. (2009). Modelling affect expression and recognition in an interactive learning environment. *International Journal of Learning Technology, 4,* 216–233.

McQuiggan, S.W., Robison, J. L., & Lester, J. C. (2010). Affective transitions in narrative-centered learning environments. *Educational Technology and Society, 13,* 40–53.

Meyer, D., & Turner, J. (2006). Re-conceptualizing emotion and motivation to learn in classroom contexts. *Educational Psychology Review, 18,* 377–390.

Millis, K, Forsyth, C., Butler, H., Wallace, P., Graesser, A., & Halpern, D. (2011) Operation ARIES! A serious game for teaching scientific inquiry. In M. Ma, A. Oikonomou, & J. Lakhmi (Eds.), *Serious games and edutainment applications* (pp.169–196). London, United Kingdom: Springer-Verlag.

Miserandino, M. (1996). Children who do well in school: Individual differences in perceived competence and autonomy in above-average children. *Journal of Educational Psychology, 88,* 203–214.

Nicaud, J. F., & Saidi, M. (1990). Explanation of algebraic reasoning: The APLUSIX System. In S. Ramani, R. Chrandrasekar, & K. Anjaneyulu (Eds.), *Knowledge based computer systems* (pp. 145–154). Berlin: Springer-Verlag.

O'Neil, H. F., & Perez, R. S. (2008). *Computer games and team and individual learning.* Amsterdam, Netherlands: Elsevier.

Ortony, A., Clore, G., & Collins, A. (1988). *The cognitive structure of emotions.* New York, NY: Cambridge University Press.

Pekrun, R. (2006). The control-value theory of achievement emotions: Assumptions, corollaries, and implications for educational research and practice. *Educational Psychology Review, 18,* 315–341.

Pekrun, R., Elliot, A., & Maier, M. (2006). Achievement goals and discrete achievement emotions: A theoretical model and prospective test. *Journal of Educational Psychology, 98,* 583–597.

Pekrun, R., Goetz, T., Daniels, L., Stupnisky, R. H., & Perry, R. P. (2010). Boredom in achievement settings: Exploring control–value antecedents and performance outcomes of a neglected emotion. *Journal of Educational Psychology, 102,* 531–549.

Piaget, J. (1952). *The origins of intelligence.* New York, NY: International University Press.

Picard, R. (1997). *Affective computing.* Cambridge, MA: MIT Press.

Picard, R. (2010). Affective Computing: From Laughter to IEEE. *IEEE Transactions on Affective Computing, 1,* 11–17.

Poh, M. Z., McDuff, D. J., & Picard, R. W. (2010). Non-contact, automated cardiac pulse measurements using video imaging and blind source separation. *Optics Express, 18,* 10762–10774.

Poh, M. Z., Swenson, N. C., & Picard, R. W. (2010). A wearable sensor for unobtrusive, long-term assessment of electrodermal activity. *IEEE Transactions on Biomedical Engineering, 57,* 1243–1252.

Reichle, E. D., Reineberg, A. E., & Schooler, J. W. (2010). Eye movements during mindless reading. *Psychological Science, 21*(9), 1300–1310.

Ritterfeld, U., Cody, M., & Vorderer, P. (Eds.). (2009). *Serious games: Mechanisms and effects.* New York, NY: Routledge, Taylor & Francis.

Russell, J. (2003). Core affect and the psychological construction of emotion. *Psychological Review, 110,* 145–172.

Ryan, K. (2001). *The incredible machine: Even more contraptions* [Computer Software]. Sierra Entertainment.

Sabourin, J., Rowe, J., Mott, B., & Lester, J. (2011). When off-task in on-task: The affective role of off-task behavior in narrative-centered learning environments. In G. Biswas, S. Bull, J. Kay, & A. Mitrovik (Eds.), *Proceedings of the 15th International Conference on Artificial Intelligence in Education* (pp. 534–536). Berlin: Springer-Verlag.

Scherer, K., Schorr, A., & Johnstone, T. (Eds.). (2001). *Appraisal processes in emotion: Theory, methods, research.* London, United Kingdom: London University Press.

Schutz, P., & Pekrun, R. (Eds.). (2007). *Emotion in education.* San Diego, CA: Academic Press.

Schwartz, D., & Bransford, D. (1998). A time for telling. *Cognition and Instruction, 16,* 475–522.

Schwarz, N., & Skurnik, I. (2003). Feeling and thinking: Implications for problem solving. In J. D. R. S. (Ed.), *The psychology of problem solving* (pp. 263–290). New York, NY: Cambridge University Press.

Strain, A., & D'Mello, S. (2011). Emotion regulation strategies during learning. In S. Bull, G. Biswas, J. Kay, & T. Mitrovic (Eds.), *Proceedings of the 15th International Conference on Artificial Intelligence in Education* (pp. 566–568). Berlin: Springer.

Tobias, S., & Fletcher, J. D. (Eds.). (2011). *Computer games and instruction.* Greenwich, CT: Information Age.

VanLehn, K., Graesser, A. C., Jackson, G. T., Jordan, P., Olney, A., & Rose, C. P. (2007). When are tutorial dialogues more effective than reading? *Cognitive Science, 31,* 3–62.

Woolf, B., Burleson, W., Arroyo, I., Dragon, T., Cooper, D., & Picard, R. (2009). Affect-aware tutors: Recognizing and responding to student affect. *International Journal of Learning Technology, 4,* 129–164.

25

TEACHER EMOTIONS

Anne C. Frenzel, University of Munich

Learning and teaching is kind of a rollercoaster. It's periods of brilliant sunshine, warm success, followed by deep valleys of depression and frustration.

(Teacher interview statement from Scott & Sutton, 2009)

Emotions are most intriguing human phenomena, as discussed in the early chapters of this book. As they are an integral part of our lives, they are ubiquitous also in classrooms, where learners and teachers come together. In the context of emotions in the classroom, the majority of research has been directed at students' experiences (cf. Schutz & Pekrun, 2007; see also Pekrun & Linnenbrink-Garcia, 2014). The present chapter, however, provides a different perspective by focusing on teachers. In educational research, teachers have typically been viewed as providers of learning contexts. A substantial amount of research has been dedicated to teaching quality or classroom climates as provided by teachers, including classroom goal structures or social interaction patterns among students and between teachers and students (Anderman & Patrick, 2012; H. Patrick, Kaplan, & Ryan, 2011; Seidel & Shavelson, 2007). Less attention has been directed towards teachers as human beings having their own motives, goals, and affective experiences (Chang, 2009; Nias, 1996; Zembylas, 2003a). One exception, however, is the relatively large body of literature on teacher burnout. Compared to other professionals, teachers have a rather high burnout risk (Hakanen, Bakker, & Schaufeli, 2006). Dropout due to psychological reasons (e.g., depression, exhaustion, or anxiety disorders) is fairly high among teachers. The literature on burnout adopts a rather clinical perspective, targeting severe states of emotional exhaustion, reduced personal accomplishment, and depersonalization (e.g., Hakanen, et al., 2006; Maslach & Jackson, 1981, 1986; Maslach, Schaufeli, & Leiter, 2001). In contrast, the present chapter seeks to explore teacher emotions from a broader perspective, examining the entire range of positive and negative emotions, from mild to intense states.

Given the relative scarcity of available research on teacher emotions, the main aims of this chapter are threefold. First, to provide an overview of the frequency of several different emotions that teachers typically experience in the classroom. Second, to compare and contrast teachers' emotions with other affective constructs addressed in the current research on teachers' personalities. Last, the chapter provides insight into what is known about correlates of teacher emotions while also presenting a model that suggests how teacher emotions may be affected by as well as affect classroom processes, including both teacher and student behaviors. The chapter closes with deliberations about methodological challenges and other controversial issues as well as their implications for future directions in the research on teacher emotions.

DISCRETE EMOTIONS RELEVANT FOR TEACHERS: DEFINITIONS AND FREQUENCIES

The existing body of literature that explicitly focuses on teacher emotions is small and dominated by studies that have used qualitative interview-based approaches. These studies have typically explored teacher emotions by using rather broadly framed questions regarding how teachers feel in relation to their jobs. Results from these studies are typically reported in terms of specific emotions: Researchers describe teachers' enjoyment or pride, their anger or contempt, rather than reporting more generally about their positive or negative affect. Since a key goal of the present chapter is to review and summarize the existing research on teacher emotions, it follows up on this research tradition and presents research findings arranged according to a number of discrete emotions, including enjoyment, pride, anger, anxiety, shame/guilt, boredom, and pity. These emotions were selected based on their salience in the literature, indicated by the number of studies that directly addressed the particular emotions, by the frequency they are reported in narrative studies, and by the frequency of their actual experience as reported in the (few) studies that used real-life assessment methods to explore the frequencies and intensities of teacher emotions.

Furthermore, the large majority of research knowledge on teacher emotions pertains to emotions experienced while teaching in class, since that is the predominating task of a teacher. Considerably less is known regarding teacher emotions in relation to preparing for teaching, giving exams, working with parents, or dealing with colleagues and supervisors, even though these activities can also arouse intense emotions in teachers. Therefore, the present chapter also focuses on emotions directly related to teaching.

Enjoyment

Enjoyment is one of the main positive emotions experienced by humans (Fredrickson & Cohn, 2008). It signals well-being and pleasure resulting either from an upcoming desirable event (anticipatory joy), from being engaged in an enjoyable activity (activity-related enjoyment), or from satisfaction and happiness derived from a desirable past event or outcome (outcome-related enjoyment). As Hargreaves emphasizes in his writings, teaching offers many emotional rewards (Hargreaves, 1998, 2005). Indeed, enjoyment can be considered one of the most salient emotions experienced by teachers during teaching (Sutton & Wheatley, 2003). Positive emotions, specifically enjoyment, also were dominant across studies that used real-life assessment methods to explore the frequencies and intensities of teachers' discrete emotions (Becker, 2011; Carson, 2006; Frenzel, Goetz, Stephens, & Jacob, 2009). Table 25.1 summarizes the frequencies of teachers' discrete emotions as reported by three studies that used a period diary or an experience-sampling approach. (For a detailed discussion of different assessment methods of teacher emotions, see below.) The data clearly indicate that enjoyment (referred to as happiness by

Carson, 2006) dominates teachers' emotions in class. This is in line with research conducted in other fields highlighting the dominance of positive emotions among humans (e.g., Tong et al., 2007). However, it is possible that when asked about their emotional experiences in class, teachers may exaggerate their experience of enjoyment. Unlike in other professions, where it might be socially acceptable to admit that work is not always fun, the teaching profession is credited with very high ideals. Emotionally, teachers may have the expectation that they should always enjoy teaching or love all of their students (e.g., Winograd, 2003; see also further on in the section on emotional labor).

Pride

Pride is a positive emotion that is closely linked to enjoyment. Typically, pride is associated with personal accomplishments or accomplishments of people to whom one feels attached (Tracy & Robins, 2007). Thus, teachers can experience pride as a result of not only their own but also their students' accomplishments. Pride as a key emotion experienced by teachers was already addressed in the 1970s by Lortie (1975). In line with this work, pride has been identified as a highly relevant emotion for teachers both in studies exploring teacher emotions through in-depth interviews (Darby, 2008; Sutton & Harper, 2009) and in those exploring the frequency and intensity of discrete emotional experiences among teachers through real-life assessment methods (Becker, 2011; Carson, 2006). Overall, this emotion can be considered the second most salient discrete emotion for teachers after enjoyment (see Table 25.1).

Table 25.1 Frequencies of Teachers' Experiences of Discrete Emotions as Observed in Studies Using a Teaching Diary or Experience-Sampling Approach

	Frenzel and Goetz (2007) Teaching Diary ($N = 59$)	Carson (2007) Experience Sampling ($N = 44$)	Becker (2011) Experience Sampling ($N = 39$)
	Period Frequency	Frequency Since Last Signal	Period Frequency
Enjoyment/happiness	79%	75%	89%
Pride	–	32%	61%
Anger	14%	17%	39%
Anxiety/nervousness	7%	16%	8%
Shame	–	2%	5%
Boredom	–	10%	26%

Notes: Different methods were used to determine the salience and frequency of emotions in the different studies, and different time samples were selected. Frenzel and Goetz (2007) and Becker (2011) sampled lesson periods, while Carson (2007) sampled entire workdays of teachers (four assessment times: before school, beginning of lunch, end of lunch, after school). Frenzel and Goetz (2007) defined period frequency by using the percentage of periods in which teachers agreed or strongly agreed to have experienced the respective emotion during the last period (answer options 3 or 4 on a 4-point scale). Carson (2007) reported the mere existence of experienced emotions since the last signal (answer option 1 on a 0/1 scale). Becker (2011) defined period frequency by using the percentage of periods in which teachers did not explicitly disagree to have experienced the respective emotion upon being signaled during the periods (answer options 2, 3, or 4 on a 5-point scale).

Anger

Anger is a rather complex emotion that can be either directed at other people or at one-self (Ellsworth & Tong, 2006; Kuppens, Van Mechelen, & Rijmen, 2008). A key deter-minant of anger is responsibility: People typically report anger when someone can be blamed for undesirable events (Kuppens, Van Mechelen, Smits, & De Boeck, 2003). In studies exploring the frequency and intensity of discrete emotional experiences among teachers through real-life assessment methods, anger is identified as the most prominent negative emotion (see Table 25.1), and this finding is supported by qualitative and nar-rative research on teachers' emotions (Chang, 2009; Sutton, 2007; Sutton & Wheatley, 2003). Teachers may experience anger toward themselves—for example, when they are unsatisfied with how they structured a lesson. They can also be angry at their students for misbehaving, for example. The latter is likely one of the most salient reasons to get angry among teachers (see the section on correlates of teacher emotions further on). However, it is important to note that experiencing and displaying anger is socially unde-sirable, particularly for teachers (Liljestrom, Roulston, & deMarrais, 2007; McPherson, Kearney, & Plax, 2003; Sutton, 2007; Sutton & Wheatley, 2003). Therefore, teachers' reports of frequency and intensity of anger experienced during teaching might be down-wardly biased.

Anxiety

A considerable amount of research has been conducted on anxiety in the classroom, with the vast majority of studies focusing on student anxiety, and more specifically, on students' test-related anxiety (see Zeidner, 2014). In contrast, very little research atten-tion has been directed toward teacher anxiety. Existing reviews on teacher anxiety date back to the 1970s (Coates & Thoresen, 1976; Keavney & Sinclair, 1978). More recent cumulative findings on teachers' anxieties and concerns are lacking. This is astounding given that anxiety is one of the key basic negative emotions that individuals experience (Oehman, 2008). Feelings of anxiety are comprised of aversive physiological and affec-tive components (sweating, shaking) as well as cognitive components (worries, desires to flee or leave the situation). Anxiety typically occurs when people are confronted with uncertainty and threat, and when they perceive their own potential to cope with the threat as low (e.g., C. A. Smith & Lazarus, 1993). Clearly, this is an emotion that is also relevant to teaching. In qualitative interview studies, teachers report feeling anxious or scared—for example, when they are unsatisfied with their own teaching performance and do not perceive themselves as being capable of improving (Darby, 2008). Feelings of anxiety can also be triggered by lack of preparedness to teach and by disciplinary issues in the classroom (Bullough, Bullough, & Mayes, 2006; Chang, 2009). Some authors sug-gest that teaching-related anxiety is particularly pronounced among young teachers and student teachers (Chang, 2009; Hart, 1987; Payne & Manning, 1990; Sutton & Wheatley, 2003).

Interestingly, the frequency and intensity of anxiety reported by teachers is compara-bly low when judged from studies using real-life assessments (see Table 25.1). One possible explanation for this is that unlike students, who regularly take formal tests and for whom failure potentially has rather serious consequences, formal feedback on teaching per-formance is rarely provided to teachers, and there are fewer and less explicit defini-tions of and formalized consequences for teacher failure. Therefore, anxiety about bad performance might really be lower for teachers than for students—even though this seems to be changing as the idea of accountability has entered schools. In the United States, the No Child Left Behind (NCLB) act federalized an approach that rewarded or punished schools for student test scores in the 1990s. More recently, there has been growing interest in pay-for-performance plans that would reward or punish individual teachers rather than entire schools. Thus, it may become more commonplace for teachers to be evaluated based on student scores on annual exams, or on observer ratings in the classroom. These evaluations may be linked to consequences relevant to teachers, such as contract renewal and merit raises (Adams, Heywood, & Rothstein, 2009). It can be speculated that teachers' performance anxiety will rise as a result of these developments. However, so far no research seems to have addressed teacher anxiety in response to being evaluated.

One specific form of anxiety that has been addressed in the context of teaching is mathematics anxiety. As Beilock, Gunderson, Ramirez, and Levine (2010) observed, in most US colleges and universities, the mathematics requirements to qualify for teacher education, specifically at the elementary level, are minimal. As a result, individuals can successfully pursue a career in teaching even if they tend to dislike math and/or suffer from mathematics anxiety. Nevertheless, they may later be required to teach mathematics—as is the case with elementary school teachers who typically teach all the core subjects. Thus, mathematics anxiety may be a relevant issue for quite a number of teachers, particularly at the elementary level (Bursal & Paznokas, 2006; Harper & Daane, 1998; Kelly & Tomhave, 1985; Wood, 1988).

Shame (and Guilt)

Shame and guilt are among the so-called self-conscious emotions. Laypeople may often use these two terms almost synonymously; however, it is worth noting that emotion researchers argue that they are distinct, with guilt reflecting a negative evaluation of one's specific behavior and shame reflecting a more global negative evaluation of the self (Lewis, 2000; Tangney & Dearing, 2002). For example, a teacher may experience guilt when he has not prepared his class well enough for a particular task on an annual state exam and thus many students failed to solve that task, whereas he may feel shame when he feels more generally inadequate in terms of providing quality instruction in a subject. As many teachers are highly committed to their jobs, they are also susceptible to experiences of shame and guilt. For example, they report experiencing feelings of shame or inadequacy for having betrayed a personal ideal, standard, or commitment (Hargeaves & Tucker, 1991; Prawat, Byers, & Anderson, 1983; van Veen, Seegers, & van de Ven, 2005).

Guilt and shame are largely social emotions, which are typically tied to the actual or imagined negative judgment of others. The practice of instructing involves having several spectators—the students. Thus, the potential threat of being negatively judged by this audience is high for teachers. Indeed, teachers do report feelings of guilt and shame in qualitative interview studies (Bibby, 2002; Hargeaves & Tucker, 1991; Zembylas, 2003b). For shame, in particular, there are scattered findings from studies using real-life assessments. Similar to anxiety, the salience of this emotion seems to be rather low based on these findings (see Table 25.1). One reason for this might be that feelings of shame (and also guilt) simply did not occur during the times sampled in these studies (lesson periods/time at school) because they may only be felt retrospectively, when reflecting about a teaching period, or in the afternoon or evening when procrastinating correction or preparation work (see, e.g., Hargeaves & Tucker, 1991).

Boredom

Boredom is an emotion that is typically characterized by low arousal and relatively low negative valence (Perkins & Hill, 1985). As such, boredom is an inconspicuous, or silent emotion (Goetz, Frenzel, Hall, Nett, & Lipnevich, 2013), which may be one reason why it so far has received scant research attention. In the context of emotions experienced while working, boredom has been studied in repetitive, blue-collar jobs (R. P. Smith, 1981) and very rarely for white-collar, intellectually demanding jobs, such as teaching. In the academic context, boredom has been studied among students (Nett & Goetz, 2011; Pekrun, Goetz, Daniels, Stupnisky, & Perry, 2010) but rarely among teachers. Is it at all conceivable that teachers would feel bored while teaching? While barely any mention of boredom could be found within the existing qualitative research on teacher emotions, two studies using real-life assessments during instruction revealed that this emotion is clearly relevant to teachers. In Becker's (2011) study, boredom was even one of the most prominent negative emotions, with teachers reporting to be bored during 26% of their periods (see Table 25.1). Thus, it appears that teacher boredom deserves more research attention than it has so far received.

Pity

Pity is a largely social emotion typically directed at persons other than the self (even though the notion of self-pity also exists; see, e.g., Stoeber, 2003). Feelings of pity involve sympathetic sorrow for someone who is suffering physically or is otherwise distressed. Teachers may experience pity toward their students. In the existing qualitative studies, there are limited references to this emotion, and the few studies using real-life assessments do not include it either. Hence, the frequency and intensity of this emotion as experienced by teachers cannot be judged from existing research.

However, the emotion of teacher pity has been the focus of quite a number of studies addressing attribution-emotion links (Georgiou, Christou, Stavrinides, & Panaoura, 2002; Graham, 1984; Graham & Weiner, 1986; Prawat et al., 1983; Weiner, 2007). According to this body of literature, teacher pity is experienced when student failure is attributed to factors beyond the control of the students, such as low ability. (In contrast, student failure attributed to factors within the control of the students is likely to trigger anger. See also the section on correlates of teacher emotions further on).

RELATED CONSTRUCTS WITH
AFFECTIVE-MOTIVATIONAL CONNOTATIONS

The following section presents affective-motivational constructs that are relevant to teachers and popular in current research. These constructs are burnout, emotional labor, teacher enthusiasm, and teacher achievement goals. Strikingly, even though all of these constructs have clearly affective connotations, they have rarely been integrated in the existing body of research that specifically focuses on teacher emotions. In the following sections these constructs are presented and how they might be related to and different from emotions is discussed.

Burnout

This is an affective teacher variable that has received considerable research attention. Burnout is typically described as a psychological syndrome in response to chronic interpersonal stressors on the job. The multidimensional theory of burnout proposed by Maslach and her colleagues (Maslach & Jackson, 1981; Maslach et al., 2001) continues to be the predominant framework in the field of burnout research. The three key dimensions in this framework are (emotional) exhaustion, feelings of cynicism and detachment from the job, and a sense of ineffectiveness and lack of professional efficacy.

Interestingly, even though burnout is clearly an emotional phenomenon and the construct has been studied for decades in relation to teachers, very few studies have attempted to analyze the link between teacher burnout and teacher emotions (Chang, 2009). Chang argues that experiences of burnout and different discrete emotions during teaching likely have common and overlapping cognitive appraisal antecedents (see also the section below on appraisal antecedents of teacher emotions), but the construct of burnout has not been examined from an appraisal-theoretical perspective. It is highly plausible, though not empirically established, that burnout is associated with the experience of discrete emotions, including decreased levels of positive emotions, such as enjoyment or pride, and increased levels of negative emotions, including anger, anxiety, or guilt.

Emotional Labor

Emotional labor has been described as the "effort, planning, and control needed to express organizationally desired emotion during interpersonal transactions" (Morris & Feldman, 1996, p. 987). The notion of organizationally desired emotions, also referred to as emotion rules or display rules (Ashforth & Humphrey, 1993; Hochschild, 1983), implies that the expression of certain emotions (typically positive, prosocial) is expected in certain jobs, and these emotions need to be up-regulated. On the other hand, emotions (typically negative and antisocial) that are not expected should not be expressed—that is, they need to be down-regulated on the job. The resulting potential incongruence between the emotion experienced (e.g., contempt for a customer) and the emotion expressed (e.g., happiness and friendliness) for the sake of complying with the emotion rules has also been referred to as emotional dissonance (Zerbe, 2000).

The existence of—at least implicit—emotion rules has also been mentioned in studies on teachers (Day, 2004; Schutz, Cross, Hong, & Osbon, 2007; Sutton, 2004; Winograd, 2003; Zembylas, 2002, 2005). As Schutz and colleagues report, teachers are typically expected to display pleasant emotions and suppress unpleasant emotions in their interactions with students in order to construct an optimal learning environment (Schutz et al., 2007). Sutton (2004) identified various sources of such implicit emotion rules for teachers, including personal role perception, family and cultural backgrounds, teacher education programs, and fellow teachers. Consistent with this,

29 out of 30 teachers interviewed by Sutton (2004) reported effortfully regulating their emotions.

Clearly, the concepts of emotional labor, emotion rules, and emotional dissonance play a key role in the context of teacher emotions. Experiencing negative emotions such as anger or anxiety is unpleasant for most individuals. However, in the teaching profession, the strain resulting from experiencing these emotions is intensified because anger and anxiety are expected to be suppressed during instruction and interaction with students. Likewise, experiencing phases on the job that are dissatisfying or provide few reasons to experience enjoyment or pride are undesirable for anyone. However, the emotion rules for teachers require that positive emotions are nevertheless displayed (i.e., faked), which may constitute a specific work stressor for them (Philipp & Schüpbach, 2010).

Enthusiasm

Teacher enthusiasm is often referred to as one of the key conditions for effective instruction and student motivation (Brophy & Good, 1986; Long & Hoy, 2006; Witcher, Onwuegbuzie, & Minor, 2001). However, this construct is defined rather inconsistently in the literature (Kunter, Frenzel, Nagy, Baumert, & Pekrun, 2011). Some researchers refer to enthusiasm as a feature of instruction in terms of a motivating, energetic teaching style (B.C. Patrick, Hisley, Kempler, & College, 2000; Turner et al., 1998). In this context, researchers also refer to teacher expressiveness or teacher immediacy (see Babad, 2007, for a review). Other researchers conceive of enthusiasm as a subjective experience of teachers themselves in terms of the excitement and enthusiasm they feel toward teaching and toward their subject(s) (Kunter et al., 2008; 2011). The latter conceptualization of enthusiasm renders it similar to teaching enjoyment. In fact, in Kunter et al.'s studies, teaching enthusiasm is among others operationalized by the item "I really enjoy teaching." An important finding of these studies is that it is worthwhile to differentiate between teachers' experiences of enthusiasm (or enjoyment) derived from teaching and enthusiasm (or enjoyment) derived from the subject being taught (Kunter et al., 2008; 2011).

To potentially distinguish between enjoyment and enthusiasm, it seems appropriate to denote a behavioral, observable teacher variable (which is strongly affectively toned) as "enthusiastic teaching," on the one hand, and a variable that depicts actual internal, subjective teacher experiences as "teacher enjoyment," on the other (see also Frenzel, Goetz, Lüdtke, Pekrun, & Sutton, 2009). Teacher enthusiasm and enjoyment can coexist independently within teachers: Some teachers may manage to display an enthusiastic teaching style without really enjoying a lesson; other teachers may actually enjoy teaching but not be able to act their enjoyment out in terms of an enthusiastic teaching style. However, it is likely that teacher enthusiasm and enjoyment positively covary within most teachers. It can be assumed that experiences of teaching enjoyment manifest in certain behaviors that are characteristic of an enthusiastic teaching style, including gestures, varied intonation, frequent eye contact, varied emotive facial expressions, movement while lecturing, and use of humor and lively examples (Collins, 1978; Gage & Berliner, 1998; Murray, 1983; Rosenshine, 1970). Existing empirical research clearly shows that teacher enthusiasm as perceived by students and enjoyment as experienced by teachers are positively correlated (Frenzel, Goetz, Lüdtke et al., 2009; Frenzel, Goetz, Stephens et al., 2009; Kunter et al., 2011).

Achievement Goals

As discussed in Linnenbrink-Garcia and Barger's (2014) and Carver and Scheier's (2014) chapters in this volume and later in this chapter, goals seem to play a crucial role as cognitive antecedents of emotions. Drawing on the large body of literature on student achievement goals, experts have recently begun to acknowledge that teachers' achievement goals may also be noteworthy variables to explore. Butler (2007) was among the first to propose that the achievement goal theory could provide a useful framework for conceptualizing qualitative differences in teachers' motives for teaching. She developed a self-report measure called "goal orientations for teaching" with items loading on four factors that reflected the desire to (a) learn and acquire professional competence (mastery goal), (b) demonstrate superior teaching ability (ability-approach goal), (c) avoid the demonstration of inferior teaching ability (ability-avoidance goal), and the desire to (d) get through the day with little effort (work-avoidance goal); however, this fourth goal would not explicitly be referred to as an achievement goal in the current literature. Butler's suggested conceptualization of teacher goals was replicated by a few recent studies. These studies showed that these teacher goals are relevant to teachers' instructional practices, interest in teaching, burnout, and help-seeking behaviors of both teachers and students (Butler & Shibaz, 2008; Dickhäuser, Butler, & Toenjes, 2007; Retelsdorf, Butler, Streblow, & Schiefele, 2010). More recently, Butler (2012) proposed that a fifth dimension of teacher goals—namely, "relational goals," may also play a crucial role. This goal corresponds to teachers' aspirations to build close and caring relationships with students. Butler (2012) showed that teachers who had strong relational goals provided not only better social support but also more mastery-oriented instruction.

Clearly, teacher goals have a strong affective connotation, and it can be speculated that the goals are systematically linked with emotions, as is the case with students (Pekrun, Elliot, & Maier, 2006). For example, teachers' avoidance goals may be related to increased anxiety or shame, whereas mastery goals may be linked to increased enjoyment and decreased anger or boredom. However, so far no empirical study seems to have examined such goal-emotion links among teachers.

CORRELATES, CAUSES, AND EFFECTS OF TEACHER EMOTIONS: EMPIRICAL FINDINGS AND A THEORETICAL MODEL

Correlates of Teacher Emotions: Empirical Evidence

Presented here is a list of constructs identified as key correlates of teacher emotions in the existing literature. In summarizing the existing evidence of correlates of teacher emotions, constructs were selected that are mentioned most often in teachers' narrative reports on their emotional lives, on the one hand, and on effect sizes reported in correlational studies, on the other.

Student Achievement Behavior

Research clearly indicates a link between students' achievement behavior and teacher emotions (Beilock et al., 2010; Hargreaves, 2000; Lortie, 1975; Scott & Sutton, 2009; Sutton & Wheatley, 2003). Much of the available empirical data support the fact that high achievement by students can serve as a source of positive experiences for teachers.

In reviewing Lortie's (1975) work and reporting about teacher interviews on emotions, Hargreaves (2000) concluded that a key source of teachers' positive emotional experiences is student success. For example, Hargreaves cites one teacher who said, "I feel very proud when they come back and say, 'We're doing very well. We've got good marks' . . . So I feel very good about that" (p. 843). Consistent with this, Frenzel et al. (2009) quantitatively assessed teaching emotions with respect to specific periods and found a positive correlation of $r = .30$ between teacher enjoyment and teacher-perceived student performance.

Conversely, a number of studies also suggest that poor achievement by students can be a cause for negative emotions in teachers. Specifically, there is quite some data that anger will be aroused if teachers perceive that their students' failure was caused by factors within the control of the students (Brophy & McCaslin, 1992; Graham, 1984; Prawat et al., 1983).

Finally, apart from student achievement eliciting positive or negative emotions within teachers, teachers' emotions can also boost or impair student achievement. Empirical evidence for the latter was recently provided by Beilock and colleagues (2010). They showed that greater math-related anxiety experienced by elementary school teachers negatively influenced the math performance of girls (but not boys). Moreover, the girls in their study were more inclined to subscribe to the stereotypical belief that "boys are good at math, and girls are good at reading," even a year after being taught by these math-anxious teachers.

Student Misbehavior

Student misbehavior and disruptions during class can be seen as one of the key factors arousing negative emotions among teachers, particularly anger and anxiety. Anger in particular is triggered when teachers perceive student misbehavior as an intentional action (Brophy & McCaslin, 1992; Graham, 1984; Graham & Weiner, 1986; Prawat et al., 1983). Hargreaves (2000) concluded from his teacher interviews that anger was caused by students' nonconformance with classroom rules, while Hart (1987) found that teachers experienced anxiety as a result of student disruptions in class. Chang and Davis (2009) studied 554 teachers' self-reported emotional responses to disruptive classroom behavior and found that the teachers' judgments regarding student behaviors influenced the unpleasant emotions they felt. The emotional responses were particularly negative if the disruptions were perceived as impeding the teachers' classroom goals, or if teachers felt incompetent at stopping or curbing these disturbances. Frenzel et al. (2009) also reported substantial correlations between teacher-perceived student discipline in the class and teachers' reports of teaching enjoyment (higher with better perceived discipline), as well as anxiety and anger (lower with better perceived discipline).

Relationships With Students

A range of findings predominantly based on narrative research confirms that teacher emotions are almost inextricably linked to the relationships they form with their students (Golby, 1996; Hargreaves, 1994, 1998, 2000; Intrator, 2006; Nias, 1989). Evidence clearly shows that teachers find the opportunity to be deeply and personally involved with students satisfying and beneficial. However, Goldstein and Lake (2000) emphasize that commitment and caring can also become a source of difficulty for teachers because of the inherently unequal nature of the teacher-student relationship. Extremely caring teachers may even feel guilty when they are unable to fulfill all the needs of their students. Failure to connect with students can also cause negative affect or pose a threat to teachers. As one teacher in Goldstein and Lake's (2000) study asserted, "I do not think I could deal with a classroom full of students who did not like me" (p. 867). Beginning teachers, in particular, experience worries about whether their students like them (Coates & Thoresen, 1976; Intrator, 2006).

Adopting a quantitative approach, Klassen and colleagues (2012) studied the relationship between teacher–student relationships and teacher engagement as well as teaching emotions based on self-report data from over 600 in-service teachers. They found that relationships with students are more relevant to teacher experiences than their relationships with colleagues. Teacher self-reported relatedness with their students correlated as highly as $r = .49$ with teaching enjoyment, $r = -.24$ with teaching anger, and $r = -.32$ with teaching anxiety.

Instructional Effectiveness

A selection of scattered findings confirms that teacher emotions are related to instructional effectiveness in terms of teachers' cognitive and motivational stimulation, classroom management, and social support. As Baird, Gunstone, Penna, Fensham, and White (2007) conclude, a balance between affect and cognition is important for effective teaching. Stough and Emmer (1998) found that beginning teachers whose students provided hostile reactions to test feedback experienced negative emotions, such as frustration and anger, and as a result, some of them altered their classroom management strategies by adopting highly structured feedback approaches to control student interactions. Detrimental effects of teacher anxiety on teaching effectiveness as evaluated by supervisors and students have also been reported by Coates and Thoresen (1976).

Teachers' own reports of teaching enjoyment have been shown to be positively linked to student ratings of monitoring, elaboration, comprehensibility, autonomy support, teacher enthusiasm, and teacher support for students (Frenzel, Goetz, Lüdtke, et al., 2009; Frenzel, Goetz, Stephens, et al., 2009; Kunter et al., 2008; Kunter et al., 2011). Conversely, negative relationships have also been found between teachers' reported anger and students' perceptions of teacher instructional behavior, including elaboration, comprehensibility, autonomy support, teacher enthusiasm, and support after failure (Frenzel, Goetz, Stephens, et al., 2009).

Personal doubts about their ability to provide effective instruction can also be a cause for teachers' negative emotions. Lack of familiarity with one's subject has been reported to be a key source of shame for teachers (Bibby, 2002). Furthermore, Coates and Thoresen (1976) summarize in their review on teacher anxiety that beginning teachers are very concerned about their ability to maintain discipline in the classroom, knowledge of subject matter, and corrective measures to be taken in case of mistakes. These findings have more recently been confirmed by Intrator (2006), who found that new teachers experience anxiety over lack of familiarity with the subject matter. Conversely, teachers' judgments of their capabilities to produce desired educational outcomes in their students, referred to as teaching efficacy in the literature (Tschannen-Moran & Hoy, 2001), can be a source of positive emotions for teachers. In line with this, Kunter and colleagues (2011) reported a correlation as high as $r = .61$ between self-reported teaching enjoyment and teaching self-efficacy.

In summarizing these findings on correlates of teacher emotions, not only teachers', but also students' well-being and the well-functioning of classrooms, seem to be related to teacher emotions. In an attempt to disentangle possible causes and effects of teacher emotions, and to better understand how teacher emotions may affect and be affected by classroom processes, Frenzel and colleagues (Frenzel, Goetz, & Pekrun, 2008; Frenzel, Goetz, Stephens, et al., 2009) have proposed a reciprocal model, which is presented in detail below.

A Reciprocal Model on Causes and Effects of Teacher Emotions

The model presented in this section is one possible approach to understanding and framing teacher emotions, and it addresses teacher emotions specifically from an achievement perspective where the pursuit of success and avoidance of failure are central processes. As such, this model addresses emotions that result from teacher judgments regarding the success or failure of their own teaching efforts, since these seem to be particularly salient for teachers. For example, the model addresses teachers' pride in catching their students' interest in a new topic thanks to the teachers' engaged introduction of it, or teachers' anger if students are inattentive and as a result, struggle with grasping a topic. However, this model does not address purely social emotions, such as empathy with a suffering child or contempt with a colleague or principle.

Basic Assumptions

The overarching theoretical frameworks that guide the model are appraisal theory and attribution theory. These theories postulate that emotions are primarily caused by individuals' cognitive judgments about situations and events rather than by the situations and events themselves (Roseman & Smith, 2001; Scherer, Schorr, & Johnstone, 2001; C. A. Smith & Lazarus, 1993; Weiner, 1986). Appraisals are general cognitive judgments about situations and events, such as whether they are considered benign (positive) or harmful (negative). Attributions, more specifically, pertain to judgments regarding the perceived causes for events. Both theories further postulate that certain constellations of cognitive judgments lead to specific emotions. For instance, feelings of gratitude are aroused in situations that are perceived as positive and caused by another individual, whereas pride is aroused in situations that are perceived as positive and caused by oneself.

Furthermore, Frenzel et al.'s model (Frenzel et al., 2008; Frenzel, Goetz, Stephens, et al., 2009) is based on general psychological insights regarding the effects of human emotions. In applying these theoretical ideas specifically to the classroom, Frenzel et al. outline reciprocal relationships between students' classroom behaviors, teacher emotions, and teachers' instructional behaviors. A revised version of the model is presented further on and is graphically illustrated in Figure 25.1.

Causes of Teacher Emotions

Based on the basic appraisal-theoretical postulation that cognitive appraisals are a primary cause of emotions, teachers' appraisals regarding events that occur in the classroom are at the heart of the model (marked in light grey in the model). The upper part of the model depicts how these appraisals may be formed (marked in white), and the lower

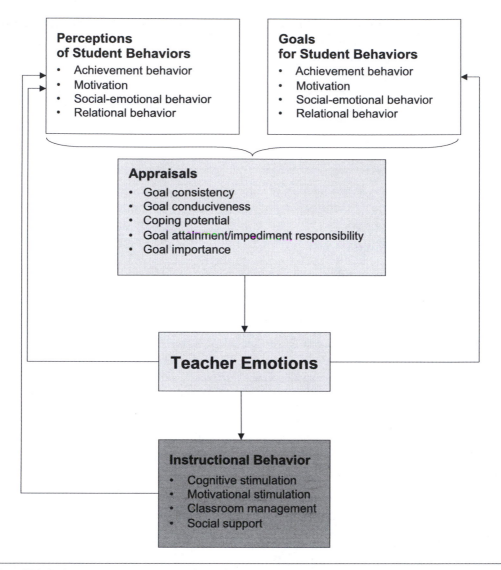

Figure 25.1 Reciprocal model on causes and effects of teacher emotions.

part of the model depicts the suggested effects of teacher emotions on their instructional behavior (marked in dark grey).

A key proposition of the model is that teachers' emotional experiences are determined based on their judgments regarding whether their classroom goals are aligned with students' behaviors in class. In other words, it is proposed that at certain points (continually during instruction, but also at the end of a period, end of an instructional unit, or end of a school year) teachers assess whether or not their set goals were achieved based on their perceptions of the students' behaviors. As part of this process, teachers cognitively appraise the activities of their classroom. This assumption that teacher emotions result from appraisals pertaining to classroom goals is in line with Lortie's assertion that teachers experience pride when they "succeed in reaching work goals"

(1975, p. 121). It is also in accordance with Sutton and Wheatley's (2003) and Chang's (2009) rationale on appraisal determinants of teacher emotions and burnout, as well as more generally with Pekrun's (2000, 2006; Pekrun & Perry, 2014) control-value theory on achievement emotions.

In order to clarify how teacher appraisals and their resulting emotions are formed (see upper, white part of the model in Figure 25.1), it is further suggested in the model that there are four broad themes that guide teachers' formation of classroom goals and their perceptions of their students' behaviors: cognitive, motivational, social-emotional, and relational.[1] The cognitive theme refers to students' acquisition of subject-specific competencies. The motivational theme pertains to students' motivational engagement in classroom activities and learning content. The social-emotional theme concerns students' development of competencies in terms of respect for themselves and others and the ability to function within a social group. Finally, the relational theme pertains to the establishment of a good relationship between the teacher and the students. For example, a teacher's goal might be for her students to be able to correctly answer certain questions about a topic (subject-specific competence), that the students show some interest in the discussed topic and actively participate in class (motivational engagement), that students abide by the classroom rules (social-emotional behavior), or that students rely on her for resolving questions or problems (relationship with the teacher).

Regarding teachers' appraisals and resulting emotions (see middle, light grey section of the model), the model proposes that there are five important appraisal dimensions. A first and key appraisal pertains to (a) whether or not teachers perceive their students' behaviors to match their goals, or in other words, if teachers feel they succeeded in meeting their goals (goal consistency appraisals). The other appraisals that seem relevant for teachers' emotional experiences include (b) goal conduciveness appraisals, which examine whether student behavior is perceived as contributing to achieving a classroom goal (i.e., approaching success even if not directly achieving it yet), (c) coping potential appraisals, which evaluate whether teachers feel capable of attaining and optimizing their goals, (d) goal attainment/impediment responsibility appraisals, which correspond with the question who is responsible if a goal is achieved or not, and (e) goal importance appraisals, which examine how important it is for teachers to attain a particular goal or avoid its impediment.

In line with appraisal-theoretical reasoning, teachers' specific emotional reactions are expected to depend on these appraisals. Generally, goal consistency and goal conduciveness appraisals should determine the valence of the emotions experienced (positive vs. negative). Goal importance appraisals should determine the intensity of the emotional experience, with higher relevance typically leading to higher intensity for both positive and negative emotions (boredom being a notable exception, since boredom is assumed to increase as relevance decreases). Coping potential and responsibility appraisals should determine both the valence and the intensity of the experienced emotion. For an emotion to arise, each of the appraisals do not have to be cognitively passed through, rather there are characteristic appraisal patterns for different emotions (see also the notion of "core relational themes" for emotions—e.g., C. A. Smith & Lazarus, 1993). For example, anxiety should result from an appraisal pattern characterized by low goal consistency or conduciveness, paired with self-responsibility and low coping potential. More specifically, a teacher may react anxiously if he or she has the impression that many students

Table 25.2 Teacher Emotions, Characteristic Appraisal Patterns, and Classroom Examples of the Experience of These Emotions Among Teachers

Emotion	Characteristic Appraisal Pattern	Classroom Example
Enjoyment	Positive goal consistency or conduciveness	A teacher tries out a new teaching method and it seems to work, students are motivated and learn the new material well
Pride	Positive goal consistency or conduciveness + internal goal attainment responsibility	A teacher is able to establish a well-functioning classroom in a class formerly known as tough thanks to his efficient classroom management
Anger	Negative goal consistency or conduciveness + external goal impediment responsibility	Many students demonstrate low interest despite the teacher's repeated and (so far usually functioning) attempts to provide interesting lessons
Anxiety	Negative goal consistency or conduciveness + low coping potential + internal goal impediment responsibility	Many students misbehave in class, and the teacher feels incapable of improving the situation
Shame	Negative goal consistency or conduciveness + internal goal impediment responsibility	Many students demonstrate a poor level of subject competence at the end of the school year, and the teacher attributes this to his own inability of providing better instruction on that subject
Boredom	Low importance of goals	A teacher has to teach a topic for several consecutive years that he personally does not find interesting nor important for the students
Pity	Negative goal consistency or conduciveness + low coping potential (*on the side of an observed person*) + external goal impediment responsibility	A student fails an important exam, and the teacher attributes the failure to the student's low ability in that content area

misbehave in class (failure to attain the social-emotional goal that students should abide with classroom rules) and that this is due to his or her lack of classroom management skills (self-responsibility) while also not knowing how to establish better classroom management (low coping potential). Table 25.2 shows proposed appraisal patterns for each of the discrete emotions discussed in this chapter, along with classroom situations that may lead to these emotions within teachers.

Effects of Teacher Emotions

In the model, it is further proposed that teacher emotions influence instructional behavior (lower, dark grey section of the model). It can generally be assumed that once teachers begin to experience emotions, irrespective of how well they may regulate these emotions, effects are bound to unfold. Specifically, it is proposed that teachers' emotions affect their behavior, in terms of the cognitive and motivational stimulation, classroom management, and social support they provide.

A specific mechanism involved in eliciting effects of teacher emotions is the expressive component of the emotions. Emotions have a deep-rooted communicative function (Anderson & Guerrero, 1998; Lazarus, 1991) and as such are related to characteristic facial expressions and postures. Therefore, emotions experienced by teachers cannot go unnoticed by their students (Sutton & Wheatley, 2003). As a consequence, the motivational stimulation a teacher provides (e.g., through displaying more or less teaching enthusiasm) should depend on the teacher's emotional experiences during teaching. In addition, it is likely that emotional contagion, a term originally coined for dyads (see, e.g., Barger & Grandey, 2006; Doherty, 1997; Hatfield, Cacioppo, & Rapson, 1994) also comes into play between teachers and their students.

Other mechanisms through which teacher emotions are likely to introduce effects can be derived from mood research and from a body of research referred to as "positive psychology" (Seligman & Csikszentmihalyi, 2000). For example, it has been shown that positive and negative moods are associated with different cognitive processing styles. According to this line of reasoning, a negative mood is associated with convergent, analytical, and detail-oriented thinking. In contrast, a positive mood is supposed to be associated with divergent, heuristic ways of thinking that enable more flexible and creative approaches (Clore, Schwarz, & Conway, 1994; Isen, 2008; Mitchell & Phillips, 2007; Sinclair & Mark, 1992). In the field of positive psychology, Fredrickson (2001), for example, proposed in her broaden-and-build theory that the experience of joy broadens one's action repertoire. According to this theory, positive emotions not only indicate success but also produce or promote success by broadening thinking and facilitating the generation of ideas when faced with obstacles.

In the classroom context, these theoretical considerations imply that teachers with predominantly positive emotional experiences may be able to effectively utilize a broad range of teaching strategies. These teachers are possibly more creative in class, more open to "riskier" (e.g., less traditional) teaching strategies, and better able to flexibly deal with unexpected obstacles that crop up during class—and as a result, provide better cognitive and motivational stimulation while teaching. In addition, they may also be more successful in building trustful relationships with their students. Conversely, teachers whose classroom experiences are dominated by negative emotions, such as anxiety and anger, may find it more difficult to deviate from the predetermined lesson plan, and they most likely use more rigid teaching strategies, such as rehearsal or rote memorization. A predominance of negative experiences during teaching can also be an obstacle to building good relationships with students.

The degree to which teachers engage in efficient cognitive and motivational stimulation, classroom management, and social support, in turn, should have effects on students' cognitive growth, motivation, social-emotional behavior in class, and their relationships with the teacher—the "input variables" considered in this model. As such, students' and teachers' behaviors in class can be viewed as both the cause and effect of teachers' emotional experiences during teaching, which is documented in the suggested reciprocity of the model. These proposed reciprocal relationships are depicted through the recursive arrows in Figure 25.1.

METHODOLOGICAL CONSIDERATIONS AND CHALLENGES

Zembylas (2003b) identified three reasons for the slow progress in research on teacher emotions. First, since teaching is typically viewed as a cognitive activity, most studies adopted a cognitive perspective, examining teachers' thoughts and beliefs, their special-ized subject-specific expertise, teaching skills, and pedagogical knowledge, rather than their affective experiences. Second, Zembylas speculated that researchers avoided study-ing emotions since they are elusive and difficult to grasp or objectively measure. Finally, he concluded that emotions were often regarded as a "soft topic," or a rather feminine subject, thus not a worthwhile research issue.

Indeed, a key methodological challenge in this line of research is the objective, reli-able, and valid measurement of emotions. While this is true for all research on emotions, it is particularly problematic when the emotions pertain to the job of teaching. First of all, studying teacher emotions calls for field-based approaches, which often lack internal validity. Laboratory-based designs seem to be conceivable only in order to identify basic related psychological mechanisms, such as attribution-emotion links (see, e.g., Clark, 1997; Graham, 1984). Second, in studying teacher emotions, the straightforward—and so far most widely adopted—approach is to directly obtain information from the teachers themselves. This is usually achieved through one-shot retrospective self-reports, whether qualitative (interview) or quantitative (questionnaire). Unfortunately, recall-based ratings of emotion do not necessarily represent the true frequencies and intensities of emotions in real-life (Robinson & Clore, 2002; Thomas & Diener, 1990). For one, recall-based self-reports of emotions might be distorted by social desirabil-ity, which can be fuelled by both self- and other-deception (impression management). This might particularly be the case for teachers, whose jobs are strongly bound by emotion rules, requiring them to overemphasize positive emotions and suppress or ignore negative emotions. Moreover, recall-based emotion ratings can be distorted by peak momentary experiences, the most recent emotional experience, or particularly salient experiences (e.g., particularly vivid experiences). Research also suggests that beliefs about one's emotionality, memory limitations, global heuristics, and implicit theories on emotions can lead to systematic biases and thus inaccurate information in retrospective emotion self-reports (Barrett, 1997; Barrett & Barrett, 2001; Robinson & Clore, 2002). In addition, in using only retrospective measures, the focus is usually on relatively stable habitual emotions, thus disregarding the highly dynamic nature of emotions (Scherer, 1984).

An alternative way to assess emotions as they occur in real-life is via the use of in-situ assessments like the experience-sampling method (Csikszentmihalyi & Larson, 1987), also referred to as ecological momentary assessment (Carson, Weiss, & Templin, 2010). Experience-sampling studies typically involve repeated assessments of data, usually col-lected several times a day (at random or fixed time points, designated by some signaling device), over a certain period of time (usually one to two weeks), asking participants to indicate their emotional state as it is "right now." By implication, the data are assessed in natural settings in the field (Carson et al., 2010). Generally, the advantage of experience sampling is that responses do not include biases stemming from retrospective memory, and the variables are assessed as they occur in real-life.

Experience sampling has been used in school contexts, but mainly to assess students' experiences and emotions (Goetz, Frenzel, Luedtke, & Hall, 2011; Nett & Goetz, 2011;

Schiefele & Csikszentmihalyi, 1995). Very few experience-sampling studies focus on teachers. A problem here is the relatively intrusive nature of this method—the disruption caused by a signal and the subsequent concentration of the teacher on answering questions on their psychological state during an actual teaching period might be untenable at times. However, it is worth noting that the few existing studies that did use experience-sampling methods in the teaching context provide reasons to believe that experience sampling is feasible and suitable also in this context (Becker, 2011; Carson et al., 2010; Totterdell & Parkinson, 1999; Zhu, 2002). Compromising between true momentary assessments and a retrospective measure, Frenzel et al. (2009) used so-called teaching diaries. Here, the teachers were asked to record the degree to which they experienced certain emotions during certain teaching periods immediately after these periods across one to two weeks. This also seems to be a promising approach to adopt with respect to situated research on teacher emotions.

Lastly, there are, of course, many other possible approaches to exploring teacher emotions from multiple methodological perspectives. Those could include observations (targeting, e.g., behavioral indicators of emotions or facial expressions), physiological indicators, or vignette studies. However, so far barely any existing studies on teacher emotions have used such alternative methods.

CONTROVERSIAL ISSUES AND FUTURE DIRECTIONS FOR RESEARCH ON TEACHER EMOTIONS

A few controversial aspects, which have already been broached in this chapter, will be elaborated on in this section. The chapter ends with a recommended research agenda regarding what can and should be done next to strengthen this new and growing field of research.

The first controversial issue pertains to the potential relationship between teacher burnout and (discrete) teacher emotions. On the one hand, there also seems to be some construct overlap, specifically between emotional exhaustion and emotions. On the other hand, it is highly plausible, though not empirically established, that these two phenomena are reciprocally related. However, research so far does not answer several questions regarding a burnout–emotion link. For instance, do experiences of burnout predominantly involve a lack of positive emotions, or increased levels of negative emotions, or both? Burnout may also result from such extreme detachment from teaching that both positive and negative emotional experiences are experienced at minimal levels and with minimal variability, implying zero-correlations between burnout and discrete emotions. Furthermore, what are the underlying psychological mechanisms for the observed correlations between experiences of burnout and emotions? Some authors speculate that it is the particularly frequent experience of negative emotions during teaching that causes teacher burnout (Carson, 2006; Chang, 2009, 2013). However, the opposite direction of causation is also conceivable: Severe symptoms of burnout may prevent teachers from deriving satisfaction and enjoyment in their work and lead them to develop intense feelings of anxiety, anger, and frustration in situations that may have initially seemed benign. Moreover, problematic personal and organizational factors and their interaction may be a common cause for both symptoms of burnout and unpleasant discrete emotions experienced during teaching. Clearly, a promising avenue for future research lies in specifying the size of relationships between dimensions of burnout and discrete emotions of teaching and shedding light on their reciprocal dependencies, as hardly any such empirical data are currently available.

A second controversial issue is determining whether emotional labor is a blessing or curse for teachers. In the original writings on emotional labor (Hochschild, 1983), it has predominantly been described as a curse of modern commercialism. Also, in the context of teaching, many authors identified the need to comply with emotion rules as a stressor for teachers (Day, 2004; Philipp & Schüpbach, 2010; Schutz et al., 2007; Sutton, 2004; Winograd, 2003; Zembylas, 2002, 2005). However, it is worth noting that the empirical evidence of teacher stress resulting from emotional labor is equivocal (Tsang, 2011). Some teachers seem to be adept at proactively regulating their emotions or truly "conjuring up" appropriate feelings within themselves during teaching (which has also been referred to as "deep acting" in Hochschild's 1983 original writings about emotional labor). As such, the existence of emotion rules for teachers, and the consequent frequent emotion regulation from their side, may also be a blessing for many teachers (Sutton & Harper, 2009; Sutton & Knight, 2006; Sutton, Mudrey-Camino, & Knight, 2009; Tsang, 2011). A concise research agenda is needed to answer several questions related to this issue: Which discrete emotions do teachers actually fake or suppress during teaching? Do they experience dissonance while doing so, and does this constitute a source of stress or act as an indicator of their own professionalism and well-being?

Finally, a third source of controversy within the current literature on teacher emotions is the need to distinguish between teacher enjoyment and enthusiasm, as well as their functional relationships. As mentioned earlier, it can be assumed, on the one hand, that teachers' experiences of teaching enjoyment manifest in certain behaviors that are characteristic of an enthusiastic teaching style. On the other hand, it is also conceivable that an enthusiastic teaching style is conducive to the experience of enjoyment during teaching because displaying enthusiasm may serve as an effective tool in up-regulating teachers' actual positive experiences. According to the "facial feedback hypothesis," a mere facial action (such as smiling) can initiate and/or modulate the subjective experience of emotion (McIntosh, 1996; Soussignan, 2004). There exist a number of questions regarding teacher enjoyment and teacher enthusiasm that remain unanswered. For instance, is some level of enjoyment toward teaching and toward the topic of instruction necessary in order to be able to show enthusiasm during teaching? Is a deliberate, controlled display of enthusiasm during teaching conducive to experiencing enjoyment during teaching? Can an enthusiastic teaching style be learned, and will this lead to interventions directed at increasing positive experiences during teaching?

The following three-point research agenda could be adopted in future research on teacher emotions (see also Chang, 2009): replicating findings, running longitudinal studies, and developing interventions. First, since much of the current scientific knowledge on teacher emotions rests on in-depth, narrative, often single-case data, it now seems important to replicate the rich qualitative knowledge that is currently available using both small-scale experimental research in the classroom and the lab and large-scale, quantitative approaches in the field. To this end, assessment tools appropriate also for use with larger samples need to be developed and validated. Those tools may involve both recall-based questionnaire approaches and ecological momentary assessments and could involve both discrete emotional experiences and molar affective variables, such as positive versus negative affect toward teaching.

Further, since many of the open questions surrounding teacher emotions pertain to unresolved cause–effect relationships, methods to disentangle such effects are needed. Those methods may involve longitudinal studies as well as intervention studies. Longitudinal data can shed light on how teachers' emotions vary across an academic year or across different stages of the teaching career, and how these variations relate to potential correlates. For example, much has been written about young teachers' anxiety and its links to lack of subject matter knowledge, but little is really known about the development of teacher anxiety across an academic year or the career span of a teacher. With intervention studies, further empirical evidence of purported causes for different teacher emotions could be obtained. For example, poor classroom management and resulting student misbehavior has often been reported to cause teacher anger, but no study so far seems to have tested whether training in classroom management can lower teachers' experiences of anger in class.

Overall, teacher emotions seem to be inextricably linked to classroom processes, including both student and teacher behaviors. However, conspicuously little is known about how to support teachers in maintaining a positive emotional attitude towards their classes and teaching or how to break vicious circles in case negative emotions predominate the classroom atmosphere. As stated above, it is not only teachers' but also students' well-being and the well-functioning of classrooms that seems to be related to teacher emotions. Clearly efforts should be made to close these research gaps in the near future. Specifically, scientifically sound and evaluated intervention studies would be called for with the goal of optimizing teachers' emotional experiences, not only for the sake of teachers but also in the interest of emotionally healthy and well-functioning classrooms.

NOTE

1. In earlier descriptions of the model (Frenzel et al., 2008; Frenzel, Goetz, Stephens, et al., 2009), these themes were referred to as teaching ideals, and only the first three were considered. Now, the so-called relational theme has been added due to recent work on teacher goals, teacher responsibility, and teacher needs that unanimously emphasize the importance of teacher–student relationships for teacher well-being and psychologically healthy classroom environments (Butler, 2012; Chang & Davis, 2009; Klassen et al., 2012; Lauermann & Karabenick, 2013).

REFERENCES

Adams, S., Heywood, J. S., & Rothstein, R. (Eds.). (2009). *Teachers, performance pay, and accountability: What education should learn from other sectors* (Vol. 1). Washington, DC: Economic Policy Institute.

Anderman, E. M., & Patrick, H. (2012). Achievement goal theory, conceptualization of ability/intelligence, and classroom climate. In S. L. Christenson, A. L. Reschly, & C. Wylie (Eds.), *Handbook of research on student engagement, Part 2* (pp. 173–191). New York, NY: Springer.

Anderson, P. A., & Guerrero, L. K. (1998). *Handbook of communication and emotion.* San Diego, CA: Academic Press.

Ashforth, B. E., & Humphrey, R. H. (1993). Emotional labor in service roles: The influence of identity. *The Academy of Management Review, 18*(1), 88–115.

Babad, E. (2007). Teachers' nonverbal behaviors and its effects on students. In R. P. Perry & J. C. Smart (Eds.), *The scholarship of teaching and learning in Higher Education: An evidence-based perspective* (pp. 201–261). New York, NY: Springer.

Baird, J. R., Gunstone, R. F., Penna, C., Fensham, P. J., & White, R. T. (2007). Researching balance between cognition and affect in science teaching and learning. *Research in Science Education, 20,* 11–20.

Barger, P. B., & Grandey, A. A. (2006). Service with a smile and encounter satisfaction: Emotional contagion and appraisal mechanisms. *Academy of Management Journal, 49,* 1229–1238.

Barrett, L. F. (1997). The relationships among momentary emotion experiences, personality descriptions, and retrospective ratings of emotion. *Personality and Social Psychology Bulletin, 23*(10), 1100–1110.

Barrett, L. F., & Barrett, D. J. (2001). An introduction to computerized experience sampling in psychology. *Social Science Computer Review, 19,* 175–185.

Becker, E. S. (2011). *Teacher's emotion in the classroom and how they relate to emotional exhaustion—An experience-sampling analysis.* Konstanz, Germany: Universität Konstanz.

Beilock, S. L., Gunderson, E. A., Ramirez, G., & Levine, S. L. (2010). Female teachers' math anxiety affects girls' math achievement. *PNAS, 107,* 1860–1863.

Bibby, T. (2002). Shame: An emotional response to doing mathematics as an adult and a teacher. *British Educational Research Journal, 28*(5), 705–721.

Brophy, J., & Good, T. L. (1986). Teacher behavior and student achievement. In M. L. Wittock (Ed.), *Handbook of research on teaching* (3rd ed., pp. 328–375). New York, NY: Macmillan.

Brophy, J., & McCaslin, M. (1992). Teachers' reports of how they perceive and cope with problem students. *Elementary School Journal, 93,* 3–68.

Bullough, R. V., Jr., Bullough, D.A.M., & Mayes, P. B. (2006). Getting in touch: Dreaming, the emotions and the work of teaching. *Teachers and teaching: Theory and practice, 12,* 193–208.

Bursal, M., & Paznokas, L. (2006). Mathematics anxiety and preservice elementary teachers' confidence to teach mathematics and science. *School Science and Mathematics, 106,* 173–180.

Butler, R. (2007). Teachers' achievement goal orientations and associations with teachers' help seeking: Examination of a novel approach to teacher motivation. *Journal of Educational Psychology, 99,* 241–252.

Butler, R. (2012). Striving to connect: Extending an achievement goal approach to teacher motivation to include relational goals for teaching. *Journal of Educational Psychology, 104,* 726–742.

Butler, R., & Shibaz, L. (2008). Achievement goals for teaching as predictors of students' perceptions of instructional practices and students' help seeking and cheating. *Learning and Instruction, 18,* 453–467.

Carson, R. L. (2006). *Exploring the episodic nature of teachers' emotions as it relates to teacher burnout.* PhD Dissertation, Purdue University, IN.

Carson, R. L., Weiss, H. M., & Templin, T. J. (2010). Ecological momentary assessment: A research method for studying the daily lives of teachers. *International Journal of Research & Method in Education, 33,* 165–182.

Carver, C. S., & Scheier, M. F. (2014). The experience of emotions during goal pursuit. In R. Pekrun & L. Linnenbrink-Garcia (Eds.), *International handbook of emotions in education* (pp. 56–72). New York, NY: Taylor & Francis.

Chang, M. L. (2009). An appraisal perspective of teacher burnout: Examining the emotional work of teachers. *Educational Psychology Review, 21,* 193–218.

Chang, M. L. (2013). Toward a theoretical model to understand teacher emotions and teacher burnout in the context of student misbehavior: Appraisal, regulation and coping. *Motivation and Emotion, 37,* 799–817.

Chang, M. L., & Davis, H. A. (2009). Understanding the role of teacher appraisals in shaping the dynamics of their relationships with students: Deconstructing teachers' judgement of disruptive behavior/students. In P. A. Schutz & M. Zembylas (Eds.), *Advantages in teacher emotion research: The impact on teachers' lives* (pp. 95–127). New York, NY: Springer.

Clark, M. D. (1997). Teacher response to learning disability: A test of attributional principles. *Journal of Learning Disabilities, 30,* 69–79.

Clore, G. L., Schwarz, N., & Conway, M. (1994). Affective causes and consequences of social information processing. In R. S. Wyer & T. K. Srull (Eds.), *Handbook of social cognition* (2nd ed., pp. 323–417). Hillsdale, NJ: Lawrence Erlbaum.

Coates, T. J., & Thoresen, C. E. (1976). Teacher anxiety: A review with recommendations. *Review of Educational Research, 46,* 159–184.

Collins, M. L. (1978). Effects of enthusiasm training on preservice elementary teachers. *Research in Teacher Education, 29,* 53–57.

Csikszentmihalyi, M., & Larson, R. (1987). Validity and reliability of the experience-sampling method. *Journal of Nervous and Mental Diseases, 175,* 526–536.

Darby, A. (2008). Teachers' emotions in the reconstruction of professional self-understanding. *Teaching and teacher education, 24,* 1160–1172.

Day, C. (2004). *A passion for teaching.* London, United Kingdom: Routledge Falmer.

Dickhäuser, O., Butler, R., & Toenjes, B. (2007). Achievement goals and attitudes to help seeking among pre-service teachers. *Zeitschrift für Entwicklungspsychologie und Pädagogische Psychologie, 39,* 120–126.

Doherty, R. W. (1997). The emotional contagion scale: A measure of individual differences. *Journal of Nonverbal Behavior, 21*, 131–154.

Ellsworth, P. C., & Tong, E.M.W. (2006). What does it mean to be angry at yourself? Categories, appraisals, and the problem of language. *Emotion, 6*, 573–586.

Fredrickson, B. L. (2001). The role of positive emotions in positive psychology: The broaden-and-build theory of positive emotions. *American Psychologist, 56*, 218–226.

Fredrickson, B. L., & Cohn, M. A. (2008). Positive Emotions. In M. Lewis & J. M. Haviland-Jones (Eds.), *Handbook of emotions* (3rd ed., pp. 777–796). New York: The Guilford Press.

Frenzel, A. C., Goetz, T., Lüdtke, O., Pekrun, R., & Sutton, R. (2009). Emotional transmission in the classroom: Exploring the relationship between teacher and student enjoyment. *Journal of Educational Psychology, 101*, 705–716.

Frenzel, A. C., Goetz, T., & Pekrun, R. (2008). Ursachen und Wirkungen von Lehreremotionen. In M. Gläser-Zikuda & J. Seifried (Eds.), *Lehrerexpertise—Analyse und Bedeutung unterrichtlichen Handelns* (pp. 189–211). Münster, Germany: Waxmann.

Frenzel, A. C., Goetz, T., Stephens, E. J., & Jacob, B. (2009). Antecedents and effects of teachers' emotional experiences: An integrated perspective and empirical test. In P. A. Schutz & M. Zembylas (Eds.), *Advances in teacher emotion research: The impact on teachers' lives* (pp. 129–152). New York, NY: Springer.

Gage, N. L., & Berliner, D.C. (1998). *Educational psychology* (6th ed.). New York, NY: Houghten Mifflin.

Georgiou, S. N., Christou, C., Stavrinides, P., & Panaoura, G. (2002). Teacher attributions of student failure and teacher behavior toward the failing student. *Psychology in the Schools, 39*(5), 583–595.

Goetz, T., Frenzel, A. C., Hall, N. C., Nett, U. E., & Lipnevich, A. A. (2013). Types of Boredom: An Experience Sampling Approach. *Motivation and Emotion.* Advance online publication. doi: 10.1007/s11031-013-9385-y

Goetz, T., Frenzel, A. C., Luedtke, O., & Hall, N. C. (2011). Between-domain relations of academic emotions: Does having the same instructor make a difference? *The Journal of Experimental Education, 79*, 84–101.

Golby, M. (1996). Teachers' emotions: An illustrated discussion. *Cambridge Journal of Education, 26*, 423–434.

Goldstein, L. S., & Lake, V. E. (2000). "Love, love, and more love for children": Exploring preservice teachers' understanding of caring. *Teaching and Teacher Education, 16*, 861–872.

Graham, S. (1984). Communicating sympathy and anger to black and white children: the cognitive (attributional) consequences of affective cues. *Journal of Personality and Social Psychology, 47*, 40–54.

Graham, S., & Weiner, B. (1986). From an attributional theory of emotion to developmental psychology: A round-trip ticket? *Social Cognition, 4*, 152–179.

Hakanen, J. J., Bakker, A. B., & Schaufeli, W. B. (2006). Burnout and work engagement among teachers. *Journal of School Psychology, 43*, 495–513.

Hargeaves, A., & Tucker, E. (1991). Teaching and guilt: Exploring the feelings of teaching. *Teaching and teacher education, 7*, 491–505.

Hargreaves, A. (1994). *Changing teachers, changing times.* London, United Kingdom: Cassell.

Hargreaves, A. (1998). The emotional practice of teaching. *Teaching and Teacher Education, 14*, 835–854.

Hargreaves, A. (2000). Mixed emotions: Teachers' perceptions of their interactions with students. *Teaching and Teacher Education, 16*, 811–826.

Hargreaves, A. (2005). The emotions of teaching and educational change. In A. Hargeaves (Ed.), *Extending educational change* (pp. 278–295). Dordrecht: Springer.

Harper, N. W., & Daane, C. J. (1998). Causes and reduction of math anxiety in preservice elementary teachers. *Action in Teacher Education, 19*, 29–38.

Hart, N. I. (1987). Student teachers' anxieties: Four measured factors and their relationships to pupil disruption in class. *Educational Research, 29*, 12–18.

Hatfield, E., Cacioppo, J. T., & Rapson, R. L. (1994). *Emotional contagion.* Cambridge, United Kingdom: Cambridge University Press.

Hochschild, A. R. (1983). *The managed heart: The commercialization of human feeling.* Berkeley, CA: University of California Press.

Intrator, S. (2006). Beginning teachers and emotional drama in the classroom. *Journal of Teacher Education, 57*, 232–239.

Isen, A. M. (2008). Some ways in which positive affect influences decision making and problem solving. In M. Lewis, J. M. Haviland-Jones, & L. Feldman Barrett (Eds.), *Handbook of emotions* (3rd ed., pp. 548–573). New York, NY: Guilford Press.

Keavney, G., & Sinclair, K. E. (1978). Teacher concerns and teacher anxiety: A neglected topic of classroom research. *Review of Educational Research, 48,* 273–290.

Kelly, W. P., & Tomhave, W. K. (1985). A study of math anxiety/math avoidance in preservice elementary teachers. *Arithmetic Teacher, 32,* 51–53.

Klassen, R. M., Perry, N. E., & Frenzel, A. C. (2012). Teachers' relatedness with students: An underemphasized component of teachers' basic psychological needs. *Journal of Educational Psychology, 104,* 150–165.

Kunter, M., Frenzel, A. C., Nagy, G., Baumert, J., & Pekrun, R. (2011). Teacher enthusiasm: Dimensionality and context specificity. *Contemporary Educational Psychology, 36,* 289–301.

Kunter, M., Tsai, Y.-M., Klusmann, U., Brunner, M., Krauss, S., & Baumert, J. (2008). Students' and mathematics teachers' perceptions of teacher enthusiasm and instruction. *Learning and Instruction, 18,* 468–482.

Kuppens, P., Van Mechelen, I., & Rijmen, F. (2008). Towards disentangling sources of individual differences in appraisal and anger. *Journal of Personality, 76,* 969–1000.

Kuppens, P., Van Mechelen, I., Smits, D.J.M., & De Boeck, P. (2003). The appraisal basis of anger: Specificity, necessity, and sufficiency of components. *Emotion, 3,* 254–269.

Lauermann, F., & Karabenick, S. (2013). The meaning and measure of teachers' sense of responsibility for educational outcomes. *Teaching and Teacher Education, 30,* 13–26.

Lazarus, R. S. (1991). *Emotion and adaptation.* New York, NY: Oxford University Press.

Lewis, M. (2000). Self-conscious emotions: Embarrassment, shame, and guilt. In M. Lewis & J. M. Haviland-Jones (Eds.), *Handbook of emotions* (2nd ed., pp. 623–636). New York, NY: The Guilford Press.

Liljestrom, A., Roulston, K., & deMarrais, K. (2007). "There is no place for feeling like this in the workplace": Women teachers' anger in school settings. In P. A. Schutz & R. Pekrun (Eds.), *Emotions in education* (pp. 275–292). San Diego, CA: Elsevier.

Linnenbrink-Garcia, L., & Barger, M. (2014). Achievement goals and emotions. In R. Pekrun & L. Linnenbrink-Garcia (Eds.), *International handbook of emotions in education* (pp. 142–161). New York, NY: Taylor & Francis.

Long, J. F., & Hoy, A. W. (2006). Interested instructors: A composite portrait of 1170 individual differences and effectiveness. *Teaching and Teacher Education, 22,* 303–314.

Lortie, D.C. (1975). *Schoolteacher.* Chicago, IL: University of Chicago Press.

Maslach, C., & Jackson, S. E. (1981). The measurement of experienced burnout. *Journal of Occupational Behavior, 2,* 99–113.

Maslach, C., & Jackson, S. E. (1986). *Maslach Burnout Inventory manual.* Palo Alto, CA: Consulting Psychologists Press.

Maslach, C., Schaufeli, W. B., & Leiter, M. P. (2001). Job burnout. *Annual Review of Psychology, 52,* 397–422.

McIntosh, D. N. (1996). Facial feedback hypotheses: Evidence, implications, and directions. *Motivation and Emotion, 20,* 121–147.

McPherson, M. B., Kearney, P., & Plax, T. G. (2003). The dark side of instruction: Teacher anger as classroom norm violations. *Journal of Applied Communication Research, 31,* 76–90.

Mitchell, R.L.C., & Phillips, L. H. (2007). The psychological, neurochemical and functional neuroanatomical mediators of the effects of positive and negative mood on executive functions. *Neuropsychologia, 45,* 617–629.

Morris, J. A., & Feldman, D.C. (1996). The dimensions, antecedents and consequences of emotional labor. *Academy of Management Review, 21,* 986–1010.

Murray, H. (1983). Low-inference classroom teaching behaviors and students' ratings of college teaching effectiveness. *Journal of Educational Psychology, 75,* 138–149.

Nett, U. E., & Goetz, T. (2011). Coping with boredom in school: An experience sampling perspective. *Contemporary Educational Psychology, 36,* 49–59.

Nias, J. (1989). *Primary teachers talking: A study of teaching as work.* London, United Kingdom: Routledge.

Nias, J. (1996). Thinking about feeling: The emotions in teaching. *Cambridge Journal of Education, 26,* 293–306.

Oehman, A. (2008). Fear and anxiety. In M. Lewis, J. M. Haviland-Jones, & L. Feldman Barrett (Eds.), *Handbook of emotions* (3rd ed., pp. 709–729). New York, NY: The Guilford Press.

Patrick, B.C., Hisley, J., Kempler, T., & College, G. (2000). "What's everybody so excited about?": The effects of teacher enthusiasm on student intrinsic motivation and vitality. *Journal of Experimental Education, 68,* 1521–1558.

Patrick, H., Kaplan, A., & Ryan, A.M. (2011). Positive classroom motivational environments: Convergence between mastery goal structure and classroom social climate. *Journal of Educational Psychology, 103,* 367–382.

Payne, B. D., & Manning, B. H. (1990). The effect of self-instructions on preservice teacher's anxiety about teaching. *Contemporary Educational Psychology Review, 15,* 261–267.

Pekrun, R. (2000). A social-cognitive, control-value theory of achievement emotions. In J. Heckhausen (Ed.), *Motivational psychology of human vevelopment* (pp. 143–163). Oxford, United Kingdom: Elsevier.

Pekrun, R. (2006). The control-value theory of achievement emotions: Assumptions, corollaries, and implications for educational research and practice. *Educational Psychology Review, 18,* 315–341.

Pekrun, R., Elliot, A. J., & Maier, M. A. (2006). Achievement goals and discrete achievement emotions: A theoretical model and prospective test. *Journal of Educational Psychology, 98,* 583–597.

Pekrun, R., Goetz, T., Daniels, L. M., Stupnisky, R. H., & Perry, R. P. (2010). Boredom in achievement settings: Exploring control-value antecedents and performance outcomes of a neglected emotion. *Journal of Educational Psychology, 102,* 531–549.

Pekrun, R., & Linnenbrink-Garcia, L. (2014). Conclusions and future directions. In R. Pekrun & L. Linnenbrink-Garcia (Eds.), *International handbook of emotions in education* (pp. 659–675). New York, NY: Taylor & Francis.

Pekrun, R., & Perry, R. P. (2014). Control-value theory of achievement emotions. In R. Pekrun & L. Linnenbrink-Garcia (Eds.), *International handbook of emotions in education* (pp. 120–141). New York, NY: Taylor & Francis.

Perkins, R. E., & Hill, A. B. (1985). Cognitive and affective aspects of boredom. *British Journal of Educational Psychology, 76,* 221–234.

Philipp, A., & Schüpbach, H. (2010). Longitudinal effects of emotional labour on emotional exhaustion and dedication of teachers. *Journal of Occupational Health Psychology, 15,* 494–504.

Prawat, R., Byers, J., & Anderson, A. H. (1983). An attributional analysis of teachers' affective reactions to student success and failure. *American Educational Research Journal, 20,* 137–152.

Retelsdorf, J., Butler, R., Streblow, L., & Schiefele, U. (2010). Teachers' goal orientations for teaching: Associations with instructional practices, interest in teaching, and burnout. *Learning and Instruction, 20,* 30–46.

Robinson, M. D., & Clore, G. L. (2002). Belief and feeling: Evidence for an accessibility model of emotional self-report. *Psychological Bulletin, 128,* 934–960.

Roseman, I. J., & Smith, C. A. (2001). Appraisal theory. Overview, assumptions, varieties, controversies. In K. R. Scherer, A. Schorr, & T. Johnstone (Eds.), *Appraisal processes in emotion* (pp. 3–19). Oxford, United Kingdom: Oxford University Press.

Rosenshine, B. (1970). Enthusiastic teaching: A review. *School Review, 78,* 499–514.

Scherer, K. R. (1984). On the nature and function of emotion: a component process approach. In P. Ekman (Ed.), *Approaches to emotion* (pp. 293–318). Hillsdale, NJ: Erlbaum.

Scherer, K. R., Schorr, A., & Johnstone, T. (Eds.). (2001). *Appraisal processes in emotion.* Oxford, United Kingdom: Oxford University Press.

Schiefele, U., & Csikszentmihalyi, M. (1995). Motivation and ability as factors in mathematics experience and achievement. *Journal for Research in Mathematics Education, 26,* 163–181.

Schutz, P. A., Cross, D. I., Hong, J. Y., & Osbon, J. N. (2007). Teacher identities, beliefs, and goals related to emotions. In P. A. Schutz & R. Pekrun (Eds.), *Emotion in education* (pp. 223–241). London, United Kingdom: Elsevier.

Schutz, P. A., & Pekrun, R. (Eds.). (2007). *Emotions in education.* San Diego, CA: Elsevier.

Scott, C., & Sutton, R. E. (2009). Emotions and change during professional development for teachers. *Journal of Mixed Methods Research, 3,* 151–171.

Seidel, T., & Shavelson, R. J. (2007). Teaching effectiveness research in the past decade: The role of theory and research design in disentangling meta-analysis results. *Review of Educational Research, 77,* 454–499.

Seligman, M.E.P., & Csikszentmihalyi, M. (2000). Positive psychology: An introduction. *American Psychologist, 55,* 5–14.

Sinclair, R. C., & Mark, M. M. (1992). The influence of mood state on judgment and action: Effects on persuasion, categorization, social justice, person perception, and judgmental accuracy. In L. L. Martin & A. Tesser (Eds.), *The construction of social judgments* (pp. 165–193). Hillsdale, NJ: Lawrence Erlbaum.

Smith, C. A., & Lazarus, R. S. (1993). Appraisal components, core relational themes, and the emotions. *Cognition and Emotion, 7,* 233–269.

Smith, R. P. (1981). Boredom: A review. *Human Factors, 23,* 329–340.

Soussignan, R. (2004). Regulatory function of facial actions in emotion processes. In S. P. Shohov (Ed.), *Advances in psychology research* (Vol. 31, pp. 173–198). Hauppauge, NY: Nova Science Publishers.

Stoeber, J. (2003). Self-pity: Exploring the links to personality, control beliefs, and anger. *Journal of Personality, 71,* 183–221.

Stough, L., & Emmer, E. T. (1998). Teacher emotions and test feedback. *International Journal of Qualitative Studies in Education, 11,* 341–362.

Sutton, R. E. (2004). Emotional regulation goals and strategies of teachers. *Social Psychology of Education, 7,* 379–398.

Sutton, R. E. (2007). Teachers' anger, frustration, and self-regulation. In P. A. Schutz & R. Pekrun (Eds.), *Emotion in education* (pp. 251–266). San Diego, CA: Academic Press.

Sutton, R. E., & Harper, E. (2009). Teachers' emotion regulation. *Springer International Handbooks of Education, 21,* 389–401.

Sutton, R. E., & Knight, C. C. (2006). Teachers' emotion regulation. In A. V. Mitel (Ed.), *Trends in educational psychology* (pp. 107–136). Hauppauge, NY: Nova Publishers.

Sutton, R. E., Mudrey-Camino, R., & Knight, C. C. (2009). Teachers' emotion regulation and classroom management. *Theory Into Practice, 48,* 130–137.

Sutton, R. E., & Wheatley, K. F. (2003). Teachers' emotions and teaching: A review of the literature and directions for future research. *Educational Psychology Review, 15,* 327–358.

Tangney, J. P., & Dearing, R. L. (2002). *Shame and guilt.* New York, NY: Guilford.

Thomas, D. L., & Diener, E. (1990). Memory Accuracy in the recall of emotions. *Journal of Personality and Social Psychology, 59,* 291–297.

Tong, E. M. W., Bishop, G. D., Enkelmann, H. C., Why, Y. P., Diong, S. M., Khader, M., & Ang, J. (2007). Emotion and appraisal: A study using ecological momentary assessment. *Cognition & Emotion, 27,* 1361–1381.

Totterdell, P., & Parkinson, B. (1999). Use and effectiveness of self-regulation strategies for improving mood in a group of trainee teachers. *Journal of Occupational Health Psychology, 4,* 219–232.

Tracy, J. L., & Robins, R. W. (2007). The self in self-conscious emotions: A cognitive appraisal approach. In J. L. Tracy, R. W. Robins, & J. P. Tangney (Eds.), *The self-conscious emotions: Theory and research* (pp. 443–467). New York, NY: Guilford.

Tsang, K. K. (2011). Emotional labor of teaching. *Educational Research, 2,* 1312–1316.

Tschannen-Moran, M., & Hoy, A. W. (2001). Teacher efficacy: Capturing an elusive construct. *Teaching and Teacher Education, 17,* 783–805.

Turner, J. C., Meyer, D. K., Cox, K. E., Logan, C., DiCintio, M., & Thomas, C. T. (1998). Creating contexts for involvement in mathematics. *Journal of Educational Psychology, 90,* 730–745.

van Veen, K., Seegers, P., & van de Ven, P.-H. (2005). Teacher's identity, emotions and commitment to change: A case study into the cognitive-affective processes of one secondary school teacher in the context of reforms. *Teaching and Teacher Education, 21,* 917–934.

Weiner, B. (1986). *An attributional theory of motivation and emotion.* New York, NY: Springer.

Weiner, B. (2007). Examining emotional diversity in the classroom: An attribution theorist considers the moral emotions. In P. A. Schutz & R. Pekrun (Eds.), *Emotions in education* (pp. 75–88). San Diego, CA: Academic Press.

Winograd, K. (2003). The functions of teacher emotions: The good, the bad, and the ugly. *Teachers College Record, 105,* 1641–1673.

Witcher, A. E., Onwuegbuzie, A. J., & Minor, L. C. (2001). Characteristics of effective teachers: Perceptions of preservice teachers. *Research in the Schools, 8,* 45–57.

Wood, E. F. (1988). Math anxiety and elementary teachers: What does research tell us? *For the Learning of Mathematics, 8,* 8–13.

Zeidner, M. (2014). Anxiety in education. In R. Pekrun & L. Linnenbrink-Garcia (Eds.), *International handbook of emotions in education* (pp. 265–288). New York, NY: Taylor & Francis.

Zembylas, M. (2002). Structures of feeling in curriculum and teaching: Theorizing the emotional rules. *Educational Theory, 52,* 187–208.

Zembylas, M. (2003a). Caring for teacher emotion: reflections on teacher self-development. *Studies in Philosophy and Education, 22,* 103–125.

Zembylas, M. (2003b). Emotions and teacher identity: A poststructural perspective. *Teachers and Teaching: Theory and Practice, 9,* 213–238.

Zembylas, M. (2005). Discursive practices, genealogies, and emotional rules: A poststructuralist view on emotion and identity in teaching. *Teaching and Teacher Education, 21,* 935–948.

Zerbe, W. J. (2000). Emotional dissonance and employee well-being. In N. M. Ashkanasy, C.E.J. Hartel, & W. J. Zerbe (Eds.), *Emotions in the workplace: research, theory, and practice* (pp. 189–214). Westport, CT: Quorum/Greenwood.

Zhu, N. Q. (2002). *The effects of teachers' flow experiences on the cognitive engagement of students* (Unpublished doctoral dissertation) University of San Diego, San Diego, CA.

26

CAREGIVING INFLUENCES ON EMOTION REGULATION

Educational Implications of a Biobehavioral Perspective

Susan D. Calkins and Jessica M. Dollar,
University of North Carolina at Greensboro

This chapter addresses the role of caregivers in the socialization of emotion and emotion regulation from a biobehavioral perspective and describes the implications of such a perspective for education. Although considerable research has sought to understand the relations between parental behavior and a range of child developmental outcomes, much of this work has been conducted at a very broad level of analysis. Psychobiological theory and research point to the need for models of caregiving that offer greater specificity regarding processes that may be implicated in the effects of these relationships (cf. Calkins, 2010). Recent animal work and some human work has focused more on the proximal mechanisms through which caregivers influence the development of children's emotion regulation skills. Such work is likely to make significant contributions for both basic and applied work that is focused on the processes through which parents provide children with the necessary emotion management skills that will facilitate the transition to school and school functioning in childhood and adolescence.

Consistent with many of our colleagues (Eisenberg, Hofer, & Vaughn, 2007; Gross & Thompson, 2007; Jacobs & Gross, 2014), we view emotion regulation processes as those behaviors, skills, and strategies, whether conscious or unconscious, automatic or effortful, that serve to modulate, inhibit, and enhance emotional experiences and expressions (Calkins & Hill, 2007). Our approach entails the examination of the child's use of specific strategies in emotionally demanding contexts and the effects of these strategies on emotion experience and expression (Calkins & Dedmon, 2000). In adopting a psychobiological approach to our work, we also measure the physiological response of the child to the emotional challenge, assuming that behavioral strategies to deal with emotional arousal are, at least, in part, dependent on biological efforts to control arousal (Calkins, 1997).

In this chapter, we use a psychobiological framework for understanding how parents influence the development of emotion regulation and address how such skills are important in school functioning. First, we provide a brief overview of the normative developments that occur in early emotion regulation from infancy to adolescence. Next, we briefly discuss the dimensions of parenting and family relationships that are important as infants and children make the transition from "other" regulation to the self-regulation of emotion, indexed by both behavior and underlying physiology. This discussion emphasizes attachment and parenting behaviors in early development and highlights some of the research that examines how caregivers affect children's acquisition of emotion regulation skills. Third, we discuss the influence of parenting on children at a more proximal physiological level and highlight some of our work on the psychophysiology of emotion regulation that focuses on the role of the autonomic nervous system in emotion regulation processes. Finally, we discuss the implications of these early emotion processes for children's adjustment in the school setting, emphasizing the importance of emotion regulation for both social and academic success and make recommendations for how this framework can be used to address school-relevant emotional functioning.

THE DEVELOPMENT OF EMOTION REGULATION

Early in development, dramatic growth occurs in the acquisition and display of emotion regulation skills and abilities. The process may be described broadly as one in which the relatively passive and reactive neonate becomes a child capable of self-initiated behaviors that serve an emotion regulatory function. The infant moves from near complete reliance on caregivers for regulation (e.g., via physical soothing provided when the infant is held) to independent emotion regulation (e.g., choosing to find another toy to play with rather than tantrumming when the desired toy is taken by a companion), although the variability in such regulation across children, in terms of both style and the efficacy, is considerable (Buss & Goldsmith, 1998; Calkins, 2009). As the infant makes this transition to greater independence, the caregiver's use of specific strategies and behaviors within dyadic interactions become integrated into the infant's repertoire of emotion regulation skills, across, we presume, both biological and behavioral levels of functioning (Calkins & Dedmon, 2000; Calkins & Hill, 2007). The child may then draw upon this repertoire in a variety of contexts in both conscious, effortful ways (e.g., walking away from a confrontation with a peer) and in nonconscious, automatic ways (e.g., averting gaze when confronted by a frightening movie scene or reducing vagal regulation of the heart to facilitate behavior coping) (Calkins, Graziano, Berdan, Keane, & Degnan, 2008).

The development of emotional, motor, language, and cognitive advances assist children to become more autonomous in their ability to regulate emotions from infancy through early childhood (Calkins, 2002; Kopp, 1989). Childhood also includes important changes within the child's social environment, as networks begin to include peers within the school and neighborhood environments and teachers. The presence of these new situations gives the child additional information regarding emotions, the social acceptability of emotions, and how to regulate arousal in given circumstances (Kopp, 1989). The ability to regulate emotional arousal continues to improve from mid- to late-childhood and into adolescence, likely due to social standards set by peers and adults (Saarni, Mumme, & Campos, 1998) and improved cognitive abilities (Steinberg, 2005). In addition, recent evidence from developmental neuroscience suggests that the regions of the brain associated with emotion regulation continue to mature through childhood into adolescence (Beauregard, Levesque, & Paquette, 2004). During this time, adolescents also develop the ability to distinguish between long- and short-term means of regulation given that they can better identify long-term consequences of their behaviors (Moilanen, 2007).

Considerable research on emotion regulation also demonstrates quite convincingly that the display of emotion and emotion regulation is a powerful mediator of interpersonal relationships and socioemotional adjustment as early as the first few years of life and continuing throughout adolescence (Thompson & Meyer, 2007). For example, Stifter, Spinrad, and Braungart-Rieker (1999) found that emotion regulation in response to frustration in infancy was related to compliance in toddlerhood. Shipman and colleagues hypothesize that while problems with emotion regulation may be broadly related to externalizing behavior problems characterized by aggression, they may differentially predict children who are prone to oppositional defiant disorder (Shipman, Schneider, & Brown, 2004). Further, children's ability to regulate emotions in order to obtain acceptance in a peer group makes emotion regulation a crucial ability with school-age children (Gottman, 2001). Thus, the degree to which the child can manage negative emotions in a constructive way versus acting-out towards parents and peers is a predictor of social success and more positive social outcomes (Howse, Calkins, Anastopoulos, Keane, & Shelton, 2003). Also, much work has explored the relations between emotion regulation and academic outcomes (e.g., Blair, Denham, Kochanoff, & Whipple, 2004; Graziano, Reavis, Keane, & Calkins, 2007; Urasache, Blair, & Raver, 2012), which will be discussed in greater detail later in this chapter. Given the central role of emotion regulation in social functioning and school success, it is useful to consider how these skills first emerge as a function of children's earliest social relationships.

CAREGIVING PRACTICES AND CHILD EMOTION REGULATION BEHAVIORS

Emotional self-regulatory processes begin to develop in the context of dyadic interactions (Sroufe, 1996). Such interactions contribute to both normative developments and individual variability in emotional self-regulation (Cassidy, 1994). Although multiple dimensions of caregiving may contribute to the development of emotion regulation (Eisenberg, Cumberland, & Spinrad, 1998; Morris, Silk, Steinberg, Myers, & Robinson, 2007), one important dimension of the dyadic caregiving relationship is the attachment relationship that develops between specific caregivers and infants over the first year of life. Current theorizing about childhood attachment and its role in emotional functioning and behavioral adjustment has its roots in the work of John Bowlby (1969/1982), whose evolutionary theory of attachment emphasized the biological adaptiveness of specific attachment behaviors displayed during the infancy period. Such behaviors permitted the infant to initiate and maintain contact with the primary caregiver, which served a survival purpose (Bowlby, 1988). In typical development, infants exhibit a repertoire of behaviors, including looking, crying, and clinging that allow them to signal, and elicit support from, the primary caregiver in times of external threat. Bowlby argued that by the end of the first year of life, the interactive history between the infant and caregiver, including during times of stress or external threat, would produce a relatively stable attachment relationship that would provide a sense of security for the infant and significantly influence the child's subsequent adaptation to a variety of challenges (Bowlby, 1988) by virtue of creating an "internal working model" of the world that guided children's expectations of self and others.

Subsequent theoretical perspectives on attachment focused on the actual biological processes involved in the regulation of attachment and emotion processes (Field, 1994; Fox & Hane, 2008). For example, Hofer (1994; Polan & Hofer, 1999) addressed the multiple psychobiological roles that the caregiver plays in regulating infant's behavior and physiology early in life. Based on his research with infant rat pups, he described these "hidden regulators" as operating at multiple sensory levels (olfactory, tactile, and oral, for example) and influencing multiple levels of behavioral and physiological functioning in the infant. So, for example, maternal tactile stimulation may have the effect of lowering the infant's heart rate during a stressful situation, which may in turn support a more adaptive behavioral response. Moreover, removal of these regulators, during separation, for example, disrupts the infant's functioning at multiple levels as well. Clearly, then, opportunities for individual differences in the development of emotional self-regulation may emerge from differential rearing conditions providing more or less psychobiological regulation. Consistent with this view, maternal holding and rocking are found to be particularly effective at reducing infant distress (Jahromi, Putnam, & Stifter, 2004) and mother-infant skin-to-skin contact has been linked with greater physiological and emotional regulation among premature infants (Feldman, Weller, Sirota, & Eidelman, 2002).

The psychobiological interpretation of attachment theory also offers insight into the mechanism by which interactive experiences across the first year of life become integrated into the internal working model that Bowlby (1969/1982) articulated. For example, Hofer (1994) described how the biological experience of infant–caregiver interactions becomes a representational structure that guides affective functioning. He argued that these early interactions are, in fact, regulatory experiences that contribute to an inner affective experience composed of sensory, physiological, and behavioral responses. Over time, these affective experiences lead to organized representations, the integration of which is the internal working model. These organized mental representations are, theoretically, what ultimately guide the child's behavior rather than the individual sensory and physiological components to which the infant responded earlier in infancy.

The pattern of findings linking attachment and specific emotion regulation behaviors suggests an important role for caregivers in this process, albeit much of this work has focused on caregivers' behaviors. For example, Diener and colleagues (Diener, Manglesdorf, McHale, & Frosch, 2002) observed that attachment classification predicted infants' regulatory strategies during a mildly stressful task in which infants were left with nothing to do while their parent completed a questionnaire. Infants in secure attachment relationships with both parents used strategies emphasizing social orientation. Likewise, in a challenging problem-solving task during which the mother was present, toddlers who were classified as secure a year earlier engaged in more maternal help seeking than did avoidant and disorganized toddlers (Schieche & Spangler, 2005). In contrast, mother-reported attachment security was unrelated to the use of mother-oriented regulation strategies during laboratory tasks designed to elicit fear and frustration but was linked with more positive and less negative affect suggesting more adaptive emotion regulation among secure children (Smith, Calkins, & Keane, 2006). Similarly, infants who were classified as secure at 15 months of age were less likely than avoidant infants to be classified as dysregulated on the basis of high negative affect and defiance during a compliance task at

24 months (NICHD ECCRN, 2004). Importantly, this effect was significant independent of a variety of demographic characteristics, infant temperament, and maternal sensitivity, indicating that the link was robust and not merely an artifact of maternal sensitivity.

Some scholars have also examined links between attachment security and emotion regulation processes beyond the infancy period. In a study of preschoolers' use of specific anger control strategies during a waiting paradigm, a secure attachment in infancy predicted greater use of attentional distraction, which was linked to successful waiting (Gilliom, Shaw, Beck, Schonberg, & Lukon, 2002). Likewise, seven year olds who had been classified as securely attached in infancy reported greater expectations that others would help them emotionally and instrumentally during peer provocations (Ziv, Oppenheim, & Sagi-Schwartz, 2004). This supports the view that children with a secure attachment history have positive expectations of others that may contribute to the use of other-oriented regulation strategies beyond infancy.

Studies examining the relations between aspects of parenting thought to be linked to attachment and emotional self-regulation are also of interest. These studies are worth noting because they are conducted with toddlers, children for whom there are clear expectations of emerging autonomous emotional control. In one study of mothers and toddlers, for example, we examined the relations between maternal behavior across a variety of different situations and child emotional self-control in frustrating situations (Calkins, Smith, Gill, & Johnson, 1998). Our analyses indicated that maternal negative, punitive, and controlling behavior (for example, pulling the child's hand away from a toy, making critical comments) was related to the use of orienting to or manipulating the object of frustration (a barrier box containing an attractive toy) and negatively related to the use of distraction techniques, which are thought to be a more adaptive way of managing emotions. Likewise, maternal nonresponsiveness and disengagement following toddler distress cues were linked with children's use of ineffective attentional control strategies during a delay of gratification task, such as visually focusing on the object that they were not supposed to touch (Rodriguez et al., 2005). These data are important in light of findings that the ability to control attention and engage in distraction has been related to the experience of less emotional arousal and reactivity (Calkins, 1997; Crockenberg & Leerkes, 2004; Grolnick, Cosgrove, & Bridges, 1996) and to fewer behavior problems characterized by acting-out (Calkins & Dedmon, 2000; Crockenberg, Leerkes, & Barrig Jó, 2008) or internalizing behavior problems (Crockenberg & Leerkes, 2006). Finally, maternal sensitivity to infant distress cues but not nondistress cues at six months was linked with less emotion dysregulation at age two among temperamentally reactive infants (Leerkes, Blankson, & O'Brien, 2009). That sensitivity to distress was a particularly salient predictor of attachment security in the same sample (McElwain & Booth-LaForce, 2006) suggests that attachment-related processes may account for this effect.

Research linking the role of parents' behavior on the development of children's adaptive emotion regulation has also been linked to children's school success. Across the domains of self-regulation, warm and responsive caregiving has been shown to enhance children's regulatory abilities. For instance, good parental scaffolding (parents who provided appropriate cognitive and emotional support while also allowing children to be autonomous) was related to better self-regulation across several domains (attentional, cognitive, and behavioral) within the preschool classroom (Neitzel & Stright, 2003). In short, children who had mothers who provided appropriate support during challenging tasks at home were better able to sustain their attention and effort on tasks, use self-talk to assist in problem solving, and comply with the rules of conduct within the classroom. In our own research, we found that for children who were at low risk of developing persistent externalizing behavior problems, those who evidenced better emotion regulation at two years of age and who had mothers who were warm and responsive were more liked by their classmates in kindergarten. In contrast, children with equally well-developed emotion regulation strategies but who had mothers who were not warm and responsive were less well liked by their classmates in kindergarten (Blandon, Calkins, & Keane, 2010). These results lend further evidence that the emotional climate of mother–child interactions is important for children to successfully use their emotion regulation strategies.

Parents continue to set a developmental context in children's ability to regulate emotions from childhood to adolescence (Bell & Calkins, 2000). In research with school-age children, mothers who responded to children's displays of negative affect with minimizing or punitive responses had children who were less likely to use constructive emotion regulation strategies (Eisenberg, Fabes, & Murphy, 1996). Based on this and similar research, it has been proposed that parents' negative reactions to children's emotions likely increases the child's arousal, leading to poorly regulated behavior by undermining the child's opportunity to experience emotions in a positive manner (Eisenberg et al., 1998). Although there is a lack of research examining the role of parents in adolescents' ability to regulate emotions, some research has focused on parents' validation or dampening of adolescents' emotions. For example, adolescents whose mothers dampened or invalidated displays of positive affect engaged in dysregulated strategies related to depressive symptomatology, and those adolescents, in turn, were likely to also engage in negative behaviors with their mothers (Yap, Allen, & Ladouceur, 2008). Additional research has shown that parental involvement in middle childhood and adolescence is positively associated with academic motivation and achievement at school (Grolnick, Kurowski, Dunlap, & Hevey, 2000; Steinberg, Lamborn, Dornbusch, & Darling, 1992), whereas high levels of parental control are damaging to students' motivation and achievement (Bronstein, Ginsburg, & Herrera, 2005). This research suggests that although there is much evidence that emotion regulation is grounded in early biological processes, these abilities are subject to environmental influence throughout development.

CAREGIVING AND THE PHYSIOLOGICAL REGULATION OF EMOTION

Although caregiving practices are often attributed in the development of emotion regulation, the specific processes by which these practices affect children's development are often discussed at a mostly global level (Fox & Calkins, 2003). Greater specificity in how caregiving affects children requires consideration of the multiple levels of child self-regulation that are emerging during early development. Clearly biological regulation is one candidate process that may allow greater specificity in understanding how caregiving affects child behavior. Theories of self-regulation that focus on underlying biological components assume that maturation of different biological support systems lays the foundation for increasingly sophisticated emotional, cognitive, and behavioral regulation that is observed across childhood.

Recent psychophysiological research highlights the role of one such system, the autonomic nervous system, in regulating many biobehavioral processes. The autonomic nervous system functions as a complex system of afferent and efferent feedback pathways that are integrated with other neurophysiological and neuroanatomical processes, reciprocally linking cardiac activity with central nervous system processes (Chambers & Allen, 2007). Pathways of the parasympathetic nervous system, in particular, are implicated in these processes, and, consequently, they play a key role in the regulation of state, motor activity, emotion, and cognition (Porges, 2003). Specifically, the myelinated vagus nerve, originating in the brainstem nucleus ambiguus, provides input to the sinoatrial node of the heart, producing dynamic changes in cardiac activity that allow the organism to transition between sustaining metabolic processes and generating more complex responses to environmental events (Porges, 2007). This central-peripheral neural feedback loop is functional relatively early in development (Porges, 2007), though there is good evidence that individual differences in the integrity of these processes are a consequence of both organic characteristics and postnatal experiences (Calkins & Hill, 2007).

Parasympathetic influences on heart rate can be easily quantified in young humans by measuring heart rate variability. Variability in heart rate that occurs at the frequency of spontaneous respiration (respiratory sinus arrhythmia, RSA) can be measured noninvasively and is considered a good estimate of the parasympathetic influence on heart rate variability via the vagus nerve. Porges and colleagues developed a method that measures the amplitude and period of the oscillations associated with inhalation and exhalation, referred to as vagal tone (Vna; Porges, 1985, 1991, 1996; Porges & Byrne, 1992). Of particular interest to researchers studying self-regulation, though, has been measurement of vagal regulation of the heart when the organism is challenged. Such regulation is indexed by a decrease in RSA or vagal tone (vagal withdrawal) during situations where coping or emotional and behavioral regulation is required (Porges, 2003, 2007). Vagal regulation in the form of decreases in RSA is often described as the functioning of "the vagal brake" because a decrease, or withdrawal, of vagal input to the heart has the effect of stimulating increases in heart rate. During demanding tasks, such a response reflects physiological processes that allow the child to shift focus from internal homeostatic demands to demands that require internal processing or the generation of coping strategies to control affective or behavioral arousal. Thus, vagal withdrawal is thought to be a physiological strategy that results in greater cardiac output in the form of HR acceleration and that supports behaviors indicative of active coping (Calkins, Graziano, & Keane, 2007; El-Sheikh, Harger, & Whitson, 2006; Porges, 1991, 1996; Propper & Moore, 2006; Wilson & Gottman, 1996).

One of the hypotheses that we have explored in our work is that although the ability to suppress RSA may be related to complex responses involving the regulation of attention and behavior, a deficiency in this ability may be related to early behavior problems, particularly problems characterized by a lack of behavioral and emotional control (Calkins & Dedmon, 2000; Porges, 1996; Wilson & Gottman, 1996). Lack of behavioral and emotional control is considered a core deficit for children with disruptive behavior problems (Gilliom & Shaw, 2004; Keenan & Shaw, 2003). Moreover, children with externalizing problems display patterns of aggressive, destructive, and undercontrolled behavior that remains stable from preschool to middle childhood (Gilliom & Shaw, 2004), that often results in more severe conduct problems in adolescence and young adulthood (Olweus, 1979), and that disrupts behavior, learning, and social relationships in the school environment. Given that such problems are believed to have both biological and socialization origins (Moffitt, 1993), one question that may be asked is whether these children display a pattern of physiological dysregulation that impairs their ability to generate and engage appropriate regulatory strategies in situations that are emotionally or behaviorally challenging.

In one study, we identified children at high risk for the development of aggressive behavior problems at age two and assessed them in a number of challenging emotion and cognitive tasks (Calkins & Dedmon, 2000). These children displayed significantly lower RSA suppression across these tasks than did children at low risk for behavior problems. In a follow-up of these same children, continued behavioral difficulties, including social problems and difficulties with emotion regulation, were characteristic of the children who displayed, across the preschool period, a stable pattern of physiological dysregulation in the form of lower RSA suppression to challenge (Calkins & Keane, 2004). Interestingly, children who displayed a pattern of lower suppression at age two, but who were observed to suppress RSA at age four, showed continued difficulties, suggesting that the early pattern of cardiac vagal regulation may have constrained the acquisition of regulatory skill that affected behavior later in the preschool period. An important issue, though, is the degree to which this regulation may be influenced by caregiver behavior.

In every study we have conducted using physiological measures of regulation, we have observed that infants and children engaged in a challenging task with a caregiver typically display a greater magnitude of RSA suppression than when they are engaged in a task alone (cf. Calkins & Dedmon, 2000; Calkins et al., 2008). Thus, the RSA suppression measure does seem to be an indicator of both the degree of challenge the task imposes on the child's regulatory ability and the extent to which the child can generate a coping response independently versus with environmental support. However, an important issue not addressed by this kind of analysis is whether caregivers contribute to the development of physiological regulation and how that regulation might influence subsequent dyadic interactions.

Much recent conceptual work and empirical research supports the view that caregiver behavior affects the development of behavioral self-regulation skills (Calkins, 2004; Crockenberg & Leerkes, 2004) as well as the functioning of numerous biological regulatory and stress systems (Calkins & Hill, 2007; Gunnar, 2006; Propper & Moore, 2006). Importantly, evidence from animal models suggests that caregiving affects infants' biological and behavioral systems of regulation through the environment the caregiver provides rather than through shared inherited traits. For example, Meeney and colleagues have shown that high levels of maternal licking/grooming and arched backed nursing in rats affects the neurological systems associated with the stress response, a process that has a long-term influence on stress-related illness, certain cognitive functions, and physiological functions (Caldji et al., 1998; Champagne & Meaney, 2001; Francis, Caldji, Champagne, Plotsky, & Meaney, 1999). Furthermore, cross-fostering studies with rats demonstrate convincingly that these maternal behaviors are transmitted behaviorally through the nursing mother and not through the biological mother, indicating that early caregiving is a crucial factor in early development and may affect the organism's level of emotional reactivity even when they reach adulthood (Calatayud, Coubard, & Belzung, 2004; Champagne & Meaney, 2001).

This psychobiological influence on emotion regulation is important because, as we have shown, children who have characteristically low thresholds for arousal, or who have difficulty managing that physiological arousal, are at a disadvantage because emergent behavioral self-regulation strategies are dependent on the basic control of physiological processes (Porges, 2003). To the extent that caregivers can provide the support for such physiological control early in development, particularly through the use of touch and physical comforting and support, children should be more successful at using attentional and behavioral strategies to control emotion, behavior, and cognitive processes. They should also be better prepared to engage in interactions with caregivers, facilitating the transactional relationship that reinforces sensitive and responsive caregiving. We have explored these issues in several cross-sectional and longitudinal studies. In one of our studies (Moore & Calkins, 2004), we found that infants who displayed a pattern of vagal regulation to challenge engaged in more positive interactions with caregivers. These infants also showed a recovery from disruption in their interactions with the caregiver by displaying less negative affect toward the caregiver after the disruption. These findings confirm our hypothesis that good physiological regulation may facilitate social interactions with others, which, in the case of caregiver–child interactions, may support the ongoing relationship that is needed for children to acquire more sophisticated regulatory skills.

Longitudinal studies that we have conducted have been more informative about the relations over time between caregiving and physiological regulation in infants. In one recent study (Propper et al., 2008), we identified children who might be at genetic risk for problems with regulation because they carried the "risk" allele of the dopamine transmitter gene DRD2. We assessed vagal regulation and caregiver sensitivity across the first year of life. We observed that infants without the risk allele displayed appropriate vagal regulation in a laboratory paradigm that was challenging to the infants, and this pattern held across the first year. Infants with the risk allele, however, displayed a different pattern of results, depending on the level of caregiver sensitivity, as measured by observing contingent responding in typical caregiver–child interactions to which they were exposed. For infants with the risk allele and mothers who were not sensitive, poor physiological regulation was observed across the first year. Infants with the risk allele and mothers who were sensitive displayed poor physiological regulation during assessments at three and six months of age, but by the end of the first year, their pattern of physiological responding to challenge was no different than the infants without the risk allele. This gene by environment interaction demonstrates convincingly that infants and caregivers each bring something to the developmental process of acquiring regulatory skills very early in development.

One final question that we have addressed concerns the effects of caregiving behavior on physiological regulation beyond infancy. The challenge to studying this question, though, is that the relations between physiological and behavioral functioning emerges quite early in development (Moore & Calkins, 2004), so disentangling the direction of effects between caregiver behavior and child biological versus behavioral functioning is difficult. We examined these effects longitudinally from the toddler period, as this is a period of rapid growth in self-regulatory abilities (Kopp, 1982), to the early childhood period, when physiological regulation has been demonstrated to support more sophisticated emotional and cognitive self-regulation skills (Calkins & Keane, 2004). Prior research indicates that there are concurrent relations between externalizing spectrum behavior problems and physiological regulation across childhood (Calkins, 1997; Calkins et al., 2007; El-Sheikh, Harger, & Whitson, 2001) and between maternal positive and negative behavior and vagal regulation (Calkins et al., 1998). In this study, we examined whether the quality of the maternal–child relationship during toddlerhood (indexed by maternal behavior characterized by low hostility, high positive affect and responsiveness, and low stress attributed to the maternal–child relationship) would affect physiological regulation at age five, beyond the effects of prior and current levels of behavioral functioning. We also controlled for earlier physiological regulation to ensure that the effects of the maternal–child relationship on the development of physiological regulation would be above and beyond the effects of prior regulation skills. The findings from this study were clear: across each of the six self-regulation tasks, whether the child was working independently or in collaboration with the caregiver, children who had harmonious relationships with their mothers in toddlerhood showed greater physiological regulation than children with less harmonious relationships, and this effect was over and above the effect of prior level of physiological regulation and prior and current behavioral problems. Earlier caregiving behavior predicted growth in physiological regulation across the toddler to preschool period of development.

An important question unaddressed in this study is whether maternal–child relationship problems during toddlerhood are a function of child or maternal difficulties. That is, it is possible that the relationship effects observed in this study were a function of manifestations of child behavioral difficulties that are observable earlier, in infancy, perhaps, and that affect parents' experiences and behaviors with their offspring. Recent work suggests that toddler behavior that is aversive, problematic, and normative affects caregiver's experience of stress in both the short (Calkins, 2002) and the long term (Williford, Calkins, & Keane, 2007). It is possible that fundamental problems in physiological regulation lead to patterns of unpredictable, unmanageable, and difficult behavior that stresses the emerging parent–child relationship. Under conditions that exacerbate such stress, such as those that accompany social and economic challenge, normative child behavioral difficulties may lead to negative, hostile, and nonsupportive parenting that undermines the acquisition of basic regulatory skills of the sort that are integral to adaptive functioning during early childhood and that may contribute to the successful transition to school and later school functioning.

PHYSIOLOGICAL AND EMOTIONAL REGULATION AND SCHOOL SUCCESS

There is a sizable body of research showing that physiological and emotional regulation is increasingly considered as an important component of school success (Urasache et al., 2012), broadly defined as social functioning and academic achievement. From a developmental perspective, the practice of early emerging emotion skills leads to greater automaticity and flexibility so that by the time the child is ready to enter the arena of formal schooling, greater effort may be directed toward more demanding academic and social challenges. Indeed, children's ability to regulate emotions with ease provides the opportunity to allocate more energy to immediate social and academic goals (Schutz, Hong, Cross, & Osbon, 2006). Importantly, these expanding interactional contexts will place demands that call on the child to integrate both emotional and cognitive skills in the service of achieving diverse academic and social goals.

Research examining biological reactivity and regulation has found that these processes are linked to skills necessary for school success. For example, researchers using a different measure of biological reactivity (salivary cortisol) found that preschoolers who evidenced moderate arousal displayed greater executive functioning (cognitive self-regulation) and were reported by their teachers to have better attentional and behavioral control within the classroom (Blair, Granger, & Razza, 2005). Also, recent research from our longitudinal study indicated that kindergarten children who had better vagal regulation tended to display more adaptive social skills as reported by their teachers and their classmates (Graziano, Keane, & Calkins, 2007). These results support the notion that regulation at the biological level facilitates one's ability to engage and disengage with the environment (Porges, Doussard-Roosevelt, Portales, Greenspan, 1996), whether that environment consists of social or cognitive challenges, both of which are critical to school success.

Considerable research on the behavioral indicators of emotion regulation also demonstrates that successful regulation of emotion influences children's functioning in both social and nonsocial domains (Blair et al., 2004; Calkins, 1994; Calkins et al., 1998; Cicchetti, Ganiban, & Barnett, 1991; Thompson, 1994). For example, the relations between emotion regulation and academic achievement have been found with children from preschool through high school. Shields and colleagues (Shields et al., 2001) found that preschoolers with good emotion regulation skills at the beginning of the school year were reported by their teachers to have better school functioning (acquired early reading, language, and math skills; adapted to routines; complied with rules) at the end of the year. In our own research, we found that toddler emotion regulation predicted kindergarten academic achievement but was mediated by behavioral self-regulation in the classroom (Howse et al., 2003). In a follow-up of these children, concurrent emotion regulation predicted academic success as measured by teacher reports of appropriate classroom behavior (Graziano et al., 2007b). Trentacosta and Izard (2007) found that, after controlling for verbal ability, children who were reported by their teachers to be able to successfully regulate their emotions in kindergarten better attended to academic tasks and subsequently had higher academic achievement in the first grade. Additionally, they found that emotion knowledge in kindergarten was directly and positively associated with academic skills in the first grade. Later in development, children with strong behavioral and emotional regulation skills when in early elementary school performed at a relatively high level academically when in middle or high school (Valiente et al., 2011). In addition, there is a fairly extensive literature outlining the importance of emotion regulation in reducing test anxiety to improve academic performance with high school and college-age students (Schutz, Davis, & DeCuir-Gunby, 2014).

One hypothesis that we have been exploring (Howse et al., 2003; Leerkes, Paradise, O'Brien, Calkins, & Lange, 2008) is that emotion control processes moderate trajectories of development of the other more sophisticated control processes. Our rationale for this hypothesis is derived from recent work in the area of self-regulation more broadly construed (Baumeister & Vohs, 2004) and from research in the area of attention development (Posner & Rothbart, 2007). First, at both a neural level and a behavioral level, emotion regulation processes recruit and integrate multiple psychological functions (attention, appraisal, affective experience, and motor responding) (Lewis & Steiben, 2004). Thus, it is clear that emotions have the capacity to organize and facilitate, or disorganize and disrupt, other psychological processes (Cole, Martin, & Dennis, 2004; Gray, 2004), both in the moment and at the level of the emergence of these skills over the course of early development (Bell & Wolfe, 2004). Second, emotion control processes appear to emerge earlier in development than do executive function processes (Blair, 2002). Recent work by Blair and Razza (2007) provides support for such a conceptualization of self-regulation and for the importance of self-regulation on children's early academic skills. Specifically, they found that attentional regulation (effortful control) and cognitive regulation (attention shifting and inhibitory control) were moderately correlated with one another. Even so, measures of both in preschool uniquely predicted academic achievement in kindergarten. To the extent that children understand and control emotions successfully, they have a greater opportunity to attend to, assimilate, and process events in the world around them, thus enhancing both social and academic competence. Therefore, from both a behavioral and a neuroscience perspective, there appears to be support for the developmental model we have proposed.

Children's emotion regulation also affects early achievement by facilitating positive interactions with teachers and peers that promote school engagement, school liking, and early learning and achievement (Hamre & Pianta, 2001; Ladd, Birch, & Buhs, 1999). For example, aggressive children who have difficulty regulating their emotions may face academic challenges because they have difficulties creating and maintaining positive relationships with their teachers (Jerome, Hamre, & Pianta, 2009). Further, Eisenberg, Fabes, and colleagues have reported in several studies that individuals who are highly emotional in response to anger-inducing events and low in regulation are likely to be aggressive with peers in the school environment (Eisenberg et al., 1993; Eisenberg, Fabes, Nyman, Bernzweig, & Pineuelas, 1994; Fabes & Eisenberg, 1992). In turn, there is a large body of research supporting the notion that various aspects of social functioning with peers are associated with children and adolescents' academic functioning (for a review, see Wentzel, 2005). Thus, it has been argued that the ability to engage in social interactions is important for children to benefit from classroom instruction and therefore perform at a high level academically (Wentzel, Baker, & Russell, 2009). In support of this position, Valiente and colleagues (2011) provided evidence that social functioning mediated the relation between behavioral and emotional regulation skills in early elementary school and academic achievement in middle or high school (six years after the assessment of emotion regulation). In sum, emotion regulation appears to play a significant role in children's school success, although questions remain about the precise role of emotion regulation in leading to the skills needed for the school environment.

SUMMARY AND IMPLICATIONS FOR EDUCATIONAL PRACTICE

The review of the research in the area of emotion regulation and parenting demonstrates that the development of emotion regulation is critical for positive social functioning and school success, both in the transition to the school environment and beyond. Accordingly, strategies that promote the development of these skills in young children should be incorporated as integral components of the instruction with research showing benefits for students from preschool through high school (Durlak, Weissberg, Dymnicki, Taylor, & Schelinger, 2011). Researchers who study self-regulation have suggested various strategies for teachers to use to facilitate its development, such as increasing children's knowledge of emotions, coaching children on understanding and identifying their own emotions, and teaching children strategies for dealing with negative emotions (Blair et al., 2004; Shields et al., 2001). It has been suggested that universal school-based programs to promote students' social and emotional learning (SEL) are a promising approach to promoting children's school success (Brackett & Rivers, 2014). A recent meta-analysis of SEL programs revealed that SEL participants showed significantly better social and emotional skills, improved teacher–child relationships and academic performance, and lower problem behavior than controls (Durlak et al., 2011). This recommendation coincides with the clear evidence of the impact that primary caregivers have in facilitating children's self-regulation.

In addition to the important role of parents in children's development of emotional regulation, some researchers have posited the importance of teachers' socialization of emotional regulation (Denham, Bassett, & Zinsser, 2012). Because teachers spend a lot of time with children and serve as sources of emotional security for children, they likely socialize emotional regulation in comparable ways to parents. For example, teachers' emotional expression and manner of responding to children's emotional expressions affect children's school success (Sutton & Wheatley, 2003).

In much the same way that caregiver practices can facilitate development in self-regulation in young children, the strategies teachers use in the classroom to encourage self-regulatory skills will be strengthened if provided within the context of a supportive teacher–child relationship (Blair et al., 2004; Meyer, 2014; Sheilds et al., 2001). In the early school years, a particularly effective student–teacher relationship is likely one that facilitates children's self-regulation in much the same way warm and responsive parents support children self-regulation (Pianta & Stuhlman, 2004). Based on attachment theory, some researchers have proposed that children will be better able to focus their energy and attention to learning if they feel emotionally secure and have effective communication with their teachers (Pianta, 1999). Research has shown that the establishment of a warm and close student–teacher relationship at the beginning of preschool is associated with better emotion regulation (Shields et al., 2001) as well as better social competence and less problem behaviors (Mashburn et al., 2008) at the end of year. However, the student–teacher relationship is one that requires the active engagement of both the teacher and the child. Given this, it is easy to understand that teachers are less likely to develop a close, positive, high-quality relationship with students who evidence significant behavior problems or difficulty with emotion regulation within the classroom (Graziano, Reavis, et al., 2007; Ladd et al., 1999). In sum, there is some support to the notion that teachers are important socializers of emotional regulation even though teachers' influence may be more attenuated than that of parents (Denham et al., 2012).

Finally, positive experiences between teachers and parents should begin early, during preschool, whereby early positive experiences may encourage parents to be actively engaged with teachers during later years. Since children will enter school with different caregiving experiences and so will come equipped with different abilities to handle the challenges they are faced with in the classroom, it seems important that teachers consider strategies for helping parents assist their children at home. This is especially important in the primary grades when children receive more homework, which often requires parents' assistance, or when parental assistance may improve children's performance on assignments. Parents can be encouraged to provide emotional support to children, especially when the child is trying to solve a difficult problem and may become frustrated. Encouraging the child for their effort ("You are working so hard on this really difficult problem."), suggesting strategies to manage frustration such as distraction ("You have been working on this for a while, why don't you take a short break or work on a different problem and come back to this in a little while"), and knowing when to offer help ("Wow, you have done a lot of this all by yourself, would you like me to help you on just this part?") are strategies that can be effective in improving parent–child interactions occurring within the context of school work. As has been observed with parents and children in the parenting literature, to the extent that teachers make concerted efforts to form positive, supportive relationships with the students (and their parents) that are evidencing significant self-regulatory failures in their classrooms, children will be more likely to develop appropriate classroom behaviors.

REFERENCES

Baumeister, R. F., & Vohs, K. D. (2004). *Handbook of self-regulation: Research, theory, and applications.* New York, NY: Guilford Press.

Beauregard, M., Levesque, J. P., & Paquette, V. (2004). Neural basis of conscious and voluntary self-regulation of emotion. In M. Beauregard (Ed.), *Consciousness, emotional self-regulation and the brain* (pp. 163–194). Amsterdam, Netherlands: Benjamins.

Bell, M. A., & Calkins, S. D. (2000). Relationships as inputs and outputs of emotion regulation. *Psychological Inquiry, 11,* 160–163.

Bell, M. A., & Wolfe, C. D. (2004). Emotion and cognition: An intricately bound developmental process. *Child Development, 75,* 366–370.

Blair, C. (2002). School readiness: Integrating cognition and emotion in a neurobiological conceptualization of children's functioning at school entry. *American Psychologist, 57,* 111–127.

Blair, K. A., Denham, S. A., Kochanoff, A., & Whipple, B. (2004). Playing it cool: Temperament, emotion regulation, and social behavior in preschoolers. *Journal of School Psychology, 42,* 419–443.

Blair, C., Granger, D., & Razza, R. P. (2005). Cortisol reactivity is positively related to executive function in preschool children attending Head Start. *Child Development, 76,* 554–567.

Blair, C., & Razza, R. P. (2007). Relating effortful control, executive function, and false belief understanding to emerging math and literacy ability in kindergarten. *Child Development, 78,* 647–663.

Blandon, A. Y., Calkins, S. D., & Keane, S. P. (2010). Predicting emotional and social competence during early childhood from toddler risk and maternal behavior. *Development and Psychopathology, 22,* 119–132.

Bowlby, J. (1969/1982). *Attachment and loss: Vol. 1. Attachment.* New York, NY: Basic Books.

Bowlby, J. (1988). *A secure base.* New York, NY: Basic Books.

Brackett, M. A., & Rivers, S. E. (2014). Transforming students' lives with social and emotional learning. In R. Pekrun & L. Linnenbrink-Garcia (Eds.), *International handbook of emotions in education* (pp. 368–388). New York, NY: Taylor & Francis.

Bronstein, P., Ginsburg, G. S., & Herrera, I. S. (2005). Parental predictors of motivational orientation in early adolescence: A longitudinal study. *Journal of Youth and Adolescence, 34,* 559–575.

Buss, K. A., & Goldsmith, H. H. (1998). Fear and anger regulation in infancy: Effects on the temporal dynamics of affective expression. *Child Development, 69,* 359–374.

Calatayud, F., Coubard, S., & Belzung, C. (2004). Emotional reactivity may not be inherited but influenced by parents. *Physiological Behavior, 80,* 465–474.

Caldji, C., Tannenbaum, B., Sharma, S., Francis, D., Plotsky, P. M., & Meaney, M. J. (1998). Maternal care during infancy regulates the development of neural systems mediating the expression of fearfulness in the rat. *Neurobiology, 9,* 5335–5340.

Calkins, S. D. (1994). Origins and outcomes of individual differences in emotional regulation. *Monographs of the Society for Research in Child Development, 59*(2), 53–72.

Calkins, S. D. (1997). Cardiac vagal tone indices of temperamental reactivity and behavioral regulation in young children. *Developmental Psychobiology, 31,* 125–135.

Calkins, S. D. (2002). Does aversive behavior during toddlerhood matter? The effects of difficult temperament on maternal perceptions and behavior. *Infant Mental Health Journal, 23,* 381–402.

Calkins, S. D. (2004). Early attachment processes and the development of emotional self-regulation. In R. Baumeister & K. Vohs (Eds.), *Handbook of self-regulation: Research, theory, and applications* (pp. 324–339). New York, NY: The Guilford Press.

Calkins, S. D. (2009). Regulatory competence and early disruptive behavior problems: The role of physiological regulation. In S. Olson & A. Sameroff (Eds.), *Biopsychosocial regulatory processes in the development of childhood behavioral problems.* New York, NY: Cambridge University Press.

Calkins, S. D. (2010). Conceptual and methodological challenges to the study of emotion regulation and psychopathology. *Journal of Psychopathology and Behavioral Assessment, 32,* 92–95.

Calkins, S. D., & Dedmon, S. A. (2000). Physiological and behavioral regulation in two-year-old children with aggressive/destructive behavior problems. *Journal of Abnormal Child Psychology, 28,* 103–118.

Calkins, S. D., Graziano, P. A., Berdan, L., Keane, S. P., & Degnan, K. (2008). Predicting cardiac vagal regulation in early childhood from maternal-child relationship quality during toddlerhood. *Developmental Psychobiology, 50,* 751–766.

Calkins, S. D., Graziano, P. A., & Keane, S. P. (2007). Cardiac vagal regulation differentiates among children at risk for behavior problems. *Biological Psychology, 74,* 144–153.

Calkins, S. D., & Hill, A. L. (2007). Caregiver influences on emerging emotion regulation: Biological and environmental transactions in early development. In J. Gross (Ed.), *Handbook of emotion regulation* (pp. 229–248). New York, NY: The Guilford Press.

Calkins, S. D., & Keane, S. P. (2004). Cardiac vagal regulation across the preschool period: Stability, continuity, and implications for childhood adjustment. *Developmental Psychobiology, 45,* 101–112.

Calkins, S. D., Smith, C. L., Gill, K. L., & Johnson, M. C. (1998). Maternal interactive style across contexts: Relations to emotional, behavioral, and physiological regulation during toddlerhood. *Social Development, 7,* 350–369.

Cassidy, J. (1994). Emotion regulation: Influences of attachment relationships. *Monographs of the Society for Research in Child Development, 59*(2-3), 228–283.

Chambers, A., & Allen, J. (2007). Cardiac vagal control, emotion, psychopathology, and health. *Biological Psychology, 74,* 113–115.

Champagne, F., & Meaney, M.J. (2001). Like mother, like daughter: Evidence for non-genetic transmission of parental behavior and stress responsivity. *Progressive Brain Research, 133,* 287–302.

Cicchetti, D., Ganiban, J., & Barnett, D. (1991). Contributions from the study of high-risk populations to understanding the development of emotion regulation. In J. Garber & K. Dodge (Eds.), *The development of emotion regulation and dysregulation* (pp. 15–48). New York, NY: Cambridge University Press.

Cole, P., Martin, S., & Dennis, T. (2004). Emotion regulation as a scientific construct: Methodological challenges and directions for child development research. *Child Development, 75,* 317–333.

Crockenberg, S., & Leerkes, E. (2004). Infant and maternal behaviors regulate infant reactivity to novelty at 6 months. *Developmental Psychology, 40,* 1123–1132.

Crockenberg, S., & Leerkes, E. (2006). Infant and maternal behavior moderate reactivity to novelty to predict anxious behavior at 2.5 years. *Development and Psychopathology, 18,* 17–34.

Crockenberg, S., Leerkes, E., & Barrig Jó, P. (2008). Predicting aggressive behavior in the third year from infant reactivity and regulation as moderated by maternal behavior. *Development and Psychopathology, 20,* 37–54.

Denham, S. A., Bassett, H. H., & Zinsser, K. (2012). Early childhood teachers as socializers of young children's emotional competence. *Early Childhood Education, 40,* 137–143.

Diener, M., Mangelsdorf, S., McHale, J., & Frosch, C. (2002). Infants' behavioral strategies for emotion regulation with fathers and mothers: Associations with emotional expressions and attachment quality. *Infancy, 3,* 153–174.

Durlak, J. A., Weissberg, R. P., Dymnicki, A. B., Taylor, R. D., & Schelinger, K. B. (2011). The impact of enhancing students' social and emotional learning: A meta-analysis of school-based universal interventions. *Child Development, 82,* 405–432.

Eisenberg, N., Cumberland, A., & Spinrad, T. L. (1998). Parental socialization of emotion. *Psychological Inquiry, 9,* 241–273.

Eisenberg, N., Fabes, R. A., Bernzweig, J., Karbon, M., Poulin, R., & Hanish, L. (1993). The relations of emotionality and regulation to preschoolers' social skills and sociometric status. *Child Development, 64,* 1418–1438.

Eisenberg, N., Fabes, R. A., & Murphy, B. C. (1996). Parents' reactions to children's negative emotions: Relations to children's social competence and comforting behavior. *Child Development, 67,* 2227–2247.

Eisenberg, N., Fabes, R. A., Nyman, M., Bernzweig, J., & Pinuelas, A. (1994). The relations of emotionality and regulation to children's anger-related reactions. *Child Development, 65,* 109–128.

Eisenberg, N., Hofer, C., & Vaughan, J. (2007). Effortful control and its socioemotional consequences. In J. J. Gross (Ed.), *Handbook of emotion regulation* (pp. 287–306). New York, NY: Guilford Press.

El-Sheikh, M., Harger, J., & Whitson, S. M. (2001). Exposure to interparental conflict and children's adjustment and physical health: The moderating role of vagal tone. *Child Development, 72,* 1617–1636.

El-Sheik, M., Harger, J., & Whitson, S. M. (2006). Longitudinal relations between marital conflict and child adjustment: Vagal regulation as a protective factor. *Journal of Family Psychology, 20,* 30–39.

Fabes, R. A., & Eisenberg, N. (1992). Young children's coping with interpersonal anger. *Child Development, 63,* 116–128.

Feldman, R., Weller, A., Sirota, L., & Eidelman, A. (2002). Skin-to-skin contact (kangaroo care) promotes self-regulation in premature infants: Sleep-wake cyclicity, arousal modulation, and sustained exploration. *Developmental Psychology, 38,* 194–207.

Field, T. (1994). The effects of mother's physical and emotional unavailability on emotion regulation. *Monographs of the Society for Research in Child Development, 59*(2-3), 208–227.

Fox, N. A., & Calkins, S. D. (2003).The development of self-control of emotion: Intrinsic and extrinsic influences. *Motivation and Emotion, 27,* 7–26.

Fox, N. A., & Hane, J. (2008). Psychophysiological measures in the study of attachment. In J. Cassidy & P. Shaver (Eds.), *The handbook of attachment* (pp. 217–240). New York, NY: Guilford Press.

Francis, D. D., Caldji, C., Champagne, F., Plotsky, P. M., & Meaney, M. J. (1999). The role of cortcotropin-releasing factor-norepinephrine systems in mediating the effects of early experience on the development of behavioral and endocrine responses to stress. *Biological Psychiatry, 46,* 1153–1166.

Gilliom, M., & Shaw, D. S. (2004). Codevelopment of externalizing and internalizing problems in early childhood. *Development and Psychopathology, 16,* 313–333.

Gilliom, M., Shaw, D. S., Beck, J., Schonberg, M., & Lukon, J. (2002). Anger regulation in disadvantaged preschool boys: Strategies, antecedents, and the development of self-control. *Developmental Psychology, 38,* 222–235.

Gottman, J. (2001). Meta-emotion, children's emotional intelligence, and buffering children from marital conflict. In C. D. Ryff & B. H. Singer (Eds.), *Emotion, social relationships, and health, Series in affective science* (pp. 23–40). New York, NY: Oxford University Press.

Gray, J. R. (2004). Integration of emotion and cognitive control. *Current Directions in Psychological Science, 13,* 46–48.

Graziano, P., Keane, S. P., & Calkins, S. D. (2007). Cardiac vagal regulation and early peer status. *Child Development, 78,* 264–278.

Graziano, P., Reavis, R., Keane, S. P., & Calkins, S. D. (2007). The role of emotion regulation in children's early academic success. *Journal of School Psychology, 45,* 3–19.

Grolnick, W., Cosgrove, T., & Bridges, L. (1996). Age-graded change in the initiation of positive affect. *Infant Behavior and Development, 19,* 153–157.

Grolnick, W., Kurowski, C. O., Dunlap, K. G., & Hevey, C. (2000). Parental resources and the transition to junior high. *Journal of Research on Adolescence, 10,* 465–488.

Gross, J. J., & Thompson, R. A. (2007). Emotion regulation: Conceptual foundations. In J. J. Gross (Ed.), *Handbook of emotion regulation* (pp. 3–24). New York, NY: Guilford Press.

Gunnar, M. R. (2006). Social regulation of stress in early child development. In K. McCartney & D. Phillips (Eds.), *Blackwell handbook of early childhood development* (pp. 106–125). Malden, NJ: Blackwell Publishing.

Hamre, B. K., & Pianta, R. C. (2001). Early teacher-child relationships and the trajectory of children's school outcomes through eighth grade. *Child Development, 72,* 625–638.

Hofer, M. A. (1994). Hidden regulators in attachment, separation, and loss. *Monographs of the Society for Research in Child Development, 59*(2-3), 192–207.

Howse, R. B., Calkins, S. D., Anastopoulos, A. D., Keane, S. P., & Shelton, T. L. (2003). Regulatory contributors to children's kindergarten achievement. *Early Education and Development, 14,* 101–119.

Jacobs, S. E., & Gross, J. J. (2014). Emotion regulation in education: Conceptual foundations, current applications, and future directions. In R. Pekrun & L. Linnenbrink-Garcia (Eds.), *International handbook of emotions in education* (pp. 183–201). New York, NY: Taylor & Francis.

Jahromi, L., Putnam, S., & Stifter, C. A. (2004). Maternal regulation of infant reactivity from 2 to 6 months. *Developmental Psychology, 40,* 477–487.

Jerome, E. M., Hamre, B. K., & Pianta, R. C. (2009). Early childhood predictors of teacher-perceived conflict and closeness. *Social Development, 18,* 915–945.

Keenan, K. & Shaw, D. S. (2003). Start at the beginning: Exploring the etiology of antisocial behavior in the first years of life. In B. B. Lahey, T. E. Moffitt, & A. Caspi (Eds.), *Causes of conduct disorder and juvenile delinquency* (pp. 153–181). New York, NY: Guilford Press.

Kopp, C. (1982). Antecedents of self-regulation: A developmental perspective. *Developmental Psychology, 18,* 199–214.

Kopp, C. (1989). Regulation of distress and negative emotions: A developmental view. *Developmental Psychology, 25,* 343–354.

Ladd, G. W., Birch, S. H., & Buhs, E. S. (1999). Children's social and scholastic lives in kindergarten: Related spheres of influence? *Child Development, 70,* 1373–1400.

Leerkes, E. M., Blankson, A., & O'Brien, M. (2009). Differential effects of maternal sensitivity to infant distress and nondistress on social-emotional functioning. *Child Development, 80,* 762–775.

Leerkes, E. M., Paradise, M., O'Brien, M., Calkins, S. D., & Lange, G. (2008). Emotion and cognition processes in preschool children. *Merrill-Palmer Quarterly, 54,* 102–124.

Lewis, M. D., & Stieben, J. (2004). Emotion regulation in the brain: Conceptual issues and directions for developmental research. *Child Development, 75,* 371–376.

Mashburn, A. J., Pianta, R. C., Hamre, B. K., Downer, J. T., Barbarin, O. A., Bryant, D., . . . Howes, C. (2008). Measures of classroom quality in prekindergarten and children's development of academic, language, and social skills. *Child Development, 79,* 732–749.

McElwain, N., & Booth-LaForce, C. (2006). Maternal sensitivity to infant distress and nondistress as predictors of infant-mother attachment security. *Journal of Family Psychology, 20,* 247–255.

Meyer, D. K. (2014). Situating emotions in classroom practices. In R. Pekrun & L. Linnenbrink-Garcia (Eds.), *International handbook of emotions in education* (pp. 458–472). New York, NY: Taylor & Francis.

Moffitt, T. E. (1993). Adolescence-limited and life-course-persistent antisocial behavior: A developmental taxonomy. *Psychological Review, 100,* 674–701.

Moilanen, K. L. (2007). The Adolescent Self-Regulatory Inventory: The development and validation of a questionnaire of short-term and long-term self-regulation. *Journal of Youth and Adolescence, 36,* 835–848.

Moore, G. A., & Calkins, S. D. (2004). Infants' vagal regulation in the still-face paradigm is related to dyadic coordination of mother-infant interaction. *Developmental Psychology, 40,* 1068–1080.

Morris, A., Silk, J., Steinberg, L., Myers, S., & Robinson, L. (2007). The role of the family context in the development of emotion regulation. *Social Development, 16,* 361–388.

Neitzel, C., & Stright, A. D. (2003). Mothers' scaffolding of children's problem solving: Establishing a foundation of academic self-regulatory competence. *Journal of Family Psychology, 17,* 147–159.

NICHD Early Child Care Research Network (2004). Affect dysregulation in the mother-child relationship in the toddler years: Antecedents and consequences. *Development and Psychopathology, 16,* 43–68.

Olweus, D. (1979). Stability of aggressive reactive patterns in males: A Review. *Psychological Bulletin, 86,* 852–875.

Pianta, R. C. (1999). *Enhancing relationships between children and teachers.* Washington, DC: American Psychological Association.

Pianta, R. C., & Stuhlman, M. (2004). Teacher-child relationships and children's success in the first years of school. *School Psychology Review, 33,* 444–458.

Polan, H. J., & Hofer, M. A. (1999). Psychobiological origins of infants attachment and separation responses. In J. Cassidy & P. Shaver (Eds.), *Handbook of attachment: Theory, research, and clinical applications* (pp. 162–180). New York, NY: Guilford Press.

Porges, S. W. (1985). Illinois classroom assessment profile: Development of the instrument. *Multivariate Behavioral Research, 20,* 141–159.

Porges, S. W. (1991). Vagal tone: An autonomic mediatory of affect. In J. A. Garber & K. A. Dodge (Eds.), *The development of affect regulation and dsyregulation* (pp. 11–128). New York, NY: Cambridge University Press.

Porges, S. W. (1996). Physiological regulation in high-risk infants: A model for assessment and potential intervention. *Development and Psychopathology, 8,* 43–58.

Porges, S. W. (2003). The polyvagal theory: Phylogenetic contributions to social behavior. *Physiology and Behavior, 79,* 503–513.

Porges, S. W. (2007). The polyvagal perspective. *Biological Psychology, 74,* 116–143.

Porges, S. W., & Byrne, E. A. (1992). Research methods for measurement of heart rate and respiration. *Biological Psychology, 34,* 93–130.

Porges, S. W., Doussard-Roosevelt, J. A., Portales, A. L., & Greenspan, S. I. (1996). Infant regulation of the vagal "brake" predicts child behavior problems: A psychobiological model of social behavior. *Developmental Psychobiology, 29,* 697–712.

Posner, M. I., & Rothbart, M. K. (2007). *Educating the human brain*. Washington, DC: American Psychological Association.

Propper, C., & Moore, G. (2006). The influence of parenting on infant emotionality: A multi-level psychobiological perspective. *Developmental Review, 26*, 427–460.

Propper, C., Moore, G., Mills-Koonce, W., Halpern, C., Hill-Soderlund, A., Calkins, S. D., . . . Cox, M. (2008). Gene-environment contributions to the development of infant vagal reactivity: The interaction of dopamine and maternal sensitivity. *Child Development, 79*, 1377–1394.

Rodriguez, M., Ayduk, O., Aber, J., Mischel, W., Sethi, A., & Shoda, Y. (2005). A contextual approach to the development of self-regulatory competencies: The role of maternal unresponsivity and toddlers' negative affect in stressful situations. *Social Development, 14*, 136–157.

Saarni, C., Mumme, D. L., & Campos, J. J. (1998). Emotional development: Action, communication, and understanding. In W. Damon & N. Eisenberg (Eds.), *Handbook of child psychology: Social, emotional, and personality development* (5th ed., Vol. 3, pp. 237–309). Hoboken, NJ: John Wiley & Sons.

Schieche, M., & Spangler, G. (2005). Individual differences in biobehavioral organization during problem-solving in toddlers: The influence of maternal behavior, infant-mother attachment, and behavioral inhibition on the attachment-exploration balance. *Developmental Psychobiology, 46*, 293–306.

Schutz, P. A., Davis, H. A., & DeCuir-Gunby, J. T. (2014). Regulating emotions related to testing. In R. Pekrun & L. Linnenbrink-Garcia (Eds.), *International handbook of emotions in education* (pp. 348–367). New York, NY: Taylor & Francis.

Schutz, P. A., Hong, J. Y., Cross, D. I., & Osbon, J. (2006). Reflections on investigating emotions among educational contexts. *Educational Psychology Review, 18*, 343–360.

Shields, A., Dickstein, S. Seifer, R., Giusti, L., Magee, K. D., & Spritz, B. (2001). Emotional competence and early school adjustment: A study of preschoolers at risk. *Early Education and Development, 12*, 73–96.

Shipman, K., Schneider, R., & Brown, A. (2004). Emotion dysregulation and psychopathology. In M. Beauregard (Ed.), *Consciousness, emotional self-regulation, and the brain* (pp. 61–85). Amsterdam, Netherlands: John Benjamins Publishing Company.

Smith, C. L., Calkins, S. D., & Keane, S. P. (2006). The relation of maternal behaviour and attachment security to toddlers' emotions and emotion regulation. *Research in Human Development, 3*, 21–31.

Sroufe, A. L. (1996). *Emotional development: The organization of emotional life in the early years*. New York, NY: Cambridge University Press.

Steinberg, L. (2005). Cognitive and affective development in adolescence. *Trends in Cognitive Sciences, 9*, 69–74.

Steinberg, L. Lamborn, L., Dornbusch, S. D., & Darling, N. (1992), Authoritative parenting, school involvement, and encouragement to succeed. *Child Development, 63*, 1266–1281.

Stifter, C. A., Spinrad, T., & Braungart-Rieker, J. (1999). Toward a developmental model of child compliance: The role of emotion regulation. *Child Development, 70*, 21–32.

Sutton, R. E., & Wheatley, K. F. (2003). Teachers' emotions and teaching: A review of the literature and directions for future research. *Educational Psychology Review, 15*, 327–358.

Thompson, R. A. (1994). Emotion regulation: A theme in search of definition. *Monographs of the Society for Research in Child Development, 59*(2), 25–52.

Thompson, R. A., & Meyer, S. (2007). The socialization of emotion regulation in the family. In J. J. Gross (Ed.), *Handbook of emotion regulation* (pp. 249–268). New York, NY: Guilford.

Trentacosta, C. J., & Izard, C. E. (2007). Kindergarten children's emotion competence as a predictor of their academic competence in first grade. *Emotion, 7*, 77–88.

Urasache, A., Blair, C., & Raver C. (2012). The promotion of self-regulation as a means of enhancing school readiness and early achievement in children at risk for school failure. *Child Development Perspectives, 6*, 122–128.

Valiente, C., Eisenberg, N., Haugen, R., Spinrad, T. L., Hofer, C., Liew, J., & Kupfer, A. (2011). Children's effortful control and academic achievement: Mediation through social functioning. *Early Education and Development, 22*, 411–433.

Wentzel, K. R. (2005). Peer relationships, motivation, and academic performance at school. In A. Elliot & C. Dweck (Eds.), *Handbook of competence and motivation* (pp. 279–296). New York, NY: Guilford Press.

Wentzel, K. R., Baker, S., & Russell, S. (2009). Peer relationships and positive adjustment at school. In R. Gilman, E. Huebner, & M. J. Furlong (Eds.), *Handbook of positive psychology in schools* (pp. 229–243). New York, NY: Routledge/Taylor & Francis Group.

Williford, A. P., Calkins, S. D., & Keane, S. P. (2007). Predicting change in parenting stress across early childhood: Child and maternal factors. *Journal of Abnormal Child Psychology, 35,* 251–263.

Wilson, B. J., & Gottman, J. M. (1996). Attention—the shuttle between emotion and cognition: Risk, resiliency, and physiological bases. In M. E. Hetherington & E. A. Blechman (Eds.), *Stress, coping, and resiliency in children and families* (pp. 189–228). Hillsdale, NJ: Lawrence Erlbaum.

Yap, M. H., Allen, N. B., & Ladouceur, C. D. (2008). Maternal socialization of positive affect: The impact of invalidation on adolescent emotion regulation and depressive symptomatology. *Child Development, 79,* 1415–1431.

Ziv, Y., Oppenheim, D., & Sagi-Schwartz, A. (2004). Social information processing in middle childhood: Relations to infant-mother attachment. *Attachment & Human Development, 6,* 327–348.

27

THE INFLUENCE OF CULTURE ON EMOTIONS

Implications for Education

Jessica T. DeCuir-Gunby and Meca R. Williams-Johnson,
North Carolina State University and Georgia Southern University

Many countries are becoming more racially and ethnically diverse. Specifically, in the United States, people of color make up nearly 35% of the population and are expected to represent nearly 50% of the population by 2050 (Fry, 2006). Subsequently, schools around the world, including in the United States, are becoming more racially and ethnically diverse. As such, the increasing global racial and ethnic diversification has caused research in the area of culture, including race and ethnicity to further expand in education (see Burlew & Smith, 1991). In doing so, researchers are beginning to examine the relationships between culture-related constructs, such as racial/ethnic identity, and a variety of educational constructs, such as emotions. It has been demonstrated that racial/ethnic issues are often related to emotionality. Specifically, issues surrounding race and ethnic differences often heighten the expressing and experiencing of emotions in schools (see DeCuir-Gunby & Williams-Johnson, 2007). Toward that end, the purpose of this chapter is to discuss the influence of culture on emotions in education with emphasis on race and ethnicity. In order to do so, we begin by discussing the concept of culture, including the differentiation between race and ethnicity as well as the dimensions of culture. Next, we examine the relationship between culture and emotions in education, focusing on the experiencing and the expressing of emotions. Last, we end the chapter by arguing for the inclusion of culturally relevant frameworks to explore emotions as well as provide implications for future research. It is important to note that while cultural and emotional interactions in schools are a global phenomena, the majority of examples presented in this chapter represent research conducted in the US context.

CULTURAL INFLUENCES ON EMOTIONS: RACE, ETHNICITY, AND IDENTITY

The construct of culture has been defined in numerous ways because it encompasses a variety of aspects (Triandis, 1996). Perhaps the most common view of culture is that it involves "shared elements" that are transferred across generations and provide "standards for perceiving, believing, evaluating, communicating, and acting among those who share a language, a historic period, and a geographic location" (Triandis, 1996, p. 408). Culture impacts the way we perceive ourselves and the manner in which we interact with others, including the perceptions of emotions. In addition, culture is dynamic in that it is learned and can change over time. The term culture can be applied to any human category, but it most often refers to societies in terms of nations, regions, religion, and racial and ethnic groups (Hofstede, 2001). As such, in examining culture, it is essential to explore the issues of race and ethnicity.

Understanding Race and Ethnicity

Although race and ethnicity are similar constructs, it is necessary to address the differences between them. This issue is particularly important to the study of racial and ethnic influences on emotions. The concept of race is a socially and historically constructed ideological system (Roediger, 1991). Specifically, race is "a concept which signifies and symbolizes social conflicts and interest by referring to different types of human bodies" (Omi & Winant, 1994, p. 55). It is largely a political characterization that is based upon classifying individuals into subgroups based upon phenotypical characteristics, such as skin color, hair texture, and nose width. Ethnicity, however, is a complex phenomenon that can be described as the characteristics shared by a particular group of people including a common name, a common ancestry (a sense of fictive kinship), a shared history, a common culture (religion, language, etc.), a link to a homeland (a physical occupation or an ancestral connection), and a sense of solidarity (Hutchinson & Smith, 1996). Some scholars argue that race and ethnicity are indeed different constructs (e.g., Helms, 1990; Helms & Talleyrand, 1997), while scholars like Phinney (1996) view that ethnicity encompasses race. We would argue there is not much distinction between the definitions of the two constructs in that the definitions are very similar. However, the words *racial* and *ethnic* carry very different political, social, and cultural connotations, as well as help to elicit different emotions. The word race usually implies physical attributes, such as skin color, and sociohistorical issues, such as oppression. Ethnic, on the other hand, generally refers to cultural elements. Because of these connotations, there are some distinctions in the usage of the constructs. For instance, within the United States, African Americans do not have a direct connection to a homeland and the homeland's cultural heritage, key aspects of ethnicity. This is a result of being stripped of cultural heritage during slavery. Because of a lack of a unified cultural heritage, African Americans are generally defined by race. In other words, African Americans' shared identity is a function of their race. Thus, we argue that racial is a more appropriate term than ethnic when discussing African Americans. However, when discussing other groups, ethnic may be appropriate. For example, the people of Cyprus are largely of Turkish or Greek descent. Although most Cypriots are racially White, they are different ethnically because of their heritage from either Turkey or Greece. As such, because of the various similarities and nuances surrounding the terms racial and ethnic, for this chapter, when discussing the research literature, we will use the terms in context, applying the constructs in the manner in which they were originally used by the authors. This distinction is necessary for better understanding how various racial and ethnic groups, within the global context, differ in the experiencing and the expressing of emotions.

Race, Ethnicity, and Dimensions of Culture

In examining the self, cultural researchers often explore a variety of concepts. Particularly, the examination of racial and ethnic identity is essential to understanding individuals' perceptions of the self. It is important to explore how those constructs help to inform individuals' overall identity or construction of the self. Identity formation is a multifaceted process that is influenced by culture (including race and ethnicity) and involves negotiating who you are through the questioning and exploration of one's present, past, and future (Melucci, 1996). There are various approaches to the examination of cultural identity, including the conceptualization of the self (independence and interdependence) and aspects of individualism and collectivism that impact the experiencing and expressing of emotions.

Independent and Interdependent Construals of the Self

The development of the self is viewed as a universal process that involves differentiating one's being from those of others (Markus & Kitayama, 1991). Every culture has some norms for how the self is developed and maintained. However, the exact foci and processes that are used varies by culture simply because culture impacts how the self and identity are conceptualized. The key issue that impacts the nature of the development of the self is the relationship between the self and others. It is within these relationships that emotions are experienced and expressed. As such, the self is often developed in terms of independent and interdependent construals.

Independent construals of the self focus on one's self and sense of autonomy and independence. It involves focusing on one's unique contributions to one's cultural group. This is not to say that interacting with the social environment is not important. It is that individual expression is more valued. This perspective is mostly adopted by Western societies that are more individualistic. For example, the United States takes pride in its rugged individualism. Self-reliance is encouraged and preferred to dependency on others or the government.

Interdependent construals of the self emphasize connectivity with others. This perspective suggests that a person constructs the self in terms of his/her relationship with the context or "self-in-relation-to-other" (Markus & Kitayama, 1991). Understanding who you are is dependent upon your relationships with others. Thus, the context plays an important role in the development of the self. This perspective is often taken by many non-Western societies that are more collectivistic. For example, many Asian countries, such as China, view achievement and success in terms of the family rather than just the individual. This distinction is important in terms of schooling in that Asian students can be impacted by their own emotions as well as the emotions of family members. This could create complex situations for both students and teachers.

Individualism and Collectivism

There is great diversity both within and between cultural groups on the development of the self. Members of particular cultural groups try to adhere to their groups' specific norms. However, cultural groups often differ on what values are emphasized because of their distinct beliefs and practices. The individualist-collectivist constructs are a useful way to examine overall cultural differences and approaches to the development of the self (Oyserman, Coon, & Kemmelmeier, 2002).

Many cultures adhere to more individualistic practices. Individualism encourages autonomy and independence from an in-group. In individualistic cultures, personal goals are more influential than the norms of the in-group (Triandis, 2001). Although this is the case, it cannot be assumed that people from individualistic cultures are always focused on themselves. Many individualist cultures do engage in activities that are more group-focused. However, emphasis is placed on the needs of the individual. Many Western cultures are considered individualistic, including the United States.

Other cultures are influenced by more collectivist practices. Collectivism implies an interdependence with an in-group (e.g., family, racial/ethnic group, etc). In collectivist cultures, behavior is largely shaped by the norms of the in-group (Triandis, 2001). Collectivists are largely concerned with the maintenance of relationships within their cultural group. Just as in individualistic cultures, it cannot be assumed that all collectivist cultures are only group-focused. They do have individualistic practices, although there is an emphasis on the needs of the group. Many Eastern and African cultures are considered collectivistic. However, there is often great variation within countries. For instance, in the United States, although largely an individualistic country, Chinese Americans tend to be collectivistic.

The individualism-collectivism constructs were initially viewed as polar opposites, but research demonstrated that there was overlap between the constructs. Few cultures are completely individualistic or collectivistic, although cultures can be influenced more by one construct than the other. This is largely the case because the individual-collectivist constructs are viewed as multidimensional. Triandis (1995) suggests that there are horizontal-vertical dimensions. The horizontal dimension focuses on issues of equality, and the vertical dimension emphasizes hierarchy. Specifically, Triandis (1995) suggests that there are four types of cultures: Horizontal Individualist (HI), Vertical Individualist (VI), Horizontal Collectivist (VC), and Vertical Collectivist (VC) (Triandis, 2001). Specifically, horizontal individualist cultures focus on autonomy with an independent self that is equal to others. Countries such as Sweden, that emphasize equality in income and services, can be described as horizontal individualistic. On the other hand, vertical individualist cultures emphasize autonomy with an independent self that is different and possibly unequal from others. Such cultures also emphasize status and competition. Examples of vertical individualism include the United States, where competition and differentiation are both encouraged and expected in order to be successful. Horizontal collectivist cultures integrate selves with in-groups, where members are similar to each other. China is a good example of this type of culture because of the equality principal associated with communist practices. Yet, vertical collectivist cultures submit to an in-group or authority and are willing to engage in self-sacrifice for the good of the group. The Japanese are best characterized as vertical collectivists in that they have a strong sense of honor, which allows them to be both serving and sacrificial.

Race, Ethnicity, Culture, and Emotions

As illustrated, these four types of culture proposed by Triandis (1995) are useful in understanding the development of the self; however, they also have a significant impact on a variety of constructs, including emotions, and are thus key for understanding cultural differences in how emotions function in educational settings. According to Haviland, Davidson, Ruesch, Gebelt, and Lancelot (1994), emotions are essential to the self in that "identity issues are associated within a differentiated network of many different emotions" (p. 504). This suggests that identity salience is influenced by the association of particular emotions. In terms of the self, according to Markus and Kitayama (1991), there are two types of emotions that people from both individualist and collectivist cultures often experience: ego-focused and other-focused emotions. Ego-focused emotions are emotions that are based upon individual experiences that are more focused on the self. These emotions are reflections of a person's internal attributes that require management. Examples of ego-focused emotions include pride, frustration, and anger. Such emotions are individually oriented and help to foster autonomy and independence. People within horizontal and vertical individualist cultures largely experience ego-focused emotions. Other-focused emotions, on the other hand, are based upon shared experiences and are more focused on others. People within horizontal and vertical collectivist cultures are more likely to experience other-focused emotions. These emotions often result from being sensitive towards others and taking others' perspectives into account. Examples of other-focused emotions include empathy and shame. These emotions help to foster connectedness and interdependence.

In education, it is important to examine how emotions such as these are experienced as well as expressed in terms of culture. It has been found that there are universal emotions (e.g., sadness, happiness, fear, and anger) that are most likely biologically based; however, the manner in which emotions are expressed and experienced differs across cultures (Elfenbein & Ambady, 2002). There is evidence to suggest that members of a cultural group have more difficulty interpreting the emotions of members outside of their cultural group (Russell, 1994). For example, within the United States, Whites can more easily interpret the emotions of other Whites rather than the emotions of African Americans and Asian Americans (Johnson & Fredrickson, 2005). This difficulty in interpreting the emotions of other racial groups is based upon the internalization of racial stereotypes and prejudices (Zebrowitz, Kikuchi, & Fellous, 2010). Since emotions are often based upon perceptions and values, as previously demonstrated, specific situations can elicit different emotional reactions among various cultural groups. For instance, racial and ethnic minority groups often experience a variety of emotions that are associated with being minority members. These emotions often stem from experiences with discrimination, prejudice, and powerlessness that are often a result of the social, economic, and political subjugation that is commonly practiced throughout many aspects of society, including the educational system (DeCuir-Gunby & Williams-Johnson, 2007). For example, there is a growing literature on racial and ethnic minority group members' experiences of racial microaggressions, which are subtle and denigrating racial/ethnic insults (Sue et al., 2007). Prior research suggests that it is common for US racial/ethnic minority groups to experience racial microaggressions in university settings from peers, faculty, and students (Gomez, Khurshid, Freitag, & Lachuk, 2011; Smith, Allen, & Danley, 2007). Over time, the experiencing of racial microaggressions can lead to race-related stress/

and the expressing of a variety of emotions including anger and sadness; it can also lead to depression (Brondolo, Brady, Pencille, Beatty, & Contrada, 2009). As such, it is necessary to examine the impact of culture, particularly issues regarding race and ethnicity, on both the experiencing and expressing of emotions in educational settings.

THE RELATIONSHIP BETWEEN CULTURE AND EMOTIONS IN EDUCATIONAL SETTINGS

Emotions are viewed as being universal internal processes that can be influenced by biology and culture (Levenson, Soto, & Pole, 2005). Nearly everyone experiences both pleasant and unpleasant emotions. However, the manner in which emotions are experienced and consequently expressed is not necessarily universal. The experiencing and expressing of emotions can be influenced by culture. For instance, it has been found that Western cultures experience and express more positive emotions than Eastern cultures (Tsai, Levenson, & McCoy, 2006). In addition, racial and ethnic groups, particularly those within the United States, experience and express emotions differently as well (Hugenberg & Bodenhausen, 2003, 2004). The differences in experiencing and expressing emotions can often be seen within the school setting.

Experiencing Emotions in Schools

One area in which there is a difference in the experiencing of emotions is in the academic area of schooling, particularly testing. Testing is a central part of schooling that often elicits a variety of emotions, especially unpleasant emotions such as anxiety. Test anxiety refers to the phenomenological, physiological, and behavioral responses that are elicited with the anticipation of not doing well on a test or exam (Zeidner, 1998, 2014). There have been several cross-cultural studies that exam test anxiety in many areas around the world. These studies have explored various areas of culture and have found both similarities and differences in the experiencing of test anxiety.

Specifically, cross-cultural studies have examined the impact of various cultural constructs, such as SES, gender, and parental influences on test anxiety. For instance, Yousefi, Redzuan, Bte, Juhari, and Talib (2010) found that family income significantly affected academic achievement and test anxiety of Iranian students. Students from families with lower incomes reported more test anxiety than families from higher incomes. In addition, it has been found that students in Islamic countries have some of the highest test anxiety, while Western European and Asian countries have the lowest levels (Bodas & Ollendick, 2005). In these same studies, women tend to experience more test anxiety than men. It is postulated that this result exists because it is more accepted for women to discuss emotions. However, Cassady, Mohammed, and Mathieu (2004) found that although women tend to experience more test anxiety, Kuwaiti and US women have distinctions in their experiencing of test anxiety. Kuwaiti women reported higher levels of affective test anxiety (feelings of nervousness), while US women experienced more anxiety regarding the impact of tests (e.g., influence on grades). Last, there has been research on the impact of parents on test anxiety. For example, Chen (2012) found that perceived parental pressure significantly impacts test anxiety in Chinese students. The more Chinese parents are perceived to stress family glory and material success, the more likely students are to experience test anxiety.

Another cultural influence on test anxiety includes the impact of race/ethnicity. The examination of test anxiety in racial and ethnic minority groups is particularly important when considering the potential extra impact of stereotype threat. According to Steele and Aronson (1995), stereotyped groups can experience stereotype threat when they identify with a particular domain and there exists a stereotype regarding their group in that domain. Specifically, when stigmatized groups experience stereotype threat, they have to exert additional resources in order to focus on the task. This pressure can become emotionally taxing because the experiencing of stereotype threat is often accompanied by feelings of perceived racism (Alliman-Brissett & Turner, 2010). As previously discussed, the experiencing of perceived racism can cause race-related stress and the experiencing of negative emotions (Mays, Cochran, & Barnes, 2007). In addition, this pressure can become physically taxing. Schmader, Johns, and Forbes (2008) found that stereotype threat disrupts performance in that the physiological stress caused by stereotype threat impairs cognitive processing, hinders the ability to monitor performance, and reduces ability to suppress negative emotions and thoughts. However, it has been found that appropriate coping strategies, such as the reappraising of the situation, can lessen the impairment, improve test performance, and reduce the experiencing of negative emotions (Johns, Inzlicht, & Schmader, 2008).

Although there has been considerable cultural work on test anxiety, there still exist many problems exploring the construct in various cultural settings. Specifically, there has been little examination on the impact of cultural variables on test anxiety, including understanding how a culture's norms and socialization practices influence test anxiety (Zeidner, 1998, 2014). Most cross-cultural test anxiety research simply examines test anxiety in various contexts without considering cultural context. In addition to the lack of exploration of cultural variables, there are issues surrounding the measurement of test anxiety in cross-cultural work. Specifically, there is a pro-Western bias, problems interpreting cross-cultural differences, and an assumption of cross-cultural equivalence (Bodas & Ollendick, 2005). Most test anxiety research takes a Western approach, including the methodology and assessments. In order to understand another culture's experiences with test anxiety, it is necessary to use methodologies and assessments that are culturally relevant. Also, it is necessary to take cultural values into consideration when comparing groups—otherwise, any interpretations made will be questionable. Last, researchers cannot assume that different cultures view and experience test anxiety in the same manner. Instruments should not be used unless construct validity has been established in that particular context. In short, in order to truly understand test anxiety in various cultures, the many dimensions of culture have to be taken into consideration in all areas of the research process.

Expressing Emotions in Schools

Although it is important to examine how emotions are experienced in schools, it is also necessary to explore how emotions are expressed in schools. One theory that helps explain the differences and similarities for expressing emotion is the theory of universal emotions (Ekman & Friesen, 1971; Ekman & Scherer, 1982). Universal emotions are described in terms of recognizing display of emotion regardless of ethnic, cultural, or racial background of the expresser and interpreter. Physical expressions of emotions, such as happiness, sadness, surprise, fear, disgust, and anger, are shown to have cross-cultural similarities. (Notice the majority of these emotions are negative expressions.) The most compelling aspects in expressing emotions are the nonverbal clues and meanings we interpret from the actions. For example, hand gestures, body movements, a simple touch from speaker to listener, and use of personal space will channel messages and provoke emotion. Two people who share the same cultural background can walk away from a nonverbal interaction with similar interpretations (Ekman & Scherer, 1982). Interpretations of messages are culturally determined and are gained from social interactions and the process of behavioral learning; our cultural perspectives impact the meaning we make from nonverbal expressions (Detweiler, 1975). When two or more people from diverse backgrounds are interacting, nonverbal and verbal expressions can create several opportunities for cross-cultural misunderstandings.

Finding ways to interact with others from a different social and cultural background has gathered considerable attention in the wake of economic globalization in the twenty-first century. Efforts in industry and education explore opportunities in aiding communication between cultures beyond language barriers and seek to understand nonverbal clues as a method to increase communication (Riberio, 2007). For example, Brazilian steel workers at an automobile factory, learning latest technologies from Japanese auto engineers, exchange communication through verbal as well as nonverbal cues to increase communication and social learning opportunities. Similarly, in schools, nonverbal support is encouraged through working with students from various cultural backgrounds. Research conducted by She and Fisher (2000) examine Taiwanese and Australian student perception of teacher communication in science and found that nonverbal cues, such as a smile, simple hand gestures, and demonstrations, positively influenced the social climate and increased teacher ratings.

Student–Teacher Interactions and Emotions

Student–teacher relationships, in particular, are fertile grounds for cross-cultural misunderstandings (Zembylas, 2003). Expressions of emotions between students and teachers can display levels of engagement and attitude. For instance, students may seem disconnected from their teachers because it is difficult to interpret the expression of emotions from their teachers. Delpit (1995) points out that teacher connectedness is critical when communicating with students verbally and nonverbally. Teacher connectedness is exhibited through shared values and level of trust (Klem & Connell, 2004). Verbal and nonverbal expressions of positive emotions, like care and compassion for students, create space for connectedness. While there are emotions illustrated through facial expressions that are globally recognized similarly, the meaning we derive from these emotional responses can vary. For instance, in classrooms, students will make sense of what the instructor is presenting by attaching meaning to what they observe the instructor doing. Thus, the action creates symbolic messages of emotional expressions that assist the hearer in interpreting the intention, intensity, and details of the message (Ekman & Scherer, 1982). To further illustrate, picture a teacher quietly giving feedback to students in a tone that is firm but caring. Some students may respond by reducing eye contact and looking down to the floor and away from the teacher. Students' feelings of shame, embarrassment, or the students' cultural belief to look away from the teacher when receiving feedback will present a physical but nonverbal response to the teacher's feedback. The teacher's intention is simply to share ways students could improve on the activity. The students' response to the feedback is based on the meaning they derive from the exchange both verbally and nonverbally. The message students will interpret considers the intention of the teacher, intensity in which the message was delivered, and details of the wording in the feedback (Elder & Brooks, 2008). Misunderstandings can occur when the components of the nonverbal and verbal cues are determined differently (Zebrowitz et al., 2010).

When teachers build relationships with students, diversity in cultural background is often met with focusing on the challenges, which are often accompanied by unpleasant emotions (Stromquist & Monkman, 2000). Differences in language and cultural rules may pose obstacles to encouraging student interaction. The attitudes of teachers often do not encourage students to participate in a pluralistic schooling environment (Stoddart, 1990). By acknowledging cultural differences instead of pretending these differences do not exist, teachers can become more culturally aware, more attentive of students' culture, and promote understanding of cultural differences (Stromquist & Monkman, 2000). Doing so will also enable both teachers and students to express more pleasant emotions surrounding cultural differences.

Students and Academic Emotions

Although there are a variety of emotions involved in teacher-student relationships, there are also many emotions associated with students and academics. Frenzel, Thrash, Pekrun, and Goetz (2007) found that student achievement emotions, such as enjoyment, hope, pride, relief, anger, anxiety, shame, and boredom, are "linked to their control and value appraisal, motivation, use of learning strategies, self-regulation of learning and academic performance" (p. 46). This suggests that emotions can profoundly impact students' performance and approach to learning in the classroom or in different settings, as is highlighted in several other chapters in this volume. Briefly, emotions are considered to influence individual behavior, interest, and curiosity, contributing to intrinsic motivation. Goal attainment toward positive ends, such as earning good grades, and other forms of extrinsic motivation are influenced by students' academic emotions. Understanding the differences, functions, and origins of student emotions is important to enhancing student engagement, learning, performance, and health. In addition, student achievement is fraught with intense emotions. Emotions such as anger, anxiety, shame, and boredom are common among students given the nature of high-stakes political policies and inattention to student interest (Pekrun, 2006). Conversely, there are also positive student emotions that display enjoyment of learning—for example, hope, pride, joy, and gratitude. All of these emotions are critically important to influencing students' academic performance and development (Pekrun, 2006).

Critical to this chapter, there are also cultural differences that exist in students' display of intense academic emotions. For example, students from collective cultural groups may display a lower frequency of intense emotions and shorter duration of intense emotions pending on the severity of the academic or social problems than students from independent cultural groups. Researchers believe this moderation for expressing intense emotions is regulated out of concern for maintaining group harmony (Bond, 1993). For instance, in North Korean culture, a facial expression such as smiling is generally considered a show of shallowness and insensitivity to others (Dresser, 1996). However, in other cultures, smiling is commonly recognized as a sign of pleasure. The show of this emotion as described by Dresser incorporates an illustration of groups' concerns beyond individually perceived emotions. Group harmony shown through physical commensuration, such as minimal facial expressions, is publically expected more so than personal praise as in smiling.

Students and Race/Ethnicity-Related Emotions

As stated earlier, social situations impact our responses and display of emotions across cultures (Lasky, 2000). Emotions are responses to social realities that may encourage effective goal-orientated action or discourage one from attempting a goal. For example, students who have felt the sting of overt discrimination based on race and express feelings of disgust may mentally withdraw from the schooling process, as suggested by low levels of achievement and high dropout rates (Sanders, 1997). On the other hand, despite the challenges and feelings of disgust, some respond to the obstacles of discrimination as an instigator to propel them toward goal achievement (Perry, Steele, & Hilliard, 2003). Not all races or persons respond to academic discrimination and inequity alike; intense emotion, political climate, social movements, and cultural influences are primary factors in public expression of emotions. The dominant picture of increasing cross-cultural differences and public display of emotions in schools fosters a need for more research on motivation and emotions in the classroom.

Also, discussions of race in schools are frequently filled with feelings, emotions, and affective dispositions. Researchers point out that the racial/ethnic discussions that are presented in the school context often minimize the intensity and display of emotions among the participants engaging in the dialogue (Nayak, 2007). For example, within schools, the celebrating of one group's ethnic heritage may result in some feeling isolated and distant from the group. Students may express frustration of being the focus of ethnic and historical discussion, especially if they are one or few in number within the class. While some schools encourage diversity and inclusion, some students are presented with fear of being considered different and under appreciating their uniqueness. As such, educational researchers that work in the paradigm of emotions and culture should begin with feelings of belonging in order to understand the process of othering. *Othering* refers to making comparisons between the self and something or someone else that exists on the outside (Delpit, 1995; Smith, 1999). As a form of social comparison, othering usually frames a perspective of one's feeling of superiority or inferiority when comparing the self to a larger group (Festinger, 1954; Taylor & Lobel, 1989). Othering can set the stage for an oppressive classification system that separates the "us" and the "them" into the dominant and subordinate groups (Tatum, 1997). Moving beyond the obvious visible differences, such as gender, age, ability or disability, language, and skin color commonly described in social comparisons, "othering" also involves social power dynamics and social relations of domination to form perceived boundaries and differences (Weis, 1995). However, the result of all comparisons, whether social comparison or complex forms of othering, will evoke emotions and impact self-image.

In an effort to challenge social comparison or othering, some teachers attempt to establish a classroom community by forming bonds of belongingness (Goodenow, 1993). To explain feelings of belonging, Sarason (1974) states it is an understanding of inclusion or kinship and a "perception of similarity to others, and acknowledge interdependence with others, a willingness to maintain this interdependence . . . and a feeling that one is part of the larger dependable and stable structure" (p. 157). Specific sites, such as the school, the classroom, the street corner, and the home, may be places of hostility to an outsider or offer specific forms of belongingness (Nayak, 2007). Triumphant emotions are also tied to sense of belonging, as Myers and Diener (1995) and Laar (1999) describe it as a "we" feeling—one of pride in and welcomed space to a group. Studies in education describing sense of belonging have explored emotions such as loneliness, depression, and anxiety while investigating perceptions of social support, motivation, conflict, racial climate, and tolerance (Anderman, 2003; Johnson et al., 2007). Students' sense of belongingness depicts their individual perceptions of acceptance within the school context. Motivation theory maintains that performance and behavior can be improved if students experience belongingness in the larger social context (Voelkl, 1995, 1997).

The dynamics of belongingness, race, ethnicity, and emotions are contextually contingent and embedded in school culture. More specific in classrooms, students report that instructional style, interpersonal interactions, peer relations, and affective regard for trust, respect, and comfort are the building blocks to belongingness (Tinto, 1997). Feelings of belonging fuel the similarities we feel and express. While students attending the same school may be ethnically, racially, and culturally different, feelings of belongingness command more of their attention than the stated differences. High levels of school belonging has shown students' increase in academic effort and attendance across different ethnic groups (Faircloth & Hamm, 2005). Additionally, students who have higher levels of sense of belongingness also have increased levels of school interest, academic competence, expectations of goal achievement, and less anxiety (Osterman, 2000).

EXPANDING CULTURE AND EMOTIONS RESEARCH IN EDUCATION

As demonstrated throughout this chapter, culture is a complicated construct to explore, mainly because it encompasses so many different elements. Race and ethnicity, components of culture, are particularly difficult to explore because of the emotionality that is associated with them. When examining issues involving race and ethnicity, it is often difficult for researchers to separate their own emotions and feelings from those of their participants. In fact, researchers' views and emotions, whether conscious or "dysconscious" (King, 1991), often overshadow the views of their participants. Dysconsciousness, as coined by King, describes the notion of pervading stereotyping and habits of mind, which include perceptions, attitudes, assumptions, and beliefs that personally justify inequity as a way of life. Further, it is a form of racism that openly accepts and validates dominate norms and privileges. To begin to understand how individual people perceive, understand, and experience culture in their contexts, particularly race and ethnicity, we need rigorous in-depth, culturally-based, research methods (Hertz-Lazarowit, Zelniker, & Azaiza, 2010) that open spaces where participants freely express their emotions and explore the complexities of how they navigate within the social world. There has been some work in this area, such as research on the Implicit Association Test (IAT), which has shown to be a useful instrument in capturing racial bias and societal assumptions to access automatic racial attitudes (Richeson & Nussbaum, 2004). However, more methodological approaches are needed. Specifically, racially grounded theoretical frameworks, such as Critical Race Theory and Intersectionality, have the potential to thoroughly and respectfully explore differences in the experiencing and expressing of emotions within the school context.

Critical Race Theory

Critical race theory (CRT) is useful in helping explain the lack of progress of social reform and racial equality (Delgado & Stefancic, 2001). Legal scholars created CRT mainly as a critique of the inadequate treatment of issues of race and racism in the United States' legal system. (Although, CRT has been embraced by researchers in countries across the world, including Canada, Great Britain, and South Africa, among others.) Creating CRT allowed for "attempting to interject minority cultural viewpoints, derived from a common history of oppression, with their efforts to reconstruct a society crumbling under the burden of racial hegemony" (Deyhle, Parker, & Villenas, 1999, p. 15). Specifically, CRT explores the relationship between race, racism, and power through the use of five major tenets: (1) *Permanence of Racism* (Bell, 1992) offers an evaluation of how racist structures are created and maintained within our everyday lives, (2) *Whiteness as Property* (Harris, 1993) examines how the evidence of the advantages to White identity is flagrantly seen in laws and policies that benefit Whites in political and social environments, such as voting, citizenship, and education, (3) *Interest Convergence* (Bell, 1980) explores how African Americans' interest in achieving racial equality has been accommodated only when this goal has converged with the interest of powerful Whites, (4) *Critique of Liberalism* (Gotanda, 1991) identifies the slow progress and innumerable delays in resolving racial inequalities in the quest for racial justice, and (5) *Counterstorytelling* (Delgado, 1989) is a method of giving voice to people of color, enabling them to describe their oppression under America's capitalist democracy. (See DeCuir and Dixson, 2004, for a detailed discussion of the tenets.)

In supporting the interdependent view of the self, CRT identifies how one may view the self in relation to others (Markus & Kitayama, 1994). Thus, it is important to have those who are oppressed, afflicted, and disheartened to speak on their experiences. CRT espouses the voicing of multiple viewpoints as a means of adding value to the political, social, and economic discourse. Thus, a major tenet of CRT is the use of counterstories, stories from the perspective of the minority that challenge the majoritarian perspective and give readers a keen insight into how race, class, and power intersect across disciplines. CRT encourages the use of counterstories or narrative voice as a means of combating the status quo. Watkins (2005) supports the use of these narratives and suggests using them as a tool to understand and eradicate dysconscious racism. These counterstories "provide the necessary context for understanding, feeling and interpreting" (Deyhle et al., 1999, p. 7). In fact, the use of counterstories as a means of expressing perspective gives voice to those who have been relegated to the margins of our society, professions, and classrooms. The counterstories used in CRT research not only describe the lived experience of the participant negotiating through inequitable circumstances, but they also share the intense emotions and feelings like loss, disempowerment, shame, and hopelessness. For example, there has been an influx of West Africans settling in European countries. Instead of focusing on White Europeans' perceptions on African immigration, counterstorytelling would focus on the experiences of the African immigrants.

CRT was initially examined within the context of education by Ladson-Billings and Tate (1995) and sought "to theorize race and use it as an analytic tool for understanding school inequity" (p. 48). These scholars acknowledged that organized schooling is a microcosm of society and is subjected to many of the same issues affecting minorities, particularly those pertaining to race and power issues. These authors marked a new beginning for CRT research and have since challenged many educational theorists to broaden the dialogue within the field of education to include the historical impact that race has on contemporary education (Kozol, 2005; Watkins, 2005), educational practices and how they are impacted by racial constructions (Delpit, 1995; Hooks, 1994; Ladson-Billings, 1994, 2009; Valdes, 1996), the effect race has on teacher expectations and bias (Gay, 2000; Paley, 2000; Tatum, 2007) as well as the investigation of the achievement gap as it relates to racial disparities (Noguera & Wing, 2006).

As an addition, we argue that the work on CRT in education should be expanded to include emotions. CRT is a useful theoretical framework to examine the relationship between culture and emotions because the theory itself is based upon aspects of racial disparities and requires that analyses are grounded in participants' experiences and contexts. Historically, CRT studies in education focus on issues that prevent equity of resources and acceptance of diversity among students and staff in schools. Several empirical studies to date describe varied emotional responses to civil rights debates and speeches in US schools (DeCuir-Gunby & Williams-Johnson, 2007; Fierros, 2006; Rychlak, 1991). Yet, many of the students' emotional experiences during these events remain disconnected to theoretical concepts. As such, CRT analyses would be useful in examining students' emotions in relation to racially/ethnically influenced events that occur at school. For example, the study conducted by DeCuir-Gunby and Williams-Johnson (2007) sought to give voice to African American private school students' emotional experience after participating in a school-wide assembly for Black History Month that featured a prominent civil rights leader. Contention and debate concerning the message from the civil rights leader and the negative response of the majority students ignited confrontational discussions about race. The African American students at the school were visibly disturbed by the negative response from their peers. A CRT analysis was used to describe racial interactions, the perceptions of race, the role of stereotypes, and the emotional response to racial injustice. CRT is an appropriate framework to elaborate on the emotions associated with experiencing racism in our social surroundings.

Intersectionality

In addition to CRT, there are other relevant theories that can be used to help explicate the relationship between racial or cultural experiences and emotions. Intersectionality, an extension of CRT, involves understanding how multiple interlocking systems and identities can operate in the lived experiences of people from day to day. The purpose of intersectionality theory is to disentangle how layered critical theoretical frames can harmoniously yet distinctly describe the sense of powerlessness individuals feel living in an oppressed and inequitable social world (Crenshaw, 1989, 1991). By weaving together gender, social class, and race, intersectionality theory also illustrates the cultural constructions of emotions that uncover women's power struggles. Intersectionality argues that identity is formed at the intersection of various identities, particularly race and gender (Pimentel, 2003). For example, an Asian woman's identity is composed of both gender and race. However, it is extremely complex to separate her gender and racial identities. Thus, her identity is the interaction between her gender and race; she is both a woman and Asian.

As an analytical approach, intersectionality also serves as a counternarrative to those individuals or systems that would support essentializing personal and professional identity into separate racial/ethnic or gender classifications (Jordan-Zachary, 2007). The origins of intersectionality framework grew out of feminist and womanist scholars of color pressing the position that most feminist scholarship at that time was about middle-class, educated, White women, and that an inclusive view of women's position should substantively acknowledge the intersections of gender with other significant social identities, most notably race (Smith,1999). Prior to the use of this analytical approach to identity development and convergence of race, gender, and class, there was no framework for interpreting the ways in which these issues are more manifested in the lives of women of color, particularly as they were related to the traditional feminist and civil rights movements. Even less visible are the emotions in which women describe their quality of life and/or their emotional health when elaborating on multiple social identities.

Although intersectionality theory has been used to examine a myriad of intersectional relationships, including gender, race, class, and sexual orientation in a broad multidisciplinary context (e.g., women's studies, education, and the social sciences), there are researchers that do not support the position of intersectionality due to the potential that the theory may diminish the power of women. It is assumed that writings of the emotionality of women and their engagement in power struggles would further regulate them to into a weaker subordinate status (Lutz and Abu-Lughod, 1990). Some further believe that women's expression of emotions will perpetuate cultural ideologies and stereotypes of the emotions of subordinated groups. On the other hand, supporters of intersectionality explain that emotions inform us, help define who we are, and clarify the roles we ascribe. Women's expressions of emotions through the lens of intersectionality strengthen women individually and collectively (Alfred, 2005; Pimentel, 2003; Purdie-Vaughns & Eibach, 2008; Settles, 2006; Thornton, 1983). Thus, we argue that the field of intersectionality should be further expanded by examining the role that multiple identities play in experiencing and expressing emotions. In order to understand how an individual experiences and expresses emotions, it is necessary to explore how multiple identities intersect and are influenced by the context. In the United States, for example, Black women teachers may have difficulty with helping increase the number of African American students in special education. The teacher's uniqueness as a professional, an African American, a woman, and possibly a mother will heighten her concern and impact her emotions. By using intersectionality as a framework, social scientists investigating this phenomenon can illustrate the complexity and relationship of identity, role construction, and emotions

CONCLUSION AND IMPLICATIONS FOR FUTURE RESEARCH

Despite the growing body of literature exploring culture and emotions, most of what we currently know is based on our individual views and limited experiences (Markus and Kitayma, 1991). Several studies document how cultural understanding and acceptance of others from different racial groups can reduce miscommunication and negative emotional responses (Haviland et al., 1994; Hugenberg & Bodenhausen, 2003, 2004; Hutchinson & Smith, 1996; Mays, Cochran, & Barnes, 2007; Schmader, Johns, & Forbes, 2008). Other studies point to differences between individualistic cultures verses collective cultural response to emotional stimuli and how these differences are presented in schools (Oyserman, Coon, & Kemmelmeier, 2002; Triandis, 2001). We also know that cultural background can impact the expression of emotions in the school setting as well as student emotional response to nonverbal and verbal cue (Ekman & Scherer, 1982; She & Fisher, 2000).

As demonstrated throughout this chapter, the relationship between culture and emotions within education is complex. Few studies directly examine culture in terms of racial/ethnic issues, suggesting we need to expand our current discussions of culture and emotions to include issues of race and ethnicity. By exploring the range of social situations and intersections between culture, emotions, and power, we can initiate meaningful conversations on the impact of social policies and its influences on educational experiences. Specifically, researchers should explore how emotions and racial and cultural differences impact our educational settings.

First, more research is needed to examine the relationships between educational experiences, emotions, and the various elements encompassed by culture. Although this chapter largely focused on issues of race and ethnicity, other areas of culture, such as religious practices, SES, gender, and sexual orientation, need to be explored. By expanding how we explore culture, we can develop a more nuanced understanding of culture as well as its relationship with various emotions (pleasant and unpleasant) within the school context.

In addition, more research is needed on race/ethnicity and emotions in terms of classroom interactions between students as well as between teachers and students. Empirical research should be conducted to better explain the connection of emotions and how it affects our classrooms. Examining these relationships would give researchers a better understanding of the reciprocal nature of emotions within the classroom. Adding emotions research would also help educators to better understand how societal problems associated with race/ethnicity are manifested and permeated within the school context.

Finally, researchers need to better frame research on culture and emotions using culturally relevant theories and frameworks. The aforementioned theories of critical race theory and intersectionality are helpful for exploring issues of race/ethnicity. However, there are numerous culturally relevant theories that can be used to explore other areas of culture, such as using queer theory to explore sexual orientation and cultural/social capital theories to examine SES. By making issues of culture central to analyses, we can develop a more contextualized understanding of emotions in education as it relates to culture.

REFERENCES

Alfred, T. (2005). *Wasase: Indigenous pathways of action and freedom.* Peterborough, Canada: Broadview Press.

Alliman-Brissett, A., & Turner, S. (2010). Racism and math-based career interests, efficacy, and outcome expectations among African American adolescents. *Journal of Black Psychology, 36,* 197–225.

Anderman, L. (2003). Academic and social perceptions as predictors of change in middle school students' sense of school belonging. *Journal of Experimental Education, 72,* 5–22.

Bell, D. A. (1980). *Brown v. Board of Education* and the interest convergence dilemma. *Harvard Law Review, 93,* 518–533.

Bell, D. A. (1992). *Faces at the bottom of the well: The permanence of racism.* New York, NY: Basic Books.

Bodas, J., & Ollendick, T. H. (2005). Test anxiety: A cross-cultural perspective. *Clinical Child and Family Psychology Review, 8,* 65–88.

Bond, M (1993). Emotions and their expression in Chinese culture. *Journal of Nonverbal Behavior, 17*, 245–262.

Brondolo, E., Brady, N., Pencille, M., Beatty, D., & Contrada, R. J. (2009). Coping with racism: A selective review of the literature and a theoretical and methodological critique. *Journal of Behavioral Medicine, 32*, 64–88.

Burlew, A. K., & Smith, L. R. (1991). Measures of racial identity: An overview and a proposed framework. *Journal of Black Psychology, 17*, 53–71.

Cassady, J. C., Mohammed, A., & Mathieu, L. (2004). Cross-cultural differences in test perceptions: Women in Kuwait and the United States. *Journal of Cross-Cultural Psychology, 35*, 713–718.

Chen, H. (2012). Impact of parent's socioeconomic status on perceived parental pressure and test anxiety among Chinese high school students. *International Journal of Psychological Studies, 4*, 235–245.

Crenshaw, K. (1989). Demarginalizing the intersection of race and sex: A Black feminist critique of antidiscrimination doctrine, feminist theory and antiracist politics. *University of Chicago Legal Forum*, 139–167.

Crenshaw, K. (1991). Mapping the margins: Intersectionality, identity politics, and violence against women of color. *Stanford Law Review, 43*, 1241–1279.

DeCuir, J. T., & Dixson, A. 2004. "So when it comes out, they aren't that surprised that it is there": Using critical race theory as a tool of analysis of race and racism in education. *Educational Researcher, 33*, 26–31.

DeCuir-Gunby, J. T., & Williams-Johnson, M. R. (2007). The impact of race and racism on students' emotions: A critical race analysis. In P. Schutz & R. Peckrun (Eds.), *Emotions in education* (pp. 205–219). New York, NY: Elsevier Publishing.

Delgado, R. (1989). Storytelling for oppositionists and others: A plea for narrative. *Michigan Law Review, 87*, 2411–2441.

Delgado, R., & Stefancic, J. (2001). *Critical race theory: An introduction*. New York, NY: New York University Press.

Delpit, L. (1995). *Other people's children: Cultural conflict in the classroom*. New York, NY: The New Press.

Detweiler, R. A. (1975). On inferring the intentions of a person from another culture. *Journal of Personality, 43*, 591–611.

Deyhle, D., Parker, L., & Villenas, S. (1999). *Race is, race isn't: Critical race theory and qualitative studies in education*. New York, NY: Westview Press.

Dresser, N. (1996). *Multicultural manners: New rules of etiquette for a changing society*. New York, NY: J. Wiley & Sons.

Ekman, P., & Friesen, W. V. (1971). Constant across cultures in the face and emotion. *Journal of Personality and Social Psychology, 17*, 124–129.

Ekman, P., & Scherer, K. R. (1982). *Emotion in the human face*. Cambridge, United Kingdom: Cambridge University Press.

Elder, B., & Brooks, D. (2008). Simple versus elaborate feedback in nursing science courses. *Journal of Science Education and Technology, 17*, 334–340.

Elfenbein, A., & Ambady, N. (2002). On the universality and cultural specificity of emotion recognition: A meta-analysis. *Psychological Bulletin, 128*, 203–235.

Faircloth, B., & Hamm, J. (2005). Sense of belonging among high school students representing four ethnic groups. *Journal of Youth and Adolescence, 34*, 293–309.

Festinger, L. (1954). A theory of social comparison processes. *Human Relations, 7*, 117–140.

Fierros, E. G. (2006). One size does not fit all: A response to institutionalizing inequity. *Disabilities Studies Quarterly, 26*(2). Retrieved from http://dsq-sds.org

Frenzel, A. C., Thrash, T. M., Pekrun, R., & Goetz, T. (2007). Achievement emotions in Germany and China: A cross-cultural validation of the Academic Emotions Questionnaire-Mathematics (AEQ-M). *Journal of Cross-Cultural Psychology, 38*, 302–309.

Fry, R. (2006). The changing landscape of American public education: New students, new schools. Retrieved from www.pewhispanic.org/2006/10/05/the-changing-landscape-of-american-public-education-new-students-new-schools

Gay, G. (2000). *Culturally responsive teaching: Theory, research, & practice*. New York, NY: Teachers College Press.

Gomez, M. L., Khurshid, A., Freitag, M. B., & Lachuk, A. J. (2011). Microaggressions in graduate students' lives: How they are encountered and their consequences. *Teaching and Teacher Education, 27*, 1189–1199.

Goodenow, C. (1993). The psychological sense of school membership among adolescents: Scale development and educational correlates. *Psychology in the Schools, 30*, 79–90.

Gotanda, N. (1991). A critique of "Our constitution is color-blind." *Stanford Law Review, 44*, 1–68.

Harris, C. (1993). Whiteness as property. *Harvard Law Review, 106*, 1707–1791.

Haviland, J. M., Davidson, R. B., Ruetsch, C., Gebelt, J. L., & Lancelot, C. (1994). The place of emotion in identity. *Journal of Research on Adolescence, 4,* 503–518.

Helms, J. (1990). *Black and White racial identity: Theory, research, and practice.* New York, NY: Greenwood Press.

Helms, J., & Talleyrand, R. (1997). Race is not ethnicity. *American Psychologist, 52,* 1246–1247.

Hertz-Lazarowitz, R., Zelniker, T., & Azaiza, F. (2010). Theoretical framework for cooperative participatory action research (CPAR) in a multicultural campus: The social drama model. *Intercultural Education, 21,* 269–279.

Hofstede, G. (2001). *Culture's consequences: Comparing values, behaviors, institutions, and organizations across nations.* Thousand Oaks, CA: Sage.

Hooks, B. (1994). *Teaching to transgress.* London, United Kingdom: Routledge.

Hugenberg, K., & Bodenhausen, G. V. (2003). Facing prejudice: Implicit prejudice and the perception of facial threat. *Psychological Science, 14,* 640–643.

Hugenberg, K., & Bodenhausen, G. V. (2004). Ambiguity in social categorization: The role of prejudice and facial affect in race categorization. *Psychological Science, 15,* 342–345.

Hutchinson, J., & Smith, A. D. (1996). *Ethnicity.* Oxford, United Kingdom: Oxford University Press.

Johns, M., Inzlicht, M., & Schmader, T. (2008). Stereotype threat and executive resource depletion: Examining the influence of emotion regulation. *Journal of Experimental Psychology: General, 137,* 691–705.

Johnson, D. R., Soldner, M., Leonard, J. B., Alvarez, P., Inkelas, K. K., Rowan-Kenyon, H. T., & Longerbeam, S. D. (2007). Examining sense of belonging among first-year undergraduates from different racial/ethnic groups. *Journal of College Student Development, 48,* 525–542.

Johnson, K. J., & Fredrickson, B. L. (2005). "We all look the same to me": Positive emotions eliminate the own-race bias in face recognition. *Psychological Science, 16,* 875–881.

Jordan-Zachary, J. (2007). Let men be men: A gendered analysis of Black ideological response to familial politics. *National Political Science Review, 11,* 177–192.

King, J. (1991). Dyconscious racism: Ideology, identity, and the miseducation of teachers. *Journal of Negro Education, 60,* 133–146.

Klem, A., Connell, J. (2004). Relationships matter: Linking teacher support to engagement and achievement. *Journal of School Health, 74,* 262–273.

Kozol, J. (2005). *The shame of the nation: the restoration of apartheid schooling in America.* New York, NY: Random House.

Laar, C. (1999). *Increasing sense of community in the military: The role of personnel support programs.* Washington, DC: Rand.

Ladson-Billings, G. (1994). *The dreamkeepers: Successful teaching for African-American students.* San Francisco, CA: Jossey-Bass.

Ladson-Billings, G. (2009). Race still matters: Critical race theory in education. In M. W. Apple, W. Au, & L. Gandin (Eds.), *The Routledge international handbook of critical education* (pp. 110–122). New York: Routledge.

Ladson-Billings, G., & Tate, W. (1995). Toward a critical race theory of education. *Teachers College Record, 97,* 161–181.

Lasky, S. (2000). The cultural and emotional politics of teacher-parent interactions. *Teacher and Teacher Education, 16,* 843–860.

Levenson, R. W., Soto, J., & Pole, N. (2005). Emotion, biology, and culture. In S. Kitayama & D. Cohen (Eds.), *Handbook of cultural psychology* (pp. 780–796). New York, NY: Guilford Press.

Lutz, C., & Abu-Lughod. (1990). *Language and politics of emotions: Studies in emotion and social interaction.* Cambridge, MA: Cambridge University Press.

Markus, H. R., & Kitayama, S. (1991). Culture and the self: Implications for cognition, emotion, and motivation. *Psychological Review, 98,* 224–253.

Mays, V. M., Cochran, S. D., & Barnes, N. W. (2007). Race, race-based discrimination, and health outcomes among African Americans. *Annual Review of Psychology, 58,* 201–225.

Melucci, A. (1996). *The playing self: Person and meaning in the planetary society.* Cambridge, United Kingdom: Cambridge University Press.

Myers, D., and Diener, E. (1995). Who is happy? *Psychological Science, 6,* 10–17.

Nayak, A. (2007). Critical whiteness studies. *Sociology Compass, 1,* 737–755.

Noguera, P. A., & Wing, J. Y. (Eds.). (2006). *Unfinished business: Closing the achievement in our schools.* San Francisco, CA: Josey Bass.

Omi, M., & Winant, H. (1994). *Racial formation in the United States from the 1960's to the 1990's* (2nd ed.). New York, NY: Routledge.

Osterman, K. (2000). Students needs for belonging in the school community. *Review of Educational Research, 70,* 323–367.

Oyserman, D., Coon, H. M., & Kemmelmeier, M. (2002). Rethinking individualism and collectivism: Evaluation of theoretical assumptions and meta-analyses. *Psychological Bulletin, 128,* 3–72.

Pekrun, R. (2006). The control-value theory of achievement emotions: Assumptions, corollaries, and implications for educational research and practice. *Educational Psychology Review, 18,* 315–341.

Perry, T., Steele, C., & Hillard III, A. (2003). *Young, gifted, and Black: Promoting high achievement among African American students.* Boston, MA: Beacon Press.

Phinney, J. S. (1996). When we talk about American ethnic groups, what do we mean? *American Psychologist, 51,* 918–927.

Pimentel, A. (2003). *Exploring racialized and gendered identities: A qualitative investigation of intersections of race and gender in the lives of a group of young black adults.* Boston, MA: Harvard Graduate School of Education.

Purdie-Vaughns, V., & Eibach, R. (2008). Intersectional invisibility: The distinctive advantages and disadvantages of multiple subordinate group identities. *Sex Roles, 59,* 377–391.

Riberio, R. (2007). The language barrier as an aid to communication. *Social Studies of Science, 37,* 561–584.

Richeson, J., & Nussbaum, R. (2004). The impact of multicultural versus color-blindness on racial bias. *Journal of Experimental Social Psychology, 40,* 417–423.

Roediger, D. R. (1991). *The wages of whiteness: Race and the making of the American working class.* London, United Kingdom: Verso.

Russell, J. A. (1994). Is there recognition of emotion from facial expression? A review of the cross-cultural studies. *Psychological Bulletin, 115,* 102–141.

Rychlak, R. (1991). Civil rights, confederate flags, and political correctness: Free speech and race relations on campus. *Tulane Law Review, 66,* 1411–1422.

Sanders, M. (1997). Overcoming obstacles: Academic achievement as a response to racism and discrimination. *Journal of Negro Education, 66,* 83–93.

Sarason, S. B. (1974). *The psychological sense of community: Prospects for a community psychology.* San Francisco, CA: Jossey-Bass.

Schmader, T., Johns, M., & Forbes, C. (2008). An integrated process model of stereotype threat effects on performance. *Psychological Review, 114,* 336–356.

Settles, I. H. (2006). Use of an intersectional framework to understand Black women's racial and gender identities. *Sex Roles, 54,* 589–601.

She, H., & Fisher, D. (2000). The development of a questionnaire to describe science teacher communication behavior in Taiwan and Australia. *Science Education, 84,* 706–726.

Smith, L. (1999). *Decolonizing methodologies: Research and indigenous peoples.* London, United Kingdom: Zed Books.

Smith, W. A., Allen, W. R., & Danley, L. L. (2007). "Assume the position . . . you fit the description": Psychosocial experiences and racial battle fatigue among African American male college students. *American Behavioral Scientist, 51,* 551–578.

Steele, C. M., & Aronson, J. (1995). Stereotype threat and the intellectual test performance of African Americans. *Journal of Personality and Social Psychology, 69,* 797–811.

Stoddart, T. (1990). The Los Angeles unified school district intern program: Recruiting and preparing teachers for an urban context. *Peabody Journal of Education, 67,* 84–122.

Stromquist, N., & Monkman, K. (2000). *Globalization and education: Integration and contestation across cultures.* New York, NY: Rowman and Littlefield.

Sue, D. W, Capodilupo, C. M., Torino, G. C., Bucceri, J. M., Holder, A., Nadal, K. L., & Esquilin, M. (2007). Racial microaggressions in everyday life: Implications for clinical practice, *American Psychologist, 62,* 271–286.

Tatum, B. (1997). *Why are all the black kids sitting together in the cafeteria? And other conversations about race.* New York, NY: Basic Books.

Tatum, B. D. (2007). *Can we talk about race? And other conversations in an era of school resegregation.* Boston, MA: Beacon Press.

Taylor, S. E., & Lobel, M. (1989). Social comparison activity under threat: Downward evaluation and upward contacts. *Psychological Review, 96,* 569–575.

Thornton, D. (1983). Race, class & gender: Prospects for an all-inclusive sisterhood. *Feminist Studies, 9,* 131–150.

Tinto, V. (1997). Classrooms as communities: Exploring the educational character of student persistence. *The Journal of Higher Education, 68,* 599–623.

Triandis, H. C. (1995). *Individualism and collectivism.* Boulder, CO: Westview.

Triandis, H. C. (1996). The psychological measurement of cultural syndromes. *American Psychologist, 51,* 407–415.

Triandis, H. C. (2001). Individualism-collectivism and personality. *Journal of Personality, 69,* 907–924.

Tsai, J. L., Levenson, R. W., & McCoy, K. (2006). Cultural and temperamental variation in emotional response. *Emotion, 6,* 484–497.

Valdes, G. (1996). *Con respeto: Bridging distances between culturally diverse families and schools.* New York, NY: Teachers College Press, Columbia University.

Voelkl, K. (1995). School warmth, student participation, and achievement. *Journal of Experimental Education, 63,* 127–138.

Voelkl, K. (1997). Identification with school. *American Journal of Education, 105,* 294–318.

Watkins, W. H. (2005). *Black protest thought and education.* New York, NY: Peter Lang.

Weis, L. (1995). Identity formation and the processes of "othering": Unraveling sexual threads. *Educational Foundations, 9,* 17–33.

Yousefi, F., Redzuan, M., Bte, M., Juhari, R. B., & Talib, M. A. (2010). The effects of family income on test-anxiety and academic achievement among Iranian high school students. *Asian Social Science, 6,* 89–93.

Zebrowitz, L. A., Kikuchi, M., & Fellous, J. (2010). Facial resemblance to emotions: Group differences, impression effects, and race stereotypes. *Journal of Personality and Social Psychology, 98,* 175–189.

Zeidner, M. (1998). *Test anxiety: The state of the art.* New York, NY: Plenum Press.

Zeidner, M. (2014). Anxiety in education. In R. Pekrun & L. Linnenbrink-Garcia (Eds.), *International handbook of emotions in education* (pp. 265–288). New York, NY: Taylor & Francis.

Zembylas, M. (2003). Interrogating "Teacher Identity": Emotion, resistance and self-formation. *Educational Theory, 53,* 107–127.

Part IV
Measurement of Emotions
in Academic Settings

28

SELF-REPORT MEASURES OF ACADEMIC EMOTIONS

Reinhard Pekrun and Markus Bühner, University of Munich

Emotions are mentally represented in the conscious mind, and humans are able to communicate these representations using verbal language. Therefore, it is not surprising that research on emotions from early on used self-report methods. This is also true for research on educationally relevant emotions. Test anxiety was the first emotion in this field to receive widespread attention by researchers, and, from the beginning, progress in test anxiety research was closely connected to advances in the self-report measurement of this emotion, as detailed below. The first systematic self-report measure of test anxiety was developed in the 1930s at the University of Chicago (Brown, 1938) and was followed by a multitude of instruments assessing this emotion. Due to the dominance of test anxiety studies over the decades, issues of test anxiety measurement were at the center of debates about measurement until the 1990s. Over the past 15 years, researchers have begun to develop self-report scales measuring students' emotions other than anxiety as well. However, to date, instruments of this type are few and far between compared to the host of test anxiety questionnaires available.

In this chapter, we first provide an overview of different types of self-report instruments that measure emotions in education and highlight the relative advantages and disadvantages of self-report instruments as compared with other methods to assess emotions. Next, we provide an overview of test anxiety questionnaires. In the subsequent sections, we address recent measures of students' academic emotions other than test anxiety as well as measures of teacher emotions (for self-report measures of emotional intelligence, see Allen, MacCann, Matthews, and Roberts, 2014). Throughout these sections, we focus on systematic self-report instruments. Furthermore, although general measures of emotion can be adapted for the purposes of educational research (see, e.g., Linnenbrink, 2007), we focus on measures assessing emotions in education specifically rather than emotions more generally. In conclusion, we address directions for future research.

DECONSTRUCTING SELF-REPORT INSTRUMENTS

Types of Instruments

The self-report of emotions can take different forms. Important dimensions that distinguish between instruments include (1) unstructured versus structured self-report, (2) state versus trait instruments, (3) retrospective versus concurrent self-report, (4) oral versus written formats, (5) qualitative versus quantitative self-report, (6) single-item versus multi-item scales, and (7) one-dimensional versus multidimensional instruments, such as instruments assessing one emotion only versus instruments assessing multiple emotions. With few exceptions, these dimensions are independent of each other. As such, multiple combinations are possible, rendering a multitude of possible types of instruments (Figure 28.1).

First, self-report instruments can range from providing no structure for the contents to be reported (unstructured), providing a set of defined questions and leaving the answers open (semistructured), or defining both questions and options to answer (fully structured). Unstructured and semistructured instruments have clear advantages for exploring emotions since they make it possible for the respondent to report phenomena that were not anticipated by the researcher. For example, Pekrun, Goetz, Titz, and Perry (2002) used semistructured interviews and questionnaires with students to explore the occurrence of emotions in academic settings; they were surprised by the broad variety of emotions reported. However, unstructured emotion report may be strongly influenced by respondents' verbal abilities. By contrast, fully structured instruments, such as systematic questionnaires, are less dependent on verbal abilities and can provide quantitative data on the frequency or intensity of emotions, thus making it easier to test a priori hypotheses on the occurrence or functional relationships of these emotions.

Second, self-report can be used to assess emotional traits or states (Cattell & Scheier, 1961; Spielberger, 1972). Emotional traits are defined as individual dispositions to frequently experience emotions of a given kind. For example, trait anxiety is defined as the

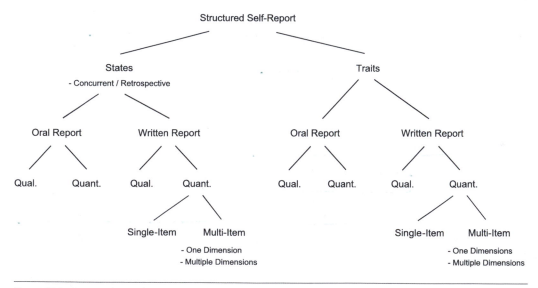

Figure 28.1 Some variants of structured self-report instruments.

individual disposition to frequently experience anxiety across various situations. State emotions are defined as emotions experienced in a given moment and situation, such as a student's anxiety the moment before an exam starts. Importantly, the trait-state distinction should not be equated with situational generality versus specificity. Whereas emotional states are situation-specific by definition (with the possible exception of free-floating emotions), emotional traits can be conceptualized in either situation-general or situation-specific ways. For example, trait anxiety can be conceived as an individual disposition to experience anxiety across various situations; by contrast, trait test anxiety is conceived as an individual's disposition to react with fear and anxiety when confronted with tests and exams specifically. For educational emotion research, both types of trait instruments can be used. However, to describe emotional processes in academic situations specifically, and to explain their impact on academic learning and performance, measures addressing contextualized, academic trait emotions may be more useful.

Third, self-report can use retrospective or concurrent formats. Any assessment of habitual emotions is retrospective because reporting about recurring emotions presupposes activating memories about these emotions. By contrast, state self-report can ask participants to report on emotions that occurred in past situations (retrospective self-report) or on current emotions (concurrent self-report). Despite its indispensability, retrospective assessment has a number of disadvantages. Any assessment that requires an individual to recall emotions may be subject to bias. For instance, momentary affective states or particularly salient experiences (such as more recent events) can influence how people report on their emotions. This is also the case for individuals' beliefs about emotionality, implicit theories about emotions, or deficits in recall that are compensated by using heuristics (Barrett, 1997; Goetz, Bieg, Lüdtke, Pekrun, & Hall, 2013; Robinson & Clore, 2002). However, concurrent self-report can also have problems, as the act of reporting itself can interrupt the situation and can alter the emotional experience (through reflection or by making emotions more salient to the individual).

Fourth, self-report can consist of interviews in which the respondent orally replies to questions, or involve pen and paper. Oral and written formats can be mixed, such as when an interviewer orally poses a question and a respondent writes a reply. Oral and written self-report have complementary advantages and disadvantages. Specifically, it may be easier and time-saving to simply talk about one's emotions rather writing an essay about one's experiences. On the other hand, written self-report has the strong advantage that emotions can be assessed in a depersonalized way, thus helping respondents to openly report their emotions. For example, in the above-mentioned exploratory research by Pekrun et al. (2002), interviewees provided numerous reports of positive emotions but few reports of some socially undesirable negative emotions such as shame. This may have been partially due to the activation of response sets such as tendencies to answer according to social desirability in an interview setting.

Fifth, self-report can result in qualitative versus quantitative data, which is partially dependent on the structure of the instrument. Specifically, unstructured and semistructured instruments render qualitative reports that can be converted into quantitative data using quantitative coding, whereas structured instruments directly provide quantitative data (in terms of binary yes/no data or data that are based on ordered response categories).

Sixth, quantitative self-report measures can consist of single or multiple items. Single items, such as binary questions or single rating scales, have the clear advantage of being less time-consuming, rendering them ideal candidates for the online assessment of emotional states during experiments or actual classroom situations (see Turner & Trucano, 2014, for an overview of instruments). However, their reliability is typically unknown and can be low, and their content validity can be low as well because it is not possible to assess multiple facets of an emotion using only one item. By contrast, multi-item scales make it possible to estimate reliability and to correct for unreliability by constructing latent variables using confirmatory factor analysis and structural equation modeling.

Regarding the validity of single versus multiple-item instruments, it is important to note that measures of emotions typically represent both emotional responses and the situation(s) that trigger these responses. Single-item instruments cannot meaningfully represent more than one category of situations and one type of response. By contrast, multi-item instruments can represent several situations, several responses, or both. Many emotion studies use a scenario approach in which one specific situation is described, and respondents are asked to report about various facets of their emotional response. Such an approach has the advantage of more fully sampling responses but fails to sample various situations. The opposite is true for instruments that sample various situations but ask for a limited set of emotional responses (e.g., experience sampling methods; Turner & Trucano, 2014). Using multiple items that represent samples of both situations and responses can, in principle, avoid both types of disadvantages but may result in instruments that are too long for practical research purposes.

Finally, self-report instruments can measure single or multiple dimensions of emotion. Self-report can assess (a) multiple dimensions of a single emotion, such as affective experience and physiological reactions related to the emotion, (b) multiple distinct emotions, such as enjoyment, pride, anger, or shame, and (c) multiple dimensions of situational stimuli that trigger these emotional responses. It is critical, both conceptually and in terms of measurement, that researchers carefully attend to matters of dimensionality when constructing emotion instruments. For example, it is not possible to explore the space of students' and teachers' distinct, discrete emotions using broad measures of affect that distinguish solely between positive and negative responses (Pekrun, Elliot, & Maier, 2006, 2009). Similarly, multidimensional instruments are needed to consider various response categories within emotions and various situational contexts that trigger emotional responses.

From a practical perspective, it is particularly important to know if an instrument measures just one emotion or multiple emotions. Test anxiety questionnaires are an example of the former, while multiple emotion scales, such as the Achievement Emotions Questionnaire (AEQ; Pekrun, Goetz, Frenzel, Barchfeld, & Perry, 2011), are an example of the latter. Although single-emotion instruments are well suited to answer research questions that pertain to only one emotion, they run the risk of underrepresenting students' emotional responses in academic settings and may lack discriminant validity. For example, as argued by Pekrun, Goetz, Perry, Kramer, and Hochstadt (2004), many test anxiety scales "measure more than [their] name[s] denote" (Nicholls, 1976, p. 976), because they assess other negative emotions, such as shame and hopelessness, in addition to anxiety, thus failing to show divergent validity. From this perspective, multiple-emotion instruments are preferable; however, since these instruments need more items, they are less easy to administer.

Benefits and Drawbacks of Self-Report

Self-report of emotions has several clear advantages. First, in contrast to other types of emotion assessment, self-report allows assessment of all of the components of emotion. Observation can assess visible expressions of emotion (Reisenzein, Junge, Studtmann, & Huber, 2014), neuroimaging the emotion-related activation of brain areas (Immordino-Yang & Christodoulou, 2014), and peripheral physiological measures the emotion-related arousal of peripheral systems (Kreibig & Gendolla, 2014). By contrast, self-report can be used to assess all of the affective, cognitive, motivational, physiological, and behavioral-expressive component processes of emotion because all of these processes can be represented in the human mind. Second, for the affective and cognitive components specifically, self-report can render a more differentiated assessment than any other method available. For a nuanced description of emotional feelings and thoughts, self-report is indispensable. Third, for practical research purposes, self-report is more economical than other methods and may be the only method applicable in some types of situations. For example, in classroom settings involving groups of students, it may be impractical to assess the emotions of all students using observation, whereas self-report methods such as experience sampling can be conveniently used to trace these emotions.

On the other hand, self-report has a number of disadvantages, suggesting that it should be complemented or substituted with other methods for many research purposes. Self-report is limited to the assessment of emotional responses that are represented in the conscious mind. Responses that cannot be represented mentally need to be assessed using other methods. For example, this is true for the activation of brain areas and of the sympathetic and parasympathetic nervous systems: Whereas the end products of activation can be consciously represented (e.g., in terms of perceived frequency of heart beat), this may not be true for the mediating physiological processes (Kreibig & Gendolla, 2014). Similarly, self-report may be of limited value for assessing emotional responses that cannot enter consciousness for individual reasons such as traumatic exposure.

A second important limitation is the use of language. Although recent research shows that emotion terms tend to be used in consistent ways across various languages (Fontaine, Scherer, & Soriano, in press), there are differences in the semantic understanding of terms between cultures. Furthermore, there can even be subtle differences between single individuals sharing the same cultural background. By implication, measurement equivalence of self-report instruments across groups should not merely be assumed but rather needs to be established empirically. This may even be true for different measurement occasions within individuals over time or in different situations. For example, Frenzel, Pekrun, Dicke, and Goetz (2012) have shown that the meaning of items measuring students' interest can change across adolescence within individual students.

Finally, another noteworthy limitation of self-report is the degree to which this particular method of emotion assessment is under respondents' control. For example, whereas it may be difficult to increase or decrease one's level of peripheral physiological activation for purposes of impression management, this may be easy when reporting about perceptions of activation. By implication, the validity of self-report is endangered by response biases that lead to an intentional or unintentional misrepresentation of the respondents' mental representations. For self-report of emotion, tendencies to bias reports towards standards of social desirability may be most important. As argued by Frenzel (2014), such bias may be fuelled by both self- and other-deception and may play a particularly important role for self-report of emotions in teachers whose jobs are strongly bound by emotion rules.

One possibility to reduce the influence of social desirability is to use forced-choice items providing options that are balanced in terms of desirability (see, e.g., Converse et al., 2010); however, such items have the disadvantage of providing ipsative scores. Second, effort can be made to generate items that are low on social desirability (Bäckström, Björklund, & Larsson, 2009), although it may be difficult to preserve content validity with such items. A third option that has been used by researchers is to control for social desirability by partialling out social desirability scores (e.g., Pekrun et al., 2006). However, the best way to deal with social desirability may be to shape the assessment setting such that participants trust that their responses are treated confidentially, making it possible for them to reveal their emotional reactions.

TEST ANXIETY QUESTIONNAIRES

Due to anxiety's long-standing renown among researchers in psychology and education, the development of instruments assessing this emotion has made significant progress over the past seven decades (Pekrun et al., 2004; Zeidner, 1998, 2014). Test anxiety measurement has been at the forefront of research on emotion assessment in personality psychology and education. Self-report instruments are the most frequently used method, including interviews, think-aloud protocols, single-item rating scales, and multi-item questionnaire scales. Among these instruments, multi-item scales are most commonly used because they are easy to administer, show good psychometric qualities (Hodapp & Benson, 1997; Zeidner, 1998), and are temporally adaptable, making it possible to assess both habitual emotional reactions to exams (*trait* test anxiety) and momentary emotional reactions (*state* test anxiety). Multi-item test anxiety scales comprise items assessing various anxiety-related emotional responses and ask students how frequently or intensely they experience these responses before or during tests and exams. Whereas these basic features of test anxiety scales have not changed, the precision of items and dimensionality of instruments showed a continuous development since the inception of test anxiety measurement.

As noted above, the first questionnaire to systematically assess students' test anxiety was developed by Brown in the 1930s (1938). Arguing that examinations had become increasingly important with the growth of universities, the change from small classes to large lectures, and the replacement of evaluations based on classroom interaction by large-scale exams, Brown wanted to assess frequency and group differences in students' exam-related anxiety. To this end, he constructed a questionnaire that comprised 70 items assessing affective, cognitive, physiological, and behavioral indicators of anxiety (e.g., "Are you nervous before an examination?", "Do you worry about an examination the night before?", "Are your hands wet and clumsy during an examination?"), with answers provided on a 5-point frequency scale ($1 = $ *always* to $5 = $ *never*). Brown did not estimate the reliability of the instrument, but he calculated (uncorrected) item-total correlations and found that 58 items passed the threshold he set for inclusion in the questionnaire ($r_{it} > .25$). Validating the instrument, he also found that mean anxiety scores differed between groups of students. Brown's findings indicate that he was successful in constructing a valid instrument measuring test anxiety.

Despite this success, Brown's questionnaire did not gain widespread acceptance. One possible reason is that his research was not theoretically based and did not fit the behaviorist Zeitgeist of the time. This was different with Mandler and S. B. Sarason's *Test Anxiety Questionnaire* (TAQ; Mandler & Sarason, 1952). Mandler and Sarason conceptualized test-related anxiety in terms of drives and posited that anxiety influences cognitive performance by triggering task-relevant and task-irrelevant behavioral responses. To test these propositions, they developed a scale with 37 items assessing affective, physiological, cognitive, and motivational components of test-related anxiety. The reliability of the scale proved to be good (split-half reliability was .91), and validity was shown by significant linkages between scale scores and intelligence test performance. Due to its theoretical underpinnings and psychometric quality, this instrument became the progenitor of many of the questionnaires developed in the six decades that followed.

Similar to Brown's questionnaire, the TAQ comprised one single scale, thus assuming that test anxiety is a homogenous, one-dimensional phenomenon. Other scales that were developed subsequently, such as I. G. Sarason's *Test Anxiety Scale* (TAS; Sarason, 1958) and S. B. Sarason's *Test Anxiety Scale for Children* (TASC; Sarason, Davidson, Lighthall, Waite, & Ruebush, 1960), shared the assumption of unidimensionality. Progress was made when these scales were subjected to factor-analytic tests of dimensionality. The findings suggested that test anxiety indeed comprises more than one dimension (e.g., Gorsuch, 1966; Sassenrath, 1964). Based on these findings, Liebert and Morris (1967) proposed distinguishing between cognitive components of test anxiety, such as worry and lack of self-confidence (referred to as "Worry"), on the one hand, and autonomic arousal (referred to as "Emotionality"), on the other hand. They used items from the TAQ to construct separate 5-item scales for worry and emotionality and found that these scales were differentially linked to students' performance expectancies; worry related negatively and emotionality proved unrelated to expectancy of success.

Research has consistently confirmed that it is possible to distinguish between affective-physiological and cognitive components of test anxiety and that these components show different relations with performance-related variables, including students' academic achievement (Zeidner, 1998, 2014). Consequently, researchers have developed two-dimensional instruments that use as their foundation the worry-emotionality distinction. Among these instruments, Spielberger's (1980) *Test Anxiety Inventory* (TAI) became the most popular. The TAI was adapted for use in different languages (e.g., Benson, Moulin-Julian, Schwarzer, Seipp, & El-Zahhar, 1992), and for many years this instrument was employed in the vast majority of test anxiety studies.

However, subsequent studies have demonstrated that it is useful to further refine the worry-emotionality distinction; a shift that is in line with current multicomponent definitions of emotion (Shuman & Scherer, 2014). An important advancement came with I. G. Sarason's (1984) *Reactions to Tests* (RTT) instrument that decomposed both the emotionality and the worry dimension. The RTT instrument contains 40 items organized in four scales measuring affective ("Tension"), physiological ("Bodily Reactions"), and cognitive ("Worry," "Task-Irrelevant Thinking") components of test anxiety. Each of the four scales contains ten items (e.g., "I feel distressed and uneasy before tests," "Before taking a test, I worry about failure," "During tests, I find myself thinking of things unrelated to the material being tested"). The scales showed sufficient reliability, with $\alpha = .78$ for the total scale and .68 to .81 for the subscales. Furthermore, documenting the validity of the instrument, worry scores were negatively related to performance on a digit symbol test and positively related to cognitive interference scores, in contrast to null relations for the other subscales.

Subsequently, a number of multidimensional test anxiety scales were developed that used Sarason's conception or a variant of it. In addition to exploratory factor analysis, confirmatory analysis was used in recent scale development to validate assumptions about dimensionality. Examples are Benson et al.'s (1992) *Revised Test Anxiety Scale* (RTA), Hodapp and Benson's (1997) integrated test anxiety scale that was based on Spielberger's TAI and Sarason's RTT, and the test anxiety scale from Pekrun et al.'s (2004, 2011) *Test Emotions Questionnaire* (TEQ), which will be discussed below. Today, researchers can choose between dozens of validated instruments assessing this particular emotion and its components. Furthermore, principles of constructing test anxiety measures have been used to create measures for other types of achievement anxiety as well, such as students' anxiety related to language classes (e.g., foreign language anxiety) or mathematics (math anxiety; e.g., *Mathematics Anxiety Rating Scale,* MARS; see Alexander & Martray, 1989).

The sophistication achieved in test anxiety measurement has enabled research on test anxiety to successfully analyze the effects and developmental trajectories of this emotion and to analyze the outcomes of treatments against its crippling effects. That said, there are still problems that remain to be solved. Specifically, there seems to be little agreement between test anxiety researchers as to the precise nature of the multidimensionality of the construct. Whereas all of the major instruments available to date assess affective, physiological, and worry components of test anxiety, there is dispute as to which additional components should be included in the construct (e.g., lack of self-confidence, task-irrelevant thinking, manifest behaviors; Zeidner, 1998).

A second major problem is that test anxiety research has disregarded other test-related emotions and has therefore disregarded problems of discriminant validity. For instance, it is often the case that items meant to measure cognitive components of test anxiety also pertain to cognitive components of hopelessness and despair (e.g., items like "Before taking a test, I worry about failure"; Sarason, 1984). Typically, these items do not differentiate between worries associated with anxiety (characterized by subjective uncertainty of failure) and worries associated with hopelessness (characterized by subjective certainty of failure; Pekrun et al., 2004). Additionally, many items tapping into the physiological components of test anxiety also assess physiological activation characteristics of other activating emotions, such as anger and shame. It is therefore possible that current test anxiety instruments still measure more than they claim to measure (Nicholls, 1976) by assessing a variety of negative emotions in addition to anxiety. Future research on the assessment of test anxiety should pay more attention to issues of discriminant validity, in addition to internal validity that has been considered over the past decades.

ASSESSING MULTIPLE ACADEMIC EMOTIONS

Students experience a wide variety of emotions while engaging in key academic contexts, such as studying, attending class, and taking tests. These include, for example, emotions like enjoyment, curiosity, hope, pride, anger, frustration, shame, hopelessness, or boredom. However, with a few recent exceptions, instruments measuring students' emotions other than test anxiety are still largely lacking. Measures that assess multiple student emotions were developed by Pekrun et al. (2004, 2011; Pekrun & Meier, 2011) and include the Achievement Emotions Questionnaire (AEQ) and the Epistemic Emotion Scales (EES). Scales measuring single emotions or ways to regulate emotions other than test anxiety have been developed for students' anger and boredom.

Achievement Emotions Questionnaire (AEQ)

In light of the shortage of instruments measuring multiple emotions, we used the findings from our exploratory research on students' emotions (Pekrun et al., 2002) to construct a multidimensional instrument that could measure a variety of major achievement emotions, including test anxiety and other achievement emotions (Achievement Emotions Questionnaire, AEQ; Pekrun et al., 2002, 2011). In its original version, the AEQ is a self-report instrument that assesses college students' achievement emotions. The instrument measures a number of discrete emotions for each of the three main categories of academic situations: attending class, studying, and taking tests and exams. Because these situations differ in terms of functions and social structures, the emotions pertaining to these situations can also differ. For example, enjoyment of classroom instruction should be differentiated from the enjoyment experienced during a challenging exam—some students may be excited when going to class, others when writing exams. Therefore, the AEQ provides separate scales for class-related, learning-related, and test-related emotions (the test emotion scales of the instrument have been published under the name *Test Emotions Questionnaire, TEQ*; Pekrun et al., 2004). Alternative versions of the AEQ measure students' emotions in specific academic domains (e.g., *AEQ-Mathematics*; Frenzel, Thrash, Pekrun, & Goetz, 2007) and in elementary school students (*AEQ-Elementary School*; Lichtenfeld, Pekrun, Stupnisky, Reiss, & Murayama, 2012).

By varying the instructions accordingly, the AEQ is able to assess students' general emotional reactions in academic situations (*trait* achievement emotions), emotional reactions in a specific course or domain (*course/domain-specific* achievement emotions), or emotions at a specific time-point (*state* achievement emotions). In its original version, the AEQ can be used to assess eight different class-related emotions, eight learning-related emotions, and eight test emotions (see Table 28.1). Specific emotions were selected based upon reported frequency and theoretical relevance (Pekrun et al., 2002).

Table 28.1 Achievement Emotions Questionnaire (AEQ): Scales and Reliabilities

	Scales					
	Class-Related Emotions		Learning-Related Emotions		Test Emotions	
	α	Items	α	Items	α	Items
Emotions						
Enjoyment	.85	10	.78	10	.78	10
Hope	.79	8	.77	6	.80	8
Pride	.82	9	.75	6	.86	10
Relief[a]	–	–	–	–	.77	6
Anger	.86	9	.86	9	.86	10
Anxiety	.86	12	.84	11	.90	12
Hopelessness	.89	11	.86	11	.87	10
Shame	.90	10	.90	11	.92	11
Boredom[b]	.93	11	.92	11	–	–

[a] Relief scale for test emotions only. [b] Boredom scale for learning-related and class-related emotions only.

The class-related emotion scales include 80 items and instruct students to report how they feel before, during, or after class with regard to class-related enjoyment (e.g., "I enjoy being in class"), hope (e.g., "I am full of hope"), pride (e.g., "I am proud of myself"), anger (e.g., "I feel anger welling up in me"), anxiety (e.g., "I feel nervous in class"), shame (e.g., "I feel ashamed"), hopelessness (e.g., "I feel hopeless"), and boredom (e.g., "I get bored"). The learning-related emotion scales include 75 items and instruct students to report how they feel before, during, or after studying with regard to the same eight emotions as above. Finally, the test-related emotion scales include 77 items and instruct students to indicate how they feel before, during, or after taking tests and exams with regard to test-related enjoyment, hope, pride, relief, anger, anxiety, shame, and hopelessness. Within each section (class-related, learning-related, test-related), the items are ordered in three blocks assessing emotional experiences before, during, and after engaging in the specified academic context. Sequencing items this way is in line with principles of situation-reaction inventories (Endler & Okada, 1975) and is intended to help respondents access their emotional memories.

The construct definitions underlying the AEQ use a multicomponent definition of emotion (Shuman & Scherer, 2014). As such, the items in each of the scales pertain to the affective, cognitive, physiological/expressive, and motivational components of each measured emotion. This is consistent with leading-edge test anxiety measures but extends test anxiety assessment in two important ways. Although most current test anxiety instruments measure affective, physiological, and cognitive components of anxiety, they neglect the motivational component. Items pertaining to this component were originally part of Mandler and S. B. Sarason's (1952) TAQ, but later motivational components were neglected. Second, effort was made to construct items that ensure discriminant content validity of scales measuring different discrete emotions; this includes differentiating between test anxiety and closely neighboring emotions like test-related shame and hopelessness.

The reliabilities of the AEQ scales range from adequate to excellent (α = .75 to .93; Table 28.1). The structural validity of the AEQ scales has been tested in two-step confirmatory factor analyses (Pekrun et al., 2004, 2011). First, we examined the dimensionality of the AEQ scales by competitively testing three models for each of the scales: (a) a unidimensional one-factor model containing one factor using all of the scale items as indicators, (b) a four-factor model containing four separate factors representing the affective, cognitive, physiological, and motivational components of the emotion, and (c) a hierarchical model containing the four component factors as well as a second-order factor representing the emotion. The findings showed that the four-factor models fit the data better than the one-factor models and that adding a second-order factor did not substantially deteriorate model fit. This documents that achievement emotions are best conceptualized in terms of hierarchical models representing emotion components as well as their linkages with the respective emotion. Second, we examined the overall structure of the instrument by evaluating various factor models for the whole set of 24 scales. The findings indicated that a two-facet approach best represented the data, with different discrete emotions (enjoyment, pride, hope, etc.) represented as separate latent factors and the three settings (class, learning, tests) represented as correlated uniquenesses. The findings confirm that the measurement of achievement emotions should attend both to the differences between discrete emotions and between the various academic settings in which these emotions occur.

As to external validity, the AEQ has been shown to predict students' academic achievement, course enrollment, and dropout rates. Also, achievement emotions as assessed by the AEQ relate to components of students' learning processes, such as study interest, achievement goals, intrinsic and extrinsic motivation to learn, cognitive and metacognitive strategies of learning, investment of study effort, and the self-regulation of academic learning (e.g., Goetz, Pekrun, Hall, & Haag, 2006; Kleine, Goetz, Pekrun, & Hall, 2005; Pekrun et al., 2006, 2009, 2011; Pekrun, Goetz, Daniels, Stupnisky, & Perry, 2010; Perry, Hladkyi, Pekrun, & Pelletier, 2001; Spangler, Pekrun, Kramer, & Hofmann, 2002). Further, gender, social feedback, teachers' instructional behavior, and the composition and social climate of classrooms have also proven important correlates of the achievement emotions assessed by the AEQ (e.g., Frenzel, Pekrun, & Goetz, 2007; Frenzel, Goetz, Lüdtke, Pekrun, & Sutton, 2009).

Epistemic Emotion Scales (EES)

Given the relevance of academic attainment for one's educational career and future employment, achievement emotions are critically important for students' academic agency. However, not all emotions occurring in academic settings are achievement emotions. Specifically, epistemic emotions that are instigated by the knowledge-generating quality of cognitive problems and mental activities are no less important for students' learning and performance, such as surprise, curiosity, or confusion triggered by cognitive disequilibrium (Pekrun & Linnenbrink-Garcia, 2014). These epistemic emotions can profoundly influence students' interest and intrinsic motivation, persistence in investing cognitive effort, use of deep-learning strategies, and ultimately their successful learning and long-term developmental trajectories. Initial empirical evidence supports the notion that epistemic emotions can facilitate knowledge acquisition (D'Mello & Graesser, 2012; D'Mello, Lehmann, Pekrun, & Graesser, 2014). Therefore, it is paramount that measures to assess these emotions are developed.

Previous research using self-report to measure students' epistemic emotions employed qualitative think-aloud procedures ("emote-aloud"; Graesser, D'Mello, & Strain, 2014), emotion checklists, or single-item rating scales for different emotions such as confusion, frustration, and boredom (Calvo & D'Mello, 2010; Graesser et al., 2014). An initial attempt to develop multi-item scales measuring epistemic emotions during learning was made by Pekrun and Meier (2011; *Epistemic Emotion Scales*, EES). The 21-item EES contain seven scales measuring epistemic emotions using emotion adjectives (3 items per scale), including surprise (e.g., "surprised," "amazed"), curiosity (e.g., "curious," "inquisitive"), enjoyment (e.g., "excited," "happy"), confusion (e.g., "confused," "puzzled"), anxiety (e.g., "anxious," "worried"), frustration (e.g., "frustrated," "dissatisfied"), and boredom (e.g., "bored," "dull"). Respondents are asked to rate how intensely they feel each emotion (1 = *not at all* to 5 = *very strong*). By varying the instructions accordingly, the scales can be used to assess either state epistemic emotions during single learning episodes or trait epistemic emotions occurring habitually during learning.

In a multinational study on the role of epistemic beliefs and epistemic emotions for students' conceptual change related to issues of climate change (N = 439 students from Canada, the United States, and Germany), the scales proved reliable despite the small number of items per scale (α range .76 to .86; Muis et al., 2013). The findings from confirmatory factor analysis showed that the scales are indeed suited to distinguish between the seven emotions. Furthermore, the scales proved externally valid by predicting students' use of learning strategies and their learning outcomes, suggesting external validity. While these initial findings are promising, more research is needed to examine whether they are replicable across studies.

Scales for Positive Academic Emotions

Self-report measures of students' positive academic emotions are largely lacking, except the AEQ and EES scales cited above. Items assessing enjoyment by using terms such as "fun," "enjoyable," or "excited" are included in many measures of students' interest; however, these measures do not clearly distinguish between enjoyment and interest (see Ainley & Hidi, 2014). This is also true for the five-item science enjoyment and interest scale used in the science-related assessments of the Programme for International Student Assessment (PISA). This scale is in part based on the learning-related enjoyment scale of the Achievement Emotions Questionnaire described earlier and measures a combination of students' enjoyment and interest in science (e.g., "I enjoy acquiring new knowledge in science," "I am interested in learning about science"; 1 = *strongly agree* to 4 = *strongly disagree;* Organization for Economic Co-operation and Development, 2009). For pride, self-report scales differentiating between authentic and hubristic pride are available, but these scales do not address students' pride in academic achievement settings (Oades-Sese, Matthews, & Lewis, 2014; Tracy & Robins, 2007). Similarly, there are a number of self-report instruments assessing curiosity; however, measures of academic curiosity seem to be lacking (for an overview, see Jirout & Klahr, 2012), except the EES curiosity scale cited previously.

Scales for Academic Anger and Boredom

In contrast to positive academic emotions, students' anger and boredom have attracted researchers' interest. Specifically, scales have been developed that measure students' anger, boredom, precursors of boredom, and coping with boredom at school. Based on evidence that students' anger can relate to various problematic outcomes, such as difficulties at school, alcohol and drug use, as well as health problems, Smith, Furlong, Bates, and Laughlin (1998; Furlong & Smith, 1998) developed the *Multidimensional School Anger Inventory* (MSAI). This instrument represents an expanded version of Smith, Adelman, Nelson, and Taylor's (1988) *School Anger Inventory.* The MSAI comprises 31 items organized in four scales derived from exploratory factor analysis. The four scales pertain to affective ("School Anger Experience"), cognitive ("Hostile Outlook"), and behavioral components of anger ("Positive Coping"; "Destructive Expression"). The School Anger Experience scale represents various anger-provoking situations at school (e.g., "You didn't notice that someone put gum on your seat and you sit on it"; 1 = *I'm not angry at all* to 4 = *I'm very angry. I'm furious*), the Hostile Outlook scale negative attitudes towards school (e.g., "School is worthless," "Grades at school are unfair"; 1 = *strongly disagree* to 4 = *strongly agree*), and the Positive Coping and Destructive Expression scales behavioral reactions (e.g., "When I get mad at school, I share my feelings," "When I'm mad, I break things"; 1 = *never* to 4 = *always*). In a revised version, items were added to the behavioral scales to increase reliability (MSAI-Revised; see Boman, Cook, Curtis,

Furlong, & Smith, 2006). Validity was documented through confirmatory factor analysis, relations with teacher ratings, and the profile of scores for students with behavior problems.

A multidimensional instrument assessing student's boredom was developed by Acee et al. (2010; *Academic Boredom Scale,* ABS). Based on theory and evidence that boredom can be caused both when skills exceed task demands and when task demands exceed skills (Czikszentmihalyi, 1975; Pekrun et al., 2010), the authors developed separate scales for boredom in under- and overchallenging academic situations. Using qualitative pilot data and exploratory factor analysis, they developed a set of 10 items assessing "task-focused boredom" (e.g., "To what extent did you find the activity dull?") and "self-focused boredom" (e.g., "To what extent did you want to do something else?") for these situations. The same items were used for under- and overchallenging situations, which were differentiated by using two different instructions ("Think of a situation in which you found academic activities too easy and not challenging," "Think of a situation in which you found academic activities too difficult and too challenging"). The final 20-item version of the ABS contains three scales: underchallenging, task-focused overchallenging, and self-focused overchallenging. In two studies with undergraduate students, the reliability of the three scales proved to be good (α range .78 to .91). Confirmatory factor analysis corroborated the three-factor structure of the instrument, and external validity was demonstrated by substantial correlations of all three scales with students' learning-related boredom as assessed by Pekrun et al.'s (2011) Achievement Emotions Questionnaire described earlier.

Expanding the assessment of situational antecedents of students' boredom beyond over- and underchallenge, Daschmann, Goetz, and Stupnisky (2011) developed the *Precursors to Boredom Scales.* Using the item stem "When I'm bored in mathematics class, it is because . . .," the scales of this 22-item instrument measure eight possible antecedents of students' boredom in mathematics, including perceived monotony (e.g., "we always do the same thing in math class"), lack of meaning ("the subject matter of math class has no meaning in my life"), opportunity costs ("I would much rather do something else"), overchallenge ("the subject matter in math is too difficult for me"), underchallenge ("the subject-matter is too easy"), lack of involvement ("my math teacher never involves us in the lesson"), teacher dislike ("I don't like my math teacher"), and generalized boredom ("I'm always bored in school"). In a study with grade five to ten students, the scales proved to be reliable (α range .69 to .88). Confirmatory factor analysis corroborated the distinctiveness of the scales, and external validity was demonstrated by linkages with the quality of classroom instruction and students' achievement in mathematics (positive and negative correlations for under- and overchallenge, respectively).

Given the prevalence and deleterious consequences of boredom in academic settings, it is important for students to be able to regulate this emotion. Adapting the two-dimensional taxonomy of coping with stress developed by Holahan, Moos, and Schaefer (1996), Nett, Goetz, and Daniels (2010) constructed scales assessing students' coping with boredom (*Boredom Coping Scales,* BCS). Using the item stem "When I'm bored in mathematics class," the four five-item scales assess "cognitive-approach coping" (cognitive reappraisal; e.g., "I make myself aware of the issue"), "behavioral-approach coping" (e.g., "I ask my teacher for more interesting tasks"), "cognitive-avoidance coping" (e.g., "I study for another subject"), and "behavioral-avoidance coping" (e.g., "I talk to my classmates"). Findings based on a sample of secondary school students showed scale reliabilities to be good (α range .83 to .92). Confirmatory factor analyses corroborated the four-factor structure of the instrument. The four ways of coping related differentially to overall boredom in math classes, suggesting external validity. Cognitive-approach coping correlated negatively with boredom, whereas the other three ways of coping correlated positively. Further confirming the positive functional role of cognitive approach coping (i.e., reappraisal), scores for this type of coping related positively to students' self-concept, interest, enjoyment, and effort in math, whereas correlations for the avoidance coping scores were negative. Overall, these findings confirm the structural and external validity of the instrument (also see Nett, Goetz, & Hall, 2011).

SELF-REPORT MEASURES OF TEACHER EMOTIONS

Whereas students' emotions have received attention from researchers, there has been considerably less research targeting the emotions experienced by teachers. A number of studies have examined teachers' achievement-related anxiety. For example, Beilock, Gunderson, Ramirez, and Levine (2010) used the *Mathematics Anxiety Rating Scale* (Alexander & Martray, 1989) to examine the negative impact of elementary teachers' math anxiety on their students' performance in mathematics. By contrast, few studies have evaluated teachers' emotions about their teaching. One possible reason is the lack of systematic instruments measuring teaching-related emotions beyond exploratory techniques such as qualitative interviews (Sutton & Wheatley, 2003). Two exceptions are scales measuring teacher anxiety and the *Achievement Emotions Questionnaire for Teachers* (AEQ-Teachers) developed by Frenzel, Pekrun, and Goetz (2010; Frenzel, 2014).

The development of instruments measuring teacher anxiety was inspired by the high levels of classroom anxiety experienced by some teachers and by the advances in test anxiety measurement described earlier. Teacher anxiety scales measure student teachers' and practicing teachers' anxiety related to preparing lessons, managing classroom instruction, and interacting with colleagues and supervisors. An example is Hart's (1987; Morton, Vesco, Williams, & Awender, 1997; Ngidi & Sibaya, 2003) *Student Teacher Anxiety Scale* (STAS). Based on a preliminary survey of student teachers' anxieties, 26 items were constructed that asked participants to indicate their anxiety levels in relation to the situational statement provided in each item (1 = *not anxious* to 7 = *very anxious*). Exploratory factor analysis was used to organize the item pool into four scales labeled "Evaluation Anxiety" (e.g., "Being observed by my TP supervisor while I am teaching"), "Pupil and Professional Concerns Anxiety" (e.g., "Setting work at the right level for the children"), "Class Control Anxiety" (e.g., "Controlling the noise level in class"), and "Teaching Practice Requirements Anxiety" (e.g., "Getting all the paperwork done in time"). Split-half reliability for the total STAS scores was high (.91), and validity was documented by positive correlations of evaluation anxiety, class control anxiety, teaching practice requirements anxiety, and total anxiety scores with observer-coded disruptive student behavior during lessons taught by the study participants.

The *Achievement Emotions Questionnaire for Teachers* (AEQ-Teachers) was developed by Frenzel, Pekrun, and Goetz (2010; Frenzel, Goetz, Stephens, & Jacob, 2009) to measure three frequently occurring teaching-related emotions, including enjoyment, anxiety, and anger. The instrument contains six scales consisting of four items each. Three of the scales measure enjoyment, anxiety, and anger as habitual reactions to teaching (e.g., "I generally enjoy teaching," "I generally feel tense and nervous while teaching," "Sometimes I get really mad while I teach"). Considering the class-specificity of teachers' emotions, the second set of three scales measures these emotions related to teaching a specific class (e.g., "I enjoy teaching these students," "I feel tense and nervous while teaching these students," "Sometimes I get really mad at these students"). In two studies with practicing elementary and secondary school teachers, respectively, reliabilities proved to be good (α range .86 to .92). Using multilevel analysis, external validity was documented by correlations with teacher-perceived student discipline and motivation (positive for enjoyment, negative for anxiety and anger) as well as student-perceived quality of classroom instruction (e.g., positive correlations for teacher enjoyment, on the one hand, and perceived teacher enthusiasm as well as elaboration and comprehensibility of instruction, on the other; negative relations for teachers' anxiety). In addition, results of multilevel longitudinal analysis suggested that teacher enjoyment during mathematics classes has a positive impact on students' enjoyment of mathematics (Frenzel et al., 2009). These findings support the validity of the instrument and suggest that teacher emotions are critically important for students' affect and learning.

CONCLUSION

Measurement of students' and teachers' emotions through self-report methods has made considerable progress since the inception of test anxiety research in the 1930s. The development of more refined, theory-based, and multidimensional instruments has substantially contributed to the progress made in educational research on emotions, as documented in the chapters of this volume. Systematic self-report instruments have a number of clear advantages, including their broad coverage of facets of emotions, differentiated account for variations in emotional contents and intensity, and easy administration. This latter advantage is especially important for assessing emotions in large-scale studies that cannot afford the use of more expensive observational or physiological measurement. On the other hand, self-report has clear limitations; self-report methods are less suited to examine emotions that cannot be consciously assessed or reported using words, they are of limited use to assess emotions in preschool and early elementary school students, and they are not well suited to examine the real-time, second-to-second dynamics of emotional processes as captured by observation and physiological analysis (see Kreibig & Gendolla, 2014; Reisenzein, Junge, Studtmann, & Huber, 2014).

Future research should strive to further improve and expand existing instruments for assessing emotions in education. For some types of academic emotions, instruments are still largely lacking. Specifically, there is an obvious shortage of instruments assessing social emotions in academic settings, such as students' admiration, contempt, or jealousy, with the exception of scales measuring anger as described earlier. Similarly, more instruments assessing a broad range of teacher emotions, beyond teachers' anxiety, are needed. Furthermore, more research should be conducted to develop useful structures for multidimensional instruments. For example, as noted earlier, at present, there is no consensus regarding which emotion components should be included in measures of achievement emotions such as test anxiety. Finally, more work on the cross-cultural equivalence of instruments is needed to ensure generalizability of findings for student and teacher emotions across languages and to examine cross-cultural similarities and differences.

REFERENCES

Acee, T. W., Kim, H., Kim, H. J., Kim, J.-I., Chu, H.-N. R., Kim, M. . . . Riekenberg, J. J. (2010). Academic boredom in under- and over-challenging situations. *Contemporary Educational Psychology, 35,* 17–27.

Ainley, M., & Hidi, S. (2014). Interest and enjoyment. In R. Pekrun & L. Linnenbrink-Garcia (Eds.), *International handbook of emotions in education* (pp. 205–227). New York, NY: Taylor & Francis.

Alexander, L., & Martray, C. (1989) The development of an abbreviated version of the Mathematics Anxiety Rating Scale. *Measurement and Evaluation in Counseling and Development, 22,* 143–150.

Allen, V., MacCann, C., Matthews, G., & Roberts, R. D. (2014). Emotional intelligence: From pop to emerging science. In R. Pekrun & L. Linnenbrink-Garcia (Eds.), *International handbook of emotions in education* (pp. 162–182). New York, NY: Taylor & Francis.

Bäckström, M., Björklund, F., & Larsson, M. R. (2009). Five-factor inventories have a major general factor related to social desirability which can be reduced by framing items neutrally. *Journal of Research in Personality, 43,* 335–344.

Barrett, L. F. (1997). The relationships among momentary emotion experiences, personality descriptions, and retrospective ratings of emotion. *Personality and Social Psychology Bulletin, 23,* 1100–1110.

Beilock, S. L., Gunderson, E. A., Ramirez, G., & Levine, S. C. (2010). Female teachers' math anxiety affects girls' math achievement. *Proceedings of the National Academy of Sciences, 107,* 1060–1063.

Benson, J., Moulin-Julian, M., Schwarzer, C., Seipp, B., & El-Zahhar, N. (1992). Cross-validation of a revised test anxiety scale using multi-national samples. In K. A. Hagtvet & T. B. Johnson (Eds.), *Advances in test anxiety research* (Vol. 7, pp. 62–83). Amsterdam, Netherlands: Swets & Zeitlinger.

Boman, P., Cook, J., Curtis, D., Furlong, M. J., & Smith, D.C. (2006). Cross-validation and Rasch analyses of the Australian version of the Multidimensional School Anger Inventory–Revised. *Journal of Psychoeducational Assessment, 24,* 225–242.

Brown, C. H. (1938). Emotional reactions before examinations: II. Results of a questionnaire. *Journal of Psychology, 5,* 11–26.

Calvo, R. A., & D'Mello, S. K. (2010). Affect detection: An interdisciplinary review of models, methods, and their applications. *IEEE Transactions on Affective Computing, 1,* 18–37.

Cattell, R. B., & Scheier, I. H. (1961). *Meaning and measurement of neuroticism and anxiety.* New York, NY: Ronald Press.

Converse, P. D., Pathak, J., Quist, J., Merbedone, M., Gotlib, T., & Kostic, E. (2010). Statement desirability ratings in forced-choice personality measure development: Implications for reducing score inflation and providing trait-level information. *Human Performance, 23,* 323–342.

Czikszentmihalyi, M. (1975). *Beyond boredom and anxiety.* San Francisco, CA: Jossey-Bass.

Daschmann, E. C., Goetz, T., & Stupnisky, R. H. (2011). Testing the predictors of boredom at school: Development and validation of the precursors to boredom scales. *British Journal of Educational Psychology, 81,* 421–440.

D'Mello, S., & Graesser, A. (2012). Dynamics of affective states during complex learning. *Learning and Instruction, 22,* 145–157.

D'Mello, S., Lehman, S., Pekrun, R., & Graesser, A. (2014). Confusion can be beneficial for learning. *Learning and Instruction, 29,* 153–170.

Endler, N., & Okada, M. (1975). A multidimensional measure of trait anxiety: The S-R Inventory of General Trait Anxiousness. *Journal of Consulting and Clinical Psychology, 43,* 319–329.

Fontaine, J.R.J., Scherer, K. R., & Soriano, C. (Eds.). (in press). *Components of emotional meaning: A sourcebook.* Oxford, United Kingdom: Oxford University Press.

Frenzel, A. C. (2014). Teacher emotions. In R. Pekrun & L. Linnenbrink-Garcia (Eds.), *International handbook of emotions in education* (pp. 494–519). New York, NY: Taylor & Francis.

Frenzel, A. C., Goetz, T., Lüdtke, O., Pekrun, R., & Sutton, R. (2009). Emotional transmission in the classroom: Exploring the relationship between teacher and student enjoyment. *Journal of Educational Psychology, 101,* 705–716.

Frenzel, A. C., Goetz, T., Stephens, E. J., & Jacob, B. (2009). Antecedents and effects of teachers' emotional experiences: An integrated perspective and empirical test. In P. A. Schutz & M. Zembylas (Eds.), *Advances in teacher emotion research: The impact on teachers' lives* (pp. 129–152). New York, NY: Springer.

Frenzel, A. C., Pekrun, R., Dicke, A. L., & Goetz, T. (2012). Beyond quantitative decline: Conceptual shifts in adolescents' development of interest in mathematics. *Developmental Psychology, 48,* 1069–1082.

Frenzel, A. C., Pekrun, R., & Goetz, T. (2007). Perceived learning environment and students' emotional experiences: A multi-level analysis of mathematics classrooms. *Learning and Instruction, 17,* 478–493.

Frenzel, A. C., Pekrun, R., & Goetz, T. (2010). *Achievement Emotions Questionnaire for Teachers (AEQ-Teachers).* Unpublished manuscript, Department of Psychology, University of Munich, Munich, Germany.

Frenzel, A. C., Thrash, T. M., Pekrun, R., & Goetz, T. (2007). Achievement emotions in Germany and China: A cross-cultural validation of the Academic Emotions Questionnaire-Mathematics (AEQ-M). *Journal of Cross-Cultural Psychology, 38,* 302–309.

Furlong, M. J., & Smith, D.C. (1998). Raging Rick to tranquil Tom: An empirically based multidimensional anger typology for adolescent males. *Psychology in the Schools, 35,* 229–245.

Goetz, T., Bieg, M., Lüdtke, O., Pekrun, R., & Hall, N. C. (2013). Do girls really experience more anxiety in mathematics? *Psychological Science, 24,* 2079–2087.

Goetz, T., Pekrun, R., Hall, N., & Haag, L. (2006). Academic emotions from a socio-cognitive perspective: Antecedents and domain specificity of students' affect in the context of Latin instruction. *British Journal of Educational Psychology, 76,* 289–308.

Gorsuch, R. L. (1966). The general factor in the test anxiety questionnaire. *Psychological Reports, 19,* 308.

Graesser, A. C., D'Mello, S. K., & Strain, A. C. (2014). Emotions in advanced learning technologies. In R. Pekrun & L. Linnenbrink-Garcia (Eds.), *International handbook of emotions in education* (pp. 473–493). New York, NY: Taylor & Francis.

Hart, N. I. (1987). Student teachers' anxieties: Four measured factors and their relationships to pupil disruption in class. *Educational Research, 29,* 12–18.

Hodapp, V., & Benson, J. (1997). The multidimensionality of test anxiety: A test of different models. *Anxiety, Stress and Coping, 10,* 219–244.

Holahan, C. J., Moos, R. H., & Schaefer, J. A. (1996). Coping, stress resistance, and growth: Conceptualizing adaptive functioning. In M. Zeidner & N. S. Endler (Eds.), *Handbook of coping. Theory, research, applications* (pp. 24–43). New York, NY: Wiley.

Immordino-Yang, M. H., & Christodoulou, J. A. (2014). Neuroscientific contributions to understanding and measuring emotions in educational contexts. In R. Pekrun & L. Linnenbrink-Garcia (Eds.), *International handbook of emotions in education* (pp. 607–624). New York, NY: Taylor & Francis.

Jirout, J., & Klahr, D. (2012). Children's scientific curiosity: In search of an operational definition of an elusive concept. *Developmental Review, 32,* 125–160.

Kleine, M., Goetz, T., Pekrun, R. & Hall, N. (2005). The structure of students' emotions experienced during a mathematical achievement test. *International Reviews on Mathematical Education, 37,* 221–225.

Kreibig, S. D., & Gendolla, G.H.E. (2014). Autonomic nervous system measurement of emotion in education and achievement settings. In R. Pekrun & L. Linnenbrink-Garcia (Eds.), *International handbook of emotions in education* (pp. 625–642). New York, NY: Taylor & Francis.

Lichtenfeld, S., Pekrun, R., Stupnisky, R. H., Reiss, K., & Murayama, K. (2012). Measuring students' emotions in the early years: The Achievement Emotions Questionnaire–Elementary School (AEQ-ES). *Learning and Individual Differences, 22,* 190–201.

Liebert, R. M., & Morris, L. W. (1967). Cognitive and emotional components of test anxiety: A distinction and some initial data. *Psychological Reports, 20,* 975–978.

Linnenbrink, E. A. (2007). The role of affect in student learning: A multi-dimensional approach to considering the interaction of affect, motivation, and engagement. In P. Schutz & R. Pekrun (Eds.), *Emotion in education* (pp. 107–124). San Diego, CA: Academic Press.

Mandler, G., & Sarason, S. B. (1952). A study of anxiety and learning. *Journal of Abnormal and Social Psychology, 47,* 166–173.

Morton, L. L., Vesco, R., Williams, N. H., & Awender, M. A. (1997). Student teacher anxieties related to class management, pedagogy, evaluation, and staff relations. *British Journal of Educational Psychology, 67,* 69–89.

Muis, K. R., Pekrun, R., Azevedo, R., Sinatra, G. M., Trevors, G., Meier, E., & Heddy, B. C. (2014). *The curious case of climate change: Epistemic emotions mediate relations between epistemic beliefs, learning strategies and learning outcomes.* Manuscript submitted for publication.

Nett, U. E., Goetz, T., & Daniels, L. (2010). What to do when feeling bored? Students' strategies for coping with boredom. *Learning and Individual Differences, 20,* 626–638.

Nett, U. E., Goetz, T., & Hall, N. C. (2011). Coping with boredom in school: An experience sampling perspective. *Contemporary Educational Psychology, 36,* 49–59.

Ngidi, D. P., & Sibaya, P. T. (2003). Student teacher anxieties related to practice teaching. *South Africa Journal of Education, 23,* 18–22.

Nicholls, J. G. (1976). When a scale measures more than its name denotes: The case of the Test Anxiety Scale for Children. *Journal of Consulting and Clinical Psychology, 44,* 976–985.

Oades-Sese, G. V., Matthews, T. A., & Lewis, M. (2014). Shame and pride and their effects on student achievement. In R. Pekrun & L. Linnenbrink-Garcia (Eds.), *International handbook of emotions in education* (pp. 246–264). New York, NY: Taylor & Francis.

Organization for Economic Co-operation and Developmend (OECD). (2009). *PISA 2006 technical report.* Paris, France: Author.

Pekrun, R., Elliot, A. J., & Maier, M. A. (2006). Achievement goals and discrete achievement emotions: A theoretical model and prospective test. *Journal of Educational Psychology, 98,* 583–597.

Pekrun, R., Elliot, A. J., & Maier, M. A. (2009). Achievement goals and achievement emotions: Testing a model of their joint relations with academic performance. *Journal of Educational Psychology, 101,* 115–135.

Pekrun, R., Goetz, T., Daniels, L. M., Stupnisky, R. H., & Perry, R. P. (2010). Boredom in achievement settings: Control-value antecedents and performance outcomes of a neglected emotion. *Journal of Educational Psychology, 102,* 531–549.

Pekrun, R., Goetz, T., Frenzel, A. C., Barchfeld, P., & Perry, R. P. (2011). Measuring emotions in students' learning and performance: The Achievement Emotions Questionnaire (AEQ). *Contemporary Educational Psychology, 36,* 36–48.

Pekrun, R., Goetz, T., Perry, R. P., Kramer, K., & Hochstadt, M. (2004). Beyond test anxiety: Development and validation of the Test Emotions Questionnaire (TEQ). *Anxiety, Stress and Coping, 17,* 287–316.

Pekrun, R., Goetz, T., Titz, W. & Perry, R.P. (2002). Academic emotions in students' self-regulated learning and achievement: A program of quantitative and qualitative research. *Educational Psychologist, 37,* 91–106.

Pekrun, R., & Linnenbrink-Garcia, L. (2014). Introduction to emotions in education. In R. Pekrun & L. Linnenbrink-Garcia (Eds.), *International handbook of emotions in education* (pp. 1–10). New York, NY: Taylor & Francis.

Pekrun, R., & Meier, E. (2011). *Epistemic Emotion Scales (EES).* Unpublished manuscript, Department of Psychology, University of Munich, Munich, Germany.

Perry, R. P., Hladkyi, S., Pekrun, R., & Pelletier, S. (2001). Academic control and action control in college students: A longitudinal study of self-regulation. *Journal of Educational Psychology, 93,* 776–789.

Reisenzein, R., Junge, M., Studtmann, M., & Huber, O. (2014). Observational approaches to the measurement of emotions. In R. Pekrun & L. Linnenbrink-Garcia (Eds.), *International handbook of emotions in education* (pp. 580–606). New York, NY: Taylor & Francis.

Robinson, M. D., & Clore, G. L. (2002). Belief and feeling: Evidence for an accessibility model of emotional self-report. *Psychological Bulletin, 128,* 934–960.

Sarason, I. G. (1958). Interrelationship among individual difference variables, behavior in psychotherapy, and verbal conditioning. *Journal of Abnormal and Social Psychology, 56,* 339–344.

Sarason, I. G. (1984). Stress, anxiety, and cognitive interference: Reactions to tests. *Journal of Personality and Social Psychology, 44,* 929–938.

Sarason, S. B., Davidson, K. S., Lighthall, F. F., Waite, R., & Ruebush, B. K. (1960). Anxiety in elementary school children. New York, NY: Wiley.

Sassenrath, J. M. (1964). A factor analysis of rating-scale items on the test anxiety questionnaire. *Journal of Consulting Psychology, 28,* 371–377.

Shuman, V., & Scherer, K. (2014). Concepts and structures of emotions. In R. Pekrun & L. Linnenbrink-Garcia (Eds.), *International handbook of emotions in education* (pp. 13–35). New York, NY: Taylor & Francis.

Smith, D. C., Adelman, H. S., Nelson, P., & Taylor, L. (1988). Anger, perceived control and school behavior among students with learning problems. *Journal of Child Psychology and Psychiatry, 29,* 517–522.

Smith, D. C., Furlong, M., Bates, M., & Laughlin, J. D. (1998). Development of the Multidimensional School Anger Inventory for Males. *Psychology in the Schools, 35,* 1–15.

Spangler, G., Pekrun, R., Kramer, K., & Hofmann, H. (2002). Students' emotions, physiological reactions, and coping in academic exams. *Anxiety, Stress and Coping, 15,* 413–432.

Spielberger, C. D. (1972). *Anxiety: Current trends in theory and research.* New York, NY: Academic Press.

Spielberger, C. D. (1980). *Test Anxiety Inventory: Preliminary professional manual.* Palo Alto, CA: Consulting Psychologist Press.

Sutton, R. E., & Wheatley, K. F. (2003). Teachers' emotions and teaching: A review of the literature and directions for future research. *Educational Psychology Review, 15,* 327–358.

Tracy, J. L., & Robins, R. W. (2007). The psychological structure of pride: A tale of two facets. *Journal of Personality and Social Psychology, 92,* 506–525.

Turner, J. C., & Trucano, M. (2014). Measuring situated emotion. In R. Pekrun & L. Linnenbrink-Garcia (Eds.), *International handbook of emotions in education* (pp. 643–658). New York, NY: Taylor & Francis.

Zeidner, M. (1998). *Test anxiety: The state of the art.* New York, NY: Plenum.

Zeidner, M. (2014). Anxiety in education. In R. Pekrun & L. Linnenbrink-Garcia (Eds.), *International handbook of emotions in education* (pp. 265–288). New York, NY: Taylor & Francis.

29

OBSERVATIONAL APPROACHES TO
THE MEASUREMENT OF EMOTIONS

Rainer Reisenzein[a], Martin Junge[a], Markus Studtmann[b], and Oswald Huber[c], University of Greifswald[a], Max Planck Institute for Human Development[b], and University of Fribourg[c]

The hallmark of psychology as an empirical science is the reliance on empirical data to support its claims. As traditionally conceived in philosophy and psychology (see, e.g., Brentano, 1874; Wundt, 1896), *empirical data* comprise all kinds of information obtained through experience, both those acquired through the "outer senses" (the sense-organs; i.e., the eyes, ears, etc.) and those acquired through the "inner sense", the self-observation of conscious mental states (also called *introspection*).[1] Common sense suggests that for obtaining empirical information about emotions, both methods—introspective self-observation and external observation—are useful. For example, to acquire empirical information about anger, one can either observe one's own feelings and thoughts during an episode of anger or ask others to report their experiences; or one can watch what other people do, say, and express nonverbally in their face, voice, and body when they are angry. In agreement with common sense, both introspection and external observation have been extensively used in emotion research since the beginnings of psychology as an independent discipline in the late 19th century (e.g., Wundt, 1896). Over the years, both methods have evolved and now exist in several more or less standardized variants. Introspection-based observation methods are today usually referred to as *self-report methods* (see Pekrun & Bühner, 2014). Their best-known incarnation in current emotion psychology is the emotion rating scale, but several other self-report based methods useful for emotion research do exist (e.g., Junge & Reisenzein, 2013). In this chapter, however, interest is on methods of emotion assessment based on external observation.

From the systematic perspective, methods of external observation in psychology comprise all methods that are based on the observation of intersubjectively accessible aspects of a psychological phenomenon (e.g., emotion), with or without the help of special observation instruments (e.g., video cameras, physiological sensors), and with or without making inferences to underlying mental states. Hence, from the systematic perspective, methods of external observation include not only assessments of behavior but also psychophysiological and neurophysiological measurements (see Immordino-Yang & Christodoulou, 2014; Kreibig & Gendolla, 2014). In this chapter, however, we focus on a subset of the methods of external observation commonly called *behavior observation methods* or simply *observational methods*. They can be defined as those methods of external observation that use human observers—or recently, machine substitutes of human observers (see the last part of this chapter)—as measurement devices and as a consequence are restricted to behaviors and events that are observable by humans, although the observers may be (and in fact typically are) asked to draw inferences to underlying mental states.[2] The following description by Wright (1960) captures the essence of behavior observation well: "One gets within seeing or hearing distance [of the target person], observes something about his behavior or situation or both, and then scores, classifies, summarizes, freely interprets, or otherwise does something with the recorded observations" (p. 71). As Wright's description also suggests, behavior observation methods rely primarily on visual and acoustic information, reflecting the fact that sight and hearing are the two most information-rich sensory channels of humans.

FOUNDATIONS OF OBSERVATIONAL APPROACHES TO THE MEASUREMENT OF EMOTIONS

We first describe the commonalities and differences of everyday and systematic behavior observations of emotions and discuss in what sense behavior observation can be regarded as a form of measurement. Then we discuss the kinds and diagnostic value of the cues to emotion that are in principle available to observers. In the central part of the chapter, we describe examples of the three main approaches to the observational measurement of emotions: objective behavior coding systems, theory-based coding methods, and the intuitive observer judgment method. Finally, we make recommendations on the practical implementation of observational emotion measurement and provide some information about recent developments in the field of behavior-based, automatic affect detection.

Everyday Versus Systematic Observations of Emotions

Observations of other people's behaviors (e.g., John smiles) and inferences from these behaviors and the context in which they occur to underlying emotions (e.g., John is amused) are commonly made by all of us in daily life (e.g., Heider, 1958; Malle, 2004; Schneider, Hastorf, & Ellsworth, 1979). Sometimes, we may even have the impression that we do not *make an inference* at all but literally *see* that another person is amused, sad, and so forth, but this shows only that the inference process can become fast and automatic to the point where it appears to be an integral part of perception. The inference of emotions is a special case of the more general phenomenon of *mindreading* or *mental state detection*—the inference of other people's mental states (which include, in addition to emotions, beliefs, desires, intentions, perceptions, and more).[3] Like its special form, emotion inference, mental state detection is routinely performed in everyday life, and the ability to engage in it is an essential component of humans' folk-psychological capacity. Mental state detection is best conceptualized as a process of *multiple-cue based, folk-theory-guided inference to the best explanation* (cf. Lipton, 2004) in which that one of several candidate mental states is attributed that best fits the available evidence (Reisenzein, 2010). The *evidence* used to infer mental states includes diverse behavioral cues discussed in more detail below, but it also includes knowledge about possible eliciting events and the personality and history of the target person (if available). Everyday mental state detection is *theory-guided* because it makes use of an implicit theory of mind that specifies the typical connections between eliciting events, mental states, and behaviors (Heider, 1958; Malle, 2004).

Let us illustrate this with an example of everyday emotion inference. Imagine you tell your colleague Ann that you have met your common friend Oscar at a recent conference, whereupon Ann seems surprised. How did you come to think that Ann is surprised? You may have noticed that, in response to your communication, Ann showed one or more of the following behaviors: Her eyebrows raised; she interrupted her typing on the computer and turned to you; she said "What?" or even "This surprises me!" You may also have recalled, either before or after you informed Ann, that she had told you earlier that Oscar could not attend the conference because of an urgent family business, and you inferred from this that Oscar's appearance at the conference would be an unexpected, and hence surprising, event for Ann. Generalizing from this case, emotion inference in everyday life seems to proceed as follows: one observes that another person reacts in a particular way to a particular event, and one then uses one's implicit knowledge about the connections between eliciting events, mental states, and diverse behavioral indicators of mental states to infer that the other person probably experiences a particular emotion.

The observational approaches to the measurement of emotions described in this chapter can be regarded as scientific versions of the sketched process of everyday emotion inference (or part of it). Compared to everyday emotion inference, the scientific methods are typically restricted to a smaller set of emotions and a limited set of cues to emotion (most often facial expressions), and some are based on an explicit psychological theory of emotion (e.g., basic emotions theory; Ekman, 1972). However, the most important difference is that, whereas everyday observations of emotion-diagnostic behaviors and inferences to underlying emotions are usually made in an unsystematic, anecdotal manner, scientific observation is *systematic*. Systematic observation is marked by three main features (e.g., Huber, 1999):

1. Its explicit aim is the observation of a defined class of phenomena (objects, behaviors, activities, processes), and ideally the observer devotes his or her full attention to this task.
2. The observation is performed in a systematic or structured way, that is, it follows an observation plan or protocol—a set of predefined rules that specify *what* is to be observed, *when* it is to be observed, and *by whom*, how the observed behavior is to be *coded*, and related to this, which (if any) *interpretations* of the directly observable behaviors are to be made (Huber, 1999; see also Bakeman, 2000).
3. The quality of the obtained data is controlled by appropriate checks to ensure an acceptable quality level. The minimum quality requirement that a scientific observation method must meet—like any scientific measurement method—is a sufficient degree of reliability. *Reliability* refers to the precision of a measurement method; in the case of behavior observation, it is usually defined operationally as the degree of inter-observer agreement. For example, a facial expression coding system for detecting emotions is reliable to the degree that different observers (or groups of observers) infer the same emotions from the same facial expressions. However, as in the case of other psychological measurements, a behavior observation

method can be reliable but have low *validity*—it may not measure what it was designed to measure. To judge the validity of a behavioral emotion indicator, one would ideally like to compare it to a "gold standard"—a standard or criterion that unambiguously indicates the person's true emotional state. Although an entirely uncontested gold standard for emotion measurement does not exist, the most frequently used validity criterion is the self-report of emotion. There are two main reasons for this. First, self-reports of emotion can claim *epistemic priority*: the primary criterion for the presence of a particular emotion in a target person is that person's subjective experience, to which the experiencer, and only he or she, has direct access.[4] Second, self-reports of emotion have unmatched *specificity*: no other emotion indicator allows to distinguish as finely between different emotions (e.g., Reisenzein & Junge, 2012). Next to the self-report of emotion, the best validity criteria for behavioral emotion indicators are face-valid emotion induction methods (e.g., Reisenzein, Bördgen, Holtbernd, & Matz, 2006). For example, unexpected events are universally surprising, and certain stimuli are disgusting for nearly everyone.

Behavior Observation as a Form of Measurement

The systematic observation of behaviors, including the inference to underlying mental states, is a form of measurement in the broad sense of "measurement" introduced by Stevens (1946). According to this broad meaning, a method of emotion measurement is any method suited to determine the quality (e.g., joy, sadness, anger, fear) or intensity of emotions, provided that the results of the assessment are numerically coded (represented as numbers) in a consistent way. Before Stevens, the term "measurement" was restricted to methods for determining the amount or degree of a quantitative attribute, yielding numerical assignments on a metric scale (i.e., an interval or a higher scale level) (Michell, 1990). In the case of emotions, a candidate quantitative attribute does exist: It is the *intensity* of emotions, such as the degree of fear or the intensity of anger.

Behavioral indicators of emotion (e.g., facial expressions) are frequently only coded as present/absent by observers and are then typically used to diagnose the presence/absence of the underlying emotions. This amounts to nominal-scale level measurement in Stevens's (1946) sense. However, most behavioral indicators of emotion actually vary in intensity (e.g., smiles can range from just visible to highly intense), and it is typically assumed, in both common-sense and scientific psychology, that their intensity reflects that of the underlying emotion (e.g., amused people smile more strongly, the more amused they are). If so, codings of the intensity of emotion indicators by observers as well as observers' direct intensity ratings of the underlying emotions, should allow the measurement of emotion intensity on at least an ordinal scale level. Furthermore, if one assumes that the *probability* of an emotion-diagnostic behavior (e.g., brow-raising) increases with the intensity of the underlying emotion (e.g., surprise), one can also derive the intensity of emotion from the probability (estimated from the relative frequency) of behavior, and hence ultimately from measurements at the nominal scale level (e.g., Reisenzein, 2000). Again, the resulting intensity scale would be at least ordinal. Whether *metric measurement* (measurement at an interval or higher scale level) of emotion intensity is possible using behavior observation methods does not seem to have been systematically investigated. However, this question could in principle be answered by testing whether emotion intensity judgments by observers fulfill certain qualitative (ordinal) conditions called measurement axioms (Junge & Reisenzein, 2013; Krantz, Luce, Suppes, & Tversky, 1971).[5]

The preceding considerations refer to the behavioral measurement of emotion intensity at a particular time point or during a short time interval. To estimate the overall intensity of an emotion experienced during a longer time interval (e.g., the overall intensity of amusement felt while watching a humorous film clip), it has been proposed to use a composite of the frequency, intensity, and duration of diagnostic behavior (e.g., smiling) (e.g., Kring & Sloan, 2007).

Finally, note that although observational methods are often associated with nonexperimental (correlational) studies and with field research, and are indeed often used in these research contexts (Fernández-Dols & Crivelli, 2013), they are not restricted to them. On the contrary, being a method of *measurement,* the observation of emotion-related behavior can be used in both experimental and nonexperimental (correlational) research, and in laboratory as well as in field studies.

A Classification of Observational Methods of Emotion Measurement

Observational methods of emotion measurement can be classified according to several criteria, including: which emotions are covered, which kinds of cues to these emotions are considered (e.g., only facial expressions versus all available cues), how much inference is required, whether the rules of inference are made explicit or not, and relatedly, to which degree a method is based on an explicit emotion theory. Based mainly on the criteria of how much inference is required by an observational method and how explicit the rules of inference are, we distinguish between objective behavior coding systems, theory-based coding systems, and intuitive observer judgments of emotions. *Objective behavior coding systems* focus on the measurement of observable behaviors potentially diagnostic of emotions but make no inferences to underlying emotions (thus they are strictly speaking not measurements of *emotions* but only of *emotion-related behaviors*).[6] In contrast, the aim of the theory-based observation methods and of the intuitive observer approach is to infer emotions from behavior. *Theory-based behavior coding systems* are based, in part or completely, on scientific emotion theories, some of which also include assumptions about how emotions relate to particular behaviors, whereas *intuitive observer judgments of emotions* rely on observers' implicit beliefs, or their implicit folk-psychological theories, about the relationship between emotions and behavior. Before describing the different behavioral approaches to emotion measurement in more detail, we first discuss the nature and diagnostic value of those cues to emotion that are in principle available to human observers.

Observable Cues to Emotion

Observable cues to another person's current emotion comprise (1) the situation, by which we mean potentially emotion-eliciting events and the context in which they occur and (2) emotion-diagnostic behaviors of the target person. The behavioral indicators of emotion that are accessible to human observers can be classified according to whether they are intentional (i.e., nonverbal and verbal actions) or nonintentional (involuntary, although typically more or less controllable) behaviors.[7] Nonintentional behaviors potentially diagnostic of emotions comprise three main classes: (1) facial displays, (2) vocal displays, which include paralinguistic features of speech as well as nonlinguistic vocalizations and vocal bursts (see further on for an explanation), and (3) bodily displays, by which we mean postures, gestures, and body movements. In addition, (4) some of the involuntary physiological changes accompanying emotions, or side-effects of these bodily changes, can become visible to observers when they are intense (e.g., sweating, trembling).

Basic research on emotion-diagnostic behaviors has focused on nonintentional behaviors and among these, on facial and to a lesser extent, on vocal expressions (Harrigan, 2005; see also Calvo & D'Mello, 2010). The reason is that facial expressions are generally considered to be the best-discriminating nonverbal channel of emotion expression, followed by vocal and bodily expression. In the following section, we briefly review the main findings of this research.

Situational Information as a Cue to Emotion

Situational information potentially diagnostic of emotions comprises information about the nature of an emotion-eliciting event and the context in which it occurs. Such information can be highly predictive of the emotions induced by the event (e.g., Reisenzein & Hofmann, 1993). For example, Reisenzein and Hofmann found that naïve judges were able to infer with high accuracy (on average, 65% correct classifications) which of 23 emotions a target person experienced from brief descriptions of the eliciting situations. Evidence from this and other studies suggests, furthermore, that information about eliciting events is often available to observers in everyday life, either because they are personal witness to an eliciting event, or because they are informed about it by others including the target person (e.g., Rimé, 2009).

Intentional Actions as Cues to Emotion

Intentional actions potentially diagnostic of emotions comprise (1) gross motor actions presumably motivated by emotions (e.g., Heider, 1958; Weiner, 1995), such as hitting in the case of anger and helping in the case of pity and (2) verbal communications (speech acts) that convey information about emotions. While both kinds of cues can be quite useful for the inference of emotions in others, verbal communications are particularly diagnostic (Reisenzein & Junge, 2012). Emotion-diagnostic utterances comprise at least three different kinds: (1) Speech acts motivated by the emotion, such as an aggressive statement in anger or a comforting remark in pity. These communications can be regarded as verbal equivalents to nonverbal emotion-motivated actions, such as hitting (anger) or helping (pity); (2) Spontaneous self-reports of emotion (e.g., "I am so surprised"); (3) Descriptions of eliciting events (e.g., the target's—but also a third party's—report about an accident), which are substitutes for the direct observation of these events. Direct observations of the events that elicited a currently experienced emotion in another person are, in fact, not possible in many cases (Reisenzein & Junge, 2012)—for example, because the events have occurred in the past and are now only remembered.

Both nonverbal and verbal intentional actions have received comparatively little attention as cues to emotion in basic emotion research. However, the content of speech has been used in clinical diagnosis systems to infer emotions such as anxiety, hostility and depression, since at least the 1960s (Gottschalk & Gleser, 1969; see also, Gottschalk, 1995). It is also considered to some extent in the SPAFF system described further on

(Coan & Gottmann, 2007) as well as in recent research on automatic affect detection (Schuller, Batliner, Steidl, & Seppi, 2011).

Nonintentional Behaviors as Cues to Emotion: The Face

Research on the nonintentional—in particular, the facial—expression of emotions has been dominated by the theory of discrete basic emotions (e.g., Ekman, 1972, 1992; Izard & Dougherty, 1982). The adherents of this theory believe that a small subset of human emotions, considered to be biologically basic, are associated with distinct patterns of involuntary behaviors, in particular facial expressions (for more information, see the section on theory-based coding systems). According to Ekman's version of basic emotions theory, the emotions associated with distinct facial expressions include at minimum happiness, sadness, fear, anger, disgust, and surprise (e.g., Matsumoto & Ekman, 2008). The prototypical expressions of these six emotions are shown in Figure 29.1.

The main evidence for Ekman's theory stems from studies in which observers were presented with pictures of posed expressions of the basic emotions together with a list of their names and were asked to indicate which emotion is expressed by which facial expression (readers can try this for themselves with Figure 29.1). Using this method,

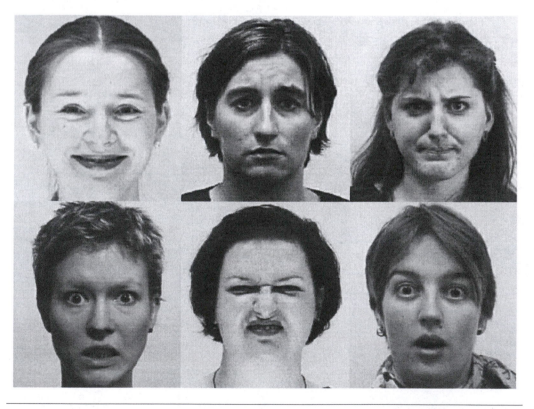

Figure 29.1 Prototypical facial expressions of six basic emotions according to Ekman (1972; see also Matsumoto & Ekman, 2008). From upper left to lower right: Happiness, sadness, anger, fear, disgust, and surprise. Photographs courtesy of Jörg Merten, Institute of Psychology, Saarland University.

average correct classification rates of more than 80% have been obtained in Western countries (e.g., Ekman et al., 1987; for reviews, see Elfenbein & Ambady, 2002; Nelson & Russell, 2013). However, accuracy is reduced if a free emotion labeling rather than a forced-choice method is used (Russell, 1994), and it also decreases with the distance to the Western culture (Nelson & Russell, 2013). Furthermore, these recognition studies show at best that if a target person shows a prototypical facial expression (which is actually not a statistical average but a high-intensity "ideal type"; Horstmann, 2002) then the correct emotion can be inferred with high accuracy. They do *not* show that people display the facial expression of a basic emotion whenever (and only) when they experience this emotion, and hence that the presence (and absence) of basic emotions can be reliably diagnosed from facial cues. Indeed, laboratory experiments (Reisenzein, Studtmann, & Horstmann, 2013) and naturalistic field studies (Fernández-Dols & Crivelli, 2013) of spontaneous emotional facial expressions suggest the opposite: Using self-reports of emotions or face-valid emotion induction methods as the criterion for the presence of emotions, these studies found that with the exception of amusement—which is usually not regarded as a basic emotion—only a minority of people who experience a discrete emotion show the facial expression presumably characteristic for it. Quite often (up to 90% in a series of studies on surprise by Reisenzein et al., 2006), no facial expression is shown at all, and if one occurs, it is typically only partial (i.e., only one or two components of the facial prototypes [Figure 29.1] are shown).

Nonintentional Behaviors as Cues to Emotion: The Voice

Speech can transmit information about emotions not only via the content of verbal messages (*what* is said, as described above) but also via *paralinguistic features* of vocal utterances (*how* something is said), such as pitch, voice intensity, and intonation. In addition, affective information can be conveyed via *nonlinguistic vocalizations*, such as breathing and laughter, and by what has been called *vocal bursts*, brief nonword utterances that arise between speech incidents and include shrieks, groans, and grunts as well as conventionalized expressions such as "wow!" (Schröder, 2003; Simon-Thomas, Keltner, Sauter, Sinicropi-Yao, & Abramson, 2009).

Basic research on emotion recognition from the voice has focused on paralinguistic features of speech and has recently also looked at vocal bursts. The findings are similar to those obtained for facial expressions. Posed paralinguistic expressions of basic emotions (most often happiness, sadness, anger, and fear), typically obtained by asking actors to speak neutral or meaningless phrases in different intonations that express the different emotions, have yielded decoding accuracies corresponding to 70% correct in a forced-choice task with five response alternatives (Juslin & Laukka, 2003; see also Juslin & Scherer, 2005, 2008). This is somewhat less than the decoding accuracy obtained for posed facial expressions in the forced-choice paradigm (see previous discussion). Actor-posed vocal bursts for basic emotions (plus a few nonbasic emotions, such as amusement and relief) can be identified with similar accuracy (Sauter, Eisner, Calder, & Scott, 2010; Schröder, 2003; Simon-Thomas et al., 2009). However, analogous to the case of facial expression, studies on spontaneous vocal affect expression suggest that the "ideal-type" vocal expressions of basic emotions occur rarely in everyday speech (e.g., Cowie & Cornelius, 2003; Laukka, Neiberg, Forsell, Karlsson, & Elenius, 2011) and that correspondingly, the detection of emotions from natural vocal expressions is possible only to a limited extent. Nevertheless, beyond-chance detection of arousal level, the valence of the emotion (positive versus negative), and some specific emotions (such as irritation) from spontaneous speech seems possible (Laukka et al., 2011; Schuller et al., 2011).

Nonintentional Behaviors as Cues to Emotion: The Body

It has long been assumed that in contrast to facial and vocal expressions, bodily expressions (i.e., gestures, postures, and body movements) provide only information about the gross quality of affective states (e.g., positive vs. negative) and about the intensity of emotions but not about specific emotions (see Dael, Mortillaro, & Scherer, 2012a). However, a recent study in which professional actors were asked to portray 12 emotions in body actions and postures (Dael et al., 2012a) obtained evidence for discriminative patterns of bodily expression for at least three emotions (anger, amusement, and pleasure). For example, a characteristic expression for anger was the forward moving of the whole body, whereas pleasure was expressed by "head tilted up and averted" and an "asymmetrical arm action" (Dael et al., 2012a, p. 1090). Other research suggests that a number of nonstandard emotions and emotion-like states that are particularly important in academic contexts, such as interest, boredom, and confusion (e.g., Pekrun, Goetz, Daniels, Stupnisky, & Perry, 2010) can be detected with beyond-chance accuracy from body movements. Specifically, Mota and Picard (2003) measured posture patterns using the *Body Pressure Measurement System* (BMPS), a thin-film pressure pad with a rectangular grid of sensing elements that can be mounted on a variety of surfaces, such as the seat and back of a chair. They found that temporal transitions of posture patterns allowed to diagnose, with beyond-chance accuracy (75%), the interest level of children (as judged by teachers) while they performed a learning task on a computer. D'Mello and Graesser (2009) have made an attempt to extend this assessment method to the diagnosis of other achievement emotions.

OBSERVATION-BASED METHODS FOR EMOTION MEASUREMENT

Having discussed the nature and diagnostic value of the cues to emotion available to human observers, we now look more closely at the three main forms of observation-based methods for emotion measurement distinguished earlier: objective behavior coding systems, theory-based coding systems, and intuitive observer judgments of emotions.

Objective Behavior Coding Systems

FACS

The Facial Action Coding System (FACS; Ekman & Friesen, 1978) is an objective, anatomically based system for the measurement of (visible) facial behavior. Based on an anatomically based description of facial actions proposed by Hjortsjö (1969), FACS is considered the state-of-the-art instrument for the manual coding of facial movements. Its most recent version is FACS 2002 (Ekman, Friesen, & Hager, 2002; see also http://face-and-emotion.com/dataface/facs/manual/TitlePage.html). In FACS, facial expressions are coded in terms of *action units* (AUs), defined as the smallest possible

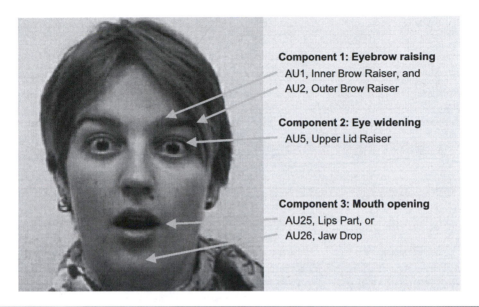

Component 1: Eyebrow raising
AU1, Inner Brow Raiser, and
AU2, Outer Brow Raiser

Component 2: Eye widening
AU5, Upper Lid Raiser

Component 3: Mouth opening
AU25, Lips Part, or
AU26, Jaw Drop

Figure 29.2 FACS coding of a prototypical surprise expression (codes according to Matsumoto & Ekman, 2008). Photograph courtesy of Jörg Merten, Institute of Psychology, Saarland University.

independent movements of facial muscles (Matsumoto & Ekman, 2008). These elementary movements can be regarded as the "phonemes" of facial expression (Littlewort et al., 2011). An overview of the FACS 2002 codes, including photographs of the action units, is given in Cohn, Ambadar, and Ekman (2007). As described there, FACS 2002 comprises 27 action units for the face (9 for the upper and 18 for the lower face), supplemented by 14 codes for head positions and movements, 9 for eye positions and movements, and several additional codes for other behaviors. Additionally, for some action units, FACS provides rules for scoring the intensity of the respective facial movements on a five-point scale. Figure 29.2 illustrates the FACS codes for a prototypical surprise face.

FACS coding can be performed comprehensively or selectively (Cohn et al., 2007). Comprehensive FACS coding considers the complete set of AUs, whereas selective FACS coding uses only a subset of AUs and ignores other facial movements. Comprehensive FACS coding is only possible for videos or still images because it is extremely time-consuming: According to Cohn et al. (2007), a well-trained FACS coder can take up to 100 minutes to code one minute of video data. However, comprehensive coding is not needed for many research purposes. If interest is restricted to Ekman's (1972) basic emotions, then EMFACS can be used (see below). If interest is still more narrowly restricted to a specific emotion (e.g., surprise, Reisenzein, 2000) or on specific facial movements (e.g., brow raising), then only the relevant subset of AUs need to be coded (see Figure 29.2 for the case of surprise). Alternatively, preliminary viewings of a set of videos may reveal that only a limited set of facial actions occur with sufficient frequency to warrant coding. Furthermore, FACS coding can be simplified by ignoring the intensities and the exact temporal onsets and offsets of AUs (which are also coded in comprehensive FACS coding)—that is, by coding only the occurrence and change of facial actions.

Cohn et al. (2007) summarize the findings of several studies on the reliability of well-trained FACS coders for 25 AUs. They found that reliability (expressed as Cohen's κ, the chance-corrected proportion of agreement) for presence/absence coding in a 0.5 sec tolerance window was good to excellent (about .70–.80) for nearly all AUs. As the tolerance window decreased in size, reliability decreased, but even with the smallest window (1/30th sec), 11 of 19 AUs had acceptable (> .60) reliabilities. High reliabilities have also been reported in studies using a strongly restricted set of AUs and coders trained only to recognize these AUs (e.g., Reisenzein, 2000). As to the validity of FACS, it is defined—because FACS is noninferential—as agreement with "what is really occurring on the face," as specified by an appropriate criterion such as an expert coding. Cohn et al. (2007) report that FACS codings agree well with several other validity criteria, such as the coding of instructed facial reactions and electromyographic (EMG) measurements of the involved facial muscles.

Objective Body Movement Coding and Voice Analysis Tools

An objective coding system analogous to FACS for the domain of *body action and posture*, the *Behavior Action and Posture coding system* (BAP), has been developed by Dael, Mortillaro, and Scherer (2012b). These authors also provide a review of other systems for coding body movement (see also, Harrigan, 2005). For *paralinguistic expressions of emotion*, a coding system using human observers analogous to FACS does not exist at present; however, as an alternative, objective acoustics-based methods are available that analyze speech waves by extracting parameters related to speech rate, voice intensity, fundamental frequency, and voice quality (e.g., Juslin & Scherer, 2005; Schuller et al., 2011). A much-used free software for the extraction of objective speech parameters is PRAAT (Boersma & Weenink, 2013).

Theory-Based Behavior Coding Systems

FACS is a tool for coding facial expressions objectively—that is, as facial movements—without making inferences to underlying emotions. In this sense, it is atheoretical (Matsumoto & Scherer, 2005). If the aim is to study whether or how particular emotions or other mental states are expressed in the face (e.g., Reisenzein et al., 2013), then no further inferences are in fact needed, and FACS is the method of choice. However, investigators of student and teacher emotions will typically not be interested in facial displays per se but in underlying emotional states. To get from facial movements to emotions, a set of inference rules is needed that connect facial behaviors (single AUs or combinations of AUs) to emotions. These rules are usually derived from a theory of emotion, such as basic emotions theory. Coding systems that contain such rules are therefore theory-based coding systems. Examples are EMFACS (Rosenberg & Ekman, 1984), the *Maximally Discriminative Facial Movement Coding System* (MAX) (Izard, 1979; Izard & Dougherty, 1982), and SPAFF (Coan & Gottman, 2007).

EMFACS (Emotion FACS)

EMFACS was developed on the basis of FACS with the aim to reduce scoring time when interest is only on emotion signals of the face. In EMFACS, only action units are coded that according to its authors are related to seven basic emotions (Ekman, 1972, 1992): the six already mentioned (happiness, sadness, anger, fear, disgust, and surprise; see Figure 29.1), plus contempt. In addition, the coding rules are simplified; in particular, whereas in standard FACS coding, the start and end time of each facial movement is coded, in EMFACS, the AUs are coded only at one time point (immediately before the point of maximum intensity). According to Ekman, Matsumoto, and Friesen (2005), coding time can be reduced to a tenth from FACS using EMFACS. Researchers considering using EMFACS should be aware, however, that the coding manual has not been published and is made available only to certified FACS coders.[8]

Although EMFACS could be regarded as a simplified version of FACS, the selection of the action units considered in EMFACS is grounded in basic emotions theory (Ekman, 1972). Furthermore, EMFACS users are typically interested in inferring basic emotions from the FACS codes and therefore use EMFACS together with a dictionary of assignment rules between FACS codes and emotions (e.g., Rosenberg, 2005). Descriptions of the assignment rules can be found, for example, in Matsumoto and Ekman (2008; see also, Ekman et al., 2002). These assignment rules, too, are based on basic emotions theory. For these reasons, EMFACS is here classified as a theory-based coding system.

The theoretical background of EMFACS, as said, is the theory of discrete basic emotions in the version proposed by Ekman (1972, 1992). According to basic emotions theory, the core of the emotion system consists of a set of discrete emotion mechanisms, each of which developed in evolution to solve a specific adaptive problem (e.g., the disgust mechanism developed to protect against poisoning by rotten food). If a basic emotion mechanism is evoked by suitable stimuli, it generates an emotion-specific pattern of responses including a specific feeling, a specific pattern of physiological reactions, and a characteristic facial expression (e.g., raising of the nose and upper lip in the case of disgust). According to Ekman, the main evolutionary function of the facial display is to communicate the emotional state to conspecifics. Although the facial expressions of the basic emotions can be deliberately suppressed or masked, as well as faked, basic emotions theory implies that spontaneous and uncontrolled displays reliably signal the presence of the corresponding basic emotions.

Assuming that the face-emotion assignment rules are unambiguous and are applied without error, the reliability of EMFACS codings depends only on the reliability of the corresponding FACS categories reported above and hence can be expected to be high. This is confirmed by the inter-coder agreements on EMFACS categories reported in several studies, which are high (e.g., Gottman & Levenson, 2002; Steimer-Krause, Krause, & Wagner, 1990). The validity of EMFACS can be gauged from the above-reported laboratory and field studies in which spontaneous expressions of basic emotions were related to self-reports of emotion or face-valid induction methods, particularly those in which EMFACS or FACS codings were made. These studies suggest that, with the exception of amusement, the validity of EMFACS is moderate to low: Expressed as a correlation, validities (not corrected for reliability) are approximately .65–.70 for amusement, < .50 for happiness, sadness, surprise, and disgust, and < .30 for anger and fear (Fernández-Dols et al., 2013; Reisenzein et al., 2013). However, note that in particular the data on anger and fear are sparse. Possible reasons for the moderate validity of facial expressions (and behavioral emotion indicators generally) as measures of emotion are discussed later.

Specific Affect Coding System (SPAFF)

The *Specific Affect Coding System* (SPAFF) was originally developed by Gottman and Krokoff (1989) for the systematic observation of "affective behavior" in marital conflict. It can be described as a theory-based coding system that (1) combines a set of explicit inference rules with an intuitive observer approach and (2) uses not only facial behaviors but also other nonverbal, as well as verbal cues including the content of utterances, to infer emotions and emotion-related action intentions (see further on). The development of SPAFF was motivated by Gottman's dissatisfaction with a previous, objective microanalytic coding system (CISS, Gottman, 1979) and similar coding systems such as FACS. According to Coan and Gottman (2007), these coding systems, which focus on physical features such as specific facial movements or gestures, often miss the forest for the trees because they are too discrete (they break up behavior in too small elements). To avoid this problem, SPAFF was devised to allow the direct coding of theoretical constructs (e.g., emotions). This is seen as a central advantage of SPAFF (Coan & Gottman, 2007, p. 267).

In its most recent version, SPAFF provides codes for 17 constructs referred to by Coan and Gottman (2007) as "positive affects" (affection, enthusiasm, humor, interest, and validation [meaning understanding and acceptance of the other]) and "negative affects" (anger, belligerence [a form of aggressive communication], contempt, criticism, defensiveness, disgust, domineering, fear/tension, sadness, stonewalling [unwillingness to listen or respond], threats, and whining). It is apparent that several of these categories (in particular validation, belligerence, criticism, defensiveness, and domineering) do not refer to emotions as typically conceived of by emotion researchers but are better described as interpersonal actions or interaction strategies, although they are probably partly motivated by emotions (e.g., defensiveness might be motivated by fear). These categories reflect SPAFF's origins as a tool to code marital interactions.

For each SPAFF construct, a hypothesized function in interpersonal encounters and a set of behavioral indicators are specified, and for a subset of the constructs, in addition a set of physical cues (facial expressions, postures, vocal features). Regarding the facial cues, SPAFF essentially incorporates EMFACS by interpreting particular combinations of FACS AUs as expressions of Ekman's basic emotions (sadness, anger, contempt, fear, disgust). However, other SPAFF categories are also linked to certain facial AUs (e.g., domineering). To illustrate, the SPAFF category *anger* is described as follows: (1) The function of anger is to "respond to perceived violations of the speaker's rights to autonomy and respect" (Coan & Gottman, 2007, p. 273); (2) Indicators of anger are frustration (a low-level form of an anger display marked by low-intensity facial expressions of anger and sometimes a lowering of the pitch and tempo of the voice), statements of being angry (e.g., "I am so angry!"), questions asked with angry affect and usually with sharp exhalations (as in "Why?!"), and commands (e.g., "Stop!") intended to stop a recent or ongoing violation of the speaker's autonomy and dignity; (3) Physical cues to anger are facial expressions of anger and changes in the voice (e.g., sudden increases in pitch, amplitude, and tempo). It is evident from this description that the indicators of SPAFF anger (and the same is true for the other categories) require considerable inference. For example, observers need to infer that frustration is present, that a question was asked with angry affect, or that a command was intended to stop a violation of the speaker's rights. To justify these inferences, Coan and Gottman (2007) refer to the so-called "cultural informants" approach to behavior observation, which assumes that experienced members of a culture are experts for the detection of emotional states from multiple nonverbal and verbal cues. This corresponds essentially to the intuitive observer approach to behavioral emotion measurement described in the next section. Hence, SPAFF combines a theory-based approach to the observational measurement of emotions with an intuitive observer approach.

SPAFF has been used in numerous studies to code affective behavior in interactions—mostly in couples, but also in children, their parents, and their peers (see Coan and Gottman, 2007; Jones, Carrère, & Gottman, 2005). Several studies found that adequate coding reliabilities can be obtained using SPAFF. For example, Carrère and Gottman (1999; see Jones et al., 2005) obtained reliabilities (Cronbach's alpha) > .70 for all SPAFF categories with the exception of contempt (.67), surprise (.56; this category was part of a previous version of SPAFF) and disgust (.37); the low reliabilities of disgust and surprise may, however, have been due to the fact that these categories occurred rarely. Similarly, Gottman and Levenson (2002) reported a chance-corrected proportion of agreement (Cohen's κ) of .75 for a 9-category version of SPAFF. Butler et al. (2003) reported an interrater reliability of $r = .90$ for a SPAFF-based index of positive emotions and .92 for negative emotions.

Although SPAFF codings have been shown to have predictive validity in being able to predict marital quality and divorce (e.g., Jones et al., 2005), data on the coherence of SPAFF emotion codings with self-reports of the same emotions are surprisingly scarce. In fact, we only found a single pertinent study (Geist & Gilbert, 1996). The authors found significant correlations to self-reported emotions for anger (.54) and sadness (.63) for wives, whereas for husbands, only the correlation for anger (.35) was significant.

Because SPAFF was explicitly designed for interaction situations, it should also be suited for use in academic contexts, although additional categories for emotions such as interest or boredom may have to be added. Finally, it may be noted that for eight SPAFF emotion categories, a behavior rating (rather than coding) system that allows nonexclusive intensity ratings has been developed (Johnson, 2002).

Facial Expression Coding System (FACES)

Developed by Kring, Smith, and Neale (1994), FACES, like EMFACS, is an exclusively face-based observational system for the measurement of emotions. Different from EMFACS and SPAFF, however, FACES does not refer to discrete basic emotions theory as its theoretical foundation but to the *dimensional approach* to emotion, specifically to pleasure-arousal theory (e.g., Russell, 1980, 2003; see also, Reisenzein, 1994). It is for this reason—the reference to pleasure-arousal theory—that we classify FACES as a theory-based observation method. However, apart from this and the fact that FACES uses some (modest) training of observers, FACES could also be classified as an intuitive observer judgment method for inferring valence (pleasure-displeasure) from facial expressions (Kring & Sloan, 2007) because it does not specify any face-emotion inference rules.

Pleasure-arousal theory assumes that emotional experiences, including basic emotions such as happiness, sadness, fear, and anger, or at least their feeling core (called "core affect" by Russell, 2003) consist of mixtures of more basic feelings—namely, feelings of pleasure or displeasure and of activation or deactivation. For example, the feeling core of anger is a mixture of displeasure and activation, whereas the feeling core of contentment is a mixture of pleasure and deactivation (see also, Reisenzein, 1994). As a consequence, pleasure-arousal theory rejects the assumption, made by some basic emotion theorists (e.g., McDougall, 1908; Oatley & Johnson-Laird, 1987), that basic emotions are characterized by unanalyzable feelings (see Reisenzein, 1995). In addition, dimensional emotion theorists reject the assumption that basic emotions are created by discrete affect programs that contain instructions for emotion-specific facial expressions (e.g., Barrett, 2006; Russell, 2003).

Approaches to emotion measurement based on pleasure-arousal theory are characterized by the attempt to measure the proposed components of emotion, either directly, by using items that ask participants to report the intensity of experienced pleasure-displeasure and arousal (e.g., Russell, Weiss, and Mendelsohn, 1989); or indirectly, by estimating the dimension values from measurements of specific affects (e.g., Smith, Vivian, & O'Leary, 1990). FACES uses the former approach; however, only the valence dimension (pleasure-displeasure) is assessed. Whenever a FACES rater detects a facial expression, defined as a change from a neutral face, he or she first makes a judgment about the valence of the expression (positive vs. negative). Next, the intensity of the facial expression (from 1 = low to 4 = high) is rated and finally its duration (in seconds).

Kring and Sloan (2007) present data on the reliability and validity of FACES. Concerning reliability, they report an average interrater agreement of ICC (intraclass correlation coefficient) = .86 in five studies, attesting to high reliability. As to the validity of FACES, (between-subject) correlations between observer ratings and self-reports of experienced pleasure/displeasure were found to depend on the nature of the emotion-eliciting event. Correlations were highest for amusing films ($r = .35$ to $r = .70$ for a composite of FACES frequency, intensity, and duration codings), moderate for happy ($r = .19$ to $r = .49$) and disgusting films ($r = .16$ to $r = .64$), and low for fearful films ($r = -.28$ to $r = .54$). This is similar to the validity of EMFACS inferences for Ekman's (1972) basic emotions, reported previously.

Intuitive Observer Judgments

An alternative to using formal behavior coding systems for the inference of mental states and traits is to use untrained raters (but possibly, and sometimes with a gain in validity [Sternglanz & DePaulo, 2004], people familiar with the target person, such as partners or staff). For example, ratings by peers are often used as observational measurements of personality traits (e.g., emotional stability, extraversion, conscientiousness) in personality psychology (Conolly, Kavanagh, & Viswesvaran, 2007). Applied to emotional states, the intuitive observer judgment method takes the intuitive observer approach already used as a component of SPAFF and FACES to its logical conclusion by dispensing completely with formal theory and relying entirely on observers' folk-psychological competence to infer emotions from behavior and context. The intuitive observer judgment method has been used in both basic research on the relation between emotions and facial expressions (e.g., Deckers, Kuhlhorst, & Freeland, 1987; see Reisenzein et al., 2013) and in more applied research, such as studies of interactions between couples (e.g., Waldinger, Schulz, Hauser, Allen, & Crowell, 2004).

Although the intuitive observer judgment method may at first sight appear to be a step backward when compared to more formal coding systems, such as SPAFF, it does have a number of advantages:

1. It is economical: Intuitive judges need not be specially trained, and the rating process takes no more time than comparable self-ratings do.
2. In principle, any emotion or emotion-related mental state can be judged by observers, including emotions such as interest and boredom, which are not considered in formal coding systems, such as EMFACS or SPAFF, but may be of particular interest to educational researchers (Pekrun et al., 2010). As a consequence, the intuitive

observer judgment method can be easily adjusted to the theoretical needs of the researcher.

3. The intuitive judgment method places no a priori restrictions on the cues used by observers to infer emotions, allowing them to use any available cue (facial, vocal, situational context, etc.) or cue combination. This maximally exploits the available information and best approximates the process of multicue emotion inference in everyday life.

4. Intuitive observer judgments avoid a potential problem of theory-based coding systems, which is the need to "reeducate" coders to define and recognize emotions in new ways that depart from their intuitive psychological understanding (Waldinger et al., 2004). In fact, Smith et al. (1990) reported that the attempt to train coders in the use of an observational coding system was partly unsuccessful, apparently because the coders' implicit theories of emotional expression were too deeply ingrained to change them in a reliable fashion.

Given these advantages of the intuitive observer judgment method, the decisive question becomes how it compares, in terms of reliability and validity, to the theory-based observational systems. Concerning reliability, the agreement between pairs of naïve judges is generally only moderate; however, reliability can be raised to adequate levels by pooling the judgments of several observers. In this way, individual biases of raters are minimized, and high agreement can be obtained (for details, see Rosenthal, 2005; see also, Schulz & Waldinger, 2005). For example, Waldinger et al. (2004) asked six judges to rate 18 emotions and emotion-related constructs (largely culled from the SPAFF) expressed in 30-second segments of interaction between couples. The reliability of the mean ratings of the six coders was on average $r = .66$, ranging from .27 (disgust) to .89 (humorous), with 14 of the 18 codings attaining reliabilities $\geq .60$ and 11 $\geq .70$. For combined indices of "hard emotions" (angry, annoyed, irritated, and aggravated) and "soft emotions" (hurt, sad, concerned, and disappointed), reliabilities around .90 were obtained by Sanford (2007). Concerning validity, Sanford (2007) reports correlations between observer ratings and self-ratings of .42 (wives) and .31 (husbands) for hard emotions, and .40 (wives) and .33 (husbands) for soft emotions. Although more research is needed, these findings suggest that the intuitive observer judgment method performs not much worse than the formal affect coding systems.

An interesting variant of intuitive observer ratings of emotion has been proposed by Levenson and Gottman (1983; see Ruef & Levenson, 2007). Observers use a dial to make near-continuous, moment-to-moment ratings of the intensity of an emotion (e.g., happiness or sadness) they perceive in the target person. These ratings can then be compared to analogous moment-to-moment self-ratings of emotion (e.g., Mauss, Levenson, McCarter, Wilhelm, & Gross, 2005).

Reasons for and Implications of the Moderate
Validity of Observational Methods

Whereas sufficient reliability can be attained for all described observational methods of emotion measurement, the validity of those methods that go beyond the observed behaviors to infer emotions (EMFACS, FACES, SPAFF, intuitive observer judgments) seems to have clear limits: With the exception of amusement (judged from facial behavior), validity as judged from agreements with self-reports typically does not exceed values of $r = .50$ for "basic emotions" (disgust, sadness, anger, fear) and is little better for pleasure-displeasure ratings. Possible reasons for the moderate coherence between emotions and their behavioral indicators have been most extensively discussed for facial expressions. The following explanations have been proposed:

1. Suboptimal designs used to estimate coherence—in particular, between-subjects rather than within-subjects designs (see, e.g., Reisenzein, 2000). Indeed, within-subjects correlations between emotion self-reports and facial expressions are usually higher than between-subjects correlations. However, with the exception of amusement, only moderate emotion-expression coherence is typically obtained even in within-subject designs (Reisenzein et al., 2013).

2. Measurement problems associated with self-reports of emotion, including the unwillingness or inability of people to accurately report the quality and intensity of their emotions (e.g., Rosenberg & Ekman, 1994). However, this is hardly the only reason: using conceptually identical self-report measures, comparatively high coherence between self-report and facial expression has been found for amusement (Reisenzein et al., 2013); conversely, low expression-experience coherence obtained for surprise was not found to increase when random measurement error in self-reports was reduced by an averaging method (Reisenzein, 2000).

3. Insufficient intensity of emotions. According to this hypothesis, emotions do not reveal themselves in facial expressions unless they exceed a threshold of intensity, which is often not reached in experimental and natural situations. Again, this is a possibility, but it explains at best part of the findings (Reisenzein et al., 2013).

4. Deliberate suppression or faking of emotional expressions (e.g., Rosenberg & Ekman, 1994). This is certainly a possibility; however, comparisons of facial expressions in social situations to those in solitary situations, where impression management should be less of an issue, suggest that expression control explains at best part of the findings (Reisenzein et al., 2013).

5. Emotions simply do not reveal themselves very clearly in facial behavior. At second thought, there may in fact be good evolutionary reasons for this: As noted by Fridlund (1994; see also Dawkins & Krebs, 1978; Russell, Bachorowski, & Fernández-Dols, 2003), the (involuntary or deliberate) truthful communication of emotions incurs potential costs to the sender, as it makes the sender more predictable and thus exploitable by others. In addition, by communicating his or her emotion to others, the sender may give away potentially useful information about the environment (e.g., that an unexpected event has occurred in the case of surprise) for free (Reisenzein & Junge, 2012). The truthful signaling of emotions to others is therefore a form of biological altruism that, like other altruistic behaviors, should have required special evolutionary conditions for its emergence. Possible evolutionary scenarios are kin selection, reciprocal altruism, group selection (Richerson & Boyd, 2005), and costly signaling. With the possible exception of costly signaling (see Dessalles, 2007), all of these scenarios require that emotions are not signaled indiscriminately but are revealed selectively to suitable targets—be it close kin, partners in a cooperative relationship, or members of a group with which the sender identifies. For other interaction partners, it would not be in the sender's interest to honestly communicate his or her emotions (and other mental states). Furthermore, it

can be argued that for the purpose of selective emotion communication, language—human's main medium of communication—is in fact much better suited than non-verbal behavior (Reisenzein & Junge, 2012).

In view of the limited validity of behavioral cues to emotion, observational emotion researchers should try to use (1) multiple behavioral cues and (2) include additional information—in particular, about eliciting events, unless doing so interferes with the goals of the study (e.g., when the goal is to test whether a particular event induces a particular emotion). For an example of the proposed multiple-cue, theory-based inference of one emotion (surprise), see Reisenzein et al. (2006). Furthermore, note that although a moderate-validity measure of emotion is of limited use for the diagnosis of emotions on the level of *individuals* (which is typically the goal of emotion measurement in applied contexts, such as counseling or therapy), it can still be useful for research questions that can be answered by comparing *groups* (e.g., does marital counseling on average decrease interpersonal anger?). In addition, instead of using behavioral observations as moderately valid indicators of a target's true emotional state, they can be used as valid measures of how that state *is perceived by* others. This information can be highly valuable in itself because how a person's emotional state is perceived by others (e.g., a student's emotional state by teachers or the emotional well-being of a nursing home resident by staff [see Kolanowski, Hoffman, & Hofer, 2007]) is presumably more important for socially relevant consequences than the target's true emotional state. A parallel argument has been made for peer ratings of personality traits (see Conolly et al., 2007).

TECHNICAL ISSUES IN THE BEHAVIORAL OBSERVATION OF EMOTIONS

Online Versus Offline Coding

Coding of emotional behaviors can be performed online, that is while the behavior occurs; or retrospectively, using recordings of the behavior. Online coding by human observers presupposes that the coding is at all possible in real time and is therefore not an option for time-consuming coding systems such as FACS, unless a strongly restricted set of AUs is used (however, as described below, online FACS coding is now becoming possible using automatic coding systems). Online coding is an option, however, for FACES valence judgment and for intuitive observer judgments of emotion.

Although nowadays offline coding is typically preferred, it deserves to be pointed out that, when it is feasible, online coding actually has some advantages (see also, Bakeman, 2000). First, it requires no technical equipment but paper and pencil.[9] Second, online coding avoids potentially intrusive recording equipment such as visible cameras. Third, it allows observers to pick up cues to the target's emotion that are not available in video recordings (e.g., olfactory cues), or that can get lost in a video recording due to, for example, low speech volume, insufficient picture resolution, or a suboptimal camera angle.

The central disadvantage of online coding is the lack of a permanent behavior record and the increased observational possibilities that such a record affords. Therefore, behavior recordings should be made additionally even when online coding is possible and preferred. Although voice-only recordings (e.g., Schuller et al., 2011) and posture measurements (e.g., D'Mello & Graesser, 2009) can be an option in special cases, video recordings are the most useful and for this reason the most widely used behavior records. Coding of video recording has several advantages over online coding. First, prior to coding, the videos can be edited with video editing software in multiple useful ways. For example, to facilitate the coding procedure, critical sections of a teacher–student interaction can be cut and saved as separate video clips, or pasted together, and multiple video recordings of the same scene (e.g., one camera focusing on the teacher and another on the student) can be synchronized to be shown side by side. Second, the videos can be coded by multiple coders (which is particularly important for intuitive observer judgments to attain adequate reliability), and additional codings can be performed should new questions arise. Third, videos can be watched repeatedly and can be played back in slow motion or framewise to detect very brief or weak expressions.

Recording and Editing

Dinkelaker and Herrle (2009) recommend the use of digital camcorders because of their small size, easy operation, and high data compatibility. Videos can be recorded on Mini-DV (digital video) or high definition (HD) cassettes and later transferred to a personal computer or notebook for further processing. Alternatively, the videos can be stored directly on a computer. For the coding of facial expressions, care must be taken to obtain a good quality picture of the face (typically, a close-up of head and shoulders or head and upper body is sufficient). In educational settings, it is often useful if not imperative to use multiple cameras to optimally capture interactions between, for example, students and teacher. One camera focuses on the student and another on the teacher. A time-code (in millisecond or frame accuracy) that is visible in the video is very helpful and often indispensable. The time code is traditionally inserted into the camera video signal at recording time, using, for example, a Vertical Time Code (VITC) generator and a linked time code reader-plus-inserter. These hardware parts are offered as internal PC cards or as external boxes by several manufacturers at affordable prices. Alternatively, some professional video editing programs (e.g., FinalCut) as well as third-party software (e.g., TokiTC, www.tokitest.fr/english/tokitc.html) allow one to insert the time code later into the digitized video.

To facilitate the coding of interactions filmed by two cameras, it is useful to combine the two video streams in such a way that the behavior of the interaction partners (e.g., students and teachers) is shown synchronously side by side. For this, a special-effects generator with a "split screen" capability can be used, but there are also special video cards that allow the synchronous recording from several cameras. Alternatively, the two videos are recorded separately and are subsequently combined into a single video using video editing software, or they can simply be played back simultaneously side-by side (although this will usually need some manual adjustment to keep the videos in sync). If students are working on a computer, it is useful to synchronize the video track of their behavior with a video capture of the computer screen to be able to identify screen events as potential elicitors of expressive behavior. Educational researchers could also exploit the wide availability of computer labs at schools and universities to simultaneously record the behavior of multiple students: By attaching inexpensive webcams and microphones to the computers, they could obtain separate close-up recordings of every student in the lab.

Software for Coding

For the coding of the videos, a good video playing software is needed. Dinkelaker and Herrle (2009) recommend the freeware VLC Media Player. We have had good experiences with Zoom Player, which is also available in a Freeware version. Codes or ratings can be noted down on a sheet of paper with labeled columns or can be directly entered into a spreadsheet opened in a second window on the same or a separate monitor. This method actually works well for the coding of brief event-locked video recordings (e.g., student's facial reactions to teacher praise in a five-second window), particularly if the exact onset and offset times of the behaviors are not important. However, for the coding of more extended behavior streams and for the measurement of exact onsets and offsets, special video coding software can be a better choice. A variety of commercial and freeware/shareware programs are available for this purpose; some of them have been reviewed in Bakeman, Deckner, and Quera (2005). General-purpose commercial behavior observation software systems suited for the coding of emotional behaviors are INTERACT® (Mangold Software and Consulting, www.mangold.de/english/intoverview.htm) and OBSERVER® XT (Noldus company, www.noldus.com). Freeware/Shareware programs include multi-purpose video annotation tools, such as ANVIL (Kipp, 2013, www.anvil-software.org) and ELAN (Lausberg, & Sloetjes, 2009; http://tla.mpi.nl/tools/tla-tools/elan/) and more specialized coding software, such as Etholog (Ottoni, 2000; www.ip.usp.br/docentes/ebottoni/EthoLog/ethohome.html) and ICODE (www-2.cs.cmu.edu/~face/index2.htm), which was specifically developed for FACS coding (see Cohn et al., 2007).

Automatic Coding and Affect Detection

Because of the time and effort required to code emotional behaviors, there have been, since the 1990s, attempts to develop computer programs that take over this task. Research on automatic coding of emotional behaviors and affect detection has increased greatly during the past decade, due in large part to the emergence of a new branch of computer science called *affective computing* that seeks to improve human-computer interaction by creating computer systems that are able to detect and appropriately respond to user emotions (Calvo, D'Mello, Gratch, & Kappas, 2014; Picard, 1997). A recent overview of automatic affect detection is provided by Calvo and D'Mello (2010).

As might be expected, a focus of this research is the development of programs that allow to detect emotion in the face (e.g., Cohn & Kanade, 2007; Pantic & Bartlett, 2007; Zeng, Pantic, Roisman, & Huang, 2009). One approach is to develop programs that first detect FACS action units in videos, from which emotions (or other mental states) can then be inferred using theoretical or empirically determined assignment rules. A second approach to automatic facial emotion recognition attempts to infer emotions directly from low-level image features (see Pantic & Bartlett, 2007). An example system that allows online coding of both FACS action units and basic emotions is the *Computer Expression Recognition Toolbox* (CERT) (Littlewort et al., 2011). Figure 29.3 illustrates the operation of CERT for the recognition of FACS AUs (for details, see Littlewort et al., 2011).

Although there has been remarkable progress in automatic FACS scoring during the past years, the performance of current automatic AU detection systems does not yet quite match that of human coders (Calvo & D'Mello, 2010). Furthermore, most automatic facial scoring systems are research prototypes. At least two real-time automatic facial

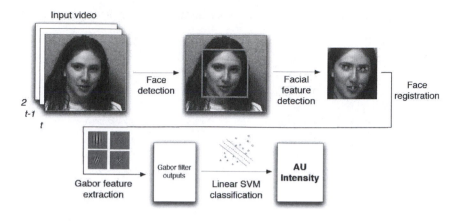

Figure 29.3 Processing pipeline of the Computer Expression Recognition Toolbox (CERT) from video to AU intensity estimates. From Littlewort et al. (2011). Courtesy of Gwen Littlewort, Machine Perception Laboratory, University of California, San Diego.

coding systems, however, are publicly available: FaceReader™ (D'Arcey, Johnson, & Ennis, 2012) and FACET™ (http://imotionsglobal.com/software/add-on-modules/attention-tool-facet-module-facial-action-coding-system-facs/), which is a commercial system based on the CERT technology (Littlewort et al., 2011).

During the past 10 years, the voice has also become a favorite target of automated affect detection systems. Several audio-based automatic emotion detection systems are reviewed by Zeng et al. (2009; see also, Calvo & D'Mello, 2010; Schuller et al., 2011). Although many of these systems focus on basic emotions (Ekman, 1992), efforts have also been made to detect other affective states, such as frustration (e.g., Laukka et al., 2011).

Automatic systems have also been developed for the detection of affect from posture (e.g., D'Mello & Graesser, 2009) and from physiological reactions (see Calvo & D'Mello, 2010). Furthermore, there is a trend to develop affect detection systems that fuse the information from several channels (Calvo & D'Mello, 2010). Although these latter systems are at present still research prototypes, educational researchers might team up with computer scientists working in the field of affective computing (see, e.g., http://emotion-research.net/) to mutual profit.

We consider it possible that within the next 10 years, automatic affect detection tools systems will reach the stage where they can compete with human observers. To achieve this, these systems will probably need to combine accurate sensing of multiple behavioral cues, including the content of speech, with knowledge about the context and the target's personality and history, and with an elaborated theory of mind component that specifies the links between behavioral cues and emotions and is possibly adjusted to the specific targets during training sessions (Reisenzein, 2010). It is conceivable that automatic affect detection systems will eventually even outperform human observers, either because they include signals (e.g., from subtle physiological changes) not available to human observers or because they use emotion inference algorithms that outperform those implicitly used by humans. In any case, the currently used observational methods of emotion measurement, described in the core section of this chapter, may soon become replaced by computer-based systems. Finally, even though there may be evolutionary limits to what can be detected about emotional states from the observation of behaviors, measurements of brain activity are not so limited: Because on the neurophysiological level, emotional states are brain states, measurements of brain activity could eventually provide precise external measurements of both the quality and intensity of experienced emotions. For an example of recent research in this area, see Wagner, Atlas, Lindquist, Roy, Woo, and Kross (2013).

NOTES

1. Empirical methods of knowledge acquisition are traditionally juxtaposed to rational methods (methods based on reasoning; e.g., Musgrave, 1993), which can be defined as all valid methods of drawing inferences from existing knowledge (e.g., deduction, induction, inference to the best explanation). Rational methods play an indispensable role in all sciences, and some sciences (e.g., logics and mathematics) use them exclusively. Inference also plays an essential role in many psychological observation methods, as illustrated in this chapter by the theory-based and intuitive observational approaches to emotion measurement.

2. This is not meant to be a precise definition. In fact, we believe with others (e.g., Cranach & Frenz, 1969) that a sharp demarcation of behavior observation from other methods of external observation is not possible. But neither is it needed.

3. Broadly understood, mental state detection also includes the inference of personality traits (Schneider et al., 1979). Many of these traits actually are, or involve, dispositions to have particular emotions (Reisenzein & Weber, 2009).

4. For a recent critique of this assumption, see Jäger (2009). Jäger argues that, as a matter of fact, we often suffer from affective ignorance, as a consequence of which observation-based ascriptions of emotions should often be credited with more rather than less authority than corresponding self-ascriptions. Although this viewpoint is a minority position among today's emotion researchers, it should be acknowledged that self-reports of emotions are subject to a number of possible biases, including reactivity (observing one's emotional state may alter this state), interindividual differences in the meanings of the emotion concepts used to report one's feelings, and unwillingness to report one's emotions (see, e.g., Mauss & Robinson, 2009).

5. Self-reports of emotion intensity on rating scales (e.g., "How happy are you right now on a scale from 0 = not at all to 10 = extremely") are thought to lie somewhere in between the ordinal and interval scale level (Krantz, Luce, Suppes, & Tversky, 1971); an interval scale level can, however, be reached with alternative self-report methods based on comparative judgments (Junge & Reisenzein, 2013). The same may be true for observer judgments of emotion intensity.

6. Note, however, that some emotion theorists consider emotion-related behaviors (at least certain involuntary behaviors) to be part of emotions, which they conceptualize as mental-behavioral syndromes (e.g., Lazarus, 1991).

7. Although the theoretical distinction between intentional and nonintentional emotion-related behaviors is widely accepted, the following classification of some kinds of emotional behavior as intentional versus unintentional could be questioned. For example, it could be argued that most gestures and some vocal bursts are intentional, whereas goal-directed actions that have become habitual should be considered unintentional. Furthermore, because most nonintentional behaviors can be deliberately simulated, the classification of *concrete instances* of emotional behaviors (e.g., Ann's smile at the joke Bill told her) as intentional versus unintentional is always more or less tentative.

8. Certified FACS coders have passed a test issued by Ekman's research group (see Ekman et al., 2002, and http://face-and-emotion.com/dataface/facs/FFT_Proc.html). It takes around 100 hours of working through the FACS manual to become competent enough to take the test (Ekman et al., 2005). Alternatively, one can participate in a FACS training course offered by several FACS researchers (Cohn et al., 2007).

9. Nevertheless, a hand-held electronic device is recommended for entering the codes because it prevents data entry errors when transferring the data from the sheets and also allows automatic storing of the time. For a review of hand-held data entry devices, see Adiguzel, Vannest, and Zellner (2009).

REFERENCES

Adiguzel, T., Vannest, K. J., & Zellner, R. D. (2009). The use and efficacy of handheld computers for school-based data collection: A literature review. *Computers in the Schools, 26,*187–206.

Bakeman, R. (2000). Behavioral observations and coding. In H. T. Reis & C. K. Judd (Eds.), *Handbook of research methods in social psychology* (pp. 138–159). New York, NY: Cambridge University Press.

Bakeman, R. Deckner, D. F., & Quera, V. (2005). Analysis of behavioral streams. In D. M. Teti (Ed.), *Handbook of research methods in developmental science* (pp. 394–420). Oxford, United Kingdom: Blackwell Publishers.

Barrett, L. F. (2006). Are emotions natural kinds? *Perspectives on Psychological Science, 1,* 28–58.

Boersma, P., & Weenink, D. (2013). Praat: Doing phonetics by computer (Version 5.4.40) [Computer program]. Retrieved Feb. 5, 2013 from www.praat.org/

Brentano, F. (1874). *Psychologie vom empirischen Standpunkte* [*Psychology from the empirical standpoint*]. Leipzig, Germany: Duncker & Humblot.

Butler, E. A., Egloff, B., Wilhelm, F. H., Smith, N. C., Erickson, E. A., & Gross, J. J. (2003). The social consequences of expressive suppression. *Emotion, 3,* 48–67.

Calvo, R. A., & D'Mello, S. K. (2010). Affect detection: An interdisciplinary review of models, methods, and their applications. IEEE *Transactions on Affective Computing, 1,* 18–37.

Calvo, R. A., D'Mello, S. K., Gratch, J., & Kappas, A. (Eds.). (2014). *Handbook of affective computing.* Oxford, United Kingdom: Oxford University Press.

Carrère, S., & Gottman, J. M. (1999). Predicting divorce among newlyweds from the first three minutes of a marital conflict discussion. *Family Process, 38,* 293–301.

Coan, J. A., & Gottman, J. M. (2007). The Specific Affect coding system (SPAFF). In J. A. Coan & J. B. Allen (Eds.), *Handbook of emotion elicitation and assessment* (pp. 106–123). New York, NY: Oxford University Press.

Cohn, J. F., Ambadar, Z., & Ekman, P. (2007). Observer-based measurement of facial expression with the Facial Action Coding System. In J. A. Coan & J. B. Allen (Eds.), *Handbook of emotion elicitation and assessment* (pp. 203–221). New York, NY: Oxford University Press.

Cohn, J. F., & Kanade, T. (2007). Automated facial image analysis for measurement of emotion expression. In J. A. Coan & J. B. Allen (Eds.), *Handbook of emotion elicitation and assessment* (pp. 222–238). New York, NY: Oxford University Press.

Conolly, J. J., Kavanagh, E. J., & Viswesvaran, C. (2007). The convergent validity between self and observer ratings of personality: A meta-analytic review. *International Journal of Selection and Assessment, 15,* 110–117.

Cowie, R., & Cornelius, R. R. (2003). Describing the emotional states that are expressed in speech. *Speech Communication, 40,* 5–32.

Cranach, M. V., & Frenz, H.-G. (1969). Systematische Beobachtung [Systematic observation]. In C. F. Graumann (Ed.), *Handbuch der Psychologie* [Handbook of psychology] (Vol 7.1; pp. 269–331). Göttingen, Germany: Hogrefe.

D'Arcey, T., Johnson, M., & Ennis, M. (2012). Assessing the validity of FaceReader using facial electromyography. *Proceedings of APS 24th annual meeting.* Retrieved from www.darcey.us/pdf/facereader.pdf

D'Mello, S., & Graesser, A. (2009). Automatic detection of learner's affect from gross body language. *Applied Artificial Intelligence, 23,* 123–150.

Dael, N., Mortillaro, M., & Scherer, K. R. (2012a). Emotion expression in body action and posture. *Emotion, 12,* 1085–1101.

Dael, N., Mortillaro, M., & Scherer, K. R. (2012b). The Body Action and Posture coding system (BAP): Development and reliability. *Journal of Nonverbal Behavior, 36,* 97–121.

Dawkins, R., & Krebs, J. R. (1978). Animal signals: information or manipulation? In J. R. Krebs & N. B. Davies (Eds.), *Behavioural ecology* (pp. 282–309). Oxford, United Kingdom: Blackwell.

Deckers, L., Kuhlhorst L., & Freeland, L. (1987). The effects of spontaneous and voluntary facial reactions on surprise and humor. *Motivation and Emotion, 11,* 403–412.

Dessalles, J.-L. (2007). *Why we talk: The evolutionary origins of language.* Oxford, United Kingdom: Oxford University Press.

Dinkelaker, J., & Herrle, M. (2009). *Erziehungswissenschaftliche Videographie: Eine Einführung* [*Educational videography: An introduction*]. Wiesbaden, Germany: VS Verlag für Sozialwissenschaften.

Ekman, P. (1972). Universals and cultural differences in facial expressions of emotion. In J. Cole (Ed.), *Nebraska symposium on motivation* (Vol. 19, pp. 207–283). Lincoln, NE: University of Nebraska Press.

Ekman, P. (1992). An argument for basic emotions. *Cognition and Emotion, 6,* 169–200.

Ekman, P., & Friesen, W. V. (1978). *Facial Action Coding System: A technique for the measurement of facial movement.* Palo Alto, CA: Consulting Psychologists Press.

Ekman, P., Friesen, W. V., & Hager, J. (2002). *Facial Action Coding System.* Salt Lake City, UT: Research Nexus.

Ekman, P., Friesen, W. V., O'Sullivan, M., Chan, A., Diacoyanni-Tarlatzis, I., Heider, K., . . . Tzavaras, A. (1987). Universals and cultural differences in the judgments of facial expressions of emotions. *Journal of Personality and Social Psychology, 53,* 712–717.

Ekman, P., Matsumoto, D., & Friesen, W. (2005). Facial expression in affective disorders. In P. Ekman & E. L. Rosenberg (Eds.), *What the face reveals: Basic and applied studies of spontaneous expression using the Facial Action Coding System* (FACS) (pp. 429–439). New York, NY: Oxford University Press.

Elfenbein, H. A., & Ambady, N. (2002). On the universality and cultural specificity of emotion recognition: A meta-analysis. *Psychological Bulletin, 128,* 203–235.

Fernández-Dols, J. M., & Crivelli, C. (2013). Emotion and expression: Naturalistic studies. *Emotion Review, 5,* 24–29.

Fridlund, A. J. (1994). *Human facial expression: An evolutionary view.* San Diego, CA: Academic Press.

Geist, R. L., & Gilbert, D. G. (1996). Correlates of expressed and felt emotion during marital conflict: satisfaction, personality, process, and outcome. *Personality and Individual Differences, 21,* 49–60.

Gottman, J. M. (1979). *Marital interaction: Experimental investigations.* New York, NY: Academic Press.

Gottman, J. M., & Krokoff, L. J. (1989). Marital interaction and satisfaction: A longitudinal view. *Journal of Consulting and Clinical Psychology, 57,* 47–52.

Gottman, J., & Levenson, R. W. (2002). A two-factor model for predicting when a couple will divorce: Exploratory analyses using 14-year longitudinal data. *Family Process, 41,* 83–96.

Gottschalk, L. A. (1995). *Content analysis of verbal behavior. New findings and clinical applications.* Hillsdale, NJ: Lawrence Erlbaum.

Gottschalk, L. A., & Gleser, G. C. (1969). *The measurement of psychological states through the content analysis of verbal behavior.* Los Angeles, CA: University of California Press.

Harrigan, J. A. (2005). Proxemics, kinesics, and gaze. In J. A. Harrigan, R. Rosenthal, & K. R. Scherer (Eds.), *New handbook of methods in nonverbal behavior research* (pp. 137–198). New York, NY: Oxford University Press.

Heider, F. (1958). *The psychology of interpersonal relations.* New York, NY: Wiley.

Hjortsjö, C. H. (1969). *Man's face and mimic language.* Lund, Sweden: Student-Litteratur.

Horstmann, G. (2002). Facial expressions of emotion: Does the prototype represent central tendency, frequency of instantiation, or an ideal? *Emotion, 2,* 297–305.

Huber, O. (1999). Beobachtung [Observation]. In E. Roth, H. Holling, & K. Heidenreich (Eds.), *Sozialwissenschaftliche Methoden: Lehr- und Handbuch für Forschung und Praxis* [*Social science methods: Textbook and handbook for research and practice*] (pp. 126–145). München, Germany: Oldenburg.

Immordino-Yang, M. H., & Christodoulou, J. A. (2014). Neuroscientific contributions to understanding and measuring emotions in educational contexts. In R. Pekrun & L. Linnenbrink-Garcia (Eds.) *International handbook of emotions in education.* New York, NY: Routledge.

Izard, C. E. (1979). *The Maximally Discriminative Facial Movement Coding System (MAX).* Newark, DE: University of Delaware Office of Instructional Technology.

Izard, C., & Dougherty, L. (1982). Two complementary systems for measuring facial expressions in infants and children. In C. Izard (Ed.), *Measuring emotions in infants and children* (pp. 97–126). New York, NY: Cambridge University Press.

Jäger, C. (2009). Affective ignorance. *Erkenntnis, 71,* 123–139.

Johnson, M. D. (2002). The observation of specific affect in marital interactions: Psychometric properties of a coding system and a rating system. *Psychological Assessment, 14,* 423–438.

Jones, S., Carrère, S., & Gottman, J. M. (2005). Specific Affect Coding System. In V. L. Manusov (Ed.), *The sourcebook of nonverbal measures: Going beyond words* (pp. 163–172). Mahwah, NJ: Erlbaum.

Junge, M., & Reisenzein, R. (2013). Indirect scaling methods for testing quantitative emotion theories. *Cognition and Emotion, 27,* 1247–1275.

Juslin, P. N., & Laukka, P. (2003). Communication of emotions in vocal expression and music performance: Different channels, same code? *Psychological Bulletin, 129,* 770–814.

Juslin, P. N., & Scherer, K. R. (2005). Vocal expression of affect. In J. A. Harrigan, R. Rosenthal, & K. R. Scherer (Eds.), *New handbook of methods in nonverbal behavior research* (pp. 65–136). New York, NY: Oxford University Press.

Juslin, P. N., & Scherer, K. R. (2008). Speech emotion analysis. Received from www.scholarpedia.org/article/Speech_emotion_analysis

Kipp, M. (2013). ANVIL: A universal video research tool. In J. Durand, U. Gut, & G. Kristofferson (Eds.), *Handbook of corpus phonology.* Oxford, United Kingdom: Oxford University Press.

Kolanowski, A., Hoffman, L., & Hofer, S. M. (2007). Concordance of self-report and informant assessment of emotional well-being in nursing home residents with dementia. *Journal of Gerontology: Psychological Sciences, 62B,* 20–27.

Krantz, D., Luce, R., Suppes, P., & Tversky, A. (1971). *Foundations of measurement, Vol. 1: Additive and polynomial representations*. New York, NY: Academic Press.

Kreibig, S. D., & Gendolla, G.H.E. (2014). Autonomic nervous system measurement of emotion in education and achievement settings. In R. Pekrun & L. Linnenbrink-Garcia (Eds.), *International handbook of emotions in education* (pp. 625–642). New York, NY: Taylor & Francis.

Kring, A. M., & Sloan, D. M. (2007). The facial expression coding system (FACES): Development, Validation and Utility. *Psychological Assessment, 19,* 210–224.

Kring, A. M., Smith, D. A., & Neale, J. M. (1994). Individual differences in dispositional expressiveness: The development and validation of the Emotional Expressivity Scale. *Journal of Personality and Social Psychology, 66,* 934–949.

Laukka, P., Neiberg, D., Forsell, M., Karlsson, I., & Elenius, K. (2011). Expression of affect in spontaneous speech: Acoustic correlates, perception, and automatic detection of irritation and resignation. *Computer Speech and Language, 25,* 84–104.

Lausberg, H., & Sloetjes, H. (2009). Coding gestural behavior with the NEUROGES-ELAN system. *Behavior Research Methods, Instruments, & Computers, 41,* 841–849.

Lazarus, R. S. (1991). *Emotion and adaptation*. New York, NY: Oxford University Press.

Levenson, R. W., & Gottmann, J. M. (1983). Marital interaction: Physiological linkage and affective exchange. *Journal of Personality and social Psychology, 45,* 587–597.

Littlewort, G., Whitehill, J., Wu, T., Fasel, I. R., Frank, M., Movellan, J. R., & Bartlett, M. S. (2011). The computer expression recognition toolbox (CERT). *Proceedings of the 9th IEEE Conference on Automatic Face and Gesture Recognition* (pp. 298–305). Santa Barbara, CA.

Lipton, P. (2004). *Inference to the best explanation*. London, United Kingdom: Routledge.

Malle, B. F. (2004). *How the mind explains behavior: Folk explanations, meaning, and social interaction*. Cambridge, MA: MIT Press.

Matsumoto, D., & Ekman, P. (2008). Facial expression analysis. *Scholarpedia, 3*(5), 4237.

Mauss, I. B., Levenson, R. W., McCarter, L., Wilhelm, F. H., & Gross, J. J. (2005). The tie that binds? Coherence among emotion experience, behavior, and physiology. *Emotion, 5,* 175–190.

Mauss, I. B., & Robinson, M. D. (2009). Measures of emotion: A review. *Cognition and Emotion, 23,* 209–237.

McDougall, W. (1908/1960). *An introduction to social psychology*. London, United Kingdom: Methuen.

Michell, J. (1990). *An introduction to the logic of psychological measurement*. Hillsdale, NJ: Erlbaum.

Mota, S., & Picard, R. (2003, June). Automated posture analysis for detecting learner's interest level. *Workshop on Computer Vision and Pattern Recognition for Human-Computer Interaction*, CVPR HCI.

Musgrave, A. (1993). *Common Sense, science and scepticism: A historical introduction to the theory of knowledge*. Cambridge, United Kingdom: Cambridge University Press.

Nelson, N. L., & Russell, J. A. (2013). Universality revisited. *Emotion Review, 5,* 8–15.

Oatley, K., & Johnson-Laird, P. N. (1987). Towards a cognitive theory of emotions. *Cognition and Emotion, 1,* 29–50.

Ottoni, E. B. (2000). EthoLog 2.2—A tool for the transcription and timing of behavior observation sessions. *Behavior Research Methods, Instruments, and Computers, 32,* 446–449.

Pantic, M., & Bartlett, M. S. (2007). Machine analysis of facial expressions. In K. Delac & M. Grgic (Eds.), *Face recognition* (pp. 377–416). Vienna, Austria: I-Tech Education and Publishing.

Pekrun, R., & Bühner, M. (2014). Self-report measures of academic emotions. In R. Pekrun & L. Linnenbrink-Garcia (Eds.), *International handbook of emotions in education*. New York, NY: Taylor & Francis.

Pekrun, R., Goetz, T., Daniels, L. M., Stupnisky, R. H., & Perry, R. P. (2010). Boredom in achievement settings: Exploring control-value antecedents and performance outcomes of a neglected emotion. *Journal of Educational Psychology, 102,* 531–549.

Picard, R. W. (1997). *Affective computing*. Cambridge, MA: MIT Press.

Reisenzein, R. (1994). Pleasure-arousal theory and the intensity of emotions. *Journal of Personality and Social Psychology, 67,* 525–539.

Reisenzein, R. (1995). On Oatley and Johnson-Laird's theory of emotions and hierarchical structures in the affective lexicon. *Cognition and Emotion, 9,* 383–416.

Reisenzein, R. (2000). Exploring the strength of association between the components of emotion syndromes: The case of surprise. *Cognition and Emotion, 14,* 1–38.

Reisenzein, R. (2010). Broadening the scope of affect detection research. *IEEE Transactions on Affective Computing, 1,* 42–45.

Reisenzein, R., Bördgen, S., Holtbernd, T., & Matz, D. (2006). Evidence for strong dissociation between emotion and facial displays: The case of surprise. *Journal of Personality and Social Psychology, 91,* 295–315.

Reisenzein, R., & Hofmann, T. (1993). Discriminating emotions from appraisal-relevant situational information: Baseline data for structural models of cognitive appraisals. *Cognition and Emotion, 7,* 271–293.

Reisenzein, R., & Junge, M. (2012). Language and emotion from the perspective of the computational belief-desire theory of emotion. In P. A. Wilson (Ed.), *Dynamicity in emotion concepts.* Lodz Studies in Language 27 (pp. 37–59). Frankfurt am Main, Germany: Peter Lang.

Reisenzein, R., Studtmann, M., & Horstmann, G. (2013). Coherence between emotion and facial expression: Evidence from laboratory experiments. *Emotion Review, 5,* 16–23.

Reisenzein, R., & Weber, H. (2009). Personality and emotion. In P. J. Corr & G. Matthews (Eds.), *Cambridge handbook of personality psychology* (pp. 54–71). Oxford, United Kingdom: Oxford University Press.

Richerson, P. J., & Boyd, R. (2005). *Not by genes alone: How culture transformed human evolution.* Chicago, IL: University of Chicago Press.

Rimé, B. (2009). Emotions elicit the social sharing of emotion: Theory and empirical review. *Emotion Review, 1,* 60–85.

Rosenberg, E. (2005). The study of spontaneous facial expressions in psychology. In P. Ekman & E. L. Rosenberg (Eds.), *What the face reveals: Basic and applied studies of spontaneous expression using the Facial Action Coding System* (FACS) (pp. 3–18). New York, NY: Oxford University Press.

Rosenberg, E. L., & Ekman, P. (1994). Coherence between expressive and experiential systems in emotion. *Cognition and Emotion, 8,* 201–229.

Rosenthal, R. (2005). Conducting judgment studies: Some methodological issues. In J. A. Harrigan, R. Rosenthal, & K. R. Scherer (Eds.), *New handbook of methods in nonverbal behavior research* (pp. 199–234). New York, NY: Oxford University Press.

Ruef, A. M., & Levenson, R. W. (2007). Continuous measurement of emotion. In J. A. Coan & J. B. Allen (Eds.), *Handbook of emotion elicitation and assessment* (pp. 286–297). New York, NY: Oxford University Press.

Russell, J. A. (1980). A circumplex model of affect. *Journal of Personality and Social Psychology, 39,* 1161–1178.

Russell, J. A. (1994). Is there universal recognition of emotion from facial expression? A review of the cross-cultural studies. *Psychological Bulletin, 115,* 102–141.

Russell, J. A. (2003). Core affect and the psychological construction of emotion. *Psychological Review, 110,* 145–172.

Russell, J. A., Bachorowski, J.-A., & Fernández-Dols, J. M. (2003). Facial and vocal expressions of emotion. *Annual Review of Psychology, 54,* 329–349.

Russell, J. A., Weiss, A., & Mendelsohn, G. A. (1989). Affect Grid: A single-item scale of pleasure and arousal. *Journal of Personality and Social Psychology, 57,* 493–502.

Sanford, K. (2007). The couples emotion rating form: Psychometric properties and theoretical associations. *Psychological Assessment, 19,* 411–421.

Sauter, D., Eisner, F., Calder, A. J., & Scott, S. K. (2010). Perceptual cues in nonverbal vocal expressions of emotion. *Quarterly Journal of Experimental Psychology, 63,* 2251–2272.

Schneider, D. J., Hastorf, A. H., & Ellsworth, P. C. (1979). *Person Perception.* Reading, MA: Addison-Wesley.

Schröder, M. (2003). Experimental study of affect bursts. *Speech Communication, 40,* 99–116.

Schuller, B., Batliner, A., Steidl, S., & Seppi, D. (2011). Recognizing realistic emotions and affect in speech: State of the art and lessons learnt from the first challenge. *Speech Communication, 53,* 1062–1087.

Schulz, M. S., & Waldinger, R. J. (2005). The value of pooling "naïve" expertise. *American Psychologist, 60,* 656–662.

Simon-Thomas, E. R., Keltner, D. J., Sauter, D., Sinicropi-Yao, L., & Abramson, A. (2009). The voice conveys specific emotions: Evidence from vocal burst displays. *Emotion, 9,* 838–846.

Smith, D. A., Vivian, D., & O'Leary, K. D. (1990). Longitudinal prediction of marital discord from premarital expressions of affect. *Journal of Consulting and Clinical Psychology, 58,* 790–798.

Steimer-Krause, E., Krause, R., & Wagner, G. (1990). Interaction regulations used by schizophrenic and psychosomatic patients: studies on facial behavior in dyadic interactions. *Psychiatry, 53,* 209–228.

Sternglanz, R. W., & DePaulo, B. M. (2004). Reading nonverbal cues to emotions: The advantages and liabilities of relationship closeness. *Journal of Nonverbal Behavior, 28,* 245–266.

Stevens, S. (1946). On the theory of scales of measurement. *Science, 103,* 677–680.

Wager, T. D., Atlas, L. Y., Lindquist, M. A., Roy, M., Woo, C.-W., & Kross, E. (2013). An fMRI-Based neurologic signature of physical pain. *New England Journal of Medicine, 368,* 1388–1397.

Waldinger, R. J., Schulz, M. S., Hauser, S. T., Allen, J. P., & Crowell, J. A. (2004). Reading other's emotions: The role of intuitive judgments in predicting marital satisfaction, quality and stability. *Journal of Family Psychology, 18,* 58–71.

Weiner, B. (1995). *Judgments of responsibility: A foundation for a theory of social conduct.* New York, NY: Guilford.

Wright, H. F. (1960). Observational child study. In P. H. Mussen (Ed.), *Handbook of research methods in child development* (pp. 71–139). New York, NY: Wiley.

Wundt, W. (1896). *Grundriss der Psychologie* [Outlines of psychology]. Leipzig, Germany: Engelmann.

Zeng, Z., Pantic, M., Roisman, G. I., & Huang, T. S. (2009). A survey of affect recognition methods: Audio, visual, and spontaneous expressions. *IEEE Transactions on Pattern Analysis and Machine Intelligence, 1,* 39–58.

30

NEUROSCIENTIFIC CONTRIBUTIONS TO UNDERSTANDING AND MEASURING EMOTIONS IN EDUCATIONAL CONTEXTS

*Mary Helen Immordino-Yang and Joanna A. Christodoulou,
University of Southern California and MGH Institute of
Health Professions*

With the advent of increasingly sophisticated neuroimaging technologies since the late 20th century, the fields of social and affective neuroscience have expanded exponentially. In parallel with the expansion of knowledge about affective and social processing in the brain (Adolphs, 1999; Adolphs & Damasio, 2000), there has been a growing emphasis in the field of education on the important roles of emotions in learning (Pekrun, Goetz, Titz, & Perry, 2002). In this chapter, we discuss how neuroscientific advances may contribute to the effort to understand and measure emotional functioning in academic contexts.

The overarching premise of this chapter is that given the current state of neuroimaging technology, as well as practical and ethical considerations, neuroscientific contributions to emotion measurement in education must be mainly indirect at this stage. In our opinion, new knowledge about brain functioning can and should inform the questions and methods employed to study emotions in educational settings, but directly measuring real-time emotion-related neural functioning in educational settings is mostly unfeasible at this point. Techniques for indirectly measuring neural functioning via measuring bodily changes associated with emotion, such as psychophysiological recording or cortisol sampling, do hold some promise. However, cortisol functioning mainly provides information about habitual responses to stress rather than about context-specific emotions, and the interpretation of psychophysiological data from real-world contexts continues to be difficult due to the need for rigid experimental designs.

For these and other reasons, we suggest that the bulk of neuroscientific research on emotions might be most usefully conducted in controlled settings like laboratories. Findings from laboratory studies, including developmental studies and studies probing neural changes associated with educational interventions, could then suggest insights that can be translated and utilized to inform educational research in the form of behavioral, psychological, and observational studies conducted in educational settings. In particular, we argue that insights from neuroscientific findings could help education psychologists to enrich or rethink theoretical models of academic emotions (Immordino-Yang, 2011) or to identify better behavioral indicators of emotions in academic contexts. Then, once these insights have been incorporated into educational theories and models and tested in educational settings, they could make their way one step further into the applied domain, where they may influence the ways in which teachers think about and design curricula to support the emotional aspects of learning. This progression from neuroscience research to educational research, and from there to educational practice, is lengthy yet important for ensuring that neuroscientific findings are responsibly translated and that inferences drawn for educational practice are legitimate. As we discuss below, the potential danger of prematurely shortcutting this lengthy trajectory is that although high-quality neuroscience research is reliable and replicable, the technological constraints on data collection methods make the validity of the findings difficult to ascertain in real-world contexts like schools. Intermediate steps aimed at translating and testing the implications for understanding emotions in educational contexts are necessary (Hirsh-Pasek & Bruer, 2007; Immordino-Yang & Fischer, 2010).

In this chapter, we first review the various technologies currently being employed to study the neurobiology of emotion in order to provide a realistic sense of their promise and limitations for addressing educational research questions for psychologists who may not be familiar with the range of techniques currently available. Of course, the majority of these instruments can only be used in laboratory settings, and therefore to use these technologies for research relevant to educational questions would require partnerships between education psychologists and affective neuroscientists (or, interdisciplinary researchers fluent in both educational and neuroscientific domains of research). We expand this review to include psychophysiological and hormone-sampling tools, as these tools hold the most promise of contributing directly to measuring neurobiological aspects of emotional functioning in educational contexts at this stage (refer also to Kreibig & Gondolla, 2014, for information on psychophysiological methods). We also include a discussion of brain lesion studies, as these provide an important source of evidence about emotional contributions to learning. We discuss the strengths, limitations, and constraints on each available technology/approach and give examples of the sorts of educationally relevant questions each has been or might be suited to help address.

We then propose three potential uses of neuroscientific evidence for measuring emotions in educational contexts. First, we argue that insights from neurobiological studies of emotion can be used to ensure that educational theories of emotion are biologically plausible and that educational models carve emotional processing into psychological components that correspond to biological mechanisms (Barrett, 2009a; Immordino-Yang, 2010). This step is critical to aligning educational questions with neurobiological methods, and, we believe, will be the key to building a future research focus in affective educational neuroscience. In this section, we take as our central example the neurobiological distinction between emotions and feelings.

Second, we propose that neurobiological indices of emotion might be useful in overcoming the current bias in educational research toward studying mainly aspects of processing that can be made conscious and that are available to be verbally reported (Karabenick et al., 2007). Third, we suggest that a new neurobiological research focus on correspondences between spontaneous behaviors and hidden neural processes can be developed to derive behavioral indices of emotion processing that could be helpful in analyzing emotion behavior in educational contexts. Here, we take the example of averting one's eye gaze during abstract thinking about emotional situations and possible relations to neural mechanisms implicated in social-emotional functioning, future-oriented thinking, and episodic memory (Immordino-Yang, Christodoulou, & Singh, 2012). We close the chapter with a prospective discussion of the future of affective educational neuroscience and a discussion of the promise of this largely futuristic research area.

RESEARCH TOOLS AND APPROACHES EMPLOYED IN THE NEUROSCIENTIFIC STUDY OF EMOTION: AN OVERVIEW

Neuroimaging tools have allowed researchers to discover the functional systems underlying emotion processing in vivo in healthy human beings as they perform active tasks (like solve math problems or react to emotionally evocative social scenarios) or rest passively. These tools offer powerful insights into the function of brain regions and systems, with few direct applications for translation to education settings at this stage. To understand the promise and potential of neuroimaging tools for understanding emotion processing, here we review the most commonly used tools and techniques and highlight their strengths and limitations. (For more information and videos of some of these tools in use, see *Neuroscience and the Classroom: Making Connections,* Unit 1, at www.learner. org/courses/neuroscience.)

Tools of modern neuroscience are typically described based on their ability to capture the temporal and spatial dimensions of functional brain activity. Generally, neuroimaging tools trade off on spatial and temporal resolution—techniques capture with high resolution either when or where activations occur in the brain but not both pieces of information. Spatial resolution describes where activity is occurring in the brain; neuroimaging tools with good spatial resolution locate activity in the brain with resolution on the order of millimeters. Temporal resolution describes when areas of the brain are engaged; neuroimaging tools with good temporal resolution describe the timing of activity with a resolution on the order of milliseconds. That said, state-of-the-art neuroimaging paradigms are beginning to combine tools together for simultaneous data acquisition, pairing tools with high spatial resolution (such as MRI; magnetic resonance imaging) with tools that provide high temporal resolution (such as MEG; magnetoencephalography). Each neuroimaging tool capitalizes on distinct physiological properties of neural activations, determining which resolution is privileged, location or timing.

A Tool With Robust Spatial Resolution: Functional Magnetic Resonance Imaging (fMRI)

Research questions that investigate the location of brain activations rely on imaging tools with high spatial resolution. Magnetic resonance imaging (MRI) scanners, which can provide both structural (i.e., information about the brain's physical characteristics) and functional information (i.e., information about how the brain is activated during tasks), are used commonly to answer such questions (Huettel, Song, & McCarthy, 2004; see further on for a description of structural MRI studies). Measurement of brain activity in fMRI is based on the BOLD (blood-oxygen-level-dependent) response. In principle, when there are high processing demands for a particular region of the brain, oxygenated blood in that area becomes initially depleted due to increased neuronal activity. A resultant rush of oxygenated blood then floods the area to compensate for the depletion. The MRI scanner detects this overflow of oxygenated blood, which occurs after a two to six second delay. Consequently, fMRI is an indirect index of brain activity and not a precise tool for understanding the time course of neural activations or the details of how sequences of regions contribute to the processing of information. However, the BOLD signal does correlate with more direct measures of neuronal firing (e.g., slow cortical potentials measured using electrophysiological techniques) and so is believed to reflect properties of neuronal communication and activity (He, Snyder, Zempel, Smyth, & Raichle, 2008).

When using MRI scanners to acquire functional data (fMRI)—that is, data on how blood flow changes in the brain during various experimental conditions, researchers typically rely on an analytic approach that involves comparing experimental and control tasks. In this approach, the experimental task is designed to elicit a specific aspect of processing, such as strong emotional feelings, that is of interest in the study. The control task is designed to incorporate all of the processing demands of the experimental task except for the main aspect of interest. For example, Immordino-Yang, McColl, Damasio, and Damasio (2009) exposed participants to a set of true social stories in the scanner, some of which resulted in participants reporting strong emotional feelings (the experimental conditions) and some of which involved equivalently complex social processing but did not result in strong emotional feelings (the control condition). By contrasting (or "subtracting") the blood flow in different areas of the brain during these conditions, the researchers were able to identify activations and deactivations (neural areas showing statistically reliably higher or lower blood flow) during strong emotional feelings. This univariate approach to analyzing fMRI data has dominated the affective and social neuroscience literatures to date.

However, other analyses of fMRI data can reveal additional information and are becoming more widely used. Some of these analysis techniques include "functional connectivity mapping," which probes the extent to which the time course of blood flow changes in a particular neural region of interest and is associated with, predicts, or is predicted by, the time course of blood flow in other regions during emotion-related tasks or rest. For instance, in a novel analysis of the dataset described above, Immordino-Yang and Singh (2013) were able to probe the ways that neural systems involved in emotional feelings and those involved in memory were influencing one another. One finding, for example, was that during admiration for virtue there was a bidirectional exchange of information between the memory-related hippocampus and the feeling-related anterior insula, while during compassion, the predominant direction of information flow was from the hippocampus to the insula. In another study, Yang, Bossman, Schiffhauer, Jordan, and Immordino-Yang (2013) demonstrated that individual differences in how and how often participants described personal memories during the interview were predicted by how tightly interconnected memory and self-related brain networks were as participants rested and daydreamed in the scanner (Yang et al., 2013). These findings together suggest a role for memory in the provocation of feelings. Alternatively, researchers can probe relations between "resting functional connectivity," or the intrinsic coordination of activity in particular brain areas during wakeful relaxation and psychological traits like IQ (Li et al., 2009; Song et al., 2009), memory ability (Wig et al., 2008), reading ability (Koyama et al., 2011), and social processing in a natural setting (Yang et al., 2013; see Immordino-Yang et al., 2012, for a review with relevance to educational questions). Finally, researchers can probe individual differences in emotion processing by correlating individuals' scores on a behavioral variable with neural activations during an emotion-related task. For example, Saxbe, Yang, Borofsky, and Immordino-Yang (2013) were able to predict individual variation in experiment participants' neural activations during emotional feelings from analyzing participants' speech during a separate qualitative interview. Murayama, Matsumoto, Izuma, and Matsumoto (2010) were able to probe the undermining effects of extrinsic rewards on motivation as participants played a video game inside and outside the fMRI scanner. And, Eisenberger, Lieberman, and Williams (2003) demonstrated that neural activations in somatosensory systems were correlated with individuals' perceptions of social exclusion during a virtual ball-toss game.

In sum, the characteristics of BOLD data make fMRI a tool that can measure with robust accuracy the location of activations in the brain, the coordination of these activations in a temporally coarse way, and relations to behavioral measures. Due to these strengths, fMRI is widely used to study how neural systems are recruited for emotion processing over the course of typical and atypical development. In the future, it could potentially be used to study how individual variability in neural functioning during tasks and rest give new insights into educationally relevant processes and the psychological variability seen in academic contexts. However, interpretation of results for educational applications will be an important consideration, as we describe in the next section.

Interpreting fMRI Results Critically

Many nonscientists encounter brain images through media outlets, in textbooks, and elsewhere. The images are deceptively simple in that they show a brain with warm or cool colored blobs as an apparent depiction of the brain regions that are responsible for a given task. However, interpreting these colored blobs is not entirely straightforward. Essentially, to produce these images, researchers first divide images of each participant's brain into myriads of three-dimensional cubes (termed voxels, short for pixels with volume), each a few millimeters across. For each voxel, blood flow during different experiment conditions is calculated. After anatomically aligning the voxel maps across participants, statistical calculations reveal the subset of voxels that were associated with different amounts of blood flow in the two experimental conditions on average across the group of participants. If activation patterns show statistically significant differences, then the cube is coded in warm colors (for relatively more activation) or cool colors (for relatively less activation). As we can see, these images reveal only those voxels that pass the strict statistical threshold for being differently engaged for one task versus another across a group. They do not reveal all the neural areas involved in completing the task. Many other areas are certainly actively involved but are equivalently active in the two conditions. As is the case for all group-level statistical comparisons, this analytic method also washes out individual differences in neural regions activated (although it can reveal individual differences in the amount of activation in a particular region).

When the analyses are described this way, it is easy to appreciate the necessity for caution in interpreting fMRI findings. Educators are concerned with supporting the development of coherent functional skills in individuals, not relative activation of isolated brain areas across groups. To understand what brain imaging findings mean for students, we must ask what the task is required of the experiment participants, what aspects of the participants' activity were being measured and recorded, whether the implicit comparison between the target and control tasks were well matched, whether the experiment participants behave like students, and what other data would be needed to build a more complete understanding of the neural systems involved. To apply the findings to education, we need additionally to ask whether the task required of subjects in the experiment has real-world validity—that is, whether it engages processing that students actually use in educational contexts (Immordino-Yang & Fischer, 2010). These are not insurmountable problems, but generally they are vastly underappreciated. This has led in the past to such egregious misapplications of neuroscientific findings as labeling students right- or left-brained learners and adjusting their programs accordingly, or teachers wearing radishes on their hats to supposedly capitalize on how the brainstem's reticular activating system detects novelty.

Millisecond Temporal Resolution but Poor Spatial Resolution: Magnetoencephalography (MEG) and Electroencephalography (EEG)

To investigate when brain activations occur and in what sequence, researchers rely on electroencephalographic neuroimaging tools that provide high temporal resolution. In particular, Magnetoencephalography (MEG) and Electroencephalography (EEG) are used to investigate how amplitude and latency of brain waves are connected to conscious and subconscious processing of information. In emotion research, both technologies provide powerful means for probing on the scale of milliseconds the elements of emotional reactions, revealing information about, for example, the development of neural processes underlying attention to particular aspects of faces when recognizing emotion (Batty & Taylor, 2006; Wessing, Fürniss, Zwitserlood, Dobel, & Junghöfer, 2011).

Unlike fMRI, MEG and EEG provide a direct index of neuronal activity (Pantazis & Leahy, 2006). MEG measures the magnetic field associated with the electrical currents that underlie cortical neuronal communication, while EEG detects traces of the electrical impulses themselves. For MEG, participants sit within a special machine that looks like a gigantic hairdryer; for EEG, electrodes are placed either on the scalp (in research with healthy subjects) or on the cortical surface directly (in neurosurgery patients). MEG and EEG signals can be measured with participants at rest or when performing a task (such as reading words). EEG is relatively portable and vastly less expensive than MEG and so has been used much more to study development of academic skills.

To measure EEG signals associated with brain activity during specific tasks, an event-related potential (ERP) is collected, which time-locks neural signals to an event or stimulus presentation, which is repeated many times. Electrical "brain waves" are averaged over multiple trials and characterized based on their amplitude and latency (Luck, 2005). Similarly, researchers use event-related magnetic fields (ERFs) to describe task-based signals in MEG (Hansen, Kringelbach, & Salmelin, 2010). Because electromagnetic impulses are generated on the brain's surface but detected outside the skull, EEG signals are subject to scattering by the intermediate layers of skull, muscle, and skin. Although MEG signals are more robust to tissue conductivity issues, for computational reasons, precise localization of the signal source is also difficult.

Poor Depth Penetration and Spatial Resolution but Portable and Robust to Movement Artifacts: Near Infrared Spectroscopy (NIRS)

For participants who are especially prone to movement during research studies, such as infants and young children, Near Infrared Spectroscopy (NIRS) provides an alternative approach to studying activity in regions of the brain that lie just under the skull (but not deep inside the head). The technique works by shining light into the head and measuring the absorption, and it is more effective with younger participants and infants since these populations have lower cranial thickness and density. Due to its relative affordability and portability, this tool offers important benefits for researchers working with young or vulnerable populations (Koizumi et al., 2003). Like fMRI, this technique relies on changes in levels of oxygenated blood in the neural tissue and is noninvasive; however, unlike fMRI, participants can move freely as they wear a lightweight cap that has lights and sensors built into it. The tool offers a high degree of temporal resolution but relatively poor spatial resolution, especially in comparison to fMRI. It has provided essential insights into brain development in infancy and early childhood, including the development of neural systems involved in emotion processing (Lloyd-Fox, Blasi, & Elwell, 2010; Nagamitsu, Yamashita, Tanaka, & Matsuishi, 2012). This tool can potentially be used to study, for example, the effects of emotional experience on brain functioning over time.

Early Neuroimaging Tools: Positron Emission Tomography and Computed Axial Tomography

Positron Emission Tomography (PET) is a method that relies on injected or inhaled radioactive material to measure brain activity (Raichle, 1998). Since nonradioactive, noninvasive MRI technology has become available, PET has largely fallen out of favor for research purposes, although it is still used in some contexts. Alternatively, Computed Axial Tomography (CAT or CT scan) is an X-ray based (i.e., radiation) method that yields structural brain images and is sometimes used for research purposes. These technologies have not, to our knowledge, been used to study educational questions. However, we mention them because educational researchers interested in neuroscientific data on emotion processing are likely to notice such studies, and PET in particular was used to conduct early neuroimaging studies of emotion (e.g., Damasio et al., 2000). In addition, the lay public often confuse neuroimaging tools that involve radiation (PET, CAT) with nonradioactive tools (fMRI and structural MRI, EEG, MEG).

Interrupting or Enhancing Neural Activity: Transcranial Magnetic Stimulation (TMS) and Transcranial Direct Current Stimulation (tDCS)

In addition to detecting the structure and function of the brain, other devices have been used to manipulate brain activity directly. Ramping activation in the brain up or down allows researchers to study the short-term effects of interrupting or heightening processing in specific brain regions. Transcranial magnetic stimulation (TMS) is a technique used to introduce a brief electric pulse associated with a magnetic field to a small region of the cortex in order to momentarily disrupt neuronal processing (Walsh & Pascual-Leone, 2003). Transcranial direct current stimulation (tDCS) uses electrodes to deliver electric currents to specific regions of the brain (Utz, Dimova, Oppenlander, & Kerkhoff,

2010). These tools are used to understand how enhancing or suppressing activation of specific brain regions can impact behavior and mental processing, including behaviors and processing that are targeted in various therapeutic interventions (Pascual-Leone, Walsh, & Rothwell, 2000). For example, one TMS study demonstrated that interfering with neuronal firing in a region of the brain implicated in social perspective-taking, the right temporo-parietal junction, caused participants' moral judgments of others' actions to become more utilitarian and less empathic (Koenigs et al., 2007). Educational applications of this tool will depend on addressing issues of invasiveness and feasibility with children.

Studying the Anatomy of the Brain and the Impact of Experiences: Structural Imaging With MRI Scanners

In addition to functional studies of brain activation, an MRI scanner can also be used to collect structural information about the brain's anatomy and relations to development and experience. Anatomical images detail the brain's white and gray matter volumes and tissue integrity and have been used to study development and neurological health (Giedd & Rapoport, 2010). Alternatively, diffusion tensor imaging (DTI), a form of data collected with an MRI scanner, advances our understanding of the brain from a static structure of discrete regions to a densely networked system by tracing the networks of white matter tracts in the brain that connect neurons from different regions. This approach has been used to study the network-level anatomical changes associated with the acquisition of particular skills, like learning to play the piano (Ellis et al., 2012), learning to meditate (Luders, Clark, Narr, & Toga, 2011; Luders et al., 2012; Tang, Lu, Fan, Yang, & Posner, 2012), or learning complex reasoning strategies (Mackey, Whitaker, & Bunge, 2012). It has also been used to investigate relations between brain development and emotional regulation and decision making in adolescence (Giedd et al., 2009), and the effects of a reading skills intervention in children (Keller & Just, 2009). In children with autism, DTI evidence has pointed to disruptions of white matter tracts associated with socioemotional processing (Ameis et al., 2011). For educational applications, DTI holds particular promise as a tool to examine the cumulative effects of emotional experience or training because it is relatively quick to collect in the scanner and robust to movement artifacts. It could eventually provide a new source of evidence about the efficacy of particular emotion-related educational interventions.

Measuring the Brain's Emotion-Related Activity Indirectly on the Body: Psychophysiological Recording and Cortisol Sampling

While neuroimaging is used to index the brain's activity by measuring physiological correlates of neural activity inside the brain itself, relevant aspects of neurobiological functioning during emotion can also be measured on the body. Emotions fundamentally involve characteristic body state changes (Damasio, 1999), such as the increased heart rate that accompanies test anxiety or the warm, flushed response that accompanies success. Longer-term changes in emotion and emotion regulation—for example, those related to chronic anxiety and stress, are associated with changes to the diurnal cycle of hormone regulation, commonly indexed using cortisol measurements from saliva samples taken over multiple hours and days (Miller, Chen, & Zhou, 2007). These body state changes can sometimes be consciously felt (that is, we can become aware of bodily feelings as part of our current emotion experience; Barrett, Mesquita, Ochsner, & Gross, 2007), but often these bodily changes remain below conscious awareness. In either case, these embodied changes influence thinking and learning (Immordino-Yang & Damasio, 2007; Immordino-Yang & Faeth, 2009), and measures of them reveal subtle information about arousal and emotional regulation (e.g., Mendes, Major, McCoy, & Blascovich, 2008), either in relation to the current context (in the case of psychophysiological recording) or over the longer term (in the case of cortisol sampling). The psychophysiological measurements potentially obtainable in classroom settings include galvanic skin response (GSR, a measure of microscopic amounts of skin sweating related to autonomic arousal, usually measured using band-aid-like electrodes glued to the skin of the hands, wrist, or feet), heart rate changes (measured using electrocardiogram monitoring belts placed around the chest or less accurately with pulse monitors worn on the finger), and breathing rates (measured by respiration belts around the chest and other means).

Measuring psychophysiological responses and hormonal regulation in educational contexts is somewhat unwieldy, although much more doable than neuroimaging and far less expensive (Rappolt-Schlichtmann & Watamura, 2010). Researchers are beginning to implement cortisol studies in classrooms—for example, to study the effects of emotion regulation interventions and quality of peer and teacher social relationships (e.g., Catherine, Schonert-Reichl, Hertzman, & Oberlander, 2012; Rappolt-Schlichtmann et al., 2009) or to study how students cope during stressful testing situations (Spangler, Pekrun, Kramer, & Hofmann, 2002).

Researchers interested in understanding emotions in educational contexts have also begun to experiment with psychophysiological recording techniques in the classroom, to some avail. For example, researchers working with middle school students measured their psychophysiological responses during a reading activity and found that better reading comprehension outcomes were associated with greater heart-rate suppressions in the moments immediately following presentation of the written materials (Daley, Willett, & Fischer, 2013). This decrease in heart rate is thought to reflect more effective cognitive appraisal of the text and a lower threat response. In a different experiment, researchers showed that teaching young adults to reappraise their stress reactions in a public speaking task positively impacted both physiological functioning over time and emotional outcomes (Jamieson, Nock, & Mendes, 2012). Applying psychophysiological techniques in classroom settings is still in the early stages, but it appears to hold some promise for measuring biological indicators of arousal with indirect but important implications for understanding emotions.

In spite of the promises, cautions are also in order, however. Interpretation of these data remains difficult because it is not yet fully understood how specific psychophysiological changes relate to particular emotions. Put another way, these measurements do not tell researchers about how the person is experiencing the arousal being measured. For example, is it related to excitement? To surprise? To anxiety? To threat? To a sense of discovery or to recognizing a correct or an incorrect answer? To a stimulus in the present physical environment or to one conjured from memory? Currently, scientists debate the meaning of these bodily signals for distinct emotion states (Lisa Feldman Barrett, 2009b; Rainville, Bechara, Naqvi, & Damasio, 2005). And in the end, differentiating emotion states from psychophysiological responses may become an intractable problem if specific emotions turn out to not neatly map onto distinct body states. In any case, the interpretability of psychophysiological data in educational contexts will likely be greatly enhanced by the simultaneous collection of behavioral and self-report measures of emotion.

Studies of Patients With Brain Damage

Previous to neuroimaging, neurobiological understanding of affect relied on patients with brain damage, generally resulting from injury generated internally (e.g., stroke) or externally (e.g., physical head trauma). Currently, lesion studies continue to provide important verifications of concepts built from neuroimaging data. Using the lesion approach, researchers aim to profile the patterns of preserved and compromised functions exhibited by patients with damage to different brain regions (Damasio & Damasio, 1989). The logic underlying this work often rests on the demonstration of *double dissociation,* or the ability of scientists to demonstrate that in patients with damage to different brain regions, a complementary set of deficits and preserved functions emerges. That is, in patients with damage to a particular brain region, a cognitive or emotional function "X" is preserved while another function "Y" is damaged; conversely, in patients with damage to a different brain region function "Y" is preserved while "X" is damaged. Such analyses give information about the interdependence of functions "X" and "Y" in the brain.

Although lesion analyses represent a special research scenario that is, for obvious reasons, not applicable to mainstream educational studies, this research approach has contributed important insights with educational relevance. One well-known example is the theory of multiple intelligences put forth by Howard Gardner (1993). Before neuroimaging was available, Gardner demonstrated with brain damaged patients that different propensities for skills, or intelligences, could be dissociated in the brain. This discovery led Gardner to formulate a highly influential developmental theory in which intelligence was not a unitary, domain-general construct. Instead, children's intelligence could be specific to a domain, such as to music, to interpersonal interaction, or to quantitative thinking. Although the details of this theory have proven problematic in some respects, arguably this work still represents an excellent example of an early attempt to use neuroscience to inform educational models.

Two additional examples with relevance to education are the case of patients with damage to a brain region just above the eyes called the ventromedial prefrontal cortex (VMPFC) and the case of high-functioning patients who have suffered hemispherectomies (the surgical removal of an entire cerebral hemisphere, amounting to half of the cortical brain, to control severe and intractable epilepsy; de Bode & Curtiss, 2000; Jonas et al., 2004). In VMPFC patients, intellect in the academic sense is preserved; these patients retain their knowledge of math, reading, language, logic, and other subjects. However, these patients show a selective disability to learn from past mistakes and a chronic insensitivity to social feedback about their behavior (Adolphs, Tranel, & Damasio, 2001). In other words, while these patients are smart in the sense recognized by educational psychologists and perform well on tasks of academic skills, they are relatively unable to adjust their behavior in accordance with newly learned information because they are emotionally insensitive to feedback. Put another way, these patients cannot use what they learn to guide their real-world functioning because their cognitive learning and their emotional functioning are relatively divorced from one another. We have argued previously that these patients provide an interesting model of what happens when students' academic learning and emotional lives are kept separate—in other words, when school learning is not relevant to children's lives outside of school (Immordino-Yang & Damasio, 2007).

Another example of lesion analyses with relevance to understanding emotions in educational contexts comes from juxtaposing the developmental histories of two young men who underwent hemispherectomy surgery, which involves removing an entire cortical hemisphere to control intractable seizures. These two young men, who have asked the scientific community to refer to them by their real first names "Nico" and "Brooke," provide some of the world's rare examples of truly right- and left-brained learners; Nico had his right hemisphere removed at age three (Battro, 2000), while Brooke had his left hemisphere removed around age eleven. Now, both young men have compensated unexpectedly well, despite residual difficulties with basic tasks like reading for Brooke and math for Nico (Immordino-Yang, 2007). The majority of children who undergo hemispherectomies are severely impaired after this life-saving surgery, but because Nico and Brooke have each compensated for skills that they would not have been expected to master, such as good spoken language for Brooke and good painting and sport-fencing skills for Nico, comparing their cases provides a new vantage point from which to understand the nature of individual differences in learning and relations to neuropsychological strengths and weaknesses.

One main insight from these young men's cases has been that while each is able to accomplish what appear to be normal skills as judged by standard behavioral and academic measures, careful analyses reveal that each has compensated by nonconsciously adapting the task into one better suited to his remaining neurological hardware, and the contributions of emotion to these adaptations seem to be strong. These young men's data suggest that normal behavior in academic-style tests may reflect very different kinds of processing and approaches in different kinds of learners; each child may not be accomplishing the academic skill in the same way, and each may need different cognitive and emotional supports to learn to accomplish the skill (Immordino-Yang, 2007). Taking together these young men's cases with studies of patients with damage to the VMPFC nicely demonstrates the importance of considering emotional goals in examining individual differences in learning, which we have described elsewhere (Immordino-Yang, 2008).

THREE IDEAS FOR INTEGRATING AFFECTIVE NEUROSCIENCE INTO EDUCATIONAL RESEARCH

One important consideration in applying neuroscientific techniques to the study of emotion in educational contexts is that neuroscience is inherently an experimental science. The techniques for neuroscience research, especially neuroimaging, are constrained by experimental designs with control conditions and active conditions, and they subject participants to highly unnatural contexts (e.g., lying still on one's back in the dark inside a loudly banging donut-shaped MRI scanner while one repeats a particular task tens to hundreds of times). EEG research, which is more portable and less expensive, also requires that a participant reliably engage in multiple sequential trials of the same mental task (typically up to a hundred trials), so that electrical signals from the brain can be averaged across these trials to identify the neural signal among the other sources of electrical noise (e.g., muscular activity in the scalp or face). Furthermore, each tool requires a decision to privilege either spatial or temporal information. As we can see, existing neuroimaging techniques do not currently provide a useful way to observe the emotional dimensions of ongoing, natural activity among children at school. Nonetheless, insights from neurobiological research can already contribute to educational research, and the future is ripe with collaborative opportunities to adapt laboratory-based experiments to inform educational questions. Below we outline three prospective avenues for such contributions and associated opportunities.

Contributions to Educational Theories and Models of Emotion

The neuroscientific study of emotion can be used by educational psychologists to understand more about the biological bases of emotion processing in order to refine models and theories of the role of emotions in academic life and to ensure that these educational theories and models are biologically plausible. The underlying premise of this argument is that all learning is biologically based and that understanding something about the logic of the biological mechanisms underlying emotions in learning could therefore usefully constrain educational models and research. One complementary benefit of this approach will be that education psychologists can use their knowledge of development and learning to help neuroscientists shape experimental questions and designs so that the findings will be maximally useful to educational researchers. The more aligned neuroscientific research is with the educational research that aims to test the real-world applicability of the neuroscientific findings, the more productive the contributions of each field will be to improving learning.

One example of a theoretical contribution from neuroscientific measurements of emotion that is educationally relevant is the distinction neurobiological models make between emotion and feeling (Damasio, 2003). While the term emotion refers to the changes in bodily and mental states that occur as concerted packages in response to environmental or internal triggers (e.g., memories), feelings involve sensations and interpretations, conscious or nonconscious, of emotions that have already happened or are ongoing. Think, for example, of a student who is nervous about an upcoming math test. This student may gradually become aware of a knot sensation in her stomach and an overall tenseness in her body. In this scenario, the bodily tenseness is automatically, nonconsciously induced by thoughts of the upcoming test, and constitutes what has been called the emotion proper (Damasio, 2003). The student's ability to subsequently become aware of this tenseness, to feel it, and to attribute its cause, reflects more complex cognitive processing and even sometimes meta-awareness on her part (Barrett, Quigley, Bliss-Moreau, & Aronson, 2004; Immordino-Yang, 2010; Immordino-Yang et al., 2012)—what has been termed the emotional feeling.

Notably, the distinction between emotions and feelings in the affective process has not generally been made in educational research because educational research on emotion processing is most concerned with the impact of bodily changes on cognition, behavior, and meaning making (neurobiological speaking, the feelings) rather than nonconscious bodily changes (neurobiologically speaking, the emotion). However, for interdisciplinary educational and neuroscientific research on emotions and feelings to move ahead, this distinction, which earlier did not matter, now should be taken into account. Neuroscientific research has been able to disentangle emotions, which happen first, from feelings, which happen later (e.g., Damasio et al., 2000) and to probe the role of arousal attributions in feelings to social emotional and academic outcomes (e.g., Mendes et al., 2008).

This distinction has two main implications for educational models: first, emotions happen before feelings, and second, feelings have the possibility of conscious and complex cognitive and affective elaboration and deliberation. It is certainly possible to regulate emotion indirectly by reshaping one's appraisal of a situation (Gross, 2008); for instance, a student can regulate her test-taking anxiety by reflecting beforehand on the implications of the test for her life more broadly (Ramirez & Beilock, 2011). But, once an emotion has been induced, students' abilities to recognize and correctly attribute their emotions—for instance, to understand that the stomach sensations relate to the upcoming math test and not to a developing viral infection, and then to reframe these feelings (e.g., as challenge/excitement rather than threat) will be critical. Indeed, curricula that teach skills not simply for emotion regulation but for social emotional awareness—in essence, skills for feeling—can significantly improve students' well-being and academic learning (Brackett, Rivers, Reyes, & Salovey, 2012; Yeager & Walton, 2011; see also Brackett & Rivers, 2014). While these curricula generally do not distinguish between emotion and feeling, doing so may help researchers to target their strategies more effectively. It might also help to better explain why students' (learned and automatic) emotional responses are so difficult to change, and to help researchers capitalize on students' developmental capacities for more adaptively "feeling" and conceptualizing one's automatic emotional reactions, as feelings may turn out to be more plastic than emotions (Immordino-Yang et al., 2012; Immordino-Yang & Sylvan, 2010). Understanding this distinction is also critical for interpreting data from future attempts to utilize neuroscientific measures of emotion in the classroom, as psychophysiological recordings and other techniques generally measure emotion but not feelings and may therefore be difficult to interpret without supplementary measures of feelings using questionnaires, interviews, or other methods. In addition, differences in how students' emotions become feelings (processes of attribution and interpretation, for instance) will also likely turn out to be important.

Contributions to Understanding the Role of Nonconscious Emotional Processing in Learning

Another benefit of incorporating insights from neurobiological findings into educational research designs and theories is that neurobiological mechanisms provide a window into the aspects of mental processing that are nonconscious (Immordino-Yang & Sylvan, 2010). Educational research as a whole relies heavily on self-report, which by definition is conscious (Karabenick et al., 2007). Related to this, the lack of methods for systematically investigating the aspects of cognition that are nonconscious has lead to a strong bias in the field toward an emphasis on the dimensions of emotions (as they relate to learning, social processing, and identity) that are most readily accessible to external observation or conscious report. While these data are useful in predicting many aspects of student learning and performance in academic and other settings, they may be unable to provide a thorough explanation of the underlying processes that give rise to emotionally relevant, socially motivated behavior. It is not that educational theories do not acknowledge the existence of nonconscious processing as a contributor to social, emotional, and memory processing; rather, there is a paucity of tools to probe the contributions of these processes. Neuroimaging research on emotion and learning in the laboratory context has the potential to help address this gap by providing new insights into the workings of nonconscious biological mechanisms. For example, work on the brain's activity during rest and social emotion suggests that people may unconsciously shift their attention inwardly, away from the immediate physical context, in order to build more abstract construals of an emotional situation (Pavarini, Yang, Schnall, & Immordino-Yang, under review; Trope & Liberman, 2010). These shifts in attention may facilitate the induction of future-oriented mindsets, including a sense of intrinsic motivation and emotions like inspiration, or a profound sense of purposeful achievement focus, both of which neuro-imaging research suggests are driven in part by neural processing that happens below the level of conscious awareness (Immordino-Yang & Sylvan, 2010; Murayama et al., 2010).

Contributions to the Creation of More Effective Behavioral Indices of Emotion Processing

One area of neurobiological research that holds promise for translation into academic settings, but is still quite exploratory, comes from neurobiological studies of relations between brain activity during fMRI scanning and natural variation in participants' spontaneous natural behaviors observed in another context, such as a private interview. Preliminary studies in this area suggest that certain behaviors can be indirect indicators of particular psychological and neural states, suggesting potentially that education researchers could be taught to identify these behaviors and would therefore not need neuroimaging to infer the neural states induced in students during particular lessons. For example, in an ongoing series of experiments in Immordino-Yang's laboratory, participants describe their genuine feelings about social stories and memories in a private videotaped interview and then react again to the same stories in the fMRI scanner (Immordino-Yang, McColl, Damasio, & Damasio, 2009; Immordino-Yang & Sylvan, 2010; Saxbe et al., 2012). Early results of a study of participants' nonverbal interview behavior reveal that participants tend to avert their gaze away from distractions in the immediate environment when they report feeling inspired or reflective in the interview. They tend to turn their eyes to the blank ceiling or nondescript wall and to incorporate long pauses into their speech. Interestingly, individual differences in the extent to which participants reported becoming inspired correlated with their tendency to avert their gaze when deliberating on the story's meaning. What is more, eye gaze aversion also correlated with individual differences in neural activity in the subsequent fMRI task, suggesting that eye gaze may be a behavioral indicator of certain patterns of thinking and certain neural systems activating (Pavarini et al., under review). Although this research is in no way ready for introduction into teacher education programs, it does provide a tantalizing suggestion that neuroscientific evidence could potentially be used to identify, in this case, instances of effortful internal reflection in academic contexts (Immordino-Yang et al., 2012). Future work may flesh out the usefulness of this insight in order to support teachers in helping students to reflect on their learning, to build more complex conceptual understandings, and to become more emotionally engaged with, and possibly even inspired by, what they are learning.

Into the Future: A Partnership Between Educational Psychologists and Affective Neuroscientists

Given the recent surge of advances in social and affective neuroscience, coupled with increased attention to the emotional aspects of academic learning, it is time to begin a serious conversation about how these two fields can inform one another. One way in which this might happen is for educational psychologists and affective neuroscientists to enter into collaborations in which neuroscientific methods are used to help address educationally relevant questions in the laboratory setting. Another way, more direct but also fraught with data interpretation difficulties, is for certain neurobiological measurement methods to be utilized for research in classroom settings. As we outline in this chapter, there are significant challenges associated with either of these ways forward, but each has potential, if done well, to be highly fruitful.

In the future that we envision, traditional educational research methods are in no way obsolete; neither are we advocating that educational explanations be replaced by biological ones. It is unreasonable and unnecessary to expect educational researchers to become amateur neuroscientists. Yet, learning theories and neuropsychological theories must be compatible, and cross-disciplinary grappling with inconsistencies or contradictions could improve thinking in both domains. Using neuroscientific conceptions in conjunction with educational approaches might make it possible to systematically probe the conscious and nonconscious biopsychological mechanisms by which our experiences, meaning-making, and emotions contribute to learning. In turn, formulating and testing hypotheses grounded in neuroscience using educational methods would also inform advances in neuroscientific thinking, by helping neuroscientists to learn about the ways that brain findings play out on larger scales in real-life settings. And if the educational hypotheses were borne out, education psychologists and social/affective neuroscientists could then work together to develop novel methods to align traditional educational self-report methods and measurements of behavioral choices with biological indexes of emotion to more deeply probe the conditions under which particular emotions are induced in educational contexts and the effects of these emotions on motivation and learning, as well as how the development of healthy academic emotions is shaped by experience, context, and biological predispositions.

In conclusion, emotions are both biological and psychological phenomena—to understand emotions in academic contexts, we should study them from both biological and psychological vantage points. Among the first steps will be for interested educational psychologists to become familiar with the range of approaches currently available in neuroscience, along with their promises and limitations, and to become familiar with the historically significant contributions of neuroscientific studies to the understanding of emotion. Our chapter aims to support readers in taking these first steps.

REFERENCES

Adolphs, R. (1999). Social cognition and the human brain. *Trends in Cognitive Science, 3*, 469–479.

Adolphs, R., & Damasio, A. R. (2000). The interaction of affect and cognition: A neurobiological perspective. In J. P. Forgas (Ed.), *Handbook of affect and social cognition* (pp. 27–49). Mahwah, NJ: Lawrence Erlbaum.

Adolphs, R., Tranel, D., & Damasio, A. R. (2001). Neural systems subserving emotion: Lesion studies of the amygdala, somatosensory cortices, and ventromedial prefrontal cortices. In G. Gainotti (Ed.), *Handbook of neuropsychology* (2nd ed., Vol. 5, pp. 89–110). New York: Elsevier.

Ameis, S. H., Fan, J., Rockel, C., Voineskos, A. N., Lobaugh, N. J., Soorya, L., . . . Anagnostou, E. (2011). Impaired structural connectivity of socio-emotional circuits in autism spectrum disorders: A diffusion tensor imaging study. *PLoS One, 6*(11), e28044.

Barrett, L. F. (2009a). The future of psychology: Connecting mind to brain. *Perspectives on Psychological Science, 4*, 326–339.

Barrett, L. F. (2009b). Variety is the spice of life: A psychological construction approach to understanding variability in emotion. *Cognition and Emotion, 23*, 1284–1306.

Barrett, L. F., Mesquita, B., Ochsner, K. N., & Gross, J. J. (2007). The experience of emotion. *Annual Review of Psychology, 58*, 373–403.

Barrett, L. F., Quigley, K. S., Bliss-Moreau, E., & Aronson, K. R. (2004). Interoceptive sensitivity and self-reports of emotional experience. *Journal of Personality and Social Psychology, 87,* 684–697.

Battro, A. (2000). *Half a brain is enough: The story of Nico.* Cambridge, United Kingdom: Cambridge University Press.

Batty, M., & Taylor, M. J. (2006). The development of emotional face processing during childhood. *Developmental Science, 9,* 207–220.

Brackett, M. A., & Rivers, S. E. (2014). Transforming students' lives with social and emotional learning. In R. Pekrun & L. Linnenbrink-Garcia (Eds.), *International handbook of emotions in education* (pp. 368–388). New York, NY: Taylor & Francis.

Brackett, M. A., Rivers, S. E., Reyes, M. R., & Salovey, P. (2012). Enhancing academic performance and social and emotional competence with the RULER feeling words curriculum. *Learning and Individual Differences, 22,* 218–224.

Catherine, N.L.A., Schonert-Reichl, K. A., Hertzman, C., & Oberlander, T. F. (2012). Afternoon cortisol in elementary school classrooms: Associations with peer and teacher support and child behavior. *School Mental Health, 4,* 181–192.

Daley, S., Willett, J. B., & Fischer, K. W. (2013). Emotional responses during reading: Physiological responses predict real-time reading comprehension. *Journal of Educational Psychology.*

Damasio, A. R. (1999). *The feeling of what happens.* New York, NY: Harcourt.

Damasio, A. R. (2003). *Looking for Spinoza: Joy, sorrow and the feeling brain.* New York, NY: Harcourt.

Damasio, A. R., Grabowski, T. J., Bechara, A., Damasio, H., Ponto, L. L., Parvizi, J., & Hichwa, R. D. (2000). Subcortical and cortical brain activity during the feeling of self-generated emotions. *Nature Neuroscience, 3*(10), 1049–1056.

Damasio, H., & Damasio, A. R. (1989). *Lesion analysis in neuropsychology.* New York, NY: Oxford University Press.

de Bode, S., & Curtiss, S. (2000). Language after hemispherectomy. *Brain and Cognition, 43,* 135–205.

Eisenberger, N. I., Lieberman, M. D., & Williams, K. D. (2003). Does rejection hurt? An fMRI study of social exclusion. *Science, 302*(5643), 290–292.

Ellis, R. J., Norton, A. C., Overy, K., Winner, E., Alsop, D.C., & Schlaug, G. (2012). Differentiating maturational and training influences on fMRI activation during music processing. *Neuroimage, 60,* 1902–1912.

Gardner, H. (1993). *Frames of mind: The theory of multiple intelligences.* New York, NY: Basic Books.

Giedd, J. N., Lalonde, F. M., Celano, M. J., White, S. L., Wallace, G. L., Lee, N. R., & Lenroot, R. K. (2009). Anatomical brain magnetic resonance imaging of typically developing children and adolescents. *Journal of the American Academy of Child and Adolescent, 48,* 465–470.

Giedd, J. N., & Rapoport, J. L. (2010). Structural MRI of pediatric brain development: What have we learned and where are we going? *Neuron, 67,* 728–734.

Gross, J. J. (2008). Emotion and emotion regulation: Personality processes and individual differences. In O. P. John, R. W. Robins, & L. A. Pervin (Eds.), *Handbook of personality: Theory and research* (3rd ed., pp. 701–723). New York, NY: Guilford Press.

Hansen, P., Kringelbach, M., & Salmelin, R. (Eds.). (2010). *MEG: An introduction to methods.* New York, NY: Oxford University Press.

He, B. J., Snyder, A. Z., Zempel, J. M., Smyth, M. D., & Raichle, M. E. (2008). Electrophysiological correlates of the brain's intrinsic large-scale functional architecture. *Proceedings of the National Academy of Sciences, 105*(41), 16039–16044.

Koizumi, H., Yamamoto, T., Maki, A., Yamashita, Y., Sato, H., Kawaguchi, H., & Ichikawa, N. (2003). Optical topography: Practical problems and new applications. *Applied Optics, 42,* 3054–3062.

Hirsh-Pasek, K., & Bruer, J. T. (2007). The brain/education barrier. *Science, 317*(5843), 1293–1293.

Huettel, S., Song, A., & McCarthy, G. (2004). *Functional magnetic resonance imaging.* Sunderland, MA: Sinauer Associates.

Immordino-Yang, M. H. (2007). A tale of two cases: Lessons for education from the study of two boys living with half their brains. *Mind, Brain and Education, 1,* 66–83.

Immordino-Yang, M. H. (2008). The smoke around mirror neurons: Goals as sociocultural and emotional organizers of perception and action in learning. *Mind, Brain, and Education, 2,* 67–73.

Immordino-Yang, M. H. (2010). Toward a microdevelopmental, interdisciplinary approach to social emotion. *Emotion Review, 2,* 217–220.

Immordino-Yang, M. H. (2011). Implications of affective and social neuroscience for educational theory. *Educational Philosophy and Theory, 1*(43), 98–103.

Immordino-Yang, M. H., Christodoulou, J., & Singh, V. (2012). Rest is not idleness: Implications of the brain's default mode for human development and education. *Perspectives on Psychological Science, 7,* 352–364.

Immordino-Yang, M. H., & Damasio, A. R. (2007). We feel, therefore we learn: The relevance of affective and social neuroscience to education. *Mind, Brain and Education, 1,* 3–10.

Immordino-Yang, M. H., & Faeth, M. (2009). The role of emotion and skilled intuition in learning. In D. A. Sousa (Ed.), *Mind, brain, and education* (pp. 66–81). Bloomington, IN: Solution Tree Press.

Immordino-Yang, M. H., & Fischer, K. W. (2010). Neuroscience bases of learning. In P. Peterson, E. Baker, & B. McGaw (Eds.), *International encyclopedia of education* (3rd ed., pp. 310–316). Oxford, United Kingdom: Elsevier.

Immordino-Yang, M. H., McColl, A., Damasio, H., & Damasio, A. (2009). Neural correlates of admiration and compassion. *Proceedings of the National Academy of Sciences, 106,* 8021–8026.

Immordino-Yang, M. H., & Singh, V. (2013). Hippocampal contributions to the processing of social emotions. *Human Brain Mapping, 34,* 945–955.

Immordino-Yang, M. H., & Sylvan, L. (2010). Admiration for virtue: Neuroscientific perspectives on a motivating emotion. *Contemporary Educational Psychology, 35,* 110–115.

Jamieson, J. P., Nock, M. K., & Mendes, W. B. (2012). Mind over matter: reappraising arousal improves cardiovascular and cognitive responses to stress. *Journal of Experimental Psychology: General, 141,* 417–422.

Jonas, R., Nguyen, S., Hu, B., Asarnow, R. F., LoPresti, C., & Curtiss, S. (2004). Cerebral hemispherectomy: Hospital course, seizure, developmental, language, and motor outcomes. *Neurology, 62,* 1712–1721.

Karabenick, S. A., Woolley, M. E., Friedel, J. M., Ammon, B. V., Blazevski, J., Bonney, C. R. . . . Musu, L. (2007). Cognitive processing of self-report items in educational research: Do they think what we mean? *Educational Psychologist, 42,* 139–151.

Keller, T. A., & Just, M. A. (2009). Altering cortical connectivity: Remediation-induced changes in the white matter of poor readers. *Neuron, 64,* 624–631.

Koenigs, M., Young, L., Adolphs, R., Tranel, D., Cushman, F., Hauser, M., & Damasio, A. (2007). Damage to the prefrontal cortex increases utilitarian moral judgements. *Nature, 446*(7138), 908–911.

Koyama, M. S., Di Martino, A., Zuo, X.-N., Kelly, C., Mennes, M., Jutagir, D. R., & Milham, M. P. (2011). Resting-state functional connectivity indexes reading competence in children and adults. *The Journal of Neuroscience, 31,* 8617–8624.

Kreibig, S. D., & Gendolla, G. H. E. (2014). Autonomic nervous system measurement of emotion in education and achievement settings. In R. Pekrun & L. Linnenbrink-Garcia (Eds.), *International handbook of emotions in education* (pp. 625–642). New York, NY: Taylor & Francis.

Li, Y., Liu, Y., Li, J., Qin, W., Li, K., Yu, C., & Jiang, T. (2009). Brain anatomical network and intelligence. *PLoS Comput Biol, 5*(5), e1000395.

Lloyd-Fox, S., Blasi, A., & Elwell, C. E. (2010). Illuminating the developing brain: the past, present and future of functional near infrared spectroscopy. *Neuroscience and Biobehavioral Reviews, 34,* 269–284.

Luck, S. J. (2005). *An introduction to the event-related potential technique.* Cambridge, MA: The MIT Press.

Luders, E., Clark, K., Narr, K. L., & Toga, A. W. (2011). Enhanced brain connectivity in long-term meditation practitioners. *Neuroimage, 57,* 1308–1316.

Luders, E., Phillips, O. R., Clark, K., Kurth, F., Toga, A. W., & Narr, K. L. (2012). Bridging the hemispheres in meditation: Thicker callosal regions and enhanced fractional anisotropy (FA) in long-term practitioners. *Neuroimage, 61,* 181–187.

Mackey, A. P., Whitaker, K. J., & Bunge, S. A. (2012). Experience-dependent plasticity in white matter microstructure: Reasoning training alters structural connectivity. *Frontiers in Neuroanaomy, 6*(32), 1–9.

Mendes, W. B., Major, B., McCoy, S., & Blascovich, J. (2008). How attributional ambiguity shapes physiological and emotional responses to social rejection and acceptance. *Journal of Personality and Social Psychology, 94,* 278–291.

Miller, G.E.C., Chen, E., & Zhou, E. S. (2007). If it goes up, must it come down? Chronic stress and the hypothalamic-pituitary-adrenocortical axis in humans. *Psychological Bulletin, 133,* 25–45.

Murayama, K., Matsumoto, M., Izuma, K., & Matsumoto, K. (2010). Neural basis of the undermining effect of monetary reward on intrinsic motivation. *Proceedings of the National Academy of Sciences, 107*(49), 20911–20916.

Nagamitsu, S., Yamashita, Y., Tanaka, H., & Matsuishi, T. (2012). Functional near-infrared spectroscopy studies in children. *Biopsychosocial Medicine, 6*(7), 1–7.

Neuroscience and the classroom: Making Connections, Unit 1, at www.learner.org/courses/neuroscience

Pantazis, D., & Leahy, R. M. (2006). Imaging the human brain with Magnetoencephalography. In A. Lazakidou (Ed.), *Handbook of research on informatics in healthcare and biomedicine* (pp. 294–302). Hershey, PA: Information Science Reference.

Pascual-Leone, A., Walsh, V., & Rothwell, J. (2000). Transcranial magnetic stimulation in cognitive neuroscience—virtual lesion, chronometry, and functional connectivity. *Current Opinion in Neurobiology, 10*, 232–237.

Pavarini, G., Yang, X., Schnall, S., & Immordino-Yang, M. H. (under review). *Verbal, nonverbal and neural indicators of psychological distance in moral elevation and admiration for skill.*

Pekrun, R., Goetz, T., Titz, W., & Perry, R. P. (2002). Academic emotions in students' self-regulated learning and achievement: A program of qualitative and quantitative research. *Educational Psychologist, 37*, 91–105.

Raichle, M. E. (1998). Behind the scenes of functional brain imaging: A historical and physiological perspective. *Proceedings of the National Academy of Sciences, 95*, 765–772.

Rainville, P., Bechara, A., Naqvi, N., & Damasio, A. R. (2005). Basic emotions are associated with distinct patterns of cardiorespiratory activity. *International Journal of Psychophysiology, 61*, 5–18.

Ramirez, G., & Beilock, S. L. (2011). Writing about testing worries boosts exam performance in the classroom. *Science, 331*(6014), 211–213.

Rappolt-Schlichtmann, G., & Watamura, S. (2010). Inter- and transdisciplinary work: Connecting research on hormones to problems of educational practice. *Mind, Brain, and Education, 4*, 157–210.

Rappolt-Schlichtmann, G., Willett, J. B., Ayoub, C., Lindsley, R., Hulette, A., & Fischer, K. W. (2009). Poverty, relationship conflict and the regulation of cortisol in small and large group contexts at child care. *Mind, Brain and Education, 3*, 131–142.

Saxbe, D., Yang, X., Borofsky, L., & Immordino-Yang, M. H. (2013). The embodiment of emotion: Language use during the feeling of social emotions predicts cortical somatosensory activity. *Social Cognitive and Affective Neuroscience, 8*, 806–812.

Song, M., Liu, Y., Zhou, Y., Wang, K., Yu, C., & Jiang, T. (2009). Default network and intelligence difference. *Conf Proc IEEE Eng Med Biol Soc, 2009*, 2212–2215.

Spangler, G., Pekrun, R., Kramer, K., & Hofmann, H. (2002) Students' emotions, physiological reactions, and coping in academic exams. *Anxiety, Stress and Coping, 15*, 413–432.

Tang, Y. Y., Lu, Q., Fan, M., Yang, Y., & Posner, M. I. (2012). Mechanisms of white matter changes induced by meditation. *Proceedings of the National Academy of Sciences, 109*, 10570–10574.

Trope, Y., & Liberman, N. (2010). Construal-level theory of psychological distance. *Psychological Review, 172*, 440–463.

Utz, K. S., Dimova, V., Oppenlander, K., & Kerkhoff, G. (2010). Electrified minds: Transcranial direct current stimulation (tDCS) and galvanic vestibular stimulation (GVS) as methods of non-invasive brain stimulation in neuropsychology—A review of current data and future implications. *Neuropsychologia, 48*, 2789–2810.

Walsh, V., & Pascual-Leone, A. (2003). *Transcranial Magnetic Stimulation: A neurochronometrics of mind.* Cambridge, MA: The MIT Press.

Wig, G. S., Grafton, S. T., Demos, K. E., Wolford, G. L., Petersen, S. E., & Kelley, W. M. (2008). Medial temporal lobe BOLD activity at rest predicts individual differences in memory ability in healthy young adults. *Proceedings of the National Academy of Sciences, 105*, 18555–18560.

Yang, X., Bossman, J., Schiffhauer, B., Jordan, M., & Immordino-Yang, M. H. (2013). Intrinsic default mode network connectivity predicts spontaneous verbal descriptions of autobiographical memories during social processing. *Frontiers in Psychology, 3*, 592.

Yeager, D. S., & Walton, G. M. (2011). Social-psychological interventions in education: They're not magic. *Review of Educational Research, 81*, 267–301.

31

AUTONOMIC NERVOUS SYSTEM MEASUREMENT OF EMOTION IN EDUCATION AND ACHIEVEMENT SETTINGS

Sylvia D. Kreibig and Guido H. E. Gendolla,
Stanford University and University of Geneva

Klara [. . .] was working on the medium difficulty problem. In the first few minutes, she experienced anxiety, which was discernible from her nonverbal expression. . . . She confirmed that she indeed was anxious. . . . The heart rate at about this time accelerated significantly. . . . Similarly, as Klara continued working on the problem she experienced anger. This was evident in her face too. . . . The heart rate measure also revealed a significantly increased heart rate. . . . As Klara completed about 75% of the task, enjoyment surfaced. Corresponding [heart rate changes] were not significant [. . .], but the clear drop from those of anger and anxiety suggests that the associated decrease was consequential. . . . Toward the end of the task, Klara reported being anxious. . . . In spite of Klara's subjective experience of anxiety, neither her nonverbal expression nor her heart rate signaled the emotion.

(Ahmed, van der Werf, & Minnaert, 2010, p. 146f)

Emotion can be conceptualized as a multicomponent response, elicited by appraising an event as relevant to personal goals, needs, or values, with coordinated effects on subjective feeling, physiology, and motor expression (Scherer, 2009). Consistent with this definition, Ahmed et al. (2010) assessed students' emotions in the classroom through a multimethod approach: Video-stimulated recall interview was used for measuring the experience of emotional feelings. Heart rate monitoring assessed the physiological response component of emotion. Video recordings of the students' face and torso were coded for nonverbal emotional expressions. Findings of this case study, as illustrated in Figure 31.1, suggest that emotionally potent events during educational episodes indeed lead to concurrent changes in emotional feelings, heart rate, and nonverbal emotional expressions.

This research was supported by the Swiss National Science Foundation (PBGEP1-125914, 100014-140251).

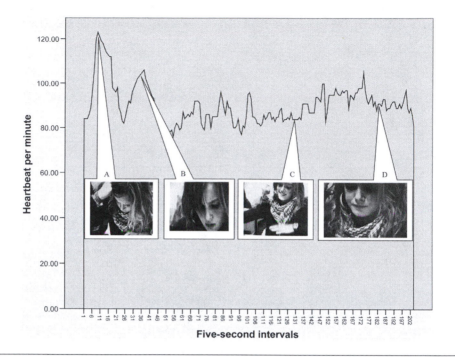

Figure 31.1 A student's emotional responses during a math exam: Feeling self-report from stimulated recall interview, nonverbal expressions, and corresponding heart rate change. From Ahmed et al. (2010). Used by permission from European Psychologist, Vol. 15(2): 142–151 © 2010 Hogrefe Publishing www.hogrefe.com DOI: 10.1027/1016-9040/a000014.

The present chapter presents an approach to studying emotion in education and achievement settings through the noninvasive measurement of autonomic nervous system (ANS) activity. Part one outlines structure and function of the ANS, introduces commonly assessed measures of cardiovascular, electrodermal, and respiratory activity and discusses how these measures index autonomic activity. Part two introduces three principles of ANS measurement to address the following questions: (1) What measurement model is adequate for assessing autonomic effects of emotion? The principle of bivariate autonomic space explicates how different branches of the ANS contribute to measurable responses at visceral organs, (2) Are autonomic responses an outcome of emotion or do they function as input to emotion? The principle of bidirectional autonomic influences illustrates how we can think about the mutual influence of emotion and ANS activity, and (3) How do emotions regulate ANS activity? The principle of allodynamic regulation suggests that emotions regulate ANS activity by fine tuning parameters of task-related ANS activity. Part three returns to Ahmed et al.'s (2010) case study to outline avenues for future research on emotion in education and achievement settings afforded by applying the three principles of ANS measurement.

THE AUTONOMIC NERVOUS SYSTEM

The ANS is a major output system of the brain. Autonomic responding in emotion is hypothesized to consist of functional activation patterns, aligned with and in support of each specific emotion's goal (Kreibig, 2010). Prediction, measurement, and interpretation of functional ANS patterns of emotion requires knowledge of the structure and functioning of the ANS and needs to be guided by appropriate selection of autonomic measures of emotional responding. We discuss each of these points in the following.

Structure and Functioning of the Autonomic Nervous System

The ANS, as illustrated in Figure 31.2, consists of a system of nerves that regulates organ functioning throughout the human body, including the viscera, vasculature, glands, and other tissues, except striated muscle fibers (Jänig, 2003; Langley, 1921).[1] Both efferent and afferent pathways are involved in autonomic regulation. Efferent, or descending, pathways relay peripherally directed motor commands to visceral target organs. Afferent, or ascending, pathways return sensory input from the viscera to central processing structures.

The ANS comprises several subsystems, including the sympathetic (SNS) and parasympathetic (PNS) nervous systems. Their distinction is based on the anatomical structure of the autonomic innervation from the central nervous system to peripheral target tissues. The SNS originates in thoracolumbar regions of the spinal cord and is relayed at

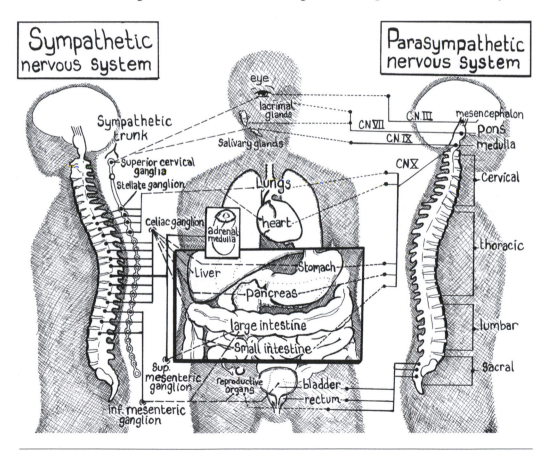

Figure 31.2 The autonomic nervous system; illustration of the sympathetic and parasympathetic branches. The enteric division, not shown separately here, consists of groups of cell bodies and nerve fibers embedded in the walls of the esophagus, stomach, and intestines. Continuous lines = preganglionic axons; dashed lines = postganglionic axons of the sympathetic nervous system; dotted lines = postganglionic axons of the parasympathetic nervous system. The sympathetic outflow to skin and deep somatic structures of the extremities (upper extremity, T2–T5; lower extremity T12–T13) and of the trunk are shown only for the lower limbs. Copyright © 2013 Sylvia Kreibig. Artist Prima Barischoff.

the paravertebral ganglia, resulting in shorter pre- and longer postganglionic neurons. It releases acetylcholine at preganglionic neurons and norepinephrine at postganglionic neurons, which activates adrenergic receptors on the target organ.

The structure of the PNS contrasts with that of the SNS. The PNS originates in craniosacral regions of the spinal cord and is relayed at ganglia close to or embedded into the target organ, resulting in longer pre- and shorter postganglionic neurons. It releases acetylcholine at both pre- and postganglionic neurons that activates nicotinic receptors at postganglionic neurons and muscarinic receptors at the target organ.

Every organ is innervated by one or both of the sympathetic and parasympathetic outflows. As shown in Figure 31.2, the SNS innervates the heart, smooth musculature of blood vessels, erector pili muscles, pupils, lungs, evacuative organs, sweat, salivary, and digestive glands, adipose tissue, liver cells, the pineal gland, and lymphatic tissues, as well as the adrenal medulla. The PNS innervates the heart's pacemaker cells and atria, smooth muscles and glands of the airways, intraocular smooth muscles, the smooth musculature, exocrine and endocrine glands of the gastrointestinal tract, pelvic organs (lower urinary tract, hindgut, reproductive organs), epithelia and mucosa throughout body, exocrine glands of the head, as well as some intracranial, uterine, and facial blood vessels not contributing to blood pressure regulation.

Autonomic regulation is normally fast, occurring within a subsecond time range. Autonomic regulation is moreover highly differentiated. A precise neural regulation of body functions is achieved by an anatomically and physiologically distinct organization of the SNS and PNS that consists of several different, functionally distinct subsystems. Each subsystem is associated with a different type of target tissue at the visceral organ. Very little or no cross-talk exists between the different peripheral pathways (Jänig & Häbler, 2000). This highly differentiated organization supports adaptive responses of the body during different types of behavior, including emotional responding. Highly differentiated effects of the SNS and PNS on target organs can thus bring about a large repertoire of distinct autonomic responses (Folkow, 2000; Jänig, 2003), constituting the basis for differentiated autonomic responses in emotion.

Measures of Autonomic Nervous System Activity

Various measures of visceral organ responses allow inferences about the state of ANS functioning. These can be organized according to the autonomic branch that controls changes in the response measure, the visceral organ that expresses the response, and the receptor type that transmits the signal between the nervous system and visceral organ. Table 31.1 gives an overview of autonomic response measures according to this organization. It also lists the type of response direction observed in the response measure based on activation of the respective pathway—that is, whether activation of the pathway has an excitatory or inhibitory effect on the measurable organ response.

The SNS innervates the heart through β-adrenergic receptors. Their stimulation leads to measurable effects that are expressed, for example, in cardiac acceleration—that is, increased heart rate. Heart rate is measured in beats per minute based on the electrocardiogram (ECG), which detects electrical activity of the heart over a period of time by electrodes attached to the surface of the skin. Although heart rate is commonly assessed, it is a relatively unspecific indicator of sympathetic influence. Because the heart is dually innervated by the SNS and PNS, both systems can evoke heart rate changes. Increases in

Table 31.1 Overview of Indicator Functions of Primary Autonomic Response Measures According to Autonomic Branch, Effector Organ, Receptor Type, and Response Direction

Autonomic Branch	Effector Organ	Receptor Type	Response Measure	Abbreviation	Response Direction
SNS	heart	β-adrenergic	heart rate[†]	HR	+
			pre-ejection period	PEP	−
			stroke volume	SV	+
			cardiac output	CO	+
			pulse transit time	PTT	−
			systolic blood pressure	SBP	+
	lungs[‡]		respiratory rate[†]	RR	+
			tidal volume[†]	V_t	+
			mean inspiratory flow rate	V_t/T_i	+
	vasculature	α-adrenergic	diastolic blood pressure	DBP	+
			total peripheral resistance	TPR	+
			finger pulse amplitude	FPA	−
			finger temperature (surface)	FT	−
	eccrine sweat glands/ electrodermal	cholinergic	skin conductance level	SCL	+
			skin conductance response amplitude	SCR	+
			skin conductance response rate	nsSCRR	+
PNS	heart/ respiration-mediated	cholinergic	heart rate[†]	HR	−
			root mean squared successive differences	RMSSD	+
			peak-valley respiratory sinus arrhythmia	p-v RSA	+
			high-frequency heart rate variability	HF-HRV	+
	heart/ baroreflex-mediated		low-frequency heart rate variability	LF-HRV	+
	lungs[‡]		respiratory rate[†]	RR	−
			tidal volume[†]	V_t	−
			inspriatory duty cycle	T_i/T_{tot}	−

SNS = sympathetic nervous system; PNS = parasympathetic nervous system; † = unspecific index due to dual control through SNS and PNS; ‡ = conjointly influenced by autonomic, cortical, and behavioral influences; + = increase with increasing autonomic influence; − = decrease with increasing autonomic influence.

heart rate can mean increased sympathetic influence, decreased parasympathetic influence, or both.

Sympathetic stimulation of the heart primarily leads to enhanced cardiac contractility. Pre-ejection period, the time interval from the beginning of electrical stimulation of the ventricles to the opening of the aortic valve—that is, electrical systole—will reflect this change by a decrease; the myocardium operates more efficiently, which shortens the time interval needed for contraction. Pre-ejection period is the most sensitive measure of sympathetic effects on the heart. Stroke volume also reflects enhanced contractility by an increase in the amount of blood expelled from the heart during one cycle. So does cardiac output, which is defined as the product of heart rate and stroke volume. These measures are obtained from impedance cardiography (ICG), a technique that applies an electrical current and detects impedance changes in the thorax for calculating various hemodynamic parameters.

Pulse transit time may also be used to index myocardial sympathetic excitation. It refers to the time it takes the pulse wave to travel between two arterial sites. It is typically measured as the time interval between the R-spike and the peripheral pulse at the finger or ear lobe. Quantification of pulse transit time requires simultaneous measurement of ECG and photoplethysmography. Similar to pre-ejection period, it will show shortened time interval with increasing activation.

Enhanced cardiac contractility also leads to increased systolic blood pressure. This is the peak pressure in the arteries that occurs at the end of cardiac contraction. Blood pressure has traditionally been measured through the oscillometric method that involves the observation of oscillations in the sphygmomanometer cuff pressure. More recent developments allow measurement of continuous noninvasive arterial pressure or indirect estimation through the principle of pulse wave velocity.

The SNS also innervates the lungs through β-adrenergic receptors. Respiratory function, among others, can be subdivided into a frequency and a volumetric component. Respiratory rate or frequency quantifies the number of breathing cycles per minute. Tidal volume quantifies inspiratory depth. Mean inspiratory flow rate is defined as the ratio of tidal volume to inspiratory time. It quantifies the velocity of contraction of respiratory muscles and is used as an index of the intensity of central respiratory drive (Gautier, 1980)—that is, centrally generated impulses to inhale in response to changing blood levels of respiratory gases. Frequency and volume measures of respiration can be obtained from piezo-electric strain gauges attached around the upper and lower torso for measuring thoracic and abdominal breathing effects.

The SNS innervates the vasculature through α-adrenergic receptors. Their stimulation leads to the narrowing of the blood vessels resulting from contraction of the muscular wall of the vessels (i.e., vasoconstriction). This effect can be assessed by various measures. Diastolic blood pressure refers to the minimum pressure in the arteries that occurs when the ventricles are filled with blood. Total peripheral resistance is the sum of the resistance of all peripheral vasculature in the systemic circulation. It is calculated as the ratio between mean arterial pressure and cardiac output and involves the joint measurement of blood pressure and ICG. Increased vasoconstriction leads to increased diastolic blood pressure and increased total peripheral resistance.

The stiffening of the arterial walls caused by vasoconstriction also leads to a decrease in the pulse wave amplitude as measured—for example, at the finger. As for the measurement of pulse transit time, this involves application of a photoplethysmograph.

Vasoconstriction also leads to decreased blood perfusion that is measurable as decreased skin temperature at the finger. This can be attained through application of a thermistor.

The SNS innervates the eccrine sweat glands, located on the palm of the hands and sole of the feet, through cholinergic receptors. If a small current is applied via two electrodes, activation of the sweat glands leads to measurable increases in conductance. Electrodermal activity is typically quantified as skin conductance level, which relates to the tonic activation component. Alternatively, skin conductance response amplitude or nonspecific skin conductance response rate may be calculated, which relate to the phasic activation component. While measures of the electrodermal system are a reliable index of sympathetic activity, it is of note that this system is solely controlled by the SNS and, in contrast to other sympathetically innervated organs, its influence is mediated by cholinergic rather than adrenergic transmitters (Schütz et al., 2008; Shields, MacDowell, Fairchild, & Campbell, 1987). Hence, inference of sympathetic functioning obtained from the electrodermal system may not apply to other organ systems.

The PNS innervates the heart through cholinergic receptors. Parasympathetic stimulation leads to cardiac deceleration (i.e., heart rate decreases). Respiration leads to variability in heart rate, a phenomenon that has been termed respiratory sinus arrhythmia. It refers to the effect that during inspiration, vagal activity is attenuated and heart rate accelerates, whereas during expiration, vagal activity is reinstated and heart rate slows. Measurement of this variability component of heart rate allows quantification of respiration-mediated parasympathetic vagal influences on the heart. Time-domain measures rely on calculation of the root mean squared successive differences of heart period series or similar variability indices. Peak-to-valley respiratory sinus arrhythmia is an alternative time-domain measure defined as the difference between the longest and shortest heart period within a given respiratory cycle. Frequency-domain measures quantify parasympathetic influences as the high-frequency component of spectral power of heart period series.

Baroreflex-mediated cardiac vagal effects impact the low-frequency component of heart rate variability (Goldstein, Bentho, Park, & Sharabi, 2011). Spectral analysis of heart rate variability allows quantification of this component. The baroreflex describes the mechanism through which increases in blood pressure lead to reflexive decreases in heart rate, cardiac output, and total peripheral resistance, illustrating the complex interaction between vascular and cardiac processes.

The PNS also innervates the lungs, through which it contributes to changes in respiratory rate and tidal volume. More specific effects can be derived from quantification of inspiratory duty cycle, defined as the ratio of inspiratory to total breath time (Gautier, 1980). It indexes a rhythm generator with variable periodicity, which cyclically switches the central inspiratory drive mechanism on and off, and may be viewed as a respiratory control mechanism. The rhythm generator is one of the main determinants of the duration of the inspiratory phase of respiration. It can also introduce marked breath-by-breath variations in respiratory rate and tidal volume.

Given the possibility of complex interactions as well as nonuniform ANS functioning at different visceral organs, multiple measures of visceral organ activity should be assessed. The underlying autonomic activation state may be more closely related to emotional states and processes than simple measures of visceral organ states. It is therefore of interest to infer the specific autonomic activation state from measuring visceral organ responses (Berntson, Sarter, & Cacioppo, 1998). Especially dually innervated organs, such as the heart, can give valuable information about the differential effects of sympathetic and parasympathetic activation components. To interpret physiological data, it is important to select the assessed ANS parameters on the basis of hypotheses about the psychophysiological meaning with regard to activation and deactivation involved in different emotions. Given availability of stationary and ambulatory monitoring systems for the measurement of the discussed cardiovascular, electrodermal, and respiratory measures (e.g., Kreibig, Schaefer, & Brosch, 2010; Wilhelm & Grossman, 2010), assessment of these measures is readily feasible in education and achievement settings.

PRINCIPLES OF AUTONOMIC NERVOUS SYSTEM MEASUREMENT FOR STUDYING EMOTION

In the following section, we introduce three fundamental principles of ANS measurement for studying emotion. We first discuss how the ANS determines the functional state of visceral organs. This leads to the formulation of the principle of bivariate autonomic space. We exemplify its application in a series of studies on the emotional effects of performance feedback. We next discuss the causal relation between autonomic change and emotion, which leads to the formulation of the principle of bidirectional autonomic influences. We illustrate its application in research on test anxiety. Finally, we discuss in what ways emotion may influence ANS regulation. This leads to the formulation of the principle of allodynamic regulation. We demonstrate its application in the context of affective influences on the mobilization of mental effort.

Autonomic Determinism of the Functional State of Visceral Organs

How does measurement of the responses of visceral organs, such as heart rate or skin conductance level, inform us of the activation state of the ANS? This measurement approach is built on the assumptions that (1) the functional state of visceral organs is governed at least in part by autonomic influences, (2) functional measures of visceral organs can provide veridical reflections of autonomic states, and (3) autonomic regulation reflects broader adaptive states of the organism (Berntson, Cacioppo, & Quigley, 1991). The model assumed to underlie autonomic organization and control of visceral target organs determines what inferences can be drawn from measures of visceral organ responses about central regulatory modes.

Visceral target organs have traditionally been viewed to be dually innervated by the two autonomic branches. These were believed to exert functionally antagonistic effects and operate in reciprocity. Autonomic control was conceptualized to vary on a single dimension from sympathetic dominance at one end to parasympathetic dominance at the other end (Cannon, 1932), operating in unity throughout the entire body. Such effects are, for example, observable at the heart, which is a dually innervated organ, and opposing effects—heart rate acceleration and deceleration—are brought about by sympathetic and parasympathetic stimulation, respectively. Reflexive responses of the heart, such as cardiac adaptation to standing upright, are characterized by this functional reciprocity—that is, increasing activity in one branch is associated with decreasing activity in the other (Berntson et al., 1991). According to this view, assessment of activity of one target organ would suffice in order to infer system-wide sympathetic or parasympathetic control dominance.

Exceptions to this model are, however, quite common (Berntson et al., 1991): Single rather than dual-system innervation is the case for most target tissues. Antagonistic effects of the SNS and the PNS are—in contrast to popular conception—rather rare (Koizumi, Terui, & Kollai, 1983). And unlike reciprocal operation, the systems typically work either synergistically or under separate functional or temporal conditions. The doctrine of functional reciprocity has consequently been superseded by the view that sympathetic and parasympathetic activity is organized within a two-dimensional space, as formalized in the model of autonomic space (Berntson et al., 1991). This model assumes that activity in the two ANS divisions may operate either coupled or uncoupled. Coupled modes include the traditional view of reciprocal functioning as well as modes of coactivation and coinhibition. In uncoupled mode, the two autonomic divisions function independently.

Berntson et al. (1998) suggested that descending influences from brain regions that give rise to emotion—the hypothalamus, amygdala, and cerebral cortex—yield nonreciprocal modes of autonomic activation in behavioral contexts. Accordingly, recruitment of flexible autonomic response modes has been documented in the context of various psychological challenges, such as painful stimulation, physical stress, or survival threats (Berntson et al., 1991).

Principle of Bivariate Autonomic Space

The principle of bivariate autonomic space holds that sympathetic and parasympathetic branches of the ANS may operate in coupled or uncoupled modes. Consequently, independent assessment of sympathetic and parasympathetic influences on dually innervated organs is required to infer autonomic activation components.

Application in the Context of Emotional Effects of Performance Feedback

The principle of bivariate autonomic space is readily illustrated in a series of studies on achievement emotions in response to performance feedback that varied in outcome relevance (i.e., relevant or irrelevant) and outcome valence (i.e., success or failure; Kreibig, Gendolla, & Scherer, 2010, 2012). It was predicted that relevant success feedback would elicit positive achievement emotions, as expressed in the experience of joy and pride and sympatho-vagal coactivation, a state of optimal activation for engaging with the environment that maximizes cardiac contractility while minimizing increases in heart rate. Relevant failure feedback was predicted to elicit negative achievement emotions, as expressed in the experience of disappointment and autonomic coinhibition, an expression of effort withdrawal and disengagement. In contrast, irrelevant feedback was expected to not lead to an emotional response, given that goal relevance is often assumed a prerequisite for the elicitation of emotion (Scherer, 2009).

Pre-ejection period was assessed as an index of sympathetic β-adrenergic cardiac activity. Respiratory sinus arrhythmia was assessed as an index of parasympathetic cardiac (vagal) activity. Based on these measures, composite indices of ANS functioning (Berntson, Norman, Hawkley, & Cacioppo, 2008) were calculated: Cardiac autonomic balance (CAB) was defined as the difference between normalized pre-ejection period and normalized respiratory sinus arrhythmia (i.e., $CAB = RSA_z - (-PEP_z)$). It considers the predominance of sympathetic or parasympathetic influences. Cardiac autonomic control (CAR) was defined as the sum over normalized pre-ejection period and respiratory sinus arrhythmia (i.e., $CAR = RSA_z + (-PEP_z)$). It considers the joint influence of sympathetic and parasympathetic influences. Additionally, measures of heart rate (given traditional assessment of this index), mean arterial blood pressure and total peripheral resistance (for probing vascular effects), and skin conductance level and response amplitude (for probing electrodermal activity) were assessed.

CAR indicated autonomic coactivation during relevant success feedback and autonomic coinhibition during relevant failure feedback, but more traditional measures of heart rate and skin conductance did not evidence this effect. This response pattern suggests a physiologically activating engagement response under positive achievement emotions and a physiologically deactivating disengagement response under negative achievement emotions. This example illustrates the importance of assessing independent indicators of sympathetic and parasympathetic effects for sensitively quantifying autonomic emotion effects.

Causal Relation of Autonomic Change and Emotion

What is the relation between emotion, feelings, and autonomic change? This question is as old as the field of emotion research but nonetheless still controversially discussed.

At the end of the nineteenth century, William James (1884, p. 189) proposed that "the bodily changes follow directly the *perception* of the exciting fact, and that our feeling of the same changes as they occur *is* the emotion." This thesis equates the sensation of bodily changes to the experience of emotional feelings. A similar relation was proposed in Lange's (1885) writings. In present-day emotion research, this afferent model of the relation between autonomic change and emotion is found, among others, in the somatic marker hypothesis (Damasio, 1996; Damasio, Tranel, & Damasio, 1991; see Dunn, Dalgleish, & Lawrence, 2006 for a comprehensive discussion of peripheral feedback theories of emotion). It suggests that afferent signals of emotion-elicited autonomic change are forwarded to higher brain regions, where such signals support decision making in complex situations. Arising gut feelings, such as anticipatory skin conductance responses to the expected outcome of the decision, may promote adaptive decision making (Bechara, Tranel, Damasio, & Damasio, 1996). Thus, central to the *afferent view* of the relation between autonomic change and emotion are the modulatory inputs of autonomic activity on the experience of feeling and the information processing demands of the emotional situation at hand.

The efferent view of the relation between autonomic change and emotion dates back at least as far as to Walter Cannon's work at the beginning of the twentieth century. Cannon (1927) vehemently questioned the capability of the ANS to provide the feedback signals assumed by the afferent view. Still, he clearly acknowledged autonomic outflows to the periphery, where these would lead to sympathetic arousal effects of emotion. Efferent effects of emotion also constitute a centerpiece of various present-day models of emotion. Discrete emotion theory assumes that innate neuromotor programs produce a distinctive physiology for each basic emotion in support of emotion-specific behaviors (Ekman, 1972; Izard, 1977; Tomkins, 1962, 1963; for recent views, see Russell, Rosenberg, & Lewis, 2011, and contributions). Motivational models of emotion suggest that emotion activates motivational brain circuits that, in turn, activate autonomic structures in preparation for defensive or appetitive actions (Lang, 1994; Lang & Bradley, 2010). Autonomic change occurring as part of emotion is also believed to protect bodily functioning (e.g., Stemmler, 2004). Thus, according to this view, emotion directly leads to autonomic change. The large majority of research on emotion has been based on this efferent conceptualization of autonomic effects of emotion.

Recent perspectives expressed within appraisal theory of emotion integrate both afferent and efferent views of the relation between autonomic change and emotion, recognizing bidirectional interactions in the control of affective and autonomic reactivity (Harrison, Kreibig, & Critchley, 2013). The efferent output role of the ANS is emphasized in the conceptualization of ANS activity as a response component of emotion (Scherer, 2009). Appraisal outcomes are believed to result in feed-forward control signals that centrally orchestrate coordinated adaptive responses in physiology, motor expression, and action tendencies. The afferent input role of the ANS is emphasized in the conceptualization of the feeling component of emotion as reflecting a "multimodal integration of synchronized changes in component processes" (Scherer, 2004, p. 148). Feelings are viewed as a central representation of the appraisal-driven changes occurring in emotion, assuming a feedback mechanism from the various emotional response components. This conceptualization also highlights the important distinction between emotion as the conceptual phenomenon under study and feeling as one observable component of emotion.

Independent of the causal direction of emotion and autonomic change, no one-to-one relation can be assumed between the two (Cacioppo & Tassinary, 1990; Kreibig, Schaefer, & Brosch, 2010). Emotion may instigate autonomic change, but so do physical activity and other nonemotional psychological factors. Autonomic afference may give rise to emotional feelings, but so do evaluative processes. Both emotion and autonomic responses then need to be viewed as multiply determined. This means that autonomic responses may only allow inference of specific emotions under standardized measurement conditions and with multivariate measurement of autonomic responses (cf. physiological response profile; Kreibig, Wilhelm, Roth, & Gross, 2007).

Principle of Bidirectional Autonomic Influences

The principle of bidirectional autonomic influences holds that signals transmitted via both efferent and afferent autonomic pathways have functional significance. Autonomic efferences generate an autonomic activation state that is believed to protect bodily functioning and support action preparation. Autonomic afferences, in contrast, transmit feedback signals of physiological changes, perception of which is believed to shape the experience of emotional feelings and lead to bottom-up modulation of cerebral function, affecting cognitive-attentional functioning.

Application in the Context of Test Anxiety

Test anxiety is a psychological condition in which a person experiences distress before, during, or after a test or other assessment. Test anxiety consists of catastrophizing thoughts, negative emotional feelings, physiological over-arousal, difficulty concentrating, and results in impaired test performance (Zeidner, 1998).

The cardiovascular afference model of cognitive effects of anxiety (Berntson et al., 1998) applies the principle of bidirectional autonomic influences to the study of anxiety. According to this model, feedback of peripheral physiological effects of anxiety generates broad cortical stimulation via the forebrain that results in impaired attention. That is, efferent pathways initiate anxiety-related changes in autonomic reactivity—including increased heart rate and blood pressure, dilation of the pupils, trachea, and bronchi, and regulation of body temperature via increased sweat gland output (e.g., Kreibig et al., 2007). Cardiovascular afferent pathways, in turn, transmit information about peripheral physiological changes back to the brain. Specifically, they activate basal forebrain cholinergic neurons, which enhances cortical evaluative processing of anxiety-related stimuli and contexts. This sensitizes the test-anxious student to detecting, selecting, and attending to anxiety-related rather than task-relevant stimuli.

To study cognitive effects of anxiety-related cardiovascular change, we can take measurements of each of the proposed processes. Anxiety may be measured as self-reported feelings or their facial expression. Anxiety-related cardiovascular changes are quantified as change scores between rest and task conditions and may involve measures, such as heart rate, heart rate variability, and pre-ejection period. Cortical stimulation can be quantified as change in regional cerebral blood flow or electroencephalographic activation. Cognitive effects can be quantified as performance outcomes on cognitive tests or school exams. Proposed interactions can be tested within an analytical framework that predicts that test anxiety results in performance decrements mediated through anxiety-related peripheral physiological changes and resulting increased cortical stimulation.

While performance impairments of test anxiety—the most intensively studied emotion in educational settings (Pekrun, 2005)—have been documented in numerous studies (e.g., Cassady, 2004; Hancock, 2001), there is paucity of research investigating interactions between central and autonomic nervous system processes in the context of test anxiety. Still, indirect links suggest anxiety-specific impairments of attentional processes (Shackman et al., 2006) as well as modulation of sensory discrimination and attentional performance by ANS states (Basile et al., 2013; Hatfield, Landers, & Ray, 1987; Saxon & Dahle, 1971). This example illustrates the potential that bidirectional conceptualizations of brain–ANS interactions offer for the explanation of emotional phenomena in education and achievement settings.

Autonomic Regulation and Emotion

How does emotion interact with autonomic regulation? That is, how does emotion "go under the skin?" Classical models of autonomic regulation view emotion as a perturber of ANS activity. The homeostasis model of autonomic regulation (Cannon, 1929, 1932) assumes that autonomic change is targeted at maintaining some internal set point of the *milieu intérieur* that has been perturbed. This basic physiological principle of equilibrium, constancy, stability, or homeostasis is instantiated as a closed negative feedback loop, returning the perturbed system to a fixed set point under fixed operating characteristics. Regulation is assumed to be exclusively compensatory in response to disturbance of a parameter.

Instead of the rigid structure of closed regulatory loops suggested by the homeostasis model, the more recently proposed model of allodynamic regulation (Berntson & Cacioppo, 2007) suggests that autonomic regulation can be adaptively varied to face anticipated or existing demands. Brain regions that give rise to emotion—the hypothalamus, amygdala, and cerebral cortex—can modulate operating characteristics (e.g., gains) and set points of brainstem homeostatic mechanisms. These regions can generate highly flexible patterns of autonomic outflow to attain adequate autonomic support. The allodynamic model of autonomic control explicitly recognizes emotion as an adaptive regulatory mechanism.

Principle of Allodynamic Regulation

The principle of allodynamic regulation of autonomic activity holds that the ANS has variable operating characteristics that are jointly determined by homeostatic and higher order controls. Adjustment of set points or operating characteristics may occur at any level.

Application in the Context of Affective Influences on Mental Effort

Motivation to learn, engage with a topic, and work on task assignments is fundamental in education and achievement settings. Motivational intensity theory (Brehm & Self, 1989) addresses effort mobilization in cognitive tasks. It postulates that motivational intensity or effort is directly related to perceived task difficulty. A maximum level of potential motivation places an upper limit on effort investment. This upper level is determined by various motivation-related appraisals, including the importance of the consequences associated with a successful outcome of the task. Beyond this upper level, success is either viewed as impossible or to require more effort than is warranted by its importance and hence, all effort is withdrawn (Figure 31.3a).

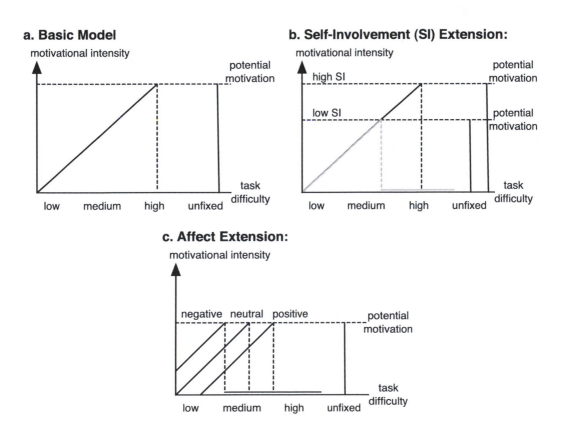

Figure 31.3 Illustration of relations between task difficulty and motivational intensity proposed by Motivational Intensity Theory.

The allodynamic principle is applied in extensions of motivational intensity theory that integrate adjustment of gains and set points by affective processes. Affect may modify the relation between effort and perceived task difficulty in two ways: First, the relation may be amplified by increased self-involvement in performance settings where instrumental behavior has implications for an individual's self-evaluation, social evaluation, or personal interests and values (Gendolla & Richter, 2010; Figure 31.3b). Students' interest or disinterest in a subject may thus modulate the maximum amount of potential motivation invested in task performance. This suggests that disinterested students will withdraw effort at lower task difficulty than interested or emotionally engaged students.

Second, the relation between effort and perceived task difficulty may be shifted over task difficulty by positive or negative feelings (Gendolla, Brinkmann, & Silvestrini, 2012; Figure 31.3c). Sad feelings lead to higher effort mobilization for tasks of low difficulty and earlier effort withdrawal for tasks of increasing difficulty as compared to that observed under neutral feelings. Happy feelings, in contrast, lead to lower effort mobilization for tasks of low difficulty and increasing effort investment for more difficult tasks up to a level superseding that observed under neutral feelings (see Gendolla et al., 2012).

Integration of motivational intensity theory with the active coping approach to cardiovascular arousal (Obrist, 1981) by Wright (1996) specifies how motivational and emotional appraisals influence autonomic reactivity. Specifically, within this framework effort is conceptualized as sympathetic β-adrenergic cardiac reactivity. Whereas preejection period is the prime noninvasive indicator of sympathetic β-adrenergic impact on the heart, systolic and diastolic blood pressure and heart rate can also reflect its influence, albeit less clearly.

Typical results demonstrate shortened pre-ejection period and increased systolic blood pressure, and—with less consistency—increased diastolic blood pressure and heart rate with increasing level of task difficulty as long as success is possible and justified: Low cardiovascular reactivity is observed for tasks that are easy, impossible, or not worth investing the necessary effort; high cardiovascular reactivity is observed in conditions of high or unspecified difficulty, interpreted to index importance of success (see Richter & Gendolla, 2009). Conditions of high self-involvement as contrasted to low self-involvement have been demonstrated to increase cardiovascular reactivity for difficult and unfixed tasks (see Gendolla & Richter, 2010); similar results have been found for emotionally engaged versus disengaged participants (Kreibig, Gendolla, & Scherer, 2010). Research has moreover demonstrated higher cardiovascular reactivity for participants with negative feelings than for participants with positive feelings at low levels of task difficulty, whereas the reverse pattern is found at high levels of task difficulty—that is, higher cardiovascular reactivity for participants with positive feelings than for participants with negative feelings (Gendolla et al., 2012). These results are typically interpreted as indicating higher perceived demand in participants with negative feelings than in participants with positive feelings, leading to higher activation at lower levels of difficulty and earlier disengagement from goal striving in participants with negative than positive feelings at higher levels of task difficulty. This example illustrates the importance of the assumed underlying model of autonomic regulation—with fixed relations and tunable parameters—for the prediction and interpretation of autonomic effects of emotion as well as for the choice of measured autonomic responses.

SUMMARY AND FUTURE DIRECTIONS

We opened the current chapter with a case description of a student's emotions—based on measurements of subjective feelings, heart rate reactivity, and facial expressions—occurring while solving actual mathematical problems in her regular classroom (Ahmed et al., 2010). We next explored the structure, functioning, and measurement of the ANS. We then introduced three central principles of ANS measurement for studying emotion—bivariate autonomic space, bidirectional autonomic influences, and allodynamic regulation. We conclude by returning to Ahmed et al.'s (2010) case study. Application of the three principles of ANS measurement to the research context of emotion in education and achievement settings opens up new directions for future research.

First, assumption of a bivariate model of autonomic space calls for differential assessment of sympathetic and parasympathetic influences on cardiac activity, such as pre-ejection period and heart rate variability. The specific assessment of autonomic activation components—and thus of autonomic modes—promises identification of specific effects of students' emotions. Positive achievement-related emotions, such as joy and pride, may be expected to lead to sympatho-vagal coactivation, whereas negative achievement-related emotions, such as disappointment, may be expected to lead to autonomic coinhibition. Addition of vascular, electrodermal, and respiratory response measures allows for a comprehensive multisystem assessment and more specific inferences regarding multisystem differentiation of autonomic emotion effects.

Second, consideration of bidirectional effects allows addressing both effects of visceral efferences in emotion—for example, as an outcome of specific events during test taking as well as effects of visceral afferences in emotion leading to specific psychological states or performance outcomes. Of course, efferent and afferent effects of emotion need not be limited to states of anxiety that may lead to sympathetic arousal and attentional impairments. Also, beneficial effects of both positive and negative emotion should be considered. As Panel C in Figure 31.1 suggests, experience of positive affect may sooth autonomic arousal and facilitate task performance (e.g., Gendolla & Krüsken, 2001).

Third, conceptualization of affective influences on mental effort from the vantage point of allodynamic regulation, as formalized in motivational intensity theory, allows us to derive specific predictions for how emotion may interact with motivation and influence ANS reactivity. Future research will need to address whether this framework can, for example, help differentiate whether students' problems result from too high task difficulty, disinterest, or negative feelings. That way, monitoring ANS responses can provide important information about emotional processes in education and achievement settings.

NOTE

1. This chapter focuses on ANS measurement of emotion. Several other physiological measures, such as central nervous system activity or facial muscular responses, are not discussed here. Information on these measures may be found, for example, in the *Handbook of Psychophysiology* (Cacioppo, Tassinary, & Berntson, 2007).

REFERENCES

Ahmed, W., van der Werf, G., & Minnaert, A. (2010). Emotional experiences of students in the classroom: A multimethod qualitative study. *European Psychologist, 15,* 142–151.

Basile, B., Bassi, A., Calcagnini, G., Strano, S., Caltagirone, C., Macaluso, E., . . . Bozzali, M. (2013). Direct stimulation of the autonomic nervous system modulates activity of the brain at rest and when engaged in a cognitive task. *Human Brain Mapping, 34,* 1605–1614.

Bechara, A., Tranel, D., Damasio, H., & Damasio, A. R. (1996). Failure to respond autonomically to anticipated future outcomes following damage to prefrontal cortex. *Cerebral Cortex, 6,* 215–225.

Berntson, G. G., & Cacioppo, J. T. (2007). Integrative physiology: Homeostasis, allostasis, and the orchestration of systemic physiology. In J. T. Cacioppo, L. G. Tassinary, & G. G. Berntson (Eds.), *Handbook of psychophysiology* (pp. 433–452). Cambridge, United Kingdom: Cambridge University Press.

Berntson, G. G., Cacioppo, J. T., & Quigley, K. S. (1991). Autonomic determinism: The modes of autonomic control, the doctrine of autonomic space, and the laws of autonomic constraint. *Psychological Review, 98,* 459–487.

Berntson, G. G., Norman, G. J., Hawkley, L. C., & Cacioppo, J. T. (2008). Cardiac autonomic balance versus cardiac regulatory capacity. *Psychophysiology, 45,* 643–652.

Berntson, G. G., Sarter, M., & Cacioppo, J. T. (1998). Anxiety and cardiovascular reactivity: The basal forebrain cholinergic link. *Behavioural Brain Research, 94,* 225–248.

Brehm, J. W., & Self, E. A. (1989). The intensity of motivation. *Annual Review of Psychology, 40,* 109–131.

Cacioppo, J. T., & Tassinary, L. G. (1990). Inferring psychological significance from physiological signals. *American Psychologist, 45,* 16–28.

Cacioppo, J. T., Tassinary, L. G., & Berntson, G. G. (Eds.). (2007). *Handbook of psychophysiology.* Cambridge, United Kingdom: Cambridge University Press.

Cannon, W. B. (1927). The James-Lange theory of emotions: A critical examination and an alternative theory. *American Journal of Psychology, 39,* 106–124.

Cannon, W. B. (1929). *Bodily changes in pain, hunger, fear, and rage* (2nd ed.). New York, NY: D. Appleton & Co.

Cannon, W. B. (1932). *The wisdom of the body.* New York, NY: Norton.

Cassady, J. C. (2004). The influence of cognitive test anxiety across the learning–testing cycle. *Learning and Instruction, 14,* 569–592.

Damasio, A. R. (1996). The somatic marker hypothesis and the possible functions of the prefrontal cortex. *Philosophical Transactions of the Royal Society London B, 351,* 1413–1420.

Damasio, A. R., Tranel, D., & Damasio, H. C. (1991). Somatic markers and the guidance of behavior: Theory and preliminary testing. In H. S. Levin, H. M. Eisenberg, & A. L. Berntson (Eds.), *Frontal lobe function and dysfunction* (pp. 217–229). New York, NY: Oxford University Press.

Dunn, B. D., Dalgleish, T., & Lawrence, A. D. (2006). The somatic marker hypothesis: A critical evaluation. *Neuroscience and Biobehavioral Reviews, 30,* 239–271.

Ekman, P. (1972). Universal and cultural differences in facial expression of emotion. In J. K. Cole (Ed.), *The Nebraska Symposium on Motivation, 1971* (pp. 207–283). Lincoln, NE: University of Nebraska Press.

Folkow, B. (2000). Perspectives on the integrative functions of the "sympatho-adrenomedullary system." *Autonomic Neuroscience: Basic and Clinical, 83,* 101–115.

Gautier, H. (1980). Control of pattern of breathing. *Clinical Science, 58,* 343–348.

Gendolla, G.H.E., Brinkmann, K., & Silvestrini, N. (2012). Gloomy and lazy? On the impact of mood and depressive symptoms on effort-related cardiovascular response. In R. A. Wright & G.H.E. Gendolla (Eds.), *How motivation affects cardiovascular response: Mechanisms and applications* (pp. 139–155). Washington, DC: APA Press.

Gendolla, G.H.E., & Krüsken, J. (2001). The joint impact of mood state and task difficulty on cardiovascular and electrodermal reactivity in active coping. *Psychophysiology, 38,* 548–556.

Gendolla, G.H.E., & Richter, M. (2010). Effort mobilization when the self is involved: Some lessons from the cardiovascular system. *Review of General Psychology, 14,* 212–226.

Goldstein, D. S., Bentho, O., Park, M.-Y., & Sharabi, Y. (2011). Low-frequency power of heart rate variability is not a measure of cardiac sympathetic tone but may be a measure of modulation of cardiac autonomic outflows by baroreflexes. *Experimental Physiology, 96,* 1255–1261.

Hancock, D. R. (2001). Effects of test anxiety and evaluative threat on students' achievement and motivation. *The Journal of Educational Research, 94,* 284–290.

Harrison, N. A., Kreibig, S. D., & Critchley, H. D. (2013). A two-way road: Efferent and afferent pathways of autonomic activity in emotion. In J. L. Armony & P. Vuilleumier (Eds.), *Handbook of human affective neuroscience* (chap. 82–106). Cambridge, England: Cambridge University Press.

Hatfield, B. D., Landers, D. M., & Ray, W. J. (1987). Cardiovascular–CNS interactions during a self-paced, intentional attentive state: Elite marksmanship performance. *Psychophysiology, 24,* 542–549.

Izard, C. E. (1977). *Human emotions.* New York, NY: Plenum Press.

James, W. (1884). What is an emotion? *Mind, 9,* 188–205.

Jänig, W. (2003). The autonomic nervous system and its coordination by the brain. In R. J. Davidson, K. R. Scherer, & H. H. Goldsmith (Eds.), *Handbook of affective sciences* (pp. 135–186). New York, NY: Oxford University Press.

Jänig, W., & Häbler, H.-J. (1999). Organization of the autonomic nervous system: Structure and function. In P. J. Vinken, G. W. Bruyn, & O. Appenzeller (Eds.), *Handbook of clinical neurology: Vol. 74. The autonomic nervous system: Part 1. Normal functions* (pp. 1–52). Amsterdam, Netherlands: Elsevier.

Jänig, W., & Häbler, H.-J. (2000). Specificity in the organization of the autonomic nervous system: A basis for precise neural regulation of homeostatic and protective body functions. *Progress in Brain Research, 122,* 351–367.

Koizumi, K., Terui, N., & Kollai, M. (1983). Neural control of the heart: Significance of double innervation reexamined. *Journal of the Autonomic Nervous System, 7,* 279–294.

Kreibig, S. D. (2010). Autonomic nervous system activity in emotion: A review. *Biological Psychology, 84,* 394–421.

Kreibig, S. D., Gendolla, G.H.E., & Scherer, K. R. (2010). Psychophysiological effects of emotional responding to goal attainment. *Biological Psychology, 84,* 474–487.

Kreibig, S. D., Gendolla, G.H.E., & Scherer, K. R. (2012). Goal relevance and goal conduciveness appraisals lead to differential autonomic reactivity in emotional responding to performance feedback. *Biological Psychology, 91,* 365–375.

Kreibig, S. D., Schaefer, G., & Brosch, T. (2010). Psychophysiological response patterning in emotion: Implications for affective computing. In K. R. Scherer, T. Baenziger, & E. Roesch (Eds.), *Blueprint for affective computing: A sourcebook* (pp. 105–130). Oxford, England: Oxford University Press.

Kreibig, S. D., Wilhelm, F. H., Roth, W. T., & Gross, J. J. (2007). Cardiovascular, electrodermal, and respiratory response patterns to fear- and sadness-inducing films. *Psychophysiology, 44,* 787–806.

Lang, P. J. (1994). The motivational organization of emotion: Affect–reflex connections. In S. VanGoozen, N. E. Van de Poll, & J. A. Sergeant (Eds.), *Emotions: Essays on emotion theory* (pp. 61–93). Hillsdale, NJ: Erlbaum.

Lang, P. J., & Bradley, M. M. (2010). Emotion and the motivational brain. *Biological Psychology, 84,* 437–450.

Lange, C. (1885). The mechanism of the emotions. In E. Dunlap (Ed.), *The emotion* (pp. 33–92). Baltimore, MD: Williams & Wilkins.

Langley, J. N. (1921). *The autonomic nervous system* (Pt. 1). Cambridge, England: Heffer.

Obrist, P. A. (1981). *Cardiovascular psychophysiology: A perspective.* New York, NY: Plenum.

Pekrun, R. (2005). Progress and open problems in educational emotion research. *Learning and Instruction, 15,* 497–506.

Richter, M., & Gendolla, G.H.E. (2009). The heart contracts to reward: Monetary incentives and preejection period. *Psychophysiology, 46,* 451–457.

Russell, J. A., Rosenberg, E. L., & Lewis, M. D. (2011). Introduction to a special section on basic emotion theory. *Emotion Review, 3,* 363.

Saxon, S. A., & Dahle, A. J. (1971). Auditory threshold variations during periods of induced high and low heart rates. *Psychophysiology, 8,* 23–29.

Scherer, K. R. (2004). Feelings integrate the central representation of appraisal-driven response organization in emotion. In A.S.R. Manstead, N. H. Frijda, & A. H. Fischer (Eds.), *Feelings and emotions: The Amsterdam Symposium* (pp. 136–157). Cambridge, England: Cambridge University Press.

Scherer, K. R. (2009). The dynamic architecture of emotion: Evidence for the component process model. *Cognition and Emotion, 23,* 1307–1351.

Schütz, B., von Engelhardt, J., Gördes, M., Schäfer, M. K.-H., Eiden, L. E., Monyer, H., & Weihe, E. (2008). Sweat gland innervation is pioneered by sympathetic neurons expressing a cholinergic/noradrenergic co-phenotype in the mouse. *Neuroscience, 156,* 310–318.

Shackman, A. J., Sarinopoulos, I., Maxwell, J. S., Pizzagalli, D. A., Lavric, A., & Davidson, R. J. (2006). Anxiety selectively disrupts visuospatial working memory. *Emotion, 6,* 40–61.

Shields, S. A., MacDowell, K. A., Fairchild, S. B., & Campbell, M. L. (1987). Is mediation of sweating cholinergic, adrenergic, or both? A comment on the literature. *Psychophysiology, 24,* 312–319.

Stemmler, G. (2004). Physiological processes during emotion. In P. Philippot & R. S. Feldman (Eds.), *The regulation of emotion* (pp. 33–70). Mahwah, NJ: Erlbaum.

Tomkins, S. S. (1962). *Affect, imagery, consciousness: Vol. 1. The positive affects.* New York, NY: Springer.

Tomkins, S. S. (1963). *Affect, imagery, consciousness: Vol. 2. The negative affects.* New York, NY: Springer.

Wilhelm, F. H., & Grossman, P. (2010). Emotions beyond the laboratory: Theoretical fundaments, study design, and analytic strategies for advanced ambulatory assessment. *Biological Psychology, 84,* 552–569.

Wright, R. A. (1996). Brehm's theory of motivation as a model of effort and cardiovascular response. In P. M. Gollwitzer & J. A. Bargh (Eds.), *The psychology of action: Linking cognition and motivation to behavior* (pp. 424–453). New York, NY: Guilford.

Zeidner, M. (1998). *Test anxiety. The state of the art.* New York, NY: Plenum.

32

MEASURING SITUATED EMOTION

Julianne C. Turner and Meg Trucano, University of Notre Dame

Attention to the situational and social nature of psychological phenomena like emotions has hovered around the edges of psychological research but these topics have never become central. In recent years, some social scientists have argued that greater attention should be paid to how phenomena change—that is, in relation to their social, cultural, and historical situations (e.g., Gergen, 1985, Hutchins, 2010; Lave, 1988; Lave & Wenger, 1991; Payr & Wallis, 2011; Rogoff, 1997). Similarly, some emotion researchers have begun to study affect as a situational process.[1] In this chapter, we will review current approaches to studying affect and emotion as arising from the specific context in which they occur. We begin by contextualizing the notion of situative psychological research and providing a rationale for the study of situative approaches to studying emotion. We continue with a discussion of methods currently used in studying situated emotions, and we evaluate the benefits and drawbacks of each. We then reflect on the conceptualization of "situativity" and its relation to the kinds of methods that researchers may choose. We close with some thoughts on future directions in methodology.

WHY TAKE A SITUATED APPROACH?

In psychology, there has long been a preference for isolating central processes for study, assuming that once processes like memory and schemata are understood, they could then be reintegrated into the social, situational, cultural, and historical contexts in which they occur. Because isolating processes is easier than situating them, progress in contextualizing processes like emotion has been slow. Both theoretical and methodological issues help explain the relatively recent attention to situational approaches to studying psychological processes like emotion.

From the theoretical perspective, psychology has favored the study of individuals as somewhat separate from the contexts in which they live and has emphasized generalizations, which are valued in natural science, in preference to contextualized explanations. In juxtaposition to this approach, Kindermann and Valsiner (1995) argued that instability and change are more representative of actual experience. They argue that we should study processes of

> individuals' adaptation to changing contexts, . . . processes of context adaptation to changing individuals, and [to] individuals' potential to instigate and shape the development of their contexts, as well as [to] contexts' potential to instigate and shape the developmental pathways of individuals.
>
> (Kindermann & Valsiner, 1995, p. 230)

Accordingly, some theorists have proposed frameworks to explain the situated relationship between persons and their environment. J. J. Gibson (1979), for example, studied psychological processes not as invariant but as ecological, or depending on features of the environment. His studies of visual perception introduced the notion of affordances and constraints. Affordances are qualities of the environment that offer resources for a certain kind of activity when the person is attuned simultaneously to its anticipated constraints. Gibson's theory highlights the situational nature of a process that many would assume to be more predictable than emotions or affect, thus illustrating the importance of studying a process like emotion as situational.

Similarly, dynamic systems theory (e.g., Thelen & Smith, 2006) endeavors to explain the stability or instability of patterns of behavior. Dynamic systems theory attempts to account for the properties of all dynamic, open systems, such as human behavioral patterns of parent-child dyads or teachers and students. A system can only be in one state at a particular moment, but different states may be available to it, and changes from state to state reflect the dynamics of the system. During certain times, the system is more sensitive, and external factors can have great influence. For example, Granic and Patterson (2006) described four affective attractor states in parent–child interaction that were related to the development of antisocial behavior: a playful, cooperative one; a mutually polite one; a mutually hostile one; and a disengaged attractor. These authors showed how interpersonal affective reactions changed in response to how the participants negotiated the situation, providing a dynamic measure of the quality and direction of interaction. These theories have rarely been applied to the study of emotion, and they offer fruitful ways of conceptualizing, and possibly, measuring, affective states (For exceptions, see J. E. Turner & Waugh, 2007, and Scherer, 2009).

Using Gibson's (1979) affordances and constraints as well as dynamic systems theory as guides, a situated approach to studying affect considers how emotion is co-constructed along with the practices and values of others in that situation, or is "scaffolded by the environment" (Griffiths, & Scarantino, 2009, p. 437). Greeno and the Middle School Mathematics Through Applications Project Group (1998) stipulate that situated affect should be studied as a "system" rather than at the individual level because "situatedness" is a characteristic of participation in a certain activity. Griffiths and Scarantino (2009) explain that a situated perspective on affect emphasizes "the role of social context in the production and management of an emotion, and the reciprocal influence of emotion on the evolving social context" (p. 348). They further note the specific methodological implications of situated affect. This perspective shifts "the theoretical focus from the intrapsychic to the interpersonal, from the unbidden to the strategic . . . from the context-independent to the context-dependent, from the static to the dynamic" (p. 448).

The importance of this view for education is that it has the potential to provide insight into how and why affect occurs and develops. Also, it might allow us to understand how affordances and constraints scaffold specific interactional patterns and lead to positive or negative educational outcomes. Affect is inextricably linked to learning and achievement, yet the complexity of its role is little understood. This suggests that measuring situated affect is an important contribution to understanding its role in education.

WHAT IS CHALLENGING ABOUT MEASURING SITUATED AFFECT?

Measuring situational affect can be much like shooting at a moving target—the question is, where to aim? Challenges for researchers include time and resources as well as meeting scientific standards. By its very nature, situated affect is co-constructed, thus changing situations and creating the need to measure at multiple time points. This consideration then prompts other considerations, such as choosing the unit of analysis. Should one sample by events, such as activity settings (Rivera & Tharp, 2004), or by time, (e.g., every minute; Vauras, Kinnunen, Kajamies, & Lehtinen, 2013), or both? The major advantage of event sampling is that one can document the activities of the people involved as sources of emotion, thus providing causal information. A disadvantage is that less perceptible changes might be difficult to capture. Time sampling, such as coding activity every 10 minutes or in continuous 30-second intervals allows one to detect trajectories of emotion but may downplay the interaction or the meaning in the activity (e.g., Granic & Patterson, 2006). Additionally, one must decide on which participants will be studied and how—should one focus on individuals as group participants, or whole groups, such as classrooms? Of course, these decisions are related to the research question, but they also pose other dilemmas. Multiple time points help determine causality but take more resources than measurement at one or two time points. Depending on the specificity of the research question, the researcher might need to focus on fewer participants, inviting the criticism of some in the scientific community that no conclusions can be drawn from small samples. Finally, there are tradeoffs between modes of experimental research and research in the field. Experimental research allows close study with simulated academic tasks, but classroom research is potentially more ecologically valid because it might involve typical learning tasks. If one opts for research in classroom settings, how does one avoid interrupting instruction and/or diverting student attention from learning? These are just a few of the decisions that investigators face as they design research to study emotion as situated in distinct tasks and settings. We address these in more depth later.

In the rest of the chapter, we describe how researchers have approached the challenges of measuring situated emotions. We have divided the chapter into two sections that represent the most typical methodologies: the use of self-reports alone and the use of multiple methods. The methodologies we discuss conform to our definition of situated affect with more or less fidelity. That is, information about the interpersonal nature of affect, its strategic nature, its context-dependence and its dynamic nature varies depending on both methodology and how the methodology is designed.

SELF-REPORT METHODOLOGY

Researchers who choose self-report methods judge that participants rather than other people are best qualified to interpret their own feelings. Of course, participants' ability to report emotions is dependent upon other factors, such as age, how they interpret items or questions, and their awareness of their affect (Schultheiss & Köllner, 2014). This may help explain why there are few studies on students younger than upper elementary school. Further support for the use of self-reports is that affective indicators, such as facial expressions, posture and physiological data, can be misinterpreted by observers (Skinner, Kindermann, & Furrer, 2009). Possibly because of their presumed validity and relatively low cost, self-reports are used very frequently, both alone and as part of multiple methods studies. There are many self-report measures of emotions (see Pekrun & Bühner, 2014), but the ones we discuss situate the self-reports in specific contexts that afford the possibility of understanding the interpersonal and contextual interplay with the reporter's affect. These self-report measures of *situated emotions* include the Experience Sampling Method, the Online Motivation Questionnaire, and the Between the Lines online measure, which are discussed below.

The Experience Sampling Method (ESM; Csikszentmihalyi & Larson, 1987; Hektner, Schmidt, & Csikszentmihalyi, 2007) provides a glimpse of the contextual landscape that comprises daily experience (Hektner et al., 2007). ESM broadly aims to connect patterns of daily experience with the contexts in which they occur while preserving temporal sequences of events. ESM can be used in numerous domains (e.g., work, school, leisure time) and with various populations (e.g., students, elderly patients). ESM typically uses some form of electronic device (beeper, watch, cell phone) that has been programmed to send a signal at random times. When alerted, the participants are to stop what they are doing and fill out an experience sampling form (ESF), thus capturing the participant's situational self-reports. The participants usually have a block of ESFs to carry around and are beeped about 15–50 times a week (e.g., Hektner et al., 2007). At the signal, the participants respond by recording where they are, what they are doing, who else is there, and what they are thinking about. Then they complete scales designed to measure affect and other states of consciousness at that moment. Measures of negative affect (e.g., angry, frustrated, irritated; Koh, 2005), positive affect (e.g. happy, cheerful, relaxed; Csikszentmihalyi, Rathunde, & Whalen, 1993), love, joy, fear, anger, shame, and sadness (Diener, Smith, & Fujita, 1995) have been collected using ESM. Some of these items or scales measure conventional emotions (e.g., excited-bored), whereas others may be more motivation related (e.g., involved-detached).

Experiences can be sampled across all daily activities in the participants' lives or simply in one situation. For example, in order to investigate the quality of middle school students' engagement in after-school activities, Shernoff and Vandell (2007) signaled students five times daily during non-school hours. Students rated their experiences on 4 point scales (1, not at all to 4, very much) for feelings (also called moods), including lonely, happy, angry, stressed, excited, bored, scared, sad, relaxed, proud, and worried. Factor analyses indicated factors for positive affect, negative affect, and apathy, which were then used as dependent variables with different activities (e.g., sports, arts enrichment) as predictors. Thus, the authors were able to demonstrate significant differences in feelings compared to other program activities in which the same person participated.

Other researchers have modified original scales to address particular research questions. For instance, Larson, Moneta, Richards, and Wilson (2002) used ESM to measure the continuity, stability, and change in daily emotional experiences in a longitudinal study from early (grades five–eight) to later adolescence (grades nine–twelve). Students completed ESFs for one week each time both in and out of school. At the moment of each signal, they rated their emotional state on seven-point semantic differential items (happy–unhappy, cheerful–irritable, friendly–angry). The authors demonstrated that emotional states were less positive and less stable in early adolescence, becoming more positive and stable by tenth grade.

Still other researchers have modified the ESM method in deference to classroom situations. Turner and her colleagues (Turner et al., 1998) used ESFs in fifth- and sixth-grade math classes over one unit of instruction. In order to avoid disrupting the class with random beeps, the researchers asked students to complete the ESF during the last five minutes of class. Although they expected student involvement to ebb and flow during class, there was rarely more than one class activity, and the intention was to measure students' overall experience during that class rather than involvement during any one phase. The researchers audio-recorded classroom activities and teacher instructional discourse. Students rated the semantic differential items with the same scale used by Csikszentmihalyi (based on pilot studies, some words were replaced with synonyms). Student reports of involvement and positive affect ("happy") differed by day and classroom and were related to aspects of teachers' instructional discourse. Researchers were able to make such claims because they had observation and audio records of classroom instruction.

Benefits of the ESM include its very situated measurement, which occurs at a particular time and place, and its ability to show fluctuations among settings such as school, leisure time, sports, extracurricular activities, and time with friends or family. Because ESM requires participants to report on contextual information, ESM is considered a highly externally valid measurement technique. While ESM values external or ecological validity over internal validity, ESM boasts higher internal validity than one-time survey measures. Measures of reliability, such as Cronbach's alpha, show that ESM scales designed to capture emotional experience range from .75–.85 (positive affect) to .90 (negative affect), indicating high levels of internal consistency for measurement of emotional experience. Measures of test-retest reliability are not applicable because ESM endeavors to capture information at each measurement occasion unique to that particular time and context. A drawback is that the situational detail is vague. Although students are asked to answer the questions "Where are you right now?" and "What are you doing right now?" students might respond "nothing." Even more detail, such as "in English" and "reading *Macbeth*" still does not provide much contextual information about why the student might report the emotions she does. Another drawback of the original ESM methodology for educational research is that it can be disruptive and distracting in classrooms as students are randomly beeped and must take time out from class work to fill out the form.

The Online Motivation Questionnaire (OMQ; Boekaerts, 2002) is another self-report measure that captures students' emotions and motivation in situ. The OMQ uses situation-specific measurement of students' appraisals and emotions before and after a familiar learning task. Boekaerts's *dual processing self-regulation model* assumes that students have two primary goals in learning contexts: to improve their competence and to maximize their well-being. Students appraise a learning task to be either congruent with their learning goal to become more competent (mastery-oriented appraisals) or congruent with their goal to maintain well-being. In the latter case, the appraisal indicates that the learning task is not a good match for the student's learning goal—that is, why the student opts instead to maintain well-being (Boekaerts, 2007). The OMQ measures students' appraisals of self-efficacy, task attraction, perceived personal relevance, perceived task difficulty, expectations of success, and their learning intentions. The OMQ measures emotions as they are related to students' appraisals, perceptions of the outcome of the task, and the effort invested in the task.

In the original version of the Online Motivation Questionnaire (Boekaerts, 2002), students' emotions related to the task are measured both before and after the task is completed, with up to eight emotion state items: joy, contentment, feeling at ease, feeling secure, feeling worried, tense, irritated, and displeased. The intensity of students' current emotional states (e.g., "How do you feel now?") is captured on a four-point scale ranging from high intensity to low intensity (e.g., "Nervous . . . not nervous"; "Happy . . . not happy"). This methodology allows researchers to understand both the students' task-related emotions as well as their relation with students' task appraisals.

A later extended version of the Online Motivation Questionnaire (Boekaerts, 2007) includes a broader range of emotions, including mood states. The inclusion of mood states reflects the need to distinguish between task-related emotion and general mood states, which may influence students' appraisals in different ways. The nine-item affect/mood scale includes measures of happy, sad, annoyed, satisfied, fed up, happily surprised, in a good mood, angry, and fine. Some versions of the OMQ also include a task anxiety scale, which includes measures of being at ease, nervousness, worry, confidence, and being concerned (Crombach, Boekaerts, & Voeten, 2003).

In summary, the OMQ method measures situation-specific motivational beliefs (appraisals), which allow the researcher to understand how the student perceives motivational and emotional cues in a specific learning situation. One benefit is that emotions are related to a specific, familiar task that is associated with a stable emotional response. A drawback is that there is no measure of emotion during the task (Schutz & DeCuir, 2002). However, Boekaerts's intention was not as much to capture the trajectory of emotion but to understand how the appraisal process (before the task) is related to students' coping and well-being (after the task). That may be why she specified that the task be a familiar one that is associated with a more stable emotional response.

The "Between the Lines" (BTL) software program (Ainley & Hidi, 2002) captures students' task-related emotions not before and after but during an academic task. In the software program, students are presented with a choice of texts in a reading task. BTL enables the researchers to measure the emotional states students experience during the reading task and explores the relationship between on-task situated emotions and interest. Interest is defined as either individual (involving relatively enduring predispositions) or situational (Ainley & Hidi, 2002) and related to students' emotions.

In the Between the Lines program, students are asked to indicate their initial level of interest in reading a 200–300 word passage (e.g., "How interesting do you expect this to be?"). As students progress through the passage, the BTL program assesses interest by recording how long it takes the student to click the "next" button to advance the screen or to select a different text altogether. Additionally, Between the Lines prompts participants with pop-up screens at critical points in the passage to indicate how they are feeling. Emotion icons on the pop-up screens represent emotions (sad, surprised, interested, scared, embarrassed, angry, happy, bored, disgusted, and neutral). Students click on the appropriate emotion icon to select the emotion that best reflects their current feeling. Immediately after clicking on an icon, another pop-up screen appears, prompting the student to rate the intensity of that emotion on a five-point scale. Students can select multiple emotions, and the whole selection process occurs rapidly. In this way, the sequence of emotions is captured in a minimally intrusive manner, allowing the researcher to assess the microlevel of students' emotional experiences and to map these experiences onto the specific portion of the task that may have elicited that emotion.

Benefits of BTL include the fact that it monitors and records what students are doing and how they are feeling about what they are doing in real time, preserving the sequence and timing of emotions (Ainley & Hidi, 2002) and providing specific emotion-related information about the tasks. One possible disadvantage of this approach is that it uses experimental tasks rather than a typical or real school task to which students may have emotion responses (as in the OMQ). Another disadvantage is the inability of researchers to disentangle mood (a longer lasting, more pervasive affective state) and dispositional information (characteristic ways of processing experiences) from the task-related affect that BTL is designed to assess. That is, students may begin the task in a certain mood or respond with a certain disposition, thus calling into question whether the emotions and intensity are related to the task or to something else.

These self-report methods have several strengths in common. One benefit to measuring emotions in this situated manner is that the process itself may make students aware of their (sometimes unconscious) cognitions and emotions. However, in making emotions explicit, it might unintentionally interfere with the appraisal process (Crombach et al., 2003). Another benefit is that self-reports provide researchers with a quick, minimally intrusive way to capture spontaneous emotional reactions. Because self-reports are more intrapsychic than interpersonal (unless they are combined with other methods), they may vary in terms of the information they provide about the situation and thus how the situation has affected the student. That is perhaps why many researchers complement self-reports with other methodologies, as we discuss in the next section.

MULTIPLE METHODS

Of course, emotion and affective states express themselves through modes other than feelings. Some researchers use additional or multiple methods, such as video, which allows analysis of situationally related facial expressions, posture, or heart rate. Together, several methods can add potentially corroborating data or provide other ways to address the researcher's questions about the situated nature of affect. In this section, we discuss two kinds of multiple method approaches, tutoring and lab-based studies and classroom studies.

Tutoring and Lab-Based Studies

Among computer tutoring programs that also measure students' affective responses is AutoTutor. AutoTutor program (Graesser, Chipman, Haynes, & Olney, 2005; Graesser et al., 2004) is a software program that provides learners with performance-related feedback (positive, negative, or neutral) during a learning task. In more recent studies, the researchers have incorporated measures of emotions along with passage comprehension. The goal is to ascertain how computer-generated feedback influences comprehension of a passage. Participants are charged with learning material presented in short training modules (approximately 35 minutes) on typically unfamiliar topics, ranging from Newtonian physics to computer operating systems. Topics are randomly assigned, and participants are given a pretest to ensure the topic's unfamiliarity. An earlier version of AutoTutor required participants to type in their responses to questions written at the top of the screen. In a later version, AutoTutor "spoke" the written response in natural language, mimicking a human tutor while still providing positive, negative, or neutral feedback to participants' answers to questions about the text. The participant's responses are video- and audio-recorded for subsequent analysis. After the training session has been completed, participants complete a posttest on the module topic.

Some studies using AutoTutor have incorporated retrospective interviews, where participants view the video of their AutoTutor session in 20-second segments (Baker, D'Mello, Rodrigo, & Graesser, 2010). Participants are then asked to recall their affective states at particular points during the training session, including immediately prior to the participants' spoken turn, immediately following positive, negative, or neutral feedback from AutoTutor, and at other randomly selected points during the AutoTutor session. Thus, researchers can collect affective information at several different points during the task in a minimally disruptive way (D'Mello & Graesser, 2012). These retrospective interviews of participants' affective states can also be used in conjunction with other affective measurement techniques and can be particularly useful given that the video recording of participants may be synchronized with the tutorial, giving the researcher a context for why a participant expressed an emotion.

One affective measurement technique that can be used with the AutoTutor program is emote-aloud (Craig, D'Mello, Witherspoon, & Graesser, 2008; see Graesser, D'Mello, & Strain, 2014). The emote-aloud training modules are constructed in much the same way as traditional AutoTutor tasks, though participants are, in this case, encouraged to vocalize emotions they experience (including anger, boredom, confusion, contempt, curiosity, disgust, eureka, and frustration) as they naturally occur during the progression of a longer dialogue with AutoTutor (approximately 90 minutes). To make emote-aloud as natural as possible, participants are encouraged before the session to report their emotions as often as they occur, but they are not prompted during the session itself.

These sessions are video-recorded. Two coders then rate the emote-aloud video and affective utterances in 10-second clips using the Facial Action Coding System (Ekman & Friesen, 1978), which uses facial cues (action units, or AUs) to code participants' emotions. Emote-aloud is considered to be a valid measure of students' emotions, and the mean Cohen's kappa reliability indicator between two independent observers of emote-aloud utterances with facial expressions is approximately .76 (Craig, D'Mello, Witherspoon, & Graesser, 2008). Emote-aloud utterances can be matched with other simultaneous and online affective measurements, such as retrospective affective judgments, facial expressions, and gross body movements.

Another method that has been used in conjunction with AutoTutor to measure situated affect involves measuring participants' body movements and posture during a tutorial. A Body Pressure Measurement System developed by Tekscan (Tekscan, 1997) captures how a participant sits and shifts throughout a tutorial. As with video capture of participants' facial expressions, body position information allows researchers to map how a participant sits and shifts as they participate in the tutorial. Body position information can also be matched with the participants' emote-alouds during the tutorial and retrospective affective judgments.

Because participants are not aware that they are being monitored in these ways (e.g., video capture of facial expressions, body position) prior to completing the AutoTutor tutorial, both video capture of facial expressions and body position monitoring offer a minimally disruptive way to measure situated emotions at multiple points (D'Mello & Graesser, 2012). The researchers have demonstrated that retrospective affective judgments (self-report) are correlated with other online affective measures (facial activity, body movements) (Craig et al., 2008; D'Mello & Graesser, 2010), thus providing more robust information about participants' affective states.

A related line of research (Dragon et al., 2008) uses sensors to detect physical behaviors linked to students' emotional states while they are using intelligent math tutors in classrooms.[2] First, the researchers observed students while using the tutor in the classroom for three weeks. They identified variables that represented (1) emotions and adaptive/maladaptive states linked to student learning and (2) physical behaviors linked to emotion states. To represent emotions, they coded valence (positive/negative), arousal, and desirability value (i.e., it is not desirable to be joyful and off task). They observed chair and head posture, movement, and face gestures and looked for expressed affect in specific facial expressions, such as smiles or nods, and verbal behavior, such as loud comments or talking with others. The researchers computed correlations between lower-level (i.e., chair movement) and higher level observations (valence, arousal, on-off task behavior) and then also between these higher level observations and student learning and attitudes. These correlations then provided information about which combinations of behaviors and affect were adaptive or not.

After observations, the authors used a low-cost multimodal sensor platform to measure what they observed. The platform included a custom produced Pressure Mouse, a Wireless Blue Tooth Skin Conductance sensor, a Posture Analysis Seat, and a Facial Expression System. Guided by the correlations from the observation phase, these data could inform the intelligent tutors so that tutors could provide feedback as needed (similar to AutoTutor).

This further work is detailed in Woolf et al. (2009). The authors describe several interventions designed to respond to a student's cognitive-affective state as well as the creation of "emotional embodied pedagogical agents" (p. 132). In relation to cognitive-affective states, the sensors can indicate whether students who are not making progress are either stuck (confused, frustrated) or still curious and working. Then the tutor can design an intervention (or not) based on the affective information (in addition to other factors such as achievement level). In addition, the researchers evaluated two "animated affective agents," Jake and Jane, who are integrated into the mathematics tutoring software program and who worked with students as learning buddies. The agents offer advice and encouragement while reflecting on the range of the student's own emotions. They also act out their own affect. For example, if the student is sad/delighted, the agent might look sad/pleased, thus visually mirroring the student's emotional state in an attempt to *empathize* with the student. The agents use full sentence expressions of cognitive, meta-cognitive, and emotional feedback, such as "You seem to know this pretty well so let's move onto something more challenging that you can learn from. Congratulations! Your effort paid off!" and "Some students are frustrated by this problem. Let's look at some similar problems already worked out" (Woolf et al., 2009, p. 152). Through these methods the researchers have developed interventions for students who are low in self-confidence, frustrated, or bored, and to support self-concept.

One advantage to using these combined methodologies is that the individual measures of emotion (e.g., posture, facial expressions, dialogue cues, and retrospective interviews) are minimally invasive and correlated with one another. Additionally, due to the situationally sensitive data points these methodologies are able to collect, researchers are better able to capture information about emotional trajectories during a task. Collectively, the data points contribute to the understanding of the shape and duration of emotions elicited during a tutorial. Individually, each data point may be matched with specific events within the tutorial that gives researchers relevant information about the relationship between the task and related emotions. The way these technologies have been able to learn about students' affective states and to respond offers promise of designing tutors that can individualize responses to support learning, motivation, affect, and metacognition. Both research programs described have been able to show that emotion- and situation-specific feedback is helpful in facilitating learning.

Practical drawbacks to the more widespread use of these technologies is their expense and the level of support (i.e., from computer scientists) they require to develop and use. Although AutoTutor has been used primarily with tasks specifically developed for research and with undergraduates, the math tutor program has been used in sixth and tenth grades in public schools.

SITUATED CLASSROOM STUDIES

A second group of multiple method studies have been conducted in naturalistic conditions within classrooms and using typical school tasks. They range from studies of individuals to small groups to whole class groups and have used both quantitative and qualitative approaches.

Linnenbrink-Garcia, Rogat, and Koskey (2011) investigated the relation between student affect and social behavioral engagement in small group contexts over time using student self-reports and codes derived from videotapes of small group interactions during mathematics tasks. After each of three group sessions, fifth- and sixth-grade students reported affect using bipolar scales (sad–happy, tense–calm, and tired–excited; low [1] to high [9]). In addition, groups were videotaped. Student behaviors from the video (facial expression, body language, tone of voice, and student comments) were coded based on a circumplex model of affect with two dimensions: valence (positive, negative) and activation (high, low). Videotapes were also coded for social behavioral engagement (quality of group interactions [positive, negative, or social loafing]). Using this information, the authors wrote extensive qualitative running records of group interaction, embedding student behavior and social behavioral engagement in descriptions of student group functioning during the mathematics task.

The quantitative measures (e.g., bipolar scales, valence/activation, and behavioral engagement) that were situated within each of the group tasks were used to examine reciprocal relations between affect and engagement during the unit. The qualitative analyses allowed a more in-depth, contextually based understanding of those relations. In particular, the qualitative analyses using affective cues (e.g., facial expressions) and talk enabled researchers to understand both when these affective states occurred during the task and how they were related to students' engaged/disengaged behavior over the duration of the task. Thus, the qualitative data highlighted the reciprocal and cyclical relations between affect and social-behavioral engagement in the small groups, enabling researchers to explain the relative effectiveness of the groups.

In a related study, Rogat and Linnenbrink-Garcia (2011), investigated the contribution of positive socioemotional interactions (affect) and collaboration and the use of social regulatory behaviors, such as planning, monitoring, and behavioral engagement on the quality of the groups studied in Linnenbrink-Garcia et al. (2011). The authors coded the videotapes using categories of interest (e.g., social regulation, positive and negative socioemotional interactions, and collaborative and noncollaborative interactions). They used the codes to write elaborated running records, which provided detailed descriptions of student interactions, (verbatim) dialogue, and behavior. The authors were able to describe a causal sequence showing that positive socioemotional interactions (affect) and collaboration set the stage for cooperative social regulatory behaviors and behavioral engagement, which then accounted for the quality of the group functioning.

Do and Schallert (2004) used a grounded theory approach to triangulate multiple sources of data in a semester-long study of the role of affect in students' experience of classroom discussion in a college classroom. The authors collected student self-reports of affective states and videotaped individuals during class discussion. They observed class and took field notes about students' gestures, facial expressions, and the general tone of the class discussion. They coded video observations for students' affective experience of classroom discussion. The authors then conducted retrospective interviews with students while students viewed their videotapes from class. During analysis, the authors studied how variation in any one dimension (e.g., motivation, cognition) was associated with variation in another (e.g., affect). The authors concluded that affect acted as a catalyst in discussion, both moment by moment and cumulatively over the semester. In a related longitudinal study, Dos Santos, Maria, and Mortimer (2003) measured teacher–student affective interaction in a high school chemistry class over the school year (71 lessons). They took field notes, coded video of classroom instruction (noting physiognomic aspects of posture and gesture of the teacher and of the students, as well as expressive intonation), and interviewed students to determine how the same teacher had very different affective interactions with two different classes. In both studies, the authors were able to measure affect in both short- and long-term situations as a function of both personal and contextual (classroom) factors and to use the methods to demonstrate the dynamic, interactive, and reciprocal processes of affect over time.

Op't Eynde, De Corte, and Verschaffel (2006) conducted a multiple-case study of 16 students that aimed to investigate their emotional processes when solving a mathematical problem in their classrooms. The researchers were interested in the joint contribution of emotion, motivation, and metacognition to problem solving. Students responded to the Mathematics Belief Questionnaire and the Online Motivation Questionnaire (OMQ) before the task. Students were videotaped and asked to think aloud as they completed the problem. They were interviewed after completing the task. The researchers labeled emotions by triangulating facial expressions, vocalizations, and body movement revealed in the videotape along with the students' interpretations and appraisals during the interview. They also interpreted students' mathematics-related beliefs in relation to their problem-solving behavior (see also Op't Eynde & Hannula, 2006).

Other studies have used various combinations of qualitative, quantitative, and computer-based methods. Ahmed, van der Werf, and Minnaert (2010) sought to determine the correspondence among three emotional response systems (nonverbal expressions, subjective feelings, and physiological reactivity [heart rate changes]) while students completed mathematics tasks in the classroom. Six students of low, average, and high achievement were given easy, average, and difficult tasks each. After skimming the tasks, students completed the Online Motivation Questionnaire (Boekaerts, 2002) to measure their appraisals of competence and value for the upcoming task. While completing the tasks, students were videotaped to capture nonverbal expressions and wore heart rate monitors. Nonverbal expressions from the videotapes were coded for six emotions:

anger, anxiety, boredom, enjoyment, pride, and shame. Videotapes were then divided into five-minute segments and shown to students during a stimulated recall session after the lesson where they were asked to describe their feelings at that time. The authors found partial correspondence among intraindividual nonverbal expressions, heart rate, and students' descriptions of their feelings (See also Dragon et al., 2008). The ratio of co-occurrence between nonverbal emotions and interview responses on experiencing emotions ranged from .19 (pride) to .50 (anger). The ratio of co-occurrence between heart rate change and nonverbal emotions ranged from 1.0 (pride and shame) to .76 (anger).

Several methodologies were common across most of these classroom studies, including self-reports of affect, video data of facial expressions, body movements, and interpersonal exchanges, and retrospective interviews. It was less common to measure physiological responses (because they are intrusive) or to use field notes (possibly because video afforded similar information). Even though the methodologies were similar, they were adapted to very different purposes based on research questions and grain size. There seems to be some convergence in this research on situated affect that some combination of self-reports and data that allow researchers to analyze external evidence (such as nonverbal expressions) is preferred. It is interesting to note that this is fairly common in studies of emotion, reflecting the history of emotion research, built partly on Eckman's (1992) work on the expression and physiology of emotion.

There are several general features of the methodologies in these classroom studies that appear to be strengths for studying situated affect. They are related to how the researchers used the methodologies. The combination of pre-task appraisals or self-reports and post-task interviews provides information about how (and potentially why) the affect has changed. Some studies used these measures to link affect to motivation and learning, showing the versatility of self-reports (e.g., Op't Eynde et al., 2006). Video data are useful to understand what happened such that pre- and post-task reports might differ and to gauge the relations between subjective and observable responses. The use of qualitative methods (e.g., Linnenbrink-Garcia et al., 2011; Do & Schallert, 2004), though time-consuming, seems especially useful when studying real-time group interaction because of its complexity. Finally, the use of typical academic tasks provides information directly related to how students experience content instruction and classroom interaction. As with any use of multiple methods, time-intensiveness remains a possible drawback for combining several methodologies.

TRADE-OFFS IN CHOICES OF METHODOLOGICAL APPROACHES

Here we take up a central question related to situated measures of affect: what counts as situated, and how are decisions about the relative situatedness of methods made? From the range of methods we reviewed, it appears that situatedness is somewhat in the eye of the beholder. Methods range from a minute analysis of affect during one task to students' emotions measured repeatedly over a semester in one course. Common to all approaches, however, is the choice to maximize external validity, as is implied in the focus on *situated* affect. Depending on research questions, researchers will make trade-offs in methodology. They include (among others) the grain size and the time, effort, and cost involved. Subsumed under these major categories are decisions about the number of data points required, the amount of information about the context, and the authenticity of the task. We discuss these trade-offs below.

Grain Size

One trade-off in making decisions about methods is grain size. Grain size refers to the specificity of the level of analysis that may be performed and is directly related to what aspect of emotion the researcher is interested in capturing. Generally speaking, a finer grain of analysis is possible as the number of data points increases. For example, pre-and post-task measures of emotion (e.g., Boekaerts, 2002) represent a larger grained analysis and permit the researcher to determine that an emotional reaction occurred sometime during the task and how the student might have coped. Longer duration can also be related to a larger grain size. If the researcher seeks to determine the development and influence of affect in a class over the semester, fewer total data points might be collected over a longer period of time (e.g., Do & Schallert, 2004). However, larger grain measures such as pre-/post-task methodologies would not be adequate for the researcher interested in the nuanced changes of emotion during one task. Capturing information about emotional trajectories during a task, for example, requires the collection of many data points. For example, D'Mello and Graesser (2012) tracked affective states at approximately 110 points in 30-minute tutoring sessions via a retrospective interview. Participants saw freeze framed video of their tutoring session at 20-second intervals and reported fixed and spontaneous judgments of affect. Finally, researchers might decide to collect data of different grain sizes that are complementary and that measure simultaneous processes such as motivation (e.g., Op't Eynde et al., 2006).

Time, Effort, Cost

Related to issues of grain size are the considerations of time, effort, and cost in both data collection and in data analysis. If research questions call for many participants or data points, researchers may consider limiting the time required to collect data. For example, ESM methodology enables the researcher to collect numerous self-reports from many participants with minimal demands on the time of participants and researchers. Collecting data using computer technology (e.g., Autotutor, Between the Lines) may be faster, but it might also require much up-front preparation (writing computer programs) and involve costly equipment. Paper/pencil measures are inexpensive but may be inadequate for answering the research question. If, however, the researcher wants participants' real-time activities or reflections, more time will be required, such as for observations and retrospective interviews (e.g., Ahmed et al., 2010; Do & Schallert, 2004). Time and effort required for data analysis may be greater if data are qualitative (e.g., coding videotapes or fieldnotes) than if data are quantitative. Triangulation of measures usually takes longer than using a single method because data from several sources must be compared and contrasted, though data triangulation can provide a more robust measure of situated emotion. Of course, some of the methods that require the most time, effort, and cost are also the ones that best help understand these complex phenomena. Unfortunately, there is no way to avoid such trade-offs, and these decisions are best guided by research questions.

FUTURE DIRECTIONS

There is wide support for situated, dynamic, and multimethod studies of emotion (e.g., Linnenbrink, 2007; Pekrun & Schutz, 2007), but they still are relatively uncommon. Nevertheless, much progress has been made in recent years in measuring situated emotions as the examples in this chapter attest. Current directions appear to lead toward more fine-grained, longitudinal, and holistic accounts of learners' emotions. Ultimately, the development of better technologies might eliminate some of the trade-offs discussed above. We expect that computer methodologies will continue to develop, perhaps becoming less intrusive so that they might be used more easily in classrooms or other authentic settings. Methodologies like those used in conjunction with AutoTutor (e.g., posture, facial expressions, dialogue cues, etc.) might be adapted for existing tutorial software in content areas like math, providing teachers with real-time data about their students' learning and emotions. Because triangulating data from multiple methods is time-consuming, expert systems might be developed that could accurately code and correlate several features of participants' situated reactions in real time. Advances in neurological methodologies that map emotional reactions onto specific areas of the brain could provide another level of analysis in the study of situated emotion (see Immordino-Yang & Christodoulou, 2014). The use of neurological techniques would have to be modified (e.g., made less intrusive and time-consuming, or made more portable) in order to capture emotion in situated learning contexts. Ultimately, we are hopeful that progress in measuring situated emotions will contribute to better understanding of human processes including motivation and learning and that it will illuminate how emotion is situated in social, cultural, and historical contexts. We believe that this kind of research will fill a gap in psychological research by illuminating how and why emotions are related to change in human learning and behavior.

NOTES

1. We will use the general term, affect, to include emotions, which are relatively brief, and moods, which last longer (Rosenberg, 1988).
2. The intelligent tutor Wayang Outpost teaches geometry and statistics and prepares students for standardized state exams. The theme and setting of Wayang Outpost is a research station on the island of Borneo featuring storylines, animated characters, and problem-solving hints. The program situates mathematics problems in investigations of the ecology and biology of tropical rainforests.

REFERENCES

Ahmed, W., van der Werf, G., & Minnaert, A. (2010). Emotional experiences of students in the classroom: A multimethod qualitative study. *European Psychologist, 15,* 142–151.

Ainley, M., & Hidi, S. (2002). Dynamic measures for studying interest and learning. In P. R. Pintrich & M. L. Maehr (Eds.) *Advances in motivation and achievement: New directions in measures and methods* (Vol. 12, pp. 43–76). Amsterdam, Netherlands: JAI Press.

Baker, R.S.J., D'Mello, S. K., Rodrigo, Ma. M. T., & Graesser, A. C. (2010). Better to be frustrated than bored: The incidence, persistence, and impact of cognitive-affective states during interactions with three different computer-based learning environments. *International Journal of Human-Computer Studies, 68,* 223–241.

Boekaerts, M. (2002). The online motivation questionnaire: A self-report instrument to assess students' context sensitivity. In P. R. Pintrich & M. L. Maehr (Eds.), *Advances in motivation and achievement, Vol. 12: New directions in measures and methods* (pp. 77–120). New York, NY: JAI.

Boekaerts, M. (2007). Understanding students' affective processes in the classroom. In P. Schutz & R. Pekrun (Eds.), *Emotion in education* (pp. 37–56). San Diego, CA: Academic Press.

Craig, S., D'Mello, S., Witherspoon, A., & Graesser, A. (2008). Emote aloud during learning with AutoTutor: applying the facial action coding system to cognitive affective states during learning. *Cognition & Emotion, 22,* 777–788.

Crombach, M. J., Boekaerts, M., & Voeten, M. J. (2003). Online measurement of appraisals of students faced with curricular tasks. *Educational and Psychological Measurement, 63,* 96–111.

Csikszentmihalyi, M., & Larson, R. (1987). The experience sampling method. *Journal of Nervous and Mental Disease, 175,* 526–536.

Csikszentmihalyi, M., Rathunde, K., & Whalen, S. (1993). *Talented teenagers: The roots of success and failure.* Cambridge, United Kingdom: Cambridge University Press.

Diener, E., Smith, H., & Fujita, F. (1995). The personality structure of affect. *Journal of Personality and Social Psychology, 69,* 130–141.

D'Mello, S., Craig, S., Sullins, J., & Graesser, A. (2006). Predicting affective states expressed through an emote-aloud procedure from AutoTutor's mixed initiative dialogue. *International Journal of Artificial Intelligence in Education, 16,* 3–28.

D'Mello, S., & Graesser, A. (2010). Multimodal semi-automated affect detection from conversational cues, gross body language, and facial features. *User Modeling and User Adapted Interaction, 20,* 147–187.

D'Mello, S., & Graesser, A. (2012). Dynamics of affective states during complex learning. *Learning and Instruction, 22,* 145–157.

Do, S. L., & Schallert, D. L. (2004). Emotions and classroom talk: Toward a model of the role of affect in students' experiences of classroom discussions. *Journal of Educational Psychology, 96,* 619–634.

Dos Santos, T., Maria, F., & Mortimer, E. F. (2003) How emotions shape the relationship between a chemistry teacher and her high school students. *International Journal of Science Education, 25,* 1095–1110.

Dragon, T., Arroyo, I., Woolf, B. P., Burleson, W., El Kaliouby, R., & Eydgahi, H. (2008, June). Viewing student affect and learning through classroom observation and physical sensors. In B.P. Woolf, E. Aimeur, R. Nkambou, & S. Lajoie (Eds.), *Intelligent tutoring systems.* Proceedings of the 9th International Conference, Montreal (pp. 29–39). Berlin, Germany: Springer-Verlag.

Ekman, P. (1992). Facial expressions of emotion: New findings, new questions. *Psychological Science, 3,* 34–38.

Ekman, P., & Friesen, W. V. (1978). *The Facial action coding system: A technique for the measurement of facial movement.* Palo Alto, CA: Consulting Psychologists Press.

Gergen, K. J. (1985). The social constructionist movement in modern psychology. *American Psychologist, 40,* 266–275.

Gibson, J. J. (1979). *The ecological approach to visual perception.* Boston, MA: Houghton Mifflin.

Graesser, A. C., Chipman, P., Haynes, B. C., & Olney, A. (2005). AutoTutor: An intelligent tutoring system with mixed-initiative dialogue. *IEEE Transactions in Education, 48,* 612–618.

Graesser, A., Chipman, P., King, B., McDaniel, B., & D'Mello, S. (2007). Emotions and learning with AutoTutor. In R. Luckin, K. Koedinger, & J. Greer (Eds.), *13th International Conference on Artificial Intelligence in Education* (pp. 569–571). Amsterdam, Netherlands: IOS Press.

Graesser, A. C., D'Mello, S. K., & Strain, A. C. (2014). Emotions in advanced learning technologies. In R. Pekrun & L. Linnenbrink-Garcia (Eds.), *International handbook of emotions in education* (pp. 473–493). New York, NY: Taylor & Francis.

Graesser, A., Lu, S., Jackson, G., Mitchell, H., Ventura, M., Olney, A., & Louwerse, M. M. (2004). AutoTutor: A tutor with dialogue in natural language. *Behavior Research Methods, Instruments, & Computers, 36,* 180–192.

Granic, I., & Patterson, G. R. (2006). Toward a comprehensive model of antisocial development: A dynamic systems approach. *Psychological Review, 113,* 101–131.

Greeno, J., & the Middle School Mathematics Through Applications Project Group. (1998). The situativity of knowing, learning and research. *American Psychologist, 53,* 5–26.

Griffiths, P., & Scarantino, A. (2009). Emotions in the wild: The situated perspective on emotion. In P. Robbins & M. Aydede (Eds.), *Cambridge handbook of situated cognition* (pp. 437–453). Cambridge, United Kingdom: Cambridge University Press.

Hektner, J. M., Schmidt, J. A., & Csikszentmihalyi, M. (2007). *Experience sampling method: Measuring the quality of everyday life.* Thousand Oaks, CA: Sage.

Hutchins, E. (2010). Cognitive ecology. *Topics in Cognitive Science, 2,* 705–715.

Immordino-Yang, M. H., & Christodoulou, J. A. (2014). Neuroscientific contributions to understanding and measuring emotions in educational contexts. In R. Pekrun & L. Linnenbrink-Garcia (Eds.), *International handbook of emotions in education* (pp. 607–624). New York, NY: Taylor & Francis.

Kindermann, T. A., & Valsiner, J. (1995). Directions for the study of developing person–context relations. In T. A. Kindermann & J. Valsiner (Eds.), *Development of person–context relations* (pp. 227–240). Mahwah, NJ: Erlbaum.

Larson, R. W., Moneta, G., Richards, M. H., & Wilson, S. (2002). Continuity, stability, and change in daily emotional experience across adolescence. *Child Development, 73,* 1151–1165.

Lave, J. (1988). *Cognition in practice.* Cambridge, United Kingdom: Cambridge University Press.

Lave, J., & Wenger, E. (1991). *Situated learning: Legitimate peripheral participation.* Cambridge, United Kingdom: Cambridge University Press.

Linnenbrink, E. A. (2007). The role of affect in student learning: A multidimensional approach to considering the interaction of affect, motivation, and engagement. In P.A. Schutz & R. Pekrun (Eds.), *Emotion in education* (pp.107–124). Amsterdam, Netherlands: Elsevier.

Linnenbrink-Garcia, L., Rogat, T. K., & Koskey, K.L.K. (2011). Affect and engagement during small group instruction. *Contemporary Educational Psychology, 36,* 13–24.

Op't Eynde, P., de Corte, E., & Verschaffel, L. (2006). "Accepting emotional complexity": A socio-constructivist perspective on the role of emotions in the mathematics classroom. *Educational Studies in Mathematics, 63,* 193–207.

Op't Eynde, P., & Hannula, M. (2006). The case study of Frank. *Educational Studies in Mathematics, 63,* 123–129.

Payr, S., & Wallis, P. (2011). Socially situated affective systems. In P. Petta, R. Cowie, & P. Pelachaud (Eds.), *Emotion-oriented systems* (pp. 501–520). Heidelberg, Germany: Springer-Verlag.

Pekrun, R., & Bühner, M. (2014). Self-report measures of academic emotions. In R. Pekrun & L. Linnenbrink-Garcia (Eds.), *International handbook of emotions in education* (pp. 561–579). New York, NY: Taylor & Francis.

Rivera, H. H., & Tharp, R. G. (2004). Sociocultural activity settings in the classroom. In H. C. Waxman, R. G. Tharp, & R. S. Hilberg (Eds.), *Observational research in U.S. classrooms: New approaches for understanding cultural and linguistic diversity* (pp. 205–230) . Cambridge, United Kingdom: Cambridge University Press.

Rogat, T. K., & Linnenbrink-Garcia, L. (2011). Socially shared collaboration in cooperative groups: An analysis of the interplay between quality and of social regulation and group processes. *Cognition and Instruction, 29,* 375–415.

Rogoff, B. (1997). Evaluating development in the process of participation: Theory, methods, and practice building on each other. In E. Amsel & K. A. Renninger (Eds.), *Change and development: Issues of theory, method, and application* (pp. 265–285). Mahwah, NJ: Erlbaum.

Rosenberg, E. (1988). Levels of analysis and the organization of affect. *Review of General Psychology, 2,* 247–270.

Rosenberg, E., & Ekman, P. (1994). Coherence between expressive and experiential systems in emotion. *Cognition and Emotion, 8,* 201–229.

Scherer, K. L. (2009). The dynamic architecture of emotion: Evidence for the component process model. *Cognition and Emotion, 23,* 1307–1351.

Schultheiss, O. C., & Köllner, M. G. (2014). Implicit motives, affect, and the development of competencies: A virtuous-circle model of motive-driven learning. In R. Pekrun & L. Linnenbrink-Garcia (Eds.), *International handbook of emotions in education* (pp. 73–95). New York, NY: Taylor & Francis.

Schutz, P. A., & DeCuir, J. T. (2002). Inquiry on emotions in education. *Educational Psychologist, 37,* 125–134.

Shernoff, D. J, & Vandell, D. L. (2007). Engagement in after-school program activities: quality of experience from the perspective of participants. *Journal of Youth and Adolescence, 36,* 891–903.

Skinner, E. A., Kindermann, T. A., & and Furrer, C. J. (2009). A motivational perspective on engagement and disaffection: Conceptualization and assessment of children's behavioral and emotional participation in academic activities in the classroom. *Educational and Psychological Measurement, 69,* 493–525.

Tekscan. (1997). *Body pressure measurement system user's manual.* South Boston, MA: Tekscan Inc.

Thelen, E., & Smith, L. (2006). Dynamic systems theories. In W. Damon & R. M. Lerner (Eds.), *Handbook of child psychology, Theoretical models of human development* (6th ed., Vol.1, pp. 258–312). Hoboken, NJ: John Wiley & Sons.

Turner, J. C., Meyer, D. K., Cox, K. E., Logan, C., DiCintio, M., & Thomas, C. (1998). Creating contexts for involvement in mathematics. *Journal of Educational Psychology, 90,* 730–745.

Turner, J. E., & Waugh, R. (2007). A dynamical systems perspective regarding students' learning processes: Shame reactions and emergent self-organizations. In P. A. Schutz & R. Pekrun (Eds.), *Emotion in education* (pp. 125–145). San Diego, CA: Elsevier.

Vauras, M., Kinnunen, R., Kajamies, A., & Lehtinen, E. (2013). Interpersonal regulation in instructional interaction: A dynamic systems analysis of scaffolding. In S. Volet & M. Vauras (Eds.), *Interpersonal regulation of learning and motivation: Methodological advances* (pp. 125–146). New York, NY: Routledge.

Woolf, B. P., Burleson, W., Arroyo, I., Dragon, T., Cooper, D., & Picard, R. (2009). Affect-aware tutors: Recognizing and responding to student affect. *International Journal of Learning Technology, 4,* 129–164.

33

CONCLUSIONS AND FUTURE DIRECTIONS

Reinhard Pekrun and Lisa Linnenbrink-Garcia,
University of Munich and Michigan State University

During the past 15 years, there has been a discernible, steady increase of investigations into the emotions experienced by students and teachers, as documented in the chapters of this volume. These investigations have produced new insights, suggesting that multiple emotions in both students and teachers should be considered when reflecting on educational problems; that these emotions are patterned in complex ways within individuals, across individuals, and over time; and that they are influenced by academic domain, gender, race, individual propensities, classroom interaction, and the sociohistorical context. Furthermore, the findings demonstrate that emotions profoundly affect students' and teachers' engagement, performance, and personality development, implying that they are of critical importance for the agency of educational institutions, and of society at large.

At the same time, however, the studies conducted so far seem to pose more new, challenging questions than they can answer. As noted by Pekrun and Schutz (2007), research on emotions in education is still at an early stage. Theories, research strategies, and measures for analyzing emotions in education are not yet fully developed. To date, studies are too scarce to allow researchers to conduct meta-analytic syntheses based on cumulative evidence or to draw any firm conclusions informing educational practitioners in evidence-based ways about how to effectively harness students' emotions, with few exceptions (e.g., evidence on test anxiety and on the linkages between students' achievement goals and emotions; Huang, 2011; Zeidner, 1998, 2014). The progress made so far is promising, but much more work is needed if educational research on emotions is to evolve in ways benefiting education and society.

In this concluding chapter, we reiterate Pekrun and Schutz's (2007) call for attending to three critically important questions in future research on emotions in education (also see Linnenbrink, 2006; Linnenbrink-Garcia & Pekrun, 2011; Pekrun, 2005; Sansone & Thoman, 2005; Schutz & DeCuir, 2002). First, how should we advance our theoretical thinking about emotions in education? Second, how should we study these emotions empirically? And third, which phenomena should be studied? In discussing answers to the first question, we address the need for developing consensus on constructs, as well as more comprehensive frameworks that work towards integrating multiple theoretical perspectives. Similarly, with regard to the methodology of empirical research, we argue that multi-methodology approaches are needed to advance this field of research. In addition, we address the need for refining the measurement of emotions. Concerning phenomena to be studied, we discuss that future advances require addressing multiple emotions, the organization of these emotions at different levels, including individuals, classrooms, institutions, and contexts, as well as the dynamics of emotional change within educational settings and over years and historical epochs. Also, the need for educational intervention research targeting emotions is addressed. In conclusion, we argue that progress in this field requires interdisciplinary perspectives and call for more interdisciplinary collaboration of researchers.

BUILDING MORE COMPREHENSIVE THEORETICAL FRAMEWORKS

In educational research and related disciplines, such as psychology, sociology, and the neurosciences, different traditions of research on emotions have been working in relative isolation, in spite of often sharing basic assumptions. Generally, whereas more comprehensive theories were developed in these disciplines in the first part of the 20th century (e.g., Allport, 1938; Lewin, 1935), there seems to be a proliferation of small constructs and theories in many research fields today, including the study of human emotions (Lewis, Haviland-Jones, & Feldman Barrett, 2008). To make things worse, authors create "new" constructs and theories that, in fact, have often been proposed previously (see, e.g., Skinner's [1996] discussion of this problem with respect to psychological constructs of control). This reinvention of existing constructs is disguised by using new terms and neglecting to cite prior work where appropriate. As a result, there is a lack of theoretical integration that has to be overcome if cumulative progress is to be made. Specifically, there is a need for consensus on constructs of emotions and integration of theoretical models that share assumptions on the structures, dynamics, and functions of emotions. At the same time, we also need debate and cross-fertilization among researchers pursuing truly divergent approaches, as well as new perspectives that enrich existing theories.

Constructs of Emotions

If researchers define their constructs in idiosyncratic ways that are not shared by others, communication between researchers and an integration of empirical findings is difficult. Fortunately, there is some consensus today as to the basic nature of human emotions. Most researchers in the affective sciences, including educational research on emotions, likely would agree that human emotions are multicomponent systems involving coordinated processes of subsystems of mind and behavior (Pekrun, 2006; Russell, 2012; Shuman & Scherer, 2014). Important components are affective processes that are physiologically bound to subcortical systems (e.g., the amygdala) and subjectively experienced as emotional feelings; emotion-specific thoughts that accompany these feelings (e.g., worries in anxiety); peripheral physiological activation (or deactivation) that prepares for action (or nonaction); emotion-specific motivational impulses, such as fight, flight, or giving up in anger, anxiety, and hopelessness, respectively; and motor movements communicating the emotion to others, such as facial expression or the prosodic features of speech.

However, the boundaries of the domain of emotions, the internal structures of this domain, and the universal versus culture-specific status of many emotions are less clear. As to *boundaries,* there is consensus that primary emotions like joy, anger, or anxiety are members of the domain, but the classification of other constructs related to feelings and affect is less clear cut. Students' interest is a case in point (Ainley & Hidi, 2014). Some researchers regard interest as an emotion (e.g., Ainley, 2007), whereas others have defined interest as a more complex construct involving several components, such as enjoyment, affectively neutral values related to the object of interest, and knowledge structures (see Schiefele, 2009). For constructing measures, comparing findings of studies, and designing educational interventions, it makes a critical difference which of the various definitions is used. Similarly, the status of affective constructs like mood (Linnenbrink, 2006), curiosity (Markey & Loewenstein, 2014), confusion (D'Mello & Graesser, 2014), or metacognitive feelings (Efklides & Petkaki, 2005), is unclear up to date.

Concerning *internal structures,* the domain of emotions can be conceptualized by using dimensional models (e.g., Linnenbrink, 2007; Russell, 2003) or concepts of discrete emotions (e.g., Pekrun, 2006; Shuman & Scherer, 2014). It seems to be clear to us that from a conceptual perspective, these two approaches are complementary rather than mutually exclusive. However, it is unclear which of the two is more appropriate for describing students' and teachers' affect, and using both of them interchangeably can make it difficult to integrate findings. For example, in studies on achievement goals and students' emotions, researchers either used a positive versus negative affect approach or a discrete emotions perspective, and the findings from these two approaches may not be entirely consistent (Huang, 2011; Linnenbrink & Pintrich, 2002; Linnenbrink-Garcia & Barger, 2014; Pekrun, Elliot, & Maier, 2006). Making the pros and cons of such divergent approaches explicit, and trying to integrate their assumptions at the theoretical or metatheoretical level, should prove useful in making progress in our understanding of the structures of emotions.

Finally, as to the *relative universality* of emotion constructs, it seems likely that basic, neuropsychologically defined processes of emotions like surprise, joy, anger, anxiety, or sadness are universal across cultures and sociohistorical contexts. Many of these basic processes are universal not only within our species but beyond our species as well. However, researchers should be aware that the specific profiles of components (e.g., cognitive contents, behavioral expression) and process parameters (e.g., frequency, intensity, duration) of these emotions can vary widely between cultures and contexts. Also, there likely is wide variability in emotions that developed during the course of cultural evolution and are unique to the human race (see Ratner, 2007). One indicator for this variability is the fact that there are emotions for which verbal labels were developed in some languages but not in others. For example, as noted by Weiner (2007), there is a term for the enjoyment of another person's harm in the German language ("Schadenfreude"), whereas no such term is available in the English language.

Researchers should attempt to reach more of a consensus on the constructs of emotions relevant for education. Consensus on constructs is a precondition for constructing consensual measures, integrating the findings of studies, and providing educational practitioners with consistent information. To the extent that different conceptions diverge in nonarbitrary ways, however, consensus should not be enforced prematurely and at all costs; a case in point is the ongoing controversy about dimensional versus discrete emotion approaches to affect (Averill, 2012; Feldman Barrett, 2006; Russell, 2012; Shuman & Scherer, 2014; Wilson-Mendenhall, Feldman Barrett, & Barsalou, 2013). In theses cases, constructive dialogue may be helpful to reduce misunderstandings and to resolve controversial issues, if possible.

Integrating Theories on Emotions

Currently, many of the theories on human emotions address isolated facets or functions of emotions or focus on one single emotion. An example is the many theoretical models on specific effects of emotions on cognitive performance that were developed since the 1970s (Fiedler & Beier, 2014). Many theories of test anxiety are examples for approaches addressing one single emotion, without taking neighboring emotions into account (Zeidner, 1998, 2014).

As with a lack of consensus on constructs, if research is built on one specific theoretical perspective only, cumulative progress may be hampered. Ignoring alternative approaches prevents the detection of commonalities and contradictions. For example, contradictory conclusions seem to follow from different social psychological theories on the cognitive effects of emotions (Aspinwall, 1998). Some of these theories imply that students' and teachers' positive affect (such as pleasant mood) is detrimental for any effortful, elaborate processing of information, whereas negative affect (such as unpleasant mood) instigates enhanced effort. As an example, safety-signal and mood-as-information approaches suggest that positive mood signals safe conditions and motivates one to relax, whereas negative mood signals unsafe conditions, thus motivating one to change the situation by investing task-related effort (see Clore & Huntsinger, 2009). Other theories, however, suggest that positive affect serves beneficial functions for problem solving (e.g., Fredrickson's, 2001, broaden-and-build model of positive emotions) and that negative affect impairs performance (e.g., models of test anxiety; Zeidner, 2014).

The contradictions between these approaches, however, may not be as real as they first appear. Empirically, each approach pertains to specific experimental conditions designed to validate the theory in the psychological laboratory. In the more complex educational reality outside the laboratory, different conditions are prevalent. The specific processes described by any laboratory-based theory may also be at work in specific situations outside the laboratory. However, it seems likely that not all of these theories are equally relevant for the real-life academic achievement of students or occupational achievement of teachers. More comprehensive theories, as well as integrative metatheories, are needed to disentangle commonalities and contradictions and to define the contextual conditions for which different propositions are valid (see Pekrun, 2006, for an attempt to integrate assumptions from some of the laboratory-based approaches to emotion and performance).

The potential fruitfulness of comprehensive theory building can be seen in research on the appraisal antecedents of emotions. In this research, consensus on some of the dimensions of appraisals seems to be emerging, as evidenced, for example, in Roseman's metatheoretical approach to synthesizing theoretical assumptions (Roseman, Antoniou, & Jose, 1996; also see Moors, Ellsworth, Scherer, & Frijda, 2013; Shuman & Scherer, 2014). While the exact contents and labeling of appraisal dimensions may still be controversial, consensus on basic structures of appraisals can enable researchers to produce cumulative evidence on the functions of these appraisals and to move on to new frontiers of research, once issues of dimensionality are settled.

Research on emotions in education, therefore, should make an attempt to construct more integrative approaches as well. Specifically, frameworks are needed that integrate perspectives on different levels and contexts of students' and teachers' emotions, including the dynamics of processes within and between levels (e.g., among components of emotions; among emotions, motivation, and cognition; between teachers and students; and between different institutional and socio-historical contexts). For creating such dynamic, multilayered, and contextualized frameworks, it would be helpful to integrate theoretical perspectives from a variety of disciplines, including education, psychology, the neurosciences, sociology, and history. Also, an integration of perspectives from different fields within these disciplines is required. For example, educational contexts and the workplace share many common features. A case in point is institution-based competitive versus cooperative goal structures that are of critical importance for students in educational organizations and employees in the business industry alike. However, educational psychology and occupational psychology have virtually ignored each other to date. Work on emotions in education is rarely cited by occupational psychologists, and vice versa (see, e.g., Grandey, 2000; Morris & Feldman, 1996; Frenzel, 2014, for work on emotional labor that should be relevant for education). The time seems ripe to integrate conceptual perspectives from the various disciplines that contribute to the emerging field of research on emotions in education.

Enlarging Theoretical Perspectives

Beyond integrating existing models, we also see the need for developing fresh perspectives. This pertains not only to the objects of theories (see the section on what to study) but also to the types of theories that need to be developed. Emotions are organized at multiple levels, change over time, and are situated in cultural contexts (Ratner, 2007). However, as noted, theories on emotions in education have yet to fully incorporate the multilevel, dynamic, and contextualized nature of students' and teachers' emotions. In order to do so, it may not be sufficient to just acknowledge these aspects of emotions. Rather, the type of theorizing used has to be adapted to these targets.

Specifically, the development of *multilevel theories* specifying the precise nature of interactions between levels is needed. For instance, theories targeting the compositional effects of schools and classrooms on students' emotions help to capture the complexity of emotional functioning in educational settings (e.g., Pekrun, Murayama, Frenzel, Goetz, & Marsh, 2011). Similarly, *dynamic theories* of emotion are needed. In research on motivation and affect, an early example of a dynamic perspective was Atkinson and Birch's (1970) dynamic theory of action which was based on differential equations modeling of affective processes. More recently, researchers have employed computational process models of emotions (Wehrle & Scherer, 2001). In contrast to black-box computational models, these computational process models specify the types of processes shaping emotions. Research on emotions in education should consider adapting dynamic models for its purposes. Propositions derived from dynamic systems theories may be particularly useful for doing so (Turner & Waugh, 2007).

Concerning cultural and sociohistorical contexts, cross-cultural, sociological, and historical perspectives are needed. *Cross-cultural theories* specifying differences of emotions in education systems around the world should be developed (DeCuir-Gunby & Williams-Johnson, 2014). To consider historical contexts, *historical theories* and collaboration with historians of education are necessary. The development of emotions over the past centuries is an emerging field of research in history (e.g., Bourke, 2005; Ratner, 2007; Stearns & Stearns, 1985). We recommend bringing this historical perspective to the study of emotions in education.

USING MULTIPLE METHODOLOGIES

In empirical research on emotions, different strategies and methods have specific advantages and disadvantages, and no single strategy is suited to answer all questions (Schutz, Chambless, & DeCuir, 2003). Traditionally, psychological research on emotions was based on deductive, quantitative, experimental approaches analyzing emotions in the laboratory by use of nomothetic strategies (Lewis et al., 2008). To fully capture the richness of emotions experienced in educational settings, however, exploratory methodology, qualitative data, nonexperimental designs, field studies, and idiographic strategies are needed as well. Therefore, rather than viewing different ways of analyzing emotions as competitive or mutually exclusive, we advocate considering different approaches as complementary. In this regard, one should also keep in mind that components of research strategies can be combined. While qualitative research that is exploratory, nonexperimental, and field-based can be contrasted with quantitative, experimental, laboratory-based hypothesis testing, many other combinations of the elements of these approaches are potentially useful. Quantitative research can serve exploratory purposes, qualitative research can be laboratory-based, and experiments can be conducted in field settings.

Thus, we believe the study of emotions in education needs a multimethod paradigm that integrates inductive (exploratory) and deductive (hypothesis-testing) strategies, qualitative and quantitative approaches, experimental and nonexperimental designs, laboratory and field studies, as well as idiographic and nomothetic strategies. In addition, advances in the measurement of emotions are also needed.

Exploration and Hypothesis Testing

In psychology, research that tests theories receives high regard, perhaps because such research makes it possible to believe that psychology is a (natural) science. All too often, however, theories are developed without observing reality in the first place, thus deriving assumptions from researchers' mental exercises instead of empirical observations. Such a strategy stands in contrast, for example, to strategies followed in the biological sciences, which often involve extended observations of the behavior of a species before deriving theoretical propositions (Lorenz, 1974).

For research on emotions in education, we recommend analyzing the richness of students' and teachers' affect using exploratory strategies. Within programs of research in this field, this may be a useful, if not necessary, first step, as theory is being developed (see, e.g., Pekrun, Goetz, Titz, & Perry, 2002). Although exploration inevitably is built on theoretical assumptions (e.g., on what and where to observe and which methods to use), these assumptions should be handled in an open-minded way, such that justice can be done to observations disconfirming preconceptions. Later on, observations can be used to create theoretical models that are tested by deductive strategies. Phases of induction and deduction can alternate, such that a program of research uses inductive-deductive loops to create, test, refine, and enlarge theories.

Exploratory strategies are often qualitative and nonexperimental in nature. However, exploratory strategies can involve any kind of empirical methods, including quantitative methods and experimental designs. For example, Ainley (2007) explored the effects of dealing with learning material on various affective processes using standardized, quantitative methods to sample affective experiences.

Qualitative and Quantitative Approaches

Qualitative research is often needed to explore emotion phenomena and to generate hypotheses. Furthermore, qualitative methods may be best suited to derive in-depth descriptions of these phenomena and to obtain explanations for unexpected findings (e.g., by asking participants why they responded in unexpected ways to an experiment on emotions). Quantitative methodology, on the other hand, is often best suited to test hypotheses and to analyze the generalizability of hypotheses across individuals and cultures. In our view, the paradigm battles about whether to prefer one or the other methodology should be disregarded in educational research on emotions in favor of multimethod approaches adapting methods in flexible ways to the research question (e.g., Immordino-Yang, McColl, Damasio, & Damasio, 2009; Johnson & Onwuegbuzie, 2004; Schutz, Chambless, & DeCuir, 2003; Schutz & DeCuir, 2002; Turner & Trucano, 2014).

Experimental and NonExperimental Designs and Laboratory and Field Studies

Controlled experiments provide the best opportunities to study causal relationships. Laboratory experiments have the potential to analyze basic processes of affect, such as the activation of different regions of the brain enhancing learning after mood induction, the impact of emotions on task-related attention (e.g., Meinhardt & Pekrun, 2003), or the influence of different types of tasks on students' emotions during computer-based collaborative learning. Similarly, field experiments and quasi-experiments can analyze the effectiveness of educational interventions targeting students' and teachers' emotions.

However, there also are clear limitations to an experimental approach to emotions in education, due to ethical constraints and problems of ecological validity. For example, as argued by Schutz and DeCuir (2002), "what principal or parent would agree to allow a researcher to create a situation in which students could become angry so that researchers could study the experience of anger in education?" (p. 125). Similarly, there are clear limitations to laboratory-based approaches. Specifically, to the extent that laboratory settings are artificial and do not represent real-life classroom situations, laboratory experiments are in danger of analyzing potential causality that can be demonstrated in the laboratory but never outside the experimental setting. For example, it is unclear to what extent the results of laboratory studies on mood and learning can be transferred to the real-life, context-bound, and often intense emotions experienced by students in the classroom. Furthermore, many aspects of emotions in education do not lend themselves to laboratory-based investigation, such as the influence of educational institutions and sociohistorical contexts.

By implication, there is a clear need to complement experimental and laboratory-based strategies with nonexperimental field studies in research on emotions. Nonexperimental field studies are limited in terms of their potential to derive causal conclusions, but they can approximate the causal power of controlled experiments by using longitudinal designs and advanced statistical techniques, such as multilevel and mediational structural equation modeling employing latent variables and controlling for autoregressive effects and confounding variables (Little, Preacher, Selig, & Card, 2007; McArdle, 2009).

Idiographic and Nomothetic Approaches

Many studies on emotions use sample-based strategies to derive conclusions about the general, nomothetic validity of theoretical propositions. In field studies, sample-based strategies typically involve observing distributions of one or more variables across individuals, as in analyzing the variation of mean values across time or groups of individuals, or in analyzing the relation between variables by using their covariances to calculate correlations and structural equations. For example, test anxiety research analyzed relations between test anxiety and students' academic performance by correlating test anxiety and performance measures across students. Similarly, in experimental laboratory investigations, groups of individuals are studied and the distributions of values of dependent variables are compared across the different experimental groups.

These sample-based strategies, however, do not allow any inferences on the psychological functioning of individuals. In fact, the resulting estimates for population parameters may not actually coincide with any single individual under study. In the methodological literature, this is a well-known issue. For example, the *interindividual* and *intraindividual* correlations between variables are known to be statistically independent (Robinson, 1950; Schmitz & Skinner, 1993), implying that any inferences from sample correlations to individual psychological mechanisms may be invalid. An example cited by Schmitz and Skinner (1993) is the positive interindividual correlation between sleep duration and frequency of migraine headaches, which seemingly implies that sleeping late can lead to headaches (or vice versa). Such a conclusion, however, would be misleading—these two variables are correlated *negatively* within individuals, implying that headaches occur in combination with *shorter* duration of sleep. Similarly, group differences in experiments can mask varying responses by participants that are due to different individual causal mechanisms rather than to one homogenous mechanism as suggested by mean value differences in the dependent variable.

Accordingly, if one wants to examine the intraindividual functioning of students' and teachers' emotions, one would need to study students and teachers individually, implying an idiographic research strategy. Idiographic analysis based on single cases, however, is problematic as well. Such an analysis has the complementary disadvantage that it is difficult to generalize the findings beyond single individuals. To summarize, we face the following dilemma: If we study *single individuals,* more general conclusions cannot be drawn, thus reducing the scientific and practical relevance of results. If, on the other hand, we study *samples of individuals,* we cannot be sure whether the resulting findings are valid for any single individual. With this strategy as well, it is unclear whether findings are generalizable and useful for reaching scientific and applied goals.

An elegant way out of this dilemma is to combine both strategies by first analyzing reality within individuals and then testing the generalizability of findings across individuals

(Schmitz & Skinner, 1993). For example, Pekrun and Hofmann (1996) used such a combined idiographic-nomothetic strategy in a diary study on student teachers' emotions before and during their final university exams. In this study, the intraindividual relations between emotions and variables of learning over days were examined first (idiographic analysis), before analyzing the generalizability of intraindividual relations across students (nomothetic analysis). One result of this study was that many functions of emotions showed generalizability across students. However, there also were relations that were more specific to individual students (e.g., relations between anxiety and students' motivation to learn; Pekrun, 2006).

Advancing the Measurement of Emotions

The measurement of students' and teachers' emotions is in its infancy. Tools need to be developed that allow an assessment of different emotions and components of emotions in reliable and valid ways (see Benson, 1998; Calvo & D'Mello, 2010). For example, whereas many test anxiety questionnaires are available today (Zeidner, 1998, 2014), self-report measures of emotions other than anxiety have to be developed as well (Pekrun & Bühner, 2014). Similarly, measures of students' regulation of, and coping with, their emotions need to be constructed (Davis, DiStefano, &. Schutz, 2008; Nett, Goetz, & Daniels, 2010). Also, there is urgent need to develop measures assessing specific emotions experienced by teachers, including their emotional labor in the classroom, beyond scales pertaining to omnibus constructs like teachers' burnout (Frenzel, 2014). Finally, measures of collective emotions and emotional climates experienced in classrooms are required.

Furthermore, we need measures that can capture the dynamic nature of students' and teachers' emotions. While self-reports of emotions can be employed to assess the development of emotions across situations (e.g., in experience sampling and diary methods), the value of self-report measures for assessing the moment-to-moment dynamics of emotions is limited. Self-report allows the assessment of emotional experiences, but it cannot render real-time estimates of emotional processes. Moreover, self-report measures are difficult to construct so that they render interval or ratio scales needed for modeling more complex, nonlinear relationships over time. They are also subject to response biases and are not well suited to assess emotional processes that have limited access to consciousness (Pekrun & Bühner, 2014).

Therefore, behavioral and neuropsychological assessment is also necessary. In research on emotions, several alternative methods are available today, including functional imaging analyzing cortical and subcortical affective processes (Immordino-Yang & Christodoulou, 2014), analysis of affect-related peripheral physiological activation (Kreibig & Gendolla, 2014), and behavioral observation of facial and postural expression of emotions and of emotion-related prosodic features of speech (Ekman & Rosenberg, 1997; Scherer, 1986; Reisenzein, Junge, Studtmann, & Huber, 2014). Studies on emotions in education should adapt these methodologies for their purposes. Research on students' affect in technology-based learning environments has made substantial progress towards this goal (Graesser, D'Mello, & Strain, 2014). Research targeting conventional learning environments could benefit from similar efforts. For example, adapting observational systems of emotions such that they can be integrated into video-based classroom studies and be used for analyzing students' and teachers' ongoing emotions in classroom discourse is critical.

EXAMINING FACETS, LEVELS, DYNAMICS, AND EDUCATIONAL CHANGE OF EMOTIONS

To date, the majority of research on emotions in education has focused on a few emotions (above all, students' test anxiety) and examined select correlates of these emotions (such as students' academic achievement) within one level of analysis (the individual student) situated in one type of sociohistorical context (North American and European education systems). In order to make progress, this nascent field of research has to take more facets, levels, and contexts of students' and teachers' emotions into account. Additionally, the situational, ontogenetic, and historical dynamics of emotions needs to be analyzed, and there is an urgent need for carefully designed educational intervention research targeting students' and teachers' emotions.

Facets, Types, and Patterns of Emotions

The chapters of this handbook document that researchers have begun to pay attention to emotions other than test anxiety, but research on these other emotions is still in its infancy. We need more evidence on important unpleasant emotions like anger, confusion, frustration, shame, hopelessness, and boredom, as well as more studies on pleasant emotions like enjoyment, hope, pride, and relief as experienced by both students and teachers (D'Mello, 2013; Pekrun et al., 2002). Furthermore, in order to gain a better understanding of the affective climate in educational institutions, we also need research on the emotions experienced by administrators, principals, and employees of these institutions.

Beyond single emotions, patterns of emotions and of emotion components should be studied as well. Typically, emotional experiences involve more than one single emotion. Currently, however, it is unclear how exactly students' and teachers' emotions are patterned, by which individuals and under which conditions patterns of emotions are experienced, and how these patterns evolve. A nonreductionist approach to emotions needs a thorough analysis of patterns of emotions and components and of their variation across individuals, contexts, and time (Sansone & Thoman, 2005).

Levels and Contexts of Emotions in Education

Emotions are organized at multiple levels. Within the individual mind, component processes of emotions are organized at different levels that are related to subsystems of the central nervous systems and of peripheral physiological and motor systems. At the level of the individual student or teacher, feedback from the component processes from these different levels is merged into a holistic emotional experience that can be verbally labeled by using categories of emotion. In education, the individual, typically, is part of an educational setting such as the classroom, implying that emotions can be conceptualized at the level of social settings as well. Indeed, emotions are seen as social rather than as individual phenomena by some researchers (see Averill, 2012; Ratner, 2007). For example, the emotional climate of classrooms is located at this level. Beyond the single classroom, relevant levels pertain to educational institutions nested within educational systems, systems nested within societies, and societies within cultures and sociohistorical macrosystems (Bronfenbrenner, 1986). Generally, from the perspective of a unit located at some specific level, the higher level units of which it is a member can be regarded as *contexts* of the unit. For example, students are situated in the context of classrooms, classrooms in the context of institutions, and both of them in broader sociohistorical contexts.

To date, research on emotions in education mainly addressed the individual and classroom levels of emotions, as shown in the chapters of this handbook. Future research should take the level of educational institutions and of different cultural and sociohistorical contexts into account as well. Two types of studies may prove to be especially important. First, *multilevel classroom studies* are needed that analyze students' and teachers' emotions from a multilevel perspective, addressing the variation of emotions between individuals, activities, and subject domains, as well as between classrooms, schools, and educational systems. For example, in which ways can the variation of emotional experiences be explained by differences between academic activities, like studying versus taking exams, or between different academic subjects (Goetz, Frenzel, Pekrun, Hall, & Lüdtke, 2007)? Also, how much of the variance in students' emotions can be attributed to teachers and classrooms, how much of the variation between different classrooms' emotional climate can be attributed to different types of schooling, and what are the critical variables at these levels influencing students' and teachers' emotions? Answers to such questions are of fundamental importance for adequately designing educational interventions.

Second, *cross-cultural* and *sociohistorical studies* are needed that analyze the variation of emotions across cultures with different values and educational practices. Conducting cross-cultural studies pertaining to cultures that are present in today's world requires researchers to specify theoretical assumptions on the nature of cross-cultural differences, to construct emotion measures that show cross-cultural equivalence (e.g., Frenzel, Thrash, Pekrun, & Goetz, 2007), and to include samples from different cultures into a single investigation. Adequate sociohistorical analyses on emotions in education are even more difficult to conduct. Such analyses can be achieved by means of oral history and by an analysis of historical documents on education, including documents such as diaries giving insights into the subjective reception of educational practices.

Dynamics Over Time: Processes, Functions, and Regulation of Emotions

Most of the extant research on emotions in education provides cross-sectional snapshots describing the phenomenology of emotions, their structures and interindividual variation, or their relation with learning and teaching. If progress regarding the dynamics of emotions is to be made, affective processes have to be studied by multiple assessments over time instead of relying on single-shot assessments. Emotion dynamics can extend over different time frames, such as fractions of seconds in the affective dynamics of emotion components, minutes and hours in the continuing development of emotions within specific educational activity settings (Graesser et al., 2014), years in ontogenetic development, and decades or centuries in historical development. For capturing these dynamics, process-oriented studies are best suited, including real-time physiological or observational analysis for dynamics of emotions over seconds or minutes, time interval or event sampling for processes within educational settings, multiwave longitudinal studies for the ontogenetic development of emotions in students' educational careers and teachers' professional development, and time series of emotion assessments across historical time intervals to capture the cultural evolution of emotions in education.

All of these possibilities are still underused to date. For example, even in the abundant research on test anxiety, there is a clear need for more longitudinal studies analyzing the linkages between students' anxiety and learning over the school years (Zeidner, 1998). Similarly, educational large-scale assessments such as the Organization for Economic Co-operation and Development's (OECD) Programme for International Student Assessment (PISA) have as yet missed the opportunity to evaluate historical stability and change in students' emotions over time and would do well to implement a stable set of core emotion variables across cycles of assessment to make such an analysis possible.

As part of a dynamic analysis of emotions, their effects on learning, teaching, and performance need to be analyzed as well. With the exception of test anxiety, not much is currently known about the specific and combined effects of different emotions on students' learning under different task conditions and on teachers' classroom instruction and professional activities. Similarly, the individual and social antecedents of students' and teachers' emotions need to be analyzed. Finally, more research on the dynamics of students' and teachers' regulation of emotions is required. There is a need to connect research on emotions in education to research on emotion regulation, coping, emotional competences, and emotional intelligence (Allen, MacCann, Matthews, & Roberts, 2014; Jacobs & Gross, 2014).

Emotional Design of Tasks and Learning Environments

Emotions are of primary practical importance in education: They affect students' and teachers' interest, engagement, and achievement, as well as their personality development, health, and well-being more generally. By implication, they can profoundly influence the productivity and quality of life in educational institutions and in society at large. The question then arises, how can we shape education in "emotionally sound" (Astleitner, 2000) ways? This is not a trivial question, as early attempts to create learning environments supporting students' adaptive emotions were only partially successful (e.g., Glaeser-Zikuda, Fuss, Laukenmann, Metz, & Randler, 2005).

Several lines of intervention research suggest, however, that it is possible to foster students' adaptive emotions and prevent or reduce their maladaptive emotions. First, over the past six decades, research on therapy for test anxiety has documented how students' anxiety can be reduced. In fact, test anxiety therapy is among the most successful types of psychotherapy available today, with effect sizes often being $d > 1$ (Zeidner, 1998). Second, beyond test anxiety, recent intervention studies have shown that attributional retraining to change students' perceptions of control can increase students' positive achievement emotions and reduce their negative emotions (Hall et al., 2007; Ruthig, Perry, Hall, & Hladkyj, 2004) and that strategies to enhance the perceived value of learning material can promote students' interest (Hulleman, Godes, Hendricks, & Harackiewicz, 2010; Hulleman & Harackiewicz, 2009). Third, recent advances in social-emotional learning programs with K–12 classrooms have demonstrated that helping students to develop emotional and social competencies can foster their general affective well-being and reduce their emotional distress (Brackett & Rivers, 2014; Durlak, Weissberg, Dymnicki, Taylor, & Schellinger, 2011).

The success story of these psychological intervention studies suggests that it is possible to design educational environments to promote students' and teachers' positive academic emotions, reduce their negative emotions at school, and enable students and teachers to calibrate more complex negative emotions, such as confusion, in ways that facilitate problem solving. Accordingly, researchers should seek to answer questions such as: How can we construct academic tasks and learning environments to prevent or reduce students' and teachers' anger, hopelessness, or boredom related to learning and teaching and to foster their academic curiosity, hope, pride, and enjoyment? In which ways should classroom instruction, tasks, assessment practices, educational institutions, and the educational climate in our societies be shaped such that the emotions experienced by students and teachers benefit individual development as well as communities and the society?

Designing cognitively activating tasks, triggering moderate levels of cognitive incongruity, tailoring task demands and goal structures to the developmental needs of students, providing autonomy support, and using informational, mastery-oriented feedback about achievement may be some of the strategies to achieve these aims (D'Mello & Graesser, 2014; Markey & Loewenstein, 2014; Pekrun, 2006, in press). Educational researchers should explore these possibilities for an affective design of learning environments. In doing so, it may prove fruitful to consider ways to enhance students' perceived control and value related to academic activities, as targeted by the aforementioned intervention studies, in routine classroom instruction. It may also prove fruitful to explore how to expand the design of subject-matter tasks and instruction to include components that help students to acquire emotional competencies, as provided by social-emotional learning programs such as the RULER program (Brackett & Rivers, 2014), and how to shape academic environments in ways that benefit cooperation with out-of-school environments influencing students' emotional development, such as the family, peers, and the neighborhood.

Constructing academic tasks, assessments, and environments in emotionally beneficial ways will not be an easy task. The best of researchers' efforts will be required to successfully design and implement interventions targeting students' and teachers' emotions, such that educational research on emotions can inform educational practitioners, administrators, and policy-makers how they might be able to shape classroom instruction and educational institutions in affectively productive ways.

CONCLUSION: A CALL FOR INTERDISCIPLINARY COLLABORATION

Researchers in this field, typically, have training in psychology or education. The program of future research outlined in this chapter, however, requires using perspectives and methodologies from a number of disciplines, some of them far removed from education research as traditionally conceived. Specifically, researching levels of emotions, from component processes within neuropsychological systems up to sociohistorical contexts, makes it necessary to integrate concepts and methods from a broad variety of disciplines. These disciplines include education and psychology, but they also include the neurosciences, computer engineering, sociology, economics, cultural anthropology, history, and philosophy.

Furthermore, it also seems necessary to transcend perspectives focused on emotions in education per se. For example, as noted earlier, structures and functions of emotions in the business world share many similarities with education. The above-cited importance of different goal structures that involve competition and cooperation, and likely exert profound effects on participants' emotions, is but one example for the many parallels between these two worlds. In spite of the many similarities of phenomena and challenges, however, there has been almost no crosstalk between affective researchers in education, on the one hand, and in work psychology and economics, on the other (Pekrun & Frese, 1992). Similar arguments can be made with regard to sports and to disciplines addressing specific institutional contexts of our youth, like family research.

More training of educational researchers by interdisciplinary programs that include instruction in the use of multiple strategies and methodologies of research would be useful to make progress along these lines. Even given extensive training and experience, however, it is likely beyond the capacities of any single researcher to develop expertise in the multitude of perspectives from all of the different disciplines mentioned. Therefore, collective interdisciplinary efforts are needed. With such efforts, it should prove possible to make the best use of collaboration between researchers of different disciplines in order to make progress in the evolving field of research on emotions in education.

REFERENCES

Ainley, M. (2007). Being and feeling interested: Transient state, mood, and disposition. In P. A. Schutz & R. Pekrun (Eds.), *Emotion in education* (pp. 147–163). San Diego, CA: Academic Press.

Ainley, M., & Hidi, S. (2014). Interest and enjoyment. In R. Pekrun & L. Linnenbrink-Garcia (Eds.), *International handbook of emotions in education* (pp. 205–227). New York, NY: Taylor & Francis.

Allen, V., MacCann, C., Matthews, G., & Roberts, R. D. (2014). Emotional intelligence in education: From pop to emerging science. In R. Pekrun & L. Linnenbrink-Garcia (Eds.), *International handbook of emotions in education* (pp. 162–182). New York, NY: Taylor & Francis.

Allport, G. W. (1938). *Personality. A psychological interpretation.* London, United Kingdom: Constable & Company.

Aspinwall, L. (1998). Rethinking the role of positive affect in self-regulation. *Motivation and Emotion, 22,* 1–32.

Astleitner, H. (2000). Designing emotionally sound instruction: The FEASP-approach. *Instructional Science, 28,* 169–198.

Atkinson, J. W., & Birch, D. (1970). *A dynamic theory of action.* New York, NY: Wiley.

Averill, J. R. (Ed.). (2012). Social-constructionist approaches to emotion [Special section]. *Emotion Review, 4*(3), 215–306.

Benson, J. (1998). Developing a strong program of construct validation: A test anxiety example. *Educational Measurement: Issues and Practices, 17,* 10–17.

Bourke, J. (2005). *Fear: a cultural history.* London, United Kingdom: Virago & Emeryville.

Brackett, M. A., & Rivers, S. E. (2014). Transforming students' lives with social and emotional learning. In R. Pekrun & L. Linnenbrink-Garcia (Eds.), *International handbook of emotions in education* (pp. 368–388). New York, NY: Taylor & Francis.

Bronfenbrenner, U. (1986). Ecology of the family as a context for human development: Research perspectives. *Developmental Psychology, 22,* 723–742.

Calvo, R. A., & D'Mello, S. K. (2010). Affect detection: An interdisciplinary review of models, methods, and their applications. *IEEE Transactions on Affective Computing, 1,* 18–37.

Calvo, R. A., & D'Mello, S. K. (Eds.). (2012). *New perspectives on affect and learning technologies* (Explorations in the learning sciences, instructional systems and performance technologies, Vol. 3). New York, NY: Springer.

Clore, G. L., & Huntsinger, J. R. (2009). How the object of affect guides its impact. *Emotion Review, 1,* 39–54.

Davis, H. A., DiStefano, C., &. Schutz, P. A. (2008). Patterns of appraisal and emotion regulation during test taking in first-year college students. *Journal of Educational Psychology, 100,* 942–960.

DeCuir-Gunby, J. T., & Williams-Johnson, M. R. (2014). The influence of culture on emotions: implications for education. In R. Pekrun & L. Linnenbrink-Garcia (Eds.), *International handbook of emotions in education* (pp. 539–557). New York, NY: Taylor & Francis.

D'Mello, S. (2013). A selective meta-analysis on the relative incidence of discrete affective states during learning with technology. *Journal of Educational Psychology, 105,* 1082–1099.

D'Mello, S. K, & Graesser, A. C. (2014). Confusion. In R. Pekrun & L. Linnenbrink-Garcia (Eds.), *International handbook of emotions in education* (pp. 289–310). New York, NY: Taylor & Francis.

Durlak, J. A., Weissberg, R. P., Dymnicki, A. B., Taylor, R. D., & Schellinger, K. B. (2011). The impact of enhancing students' social and emotional learning: A meta-analysis of school-based universal interventions. *Child Development, 82*, 405–432.

Efklides, A., & Petkaki, C. (2005). Effects of mood on students' metacognitive experiences. *Learning and Instruction, 15*, 415–431.

Ekman, P., & Rosenberg, E. L. (Eds.). (1997). *What the face reveals: Basic and applied studies of spontaneous expression using the Facial Action Coding System (FACS).* New York, NY: Oxford University Press.

Feldman Barrett, L. (2006). Are emotions natural kinds? *Perspectives on Psychological Science, 1*, 28–58.

Fiedler, K., & Beier, S. (2014). Affect and cognitive processes in educational contexts. In R. Pekrun & L. Linnenbrink-Garcia (Eds.), *International handbook of emotions in education* (pp. 36–55). New York, NY: Taylor & Francis.

Fredrickson, B. L. (2001). The role of positive emotions in positive psychology: The broaden-and-build theory of positive emotions. *American Psychologist, 56*, 218–226.

Frenzel, A. C. (2014). Teacher emotions. In R. Pekrun & L. Linnenbrink-Garcia (Eds.), *International handbook of emotions in education* (pp. 494–519). New York, NY: Taylor & Francis.

Frenzel, A. C., Thrash, T. M., Pekrun, R., & Goetz, T. (2007). Achievement emotions in Germany and China: A cross-cultural validation of the Academic Emotions Questionnaire-Mathematics (AEQ-M). *Journal of Cross-Cultural Psychology, 38*, 302–309.

Glaeser-Zikuda, M., Fuss, S., Laukenmann, M., Metz, K., & Randler, C. (2005). Promoting students' emotions and achievement—Instructional design and evaluation of the ECOLE-approach. *Learning and Instruction, 15, 481–495.*

Goetz, T., Frenzel, A. C., Pekrun, R., Hall, N. C., & Lüdtke, O. (2007). Between- and within-domain relations of students' academic emotions. *Journal of Educational Psychology, 99*, 715–733.

Goetz, T., & Hall, N. C. (2014). Academic boredom. In R. Pekrun & L. Linnenbrink-Garcia (Eds.) *International handbook of emotions in education* (pp. 311–330). New York, NY: Taylor & Francis.

Graesser, A. C., D'Mello, S. K., & Strain, A. C. (2014). Emotions in advanced learning technologies. In R. Pekrun & L. Linnenbrink-Garcia (Eds.) *International handbook of emotions in education* (pp. 473–493). New York, NY: Taylor & Francis.

Grandey, A. A. (2000). Emotional regulation in the work place: A new way to conceptualize emotional labor. *Journal of Occupational Health Psychology, 5*, 95–110.

Huang, C. (2011). Achievement goals and achievement emotions: A meta-analysis. *Educational Psychology Review, 23*, 359–388.

Hulleman, C.S., Godes, O., Hendricks, B., & Harackiewicz, J. M. (2010). Enhancing interest and performance with a utility value intervention. *Journal of Educational Psychology, 102*, 880–895.

Hulleman, C. S., & Harackiewicz, J. M. (2009). Promoting interest and performance in high school science classes. *Science, 326*, 1410–1412.

Immordino-Yang, M. H., & Christodoulou, J. A. (2014). Neuroscientific contributions to understanding and measuring emotions in educational contexts. In R. Pekrun & L. Linnenbrink-Garcia (Eds.), *International handbook of emotions in education* (pp. 607–624). New York, NY: Taylor & Francis.

Immordino-Yang, M., McColl, A., Damasio, H., & Damasio, A. (2009). Neural correlates of admiration and compassion. *Proceedings of the National Academy of Sciences, 106*, 8021–8026.

Jacobs, S. E., & Gross, J. J. (2014). Emotion regulation in education: Conceptual foundations, current applications, and future directions. In R. Pekrun & L. Linnenbrink-Garcia (Eds.), *International handbook of emotions in education* (pp. 183–201). New York, NY: Taylor & Francis.

Johnson, R., & Onwuegbuzie, A. J. (2004). Mixed methods research: A research paradigm whose time has come. *Educational Researcher, 33*, 14–26.

Kreibig, S. D., & Gendolla, G.H.E. (2014). Autonomic nervous system measurement of emotion in education and achievement settings. In R. Pekrun & L. Linnenbrink-Garcia (Eds.), *International handbook of emotions in education* (pp. 625–642). New York, NY: Taylor & Francis.

Lewin, K. (1935). *A dynamic theory of personality.* New York, NY: McGraw-Hill.

Lewis, M., & Haviland-Jones, J. M., Feldman Barrett, L. (Eds.). (2008). *Handbook of emotions* (3rd ed.). New York, NY: Guilford Press.

Linnenbrink, E. A. (2007). The role of affect in student learning: A multi-dimensional approach to considering the interaction of affect, motivation, and engagement. In P. A. Schutz & R. Pekrun (Eds.), *Emotion in education* (pp. 107–124). San Diego, CA: Academic Press.

Linnenbrink, E. A., & Pintrich, P. R. (2002). Achievement goal theory and affect: An asymmetrical bidirectional model. *Educational Psychologist, 37*, 69–78.

Linnenbrink, L. (Ed.). (2006). Emotion research in education [Special issue]. *Educational Psychology Review, 18*(4).

Linnenbrink-Garcia, L., & Barger, M. M. (2014). Achievement goals and emotions. In R. Pekrun & L. Linnenbrink-Garcia (Eds.) *International handbook of emotions in education* (pp. 142–161). New York, NY: Taylor & Francis.

Linnenbrink-Garcia, L., & Pekrun, R. (2011). Students' emotions and academic engagement: Introduction to the special issue. *Contemporary Educational Psychology, 36*, 1–3.

Little, T. D., Preacher, K. J., Selig, J. P., & Card, N. A. (2007). New developments in latent variable panel analyses of longitudinal data. *International Journal of Behavioral Development, 31*, 357–365.

Lorenz, K. (1974). Analogy as a source of knowledge. *Science, 185*, 229–234.

Markey, A., & Loewenstein, G. (2014). Curiosity. In R. Pekrun & L. Linnenbrink-Garcia (Eds.), *International handbook of emotions in education* (pp. 228–245). New York, NY: Taylor & Francis.

McArdle, J. J. (2009). Latent variable modeling of differences and changes with longitudinal data. *Annual Review of Psychology, 60*, 577–605.

Meinhardt, J., & Pekrun, R. (2003). Attentional resource allocation to emotional events: An ERP study. *Cognition and Emotion, 17*, 477–500.

Moors, A., Ellsworth, P., Scherer, K. R., & Frijda, N. (Eds.). (2013). Appraisal [Special section]. *Emotion Review, 5*, 119–224.

Morris, J. A., & Feldman, D.C. (1996). The dimensions, antecedents, and consequences of emotional labor. *Academy of Management Review, 21*, 986–1010.

Nett, U., Goetz, T., & Daniels, L. (2010). What to do when feeling bored? Students' strategies for coping with boredom. *Learning and Individual Differences, 20*, 626–638.

Pekrun, R. (2005). Progress and open problems in educational emotion research. *Learning and Instruction, 15*, 497–506.

Pekrun, R. (2006). The control-value theory of achievement emotions: Assumptions, corollaries, and implications for educational research and practice. *Educational Psychology Review, 18*, 315–341.

Pekrun, R. (in press). *Emotions and learning.* Geneva, Switzerland: International Academy of Education (IAE) and International Bureau of Education (IBE) of the United Nations Educational, Scientific and Cultural Organization (UNESCO).

Pekrun, R., & Bühner, M. (2014). Self-report measures of academic emotions. In R. Pekrun & L. Linnenbrink-Garcia (Eds.), *International handbook of emotions in education* (pp. 561–579). New York, NY: Taylor & Francis.

Pekrun, R., Elliot, A. J., & Maier, M. A. (2006). Achievement goals and discrete achievement emotions: A theoretical model and prospective test. *Journal of Educational Psychology, 98*, 583–597.

Pekrun, R., & Frese, M. (1992). Emotions in work and achievement. In C. L. Cooper & I. T. Robertson (Eds.), *International review of industrial and organizational psychology* (Vol. 7, pp. 153–200). Chichester, United Kingdom: Wiley.

Pekrun, R., Goetz, T., Titz, W., & Perry, R. P. (2002). Academic emotions in students' self-regulated learning and achievement: A program of quantitative and qualitative research. *Educational Psychologist, 37*, 91–106.

Pekrun, R., & Hofmann, H. (1996, April). *Affective and motivational processes: Contrasting interindividual and intraindividual perspectives.* Paper presented at the annual meeting of the American Educational Research Association, New York, NY.

Pekrun, R., Murayama, K., Frenzel, A. C., Goetz, T., & Marsh, H. W. (2011, September). *Origins of achievement emotions: The impact of individual and class-level ability.* Paper presented at the 14th biannual conference of the European Association for Research on Learning and Instruction, Exeter, United Kingdom.

Pekrun, R., & Schutz, P. A. (2007). Where do we go from here? Implications and future directions for inquiry on emotions in education. In P. A. Schutz & R. Pekrun (Eds.), *Emotion in education* (pp. 313–331). San Diego, CA: Academic Press.

Ratner, (2007). A macro cultural-psychological theory of emotions. In P. A. Schutz & R. Pekrun (Eds.), *Emotion in education* (pp. 89–104). San Diego, CA: Academic Press.

Reisenzein, R., Junge, M., Studtmann, M., & Huber, O. (2014). Observational approaches to the measurement of emotions. In R. Pekrun & L. Linnenbrink-Garcia (Eds.), *International handbook of emotions in education* (pp. 580–606). New York, NY: Taylor & Francis.

Robinson, W. S. (1950). Ecological correlations and the behavior of individuals. *American Sociological Review, 15*, 351–356.

Roseman, I. J., Antoniou, A. A., & Jose, P. E. (1996). Appraisal determinants of emotions: Constructing a more accurate and comprehensive theory. *Cognition and Emotion, 10,* 241–277.

Russell, J. A. (2003). Core affect and the psychological construction of emotion. *Psychological Review, 110,* 145–172.

Russell, J. A. (Ed.). (2012). Defining emotion [Special section]. *Emotion Review, 4*(4).

Ruthig, J. C., Perry, R. P., Hall, N. C., & Hladkyj, S. (2004). Optimism and attributional retraining: Longitudinal effects on academic achievement, test anxiety, and voluntary course withdrawal in college students. *Journal of Applied Social Psychology, 34,* 709–730.

Sansone, C., & Thoman, D. B. (2005). Does what we feel affect what we learn? Some answers and new questions. *Learning and Instruction, 15,* 507–515.

Scherer, K. R. (1986). Vocal affect expression: A review and a model for future research. *Psychological Bulletin, 99,* 143–165.

Schiefele, U. (2009). Situational and individual interest. In K. R. Wentzel & A. Wigfield (Eds.), *Handbook of motivation at school* (pp. 197–222). New York, NY: Taylor & Francis.

Schmitz, B., & Skinner, E. (1993). Perceived control, effort, and academic performance: Interindividual, intraindividual, and multivariate time series analyses. *Journal of Personality and Social Psychology, 64,* 1010–1028.

Schutz, P. A., Chambless, C. B., & DeCuir, J. T. (2003). Multimethods research. In K. B deMarrais & S. D. Lapan (Eds.), *Foundations for research: Methods of inquiry in education and the social sciences* (pp. 267–282). Hillsdale, NJ: Lawrence Erlbaum.

Schutz, P. A., & DeCuir, J. T. (2002). Inquiry on emotions in education. *Educational Psychologist, 37,* 125–134.

Schutz, P. A., DiStefano, C., Benson, J., & Davis, H. A. (2004). The development of a scale for emotional regulation during test taking. *Anxiety, Stress and Coping, 17,* 253–269.

Shuman, V., & Scherer, K. R. (2014). Concepts and structures of emotions. In R. Pekrun & L. Linnenbrink-Garcia (Eds.), *International handbook of emotions in education* (pp. 13–35). New York, NY: Taylor & Francis.

Skinner, E. A. (1996). A guide to constructs of control. *Journal of Personality and Social Psychology, 71,* 549–570.

Stearns, P. N., & Stearns, C. Z. (1985). Emotionology: Clarifying the history of emotions and emotional standards. *American Historical Review, 90,* 813–836.

Turner, J. C., & Trucano, M. (2014). Measuring situated emotion. In R. Pekrun & L. Linnenbrink-Garcia (Eds.), *International handbook of emotions in education.* New York, NY: Taylor & Francis.

Turner, J. E., & Waugh, R. M. (2007). A dynamical systems perspective regarding students' learning processes: Shame reactions and emergent self-organizations. In P. A. Schutz and R. Pekrun (Eds.), *Emotions in education* (pp. 125–145). San Diego, CA: Elsevier.

Weiner, B. (2007). Examining emotional diversity in the classroom: An attribution theorist considers the moral emotions. In P. A. Schutz and R. Pekrun (Eds.), *Emotion in education* (pp. 75–88). San Diego, CA: Academic Press.

Wehrle, T., & Scherer, K. R. (2001). Toward computational modeling of appraisal theories. In K. R. Scherer, A. Schorr, & T. Johnstone (Eds.), *Appraisal processes in emotion* (pp. 350–365). New York, NY: Oxford University Press.

Wilson-Mendenhall, C. D., Feldman Barrett, L., & Barsalou, L. W. (2013). Neural evidence that human emotions share core affective properties. *Psychological Science, 24,* 947–956.

Zeidner, M. (1998). *Test anxiety: The state of the art.* New York, NY: Plenum.

Zeidner, M. (2014). Anxiety in education. In R. Pekrun & L. Linnenbrink-Garcia (Eds.), *International handbook of emotions in education* (pp. 265–288). New York, NY: Taylor & Francis.

CONTRIBUTORS LIST

Mary Ainley, PhD, Honorary Fellow, Melbourne School of Psychological Sciences, University of Melbourne, Melbourne, Australia

Veleka Allen, PhD, Postdoctoral Fellow in Psychometric Research, Law School Admission Council, Newtown, Pennsylvania

Michael M. Barger, BS, Doctoral Student in Developmental Psychology, Department of Psychology and Neuroscience, Duke University, Durham, North Carolina

Susanne Beier, PhD, Research Assistant, Institute of Psychology, University of Heidelberg, Heidelberg, Germany

Catherine M. Bohn-Gettler, PhD, Associate Professor of Educational Psychology, Wichita State University, Wichita, Kansas

Marc A. Brackett, PhD, Director of the Yale Center for Emotional Intelligence, Senior Research Scientist in the Department of Psychology, and Faculty Fellow in the Edward Zigler Center in Child Development and Social Policy, Yale University, New Haven, Connecticut

Suzanne H. Broughton, PhD, Assistant Professor of Literacy, Emma Eccles Jones College of Education and Human Services, Utah State University, Logan, Utah

Heather Brule, Graduate Student, Department of Psychology, Portland State University, Portland, Oregon

Markus Bühner, PhD, Professor of Psychological Methodology and Assessment and Head of the Department, Department of Psychology, University of Munich, Munich, Germany

Susan D. Calkins, PhD, Bank of America Excellence Professor, Department of Human Development and Family Studies and Department of Psychology, University of North Carolina at Greensboro, Greensboro, North Carolina

Charles S. Carver, PhD, Distinguished Professor of Psychology, Department of Psychology, University of Miami, Miami, Florida

Joanna A. Christodoulou, PhD, Assistant Professor, Department of Communication Sciences and Disorders, MGH Institute of Health Professions, Boston, Massachusetts

Heather A. Davis, PhD, Associate Professor of Educational Psychology, Department of Curriculum, Instruction, and Counselor Education, North Carolina State University, Raleigh, North Carolina

Jessica T. DeCuir-Gunby, PhD, Associate Professor of Educational Psychology, Department of Curriculum, Instruction, and Counselor Education, North Carolina State University, Raleigh, North Carolina

Sidney K. D'Mello, PhD, Assistant Professor, Department of Computer Science and Department of Psychology, University of Notre Dame, Notre Dame, Indiana

Jessica M. Dollar, PhD, Postdoctoral Fellow, Department of Human Development and Family Studies, University of North Carolina at Greensboro, Greensboro, North Carolina

Klaus Fiedler, PhD, Chair in Social Psychology, Institute of Psychology, University of Heidelberg, Heidelberg, Germany

Anne C. Frenzel, PhD, Associate Professor of Psychology, Department of Psychology and Munich Center of the Learning Sciences, University of Munich, Munich, Germany

Guido H. E. Gendolla, PhD, Chair for Motivation Psychology, Section of Psychology, University of Geneva, Geneva, Switzerland

Thomas Goetz, PhD, Professor of Psychology, Department of Empirical Educational Research, University of Konstanz, Konstanz, Germany, and Thurgau University of Teacher Education, Kreuzlingen, Switzerland

Gerald A. Goldin, PhD, Professor of Mathematics, Physics, and Education, Rutgers University, Piscataway, New Jersey

Arthur C. Graesser, PhD, Professor, Department of Psychology and Institute for Intelligent Systems, University of Memphis, Memphis, Tennessee, and Senior Research Fellow, Department of Education, University of Oxford, Oxford, United Kingdom

Sandra Graham, PhD, Professor and Presidential Chair in Education and Diversity, Department of Education, University of California at Los Angeles, Los Angeles, California

James J. Gross, PhD, Professor of Psychology and Director of the Stanford Psychophysiology Laboratory, Department of Psychology, Stanford University, Stanford, California

Nathan C. Hall, PhD, Assistant Professor, Department of Educational and Counseling Psychology, McGill University, Montreal, Canada

Suzanne Hidi, PhD, Senior College, University of Toronto, Toronto, Canada

Oswald Huber, PhD, Professor Emeritus of General Psychology, University of Fribourg, Fribourg, Switzerland

Mary Helen Immordino-Yang, EdD, Assistant Professor of Education, Psychology and Neuroscience, Brain and Creativity Institute and Rossier School of Education, University of Southern California, Los Angeles, California

Scott E. Jacobs, PhD, Department of Psychology, Stanford University, Stanford, California

Martin Junge, MSc, Doctoral Student, Institute of Psychology, University of Greifswald, Greifswald, Germany

Martin G. Köllner, MSc, Research Associate, Department of Psychology, Friedrich-Alexander University Erlangen, Erlangen, Germany

Sylvia D. Kreibig, PhD, Postdoctoral Research Fellow, Department of Psychology, Stanford University, Stanford, California

Michael Lewis, PhD, University Distinguished Professor of Pediatrics and Psychiatry and Director of the Institute for the Study of Child Development, Robert Wood Johnson Medical School, Rutgers University, New Brunswick, New Jersey

Lisa Linnenbrink-Garcia, PhD, Associate Professor of Educational Psychology, Department of Counseling, Educational Psychology, and Special Education, Michigan State University, East Lansing, Michigan

George Loewenstein, PhD, Herbert A. Simon University Professor of Economics and Psychology, Department of Social and Decision Sciences, Carnegie Mellon University, Pittsburgh, Pennsylvania

Doug Lombardi, PhD, Assistant Professor of Science Education, College of Education, Temple University, Philadelphia, Pennsylvania

Carolyn MacCann, PhD, Psychology Lecturer, The University of Sydney, Sydney, Australia

Amanda Markey, MSc, Doctoral Student, Department of Social and Decision Sciences, Carnegie Mellon University, Pittsburgh, Pennsylvania

Gerald Matthews, PhD, Research Professor, Institute for Simulation and Training, University of Central Florida, Orlando, Florida

Tara Ann Matthews, MD, American Academy of Pediatrics Board-certified Pediatrician and Developmental Behavioral Pediatrics Fellow, Institute for the Study of Child Development, Robert Wood Johnson Medical School, Rutgers University, New Brunswick, New Jersey

Debra K. Meyer, PhD, Professor of Education, Department of Education, Elmhurst College, Elmhurst, Illinois

Geraldine V. Oades-Sese, PhD, Assistant Professor of Pediatrics and Associate Director of the Institute for the Study of Child Development, Robert Wood Johnson Medical School, Rutgers University, New Brunswick, New Jersey

Reinhard Pekrun, PhD, Professor and Research Chair for Personality and Educational Psychology, Department of Psychology, University of Munich, Munich, Germany

Raymond P. Perry, PhD, Distinguished Professor of Psychology, Department of Psychology, University of Manitoba, Winnipeg, Canada

Jennifer Pitzer, Graduate Student, Department of Psychology, Portland State University, Portland, Oregon

David N. Rapp, Associate Professor in the Learning Sciences, School of Education and Social Policy and Department of Psychology, Northwestern University, Evanston, Illinois

Rainer Reisenzein, Professor of General Psychology, Institute of Psychology, University of Greifswald, Greifswald, Germany

Susan E. Rivers, PhD, Deputy Director of the Yale Center for Emotional Intelligence and Research Scientist in the Department of Psychology, Yale University, New Haven, Connecticut

Richard D. Roberts, PhD, Managing Principal Research Scientist, Center for Academic and Workforce Readiness and Success, Educational Testing Service, Princeton, New Jersey

Michael F. Scheier, PhD, Professor and Department Head of Psychology, Department of Psychology, Carnegie Mellon University, Pittsburgh, Pennsylvania

Klaus R. Scherer, PhD, Professor of Psychology, Swiss Center for Affective Sciences and University of Geneva, Geneva, Switzerland, and University of Munich, Munich, Germany

Oliver C. Schultheiss, PhD, Professor and Chair of Affective Neuroscience, Department of Psychology, Friedrich-Alexander University Erlangen, Erlangen, Germany

Paul A. Schutz, PhD, Professor of Educational Psychology, Department of Educational Psychology, University of Texas at San Antonio, San Antonio, Texas

Vera Shuman, PhD, Senior SNF Researcher, School of Business and Economics, University of Lausanne, Lausanne, Switzerland

Gale M. Sinatra, PhD, Professor of Education and Psychology, Rossier School of Education, University of Southern California, Los Angeles, California

Ellen Skinner, PhD, Professor of Psychology, Department of Psychology, Portland State University, Portland, Oregon

Amber C. Strain, MSc, Doctoral Student, Department of Psychology and Institute for Intelligent Systems, University of Memphis, Memphis, Tennessee

Markus Studtmann, PhD, Postdoctoral Research Fellow, Max Planck Institute for Human Development, Berlin, Germany

April Z. Taylor, PhD, Associate Professor, Department of Child and Adolescent Development, California State University, Northridge, California

David Tillman, PhD, Assistant Professor of Public Health, College of Pharmacy and Health Sciences, Campbell University, Buies Creek, North Carolina

Meg Trucano, MSc, Graduate Student in Developmental Psychology, Department of Psychology, University of Notre Dame, Notre Dame, Indiana

Julianne C. Turner, PhD, Associate Professor of Psychology, Department of Psychology, University of Notre Dame, Notre Dame, Indiana

Meca R. Williams-Johnson, Associate Professor of Educational Research Methods, Department of Curriculum, Foundations, and Reading, Georgia Southern University, Statesboro, Georgia

Moshe Zeidner, PhD, Professor of Educational Psychology and Human Development, Laboratory for Personality and Emotions, University of Haifa, Haifa, Israel

INDEX

A *t* or *f* following a page number indicates a table or figure, respectively.

ability tracking 256–7, 283
abstraction levels 57–8
academic achievement: boredom and 316; emotions and 131–5; and emotional intelligence 168, 178; interest and 215–16; interest and enjoyment as contributors to 220–3; in mathematics 399; measurement of 369–71
academic boredom 311–12; antecedents of 316–19, 323–4; assessment of 321–2, 324; classification of students' strategies for coping with 319*t*; consequences of 323–4; and the control-value theory 316–17; coping with 319–20, 323, 324; effects of on learning behavior and achievement 315–16; empirical findings on 316, 318–19, 320; frequency and intensity of 314–15, 323; future research on 323–4; General Boredom Model 317; intervention programs for 324; levels of 314*f*; measurement of 572–3; Model of Academic Boredom 317; prevention/reduction of 322–3; *see also* boredom
Academic Boredom Scale (ABS) 573
academic emotions 416–18; anger 572–3; assessment of 568–74; classification of 478; development of 621; neuroscientific measurement of 608; positive 572; research on 431; and science 422; self-report of 561–75; students and 547–9, 670; of teachers 670; *see also* academic achievement; academic boredom
academic health, effect of discrimination on 111
academic success 3–4, 36, 88–90, 131–5, 115–26, 339, 345, 368, 369, 437, 521; emotional intelligence and 174–5, 178; noncognitive factors in 162; physiological and

emotional regulation and 529–31; preconditions for 331
accommodation 38–40, 47, 50; cognitive 6
achievement: consequences of 131; educational 120–2; effects of boredom on 315–16; feedback for 131; interest and enjoyment as contributors to 220–3; and mood 51; motivation for 6, 74, 76, 132; nonachievement 5; pride, hubris and 254–6; social 5; student 547; *see also* academic achievement; achievement emotions; achievement goals; n Achievement
achievement emotions 3–4, 6; attributional antecedents of 2; attributional theory of 125; concept of 121; distal individual antecedents of 129; impact of 120–1; influence of tasks and learning environments on 129–30; origins and outcomes of 124; research on 120–1, 137; situational specificity of 128–9; three-dimensional taxonomy of 121*t*; *see also* control-value theory of achievement emotions; attributional theory of achievement emotions
Achievement Emotions Questionnaire (AEQ) 216, 564, 568–71, 572, 573; scales and reliabilities 569*t*
Achievement Emotions Questionnaire for Teachers (AEQ-Teachers) 574–5
Achievement Emotions Questionnaire-Mathematics (AEQ-M) 392
achievement gap 111, 112, 551
achievement goals 3, 129; asymmetrical bidirectional model 143–5, 144*f*; and emotions 142; function of 142; of teachers 502; theoretical background 142–3; *see also* control-value theory of achievement emotions; goals

achievement priming 50
action control, feedback-based 56
action loops 58
action-outcome expectancies 125
action programs 58
actions, motivated 81
action tendencies 108
action units (AUs) 588–9, 599
activation: autonomic 626, 628, 631, 632, 635, 639; brain 122, 234, 565, 611–14, 665; electroencephalographic 636; physiological 3, 4, 27, 63, 79, 82, 114, 143, 147, 157, 185, 188, 207, 208, 210, 211, 216, 217, 266, 291, 297, 350–1, 353, 357–8, 405, 418, 442–3, 444, 446, 448, 449, 451, 468, 563, 565, 568, 593, 632, 638, 652, 660, 667; sympathetic and parasympathetic 632
adaptive functions 38
adjustment to school, relatedness and 464–5
administrators 1, 114, 163, 379, 428, 668, 671
admiration 5, 31, 106, 110, 121, 575, 610
Adolescent Swinburne University Emotional Intelligence Test 174–5
advanced learning technologies: emotions in 473–5; manipulating and responding to emotions in 484–8
affect: and action 61–2; amplification of 77–9; architecture of 397; circumplex models of 3; and cognition 36, 38, 90, 214; components of 2, 565; core 22–5, 350–2, 593; as core of emotion 56, 58; and curiosity 242n1; defined 2–3, 442; depressed 68; dimensionality of 6, 60–3; as dynamic process 350; and emotion 143, 206; esteem-related 111; and goals 152; and implicit motivation 77–9; and learning 1; local 395; and mathematics 7, 391, 393; negative 592; and persistence 43–4; positive 6, 65, 88, 208, 209; positive vs. negative 3, 157; powerful 408–9; scope of 15; situated 645–9; unipolar dimensions of 62, 63; use of term 37; *see also* affective states; affective structures; affective tendencies; global affect
affect dispositions, compared to emotions 18–19
affect infusion model 42, 444, 446
affection 340, 393, 592
Affective AutoTutor 484–5
affective climate 462
affective computing 599
Affective Computing (Picard) 305
affective cues 49
affective experiences 222, 350
affective influences on mental effort 637–8
affective priming 49–50
affective reactions, velocity function 59–60
affective states: and learning 39–40; negative vs. positive 50–1; positive 133, 592; resulting from learning experience 39–40; types of 37

affective structures, emotions within 407
affective tendencies 351–2; relationship with emotional episodes and core affect 350f
affect programs 24
affect-sensitive learning technologies 473–4
affect transitions 299f
afferent view 634–5
affiliation 77–8, 83, 86, 97; motive for 75, 88; *see also* n Affiliation
affordances 644
agency 124; and testing 354
aggression *see* children, aggressive
alexithymia 168
allodynamic regulation 637
American Educational Research Association 2
amusement: bodily expression of 588; vocal expression of 587
amygdala 80f, 80–3
anger 3, 15, 103–4, 105, 106, 109, 112, 114–15, 120, 126, 127, 152, 349, 397, 661; academic 572–3; and aggression 18–19; bodily expression of 588; self-report on 572; in teachers 497
anterograde amnesia 81
antisocial delinquency 48
ANVIL 599
anxiety 1, 2, 3, 4, 45, 120, 126, 127, 132, 145, 146, 149, 150, 151, 153, 369, 661; in academic domains 314f; biological factors 271–2; and cognitive performance 274–7; conceptualization of 281–2; and culture 362–3; determinants of 270–4; different levels of analysis 282; distal factors 271–3; in education 265, 281–4; empirical research in natural settings 283; family environment and primary socialization 272–3; historical studies of 266–7; information processing deficits in anxious students 276t; interactional model of 267–8; interventions for 279–81; and mathematics 398–401; mediating and moderating effects 275–7; normal vs. abnormal 278–9; proximal factors 273–4; relationship with performance 283–4; research methodology 283; and resilient students 284; and science 422–3; self-regulation model of 268–9; in self-reports 564; in teachers 497–8; as trait 266; trait vs. state 266, 349; viable taxonomies for 282; vs. worry and emotionality 266–7; and the writing process 446; *see also* state anxiety; test anxiety; trait anxiety
apathy 45, 101, 127, 257, 336, 338, 646
Aplusix II Algebra Learning Assistant 479
apologies 105
appraisal biases 19
appraisal theory of emotion 172, 635; and achievement emotions 124–8; appraisal objectives 25–6; complementary approach 27; decision tree 26–7; stimulus evaluation checks 26; and teacher emotions 505

apprehension 266, 274, 363, 398, 407, 408; *see also* anxiety; nervousness; worry

approach system 62–3

arousal 28*f*, 615; affective 89, 121; and boredom 313; emotional 84, 86; in reading and writing 449–50; valence and 22, 23, 25, 27, 30, 31, 131, 134, 325, 450, 476, 651

Asians, in the United States 110–11

assessments: of emotions 8; forced-choice 170; of emotions and goals 153; of implicit motives 75; standardized 177–8; *see also* emotional intelligence assessment; measurement of emotions; testing

assimilation 38–9, 42–3, 47, 50; cognitive 6

assymetrical bidirectional model 149–51, 158

attachment 75, 272, 333, 521, 522–4, 532

attention 131, 194, 197

attention impairments 46; *see also* boredom

attitudes: compared to emotions 18; about mathematics 391

attractor states 23

attributional bias 104

attributional retraining 136

attributions: causal 125; gender differences in 254; global and specific 249–50, 253–4; and other-directed emotions 98*f*, 102–7; and self-directed emotions 97*f*, 99–102, 249

attributional theory of achievement emotions 6, 96, 112, 114, 115, 125, 459; causal attributions 97–9; causal dimensions 99; other-directed emotions 98*f*; self-directed emotions 97*f*; and teacher emotions 505

autonomic change, and emotion 634–5

autonomic influences, bidirectional 635

autonomic nervous system (ANS): activity 525–6, 616, 629*t*, 632, 633, 635, 639; explained 626–7; measurements of activity 628–32;measurement for studying emotion 632–9; measurement of emotion in education 625; structure and functioning of 627*f*, 627–8, 630; student's emotional responses during a math exam 626*f*

autonomic regulation: and emotion 636; homeostasis model 636

autonomic space, bivariate 633–4

autonomy: and motivation 333, 337; and motivational resilience 341

AutoTutor Multiple Judge Study 222, 295–7, 299, 478–81, 484, 649–50, 652

avoidance system 62–3

behavior: adult and child 20–1; affective 47–8; assessment of 667; coding systems for 584; incentives for 79; nonintentional 586–8; observation of 583–4; and positive emotions 208; rates of 61; regulation of 49, 77; social 65, 76, 652

Behavior Action and Posture coding system (BAP) 590

beliefs: and academic goals 355; and affect 3; as antecedents of emotion 123, 129; and attitudes 18; causal 113, 115; challenges to 242, 258; cognitive 418; cultural 542, 549; entity 143; epistemic 571; inference of 581, 584; in literacy education 440, 441, 448; in mathematics education 391–2, 394–8, 402, 403, 405, 407, 653; motivational 77, 112, 648; about outcomes 116; in science education 418, 421, 422, 427; self-attribution 249–50; and stereotypes 113; of students 282, 342, 403, 460; subjective 322, 510, 563; of teachers 391, 510; unconscious 114; value 317

belongingness 548–9

Between the Lines (BTL) online measure 646, 648–9

bidirectional autonomic influences 635

biological reactivity 529–30

biopsychology 77, 86

bivariate autonomic space, principle of 633–4

blood-oxygen-level-dependent (BOLD) response 610, 611

bodily expressions and movements 296, 393, 444, 588

Body Pressure Measurement System 588, 650

boredom 1, 4, 7, 46, 120, 127–30, 132, 152, 153, 183, 478–9, 488, 588; and academic achievement 316; assumed antecedents of 318*t*; defined 311–14, 325; and mathematics 393–4; in reading and writing 450; self-report measures of 321*t*, 572; in teachers 499; types of 313; *see also* academic boredom

Boredom Coping Scales (BCS) 573

boundaries 19, 217, 305, 548, 661

brain physiology 211, 610, 612, 633, 636, 660; damage to the brain 616–17

broaden-and-build model of positive emotions 30, 86–7, 207, 223, 509, 662

bullying 14, 163, 257, 369, 468; *see also* children, aggressive

burnout, and teachers 500, 511–12, 667

calm 145, 146, 155, 157, 449, 450, 652

cardiac autonomic control (CAR) 633–4

career success, predictions of 76, 87–8, 163, 177, 178, 374, 437

caregivers: influence of on emotional regulation 8, 520–5; and the physiological regulation of emotion 525–9

catastrophizing 337

causal controllability 113–14, 124–8

causal thinking 114–15

change: autonomic 634–5; cognitive 194, 197; conceptual 420–2; *see also* climate change

child development *see* attachment; children

children: academic development of 248; aggressive 19, 74, 104–5, 109, 374, 467, 526–7, 531; anxiety in 272; attitudes of toward reading and writing 219–20; development of emotion regulation in 189–91, 520–5; emotional development of 107–8, 108*f*,

109–10, 110*f*, 248–50; high-risk 373, 527; interest and enjoyment in 214, 237; interest development of 219–20; low-risk 525, 527; physiological regulation of emotion in 525–9; racial/ethnic minority 110–14; self-attribution in 253; social-emotional development 248; writing development of 215; *see also* students

circumplex models 3, 25, 26*f*, 27, 28*f*

Classroom Assessment Scoring System (CASS) framework 465

classroom climate 460; effect of 451–2; emotional 668; and emotional support 462–3

classroom practices 508, 509; and achievement emotions 130–1; coping with unpleasant emotions 467–8; and emotional competence 466–8; emotions in 458–9; future research on 469, 669; instructional challenge 460–1; and motivation 459; and peer interactions 466–7; sustaining enjoyment 467–8; and teacher emotions 512

climate change 416–18, 422, 427–30, 571

coasting 64–6, 67

cognition: and affect 36, 38, 58, 90; antecedents of 129; components of 2, 565; and emotion 475; and mood 40–1, 50–1; *see also* cognitive processes; learning

Cognitive-Affective Model of Conceptual Change (CAMCC) 421

cognitive appraisals, related to testing 354–5; *see also* appraisal theory of emotion

cognitive disequilibrium 7, 289–90, 292, 300, 302, 424, 450, 475, 479, 481, 481*f*, 571; augmenting with traits and moods 483; stimulating 485–7; theoretical perspective 482–3; *see also* confusion

cognitive disequilibrium framework 481*f*, 482, 484, 488–9

cognitive dissonance 290; *see also* confusion

cognitive incongruity 4; *see also* cognitive disequilibrium

cognitive-motivational model of emotion effects 131

cognitive processes 6, 247; affect infusion model 444, 446; impact of emotion on 442; problem-solving 131; and reading 438–9; resource allocation models 443–4; semantic network theories 442–3, 445; and writing 440–1; *see also* cognition; learning

Cognitive Reconstruction of Knowledge Model (CRKM) 422

cognitive reflection 49–50

cognitive reflection test (CRT) 49–50

cognitive resources 132; allocation of 444, 446; effects of boredom on 315

Coh-Metrix 298

collaborative argumentation 429

Collaborative for Academic, Social, and Emotional Learning (CASEL) 370, 372

collectivism 542

compassion 14, 546, 610

competence and competencies 145; development of 86; and implicit motives 87; and motivation 332–3, 337; social and emotional learning 370*f*; subject-specific 507

component process model 25–6

computed axial tomography (CAT) 613

Computer Expression Recognition Toolbox (CERT) 599–600; processing pipeline of 600

conceptual novelty 293

confidence 43, 47, 49, 101, 183, 206, 233, 235–6, 241, 282, 353, 354, 357, 358, 371, 403, 406, 426, 427, 474, 477, 648; *see also* self-confidence

confusion 7, 290, 450, 479, 488, 588, 661; appraisals of 292–4; as beneficial to learning 303–4, 306; and bodily response systems 291–2; body movements suggesting 296; and communication 297; contextual cues 298; definition of 290–1; discourse features 298; as emotion 291–2, 305; expression of 294–8; growth and decay dynamics 301*f*; and learning 485–7; facial expressions of 295–6; physiology of 297; regulation of 300–1; relevance to learning 302–3; and science education 424–5; and surprise 292; temporal dynamics of 298–300; zone optimal 299, 306, 489

conscientiousness 162, 255, 483, 594

contempt 5, 121, 302, 304, 393, 480, 495, 500, 505, 575, 590, 592, 593, 650

contradictions 290, 293–4, 303–4, 424, 446, 482, 486–7, 621, 662

control, perceived 124–5

control appraisals 122; and achievement emotions 126–8; types of 124–5

controllability 99, 100, 106, 124; causal 101–2, 104; of success and failure 126

Control-Value Theory of Achievement Emotions 6, 45–7, 121, 131, 135–8, 151, 451, 459; basic propositions of 123*f*, 124–8; and boredom 315, 316–17; interest in 217; structure of 122–4; types of control and value appraisals 124–5

coping strategies/styles 7, 175, 185, 267, 353–4; for academic boredom 319–20, 323, 324; cognitive-approach 574; emotion-focused 193; model of 7; problem-focused 193; with stress 335

Coping with Boredom Scale 320

core affect 22–5, 350–2, 593; relationship with emotional episodes and affective tendency 350*f*

corrugator muscle 79

cortisol sampling 607, 614–16

counterstorytelling 550

creativity 43, 86, 133, 178, 207, 247, 275, 324, 446, 450

Critical Race Theory (CRT) 549–51

critique of liberalism 550

cross-cultural studies 669

Crystal Island 481, 487–8

culture: and anxiety 273; dimensions of 541–2; and emotion experience 30–1; and emotion expression

20–2, 23; and emotion expression in schools 545–6; and emotions 115–16, 363, 539, 543–4, 547–8; and emotions in educational settings 544–9; and facial expressions 30; and independent/interdependent construals of self 541; influence on student-teacher interactions 546–7; and implicit motives 78; individualism/collectivism in 542; perspective of 14; and test anxiety 278, 362, 544–5

curiosity 1, 4, 5, 7, 14, 17, 23, 209–11, 228–9, 240–2, 297, 302, 333, 342, 392, 394, 396, 397, 404, 406, 417, 421, 430, 450, 475, 480, 488, 547, 568, 571, 572, 650, 661, 671; cultivation of 236–40; defined 229–30; dimensionality of 229–30; and education 228–9, 234–6; importance, salience and surprise 236–40, 242; increasing 240–1; information-gap account of 230–4, 235, 239; neurophysiological correlates of 241; potential harms of 241; research on 240–2; self-report on 572; trait scales for 230

decision-making 125, 131
delay of gratification 191–2
delight 4, 214, 222, 295, 302, 450, 457, 478, 479, 480, 482, 484, 487, 488
depression 18, 45, 48, 68, 78, 101, 152, 154, 168, 272, 369, 544
determination 162, 268, 331, 393; *see also* self-determination
Diagnostic Analysis of Nonverbal Accuracy Scales (DANVA, DANVA-2) 171–2
Diagnostic and Statistical Manual of Mental Disorders, Fifth Edition (DSM-5) 266
diffusion tensor imaging (DTI) 614
disappointment 36, 101, 121, 126, 357, 375–6, 395, 633, 639
discrimination 111, 115, 543, 548
disequilibrium, cognitive *see* cognitive disequilibrium
disgust 14, 17, 30, 290, 291, 297, 302, 304, 305, 393, 478, 480, 545, 548, 586, 590, 591, 592, 593, 595, 596, 650
disincentives 73, 79, 85
distractibility 67, 270, 276, 316
distrust 50
diversity 111, 547, 548, 551
dominance 27, 74, 82, 87, 632
dopamine 247, 528
dopaminergic midbrain 211
drive states 241
drive theory 231
dynamic systems theory 644

eagerness 60, 357, 392, 393
eccrine sweat glands 631
ecological systems theory 369, 371, 377
ecstasy 25

education: defined 36–7; emotion regulation and 197; salience in 237–9; structure in 341; *see also* emotion, in education; learning
educational achievement *see* academic achievement
effort expenditure 43–4, 64, 65
ego-involvement 150
ELAN 599
electrocardiogram (ECG) 628, 630
electroencephalography (EEG) 8, 612, 617
electromyography (EMG) 79
embarrassment 37, 102, 185, 186, 249, 250, 404, 405, 489, 546; compared to shame 251–2; exposure embarrassment 252; types of 252
emotion/emotions: and academic performance 6; in advanced learning technologies 473–5; antecedents of 6, 15; assessment of 8, 153; and autonomic change 634–5; as calls for reprioritization 66; characteristics of 291; and cognition 475; communicative functions of 406, 509; during complex learning 475–82; as conceptual act 23; and conceptual change learning 420–2; constructs of 660–1; control processes 530–1; cultural perspectives on 14, 124; and curiosity 242n1; curricula 459; in deep learning 477–80; defined 2, 184, 247; differentiation from other affective phenomena 18–19; dimensionality of 6; expressive components of 294–5; domain specificity of 128; duration and sequences of 480; in education 2, 7, 8–9, 96–7, 184, 304, 331, 460, 463, 469, 470, 475, 478–9, 488; evolutionary perspective on 14; expression of in schools 545–6; and feelings 608, 618–19; function of 30; functional mechanisms of 132; and goal pursuit 6, 66–7; higher order dimensions 27; impact of on cognitive processes 442; inferences about 445; intentional actions as cues to 585–6; internal structures of 661; learning about 466–8; levels and contexts in education 668–9; modal model of 184f; and mood 2, 37; psychological needs as source of 333–5; applied to reading and writing 7, 445–7; as representational 406; research (*see* research); role of in learning 247–8; rules 500–1; schemas 21, 24, 42, 214, 397; situational information as cues to 585–6; structural models 25–6; as subjective experience 15–16; terms 27; theoretical perspectives on 13, 662–4; underlying dynamics of 31; vocal expressions of 587–8; *see also* academic emotions; emotion types; emotion regulation; emotion studies; emotion theories; emotions related to testing; epistemic emotions; feelings; measurement of emotions; moods; *see also* individual emotions by name
emotional climate 362, 373–4, 378, 380, 383, 525, 668–9; social 343
emotional components 14–19, 27; action tendency component 15–17, 16t; appraisal component 15–16, 16t; in constructionist theories 22; levels

of analysis 17; measurement paradigms 17–18; modal patterns of 22; motor component 15–17 16t; physiological component 15–17, 16t; subjective feeling component 15–16, 16t

emotional development see children, emotional development of

emotional distance 500–1

emotional engagement 336, 338, 340

emotional episodes 350–1; relationship with core affect and affective tendency 350f

emotional intelligence (EI) 6; ability-based 175; as ability construct 167–8; and academic achievement 174–5,178; defined 162–3; enhanced 378, 380; four-branch hierarchical model 167; high-stakes applications of 176–7; historical overview 163–5; mixed model of 165–7; as predictor of educational outcomes 174–5; standards for 177; and the standards movement 177–8; testing for competence 176; theoretical models of 163; theoretical principles of 165–8; three-branch ability model 167; trait model of 165–7; see also emotional intelligence assessment

Emotional Intelligence: Why It Can Matter More than IQ (Goleman) 163

emotional intelligence assessment 178; constructed response 173–4; correlation with academic success 174–5; development of 176; emotional management 172–3; emotional perception 171–2; emotional understanding 172; in MBA programs 176–7; in medical school applicants 176; multimedia situational judgment tests 173, 178; multiple choice 170–3; multiple mini-interview (MMI) 176; other-report approaches 174; self-report approaches 168–70; and social and emotional learning (SEL) programs 175–6

emotional labor 500–1, 512

emotional meta-experience 22, 24

emotional recovery 337–8

emotional resilience 7, 342

emotional salience 445–6

emotional support, and classroom climate 462–3

emotional well-being 78–9; and facial affect 79; self-reporting of 78

Emotion Facial Action Coding System (EMFACS) 590–2

emotion regulation 6, 7, 135–6, 351, 615; adaptive 190–1; attention deployment 186–7, 186f; behavioral indicators of 530; cognitive change 186f, 187; cognitive reappraisal 187–8; current applications 188–95; defined 185–7; development of 51, 189–91, 521–2; dysregulation 189; expressive suppression 187–8, 197; goals for 195–6; implications for education 531–3; individual differences 196–7; influence of caregivers on 520–1; interventions for 196; intrinsic vs. extrinsic 185; key findings on 187–8; management of

temptations 6, 184, 189, 191–2; physiological 525–9; process model of 186f; research on 24, 615; response modulation 186f, 187; situation modification 186, 186f; situation selection 186, 186f; and test anxiety 192–5

Emotion Regulation During Testing measure (ERDT) 364

emotion schemas 21, 24, 214

emotions related to testing 348–9, 350; cognitive appraisals 354–5; emotion-focusing processes 356; four dimensions of regulation 353–4; regaining task-focusing processes 356–7; regulating 352–3; task-focusing procedures 355; see also test anxiety

emotion studies 5; cross-cultural 663–4, 669; dynamic 663; in educational settings 45–6; experimental and nonexperimental designs 665–6; exploration and hypothesis testing 664–5; idiographic and nomothetic approaches 666–7; laboratory and field studies 665–6; multilevel 663, 669; multiple methodologies 664–7; qualitative and quantitative approaches 665; sociohistorical 669; see also situated emotion studies

emotion theories: appraisal 20f, 21–2, 24–5, 30; basic 19–21, 20f, 24; broaden-and-build 30, 86–7, 207, 223, 509, 662; circumplex models 3, 25, 26f, 27, 28f; comparison chart 20f; discrete 19–21, 20f, 24; and emotion regulation 24–5; and emotion space 25–6; Geneva Emotion Wheel 28–9, 29f; implications for 29–30; and measurements of emotions 25–6; multidimensional scaling 28f; nonlinear dynamic systems 20f, 23–4, 25, 31; psychological constructionist 20f, 22–3, 24, 25, 27, 30

emotion types: achievement 45–6, 216–17, 575, 588, 633–4, 670; activity-related 4, 126–7; adaptive 13; aesthetic 31–2; attraction 26; attribution-related 26, 107, 108–10, 115–16, 499, 510; basic 19–21, 214, 393, 586f, 590; categories/types 3, 26–7; control-independent 126; controllability-related 105–6; discrete 6, 19, 25, 27, 143, 157, 209, 376, 450–1, 495–9, 496t, 500, 508, 511–12, 564, 569, 570, 661; ego-focused 543; empathetic 4; epistemic 3–4, 7, 31–2, 121, 417, 571; exam-related 127; expectancy-related 100–1; facets, types and patterns of 668; incidental 3; incidental 3; in-the-moment 402–6; low-intensity 2; maladaptive 129; mixed positive-negative 2, 27; moment-to-moment 476–7; other-directed 98f, 102–7, 534; outcome-dependent 4, 26, 108, 110; primary 248; race/ethnicity-related 543–4, 548–9; retrospective 126; self-conscious 7, 249, 250–1; self-directed 97f, 99–102; self-reported 402; situated 643–5; subject matter 121; universal 543, 545; utilitarian 31; see also academic emotions; achievement emotions; negative emotions; positive emotions; social emotions; state emotions; topic emotions; trait emotions empathy 5, 165, 166, 169, 170, 171, 175–7, 251, 376, 380, 381, 448, 505, 543

energy, psychological needs as source of 333–5

engagement: academic 374; affective 402; of the approach system 62; of the avoidance system 62; behavioral 336, 338, 340, 407, 652–3; boredom and 315, 323; civic 371; defined 222; and disaffection 336; emotional 336, 338, 340; and flow 478, 488; in infants 248; mathematical 7, 391, 396–7, 402, 404–5, 407; motivational 507; physiological 634; re-engagement 334–5, 337–8, 339, 344; research on 295, 299, 302; in science 223, 416–18, 421, 423, 424, 426–7, 430, 432; of students 5, 125, 149, 157, 190, 205, 216, 231, 238, 323, 331, 332, 333, 335, 341, 343, 345, 378, 450, 464, 469, 531, 532, 547, 646, 670; of teachers 3, 5, 343–5, 504, 532, 659, 670; and technology 474, 475, 478–82, 484, 487, 488; *see also* flow

enjoyment 1, 3, 4, 6, 120, 127, 145, 153, 661; in academic domains 314*f*; as an achievement emotion 216–17; in classroom practices 467–8; compared to interest 206–9; as contributor to learning and achievement 220–3; hierarchical structure of 213; and interest 205–6, 214–15, 223; of learning 47; measuring 217–20; neuroscience on 209–12; and science 423–4; self-report on 572; in teachers 495–6, 501, 512

enthusiasm 192, 234, 331, 333, 336, 337, 338, 341, 342, 392, 407, 464, 465, 501, 592; in teachers 130, 195, 318, 323, 344, 361, 431, 451, 461–3, 501, 504, 509, 512, 575

entrepreneurs 87

envy 5, 106, 110, 121, 251, 284; *see also* jealousy

epistemic emotions 3–4, 7, 31, 32, 121, 230, 290, 292, 417, 431, 478, 568, 571, 583

Epistemic Emotion Scales (EES) 568, 571–2

epistemic feeling, and curiosity 242n1

EQ-i 165, 166, 168–9, 174–5

eureka 302, 475, 480, 650

European Association for Research on Learning and Instruction 2

evaluative anxiety *see* test anxiety

evaluative embarrassment 252; *see also* embarrassment

Evaluative Space Grid 27

event focus 15

evolution: human 14, 20, 30; teaching in science classrooms 416–17, 426–7, 429–30, 431

excitement 1, 3, 60, 122, 143, 189, 195, 206, 207, 213–13, 217–20, 222, 304, 333, 345, 351, 376, 377, 393, 449, 463, 469, 501, 615, 619

exhilaration 357

expectancy-value theories 125, 218

experience sampling method (ESM) 646–7

Expression of Emotions in Man and Animals, The (Darwin) 164, 289

expressive suppression 187–8, 197

expulsions 113

External Assessment Questionnaire (EAQ) 177

FaceReader 600

FACET 600

Facial Action Coding System (FACS) 30, 208, 588–90, 597, 599, 650; coding of surprise expression 589*f*

facial affect 79; *see also* facial expressions

Facial Expression Coding System (FACES) 593–4, 597

facial expressions: of anger 82; of anxiety 636; automated detection of 477; in AutoTutor 485; of basic emotions 586*f*, 586–7; of confusion 291, 295–6; cultural differences in 547; and emotion 2, 124, 375–6, 444; and emotion-diagnostic behaviors 585; and implicit learning 83; as indicators of emotion 393, 582–3, 586–7, 589–94, 596, 661; and interest/enjoyment 208; and positive emotions 208–9; and regulation of emotion 190; smiling 16, 17, 23, 48, 79, 88, 185, 241, 376, 547–8, 584; study of 30, 32, 652; of surprise 23, 589*f*; of teachers 512

failure 3, 131, 145, 215–16; academic 4; controllability of 126; fear of 45, 126, 143, 273, 282, 408; and test anxiety 274; *see also* achievement 131

false-memory paradigm 40

family problems 5, 272–3

fantasies 44–5

fascination 392

fatigue 90, 311, 449, 474, 475, 478

fear 14–17, 19, 27, 30, 45, 61, 63, 127, 148*f*, 164, 172, 242n1, 248, 256, 297, 302, 304, 306, 357–8, 373, 382, 392–3, 408, 415, 417, 421, 427, 429, 448, 449, 478, 480, 523, 543, 545, 548, 563, 583, 586, 587, 590–3, 596, 646; of failure 45, 126, 143, 273, 282, 408; fear conditioning 80–1; of mathematics 398–400, 402, 404; of punishment 270, 363; of tests 361

feedback: and affect 58–9, 64; from AutoTutor 485; and behavior 56–8; communicating anger 104; confusion and 304; delicate balance of 100; and emotion 56–7; emotional 214; from instructors 451–2; and learning 293; in mathematics instruction 394; physiological 124; proprioceptive 50; sensory 124; tandem systems 61–2; "wise" 112; *see also* feedback loops

feedback loops 87, 124, 217; central-peripheral neural 526; and motivation 340; negative 636; and test anxiety 268–9

feelings: defined 37; and emotions 608, 618–19; negative 68; positive and negative 195; and reprioritization 66–7

Feeling Words curriculum (RULER) 381–2

feminism 552

Fennema-Sherman Mathematics Attitude Scale 398

flexibility 17, 41, 133, 247, 483, 529

flow 51, 88, 120, 132, 222, 241, 295, 302, 317, 318, 353, 405, 461, 474–5, 478–82, 484, 487–9; *see also* engagement; flow theory
flow theory 459, 460
fluency 37, 48, 49–51, 373, 394, 438; and disfluency 49–50
Four-Phase Model of Interest Development 212–17
frowns 186, 289, 295
frustration 1, 3, 4, 16, 36, 59, 60, 61, 63, 64, 68, 120, 127, 145, 186, 189, 216, 221, 222, 265, 295, 302, 304, 336, 337, 338, 377, 392–7, 402–4, 408, 409, 417, 421, 449, 450, 461, 463, 464, 475, 476, 478, 479–80, 482–4, 487–8, 504, 511, 522, 523, 524, 532, 543, 548, 568, 571, 592, 600, 650, 668
functional connectivity mapping 610
functional magnetic resonance imaging (fMRI) 8, 210, 609–11, 620; interpretation of results 611–12
future research 659–60; on academic boredom 323–5; on achievement goals and emotions 155–8; on anxiety 281–5; on confusion 304–6; on culture and emotions 552–3; on curiosity 240–3; on emotion and emotion in education 31–2; on emotion in mathematical education 406–9; on emotion regulation in education 195–7; on emotions 668–9; on emotions in advanced learning technologies 489; on emotions in classroom practice 469–70; on emotions in education 663; on emotions and science learning 431–2; interdisciplinary collaboration 671–2; on intervention 670; on neurobiology 639; partnership between educational psychologists and affective neuroscientists 620; on self-report measures 575; on situated emotions 655–6; on teacher emotions 511–13

galvanic skin response (GSR) 615
gaming the system 479
gender: differences in attribution orientation 254; effect on emotion 129, 137; and identity 551–2; and test anxiety 277, 544
Geneva Emotion Wheel (GEW) 28–9, 29f
gestural expressions 124; *see also* gestures
gestures 107, 172, 546, 585, 588, 592, 651, 653
global affect 395; positive 208
globality 99
goal attainment 57, 84–8
goal congruence 124, 125
goal orientations 145
goal pursuit 44–5, 65–6; and emotions 56–8; evaluation of progress 145; implicit motives and 87, 89–90; successful 57, 84–8
goal relevance 124–5
goals: and abstraction 57–8; and achievement 120; and affect 146–7; and appraisal standards 354; assessment of 153; in education 69; and emotion appraisal 21; and emotions 1, 3, 6, 152; envisioning 1; and feedback loops 87; and

motives 78; *see also* goal orientations; goal profiles; goals and emotion
goals and emotion: further research 155–8; person-centered view 152–5; variable-centered view 147–8, 148f, 149–52
goal types 152–3; amotivated 152, 154–5; approach oriented 153; mastery 44, 146–7, 148–9, 152–3, 156; mastery-avoidance 146–7, 149–50, 157; motive-congruent 84; multiple goals 152, 156; performance-approach 146–7, 150–1, 153, 156, 157; performance-avoidance 146–7, 151, 153; performance-oriented 44, 153; 2 × 2, 154; trichotomous 145, 153
gratification, delayed 191–2
gratitude 15, 105–8, 110, 126
grief 68, 164
grounded theory approach 653
guilt 101–2, 106, 107–8, 109–10, 115–16, 127; compared to shame 251–2; in teachers 498–9

habituation 15, 48
Handbook of Self-Regulation (Zeidner, Boekaerts, Pintrich) 2
happiness 3, 16, 17, 22, 23, 25, 27, 30, 39, 43, 45, 48, 67, 97, 127, 164, 166, 169, 187, 209, 302, 305, 311, 354, 357, 393, 394, 404, 429, 449, 460, 461, 463, 464, 469, 478, 480, 488, 495, 500, 505, 543, 545, 586, 587, 590, 591, 593, 595
hatred 5, 392, 403
health problems, related to anger 572; *see also* physical health
heart rate 2, 156, 352, 477, 523, 526, 614, 615, 625–6, 628–9, 634–6, 639, 649, 653–4
hedonic responses/biases 37–8, 48, 78, 85–7, 100, 211
hedonic tone scale 78
helplessness 99, 253, 332, 338, 404
hemispherectomy surgery 617
hippocampus 80f, 81, 83, 211, 610
hope 3, 4, 120, 127, 135, 136, 145, 146, 165, 349
hopelessness 4, 101, 106, 120, 126, 127, 132, 145, 568, 661
How Learning Works (Ambrose) 239
hubris 254–6; *see also* pride
humiliation 102, 184, 274, 392, 393, 395, 403, 404, 463; *see also* shame
humor 393, 461, 463, 501, 592

ICODE 599
identity: academic 340, 342, 345; and achievement 125; and attentional deployment 194; and class 552; and emotions 619; identity salience 543; and intersectionality 551–2; mathematical self- 395, 404, 407; racial/ethnic 539, 540–1, 543, 551–2; science 423; social 111, 325; threat to 425
immigration 110–11
impasse 391–2, 394

impedance cardiography (ICG) 630
implicit motives 73–7; and adaptive behavior 87–8; assessment of 75; vs. explicit motives 76–7; in instruction 89; and learning 79–84, 80f; and learning and memory 82–4; as predictors of behaviors 76–7; reliability and validity of 75–6; and the virtuous-circle model 84–8, 85f
incentive cues 75, 77
incentives 43, 56, 60, 67, 73, 76–80, 83–6, 88, 132, 211–12, 341, 478; economic 470; motivational 89; motive-specific 86; nonverbal 77; positive 69; situational 84; verbal 77
incentive value 127
inclusion 548
Incredible Machine, The: Even More Contraptions 479
individualism 542
infants, interest and enjoyment in 214; see also children
inference, of mental states 580–2
information gap theory of curiosity 7, 230–4, 235, 239
information processing 133
instrumental conditioning 84
intelligence: abstract 164; interpersonal 164; intrapersonal 164; mechanical 164; multiple 164; social 164; theories of 113; see also emotional intelligence
intentional actions, as cues to emotion 585–6
INTERACT 599
interest 5, 6, 183, 208, 450, 588, 661; as an achievement emotion 216–17; compared to enjoyment 206–9; as contributor to learning and achievement 220–3; definition of 231; and enjoyment 205–6, 214–15, 223; Four-Phase model of interest development 212–16; in-the-moment experience of 213, 214; measuring 217–20; neuroscience on 209–12; research on students and 221–2; in science 423–4; self-report on 572; situational (SI) 219; in socioscientific issues 430
interest convergence 550
interest-excitement 206, 217, 219; see also excitement; interest
International Society for Research on Emotions 171
interruption (discrepancy) theory 292
intersectionality 549, 551
interventions 7, 9, 111, 189; for anxiety 279–81, 284–5; attribution 104–5; for boredom 324; cognitive-focused 280; and control-related appraisal 136–7; designing 651; for emotion regulation 135–6, 196–7; reading skills 614; research 112–13, 660, 668, 670–1; for RULER 378; SEL programs 369; study skills training 280–1; taxonomies for 282; for teacher emotions 513, 668
introspection 580
intuitive observer judgments 594–5
ipsative scores 170
item-specific processing 133

Japanese and Caucasian Brief Affect Recognition Test (JACBART) 171–2
jealousy 106, 110, 189, 407, 575; see also envy
joy 15, 25, 67, 86, 121, 126, 127, 164, 172, 206–9, 216–17, 219, 256, 284, 333, 345, 361, 376, 377, 382, 393, 402, 408, 415, 430, 509, 547, 583, 633, 639, 646, 648, 661; anticipatory 216–17, 495; see also enjoyment; pleasure
judgments, evaluative 114

knowledge: acquisition of 36, 40, 215, 247, 571; and anxiety 282; background 439–40, 450; cognitive generation of 3–4, 13, 14, 207, 571; conceptual 22–3, 392, 394, 400; and confusion 290, 291–4, 297; content 437; creative 39; crystallized 165; and curiosity 228, 231–3, 235, 236, 239–40, 242; emotional 16, 22–5, 30, 343, 374–5, 376, 467–8, 530, 531; emotions related to 32; enjoyment of 205, 207, 212–16, 218, 223; implicit 582; internalized 38, 43; intuitive 85; mathematical 483; in memory 41; metacognitive 276; neuroscientific 607; pedagogical 510; scientific 418, 420–1, 423, 424, 426, 427, 429–30, 431, 512, 572; semantic 438, 442; of students 177, 478, 483, 484–5; subject matter 489, 504, 513; and testing 349, 353, 400; vocabulary 438;
Know-Want-to-Know-Learned chart (KWL) 238–9

lab-based studies 649–52
language: and confusion 297–8; and self-report 565
Latino/as, in the United States 110
law school admissions test (LSAT), preparation for 480
leadership 74, 162, 176, 178, 370, 380, 382
learning: declarative 84; emotional 6; memory organization and 41–2; motive-driven 84–8; neurobiological substrates of 81–4; see also academic achievement; cognition; education; knowledge; memory
learning environments 670–1
learning programs, social-emotional 7
learning technologies 7–8; affect-sensitive 473–4
lesion analyses 616–17
Levels of Emotional Awareness Scale (LEAS) 173–4
Linguistic Inquiry and Word Count (LIWC) 174, 298
literacy skills 438–40; see also literacy tasks; reading; writing
literacy tasks: and emotion 445; individual differences in 447; processing during 446–7; see also literacy skills; reading; writing
locus of causality 97, 99–101, 106–7, 111, 127, 262, 354
loops: affect 59; discrepancy-enlarging 60–2; discrepancy-reducing 57–60; see also feedback loops
love 5, 14, 25, 26, 30, 86, 88, 219, 220, 228, 242n1, 392, 408, 427–8, 496, 646

magnetic resonance imaging (MRI) 614, 617; *see also* functional magnetic resonance imaging (fMRI)
magnetoencephalography (MEG) 8, 612
maladaptive causal thinking 136
mastery-approach goals 44, 146–7, 148–9, 152–3, 156
mastery-avoidance goals 146–7, 149–50, 157
Math Anxiety Questionnaire (MAQ) 399
mathematical caring relations 407
mathematics anxiety 398–402, 498; *see also* test anxiety
Mathematics Anxiety Rating Scale (MARS) 398–9, 568, 574
Mathematics Anxiety Scale for Children (MASC) 399
Mathematics Belief Questionnaire 653
mathematics education 391–409; affect and emotion in 7; anxiety in 398–402, 498; attitudes toward 393; boredom in 314, 319, 321–2, 394; coding scheme for emotions in 392–3; competing emphases in 397–8; concept development in 394; emotional experience in 46, 137, 218, 222; emotions in learning and teaching 391–5; feedback in 394; impasse in 391–2, 394; interest in 215–16, 218–20, 222; in-the-moment emotion toward 402–6; maladaptive emotions in 129; positive attitude and 42; problem solving in 394; research on emotions in 406–9; state emotions in 396, 404; success and failure in 215; trait emotion in 398–401
Maximally Discriminative Affect Coding System (MAX) 208
Mayer Salovey Caruso Emotional Intelligence Test (MSCEIT) 170–1, 173
MBA programs, emotional intelligence assessment in 176–7
measurement of emotions 510, 667; interest and enjoyment 217–20; moment-to-moment emotions 476–7; observational approaches to 580–1; observation-based methods 588–97
medical school applicants, and emotional intelligence assessments 176
memory/memories 611; and affective arousal 89; effect of mood on 40–1; emotion information and 443; explicit 83; false-memory paradigm 40; generation effect 40–1; long-term 247; mood-congruent 42; organization of 41–2; and reading fluency 440; retrieval of 131; semantic 442–3; storage 131; working 447; working reserves 132; and writing fluency 441
mental effort, affective influences on 637–8
mental health 76, 111
mental state detection 581
meta-affect 407–8
metacognitive feelings 661
methodology, vignette 114
microaggressions, racial 543–4
Middle School Mathematics Through Applications Project Group 644

mindreading 581
minorities, and science 415–16
Model of Academic Boredom 317
mood 2, 3, 13, 15; as affective construct 662; categories of 3; and cognition 40–1, 50–1; creation or maintenance of 63; and creativity 43; effect of on reading and writing 447–9; and effort expenditure 43–4, 64, 65; and emotions 18, 37; and goals pursuit 44–5, 147; influence of on learning 444; and motivation 51; not tied to academic activity 5; and persistence 43–4; positive vs. negative 42–3, 444, 446, 483; self-regulation of 49; *see also* mood congruency; mood regulation; mood states
mood congruency 42–3, 49, 445–6; effects of 442–3
mood regulation 48–50; of affective behavior 47–8
mood repair 49
mood states 39, 395
mother-child relationships 523–5, 527–9
motivation 3, 5, 125, 162, 212; academic work and 341–2; to achieve 132; and affect 77; and autonomy 333, 337; and belongingness 549; in the classroom 459, 461; and competence 332–3, 337; components of 2; and curiosity 242n1; and emotional intelligence 165; and emotions 247; interest and 217; intrinsic 100; and mood 51; and reading instruction 440; and relatedness 333, 337; *see also* achievement goals; action tendencies; attributions; implicit motives; motivation systems theory; motivational intensity; motivational resilience; motives
motivational intensity, and task difficulty 637f
motivational resilience 331–2; and academic work 341–2; and autonomy 341; coping with stress 335, 336–7; counteracting disaffection 342–3; emotion as central to 335f, 335–6, 338; and emotional engagement 340; emotional recovery 337; engagement and disaffection 336; and emotional resilience 342; external dynamics of; motivational vulnerability 331, 339; re-engagement 337; self-determination theory (SDT) model of 332–5; and structure 341
motivational vulnerability 331, 339
motivation systems theory 459
motive assessment 73–7, 76–7; content-coding approach 75–6; by questionnaire 76–7
motives: achievement 6, 74, 76, 132; affiliation 75, 88; defined 77–8; and goals 78; power 74, 82–3; and the virtuous-circle model 86; *see also* motive assessment
motor activities, observable 16, 17, 25
Multidimensional School Anger Inventory 572
Multifactor Emotional Intelligence Scale (MEIS) 170–1
Multiple Mini-Interview (MMI) assessment 176

n Achievement 73, 74, 76, 77–8, 79, 83, 87, 89; *see also* achievement; implicit motives n Affiliation 73, 75, 79, 83, 87, 89; *see also* affiliation; implicit motives

n Intimacy 88; *see also* implicit motives

n Power 73, 74, 79, 82, 87; *see also* implicit motives; power

National Research Council (NRC) 177

near infrared spectroscopy (NIRS) 8, 613

negative emotions 1, 3, 14, 27, 30; and academic boredom 312, 317, 319, 499; achievement effects of 134–5; and autonomy 130–1; avoidance of 192; in classroom 464; and confusion 300; cultural determinants of 376; and fear of failure 45; in interest development 212; in literacy education 446–7, 449; LIWC approach 174; management of 522, 531; and mastery-approach goals 147–8, 152, 154, 157; and mastery-avoidance goals 146–7, 149; in mathematics education 402, 406, 409; measurement of 593; and memory 133; and motivation 247; negative activated emotions 151; negativity bias 446; and perceived control and value appraisals 128, 135–6; and performance-approach goals 146–7, 150–2; reducing 44, 144, 670–1; in school 138, 670–1; in science education 417, 420, 421, 425–6, 430; self-reported 563, 564; shame and guilt 101; specific 44; and stereotypes 545; of students 334, 337, 338, 342, 425, 429, 430, 467, 475; and teacher burnout 500; in teachers 343, 427–8, 494, 497, 501, 503, 504, 507, 509, 510, 511, 513; in testing situations 284, 568 (*see also* test anxiety)

nervousness 266, 392, 394, 398, 400, 402, 404, 496, 544, 648; *see also* anxiety; worry

neural functioning 607

neurobiology 58; of emotion 608; of learning and memory 80–4

neurohormonal processes 124

neuroimaging techniques 8, 565, 607

neuroimmunological function 247

neuropsychological assessments 667

neuroscience: developmental 521–2; emotion and 2, 31; on interest and enjoyment 209–12; and the virtuous-circle cycle 86

Neuroscience and the Classroom: Making Connections 609

neuroscientific study of emotion 8, 607–9; contributions to educational theories and models of emotion 618–19; and the creation of more effective behavioral indices of emotion processing 620; in educational research 617–21; and the role of nonconscious emotional processing in education 619–20; *see also* neuroscientific techniques

neuroscientific techniques: computed axial tomography (CAT) 613; cortisol sampling 614–16; electroencephalography (EEG) 8, 612, 617; functional magnetic resonance imaging (fMRI) 8, 210, 609–12, 620; magnetoencephalography (MEG) 8, 612; MRI scanners 614, 617; near infrared spectroscopy (NIRS) 8, 613; in patients with brain damage 616–17; positron emission tomography (PET) 8, 613; psychophysiological recording 614–16; research tools and approaches 609–17; transcranial direct current stimulation (tDCS) 613–14; transcranial magnetic stimulation (TMS) 8, 613–14

New Perspectives on Affect and Learning Technologies 305

Newtown school tragedy 97

nonlinguistic vocalizations 587

object focus 3–4, 121–2

observational methods 8, 581; *Behavior Action and Posture coding system* (BAP) 590; classification of 584–5; cues to emotion 584–5; *Emotion Facial Action Coding System* (EMFACS) 590–2; everyday vs. systematic 581–3; *Facial Action Coding System* (FACS) 588–90; *Facial Expression Coding System* (FACES) 593–4; intuitive observer judgments 594–5; moderate validity of 595–7; objective behavior coding systems 588–90; recording and editing 598; *Specific Affect Coding System* (SPAFF) 591–3; technical issues 597–601; theory-based behavior coding systems 590–4; validity of 583, 595–7

OBSERVER 599

On-line Motivation Questionnaire (OMQ) 646, 647–8, 653

Operation ARA 486

Operation ARIES 485–7

optimism 48, 166, 169, 358, 448

Organization for Economic Co-operation and Development (OECD) 670

organizational psychology 163

othering 548

outcomes: cognitive 2; unexpected 101

panic 21, 279, 393

paralinguistic features and expressions 587, 590

parasympathetic nervous system (PNS) 526, 627–8, 631, 633

parent-child relationships 248, 251; and anxiety 272–3

parents: and emotion regulation 197, 525–9; importance of 8; influence of 248; influence of on emotional regulation 520–5; influence on test anxiety 544; positive experiences with teachers 532–3; role of in emotional regulation 532; *see also* parent-child relationships

Partnership for 21st Century Skills 177–8

passion 1, 415

Pavlovian learning 81, 84, 85, 86

peer aggression 104; *see also* children, aggressive

perceived control 124–5

perceived responsibility: controllability-related emotions 105–6; impression management strategies 105; indirect low-ability cues 104; peer-directed aggression 104

perceived value 125

performance-approach goals 146–7, 150–1, 153, 156, 157

performance-avoidance goals 146–7, 151, 153

peripheral physiology 565, 660

permanence of racism 550

perseverance 162, 259, 368

persistence 43–4, 49, 67, 125, 209, 215, 221, 259, 315, 331, 332, 335, 336, 458, 463, 475, 483, 489, 571

personality, and emotional intelligence 165–6, 175

photoplethysmography 630

physical health 1, 76, 88, 369

physiology/physiological: activations 185; components 2, 3; and confusion 297; emotion regulation 525–9

Picture Story Exercise (PSE) 75–6

pity 103–4, 105, 106, 109, 112, 499

pleasure 47, 65, 74, 79, 81, 84, 86, 145, 192, 206, 209, 211, 212, 215, 216, 219, 223, 231, 357, 392, 393, 408, 409, 495, 547, 593; anticipatory 408, 495; bodily expression of 588; and displeasure 593–4, 596; pleasure-arousal theory 593–4; pleasure response 85

Plutchik's emotion circumplex see circumplex models

Positive and Negative Affect Schedule (PANAS) 27, 208

positive emotions 14, 27, 30, 45; and academic boredom 312, 325, 450; achievement effects of 133–4; broaden-and-build model of 30, 86–7, 207, 223, 509, 662; and classroom engagement 338, 463; control-value appraisals and 128; cultural determinants of 544; and emotion regulation 192; engagement/flow 478, 482; enjoyment 495–6, 500; and expressive suppression 188; and facial patterning 209; and interest 212, 223; in literacy instruction 440, 447; and mastery-approach goals 147, 149, 154; and mastery-avoidance goals 146; in mathematics instruction 403; measurement of 593; and optimistic control appraisals 135; and performance-approach goals 150, 154, 157; pride 500; in science instruction 417, 418, 421, 425, 426, 427, 430, 431; self-reported 402, 462, 563; specific 208–9; in students 145, 164, 475; in teacher-student relationships 247, 546; of teachers 440, 501, 504, 510, 511

positive psychology 164, 509

positron emission tomography (PET) 8, 613

posture 16, 124, 173, 222, 254, 294–6, 324, 477, 484, 488, 588, 590, 597, 600, 646, 649–51, 653, 656

power/control 27, 28

powerful affect, in mathematics 408–9

power motive 74, 82–3; *see also* n Power

praise 104, 112, 256, 274, 548, 599; process vs. person 100

Precursors to Boredom Scales 573

predictions, educational value of 239

preferences, compared to emotions 18

prejudice 18

pride 3, 4, 7, 106, 107–8, 109–10, 115–16, 120, 126, 127, 136, 349; and achievement 254–6; authentic 572; authentic vs. hubristic 100, 254–6; in classrooms 259–60; engendering 258–9; hubristic 572; self-report on 572; in teachers 496

primary autonomic response measures 629t

primary socialization, and anxiety 272–3

priming 49–50

principals *see* administrators

principle of bivariate autonomic space 633–4

priority management 66–8

probability 124, 125

procedural emotion schematas 127

Programme for International Student Assessment (PISA) 222–3, 572, 670

Promoting Alternative Thinking Strategies (PATHS) 373

psychobiological research/theory 520; on attachment 523; on emotion regulation 526–8

psychological defenses 185

psychological health 1, 247, 369

psychological needs 332–5

psychophysiological recording 607, 614–16

pulse transit time 630

punishment 46, 74, 79–80, 81, 84, 103, 104, 113, 270, 341; and motive-driven learning 85–6

purpose, as motivational resource 338–9

questioning: critical 429; strategies 238

questionnaires, on test anxiety 566–8

race/ethnicity 540–1; and dimensions of culture 541–2; and emotions 543–4; and identity 551–2; and test anxiety 545

racial microaggressions 543–4

racism 545, 549–51

rapture 31

Reaction to Tests (RTT) instrument 567

reading: and emotions 7; models of 438–40; and mood congruency 446; tripartite theory of 438–9; *see also* reading and writing

reading and writing: discrete emotions and 450–1; effect of mood on 447–9; emotion applied to 7, 445–7; future research directions 449–52; role of arousal in 449–50

Reading, Writing, Respect, and Resolution (4Rs) program 374

reciprocal causation 135

regulation *see* emotion regulation

relatedness: and motivation 333, 337; and student-teacher relations 463–6

relational processing 133

relative universality 661

relief 3, 61, 63, 67, 74, 101, 122, 126, 131, 132, 134, 144, 145, 149, 157, 172, 194, 350, 357, 360, 375, 394, 397, 418, 449, 450, 451, 547, 570, 587, 668

reprioritization 66–7

research: on culture and emotions in education 549–52; dynamics of 669–70; on emotions 1–2, 5–6, 31–2, 659, 660, 668; experience-sampling studies 510–11; interdisciplinary 305; on intervention 670; neuroscientific 607–9; on text anxiety 7, 568, 670; see also future research

resiliency 7, 274, 284, 344

resource allocation: cognitive 444, 446; models for 443–4

respiratory sinus arrhythmia (RSA) 526–7, 633

responsibility 99, 102–7

response modification 194–5

Responsive Classroom (RC) 373–4

Revised Test Anxiety Scale (RTA) 568

reward 74, 79, 80–2, 84–6, 103, 105, 108, 191–2, 206, 228, 230, 405, 474, 498; reward system 219–12

risk: academic 300, 462, 483, 489; at-risk students 339; of being wrong 408; of burnout 332, 344, 494; of data errors 294; of dropping out 306; of failure 152, 257; of frustration/disengagement 299, 482, 484; of helplessness 338; high-risk children 373, 527; low-risk children 525, 527; multiple factors of 340; of negative affect 153; perceptions of 114; reducing 371; "risk" allele 528

RULER program 7, 374–5; anchor tools 380–1, 381t; components of 380–2; Feeling Words curriculum 381–2; impact of 382–3; implementation of 378–80, 379f; skills of 375–7; theory of change 377f, 377–8; training for 379–80

sadness 3, 15, 16, 25, 27, 30, 60, 63, 68, 97, 101, 115, 126, 144–6, 149, 151, 152, 172, 258, 284, 302, 305, 332, 351, 357, 376, 393, 417, 421, 447, 449, 478, 480, 544, 545, 583, 586, 587, 590–3, 595, 596, 661

satisfaction 3, 27, 39, 60, 73–5, 77–9, 86–8, 122, 164, 170, 171, 173, 174, 188, 206, 215, 220, 222, 223, 231, 255, 260, 336, 338, 392, 394, 396, 397, 403, 409, 495, 511

saturation 48, 164

School Anger Inventory 572

school success see academic success

school transitions, relatedness and 465–6

Schutte Self-Report Scale (SSRS) 169–70

science anxiety 422–3

science education: attitudes toward science in 418–20; cognitive engagement and 417–18; and confusion 424–5; controversial topics in 422, 427–8, 430–1; and curiosity 234; emotions and 7, 415–17, 439, 431–2, 437, 452; emotions research in 428–9; enjoyment in 423–4, 572; interest in 423–4, 572

science, technology, engineering, and mathematics (STEM) education 423, 477–8

SEEKING system 209–10

selective attention 39, 114

self, construals 541

self-appraisal, on emotions and mathematics 393

Self-Assessment Manikin 27

Self-Assessment Questionnaire (SAQ) 177

self-attributions 42, 248–53

self-awareness 101, 165, 176, 370

self-concepts 3, 127–9; of ability 123, 125, 135

self-confidence 42–3, 49, 165, 233, 247, 332, 394, 399, 567, 568, 651; see also confidence

self-control 169, 177, 192, 280, 368, 373, 458, 524

self-determination theory (SDT) 260, 371, 465; and motivational resilience 332–5

self-esteem 163, 166, 169, 233, 267, 285, 333; in African Americans 111; and locus 99–100, 111

self-ratings, in emotional intelligence assessments 166, 168–70

self-regulation 1, 7, 56, 77, 165, 370–1, 525–6, 529–30, 531; and boredom 315; dual processing 647; and testing 352, 355; two orthogonal dimensions of 61f

self-report measures 561, 575, 580; assessment of emotional traits or states 562–3; benefits and drawbacks of 565–6; interviews vs. written 563; qualitative vs. quantitative 563; retrospective vs. concurrent 563; single or multiple dimensions of emotion 564; single vs. multiple items 563–4; on teacher emotions 574–5; types of instruments 562–4; unstructured vs. structured 562; variants of structured self-report instruments 562f

self-reporting 15, 17, 25, 32, 76, 174–5; of emotional intelligence 178; and emotional well-being 78; of situated affect 645–9; see also self-report measures

semantic network theories 442–3, 445

sensor platform, multimedia 651

serenity 25

shame 3, 4, 7, 101–2, 106, 115–16, 120, 126, 127, 132, 145, 152; compared to guilt and embarrassment 251–2; defined 250; in teachers 498–9; reparation of 257–8; role of in achievement 252–4; see also shaming

shaming 256–7, 258–60

situated affect: measurement of 645; self-reporting of 645–9

situated emotion studies: classroom studies 652–4; grain size 655; methodological approaches 654–6; multiple methods of measurement 649–52; time, effort, cost 655

situational information 585–6

situational interest (SI) 4, 219

situational judgment tests (SJTs) 172, 174, 176

situational perceptions 124

Situational Test of Emotional Management (STEM) 172–3

Situational Test of Emotional Management-Youth (STEM-Y) 172–4
Situational Test of Emotional Understanding (STEU) 172
situation modification 193–4
skin conductance response 631
social and emotional learning (SEL) 164, 175–6, 368–9, 531–2; competencies 370*f*; defined 369–71; examples of 372–5; theoretical foundations of 371–2
social constructs and theories: alliances 86; behavioral engagement 652; comparison theory 274; desirability scores 566; intelligence 164; interactions 3; learning theory 99; psychology 99, 112, 114, 420; skills 90n1; stigma 109, 111
social-emotional behavior 507
social emotions 3, 5, 121, 498–9
socialization 8
sociocultural contexts 8
socioemotional interactions 652
socio-emotional learning programs 670
sociohistorical studies 669
software, for video coding 599
Specific Affect Coding System (SPAFF) 585–6, 591–3
speech contours, and confusion 296
SSRI 175
stability 99, 100–1, 106; causal 99–101
standardized assessments 177–8
state anxiety 266–8, 270, 282, 349, 296, 399, 408
state emotions 563; in mathematics education 404–7; vs. trait emotions 395–7; *see also* state anxiety
stem cell research 422, 429, 431
stereotypes: cultural 113; racial 113–14; stereotype threat 363
stigmas, social 109, 111
stimuli 15, 23; anxiety-evoking 265; emotional reactions to 81; incentive 84; input of 38; motivation and 77; and motor behavior 81; novelty of 293; and the reward system 211–12; stimulus evaluation checks 26
stimulus-response associations 82
stimulus-stimulus associations 82
strategic account giving 105
stress: and anxiety/emotionality 267; in caregivers 529; causes of 489; coping with 136, 163, 175, 176, 281, 335–6, 363, 573; and education 265; effects of 469; and EI 163, 165, 166, 168, 169; Lazarus's transactional theory of 267; neurological processes of 81; outside of school 5; physical reactions to 188, 527, 614–15; race-related 543, 545; research on 319, 353; responses to 85, 271, 279, 281, 527, 607; in science education 427; in teachers 427, 429, 512; and testing; *see also* test anxiety
striatum 80*f*, 81, 82
students: and academic emotions 547–8; achievement behavior of 502–3; affective development of 7;

African-American 111–13; anxious 276*t*; behavior of 505–7; diversity of emotions in 8, 392; effect of teachers' emotions on 461–2; emotions of 2, 6, 7, 392, 458–9, 667; emotions of during exams 357; interactions with teachers 467, 546–7; misbehavior of 259, 497, 503, 508, 513; racial and ethnic minority 6, 97, 110–13, 277, 543, 545, 550; resilient 284; and stress 335; *see also* children; student-teacher relationships
Student Teacher Anxiety Scale (STAS) 574
student-teacher relationships 7, 246–8, 460, 463–6, 503–4, 507, 532, 546–7
subcortical systems 660
substantianigra and ventral tegmental area (SN/VTA) 211
success 4, 5, 14, 38, 39, 43, 57, 69, 74, 78, 83, 97–100, 104, 105, 107, 112, 115, 120–1, 122, 124, 128–9, 131, 132, 135–6, 138, 145, 146, 191, 208, 215, 248–50, 252, 254–6, 260, 271, 273, 278, 282, 284, 292, 315, 352, 421, 437, 460, 469, 505, 507, 509, 613, 633; career/life 76, 87–8, 163, 177, 178, 374, 437; cultural views of 541, 544, 637–8; expectations of 45, 101, 126, 216, 358, 567, 647; feedback for 633–4; lifelong 370, 470; with mathematics 394–6, 407; in school 331, 332, 335, 339, 342, 349, 503, 522, 524, 529–32; valuing 125; *see also* academic success
suicide 1, 163
surprise 4, 17, 23, 27, 30, 97, 98, 101, 106, 228, 232, 234, 236, 239, 240, 242, 269, 292, 294, 295, 302, 305, 392, 393, 404, 415, 430, 448–50, 478–80, 482, 484, 488, 545, 571, 583, 586, 587, 589*f*, 590, 591, 593, 596, 597, 615, 661
suspensions 113
sympathetic nervous system (SNS) 627–8, 630–1, 633
sympathy 103, 109, 112, 115

task avoidance 62–3
task difficulty, and motivational intensity 637*f*
task-focusing processes 355–6
task information, processing 4
task performance: prediction of 76; self-attributions 249–50
tasks: cognitive quality of 130; designing 671; emotional design of 670–1; goal structures of 130–1; motivational quality of 130; social expectations of 130–1; supporting autonomy 130; *see also* task performance
teacher emotions 2–5, 8, 494–5; achievement goals 502; anger 497; antecedents to 670; anxiety 497–8, 574; boredom 499; and burnout 500, 511–12, 667; causes of 505–8; characteristic appraisal patterns and classroom examples 508*t*; and classroom processes 512; controversial issues 511–13; correlates of 502–5; discrete emotions 495–9, 496*t*; during instruction 461–2; effects of 508–9;

emotional labor 500–1, 512; enjoyment 495–6, 501, 512; enthusiasm 501, 512; expressiveness 501; fear of failing 3; guilt 498–9; immediacy 501; measurement of 667; pity 499; pride 496; reciprocal model of 8, 505–8; reciprocal model on causes and effects of 506f; regulation of 197, 351–2; research on 510–11; self-report measures 574–5; shame 498–9; and student emotions 361–2

teachers: achievement goals of 502; affective states of 36; classroom goals of 507; coping, re-engagement, and emotional recovery 344; countering disaffection by 342–3; effect of 362–3; emotional complexity of 8; emotional needs of 343–5; emotional reaction to students by 344–5; enthusiasm of 130, 195, 318, 323, 344, 361, 431, 451, 461–3, 501, 504, 509, 512, 575; feedback from 451–2; influence of 246–7, 372; instructional effectiveness of 504–5; instructional methods of 259–60; interaction of with colleagues, parents, and supervisors 5; and low-ability cues 112; nonverbal cues by 546; positive experiences with parents 532–3; role of in emotional regulation 532; and student motivation 89, 339, 340–1; success of 120, 122; and test anxiety 273–4; see also teacher emotions; teacher-student relationships

teacher-student relationships 7, 246–8, 460, 463–6, 503–4, 507, 532, 546–7

Teaching for Transformative Experience in Science (TTES) 425–6

technology: automatic coding and affect detection 599–601; in behavioral observation of emotions 597–601; educational 473–4; future developments 600–1; recording and editing 598; software for coding 599

temptation resistance 6, 184, 189, 191–2

tension 27, 266, 270, 352, 392, 393, 395, 400, 567, 592; reduction of 356–7

test anxiety 2, 19, 46–7, 127, 192–5, 269–70, 272, 273, 635–6, 668; avoiding 377; cognitive-focused interventions 28; cultural variables 277, 278, 544–5; emotion-focused interventions 279–80; future research on 281–4; gender differences 277, 544; influences on 544; information processing deficits in anxious students 276t; management of 196; questionnaires on 566–8; racial/ethnic factors 545; research on 7, 349, 670; and the school environment 273–4; study skills training 280–1; see also anxiety

Test Anxiety Inventory (TAI) 567

Test Anxiety Scale (TAS) 567

Test Anxiety Scale for Children (TASC) 567

Test Emotions Questionnaire (TEQ) 568

testing: cognitive appraisals related to 354–5; emotions related to 348–9; high-stakes 265, 269, 274, 372; social–contextual constraints 361; testing

problem efficacy 354; see also test anxiety; testing process

testing process: forethought phase 468–8; performance phase 358–60; regulation in 356; self-reflection phase 360

Thematic Apperception Test 75

threat avoidance 62

topic emotions 3–5, 416–17, 422, 431; of students 425–7; of teachers 427–8

trait anxiety 266–8, 270–2, 275, 282, 399, 422, 562–3

trait emotional intelligence 175

Trait Emotional Intelligence Questionnaire (TEIQue) 169, 174

trait emotions: and affect 351, 397, 407; as antecedents of emotions 129; defined 18–19; in global affect 395, 409; and mathematics 392, 396–404, 406, 408; research on 392, 396–8, 401–4, 563; vs. state emotions 395–7; see also affect dispositions; trait anxiety; trait emotional intelligence

traits: attributional 115; emotional 562; see also trait emotions

Transactions in Affective Computing 305

transcranial direct current stimulation (tDCS) 613–14

transcranial magnetic stimulation (TMS) 8, 613–14

tutoring programs 649–52

twenty-first-century skills 177

uncertainty 238, 292–3, 296, 482, 487, 497; see also confusion

underserved populations 363

valence: and activation 3, 4; and affect 18, 22, 25, 59, 62, 63, 143, 352, 462; and affective priming 49; and arousal 22, 23, 25, 27, 30, 31, 131, 134, 325, 450, 476, 651; bipolar vs. bivariate 27; change in 448; dimensions of 27, 29, 30, 313, 351, 418, 652; and emotions 23, 30, 122, 147, 157, 216, 292, 297, 312, 402, 407, 408, 409, 422, 423, 425, 432, 449, 451, 499, 507, 588; and facial expression 593–4, 597; outcome 63

value appraisals 122; and achievement emotions 126–8; types of 124–5

values: intrinsic vs. extrinsic 125; and mathematics 391

vasoconstriction 630–1

velocity function 59–61

ventromedial prefrontal cortex (VMPFC) 616

Vertical Time Code (VTC) generator 598

videos, recording 598

virtuous-circle model 6, 73, 84–8, 85f; and education 88–90

visceral organ function 632–3

VLC Media Player 599

vocabulary knowledge 438, 441

vocal bursts 587

vocal expressions of emotion 32, 393, 587–8
vocalizations 587

whiteness as property 550
womanism 552
women: identity issues of 552; and science 415–16; and science anxiety 422; and test anxiety 277, 544
Wong and Law Emotional Intelligence Scale (WLEIS) 169–70, 175

worry 207, 266–71, 275, 279, 280, 282, 283, 337, 338, 357, 361, 375, 392, 393, 400, 402, 567, 568, 648; *see also* anxiety; test anxiety
writing: and emotions 7, 437, 445–7, 452; models of 438–9; and mood congruency 445, 446; process of 440–1; *see also* reading and writing

Zero Tolerance 113
zone of optimal confusion 299, 306, 489